THE NEW INTERNATIONAL COMMENTARY
ON THE
OLD TESTAMENT

General Editors

R. K. HARRISON
(1968–1993)

ROBERT L. HUBBARD, JR.
(1994–)

The First Book of
SAMUEL

DAVID TOSHIO TSUMURA

William B. Eerdmans Publishing Company
Grand Rapids, Michigan / Cambridge, U.K.

Published 2007 by
Wm. B. Eerdmans Publishing Co.
2140 Oak Industrial Drive N.E., Grand Rapids, Michigan 49505 /
P.O. Box 163, Cambridge CB3 9PU U.K.

Printed in the United States of America

18 17 16 10 9 8 7 6 5

Library of Congress Cataloging-in-Publication Data

Tsumura, David Toshio.
The First book of Samuel / David Toshio Tsumura.
p. cm. — (The new international commentary on the Old Testament)
Includes bibliographical references and indexes.
ISBN 978-0-8028-2359-5 (cloth : alk. paper)
1. Bible. O.T. Samuel, 1st — Commentaries. I. Title.

BS1325.53.T78 2007
222′.43077 — dc22

2006039029

www.eerdmans.com

For

Susan, Michio, and Makoto

and in memory of

My parents and Jean Harter

CONTENTS

TEXT AND COMMENTARY

INDEXES

GENERAL EDITOR'S PREFACE

Long ago St. Paul wrote: "I planted, Apollos watered, but God gave the growth" (1 Cor. 3:6, NRSV). He was right: ministry indeed requires a team effort — the collective labors of many skilled hands and minds. Someone digs up the dirt and drops in seed, while others water the ground to nourish seedlings to growth. The same team effort over time has brought this commentary series to its position of prominence today. Professor E. J. Young "planted" it forty years ago, enlisting its first contributors and himself writing its first published volume. Professor R. K. Harrison "watered" it, signing on other scholars and wisely editing everyone's finished products. As General Editor, I now tend their planting, and, true to Paul's words, through four decades God has indeed graciously "[given] the growth."

Today the New International Commentary on the Old Testament enjoys a wide readership of scholars, priests, pastors, rabbis, and other serious Bible students. Thousands of readers across the religious spectrum and in countless countries consult its volumes in their ongoing preaching, teaching, and research. They warmly welcome the publication of each new volume and eagerly await its eventual transformation from an emerging "series" into a complete commentary "set." But as humanity experiences a new century of history, an era commonly called "postmodern," what kind of commentary series is NICOT? What distinguishes it from other similarly well-established series?

Its volumes aim to publish biblical scholarship of the highest quality. Each contributor writes as an expert, both in the biblical text itself and in the relevant scholarly literature, and each commentary conveys the results of wide reading and careful, mature reflection. Ultimately, its spirit is eclectic, each contributor gleaning interpretive insights from any useful source, whatever its religious or philosophical viewpoint, and integrating them into his or her interpretation of a biblical book. The series draws on recent methodological innovations in biblical scholarship, for example, canon criticism, the so-called "new literary criticism," reader-response theories, and sensitivity to gender-based and ethnic readings. NICOT volumes also aim to be irenic in tone, summarizing and critiquing influential views with fairness while defending their own. Its list of contributors includes male and female scholars from a number of Christian faith-groups. The diversity of contributors and their freedom to draw on all relevant methodologies give the entire series an exciting and enriching variety.

What truly distinguishes this series, however, is that it speaks from within that interpretive tradition known as evangelicalism. Evangelicalism is an informal movement within Protestantism that cuts across traditional denominational lines. Its heart and soul is the conviction that the Bible is God's inspired Word, written by gifted human writers, through which God calls humanity to enjoy a loving personal relationship with its Creator and Savior. True to that tradition, NICOT volumes do not treat the Old Testament as just an ancient literary artifact on a par with the *Iliad* or *Gilgamesh.* They are not literary autopsies of ancient parchment cadavers but rigorous, reverent wrestlings with wonderfully human writings through which the living God speaks his powerful Word. NICOT delicately balances "criticism" (i.e., the use of standard critical methodologies) with humble respect, admiration, and even affection for the biblical text. As an evangelical commentary, it pays particular attention to the text's literary features, theological themes, and implications for the life of faith today.

Ultimately, NICOT aims to serve women and men of faith who desire to hear God's voice afresh through the Old Testament. With gratitude to God for two marvelous gifts — the Scriptures themselves and keen-minded scholars to explain their message — I welcome readers of all kinds to savor the good fruit of this series.

ROBERT L. HUBBARD JR.

AUTHOR'S PREFACE

Writing a commentary, however modest, is a hard task. Only by the grace of God can one complete the work. For a student of the Bible it is certainly a great privilege as well as a heavy responsibility. The task is done by continually learning from the vast information gathered by preceding commentaries and scholarly works, while facing directly the original text of the book. Because I tried to respond to their views as well as keep abreast of new discoveries, both archaeological and philological, the present volume has become more voluminous than I originally expected. Among the many commentaries, I have learned from those of P. K. McCarter and R. P. Gordon, though I often disagree with them.

When dealing with the Hebrew text, my training in Semitic philology, especially in Ugaritic as well as in Canaanite religion, by the late Prof. C. H. Gordon prepared me to make some new suggestions for better understanding of the text of 1 Samuel. Prof. A. Millard of Liverpool University read many parts of the draft, providing valuable information and comments. Prof. T. Ishida, my former colleague at the University of Tsukuba, also gave me a number of significant comments, especially on the introductory section. The series editor Prof. R. L. Hubbard was most helpful in improving the style and content of this commentary. I am grateful to his patience and encouragement. However, I am fully responsible for what I wrote in this book.

In this commentary I have stuck to the MT as much as possible, without easy recourse to emendation on the basis of the LXX and other ancient versions, not because the MT is perfect, but because it is time again to read the MT straightforwardly and determine whether, with the present knowledge of Hebrew grammar and style, we can make good sense out of the MT itself — the grammar includes, of course, discourse grammar, that is, supra-sentential grammatical analysis, as well as the styles.

This is a comparatively literal translation. For instance, *waw* is translated as "and" where possible, instead of using various subordinate clauses to express the relationship. Also, where possible, the original word order is reflected in the English translation. On the other hand, some idiomatic expressions and formulae are translated non-literally, for example, "and said" is left out of expressions like "And Hannah prayed and said" (1 Sam. 2:1) or "answered and said,"[1] thus "answered" (see 1 Sam. 4:17; 9:12, 19; 16:18; 22:14; 23:4; 29:9). But, see 1 Sam. 26:6. For the translation of perfect verbs, see on 1 Sam. 2:1b.

When citing commentaries, we noted only the author's family name with page numbers, after its second occurrence. So, Caquot and de Robert, p. 12 is from A. Caquot and P. de Robert, *Les Livres de Samuel* (1994). The full information on these commentaries can be found in "Select Bibliography" at the end of the "Introduction."

While the MS of this commentary was in the process of editing, important archaeological discoveries were being made. For example, according to the *Jerusalem Post,* Nov. 10, 2005, Bar-Ilan University archaeologists found at Tel eṣ-Ṣâfī, "Gath of the Philistines," the earliest known Philistine inscription, which reportedly mentions two names similar to "Goliath." Another news item in March 2006 stated that the Israeli archaeologist Eilat Mazar believes that she has found the 10th-century remains of King David's palace just south of Jerusalem's Temple Mount.

Also, F. M. Cross, D. W. Parry, R. J. Saley, and E. Ulrich, *Qumran Cave 4:* XII: *1-2 Samuel* (Discoveries in the Judaean Desert 17; Oxford: Clarendon, 2005), appeared too late to consult in this commentary, though the Qumran texts themselves have been available for some time and the relevant passages have been examined. Their work will be thoroughly evaluated in my forthcoming commentary on 2 Samuel.

Many persons, family and friends, both in Japan and abroad have prayed for this project and encouraged me. Faculty members and students (many now graduates) of Japan Bible Seminary have encouraged me on various occasions. Hamadayama Church members have also remembered me in their prayers.

Susan and my two sons, Michio and Makoto, have been faithful supporters and have experienced the frustration and joy of writing this commentary with me for more than a decade. Susan's criticisms, often very sharp but always constructive, helped me to improve content and style, as well as English grammar. To her and my sons I dedicate this book with love.

ἀρκεῖ σοι ἡ χάρις μου, ἡ γὰρ δύναμις ἐν ἀσθενείᾳ τελεῖται. (2 Cor. 12:9)

1. See C. L. Miller, "Introducing Direct Discourse in Biblical Hebrew Narrative," in *Biblical Hebrew and Discourse Linguistics,* ed. R. D. Bergen (Dallas: Summer Institute of Linguistics, 1994), pp. 219-20.

ABBREVIATIONS

*	* (Semitic verbal root)
AASF	Annales Academiae Scientiarum Fennicae
AB	Anchor Bible
ABD	D. N. Freedman (ed.), *The Anchor Bible Dictionary.* 6 vols. New York: Doubleday, 1992.
ABRL	Anchor Bible Reference Library
AbrN	*Abr-Nahrain*
AdvPh	adverbial phrase
AfO	*Archiv für Orientforschung*
AGE	K. Tallqvist, *Akkadische Götterepitheta* (SO 7). Helsinki: Societas Orientalis Fennica, 1938.
AHw	W. von Soden, *Akkadisches Handwörterbuch.* Wiesbaden: Otto Harrassowitz, 1965-81.
AJBA	*Australian Journal of Biblical Archaeology*
AJBI	*Annual of the Japanese Biblical Institute*
AJSL	*Americal Journal of Semitic Languages and Literatures*
AnBib	Analecta Biblica
Andersen	F. I. Andersen, *The Sentence in Biblical Hebrew.* The Hague/Paris: Mouton, 1974.
ANE	Ancient Near East
ANEP	J. B. Pritchard (ed.), *The Ancient Near East in Pictures Relating to the Old Testament.* Princeton: Princeton University Press, 1954, 1968.
ANET	J. B. Pritchard (ed.), *The Ancient Near Eastern Texts Relating to the Old Testament.* 3rd edition. Princeton: Princeton University Press, 1969.
AnOr	Analecta Orientalia
AOAT	Alter Orient und Altes Testament
AOS	American Oriental Series

ARM	Archives royales de Mari
AS	Assyriological Studies (University of Chicago)
ATD	Das Alte Testament Deutsch
ATDa	Acta Theologica Danica
ATSAT	Arbeiten zu Text und Sprache im Alten Testament
AuOr	*Aula Orientalis*
AusBR	*Australian Biblical Review*
AUSS	*Andrews University Seminary Studies*
B-L	H. Bauer & P. Leander, *Historische Grammatik der Hebräischen Sprache des Alten Testaments.* Hildesheim: G. Olms, 1962 [orig. 1922].
BA	*Biblical Archaeologist*
BAR	*Biblical Archaeology Review*
BASOR	*Bulletin of the American Schools of Oriental Research*
BDB	F. Brown, S. R. Driver & C. A. Briggs, *A Hebrew and English Lexicon of the Old Testament.* Oxford: Clarendon Press, 1907.
BEATAJ	Beiträge zur Erforschung des Alten Testaments und des Antiken Judentums
BeO	Bibbia e Oriente
Berg	G. Bergsträsser, *Hebräische Grammatik.* I/II. Hildesheim: G. Olms, 1962 [orig. 1918].
BHK	Biblia Hebraica Kittel
BHQ	Biblia Hebraica Quinta
BHS	Biblia Hebraica Stuttgartensia
Bib	*Biblica*
BibInt	*Biblical Interpretation*
Biella	J. C. Biella, *Dictionary of Old South Arabic: Sabaean Dialect* (HSS 25). Chico: Scholars Press, 1982.
BIOSCS	*Bulletin of the International Organization for Septuagint and Cognate Studies*
BIS	Biblical Interpretation Series
BKAT	Biblischer Kommentar Altes Testament
BLS	Bible and Literature Series
BMECCJ	Bulletin of the Middle Eastern Culture Center in Japan
BN	*Biblische Notizen*
BR	*Bible Review*
BS	*Bibliotheca Sacra*
BT	*The Bible Translator*
BTB	*Biblical Theology Bulletin*
BToday	*Bible Today*
BWANT	Beiträge zur Wissenschaft vom Alten und Neuen Testament

BZ	*Biblische Zeitschrift*
BZAW	Beihefte zur *ZAW*
CAD	*Chicago Assyrian Dictionary*
CAT	Commentaire de l'Ancien Testament
CB	Coniectanea Biblica
CBC	Cambridge Bible Commentary
CBQ	*Catholic Biblical Quarterly*
CH	Code of Hammurabi
CML	G. R. Driver, *Canaanite Myths and Legends.* Edinburgh: T. & T. Clark, 1956.
CML[2]	J. C. L. Gibson, *Canaanite Myths and Legends.* New ed. Edinburgh: T. & T. Clark, 1978.
COT	Commentaar op het Oude Testament
CPTOT	J. Barr, *Comparative Philology and the Text of the Old Testament.* Oxford: Clarendon Press, 1968.
CRB	Cahiers de la Revue Biblique
CS	W. W. Hallo (ed.), *The Context of Scripture.* Vol. I: *Canonical Compositions from the Biblical World.* Leiden: E. J. Brill, 1997; Vol. II: *Monumental Inscriptions from the Biblical World.* Leiden: E. J. Brill, 2000.
CTCA	A. Herdner, *Corpus des tablettes en cunéiformes alphabétiques.* Paris: Impr. Nationale, 1963.
Davidson	A. B. Davidson, *An Introductory Hebrew Grammar.* 26th edition. Edinburgh: T. & T. Clark, 1966.
DBSup	Supplement au *Dictionnaire de la Bible*
DCH	D. J. A. Clines (ed.), *The Dictionary of Classical Hebrew.* Vol. I: (א)-. Sheffield: Sheffield Academic Press, 1993-.
DDD	K. van der Toorn, B. Becking, and P. W. van der Horst, *Dictionary of Deities and Demons in the Bible.* Leiden: E. J. Brill, 1995.
DJPA	M. Sokoloff, *A Dictionary of Jewish Palestinian Aramaic of the Byzantine Period.* Ramat-Gan: Bar Ilan University, 1990.
DN	divine name
DNWSI	J. Hoftijzer and K. Jongeling, *Dictionary of the North-West Semitic Inscriptions.* Leiden: E. J. Brill, 1995.
DOTT	D. W. Thomas (ed.), *Documents from Old Testament Times.* New York: Harper & Row, 1958.
EA	El-Amarna tablets
EB	Études bibliques
EBC	*Expositor's Bible Commentary*
EI	*Eretz Israel*
EQ	*Evangelical Quarterly*

ET	English translation
ETL	*Ephemerides Theologicae Lovanienses*
EvT	*Evangelische Theologie*
ExTi	*Expository Times*
FB	Forschung zur Bibel
FRLANT	Forschungen zur Religion und Literatur des Alten und Neuen Testaments
GB	F. Buhl, *Wilhelm Gesenius hebräisches und aramäisches Handwörterbuch über das Alte Testament.* 17th ed. Berlin: Springer, 1915.
Gibson	J. C. L. Gibson, *Davidson's Introductory Hebrew Grammar: Syntax.* 4th edition. Edinburgh: T. & T. Clark, 1994.
GKC	E. Kautszch and A. E. Cowley, *Gesenius' Hebrew Grammar.* Second English edition. Oxford: Clarendon Press, 1910.
GMD	R. Meyer and H. Donner, *Wilhelm Gesenius hebräisches und aramäisches Handwörterbuch über das Alte Testament.* 18th ed. Berlin: Springer, 1987.
GN	geographical name
GVG	Carl Brockelmann, *Grundriss der vergleichenden Grammatik der semitischen Sprachen.* 2 vols. Hildesheim: G. Olms, 1966 [orig. 1908 and 1913].
HAHE	J. Renz and W. Röllig, *Handbuch der althebräischen Epigraphik,* I. Darmstadt: Wissenschaftliche Buchgesellschaft, 1995.
HAL	W. Baumgartner, *Hebräisches und aramäisches Lexikon zum Alten Testament.* Leiden: E. J. Brill, 1967-.
HALOT	L. Koehler and W. Baumgartner, *The Hebrew and Aramaic Lexicon of the Old Testament.* Trans. by M. E. J. Richardson. Leiden: E. J. Brill, 1994-2000.
HAR	*Hebrew Annual Review*
HAT	Handbuch zum Alten Testament
HbO	Handbuch der Orientalistik
HKAT	Handkommentar zum Alten Testament
HSAT	Die heilige Schrift des Alten Testaments
HSM	Harvard Semitic Monographs
HSS	Harvard Semitic Studies
HTR	*Harvard Theological Review*
HUCA	*Hebrew Union College Annual*
IB	*The Interpreter's Bible*
IBD	*The Illustrated Bible Dictionary.* 3 vols. 1980.
ICC	International Critical Commentary
IDB	*The Interpreter's Dictionary of the Bible*

IDBSup	Supplement to *IDB*
IEJ	*Israel Exploration Journal*
Iliad 1–12	Homer, *Iliad* I: Books 1–12. With an English Translation by A. T. Murray, revised by W. F. Wyatt. 2nd ed. Loeb Classical Library 170. Cambridge, Mass.: Harvard University Press, 1999.
Iliad 13–24	Homer, *Iliad* II: Books 13–24. With an English Translation by A. T. Murray. Loeb Classical Library 171. Cambridge, Mass.: Harvard University Press, 1925 [repr. 1985].
inf. abs.	infinitive absolute
Int	*Interpretation*
IOS	Israel Oriental Studies
IOSCS	International Organization for Septuagint and Cognate Studies
IrBS	Irish Biblical Studies
ISBE	G. W. Bromiley (ed.), *The International Standard Bible Encyclopedia.* 4 vols. Grand Rapids: Eerdmans, 1979-88.
ITC	International Theological Commentary
J-M	P. Joüon–T. Muraoka, *A Grammar of Biblical Hebrew.* Part One: Orthography and Phonetics. Part Two: Morphology. Part Three: Syntax. Subsidia Biblica 14/I-II. Rome: Editrice Pontificio Istituto Biblico, 1991.
JAAR	*Journal of the American Academy of Religion*
JANES	*The Journal of the Ancient Near Eastern Society*
JAOS	*Journal of the American Oriental Society*
Jastrow	M. Jastrow, *A Dictionary of the Targumim, the Talmud Babli and Yerushalmi, and the Midrashic Literature.* New York: Pardes, 1950.
JBL	*Journal of Biblical Literature*
JBQ	*The Jewish Bible Quarterly*
JBR	*Journal of Bible and Religion*
JCS	*Journal of Cuneiform Studies*
JDS	Judean Desert Studies
JETS	*Journal of the Evangelical Theological Society*
JHNES	Johns Hopkins Near Eastern Studies
JJS	*Journal of Jewish Studies*
JNES	*Journal of Near Eastern Studies*
JNSL	*Journal of Northwest Semitic Languages*
JPOS	*Journal of the Palestine Oriental Society*
JPS	Jewish Publication Society
JQR	*Jewish Quarterly Review*
JRAS	*Journal of the Royal Asiatic Society*

JSOT	*Journal for the Study of the Old Testament*
JSOTSS	*JSOT,* Supplement Series
JSS	*Journal of Semitic Studies*
JTS	*Journal of Theological Studies*
K.	Ketib
KAI	H. Donner and W. Röllig, *Kanaanäische und aramäische Inschriften.* 3 vols. Wiesbaden: Otto Harrassowitz, 1962, 1964, 1973.
KAT	Kommentar zum Alten Testament
KHCAT	Kurzer Hand-Commentar zum Alten Testament
KJV	King James Version
König	E. König, *Stilistik, Rhetorik, Poetik in Bezug auf die biblische Litteratur.* Leipzig: Theodor Weicher, 1900.
KTU	M. Dietrich–O. Loretz–J. Sanmartin, *Die keilalphabetischen Texte aus Ugarit.* AOAT 24. Neukirchen-Vluyn: Neukirchener, 1976.
Lambdin	T. O. Lambdin, *Introduction to Biblical Hebrew.* London: Darton, Longman & Todd, 1973.
Lane	E. W. Lane, *An Arabic-English Lexicon.* London: Williams and Norgate, 1863 [repr. 1968].
LAPO	Littératures anciennes du Proche-Orient
LB	Late Bronze Age
LBH	Late Biblical Hebrew
Lesh	*Leshonenu*
LXX	Septuaginta
LXX^{A}	Septuagint Codex Alexandrinus
LXX^{B}	Septuagint Codex Vaticanus
LXX^{L}	Septuagint Lucianic Manuscripts
MB	Middle Bronze Age
MR	Map Reference, based on *Student Map Manual: Historical Geography of the Bible Lands.* Jerusalem: Pictorial Archive (Near Eastern History) Est. Distributed by Grand Rapids: Zondervan, 1980. E.g., [MR 169-123] = Map Reference to Bethlehem according to the Grid [EW-NS].
MT	Masoretic Text
NAB	New American Bible
NABU	*Nouvelles Assyriologiques Brèves et Utilitaires*
NAC	New American Commentary
NASB	New American Standard Bible
NB	Neo-Babylonian
NCB	New Century Bible

NDBT	T. D. Alexander and B. S. Rosner (eds.), *New Dictionary of Biblical Theology.* Leicester: InterVarsity Press, 2000.
NEA	*Near Eastern Archaeology*
NEAEHL	E. Stern (ed.), *The New Encyclopedia of Archaeological Excavations in the Holy Land.* 4 vols. Jerusalem: Israel Exploration Society & Carta, 1993.
NEB	New English Bible
neg.	negative
NICOT	New International Commentary on the Old Testament
NIDOTTE	W. A. VanGemeren (ed.), *The New International Dictionary of Old Testament Theology and Exegesis.* Grand Rapids: Zondervan, 1996.
NIV	New International Version
NJB	New Jerusalem Bible
NJPS(V)	New Jewish Publication Society (Version)
NKJB	New King James Bible
NovT	*Novum Testamentum*
NP	noun phrase
NRSV	New Revised Standard Version
NRT	Nouvelle revue théologique
OBL	Orientalia et biblica Lovaniensia
OBO	Orbis Biblicus et Orientalis
OEANE	E. M. Meyers (ed.), *The Oxford Encyclopedia of Archaeology in the Near East.* 5 vols. Oxford: Oxford University Press, 1997.
OIP	Oriental Institute Publications
OL	Old Latin
OLA	Orientalia Lovaniensia Analecta
OLZ	*Orientalistische Literaturzeitung*
Or	*Orientalia*
OTA	*Old Testament Abstracts*
OTE	*Old Testament Essays*
OTG	Old Testament Guides
OTL	Old Testament Library
OTS	Oudtestamentische Studiën
OTWSA	*Die Ou-Testamentiese Werkgemeenskap in Suid-Afrika*
PEQ	*Palestine Exploration Quarterly*
PLMU	C. H. Gordon, "Poetic Legends and Myths from Ugarit." *Berytus* 25 (1977), pp. 5-133.
PN	personal name
POS	Pretoria Oriental Series

POTT	D. J. Wiseman (ed.), *Peoples of Old Testament Times.* Oxford: Clarendon Press, 1973.
POTW	A. J. Hoerth, G. L. Mattingly, and E. M. Yamauchi (eds.), *Peoples of the Old Testament World.* Grand Rapids: Baker, 1994.
PTU	F. Gröndahl, *Die Personennamen der Texte aus Ugarit.* SP 1. Rome: Pontifical Biblical Institute, 1967.
Q.	Qere
qtl	"perfect"
RA	*Revue d'assyriologie et d'archéologie orientale*
RB	*Revue Biblique*
REB	Revised English Bible
RlA	*Reallexikon der Assyriologie*
RQ	*Revue de Qumran*
RSO	Revista degli Studi Orientali
RSP	L. R. Fisher (ed.), *Ras Shamra Parallels.* Vol. 1, AnOr 49. Rome: Pontifical Biblical Institute, 1972; vol. 2, AnOr 50, 1975. S. Rummel (ed.), *Ras Shamra Parallels.* Vol. 3, AnOr 51, 1981.
RSR	*Religious Studies Review*
RSV	Revised Standard Version
RV	Revised Version
S	subject
SAA	State Archives of Assyria
SBLDS	Society of Biblical Literature Dissertation Series
SBLMS	Society of Biblical Literature Monograph Series
SBTS	Sources for Biblical and Theological Study
SEL	*Studi epigrafici e linguistici sul vicino Oriente Antico*
SFSHJ	South Florida Studies in the History of Judaism
SHCANE	Studies in the History and Culture of the Ancient Near East
SJOT	*Scandinavian Journal of the Old Testament*
SLOCG	E. Lipiński, *Semitic Languages: Outline of a Comparative Grammar.* OLA 80. Leuven: Uitgeverij Peeters, 1997.
SP	Studia Pohl
SSI	J. C. L. Gibson, *Textbook of Syrian Semitic Inscriptions.* I-III. Oxford: Clarendon Press, 1971-82.
SSN	Studia Semitica Neerlandica
ST	Studia Theologica
STDJ	Studies on the Texts of the Desert of Judah
StOr	Studia Orientalia
SVT	Supplement to *VT*
TDOT	G. J. Botterweck and H. Ringgren (eds.), *Theological*

	Dictionary of the Old Testament. Vol. I-. Grand Rapids: Eerdmans, 1974-.
Temp-ph	temporal phrase
THAT	*Theologisches Handwörterbuch zum Alten Testament.* 2 vols. Munich: Chr. Kaiser, 1971-1976.
TICP	Travaux de l'Institut Catholique de Paris
Tiq. soph.	Tiqqun sopherim ("corrections of scribe")
TLZ	*Theologische Literaturzeitung*
TO	A. Caquot, M. Sznycer, and A. Herdner, *Textes ougaritiques,* I: *Mythes et légendes.* LAPO 7. Paris: Cerf, 1974.
TOTC	Tyndale Old Testament Commentaries
TrinJ	*Trinity Journal*
TWAT	*Theologisches Wörterbuch zum Alten Testament.* Stuttgart: W. Kohlhammer, 1970-.
TWOT	R. L. Harris, G. L. Archer, Jr., and B. K. Waltke (eds.), *Theological Wordbook of the Old Testament.* 2 vols. Chicago: Moody, 1980.
TynB	*Tyndale Bulletin*
TZ	*Theologische Zeitschrift*
UCOP	University of Cambridge Oriental Publications
UF	*Ugarit-Forschungen*
Ug	*Ugaritica*
UMM	University Museum Monograph
UnSemQ	*Union Seminary Quarterly Review*
UT	C. H. Gordon, *Ugaritic Textbook.* AnOr 38. Rome: Pontificium Institutum Biblicum, 1965.
UTS	Supplement to C. H. Gordon, *UT*
VigChr	*Vigiliae Christianae*
VP	verb phrase
VT	*Vetus Testament*
VTS	*VT* Supplement Series
w	simple *waw* (w^e)
W–O	B. K. Waltke and M. O'Connor, *An Introduction to Biblical Hebrew Syntax.* Winona Lake: Eisenbrauns, 1990.
Watson	W. G. E. Watson, *Classical Hebrew Poetry: A Guide to Its Techniques.* JSOTSS 26. Sheffield: JSOT Press, 1984.
wayhy	*waw* consecutive + Qal "imperfect" 3 m s *hyh ("to be")
wayqtl	*waw* consecutive + "imperfect" *(yqtl)*
WBC	Word Biblical Commentary
Williams	R. J. Williams, *Hebrew Syntax: An Outline.* 2nd ed. Toronto: University of Toronto Press, 1976.

WMANT	Wissenschaftliche Monographien zum Alten und Neuen Testament
WO	*Die Welt des Orients*
WTJ	*The Westminster Theological Journal*
yqtl	"imperfect"
ZA	*Zeitschrift für Assyriologie*
ZAH	*Zeitschrift für Althebräistik*
ZAW	*Zeitschrift für die alttestamentliche Wissenschaft*
ZDMG	*Zeitschrift der Deutschen Morgenländischen Gesellschaft*
ZDMGSup	Supplement to *ZDMG*
ZDPV	*Zeitschrift des Deutschen Palästina-Vereins*
ZKT	*Zeitschrift für katholische Theologie*

INTRODUCTION

1-2 Samuel is one of the most fascinating sections of the Bible. Stories such as "David and Goliath" (1 Sam. 17:1-54), "Call of Samuel as a Prophet" (1 Sam. 3:1-21), "Witch of Endor" (1 Sam. 28), and "David and Bathsheba" (2 Sam. 11:2–12:25) are among the most famous from the entire ancient world. Many works of literature and music and art have been produced based on these stories. Figures such as Hannah, Jonathan, Abigail, Joab, and Barzillai, though not main *dramatis personae* like Samuel, Saul, and David, still took a major role in each stage of God's unfolding plan of salvation. The stories are easy to follow, and even children can appreciate and enjoy reading and re-reading them.

Yet, the books are among the most difficult ones in the Hebrew Bible. The Hebrew text is widely considered corrupt and sometimes even unintelligible. The socio-religious customs are often strange and seemingly divergent from the Mosaic traditions. To write a commentary on 1-2 Samuel is certainly a hard and never-ending task. The present effort is just a small contribution toward a better understanding and appreciation of the fascinating drama of the Bible.

Before commenting on the individual sections, some general introductory notes are in order. Below we summarize the present state of the study of 1-2 Samuel in the areas of Title, Text, Date and Authorship, Literary Approach, Historiography, Historical and Religious Background, Grammar and Syntax, Discourse Analysis, Prose and Poetry, Literary Structure and Themes, and Theology.

I. TITLE

In the Hebrew Bible, the First and Second Books of Samuel are counted among the "Former Prophets" (Joshua–2 Kings). The Greek translation, the

Septuagint (LXX), divides Samuel and Kings into the four "Books of Kingdoms" *(basileiōn A-D);* thus 1-2 Samuel are 1-2 Kingdoms — in the Vulgate, 1-2 Kings.[1]

1 Chr. 29:29 says, "As for the events of King David's reign, from beginning to end, they are written in the records of Samuel the seer, the records of Nathan the prophet and the records of Gad the seer. . . ." It implies the existence of the written records of Samuel on which the Chronicler presumably drew. Of course, Samuel could not have written the whole of even the first book since it refers to his death (1 Sam. 25:1; 28:3) and records the subsequent history of Saul and David. Some parts of 1 Samuel might have been written (see 1 Sam. 10:25) or preserved by the prophet himself or his disciples, however; see below on "Date and Authorship."

Nevertheless the Hebrew title "Samuel" most likely refers to Samuel not as the author, but as the key figure, the one who established the monarchy in Israel by anointing first Saul and then David; Samuel was the king-maker in the history of ancient Israel. Thus, it was reasonable to name the books after him.

II. TEXT

Besides the traditional Hebrew "Masoretic Text" (MT) known from manuscripts of the 10th and 11th centuries A.D., various ancient textual traditions for the books of Samuel are known. The three Hebrew texts of Samuel among the Dead Sea Scrolls (ca. 3rd century to 1st century B.C.), $4QSam^a$, $4QSam^b$, and $4QSam^c$, are extremely important for the textual study of the books.[2]

Ancient versions are also helpful for understanding the textual history of the Hebrew Bible. Among the versions, the most important is the Greek one, the Septuagint (LXX) of ca. 2nd century B.C., which has been preserved in three major manuscript traditions, the Codex Vaticanus (LXX^B), the Codex Alexandrinus (LXX^A) and the Lucianic Manuscripts (LXX^L).[3] Other known ancient versions are the Old Latin (OL),[4] the Aramaic Targum Jona-

1. See R. P. Gordon, *I & II Samuel* (Exeter: Paternoster, 1986), pp. 19-20; A. Caquot and P. de Robert, *Les Livres de Samuel* (CAT VI; Geneva: Labor et Fides, 1994), p. 7.

2. See below.

3. A. Aejmelaeus, "The Septuagint of 1 Samuel," in *VIII Congress of the IOSCS: Paris 1992,* ed. L. Greenspoon and O. Munnich (Atlanta: Scholars Press, 1995), p. 110. Also S. Jellicoe, *The Septuagint and Modern Study* (Oxford: Clarendon, 1968), pp. 283-87.

4. See E. C. Ulrich, "The Old Latin Translation of the LXX and the Hebrew

than (Targ.),[5] the Syriac Peshitta (Syr.),[6] and the Latin Vulgate (Vulg.). Josephus's *Jewish Antiquities* (Ant.) also provides useful information.[7]

The MT of 1-2 Samuel has suffered from transcriptional corruption and is allegedly "in extremely poor condition"[8] because of its peculiar and often unintelligible spellings and grammatical forms. Hence, scholars have "corrected" it in the light of LXX and other versions, and recently using the Qumran biblical texts.[9]

A. HISTORY OF RESEARCH

1. Before the Discovery of the Dead Sea Scrolls

The first systematic attempt at correction was made by Otto Thenius, *Die Bücher Samuelis* (1842), who used the LXX to recover the "original readings" at many points where the MT was taken as corrupt. The major work by Wellhausen[10] compared the MT, LXX, and other versions and produced "the outline of an eclectic text" of Samuel. His work influenced subsequent studies by H. P. Smith, Budde, Dhorme, and others,[11] as well as S. R.

Scrolls from Qumran," in *The Hebrew and Greek Texts of Samuel,* ed. E. Tov (Jerusalem: Academon, 1980), pp. 123-65.

5. A scholarly work on the Targum of Samuel is E. van Staalduine-Sulman, *A Bilingual Concordance to the Targum of the Prophets,* vol. 3: *Samuel, 1* (Leiden: E. J. Brill, 1996).

6. See R. P. Gordon, "Translational Features of the Peshitta in 1 Samuel," in *Targumic and Cognate Studies: Essays in Honour of Martin McNamara,* ed. K. J. Cathcart and M. Maher (Sheffield: Sheffield Academic Press, 1996), pp. 163-76. On the Peshitta in general, see M. P. Weitzman, *The Syriac Version of the Old Testament: An Introduction* (Cambridge: Cambridge University Press, 1999).

7. L. H. Feldman, "Josephus' Portrait of Saul," *HUCA* 53 (1982) 45-99; "Josephus' Portrait of David," *HUCA* 60 (1989) 129-74; "Josephus' Portrait of Samuel," *AbrN* 30 (1992) 103-45.

8. B. C. Birch, "The First and Second Books of Samuel: Introduction, Commentary, and Reflections," in *The New IB,* vol. II, ed. L. E. Keck et al. (Nashville: Abingdon, 1998), p. 950.

9. For example, see S. R. Driver, *Notes on the Hebrew Text of the Books of Samuel* (Oxford: Clarendon, 1890), p. v; Jellicoe, *The Septuagint and Modern Study,* p. 283; P. K. McCarter, Jr., *1 Samuel: A New Translation with Introduction, Notes and Commentary* (AB 8; Garden City, N.Y.: Doubleday, 1980), p. 5; cf. R. W. Klein, *1 Samuel* (WBC 10; Waco, Tex.: Word Books, 1983), p. xxvii; etc.

10. J. Wellhausen, *Die Text der Bücher Samuelis Untersucht* (Göttingen: Vandenhoeck & Ruprecht, 1871).

11. H. P. Smith, *A Critical and Exegetical Commentary on the Books of Samuel* (ICC; Edinburgh: T. & T. Clark, 1899); K. Budde, *The Books of Samuel: Critical Edition*

Driver,[12] who, however, paid more attention to the details of Hebrew grammar and syntax. By 1913 when the second edition of Driver's *Notes* . . .[13] was published, knowledge of Hebrew language and orthography as well as of the characteristics of the versions and text families had increased. Nevertheless, conjectural emendations continued to be suggested to solve many difficult passages.

The comparative use of the LXX and other versions for clearing up the problems in the MT faced sharp criticisms and questions, for it was questioned whether the LXX readings really reflected the details of a divergent Hebrew original text. It was pointed out that there was a strong possibility that the LXX had artificially corrected a difficult text that was close to the MT. P. A. H. de Boer,[14] for example, was completely negative toward the use of LXX to "correct" the MT.

2. Discovery of the Qumran Biblical Scrolls

With the discovery of the Qumran biblical texts, however, a revolution began in the study of the text of Samuel. These texts are older by a millennium than any extant MT manuscripts. Among them, 4QSam[a] is a large and fairly well preserved scroll, dated 50-25 B.C. It includes parts of much of 1-2 Samuel and has now finally been published.[15] 4QSam[b] is a group of fragments of a small part of 1 Samuel, that is, 16:1-11; 19:10-17; 21:3-10; and 23:7-17. According to McCarter,[16] it is probably the oldest biblical manuscript found at Qumran, and is dated mid-3rd century B.C. It was published partially by Cross and has now been published fully by Cross and Parry.[17] 4QSam[c] is a

of the Hebrew Text (Leipzig: Hinrichs'sche, 1894); *Die Bücher Samuel erklärt* (Tübingen: J. C. B. Mohr, 1902); É. P. Dhorme, *Les livres de Samuel* (Paris: J. Gabalda, 1910).

12. S. R. Driver, *Notes on the Hebrew Text of the Books of Samuel* (Oxford: Clarendon, 1890).

13. S. R. Driver, *Notes on the Hebrew Text and the Topography of the Books of Samuel* (Oxford: Clarendon, 1913).

14. P. A. H. de Boer, *Research into the Text of I Samuel i–xvi* (Amsterdam: H. J. Paris, 1938); "Research into the Text of I Samuel xviii–xxxi," *OTS* 6 (1949) 1-100.

15. E. C. Ulrich, Jr., *The Qumran Text of Samuel and Josephus* (HSM 19; Missoula, Mont.: Scholars Press, 1978); F. M. Cross, "The Ammonite Oppression of the Tribes of Gad and Reuben: Missing Verses from 1 Samuel 11 Found in 4QSamuel[a]," in *History, Historiography and Interpretation: Studies in Biblical and Cuneiform Literatures,* ed. H. Tadmor and M. Weinfeld (Jerusalem: Magnes Press, 1983), pp. 148-58. Most recently by E. D. Herbert, *Reconstructing Biblical Dead Sea Scrolls: A New Method Applied to the Reconstruction of 4QSam[a]* (STDJ 22; Leiden: E. J. Brill, 1997).

16. McCarter, p. 6.

17. F. M. Cross, Jr., "The Oldest Manuscripts from Qumran," *JBL* 74 (1955) 147-72; F. M. Cross and D. W. Parry, "A Preliminary Edition of a Fragment of 4QSam[b]

group of small fragments of 1 Sam. 25:30-32 and 2 Sam. 14:7-21; 14:22–15:4; 15:4-15, dated early 1st century B.C. and published by Ulrich.[18]

These biblical scroll and fragments diverge widely from the MT and, according to Cross,[19] are consistently close to what is reflected by LXX. So, it has been claimed that the LXX does actually reflect a different manuscript tradition and needs to be taken into account in textual criticism.

3. Cross's "Local Texts Theory"

Since these Qumran Samuel manuscripts are closer in detail to the LXX^L (Lucian) text[20] than to the text of the LXX^B, which preserves the oldest Greek translation (OG), Cross assumes the OG was at some point revised in accordance with Hebrew texts from Palestine, which were similar to the Qumran Samuel scrolls. Then the final stratum of the Lucian text tried to bring this text into harmony with the current Hebrew text, a forerunner of the MT.

Thus, he proposes a "local texts theory," taking this Palestinian text type to be a third tradition beside the Babylonian (MT) and the Egyptian (OG in LXX^B) text types.[21] However, recent studies by Aejmelaeus,[22] Saiz,[23] and Herbert[24] certainly cast significant doubt on Cross's theory that the proto-Lucianic recension was based on a 4QSam^a-like text.

(4Q52)," *BASOR* 306 (1997) 63-74. See also F. I. Andersen and D. N. Freedman, "Another look at 4QSam^b," *RQ* 14 (1989) 7-29; E. M. Cook, "1 Samuel xx 26–xxi 5 According to 4QSam^b," *VT* 44 (1994) 442-54.

18. E. C. Ulrich, Jr., "4QSam^c: A Fragmentary Manuscript of 2 Samuel 14–15 from the Scribe of the Serek Hay-yaḥad," *BASOR* 235 [= in *The Hebrew and Greek Texts of Samuel* (1980 Proceedings IOSCS — Vienna), ed. E. Tov, pp. 166-88] (1979) 1-25.

19. F. M. Cross, Jr., "A New Qumran Biblical Fragment Related to the Original Hebrew Underlying the Septuagint," *BASOR* 132 (1953) 15-26; "The Oldest Manuscripts from Qumran," *JBL* 74 (1955) 147-72; E. Tov, "The Textual Affiliation of 4QSam^a," *JSOT* 14 (1979) 37-53.

20. See E. Tov, "Lucian and Proto-Lucian: Toward a New Solution of the Problem," *RB* 79 (1972) 101-13; B. A. Taylor, *The Lucianic Manuscripts of 1 Reigns 1: Majority Text* (HSM 50; Atlanta: Scholars Press, 1992); *The Lucianic Manuscripts of 1 Reigns 2: Analysis* (HSM 51; Atlanta: Scholars Press, 1993).

21. For a summary of Cross's "Local texts" theory, see F. M. Cross, "The Evolution of a Theory of Local Texts," in *Qumran and the History of the Biblical Text*, ed. F. M. Cross and S. Talmon (Cambridge, Mass.: Harvard University Press, 1975), pp. 306-20; McCarter, pp. 7-8 and n. 15.

22. Aejmelaeus, "The Septuagint of 1 Samuel," in *VIII Congress of the IOSCS*, p. 112.

23. J. Busto Saiz, "The Antiochene Text in 2 Samuel 22," in *VIII Congress of the IOSCS*, p. 142.

24. E. D. Herbert, "4QSam^a and Its Relationship to the LXX: An Exploration in

4. Conventional Textual Criticism of 1-2 Samuel

Following his mentor Cross, McCarter reconstructs the text of Samuel eclectically. He thinks the MT tends to skip text and the Qumran-type text tends to expand it.[25] However, there are strong objections to the validity of such an eclectic text. One major one is that, unlike the case of the NT, there are not enough manuscript witnesses to reconstruct a primitive text of Samuel. Walters notes that at times there is no way to account for the readings based on textual evidence, and so decisions are made *ad sensum*.[26] Especially in the case of the Qumran texts, we really have only one manuscript ("scroll"), since only in the case of 4QSam^{a} can we be reasonably sure that we have what could be called a biblical text. The other two texts are so fragmentary that we cannot rule out that they are some type of paraphrase, similar to other biblical paraphrases that have been found.

As Tov summarizes, there are two theories among scholars concerning the original shape of the biblical text.[27] The first is the single original text hypothesis, accepted by the majority of scholars, including McCarter, Tov, R. Klein, and Stoebe. This position accepts the possibility that one of the readings was the original, even if it is often impossible to decide among textual variants. The second is the different pristine texts hypothesis, held by scholars such as Kahle, Barthélemy, Goshen-Gottstein, Talmon, Greenberg, and Walters.[28] This approach does not try to reach a single original text.[29]

When there is so little evidence, it is certainly wise not to jump to hasty generalizations. Nevertheless, the present writer holds that one of the available readings could be nearer to the original than the others. Though there is not enough evidence available now to make final decisions, it is also wise not to give up the possibility of approaching a more original text in the future. See further the commentary on 1 Samuel 11 and 17.

Stemmatological Analysis," in *IX Congress of the IOSCS, 1995,* ed. B. A. Taylor (Atlanta: Scholars Press, 1997), pp. 37, 44.

25. McCarter, p. 8.

26. S. D. Walters, "Review of P. Kyle McCarter, *I Samuel: A New Translation with Introduction, Notes, and Commentary* (AB 8; Garden City, N.Y.: Doubleday, 1980)," *JBL* 101 (1982) 437-38.

27. E. Tov, *Textual Criticism of the Hebrew Bible* (Minneapolis: Fortress, 1992), pp. 155-97.

28. S. D. Walters, "Hannah and Anna: The Greek and Hebrew Texts of 1 Samuel 1," *JBL* 107 (1988) 385-412.

29. For a combination of these two approaches, see J. Cook, "Hannah and/or Elkanah on Their Way Home (1 Samuel 2:11)? A Witness to the Complexity of the Tradition History of the Samuel Texts," *OTE* 3 (1990) 247-62.

B. NEW DEVELOPMENTS IN TEXTUAL STUDIES

1. Reconstructing the Qumran Text

In recent years scholars have been engaged in more scientific and objective studies of the text of the Qumran scrolls. Until recently no clear method had been developed for reconstructing the text of scrolls, and scholars had to use their judgment and common sense. However, this scholarly common sense can often be very subjective.

Herbert recently proposed measuring the average column width and the average letter widths for 4QSam[a] in order to reconstruct the text more objectively. The usefulness of this study is clear when one compares Herbert's work[30] with the most recent article by F. M. Cross and D. W. Parry.[31] While there is no way for a reader to check the latter's *ad hoc* remarks such as "spacing requires," "the reconstruction required by the limited space," "there is no room," and "this line is long," Herbert's method is empirical and open to the reader's scrutiny.[32]

2. LXX's Limitations

One should also not forget that the LXX is a translation and is itself not exempt from textual corruptions.[33] McCarter and others seem to go very easily to the ancient versions when they deal with difficult Hebrew texts. However, in many of the places where the LXX is clear and the MT very difficult, it is probably not because the translators worked from an "uncorrupted" text, but because the LXX translators were working from an MT-like text which they also found difficult, and they made their own best guess as to what it meant. After all, as translators they felt they had to produce meaningful Greek. Going to the LXX is often against the principle of *lectio difficilior,* that is, "the more difficult reading is to be preferred."

For example, the MT in 1 Sam. 1:24, *pārîm š*ᵉ*lōšāh,* usually translated as "three bulls," is often emended to mean "a three-year-old bull," based on

30. Herbert, *Reconstructing Biblical Dead Sea Scrolls.*

31. Cross and Parry, "A Preliminary Edition of a Fragment of 4QSam[b] (4Q52)," *BASOR* 306 (1997) 63-74.

32. See my review, D. T. Tsumura, "Review of Edward D. Herbert, *Reconstructing Biblical Dead Sea Scrolls: A New Method Applied to the Reconstruction of 4QSam*[a] (Leiden: E. J. Brill, 1997)," *JETS* 43 (2000) 315-16. On stemmatology, i.e., the study of the family tree of a text, see Herbert, "4QSam[a] and Its Relationship to the LXX," in *IX Congress of the IOSCS,* pp. 37-55, esp. on Fig. 1 (Stemma for 1 Sam 1–2 Sam 9). See below on 1 Sam. 20:27 for a concrete example.

33. See Caquot and de Robert, p. 11.

the LXX, 4QSam[a], and the Peshitta, because "three bulls" seem to be too much for the dedication of a little boy. However, the term *pārîm* here probably has the older meaning "younglings." So, the animals which Hannah brought to Shiloh were not necessarily adult "bulls," but the "younglings" of cows or sheep; see on 1 Sam. 1:24. Thus, it seems that it is incorrect in this case to emend the MT in the light of LXX and other versions. The primary task of exegetes of ancient texts, whether biblical or extra-biblical, is to interpret data in its original context, not to alter the data so that they can explain it easily.

3. Reevaluation of the MT

While it is often true that the LXX and other versions are sought out "only when the MT is unintelligible,"[34] many textual critics too easily give up seeking solutions to difficult and obscure passages in MT and turn to various ancient versions too soon. In recent years such an overemphasis on the LXX as against MT has been criticized by Barthélemy and his followers, notably Pisano, and others.[35] The most recent trend is a higher regard for the Masoretic tradition, as can be seen by comparing *BHQ* with previous editions.[36]

Compared with the days of S. R. Driver, a century ago, we have much more information about the ancient writing system and its cultural back-

34. T. J. Lewis, "The Textual History of the Song of Hannah: 1 Samuel II 1-10," *VT* 44 (1994) 18.

35. D. Barthélemy, "La qualité du texte massorétique de Samuel," in *The Hebrew and Greek Texts of Samuel (1980 Proceedings IOSCS — Vienna),* ed. E. Tov (Jerusalem: Academon, 1980), pp. 1-44; *Critique Textuelle de l'Ancien Testament I* (OBO 50/1; Fribourg: Éditions Universitaires, 1982); S. Pisano, *Additions or Omissions in the Books of Samuel: The Significant Pluses and Minuses in the Massoretic, LXX and Qumran Texts* (OBO 57; Freiburg: Universitätsverlag, 1984). See the review by R. P. Gordon, in *VT* 37 (1987) 383-84. See also G. L. Archer, "Reassessment of the Value of the Septuagint of 1 Samuel for Textual Emendation, in the Light of the Qumran Fragments," in *Tradition and Testament: Essays in Honor of Charles Lee Feinberg* (Chicago: Moody, 1981), pp. 223-40; A. A. Anderson, *2 Samuel* (WBC 11; Dallas: Word Books, 1989); D. G. Deboys, "1 Samuel xxix 6," *VT* 39 (1989) 214-19 on 1 Sam. 29:6; A. L. Warren, "A Trisagion Inserted in the 4QSam[a] Version of the Song of Hannah, 1 Sam. 2:1-10," *JJS* 45 (1994) 278-85 on 2 Sam. 2:2.

36. A sample volume of BHQ (= *Biblia Hebraica Quinta*) on Ruth (by Jan de Waard) was published in 1998; see H. P. Scanlin, "The Presupposition of HOTTP and the Translator," *BT* 43 (1992) 101-16. Note also that recently J. R. Lundbom, *Jeremiah 1-20: A New Translation with Introduction and Commentary* (AB 21A; Garden City, N.Y.: Doubleday, 1999), p. 62, concludes that in the case of Jeremiah, at least in chs. 1-20, it is "simply not the case" that the shorter text (LXX) is better than the MT. The recent commentary by Caquot and de Robert takes the MT as the best-preserved text.

ground. However, the correct reading is still lacking for many obscure passages in the MT Samuel. In some cases their obscurity is not due to the corrupted nature of the text but to phonetic spelling.

4. Scribal Errors or Phonetic Spellings?

Textual critics have a tendency to watch carefully the formal aspects of the text (i.e., shapes of letters, words spelt similarly, phrases, etc.) and often suggest that there were deliberate "corrections," but they often overlook phonological and grammatical features. The present author believes as a result of his study that many of the "scribal errors" in 1-2 Samuel suggested by textual critics may be in fact phonetic spellings or Hebrew grammatical constructions that have been misunderstood.[37]

For example, in 2 Sam. 22:40, the MT *wattazrēnî* וַתַּזְרֵנִי is usually taken to be corrupt. However, actually, the spelling probably reflects the phonetic realization of the word, that is, how it was actually pronounced, rather than a copyist's misreading. Since the form וַתְּאַזְּרֵנִי: *watt^{e}ʾazz^{e}rēnî* seems to be the original and normal form, as attested in Ps. 18:40 (MT) and 2 Sam. 22:40 (4QSam^{a}), the MT form might be explained as a *sandhi* spelling, as follows:

watt^{e}ʾazz^{e}rēnî
- (loss of the intervocalic aleph) → watt^{e}+azz^{e}rēnî
- (vowel *sandhi*)[38] → wattazz^{e}rēnî
- (shorter form) → wattazrēnî

Hence, there is no need to reckon the MT Samuel here as textually defective.[39]

Another example is the form *n^{e}mibzāh* in 1 Sam. 15:9, which many critics deem unintelligible. However, this form might be explained phonologically as follows:

Ni. ptc. f.s. nibzāh
- (*m*-glide) → nimbzāh —(anaptyxis)→ nimibzāh
- (vowel reduction) → *n^{e}mibzāh*

37. See D. T. Tsumura, "Scribal Errors or Phonetic Spellings? Samuel as an Aural Text," *VT* 49 (1999) 390-411.

38. I.e., the fusion of two adjacent vowels. See D. T. Tsumura, "Vowel sandhi in Biblical Hebrew," *ZAW* 109 (1997) 575-88.

39. See D. T. Tsumura, "Some Problems Regarding Psalm 18," *Exegetica* 3 (1992) 63 [Japanese with an English summary].

The form nibzāh, Ni. ptc. f.s. of *bzh ("to despise"), which is most suitable to the context, experienced a change of form by the insertion of an *m*-glide (cf. the insertion of a *p*-glide in *Sampson* from the original Samson)[40] and by the subsequent restructuring of the term. Thus, the spelling seems to reflect the actual pronunciation of the word, not a scribal error.

These examples[41] warn us against too easily emending the Hebrew texts when they look peculiar or even "unintelligible" to the eyes of a modern reader. A narrative like 1-2 Samuel could have been written, at least partly, as if it was heard or spoken. Therefore, one should take "aural" features of the narrative into consideration when spellings seem peculiar or even impossible.[42]

5. Idiomatic Expressions

A textual irregularity is also sometimes due to an idiomatic expression. For example, usually the verb *npl appears in the idiomatic phrase "Cast the lot(s)" *npl (Hi.) + *gôrāl.* But in 1 Sam. 14:42 *happîlû* "decide" (lit. "cause to fall") is used without the object noun. McCarter thinks that MT suffered a long haplography here. Such "text-critical" solutions miss the characteristics of linguistic phenomena such as brachylogy, which is an ellipsis of the noun (here, "lots") in an idiom (see below [VII, D]); so, the verb (here, *happîlû*) by itself retains the idiomatic meaning (here, "to decide").[43] Thus, students of the Hebrew text should be prepared to seek phonological and grammatical explanations of any unusual Hebrew forms, not just orthographic explanations.

When there is not enough evidence to draw the solid conclusion that the text is corrupt, the best thing to do is to leave the MT, an ancient artifact, unaltered, and to explain it with minimal speculation.

While there are passages where the MT still seems unintelligible in 1 Samuel, as 13:21 and 17:12, and several where the meaning seems strange, as 9:24; 13:1, 8; and 20:14, the present author feels he has shown in this commentary that the majority of proposed emendations are needless.

40. Note that the consonants *m, b,* and *p* are all pronounced at the same point of articulation, being bilabial.

41. Also, 1 Sam. 1:17; 10:7; 14:27, 32; 15:9; 2 Sam. 5:13; 21:9; 22:36, 40, 46; etc.

42. On the aural features of the text of 2 Sam. 22 in comparison with Ps. 18; see Tsumura, "Some Problems Regarding Psalm 18," 57-64; "Scribal Errors or Phonetic Spellings?" 390-411.

43. See on 1 Sam. 14:42.

III. DATE AND AUTHORSHIP

Scholars have long studied the problem of the authorship of the books of Samuel. To state the conclusion first, we do not know who wrote the books of Samuel. There is no explicit and objective evidence indicating the author. Since Samuel's death is mentioned in 1 Sam. 25:1 (also 28:3), the name "Samuel" was not intended to imply authorship. As discussed below, the books of Samuel seem to have been composed and edited in several stages. The "Story of the Ark of God" (1 Sam. 4:1–7:1) could have originated very early, even from the pre-Davidic era; others, such as the "Story of Saul and David" (1 Samuel 16–31) and the "Story of King David" (2 Samuel 1–20), must have been composed later, at the earliest during the early part of David's reign in Jerusalem and during the later part of David's reign or the Solomonic era, respectively. The final editing of 1-2 Samuel, with minor adjustments, was probably made no later than the late 10th century B.C. in view of 1 Sam. 27:6 ("Therefore Ziklag has belonged to the kings of Judah to this day"). See below for details.

A. THREE PUTATIVE SOURCES

In modern critical study,[44] some earlier scholars (e.g., Cornill 1885, 87, Budde 1890) saw two strata in the books of Samuel, an early, pro-monarchic source associated with the Pentateuchal "J" and a late, anti-monarchic source associated with "E," while the others, such as Smend and Eissfeldt,[45] saw also a third, "L" (= Lay). However, the difference between the pro-monarchic and anti-monarchic passages has been somewhat overemphasized (see on 1 Sam. 8:4-6a), and the existence of "J" and "E" sources in the Pentateuch, hence also in the Historical books, has become suspect these days.[46]

However, H. Gressmann's "fragmentary hypothesis," which claims that various short narrative units were eventually combined by an editor, has remained influential among scholars.[47] Rost's *Die Überlieferung von der*

44. For a useful summary of research, see Baldwin, pp. 20-32; R. P. Gordon, *1 & 2 Samuel* (OTG; Sheffield: JSOT Press, 1984); Caquot and de Robert, pp. 15-19; J. W. Flanagan, "Samuel, Book of 1-2," in *ABD,* V, pp. 957-65. For pre-modern Jewish and Christian interpretations, see Caquot and de Robert, pp. 12-14.

45. O. Eissfeldt, *The Old Testament: An Introduction,* trans. P. R. Ackroyd (New York: Harper and Row, 1965), p. 271.

46. See G. J. Wenham, *Genesis 1–15* (WBC 1; Waco, Tex.: Word Books, 1987), pp. xxx-xxxi.

47. See McCarter, p. 13. For an English translation of Gressmann's article, "The Oldest History Writing in Israel," see D. M. Gunn, ed., *Narrative and Novella in Samuel:*

Thronnachfolge Davids (1926)[48] also advocated the composite nature of the older materials. He isolated distinct and originally independent narrative sources within the early stratum — especially an old history of the succession to David in 2 Samuel 9–20 and 1 Kings 1–2 and an even more ancient "ark narrative" in 1 Sam. 4:1b–7:1 and 2 Samuel 6.

It is widely accepted that there were originally three major compositions before the final editing of 1-2 Samuel, though there are some differences in detail. However, actually, whether these proposed "blocks" ever existed as single works is still in doubt.

1. "Ark Narrative"

The so-called "Ark Narrative" (AN),[49] according to Rost, followed by many scholars, consists principally of 1 Sam. 4:1b–7:1 together with parts of 2 Samuel 6. However, the similarity in vocabulary and style between the two sections is not decisive to support his theory, as Miller and Roberts observe.[50] The same geographical place is referred to both as Kiriath-jearim (1 Sam. 6:21) and as Baalah of Judah (2 Sam. 6:2), and thus one can question whether 2 Samuel 6 was originally part of this narrative.[51] Moreover, in the latter story Yahweh and the ark are no longer the major actors; David "takes the initiative for transferring the ark to Jerusalem."[52] So, it is difficult to prove that these sections originally constituted a single story.

The story in 1 Samuel 4–6 is probably among the oldest compositions in the books of Samuel, because it does not envisage a royal cult in Jerusalem. It is possible that 1 Sam. 4:1–7:1 is from a source that was contemporary with Samuel, while 2 Samuel 6 is taken from a later, that is, early Davidic, source.

As Alter holds, the story "has to be read in the context of the compre-

---

Studies by Hugo Gressmann and Other Scholars, 1906-1923 (JSOTSS 116; Sheffield: Almond, 1991), pp. 9-58.

48. English translation: L. Rost, *The Succession to the Throne of David* (Sheffield: Almond, 1982).

49. For detailed discussions, see F. Schicklberger, *Die Ladeerzählung des ersten Samuel-Buches: Eine literaturwissenschaftliche und theologiegeschichtliche Untersuchung* (FB 7; Würzburg: Echter, 1973); A. F. Campbell, *The Ark Narrative (1 Sam 4-6; 2 Sam 6): A Form-Critical and Traditio-Historical Study* (SBLDS 16; Missoula, Mont.: Scholars Press, 1975).

50. P. D. Miller, Jr. and J. J. M. Roberts, *The Hand of the Lord: A Reassessment of the "Ark Narrative" of 1 Samuel* (JHNES; Baltimore: Johns Hopkins University Press, 1977), p. 23.

51. See R. P. Gordon, *1 & 2 Samuel,* pp. 32-34.

52. Miller and Roberts, *The Hand of the Lord,* p. 24.

hensive literary structure into which it has been integrated, whether by editorial ingenuity or by the allusive artistry of the author of the David story."[53] Certainly, the story of the "Ark of God" (4:1–7:1) is embedded into the "Story of Samuel" (1:1–7:17), while the other story of the ark, that in 2 Samuel 6, is placed there so as to fit in the context both chronologically and thematically. However, it has still not been proved that the AN as such ever existed as an independent composition.

2. "History of David's Rise"[54]

Many scholars believe there was originally an independent narrative "History of David's Rise" (HDR),[55] which is generally held to begin in 1 Samuel 15 or 16 and continue until 2 Samuel 5 or 7. Some think that this history itself is a composite. Most commentators say its purpose was to legitimatize King David, that is, to show that David's succession to Saul's throne was lawful. Certain passages such as David's sparing of Saul's life (1 Samuel 24 and 26), his reaction to the news of Saul's death (2 Samuel 1), and the deaths of Abner (ch. 3) and Ishbosheth (ch. 4) seem written or selected to emphasize that David was guiltless of murderous intentions towards Saul's house.

This might suggest that it was composed at a time when David's rule was being challenged, perhaps soon after the death of Solomon when the northern tribes were challenging Davidic national sovereignty.[56] Comparing it with the 13th century B.C. Hittite "Apology of Hattušiliš," McCarter even dates the earliest versions to the reign of David himself, that is, during the early part of the 10th century B.C., especially in the context of Shimei's rebellion (see 2 Sam. 16:7) and pro-Saulide sentiment.[57]

53. R. Alter, *The David Story: A Translation with Commentary of 1 and 2 Samuel* (New York: W. W. Norton, 2000), p. xi.

54. For a useful summary on this "narrative," see McCarter, pp. 27-30.

55. See D. M. Howard, Jr. on "David" in *ABD,* II, pp. 41-49. There is considerable disagreement among scholars concerning the beginning and the end of HDR. For various views, see Gordon, *1 & 2 Samuel,* pp. 61-63; J. C. VanderKam, "Davidic Complicity in the Deaths of Abner and Eshbaal: A Historical and Redactional Study," *JBL* 99 (1980) 521-22.

56. J. H. Grønbaek, *Die Geschichte vom Aufstieg Davids (1. Sam. 15–2. Sam. 5): Tradition und Komposition* (ATDa 10; Copenhagen: Prostant apud Munksgaard, 1971); T. N. D. Mettinger, *King and Messiah: The Civil and Sacral Legitimation of the Israelite Kings* (CB: OT Series 8; Lund: C. W. K. Gleerup, 1976), pp. 38-41.

57. P. K. McCarter, Jr., "The Apology of David," *JBL* 99 (1980) 489-504; McCarter, p. 29. A. van der Lingen, *David en Saul in I Samuel 16–II Samuel 5: Verhalen in Politiek en Religie* (Gravenhage: Uitgeverij Boekcentrum, 1983), also dates the story basically to the tenth century B.C. See also T. Ishida, *The Royal Dynasties in Ancient Israel: A Study on the Formation and Development of Royal-Dynastic Ideology* (BZAW

It is certainly possible that the section or story was written as political justification for the Davidic kingship during the time of David himself, especially since "a defense of the Davidic dynasty is conspicuously lacking."[58] However, this author would take 1 Samuel 16–31, rather than 1 Samuel 15/16–2 Samuel 5/-7, as a literary unit:[59] that is, the "Story of Saul and David," in which Saul is still a reigning king while David is rising toward his throne. To this, the "Story of King David" (2 Samuel 1–20) is linked by means of an episode about the report of Saul's death and David's elegy (2 Samuel 1), which functions as "a" of the A/aB pattern of the transitional technique; see below (Section VI, B). As Alter holds, to posit an independent story HDR may be "to do palpable violence to the beautiful integrity of the story as the probing representation of a human life."[60] In fact, in a recent study, Dietrich and Naumann support Ficker's view that HDR "probably never existed as a single work on its own but was conceived as an additional layer to the Succession Narrative."[61]

3. "Succession Narrative" or "Court History"?

Among the three putative extended sources, the "Succession Narrative" (SN),[62] that is, 2 Samuel 9–20 and 1 K. 1–2, has received the most scholarly scrutiny and acclaim on account of its high literary quality and presumed homogeneity and historical value.

Rost advocated the view that this section was a pro-Solomonic succession narrative written by an eyewitness not only to validate the Davidic monarchy but specifically to defend the accession of Solomon to the throne. However, scholars like Eissfeldt have taken it to be rather a "Court History" (CH).[63] They point out that the story of David and Bathsheba and the court

---

142; Berlin: de Gruyter, 1977); H. Tadmor, "Autobiographical Apology in the Royal Assyrian Literature," in *History, Historiography and Interpretation,* p. 56.

58. McCarter, p. 29.

59. Also Birch, p. 1094.

60. Alter, *The David Story,* p. xi.

61. W. Dietrich and T. Naumann, "The David-Saul Narrative," in *Reconsidering Israel and Judah: Recent Studies on the Deuteronomistic History,* ed. G. N. Knoppers and J. G. McConville (SBTS 8; Winona Lake, Ind.: Eisenbrauns, 2000), p. 313.

62. For a detailed discussion of the SN, see the "Introduction" to the second volume of this commentary. For a recent and comprehensive treatment, see T. Ishida, *History and Historical Writing in Ancient Israel: Studies in Biblical Historiography* (SHCANE 16; Leiden: E. J. Brill, 1999), pp. 102-85; also J. van Seters's rather unduly negative review of this book in *JAOS* 121 (2001) 505-6.

63. Eissfeldt, *The Old Testament: An Introduction,* pp. 137-39; see J. van Seters, *In Search of History: Historiography in the Ancient World and the Origins of Biblical History* (New Haven: Yale University Press, 1983), pp. 277-91.

intrigue scene in 1 Kings 1 hardly seem designed to prove Solomon's legitimacy as a successor.[64] In addition, there is no prophetic announcement of God's choice of Solomon in this section.

For Gunn[65] the CH is neither a succession narrative nor propaganda nor wisdom. It is a novel whose purpose is serious entertainment.[66] Similarly, from literary analytical perspectives, Ackerman says the CH was written by a true artist showing the complexity of life, with good and evil mingled in the characters, "a profound meditation on how life works, envisioning an intricate balance between human freedom and divine sovereignty."[67] Alter also questions "whether the succession to the throne is actually the central concern of this sequence of episodes."[68] He notes the works of J. P. Fokkelman, R. Polzin, and S. Bar-Efrat, which "illuminate the fine and complex interconnections among the various phases of the story of David, Saul, and Samuel."[69]

Yet those who take the narrative as "succession narrative" or "court history" usually treat the final four chapters of 2 Samuel, that is, chs. 21–24, as "Appendices," which interrupt the flow of historical narrative from 2 Samuel 20 to 1 Kings 1. To be sure, those four chapters provide materials that are not in a chronological order. 2 Samuel 21 mentions the incident of the sacrifice of Saul's seven sons for his blood-guilt against the Gibeonites (vv. 1-14) as well as David's encounters with the Philistine heroes (vv. 15-22). Chapter 22, a slightly different version of Psalm 18, is a thanksgiving psalm of David. 2 Sam. 23:1-7 is "the last words of David," while vv. 8-39 are a list of David's heroes, "the three" and "the thirty." The final chapter, 2 Samuel 24, refers to David's census and the subsequent plague as well as to the purchase of the threshing floor of Araunah the Jebusite for building an altar to Yahweh.

However, generally speaking, while an "appendix" implies a later addition to the main part, an "epilogue" constitutes a structurally integral part of the entire story. In fact, the final episode of purchasing Araunah's threshing floor prepares for the subsequent story of Solomon, who will build the temple for Yahweh at the very same place. As discussed later in Section VIII,

64. J. S. Ackerman, "Knowing Good and Evil: A Literary Analysis of the Court History in 2 Samuel 9–20 and 1 Kings 1–2," *JBL* 109 (1990) 55.

65. D. M. Gunn, "Traditional Composition in the 'Succession Narrative,'" *VT* 26 (1976) 214-29; *The Story of King David: Genre and Interpretation* (JSOTSS 6; Sheffield: JSOT Press, 1978).

66. On the literary character of the Narrative, see also C. Conroy, *Absalom, Absalom! Narrative and Language in 2 Sam 13–20* (AnBib 81; Rome: Pontifical Biblical Institute, 1978).

67. Ackerman, "Knowing Good and Evil," p. 59.

68. Alter, *The David Story,* p. xi.

69. Alter, *The David Story,* p. xii.

"Literary Structure and Themes," the epilogues in 2 Samuel 21–24 nicely correspond to 1 Samuel 1–2. It is most reasonable to take 2 Samuel 1–20 as a unified "Story of King David," with 2 Samuel 1 as the link to 1 Samuel.

In any history writing (i.e., historiography) the author must certainly select sources of information and put them in order for his own purpose. The author of Samuel must have had sources of information when he edited and wrote the historical narrative of 1-2 Samuel. However, he seems to present the entire book as a unified and cohesive piece of literature concerning the establishment of David's kingly throne. Thus, the issue is when the editing or "redacting" of this unified and cohesive piece of historical narrative was performed.

B. TWO RECENT APPROACHES

1. Noth's Hypothesis

In his *Überlieferungsgeschichtliche Studien* M. Noth advocated that a single person or persons compiled a continuous history of Israel from the time of the settlement of Canaan to the Babylonian exile, that is, the books of Joshua-Kings. He was not merely an editor, but the author of the history which is usually designated as the "Deuteronomistic history" (DH). According to Noth,[70] the Deuteronomistic historian(s) (Dtr) took over extensive collections of traditions available to him(them), such as the three narratives (AN, HDR, and SN/CH) mentioned above and traditions concerning Saul. Surprisingly, Noth considered Dtr's contributions in the case of 1-2 Samuel to be limited to 1 Samuel 7–8, 12, part of ch. 10, 2 Sam. 5:6-12, and some chronological notes. Noth's view and the recent emphasis on the holistic approach are taken up in Polzin's study,[71] in which he takes the entire 1-2 Samuel as written by one author/redactor during the exilic period.

Against Noth, Cross advocates two editions of the Deuteronomistic history, mainly based on the treatment of Josiah in the books of Kings. He says that since Josiah is portrayed as a second David who reactivates the dynastic promise, the first edition originated in the reign of Josiah (ca. 640-609

70. M. Noth, *Überlieferungsgeschichtliche Studien: Die sammelnden und bearbeitenden Geschichtswerke im Alten Testament* (Tübingen: Niemeyer, 1943; 2d ed. 1957); *The Deuteronomistic History,* trans. J. Doull et al. (JSOTSS 15; Sheffield: Sheffield Academic Press, 1981). For a useful summary and analysis of Noth's view and many new directions, see G. N. Knoppers's "Introduction" in *Reconsidering Israel and Judah,* pp. 1-18.

71. R. Polzin, *Samuel and the Deuteronomist: A Literary Study of the Deuteronomic History, Part II: 1 Samuel* (Bloomington: Indiana University Press, 1989).

B.C.), and the second, in the Exilic era (ca. 550 B.C.).[72] Other scholars also have suggested two or more stages for compiling the Deuteronomistic history.[73] Some scholars posit a stage of a prophetic revision before the Deuteronomic redaction(s).[74] Still more recently, Caquot and de Robert, who doubt the existence of a prophetic redaction, have proposed three stages of composition, that is, one by Abiathar, one by a Zadokite author, and one by an exilic Deuteronomist.[75]

But on what grounds are parts of Samuel considered to have been written or redacted by a Josiah or post-Josiah Deuteronomist (circle) or by others? One ground is the use of language considered to be Deuteronomistic. However, when we look at the individual phrases, we have no reason to suggest that they are so late. That a phrase occurs in certain unquestionably later passages does not automatically mean it could not have been used earlier.

For example, the phrase "to this day" is often taken as "Deuteronomistic" in 2 K. 8:22 and 16:6. However, the phrase is used in 1 Sam. 6:18b,

> As for the great platform of Abel on which they laid the ark of the Lord, it is in the field of Joshua the Bethshemeshite until this day,

72. F. M. Cross, Jr., *Canaanite Myth and Hebrew Epic* (Cambridge, Mass.: Harvard, 1973), pp. 274-89. His view has been accepted by R. G. Boling, *Judges: A New Translation with Introduction and Commentary* (AB 6A; Garden City, N.Y.: Doubleday, 1975); R. D. Nelson, *The Double Redaction of the Deuteronomistic History* (JSOTSS 18; Sheffield: JSOT Press, 1981).

73. E.g., R. Smend, "Das Gesetz und die Völker: Ein Beitrag zur deuteronomistischen Redaktionsgeschichte," in *Probleme biblischer Theologie (Gerhard von Rad volume),* ed. H. W. Wolff (Munich: C. Kaiser, 1971), pp. 494-50; T. Veijola, *Die ewige Dynastie: David und die Entstehung seiner Dynastie nach der deuteronomistischen Darstellung* (Annales Academiae Scientiarum Fennicae Series B 193; Helsinki: Suomalaisen tiedeakatemian kustantama, 1975); W. Dietrich, *Prophetie und Geschichte: Eine redaktionsgeschichtliche Untersuchung zum deuteronomistischen Geschichtswerk* (FRLANT 108; Göttingen: Vandenhoeck und Ruprecht, 1972); *David, Saul und die Propheten: Das Verhältnis von Religion und Politik nach den prophetischen Überlieferungen vom frühesten Königtum in Israel* (Stuttgart: W. Kohlhammer, 1987).

74. E.g., A. Weiser, *Samuel: seine geschichtliche Aufgabe und religiöse Bedeutung: Traditionsgeschichtliche Untersuchungen zu 1 Samuel 7–12* (FRLANT 81; Göttingen: Vandenhoeck und Ruprecht, 1962); McCarter, pp. 18-23; B. C. Birch, *The Rise of the Israelite Monarchy: The Growth and Development of I Samuel 7–15* (SBLDS 27; Missoula, Mont.: Scholars Press, 1976; W. E. Evans, "An Historical Reconstruction of the Emergence of Israelite Kingship and the Reign of Saul," in *Scripture in Context II: More Essays on the Comparative Method,* ed. W. W. Hallo, J. C. Moyer, and L. G. Perdue (Winona Lake, Ind.: Eisenbrauns, 1983), pp. 61-77.

75. Caquot and de Robert, pp. 19-20.

which probably goes back to the pre-Davidic time, for the description of the field as belonging to "Joshua the Bethshemeshite" here (also v. 14) is more meaningful to the contemporary readers of the story of the ark than to the post-Exilic readers. In fact, this part of the story of the ark seems to be earlier than the Davidic era (see on 1 Sam. 4–6). On the other hand, 1 Sam. 27:6 ("Therefore Ziklag has belonged to the kings of Judah to this day") seems to have been written early in the Divided Monarchy, probably during the early days of Rehoboam's era, not later than the late 10th century B.C., for after Shishak's campaign (925 B.C.) the city would not have belonged to Judah; see the commentary on this verse. Therefore, the use of the phrase "to this day" should not automatically be taken to mean that the passages are "Deuteronomistic."

In Gen. 47:26 as well as in 1 Sam. 30:25, certain legal customs were said still to be in force at the time of the narrator. The phrase *from the day when I brought them up from Egypt to this day* (1 Sam. 8:8) refers to the entire past history of Israel, from their beginning as the covenant people until now, that is, to the time of Samuel. In fact this phrase is a widely used expression in the Bible and appears most often in historical narratives including Chronicles.[76] The Israelites surely had used such an expression in reviewing their own history from time to time ever since they settled in the "present" location. So, if the "Deuteronomist" could have used this expression, Samuel himself could have also. It should be noted that the phrases *adi inanna, adi anni, adi enna, adi akanni, adi udīna* "until now" are frequent in Akkadian literature from Old Babylonian times.[77] See also the comments on 1 Sam. 7:3; 29:3, 8.

Some other expressions, such as "to abandon Yahweh" and "to serve other gods," though sometimes argued as being instances of "Deuteronomistic interpolation,"[78] are not necessarily characteristically "Deuteronomistic" expressions. For one thing, "to abandon" *(ʿzb)* and "to serve" *(ʿbd)* are a word pair in the Hebrew Bible,[79] like the pair "to abandon" (*ʿzb) and "to worship" (Hišt. *ḥwh), which appears in Judg. 2:12; 1 K. 9:9; 11:33; 2 K. 17:16; Jer. 1:16; 16:11; 22:9; 2 Chr. 7:19, 22. These word pairs could have been used by any biblical author.

Moreover, some expressions that had been considered typically "Deuteronomistic" occur also in other parts of the Old Testament and have turned up in the ancient Near Eastern literature from much earlier times. For

76. The phrase *to this day* (*ʿad-hayyôm hazzeh;* i.e., "until now") appears 84 times: Gen. (4), Exod. (1), Num. (1), Deut. (6), Josh. (16), Judg. (7), 1 Sam. (9), 2 Sam. (4), 1 K. (5), 2 K. (9), Isa. (1), Jer. (9), Ezek. (1), Ezra (1), Neh. (1), 1 Chr. (5), 2 Chr. (4).

77. See *CAD,* A/1 (1964), pp. 119-20.

78. McCarter, p. 157.

79. It appears in Josh. (2x), Judg. (4x), 1 Sam. (2x), K. (2x), Jer. (3x), and Chr. (4x).

example, the expression **ntn byd* "to give (deliver) into the hand (of)" as in 1 Sam. 14:12 appears frequently in the "Deuteronomistic history" but also appears in other parts of the Old Testament: for example, Gen. 14:20; Ex. 23:31; Num. 21:34; Ezek. 7:21; Ps. 106:41; Neh. 9:27; 2 Chr. 16:8. The same expression appears also in the Amarna letters (14th century B.C.) and in a building inscription of Nebuchadnezzar II (6th century B.C.).[80] So, any biblical author from any time could use the expression, and there is no reason why it could not have been used early. For the "early" terms in Samuel, see below (Section III, C, 5).

Thus, the conventional theories of "redaction" rest on questionable assumptions concerning the nature of language, often overlook the real situation of languages and styles, and treat the language of the Bible too mechanically. Much of the reasoning seems circular. Certain passages are taken as normative and late, and any similar ideas or words in apparently earlier works were written or interpolated at that later time. What is really needed is more research into the methods of composition and recensions and the historiography of the ancient Near Eastern and Greek historians.[81] Before surveying the recent development on historiography and making tentative conclusions on authorship and date, let us survey the recent history of the holistic literary approaches.

2. Holistic Literary Approaches

During the second half of the 20th century, and especially since the 1970s, scholarly interest has been moving away from historical-critical study.[82] Instead of isolating units and tracing compilation and redaction processes, scholars are more and more concerned with the themes and final forms of the canonical text and with the relationship between the texts and the social world that yielded them. In fact, the trend has moved so far that many scholars who are engaged in literary-rhetorical study have almost no interest in history at all.

This shift initially came about under the influence of linguist F. de Saussure's emphasis on synchrony and by the application of "structuralism" to literary criticism, which resulted in an anti-historical tendency and an em-

80. B. Albrektson, *History and the Gods: An Essay on the Idea of Historical Events as Divine Manifestations in the Ancient Near East and in Israel* (Lund: CWK Gleerup, 1967), p. 39.

81. B. O. Long, "Review of Richard D. Nelson, *The Double Redaction of the Deuteronomistic History* (JSOT Sup. 18; Sheffield: JSOT Press, 1981)," *JBL* 102 (1983) 455.

82. See especially R. Polzin, *Moses and the Deuteronomist: A Literary Study of the Deuteronomic History, Part 1* (New York: Seabury, 1980).

phasis on holistic, as opposed to analytical, interpretation of texts. Such literary approaches are therefore not very concerned with "date and authorship" problems, since literary analyses by themselves cannot date sources or determine their historicity, that is, spatio-temporal reality. However, we cannot fully understand a text unless we know the starting point for the authors and redactors, their languages, conventions, and genres, and our knowledge of these depends upon historical research.[83]

a. The So-Called New Literary Criticism

Dissatisfied with the historical critical attempts to account for discrepancies by postulating different sources or editorial additions, scholars since the 1970s have emphasized the "close reading" of the biblical text as it stands. Gunn,[84] Jobling,[85] Fokkelman,[86] Sternberg, Eslinger, and others[87] focus solely on the text of Samuel in its final form, though they use different perspectives and methods to approach the text.

Gunn's (1980) work on the Saul story, *The Fate of King Saul,* is one of the most important of the earlier works which apply literary criticism to bib-

83. On the failure of Biblical scholarship to engage with contemporary humanistic scholarship, see R. Polzin, "1 Samuel: Biblical Studies and the Humanities," *RSR* 15 (1989) 297-306.

84. Gunn, *The Story of King David; The Fate of King Saul* (JSOTSS 14; Sheffield: JSOT Press, 1980).

85. D. Jobling, *The Sense of Biblical Narrative: Three Structural Analyses in the Old Testament (I Samuel 13–31, Numbers 11–12, I Kings 17–18)* (JSOTSS 7; Sheffield: JSOT Press, 1978); see also his most recent study, *1 Samuel* (Berit Olam: Studies in Hebrew Narrative & Poetry; Collegeville, Minn.: Liturgical Press, 1998).

86. J. P. Fokkelman, *Narrative Art and Poetry in the Books of Samuel: A Full Interpretation Based on Stylistic and Structural Analysis,* vol. I: *King David (II Sam. 9–20 & I Kings 1–2)* (SSN 20; Assen: Van Gorcum, 1981); vol. II: *The Crossing Fates (I Sam. 13–31 & II Sam. 1)* (SSN 23; Assen: Van Gorcum, 1986); vol. III: *Throne and City (II Sam. 2–8 & 21–24)* (SSN 27; Assen: Van Gorcum, 1990); vol. IV: *Vow and Desire (I Sam. 1–12)* (SSN 31; Assen: Van Gorcum, 1993). His detailed analysis of the Samuel texts is typical of a structuralist approach, lacking in any historical perspective; see Polzin, "1 Samuel," *RSR* 15 (1989) 301-3.

87. M. Sternberg, *The Poetics of Biblical Narrative: Ideological Literature and the Drama of Reading* (Bloomington: Indiana University Press, 1985); L. Eslinger, *Kingship of God in Crisis: A Close Reading of 1 Samuel 1–12* (BLS 10; Sheffield: Almond, 1985), applies "New Criticism" to 1 Sam. 1–12; also L. Eslinger, "Viewpoints and Points of View in 1 Samuel 8–12," *JSOT* 26 (1983) 61-76. Also see Polzin, *Samuel and the Deuteronomist;* M. Garsiel, *The First Book of Samuel: A Literary Study of Comparative Structures, Analogies and Parallels* (Jerusalem: Rubin Mass, 1990 [orig. 1983, 1985]); W. Brueggemann, "Narrative Coherence and Theological Intentionality in 1 Samuel 18," *CBQ* 55 (1993) 225-43.

lical narrative and emphasize "a closer look" at the biblical story. While many of the scholars of this type come up with interpretations completely separated from the original historical-cultural setting, Gunn does try to combine the literary and historical spheres. But he probably moves too far away from the writer's world. With the publication of R. Alter's *Art of Biblical Narrative* in 1981, the literary approach "reordered priorities so that biblical texts were examined in their final context as a literary whole,"[88] without rejecting diachronic methods. Alter is not completely free from the assured "fact" resulting from the diachronic approaches, as seen in his treatment of "two different creation stories" in Gen. 1:1–2:4a ("P") and 2:4bff. ("J").[89] However, it has been an axiom of structural linguistics and literary studies since de Saussure's work that a synchronic approach, which deals with the text as it stands, should have a priority over a diachronic approach.

Fokkelman's massive four-volume work on 1-2 Samuel is a formalistic and fully synchronic approach to the text as it stands, without trying to go behind the text. He too emphasizes holistic interpretations of the text, but with some psychologizing and an allegorizing tendency, occasionally suggesting, in Polzin's words, "what is supposed to be happening within Saul's sub- or unconscious."[90] Sternberg also takes a similar position, according to which all texts are structured with coherence and every utterance presupposes a "speaker" who has in mind an implicit addressee and a goal to be achieved by the address.[91] These scholars are, broadly speaking, taking a structuralist ap-

88. T. Longman, III, "Literary Approaches to Old Testament Study," in *The Face of Old Testament Studies: A Survey of Contemporary Approaches,* ed. D. W. Baker and B. T. Arnold (Grand Rapids: Baker Books, 1999), p. 98. See also his earlier work, *Literary Approaches to Biblical Interpretation* (Foundations of Contemporary Interpretation 3; Grand Rapids: Zondervan, 1987).

89. R. Alter, *The Art of Biblical Narrative* (London: George Allen & Unwin, 1981), p. 141. See, however, D. T. Tsumura, "Genesis and Ancient Near Eastern Stories of Creation and Flood: An Introduction," in *"I Studied Inscriptions from Before the Flood": Ancient Near Eastern, Literary, and Linguistic Approaches to Genesis 1–11,* ed. R. S. Hess and D. T. Tsumura (SBTS 4; Winona Lake, Ind.: Eisenbrauns, 1994), pp. 27-30.

90. Polzin, "1 Samuel," *RSR* 15 (1989) 303. Note that Fokkelman's "metaphorical reading" would see the "two climaxes in Samuel's life" in the dual form of the place-name *Ramathaim* (1 Sam. 1:1; lit. "two heights"). See Fokkelman, IV (1993), p. 8, n. 18.

91. Sternberg's theory of "gapping" is fully utilized by V. P. Long on 1 Sam. 13; see V. P. Long, *The Reign and Rejection of King Saul: A Case for Literary and Theological Coherence* (SBLDS 118; Atlanta: Scholars Press, 1989); "How Did Saul Become King? Literary Reading and Historical Reconstruction," in *Faith, Tradition, and History: Old Testament Historiography in Its Near Eastern Context,* ed. A. R. Millard, J. K. Hoffmeier, and D. W. Baker (Winona Lake, Ind.: Eisenbrauns, 1994), pp. 280-84; *The Art of Biblical History* (Grand Rapids: Zondervan, 1994), pp. 214-23. But see the commentary on 1 Sam. 13:9.

proach, in which, as Longman summarizes, "the meaning of a text is found not in the author's intention but in the text's conventional code."[92]

b. Post-modern/Post-structuralist Approach

In the late 1980s and 1990s, studies in 1-2 Samuel were not immune to influence by post-modern hermeneutics, which has declared authors irrelevant and "meaning" meaningless. What is important is what the readers past and present have made of the text.[93]

Miscall[94] takes a typically post-modern approach to the biblical narratives and accepts the multivocal and polysemous quality of the text and hence does not admit any "correct" interpretation. This post-modern approach is characterized by *deconstruction* and *intertextuality.*[95] According to him, one aim of deconstruction is "the questioning of metaphysical thought — the attempt to undermine it and its founding concepts, particularly the ubiquitous use of conceptual dyads (Gasché) or dichotomies that present themselves as hierarchies, that is, one pole is granted privilege and primacy, while the other is considered secondary and irrelevant."[96] At the same time, he sees almost any similarity as significant. For example, he sees in Jonathan's warning to David to stay "in a secret place" (1 Sam. 19:2) an intertextual association with 2 Sam. 12:12, a foreshadowing of the relationship between David and Bathsheba "in a secret place" (2 Sam. 12:12).[97] His approach to the text well illustrates the deconstructive analysis associated with the work of J. Derrida.

Derrida, the formulator of post-modernism,[98] emphasizes the "intertextual" associations among the elements of the text and the literary traditions in the society where it was produced, with the post-modern claims for relativity, multivalency, and indeterminacy. According to Lyke, interpretation is not attained by "univocal readings," that is, what the author or redactor intends the

92. Longman, "Literary Approaches to Old Testament Study," p. 104.

93. On the "reader-response approach," see Longman, "Literary Approaches to Old Testament Study," pp. 105-7.

94. P. D. Miscall, *The Workings of Old Testament Narrative* (Semeia Studies; Chico, Calif.: Scholars Press, 1983); *1 Samuel: A Literary Reading* (Bloomington: Indiana University Press, 1986).

95. Jobling, *1 Samuel,* p. 11.

96. Miscall, *1 Samuel: A Literary Reading,* p. xx.

97. Miscall, *1 Samuel: A Literary Reading,* p. 96. A similar "intertextual" association is expressed with regard to David's baggage left with the equipment keeper (1 Sam. 17:22) in his comment: "Would Saul have been hiding in the baggage? 10:22"; see Birch, p. 1110.

98. C. G. Bartholomew, "Babel and Derrida: Postmodernism, Language and Biblical Interpretation," *TynB* 49 (1998) 305-28; T. J. Keegan, "Biblical Criticism and the Challenge of Postmodernism," *BibInt* 3 (1995) 1-14, esp. 3.

texts to mean, but by "multiple readings" which accrue over an extended period of time, since "the texts represent the social and communal process of articulating core idioms and conceptualizations."[99] However, while intertextuality can be intended by later writers or editors, it should be distinguished from diachronic approaches such as typology and allusions. It is fully synchronic without any intention of discussing the text's author or origin.[100]

If this is carried to its logical conclusion, however, one might wonder how one is supposed to know what other people have thought of a certain text, or indeed of anything, if when one reads what they said about it one cannot determine what they intended to say. In biblical studies, intertextuality ignores how the author intended his text to be understood, an all-significant concern, especially for biblical hermeneutics.[101] What is needed is the "competence" to read the biblical text in its original cultural and historical settings, the ancient Near East, and to notice its uniqueness and then to consider its meaning for today.

To be sure, a literary-rhetorical approach can be useful in viewing the text that we have without having to base our work on hypotheses about the pre-history, and some controlled intertextuality could become a useful method of exegesis. Moreover, to pay attention to literary strategy in the narrative would advance our "theological understanding of the text."[102] However, for the Hebrew text, as for all foreign and ancient texts, it is only when one has first analyzed it linguistically in its immediate context and learned as much as possible about the historical background that one can appreciate the content of the story properly.

C. HISTORIOGRAPHY

In studies of the Historical Books such as 1-2 Samuel, recently scholarly concern has focused on how history was written (i.e., historiography) rather

99. See L. L. Lyke, *King David with the Wise Woman of Tekoa: The Resonance of Tradition in Parabolic Narrative* (JSOTSS 255; Sheffield: Sheffield Academic Press, 1997), p. 192.

100. See B. D. Sommer, "Exegesis, Allusion and Intertextuality in the Hebrew Bible: A Response to Lyle Eslinger," *VT* 46 (1996) 479-89.

101. See, for example, F. Watson, *Text and Truth: Redefining Biblical Theology* (Edinburgh: T. & T. Clark, 1997), ch. 3; see D. T. Tsumura, "Review of Larry L. Lyke, *King David with the Wise Woman of Tekoa: The Resonance of Tradition in Parabolic Narrative* (JSOTSS 255; Sheffield: Sheffield Academic Press, 1997)," *Themelios* 24/3 (1999) 48-49.

102. W. Brueggemann, "Narrative Coherence and Theological Intentionality in 1 Samuel 18," *CBQ* 55 (1993) 243.

than what actually happened (i.e., historicity). Such a shift of focus from historicity to historiography has been a notable trend in the scholarly world for the last twenty years. M. Brettler explains this as "a movement from history in the sense of a reconstruction of the past to history as a narrative which is influenced by its authors' religious and political ideologies."[103] Thus, literary and rhetorical concerns, rather than historical concerns, are the focus of studies of 1-2 Samuel.

According to Rainey, in the 1980s OT scholarship wasted much of its time explaining away the Israelites as former Canaanite peasants.[104] But in the 1990s, it appears that the new fashion was explaining away the monarchies of the United Kingdom and any records that may have survived from then.[105] In other words, the historicity, not just the historiography, of the books of Samuel became the hottest issue in recent scholarship.

In particular, the historicity of David and Solomon has been questioned[106] because there is no extra-biblical evidence for them. This "minimalist" approach[107] to the history of Israel denies any biblical statement for which there is no extra-biblical evidence. Thus, the existence of an Israelite state during the 10th century B.C. has been denied. Davies[108] even denies that there was a Josianic reform and discounts incidents such as Jehu's seizure of power in 841 B.C. and Shishak's campaign in 925 B.C. despite the existence of an Egyptian monument referring to the latter. Such agnostic attitudes to history are in keeping with the "post-modern" approach to literature in general, as noted in the preceding section.

Moreover, any accounts that show literary traits tend to be considered unhistorical. Provan[109] notes that recent historiographies, such as those by

103. M. Z. Brettler, *The Creation of History in Ancient Israel* (London: Routledge, 1995), p. 3 [= V. P. Long, ed., *Israel's Past in Present Research: Essays on Ancient Israelite Historiography* (Winona Lake, Ind.: Eisenbrauns, 1999), p. 44]. See also van Seters, *In Search of History,* ch. 7 ("Israelite Historiography"), pp. 209-48.

104. For a helpful survey of OT historiographical studies in the 1980s, see E. Yamauchi, "The Current State of Old Testament Historiography," in *Faith, Tradition, and History,* pp. 21-25.

105. A. F. Rainey, "Uncritical Criticism," *JAOS* 115 (1995) 101-4.

106. On the historicity of King Solomon, see A. Millard, "King Solomon in His Ancient Context," in *Age of Solomon: Scholarship at the Turn of the Millennium,* ed. L. K. Handy (Leiden: E. J. Brill, 1997), pp. 30-53.

107. For example, see V. Fritz and P. R. Davies, eds., *The Origins of the Ancient Israelite States* (JSOTSS 228; Sheffield: Sheffield Academic Press, 1996); also see B. Halpern, "Erasing History: The Minimalist Assault on Ancient Israel," *BR* 11, no. 6 (1995) 26-35, 47.

108. P. R. Davies, *In Search of Ancient Israel* (JSOTSS 148; Sheffield: Sheffield Academic Press, 1992).

109. I. W. Provan, "Ideologies, Literary and Critical: Reflections on Recent Writ-

Whitelam and Thompson, are distinguished by the characterization of previous scholarship as compromised by ideology, and by the marginalization of the biblical texts. These historiographies claim that "the creative art" of the authors and the late date of the texts prevent them from giving information about "the 'real' world of the past." Provan questions[110] this recent assumption that narrative shaped by literary and ideological considerations is somehow less worthy of consideration as source material for modern historiographers than other sorts of data from the past. He also questions the assertion that traditions are not useful sources of information about the past.

Recently there has been a debate or "quarrel" between W. Dever and K. Whitelam. According to Dever, Whitelam claims that there is almost nothing we can know about the early history of Israel.[111] D. Jobling explains the situation as follows:

> Dever is working more as an archaeologist, Whitelam more as an ideological critic, and these roles tend to produce mutual suspicion. What Whitelam is rejecting is not the possibility of writing a history along Dever's lines but rather certain outmoded assumptions in the writing of history. . . . Both are interested in the new systemic kind of history, though from different perspectives.[112]

Both historicity (what actually happened) and historiography (how the history is written) are very crucial problems, especially in the studies of 1-2 Samuel.

1. Problems of the Historicity of David

In 1993 David-denying historians received a jolt. A late-9th-century Aramaic inscription was discovered at Tel Dan containing the phrase *bytdwd.*[113] This is most probably to be read as "the House of David," despite the dissenting voices of Davies and others, and thus for the first time the name "David" has

---

ing on the History of Israel," *JBL* 114 (1995) 585-606; "The End of (Israel's) History? K. W. Whitelam's *The Invention of Ancient Israel:* A Review Article," *JSS* 42 (1997) 284.

110. Provan, "The End of (Israel's) History?" 289.

111. W. Dever, "The Identity of Early Israel: A Rejoinder to Keith W. Whitelam," *JSOT* 72 (1996) 3-24; K. W. Whitelam, "Prophetic Conflict in Israelite History," *JSOT* 72 (1996) 25-44.

112. Jobling, *1 Samuel,* pp. 17-18, n. 21.

113. See A. Biran and J. Naveh, "An Aramaic Stele Fragment from Tel Dan," *IEJ* 43 (1993) 81-98; "The Tel Dan Inscription: A New Fragment," *IEJ* 45 (1995) 1-18; A. Biran, "Sacred Spaces: Of Standing Stones, High Places and Cult Objects at Tel Dan," *BAR* 24 (1998) 38-45, 70; A. Lemaire, "The Tel Dan Stela as a Piece of Royal Historiography," *JSOT* 81 (1998) 3-14; most recently translated by A. R. Millard, in *CS,* II, pp. 161-62.

been attested.[114] This inscription furnishes epigraphic evidence that in the late 9th century surrounding countries knew that the southern dynasty was founded by "David" and was named after him, as many other dynasties were named after their founders. It shows that he was not just a figment of the imagination of someone who lived centuries later.[115] Line 31 of the "Mesha Stela" may contain another 9th-century reference to the "House of David" if Lemaire's recently proposed reading *b(y)t-[d]wd* is correct.[116] Furthermore, Kitchen calls scholars' attention to a possible reference to "highland/heights of David" in the Egyptian name list of Shoshenq I (ca. 924 B.C.).[117] This would be the earliest attestation of David, "barely 50 years after his death."

2. Comparative and Contextual Approach

Archaeological discoveries have tended to be misused, whether for proving or for disproving the accuracy of the Bible. However, while archaeology does not necessarily prove the Bible, it often illuminates or illustrates it.[118] Also, even though it may not prove that a biblical text is from a particular date, it may be able to show that an early date is not impossible. For example, see the arguments for an early date for the "Ark Narrative" (Miller and Roberts),[119] for the "History of David's Rise" in the light of the Apology of Hattusilis (McCarter),[120] and for the "Succession Narrative" in the light of Esarhad-

114. See K. A. Kitchen, "A Possible Mention of David in the Late Tenth Century BCE, and Deity *Dod as Dead as the Dodo?" *JSOT* 76 (1997) 29-44.

115. W. W. Hallo, "New Directions in Historiography (Mesopotamia and Israel)," in *dubsar anta-men: Studien zur Altorientalistik: Festschrift für Willem H. Ph. Römer,* ed. M. Dietrich and O. Loretz (AOAT 253; Münster: Ugarit-Verlag, 1998), pp. 109 and 122.

116. A. Lemaire, "'House of David': Restored in Moabite Inscription," *BAR* 20 (1994) 30-37.

117. Kitchen, "A Possible Mention of David in the Late Tenth Century BCE," *JSOT* 76 (1997) 42; "Egyptians and Hebrews, from Ra'amses to Jericho," in *The Origin of Early Israel — Current Debate: Biblical, Historical and Archaeological Perspectives: Irene Levi-Sala Seminar, 1997,* ed. S. Aḥituv and E. D. Oren (Beer-Sheva: Ben-Gurion University of the Negev Press, 1998), p. 100.

118. K. A. Kitchen, *Ancient Orient and Old Testament* (Chicago: Inter-Varsity Press, 1966), p. 153. There has been an ongoing debate recently over the relationship between archaeology and the Bible; e.g., the negative view toward the use of archaeology for biblical studies as seen in T. L. Thompson, "Historiography of Ancient Palestine and Early Jewish Historiography: W. G. Dever and the Not So New Biblical Archaeology," in *The Origins of the Ancient Israelite States,* pp. 26-43, as against the more positive views as those in B. Halpern, "The Construction of the Davidic State: An Exercise in Historiography," in *The Origins of the Ancient Israelite States,* pp. 44-75.

119. See above; also on 1 Sam. 5.

120. See above; also on 1 Sam. 16.

don's Apology (Ishida).[121] Redaction critical scholars often say that the idea of an "eternal dynasty" in 2 Samuel 7 is postexilic.[122] Yet, according to Laato, early Assyrian royal building inscriptions from around the time of David refer to such a concept, and so it is entirely possible that it "played an important role in Israelite royal ideology already during the time that David planned to build a Temple for Yhwh."[123]

C. H. Gordon notes that both the OT and Homer's works are the culmination of long literary development in the East Mediterranean milieu. In fashioning the Homeric epics, the creative poet could choose and use existing material and shape it to create a masterpiece.[124] Likewise, we can assume that 1-2 Samuel was composed as the culmination of long literary development which incorporated earlier works such as "the Book of Jashar" (2 Sam. 1:18; also in Josh. 10:13), just as the Pentateuch quotes "the Book of the History of Man" (Gen. 5:1) and "the Book of the Wars of Yahweh" (Num. 21:14).[125]

Here, we need to consider comparative studies of ANE historiographies, for Israelite historiography after all is an ANE historiography, just as Hittite historiography is.[126] In the 1960s C. H. Gordon argued convincingly for the use of both comparison and contrast to illuminate the entire Near Eastern context.[127] Kitchen and Hallo have also demonstrated the importance of the same comparative and contextual approach to the Bible.[128] In contrast

121. See T. Ishida, "The Succession Narrative and Esarhaddon's Apology: A Comparison," in *Ah, Assyria . . . Studies in Assyrian History and Ancient Near Eastern Historiography Presented to Hayim Tadmor,* ed. M. Cogan and I. Eph'al (Jerusalem: Magnes Press, 1991), pp. 166-73; also H. Tadmor, "Autobiographical Apology in the Royal Assyrian Literature," in *History, Historiography and Interpretation,* pp. 36-57.

122. For example, van Seters, *In Search of History,* pp. 271-77.

123. A. Laato, *A Star Is Rising: The Historical Development of the Old Testament Royal Ideology and the Rise of the Jewish Messianic Expectations* (Atlanta: Scholars Press, 1997), p. 40. See also Ishida, *History and Historical Writing in Ancient Israel,* pp. 137-50 on "Nathan's prophecy," whose purpose, Ishida holds, is to confirm the legitimacy of Solomon's kingship.

124. C. H. Gordon, *The Common Background of Greek and Hebrew Civilizations* (New York: W. W. Norton, 1965), pp. 225-26.

125. Gordon, *The Common Background,* p. 226.

126. See H. M. Wolff, "The Apology of Ḫattušiliš Compared with Other Political Self-Justifications of the Ancient Near East" (Unpublished Ph.D. dissertation, Brandeis University, 1967); H. A. Hoffner, Jr., "Propaganda and Political Justification in Hittite Historiography," in *Unity and Diversity: Essays in the History, Literature, and Religion of the Ancient Near East,* ed. H. Goedicke and J. J. M. Roberts (Baltimore: Johns Hopkins, 1975), pp. 49-62; C. H. Gordon, *The Common Background,* p. 7.

127. C. H. Gordon, *The Ancient Near East* (New York: W. W. Norton, 1965).

128. K. A. Kitchen, *The Bible in Its World: The Bible and Archaeology Today* (Exeter: Paternoster Press, 1977); C. D. Evans, W. W. Hallo, and J. B. White, eds., *Scrip-*

to the "minimalist view" represented by T. L. Thompson, P. R. Davies, and others, Hallo is a "maximalist" because he says "the historian of antiquity has no alternative but to use every scrap of evidence available."[129] It seems obvious we should make full use of these precious pieces of evidence from the ancient Near East, not so much because they can prove that the Bible is true but because they can illuminate and illustrate the biblical account of Israel and her history.

3. Methodological Principles

A major problem with "proving" the Bible is that, like most events of the past, much of the content is of the type that leaves no remains. Furthermore, much physical evidence has been lost forever, and much has not yet been excavated. With regard to archaeological evidence, one should keep in mind the following principle: "The absence of evidence is not evidence of absence."[130]

Some historians claim that the "religious" nature of the biblical historical narrative automatically makes it "unhistorical," but biblical authors are not the only ancient record-makers to refer to gods. For example, the Assyrian kings such as Tiglath-pileser I believed that their gods were active in the world and referred to this activity in their inscriptions. Also, in the Mesha Stele and the Zakir Inscription, historical reminiscences refer to both divine and human activities. Yet modern historians use these inscriptions to determine the history of the ancient Near East.[131] Cogan says: "a specific

---

ture in Context: Essays on the Comparative Method (Pittsburgh: Pickwick Press, 1980); W. W. Hallo, J. C. Moyer, and L. G. Perdue, eds., *Scripture in Context II: More Essays on the Comparative Method* (Winona Lake, Ind.: Eisenbrauns, 1983). See also Hallo's recent significant efforts in W. W. Hallo, ed., *The Context of Scripture,* vol. I: *Canonical Compositions from the Biblical World* (Leiden: E. J. Brill, 1997); *The Context of Scripture,* vol. II: *Monumental Inscriptions from the Biblical World* (Leiden: E. J. Brill, 2000).

129. Hallo, "New Directions in Historiography," in *dubsar anta-men,* p. 122; also see "Biblical History in Its Near Eastern Setting: The Contextual Approach," in *Scripture in Context,* pp. 1-26. On the historiographical validity of the biblical text, see A. R. Millard, "Story, History, and Theology," in *Faith, Tradition, and History,* pp. 37-64; "King Solomon in His Ancient Context," in *Age of Solomon: Scholarship at the Turn of the Millennium,* ed. L. K. Handy (Leiden: E. J. Brill, 1997), pp. 30-53; K. A. Kitchen, "New Directions in Biblical Archaeology: Historical and Biblical Aspects," in *Biblical Archaeology Today, 1990: Proceedings of the Second International Congress on Biblical Archaeology: Jerusalem, June-July 1990* (Jerusalem: Israel Exploration Society, 1993), pp. 34-52; Yamauchi, "The Current State of Old Testament Historiography," in *Faith, Tradition, and History,* pp. 1-36.

130. Kitchen, *Ancient Orient and Old Testament,* pp. 30-32; Yamauchi, "The Current State of Old Testament Historiography," in *Faith, Tradition, and History,* pp. 34-36.

131. Millard, "Story, History, and Theology," in *Faith, Tradition, and History,* pp.

event may be presented in one case as divine intervention, in another as human action."[132]

4. History Writing in the ANE

Scribes in Assyria and Babylonia kept "some sort of running records"[133] or "diaries"[134] of important events. It is possible that they wrote the Babylonian Chronicles and Assyrian Eponym Chronicles on the basis of these records. Millard thinks that they probably kept their logbooks on wooden tablets (Hebrew *lūaḥ)* covered by wax. (These have now disintegrated, but there are reliefs of scribes using them, and some ivory tablets still exist.)[135] By analogy, there were probably Hebrew sources many generations old on wax or papyrus that could have been used by Hebrew historians.

Millard[136] points out that the Assyrian royal inscriptions use the same style over centuries. For example, phraseology used in the "annals" of king Tiglath-pileser I (*ca.* 1100 B.C.) is used with minor variation in the monuments of Sargon II four hundred years later, and in the "annals" of Sargon's successors Sennacherib and Ashurbanipal. Thus, here one certainly cannot claim that because certain phraseology appeared in "late" sources, any source with that phraseology must be late. The "Deuteronomistic" style has many parallels to the Assyrian royal inscriptions. In the same way, it seems mistaken to claim that just because certain "Deuteronomistic" phrases appear in undeniably late Hebrew texts, any text containing these phrases must have been written about the same time.[137]

5. Linguistic Data and Dating of Texts

Besides noting the historiographical practices in the neighboring countries, linguistic study of the Hebrew text itself may shed light on "date and author-

---

53-54; R. P. Gordon, "Who Made the Kingmaker? Reflections on Samuel and the Institution of the Monarchy," in *Faith, Tradition, and History,* p. 256.

132. M. Cogan, "A Plaidoyer on behalf of the Royal Scribes," in *Ah, Assyria . . . Studies in Assyrian History,* p. 126. Note also A. Millard, "On Giving the Bible a Fair Go," *Buried History: Quarterly Journal of the Australian Institute of Archaeology* 35/4 (1999) 8.

133. Millard, "King Solomon in His Ancient Context," in *Age of Solomon,* pp. 49-51.

134. Cogan, "A Plaidoyer on behalf of the Royal Scribes," in *Ah, Assyria . . . Studies in Assyrian History,* p. 127.

135. See *ANEP,* fig. 803.

136. Millard, "King Solomon in His Ancient Context," in *Age of Solomon,* pp. 49-51.

137. See above on "criticism" of redaction theories.

ship" problems. Avi Hurvitz compared some words and expressions in "P" and Ezekiel and succeeded in showing that the "P" words were older.[138] On the same principle, one can gain some insight by comparing the language of Samuel with that of postexilic literatures. There are several probably early terms that can be understood with the help of Ugaritic or Akkadian, but which have caused trouble with translators or critics ever since. If Samuel was really written or "redacted" by a postexilic "Deuteronomistic historian(s)," one wonders why he used certain terms which must have become obsolete by that time.

We offer some examples here.

ḥămôr leḥem (1 Sam. 16:20) "one ass-measure of bread"

The term *ḥămôr,* literally "ass," has usually been emended to one of the measurements, "omer" or "homer." However, the word is better explained as a loan translation (or calque) of the Akkadian dry measurement term *imēru,* literally, "ass."[139] A postexilic "redactor" would not have used such an obsolete term of measurement in this dramatic story since by his days the term "homer" had become the standard word for measurement.[140] The Greek translator in the 3rd or 2nd century B.C., who took it as "omer," evidently did not understand this by then already archaic term.

ṣemed (1 Sam. 14:14) "one yoke-measure"

The term *ṣemed* in the phrase "a yoke of field" is a unit of area measure equivalent to the Akkadian *ṣimdu,* which was reckoned as "1 day's seeding with the seeder plow" in the Kassite-NB system.[141] The term may have been an early Akkadian loanword and had nothing to do with a yoke of oxen when it entered the Hebrew vocabulary. 1 Sam. 14:14 would mean "in about a half of a plowing field, namely, a *yoke* of field." It is usually translated as "acre" (also in Isa. 5:10). McCarter thinks that the MT is "plainly corrupt" and unnecessarily omits this part of the verse.[142]

Several more examples will be briefly mentioned. In 1 Sam. 1:24 *pār*

138. A. Hurvitz, *A Linguistic Study of the Relationship Between the Priestly Source and the Book of Ezekiel: A New Approach to an Old Problem* (CRB 20; Paris: J. Gabalda, 1982).

139. From LB (ca. 1600) on, the "assload" *(imēru)* was the most commonly attested capacity system in northern Mesopotamia; see *RlA* 7, p. 499; D. T. Tsumura, "*ḥămōr leḥem* (1 Sam xvi 20)," *VT* 42 (1992) 412-14.

140. See M. Powell, "Weights and Measures" in *ABD,* VI, pp. 897-908, especially "E. Capacity. 1. OT Capacity Measures."

141. See *RlA* 7, p. 482.

142. Following S. R. Driver, pp. 108-9.

may have an older meaning of "youngling" rather than "bull." In 1 Sam. 2:13 *naʿar* seems to have the meaning of a "young" or "offspring," rather than a "servant." Also *sēper* is used for "letter" (epistle) in 2 Sam. 11:14 instead of the LBH word *ʾiggeret*.[143] For more on all of the above words, see the commentary.

These early words suggest that the author was writing in an early period, much earlier than exilic or postexilic times. While the oldness of these terms does not necessarily indicate early redaction, if they had become obsolete by the time of redaction, the redactor would have modernized them, especially such measurement terms as "an ass-measure," replacing it with "homer." The fact that the redactor/editor kept using those "old" terms indicates that he was editing the narrative probably from the time of the early monarchic period.

6. Tentative Conclusions

In the light of the above, I tentatively suggest that individual sections in 1-2 Samuel, such as the "Story of Samuel" (1 Samuel 1–7), the chapter on the introduction of monarchy (ch. 8), the "Story of Saul" (chs. 9–15), the "Story of Saul and David" (chs. 16–31), and the "Story of King David" (2 Samuel 1–20), as well as the Epilogues (chs. 21–24), existed during the era of the United Monarchy before the entire book was edited into a unified whole.

Moreover, it is possible that the "Story of Samuel," in which the ancient story of "the Ark of God" (4:1–7:1) was embedded, and the transitional chapter which includes the "Right of the King" (1 Sam. 8:11-18) came from the early time of Samuel's ministry, while the "Story of Saul" (chs. 9–15) came from a later time of Samuel's era. The "Story of Saul and David," which deals with the tension and contrast between Saul and David, was probably composed during the early part of David's era when David still needed to justify his kingship as divinely ordained in response to the Saulide family. The "Story of King David" in 2 Samuel 1–20 must have come from the later part of his reign (or the early part of Solomon's), since the principal purpose of the story is probably "to acquit David of charges of serial murder," as Halpern argues.[144]

The final editors presumably did "no more with the inherited narrative

143. See A. Hurvitz, "The Historical Quest for 'Ancient Israel' and the Linguistic Evidence of the Hebrew Bible: Some Methodological Observations," *VT* 47 (1997) 311-14.

144. B. Halpern, "Erasing History," p. 47; "Text and Artifact: Two Monologues?" in *The Archaeology of Israel: Constructing the Past, Interpreting the Present,* ed. N. A. Silberman and D. Small (JSOTSS 237; Sheffield: Sheffield Academic Press, 1997), pp. 311-41.

than to provide some minimal editorial framing and transition (far less than in the book of Judges) and to interpolate a few brief passages," as R. Alter holds.[145] Therefore, the major responsibility of the final editors was to combine the already existing stories and the "Epilogues" into a unified whole, not simply adding the "Appendices," as is often advocated. They probably worked around a time not later than the late 10th century, that is, the early period of Rehoboam's reign, in light of the comment "Therefore Ziklag has belonged to the kings of Judah to this day" in 1 Sam. 27:6. Certainly, one does not need wait many generations to compile a history of the period. A generation or two[146] after the death of the founder of a dynasty is certainly a reasonable time for an official historian(s) to write its history. However, this view remains hypothetical. There is much variation in the redaction theories, especially as to which sections are assigned to which sources. Dividing sources is made even more difficult by the frequent use of "transitional techniques" (see below, Section VI, B) between sections.

Early in the last century Gressmann[147] suggested that while history writing might be easily transformed into saga with the aid of a good imagination, in the time of David the historical narrative was given added depth along the line of novella. A half century later C. H. Gordon, comparing David's elegy in 2 Sam. 1:17-27 with the 13th-century Ugaritic epic of Aqhat, posits the origin of Hebrew historiography in the epic traditions which reached their height under David. He says:

> The Hebrews achieved true historical composition by transferring human values from the epic to current events. In reading the account of the Battle of Gilboa, we see that while the political and military developments are mentioned, the real interest is in the fate of Saul and Jonathan, and in how their fate affected the hero David.[148]

Such history writing did not have to wait in ancient Israel until the appearance of 7th-century or postexilic "Deuteronomistic" historian(s).

For a detailed discussion of 2 Samuel 7 and its place in the Hebrew historiography, see the "Introduction" to my commentary on 2 Samuel.

145. Alter, *The David Story,* p. xii.

146. R. Alter recently wrote: "If . . . the bulk of the story was actually composed within a generation or two, or perhaps three, after the reported actions, it is hard to imagine how such encompassing national events as a civil war between the house of Saul and the house of David, the Davidic campaigns of conquest east of the Jordan, and the usurpation of the throne by Absalom with the consequent military struggle, could have been invented out of whole cloth" (Alter, *The David Story,* p. xvii).

147. Gunn, ed., *Narrative and Novella in Samuel,* pp. 15-16.

148. Gordon, *The Ancient Near East,* pp. 166-67; also p. 181.

IV. HISTORICAL AND RELIGIOUS BACKGROUND

The historical background of the books of Samuel is known from two sources, the Old Testament and archaeological findings. Historiography helps us use the biblical material correctly, and archaeology gives us data with which to develop historiographical understanding and on which to base judgments. For the study of the Bible, comparative and contextual approaches to the biblical and ancient Near Eastern literatures are very important and useful. In the case of Samuel, archaeology can give information especially about the Philistines and the Canaanites.

The books of Samuel deal with a transitional period in the history of ancient Israel — the transition, first, from the priest Eli to the judge Samuel, then from the judge Samuel to the king Saul, then from Saul to David, who founded the dynasty which would last as long as the kingdom of Judah. The prophet Samuel thus functions as the link between the judgeship and the kingship. The kingdom of Saul was "transitional."[149] It was more than a loose confederation which gathered together when there was a common threat, but it was not a period of strong central rule such as existed later. Then, the story of the rise of David in 1 Samuel 16–31 prepares the reader for the full kingship of David in 2 Samuel.[150]

A. EARLY IRON AGE, CA. 1200-1000 B.C.

The Early Iron Age was, according to B. Mazar, "a historically-momentous period of transformations in the ethnic, social and cultural character of the populations"[151] in the East Mediterranean, and many small kingdoms (e.g., Israel, Moab, Ammon, Edom) were formed, no longer under the control of the great empires of the preceding period, such as the Egyptian and Hittite. Especially in this part of the ancient world, "the fateful transition" occurred at the end of the 13th century and beginning of the 12th century B.C., that is, at the change from LB to the Iron Age, which brought about a complete change in Canaan. Ancient Israel witnessed also the transition from the city-states of Canaan to the (United) Monarchy.[152]

149. C. H. Gordon and G. A. Rendsburg, *The Bible and the Ancient Near East,* 4th ed. (New York: W. W. Norton, 1997), p. 184.

150. On the topic of "kingship," see the introduction to the second volume of this commentary.

151. B. Mazar, *Biblical Israel: State and People,* ed. S. Ahituv (Jerusalem: Magnes Press, 1992), p. 11.

152. See the recent article on this period: Elizabeth Bloch-Smith and Beth Alpert

One of the major factors in this change was the so-called Sea Peoples,[153] who migrated from the Aegean, the realm of the Mycenaean civilization, to the coasts of Anatolia and Syria-Palestine. One of the groups, the biblical Philistines,[154] settled in southern Palestine ca. 1200 B.C., establishing city-states, as they did also in Phoenicia.

This period was characterized by the introduction of iron into daily life. In the ancient Near East smelted iron had appeared by the 3rd millennium B.C., but iron objects were still "noteworthy" in LB,[155] though references to both iron religious objects and iron weapons such as daggers and knives can often be noted from 16th-century Hittite texts.[156] However, it was not until ca. 1200 B.C. that iron technology influenced every phase of life. With this as the historical background, the First Book of Samuel begins.

B. ISRAEL AND THE PHILISTINES[157] IN PHILISTIA

While some hold that the Sea Peoples came from western Anatolia, Wolf-Dietrich Niemeier suggests that they came from "the Mycenaeanized Aegean

---

Nakhai, "A Landscape Comes to Life: The Iron I Period," *NEA* 62 (1999) 62-92, 101-27 [with good bibliography and charts].

153. Most recently, see E. D. Oren, ed., *The Sea Peoples and Their World: A Reassessment* (UMM 108, University Museum Symposium Series 11; Philadelphia: University of Pennsylvania Museum, 2000).

154. See K. A. Kitchen, "The Philistines," in *POTT,* pp. 53-78; D. M. Howard, Jr., "Philistines," in *POTW,* pp. 231-50.

155. A. R. Millard, "King Og's Bed and Other Ancient Ironmongery," in *Ascribe to the Lord: Biblical and Other Studies in Memory of Peter C. Craigie,* ed. L. Eslinger and G. Taylor (Sheffield: Sheffield Academic Press, 1988), p. 487.

156. See P. R. S. Moorey, "The Craft of the Metalsmith in the Ancient Near East: The Origins of Ironworking," in *From Gulf to Delta and Beyond,* ed. E. D. Oren (Beer-Sheva 8; Beersheva: Ben-Gurion University of the Negev Press, 1995), p. 59.

157. For useful introductions to the Philistines, see T. Dothan and M. Dothan, *People of the Sea: The Search for the Philistines* (New York: Macmillan, 1992); N. Bierling, *Giving Goliath His Due: New Archaeological Light on the Philistines* (Grand Rapids: Baker, 1992); Howard, "Philistines," in *POTW,* pp. 231-50. Also Kitchen, "The Philistines," in *POTT,* pp. 53-78; B. Mazar, "The Philistines and the Rise of Israel and Tyre," in *The Early Biblical Period: Historical Studies,* ed. A. Ahituv and B. A. Levine (Jerusalem: Israel Exploration Society, 1986), pp. 63-82; C. S. Ehrlich, *The Philistines in Transition: A History from ca. 1000–730 BCE* (SHCANE 10; Leiden: E. J. Brill, 1996). The study of the Philistines and their culture has been rekindled recently by the excavations at Ekron and other Philistine cities. See S. Gitin, A. Mazar, and E. Stern, eds., *Mediterranean Peoples in Transition: Thirteenth to Early Tenth Centuries BCE: In Honor of Professor Trude Dothan* (Jerusalem: Israel Exploration Society, 1998).

(probably via Cyprus)."[158] Margalith even tries to identify the homeland of the Philistines as the province of Pylos in Greece. Two of the cities of Pylos, A-pe-ke-e and Asiatia, were "centres of metalworkers and armourers."[159] See on "Aphek" the commentary at 1 Sam. 4:1.

Arriving in East Mediterranean areas, those immigrants from the sphere of Mycenaean traditions culturally assimilated to the native Canaanite population.[160] T. Dothan concludes: "Philistine material culture lost its uniqueness when the Philistines reached the peak of their prosperity and their political and military power at the end of the 11th century B.C.E. This period was one in which older Aegean traditions were abandoned, not only at Ekron but in the rest of Philistia, and new cultural influences, primarily Egyptian and Phoenician, took their place."[161]

The Philistines had probably adopted the native Canaanite language for communication in southern Palestine right after their settlement.[162] Moreover, it is possible that the Philistines had also adopted "the fully standardized Phoenician alphabet of twenty-two letters," as the Greeks did around 1100 B.C.[163] First, the Philistines established three coastal city-states, Gaza, Ashdod and Ashkelon. Later, Gath and Ekron in the Shephelah (the Lowland) were added to them, thus establishing a pentapolis, a confederation of five cities in the Philistine Plain.

158. W.-D. Niemeier, "The Mycenaeans in Western Anatolia and the Problem of the Origins of the Sea Peoples," in *Mediterranean Peoples in Transition,* pp. 17-65. See also A. Mazar, "The Emergence of the Philistine Material Culture," *IEJ* 35 (1985) 105-6; Mazar, *Biblical Israel,* pp. 13-14.

159. O. Margalith, "Where Did the Philistines Come From?" *ZAW* 107 (1995) 107.

160. The earlier "Philistines" in the Patriarchal days had Semitic names such as Abimelech, though the non-Semitic name Phicol is still preserved for a captain (Gen. 21:22). Note that these "Philistines" were distinct from those who confronted Saul and David. The former were friendly to Abraham and dwelt around Gerar and had not organized a pentapolis as in the later time. No later author of the Iron Age would depict the Philistines like this. The term "Philistines" itself might be "a thirteenth- to twelfth-century term used of an earlier Aegean group such as the Caphtorim by the narrator"; see Kitchen, "The Philistines," in *POTT,* p. 56.

161. On the cultural assimilation, see Kitchen, "The Philistines," in *POTT,* pp. 69-70.

162. See J. Naveh, *Early History of the Alphabet: An Introduction to West Semitic Epigraphy and Palaeography,* 2d rev. ed. (Jerusalem: Magnes Press, 1987), pp. 175-86. But see also A. R. Millard, "The Canaanite Linear Alphabet and Its Passage to the Greeks," *Kadmos* 15 (1976) 130-44.

163. T. Dothan, "Tel Miqne-Ekron: The Aegaean Affinities of the Sea Peoples' (Philistines') Settlement in Canaan in Iron Age I," in *Recent Excavations in Israel: A View to the West,* ed. S. Gitin (Dubuque, Iowa: Archaeological Institute of America, 1995), p. 53.

The purpose of the Philistines in extending control in Canaan was not only to dominate the native inhabitants and to exact corvée and taxes, but also to control the vital overland routes by establishing military posts and garrisons (see 1 Sam. 13:3; 2 Sam. 23:14).[164]

For details on the location of the Philistine cities, see the commentary at the following passages: 1 Sam. 6:17 (Gaza); 5:1 (Ashdod); 6:17 (Ashkelon); 5:8 (Gath); and 5:10 (Ekron).

During the period of Judges, the Philistines were one of Israel's major enemies (Judg. 3:3, 31; 13:5; 14:4). They especially appear in the stories of Samson (Judges 14–16), which are probably set in the 12th century. Later, about the mid-11th century B.C., the Philistines won a major conflict with Israel during the time of Eli (1 Sam. 4:1-10).

1. Samuel and the Philistines

After this victory at Ebenezer (near Aphek in the Sharon Valley), the Philistines were able to use the road into the Ephraim mountains and secured their domination of the *Via Maris.* Then, in 1 Sam. 7:7-11, Samuel gained a victory over the Philistines near Mizpah in the southern mountains of Ephraim. On the historical background of the emergence of the monarchy in Israel, see the commentary on 1 Samuel 8.

2. Saul and the Philistines

Before and during the reign of Saul the Philistines established their garrisons at strategic points (see 1 Sam. 10:5 on *Gibeath-elohim*) and on the main roads (1 Sam. 13:17; 14:15). When necessary, they could send a *mašḥit,* a military unit that included chariots, to aid a garrison. In this way they could control and tax large areas. They also could conscript units from the subjugated population (1 Sam. 14:21). However, Saul conquered the Philistine fortress at Geba in 1 Sam. 13:3 and brought Philistine domination in the territory of Benjamin to an end.

At least at the end of the 11th century B.C., the Philistines had a monopoly on iron metallurgy.[165] What the Philistines did, however, was to prevent Israelite craftsmen from learning the new skills, though presumably

164. Mazar, "The Philistines and the Rise of Israel and Tyre," in *The Early Biblical Period,* p. 73; Mazar, *Biblical Israel,* p. 34.

165. J. D. Muhly, "How Iron Technology Changed the Ancient World and Gave the Philistines a Military Edge," *BAR* 8, no. 6 (Nov./Dec. 1982) 40-54. See the recent article, Moorey, "The Craft of the Metalsmith in the Ancient Near East," in *From Gulf to Delta and Beyond,* pp. 53-68. Also, Millard, "King Og's Bed" in *Ascribe to the Lord,* pp. 481-92.

they continued working in bronze.[166] Thus, they subjugated the Israelites economically; see 1 Sam. 13:19-21. The Philistine military organization and the quality of their weapons were superior to those of the Israelites; see on Goliath's weapons in 1 Samuel 17. The Philistine material culture was highly developed with well-planned urban centers. It was prosperous, and they increasingly imported goods from Egypt, Phoenicia, and Cyprus.[167] It may be that David learned something of Philistine military and administrative techniques during his stay in Gath and Ziklag; see 1 Samuel 27–30.

Saul seems to have been successful in the hill country, but his troops could not win a battle in the open plain. In 1 Samuel 23 the war shifted from the mountains to the lowland Shephelah, which was the border between the Israelite towns and Philistia proper. Then, in 1 Samuel 28–31, the Philistines attacked Israel from bases in the Jezreel Valley on the Via Maris and destroyed the Israelite army and killed King Saul on Mt. Gilboa.

3. David and the Philistines

"Achish"[168] in 1 Sam. 27:2 employed the ancient tactic of "divide and rule" by supporting David against the House of Saul in Israel.[169] But then, when David became king, he was able to defeat the Philistines and control territory in the northern plain and in the Jezreel Valley and large sections along the Via Maris. He captured the cities of Dor, Megiddo, and Beth-shean. Thus, he broke Philistine military, political, and economic power over Israel, though he could not destroy the major cities on the southern coast.

David used mercenaries such as the Cherethites, Pelethites, and Gittites (2 Sam. 15:18). All these peoples were either Philistine or closely related Aegean groups.

Those Philistines were certainly "uncircumcised," but they were not the uncultivated and unsophisticated people that medieval Europe once thought them to be.[170] They had a highly developed technology and civilization when Saul and David were confronted by them around the 11th and 10th centuries B.C.

166. A. R. Millard, personal communication.

167. Mazar, *Biblical Israel,* p. 36.

168. On the name or title "Achish," see the Ekron Inscription (*CS,* II, p. 164); see on 21:11.

169. See Mazar, "The Philistines and the Rise of Israel and Tyre," in *The Early Biblical Period,* pp. 74-75.

170. Modern dictionaries list as the first meaning of "Philistine" "a person who is unreceptive to or hostile towards culture, the arts, etc.; a smug boorish person," before the meaning of a proper noun "Philistine"; see *Collins Dictionary of the English Language,* 2d ed. (London: Collins, 1986), p. 1152.

C. CANAAN AND THE CANAANITES

Study of the land of Canaan and its culture[171] is vital for understanding the background of the Old Testament. Hebrew is a branch of the Canaanite languages, and classical Hebrew has strong affinities in language and literary form with other Canaanite languages of the Iron Age. Israelites early on adopted the Canaanite-Phoenician alphabetic script[172] for writing their literature. (During or after the Exile, however, they adopted the Aramaic form of the alphabet, the "square" letters, which was used in the Persian empire. This script was used in the Dead Sea Scrolls — except for the name of God, which was written in the old script — and developed into the modern "Hebrew script.") For the background of Samuel, an understanding of Canaanite religion is important because of its influence on Israel, both through the Canaanites and through the Philistines, who had become assimilated to Canaanite religion and culture.

For example, the "Witch of Endor" story clearly mirrors many Canaanite ideas.[173] Such practices in the cult of the dead have been elucidated in detail in recent years with the help of religious and liturgical texts from ancient Ugarit and other places. The names of gods and goddesses in 1-2 Samuel such as Baal, Astarte, and Dagon also are all known from those "Canaanite" documents.

1. Canaanite Religion

As will become evident below, the influence of Canaanite religion,[174] especially of Baal worship, had been strong, at least on the popular level, ever since the Israelite people came and lived in the land of Canaan. Ugaritic and Akkadian documents from the LB city-state of Ugarit as well as Akkadian texts from Emar provide rich sources for understanding religious life in pre-Israelite Canaan, though strictly speaking these cities were geographically not located in Canaan.[175] Evidence from southern Canaan is meager because texts were written on perishable papyrus or parchment.

171. See A. R. Millard, "The Canaanites," in *POTT,* pp. 29-52; K. N. Schoville, "Canaanites and Amorites," in *POTW,* pp. 157-82.

172. See Naveh, *Early History of the Alphabet,* pp. 65-78. The earliest known example of alphabetic script is now attested from Wadi el-Ḥol of the mid-Nile as early as ca. 1900 B.C. See the 1998-99 season report of the *Theban Desert Road Survey,* by J. C. Darnell (Cairo: Supreme Council for Antiquities in Egypt, 1999), pp. 108-11 and 122.

173. Gordon and Rendsburg, *The Bible and the Ancient Near East,* p. 190, n. 16.

174. See, for example, A. Caquot and M. Sznycer, *Ugaritic Religion* (Leiden: E. J. Brill, 1980); J. Day, "Religion of Canaan," in *ABD,* I, pp. 831-37.

175. On Ugarit and its significance for the Old Testament study, see, for example,

Since religious traditions do not change quickly and were probably somewhat "homogeneous"[176] throughout Syria-Palestine, this northern LB evidence from Ugarit and Emar sheds valuable light on the Canaanite religious practices at the beginning of the Iron Age, that is, the period of 1-2 Samuel, though it would be subject to correction should evidence be found from more southern sites.

2. The Canaanite Pantheon

In pre-Israelite Canaan, the sky, the earth, the sea, the sun, the moon, and other natural entities were deified. There were many gods, but they were ranked. The "official" pantheon list from the city of Ugarit (*KTU* 1.47 and 118 [= RS 24.264 and 24.280]//RS 20.24), which is known from several copies and in several languages, that is, Ugaritic, Akkadian, and Hurrian, lists some thirty gods and goddesses in a particular order. Because the Ugaritic system is the Canaanite one about which we have the most evidence, below we will describe some of its features.

a. Divine Ancestor (ilib)

At the top of the Ugaritic pantheon list is *ilib,* "the divine ancestor," the ancestor *par excellence,* which means that ancestor worship was of greatest importance among their religious activities. The same is possibly true on the popular level in Israel during the period of 1-2 Samuel.[177] One text (*KTU*

P. C. Craigie, *Ugarit and the Old Testament* (Grand Rapids: Eerdmans, 1983). For translations of Ugaritic myths and legends, see *CS,* I, pp. 241-358. On Emar, see *CS,* I, pp. 427-43; D. E. Fleming, "More Help from Syria: Introducing Emar to Biblical Study," *BA* 58 (1995) 139-47.

176. According to W. F. Albright, during MB-LB ages, "the civilization of Phoenicia, southern Syria and Palestine was quite homogeneous"; see W. F. Albright, *Yahweh and the Gods of Canaan* (Garden City, N.Y.: Doubleday, 1969), p. 111. Also see the following comment by W. G. Lambert: "The area of roughly the modern Syria and Lebanon was, it seems, more or less homogeneous in religion over the second half of the third millennium," in the "Postscript," added to the reprinted article, "A New Look at the Babylonian Background of Genesis," *JTS* 16 (1965) 287-300, in *Babylonien und Israel: Historische, religiöse und sprachliche Beziehungen,* ed. H.-P. Müller (Darmstadt: Wissenschaftliche, 1991), pp. 112-13; also Hess and Tsumura, eds., *"I Studied Inscriptions from before the Flood,"* p. 110.

177. See, for example, T. J. Lewis, *Cults of the Dead in Ancient Israel and Ugarit* (HSM 39; Atlanta: Scholars Press, 1989); B. B. Schmidt, *Israel's Beneficent Dead: Ancestor Cult and Necromancy in Ancient Israelite Religion and Tradition* (Tübingen: J. C. B. Mohr, 1994). The cult of the dead was known in ancient Mesopotamia as the *kispu* ritual, in which the name of the dead was invoked and a presentation of food and a libation of water were made.

1.17:I:26-33) refers to the duty of a son "to set up the stele of his [father's] divine ancestor *(ilib)* in the shrine" as well as "to send out his incense from the dust." *Ilib* was frequently offered sacrifices in various rituals. Another Ugaritic text *KTU* 1.113:13-26 refers to the royal ancestors as "gods": for example, "god Niqmaddu" *(il nqmd),* "god Yaqaru" *(il yqr),* etc. Thus, in ancient Ugarit the practice of the *postmortem deification*[178] of kings existed.

The royal funerary ritual *KTU* 1.161 is of prime importance in understanding the cult of the dead in ancient Ugarit.[179] It sends the dead king to join his royal ancestors in the underworld and prays for the welfare of Ugarit and the new king. In this ritual, the "spirits of the ancestors," the *rpum* and *mlkm,* are invoked. The *rpum,* whose Old Testament counterparts are the Rephaim (e.g., Isa. 14:9), are "the ancestral line of dead heroes and kings," and are distinguished from the *mlkm,* the "spirits" of recently dead kings.[180] There is no mention of such a practice or belief in the official Yahwistic religion in ancient Israel. On *'ĕlōhîm* (1 Sam. 28:13) as the spirits of the dead, see below.

The *marzēaḥ,* an institution which has been known as a drinking festival and sometimes was associated with funerary feasts,[181] was widely practiced from Syria to North Africa, and chronologically from Ugarit in the Late Bronze Age, to Palmyra in the 3rd century A.D.[182] It seems to have been widely known among the Israelites, too, as in Amos 6:7 and Jer. 16:5. In many Ugaritic houses there were pipes leading from the ground level into basement tombs, evidently used to provide the deceased with water. It seems the cult of the dead was practiced daily in Ugaritic society.[183]

178. I.e., kings were deified after death.

179. D. T. Tsumura, "The Interpretation of the Ugaritic Funerary Text KTU 1.161," in *Official Cult and Popular Religion in the Ancient Near East,* ed. E. Matsushima (Heidelberg: C. Winter, 1993), pp. 40-55; also *CS,* I, pp. 357-58.

180. In the Old Testament they are frequently described as "the dead who dwell in the underworld" (Ps. 88:11) as well as "dead kings" (Prov. 2:18; 9:18; 21:16; Job 26:5; and Isa. 14:9). See M. S. Smith, "Rephaim," in *ABD,* V, p. 675. In the Phoenician Sarcophagus Inscriptions of Tabnit and Eshmunazor (*CS,* II, pp. 181-83), Rephaim also refers to deified royal ancestors.

181. See T. J. Lewis, "Banqueting Hall/House," *ABD,* I, p. 582. See also Lewis, *Cults of the Dead in Ancient Israel and Ugarit,* pp. 80-94; D. Pardee, "Marzihu, Kispu, and the Ugaritic Funerary Cult: A Minimalist View," in *Ugarit, Religion and Culture: Essays Presented in Honour of Professor John C. L. Gibson* (Münster: Ugarit-Verlag, 1996), pp. 273-78.

182. J. C. Greenfield, "Aspects of Aramean Religion," in *Ancient Israelite Religion. Essays in Honor of Frank Moore Cross,* ed. P. D. Miller, Jr., P. D. Hanson, and S. D. McBride (Philadelphia: Fortress Press, 1987), p. 71.

183. See J. Margueron, "Quelques réflexions sur certaines pratiques funéraires d'Ugarit (fig. 1-17)," *Akkadica* 32 (1983) 5-31.

In the biblical religion, however, unlike in Canaan,[184] kings are not considered divine. There is no practice of *postmortem deification* in 1-2 Samuel. Even King David and great figures such as Abraham and Samuel were not deified after death. It was an abomination for the Israelites to eat the "sacrifices for the dead," since if they did, they were identifying themselves with the Canaanite god Baal-peor (Ps. 106:28). When the people buried Samuel "in his house" in Ramah (1 Sam. 25:1), there is no hint either of worshipping his dead spirit or of holding a *marzēaḥ* for his sake, though in ancient Ugarit the burial was performed in the house and the ancestor spirits were worshipped in the liturgy.

b. Dagan

The god Dagan was third in the pantheon following the god El, but he does not appear in extant myths except in Baal's epithet "son of Dagan." One of the two temples in Ugarit was dedicated to him. He is known from Early Bronze Age Mesopotamia and northern Syria, especially Mari and Ebla.[185] The Philistines apparently adopted this god as their national deity soon after they arrived in Palestine early in the Iron Age (Judg. 16:23; 1 Sam. 5:2). This illustrates the continuing role of Dagan among the religions of Syria-Palestine.[186]

c. Baal

Baal, the most popular god among the Canaanites, is next in order. He was the god of fertility and the god of storm, a figure in many myths. He conquered the chaotic Sea (Yam), and thus became the king of deities. He also conquered the power of Death, though he was defeated by the god Death and needed to be revived. He was also locally manifested as, for example, "Baal of Aleppo," "Baal of Ugarit," etc.[187] The biblical Baal-Peor, or "Baal of Peor," who was one of the leading gods of the Moabites, Midianites, and Ammonites, is probably the Canaanite Baal who was locally manifested; see Numbers 25.

Baal worship was thus a real temptation to the Israelites from the beginning of their life in Canaan, as can be seen from the Baal-Peor incident

184. See T. Kleven, "Kingship in Ugarit (*KTU* 1.16 I 1-23)," in *Ascribe to the Lord,* pp. 29-53.

185. See *CS,* II, p. 248; J. F. Healey, "Dagon" in *DDD,* pp. 407-13.

186. See P. D. Miller, Jr., "Aspects of the Religion of Ugarit," in *Ancient Israelite Religion,* pp. 57-58. See the commentary on 1 Sam. 5:2.

187. See also "Baal of Sidon" in the Phoenician Sarcophagus Inscription of Eshmunazor (*CS,* II, p. 183).

(Num. 23:28-30).[188] During Samuel's time the Israelite people turned back from serving these Canaanite gods (lit. "the Baals") and goddesses (lit. "the Astartes") in 1 Sam. 7:4 (also 1 Sam. 12:10). Astarte corresponds to Ugaritic fertility goddess *ʿṯtrt*.[189] She may have been the principal goddess of Beth-shan (1 Sam. 31:10).

Male-female pairs of divinities can be recognized also in the Ugaritic mythology such as the divine pairs "El and Asherah"[190] and "Baal and Anath." Sometimes composite divine names such as Lṭpn-w-Qdš and "Mountains-and-Valley" (Ugar. *ġrm w [ʿmqt]* = Akk. *dḫuršānu u amutu[m]*) appear in various religious texts. But in 1-2 Samuel, Baal is paired with Astarte (1 Sam. 7:4; 12:10), while during Ahab's time he is seemingly paired with Asherah (1 K. 18:19). As in 1 Sam. 7:4, in Emar the storm god called Baal is paired with the goddess Aštart at Emar's western temples.[191]

The fertility cult[192] of Baal and Astarte was attractive to the people of Israel because it appeared to promise them material blessings. When they did not listen to the word of God, even the covenant people easily fell prey to Baal worship. The heyday of Baal worship in the history of Israel was the era of King Ahab in the 9th century, although Baal worship had constantly been a temptation during the earlier historical era, which 1-2 Samuel relates. Material abundance and social stability are always a danger to the covenant people at any time and in any society.

d. Solar Worship

The solar deity, Ugar. *špš* = Akk. *dšamaš* (UTU), is also among the Ugaritic pantheon. A stela for a solar deity has been found in Ugarit,[193] and the goddess Shapshu often appears in Ugaritic myths as well as in the cult; its frequent appearance in personal names indicates its popularity in Ugaritic reli-

188. See on Baal-Peor in *DDD,* pp. 279-81 (K. Spronk). In Ugaritic myths, fertility is the major theme not only in the Baal cycle but also in *KTU* 1.23, which is concerned with the birth of the good gods of fertility; see D. T. Tsumura, *The Ugaritic Drama of the Good Gods: A Philological Study* (Ann Arbor: University Microfilms, 1973).

189. For Astarte, see *HALOT,* p. 899; N. Wyatt, "Astarte," in *DDD,* pp. 203-13. See the commentary on 1 Sam. 31:10.

190. On Yahweh and "his Asherah" (or "his asherah"), see the Kuntillet Ajrud Inscriptions in *CS,* II, pp. 171-72; J. A. Emerton, "'Yahweh and His Asherah': The Goddess or Her Symbol?" *VT* 49 (1999) 315-37. For a comprehensive treatment of these inscriptions, see J. M. Hadley, *The Cult of Asherah in Ancient Israel and Judah: Evidence for a Hebrew Goddess* (UCOP 57; Cambridge: Cambridge University Press, 2000).

191. See Fleming, *CS,* I, p. 439, n. 37.

192. For Ugaritic fertility cults, see Miller, "Aspects of the Religion of Ugarit," in *Ancient Israelite Religion,* pp. 59-60.

193. See Caquot and Sznycer, *Ugaritic Religion,* plate XXVI.

gious life.[194] Considering the popularity of the solar cult in the ancient Near East,[195] it would be astonishing if it were not practiced somewhat among the Israelites, and the polemical references in Deut. 4:19; 17:3; Jer. 8:2; and Job 31:26-28 show that many Israelites were indeed attracted to the worship of the sun.

The place-name Beth-shemesh "House of the Sun" (see 1 Sam. 6:9-15) as well as the occasional femine gender of the sun in Hebrew (see on 1 Sam. 20:19) probably reflect the pre-Israelite solar worship in Canaan.[196]

The cult of the sun[197] seems to have existed alongside the cult of the dead in ancient Israel from before the monarchic era.[198] For example, it is possible that the female necromancer[199] *('ēšet baʿălat 'ôb)* in 1 Sam. 28:7 was "a woman who serves the Lady of the 'ob-spirits," "the Lady" referring to the sun goddess as ruler or guide of the spirits in the netherworld, like the Mesopotamian Shamash, who is called "the lord or king of the spirits of the dead" *(eṭemmi)*.[200]

The sun cult especially flourished in Manasseh's time, and even after. See 2 K. 23:5, 11 and Ezek. 8:16. Since the cult of the sun was well established traditionally in Syria and Palestine, van der Toorn is probably right when he says that "there is no need to assume that it was a 7th-century innovation on the part of the Assyrian overlords."[201]

3. Spirits of the Dead

There was popular belief in the spirits of the dead, as is shown by the existence of necromancy.[202] In the necromantic situation/context in 1 Sam. 28:13

194. See Miller, "Aspects of the Religion of Ugarit," in *Ancient Israelite Religion,* p. 57; E. Lipinski, "Shemesh," in *DDD,* pp. 1445-52.

195. The sun was the most popular deity in Mesopotamia from Akkadian times onwards. It is often depicted in cylinder seals: see D. Collon, *First Impressions: Cylinder Seals in the Ancient Near East* (London: British Museum, 1987), p. 167.

196. See D. T. Tsumura, "שֶׁמֶשׁ — sun," in *NIDOTTE,* 4, pp. 185-90.

197. See J. G. Taylor, *Yahweh and the Sun: Biblical and Archaeological Evidence for Sun Worship in Ancient Israel* (JSOTSS 111; Sheffield: Sheffield Academic Press, 1993).

198. Tsumura, "שֶׁמֶשׁ — sun," in *NIDOTTE,* 4, p. 188.

199. See below on "necromancy."

200. See *CAD* E, p. 398; also Tallqvist, *AGE,* pp. 458-59. See D. T. Tsumura, "The Interpretation of the Ugaritic Funerary Text KTU 1.161," in *Official Cult and Popular Religion in the Ancient Near East,* pp. 40-55. See also the commentary on 1 Sam. 28:7 and the excursus.

201. Van der Toorn, "Sun," *ABD,* VI, p. 238.

202. I.e. the art or practice of supposedly conjuring up the dead, esp. in order to obtain from them knowledge of the future.

the woman refers to *'ĕlōhîm* "gods," that is, the spirits of the dead or a "preternatural being"[203] like Ugaritic *rpim — ilnym* and *ilm — mtm* (*KTU* 1.6:VI:46-48) or *ilu,* which refers to the deceased, in the ancient Near Eastern texts.[204] Another biblical example in which *'ĕlōhîm* can be interpreted as referring to the dead *(mētîm)* is Isa. 8:19, where the prophet Isaiah mocks the people's desire to consult mediums.[205] There is also a parallel use of these terms in Ps. 106:28 *(mētîm)* and Num. 25:2 *('ĕlōhîm),* where the daughters of the Moabites invited the people of Israel to eat the sacrifices to dead ancestors.

Strictly speaking, the story of Endor is not concerned with ancestor worship but with necromancy, since it has nothing to do with Saul's ancestors. It should also be noted that this biblical episode is briefer and much less elaborate than Mesopotamian texts of necromancy.[206] However, necromancy seems to have been widespread in ancient Israel. 1 Sam. 28:3 reports that "Saul had put the mediums and the wizards out of the land." In Isa. 29:4 the prophet even uses necromantic imagery ironically ("your voice shall come from the ground like the voice of a ghost").

The Old Testament, however, forbids as abominations *(tô'ēbōt)*[207] mediums, wizards, necromancers, who consult the spirits of the dead (Deut. 18:11; Lev. 19:31; 20:6, 27), offerings to the dead (Deut. 26:14; Ps. 106:28), and self-laceration rituals for the dead (Lev. 19:28; Deut. 14:1; Jer. 16:6). The very need for such prohibitions is an indication that the problem of necromancy was persistent on the popular level in ancient Israel.

However, despite the best efforts to eradicate the existence of "pagan" cults of the dead, as done by Saul in 1 Sam. 28:3, they existed in ancient Israel throughout the monarchic era. For example, Jer. 16:5-8 speaks against those who go to the funeral banquet house (*bêt marzē aḥ* "house of mourning" in v. 5 = *bêt mišteh* "house of feasting" in v. 8; cf. Ugaritic *mrzḥ*) and those who lacerate themselves for the dead. The "revelry" *(mirzaḥ)* mentioned in Amos 6:7 also seems to be related to a certain aspect of the cult of the dead. Also, Ezek. 43:7-9 refers to an abomination practiced upon the death of kings, namely, "the practice of placing either their corpses or their

203. T. J. Lewis, "The Ancestral Estate (נַחֲלַת אֱלֹהִים) in 2 Samuel 14:16," *JBL* 110 (1991) 602-3 and "Ancestor Worship," *ABD,* I, p. 241.

204. See Lewis, "The Ancestral Estate," pp. 600-602. On Nuzi and Emar, see K. van der Toorn, "Gods and Ancestors in Emar and Nuzi," *ZA* 84 (1994) 38-59. See also on 2 Sam. 14:16.

205. See Lewis, "The Ancestral Estate," p. 602; E. M. Bloch-Smith, "The Cult of the Dead in Judah: Interpreting the Material Remains," *JBL* 111 (1992) 220-21.

206. See, for example, I. L. Finkel, "Necromancy in Ancient Mesopotamia," *AfO* 29/30 (1983/84) 1-17. See Lewis, *DDD,* p. 436.

207. J. Lust, "On Wizards and Prophets," in *Studies on Prophecy: A Collection of Twelve Papers* (SVT 26; Leiden: E. J. Brill, 1974), p. 140.

royal mortuary steles in close proximity to the temple precinct, resulting in its defilement."[208]

The paucity of the biblical references to the spirits of the dead and life after death was probably a conscious reaction against the pagan practices of neighboring peoples. The story of the "Witch of Endor" teaches us how futile it is to call upon the practice of necromancy, since conjuring the dead resulted in an announcement of death for Saul. At the same time, the story reports that something unusual happened, presumably by God's power, beyond the female necromancer's control; see the commentary on 1 Samuel 28.

The biblical expression "slept with his ancestors," which means "died and was buried," used for David (1 K. 2:10), Solomon (11:43), Jeroboam (14:20), Rehoboam (14:31), and others, has nothing to do with the ancestor worship. The Israelite religion does not prohibit people from lamenting for the dead and having burial services, as with the case of the great prophet Samuel (1 Sam. 28:3). However, they did not worship his dead spirit. In the biblical religion it is Yahweh who holds authority over life and death, for, as Hannah said, "The LORD kills and makes alive; He brings down to Sheol and raises up" (1 Sam. 2:6).[209]

4. Role of the King in the Royal Dynastic Cults

Saul seems to have presided over the New Moon festival meal as the head of the royal family, and men considered part of the royal family and perhaps some others were expected to take part (1 Sam. 20:5),[210] though there is no indication that Saul took any priestly role.

On the other hand, the king in Ugarit played a sacral role in the royal dynastic rituals observed monthly in his court, such as the Full Moon or New Moon festivals,[211] purifying himself and officiating during some part of the liturgy. He sacrificed to "the divine ancestor" *(ilib),* "Lady of the House(s)," and other major deities such as Baal and Anath, and offered prayers, thus fulfilling his filial duty to the dynastic ancestor spirits, in order that he and his family together with the city and the people might receive

208. Lewis, "Ancestor Worship," in *ABD,* I, p. 242. See also Isa. 57:6 and 65:4.

209. See E. Yamauchi, "Life, Death, and the Afterlife in the Ancient Near East," in *Life in the Face of Death: The Resurrection Message of the New Testament,* ed. by R. N. Longenecker (Grand Rapids: Eerdmans, 1998), pp. 21-50.

210. In a ritual from Emar — the Installation of the Storm God's High Priestess — the clan head slaughters one sheep at his house and cooks and serves it. See *CS,* I, p. 428.

211. See D. T. Tsumura, "Kings and Cults in Ancient Ugarit," in *Priests and Officials in the Ancient Near East,* ed. K. Watanabe (Heidelberg: C. Winter, 1999), pp. 215-38; Miller, "Aspects of the Religion of Ugarit," In *Ancient Israelite Religion,* pp. 60-63.

blessings and protection from the ancestors.[212] Thus, kings in ancient Canaan, as in other parts of the ancient Near East, were responsible for performing royal ancestor cults. In ancient Israel, however, all blessings and protection came from the only god Yahweh himself; see 1 Sam. 2:6. Hence, there was no need for the Israelite kings to induce divine blessings from their ancestors through the cults.

V. GRAMMAR AND SYNTAX

For a balanced exegesis, the linguistic aspects of the relevant text need to be understood as much as possible before attempting to reconstruct the history or theology. However, Samuel is particularly difficult linguistically as there are certain peculiarities in the Hebrew grammar and style that are impossible according to the standard Hebrew grammar. While textual critics tend to emend such passages with the help of ancient versions, scholars must admit that some grammatical constructions may have been forgotten, or that a construction is actually ambiguous and they have used the wrong analysis. So, before deciding that some forms are impossible and unintelligible, one ought to note those unusual forms and usages and explain their linguistic phenomena as objectively as possible, as I have discussed in "Linguistic Data and Dating of Texts" (III, C, 5, above). The following section illustrates some noteworthy features.

A. UNUSUAL TOPICALIZATION

In a sentence a prominent term or phrase may be "topicalized" or "focused" by being placed at the head of a clause in order to indicate first what the speaker is going to talk about. Such topicalization[213] is often expressed by a disjunctive clause[214] (i.e., a simple conjunctive *waw* followed by a nonverbal phrase) in biblical Hebrew. However, there are some unusual ways that topicalization appears in 1-2 Samuel. There are a few cases where *wayhî* (lit.

212. The king acted as the officiant in rituals in the Ugaritic Keret epic (*KTU* 1.14:III:50-IV:8).

213. See, for example, F. R. Palmer, *Semantics,* 2d ed. (Cambridge: Cambridge University Press, 1981), pp. 158-61. Traditionally, our "topicalization" has been called "casus pendens" (Gibson, pp. 180-83; W. Groß, *Die Pendenskonstruktion im Biblischen Hebräisch* [ATSAT 27; St. Ottilien: EOS Verlag, 1987]). It is sometimes resumed by a "resumptive" pronoun or pronominal suffix in Hebrew.

214. Lambdin, §132.

"and it was") introduces a topic or a "focused" noun phrase, as in *wayhî hanniš'ārîm wayyāpūṣû* "As for those who survived, they were scattered"; (lit. "*And it was* those who survived *and* they were scattered") in 1 Sam. 11:11. Since a plural noun phrase like *hanniš'ārîm* "those who survived" is not normally the subject of a singular verb, *wayhî* (3 m.s.) is usually taken as corrupt.[215] However, the phrase *wayhî* seems to play a topicalizing or focusing role here; see also 1 Sam. 10:11; 2 Sam. 2:23.[216]

Also, in the books of Samuel, there are several examples of a "topicalized" noun phrase before a *waw*+V form. This is a very unusual construction in Hebrew, and usually the passages in which they occur are emended by scholars.

Several of these examples are of a topic before a *wayqtl* construction. For example, in 2 Sam. 19:41 (K.), *w^ekol-ʿam y^ehûdāh wyʿbrw* [*wayyaʿăbīrū*] *'et-hammelek. . . .* "As for all the people of Judah, they accompanied the king" (lit. "*And* all the people of Judah *and* they accompanied the king"), the phrase "all the people of Judah" is "topicalized," being placed before *waw*+V. The same pattern can be seen in 1 Sam. 14:20; 17:24. See also 2 Sam. 20:14.

Topicalization also occurs with the "*waw*+pf." construction. For example, in 2 Sam. 19:17, *w^eṣîbā' naʿar bêt šā'ûl waḥămēšet ʿāśār bānâw w^eʿeśrîm ʿăbādâw 'ittô w^eṣāl^eḥû hayyardēn lipnê hammelek* "As for Ziba, the servant of the house of Saul, and his fifteen sons and his twenty servants with him, they rushed down to the Jordan ahead of the king" (lit. "*And* Ziba . . . and his fifteen sons . . . *and* they rushed down . . ."), the composite noun phrase "Ziba . . . with him" is "topicalized," being placed before the nucleus of the sentence, which begins with "they rushed" ("*waw*+pf.").[217] See also 1 Sam. 17:20; 2 Sam. 20:12.

A topic with the "*waw* + jussive" pattern is attested in 2 Sam. 5:8: *kol-*

215. See H. P. Smith, *A Critical and Exegetical Commentary on the Books of Samuel,* p. 80; H. J. Stoebe, *Das erste Buch Samuelis* (KAT VIII/1; Gütersloh: Gerd Mohn, 1973), p. 222.

216. See GKC, §111g and §116w; Gibson, §80, Rem. 1 (p. 99). A similar case is recognizable in Num. 9:6, where the phrase *wayhî* introduces the plural noun "men" *('ănāšîm)* and is followed by a plural verbal phrase. While J. Milgrom, *Numbers* (JPS Torah Commentary; Philadelphia: Jewish Publication Society, 1990), p. 306, like P. J. Budd, *Numbers* (WBC 5; Waco, Tex.: Word Books, 1984), p. 95, and G. B. Gray, *A Critical and Exegetical Commentary on Numbers* (ICC; Edinburgh: T. & T. Clark, 1903), p. 85, emends the phrase *wayhî* to the plural *wayihyû,* based on LXX, Targums, and others, B. A. Levine, *Numbers 1-20: A New Translation with Introduction and Commentary* (AB 4; Garden City, N.Y.: Doubleday, 1993), p. 296, thinks that it is "most likely, an instance of narrative style: 'It happened that — .'" See also 2 Sam. 2:23.

217. GKC, §112*tt* takes this as an error for *wayqtl.*

makkēh y^{e}būsî w^{e}yigga‘ baṣṣinnôr w^{e}’et-happisḥîm w^{e}’et-ha‘iwrîm śn’w [ś^{e}nū’ê] nepeš dāwīd “As for every one who strikes a Jebusite, let him strike down the ‘lame and blind’, those hated by the soul of David, going through the water tunnel!” (lit. “Every one who strikes a Jebusite *and* let him strike down . . .”). Here also the phrase *kol-makkēh y^{e}būsî* is placed before the *waw* + jussive *(w^{e}yigga‘)*.[218] Also see 1 Sam. 20:4; 2 Sam. 22:41.

B. RELATIVE CLAUSE INSERTED INTO THE MAIN CLAUSE

Sometimes a relative clause which is inserted into the main clause causes an ambiguity in the latter’s syntactical structure. In the case of the structure, “Verb + Subject + Object + <*’ăšer*-clause> + Adverbial Phrase,” the adverbial phrase often appears to be a part of the relative clause, though in fact it belongs to the main clause. For example, in 2 Sam. 11:27, *wayyēra‘ haddābār ’ăšer-‘āśāh dāwīd b^{e}‘ênê YHWH* (lit. “and the matter was evil which David did in the eyes of the Lord”), it is clear from the idiomatic expression, “be evil in the eyes of . . . ,” that the adverbial phrase “in the eyes of the Lord” modifies the main verb, “was evil,” not the subordinate verb, hence the translation: “And the matter that David did was evil in the eyes of the Lord.”

In 1 Sam. 26:3, the text is ambiguous, but the geographical context suggests that the adverbial phrase belongs to the main clause, not the relative clause. See the commentary. If we realize such possible ambiguities, we can solve several *cruces interpretatum* in 1-2 Samuel.[219]

C. SPEAKER-ORIENTED *KÎ*

There are two usages of the particle *kî* (for): (1) the “causal” *kî,* denoting causal relationship between the preceding clause [A] and the following clause [B]: that is, [A] happened because [B] happened; (2) “speaker-oriented” *kî,* which means “the reason I said [A] is [B],” for example, “They are away from home, for their mail has been piling up.”[220] 1 Sam. 2:1 has the particle *kî,* “for,” which is sometimes taken as “a prosaic addition.” However,

218. The syntax of the present sentence has been interpreted variously; see on 2 Sam. 5:8. GKC, §167*a* takes the text as being “very corrupt.”

219. For example, in 1 Sam. 2:29, the AdvPh “at (my) shrine” could be a part of the main clause, modifying “despise”; in 1 Sam. 20:19, the AdvPh “on the working day” probably modifies the main verb “come.” Also 2 Sam. 2:24; 13:16; 15:7.

220. See W. T. Claasen, “Speaker-oriented Functions of kî in Biblical Hebrew,” *JNSL* 11 (1983) 29-46.

it denotes the reason for the preceding three *performative* utterances.[221] By understanding the "speaker-oriented" *kî* we can understand the structure of narrative discourses such as those in 1-2 Samuel better than before.

VI. DISCOURSE ANALYSIS

Discourse analysis is the analysis of linguistic expressions beyond the sentence unit. Such a method is especially useful and necessary for a study of Hebrew narratives like Samuel. However, it is not easy in practice, especially in an ancient foreign language, since in particular the prosodic information of pitch, tempo, and pause is usually unrecoverable. Within this limitation, however, one can still gain valuable insight into the text and clarify some of the difficulties.

Discourse analysis is still a new and growing area of research.[222] Especially in America, it has usually followed the lines of Paul Hopper's theory.[223] He distinguished between the events of the main story (the "foreground") and the supporting material (the "background"). Several scholars have enthusiastically applied this method to the Hebrew Bible. In the last decade, some scholars trained in general linguistics have continued this field.[224]

Longacre's study on the Joseph story[225] published in 1989 was a milestone in the study of Hebrew discourse. In his analysis, the "main line" is taken by sentences with verb-initial *wayqtl*s, and other sentences are distinguished according to how near or far they are to the "main line." The present

221. Cf. Luke 1:46b-48 ("My soul magnifies the Lord, . . . for he has regarded . . .").

222. In 1989, Cotterell and Turner noted its tentative nature: "at the present there are no firm conclusions, no generally accepted formulae, no fixed methodology, not even an agreed terminology"; P. Cotterell and M. Turner, *Linguistics and Biblical Interpretation* (Downers Grove, Ill.: Inter-Varsity Press, 1989), p. 233.

223. P. J. Hopper, "Aspect and Foregrounding in Discourse," in *Discourse and Syntax,* ed. T. Givón (Syntax and Semantics 12; New York: Academic, 1979), pp. 213-14.

224. See R. D. Bergen, ed., *Biblical Hebrew and Discourse Linguistics* (Dallas: Summer Institute of Linguistics, 1994); W. R. Bodine, ed., *Discourse Analysis of Biblical Literature: What It Is and What It Offers* (SBL Semeia Studies; Atlanta: Scholars Press, 1995). For the value of discourse analysis for studies in Hebrew Bible, see W. R. Bodine, "Discourse Analysis of Biblical Literature: What It Is and What It Offers," in *Discourse Analysis of Biblical Literature,* pp. 7-11; D. A. Dawson, *Text-Linguistics and Biblical Hebrew* (JSOTSS 177; Sheffield: Sheffield Academic Press, 1994).

225. R. E. Longacre, *Joseph: A Story of Divine Providence: A Text Theoretical and Textlinguistic Analysis of Genesis 37 and 39–48* (Winona Lake, Ind.: Eisenbrauns, 1989).

author also has worked with this theory, especially on how to treat different types of *wayqtls*.[226] The validity of the theoretical basis of foreground/background theory is being continually discussed and revised,[227] though it is almost unanimously recognized that the basic function of the *wayqtl* clause is to push along the plot or mainline story.[228]

In the fourth edition of *Davidson's Introductory Hebrew Grammar: Syntax* (1994), Gibson adopts these recent developments in discourse grammar, as can be seen in descriptions like the following:

> The narrative usually opens with a statement of circumstances, the subj. coming first, or a statement of time, with or without an impersonal וַיְהִי. . . . The story line begins thereafter with *Vav* cons. YIQTOL and is continued with other *Vav* cons. YIQTOLs, identifying the main successive events. (§80)

Thus, the discourse grammatical approach has become one of the standard methods in studying biblical Hebrew narrative. However, no commentary has appeared which applies this analysis thoroughly to the Hebrew text of 1-2 Samuel.[229] Since the present volume pursues such an analysis, the following is a brief, greatly simplified, explanation of the way narrative discourses are analyzed in this commentary.

A. BASIC STRUCTURE

The narrative as a whole is a series of episodes, often connected by formal "links"; see below. The basic structure of an episode is SETTING-EVENT-TERMINUS-(TRANSITION). The SETTING provides the preliminary information for the following EVENT,[230] while the TERMINUS ends the epi-

226. D. T. Tsumura, *The Earth and the Waters in Genesis 1 and 2: A Linguistic Analysis* (JSOTSS 83; Sheffield: Sheffield Academic Press, 1989), p. 119, n. 9; see also pp. 85-86 and 119-20. See below.

227. See Y. Endo, *The Verbal System of Classical Hebrew in the Joseph Story: An Approach from Discourse Analysis* (Assen: Van Gorcum, 1996), on his "sequence vs. non-sequence" theory; A. Niccacci, "Analysing Biblical Hebrew Poetry," *JSOT* 74 (1997) 92, n. 61; E. van Wolde, ed., *Narrative Syntax and the Hebrew Bible: Papers of the Tilburg Conference 1996* (BIS 29; Leiden: E. J. Brill, 1997).

228. See Niccacci, "Analysis of Biblical Narrative," in *Biblical Hebrew and Discourse Linguistics,* p. 176; G. Long, "The Written Story: Toward Understanding Text as Representation and Function," *VT* 49 (1999) 171.

229. Bergen's recent commentary talks about it, but not in detail.

230. Thus, Gen. 1:1-2 is the SETTING for the following EVENT in vv. 3ff. See Tsumura, *The Earth and the Waters in Genesis 1 and 2,* p. 85.

sode and an optional TRANSITION prepares for the next episode. The EVENT carries the main line, and the others are "off-line." There can be complex structures, especially in the SETTING, with some sentences being explained or expanded upon by other sentences.

The EVENT begins with a verb-initial *wayqtl* verb, normally with a stated subject (i.e., the subject is not just implied by the verb), and consists of one or more "subparagraphs."[231] Each subparagraph begins with a *wayqtl* verb and has a stated subject. The *waw* here is "initial." In other words, such an "initial" *waw* initiates a subparagraph. The first sentence in the subparagraph may be followed by a series of *wayqtl* verbs without a stated subject. This construction indicates that the action or event is in sequence with the previous action or event; *waw* here is "sequential."[232] In principle, such a "sequential" *waw* simply carries on the action or event within the subparagraph.

Longacre proposed a "verb rank" system in Hebrew narrative discourse.[233] In this system, a verb initial *wayqtl* sentence has the highest rank since it is in the mainline of narrative discourse. Then come perfect sentences[234] and focused noun + perfect as "backgrounded actions" and participles as "backgrounded activities," which can appear as part of the SETTING or inserted into the EVENT. Verbless sentences and the perfect or *wayqtl* form of *hyh ("to be") are typically part of the SETTING. However, I have noted that even the *wayqtl* forms of certain types of verbs are usually not part of the EVENT and must be ranked according to the "principle of relativity," namely, how near they are to the main line either logically or psychologically, and that other factors such as whether the agent is personal or impersonal, focused or defocused,[235] singular or plural, also have to be con-

231. Longacre's "complex links" are also the chains of preterites, in which verbs of speech, of sensation, and of motion are combined with other preterites to constitute "subparagraphs"; see Longacre, *Joseph: A Story of Divine Providence,* pp. 70-73.

232. See Tsumura, *The Earth and the Waters in Genesis 1 and 2,* p. 119, n. 9. Niccacci also distinguishes between the *initial* forms, which introduce a mainline of communication, and the *continuative* forms, which have no tense value of their own; Niccacci, "Analysis of Biblical Narrative," in *Biblical Hebrew and Discourse Linguistics,* pp. 175-98; see C. H. J. van der Merwe, "Discourse Linguistics and Biblical Hebrew Grammar," in *Biblical Hebrew and Discourse Linguistics,* p. 24.

233. For other types of discourse, see 1 Sam. 2:12-21; 8:11-18 ("procedural"); and 10:2-6 ("predictive"). However, non-narrative materials have not been studied much from a discourse grammatical point of view. See van der Merwe, "Discourse Linguistics and Biblical Hebrew Grammar," in *Biblical Hebrew and Discourse Linguistics,* p. 41.

234. R. E. Longacre, "Weqatal Forms in Biblical Hebrew Prose," in *Biblical Hebrew and Discourse Linguistics,* pp. 50-98, esp. pp. 51-52, 60-64 on 1 Sam. 2:12-21; 10:2-6.

235. When the question "Who did . . . ?" is asked, the agent is "focused." On the other hand, when the question "What is done . . . ?" is asked, the agent is "defocused."

sidered. For example, the *wayqtl* of a movement verb, such as "to go" (*hlk) and "to run" (*rwṣ), or a stative verb, such as "to be heavy" (*kbd), is usually not on the main line, but is part of the SETTING. Impersonal sentences or 3 m.p. verbs without subject are often part of the TERMINUS or TRANSITION. See 1 Sam. 1:25, 28; 2:20; etc.

As a simple example, take 1 Sam. 18:5.

Setting	And David went out *(wayqtl)* (for battle);
	wherever Saul would send *(yqtl)* him,
	he was successful *(yqtl)*.
Event	And Saul appointed *(wayqtl)* him over the men of the war.
Terminus	And it was good *(wayqtl)* in the eyes of the whole people
	and even in the eyes of the officials of Saul.

(In Hebrew, the *wayqtl* verbs are all sentence-initial.)

Since the *wayqtl* of a movement verb ("and he went out") is transitional, the first sentence provides the background information (SETTING) for the following EVENT ("And Saul appointed . . ."), which begins with a *wayqtl* followed by a stated subject. The clause "And it was good" with an impersonal subject, though in a *wayqtl* form, points to the end of an episode (TERMINUS). So, v. 5 is itself a short episode. The clause "wherever Saul would send him *(yqtl),* he was successful *(yqtl),*" with two non-*wayqtl* forms, is circumstantial and so is a part of SETTING but subordinate to "And David went out." Even in the SETTING there is thus a relative order in terms of the nearness to the mainline story (i.e., "the principle of relativity"). The overall meaning is: "And David marched out for battle, with the result that wherever Saul sent him David was successful. So Saul appointed him over the army. That pleased everybody, even Saul's officials." Thus, a grasp of the discourse structure of even one verse clarifies the meaning of the text.

This use of the *wayqtl* of a motion verb as part of the SETTING or TRANSITION rather than part of the EVENT is normal in Hebrew, and occurs also in Samuel. This is clear in 1 Sam. 11:1, for example, where a new stage (SETTING) on which a new event with new dramatis personae will take place is thus introduced. Such a usage can be recognized in 1 Sam. 17:1; 20:1; 22:1; 26:1; 29:1; 2 Sam. 5:1; etc.[236]

For other references to the structure of episodes, see the commentary at 1 Sam. 5:2; 14:13-15; 2 Sam. 7:8-16, 22; 17:1-3; etc.

236. Also Gen. 20:1; 34:1; Exod. 2:1; Deut. 34:1; Judg. 2:1; 9:1; 16:1.

B. LINK: "TRANSITIONAL TECHNIQUES"

One of the most significant contributions made by discourse analysis to the study of the Bible comes from Parunak's work on "transitional techniques,"[237] or "links." According to him, when two units of narrative discourse are linked, there are usually formal similarities in the beginning and/ or at the end of the two units in terms of similar sounds, similar grammatical forms, or similar words or phrases.

For example, when a key term (a) of the first unit (A) is repeated in the beginning of the second unit (B), the linkage is formulated as the <A/aB> pattern.[238] On the other hand, sometimes a key term (b) of the second unit (B) is anticipated at the end of the first (A); thus we have the <Ab/B> pattern. More complicated patterns are <Ab/aB>, <A/ab/B> or <A/ba/B>. In the latter two, the /ab/ or /ba/ forms an independent discourse unit called a "hinge" which links the two units (A and B) in both directions.

For example, in 1 Sam. 3:1, "Now the boy Samuel was ministering to the Lord before Eli. And the word of the Lord was rare in those days; the vision was not frequent," the first clause *the boy Samuel was ministering to the Lord* functions as a link to the preceding chapter, repeating the key words "boy" and "ministering" from 1 Sam. 2:11 and 18. Thus, these two chapters are linked by the transitional technique of the <A/aB> pattern.

In 1 Sam. 4:1, understanding the role of links helps us to decide whether the verse goes with ch. 3 or ch. 4. See the commentary. This transitional technique (link) can be attested in other places in 1-2 Samuel. See for example the comments on 1 Sam. 7:17; 13:23; 16:1; 17:31; 24:1; etc.

C. TEMPO

In a narrative discourse the writer can cause the story's tempo to vary according to the context by his grammatical structure and choice of words. For example, in 1 Sam. 17:41-44, the phrase "the Philistine" appears as the subject five times; it is repeated for almost every verb which has Goliath as its subject. This repetition is quite unnecessary for meaning, but it suggests his heavy, ponderous motions. In contrast, 1 Sam. 17:48 says David "ran quickly." With these words, the tempo of the narrative increases greatly, as the successive actions in the sequence of *wayqtl* "narrative" tense show:

237. H. van Dyke Parunak, "Transitional Techniques in the Bible," *JBL* 102 (1983) 525-48.

238. This pattern can be noted in Gen. 1–2. Namely, A (1:1–2:3)/a (2:4a) B (2:4b-). See D. T. Tsumura, "Evangelical Biblical Interpretation: Towards the Establishment of Its Methodology," *Evangelical Theology* 17 (1986) 40-57 [Japanese with English summary].

v. 48b	David made haste —	ran	
v. 49	David	sent → took → slung →	struck (on the forehead)
v. 50	David		struck
			→ killed (-sword)
v. 51	David		ran → stood → took → drew → killed → cut (+sword)

Note that 14 *wayqtl* forms appear in these four verses. Thus, the contrast between the two men is expressed in the structure. See also 1 Sam. 28:24-25.

The author also often intentionally slows down the flow of discourse by the insertion of a parenthetical expression. For example, 2 Sam. 13:18a, a description of Tamar's robe, is probably intentionally placed between the utterance of Amnon's command and its fulfillment in order to slow down the flow of discourse. The audience may easily guess at the resistance of Tamar as she was forced outside. Another example is in 1 Sam. 7:10f., on which see the commentary.

D. VIEWPOINT

In a discourse analytical study, it is important to grasp the viewpoint, the vantage point from which the narrator is seeing the actions on the stage. The verbs "to come" and "to go" are the clearest indicators of such features. The former is always concerned with the movement "to this place," that is, to the narrator's vantage point, while the latter is concerned with the movement "from this place," that is, away from it.

For example, in the expression "take and go" the narrator's viewpoint is still on this side, that is, at the location before the movement (e.g., 1 Sam. 9:3; 24:2; 26:11, 12; 2 Sam. 4:7), while in "take and come" his viewpoint is already on that side, that is, at the location after the movement (e.g., 1 Sam. 5:1, 2; 9:22; 17:54, 57; 20:21; 2 Sam. 1:10; 8:7; 13:10). In the story of the ark in chs. 4–6, the narrator's viewpoint shifts several times as the ark is moved around. See also on 1 Sam. 1:19; 17:22; 25:12; 28:4; 2 Sam. 11:22; etc.

With viewpoint in mind, certain ambiguities in expressions such as *bā' y*^{e}*rûšālaim* "came (from/to) Jerusalem" (2 Sam. 19:25) might be clarified. McCarter, who translates it here as "came to Jerusalem," holds that the events of vv. 25-30 occur later than the previous events, after Mephibosheth came back to (!) Jerusalem. However, the use of the verb "came" rather suggests that the narrator's viewpoint is still near the Jordan, hence the translation "came from Jerusalem" (so NIV, JPS, NRSV, NASB) is preferable.

Change of viewpoint can also explain unusual combinations such as "set out and came" in 1 Sam. 26:5 (see the commentary).

Discourse grammar of the Hebrew language thus helps to solve some long-standing exegetical problems by directing the reader's attention to linguistic units larger than a sentence and focusing on the narrative flow. While such discourse grammatical features might have been natural and intuitive matters to the native speaker, modern readers must observe, analyze, and interpret the formal side of the Hebrew narrative, which is primarily an "aural" text (i.e., one that is to be heard) and written as if it were to be read aloud.[239]

VII. PROSE AND POETRY

1-2 Samuel is not only an ancient Hebrew prose narrative in which several poems are quoted (e.g., 1 Sam. 2:1-10; 2 Sam. 1:19-27; 3:33-34; 22; 23:1-7); many prose texts in 1-2 Samuel can be subjected to poetic analysis. In fact, it is often impossible to clearly distinguish between prose and poetry.[240] Not only direct speeches but also the narrative parts reflect poetic style. However, within the ancient narrative story, it is often impossible to distinguish between "direct" speech and narration.[241] Before discussing the poetic nature of Hebrew narrative, the principles of parallelism, which is the basic grammar and style of Hebrew poetry, needs to be summarized.

A. VERTICAL GRAMMAR — THE GRAMMAR OF PARALLELISM[242]

Parallelism is the poetic device of expressing "one through two lines." This is the shortest definition of parallelism. Its basic features are repetition and cor-

239. See Tsumura, "Scribal Errors or Phonetic Spellings?" *VT* 49 (1999) 390-411.

240. Kugel even holds that the distinction between "poetry" and "prose" is not native to the biblical texts; see J. A. Kugel, *The Idea of Biblical Poetry: Parallelism and Its History* (New Haven: Yale University Press, 1981), pp. 59-95. Also Watson, pp. 44-62.

241. It is a modern convention to distinguish them by introducing quotation marks, sometimes both double and single quotation marks, for the clarity of the logical flow of discourse. Our translation of 1-2 Samuel also follows this convention, though the original Hebrew text has no such markers. On the problem of relationship between narration and "direct" speeches in narrative, see S. Hayashi, *Bunshōron no Kiso Mondai* [= *Basic Problems of Discourse Grammar*] (Tokyo: Sanseido, 1998), pp. 249-80, based on ancient Japanese narrative stories.

242. For a detailed discussion of this topic, see D. T. Tsumura, "Vertical Gram-

respondence between two parallel lines (or cola).[243] For example, look at 1 Sam. 2:10b:

wᵉyitten-ʿōz lᵉmalkô	May-he-give power to-his-king;
wᵉyārēm qeren mᵉšîḥô	may-he-raise the horn of-his-anointed!

In this bicolon, or two-line parallelism, the paired words "king" and "anointed" (also in 2 Sam. 22:51 [= Ps. 18:50]) occur in two lines and correspond to each other. Though the syntax is not same in the two lines (V-O-prepPh//V-O),[244] the two lines are synonymously parallel in meaning, expressing one and the same idea: "May the Lord strengthen his king, the anointed one!"

In 1 Sam. 2:4

qešet gibbōrîm ḥattîm	of the bow — the mighty — are broken;
wᵉnikšālîm ʾāzᵉrû ḥāyil	and the feeble — are girded — with strength

the two lines correspond to each other in meaning but in a chiastic[245] structure a-b-c//b′-c′-a′. In this structure, two antithetical TOPICs "the mighty" (b) and "the feeble" (b′) are given antithetical COMMENTs, "be broken (c) of bow (a)"[246] and "be girded (b′) with strength (c′),"[247] and the word order is changed between the two lines, so the parallelism is chiastic, ab//b′a′.

A suggested translation would be:

The mighty, their bows are broken;
the feeble are girded with strength,

mar — the Grammar of Parallelism in Biblical Hebrew" in *Hamlet on a Hill: Semitic and Greek Studies Presented to Professor T. Muraoka on the Occasion of His Sixty-fifth Birthday,* ed. M F. J. Baasten and W. Th. van Peursen (Leuven: Peeters, 2003), 487-97.

243. For useful introduction, see Watson, *Classical Hebrew Poetry;* A. Berlin, *The Dynamics of Biblical Parallelism* (Bloomington: Indiana University Press, 1985); W. W. Klein, C. L. Blomberg, and R. L. Hubbard, Jr., *Introduction to Biblical Interpretation* (Dallas: Word Publishing, 1993), pp. 225-41.

244. V: verb, O: object, prepPh: prepositional phrase.

245. "Chiasmus" is a term for an inverted parallelism, in which the order of corresponding elements in the first line is inverted in the second line: e.g., a-b//b′-a′.

246. Since the predicate *are broken* is m.pl., its subject is most naturally *mighty men* (m.pl.) rather than *bow* (f.s.), despite some English translations such as "The bows of the mighty are broken" (NRSV, JPS, etc.). Note the pattern singular *(bow)*–plural *(the mighty are broken)*//plural *(the feeble are girded)*–singular *(strength)* here.

247. See D. T. Tsumura, "'The mighty are broken of the bow' (I Sam 2:4)," *Exegetica* 8 (1997) 83-87 [Japanese with an English summary] and on 1 Sam. 2:4.

though one loses the chiastic word order in English. The bicolon as a whole expresses the same truth from two opposite sides: "human fate is reversed by God's will."

However, poetic texts should be analyzed not only stylistically but also grammatically. While the grammar of prose is characterized by the sequential (syntagmatic) combination of various linguistic elements, the grammar of poetic parallelism[248] is characterized by "vertical grammar," in which the elements of lines have grammatical dependency on each other "vertically" as well as "horizontally."[249] Here my definition of parallelism as "one through two lines" proves itself most effectively.

There are cases where there are two parallel lines, but where (1) an element in the second line (often the verb) is omitted by ellipsis or (2) a construction has been split between two lines. To understand the grammatical relations, one must look either up to the previous line or down to the next one; in other words, one must look vertically.

For example, in 2 Sam. 22:15,

wayyišlaḥ ḥiṣṣîm waypîṣēm	and he sent out — arrows — and he scattered them,
bārāq wayyāhōmem	lightning — and he routed them

there are two synonymously parallel lines, but the verb "sent out" in the second sentence is omitted by ellipsis and can only be understood by reference to the previous line (1). Thus we have the two parallel lines "He sent out arrows and scattered them; He sent out lightning and routed them." Both "arrows" and "lightning" are the object of "sent out." For a case where the subject is repeated with variation in the second line while the verb is omitted by ellipsis, see Ps. 105:20: "The king sent and released him; the ruler of peoples [sent] and set him free."

There are also examples of two parallel lines where a phrase is split between two lines (2). Thus in Hab. 3:16 we have:

šāmaʿtî wattirgaz biṭnî	I listened — and trembled — my internal organs
lᵉqôl ṣālălû śᵉpātay	to the sound — quivered — my lips.[250]

Clearly "my internal organs trembled" is parallel to "my lips quivered" (x//

248. See R. Jakobson, "Grammatical Parallelism and Its Russian Facet," *Language* 42 (1966) 400-401.

249. The term "vertical grammar" is my own. See Niccacci, "Analysing Biblical Hebrew Poetry," pp. 77-93.

250. Cf. "I heard and my heart pounded,/my lips quivered at the sound" (NIV).

x′).[251] But the phrase "I listened to the sound" (ab)[252] is split between two lines as a//b. Hence, the bicolon is ax//bx′. Thus, it seems that the meaning consists of the synonymous parallelism "I listened to the sound and my internal organs trembled;//I listened to the sound and my lips quivered." See also Ps. 8:4; Num. 23:19a.

2 Sam. 22:42 has the same structure, ax//bx′.

yišʿû wᵉʾên mōšîaʿ	They looked for help — but there was not — one to save
ʾel-YHWH wᵉlōʾ ʿānām	to the Lord — but not — he answered them.

"To the Lord" (b) in the second line modifies vertically "They looked for help" (a) in the first line, while the clause "but he did not answer them" (x′) in the second line is a further specification of "but there was none to save" (x). See also on 1 Sam. 12:17 for this pattern in a poetic narrative.

This pattern is sometimes chiastically structured, as in Ps. 24:6,

zeh dôr dōrᵉšāw	This is — generation — those who seek Him,
mᵉbaqšê pāneykā yaʿăqōb	those who seek — your face — of Jacob.

Here, the construct chain *dôr yaʿăqōb,* "the generation of Jacob"[253] (ab), is divided between two separate lines (a//b).[254] The phrase "those who seek Him" (x) is parallel to "those who seek your face" (x′). In the first line "those who seek him" is the last item in the Hebrew, while "those who seek your face" comes first in the second line; therefore, the order is chiastic. The verse constitutes an ax//x′b pattern. See below on 1 Sam. 2:14 in the following section ("Poetic Prose").

Thus, the relationship between two parallel lines is not only stylistic but also grammatical. In other words, poetic texts in the OT are governed by "vertical" grammatical rules between the parallel lines[255] as well as charac-

251. I use "x" and "x′" here instead of "a" and "a′," for x′ is a restatement of x, while "a" is used for the first element of a sequential (syntagmatic) phrase ab, whose two elements are split and paralleled in two lines as "a"//"b." The grammatical relationship between the coresponding elements is different between "x"//"x′" and "a"//"b."

252. Also in Gen. 3:17; 1 Sam. 2:25; 15:1; 28:23; etc.

253. For similar examples, see *dôr ṣaddîq* "the generation of the righteous" (Ps. 14:5), *dôr ʾăbôtâw* "the generation of his fathers" (49:20), *dôr yᵉšārîm* "the generation of the upright" (112:2); also Ugaritic *dr. il* (*KTU* 1.15:III:19) "the generation of El," etc.

254. D. T. Tsumura, "Literary Insertion (AXB Pattern) in Biblical Hebrew," *VT* 33 (1983) 471-72.

255. See D. T. Tsumura, "Literary Insertion, AXB Pattern, in Hebrew and Ugaritic: A Problem of Adjacency and Dependency in Poetic Parallelism," *UF* 18 (1986) 351-61.

terized by stylistic repetition and correspondence. With this basic understanding of the nature of poetic parallelism, we now proceed to the problem of the poetic nature of Hebrew narratives such as 1-2 Samuel.

B. POETIC PROSE

One might be surprised at the assertion that "vertical grammar" can be also recognized in a narrative like 1 Sam. 2:12-17, the embedded story of Eli's sons, which everybody would normally consider written in prose in contrast to the preceding Song of Hannah.[256] However, by reading this prose text as if it were poetic, we may possibly solve some problems in interpretation.

For example, 1 Sam. 2:14 has:

kākāh ya'ăśû lekol-yiśrā'ēl	*habbā'îm šām bešīlōh*
"Such was done to all Israel,	to those who came there at Shiloh."

According to the normal prose grammar, the phrase "at Shiloh" is to be understood as modifying "those who came" *habbā'îm* (so REB; NIV). McCarter, holding *šām* ("there") to be unlikely before *bešīlōh* ("at Shiloh"), emends *šām* to read "to sacrifice to Yahweh."

However, the MT as it stands might be better explained if we take v. 14 as constituting a "bicolon."

kākāh ya'ăśû lekol-yiśrā'ēl	Such — was done — to all Israel,
habbā'îm šām bešīlōh	those who came — there — at Shiloh.

In this "bicolon," the basic meaning is "Such was done at Shiloh to all Israel// to those who came there." Thus, the prepositional phrase "at Shiloh" (b) in the second line modifies the verb *ya'ăśû* "was done (lit. they do)" (a) (so NRSV; NASB; JPS) in the first line and is related to it vertically, not to the preceding verbal phrase "those who came" *horizontally.* On the other hand, *lekol-yiśrā'ēl* "to all Israel" (x) is restated as "those who came there" (x′) in the second line. Such parallelism might be explained, like Ps. 24:6 (see above), as ax//x′b.

Another example of poetic narrative can be seen in 1 Sam. 28:19,

weyittēn YHWH gam 'et-yiśrā'ēl 'immekā beyad-pelištîm
And will give — the Lord — even — Israel — with you — in the hand — of the Philistines

256. See D. T. Tsumura, "Poetic Nature of the Hebrew Narrative Prose in I Samuel 2:12-17," in *Verse in Ancient Near Eastern Prose,* ed. J. C. de Moor and W. G. E. Watson (AOAT 42; Neukirchen-Vluyn: Neukirchener, 1993), pp. 293-304.

ûmāḥār 'attāh ûbāneykā 'immî
and tomorrow — you — and your sons — (are) with me
gam 'et-maḥănēh yiśrā'ēl yittēn YHWH bᵉyad-pᵉlištîm
even — the camp — of Israel — will give — the Lord — in the hand — of the Philistines

so that the Lord might give even Israel (who is) with you
into the hand of Philistines
— tomorrow you and your sons shall be with me —
(so that) even the camp of Israel the Lord might give
into the hand of Philistines!

McCarter thinks that the text is "corrupt in all witnesses, conflating two versions of one clause."[257] However, it can probably be taken as constituting a "tricolon," namely, a three-line parallelism, in which the first and the third lines are in chiastic parallelism : a-b-c//b′-a-c. While the exact phrases, "the Lord might give" (a) and "into the hand of Philistines" (c) are repeated in both lines, the third element is repeated with a slight variation (b//b′). The second line constitutes the X-line of the A//X//B pattern (see below). In direct speech, prose is often highly poetic and repetitive, and hence a text such as this should be kept as it stands.[258]

Poetic features of narrative prose are recognizable also in 1 Sam. 2:12, 17; 12:17; 16:18; 17:6; 18:2, 6; 20:13; 26:2; 2 Sam. 3:22; 14:9; 22:15; etc. When we take into consideration that narrative like 1-2 Samuel is basically an "aural" text,[259] we can detect more examples of poetic features in such a historical narrative story.[260]

C. LITERARY INSERTION: AXB PATTERN

Repetition and correspondence are two stylistic features of poetic expression in language. Elements (words, phrases, sentences, or even paragraphs) can be repeated, often with variation. One very common use of repetition is the *inclusio,* or envelope pattern, where something is repeated at the beginning

257. McCarter, p. 419.

258. D. T. Tsumura, "Coordination Interrupted, or Literary Insertion AX&B Pattern, in the Books of Samuel," in *Literary Structure and Rhetorical Strategies in the Hebrew Bible,* ed. L. J. de Regt, J. de Waard, and J. P. Fokkelman (Assen: Van Gorcum, 1996), pp. 126-27.

259. See above.

260. See the articles in de Moor and Watson, eds., *Verse in Ancient Near Eastern Prose.*

and end of a unit. For example, the repetition of "horn" in the beginning and end of Hannah's song (1 Sam. 2:1, 10) forms an *inclusio.* Repetition in a different order, as seen above in 1 Sam. 2:4 (ab//b′a′) or 1 Sam. 2:14 and Ps. 24:6 (ax//x′b), is chiasmus. Sometimes the first and the last, the second and the second to the last, etc., correspond to each other in a concentrism or palistrophe, as in Lev. 24:16-22.

While chiasmus or *inclusio* is a typical stylistic phenomenon, especially in ancient Near Eastern literatures,[261] one that has not been noted until recently is the "literary insertion" or "AXB pattern."[262] This refers to the phenomenon of literary or rhetorical insertion in which a grammatically or semantically "different" element (X) is inserted into a linguistic complex (AB) which is not normally separated. "A" and "B" keep their grammatical unity even after the insertion of "X," and "X" holds a linguistic relationship with the "A-B" unit as a whole rather than with either of the two (A, B). This "insertion" of X is a rhetorical technique of an author, not a compositional one, which assumes that someone inserted an element into a text later. Such an insertion has the rhetorical effect of slowing down the tempo of the narrative discourse in order to keep the audience in suspense. As will be seen in the commentary, recognizing this technique can solve many *cruces interpretum* in Samuel.

This pattern (AXB) may be seen in structures such as the "broken construct chain,"[263] the "interrupted hendiadys or merismus," the unique tricolon A//X//B, or the "inserted bicolon" (A//x//y//B). For example, in Hos. 6:9, *derek yᵉraṣṣᵉḥû-šekmāh* "They commit murder on the road to Shechem," the construct chain *derek šekmāh* "the road to Shechem" is interrupted by the insertion of the verb *yᵉraṣṣᵉḥû.*[264] In Ps. 11:5, *YHWH ṣaddîq yibḥān wᵉrāšāʿ// wᵉʾōhēb ḥāmās śānᵉʾāh napšô* "The Lord examines the righteous and the wicked; he who loves violence His soul hates [him]," a merismatic word pair "the righteous and the wicked" *ṣaddîq wᵉrāšāʿ* is interrupted by the insertion of the verb *yibḥān* "he examines."[265] In both cases the intruding element, the

261. Watson, pp. 282-87.

262. For the AXB pattern, see D. T. Tsumura, "Literary Insertion (AXB) Pattern in Biblical Hebrew," in *Proceedings of the Eighth World Congress of Jewish Studies, 1981: Division a: The Period of the Bible* (Jerusalem: World Union of Jewish Studies, 1982), pp. 1-6; "Literary Insertion (AXB Pattern) in Biblical Hebrew," pp. 468-82; "Literary Insertion, AXB Pattern, in Hebrew and Ugaritic," pp. 351-61; "'Inserted Bicolon,' the AXYB Pattern, in Amos I 5 and Psalm IX 7," *VT* 38 (1988) 234-36; "Coordination Interrupted, or Literary Insertion AX&B Pattern," in *Literary Structure and Rhetorical Strategies in the Hebrew Bible,* pp. 117-32.

263. D. N. Freedman, "The Broken Construct Chain," *Bib* 53 (1972) 534-36.

264. Tsumura, "Literary Insertion (AXB Pattern) in Biblical Hebrew," p. 469.

265. Tsumura, "Literary Insertion (AXB Pattern) in Biblical Hebrew," p. 476;

verb (x), governs the construct chain (ab) or a merismatic pair (a&b) as a whole, even though a and b are interrupted by the insertion of x. Let us cite a few examples from 1-2 Samuel. First, 1 Sam. 2:2:

'ên-qādôš kaYHWH	(A)	There is no holy one like the Lord;
kî 'ên bilteka	(X)	indeed there is none but you;
w^{e}'ên ṣûr kē'lōhênû	(B)	there is no rock like our God.

Scholars often take it as being originally a synonymous bicolon, omitting the second line, following LXX. According to McCarter,[266] it is conflate in all witnesses; Lewis takes the second line as "a theological gloss added by a later editor."[267] But if this were the case, it is strange that this editor should use the second person for God only in his gloss. Rather, this tricolon constitutes an example of "AXB pattern," in which the second line (X) is inserted between the lines of a bicolon, A//B, for a rhetorical purpose.

According to the MT punctuation, the scansion of 2 Sam. 3:33b-34a is as follows:

hakk^{e}môt nābāl yāmût 'abnēr	Like a fool dies should Abner die?
yādekā lō'-'ăsūrôt	Your hands were not bound,
w^{e}ragleykā lō'-linḥuštayim huggāšû	your feet were not fettered;
kinpôl lipnê b^{e}nê-'awlāh nāpāltā	Like a falling before sons of injustice have you fallen?

However, the middle two lines do not balance each other: the second line has 2 words and 7 syllables [2 (7)], while the third line has 3 words and 12 syllables [3 (12)]. Hence, McCarter, Freedman, and A. A. Anderson[268] add "by manacles" or "in chains" at the end of the second line, based on the 4QSam^{a} *bzqym,* to improve balance within the parallelism.

But instead of adding another phrase for balance, a better analysis is to analyze the first word of the third line *w^{e}ragleykā* as being the last word of the second. Then the scansion of the passage would be 4 (9)//3 (11)//2 (8)//4 (11).

"Literary Insertion, AXB Pattern, in Hebrew and Ugaritic," p. 357; also see my "Coordination Interrupted, or Literary Insertion AX&B Pattern," in *Literary Structure and Rhetorical Strategies in the Hebrew Bible,* pp. 117-32.

266. McCarter, pp. 68-69.

267. T. Lewis, "The Textual History of the Song of Hannah," *VT* 44 (1994) 28.

268. McCarter, II, pp. 110-11; D. N. Freedman, "On the Death of Abner," in *Love and Death in the Ancient Near East: Essays in Honor of M. H. Pope,* ed. J. H. Marks and R. M. Good (Guilford, Conn.: Four Quarters, 1987), pp. 125-27; Anderson, *2 Samuel,* p. 54.

hakk^{e}môt nābāl yāmût 'abnēr	As a fool dies should Abner die?
yādekā lō'-'ăsūrôt w^{e}ragleykā	Neither your hands nor your feet were bound;
lō'-linḥuštayim huggāšû	they were not put in fetters.
kinpôl lipnê b^{e}nê-'awlāh nāpāltā	Like a falling before sons of injustice have you fallen?

The second line, *yādekā lō'-'ăsūrôt w^{e}ragleykā* (lit. "your hands were not bound and your feet") is most probably an interrupted coordination (AX&B);[269] thus, Abner's "hands and feet" as a whole are the subject of the verb. Moreover, the entire unit, vv. 33b-34a, follows the AXB pattern, realized as A//x//y//B in which the middle two lines are an inserted bicolon, as in Amos 1:5; Ps. 9:7; 17:1; Job 12:24-25.[270] This inserted bicolon has a *qinah* pattern (3:2), which is most suitable for a lament; see 2 Sam. 19:1.

Another example is 1 Sam. 10:2, *'im-q^{e}būrat rāḥēl bigbûl binyāmīn b^{e}ṣelṣaḥ* (lit. "near Rachel's tomb in the territory of Benjamin in Zelzah"). Since Benjamin is not likely to be located within the unknown Zelzah, McCarter conjectures *bṣl'm bmqlwt* (lit. "in their limping on staffs") to be original, following the LXX and other Greek manuscripts. However, this passage can be explained as the "AXB" pattern, in which the phrase "Rachel's tomb in Zelzah" is modified by "in the territory of Benjamin," but the latter phrase is inserted between the two parts of the former. Such a literary phenomenon is not impossible in a piece of literature like a narrative which is essentially to be heard — "aural" — rather than to be read.[271] See also 1 Sam. 1:9; 2:3a, 13; 3:1; 6:11; 7:3, 16; 8:16; 24:8; 26:11; 2 Sam. 1:21; 6:17c; 12:9, 11; etc.

Such a rhetorical or literary phenomenon may also be recognized in much larger parts of 1-2 Samuel. For example, the narrator of 1 Samuel alternates the account of David (A-B) and that of Saul (X-Y), thus following the pattern AXBY in the story of 1 Samuel 28–31 (also see on 1 Samuel 17). Namely, 28:1-2 (A) — 28:3-25 (X) — 29–30 (B) — 31 (Y). Here, the story of David moves from 28:1-2 to 29:1 onward, while that of Saul, from 28:3-25 to ch. 31.[272]

269. Tsumura, "Coordination Interrupted, or Literary Insertion AX&B Pattern," in *Literary Structure and Rhetorical Strategies in the Hebrew Bible,* pp. 117-32.

270. See Tsumura, "'Inserted Bicolon,' the AXYB Pattern," pp. 234-36.

271. On the essential nature of the Biblical texts as "aural," see H. van Dyke Parunak, "Some Axioms for Literary Architecture," *Semitics* 8 (1982) 2-4. Such aural features can be recognized in the "phonetic" spellings of the MT; see Tsumura, "Scribal Errors or Phonetic Spellings?" pp. 390-411. Generally speaking, the narrative is meant for comprehension by listening rather than reading; see Hayashi, *Bunshōron no Kiso Mondai* [= *Basic Problems of Discourse Grammar*], p. 252.

272. Such an alternation in the literary structure can be noted in many narrative

David 28:1-2 (A) → 29:1–30:31 (B)
Saul 28:3-25 (X) → 31 (Y)

One must constantly keep in mind that any linguistic description is mono-dimensional, as compared with the real, multi-dimensional world, where many events concur simultaneously. The narrator could choose freely which event, that of David or that of Saul, to describe first and afterward come back to the other. Hence, he often goes chronologically backward and describes a preceding event; see commentaries on 1 Sam. 15:32-33; 22:20; etc. Such description has usually nothing to do with a mixture of literary "sources"; it simply reflects a basic nature of linguistic phenomena.

D. BRACHYLOGY AND IDIOM

Brachylogy is the omission of key words in "idiomatic" expressions. Before discussing brachylogy in 1-2 Samuel, however, we should pay attention to idioms in Hebrew language. Generally speaking, an idiom involves collocation of several words, like *kick the bucket,* and its meaning "is not related to the meaning of the individual words, but is sometimes (though not always) nearer to the meaning of a single word (thus *kick the bucket* equals *die*)."[273] A. Gibson explains this fact differently:

> The features of ossification, fossilization, non-substitutivity of components and unpredictability of relations of idioms to their components' prehistory or synchronic homonyms are properties of idioms which can be adduced.[274]

Sometimes an important element of an idiom is missing. Such an omission is called "brachylogy," which is a type of "ellipsis."[275] One obvious example of brachylogy is 1 Sam. 22:8, where the expression *made a covenant* (*bikrot;* lit. "in cutting") has only the verb *krt, the noun *brt* "a covenant" being omitted by brachylogy as in 1 Sam. 11:2; 20:16; also 1 K. 8:9 = 2 Chr. 5:10. Also, in 1 Sam. 14:42 the term *decide* (*happîlû;* lit. "cause to fall") is without an object noun. Usually the verb (*npl) appears with the

stories; e.g., John 1:1-18, where AXB pattern is repeated twice: vv. 1-5 (A), vv. 6-8 (X), vv. 9-13 (B); v. 14 (A′), v. 15 (X′), vv. 16-18 (B′).

273. Palmer, *Semantics,* p. 80.

274. A. Gibson, *Biblical Semantic Logic: A Preliminary Analysis* (Oxford: Blackwell, 1981), p. 122.

275. See on 1 Sam. 11:2. The term is used in König, p. 188; also Tsumura, "Literary Insertion (AXB Pattern) in Biblical Hebrew," p. 474; idem, "Niphal with an Internal Object in Hab 3,9a," *JSS* 31 (1986) 14, n. 10.

term *gôrāl* ("lot") as in the phrase "cast the lot(s)" *npl (Hi.) + *gôrāl*.[276] Here, there is a brachylogy, namely, an ellipsis of the noun "lots." The phrase "to cause the lots to fall" became an idiom which means "to decide." Hence, even after the ellipsis of "the lots," the verb *npl (Hi.) keeps this idiomatic sense.[277]

So far, the examples given involve brachylogy of the object (also 1 Sam. 2:5; 8:3; 12:6; 18:11; 20:42). However, a subject that is a part of an idiom may also be omitted by brachylogy. For example, in 1 Sam. 24:11 the verb *I pitied* (*wattāḥos;* 3 f.s.) is literally "(my eye) looked upon with compassion" with a brachylogy of the f.s. subject, "my eye." It is unnecessary to restore *ʿyny* before *ʿlyk,* since body terms are often omitted from idiomatic expressions. So, its omission is not due to accidental "loss" in the history of textual transmission but is an example of brachylogy. See also 1 Sam. 20:19; 23:8.

Thus, these unusual phenomena in both prose and poetry are important for the better understanding of Hebrew narrative, especially for 1-2 Samuel, whose "peculiar" grammatical forms and usages have been often explained as due to textual "corruption." To note those stylistic and grammatical features and to clarify their functions are very important for interpreting narrative prose, which is primarily an "aural" text and subject to poetic analysis. Before treating the texts of 1-2 Samuel as "corrupt," we ought to read them according to their own style and grammar, as the examples noted in the preceding sections demonstrate.

VIII. LITERARY STRUCTURE AND THEMES

A. LITERARY STRUCTURE OF 1 SAMUEL

The First Book of Samuel is composed of three major stories, that is, the "Story of Samuel" (1:1–7:17), the "Story of Saul" (9:1–15:35), and the "Story of Saul and David" (16:1–31:13), and a transitional section on the introduction of the monarchy (ch. 8). Each story consists of a number of epi-

276. In Isa. 34:17; Ezek. 24:6 (Qal); Jonah 1:7 (Hi. & Q.); Ps. 22:18; Prov. 1:14; Esth. 3:7; 9:24; Neh. 10:34; 11:1; 1 Chr. 24:31; 25:8; 26:13, 14 (Hi. and Qal); cf. *šlk (Hi.) + *gôrāl* in Josh. 18:8, 10.

277. See D. T.sumura, "Exegetical Notes (1)," *Exegetica* 1 (1990) 27-28 [Japanese]. For other examples, see D. T. Tsumura, "Literary Insertion (AXB Pattern) in Biblical Hebrew," p. 474 on Ps. 58:8; 64:4. Also note the omission of *ʾōzen* from the idiom *glh (Qal) + *ʾōzen* (lit., "to uncover the ear") by brachylogy in Amos 3:7 and Prov. 20:19.

sodes, selected and arranged according to the themes and purposes of the story. Individual sections were probably composed on different occasions and originated with various backgrounds, yet the transition from one section to another and from one episode to another is well planned. Consequently the entire narrative has a cohesive literary unity.[278]

- I. "Story of Samuel" — with the embedded story of "the Ark of God" (1 Sam. 1:1–7:17)
  - A. Rise of Samuel as prophet (1:1–3:21)
  - B. Story of the Ark of God (4:1–7:1)
  - C. Judgeship of Samuel (7:2-17)
- II. — transition to the monarchy — (1 Sam. 8:1-22)
  "Appoint us a king" (8:1-22)
- III. "Story of Saul" (1 Sam. 9:1–15:35)
  - A. Saul made king (9:1–11:15)
  - B. Samuel's address to Israel (12:1-25)
  - C. Reign of Saul (13:1–15:35)
- IV. "Story of Saul and David" (1 Sam. 16:1–31:13)
  - A. Introduction of David (16:1-23)
  - B. David and Goliath: Battle at the Valley of Elah (17:1-54)
  - C. Saul, Jonathan, and David (17:55–18:5)
  - D. Saul becomes David's enemy (18:6-30)
  - E. Saul's attempts to kill David (19:1–20:42)
  - F. David's Escape from Saul (21:1–26:25)
    1. Early escapes (21:1–22:5)
    2. Saul's massacre of Nob's priests (22:6-23)
    3. David's further escapes (23:1-14)
    4. Jonathan, Saul, and David (23:15–24:1)
    5. David spares Saul at En-gedi (24:1–25:1)
    6. David marries Abigail (25:2-44)
    7. David spares Saul at the hill of Hachilah (26:1-25)
  - G. David in Philistia (27:1–30:31)
    1. David and Achish (27:1–28:2)
    2. "Witch of Endor" (28:3-25)
    3. Philistine rulers and David (29:1-11)
    4. Amalekite raid on Ziklag (30:1-31)
  - H. Death of Saul and Jonathan (31:1-13)
- V. "Story of King David" (2 Sam. 1:1–20:26)
- VI. Epilogues (2 Sam. 21:1–24:25)

278. See on "Date and Authorship" (Section III) above, especially "C.6. Tentative Conclusions."

The overall structure of 1-2 Samuel[279] is delimited by the presence of poetic sections. At both the beginning and the end of the entire narrative are poems, namely, the Song of Hannah (1 Samuel 2) and the Song of David (2 Samuel 22) and his Last Words (2 Samuel 23). Similarly, 2 Samuel begins with David's Elegy for Saul and Jonathan (2 Sam. 1:19-27) and ends with the poems in chs. 22 and 23. Such a literary structure is not an accident; the poetic texts constitute an *inclusio* or framing of the entire narrative.[280]

With Hertzberg and others, one might take 2 Samuel 1 to be a part of the preceding section,[281] with the songs at both the beginning and the end of the first division, 1 Sam. 1:1–2 Sam. 1:27. However, in the present commentary, I would rather take 2 Samuel 1, with the Elegy of David (vv. 17-27), as a transitional section which functions as a LINK ("a" of the A/aB pattern; see above [VI,B]) between two divisions, that is, A (1 Sam. 1:1–31:13) and B (2 Samuel 2–20). This transitional chapter of 2 Samuel 1 consists of a narrative section (vv. 1-16) and a poem (vv. 17-27), just as Hannah's story begins with a narrative (1 Sam. 1:1-28), followed by a poem (2:1-10).

The final four chapters, 2 Samuel 21–24, constitute a concentric structure, the ABCBA pattern,[282] and are an integral part of 1-2 Samuel, not a secondary addition as an "Appendix."[283] They are rather a series of "Epilogues" which provide a thematic closure for 1-2 Samuel.[284] The very final chapter (2 Samuel 24) prepares the way to Solomon's building of the temple in 1 Kings 5–6 and hints at why David was not allowed to build the temple (2 Sam. 7:5); see 1 K. 5:3; cf. 1 Chr. 22:8; 28:3.[285]

The first two chapters of 1 Kings are not the concluding section of the

279. Cf. Caquot and de Robert's analysis (pp. 8-9): (I) "Samuel, Eli and the Ark" (1 Sam. 1–7); (II) "Origins of the monarchy" (1 Sam. 8–12); (III) "Saul and Jonathan" (1 Sam. 13–14); (IV) "Rejection of Saul and the election of David" (1 Sam. 15–16); (V) "Rise of David" (1 Sam. 17–2 Sam. 4); (VI) "David the founder of the state" (2 Sam. 5–8); (VII) "Succession of David" (2 Sam. 9–20); (VIII) "Appendices" (2 Sam. 21–24).

280. See R. C. Bailey, "The Redemption of Yahweh: A Literary Critical Function of the Songs of Hannah and David," *BibInt* 3 (1995) 213-31; Birch, p. 980.

281. Hertzberg, p. 236; Fokkelman, II, p. 631.

282. R. P. Gordon, *1 & 2 Samuel,* p. 94.

283. See H. H. Klement, *II Samuel 21–24: Context, Structure and Meaning in the Samuel Conclusion* (Europösche Hochschulschriften Reihe 23; Frankfurt am Main: Peter Lang, 2000).

284. V. P. Long, "First and Second Samuel," in *A Complete Literary Guide to the Bible,* ed. L. Ryken and T. Longman III (Grand Rapids: Zondervan, 1993), p. 170.

285. 1 Chr. 22:8 mentions the "pouring" of the blood of many "before the Lord" as the reason why David was disqualified to build the temple. This "pouring" refers not only to "great wars" but also probably to the death of 70,000 people for the atonement of David's sin of counting the people (census) in 2 Sam. 24. See R. P. Gordon, *1 & 2 Samuel,* p. 96.

"Succession Narrative," which is interrupted by the secondary insertion of the "Appendices."[286] They are rather the "interleaving of the biographies of David and Solomon."[287] Here again a "transitional technique" can be recognized: 1 Kings 1–2 probably functions as a LINK (a) of the "A/aB pattern" to connect the "Story of King David" (A: 2 Samuel 1–20) and the "Story of King Solomon" (B: 1 Kings 3ff.). One might surmise that these two chapters were written by the editor(s) of the "Story of King Solomon" who had the complete books of Samuel in hand. Hence, the editor(s) could have lived a little later than the late 10th century, that is, the latter part of Rehoboam's reign.[288]

B. THEMES OF 1 SAMUEL

The Song of Hannah, which became the prototype of the Magnificat (Luke 1:46-55), is placed at the beginning of the entire narrative; as Bailey remarks, it serves as "a thematic and structural introduction to Samuel."[289] In other words, the literary themes of the books 1-2 Samuel seem to be built into the Song of Hannah, into the initial section of the first story of the books. They are (1) Yahweh's holy sovereignty (vv. 1-3, 6-7, 8b-10a), (2) the reversal of human fortunes (vv. 4-5, 8b), and (3) the theme of kingship (v. 10b). All these themes appear and reappear in the entire book of 1-2 Samuel. We will deal with the second one here and discuss the other two in the section "Theology of 1 Samuel." The last theme, that of kingship in Israel, will be dealt with again more thoroughly in the "Introduction" to 2 Samuel.

The Reversal of Human Fortune

Hannah's Song praises the Lord of the universe and his dealings with humankind: "human fate is reversed by God's will" (vv. 4-5, 8b). Such reversals[290] occurred in the lives of Hannah, Samuel, Saul, and David. Samuel was a little boy when he went to Eli's place, while Eli's two sons were already "junior" priests (see 2:13, 15). The house of Eli kept falling while Samuel arose to be-

286. See above, Section III (Date and Authorship).

287. R. P. Gordon, *1 & 2 Samuel,* p. 95.

288. See our "Tentative Conclusions" on the Date and Authorship of 1-2 Samuel above (Section III.C.6).

289. Bailey, "The Redemption of Yahweh," pp. 213-31; also W. Brueggemann, "1 Samuel 1: A Sense of a Beginning," *ZAW* 102 (1990) 43; R. P. Gordon, p. 26. See Klement, *II Samuel 21–24*.

290. Prof. Stanley D. Walters's unpublished manuscript on Samuel, which was kindly sent to me in April 1998, is named "Book of Reversals."

come the national leader. Saul's family was not from an important clan in Israel, but he was chosen to be the first king in ancient Israel.

In David's case, he was the youngest in the family but was chosen rather than his "seven" elder brothers to be anointed; see at 1 Sam. 16:1-13. As the king's son-in-law, David was inferior in rank to Jonathan, the crown prince, but Jonathan acknowledged that it was he who was inferior in rank to David. The spirit of the Lord departed from Saul and was poured on David, who was to sit on the royal throne of Israel. The divine presence with David (see 1 Sam. 16:18) is the *leitmotiv* of the "Story of Saul and David." Divine favor, *ḥesed,* is God's unmerited favor to humankind (see 1 Sam. 20:8, 14-15). J. A. Martin even analyzes the whole of Samuel according to the "reversal-of-fortune" motif, though some of his examples are somewhat forced.[291]

IX. THEOLOGY OF 1 SAMUEL

A. KINGSHIP OF GOD

According to the biblical tradition, God is the King of the Universe; no human king can assume kingship except as the deputy of the divine King; see the commentary on 8:7. God has been enthroned as King from "before the Flood" (Ps. 29:10),[292] that is, from eternity. This view is expressed early — even in the premonarchic period — in Exod. 15:18, "The Lord will reign forever and ever."[293]

The first occurrence of the word "king" in the books of Samuel is at 1 Sam. 2:10, where Hannah expresses her conviction that the Lord is the one who gives "power" *(ʿōz)* to his human deputy (the king) and lifts up the "horn of his anointed." Here, though the Lord is not explicitly described as king, he is the one who "judges the ends of the earth." While the term "to judge" here is from the root *dyn, not *špṭ (as in 8:6;//*mlk in v. 7), the expression "to judge the ends of the earth" is certainly suitable to the God who is king. In short, the kingship of Yahweh is here expressed clearly. In fact, in Ps. 96:10,

291. J. A. Martin, "The Literary Quality of 1 and 2 Samuel: Part 2," *BS* 141 (1984) 28-42.

292. D. T. Tsumura, "'The Deluge' *(mabbûl)* in Psalm 29:10," *UF* 20 (1988) 351-35.

293. See M. Z. Brettler, *God Is King* (JSOTSS 76; Sheffield: Sheffield Academic Press, 1989), p. 14. Brettler cites Num. 23:21 and Deut. 33:5 as other "possibly premonarchical texts where God may be explicitly depicted as king" (p. 171, n. 4).

Say among the nations,
"The Lord is king!
  The world is firmly established;
  it shall never be moved.
He will judge the peoples with equity." (NRSV)

the Lord is said to judge (*dyn) the peoples as king.

According to the creation narratives in Genesis, in a sense, all human beings were created as "royal" figures,[294] unlike in other ancient Near Eastern traditions where only kings represent deities as their "image." In the biblical tradition, humankind, *the image of God,* was made as a deputy for the King of the Universe that he might rule and control other creatures for the King's sake. So, when God allowed the people of Israel to have a human king (1 Sam. 8:6b-9), he gave them a king only as God's earthly vice-regent or deputy.[295]

Yahweh's holy sovereignty is asserted at the very beginning of the narrative, not only in the Song of Hannah (esp. 2:6-10) but also in his title *the Lord of Hosts who sits on the cherubim* (4:4).[296] See the commentary on 1:3. He is sovereign not only over Israel but also over the Philistines (see 7:13: *The hand of the Lord was upon the Philistines all the days of Samuel,* etc.). Yahweh controls the entire history of the world, even the Philistine "exodus" (Amos 9:7), as well as that of the covenant people Israel. However, the kingship of Yahweh was his by his nature and the fact of creation; it was not attained as the result of any victory over the power of chaos, as was that of Marduk or Baal.[297]

B. GOD'S PROVIDENTIAL GUIDANCE

The New Testament passage Romans 8:28, "We know that all things work together for good for those who love God, who are called according to his pur-

294. See, for example, P. A. Bird, "'Male and Female He Created Them': Genesis 1:27b in the Context of the Priestly Account of Creation," *HTR* 74 (1981) 129-59 [reprinted in *"I Studied Inscriptions from before the Flood,"* pp. 329-61].

295. M. Tsevat, "The Biblical Account of the Foundation of the Monarchy in Israel," in *The Meaning of the Book of Job and Other Biblical Studies: Essays on the Literature and Religion of the Hebrew Bible* (New York: Ktav, 1980), p. 88.

296. Satterthwaite, "Samuel," in *NDBT,* p. 183.

297. On the "chaos" motif in the ancient Near East, see Tsumura, *The Earth and the Waters in Genesis 1 and 2,* esp. ch. 3 and its revised and enlarged edition *Creation and Destruction: A Reappraisal of the Chaoskampf Theory in the Old Testament* (Winona Lake, Ind.: Eisenbrauns, 2005).

pose" (NRSV), summarizes well what the author of 1 Samuel means to convey to readers. God is certainly the One who guided providentially the lives of the God-chosen individuals such as Hannah, Samuel and David. He guided each one's life in a unique and special way; even the life of Saul was in God's providential care (see 1 Sam. 9:16), though he was rejected by God for his failure to obey the commandment of the Lord (1 Sam. 13, 15).

The course of life is different for each individual — even each moment is different — but the same God, not "Fate," guides one's life consistently and graciously. And God's timing is always perfect (see 1 Sam. 9 and 23), though it is often not realised by the human agents themselves, for he is the Lord of history, controlling time and space — the when and where — of his chosen individuals as well as of his corporate people.

God's saving plan is fulfilled in the normal day-to-day life of human beings. For example, God uses the hardship in Hannah's relation with Peninnah (1 Sam. 1); he manages Saul's donkey-searching journey to lead to the encounter with the prophet Samuel (1 Sam. 9); David's chore of bringing food to his brothers in the Valley of Elah during the war enables him to see Goliath, the enemy of God's covenant people Israel (1 Sam. 17). Hence, the ordinary life situation is the most meaningful to human life, and it is there that God "works for good." God proceeds with his saving plan in the very real lives of men and women, not in some virtual reality.

Later, God uses King David's earnest plea to build a house for the Lord God to dwell in (see 2 Sam. 7:5) as an occasion to further his eternal plan of salvation by chosing David's line to be that of the Messiah king who would sit on the throne of David forever. In v. 16 God says to David:

> Your house and your kingdom shall be made sure forever before me; your throne shall be established forever. (NRSV)

In other words, in 2 Samuel 7, Yahweh, King of Universe, promises David to establish David's house, that is, his dynasty, as eternal. Thus, this promise to, or "covenant" with, David was a turning point in the outworking of God's saving purposes. Matt. 1:1 in fact summarizes God's whole plan of salvation, placing David at the middle point, as follows:

> An account of the genealogy of Jesus the Messiah, the son of David, the son of Abraham. (NRSV)

C. GOD'S SOVEREIGN WILL AND POWER

As Hannah phrases it, God is the all-knowing God, "the God of true knowledge" (1 Sam. 2:3b). He is certainly the "God who knows truly well about everything by experience as the owner and creator of the world." And he chooses or rejects people according to his absolute sovereign will, "according to his purpose." Sometimes, to human eyes, it looks as if God has changed his decision, but God "does not change his mind, for he is not a man that he should change his mind" (1 Sam. 15:29). To be sure, the Lord as the sovereign deity may change his way of dealing with individuals according to his plan and purpose. But his decision is always just and right; at the same time, he is merciful and gracious to sinful human beings.

Therefore, obedience to God's word is of prime importance in human life. The books of Samuel provide many examples of the importance of hearkening to the word of God. The boy Samuel listens to the word of God (1 Samuel 3), but Saul fails in this matter, rejecting God's commandment (1 Samuel 13, 15). David fights bravely with Goliath for the honor of Yahweh's name (1 Samuel 17) but later fails to keep the commandments, committing adultery and murder (2 Samuel 11). God gives David a second chance by sending the prophet Nathan (2 Samuel 12), while Saul is refused a chance of repentance (1 Samuel 15). Only God's grace upholds the human being who is sinful in nature before the holy God.

"Who can stand before the Lord, this holy God?" (1 Sam. 6:20) — the words of the men of Beth-shemesh express well the human reality, though their understanding of God's "holiness" is not adequate (see Leviticus 19). Only the God-given way of approaching him through sacrifice can prepare sinful human beings to come closer to the holy God.

God spontaneously reveals his will in words to humankind, and his word through the mouths of prophets "exercises a determinative influence upon historical events."[298] But not every matter is revealed to human beings — for example, 1 Samuel 3; 9:15-21; 16:1-13. We can only wait on God, who will act according to his own will.

For fighting God's battle against his enemy, Jonathan (1 Sam. 14:6), David (1 Sam. 17:45-47), and Abigail (1 Sam. 25:28-29) called on God's power. God uses human urges and enthusiasms for his honor — often beyond common sense. God is the one who works wonders and uses even his enemies, Philistine kings, Achish, and so forth, in order to fulfill his plan and purpose. Thus, humanly impossible matters are in fact divinely possible and hence challenge us to put our faith on the One who is sovereign over the entire creation.

The story of the books of Samuel begins with Samuel and ends with David. These two figures make "a frame round the dark, problematical figure of King Saul." These three are certainly central figures in the history of the kingdom of God and "much of the message of the Bible is embodied in their lives

298. R. P. Gordon, "Theology of Samuel" in *NIDOTTE,* 4, pp. 1168-69.

and in their struggles; and all three, each in his own way, are forerunners and heralds of the real King."[299] However, in God's dealings with Saul and David, one might see God's "justice" and his "mercy," respectively; both aspects will be fulfilled, according to the NT, in the person of Jesus Christ, who died on the cross.[300] On the Messianic promise, see "Introduction" in the second volume.

X. PURPOSE OF 1 SAMUEL

The purpose of the book of 1 Samuel is to highlight two major events: first, the establishment of the monarchy in Israel (chs. 8–12) and, then, the preparation of David to sit on the royal throne after Saul (chs. 16–31). Saul ruled Israel for only "two years" (see on 1 Sam. 13:1) even though, humanly speaking, he kept sitting on the throne until his death at Mt. Gilboa (ch. 31). In God's eye, Saul had long been rejected from being the king, that is, the vice-regent of Yahweh, the King of the Universe (see on 16:1). Later, in 2 Samuel 7, God promises David and his house an eternal dynasty; see the discussion of the "Davidic covenant" in vol. 2. In relation to these two central events, the prophet Samuel took the very important role as the kingmaker, anointing first Saul, then David, as king over the covenant people. Thus, 1 Samuel sets the principle that the king in Israel is to be subject to the prophet through whom God conveys his word. In other words, the obedience to the word of God is the necessary condition for a king acceptable to the God of Israel. This is what Jesus the Messiah-king did in his life of obedience to God the Father, "even unto the death of the cross" (Phil. 2:8).

XI. OUTLINE OF 1 SAMUEL

The following analysis is given in order to help the reader to grasp the entire literary structure and flow of narrative discourse in the book of 1 Samuel. The book consists of three major stories: the "Story of Samuel" with the embedded story of "the Ark of God" (1 Sam. 1:1–7:1); the "Story of Saul" (1 Sam. 9:1–15:35); and the "Story of Saul and David" (1 Sam. 16:1–31:13). The book includes a chapter about the transition to the monarchy (1 Sam. 8:1-22). The book is succeeded by another story, the "Story of King David" (2 Sam. 1:1–20:26), which is followed by "Epilogues" (2 Sam. 21:1–24:25).

299. Hertzberg, p. 20.
300. See the commentary on 1 Sam. 15:35.

I. “Story of Samuel” — with the embedded “Story of the Ark of God” (1:1–7:17)
A. Rise of Samuel as prophet (1:1–3:21)
1. Birth and dedication of Samuel (1:1-28)
a. Elkanah and his two wives (1:1-3)
b. Hannah’s prayer and vow (1:4-19)
(1) Hannah and her tormenter (1:4-8)
(2) Hannah’s prayer and vow (1:9-11)
(3) Background information (1:12-13)
(4) Dialogue between Eli and Hannah (1:14-18)
(5) Back to Ramah (1:19)
c. Dedication of Samuel (1:20-28)
<Hannah’s song> (2:1-10)
(1) Title (2:1a)
(2) Song (2:1b-10)
d. Return of Elkanah (2:11)
2. Eli’s two sons (2:12-17)
3. Samuel (2:18-21)
4. Eli’s two sons (2:22-26)
5. Warning of a man of God (2:27-36)
6. Call of Samuel as a prophet (3:1-21)
a. Setting (3:1-3)
b. The Lord calls Samuel (3:4-14)
(1) First call (3:4-5)
(2) Second call (3:6-7)
(3) Third call (3:8-9)
(4) Fourth call and His message (3:10-14)
c. Eli calls Samuel (3:15-18)
d. Terminus (3:19-21)
B. Story of the Ark of God (4:1–7:1)
1. Capture of the Ark (4:1-22)
a. Defeat of Israel (4:1-11)
b. Death of Eli (4:12-18)
c. Birth of Ichabod (4:19-22)
2. The Ark in Philistia (5:1-12)
a. The Ark in Dagon’s temple (5:1-5)
b. The Hand of the Lord (5:6-12)
3. Return of the Ark (6:1–7:1)
a. Priests and diviners (6:1-9)
b. The Ark to Bethshemesh (6:10-16)
c. Summary Statement (6:17-18a)
d. The Ark to Kiriath-jearim (6:18b–7:1)

C. Judgeship of Samuel (7:2-17)
   1. After twenty years (7:2-4)
   2. Samuel at Mizpah (7:5-12)
   3. Samuel judges (7:13-17)

II. — transition to the monarchy — (8:1-22)
"Appoint us a king" (8:1-22)
   1. Aged Samuel and his two sons (8:1-3)
   2. The Elders' request for a king (8:4-6a)
   3. The Lord's answer to Samuel (8:6b-9)
   4. "The right of the king" (8:10-18)
   5. People's demand for a king (8:19-22)

III. "Story of Saul" (9:1–15:35)
A. Saul made king (9:1–11:15)
   1. Lost donkeys (9:1-14)
      a. Kish and his son Saul (9:1-2)
      b. Kish's donkeys lost (9:3-4)
      c. Saul and his servant (9:5-10)
      d. They meet guides (9:11-14)
   2. Saul's meeting with Samuel (9:15-27)
      a. The Lord's revelation to Samuel (9:15-17)
      b. Saul meets Samuel (9:18-21)
      c. Saul as the main guest (9:22-24)
      d. Back to the city (9:25-27)
   3. Anointing of Saul (10:1)
   4. Return of Saul (10:2-16)
      a. Samuel's prediction (10:2-6)
      b. Samuel's order (10:7-8)
      c. Saul's departure (10:9-13)
      d. Saul's uncle (10:14-16)
   5. Election of Saul at Mizpah (10:17-27)
   6. Saul's first war (11:1-13)
      a. Nahash's threat to Jabesh (11:1-3)
      b. Messengers to Gibeah (11:4-9a)
      c. Messengers come back (11:9b-10)
      d. Saul's victory over Ammon (11:11-13)
   7. Making Saul king at Gilgal (11:14-15)
B. Samuel's address to Israel (12:1-25)
   1. "Testify against me!" (12:1-6)
   2. "Behold the King!" (12:7-15)
   3. "Take your stand and see!" (12:16-17)
   4. "Fear the Lord and serve him!" (12:18-25)
C. Reign of Saul (13:1–15:35)

1. Saul and the Philistines (13:1-23)
    a. Summary statement (13:1)
    b. Saul and Jonathan (13:2-3a)
    c. Philistines and the Israelite troops (13:3b-7a)
    d. Saul waits seven days at Gilgal (13:7b-9)
    e. Saul and Samuel (13:10-15)
    f. Philistine raiders & garrison (13:16-23)
        (1) Raiders come out (13:16-18)
        (2) Philistine monopoly of metal (13:19-22)
        (3) The garrison comes out (13:23)
2. Saul and Jonathan (14:1-46)
    a. Jonathan attacks the Philistine garrison (14:1-15)
        (1) Initial statement (14:1)
        (2) Background information (14:2-5)
        (3) Jonathan and his servant (14:6-15)
            (a) "Let us go across!" (14:6-7)
            (b) "Come up toward us!" (14:8-12)
            (c) Philistines fall before Jonathan (14:13-15)
    b. The Lord saves Israel (14:16-23)
        (1) Saul at Gibeah (14:16-20)
        (2) Hebrews and the men of Israel (14:21-23)
    c. The people save Jonathan (14:24-46)
        (1) Saul's ban (14:24-30)
            (a) People under oath (14:24)
            (b) Jonathan tastes honey (14:25-27)
            (c) Jonathan is informed of the oath (14:28-30)
        (2) The sin of the troops (14:31-35)
            (a) Troops eat blood (14:31-32)
            (b) Saul builds an altar (14:33-35)
        (3) Saul makes inquiry of God (14:36-46)
            (a) No answer on that day (14:36-37)
            (b) Saul's oath (14:38-39)
            (c) Jonathan is "taken" (14:40-42)
            (d) The people rescue Jonathan (14:43-45)
            (e) Saul returns (14:46)
3. Summary statements (14:47-52)
    a. Saul against his enemies (14:47-48)
    b. Saul's family and his general (14:49-51)
    c. Recruitment of soldiers for Saul's army (14:52)
4. Saul and the Amalekites (15:1-35)
    a. "Go and strike Amalek" (15:1-3)
    b. Saul spares Agag and livestock (15:4-9)

c. The Lord's word to Samuel (15:10-11)
d. Samuel and Saul (15:12-31)
(1) Saul erects a monument (15:12)
(2) "I have carried out the word of the Lord" (15:13-16)
(3) "Because you have rejected the word of the Lord" (15:17-23)
(4) "The Lord has rejected you" (15:24-26)
(5) "The Lord has given the kingdom of Israel to your neighbor" (15:27-31)
e. Samuel kills Agag (15:32-33)
f. Samuel returns home (15:34-35)

IV. "Story of Saul and David" (16:1–31:13)
A. Introduction of David (16:1-23)
1. Anointing of David (16:1-13)
a. The Lord sends Samuel to Bethlehem (16:1-4a)
b. Samuel chooses David (16:4b-13)
(1) Elders of the city (16:4b-5a)
(2) The Lord rejects the elder sons (16:5b-11)
(3) Samuel anoints David (16:12-13)
2. David at Saul's court (16:14-23)
a. Spirit for evilness (16:14)
b. Saul is informed about David (16:15-18)
c. David attends Saul (16:19-22)
d. Summary statement (16:23)
B. David and Goliath: Battle at the Valley of Elah (17:1-54)
1. Battle in the Valley of Elah (17:1-11)
a. Philistines and Israel (17:1-3)
b. Goliath the champion (17:4-11)
(1) Goliath from Gath (17:4)
(2) Goliath's weapons (17:5-7)
(3) Challenge to a duel (17:8-11)
2. David in Bethlehem (17:12-19)
a. David son of Jesse (17:12-15)
b. Goliath the champion (17:16)
c. Jesse sends David to the valley (17:17-19)
3. David's victory over Goliath (17:20-54)
a. David comes to the valley (17:20-23)
b. Goliath the champion (17:24)
c. "Who is this uncircumcised Philistine?" (17:25-30)
d. David appears before Saul (17:31-40)
e. Duel between Goliath and David (17:41-51a)
(1) "For the battle is the Lord's!" (17:41-47)

(2) David kills Goliath (17:48-51a)
f. Israelites defeat the Philistines (17:51b-54)
C. Saul, Jonathan, and David (17:55–18:5)
1. Saul and David: "Whose son are you?" (17:55-58)
2. Jonathan and David: covenant (18:1-4)
3. Summary statements (18:5)
D. Saul becomes David's enemy (18:6-30)
1. Saul's anger (18:6-9)
2. Saul's first attack on David (18:10-11)
3. The Lord is with David (18:12-16)
4. David as Saul's son-in-law (18:17-28)
a. Merab for David (18:17-19)
b. Michal as David's wife (18:20-28)
(1) A: Michal loves David (18:20)
(2) B: Saul sends messengers to David (18:21-26a)
(3) A′: The matter is right in David's eyes (18:26b-28)
5. Saul as David's enemy (18:29-30)
E. Saul's attempts to kill David (19:1–20:42)
1. Saul orders that David be killed (19:1-7)
a. Saul gives the order (19:1)
b. Jonathan informs David (19:2-3)
c. Jonathan speaks with Saul (19:4-7)
2. David's victory over the Philistines (19:8)
3. Saul's second attack on David (19:9-10)
4. David escapes from Saul (19:11-24)
a. David goes home (19:11-17)
(1) Michal helps David to escape (19:11-13)
(2) Saul sends men to capture David (19:14-17)
b. David goes to Samuel at Ramah (19:18-24)
(1) David informs Samuel (19:18-19)
(2) Saul sends messengers to Naioth (19:20-21)
(3) Saul himself goes to Naioth (19:22-24)
5. David meets Jonathan (20:1-24a)
a. "What did I do?" (20:1-4)
b. "Let me hide in the field" (20:5-11)
c. Covenant between Jonathan's house and David's house (20:12-17)
d. "You shall spend three days" (20:18-24a)
6. New Moon Festival (20:24b-34)
a. First day of the New Moon (20:24b-26)
b. Second day of the New Moon (20:27-34)
(1) David's place is empty (20:27-29)

        (2) Saul's anger against Jonathan (20:30-34)
    7. Jonathan informs David in the field (20:35-42)
      a. Jonathan shoots arrows (20:35-41a)
      b. Jonathan sends David off (20:41b-42)
F. David's escape from Saul (21:1–26:25)
    1. Early escapes (21:1–22:5)
      a. To Nob (21:1-9)
        (1) David requests five loaves of bread (21:1-6)
        (2) Doeg the Edomite (21:7)
        (3) David requests a weapon (21:8-9)
      b. To Gath (21:10-15)
      c. To the cave of Adullam (22:1-2)
      d. To Mizpeh of Moab (22:3-4)
      e. To the Forest of Hereth (22:5)
    2. Saul's massacre of Nob's priests (22:6-23)
      a. Saul in Gibeah (22:6-10)
      b. Saul kills the priests of Nob (22:11-19)
      c. Abiathar escapes to David (22:20-23)
    3. David's further escapes (23:1-14)
      a. To Keilah (23:1-13)
        (1) David inquires of the Lord (23:1-4)
        (2) David saves Keilah (23:5-6)
        (3) Saul is informed (23:7-8)
        (4) David again inquires of the Lord (23:9-12)
        (5) David leaves Keilah (23:13)
      b. To the wilderness of Ziph (23:14)
    4. Jonathan, Saul, and David (23:15-29)
      a. Jonathan comes to Horesh (23:15-18)
      b. Ziphites inform Saul (23:19-24a)
      c. David in the wilderness of Maon (23:24b-28)
      Hinge (23:29)
    5. David spares Saul at En-gedi (24:1–25:1)
      a. Saul enters the cave (24:1-3)
      b. David cuts off the skirt of Saul's robe (24:4-7)
      c. David's long speech (24:8-15)
      d. Saul's response (24:16-22)
      e. Death of Samuel (25:1)
    6. David marries Abigail (25:2-44)
      a. Nabal in Maon (25:2-3)
      b. David sends to Nabal (25:4-8)
      c. Nabal responds (25:9-11)
      d. David gets ready to fight (25:12-13)

e. Abigail is informed (25:14-17)
f. Abigail gets ready (25:18-19)
g. Abigail meets David (25:20-23)
parenthetical clause (25:21-22)
h. Abigail's long speech (25:24-31)
i. David's response to Abigail (25:32-35)
j. Death of Nabal (25:36-39a)
k. Abigail becomes David's wife (25:39b-44)
7. David spares Saul at the hill of Hachilah (26:1-25)
a. Ziphites inform Saul (26:1)
b. Saul goes to the wilderness (26:2-3a)
c. David goes to Saul's camp (26:3b-5)
d. David and Abishai (26:6-12)
e. David and Abner (26:13-16)
f. Saul and David (26:17-25)
(1) Saul speaks (26:17a)
(2) David responds (26:17b-20)
(3) Saul speaks (26:21)
(4) David responds (26:22-24)
(5) Saul returns (26:25)
G. David in Philistia (27:1–30:31)
1. David and Achish (27:1-12)
a. Escape to Gath (27:1-4)
b. David at Ziklag (27:5-12)
2. The Philistines gather for war (28:1-2)
<"Witch of Endor"> (28:3-25) [embedded story]
a. Setting (28:3-4a)
b. Events (28:4b-23)
(1) No answer from the Lord (28:4b-6)
(2) "Search for me a woman" (28:7-8a)
(3) "Divine for me" (28:8b-12a)
(4) "I saw gods coming up" (28:12b-14a)
(5) Saul and Samuel (28:14b-19)
(6) Saul falls down (28:20-23)
c. Terminus (28:24-25)
3. The Philistine rulers and David (29:1-11)
a. Setting (29:1-2)
b. Philistine rulers and Achish (29:3-5)
c. Achish and David (29:6-10)
d. Terminus (29:11)
4. Amalekite raid on Ziklag (30:1-31)
a. Raid of Ziklag (30:1-8)

(1) The Amalekites raid Ziklag (30:1-2)
(2) David enters the city (30:3-6)
(3) David inquires of the Lord (30:7-8)
b. Pursuit of the Amalekites (30:9-25)
(1) To Wadi Besor (30:9-10)
(2) David finds an Egyptian (30:11-15)
(3) David strikes the Amalekites (30:16-20)
(4) David comes back to Wadi Besor (30:21-25)
c. Gifts to the elders of Judah (30:26-31)
(1) Narrative (30:26)
(2) List (30:27-31)
H. Death of Saul and Jonathan (31:1-13)
1. Saul's three sons fall (31:1-2)
2. Saul dies (31:3-6)
3. The Israelites flee (31:7)
4. The Philistines expose Saul's corpse (31:8-10)
5. The Jabeshites bury the corpses (31:11-13)

XII. SELECT BIBLIOGRAPHY

Ackroyd, P. R. *The First Book of Samuel* (CBC). Cambridge: Cambridge University Press, 1971.

Aharoni, Y. *Arad Inscriptions* (JDS). Jerusalem: Israel Exploration Society, 1981.

Albrektson, B. *History and the Gods: An Essay on the Idea of Historical Events as Divine Manifestations in the Ancient Near East and in Israel.* Lund: CWK Gleerup, 1967.

Albright, W. F. *Yahweh and the Gods of Canaan.* Anchor Books. Garden City, N.Y.: Doubleday, 1969.

Alter, R. *The Art of Biblical Narrative.* London: George Allen & Unwin, 1981.

Althann, R. "Northwest Semitic Notes on Some Texts in 1 Samuel." *JNSL* 12 (1984) 27-34.

Andersen, F. I. *The Sentence in Biblical Hebrew.* The Hague: Mouton, 1974.

Arnold, P. M. *Gibeah: The Search for a Biblical City* (JSOTSS 79). Sheffield: JSOT Press, 1990.

Avigad, N. "The Contribution of Hebrew Seals to an Understanding of Israelite Religion and Society." In *Ancient Israelite Religion: Essays in Honor of Frank Moore Cross,* ed. P. D. Miller, Jr., P. D. Hanson, and S. D. McBride, pp. 195-208. Philadelphia: Fortress, 1987.

Avigad, N., and B. Sass. *Corpus of West Semitic Stamp Seals.* Jerusalem: Israel Academy of Sciences and Humanities, 1997.

Baker, D. W. "Further Examples of the *wāw* explicativum." *VT* 30 (1980) 129-36.

Baldwin, J. G. *1-2 Samuel* (TOTC). Leicester: InterVarsity, 1988.

Bar-Efrat, S. *Narrative Art in the Bible.* Sheffield: JSOT Press, 1989.

Barr, J. *Comparative Philology and the Text of the Old Testament.* Oxford: Clarendon, 1968.

Barthélemy, D. *Critique Textuelle de l'Ancien Testament I* (OBO 50/1). Fribourg: Éditions Universitaires, 1982.

Barthélemy, D., et al. *The Story of David and Goliath: Textual and Literary Criticism: Papers of a Joint Research Venture* (OBO 73). Fribourg: Éditions Universitaires, 1986.

Bergen, R. D. *1, 2 Samuel* (NAC 7). Nashville: Broadman & Holman, 1996.

Berlin, A. *The Dynamics of Biblical Parallelism.* Bloomington: Indiana University Press, 1985.

Beuken, W. A. M. "I Samuel 28: The Prophet as 'Hammer of Witches.'" *JSOT* 6 (1978) 3-17.

Bierling, N. *Giving Goliath His Due: New Archaeological Light on the Philistines.* Grand Rapids: Baker Book House, 1992.

Biran, A., and J. Naveh. "An Aramaic Stele Fragment from Tel Dan." *IEJ* 43 (1993) 81-98.

Birch, B. C. "The First and Second Books of Samuel: Introduction, Commentary, and Reflections." In *The New Interpreter's Bible,* vol. II, ed. L. E. Keck et al., pp. 947-1383. Nashville: Abingdon, 1998.

———. *The Rise of the Israelite Monarchy: The Growth and Development of I Samuel 7–15* (SBLDS 27). Missoula, Mont.: Scholars Press, 1976.

Block, D. I. "Empowered by the Spirit of God: The Holy Spirit in the Historiographic Writings of the Old Testament." *Southern Baptist Journal of Theology* 1 (1997) 42-60.

Bodine, W. R., ed. *Discourse Analysis of Biblical Literature: What It Is and What It Offers* (SBL Semeia Studies). Atlanta: Scholars Press, 1995.

Boer, P. A. H. de. *Selected Studies in Old Testament Exegesis,* ed. C. van Duin (OTS 27). Leiden: E. J. Brill, 1991.

Brettler, M. Z. "The Composition of 1 Samuel 1–2." *JBL* 116 (1997) 601-12.

———. *The Creation of History in Ancient Israel.* London: Routledge, 1995.

Brichto, H. C. "Kin, Cult, Land and Afterlife — A Biblical Complex." *HUCA* 44 (1973) 1-54.

Brueggemann, W. *First and Second Samuel.* Louisville: John Knox, 1990.

———. "1 Samuel 1: A Sense of a Beginning." *ZAW* 102 (1990) 33-48.

Bryce, T. *The Kingdom of the Hittites.* Oxford: Clarendon, 1998.

Caird, G. B. "The First and Second Books of Samuel." In *IB,* vol. 2, pp. 853-1176. Nashville: Abington, 1953.

Campbell, A. F. *The Ark Narrative (1 Sam 4–6; 2 Sam 6): A Form-Critical and Traditio-Historical Study* (SBLDS 16). Missoula, Mont.: Scholars Press, 1975.

———. *Of Prophets and Kings: A Late Ninth-Century Document (1 Samuel 1–2 Kings 10)* (CBQ Monograph Series 17). Washington: Catholic Biblical Association, 1986.

Caquot, A., and M. Sznycer. *Ugaritic Religion.* Leiden: E. J. Brill, 1980.

Caquot, A., M. Sznycer, and A. Herdner. *Textes Ougaritiques I: Mythes et Légendes* (LAPO 7). Paris: Cerf, 1974.

Caquot, A., and P. de Robert. *Les Livres de Samuel* (CAT VI). Geneva: Labor et Fides, 1994.

Claasen, W. T. "Speaker-oriented Functions of *kî* in Biblical Hebrew." *JNSL* 11 (1983) 29-46.

Clines, D. J. A., and T. C. Eskenazi. *Telling Queen Michal's Story: An Experiment in Comparative Interpretation* (JSOTSS 119). Sheffield: JSOT Press, 1991.

Collins, N. "The Start of the Pre-exilic Calendar Day of David and the Amalekites: A Note on 1 Samuel 30:17." *VT* 41 (1991) 203-10.

Collon, D. *First Impressions: Cylinder Seals in the Ancient Near East.* London: British Museum, 1987.

Cook, E. M. "1 Samuel xx 26–xxi 5 According to 4QSam^{b}." *VT* 44 (1994) 442-54.

Cook, J. E. *Hannah's Desire, God's Design: Early Interpretations of the Story of Hannah* (JSOTSS 282). Sheffield: Sheffield Academic Press, 1999.

Cook, S. L. "The Text and Philology of 1 Samuel xiii 20-1." *VT* 44 (1994) 250-54.

Cross, F. M. "The Ammonite Oppression of the Tribes of Gad and Reuben: Missing Verses from 1 Samuel 11 Found in 4QSamuel^{a}." In *History, Historiography and Interpretation: Studies in Biblical and Cuneiform Literatures,* ed. H. Tadmor and M. Weinfeld, pp. 148-58. Jerusalem: Magnes, 1983.

———. *Canaanite Myth and Hebrew Epic.* Cambridge, Mass.: Harvard University Press, 1973.

Cross, F. M., and D. W. Parry. "A Preliminary Edition of a Fragment of 4QSam^{b} (4Q52)." *BASOR* 306 (1997) 63-74.

Cross, F. M., and S. Talmon, eds. *Qumran and the History of the Biblical Text.* Cambridge, Mass.: Harvard University Press, 1975.

Cryer, F. H. *Divination in Ancient Israel and Its Near Eastern Environment: A Socio-historic Investigation* (JSOTSS 142). Sheffield: Sheffield Academic Press, 1994.

De Moor, J. C., and W. G. E. Watson, eds. *Verse in Ancient Near Eastern Prose.* Neukirchen-Vluyn: Neukirchener, 1993.

De Regt, L. J. "The Order of Participants in Compound Clausal Elements in the Pentateuch and Earlier Prophets: Syntax, Convention or Rhetoric?" In *Literary Structure and Rhetorical Strategies in the Hebrew Bible,* ed. L. J. de Regt, J. de Waard, and J. P. Fokkelman, pp. 79-100. Assen: Van Gorcum, 1996.

De Ward, E. F. "Mourning Customs in 1, 2, Samuel." *JJS* 23 (1972) 1-27, 145-66.

Dietrich, W. "Die Erzählungen von David und Goliat in 1 Sam 17." *ZAW* 108 (1996) 172-91.

Dothan, T., and M. Dothan. *People of the Sea: The Search for the Philistines.* New York: Macmillan, 1992.

Driver, G. R. "Old Problems Re-examined." *ZAW* 80 (1968) 174-83.

———. "Problems of the Hebrew Text and Language." In *Alttestamentliche Studien, Friedrich Nötscher zum 60. Geburtstag gewidmet,* ed. H. Junker and J. Botterweck, pp. 46-61. Bonn: Peter Hanstein, 1950.

Driver, S. R. *Notes on the Hebrew Text and the Topography of the Books of Samuel.* Oxford: Clarendon, 1913.

Edelman, D. V. *King Saul in the Historiography of Judah* (JSOTSS 121). Sheffield: Sheffield Academic Press, 1991.

———. "Saul ben Kish in History and Tradition." In *The Origins of the Ancient Israelite States,* ed. V. Vritz and P. R. Davies (JSOTSS 228), pp. 142-59. Sheffield: Sheffield Academic Press, 1996.

Ehrlich, C. S. *The Philistines in Transition: A History from ca. 1000-730 BCE* (SHCANE 10). Leiden: E. J. Brill, 1996.

Emerton, J. A. "Sheol and the Sons of Belial." *VT* 37 (1987) 214-18.

———. "Two Issues in the Interpretation of the Tel Dan Inscription." *VT* 50 (2000) 27-37.

Endo, Y. *The Verbal System of Classical Hebrew in the Joseph Story: An Approach from Discourse Analysis.* Assen: Van Gorcum, 1996.

Eskenazi, T. C. "A Literary Approach to Chronicler's Ark Narrative in 1 Chronicles 13–16." In *Fortunate the Eyes That See: Essays in Honor of David Noel Freedman in Celebration of His Seventieth Birthday,* ed. A. B. Beck et al., pp. 258-74. Grand Rapids: Eerdmans, 1995.

Eslinger, L. *Kingship of God in Crisis: A Close Reading of 1 Samuel 1–12* (BLS 10). Sheffield: Almond, 1985.

Evans, C. D., W. W. Hallo, and J. B. White, eds. *Scripture in Context: Essays on the Comparative Method.* Pittsburgh: Pickwick, 1980.

Fenton, T. L. "Deuteronomistic Advocacy of the *nābî'*: 1 Samuel ix 9 and Questions of Israelite Prophecy." *VT* 47 (1997) 23-42.

Finkel, I. L. "Necromancy in Ancient Mesopotamia." *AfO* 29/30 (1983/84) 1-17.

Finkelstein, I. "The Emergence of the Monarchy in Israel: The Environmental and Socio-economic Aspects." *JSOT* 44 (1989) 43-74.

Finkelstein, J. J. "Cutting the *sissiktu* in Divorce Proceedings." *WO* 8 (1975) 236-40.

Fisher, L. R., ed. *Ras Shamra Parallels I* (AnOr 49). Rome: Pontifical Biblical Institute, 1972.

———, ed. *Ras Shamra Parallels II* (AnOr 50). Rome: Pontifical Biblical Institute, 1975.

Fleming, D. E. "The Biblical Tradition of Anointing Priests." *JBL* 117 (1998) 401-14.

———. "The Etymological Origins of the Hebrew *nābîʾ*: The One Who Invokes God." *CBQ* 55 (1993) 217-24.

———. *The Installation of Baal's High Priestess at Emar: A Window on Ancient Syrian Religion* (HSS 42). Atlanta: Scholars Press, 1992.

———. "The Israelite Festival Calendar and Emar's Ritual Archive." *RB* 106 (1999) 8-34.

———. "Mari's Large Public Tent and the Priestly Tent Sanctuary." *VT* 50 (2000) 484-98.

———. "More Help from Syria: Introducing Emar to Biblical Study." *BA* 58 (1995) 139-47.

———. "The Seven-Day Siege of Jericho in Holy War." In *Ki Baruch Hu: Ancient Near Eastern, Biblical, and Judaic Studies in Honor of Baruch A. Levine,* ed. R. Chazan, W. W. Hallo, and L. H. Schiffman, pp. 211-28. Winona Lake, Ind.: Eisenbrauns, 1999.

Fokkelman, J. P. *Narrative Art and Poetry in the Books of Samuel,* vol. II: *The Crossing Fates (I Sam. 13–31 and II Sam. 1)* (SSN 23). Assen: Van Gorcum, 1986.

———. *Narrative Art and Poetry in the Books of Samuel,* vol. IV: *Vow and Desire (I Sam. 1–12)* (SSN 31). Assen: Van Gorcum, 1993.

Fontaine, C. R. *Traditional Sayings in the Old Testament, A Contextual Study* (BLS 5). Sheffield: Almond, 1982.

Frankfort, H. *Kingship and the Gods: A Study of Ancient Near Eastern Religion as the Integration of Society and Nature.* Chicago: University of Chicago Press, 1948, 1978.

Freedman, D. N. "Psalm 113 and the Song of Hannah." *EI* 14 (H. L. Ginsberg Volume) (1978) 56*-69*.

———, ed. *The Leningrad Codex; A Facsimile Edition.* Grand Rapids: Eerdmans, 1998.

Fritz, V., and P. R. Davies, eds. *The Origins of the Ancient Israelite States* (JSOTSS 228). Sheffield: Sheffield Academic Press, 1996.

Galil, G. "The Jerahmeelites and the Negeb of Judah." *JANES* 28 (2001) 33-42.

Galling, K. "Goliath und seine Rüstung." In *Volume du Congrès: Genève 1965* (SVT 15), pp. 150-69. Leiden: E. J. Brill, 1966.

Garsiel, M. *The First Book of Samuel: A Literary Study of Comparative Structures, Analogies and Parallels.* Jerusalem: Rubin Mass, 1990 [orig. 1983, 1985].

———. "Wit, Words, and a Woman: 1 Samuel 25." In *On Humour and the Comic in the Hebrew Bible,* ed. Y. T. Radday and A. Brenner (BLS 23/JSOT 92), pp. 161-68. Sheffield: Almond, 1990.

George, M. K. "Yhwh's Own Heart." *CBQ* 64 (2002) 442-59.

Gibson, A. *Biblical Semantic Logic: A Preliminary Analysis.* Oxford: Blackwell, 1981.

Gitin, S., A. Mazar, and E. Stern, eds. *Mediterranean Peoples in Transition: Thirteenth to Early Tenth Centuries* BCE. *In Honor of Professor Trude Dothan.* Jerusalem: Israel Exploration Society, 1998.

Gitin, S., T. Dothan, and J. Naveh. "A Royal Dedicatory Inscription from Ekron." *IEJ* 47 (1997) 1-16.

Gnuse, R. K. "A Reconsideration of the Form-Critical Structure in I Samuel 3: An Ancient Near Eastern Dream Theophany." *ZAW* 94 (1982) 379-90.

Gooding, D. W. "An Approach to the Literary and Textual Problems of . . . 1 Sam 16–18." In *The Story of David and Goliath: Textual and Literary Criticism: Papers of a Joint Research Venture,* ed. D. Barthélemy, D. W. Gooding, J. Lust, and E. Tov (OBO 73), pp. 55-86, 114-20, 121-28, 145-54. Göttingen: Vandenhoeck and Ruprecht, 1986.

Gordon, C. H. *The Common Background of Greek and Hebrew Civilizations.* New York: W. W. Norton, 1965.

———. "Fratriarchy in the Old Testament." *JBL* 54 (1935) 223-31.

———. *Ugaritic Textbook* (AnOr 38). Rome: Pontifical Biblical Institute, 1965.

Gordon, C. H., and G. A. Rendsburg. *The Bible and the Ancient Near East.* 4th ed. New York: W. W. Norton, 1997.

Gordon, R. P. *I & II Samuel.* Exeter: Paternoster, 1986.

———. *1 & 2 Samuel* (OTG). Sheffield: JSOT Press, 1984.

———. "From Mari to Moses: Prophecy at Mari and in Ancient Israel." In *Of Prophets' Visions and the Wisdom of the Sages,* ed. H. McKay and D. J. A. Clines (JSOTSS 162), pp. 63-79. Sheffield: Sheffield Academic Press, 1993.

———. "Who Made the Kingmaker? Reflections on Samuel and the Institution of the Monarchy." In *Faith, Tradition, and History: Old Testament Historiography in Its Near Eastern Context,* ed. A. R. Millard, J. K. Hoffmeier, and D. W. Baker, pp. 255-69. Winona Lake, Ind.: Eisenbrauns, 1994.

———, ed. *"The Place Is Too Small for Us": The Israelite Prophets in Recent Scholarship* (SBTS 5). Winona Lake, Ind.: Eisenbrauns, 1995.

Greenfield, J. C. "Aspects of Aramean Religion." In *Ancient Israelite Religion:*

Essays in Honor of Frank Moore Cross, ed. P. D. Miller, Jr., P. D. Hanson, and S. D. McBride, pp. 67-78. Philadelphia: Fortress, 1987.

———. "The Hebrew Bible and Canaanite Literature." In *The Literary Guide to the Bible,* ed. R. Alter and F. Kermode, pp. 545-60. Cambridge, Mass.: Belknap, 1987.

Grønbaek, J. H. *Die Geschichte vom Aufstieg Davids (1. Sam. 15–2. Sam. 5): Tradition und Komposition* (ATDa 10). Copenhagen: Prostant apud Munksgaard, 1971.

Gröndahl, F. *Die Personennamen der Texte aus Ugarit* (SP 1). Rome: Pontifical Biblical Institute, 1967.

Gruber, M. I. "Fear, Anxiety and Reverence in Akkadian, Biblical Hebrew and Other North-West Semitic Languages." *VT* 40 (1990) 411-22.

Gunn, D. M. *The Fate of King Saul* (JSOTSS 14). Sheffield: JSOT Press, 1980.

———, ed. *Narrative and Novella in Samuel: Studies by Hugo Gressmann and Other Scholars 1906-1923* (JSOTSS 116). Sheffield: Almond, 1991.

Hadley, J. M. *The Cult of Asherah in Ancient Israel and Judah: Evidence for a Hebrew Goddess* (UCOP 57). Cambridge: Cambridge University Press, 2000.

Hallo, W. W. "Biblical History in Its Near Eastern Setting: The Contextual Approach." In *Scripture in Context: Essays on the Comparative Method,* ed. C. D. Evans, W. W. Hallo, and J. B. White, pp. 1-26. Pittsburgh: Pickwick, 1980.

———. "New Directions in Historiography (Mesopotamia and Israel)." In *dubsar anta-men: Studien zur Altorientalistik: Festschrift für Willem H. Ph. Römer,* ed. M. Dietrich and O. Loretz (AOAT 253), pp. 109-28. Münster: Ugarit-Verlag, 1998.

———. *Origins: The Ancient Near Eastern Background of Some Modern Western Institutions* (SHCANE 6). Leiden: E. J. Brill, 1996.

———. "Proverbs Quoted in Epic." In *Lingering Over Words: Studies in Ancient Near Eastern Literature in Honor of William L. Moran,* ed. T. Abusch, J. Huehnergard, and P. Steinkeller, pp. 203-17. Atlanta: Scholars Press, 1990.

———, ed. *The Context of Scripture,* vol. I: *Canonical Compositions from the Biblical World.* Leiden: E. J. Brill, 1997.

———, ed. *The Context of Scripture,* vol. II: *Monumental Inscriptions from the Biblical World.* Leiden: E. J. Brill, 2000.

Hallo, W. W., J. C. Moyer, and L. G. Perdue, eds. *Scripture in Context II: More Essays on the Comparative Method.* Winona Lake, Ind.: Eisenbrauns, 1983.

Halpern, B. *The Constitution of the Monarchy in Israel* (HSM 25). Chico, Calif.: Scholars Press, 1981.

———. "The Construction of the Davidic State: An Exercise in Historiography."

In *The Origins of the Ancient Israelite States,* ed. V. Vritz and P. R. Davies (JSOTSS 228), pp. 44-75. Sheffield: Sheffield Academic Press, 1996.

———. "Erasing History: The Minimalist Assault on Ancient Israel." *BR* 11, no. 6 (1995) 26-35, 47.

Haran, M. *Temples and Temple-Service in Ancient Israel: An Inquiry into Biblical Cult Phenomena and the Historical Setting of the Priestly School.* Winona Lake, Ind.: Eisenbrauns, 1985.

Harland, P. J. "**בצע**: Bribe, Extortion or Profit?" *VT* 50 (2000) 310-22.

Healey, J. F. "Grain and Wine in Abundance: Blessings from the Ancient Near East." In *Ugarit, Religion and Culture: Proceedings of the International Colloquium on Ugarit, Religion and Culture, Edinburgh, July 1994: Essays presented in honour of Professor John C. L. Gibson,* ed. N. Wyatt, W. G. E. Watson, and J. B. Lloyd, pp. 65-74. Münster: Ugarit-Verlag, 1996.

Herbert, E. D. "4QSam[a] and Its Relationship to the LXX: An Exploration in Stemmatological Analysis." In *IX Congress of the International Organization for Septuagint and Cognate Studies: Cambridge, 1995,* ed. B. A. Taylor, pp. 37-55. Atlanta: Scholars Press, 1997.

———. *Reconstructing Biblical Dead Sea Scrolls: A New Method Applied to the Reconstruction of 4QSam[a]* (STDJ 22). Leiden: E. J. Brill, 1997.

Hertzberg, H. W. *I and II Samuel: A Commentary* (OTL). Philadelphia: Westminster, 1964 [orig. 1960].

Hess, R. S. *Joshua: An Introduction and Commentary* (TOTC). Leicester: InterVarsity, 1996.

Hess, R. S., and D. T. Tsumura, eds. *"I Studied Inscriptions from Before the Flood": Ancient Near Eastern, Literary, and Linguistic Approaches to Genesis 1–11* (SBTS 4). Winona Lake, Ind.: Eisenbrauns, 1994.

Hobbs, T. R. "Reflections on Honor, Shame, and Covenant Relations." *JBL* 116 (1997) 501-3.

Hoerth, A. J., G. L. Mattingly, and E. M. Yamauchi, eds. *Peoples of the Old Testament World.* Grand Rapids: Baker Book House, 1994.

Hoffner, H. A., Jr. "A Hittite Analogue to the David and Goliath Contest of Champions?" *CBQ* 30 (1968) 220-25.

———. "Propaganda and Political Justification in Hittite Historiography." In *Unity and Diversity: Essays in the History, Literature, and Religion of the Ancient Near East,* ed. H. Goedicke and J. J. M. Roberts, pp. 49-62. Baltimore: Johns Hopkins University Press, 1975.

Hoftijzer, J., and K. Jongeling. *Dictionary of the North-West Semitic Inscriptions.* Leiden: E. J. Brill, 1995.

Horowitz, W., and V. A. Hurowitz. "Urim and Thummim in Light of a Psephomancy Ritual from Assur (LKA 137)." *JANES* 21 (1992) 95-115.

Houtman, C. "The Urim and Thummim: A New Suggestion." *VT* 40 (1990) 229-32.

Howard, D. M., Jr. "The Case for Kingship in Deuteronomy and the Former Prophets." *WTJ* 52 (1990) 101-15.

Humphreys, C. J. "The Number of People in the Exodus from Egypt: Decoding Mathematically the Very Large Numbers in Numbers I and XXVI." *VT* 48 (1998) 196-213.

Hurowitz, V. A. "Temporary Temples." In *kinattūtu ša dārâti:* Raphael Kutscher Memorial Volume, ed. A. F. Rainey (Occasional Publications No. 1), pp. 37-50. Tel Aviv: Tel Aviv University, 1993.

Hurvitz, A. "The Historical Quest for 'Ancient Israel' and the Linguistic Evidence of the Hebrew Bible: Some Methodological Observation." *VT* 47 (1997) 301-15.

———. "Originals and Imitations in Biblical Poetry: A Comparative Examination of 1 Sam 2:1-10 and Ps 113:5-9." In *Biblical and Related Studies Presented to Samuel Iwry,* ed. A. Kort and S. Morschauser, pp. 115-21. Winona Lake, Ind.: Eisenbrauns, 1985.

Isaksson, B. " 'Aberrant' Usages of Introductory *wᵉhāyā* in the Light of Text Linguistics." In *"Lasset uns Brücken bauen . . .": Collected Communications to the XVth Congress of the International Organization for the Study of the Old Testament, Cambridge 1995,* ed. K.-D. Schunck and M. Augustin, pp. 9-25. Frankfurt am Main: Peter Lang, 1998.

Ishida, T. *History and Historical Writing in Ancient Israel: Studies in Biblical Historiography* (SHCANE 16). Leiden: E. J. Brill, 1999.

———. *The Royal Dynasties in Ancient Israel: A Study on the Formation and Development of Royal-Dynastic Ideology* (BZAW 142). Berlin: de Gruyter, 1977.

———, ed. *Studies in the Period of David and Solomon.* Tokyo: Yamamoto Shoten/Winona Lake, Ind.: Eisenbrauns, 1982.

Jacobsen, T. "The Eridu Genesis." *JBL* 100 (1981) 513-29.

———. "The Historian and the Sumerian Gods." *JAOS* 114 (1994) 145-53.

Japhet, S. *I & II Chronicles* (OTL). London: SCM, 1993.

Jobling, D. *1 Samuel: Berit Olam: Studies in Hebrew Narrative & Poetry.* Collegeville, Minn.: Liturgical, 1998.

Joosten, J. "Biblical Hebrew *wᵉqātal* and Syriac *hwā qātel:* Expressing Repetition in the Past." *ZAH* 5 (1992) 1-14.

Keel, O. *Goddesses and Trees, New Moon and Yahweh: Ancient Near Eastern Art and the Hebrew Bible* (JSOTSS 261). Sheffield: Sheffield Academic Press, 1998.

Kinnier-Wilson, J. V. "Medicine in the Land and Times of the Old Testament." In *Studies in the Period of David and Solomon and Other Essays: Papers Read at the International Symposium for Biblical Studies, Tokyo, 5-7 De-*

cember, 1979, ed. T. Ishida, pp. 337-65. Tokyo: Yamakawa-Shuppansha, 1982.

Kitchen, K. A. "Egyptians and Hebrews, from Ra'amses to Jericho." In *The Origin of Early Israel — Current Debate: Biblical, Historical and Archaeological Perspectives: Irene Levi-Sala Seminar, 1997,* ed. S. Aḥituv and E. D. Oren, pp. 65-131. Beer-Sheva: Ben-Gurion University of the Negev Press, 1998.

———. "New Directions in Biblical Archaeology: Historical and Biblical Aspects." In *Biblical Archaeology Today, 1990: Proceedings of the Second International Congress on Biblical Archaeology: Jerusalem, June-July 1990,* pp. 34-52. Jerusalem: Israel Exploration Society, 1993.

———. "The Philistines." In *POTT,* pp. 53-78.

———. "A Possible Mention of David in the Late Tenth Century BCE, and Deity *Dod as Dead as the Dodo?" *JSOT* 76 (1997) 29-44.

Kitz, A. M. "The Plural Form of ûrîm and tummîm." *JBL* 116 (1997) 401-10.

Kiuchi, N. *The Purification Offering in the Priestly Literature: Its Meaning and Function* (JSOTSS 56). Sheffield: JSOT Press, 1987.

Klein, R. W. *1 Samuel* (WBC 10). Waco, Tex.: Word Books, 1983.

Klement, H. H. *II Samuel 21–24: Context, Structure and Meaning in the Samuel Conclusion.* Frankfurt am Main: Peter Lang, 2000.

Klingbeil, G. A. "Ritual Time in Leviticus 8, with Special Reference to the Seven Day Period in the Old Testament." *ZAW* 109 (1997) 500-513.

Klingbeil, M. *Yahweh Fighting from Heaven: God as Warrior and as God of Heaven in the Hebrew Psalter and Ancient Near Eastern Iconography.* Göttingen: Vandenhoeck, 1999.

Knoppers, G. N. "Dissonance and Disaster in the Legend of Kirta." *JAOS* 114 (1994) 572-82.

Knoppers, G. N., and J. G. McConville, eds. *Reconsidering Israel and Judah: Recent Studies on the Deuteronomistic History* (SBTS 8). Winona Lake, Ind.: Eisenbrauns, 2000.

Kochavi, M. *Aphek-Antipatris: Five Seasons of Excavation at Tel Aphek-Antipatris (1972-1976).* Tel Aviv: Tel-Aviv University, 1977.

Kooij, A. van der. "The Story of David and Goliath: The Early History of Its Text." *ETL* 68 (1992) 118-31.

König, E. *Stilistik, Rhetorik, Poetik in Bezug auf die biblische Literatur.* Leipzig: Theodor Weicher, 1900.

Laato, A. *A Star Is Rising: The Historical Development of the Old Testament Royal Ideology and the Rise of the Jewish Messianic Expectations.* Atlanta: Scholars Press, 1997.

Labuschagne, C. J. *The Incomparability of Yahweh in the Old Testament* (POS 5). Leiden: E. J. Brill, 1966.

Lawergren, B. "Distinctions among Canaanite, Philistine, and Israelite Lyres, and Their Global Lyrical Contexts." *BASOR* 309 (1998) 41-68.

Layton, S. C. *Archaic Features of Canaanite Personal Names in the Hebrew Bible* (HSS 47). Atlanta: Scholars Press, 1990.

Lemaire, A. "The Tel Dan Stela as a Piece of Royal Historiography." *JSOT* 81 (1998) 3-14.

Lewis, T. J. *Cults of the Dead in Ancient Israel and Ugarit* (HSM 39). Atlanta: Scholars Press, 1989.

———. "The Textual History of the Song of Hannah: 1 Samuel II 1-10." *VT* 44 (1994) 18-46.

Lipiński, E. *Semitic Languages: Outline of a Comparative Grammar* (OLA 80). Leuven: Uitgeverij Peeters, 1997.

Livingstone, A. *Mystical and Mythological Explanatory Works of Assyrian and Babylonian Scholars.* Oxford: Clarendon, 1986.

Long, B. O. "Framing Repetitions in Biblical Historiography." *JBL* 106 (1987) 385-99.

Long, G. "The Written Story: Toward Understanding Text as Representation and Function." *VT* 49 (1999) 165-85.

Long, V. P. "How Did Saul Become King? Literary Reading and Historical Reconstruction." In *Faith, Tradition, and History: Old Testament Historiography in Its Near Eastern Context,* ed. A. R. Millard, J. K. Hoffmeier, and D. W. Baker, pp. 271-84. Winona Lake, Ind.: Eisenbrauns, 1994.

———. *The Reign and Rejection of King Saul: A Case for Literary and Theological Coherence* (SBLDS 118). Atlanta: Scholars Press, 1989.

———, ed. *Israel's Past in Present Research: Essays on Ancient Israelite Historiography* (SBTS 7). Winona Lake, Ind.: Eisenbrauns, 1999.

Longacre, R. E. "Weqatal Forms in Biblical Hebrew Prose." In *Biblical Hebrew and Discourse Linguistics,* ed. Robert D. Bergen, pp. 50-98. Dallas: Summer Institute of Linguistics, 1994.

Lust, J. "The Story of David and Goliath in Hebrew and in Greek." In *The Story of David and Goliath: Textual and Literary Criticism: Papers of a Joint Research Venture,* ed. D. Barthélemy et al. (OBO 73), pp. 5-18, 87-91, 121-28, 155f. Freiburg: Universitätsverlag, 1986.

Mabee, C. "Judicial Instrumentality in the Ahimelech Story." In *Early Jewish and Christian Exegesis: Studies in Memory of William H. Brownlee,* ed. C. A. Evans and W. F. Stinespring, pp. 17-32. Atlanta: Scholars Press, 1987.

McCarter, P. K., Jr. "The Apology of David." *JBL* 99 (1980) 489-504.

———. "Aspects of the Religion of the Israelite Monarchy: Biblical and Epigraphic Data." In *Ancient Israelite Religion: Essays in Honor of Frank Moore Cross,* ed. P. D. Miller, Jr., P. D. Hanson, and S. D. McBride, pp. 137-55. Philadelphia: Fortress, 1987.

———. *I Samuel: A New Translation with Introduction, Notes and Commentary* (AB 8). Garden City, N.Y.: Doubleday, 1980.

———. *II Samuel: A New Translation with Introduction, Notes and Commentary* (AB 9). Garden City, N.Y.: Doubleday, 1984.

McCarthy, C. *The Tiqqune Sopherim and Other Theological Corrections in the Masoretic Text of the Old Testament* (OBO 36). Freiburg: Universitätsverlag, 1981.

McCarthy, D. J. *Treaty and Covenant: A Study in Form in the Ancient Oriental Documents and in the Old Testament.* New ed. Rome: Biblical Institute Press, 1963, 1978.

McConville, J. G. "Priesthood in Joshua to Kings." *VT* 49 (1999) 73-87.

Malamat, A. "The Ban in Mari and in the Bible." *OTWSA* 9 (1966) 40-49.

———. *Mari and the Bible* (SHCANE 12). Leiden: E. J. Brill, 1998.

———. "Military Rationing in Papyrus Anastasi I and the Bible." In *Mélanges bibliques rédigés en l'honneur de André Robert* (TICP 4), pp. 114-21. Paris: Bloud & Gay, 1956.

Maul, S. M. "Der assyrische König — Hüter der Weltordnung." In *Priests and Officials in the Ancient Near East: Papers of the Second Colloquium on the Ancient Near East — The City and Its Life Held at the Middle Eastern Culture Center in Japan (Mitaka, Tokyo), March 22-24, 1996,* ed. K. Watanabe, pp. 201-14. Heidelberg: C. Winter, 1999.

Mazar, A. *Archaeology of the Land of the Bible, 10,000–586 B.C.E.* (ABRL). New York: Doubleday, 1990, 1992.

Mazar, B. *Biblical Israel: State and People,* ed. S. Ahituv. Jerusalem: Magnes, 1992.

———. "The Philistines and the Rise of Israel and Tyre." In *The Early Biblical Period: Historical Studies,* ed. A. Ahituv and B. A. Levine, pp. 63-82. Jerusalem: Israel Exploration Society, 1986.

Merwe, C. H. J. van der. "Discourse Linguistics and Biblical Hebrew Grammar." In *Biblical Hebrew and Discourse Linguistics,* ed. R. D. Bergen, pp. 13-49. Dallas: Summer Institute of Linguistics, 1994.

Mettinger, T. N. D. *King and Messiah: The Civil and Sacral Legitimation of the Israelite Kings* (CB: OT Series 8). Lund: C. W. K. Gleerup, 1976.

———. "YHWH SABAOTH — The Heavenly King on the Cherubim Throne." In *Studies in the Period of David and Solomon and Other Essays: Papers Read at the International Symposium for Biblical Studies, Tokyo, 5-7 December, 1979,* ed. T. Ishida, pp. 109-38. Tokyo: Yamakawa-Shuppansha, 1982.

Meyers, C. "An Ethnoarchaeological Analysis of Hannah's Sacrifice." In *Pomegranates and Golden Bells: Studies in Biblical, Jewish, and Near Eastern Ritual, Law, and Literature in Honor of Jacob Milgrom,* ed. D. P. Wright,

D. N. Freedman, and A. Hurvitz, pp. 77-91. Winona Lake, Ind.: Eisenbrauns, 1995.

Meyers, E. M., ed. *The Oxford Encyclopedia of Archaeology in the Near East.* 5 vols. Oxford: Oxford University Press, 1997.

Milgrom, J. *Cult and Conscience: The Asham and the Priestly Doctrine of Repentance.* Leiden: E. J. Brill, 1976.

Millard, A. R. "The Canaanites." In *POTT,* pp. 29-52.

———. "On Giving the Bible a Fair Go." *Buried History: Quarterly Journal of the Australian Institute of Archaeology* 35, no. 4 (1999) 5-12.

———. "Story, History, and Theology." In *Faith, Tradition, and History: Old Testament Historiography in Its Near Eastern Context,* ed. A. R. Millard, J. K. Hoffmeier, and D. W. Baker, pp. 37-64. Winona Lake, Ind.: Eisenbrauns, 1994.

———. "Strangers from Egypt and Greece — The Signs for Numbers in Early Hebrew." In *Immigration and Emigration within the Ancient Near East: Festschrift E. Lipiński,* ed. K. van Lerberghe and A. Schoors (OLA 65), pp. 189-94. Leuven: Uitgeverij Peeters, 1995.

Miller, C. L. "Introducing Direct Discourse in Biblical Hebrew Narrative." In *Biblical Hebrew and Discourse Linguistics,* ed. R. D. Bergen, pp. 199-241. Dallas: Summer Institute of Linguistics, 1994.

Miller, P. D., Jr. "Aspects of the Religion of Ugarit." In *Ancient Israelite Religion: Essays in Honor of Frank Moore Cross,* ed. P. D. Miller, Jr., P. D. Hanson, and S. D. McBride, pp. 53-66. Philadelphia: Fortress, 1987.

Miller, P. D., Jr., and J. J. M. Roberts. *The Hand of the Lord: A Reassessment of the "Ark Narrative" of 1 Samuel* (JHNES). Baltimore: Johns Hopkins University Press, 1977.

Miscall, P. D. "Introduction to Narrative Literature." In *The New Interpreter's Bible,* ed. Leander E. Keck, pp. 539-52. Nashville: Abingdon, 1998.

Mitchell, T. C. *The Bible in the British Museum: Interpreting the Evidence.* London: British Museum Publications, 1988.

———. "The Music of the Old Testament Reconsidered." *IEJ* (124th year) (1992) 124-43.

Moberly, R. W. L. "'God is not a human that he should repent' (Numbers 23:19 and 1 Samuel 15:29)." In *God in the Fray: A Tribute to Walter Brueggemann,* ed. T. Linafelt and T. K. Beal, pp. 112-23. Minneapolis: Fortress, 1998.

Moorey, P. R. S. "The Craft of the Metalsmith in the Ancient Near East: The Origins of Ironworking." In *From Gulf to Delta and Beyond,* ed. E. D. Oren (Beer-Sheva 8), pp. 53-68. Beersheva: Ben-Gurion University of the Negev Press, 1995.

Muchiki, Y. *Egyptian Proper Names and Loanwords in North-West Semitic* (SBLDS 173). Atlanta: Scholars Press, 1999.

Muhly, J. D. "How Iron Technology Changed the Ancient World and Gave the Philistines a Military Edge." *BAR* 8, no. 6 (Nov./Dec. 1982) 40-54.

Muraoka, T. "The Status Constructus of Adjectives in Biblical Hebrew." *VT* 27 (1977) 375-80.

Muraoka, T. "The Tripartite Nominal Clause Revisited." In *The Verbless Clause in Biblical Hebrew: Linguistic Approaches,* ed. C. L. Miller, pp. 187-213. Winona Lake, Ind.: Eisenbrauns, 1999.

Naveh, J. "Achish-Ikausu in the Light of the Ekron Dedication." *BASOR* 310 (1998) 35-37.

Nelson, R. D. "*ḥerem* and the Deuteronomic Social Conscience!" In *Deuteronomy and Deuteronomic Literature: Festschrift C. H. W. Brekelmans,* ed. M. Vervenne and J. Lust, pp. 39-54. Leuven: Leuven University Press, 1997.

———. "The Role of the Priesthood in the Deuteronomistic History." In *Congress Volume: Leuven 1989,* ed. J. A. Emerton (SVT 43), pp. 132-47. Leiden: E. J. Brill, 1991.

Niccacci, A. "Analysing Biblical Hebrew Poetry." *JSOT* 74 (1997) 77-93.

———. "Analysis of Biblical Narrative." In *Biblical Hebrew and Discourse Linguistics,* ed. R. D. Bergen, pp. 175-98. Dallas: Summer Institute of Linguistics, 1994.

———. *The Syntax of the Verb in Classical Hebrew Prose* (JSOTSS 86). Sheffield: Sheffield Academic Press, 1990.

Nielsen, K. *Incense in Ancient Israel* (SVT 38). Leiden: E. J. Brill, 1986.

Noth, M. *The Deuteronomistic History,* trans. J. Doull et al. (JSOTSS 15). Sheffield: JSOT Press, 1981.

O'Connor, M. "War and Rebel Chants in the Former Prophets." In *Fortunate the Eyes That See: Essays in Honor of David Noel Freedman in Celebration of His Seventieth Birthday,* ed. A. B. Beck, A. H. Bartelt, P. R. Raabe and C. A. Franke, pp. 322-37. Grand Rapids: Eerdmans, 1995.

Olyan, S. M. "Honor, Shame, and Covenant Relations in Ancient Israel and Its Environment." *JBL* 115 (1996) 201-18.

Oren, E. D., ed. *The Sea Peoples and Their World: A Reassessment* (UMM 108). Philadelphia: University of Pennsylvania Museum, 2000.

Pardee, D. "Marzihu, Kispu, and the Ugaritic Funerary Cult: A Minimalist View." In *Ugarit, Religion and Culture: Essays presented in honour of Professor John C. L. Gibson,* pp. 273-87. Münster: Ugarit-Verlag, 1996.

Parker, S. B. "Did the Authors of the Books of Kings Make Use of Royal Inscriptions?" *VT* 50 (2000) 357-78.

Parunak, H. van D. "Some Axioms for Literary Architecture." *Semitics* 8 (1982) 2-4.

———. "Transitional Techniques in the Bible." *JBL* 102 (1983) 525-48.

Penkower, J. S. "Verse Divisions in the Hebrew Bible." *VT* 50 (2000) 379-93.

Pisano, S. *Additions or Omissions in the Books of Samuel: The Significant Pluses and Minuses in the Massoretic, LXX and Qumran Texts* (OBO 57). Freiburg: Universitätsverlag, 1984.

Provan, I. W. "Ideologies, Literary and Critical: Reflections on Recent Writing on the History of Israel." *JBL* 114 (1995) 585-606.

Rainey, A. F. *Canaanite in the Amarna Tablets: A Linguistic Analysis of the Mixed Dialect Used by the Scribes from Canaan.* 4 vols. (HbO). Leiden: E. J. Brill, 1996.

———. "The Identification of Philistine Gath: A Problem in Source Analysis for Historical Geography." *EI* 12 [Nelson Glueck Memorial Volume] (1975) 63*-76*.

———. "Uncritical Criticism." *JAOS* 115 (1995) 101-4.

———, ed. *Kinattūtu ša dārâti: Raphael Kutscher Memorial Volume* (Occasional Publications No. 1). Tel Aviv: Tel Aviv University, 1993.

Rendsburg, G. A. *Diglossia in Ancient Hebrew* (AOS 72). New Haven: American Oriental Society, 1990.

———. "Linguistic Variation and the 'Foreign' Factor in the Hebrew Bible." In *Language and Culture in the Near East,* ed. S. Izre'el and R. Drory (IOS 15), pp. 177-90. Leiden: E. J. Brill, 1995.

———. "Some False Leads in the Identification of Late Biblical Hebrew Texts: The Cases of Genesis 24 and 1 Samuel 2:27-36." *JBL* 121 (2002) 23-46.

Rendtorff, R. "Samuel the Prophet: A Link between Moses and the Kings." In *The Quest for Context and Meaning: Studies in Biblical Intertextuality in Honor of James A. Sanders,* ed. C. A. Evans and S. Talmon, pp. 27-36. Leiden: E. J. Brill, 1997.

Renz, J., and W. Röllig. *Handbuch der althebräischen Epigraphik I.* Darmstadt: Wissenschaftliche Buchgesellschaft, 1995.

Revell, E. J. "The Repetition of Introductions to Speech as a Feature of Biblical Hebrew." *VT* 47 (1997) 91-110.

Reviv, H. *The Elders in Ancient Israel.* Jerusalem: Magnes, 1989.

Roberts, J. J. M. "In Defense of the Monarchy: The Contribution of Israelite Kingship to Biblical Theology." In *Ancient Israelite Religion: Essays in Honor of Frank Moore Cross,* ed. P. D. Miller, Jr., P. D. Hanson, and S. D. McBride, pp. 377-96. Philadelphia: Fortress, 1987.

Rooy, H. F. van. "Prophetic Utterances in Narrative Texts, with reference to 1 Samuel 2:27-36." *OTE* 3 (1990) 203-18.

Rost, L. *The Succession to the Throne of David.* Sheffield: Almond, 1982.

Sasson, J. M. "The Numeric Progression in Keret 1:15-20: Yet Another Suggestion." *SEL* 5 [= *Cananea Selecta: Festschrift für Oswald Loretz zum 60. Geburtstag*] (1988) 181-88.

Sasson, V. "The Inscription of Achish, Governor of Ekron, and Philistine Dialect, Cult and Culture." *UF* 29 (1997) 627-39.

Schenker, A. "Once Again, the Expiatory Sacrifices." *JBL* 116 (1997) 697-99.

Schicklberger, F. *Die Ladeerzählung des ersten Samuel-Buches: Eine literaturwissenschaftliche und theologiegeschichtliche Untersuchung* (FB 7). Würzburg: Echter, 1973.

Schmidt, B. B. *Israel's Beneficent Dead: Ancestor Cult and Necromancy in Ancient Israelite Religion and Tradition.* Tübingen: J. C. B. Mohr, 1994.

Schniedewind, W. M. "The Geopolitical History of Philistine Gath." *BASOR* 309 (1998) 69-77.

Schunck, K.-D. M. A .H. *"Lasset uns Brücken bauen . . .": Collected Communications to the XVth Congress of the International Organization for the Study of the Old Testament, Cambridge 1995* (BEATAJ 42). Frankfurt am Main: Peter Lang, 1998.

Scolnic, B. E. *Theme and Context in Biblical Lists* (SFSHJ 119). Atlanta: Scholars Press, 1995.

Sivan, D. *A Grammar of the Ugaritic Language.* Leiden: E. J. Brill, 1997.

Ska, J. L. "Quelques exemples de sommaires proleptiques dans les récits bibliques." In *Congress Volume: Paris 1992,* ed. J. A. Emerton, pp. 315-26. Leiden: E. J. Brill, 1995.

Smith, H. P. *A Critical and Exegetical Commentary on the Books of Samuel* (ICC). Edinburgh: T. & T. Clark, 1899.

Smith, M. S. "Anat's Warfare Cannibalism and the West Semitic Ban." In *The Pitcher Is Broken: Memorial Essays for Gosta W. Ahlstrom,* ed. S. W. Holloway and L. K. Handy (JSOTSS 190), pp. 368-86. Sheffield: Sheffield Academic Press, 1995.

Sokoloff, M. *A Dictionary of Jewish Palestinian Aramaic of the Byzantine Period.* Ramat-Gan: Bar Ilan University, 1990.

Stern, E., ed. *The New Encyclopedia of Archaeological Excavations in the Holy Land.* 4 vols. Jerusalem: Israel Exploration Society and Carta, 1993.

Sternberg, M. *The Poetics of Biblical Narrative: Ideological Literature and the Drama of Reading.* Bloomington: Indiana University Press, 1985.

Stoebe, H. J. *Das erste Buch Samuelis* (KAT VIII/1). Gütersloh: Gerd Mohn, 1973.

———. "Die Goliathperikope 1 Sam. XVII 1–XVIII 5 und die Textform der Septuaginta." *VT* 6 (1956) 397-413.

Tadmor, H., and M. Weinfeld, eds. *History, Historiography and Interpretation: Studies in Biblical and Cuneiform Literatures.* Jerusalem: Magnes, 1983.

Talmon, S. "The Biblical Idea of Statehood." In *The Bible World: Essays in Honor of Cyrus H. Gordon,* ed. G. Rendsburg, R. Adler, M. Arfa, and N. H. Winter, pp. 239-48. New York: Ktav, 1980.

———. *Literary Studies in the Hebrew Bible: Form and Content: Collected Studies.* Jerusalem: Magnes, 1993.

Tarragon, J.-M. d. *Le Culte à Ugarit: D'après les Textes de la Pratique en Cunéiformes Alphabétiques* (CRB 19). Paris: J. Gabalda, 1980.

Taylor, J. G. *Yahweh and the Sun: Biblical and Archaeological Evidence for Sun Worship in Ancient Israel* (JSOTSS 111). Sheffield: Sheffield Academic Press, 1993.

Thenius, O. *Die Bücher Samuels.* Leipzig: Hirzel, 1842 [2d ed., 1864; 3d ed. (Max Löhr), 1898].

Thompson, T. L. "Historiography of Ancient Palestine and Early Jewish Historiography: W. G. Dever and the Not So New Biblical Archaeology." In *The Origins of the Ancient Israelite States,* ed. V. Vritz and P. R. Davies (JSOTSS 228), pp. 26-43. Sheffield: Sheffield Academic Press, 1996.

Toorn, K. van der. *Family Religion in Babylonia, Syria and Israel: Continuity and Change in the Forms of Religious Life* (SHCANE 7). Leiden: E. J. Brill, 1996.

———. "The Nature of the Biblical Teraphim in the Light of the Cuneiform Evidence." *CBQ* 52 (1990) 203-22.

Tov, E. "The Composition of 1 Samuel 16–18 in the Light of the Septuagint Version." In *Empirical Models for Biblical Criticism,* ed. J. H. Tigay, pp. 97-130. Philadelphia: University of Pennsylvania Press, 1985.

———. *Textual Criticism of the Hebrew Bible.* Minneapolis: Fortress, 1992.

———, ed. *The Hebrew and Greek Texts of Samuel. 1980 Proceedings IOSCS — Vienna.* Jerusalem: Academon, 1980.

Tropper, J. *Nekromantie* (AOAT 228). Neukirchen-Vluyn: Neukirchener, 1989.

Tsevat, M. "Assyriological Notes on the First Book of Samuel." In *Studies in the Bible presented to M. H. Segal,* ed. J. M. Grintz and J. Liver, pp. 77-86. Jerusalem: Kiryat Sepher, 1964.

———. "The Biblical Account of the Foundation of the Monarchy in Israel." In *The Meaning of the Book of Job and Other Biblical Studies: Essays on the Literature and Religion of the Hebrew Bible,* pp. 77-99. New York: Ktav, 1980.

———. "Was Samuel a Nazirite?" In *"Sha'arei Talmon": Studies in the Bible, Qumran, and the Ancient Near East presented to Shemaryahu Talmon,* ed. M. Fishbane and E. Tov, pp. 199-204. Winona Lake, Ind.: Eisenbrauns, 1992.

Tsumura, D. T. "Coordination Interrupted, or Literary Insertion AX&B Pattern, in the Books of Samuel." In *Literary Structure and Rhetorical Strategies in the Hebrew Bible,* ed. L. J. de Regt, J. de Waard, and J. P. Fokkelman, pp. 117-32. Assen: Van Gorcum, 1996.

———. "The Interpretation of the Ugaritic Funerary Text KTU 1.161." In *Official Cult and Popular Religion in the Ancient Near East,* ed. E. Matsushima, pp. 40-55. Heidelberg: C. Winter, 1993.

———. "Kings and Cults in Ancient Ugarit." In *Priests and Officials in the An-*

cient Near East, ed. K. Watanabe, pp. 215-38. Heidelberg: C. Winter, 1999.

———. "List and Narrative in I Samuel 6,17-18a in the Light of Ugaritic Economic Texts." *ZAW* 113 (2001) 353-69.

———. "Literary Insertion (AXB Pattern) in Biblical Hebrew." *VT* 33 (1983) 468-82.

———. "Poetic Nature of the Hebrew Narrative Prose in I Samuel 2:12-17." In *Verse in Ancient Near Eastern Prose,* ed. J. C. de Moor and W. G. E. Watson (AOAT 42), pp. 293-304. Neukirchen-Vluyn: Neukirchener, 1993.

———. "Scribal Errors or Phonetic Spellings? Samuel as an Aural Text." *VT* 49 (1999) 390-411.

———. "Vowel sandhi in Biblical Hebrew." *ZAW* 109 (1997) 575-88.

Ulrich, E. C., Jr. *The Qumran Text of Samuel and Josephus* (HSM 19). Missoula, Mont.: Scholars Press, 1978.

Van Dam, C. *The Urim and Thummim: A Means of Revelation in Ancient Israel.* Winona Lake, Ind.: Eisenbrauns, 1997.

Van Seters, J. *In Search of History: Historiography in the Ancient World and the Origins of Biblical History.* New Haven: Yale University Press, 1983.

Van Wolde, E., ed. *Narrative Syntax and the Hebrew Bible: Papers of the Tilburg Conference 1996* (BIS 29). Leiden: E. J. Brill, 1997.

Vannoy, J. R. *Covenant Renewal at Gilgal: A Study of 1 Samuel 11:14–12:25.* Cherry Hill, N.J.: Mack, 1978.

Walters, S. D. "After Drinking (1 Sam 1:9)." In *Crossing Boundaries and Linking Horizons: Studies in Honor of Michael C. Astour on His 80th Birthday,* ed. G. D. Young, M. W. Chavalas, and R. E. Averbeck, pp. 527-45. Bethesda: CDL, 1997.

———. "Childless Michal, Mother of Five." In *The Tablet and the Scroll: Near Eastern Studies in Honor of William W. Hallo,* ed. M. Cohen, D. Snell, and D. Weisberg, pp. 290-96. Bethesda, Md.: CDL, 1993.

Watson, W. G. E. *Classical Hebrew Poetry: A Guide to Its Techniques* (JSOTSS 26). Sheffield: JSOT Press, 1984.

Watson, W. G. E., and N. Wyatt, eds. *Handbook of Ugaritic Studies* (HbO). Leiden: E. J. Brill, 1999.

Weinfeld, M. *Social Justice in Ancient Israel and in the Ancient Near East.* Jerusalem: Magnes, 1995.

Wellhausen, J. *Die Text der Bücher Samuelis Untersucht.* Göttingen: Vandenhoeck and Ruprecht, 1871.

Whitelam, K. W. "Israelite Kingship: The Royal Ideology and Its Opponents." In *The World of Ancient Israel: Sociological, Anthropological and Political Perspectives: Essays by Members of the Society for Old Testament Study,* ed. R. E. Clements, pp. 119-39. Cambridge: Cambridge University Press, 1989.

Willis, J. T. "Samuel versus Eli, I. Sam. 1–7." *TZ* 35 (1979) 201-12.

Wilson, R. R. *Prophecy and Society in Ancient Israel.* Philadelphia: Fortress, 1980.

Wiseman, D. J. "'Is It Peace?' — Covenant and Diplomacy." *VT* 32 (1982) 311-26.

Wright, D. P. "The Gesture of Hand Placement in the Hebrew Bible and in Hittite Literature." *JAOS* 106 (1986) 433-46.

Yamauchi, E. "The Current State of Old Testament Historiography." In *Faith, Tradition, and History: Old Testament Historiography in Its Near Eastern Context,* ed. A. R. Millard, James K. Hoffmeier, and David W. Baker, pp. 1-36. Winona Lake, Ind.: Eisenbrauns, 1994.

TEXT AND COMMENTARY

I. "STORY OF SAMUEL" — WITH THE EMBEDDED "STORY OF THE ARK OF GOD" (1:1–7:17)

The beginning of the First Book of Samuel is placed late in the period of the judges, which is probably the mid-eleventh century B.C. It is set against the background of "the grand finale" of the book of Judges, chapters 17–21, which gives "a disconcerting picture of cultic and moral chaos," as described in the formulaic expression: "In those days there was no king in Israel; everyone did what was right in his own eyes" (Judg. 17:6; 21:25).[1] In this dark time in the history of Israel, Yahweh chose as his prophet Samuel, who was destined to appoint the first kings in Israel. Thus, the first seven chapters, chs. 1–7, constitute a unified whole, dealing with the transitional period from the end of judgeship to the new era of kingship.[2]

The story of the ark (4:1–7:1), which constitutes itself a unified episode, is embedded in the entire story of Samuel (1:1–7:17). Its embedding, however, is intentional and well planned, as the very first verse (4:1a) refers back to the preceding section (ch. 3). Recent scholarly emphasis on the unity and "interconnections" between the embedded story of the ark and its surrounding chapters in 1 Samuel 1–7 is a welcome feature, though one need not wait until the exilic era, as Polzin and Birch do,[3] in order to write out this early event in the history of Israel. The present writer is inclined to take the account in chs. 4–6 as pre-Davidic, though its final editing into a wider section, chs. 1–7, could be during the early Davidic era; see "Introduction."

A. RISE OF SAMUEL AS PROPHET (1:1–3:21)

1 Samuel 1–3 deals with the rise of the prophet Samuel in contrast to the decline of the Shilonite priesthood. This is reflected in the alternating literary structure ABABBA.

1. J. P. Fokkelman, *Narrative Art and Poetry in the Books of Samuel,* vol. IV: *Vow and Desire (I Sam. 1–12)* (SSN 31; Assen: Van Gorcum, 1993), p. 1.

2. For the essential unity of chs. 1–7, see J. T. Willis, "An Anti-Elide Narrative Tradition from a Prophetic Circle at the Ramah Sanctuary," *JBL* 90 (1971) 288-308; "Samuel versus Eli, I. Sam. 1–7," *TZ* 35 (1979) 201-12.

3. R. Polzin, *Samuel and the Deuteronomist: A Literary Study of the Deuteronomic History, Part II: 1 Samuel* (Bloomington: Indiana University Press, 1989), pp. 5, 55-79; B. C. Birch, "The First and Second Books of Samuel: Introduction, Commentary, and Reflections," in *The New Interpreter's Bible,* vol. II, ed. L. E. Keck et al. (Nashville: Abingdon, 1998), p. 996.

(A) Birth of Samuel, with the embedded prayer of Hannah (1:1–2:11)
(B) Sins of Eli's sons (2:12-17)
(A) Samuel and his family (2:18-21a), with a note of Samuel's growth (2:21b)
(B) Sins of Eli's sons (2:22-25), with a note of Samuel's growth (2:26),

followed by

(B) A divine message to Eli through "a man of God" (2:27-36)
(A) The prophetic call of Samuel (3:1-21).

There is a "resumptive repetition" of the expression, "the boy/Samuel was ministering to/before the Lord," in 1 Sam. 2:11, 18.

In this section, Hannah, Elkanah, and Samuel are sharply contrasted with Eli and his two sons, Hophni and Phinehas. At that time the ark of God was still at Shiloh, the chief Israelite sanctuary, and was the symbol of Yahweh's presence in the midst of the covenant people, though it was soon to be carried away by the Philistines (1 Sam. 4). Such a dreadful thing had never happened in the history of the covenant people Israel. It was surely one of the darkest times of its history when Samuel was called to be a prophet of the Lord (1 Samuel 3). This teaches us that regardless of how desperate the situation looks outwardly, God is certainly preparing his chosen individuals in order to fulfill his plan and purpose according to his sovereign will and gracious concern for his people.

1 Sam. 1:1–2:11

The birth of Samuel (1 Samuel 1) inaugurated "a decisive period" like the birth of Moses (Exodus 1–2) or of Jesus (Luke 1–2).[4] A new era — the era of the monarchy — was brought about by the birth of the kingmaker. The story is not just about a devout woman whose prayer was heard. In the midst of an ordinary family life situation, God directed Hannah's life so she played a crucial role as mother of the kingmaker. The one who was to be born to her was not only a prophet of Israel but the one who would establish kingship in Israel, appointing first Saul, then David. This Samuel takes the decisive role in the period of transition from the days of the judges to the monarchical era, leading to the establishment of the House of David and the beginning of the worship of Yahweh in Jerusalem. If an incident in a woman's ordinary family life could be such a significant step in the eternal

4. A. Caquot and P. de Robert, *Les Livres de Samuel* (CAT VI; Geneva: Labor et Fides, 1994), p. 36.

plan of a saving God, each day can be no less significant to a believer for God's plan and purpose.

Although Hannah's prayer for a son (1 Sam. 1:11) does not involve the need of an heir for her husband, C. H. Gordon is right: "Preoccupation with the birth of a son is part of the repertoire of what was worth recording down through the period of the Judges and Samuel, but not thereafter."[5] But, the "song" (2:1b-10) that Hannah prayed is not so much a thanksgiving for the son as a "hymn" to the sovereign God Yahweh, a song which became the prototype of the Magnificat (Luke 1). Thus, the story of Samuel's birth reaches its climax with the "song" of Hannah in the story unit, 1:1–2:11.[6]

1. Birth and Dedication of Samuel (1:1-28)

A look at the discourse structure, based on the analysis of the "verbal sequence" of the text as it stands (see "Introduction" [Section VI, A]), shows that vv. 1-3 give the background information ("Elkanah and his two wives": SETTING) for the following two EVENTs, that is, "Hannah's prayer and vow" (vv. 4-19: EVENT 1) and the "Dedication of Samuel" (vv. 20-28: EVENT 2). And v. 28 is a transition leading toward the TERMINUS at 2:11, with the embedded "Hannah's song" (2:1b-10). It is noteworthy that the entire chapter begins (v. 3: *This man used to go up*) and ends (v. 28: *they worshipped*) with Elkanah's family worshipping God, and with a focus on Hannah, who will give praise to Yahweh.

a. Elkanah and His Two Wives (1:1-3)

1 *There was a man, one of the Zuphites from Ramathaim,*
from the hill country of Ephraim;
his name was Elkanah,
son of Jeroham, son of Elihu,
son of Tohu,[7] *son of Zuph*
an Ephrathite.

5. C. H. Gordon, *The Common Background of Greek and Hebrew Civilizations* (New York: W. W. Norton, 1965), p. 156.

6. For various views on the literary structure of this section, see Fokkelman, *Narrative Art and Poetry,* vol. IV; Caquot and de Robert, p. 36; S. Bar-Efrat, "Some Observations on the Analysis of Structure in Biblical Narrative," *VT* 30 (1980) 159; M. Brettler, "The Composition of 1 Samuel 1–2," *JBL* 116 (1997) 607.

7. PN *tōḥû; tôaḥ* in 1 Chr. 6:19 is simply a shorter variant. See the variation of *thw and *twh, both meaning "desert" (D. T. Tsumura, *The Earth and the Waters in Genesis 1 and 2: A Linguistic Analysis* [JSOTSS 83; Sheffield: Sheffield Academic Press, 1989], p. 17, n. 3).

2 *He had two wives:*
the name of the first was Hannah
and the name of the second was Peninnah;
Peninnah had children,
but Hannah had no children.
3 *This man used to go up from his city annually*[8]
to worship and sacrifice to the Lord of Hosts at Shiloh,
where Eli's[9] *two sons, Hophni and Phinehas,*[10]
were [acting as] priests for the Lord.

1-3 In terms of discourse grammar the first three verses constitute the SETTING. While vv. 1-2 introduce the major *dramatis personae,* Elkanah and his wife Hannah, v. 3 explains what this man used to do and where. The mention of Shiloh and the priestly family of Eli as well as *the Lord of Hosts,* the hidden but ultimate agent of the events, foreshadows the entire narrative to come.

1 Like the stories of Saul and of Samson, the story of Samuel starts with the expression: *There was a man* (cf. 1 Sam. 9:1, "There was a man from Benjamin," and Judg. 13:2, "There was a certain man of Zorah, of the tribe of the Danites"). The MT *ʾîš ʾeḥād* is usually translated as "a certain man" (NRSV; NASB; NIV; REB) as in 2 Sam. 18:10. But with this translation, the plural of *ṣôpîm* (Zuphite) cannot be explained satisfactorily. Hence, most scholars take the pl. *mem* of *ṣôpîm* as dittography of the following *m* and read *ṣwpy mhr ʾprym:* for example, "a certain man from Ramathaim, a Zuphite from . . ." (REB).[11] Another suggestion is to take *ṣôpîm* without emendation as plural and to connect it with Ramathaim: for example, "Ramathaim-zophim" (KJV; NASB);[12] "Ramathaim of the Zuphites" (JPS). However, it is also possible to see here an instance of the AXB pattern, in

8. Lit., "from days to days"; also Exod. 13:10; Judg. 11:40; 21:19; 1 Sam. 2:19.

9. "Eli" is possibly a short form of *yḥwʿly* (Samaria Ostracon, 55:2) "May the Exalted One preserve alive" (?); see *RSP* 3 (1981), p. 457; also on a Hebrew seal, N. Avigad and B. Sass, *Corpus of West Semitic Stamp Seals* (Jerusalem: Israel Academy of Sciences and Humanities, 1997), no. 181. See 1 Sam. 2:10 on *ʿlw,* which might be a divine epithet, "the Exalted One." However, the divine element usually drops from theophoric names like *Nathan, Baruch,* etc.

10. The sons' names are probably Egyptian names; see Y. Muchiki, *Egyptian Proper Names and Loanwords in North-West Semitic* (SBLDS 173; Atlanta: Scholars Press, 1999), pp. 211, 222.

11. E.g., P. K. McCarter, Jr., *I Samuel: A New Translation with Introduction, Notes and Commentary* (AB 8; Garden City, N.Y.: Doubleday, 1980), p. 51; also Fokkelman, *Narrative Art and Poetry,* vol. IV, p. 558.

12. Caquot and de Robert, p. 33.

which AB: *'eḥād ṣôpîm* (one of the Zuphites) is interrupted by the insertion of X: *min-hārāmātayim* (from Ramathaim) while keeping the relationship between A and B; hence, X modifies A . . . B as a whole; see "Introduction" (Section VII, C). With this explanation, the pl. form of *ṣôpîm* causes no problem, and the phrase is translated *one of the Zuphites from Ramathaim.*

This man is described as *one of the Zuphites,* a description in harmony with the *son of Zuph an Ephrathite* of the end of this verse. It is also in keeping with 1 Sam. 9:5, which places Samuel's home town in "the land of Zuph." Zuph is the ancestor of a local clan, while Ephraim is the tribal ancestor.[13]

The location of *Ramathaim* is a matter of dispute. McCarter identifies it with modern Rentis, about 16 miles east of Tel Aviv on the western slope of the hills of Ephraim.[14] Later in the book it is called *Ramah* (1 Sam. 1:19; 2:11; 8:4; 25:1; 28:3), the usual name for Samuel's home town (7:17), which is presumably "the city where the man of God was" (9:10), the Zuphite Ramah (9:5). Eusebius associated it with Arimathea of the NT and identified it with the village of Rempthis, whereas Jerome located it in the region of Timnah, about 9 miles northwest of Bethel. On the identification of Ramah, see on 1:19. The city was called *Ramathaim* (lit. "two hills") probably because there were two hills associated with it; one for the city itself and the other for a high place. According to 1 Samuel 9, the high place, which was presumably on a hilltop (see 9:25), was located outside the city, which was itself on the top of a hill (see 9:11f.).

Elkanah ("God created"; cf. Gen. 14:19) must have been from a well-to-do family (see on 1 Sam. 1:24), as suggested by his pedigree and his dual marriage.[15] The phrase "the Ephrathites" can refer either to "those hailing from Ephrath" (i.e., Bethlehem) or "Ephraimites," members of the northern tribe of Ephraim (Judg. 12:5; 1 K. 11:26).[16] According to Haran, *'eprāt* or *'eprātāh* is an "appellative" of the city Bethlehem (Gen. 35:16; 48:7; Ruth 4:11; Mic. 5:2; etc), whereas the gentilic *'eprātî* denotes either a member of the tribe of Ephraim (Judg. 12:5; 1 K. 11:26) or an inhabitant of Bethlehem (1 Sam. 17:12; Ruth 1:2).[17] Elkanah might have been of Bethlehemite stock rather than being an "Ephraimite," even though he dwelt in *the hill country of Ephraim.*

13. See on 1 Sam. 10:21 for the relationship: "people" — "tribe" — "clan" — "family."

14. On *Ephraim,* see S. Herrmann, "Ephraim," in *ABD,* II, pp. 551-53.

15. On *qnh "to create," see *HALOT,* pp. 1111-12. Cf. "a man of means" (R. P. Gordon, *I & II Samuel* [Exeter: Paternoster, 1986], p. 72).

16. See R. L. Hubbard, Jr., *The Book of Ruth* (NICOT; Grand Rapids: Eerdmans, 1988), pp. 90-91; L. M. Luker, "Ephrathah," in *ABD,* II, pp. 557-58.

17. M. Haran, *Temples and Temple-Service in Ancient Israel: An Inquiry into Biblical Cult Phenomena and the Historical Setting of the Priestly School* (Winona Lake, Ind.: Eisenbrauns, 1985), pp. 307-8.

2 In the ancient Near East, having an heir was very important, for lacking an heir meant the end of one's "house." For example, King Keret of the Ugaritic epic, though he had gold and silver, lost all his male children and so his dynasty was about to be extinguished.[18] It was common in real life for a well-to-do man to take a second wife if the first did not bear him an heir. Sarah, of course, advised Abraham to take her slave-girl Hagar as his second "wife" (NEB; or concubine) so that he might have an heir (Gen. 16:1-6). One can easily guess that there was tremendous tension because of jealousy and enmity in a household where a man had *two wives*. In the light of the above, the term *'aḥat* in this context probably means *first*.[19] The construction *the first . . . the second . . .* appears in Gen. 4:19; Exod. 1:15; Ruth 1:4; cf. 1 Sam. 8:2; 25:3.

Hannah, the central figure in this chapter, appears for the first time. C. Meyers even suggests that "the narrative of Samuel's birth could just as well be called the Hannah Narrative."[20] The names *Hannah* ("favor [with God?]") and *Peninnah*[21] appear in chiastic order, that is, Hannah — Peninnah — Peninnah — Hannah. However, the focus here is on Hannah.

3 This verse, which begins with a *wqtl* NP *(This man used to go up),* fills in more of the SETTING.[22]

Elkanah went *annually* to Shiloh to perform the seasonal sacrifice (see 1 Sam. 1:21). The three annual festivals — the Feast of Unleavened Bread, the

18. See D. T. Tsumura, "The Problem of Childlessness in the Royal Epic of Ugarit," in *Monarchies and Socio-Religious Traditions in the Ancient Near East* (Wiesbaden: Otto Harrassowitz, 1984), pp. 11-20.

19. So McCarter, p. 51. See Gen. 1:5 "the first day" *(yôm 'eḥād)*. Note that Ugaritic *aḥd* was also used as an ordinal number; see C. H. Gordon, *UT,* p. 550.

20. C. Meyers, "An Ethnoarchaeological Analysis of Hannah's Sacrifice," in *Pomegranates and Golden Bells: Studies in Biblical, Jewish, and Near Eastern Ritual, Law, and Literature in Honor of Jacob Milgrom,* ed. D. P. Wright, D. N. Freedman, and A. Hurvitz (Winona Lake, Ind.: Eisenbrauns, 1995), p. 80; also C. Meyers, "Hannah and Her Sacrifice: Reclaiming Female Agency," in *A Feminist Companion to Samuel and Kings,* ed. A. Brenner (Feminist Companion to the Bible 5; Sheffield: Sheffield Academic Press, 1994), pp. 93-104.

21. The etymology of the name Peninnah ("the fruitful woman"?) is not certain; see *HALOT,* p. 946.

22. This form, *wqtl,* expresses "habitual aspect in story-past"; also vv. 4, 6. G. Long, "The Written Story: Toward Understanding Text as Representation and Function," *VT* 49 (1999) 180. For this "frequentative" meaning of <*waw* + pf.>, see also 1 Sam. 2:20, Gen. 2:6; J. Joosten, "Biblical Hebrew *w^{e}qātal* and Syriac *hwā qātel* Expressing Repetition in the Past," *ZAH* 5 (1992) 1-14; also R. E. Longacre, "Weqatal Forms in Biblical Hebrew Prose," in *Biblical Hebrew and Discourse Linguistics,* ed. R. D. Bergen (Dallas: Summer Institute of Linguistics, 1994), pp. 50-98. See also S. R. Driver, *Notes on the Hebrew Text and the Topography of the Books of Samuel* (Oxford: Clarendon, 1913), p. 11.

Feast of Weeks and the Feast of Booths (see Exod. 23:14-17; Lev. 23:15-20) — are not mentioned in 1 Samuel. Elkanah's visit to Shiloh was made only once a year (1 Sam. 1:7, 21f.), and according to Haran his annual sacrifice was "a family or clan feast, confined to the family and celebrated by all its members, women and children included."[23] 1 Sam. 20:6 also refers to "a yearly feast . . . for the entire family" of David; see on "a family feast" in 1 Sam. 20:29.[24]

Elkanah's visit could have been connected to the feast of the Lord in Shiloh mentioned in Judg. 21:19. About this feast there are two opposing views: one view takes it as the autumnal vintage festival;[25] the other view denies any connection with such a festival.[26] The view that sacrifices were offered to the dead at Shiloh with the assistance of the priest Eli is, however, sheer speculation.[27] Regardless of the exact origin of this feast, Elkanah's annual visit to Shiloh may well have had a historical significance for a member of the covenant people.

The phrase *the Lord of Hosts (YHWH ṣᵉbāʾôt)* is a construct chain, with a proper noun as the first noun in *status constructus* like the Ugaritic DN *il brt* "El of covenant" (*KTU* 1.128:14-15) and *il dn* "El of judgment" (128:16). Such a genitival explanation can be supported by the phrases "Yahweh of Teman" and "Yahweh of Samaria" in the Kuntillet ʿAjrud inscriptions.[28] The "hosts" *(ṣᵉbāʾôt)* can refer to heavenly bodies (Judg. 5:20; Isa. 40:26), angelic beings (Josh. 5:14f.), the armies of Israel (1 Sam. 17:45), or all creatures (Gen. 2:1). The noun (f.pl.) has probably an abstract meaning such as "plentifulness, numberlessness" and is intensified by plural form. Hence, it refers to numerous entities such as heavenly bodies and earthly armies. As 1 Sam. 1:3, 11 imply, "the original connection was evidently with worship rather than with battles, in which case the 'hosts' were angelic beings."[29]

23. Haran, *Temples and Temple-Service in Ancient Israel,* p. 306.

24. For dynastic monthly rituals held in the royal palace of Ugarit, which are a more "private" family cult than those held in the national temples, see D. T. Tsumura, "Kings and Cults in Ancient Ugarit," in *Priests and Officials in the Ancient Near East,* ed. K. Watanabe (Heidelberg: C. Winter, 1999), pp. 215-38.

25. E.g., R. P. Gordon, p. 72.

26. E.g., Haran, *Temples and Temple-Service in Ancient Israel,* p. 299.

27. See E. M. Bloch-Smith, "The Cult of the Dead in Judah: Interpreting the Material Remains," *JBL* 111 (1992) 220-21.

28. As discussed by J. A. Emerton, "New Light on Israelite Religion: The Implications of the Inscriptions from Kuntillet ʿAjrud," *ZAW* 94 (1982) 2-20; R. P. Gordon, p. 331, n. 8. On the Kuntillet ʿAjrud inscriptions, see J. Renz and W. Röllig, *Handbuch der althebräischen Epigraphik I* (Darmstadt: Wissenschaftliche Buchgesellschaft, 1995), pp. 59-64; also J. M. Hadley, "Kuntillet ʿAjrud: Religious Centre or Desert Way Station?" *PEQ* 125 (1993) 115-24; also see "Introduction" (Section IV, C, 2, *c*).

29. See J. G. Baldwin, *Haggai, Zechariah, Malachi: Introduction and Commentary* (TOTC; London: IVP, 1972), pp. 44-45; also *NIDOTTE,* 4, pp. 1297-98.

This is the first occurrence in the Bible of the phrase.[30] It may originally have been specially connected with the Shiloh sanctuary (also v. 11; 4:4). Mettinger goes further and even hypothesizes that the phrase refers to the heavenly king who sits on his cherubim throne in the temple and that the notion of the Lord as king was seemingly current among the priests at Shiloh. Moreover, he makes the assumptions that the designation "originated in connection with the meeting of religions in Canaan" and that the original form of the name was *'el ṣᵉbā'ôt.*[31] However, it is not easy to see exactly how and when this "meeting" happened. Similarity in matters of language and symbolism is not necessarily the result of a religious syncretism or influence.[32] Mettinger's view is highly conjectural,[33] though his view that the kingship of Yahweh was seemingly current in the Shilonite cult might be supported in view of Hannah's song; see "Introduction" (Section IX, A).

Shiloh, the modern site Khirbet Seilun [MR177-162], is situated 1.5 miles east of the Jerusalem-Nablus (Arabic name for Shechem) road and 20 miles north of Jerusalem. The first occurrence of this name in the OT is Josh. 18:1. As A. Mazar notes, "Shiloh seems to have been a sacred place long before the Iron Age, and perhaps this tradition led to its choice as the religious center of the Israelites during the period of the Judges."[34] It remained so dur-

30. See M. Tsevat, *"Yhwh Ṣeḇa'oṯ,"* in *The Meaning of the Book of Job and Other Biblical Studies: Essays on the Literature and Religion of the Hebrew Bible* (New York: Ktav, 1980), pp. 119-29.

31. T. N. D. Mettinger, "YHWH SABAOTH — The Heavenly King on the Cherubim Throne," in *Studies in the Period of David and Solomon and Other Essays: Papers Read at the International Symposium for Biblical Studies, Tokyo, 5-7 December, 1979,* ed. T. Ishida (Tokyo: Yamakawa-Shuppansha, 1982), pp. 126, 130, 134; also pp. 109-38; "Yahweh Zebaoth," in *DDD,* pp. 1730-40.

32. See D. T. Tsumura, "Ugaritic Poetry and Habakkuk 3," *TynB* 40 (1988) 24-48. Since the title *the Lord of Hosts,* which appears more than 280 times in the OT, does not occur in Ezekiel, T. N. D. Mettinger (*The Dethronement of Sabaoth: Studies in the Shem and Kabod Theologies* [Lund: CWK Gleerup, 1982]) advocates the theory that the older "Yahweh-Sabaoth" designation was *dethroned* from its place in temple tradition in later periods and replaced by "Name" in the Deuteronomistic historical work and "Glory" in Ezekiel or the Priestly tradition. As for the so-called "Name Theology," see Wilson's recent work (I. Wilson, *Out of the Midst of the Fire: Divine Presence in Deuteronomy* [SBLDS 151; Atlanta: Scholars Press, 1995]), which says "the claim that the Deuteronomic cult envisages Yahweh as being *only* in heaven" should be modified.

33. See R. P. Gordon, p. 72. Compare Jerusalem as "the city of the Lord of hosts" (Ps. 48:8).

34. A. Mazar, *Archaeology of the Land of the Bible, 10,000–586 B.C.E.* (ABRL; New York: Doubleday, 1990, 1992), p. 348; also D. G. Schley, *Shiloh: A Biblical City in Tradition and History* (JSOTSS 63; Sheffield: Sheffield Academic Press, 1989); I. Finkelstein, *Shiloh: The Archaeology of a Biblical Site* (Tel Aviv: Institute of Archaeology, 1993).

ing the period of tribal history (e.g., Josh. 21:2; Judg. 21:12), and a yearly feast of the Lord was held there (Judg. 21:19-21). Its destruction in the eleventh century B.C. is later mentioned in Jer. 7:12-14 and Ps. 78:60, and traces of the destruction have been discovered in excavations.[35]

The Hebrew phrase *kōhănîm laYHWH* (lit., "priests of the Lord") appears only in this verse. Usually the phrase *kōhănê YHWH* "the priests of Yahweh" (1 Sam. 22:17, 21; Isa. 61:6; 2 Chr. 13:9) is used. The author may have had reservations about accepting them as "*the* priests of Yahweh"; hence, the translation *[acting as] priests for the Lord* may be preferred here. R. P. Gordon sees already at this stage the narrator's "ominous note in relation to the ensuing narrative."[36]

b. Hannah's Prayer and Vow (1:4-19)

(1) Hannah and Her Tormenter (1:4-8)

4 *On such a day*[37]
Elkanah made a sacrificial banquet[38]
— he used to[39] *give shares (of the meat) to his wife Peninnah*
and all her sons and daughters;
5 *but to Hannah he used to give two noses*[40] *(of sheep) as one share,*
for it was Hannah whom he loved,
though the Lord had closed her womb.
6 *And her tormentor used to provoke her severely*[41]

35. See A. I. F. Kempinski, "Shiloh," in *NEAEHL,* pp. 1364-70.

36. R. P. Gordon, p. 73.

37. Lit., "on the day."

38. Usually, "sacrificed" (NASB; NRSV) or "slaughtered"; see *HALOT,* pp. 261-62. However, *zbḥ here is translated as "made a sacrificial banquet" in the light of Ugar. *dbḥ,* an Akkadian equivalent of which is *isinnu* "feast, festival" in the polyglot vocabularies; see Pardee in *CS,* I, p. 258, n. 142.

39. For the "frequentative" verb *used to . . .* (*wqtl* "to PN"), see v. 3.

40. D. Aberbach ("mnh 'ḥt 'pym (1 Sam. I 5): A New Interpretation," *VT* 24 [1974] 350-53) explains the form as coming from a *prosthetic aleph* followed by *pym; F. Deist ("'APPAYIM (1 Sam. i 5) <*PYM?," *VT* 27 [1977] 206) emends to *'ăbusā* "fattened." But neither of these explanations is convincing. McCarter's reading *kpym* "proportionate to them" (p. 52) is also not without difficulty morphologically. J. Barr interprets it as meaning "but" in the light of Ugar. *aphn, apn, apnk,* meaning "then, thereafter, also" (see J. Barr, "Semitic Philology and the Interpretation of the Old Testament," in *Tradition and Interpretation: Essays by Members of the Society for Old Testament Study,* ed. G. W. Anderson [Oxford: Clarendon, 1979], p. 48), but it does not explain the dual form. For its meaning see the commentary.

41. Taking *gam-kaʿas* as a cognate accusative (or *internal object*) with an emphatic particle *gam* (Andersen, p. 166); see D. T. Tsumura, "Niphal with an Internal Ob-

with the result that[42] *she would aggravate her,*
for the Lord had shut her womb.
7 *Such things had been done*[43] *year after year,*
as often as she went up to the house of the Lord,
and in such a manner she kept provoking[44] *her to anger —*
and Hannah began to weep and would not eat.
8 *Elkanah, her husband, said to her,*
"Hannah, why[45] *are you weeping?*
Why aren't you eating?
Why do you let your heart be troubled?
Am I not better than ten sons to you?"

4 This verse opens with first narrative tense *(wayqtl),* a linguistic signal that here the main story begins.

On such a day (wayhî hayyôm) refers to a day like one mentioned in the previous information (the SETTING); see also on 1 Sam. 14:1. It is the report of a specific incident on a particular occasion: *On such a day Elkanah made a sacrificial banquet . . . and she began to weep . . .* (vv. 4a, 7b). The sacrifice is usually followed by a banquet feast, and "sacrificing" and "banqueting" became almost one and the same event; hence, the translation *made a sacrificial banquet.*[46] As C. H. Gordon notes, slaughtering beasts for food normally was done only as part of a sacrifice, and so gods and men both received shares of the feast.[47]

The section vv. 4b-7a, which is inserted between two *wayqtl* (vv. 4a, 7b), is parenthetical, giving background information about customary actions. These "shares" would have been taken from the worshipper's share of the "peace offering" (Lev. 7:11-18).[48] In Ugarit, the ideal son is supposed to eat his "portion" in the "house" of El *(bt. il).*[49]

---

ject in Hab 3,9a," *JSS* 31 (1986) 11-16. There is no need to emend it to a verb with most commentators.

42. The phrase *baʿăbûr* introduces a result clause here rather than a purpose clause.

43. The verb *yaʿăśeh* (3 m.s.) is here an impersonal "passive" usage; see J-M, §155*b* N. See "it went on" (NRSV); "it happened" (NASB).

44. Hi. impf. 3 f.s. with suffix (3 f.s.): the imperfect is used here to express the repeated action; see J-M, §113*e.*

45. The threefold "why" is Heb. *lāmeh,* rather than the standard *lammāh.* This might be a northern dialectal form; see G. A. Rendsburg, "Morphological Evidence for Regional Dialects in Ancient Hebrew," in *Linguistics and Biblical Hebrew,* ed. W. R. Bodine (Winona Lake, Ind.: Eisenbrauns, 1992), p. 71.

46. See *KTU* 1.114:1-2.

47. C. H. Gordon, *The Common Background,* p. 150.

48. R. P. Gordon, p. 73.

49. Aqhat epic (*KTU* 1.17:I:31-32); see *CS,* I, p. 344.

Here, "Peninnah" is mentioned before Hannah so that the focus can remain on "Hannah" (v. 5); see 1 Sam. 1:2b. This literary device of dealing with the secondary figure first in order to focus on the primary figure can be seen in other biblical narratives: for example, Gen. 10 (Japheth — Ham — Shem); 11:28-29 (Haran — Abram).

5 The term *'appāyim* (dual; lit., "two noses"; or "face," e.g. 1 Sam. 25:23)[50] has been translated variously: for example, "a double portion" (NASB; NRSV); "a worthy portion" (KJV); "choice portion" (Targum); also "une unique part d'honneur" (Caquot and de Robert, p. 33). It has often been emended to *'epes* ("except") from the LXX *plēn hoti,* but this equivalence is not securely established.[51] There are many other suggestions, but none seems convincing. It seems best to keep the literal meaning "two noses" and, with Barthélemy, to read the MT form as a technical term of the sacrificial ritual.[52] It is interesting to note that the Ugaritic *ap* "nose" appears together with *npš* "lung" as an offering to deities in ritual texts.[53] The dual form might reflect the practice that animals were sacrificed in pairs in ancient Canaan because the sheep was an animal often offered in pairs (*ṯn šm,* "two [heads of] sheep") at Ugarit.[54] Two or seven (or twice-seven) sheep were sacrificed in Israel (see Numbers 28f.).

Elkanah gave to Hannah two of the choicest parts of sheep, that is, two noses "as one share" (MT accentuation: *mānāh 'aḥat*). Or, Elkanah gave "one of two noses" *('aḥat 'appāyim)* to Hannah as a share.[55] In the Emar rituals, the head of the sacrificed animal was treated as a favored part, reserved for the deity, for the diviner, and, sometimes, for the king.[56] It may be that

50. See BDB, p. 60; *HALOT,* p. 77.

51. See S. D. Walters, "Hannah and Anna: the Greek and Hebrew Texts of 1 Samuel 1," *JBL* 107 (1988) 390. See n. 40 (above) for other views.

52. D. Barthélemy, *Critique Textuelle de l'Ancien Testament I.* (OBO 50/1; Fribourg: Éditions Universitaires, 1982), p. 138.

53. E.g., *ap w npš* (*KTU* 1.43:12, 15; 1.90:2-3), *ap//npš* (1.40:14, 22). Cf. J. C. de Moor, *An Anthology of Religious Texts from Ugarit* (NISABA 16; Leiden: E. J. Brill, 1987), p. 170: "a snout and a throat" (n. 17: These parts of the victim were often sacrificed to the gods).

54. See J.-M. de Tarragon, *Le Culte à Ugarit: D'après les Textes de la Pratique en Cunéiformes Alphabétiques* (CRB 19; Paris: J. Gabalda, 1980), p. 34.

55. Taking *ntn + *mānāh* as a verbal idiom, "to give a share/portion" (e.g., 1 Sam. 1:4, 5; 9:23; Esth. 2:9; 2 Chr. 31:19), which takes "one of two noses" as another object: [Verb + Internal Object] + Object; see Tsumura, "Niphal with an Internal Object in Hab 3,9a," pp. 11-16. For the f. numeral *'aḥat* followed by a m.pl. noun, see *bᵉ'aḥat happᵉḥātîm* "in one of the caves" (2 Sam. 17:9; also cf. the m. numeral followed directly by a m. noun) and 2 Sam. 17:12 (K.); 23:8 (Q.).

56. See D. E. Fleming, *The Installation of Baal's High Priestess at Emar: A Window on Ancient Syrian Religion* (HSS 42; Atlanta: Scholars Press, 1992), pp. 136, 155-56;

two noses in our text stands for two heads of sheep. Most translations (KJV; NIV; NRSV; etc.) take the giving to Hannah of the *'appāyim* as a mark of love and favor and translate "he gave her . . . for he loved her . . . , though. . . ." However, some interpreters think that the distribution favored Peninnah since she had children, and they translate it "he gave her . . . although he loved her, because. . . ."[57] The former interpretation is preferable, for she could hardly expect to have as much as a large group.

6 Peninnah is *her tormentor;*[58] compare "her rival" (NASB; NRSV); "her adversary" (KJV); "co-wife" (Walters).[59] The name "Peninnah" no longer appears after v. 5, but while she thus keeps silence in the scene, she is "powerfully present in the background."[60] The plural marriage thus created severe tensions in this family as it did in Abraham's (Gen. 16:4-5); see also "rival-wife" (NEB) in Lev. 18:18. Because Hannah was childless, Peninnah tormented Hannah, as Hagar despised the childless Sarah after Ishmael was born (Gen. 16:4-6); later, it was Sarah who afflicted Hagar, with the approval of her husband. It is noteworthy that the Lord's closing of Hannah's womb was the reason why Peninnah used to provoke her severely, while, on the other hand, despite it, Elkanah loved her (v. 6).

7 It is often argued that the sanctuary of Shiloh was "a temple" (see v. 9; also 1 Sam. 3:3) built of stone,[61] while 2 Sam. 7:6 states that the Lord had never lived in "a house" before the time of David but had been moving about in "a tent." Hence, some conclude that the traditions are contradictory. However, there is no evidence in the biblical text that this "temple" at Shiloh was made of stone. The term *house* in this verse simply refers to a dwelling place without reference to its material; on the other hand, the "house" in the context of 2 Sam. 7:6-7 refers to the "house of cedar," that is, a wooden shrine surrounded by a stone structure. The reference to *the entrance of the Tent of Meeting* (1 Sam. 2:22) rather suggests that the central part of *the*

CS, I, p. 437. In nomadic societies, the head of a sheep is a special portion set apart for a special person or guest. Recently van Zyl supports Targ. "a choice portion" by reading the MT term as referring to "face or nose" of the sacrificial animal. He refers to South African practices of giving a special portion to a special person; see D. C. van Zyl, "Hannah's Share, Once More 1 Samuel 1:5," *OTE* 6 (1993) 364-66. See 1 Sam. 9:24 below on "a proportionate feast."

57. JPS; C. Meyers, "An Ethnoarchaeological Analysis of Hannah's Sacrifice," in *Pomegranates and Golden Bells,* p. 80; W. Brueggemann, "1 Samuel 1: A Sense of a Beginning," *ZAW* 102 (1990) 35.

58. Cf. Ugar. *ṣrt* "enemy"; an Akkadian term in "the lady will have a rival *(ṣerreta)*" (*CAD,* B, p. 190).

59. Walters, "Hannah and Anna," p. 389.

60. W. Brueggemann, "1 Samuel 1: A Sense of a Beginning," *ZAW* 102 (1990) 34.

61. H. Kruse, "David's Covenant," *VT* 35 (1985) 144.

house of the Lord at Shiloh was in fact made of cloth. It may be that a more stable structure was built around the tent-shrine.[62]

The *door post* in v. 9 suggests that this *house* was apparently set up more like a temple than a portable tent. The doors are also mentioned in 3:15. In v. 9 *the temple of the Lord (hêkāl YHWH),* the word *hêkāl,* whose etymology goes back to the Sumerian word É.GAL "a large house," appears for the first time in the OT. The term *temple* definitely signifies a large structure; it could in fact refer to a large tent structure as in Ugaritic and Mari documents.[63] Though one might see in these expressions "anachronistic touches based on conditions existing during the monarchical period,"[64] such an explanation is unnecessary in the light of these second millennium evidences.

8 The pharase *ten sons* here is a literary cliché like "seven sons"; see on 1 Sam. 2:5. One might think that Elkanah conveys here his thought that "a husband . . . can more than make up for the lack of natural offspring."[65] Also, the form of the question, the four-fold question with three "why's," conveys Elkanah's concern for his beloved wife. However, despite his love, he cannot give her children, and so all depends on Hannah's actions and God's response.

(2) Hannah's Prayer and Vow (1:9-11)

9 *Hannah arose*[66] *after the eating and drinking*[67] *at Shiloh*
— Now Eli the priest was sitting on his chair
by the door post of the temple of the Lord;

62. Note that the term *bt* sometimes refers to "a tent." See *HALOT,* p. 124; see also the GN Bethel ("House of God/El") and the commentary on v. 4 (above). Note that Ug. *bt* refers to El's residence in *KTU* 1.23:36 (see *CS,* I, p. 280 "house") which was presumably a tent (*ḏd//qrš* in *KTU* 1.3 V 7-8). The Akkadian *bītu* sometimes means "a tent," though very rarely; see *AHw,* p. 133. See D. T. Tsumura, *The Ugaritic Drama of the Good Gods: A Philological Study* (Ann Arbor: University Microfilms, 1973), p. 65. In fact, the Timnah "shrine" had a stone footing and apparently a cloth roof; see *NEAEHL,* pp. 1482-83. For a temple structure at Arad from the Iron Age, see Ackroyd, p. 24. See on 1 Sam. 1:9; 3:3; 2 Sam. 7:6; 12:20.

63. See D. E. Fleming, "Mari's Large Public Tent and the Priestly Tent Sanctuary," *VT* 50 (2000) 484-98.

64. Haran, *Temples and Temple-Service,* p. 202.

65. See R. Westbrook, "1 Samuel 1:8," *JBL* 109 (1990) 115; Y. Amit, "'Am I Not More Devoted to You Than Ten Sons?' (1 Samuel 1:8): Male and Female Interpretations," in *A Feminist Companion to Samuel and Kings,* ed. A. Brenner (Feminist Companion to the Bible 5; Sheffield: Sheffield Academic Press, 1994), pp. 68-76.

66. This *wayqtl* of a movement verb signifies a TRANSITION a little "off" from the mainline story line.

67. *'oklāh* is an infinitive construct with a feminine ending; J-M, §49*d.* The Hebrew *wᵉ'aḥărê šātōh* (lit., "and after drinking") has been taken as "impossible" and "a late

10 *as for her, she was bitter in spirit*[68] —
and prayed to the Lord, weeping hard,
11 *and made a vow:*[69]
"O Lord of Hosts!
If you will indeed[70] *pay attention to the affliction of your maidservant*
and remember me and do not forget[71] *your maidservant*
and give your maidservant a child,[72]
I will give[73] *him to the Lord all the days of his life,*
his head no razor shall touch."

9 Hannah, the future mother of Samuel, here encounters Eli, the father of Hophni and Phinehas, sitting on his *chair*[74] of high-priesthood. A chair was a sign of honor in a society where most people sat on the ground. This prepares the way toward the contrast between their sons in 1 Samuel 2. Verses 9b-10a are parenthetical and "break into the main narrative to supply information relevant to or necessary for the narrative."[75]

---

addition" as LXX omits it (GKC, §113e, n. 3); see Driver, p. 12. However, the infinitive absolute, *šātōh,* governed by a preposition (here *'aḥărê*) is indeed "abnormal," but W-O, §35.3.3 lists this as an example of a nominal use of the inf. abs. (also 25:33) as "the object of a preposition" (p. 591; see also p. 597: a use of inf. abs. as an inf. cstr.). The subject of these verbs is indefinite, not necessarily Hannah herself (cf. vv. 7, 15).

68. *mārat nāpeš:* i.e., embittered; also 1 Sam. 22:2; see *HALOT,* p. 629; adj. f.s. cstr. with "receding of the stress" (J-M, §31c), followed by a noun in pause; see T. Muraoka, "The Status Constructus of Adjectives in Biblical Hebrew," *VT* 27 (1977) 375-80, for uses of an adj. in construct.

69. Lit., "made a vow and said"; see "Introduction." Note that "making a vow" is a verbal action which accompanies an utterance, "saying."

70. The vow formula of *'im* + inf. abs. + *yqtl* (2 m.s.) . . . *w-qtl* (1 c.s.). Num. 21:2; Judg. 11:30-31; 2 Sam. 15:8(Q.) are the only other examples.

71. A paired expression, "remember" + "not forget," is an "A not B" pattern ("negated antonym"); e.g., Hab. 2:3-4; etc. (see D. T. Tsumura, "An Exegetical Consideration on Hab 2:4a," *Tojo* 15 (1985) 14 [Japanese]; R. E. Longacre, *The Grammar of Discourse* (New York: Plenum, 1983), pp. 116-19.

72. Either son or daughter; or "offspring" (McCarter, p. 61). Lit., "a seed of men" *zeraʿ 'ănāšîm;* cf. Akk. *zēr amēlûti* "semence d'humanité" for signifying "progéniture" (Dhorme, p. 20). *CAD,* Z, p. 96 has an idiom for expressing "a child, human being, human extraction, living man," originally "semen" in Akkadian (*CAD,* Z, p. 93), and there is a Japanese idiom *ko-dane* ("offspring-seed").

73. *qtl* preceded by *waw.* This 1 c.s.pf. in an utterance in a vow is certainly performative; see 2 Sam. 19:29; Ps. 2:7b.

74. In Emar the high priestess sat on her throne; see Emar ritual text of "The Installation of the Storm God's High Priestess" (*CS,* I, p. 429). Also 1 Sam. 4:13.

75. W-O, §39.2.3c.

For the paired expression, *eating and drinking,* see Gen. 24:54; 25:34; 26:30; Exod. 24:11; etc. Since these two verbal phrases are so commonly paired, the phrase after *the eating and drinking* probably simply denotes "after dinner" or the like, without specifying whether Hannah had drunk wine or other alcohol; see v. 14.

Why is *Shiloh* mentioned here when the audience already knows the setting? It may be "intended to formalize the turn of events."[76] Or it may be that "Shiloh" is mentioned in order to officially introduce Eli, the priest there. Or it may simply be a reminder that this scene is set there, since it has not been mentioned since v. 3. The initial *waw* of the directly following clause *(wᵉʿēlî . . .)* introduces a circumstantial clause *(Now Eli . . .)* and explains the situation of that place at that moment. So, mention of Shiloh as Eli's sphere of activity here is not odd. This background information continues to v. 10a; thus, vv. 9b-10a are parenthetical, the main thought resuming at v. 10b ("and prayed to the Lord . . ."). On *the door post of the temple of the Lord,* see above (v. 7).

10 With the *wayqtl (and prayed)* in v. 10b, the main line of the story resumes, picking up Hannah's previous action "she arose" (*wayqtl* in v. 9). As a person with *a struggling spirit* (see v. 15), Hannah here takes refuge in the Lord, bringing her problem directly to her God by prayer. Affliction (v. 11) can often direct believers closer to their holy God.

11 Hannah's agony finally finds words in the form of a vow. The only other example of "making a vow" in Samuel is 2 Sam. 15:7-8. According to Parker, a comparison with the Ugaritic *Keret Epic* shows a common form for vows in both Israel and Late Bronze Age Syria.[77] Van der

76. R. P. Gordon, p. 74. Cf. J. Wellhausen, *Die Text der Bücher Samuelis Untersucht* (Göttingen: Vandenhoeck & Ruprecht, 1871), p. 38; Driver, p. 12; H. P. Smith, *A Critical and Exegetical Commentary on the Books of Samuel* (ICC; Edinburgh: T. & T. Clark, 1899), p. 10; H. W. Hertzberg, *I and II Samuel: A Commentary* (OTL; Philadelphia: Westminster, 1964 [orig. 1960]), p. 22; R. W. Klein, *1 Samuel* (WBC 10; Waco, Tex.: Word Books, 1983), p. 3; and others, who divide MT as *ʾḥry ʾkl hbšlh* "after eating *the boiled meat*" (see 1 Sam. 2:13). McCarter (p. 53) emends to *bšly* "privately, quietly," for he also thinks that "the mention of Shiloh seems oddly repetitious here." However, as R. P. Gordon notes, "the versional support for MT is very strong" (p. 74). A better solution would be to recognize an AX&B pattern here: "at Shiloh" (X: adv. phr.) is inserted between two prepositional phrases which are usually combined as a unit (A and B); see D. T. Tsumura, "Coordination Interrupted, or Literary Insertion AX&B Pattern, in the Books of Samuel," in *Literary Structure and Rhetorical Strategies in the Hebrew Bible,* ed. L. J. de Regt, J. de Waard, and J. P. Fokkelman (Assen: Van Gorcum, 1996), p. 124; also "Introduction" (Section VII, C).

77. On the formal similarity between the present verse and the vow in Ugaritic, see S. B. Parker, "The Vow in Ugaritic and Israelite Narrative Literature," *UF* 11 (1979) 693-96. On "curse," see on 1 Sam. 14:24, etc. For "Oath and Vow," see T. W. Cartledge,

Toorn[78] notes in the expression "son of my vows" (Prov. 31:2) apparently another biblical case in which a child is the result of a mother's vow.[79] In her plea that Yahweh *remember me,* Hebrew *zkr *(remember)* has much stronger nuance than simply putting something into one's memory; it includes positive actions toward the one "remembered"; for example, Ps. 8:4 (//*pqd "to care for").

The sentence *I will give him to the Lord* has a "performative" force; it shows not only that Hannah promises it but also that she has already given him by faith. Usually a woman who had suffered so from not having a child would not give him up once he was born, but Hannah, a dedicated woman, was willing. Compare Abraham in Genesis 22. Here Hannah promised and gave; there Abraham was promised and was ordered to give. Both acted on faith. See vv. 27-28.

The phrase *all the days of his life* signifies life-long dedication, though the Nazirite consecration was normally a temporary one (see Numbers 6). See 1 Sam. 27:12 on the expression "an eternal servant" (also Ugaritic *ʿbd ʿlm*). Scholars are divided as to whether the MT here describes Samuel as a Nazirite. Some say it does, for there are correspondences between the present episode and that of the birth of Samson the Nazirite in Judges 13. For *No razor shall touch his head,* see Judg. 13:5; 16:17; cf. *taʿar lōʾ-yaʿăbōr ʿal-rōʾšô* (Num. 6:5). McCarter, based on the LXX and 4QSam[a], even restores before *the razor* the phrase: "and wine and strong drink he will not drink."[80] But others argue that the Naziritism was due to the later growth in LXX and 4QSam[a].[81] The fact remains that explicit reference to the Nazirite is not made and the abstinence from grape products (see Num. 6:3-4) is not mentioned here in the MT.[82]

Without contesting the first possibility, R. P. Gordon suspects that the narrator presents here "a deliberate contrast" with the Samson story. He holds that "Hannah's reference to the razor . . . may be expressing the conviction that the same depilatory disaster as befell Samson (Judg. 16:17-21) will not overtake [her] son." However, one might need to read the text in a more immediate context before reading it in a wider context "with an eye on

---

Vows in the Hebrew Bible and the Ancient Near East (JSOTSS 147; Sheffield: JSOT Press, 1992).

78. K. v. d. Toorn, "Female Prostitution in Payment of Vows in Ancient Israel," *JBL* 108 (1989) 196.

79. See *NIDOTTE,* #2349; *HALOT,* pp. 269-70.

80. McCarter, pp. 53-54; also Klein, p. 3.

81. See M. Tsevat, "Was Samuel a Nazirite?" in *"Shaʿarei Talmon": Studies in the Bible, Qumran, and the Ancient Near East presented to Shemaryahu Talmon,* ed. by M. Fishbane and E. Tov (Winona Lake, Ind.: Eisenbrauns, 1992), pp. 199-204.

82. Caquot and de Robert, p. 39.

intertextual concerns."[83] Taking note of the "aural" feature of the narrative (see "Introduction" [Section VI, D; VII, B]), especially in direct speech, it would not be strange if Hannah mentioned only a part of the Nazirite customs. A sentence may stop even in the middle of an utterance and hence be grammatically incomplete, leaving an incomplete feeling: that is, "aposiopesis" (see v. 22 below). Also, perhaps she limits herself to the hair provision because the prohibition of cutting his hair would begin in infancy, while the prohibition on wine drinking would come into force later.

(3) Background Information (1:12-13)

12 *While*[84] *she continued praying before the Lord,*
Eli was watching her mouth.
13 *As for Hannah, she was speaking in her heart;*
only her lips were quivering but her voice could not be heard.
So Eli thought she was drunk.

12-13 Verses 12-13 parenthetically provide background information to the following EVENT. The expression *praying before* occurs here for the first time in the OT. The sense is that Hannah was fully absorbed in the presence of the Lord (also v. 15: "pouring out my soul before the Lord"), forgetting herself and, for a long time, not knowing that Eli was watching.[85] Note that

83. R. P. Gordon, "Who Made the Kingmaker? Reflections on Samuel and the Institution of the Monarchy," in *Faith, Tradition, and History: Old Testament Historiography in Its Near Eastern Context,* ed. A. R. Millard, J. K. Hoffmeier, and D. W. Baker (Winona Lake, Ind.: Eisenbrauns, 1994), p. 265.

84. *w^{e}hāyāh: waw* + pf. (*hyh); lit., "and it will be"; the expression is usually explained as "abnormal" (J-M, §119z; cf. GKC §112*uu;* Berg II, 43, n. *b-k.* In Josh. 9:12; 1 Sam. 1:12; 10:9; 13:22; 17:48; 25:20; 2 Sam. 6:16; 2 K. 3:15; Jer. 37:11; and Amos 7:2 they assert *wyhy* "is to be read" instead of *whyh;* but see B. Isaksson, "'Aberrant' Usages of Introductory *w^{e}hāyā* in the Light of Text Linguistics," in *"Lasset uns Brücken bauen . . .": Collected Communications to the XVth Congress of the International Organization for the Study of the Old Testament, Cambridge 1995,* ed. K.-D. Schunck and M. Augustin (Frankfurt am Main: Peter Lang, 1998), pp. 9-25; also Y. Endo, *The Verbal System of Classical Hebrew in the Joseph Story: An Approach from Discourse Analysis* (Assen: Van Gorcum, 1996), pp. 184-86, 274. Longacre explains that this unusual expression functions as "marking significant background or important events to follow (cataphoric)"; see "Weqatal Forms in Biblical Hebrew Prose," in *Biblical Hebrew and Discourse Linguistics,* pp. 84-91; but also see C. H. J. van der Merwe, "Discourse Linguistics and Biblical Hebrew Grammar," in *Biblical Hebrew and Discourse Linguistics,* pp. 28-29.

85. See the useful summary of the discussion of *lipnê YHWH* in Wilson, *Out of the Midst of the Fire,* pp. 131-42. Fowler argues against the view that *lipnê YHWH* implies

"to pray before the Lord" in the present context is distinct from "to pray to the Lord." While the former emphasizes the prayer in the presence of Yahweh, the latter emphasizes the direction of prayer, implying more distance from him. Though closer, Eli misread her quivering mouth as the mild derangement of a drunk.

(4) Dialogue between Eli and Hannah (1:14-18)

14 *And Eli said to her,*
"How long will you make yourself drunken?
Put aside your wine away from you!"
15 *And Hannah answered:*[86]
"No, my lord!
I am a woman struggling in spirit;[87]
I have drunk neither wine nor strong drink.[88]
I have been pouring out my soul before the Lord.
16 *Do not deliver up*[89] *your maidservant*
to the Daughter of Beliyaal,
for because of my great anguish
and my vexation
I have spoken until now."
17 *And Eli answered:*

---

the existence of a permanent sanctuary or a temple. As he rightly notes, the expression is often used without direct reference to a shrine of any sort (1) to mean "in the sight (estimation) of YHWH"; (2) to depict "the omnipresence of YHWH"; (3) "in a heightened metaphorical sense to express the direct and personal communication between God and man." See M. D. Fowler, "The Meaning of *lipne YHWH* in the Old Testament," *ZAW* 99 (1987) 384-90.

86. Lit., "answered and said"; see "Introduction."

87. *qᵉšat rûaḥ* (lit., "hard/firm of spirit") is an example of the construct chain of adj. and noun; see Muraoka, "The Status Constructus of Adjectives," pp. 375-80; cf. "oppressed in spirit" (NASB); "deeply troubled" (NRSV); "unfortunate" (McCarter, p. 54), lit., "hard of day," following LXX. Ahlström suggests "hard, obstinate or stubborn" for this idiom; G. W. Ahlström, "1 Samuel 1,15," *Bib* 60 (1979) 254; this is followed by Klein, p. 2 ("persistent"). But there is no reason to take the LXX reading as superior to MT's.

88. This word pair, *yayin* and *šēkār,* appears often as in Lev. 10:9; Judg. 13:4; Isa. 5:11; Mic. 2:11; Prov. 20:1; etc. See M. Malul, "Strong Drink," in *DDD,* pp. 1550-53. Note that a strong and intoxicating drink was "purportedly used to elicit a divine oracle" in the ancient Near East; see *DDD,* p. 1551. Eli may have been especially sensitive to such behavior because of misbehavior at Shiloh, especially his son's misbehavior with women.

89. Lit., "give . . . before . . ."; cf. "take . . . for . . ." (NIV; JPS), "regard . . . as . . ." (NRSV).

"Go in peace!
May the God of Israel grant (you) the request[90]
you have made of him!"
18 *And she said,*
"May your handmaid[91] *find favor in your eyes!"*
And the woman went her way and ate;[92] *she no longer looked miserable.*[93]

14 Here begins a dialogue between Eli and Hannah. Eli's approach to her marks the decisive start of a new development in the story. Naturally, it is Eli, a senior male and a priest, who initiates the dialogue. By mistaking Hannah as being drunken, he commands her to *put aside* her wine.

15 Hannah replies to Eli's irritated rebuke by explaining herself. She is *a woman struggling in spirit.* Muraoka compares the expression *who is struggling in spirit* with the "determinedness" of Sihon in Deut. 2:30 and explains that Hannah was "firmly determined to take up the matter with her God."[94]

The expression *pouring out my soul* denotes not simply an inward state of one's heart or mind, but an involvement of the whole being.[95] Hannah's prayer completely consumes her. The verbal root *špk means "to pour (some thing) out of (its container) into (some place)."[96] Here, with this expression, Hannah rephrases the narrator's comment "she was praying before the Lord" (v. 12). Hannah "pours out" words of agonizing petition. In both passages *before the Lord* means more than just being in a temple; it refers to the divine presence where she faced the holy God in person.

16 The first half of this verse *(deliver up . . . to . . .)* is a *crux*

90. Lit. "your request"; *šēlātēk* is a *sandhi* spelling, in which two contiguous vowels fused as a result of the loss of /ʾ/ in the intervocalic position: *šeʾēlāt-* → *šeēlāt-* → *šēlāt-*. See D. T. Tsumura, "Vowel sandhi in Biblical Hebrew," *ZAW* 109 (1997) 575-88. This *sandhi* spelling and the full spelling *šeʾēlātî* (1 Sam. 1:27) are thus to be reckoned as "free variations"; see S. J. Lieberman, "Toward a Graphemics of the Tiberian Bible," in *Linguistics and Biblical Hebrew,* ed. W. R. Bodine (Winona Lake, Ind.: Eisenbrauns, 1992), p. 270.

91. *šipḥātekā.* The term is never used in addressing God, for which *ʾāmāh* "maidservant" (vv. 11, 16) is used (see BDB, pp. 51, 1046).

92. Cf. "ate and drank with her husband" (NRSV), following LXX, which adds "when she came to the chamber, she [ate] with her husband and drank." For a defense of MT, see Weingreen (cited by McCarter, p. 55).

93. Lit., "as for her face, it was no longer (belonging) to her" = "she no longer had such a face."

94. T. Muraoka, "1 Sam 1,15 Again," *Bib* 77 (1996) 98-99.

95. See also Ps. 42:4 ("I pour out my soul within me"; cf. Job 30:16 ("my soul is poured out within me"//"Days of affliction have seized me"); cf. the petition in Lam. 2:19.

96. See BDB, pp. 1049-50.

interpretum, and all ancient witnesses are taken as "unintelligible." Since comparison with Job 3:24 and 4:19 is hardly sufficient to establish the meaning of *nātan lipnê* as "regard as, treat as," McCarter suggests reading *lpnyk lbt . . .* instead of *lpny bt . . .* and translates: "Do not set your maidservant before you as a worthless woman," that is, "Do not reckon your maidservant a worthless woman." However, the most natural translation of MT is: *Do not deliver up your maidservant to bt blyʿl.* Hence, our passage has something to do with delivering up Hannah to someone. The real issue is how to interpret the phrase "the daughter of Beliyaal" *(bt blyʿl).* Most modern scholars take it for granted that it means "a worthless woman," but the "Excursus" (below) defends the preferred *Daughter of Beliyaal.*

17 The expression *Go in peace!* marks "a successful conclusion of negotiation or assurance that the request for a desired state of relationships has been granted";[97] see also 1 Sam. 20:42; 2 Sam. 15:9. It is noteworthy that Eli invokes here the blessing of the *God of Israel,* while Hannah prayed to and before *the Lord of Hosts,* citing this intimate name of the covenant, Yahweh, quite frequently (vv. 11[x2], 15, 20, 22, 26, 27, 28a[x2]). The narrator seems to emphasize the personal and intimate relationship of Hannah and Elkanah with Yahweh (see vv. 3[x2], 5, 6, 10, 12, 19[x2], 21, 23, 28b) in contrast with Eli's formal association with the cult of Yahweh. The word *the request* anticipates the wordplay in vv. 27f. R. P. Gordon notes that this is the only place in the OT where a priest blesses an individual.[98]

18 Hannah responds positively to Eli, wishing to enjoy his good will always. Note the contrast between *and she would not eat* in v. 7 and *and she ate* here. Evidently, she was deeply encouraged by Eli's words, which she took as God's promise. She ate because she was confident that her request had been heard. Now *she no longer looked miserable,* of course, not because she ate, but because she put her complete trust on Eli's words. Her confidence clearly shone on her contented face.

EXCURSUS: "DAUGHTER OF BELIYAAL" (1 SAM. 1:16)

Various translations have attempted to render the phrase *bt blyʿl:* for example, "a wicked woman" (NIV); "a worthless woman" (NASB, NRSV, JPS); *"base woman"* (NEB "degraded").[99] The term *blyʿl* appears nine times in

97. D. J. Wiseman, "'Is it peace?' — Covenant and Diplomacy," *VT* 32 (1982) 324.

98. R. P. Gordon, p. 75.

99. *Beliyaal* in the intertestamental era is taken as the prince of evil (so Beliar/Belial in 2 Cor. 6:15). See S. D. Sperling, "Belial," in *DDD,* pp. 322-27; also T. J. Lewis, "Belial," in *ABD,* I, pp. 654-56.

Samuel besides this verse. "Son(s) of B." (1 Sam. 2:12; 10:27; 25:17), "man/men of B." (1 Sam. 25:25; 30:22; 2 Sam. 16:7; 20:1), "the torrents of B." (2 Sam. 22:5), and "B." (2 Sam. 23:6). In 2 Sam. 22:5 the term is in parallel to "death," though "the verse is not proof that the word means Sheol."[100] In its twenty-seven occurrences in the OT it never appears in the plural, but sometimes with a definite article (1 Sam. 25:25; 2 Sam. 16:7; 1 K. 21:13).

For the etymology of the term *Beliyaal,* there are basically two possibilities: one analyzes it as a noun with a negative particle *bl;* the other posits a verbal root *blʿ.

1. b^{e}lî + yāʿal "without worth" or "worthlessness"; cf. Ugar. *blmt* "immortality" (Gordon, *UT,* §19.466). McCarter, following Cross and Freedman, takes it to be a "(place of) not-coming-up," which refers to "hell, the underworld"; this is refuted by Emerton.[101]
2. For the verbal root *blʿ, various translations have been suggested: "to confuse" (G. R. Driver), yielding the noun "confusion" (with an afformative *-l*); "to swallow" (Thomas 1963), yielding "the swallower" (cf. Prov. 1:12; the idea of Sheol swallowing people[102]); or "to destroy" (Emerton) yielding "destructiveness." In Emerton's words, "The sons of Belial are . . . those whose characters are destructive, harmful, evil."[103]

Thomas thinks that the phrase "indicates one whose actions or words engulf a man, bring him to the abyss, to the underworld."[104] McCarter suggests similarly "fiend of hell."[105] However, as Emerton notes, Sheol in the OT is "not the place of torment or the abode of fiends. It is not a pleasant place,

100. J. A. Emerton, "Sheol and the Sons of Belial," *VT* 37 (1987) 217.

101. P. K. McCarter, Jr., *II Samuel: A New Translation with Introduction, Notes and Commentary* (AB 9; Garden City, N.Y.: Doubleday, 1984), p. 373 on 2 Sam. 16:7; F. M. Cross and D. N. Freedman, "A Royal Song of Thanksgiving: II Samuel 22 = Psalm 18," *JBL* 72 (1953) 22. See Emerton, "Sheol and the Sons of Belial," pp. 214-17.

102. See Sperling, *DDD,* p. 323.

103. Emerton, "Sheol and the Sons of Belial," p. 217. See M. Autexier, "Bly'l: Implications d'un champ sémantique clos," in *"Lasset uns Brücken bauen . . .": Collected Communications to the XVth Congress of the International Organization for the Study of the Old Testament, Cambridge 1995,* ed. K.-D. Schunck and M. Augustin (Frankfurt am Main: Peter Lang, 1998), pp. 45-57.

104. D. W. Thomas, "בְּלִיַּעַל in the Old Testament," in *Biblical and Patristic Studies in Memory of Robert Pierce Casey,* ed. J. N. Birdsall and R. W. Thomson (Freiburg/New York: Herder, 1963), p. 19; Emerton, "Sheol and the Sons of Belial," p. 215.

105. McCarter, II, p. 373.

but it is the place to which everyone goes. . . ."[106] Emerton thinks that *b*^{e}*lîyāʿal* does not mean "hell" but probably "destructiveness" or the like.

Whatever its etymology, the term seems to have experienced the following semantic change:

(1) a common noun: "worthlessness" *(b*^{e}*lî + yāʿal)* or "utter destructiveness" *(blyʿ + l)* with a superlative *(')l* "god"
(2) a divine name: *B*^{e}*lîyāʿal*
(3) idiomatic expressions: "sons of Beliyaal" = "utterly destructive men"; "daughter of Beliyaal" = "utterly destructive woman"

I propose that here the phrase *bat b*^{e}*lîyāʿal* is an archaic phrase reflecting the second stage and probably means "the Daughter of Beliyaal," which refers to the Queen of the underworld, like Eresh-ki-gal of the Mesopotamian tradition.[107] This fits the context of the MT: "Do not deliver up your maidservant before/to the presence of the Daughter of Beliyaal." In other words, the expression "to deliver up someone to the presence of Beliyaal's daughter" is an idiom which means "to bring someone for judgment by Beliyaal's daughter," that is, "to destroy someone utterly."

(5) Back to Ramah (1:19)

19 *And they got up early in the morning and worshipped before the Lord and came back to their home in Ramah.*
And Elkanah knew[108] *Hannah his wife.*
And the Lord remembered her.

19 Here the stage shifts from Shiloh to Ramah, so the narrator's viewpoint moves from *šwb "returned (from Shiloh)" to *bw' "came (to Ramah)"; hence *came back* rather than simply "came." See "Introduction" (Section VI, D) on the use of "come" and "go." This change of location signals the transition of this narrative toward the next stage.

Ramah here is that of Benjamin, probably modern er-Rām, 7-8 kilometers north of Jerusalem.[109] The biblical tradition names both Ramathaim

106. Emerton, "Sheol and the Sons of Belial," p. 217.

107. Sheol (fem. noun), the realm of the dead, is sometimes personified (e.g., Prov. 1:12), but there is no evidence that it is a deity. See H. M. Barstad, "Sheol," in *DDD,* pp. 1452-57.

108. I.e., "had sexual intercourse" with his wife.

109. See Arnold, "Ramah" in *ABD,* V, pp. 613-14. Cf. D. Edelman, "Saul's Journey through Mt. Ephraim and Samuel's Ramah (1 Sam. 9:4-5; 10:2-5)," *ZDPV* 104 (1988) 56, who identifies it with Khirbet Raddana, on the western edge of Ramallah.

and Ramah of Benjamin as Samuel's home town (1 Sam. 1:1 and 7:17). Perhaps the city's name proper was "Ramah" (also 1 Sam. 2:11) and was sometimes called by its descriptive name, Ramathaim "Two Hills" (see above on 1 Sam. 1:1).

That God *remembered* means he "fulfilled" his agreed promises. As McCarter comments, "Remembering in the religious terminology of Israel and other Northwest Semitic societies referred to the benevolent treatment of an individual or group by a god, often, as in this case, in response to a specific plea."[110] With the short sentence, *And the Lord remembered her (wayyizk^{e}rehā YHWH),* this part of the narrative ends (i.e., the TERMINUS). See on 1 Sam. 1:11. The actions which implement that remembering are soon to follow.

c. Dedication of Samuel (1:20-28)

20 *A year later,*[111]
Hannah conceived and bore a son; and she called his name Samuel, because (she said) "From the Lord I have requested him."[112]
21 *And her husband Elkanah and all his house went up to carry out the yearly sacrifice and his vow*[113] *to the Lord.*
22 *But Hannah did not go up,*
for she had said to her husband,
"[Not] until the child is weaned and I bring him
and he appears[114] *before the Lord*
and stays there for ever."[115]
23 *And Elkanah, her husband, said to her,*
"Do what is good in your eyes!

110. McCarter, p. 62.

111. Lit., "at the circuits of the days"; cf. Ug. *nqpt* "year(s)" (*//šnt*); see *KTU* 1.23:66-67. More accurately it refers to a full cycle of the calendar.

112. *š^{e}ʾiltîw;* on this form with [i] as a theme vowel, see GKC §64f. For the wordplay on the verb *šʾl* "ask, request," see vv. 27-28.

113. On *the yearly sacrifice,* see Haran, *Temples and Temple-Service in Ancient Israel,* pp. 304-5; also 1 Sam. 20:6, 29 (below). See on v. 3. For *vow,* see Hannah's vow in 1 Sam. 1:11.

114. Niphal (= "passive") transformation of the original phrase [to see the face of the Lord] → "to appear before the Lord."

115. Unlike MT and LXX, 4QSam^{a} has an additional line (see Josephus, *Ant.* v. 10, 3). McCarter takes the shorter text in MT and LXX as having lost the original phrase "and I will dedicate him as a Nazirite forever," while he takes the phrase "all the days of his life" in 4QSam^{a} as secondary (p. 56). However, expansion is typical of 4QSam^{a}, so MT is preferred as the more original.

Stay until you wean him!
Only[116] *may the Lord establish his word!"*
And the wife stayed and nursed her son until she weaned him;
24 *she brought him up with her, when she had weaned him,*[117]
with three younglings[118]
and one ephah of flour[119]
and a jar of wine
and brought him to the House of the Lord in Shiloh.
And the boy was young.[120]
25 *And the younglings were slaughtered and the boy was brought to Eli.*[121]
26 *And she said,*
"Pardon me, my lord!
As your soul lives, my lord,
I am the woman who stood here with you
to pray to the Lord.

116. This is a clause "adverb" with emphatic meaning; see Andersen, p. 177.

117. *g^{e}mālattû* < *g^{e}mālat-hû* < *gām^{e}lah* + *-hû* is a progressive assimilation of /h/ to /t/; see Bauer and Leander, §15*b.*

118. *par* is often explained as *ben-bāqār,* lit., "son of cattle" (Exod. 29:1; Lev. 4:3; Num. 7:15; Ezek. 43:19; 2 Chr. 13:9; etc), though the expression does not necessarily refer to a youngling; see R. Péter, "*pr* et *šwr:* Note de Lexicographie hébraïque," *VT* 25 (1975) 491-92.

119. The MT reading should be retained as *lectio difficilior,* while McCarter, who takes MT as "a simple corruption," has to delete "one" as an expansion. *Ephah ('yph)* is an Egyptian loanword; see Muchiki, *Egyptian Proper Names and Loanwords,* pp. 239-40. For *flour,* see Meyers, "An Ethnoarchaeological Analysis of Hannah's Sacrifice," in *Pomegranates and Golden Bells,* p. 84, referring to O. Borowski, *Agriculture in Iron Age Israel* (Winona Lake, Ind.: Eisenbrauns, 1987), pp. 88-90; also in 1 Sam. 28:24; 2 Sam. 17:28; see *RlA* 8 (1993) 22-31 on "Mehl": "[in Sumero-Akkadian religious practice]."

120. According to McCarter, all witnesses "point to a reading similar to that of the *Vorlage* of LXX": "and the boy was with them. And they came before the Lord, and his father killed the sacrifice as he did year by year before the Lord, and she brought the boy . . ." (translation by R. P. Gordon, p. 78). But he thinks that "this long, repetitious text is manifestly a conflation of two shorter variants"; see Walters, "Hannah and Anna," pp. 403-4 for detailed discussion. Walters holds that the MT is "deliberate" since "the arguments of both text criticism and narrative coherence are against this suggestion"; he sees in the expression "paronomasia in the noun clause" and translates "lad though he was," since it is a disjunctive clause (p. 404).

121. LXX and probably also 4QSam^{a} have a long addition; see S. Pisano, *Additions or Omissions in the Books of Samuel: The Significant Pluses and Minuses in the Massoretic, LXX and Qumran Texts* (OBO 57; Freiburg: Universitätsverlag, 1984), pp. 157-63.

27 *For this boy I prayed!*
And the Lord granted me the request I had made of him.
28 *And I also entrust him to the Lord all his life,*[122]
since[123] *he was entrusted to the Lord (all his life)!"*
And they worshipped the Lord there.

20 Here begins the third section (EVENT 2), as indicated by *wayhî* (see also vv. 1 and 4). Their "knowing" (v. 19) eventually produced happy results — conception and birth. In the series of three *wayqtl,* that is, "and she conceived," "and she bore," and "and she called," the second one ("and she bore") is a direct sequel to the first, forming a word pair, "conceived and bore"; the MT punctuation sets a pause *(atnaḥ)* after *a son.* In such a construction, emphasis is given on the final action "she called"; see "Introduction." In this case, the mother named the child, as with the cases of Ichabod (1 Sam. 4:21) and Solomon (2 Sam. 12:24).

The name *Samuel* and the narrator's reason, that is, *because (she said) from the Lord I have requested him,* do not match etymologically, for it is impossible to explain the etymology of the name Samuel *(šᵉmû'ēl)* as being from the root *š'l ("to ask, request") and thus to mean something like *šā'ûl mē'ēl* "Asked-of-God" (Qimhi). As S. R. Driver[124] notes, the association of the two is probably meant to be conveyed by assonance, not by etymology.

The name *Samuel* itself has been explained etymologically in various ways: (1) **šᵉmû'ă'ēl* "Heard-of-God"; (2) **šemē'ēl* "He-who-is-from-God"; (3) **šimuhū-'il* "His-name-is-El" (McCarter, p. 62); (4) *šᵉmû'ēl* "Name-of-God" (Gesenius, Driver).[125] But the last view is most natural and does not require emendation. R. P. Gordon accepts the last view and translates "Name of El" or "El is exalted," though he takes El as a divine name "in vogue in pre-Israelite Canaan."[126] Mettinger explains that the name "Samuel" contains a reference to the hypostatized name of YHWH-EL.[127] Another possible way to explain its etymology is "The Name is God," like the royal names in the First Dynasty of Babylon: *Sumu-la-ilu* "The Name is verily God" and *Sumu-Abu* "The Name is Father" (cf. Eliab in 1 Sam. 16:6).[128]

122. Lit., "all the days."

123. *'ăšer = ka'ăšer;* see BDB, p. 83, 8c.

124. Driver, p. 16.

125. See Driver, pp. 16-19. Note in Phoenician Sidon the goddess Ashtart had an epithet "Name of Baal" (see *CS,* II, p. 183).

126. R. P. Gordon, p. 76.

127. Mettinger, *The Dethronement of Sabaoth,* p. 131.

128. See C. H. Gordon, "Eblaitica," *Eblaitica: Essays on the Ebla Archives and Eblaite Language* 1 (1987) 25-26. Also S. C. Layton, *Archaic Features of Canaanite Personal Names in the Hebrew Bible* (HSS 47; Atlanta: Scholars Press, 1990), pp. 78-87.

However, the context has something to do with the meaning of the name, even if not etymologically. One might surmise that Samuel, the "child" (lit., "seed of men"; v. 11 and fn.) whom God gave Hannah as the requested gift, would bear the name, that is, the essence, of God, who gave Samuel. Though she conceived by her human husband Elkanah (v. 19), not by Yahweh, Samuel was given to the childless woman Hannah by God's grace.[129] Hence, the name Samuel ("name" or "offspring"[130] of God) would signify the God-given child.[131] Though it is often said that the name *Samuel* displays archaic features and may already have been an ancient name in the time when the present story is set, there is no evidence for McCarter's claim that "Samuel's birth narrative has absorbed elements from another account describing Saul's birth."[132]

22 This year Hannah decided not to accompany Elkanah to Shiloh. She preferred to wait until the time came for her to present Samuel to God. The expression *[Not] until* (i.e., "I will not go until . . .") is a case of aposiopesis, the device of suddenly breaking off in the middle of a sentence as if unwilling to continue.[133] McCarter explains this as "an elliptical expression with *ʿad*" which is "unusual but not unexampled elsewhere," and he cites Judg. 16:2 as another example. A similar case is attested in *ʿad-bêt lāḥem* ("(up) to Bethlehem") in 1 Sam. 20:28, where some movement verb is to be understood: thus, *[to go] to Bethlehem.* Compare *lārûṣ bêt-leḥem ʿîrô* "in order to run to Bethlehem his city" (v. 6). An aposiopesis is also attested in 2 Sam. 13:16, where no particle *ʿad* appears. See also Ps. 6:3.

A child might not be weaned until three or four years old (2 Macc. 7:27); breastfeeding for three years is mentioned in the Egyptian "Instruction

129. On the theological issue of "childlessness," see K. T. Magnuson in *NDBT,* pp. 404-7.

130. Note that Akkadian *šumu* sometimes means "offspring" and is paired with *aplu* "heir" (CH, Epilogue); see W. G. E. Watson, "Some Additional Word Pairs," in *Ascribe to the Lord: Biblical and Other Studies in Memory of Peter C. Craigie,* ed. L. Eslinger and G. Taylor (JSOTSS 67; Sheffield: Sheffield Academic Press, 1988), pp. 192-93. It appears in personal names such as *Šumumliṣi* "May-a-Son-Come-Out"; see *CAD,* Š/iii, p. 295.

131. See 1 Sam. 2:20 ("grant . . . offspring") for a similar expression. Note also ^{d}Sin *nādin* NUMUN *nišī rapšāti* (*CAD,* Z, p. 93). "Sin gives numerous 'seeds of men'" (?); in another text, it is said, "without you (Sin) the childless woman cannot conceive (from) semen and become pregnant" (*CAD,* Z, p. 93). In Mesopotamia the god Sin was believed to be the deity who gave offspring to a childless woman. On the word pair "seed" and "name" in the ancient Near East, see on 1 Sam. 24:21.

132. McCarter, p. 62. See also on vv. 27-28 below.

133. GKC, §167*a* defines aposiopesis as "the concealment or suppression of entire sentences or clauses, which are of themselves necessary to complete the sense, and therefore must be supplied from the context."

of Any."[134] As for *appears before the Lord,* R. P. Gordon notes that the text may have originally read, "that we (or possibly 'he') may see the face of the Lord," as it was apparently a very early scribal practice to de-anthropomorphize phrases like this that were originally acceptable.[135] On the phrase *for ever,* see above (v. 11).

23 In Num. 30:13 it is the husband's responsibility to decide whether he should "confirm" his wife's oath or "annul" it; here it is the husband who wants the vow to be confirmed. It should be noted that when God is the subject of the verb "to establish," its object is usually either *his* word or promise or the words of his prophets: for example, God is to fulfill his promise (Deut. 9:5; 2 Sam. 7:25; etc.). The only two passages where *hēqîm* with God as subject and human *dābār* occur are "may the LORD confirm your words which you have prophesied" (Jer. 28:6) — in Jeremiah's ironical word against Hananiah — and Isa. 44:26.[136]

For *his word,* NEB translates "your vow," since the MT reading appears to be strange, considering that God has already fulfilled Hannah's wish. Hence, McCarter reads it as "what you have said" (lit., "that which goes forth from your mouth"), following LXX *(to exelthon ek tou stomatos sou)* and 4QSam^a^ *(hywṣ' mpyk).* However, what Elkanah is saying is that his wife may do whatever she thinks best, as long as the Lord does his own will (lit., "his word"). Here *word* refers to the will of God in general rather than a specific divine promise to her. Birch sees here the beginning of "the story of God's Word working through Samuel in Israel"; see 15:11.[137] The particle *'ak* (only) functions here restrictively. Hence, McCarter's comment, "as yet there has been no word from Yahweh," is not appropriate in this context.

While Elkanah has stayed in the background, he has been present with her all along (see below on vv. 25, 28; also 1 Sam. 2:11).

24 When the time for presentation of the child came, a votive offering of generous proportions accompanied the family to Shiloh.[138]

The Hebrew phrase *pārîm šᵉlōšāh* (MT) is normally translated as "three bulls" (JPS; also Caquot and de Robert) or emended to mean "a three-year-old bull" (NRSV; NASB; NIV). Since three bulls seem to be too much for the occasion of dedicating a little boy, almost all scholars, following LXX, 4QSam^a^, and the Peshitta, accept "a three-year-old bull." R. P. Gordon

134. See *CS,* I, p. 113.

135. R. P. Gordon, p. 77.

136. See Walters, "Hannah and Anna," p. 410.

137. Birch, p. 976.

138. G. L. Archer, "Reassessment of the Value of the Septuagint of 1 Samuel for Textual Emendation, in the Light of the Qumran Fragments," in *Tradition and Testament: Essays in Honor of Charles Lee Feinberg* (Chicago: Moody Press, 1981), pp. 223-40; McCarter, p. 56.

thinks, "As in Genesis 15:9, it is a question of maturity and, therefore, of cultic acceptability."[139]

However, why should the MT be considered problematic? C. Meyer lists three reasons: (1) the word order, (2) the inconsistency with the mention in v. 25 of a single animal, and (3) its economic extremity, that is, the representation of "a sacrificial element disproportionately larger and more costly than the other two items."[140]

The word order should be no problem, for countable items in a list are often followed by numerals, sometimes as opposed to measured items. Compare this list

younglings 3
and 1 ephah of flour
and "jar" of wine

with 1 Sam. 16:20:

An "ass"[141] of bread
and "skin" of wine
and kid of she-goats 1

These examples are not formal lists, but in one of the ancient Near Eastern formal list-types, the lines consist of the type of item followed by the numeral.[142] See also 1 Sam. 6:17; 2 Sam. 10:6; cf. 1 Sam. 25:18; 2 Sam. 6:19; 10:18 for lists.

As for the next objection, a singular noun is often used collectively.

For "economic extremity," at first glance, three animals does seem disproportionate. However, not only the animal offering but also the flour offering is substantial; see below. It is reasonable to think that Hannah made a generous sacrifice to the Lord for the lifelong consecration of her son, who may have been three years old by then (see above, v. 22). As R. L. Hubbard, Jr. personally suggested, the gift might seek to offset the added expenses of Samuel's joining the staff. Or, as Walters suggests, three animals were presented, "one for each person," as in 1 Sam. 10:3, "where three men on a pilgrimage to Bethel have three kids with them."[143]

139. On "legal maturity for sacrifice," see E. A. Speiser, "The Nuzi Tablets Solve a Puzzle in the Books of Samuel," *BASOR* 72 (1938) 15-17; McCarter, p. 63.

140. Meyers, "An Ethnoarchaeological Analysis of Hannah's Sacrifice," in *Pomegranates and Golden Bells,* p. 82.

141. Here, the term "ass" is a dry measure, see below on 1 Sam. 16:20.

142. See D. T. Tsumura, "List and Narrative in I Samuel 6,17-18a in the Light of Ugaritic Economic Texts," *ZAW* (2001) 353-69.

143. Walters, "Hannah and Anna," p. 401; see also on v. 28 below.

Moreover the term *pārîm* probably means "younglings." As Judg. 6:25 *par-haššôr* (lit., "*par* of the bull") suggests, *pār* originally meant "young (one)" (adj./n.), like *naʿar* in 1 Sam. 2:13, and refers to any kind of young animal (cf. Akk. *parru* "lamb, young sheep").[144] In fact, in Ugaritic, the terms *pr* and *prt* in *KTU* 1.86:3-4 probably mean "young bull" and "heifer," respectively.[145] So, the animals which Hannah brought to Shiloh were not necessarily adult "bulls," but the *younglings* of cows or sheep; see also on *calves* (1 Sam. 8:16). Then, in the present list-like expression, it may be that the term *pārîm* is used with an older meaning "young sheep"; see another list-like expression in 1 Sam. 16:20.

One ephah of flour is a tenth of a homer, probably about 3/5 bushel (about 22 liters). The flour represents a substantial offering. The priestly regulations regarding accompanying grain offerings specify 1/10 ephah for each lamb sacrificed (Lev. 14:10; 14:21; Num. 15:4; 28:4-9, 13; Lev. 23:13 states 2/10 ephah), 2/10 for each ram (Num. 15:6; 28:20, 28), and 3/10 for each bull (Num. 15:9; 28:12, 20, 28). So with three bulls, one would expect an offering of 9/10 ephah, just a little less than what Hannah offered. Hannah's husband, Elkanah, was presumably a well-to-do person who was capable of a substantial offering on the special occasion of the life-long dedication of the first son of his beloved first wife.

The word for "jar," which is also translated as "skin," may refer to a large vessel for holding wine, oil, grain, etc. The *nbl*-jar could be quite large, holding a bath, a measure apparently equal to an ephah. For "a skin" *(n'd),* see 1 Sam. 16:20. Against Meyers, nothing is strange or "aberrant" in offering only two items of agricultural products, grain and grapes without oil, for bread and wine were the basic food-and-drink in ancient Canaan.[146]

The boy was young or "the child was young" (NASB; RSV). McCarter considers the phrase *whnʿr nʿr* as "unintelligible" and translates the MT as "and the child was a child (?)." Thenius's proposal in 1842 to posit a haplography in the MT, based on LXX's longer text, now appears to be supported by 4QSam[a] and is followed by many scholars (e.g., R. P. Gordon). But the MT makes sense. For one thing, the first word, the noun *naʿar,* can mean "servant, steward" (1 Sam. 9:3; 2 Sam. 9:9; 13:17; 16:1; 19:17) as well as "boy, child." The second word is most naturally the adjective "young" as in 1 Sam. 2:13, 15, 17, 18.[147]

144. See *AHw,* p. 834; also see *HALOT,* p. 960.

145. Pardee, in *CS,* I, p. 293, n. 2.

146. Cf. Meyers, "An Ethnoarchaeological Analysis of Hannah's Sacrifice," in *Pomegranates and Golden Bells,* p. 85. In Ugaritic, *lḥm* and *yn* are the basic food and drink; see *KTU* 1.23:6; Tsumura, *The Ugaritic Drama of the Good Gods,* pp. 28-29.

147. See D. T. Tsumura, "Poetic Nature of the Hebrew Narrative Prose in I Samuel 2:12-17," in *Verse in Ancient Near Eastern Prose,* ed. J. C. de Moor and W. G. E. Wat-

Therefore, the phrase "the *naʿar* was young" is perfectly legitimate, since the noun *naʿar* could refer to an older person such as Ziba, Saul's *naʿar,* who had fifteen sons (2 Sam. 19:17). Thus, the term *naʿar* indicates someone, of whatever age, who was under the authority of another person and not free, legally, to act as an independent individual.[148] Furthermore, the clause is a key expression, denoting "the boy" Samuel's early stage of growth; in other words, Samuel began his dedicated life in his extreme youth. The reference to the "boy" anticipates those in 1 Sam. 2:11, 18, 21, 26, thus connecting two narrative sections interrupted by the insertion of Hannah's prayer (1 Sam. 2:1-10); see the commentary on 9:3.

25 The verbs *were slaughtered* and *was brought* are impersonal passives, as they are often in the context of slaughtering animals: for example, Lev. 1:11; 3:2, 8, 13; etc. — in this flow of discourse the agent is *defocused,* that is, the emphasis is on what was done, rather than on who did it. In the narrative discourse this is transitional and a little "off-the-story-line."[149]

As for *the younglings,* the singular adjective with a definite article (*happār;* lit., "the young [one]") is used as a collective (see above v. 24).

26-27 With *And she said,* the spotlight goes back to the main actor. Hannah invokes an oath to remind Eli of who she was — the woman he saw praying desperately to God for a son. For the oath formula, *As your soul lives, my lord,* see 1 Sam. 14:39 ("as the Lord lives"). On *pray to,* see on 1 Sam. 1:10; compare "pray before" in 1 Sam. 1:12. *And the Lord granted me the request I had made of him* is almost verbatim the repetition of Eli's blessing in 1 Sam. 1:17. Joyously, Hannah points to *this boy* as the answer to that prayer.

28 *I also entrust . . . to . . . :* The verb (Hi. pf. 1 c.s.) is a *performative* perfect: that is, by uttering these words Hannah performed the act of dedication; see on 17:10. Hannah entrusts her requested son to the Lord, giving him back to the Giver in a true act of worship.

Walters[150] translates "was asked for/by YHWH," taking the preposition *le* as polysemous, that is, as having multiple meanings. According to him, the boy was "asked for YHWH" by Hannah as well as "asked by

---

son (AOAT 42; Neukirchen-Vluyn: Neukirchener, 1993), pp. 293-304 and below. Caquot and de Robert take the second term as a denominative verb and translate the clause as "the boy became servant" (p. 34).

148. A. R. Millard, personal communication.

149. See also 1 Sam. 2:20. R. E. Longacre uses "goal oriented" in contrast with "agent oriented"; see "Building for the Worship of God: Exodus 25:1–30:10," in *Discourse Analysis of Biblical Literature: What It Is and What It Offers* (SBL Semeia Studies; Atlanta: Scholars Press, 1995), p. 23; see Endo, *The Verbal System of Classical Hebrew in the Joseph Story,* p. 247. See also on 2 Sam. 13:32.

150. Walters, "Hannah and Anna," p. 405.

YHWH"; Samuel was "asked — by both Hannah and YHWH — and both requests are now satisfied." However, note that the prepositions connected with the verbal root *š'l are different:

> *š'l (Qal) + *min:* "request (a request) from . . ." (vv. 17, 20, 27; 1 Sam. 8:10)
> *š'l (Qal) + *l:* "request (a request) to . . ." → "be entrusted to . . ." (1 Sam. 2:20)
> *š'l (Qal pass.) + *l:* "requested to . . ." → "entrusted to . . ." (v. 28)
> *š'l (Hi.) + *l:* "entrust . . . to . . ." (v. 28)

The semantic structure of these two stems may be explained as follows:

> Qal = A requests X (to B and expects response) *from* B
> Hi. = A causes X to be requested *to* B = A entrusted X *to* B.

Thus, in vv. 27-28 there is certainly a wordplay on the root *š'l. Hannah here says, *I entrust* (*š'l: Hi.) Samuel *to the Lord,* for the Lord granted her *the request* she "requested from" (*š'l: Qal + *min*) him.

The form *šā'ūl* (*was entrusted*[151]) in this verse is exactly the same as the name Saul. There is also a formal similarity between the introductory verse of this story (1:1) and that of the tale of the lost asses of Kish, Saul's father (9:1). Hence, some suspect that the narrative about Samuel's birth originally concerned Saul.[152] Walters holds that while it is possible that the wordplay in vv. 27-28 was originally connected with Saul, in the present context it was not a king, but a prophet, who was "asked" by God.[153] If so, Gordon is right: "the logic of the section that culminates in 1:28 would require that Saul spent his youth in the service of the Shiloh sanctuary."[154] Such

151. Qal, pass. ptc., here functioning as the participle of Hi. "to entrust . . . to." For a case that Qal, ptc. functions as the participle of Pi. stem, see *dōbēr* for *dbr (Pi) "to speak." Note that a PN *š'l* appears on several Hebrew seals; see N. Avigad and B. Sass, *Corpus of West Semitic Stamp Seals* (Jerusalem: Israel Academy of Sciences and Humanities, 1997), nos. 56, 383, 1175. They explain the name to be related to the meaning, "lent to (God)."

152. McCarter, pp. 63, 65-66; M. Brettler, "The Composition of 1 Samuel 1–2," *JBL* 116 (1997) 602; see also D. G. Schley, *Shiloh: A Biblical City in Tradition and History* (JSOTSS 63; Sheffield: Sheffield Academic Press, 1989), pp. 152-53; J. S. Ackerman, "Who Can Stand Before YHWH, This Holy God? A Reading of 1 Samuel 1–15," *Prooftexts* 11 (1991) 3-4.

153. Walters, "Hannah and Anna," p. 406.

154. R. P. Gordon, "Who Made the Kingmaker?" in *Faith, Tradition, and History,* p. 266.

an association between Saul and Shiloh cannot be supported by the biblical text. He aptly notes that many scholars assume the original existence of a birth narrative of Saul here "when no one in biblical antiquity seems to have thought to devise one for David."[155] This kind of similarity does not necessarily support literary interdependence. The verbal form certainly reminds readers of the person Saul, but the name seems to be a common NW Semitic name.[156]

The verbal phrase *wayyištaḥû (they worshipped)* is traditionally taken as singular (so KJV; NASB; NIV; JPS note).[157] If this is so, "[Elkanah] worshipped" will be followed by 1 Sam. 2:11 ("And Elkanah went back to Ramah, to his house"), just interrupted by Hannah's "prayer." Walters takes Samuel as the subject and translates: "he bowed low there to YHWH," though he agrees that Elkanah was probably with Hannah "all along" since "the mother and the child would probably not travel alone."[158] However, the plural subjects are expected for this act of worshipping from the context (so "they . . ." in JPS; RSV; NEB; REB), for not only Elkanah (see also 1 Sam. 2:11) but also Hannah must have worshipped the Lord. As Hannah and Samuel and Elkanah (1 Sam. 2:11) were all there and would have worshipped, we would expect a plural verb. Also, from a discourse-grammatical point of view, a 3 m.pl. form *they worshipped* would certainly serve as transitional in the narrative, with agent defocusing, that is, with emphasis on what was done rather than who did it, as in v. 25 (also *wayyištaḥăwû* 3 m.pl. in 1:19). The term *wayyištaḥû* then might possibly be explained as a shortened form of the original 3 m.pl., with the accent on the penultimate syllable:

wayyištáḥwû → *wayyištáḥ^{u}û* → *wayyištáḥû*

This variant form could be another example of "phonetic spellings," which the MT of Samuel occasionally exhibits and preserves; see "Introduction" (Section II, B, 4).

In this initial chapter of the books of Samuel, the future mother of the kingmaker, Samuel, is introduced. The reader learns who she was, why and how she requested a son from the Lord, and how, after the request was granted her, she entrusted him to the Lord. Like Hannah, believers too are called to approach God through prayer and worship, to ask him to grant his

155. R. P. Gordon, "Who Made the Kingmaker?" in *Faith, Tradition, and History,* p. 269.

156. E.g., F. Gröndahl, *PTU,* p. 191.

157. Based on 4QSam[a], McCarter translated "Then she left him there and worshipped Yahweh" (p. 50). Also "She left him there for the Lord" (NRSV).

158. Walters, "Hannah and Anna," p. 401.

gift to us, and to dedicate that gift to his service. God certainly guides the life of worship according to his plan and purpose. Though the world becomes darker and darker, God in Christ is surely still working through the lives of individuals who fear and honor him.

<Hannah's Song> (2:1-10)

Verses 1-11 of this chapter continue the section on Hannah's family. The episode about the birth and dedication of Samuel finally terminates at 2:11, which states that Elkanah (and presumably Hannah) returned to their home at Ramah and gives a brief summary of Samuel's "ministering to the Lord before Eli, the priest." The "prayer" or Song of Hannah in vv. 1b-10a (or 10b) is thus embedded into the narrative, and so v. 11 is sequential to 1:28 ("And they worshipped the Lord there").[1]

The song, which became the prototype of the Magnificat (Luke 1:46-55),[2] fits as well into the narrative, as does David's elegy for Saul and Jonathan in 2 Sam. 1:19-27. It serves as the TERMINUS[3] to the story of Samuel's birth. At the other end of the grand narrative of the books of Samuel are the "songs" of David (2 Samuel 22; 23). Hannah's "song" and David's "songs" serve as a frame or *inclusio* around the entire narrative of 1-2 Samuel. Thus, the Song of Hannah serves as "a thematic and structural introduction to Samuel."[4]

1. The most recent thorough study of the Song of Hannah is T. J. Lewis, "The Textual History of the Song of Hannah: 1 Samuel II 1-10," *VT* 44 (1994) 18-46; see p. 21, n. 12, for a bibliography. See also R. Tournay, "Le cantique d'Anne: I Samuel II.1-10," in *Mélanges Dominique Barthélemy: Études bibliques offertes a l'occasion de son 60e anniversaire,* ed. P. Casetti, O. Keel, and A. Schenker (OBO 38; Fribourg: Éditions Universitaires, 1981), pp. 553-76; J. W. Watts, *Psalm and Story: Inset Hymns in Hebrew Narrative* (JSOTSS 139; Sheffield: JSOT Press, 1992). For linguistic and stylistic analyses, see R. Bartelmus, "Tempus als Strukturprinzip: Anmerkungen zur stilistischen und theologischen Relevanz des Tempusgebrauchs im 'Lied der Hanna' (1 Sam 2,1-10)," *BZ* 31 (1987) 15-35.

2. A tenth-century date has been proposed by D. N. Freedman, "Psalm 113 and the Song of Hannah," *EI* 14 (H. L. Ginsberg Volume) (1978) 56-69 [English section]; see C. Meyers, "An Ethnoarchaeological Analysis of Hannah's Sacrifice," in *Pomegranates and Golden Bells: Studies in Biblical, Jewish, and Near Eastern Ritual, Law, and Literature in Honor of Jacob Milgrom,* ed. D. P. Wright, D. N. Freedman, and A. Hurvitz (Winona Lake, Ind.: Eisenbrauns, 1995), p. 81, n. 8. Caquot and de Robert, p. 60, think it is a lyric of the First Temple period. For the "resignification" of the Song in the later Jewish and NT traditions, see J. E. Cook, *Hannah's Desire, God's Design: Early Interpretations of the Story of Hannah* (JSOTSS 282; Sheffield: Sheffield Academic Press, 1999).

3. For the terminology, see "Introduction" (Section VI, A).

4. R. C. Bailey, "The Redemption of Yahweh: A Literary Critical Function of the Songs of Hannah and David," *BibInt* 3 (1995) 213-31. See H. H. Klement, *II Samuel 21–*

The song is not a prayer of supplication but a psalm of thanksgiving.[5] Yet it is not simply thanksgiving for the birth of a son. In fact, the subject of barrenness and birth-giving is mentioned only in v. 5. It is really a song of praise, or a hymn,[6] to the God who reverses human fortunes by his mighty power. As Labuschagne says, "The main emphasis is on the help received from Yahweh by one involved in an unequal struggle. For this reason, the song fits excellently in the mouth of Hannah as a woman involved in an unequal struggle."[7]

The concluding remark on *king* in v. 10b makes Hannah's song a worthy candidate for the so-called "royal psalms" (e.g. Psalms 45, 72), and the song is often compared with Psalm 113.[8] Because of the militaristic moments in the song, it is sometimes proposed that its composition was occasioned by an Israelite victory over an external enemy. But, whatever its original life situation may be, the Song fits well into the story of Hannah, and its universality makes it "an ideal introit to the history of the early monarchy as recounted in the books of Samuel."[9]

(1) Title (2:1a)

1a *And Hannah prayed:*[10]

1a The flow of narrative moves from the end of ch. 1 (v. 28b: "And they worshipped the Lord there.") to 2:11a ("And Elkanah went back to Ramah, to his house"), which Hannah's prayer interrupts, as an embedded discourse, introduced by the formula "*And Hannah prayed* and said" (v. 1a). The prayer here involves praise (v. 1b) and prophecy (v. 10b), just as in Hab. 3:1 where the title, *tᵉpillāh laḥăbaqqûq* "a prayer of Habakkuk," is followed by a song in an archaic hymnic style.[11]

24: Context, Structure and Meaning in the Samuel Conclusion (Europäische Hochschulschriften Reihe 23; Frankfurt am Main: Peter Lang, 2000).

5. R. P. Gordon, p. 78. The prayer of Hannah is called "the Song of Hannah" for reasons summarized by McCarter, p. 74.

6. See Caquot and de Robert, pp. 57-58.

7. C. J. Labuschagne, *The Incomparability of Yahweh in the Old Testament* (POS 5; Leiden: E. J. Brill, 1966), p. 117, n. 2.

8. See, for example, Freedman, "Psalm 113 and the Song of Hannah," pp. 56-69.

9. R. P. Gordon, p. 79.

10. Lit., "prayed and said"; see "Introduction." Lewis ("The Textual History of the Song of Hannah," p. 19) applies the principle of *lectio brevior* here and drops *and said* as an addition.

11. See T. Hiebert, *God of My Victory: The Ancient Hymn in Habakkuk 3* (HSM 38; Atlanta: Scholars Press, 1986).

(2) Song (2:1b-10)

(a) Yahweh's Holy Sovereignty

1b *My heart exults*[12] *in the Lord,*
my horn rises[13] *in the Lord;*
my mouth opens wide against my enemies,
for[14] *I have rejoiced in your salvation.*
2 *There is no holy one like the Lord;*
indeed[15] *there is none but you;*[16]
there is no rock like our God.
3 *Do not speak too much,*[17]
very haughtily,[18]

12. Or "rejoices" (NIV) ; Akk. *elēṣu* "to rejoice" (see *īliṣ libbašuma* [Gilg. P. iii 20 (OB), etc.], "his heart rejoiced" [*CAD,* E, 88]). It shows "unlimited, unrestrained joy." See A. R. Millard, "*ʿlṣ* 'to exult,'" *JTS* 26 (1975) 88.

13. *rāmāh* (*rwm); not passive, but a middle, intransitive verb. The preposition should be translated not as an agent with "by" (McCarter), but with "in." McCarter notes (p. 72) that the idiom "exalt the horn" sometimes refers to "the establishment of the lasting distinction of posterity." However, what is characteristic of this verse is that the expression "my horn" is used by a female, as against the cases in all passages cited by McCarter.

14. Lewis takes this *ki* as "a prosaic addition" ("The Textual History of the Song of Hannah," p. 26).

15. See M. Dahood, in *RSP* 3, p. 88, who sees here an emphatic particle. Cf. LXX, which deletes the second colon, followed by BHK. Lewis ("The Textual History of the Song of Hannah," p. 28) takes this particle *ki* as "a prosaic addition."

16. According to McCarter, pp. 68-69, this verse is conflate in all witnesses; Lewis takes the second line, which he reads *ʾên (qādôš) biltekā,* as "a theological gloss added by a later editor" ("The Textual History of the Song of Hannah," p. 28). But if this were the case, it is strange that the later editor should use the second person for God only in his gloss. However, this unique feature should be explained as an exact symmmetry of person in a tricolon: 3 m.s.–2 m.s.–3 m.s. And this tricolon constitutes an "AXB pattern," in which the second line (X) is inserted between a bicolon, A//B, for a rhetorical purpose; see "Introduction" (Section VII, C).

17. Lit., "you do much/many" and "you speak," connected asyndetically as a verbal hendiadys; see also J-M, §177g: "asyndesis where the first verb expresses an adverbial notion": "Talk no more so very proudly."

18. One might feel that "the line is unduly long" (Driver, p. 24); hence, some scholars take it as a bicolon: "Do not speak haughtily//Or let arrogance out of your mouth!" (McCarter, p. 69); "Do not multiply haughtiness//Let not arrogance come from your mouths" (Lewis, "The Textual History of the Song of Hannah," p. 23). However, it is reasonable to recognize a tricolon of the "AXB pattern" here, like the preceding verse. The second line (X), "haughty (and) haughty," seems to be inserted between a bicolon (A//B): "Do not speak too much"//"let no arrogant word go out of your mouths," and modifies the bicolon as a whole adverbially.

let no arrogant word go out of your mouths!
For the Lord is the God of true knowledge;
and (his) deeds are immeasurable.[19]

(b) Reversal of Human Fortunes (vv. 4-5)

4 *The mighty, their bows are broken;*[20]
the feeble are girded with strength.
5 *Those who were sated with*[21] *bread are hired;*[22]
and those who were hungry need not be so[23] *for ever.*[24]
A barren woman bears seven;
but a woman with many sons[25] *becomes childless.*

19. Following the Ketib l' ntknw: *lō' nitkᵉnû* "are not measured"; cf. Qere: *lô nitkᵉnû* "to/by him are measured."

20. In both the LXX and 4QSam^a the predicate is m.s., and so "God" is the agent and "the bow of the mighty" is the object of the verb. However, the MT makes good sense as it stands, both grammatically and stylistically. Note that the term *bow* (s.) here is adverbial accusative. See "Introduction" (Section VII, A) for the analysis of this verse.

21. The preposition *(b-)* can go either with the verb "be sated" (*śbʿ) as in Ps. 65:4; 103:5 (cf. often with *min*), or with the verb "be hired" (*śkr: Ni.) as in Gen. 30:16; Judg. 9:4; 2 Chr. 25:6 and most modern translations such as NRSV ("have hired themselves out for bread"); NIV; JPS; and NASB. Lewis thinks that the preposition *b-* is that of "price or exchange," translating "The well-fed hire themselves out *in exchange for* food" ("The Textual History of the Song of Hannah," p. 33). The parallelism should be either abc//acd or Ab//abc (e.g., Ps. 2:4). The former directs us to either syntax, but the latter leads to the translation: "those who are hungry (for the bread)," *balleḥem* being double-duty (cf. Jer. 42:14 *rʿb l-).

22. Ni. *śkr or "hire oneself out." Cf. Ugar. *almnt. škr tškr* "The widow will indeed hire herself out" (*KTU* 1.14 II 44-45, IV 22-23).

23. In Isa. 24:8 the verb *ḥdl parallels *šbt "cease, desist, rest." T. J. Lewis ("The Song of Hannah and Deborah: *ḥdl* — II [Growing plump]," *JBL* 104 [1985] 107f.) translates the bicolon as follows:

"The well-fed hire themselves out for food,
But the hungry do not do so anymore." (repointing to *ʿōd)*

Some scholars rather take it as a second root, *ḥdl "to be fat, well-nourished" (e.g., R. P. Gordon, p. 80 ["The hungry are to be 'fattened with food'"]). But this is not necessary. For many ways of emending the text, see Lewis, "The Song of Hannah and Deborah," pp. 105-6.

24. Lit., "perpetuity." Here it appears as adverbial accusative; also Gen. 49:26 (against MT cantillation; see G. A. Rendsburg, "Janus Parallelism in Gen 49:26," *JBL* 99 [1980] 291-93). McCarter (p. 72) compares this term *ʿad* with Ugaritic *mġd* "food" (*//lḥm*) and translates it as "food." But, the Arabic cognates *maġḏā* and *ġiḏā'* (*UT* 19.1519) suggest that the Hebrew correspondence is *ʿaz* rather than *ʿad.*

25. Lit., "(a woman) abounding in sons" or "(she who is) abundant of sons" (McCarter, pp. 72-73): <adj. f.s. cstr. + genitive>; see GKC, §128x-y.

(c) Yahweh's Holy Sovereignty (vv. 6-7)

6 *The Lord is the one who brings death and makes alive,*
the one who brings down to Sheol[26] *and brings up.*[27]
7 *The Lord is the one who makes poor*[28] *and makes rich,*
the one who makes low and also makes high.

(d) Reversal of Human Fortunes (v. 8a)

8 *He is the one who raises the poor from the dust;*
from the dunghill he is able to lift[29] *the needy,*
so that he may make (them) sit with noblemen,[30]
and a chair of honor[31] *grant them.*

26. "Sheol" is here used adverbially, modifying both the preceding and following verb; thus, it functions as X of AX&B pattern, in which X is inserted into a coordinated phrase ("to bring down" and "to bring up"); see "Introduction" (Section VII, C).

27. Lewis thinks that we should expect here "another participle or a durative *(yaqtulu)* form **wa-yaʿleh*" ("The Textual History of the Song of Hannah," p. 36). However, there are a number of cases where *wayqtl* follows the preceding participle in poetic texts: e.g., Ps. 18:33; 18:48; 29:5; 104:32; 107:40;, Amos 6:3; Nah. 1:4; 2:13; Job 12:22, 23; 14:20; Prov. 20:26; also *KTU* 1.6:I:48; see also Driver, p. 25. Moreover, this *wayqtl* seemingly is sequential to the perf. of the preceding verse. Hence, there is no need to reconstruct **wa-yaʿl <eh>,* with Lewis. See on 1 Sam. 2:8 (below).

28. Factitive Hi. *yrš (orig., *wrš). This root is a byform of *rwš (to be poor), and both originate from a bi-consonantal root *rš; hence, no "confusion" should be seen here. Cf. Driver, p. 26: "we should expect *mērîš; yrš* (Qal) means, however, to *impoverish* in Judg. 14,5."

29. This is a simple impf. verb after five consecutive participles in vv. 7-8a; cf. v. 6 above. Such an impf. might be taken as having a modal sense (hence, "is able to lift").

30. Adj. *nādîb* "willing, one who is generous, noble"; see J. P. Weinberg, "The Word ndb in the Bible: A Study in Historical Semantics and Biblical Thought," in *Solving Riddles and Untying Knots: Biblical, Epigraphic, and Semitic Studies in Honor of Jonas C. Greenfield,* ed. Z. Zevit, S. Gitin, and M. Sokoloff (Winona Lake, Ind.: Eisenbrauns, 1995), p. 369; cf. Prov. 8:16 "noblemen"//18 "honor"; also Job 30:15 ("nobility" = honor, cf. BDB, p. 622). "Needy" — "noblemen" is a word pair in Ps. 113:7-8 and, in reverse order, in Ps. 107:40-41. This may also support the view that the text constitutes a four-line parallelism, instead of two two-line parallelisms.

31. Lewis ("The Textual History of the Song of Hannah," p. 37) reconstructs *nĕdîbê ʿam* "the nobility of the people" in light of the LXX and a Syro-Hexaplar text. But the MT *nĕdîbîm* has an exact parallel to Ps. 113:8. For a comparative study of 1 Sam. 2:1-10 and Ps. 113:5-9, see A. Hurvitz, "Originals and Imitations in Biblical Poetry: A Comparative Examination of 1 Sam 2:1-10 and Ps 113:5-9," in *Biblical and Related Studies Presented to Samuel Iwry,* ed. A. Kort and S. Morschauser (Winona Lake, Ind.: Eisenbrauns, 1985), pp. 115-21.

(e) Yahweh's Holy Sovereignty (vv. 8b-10a)

For the pillars of the earth are the Lord's;
and he placed on them the world.[32]
9 *He guards the feet of his faithful;*
but the wicked perish in darkness,[33]
for no one can prevail by his own ability.
10 *As for the Lord,*[34] *his antagonists*[35] *are shattered;*
against them[36] *he thunders from*[37] *the heaven.*
The Lord judges the ends of the earth.

(f) Theme of Kingship (v. 10b)

May he give power to his king;
may he raise the horn of his anointed![38]

32. Always without an article; *tēbēl* *ybl (BDB, p. 385; *HALOT,* pp. 1682-83); cf. Akk. *tābalu* "trockenes Land" (*AHw,* p. 1298); "foundations of the world" (2 Sam. 22:16); <word pair>: "earth" — "world" (hence "world" of the earth) and "poetic synonym" (BDB) of "earth" (also Ps. 24:1).

33. The first two lines make up a good bicolon in the deep grammar, though the elements of each line do not correspond well in the surface grammar: i.e., a (feet of) b (his faithful) c (he guards)//b′ (the wicked) d′ (in darkness) c′ (perish). Though b and b′ do not correspond to each other on the surface, both have the same grammatical relation to the verbs of each line: they are *recipients* (PATIENTS) of the verbs "to guard" (transitive) and "to perish" (intransitive). In the deep grammar, the two lines correspond thus: "God PROTECTS his faithful"//"but (God) DESTROYS the wicked"; also see Ps. 1:6.

34. *Casus pendens,* so McCarter, p. 70; Lewis ("The Textual History of the Song of Hannah," p. 40). Hence, most likely this is the head of the first line of parallelism, contra NIV.

35. A singular form (Hi. ptc.) is used here as collective, following Ketib; cf. "my enemies" (v. 1).

36. Q. *ʿālâw,* the suffix is s., referring to "them"; so Caquot and de Robert, p. 48. However, the Lord's enemies were already referred to in the plural; hence, K. *ʿlw,* which is in parallel with Yahweh, might be taken as a divine epithet, "the Exalted One" (e.g., "the Most High" [NRSV]; "Eli" [McCarter]), like the Ugaritic *ʿly* for Baal (see Gordon, *UT,* §19.1855; *RSP* 3, p. 456) and the Akkadian *elû* (*CAD,* E, p. 111). For the divine name *ʿal* here, see G. R. Driver, "Hebrew ʿal ('high one') as a Divine Title," *ExTi* 50 (1938) 92-93; J. Barr, *CPTOT,* p. 283; R. P. Gordon, p. 333, n. 53. See also Gibson, *CML*^{2}, p. 98, n. 4; Pardee in *CS,* I, p. 341; B. Schmidt, "Al" in *DDD,* pp. 23-28. But, see the commentary on the name Eli (1:3) above.

37. The preposition *b* means "from" in this context and also in Ps. 18:23. Cf. *min* in 2 Sam. 22:14; see 1 Sam. 12:3 (below). Yahweh's destructive intervention is *from* where he is, not *in* where he is.

38. "King" and "anointed" are a word pair; also in 2 Sam. 22:51 [= Ps. 18:50].

In this hymn of praise Caquot and de Robert recognize the following "concentric structure":[39]

v. 1	Elevation of the weak ("I")/abasement of the strong ("enemies")
vv. 2-3	Who is Yahweh? (the Holy One; the God who knows)
vv. 4-5	Abasement of the strong/elevation of the weak
vv. 6-7	Who is Yahweh? (the One who abases and elevates)
v. 8a	Elevation of the weak/(abasement of thc strong)
vv. 8b-9	Who is Yahweh? (the Creator)
v. 10	Abasement of the strong ("enemies")/elevation of the weak ("king")

However, their analysis seems to be a little forced; it might be better analyzed as follows:

(1) Yahweh's holy sovereignty (vv. 1b-3)
(2) Reversal of human fortunes (vv. 4-5)
(3) Yahweh's holy sovereignty (vv. 6-7)
(4) Reversal of human fortunes (v. 8a)
(5) Yahweh's holy sovereignty (vv. 8b-10a)
(6) The theme of kingship (v. 10b).

The literary structure is a rondo form (ABABAC)[40] rather than a concentric pattern.

(1) "Yahweh's Holy Sovereignty" (vv. 1b-3)

1b Verse 1b has four parallel lines, and the opening statement, with YHWH *(the Lord)* twice, forms an *inclusio* with the final verse (v. 10a). The song begins with very personal emotion (*my* [3 x]), but that emotion is soon dropped. After the *our God* in v. 2, the first person disappears completely.

While here Hannah confesses that her horn *rises in the Lord,* at the end, she (or the narrator) makes supplication that the Lord *raise the horn of his anointed.* The phrase, *rwm + "horn," thus forms an *inclusio.* The Song of Hannah thus makes a perfect introduction to the institution of monarchy in Israel. The animal horn here symbolizes both strength and pride, possibly of kingship, but not of divinity as sometimes in the ancient Near East. Here,

39. Caquot and de Robert, p. 60.

40. Like Psalm 46, which has a rondo pattern of ABA′CA′; see D. T. Tsumura, "Literary Structure of Psalm 46,2-8," *AJBI* 6 (1980) 55, n. 91.

Hannah's *horn* symbolizes her dignity. Verbal forms of *rwm ("to rise") also appear in vv. 7, 8, 10, and the verb is "the theme verb of the poem."[41] YHWH *(the Lord)* appears twice in this verse.[42] Thus, the repetition of YHWH both in the beginning and at the end of the prayer constitutes a perfect framing.[43] As R. P. Gordon observes, "God is the ground of rejoicing as he is the object of praise."[44]

The phrase *my mouth opens wide* has been interpreted in various ways:

(a) "swallowing enemies," figuratively to stand for triumphing over one's enemies (so BDB; NAB);
(b) gloating over or deriding one's enemies (so JPS; RSV);
(c) an expression of joy in parallel with v. 1d.[45]

The first (a) seems to be the best fit for the parallelistic structure; see below.

With the expression *against my enemies,* Hannah is not making a personal attack on Peninnah (s.) here, but "against" God's enemies. His enemies are Hannah's enemies too (see Ps. 139:21-22), because his *enemies* attack her trust in God and his dealings with her. See on 17:47b. Note that *against my enemies* (pl.) is contrasted with *in the Lord* (s.) of the first two lines; both elements, that is, both the preposition and the noun, are complete opposites. This contrast, together with the repetition of "heart" — "horn" — "mouth," supports the view that this is a quadracolon, in which the first three lines (or cola) have a close association to each other.

Hannah gives the reason for her joy: *I have rejoiced,* a reference to Hannah's intimate ("I" — "you") relation with the covenant God Yahweh. At the climax of the quadracolon the key word *salvation* appears, which here means the "victory" of the Lord over his enemies.

2 Hannah affirms several convictions about the Lord. The verse's poetic structure ties them together and gives her words added rhetorical power. The parallelism between the first line and the third is firmly estab-

41. Hamilton, cited by Lewis, "The Textual History of the Song of Hannah," p. 25, n. 30.

42. McCarter takes the second Yahweh as "poetically inferior" and reads "my God" *('ĕlōhāy),* following the versions (McCarter, p. 68; Lewis, "The Textual History of the Song of Hannah," p. 26), though MT and 4QSam[a] have *yhwh,* which Lewis thinks is assimilatory. However, v. 10a also repeats YHWH twice.

43. See B. O. Long, "Framing Repetions in Biblical Historiography," *JBL* 106 (1987) 385-99.

44. R. P. Gordon, p. 79.

45. See Lewis, "The Textual History of the Song of Hannah," p. 23, n. 20. See also Isa. 57:4 "open your mouth wide."

lished by their grammatical structure. Note the word pair, *the Lord — our God* (also 2 Sam. 22:32; Ps. 18:31).[46] The other pair, "holy one" *qādôš*// "rock" *ṣûr* occurs only here in OT, but it may be a formulaic pair.[47]

The formula "there is no . . . like . . ." denotes *incomparability,* which "presupposes uniqueness and implies the exclusion of rivals";[48] see 1 Sam. 10:24; 21:9 for the expression of "comparative negation" in ordinary life. As Labuschagne notes, it is "Yahweh's *holiness,* revealed through His intervention in human history as the redeeming God, that is given special prominence with regard to His incomparability."[49] See also on 1 Sam. 6:20.

There is none but you: or "there is no (holy) one but you." In the latter translation, *qādôš* is understood as elided for the parallelistic style. As Warren proposes, the MT "must be original," for the *trisagion* (i.e., "liturgically significant triple use of the divine attribute 'holy' ") is not yet recognizable in the MT as it is in the Vorlage of LXX and, possibly, in the Qumran version 4QSam^a.[50] The text expresses the idea that there is only one God (i.e., "monotheism"; see Deut. 4:35; 32:39; 2 Sam. 22:32), for the "holy one" here is synonymous with "God" as in Hab. 1:12; 3:3. Thus, 1 Sam. 2:2, as in Deut. 4:34-35; 2 Sam. 7:22; etc., juxtaposes "incomparability and uniqueness."[51] The idea that Yahweh was incomparable appears also in Exod. 15:11 as well as in the Song of Moses (Deuteronomy 32), so it comes probably from the earliest period of Mosaic Yahwism, if these Songs are that early.[52] R. P. Gordon thinks that there are "intimations of pure monotheism here (cf. Isa. 45:21f)."

Hannah says that no other rock compares to Yahweh. The term *rock* (also 2 Sam. 22:2; 23:3) is a common epithet of God in the OT (e.g., Deut. 32:4, 15, etc., in a section which has various parallels with our text), and it implies God's protection and strength. R. P. Gordon notes that Isa. 8:14; 28:16; and Ps. 118:22 give the figure "a messianic significance which is re-

46. See also Lewis, "The Textual History of the Song of Hannah," p. 28.

47. Cf. "God" *'ĕlôah*//"the holy One" *qādôš* (Hab. 3:3), "my God" + "my holy One" *'ĕlōhay q^{e}dōšî* (1:12). and "YHWH"//"rock" *ṣûr* (Deut. 32:30; 2 Sam. 22:47; Isa. 26:4; Hab. 1:12; Ps. 18:2, 46; 19:14; 28:1; 92:16; 95:1; 144:1). On the etymology of holy one *(qādôš),* see *HALOT,* pp. 1072-78. Note that in Ugaritic the "sons of Holiness" means "deities," since the goddess Athirat is called "Holiness" (Qudshu).

48. Labuschagne, *The Incomparability of Yahweh,* p. 10.

49. Labuschagne, *The Incomparability of Yahweh,* p. 99.

50. A. L. Warren, "A Trisagion Inserted in the 4QSam^a Version of the Song of Hannah, 1 Sam. 2:1-10," *JJS* 45 (1994) 283-84.

51. Labuschagne, *The Incomparability of Yahweh,* p. 115. Labuschagne deals also with Deut. 32:31, 39; Ps. 18:31; 86:8-10; 1 K. 8:23; Jer. 10:10; Isa. 40:12-26; 44:7-8; 46:5-9.

52. Labuschagne, *The Incomparability of Yahweh,* p. 146. See also on 2 Sam. 22:32.

flected in the New Testament (e.g. 1 Pet 2:6–8)."[53] With *our God,* with the plural pronoun, Hannah speaks here as a member of the covenant community of Yahweh.

3 After addressing Yahweh her covenant God in vv. 1b-2, she now speaks to the other members (*your* [2 m.pl.]) of the community and admonishes them how to behave before the all-knowing and holy sovereign God.

As for *very haughtily* (lit., "haughty (and) haughty"), the nominal "plurality," usually formulated by the addition of plural endings (see below on *dēʿôt*), is sometimes expressed by the repetition of the same word: for example, "very unclean" (*ṭāmēʾ ṭāmēʾ;* Lev. 13:45), "truly living" (*ḥay ḥay;* Isa. 38:19), etc.[54]

The plurality of the abstract noun *knowledge* here denotes its degree, not its number.[55] The phrase may mean "an all-knowing God" (so NAB; JPS). But, the connotation here seems to be more on the quality of his knowledge than on the quantity (hence, *true knowledge,* i.e., "God who knows truly well about everything by experience as the owner and creator of the world"; see 1 Sam. 2:8b).

Deeds may refer either to God's deeds (as in Ps. 66:5) or to human deeds that are evaluated by God. However, the latter interpretation is based on the Qere, which reads "to him" instead of the negative particle "not" (so BDB: "by him are actions estimated," followed by NRSV; JPS; NASB; NIV). Since *deeds* is in parallel with God's knowledge in this poetic text, it is more reasonable to take it as referring to Yahweh's "awesome or terrible deeds" rather than "deeds" of men. In fact, the term is never used for human deeds in the Bible.

Lewis holds that the Ketib reading should be translated as "(violent) actions are not weighed/measured" and says while that might make sense in a discussion of theodicy, it does not make sense in a song of praise.[56] However, the question here is the sense of the term *deeds.* The term denotes not so much violence of divine actions as awesomeness of divine deeds. Since the extremeness of God's knowledge and actions is expressed in a parallelistic structure — the

53. See Korpel, "Rock," in *DDD,* pp. 1338-40.

54. Also "very bad" (*raʿ raʿ;* Prov. 20:14); "very deep" (*ʿāmōq ʿāmōq;* Eccl. 7:24); cf. *rāšāʿ rāšāʿ* (Ezek. 33:8; cf. 3:18); *qādôš qādôš qādôš* (Isa. 6:3); cf. GKC, §133k. Cf. "so proudly" (W-O, §12.5; but as a <repetitive apposition>); as a poetic "repetition" (J. T. Willis, "The Song of Hannah and Psalm 113," *CBQ* 35 [1973] 145-46); "a dittography or a conflated text" (Lewis, "The Textual History of the Song of Hannah," p. 29).

55. See J-M, §136g; W-O, §7.4.2.a ("abstract nouns specifying qualities"). Cf. *ʾl hdʿwt* "God of knowledge" in Qumran; see L. H. Schiffman, "4QMysteries[a]: A Preliminary Edition and Translation," in *Solving Riddles and Untying Knots,* p. 238; also Lewis, "The Textual History of the Song of Hannah," p. 24.

56. Lewis, "The Textual History of the Song of Hannah," p. 31, n. 44.

former by the plural form and the latter by the negation of the verbal form, following the <A not B> pattern[57] in its deep structure — the Ketib (*immeasurable,* lit., "not measured")[58] does make sense in the immediately preceding context where human arrogance in speech (not in action) is warned against: *For* the Lord's knowledge and deeds are beyond human comprehension.

(2) "Reversal of Human Fortunes" (vv. 4-5)

4 Hannah now recalls the results of Yahweh's *deeds.* She contrasts the fates of the *mighty* and the *feeble,* that is, the reversal of their fortunes.

The *mighty, their bows are broken* (lit., "The mighty are broken with respect to their bow") has the m.pl. adj. from *ḥtt (also in v. 10), whose subject is most naturally *mighty men* (m.pl.) rather than *bow* (f.s.). The verse constitutes a bicolon, in which "the mighty" corresponds with "the feeble," and "bow" with "strength." In this structure, two TOPICs "the mighty" and "the feeble" are given COMMENTs, that is, "be broken of bow" and "be girded with strength."[59] The poetic structure is thus chiastic: a-b-c//b′-c′-a′.[60] Here as in vv. 5, 8a, one of the Lord's immeasurable deeds is the reversal of life situations. He is the one who acts according to his sovereign will, often beyond human understanding and common sense.

5 In a series of perfect verbs Hannah expresses her *confidence* in Yahweh's knowledge and deeds (v. 3b). "A barren woman" is the most direct reference in Hannah's song to her experience.

The "seven sons" motif is popular in the ancient Near East (Jer. 15:9; Ruth 4:15),[61] and the number seven is used here as a poetic idiom for perfection. So, even *a barren woman* like Hannah would be able to have the ideal number of children. In fact, Hannah had only six children.[62] See on 1 Sam. 1:8 ("ten sons") and on 16:10-11 ("eight" sons; cf. "seven" sons in 1 Chr. 2:13-15).

57. For "negated antonyms," see on 1 Sam. 1:11; 3:2; 2 Sam. 1:21; 22:39; etc.

58. On various suggestions for the meaning of the verb *tkn, see *HALOT,* pp. 1733-34.

59. See D. T. Tsumura, "'The Mighty Are Broken of the Bow' (I Sam 2:4)," *Exegetica* 8 (1997) 83-87 [Japanese with an English summary].

60. For a bow and a mighty man, see Aqhat story in Ugaritic; see C. H. Gordon, *The Common Background of Greek and Hebrew Civilizations* (New York: W. W. Norton, 1965), pp. 159-60.

61. See D. T. Tsumura, *The Ugaritic Drama of the Good Gods: A Philological Study* (Ann Arbor: University Microfilms, 1973); Klein, p. 17; also Gordon, *The Common Background,* p. 145.

62. W. W. Hallo, *Origins: The Ancient Near Eastern Background of Some Modern Western Institutions* (SHCANE 6; Leiden: E. J. Brill, 1996), p. 169.

The verb *'umlālāh* means usually "become a widow," but here "become childless," but not "become barren, infertile," for the contrastive parallelism requires the idea of losing all her sons, like the king losing all his sons, "seven"//"eight," in the Keret epic.[63] Note the word pair "loss of children" and "widowhood," which is common to Hebrew and Ugaritic; see Isa. 47:8-9 as well as *ṯkl* and *ulmn* in *KTU* 1.23:8-9.[64]

Thus, in these two verses, the motif of the "reversal of human fortunes" can be clearly seen; it also appears in v. 8a. In v. 4, Hannah contrasts the fate of the *mighty* and that of the *feeble,* while in v. 5 she contrasts those who have enough food and many children with those who have no food and no child. Though the agent of this reversal is not explicitly mentioned, it is clear that it is the holy and sovereign God, who holds everyone's fate in his mighty hand and can certainly reverse human fortune according to his own will. The next five verses (vv. 6-10a) extol the character of Yahweh as displayed in his actions.

(3) "Yahweh's Holy Sovereignty" (vv. 6-7)

6 The phrase *brings death and makes alive* is a merismus which claims that Yahweh holds total authority over life and death and the entire course of a human's life (cf. "It is I who bring death and make alive" [Deut. 32:39b]). The term *Sheol* refers to "the grave" (NIV) or "the realm of the dead, both as a place of judgment and a final residence" (McCarter), or "the resting-place of the shades."[65] In the Bible, the term usually appears in idiomatic phrases such as "going down to Sheol" or "coming up from Sheol." Hence, the term "Sheol" had already become fossilized as a place-name and was used in a metaphorical sense.[66]

The Lord *brings down to Sheol* (i.e., he dispatches the dead to their proper place) and *brings up* one's soul from Sheol (e.g., Ps. 30:4 [3] "O LORD, you brought up my soul from Sheol, restored me to life from among those gone down to the Pit" [NRSV]). In the ancient Near East the sun god(dess) is considered to be the *psychopompe, the guide of the dead,* in the

63. See D. T. Tsumura, "The Problem of Childlessness in the Royal Epic of Ugarit," in *Monarchies and Socio-Religious Traditions in the Ancient Near East* (Wiesbaden: Otto Harrassowitz, 1984), pp. 11-20.

64. See Tsumura, *The Ugaritic Drama of the Good Gods,* pp. 31-33; D. T. Tsumura, "A Ugaritic God, Mt-w-šr, and His Two Weapons (UT 52:8-11)," *UF* 6 (1974) 407-13.

65. On "Sheol," see *NIDOTTE,* 4, pp. 6-7; H. M. Barstad, "Sheol," in *DDD,* pp. 1452-57.

66. For the semantics of Hebrew idioms, see A. Gibson, *Biblical Semantic Logic: A Preliminary Analysis* (Oxford: Blackwell, 1981).

death cult; see "Excursus" (1 Samuel 28). For example, in the Ugaritic funerary cult (*KTU* 1.161), the newly dead king Niqmaddu[67] was sent to the netherworld with the assistance of the sun goddess Shapshu. However, Yahweh the creator of heaven and earth, that is, the creator of the sun (see Psalm 19), is the Lord of "the quick and the dead" who brings men down to or up from Sheol. He holds absolute authority over the world of the dead as well as of the living. Yahweh is the one who holds the key to Job's question: "If a man dies, will he live again?" (Job 14:14). While Gilgamesh finally gave up any hope of immortality for himself, Job remains confident: "I know that my Redeemer lives, and that in the end he will stand upon the earth" (Job 19:25 [NIV]). Hannah affirms that same confidence in her sovereign Lord.

7 Here two merismatic pairs explain that Yahweh is the one who controls the material and social life of humans. This means both that he makes some poor and some rich (v. 7a) and that he makes one sometimes rich and sometimes poor (see v. 8a). He demotes the socially prominent to insignificance and promotes the socially insignificant to high prominence (v. 7b).

(4) "Reversal of Human Fortunes" (v. 8a)

Verse 8a constitutes a quadricolon rather than two bicola. The first two lines constitute a chiasmus: a-b-c//b′-a′-c′; with two sets of synonymous word pairs: "poor" — "needy" and "dust" — "dunghill." The third line is grammatically governed by the verbs "raises" and "lift"; the infinitive functions as a result clause: *so that. . . .* The fourth line corresponds well to the third semantically if not formally grammatically: a — B//C — a′, <inf.cstr.>//<impf.>. Thus, the quadricolon as a whole expresses the following idea: it is the Lord who reverses human fortunes, by raising *the poor* from his lowly position to an honorable one.

(5) "Yahweh's Holy Sovereignty" (vv. 8b-10a)

8b *For* is a speaker-oriented particle (see "Introduction" [Section V, C]) that expresses the reason why I have said that Yahweh *raises the poor . . . needy* from the dust/dunghill — the Lord is sovereign, for he is the "owner" and "creator" of the world. Since the Lord founded the world, "he has the right to intervene in the social order."[68]

The exact meaning of the term *pillars* (so NASB; NRSV; JPS;

67. I.e., Niqmaddu III (ca. 1225/1220-1215); see I. Singer, "A Political History of Ugarit," in *Handbook of Ugaritic Studies,* ed. W. G. E. Watson and N. Wyatt (HbO; Leiden: E. J. Brill, 1999), pp. 691-704.

68. R. P. Gordon, p. 80.

m^{e}ṣûqîm) is unknown; cf. "foundations" (NIV; NEB; REB). *HALOT* translates it as "arrows" on the bases of the Peshitta and Vulgate, while it suggests to delete the term from 1 Sam. 14:5 as dittography.[69] For an expression similar to *the pillars of the earth (m^{e}ṣūqê 'ereṣ),* see *'ammûdîm* ("pillars") of the earth in Job 9:6, Ps. 75:3; also on 2 Sam. 22:16 (*mōs^{e}dôt tēbēl* "the foundations of the world"). The phrase always appears in poetic texts, used idiomatically. However, the reference to the foundation or support ("pillars") of the earth is meaningful here, for the Lord is the one who upholds the place where we live as well as the moral order of this world; he protects his faithful while he destroys the wicked (v. 9); see Ps. 10:3.

9 Yahweh, who stabilized the earth on its *pillars,* also gives *his faithful* protective stability. *Darkness* here refers to "the nether gloom which engulfs the wicked at death and which may be experienced already in this life (Ps. 35:6)."[70] Nobody can prevail *by his own ability.* Only when God *guards* their feet can the faithful ones stand and *prevail* against the power of *darkness.*

10a The scansion of vv. 9-10 has been somewhat unsettled among modern translations. For example, NIV joins the third line of v. 9 with the first of v. 10 and takes the second and third lines of v. 10 as a bicolon, rendering vv. 9c-10 as three bicola. On the other hand, NRSV joins the third line with the following two lines, thus taking v. 10 as <bicolon> — <tricolon>, while JPS takes v. 10 as <bicolon> — <monocolon> — <bicolon>. Since the monocolon appears often at a significant position such as at the beginning (e.g., Ps. 23:1; 139:1b) or at the end or at a poem's climax,[71] the JPS scansion seems preferable.

The phrase *his antagonists* refers to those who attack Yahweh with reproaches.[72] The root *ryb often has a legal connotation, meaning "to contest a lawsuit," but here it is used in a non-legal situation. So, Yahweh's enemies (see on v. 1b) *are shattered* (i.e., completely destroyed by him), for he is not simply a God of the covenant people Israel, but the creator and upholder of the entire world (see v. 8b). He intervenes from heaven against the evil doings of his enemies; see also 1 Sam. 7:10 ("thundered . . . against the Philistines"). Here the metaphor of thunder expresses Yahweh's destructive power, as it often appears in the context of battle. There is no allusion to or dependence on Baal myths. Storm terminology is often used in the OT to describe battles, and battle terminology is used for describing storms.[73]

69. *HALOT,* p. 623. See on 1 Sam 14:5.

70. R. P. Gordon, p. 80.

71. Watson, pp. 168-72.

72. See *HALOT,* p. 1225.

73. See now D. T. Tsumura, *Creation and Destruction: A Reappraisal of the* Chaoskampf *Theory in the Old Testament* (Winona Lake, Ind.: Eisenbrauns, 2005), pp. 184-87. See on 1 Sam. 7:10; also M. Weinfeld, "Divine Intervention in War in Ancient Is-

The term *šāmayim* can mean either "heaven" (i.e., God's dwelling) or "sky." The latter would lead us to take the whole expression "to thunder from the sky" as a metaphor, while in the former translation "heaven" refers to the heavenly domain where God resides.[74] The source of this thunder would be higher than the "sky" (i.e., the clouds). The context seems to support "heaven" rather than "sky."

The Lord judges the ends of the earth is a monocolon. According to MT punctuation, v. 10 is divided here into two sections. It is not unreasonable to end the major body of the poem by a monocolon[75] and with a double usage of the divine name Yahweh, corresponding as an *inclusio* to v. 1. Yahweh *judges* (*dyn) the whole world. This is a claim that assumes the kingship of Yahweh (see on 8:5). The expression *the ends of the earth ('apsê-'āreṣ),*[76] which refers to the entire world, appears almost always in the context which describes Yahweh's uniqueness, majesty, and dominion (e.g., Isa. 45:22; 52:10; Mic. 5:4; Zech. 9:10; Ps. 2:8; 22:27; 67:7; 72:8; 98:3; Prov. 30:4). On the kingship of the Lord and his role as judge, see Ps. 96:10 (*dyn). See "Introduction" (Section IX, A).

(6) "Theme of Kingship" (v. 10b)

It has been often suggested that v. 10b is a secondary and pro-monarchic addition. Yet it surely has correlations with the song and fits the context too well to take it as a simple addition. It is noteworthy that v. 1b and v. 10b constitute an *inclusio* or "envelope construction" with the use of the theme verb *rwm* (vv. 1b, 7b, 8a, 10b) and the term "horn."

---

rael and in the Ancient Near East," in *History, Historiography and Interpretation: Studies in Biblical and Cuneiform Literatures,* ed. H. Tadmor and M. Weinfeld (Jerusalem: Magnes, 1983), pp. 141-42, and M. Klingbeil, *Yahweh Fighting from Heaven: God as Warrior and as God of Heaven in the Hebrew Psalter and Ancient Near Eastern Iconography* (Göttingen: Vandenhoeck, 1999).

74. For the metaphorical uses of "heaven," especially of "from the heaven," see D. T. Tsumura, "*šmym — Heaven, Sky, Firmament, Air," in NIDOTTE,* 4, pp. 160-66.

75. On the *closing monocolon,* see Watson, p. 170.

76. Taking *the heaven* and *the ends of the earth* as "an antithetical pair," Lewis holds that the second and third lines of v. 10 form "a couplet" ("The Textual History of the Song of Hannah," p. 41) and restores a line ("Who is holy like Yahweh?") to be coupled with the first line, based on the LXX^B text and $4QSam^a$. However, while "heaven" — "earth" makes a good word pair, *heaven* and *the ends of the earth* are *not* paired even in Prov. 30:4. Also, the phrase "from the heaven" would rather correspond to the first line; the bicolon of the first two lines refers to Yahweh's destructive acts toward his enemies. The third line, which constitutes a monocolon, being sandwiched with two bicola, describes Yahweh's universal rule as judge. Cf. the role of King Keret as a just judge in the Ugaritic epic; see *CS,* I, p. 342.

However, it could be a comment by the narrator rather than a part of Hannah's prayer since it is outside of the *inclusio* formed by the repetition of YHWH in v. 1b and v. 10a. Moreover, the monocolon in the third line (v. 10a) possibly *closes* the actual "prayer" of Hannah. None of these formal structural arguments is decisive. Besides, the two imperfect verbs with a modal sense could have been used even by the author of this song, without a specific king in mind.

The text must be very early, even pre-Davidic, if Hannah, by the spirit of God (like David in 2 Sam. 23:2), prophesied about the future before the actual institution of kingship was introduced to Israel. Note that Hannah does not mention any proper name such as David (cf. 2 Sam. 22:51 "king// anointed, David and his seed") and that the institution of kingship had been well known to Hannah and her contemporaries through Canaanite examples, as well as the Israelite institution of "theocracy." Expectations for a monarchy had arisen even before Hannah — as in the cases of Gideon (Judg. 8:22) and Abimelech (9:6) — though they never materialized; see on 1 Samuel 8.

It is Yahweh, who *judges* the entire world, who can grant power to *his king* to let him judge or rule as his human representative or vice-regent. The term *ʿōz* refers to the divine power; compare "strength" (v. 4) and "ability" (v. 9). On the "power" *(ʿōz)* that is given to a king *(melek)* from God, see Ps. 21:1 ("In your power the king rejoices, O Lord"). The metaphor of a kingly *horn* in v. 10b may have arisen from the depiction of the king as a wild bull.[77]

The phrase *his anointed (mᵉšîḥô)* appears for the first time. This makes Hannah's Song more meaningful and indispensable in the history of salvation. The pronominal suffix, "his" or "my," always refers to the Lord. In the OT, "anointed ones" may be priests, kings, and prophets, though references to royal cases are numerous as in 1-2 Samuel.[78] Though the anointing of kings is known from the ancient Near East, the title *māšîaḥ* as a royal appellation is attested only in the Bible.[79] See also on 1 Sam. 9:16.

In sum, the Song concludes with a two-fold plea for Yahweh — the incomparably holy one, the rock (v. 2), the truly knowledgeable one (v. 3), the lord of life and death (v. 6), the maker of rich and poor (v. 7), the greater

77. W. F. Albright, *Yahweh and the Gods of Canaan* (Garden City, N.Y.: Doubleday, 1969), p. 18.

78. For a recent study of Messiah, see P. E. Satterthwaite, R. S. Hess, and G. J. Wenham, *The Lord's Anointed: Interpretation of Old Testament Messianic Texts* (Carlisle: Paternoster, 1995); M. de Jonge, "Christ," in *DDD,* pp. 368-84, esp. pp. 370-71; A. Laato, *A Star Is Rising: The Historical Development of the Old Testament Royal Ideology and the Rise of the Jewish Messianic Expectations* (Atlanta: Scholars Press, 1997).

79. See S. Talmon, "The Biblical Idea of Statehood," in *The Bible World: Essays in Honor of Cyrus H. Gordon,* ed. G. Rendsburg et al. (New York: KTAV, 1980), p. 246.

demoter and promoter (v. 8) — to raise the king of Israel to a position of power and prominence worthy of the Great God who appointed him.

d. Return of Elkanah (2:11)

11 *And Elkanah went back to*[80] *Ramah, to his house. As for the boy, he was ministering to the Lord before Eli, the priest.*

11 With the resumption of past narration and the reintroduction of *Elkanah,* this sub-paragraph resumes the story line where the narrator left it at the beginning of this chapter (1 Sam. 2:1: *And Hannah prayed:*) and serves as a transition toward a new episode. The use of a *movement* verb ("to go") signals a transition. The narrator's viewpoint is still in Shiloh (Elkanah hence *went back,* not "came back"), and so he prepares the audience for hearing about the situation in Shiloh after Elkanah left. (See "Introduction" on the use of "come" and "go" in the narrative transition.)

It is often asserted that the Song of Hannah was not included in the early stage of the tradition history of the present narrative.[81] However, the Song is integrated into the present narrative with no trace of artificial or mechanical "later insertion" into its context. As is often the case, both narrative and poem were put together in the narrative story of Hannah as a cohesive discourse unit. Also see on 1:28.

The phrase *As for the boy* recalls *the boy* of 1 Sam. 1:24 and reintroduces him after the narrative interruption through the insertion of Hannah's Song. After describing Elkanah's departure for Ramah the narrator does not concern himself with the arrival at Ramah, but the focus is now on *the boy,* who was still "young" (see 1 Sam. 1:24).

Samuel was serving the Lord, not Eli, though he did it *before Eli.* The phrase *before Eli* points to Samuel's apprenticeship under Eli's guidance. The narrator emphasizes the relationship between Samuel and Yahweh, though inconspicuously. This contrasts with the ignorance of Eli's sons about the Lord and his commandments in v. 12. The audience already knows that Eli is the priest; nevertheless, the title *priest* is added to Eli since it is important to remind them that he was the official and chief priest to the Lord at that time.

In the following episodes Samuel and Eli's sons are contrasted

80. On the directive *ʿal,* see 2 K. 23:29 "(Pharaoh Neco . . . went up) to(ward) the king of Assyria to(ward) the river Euphrates" *(ʿal-melek ʾaššûr ʿal-nᵉhar-pᵉrāt),* no longer "against . . . to . . ." (so KJV; JPS) in the light of the Babylonian Chronicles (see A. R. Millard, in *CS,* I, p. 467).

81. For example, J. Cook, "Hannah and/or Elkanah on Their Way Home (1 Samuel 2:11)? A Witness to the Complexity of the Tradition History of the Samuel Texts," *OTE* 3 (1990) 253.

sharply. Through the development of the story, however, Samuel's growth and preparation for his future task are the main themes under the surface. The narrative structure serves to highlight that contrast:

11	Samuel	"the boy" *(hannaʿar)*
12-17	Eli's sons	"the young men" *(hann^{e}ʿārîm)*
18-21	Samuel and his parents	"Samuel . . . the boy Samuel"
22-25	Eli and his sons	
26	Samuel	"the boy Samuel"

With Elkanah (and presumably Hannah) home in Ramah and Samuel now serving at Shiloh, we are ready to watch this contrast unfold.

2. Eli's Two Sons (2:12-17)[82]

12 *Now the sons of Eli were*
sons of Beliyaal;[83]
they did not know the Lord,
13 *or even*[84] *the rights of the priests in dealing with the people.*
When anyone was offering a sacrifice,[85]
the young priest would come,[86]

82. For a poetic analysis of vv. 12-17, see D. T. Tsumura, "Poetic Nature of the Hebrew Narrative Prose in I Samuel 2:12-17," in *Verse in Ancient Near Eastern Prose,* ed. J. C. de Moor and W. G. E. Watson (AOAT 42; Neukirchen-Vluyn: Neukirchener, 1993), pp. 293-304; also see "Introduction" (Section VII, B).

83. The initial expression *(ûbnê ʿēlî b^{e}nê b^{e}lîyāʿal)* constitutes either a monocolon with four feet (4) or a bicolon with two feet each (2//2). Note the alliteration of "b" and "ʿ" sounds and the parallelism of the two halves.

84. V. 12b seems to continue into v. 13. S. R. Driver holds that the omission of the particle *ʾt* between *waw* and *mšpṭ* (cf. *ʾt YHWH*) is acceptable for there are exceptions to the rule that "when the first of two or more nouns has *ʾt,* all must have it" (Driver, p. 29). McCarter thinks this omission is the result of the "intrusion of *yhwh* into a text which originally read *lʾ ydʿw ʾt mšpṭ hkhn,* etc." (McCarter, p. 78). However, if we understand the poetic nature of this narrative, the existence of an initial *w* without *ʾt* in v. 13a is no hindrance to understanding the grammatical dependency between *ydʿw* and *mšpṭ.*

85. The phrase *w^{e}hāyāh,* which normally introduces a temporal (non-past) setting in narrative prose, does not appear either here or in v. 15a. This could be a sign of the poetic nature of this narrative, not an example of *casus pendens,* though Niccacci takes it as such; see A. Niccacci, *The Syntax of the Verb in Classical Hebrew Prose* (JSOTSS 86; Sheffield: Sheffield Academic Press, 1990), p. 145.

86. After a temporal clause with a participle ("When . . . offering . . ."), one expects some habitual tense ("would come") even though the verb is a perfect with *waw.* On "narrative frequentatives" for *weqatal,* see R. E. Longacre, "Weqatal Forms in Biblical

while the meat was boiling,
with a three-pronged fork[87] *in his hand,*
14 *and he would plunge it into the pan or kettle,*
or caldron[88] *or pot;*
all that the fork brought up
the priest took away with it.[89]
Such was done to all Israel,
to those who came there at Shiloh.[90]
15 *Also, before the fat was burned*[91] *—*
The young priest would come[92]
and say to the man who was sacrificing:
"Give meat for roasting to the priest;
he will not accept from you boiled meat,
but only raw."
16 *Then the man would say*[93] *to him:*

Hebrew Prose," in *Biblical Hebrew and Discourse Linguistics,* ed. R. D. Bergen (Dallas: Summer Institute of Linguistics, 1994), pp. 56-66, though he wrongly takes this verbal form as a participle.

87. The entire noun phrase is probably adverbial ("with a . . . fork . . ."). For the grammar of (lit.) "the fork which is three (cstr.) of the teeth," see J-M, §91e ("the dual is used for the plural"); §131b. See also W-O, §6.4.1e, §12.3b.

88. The term *caldron (qallaḥat)* also appears in Mic. 3:3. The Ugar. term *qlḫt* suggests that it was an old loanword from Egyptian *ḳrḥ.t* "vessel." See E. Lipinski, "The Inscribed Marble Vessels from Kition," in *Solving Riddles and Untying Knots,* p. 435; Y. Muchiki, *Egyptian Proper Names and Loanwords in North-West Semitic* (SBLDS 173; Atlanta: Scholars Press, 1999), pp. 254, 282f.

89. *bw* "it" is often emended to *lw* ("for himself"; e.g., McCarter, p. 79), following ancient versions. But, this is without any support from Hebrew MSS and is unnecessary. The "it" refers to the "fork."

90. The phrase "at Shiloh" has been understood as modifying either *yʿśw* "they did" (so NRSV; NASB; JPS) or *hbʾym* "those who came" (so REB; NIV). McCarter thinks that *šm* seems unlikely before "in Shiloh" (McCarter, p. 79). This is true if the text is taken as straight prose, but it is acceptable in a poetic narrative. In this bicolon, the prepositional phrase *bšlh* is related *vertically* to the verb *yʿśw,* not *horizontally* to the preceding term *šm* "there." See "Introduction" (Section VII, B).

91. Lit., "they burn"; impersonal passive.

92. The *waw* + perfect is certainly sequential with the habitual tense. Cf. "came and said" (Niccacci, *The Syntax of the Verb,* p. 131).

93. The *waw* + imperfect here is hard to explain by the usual grammatical rules of Hebrew narrative prose; hence, it is often emended to *wʾmr* "And (the man) would say" (McCarter, p. 79). The text's various poetic features, however, remove the need to read it as strict prose grammar. A. Niccacci, "Analysing Biblical Hebrew Poetry," *JSOT* 74 (1997) 92, n. 61: "The puzzling ויאמר in 2.16 . . . can be explained as continuation (non-narrative) Wayyiqtol"; cf. Niccacci, *The Syntax of the Verb* (1990) §146.2.

"Let the fat be burned up first,
and then take for yourself according to the desire of your appetite!"
But he would say[94] *to him:*
"Now! You must give it to me!
If you don't, I will take[95] *it by force!"*
17 *The sin of the young men was*
very great
before the Lord;
for the men treated with contempt
the offering to the Lord.

12-21 Here follow what Longacre calls three "how-it-was-done procedural discourses"[96] (vv. 13-14, 15-16, 19-20) dominated by *waw* + perfects. In v. 21, with the *wayqtl* form *(she conceived),* a shift occurs from the embedded "procedural" discourse to the larger narrative framework. See also Gen. 29:2-3; 2 K. 25:29-30; etc. Verses 12-17[97] contrast the conduct of Eli's sons with that of Samuel. Directly after the verse about Samuel's service in 1 Sam. 2:11b comes the harsh criticism of Eli's sons. This juxtaposes "the person who serves the Lord and those who do not."[98] This contrast appears again in vv. 17, 18, 21b, and 22. The use of the word *naʿar* for both groups further highlights this contrast.

Structurally, vv. 12-17 comprise an embedded discourse within the broader context of chs. 2–3. After the introductory remarks about Eli's sons (vv. 12-13a), the story itself is divided into two parts, each with a short temporal clause (i.e., "monocolon") in vv. 13b and 15a as the SETTING for the following EVENTS, vv. 13c-14 and 15b-16. Then, v. 17 concludes the section.

12 Eli's sons *did not know* the Lord, that is, did not regard or pay due respect to the Lord; their "knowledge" of God remained only a superfi-

94. The verb *w'mr* carries on the habitual tense in v. 15.

95. The perfect without a "conversive" *waw* is another example of the use of "perfect" for a future action as in Ugaritic; see also on 1 Sam. 14:10; 2 Sam. 5:24; T. L. Fenton, "The Hebrew 'Tenses' in the Light of Ugaritic," in *Proceedings of the Fifth World Congress of Jewish Studies, held in 1969,* vol. 4 (Jerusalem: World Union of Jewish Studies, 1973), p. 37.

96. Longacre, "Weqatal Forms in Biblical Hebrew Prose," pp. 60-64.

97. Compare this section with "Hittite Instructions to Priests and Temple Officials" (*CS,* I, p. 218, §5); also Mal. 1:6-13.

98. M. Garsiel, *The First Book of Samuel: A Literary Study of Comparative Structures, Analogies and Parallels* (Jerusalem: Rubin Mass, 1990 [orig 1983, 1985]), p. 38. See also R. P. Gordon, *1 & 2 Samuel* (OTG; Sheffield: JSOT Press, 1984), pp. 24-25.

cial formality. Not only did they, being *sons of Beliyaal,* that is, "utterly destructive men" (see Excursus on 1:16), lack an intimate relationship with Yahweh whom they served, but they did not even recognize (hence, obey) the divine instruction, the law (see below; Deut. 18:3). The phrase *sons of Beliyaal* harks back to the words, *Daughter of Beliyaal,* of Hannah to Eli in 1 Sam. 1:16 and emphasizes the contrast between their sons.

The divine name (YHWH) appears again in v. 17, thus making an *inclusio* for the entire section as it did in vv. 1b, 10a; see also Psalm 23, where YHWH appears both in the beginning and at the end of the psalm.

13-14 The wording of v. 13 closely parallels Deut. 18:3, which distinguishes "the priests' right from that of the people, from those offering a sacrifice."[99] The term *mišpāṭ, the rights,* is also translated as "duties" (NRSV), "custom" (NASB), "practice" (NIV), "how the priests used to deal with the people" (JPS), or "due portion" (McCarter). However, Deut. 18:3 and our verse seem to refer to regulations about the allotment of offerings to priests.[100] The priests were to be provided for from the sacrifices (see Lev. 2:3, 10; 7:31-36; Num. 18:8; 1 Cor. 9:13f.; 1 Tim. 5:17f.), but the practice outlined in vv. 13-14 has little in common with the regulations on priestly rights in, for example, Lev. 7:31-36,[101] although the narrator probably knew about the levitical regulations. Samuel's sons, who perverted "justice" (the same word) in 1 Sam. 8:3, have despicable peers in Eli's sons.

Opinion is divided as to whether vv. 13-14 represent part of the abuse of Eli's sons or give background information on the accepted (but degenerate) practices of the time, which the sons further perverted. Certainly, "the priests' subsistence at Shiloh depended more on 'pot luck,' perhaps in the belief that the hand of God decided the trident's catch."[102] It was because *they did not know the Lord* that they disregarded his law without any guilty feeling. Such a cultic "procedure" could have emerged out of the common Canaanite cultic traditions, while the people, including the priests, had forgotten the existence of the law completely as later in the time of Josiah and his predecessors (see 2 K. 22:8-13). NEB and REB clearly take vv. 13-14 as normal and vv. 15-16 as abnormal. However, the occurrence of "also" *(gam)*

99. Note that the MT spelling in 1 Sam. 2:13 exhibits a shorter phonetic representation as a result of *sandhi.* See D. T. Tsumura, "Vowel sandhi in Biblical Hebrew," *ZAW* 109 (1997) 575-88.

100. See "Punic Sacrificial Tariff" in *CS,* I, pp. 305-9. The term for "tariff," *bʿt,* is from the root *bʿh and is related to "demand, requirement" in Arabic and Aramaic (also Akk. *buʾʾu* "to seek"); see *CS,* I, p. 305, n. 2.

101. According to a Nabataean religious law about the allotment of offerings, priests seem to have received the half amount; see *CS,* II, p. 166. For Akkadian regulations on the grant to the priest, see *CS,* II, p. 367 and n. 40.

102. R. P. Gordon, p. 82.

at the beginning of v. 15 rather suggests that both practices were abnormal, and RSV and NRSV as well as NASB take it as such.

Since the agent of the various evil actions in the preceding verses is *the young priest* (*naʿar hakkōhēn,* literally, "the young one of the priest"; see below) and his actions are explained by singular verbs *(would come, would plunge, took away),* it may well be that the plural verb *yaʿăśû* (3 m.) is being used impersonally (*Such was done to all Israel;* cf. "This was the practice at Shiloh with all the Israelites who came there" [JPS]; "This should have been their practice whenever Israelites came to sacrifice at Shiloh" [REB]).

15 The *fat* was supposed to be burned first as "an aroma pleasing to the Lord" (Lev. 3:5). So, here the phrase *before the fat was burned* is concerned with the timing of the priest's conduct. *Give meat . . . to the priest* marks the first speech of the priest. The speaker uses the third person, "to the priest" and "he will not take," rather than the first person, "to me" and "I will not take." As discussed below, if the speaker is "the young priest" himself and not a "servant" of the priest, this might be a reserved or modest speech, at least in tone. Or, is this young [junior] priest acting, at least on the surface, for Eli the "old [senior] priest" or for the priest's family? On *boiled meat,* see Num. 6:19.

16 We have the extraordinary situation where the priest, who was supposed to know the rules of sacrifice, was engaging in behavior that shocked even the ordinary worshipper. The *fat* was normally removed from certain internal organs and offered as a burnt offering to God (see Exod. 23:18; 29:13; Lev. 3:3-5). In the Punic sacrificial system, that was the portion which the priest should receive, though "the proper disposal of the fat did not have the same ideological significance as in the Israelite cult."[103] It is interesting to note that the "Punic Sacrificial Tariff" states that the oppressive priest who "requires a fee deviating from what is set down in (the text on) this plaque shall be fined";[104] see Exod. 21:22; Deut. 22:19. Here, a lay Israelite protests this priest's freelancing approach, only to be told, *Now! You must give it to me!* a demand backed up by the threat that *I will take (it) by force.* The short lines of the speech hint at the priest's growing irritation. The initial *ky (Now!)* emphasizes the "immediateness" of his demand. His forceful words imply that an embarrassing row will ensue if he doesn't get his way.

17 All these selfish demands and aggressive threats amounted to *sin . . . very great* in the Lord's opinion. The term *offering* is usually used for grain offerings and other bloodless offerings, but it can be used for animal

103. See Pardee in *CS,* I, p. 308 and n. 37.
104. *CS,* I, p. 309.

offerings (Gen. 4:4).[105] Whatever its nature, these *young men* treated it not with sober respect or sacred awe, but with *contempt,* as if they resented both their dependence on offerings for food and the religious rigmarole that went with it.

The divine name YHWH appears twice in this verse, emphasizing the importance of the priest's relationship with his God. As noted above, as YHWH appeared also in the introductory remark, this finished the frame of the entire section as an *inclusio.* Subtly, the author invokes the sacred name of the one in whose honor all offerings are given and whose generosity in sharing those gifts has spread many a rich feast across the priests' tables. For *the young men,* see below.

EXCURSUS: *nʿr hkhn* AND THE POETIC STRUCTURE

Scholars disagree about to whom the phrase *naʿar hakkōhēn* (lit. "the young one of the priest") (vv. 13, 15) refers. The issue is whether *naʿar* (vv. 13, 15) and *nᵉʿārîm* (*the young men;* v. 17) all refer to Eli's sons or not. KJV, RSV, NEB, NIV, JPS, and others seem to treat the first two cases as "servants" and the *nᵉʿārîm* as Eli's sons.[106] However, it seems strange after decrying the behavior of the *naʿar* to suddenly change the reference of *naʿar* in v. 17 ("the sin of the *nᵉʿārîm* was great"). However, it is unlikely that v. 17 would be criticizing just the temple servants (as McCarter seems to imply), especially when one considers the repeated contrast in v. 12 and v. 29 between Samuel, the *naʿar* who *ministered to the Lord* (v. 11), and Eli's sons who *do not know the Lord* (v. 12). Therefore, all three instances probably refer to Eli's sons. It does seem strange though that Eli's sons who were already "priests" (see 1:3) should be called "attendants" (so Klein).[107]

It seems that the clue for solving this crux is grammatical. While the phrase *naʿar hakkōhēn* is usually translated as "the lad (or servant) of the priest," this construct chain probably means "the young [or, junior] priest" (lit., "the young [one] of the priest") since the term *naʿar* can be an adjective, meaning "young,"[108] and the genitive noun (here, "the priest") is "character-

105. See K. Nielsen, *Incense in Ancient Israel* (SVT 38; Leiden: E. J. Brill, 1986), pp. 73-74.

106. Similarly Garsiel, though translating all three as "lad" or "lads," takes the first two as referring to the priest's lad "sent by Eli's sons" and the third as referring to Eli's sons themselves.

107. Recent commentators such as McCarter (p. 77) and Klein (p. 21) translate all three *naʿar* in the same way ("servant" or "attendant").

108. For *naʿar* in the sense of "young," see 1 Sam. 17:33; Jer. 1:6; Judg. 8:20; 1 Chr. 12:28 [29]; 2 Chr. 13:7; 34:3; Prov. 7:7; and its use in a merismatic pair with *zqn* "old" (e.g., Lam. 2:21). See 1:24 (also 9:3) on *naʿar* for "servant, steward."

ized by" the construct adjective ("young") as in the cases of "stiff-necked" *(q^ešēh-ʿōrep)* in Exod. 32:9 and others.[109] For a similar grammatical structure, see "a heifer" *ʿeglat bāqār* (lit., "a young female [one] of cattle") in 1 Sam. 16:2. If this interpretation is correct, we can see the cohesion of the entire section of the present narrative discourse.

The poetic nature of this narrative discourse influences its presentation of the conduct of the young priests in two separate parts, vv. 13b-14 and vv. 15-16. The fact that only one *young priest* is mentioned in each part, and yet at the end (v. 17a) they are mentioned as *the young* [priests] (pl.), supports the idea the entire section is "poetical" in nature.

1 Sam. 2:12-17, which is usually taken as a prose narrative, seems to exhibit a number of poetic features and can be read as poetic prose or narrative poetry, which is characterized by a *vertical* grammar.[110] This poetic nature is recognized not only in smaller units such as cola or verses, but also in larger units such as strophes or canticles. This section is thus narrative poetry embedded within a larger story in which Eli's sons and Hannah's son are sharply contrasted.

3. Samuel (2:18-21)

18 *Now Samuel was ministering before the Lord as a boy wearing a linen ephod.*
19 *His mother made it a custom*[111] *to make a little robe for him and bring it to him each year when she went up with her husband to offer the yearly sacrifice.*
20 *Then Eli would bless Elkanah and his wife:*
"May the Lord grant you offspring[112] *of this woman*
in place of the one who was entrusted to the Lord!"[113]

109. See J-M, §129*i-ia.*

110. On *vertical grammar,* see "Introduction" (Section VII, A).

111. Here the impf. *(taʿăśeh)* stands for customary action in the past, followed by the *waw* + perfect constructions in vv. 19-20, i.e., *w^ehaʿaltāh (bring), ûbērak (would bless), ûbērak . . . w^eʾāmar* (lit., *would bless . . . and say)* and *w^ehāl^ekû (would go back).* These repetitive actions are complemented by the expression *each year* (lit., "from year to year"). See also on 1 Sam. 1:3.

112. MT has *yāśēm* ("put"); cf. 4QSam^a, LXX, which have *yšlm* ("repay"). However, the following comparison makes the MT reading more plausible:

> God *ŚYM *zeraʿ* (a descendant) to you (a husband) from this woman a descendant who carries on his father's name: see 1 Sam. 24:22 (below).
> God *NTN *zeraʿ ʾănāšîm* (a child; lit., "a seed of men") to me (a woman) (1 Sam. 1:11).

113. Lit., "he requested to the Lord" *(šāʾal lYHWH).* See on *šāʾûl lYHWH* "(was)

and they would go back home.
21 *Because the Lord took note of*[114] *Hannah, she conceived and bore three sons and two daughters.*
And the boy Samuel grew up in the Lord's presence.

Now the focus of the story changes from "the (young) men," that is, Eli's sons, to "a (servant) boy," that is, Samuel, and his parents. The Lord blesses this dedicated couple with three more sons and two daughters, a total of six children. They gave one to God and received five more without losing the first, just as Abraham gave Isaac and received many offspring without losing Isaac! Though this prosperity is certainly connected with Eli's priestly blessing, the Lord generously responded to Hannah's request made in her trust and hope in him. He gave her back far more than she had given him. God still works in the same way for those who love him and seek to live according to his plan and purpose.

Now (v. 18) is a disjunctive *waw,* which signals a change of topic in the story. Since the first narrative "tense" verb appears in the final verse ("and she conceived and bore"; v. 21b), vv. 18-21a present the background information to that EVENT.

This section, vv. 18-21, begins with *Samuel* and ends with *the boy Samuel* (v. 21), which picks up *the boy* from v. 11. Thus, the story of "the boy Samuel" consists of two parts (AB) and is interrupted by the insertion of the episode (X) of the "young" priests, Eli's sons, in vv. 12-17. The whole constitutes an AXB pattern.

18 With this verse, Samuel's story line resumes with an expression, *Samuel was ministering before the Lord,* similar to that in v. 11b. However, here he is ministering *before the Lord* instead of "before Eli." The narrator possibly emphasizes Samuel's direct relationship with God as well as his growth *in the Lord's presence* (v. 21).

The *linen ephod* (*'ēpôd bād;* also 1 Sam. 22:18; see 2:28 on the ephod worn by the high priest) refers to a simple linen garment, perhaps a white tu-

---

entrusted to the Lord" (1 Sam. 1:28), with Qal, passive ptc. McCarter (p. 80) holds that the MT reading is "impossible" and alters the text to "she has dedicated" *(hš'lh).* However, this is a case of impersonal passive 3 m.s., which is a "patient-oriented" grammar (i.e., a grammar whose primary concern is what is done rather than who does it); also on 1 Sam. 1:28. As for similar cases, see Lev. 1:4, 5; 4:15, 24; 8:14, 18, 22 (New JPS translation); J. Milgrom, *Leviticus 1–16* (AB 3; New York: Doubleday, 1991), pp. 154, 244, 248; B. Levine, *Leviticus* (JPS Torah Commentary; Philadelphia: Jewish Publication Society, 1989), p. 52.

114. So NRSV; JPS; cf. "was gracious to" (NIV); "favored" (McCarter, p. 80). On the veral root *pqd "to determine someone's destiny," see T. F. Williams, *"pqd,"* in *NIDOTTE,* 3, pp. 657-63.

nic or long shirt. In 2 Sam. 6:14, King David wore it in his dance before the ark.[115] On its etymology, see *HALOT,* p. 77. "Samuel is thus depicted virtually as a little priest."[116]

19 *The small robe* which Hannah made for Samuel may be a special garment for priests like the Akkadian *tēlītu* garment[117] (cf. 1 Sam. 15:27; 28:14).

20-21 The blessing by the priest Eli concerning the offspring was effective only because *the Lord* himself *took note of* (*pqd) Hannah. Eli, though he is said to have *always* despised the offering made to his God (see 2:29), was certainly used to deliver God's blessing to the worshipper through his spoken words.

4. Eli's Two Sons (2:22-26)

22 *Now Eli had become very old. He kept hearing*[118] *about everything that his sons had been doing to all Israel, even*[119] *about the matter that they had been sleeping with the women who were serving*[120] *at the entrance of the Tent of Meeting.*

23 *He said to them,*
"Why have you been doing[121] *such things?*
For[122] *I am hearing about your evil deeds from all these people.*
24 *No, my sons!*
For the report which I hear the people of the Lord spreading is not good.
25 *If a man sins against a man, God*[123] *will mediate for him;*

115. See N. L. Tidwell, "The Linen Ephod," *VT* 24 (1974) 505-7.

116. Budde, quoted by Hertzberg, p. 35.

117. See V. Hurowitz, "The 'Sun Disk' Tablet of Nabû-apla-iddina," in *CS,* II, p. 367.

118. So McCarter, p. 77; or "he heard from time to time" (Driver, p. 33); in any case, a frequentative perfect.

119. Emphatic *waw.* Verse 22b is absent from 4QSam^a and from part of the LXX tradition; hence, some take it as a "late interpolation" (H. P. Smith, *A Critical and Exegetical Commentary on the Books of Samuel* [ICC; Edinburgh: T. & T. Clark, 1899], p. 20; also McCarter, p. 81). However, this less-than-flattering information is more likely to have been deleted than to have been added.

120. *ṣb' "to serve"; those who serve at the sacred tent are the Levites (Num. 4:23; 8:24) and women (Exod. 38:8).

121. Impf. habitual sense, from the context in which Eli *kept hearing* (v. 22).

122. The particle *'ăšer* here functions almost the same as the speaker-oriented *kî* of reason.

123. Or "the judges" (NIV, note) with a plural verb: *pllw.* See Exod. 18:19-22; 21:6; 22:8-9 (J. G. Baldwin, *1-2 Samuel* [TOTC; Leicester: InterVarsity, 1988], p. 61).

but if a man sins against the Lord, who will intercede for him?"
But they would not listen to their father, because the Lord intended to kill them.
26 *Meanwhile the boy Samuel was continually growing and was pleasing both to the Lord and to people.*

A new episode begins with a SETTING (v. 22) to introduce Eli's direct discourse. The first *wayqtl,* "And he said," in v. 23 signals the EVENT, though the phrase itself functions as an introductory formula to the following direct discourse.

22 It seems that some time has passed since the last episode. Eli is now already very old.

These women with whom Eli's sons are *sleeping* are not the Canaanite cult prostitutes. They were probably those who performed menial duties in the pre-monarchical Israelite sanctuaries (see Exod. 38:8). They illustrate here "the degeneracy of Eli's sons."[124] *The Tent of Meeting* is the place where the holy God arranged to meet his people "outside the curtain that is in front of the Testimony" where "Aaron and his sons are to keep the lamps burning before the LORD from evening till morning" (Exod. 27:21).

25 In the Bible, "sin" (*ḥṭʾ) is always primarily against the Lord, who is the creator and covenant God. But "high-handed sin against God, unlike offences against one's fellow, leaves no room for mediation."[125]

The terms *mediate* and *intercede* here primarily refer to the ordinary relationships among human beings in a legal context. *If a man sins against a man,* it is *God,* or *the judges* who represent him, who *will mediate for him.* But, *if a man sins against the Lord,* there is nobody *who will intercede for him.*[126] Eli's words of warning had no effect on his "worthless" sons who had no ears to listen. For God had decided the destiny of Eli's sons: *the Lord intended to kill them,* because of their willful rejection of God. When God determined to destroy them, no human intercession was effective. Only when God is willing to listen to supplications and requests, can such human intercessions calm God's anger as in Exod. 32:7-14. Only when and because God is willing to listen to the supplications and intercessions — for he is gracious — is there hope for sinful human beings.

For the writers of the Bible, the fact that divine providence and human destinies mingle means destinies are regarded as the result of divine will. The most obvious example is the Pharaoh in Exodus. However, this does not

124. R. P. Gordon, p. 83.

125. R. P. Gordon, p. 84.

126. For various views on the meanings of the verb *pll and the noun *ʾĕlōhîm,* see E. F. de Ward, "Eli's Rhetorical Question: I Sam. 2:25," *JJS* 27 (1976) 117-37.

mean that humans are not accountable. As Gordon says, "on the contrary, it is assumed that the cause of the downfall of Hophni and Phinehas was their own willful rejection of God (cf. Luke 7:30)."[127]

Not only were Eli's sons' deeds with the women bad enough, but their refusal to listen to their father's warning was inexcusable. Such a hardening of their heart was the sign of the Lord's judgment.[128]

But if a man sins against the Lord, who will intercede for him? This question of Eli's has a deeper implication in the framework of salvation history. Since every human being is a sinner and sins against the Lord (see Ps. 51:4), does not Eli's rhetorical question suggest that there is no hope of sinners being interceded for? But, Job did not give up seeking a mediator between himself and God, when he said "If only there were someone to arbitrate between us, to lay his hand upon us both" (Job 9:33). Paul's conviction is that Job's question was answered in Jesus: "For there is one God and one mediator between God and people, the human Christ Jesus" (1 Tim. 2:5).

26 *Meanwhile* marks the mid-point in the macrostructure of the narrative which describes the growth of Samuel in 2:18, 26, and 3:1.

> 2:18 (Now Samuel was ministering before the Lord . . .)
> 2:26 (Meanwhile the boy Samuel was continually growing and was pleasing both to the Lord and to people.)
> 3:1 (Now the boy Samuel was ministering to the Lord before Eli.)

The growth of Samuel is contrasted with the evil behaviors of Eli's sons: 2:12 (Now the sons of Eli were sons of Beliyaal) → 2:22f. → 2:27f. Eli's successor will not be his sons, but Samuel. The phrase *the boy Samuel* reappears after v. 21. Thus, the term "boy" is a key word, which frames the story line and keeps reminding the reader of Samuel, and as a stark contrast, during the episodes describing Eli and his sons.

5. Warning of a Man of God (2:27-36)

27 *And a man of God came to Eli and said to him,*
"Thus says the Lord:
'Indeed[129] *I revealed myself to the house of your ancestor,*

127. R. P. Gordon, p. 84.

128. On the divine hardening of the human heart, see M. Tsevat, "The Death of the Sons of Eli," *JBR* 32 (1964) 355-58.

129. Usually <interrogative>, but here <conviction> (GKC, §150e; also J-M, §161b).

when they belonged to[130] *the house of Pharaoh in Egypt,*
28 *and chose*[131] *it as my priest from all the tribes of Israel*
to go up to my altar,
to burn incense,
to wear the ephod before me,
and gave to the house of your ancestor
all the food-offerings of the Israelites.
29 *Why do you always despise*[132] *the sacrifice and offering made to me,*[133]
which I have commanded, at (my) shrine
and honor[134] *your sons more than me,*
to enrich yourselves[135] *with the first part of all the offerings of Israel, my people?'*
30 *Therefore, the oracle of the Lord, God of Israel:*
'Indeed I said
that your house and your ancestor's house would walk before me forever.
But now — the oracle of the Lord —
far be it from me!
For those who honor me I will honor;
those who despise[136] *me will be humiliated.*[137]
31 *Behold the days are coming*

130. Or "were subject to" (JPS).

131. This use of the infinitive absolute in place of the finite verb might be a northern Israelite dialectal feature; see Gary Rendsburg, "Some False Leads in the Identification of Late Biblical Hebrew Texts: The Cases of Genesis 24 and 1 Samuel 2:27-36," *JBL* 121 (2002) 37-38.

132. A "habitual" imperfect verb.

133. Lit., "my sacrifice and my offering"; objective genitive, "to me."

134. *Wayqtl* here is sequential to the preceding "habitual" *yqtl,* and hence read "honor" rather than "honored"; see W-O, §33.3.3c (p. 559); C. H. J. van der Merwe, "Discourse Linguistics and Biblical Hebrew Grammar," in *Biblical Hebrew and Discourse Linguistics,* p. 24.

135. Lit., "to fatten you (pl. = 'you and your sons')"; = "to feather your own nest; line your pockets." Cf. *HALOT,* p. 154; also in Arabic (so M. Brettler, "The Composition of 1 Samuel 1–2," *JBL* 116 [1997] 609, n. 36). The fact that the root is a *hapax legomenon* in the Bible but attested commonly in Aramaic does not make it a later word; so Brettler (pp. 609-10). G. Rendsburg takes this as Israelite (northern) Hebrew; see Gary Rendsburg, "Some False Leads in the Identification of Late Biblical Hebrew Texts: The Cases of Genesis 24 and 1 Samuel 2:27-36," *JBL* 121 (2002) 38-39.

136. *bzh; in contrast with *kbd (to honor < to be heavy). See above on other terms for "despise" (*bʿṭ) in v. 29.

137. Or "dishonored" (JPS); "disdained" (NIV); cf. "accursed" (McCarter, p. 86).

when I will cut off[138] *your strength (lit., "arm")*
and the strength of your ancestor's house
so that there may not[139] *be an old man in your house.*
32 *You shall see a decline*[140] *of my dwelling*
whenever things go well with Israel;
no old man shall be in your house at any time.
33 *All but one man of you shall I cut off from my altar*
so that I may wear out your eyes[141]
and cause your life to waste away,[142]
but all the new children[143] *of your house will die by the hands of men.*
34 *And this*[144] *is the sign for you,*
which will happen to your two sons,
to Hophni and Phinehas:
on the same day[145] *both of them will die.*
35 *And I will raise up for me a faithful priest;*
he will act according to that which is in my heart and in my soul
and I will build for him an enduring house,
and he will serve[146] *before my anointed all the time.*[147]
36 *Whoever remains in your house will come to bow to him*
for a small piece of silver[148] *and a loaf of bread*
and say,

138. Heb. *gdʿ, lit., "hew off"; its collocation requires something like a long and narrow object as its object, e.g., Asherah (wooden) pole (Deut. 7:5; 2 Chr. 14:2), tree (Isa. 9:9; 10:33), also "tribe (of Israel)" (Judg. 21:6) and "morning star" (Isa. 14:12).

139. Privative *min* "without" result.

140. McCarter, pp. 88-89, following Cross and Wellhausen, takes the *Vorlage* of LXX^{B} and 4QSam^{a} as "primitive" and omits the whole of vv. 31b and 32a. See Comment.

141. For *klh + "eyes," see also Lev. 26:16 (Pi.: "waste away the eyes"); Deut. 28:65 ("failing of eyes"); Job 11:20 (Qal: "the eyes of the wicked will fail").

142. For *laʾădîb* "to languish" (prep. *la* = Hi. inf. const. *ʾdb),* cf. Lev. 26:16 ("cause life to pine away": Hi. part. *dwb*) and Deut. 28:65 (noun *daʾăbôn* < **dʾb*). All three roots, *ʾdb, *dwb, and *dʾb, may go back to an original bi-consonantal *db.

143. See *HALOT,* p. 631: "new children" in the family; *marbît* "largest part; increase" < *rbh; "increase" (NASB; RSV); "members" (NRSV).

144. Namely, the following matter.

145. Lit., "in one day"; see 1 Sam. 4:11.

146. Hith., lit., "walk around," i.e., serve as priest ("go in and out" [NRSV]; "minister" [NIV]). See 1 Sam. 2:30 (before Yahweh).

147. Lit., "all the days" or "always" (NASB; NIV); cf. "forever" (NRSV), "evermore" (JPS). Cf. "forever" *ʿad-ʿôlām* (1 Sam. 2:30).

148. *ʾăgôrat kesep,* "a bit of money" (McCarter, p. 89).

"Please admit me to one of the priestly offices to eat a morsel of bread!" '"

This section concerns the prophetic message to Eli about the destiny of him and his household. It is a message of judgment on the Shilonite priesthood, and it reveals a new plan of God for his cultic tradition. This passage gives the rationale for the later replacement of the house of Eli by the house of Zadok. Solomon exiled Eli's descendant Abiathar to Anathoth (1 K. 2:26-27) at the beginning of his reign, and, after that, Zadok's family controlled the priesthood in the Jerusalem temple until the Exile.

27 The phrase *a man of God (ʾîš-ʾĕlōhîm)* is a synonym for "prophet" (e.g., 2 K. 1:9). The "prophet" sent to criticize the priest and the cult is in contrast to Mari's "prophets" who spoke for the cult. See 1 Sam. 9:6.

Thus says the Lord is the so-called prophetic "messenger formula" where the verb is pf. of *performative,* the messenger speaking now as Yahweh who sent him. In Samuel this formula appears in 1 Sam. 2:27; 10:18; 15:2; 2 Sam. 7:5, 8; 12:7, 11; 24:12. In the ancient world, the messengers were supposed to recite their messages verbatim, and so the messenger would start "[The sender] has spoken thus:" and use the first person in the body of the message (Gen. 45:17-20; etc.).

The translation *when they belonged to the house of Pharaoh in Egypt* is based on the MT as it stands: *bihyôtām bᵉmiṣrayim lᵉbêt parʿōh* (lit., "in their being in Egypt to the house of Pharaoh"). The first two words are normally translated as "when they were in Egypt."[149] McCarter renders "when they were in Egypt, slaves to the house of Pharaoh," recovering *ʿbdym* with 4QSamᵃ and LXX.[150] But this unusual word order is due to the "AXB pattern,"[151] in which "in Egypt" (X) is inserted into a nucleus of the temporal phrase, "in their belonging to (*hyh + l-) the house of Pharaoh" *bihyôtām — lᵉbêt parʿōh* (A-B). This is confirmed by Deut. 6:21 *ʿăbādîm hāyînû — lᵉparʿōh bᵉmiṣrāyim* (usually translated, "we were slaves of Pharaoh in Egypt"; but rather, literally, "[as slaves] we belonged to Pharaoh in Egypt"), which follows ABX. In both cases, the sense is that the Israelites were slaves owned by the royal house in Egypt![152]

28 The chief duties of the priesthood are summarized here:

149. GKC, §114e.

150. McCarter, p. 87; also Driver, p. 36.

151. See "Introduction" (Section VII, C).

152. Cf. JPS that moves the phrase "in Egypt" out of the temporal phrase and translates: "Lo, I revealed Myself to your father's house in Egypt when they were subject to the House of Pharaoh." But this is not necessary with our understanding.

1. *to go up to my altar:* the sum of actions performed on the altar, including burning offerings as "an aroma pleasing to the Lord" (Lev 1:9; etc.).
2. *to burn incense* (Exod. 30:7; Num. 16:40): in the holy place, "before the Lord" (Lev. 16:13). Note that the incense *(qᵉṭōret)* was "burned" (always Hi. *hiqṭîr*) on a special altar, not on that of "the food-offering" (see below).[153] Its purpose is to make "the cloud" to "conceal the atonement cover above the Testimony, so that [the high priest] will not die" (Lev. 16:13).
3. *to wear the ephod* (Lev. 8:7): this *ephod* is to be distinguished from Samuel's linen ephod (v. 18). It refers to the high priest's ephod of Exod. 28:5-30, which included the jeweled breastplate and the Urim and Thummim. It appears in 1 Sam. 23:6 and 30:7 in connection with oracular decisions. Also see on 1 Sam. 14:3.

The food-offering *('iššê)*[154] is usually explained as "an offering made by fire,"[155] but its association with *'ēš,* "fire," has been considered doubtful. Its etymology is sometimes sought in Ugaritic *'iṯt,* "(votive) offering,"[156] but the identification of Heb. *'iššê* with Ugar. *'iṯt* has been questioned in recent years.[157] In Lev. 2:2-3, "After taking from [the grain offering] a handful of the choice flour and oil, with all its frankincense, the priest shall cause this memorial portion to go up in smoke on the altar, as an *'iššê*-offering, an aroma pleasing to the Lord. The rest of the grain offering belongs to Aaron and his sons; it is a most holy part of the *'iššê*-offering to the Lord" (Lev. 2:2-3; also 10), so the *'iššê*-offering is not totally consumed by fire. Most of it was eaten by the priests. So, Akk. *eššešu* "offering" (*CAD,* E, pp. 371-73) (a loanword from Sumerian) might be a better candidate for the etymology.

29 Despite God's provisions for the priests, Eli has closed his eyes

153. See D. Edelman, "The Meaning of qiṭṭēr," *VT* 35 (1985) 400; Nielsen, *Incense in Ancient Israel,* pp. 73, 102. H. J. Stoebe (*Das erste Buch Samuelis* [KAT VIII/1; Gütersloh: Gerd Mohn, 1973], p. 116), following Budde, takes this burning to be that of sacrifices on the altar; hence, only two duties — "to go up to my altar to burn sacrifices" and "to wear the ephod" — are mentioned here. See Nielsen, *Incense in Ancient Israel,* p. 54.

154. So NEB; G. J. Wenham, *The Book of Leviticus* (NICOT; Grand Rapids: Eerdmans, 1979), p. 56, n. 8; Edelman, "The Meaning of qiṭṭēr," p. 396.

155. BDB; also *HALOT,* p. 93.

156. See G. R. Driver, "Ugaritic and Hebrew Words," *Ug* VI (1969), pp. 181-84; also McCarter, p. 90.

157. M. Dietrich, O. Loretz, and J. Sanmartín, "Ein Brief des Königs an die Königin-Mutter," *UF* 6 (1974) 460-62; see D. T. Tsumura, *The Earth and the Waters in Genesis 1 and 2: A Linguistic Analysis* (JSOTSS 83; Sheffield: Sheffield Academic Press, 1989), p. 105, n. 63.

to his sons' devices, and Eli is responsible. His responsibility is emphasized by the references to "honor" in vv. 29-30.

The term *despise* (*bʿṭ)[158] is contrasted with *honored* (see below). In this context to despise means to ignore God's commandment and dishonor him. God criticizes such contempt of the divinely ordained sacrificial system, rather than the emptiness of the sacrifices as the later prophets do (e.g., Hos. 8:13; Amos 4:4f). But, both emptiness and contempt are serious offenses against the God who commanded the sacrifice.

The terms *sacrifice* and *offering,* being m. and f. nouns, respectively, are a merismus which refers to the entire sacrificial system; see also 1 Sam. 3:14. Note that the Lord does not discard the sacrificial system here any more than he does in 1 Sam. 15:22.

The term *māʿôn* (lit., "dwelling place") is a poetic designation of sanctuary.[159] Since the syntactic structure of the sentence is not so clear, the text has been taken as "unintelligible" (BDB, p. 733). McCarter emends it on the basis of LXX^B, following Wellhausen.[160] However, the term might be taken adverbially, *at (my) shrine,* as a locative noun which modifies the main verb *despise,* not the verb *commanded* of the relative clause. Such examples where a relative clause is followed by a word or phrase belonging to the main clause can be noted in 1 Sam. 20:19; 26:3; 2 Sam. 2:24; 11:27; 13:16; and 15:7. Hence, no emendation is necessary. See the "Introduction" (Section V, B).

Honored is contrasted with *despise* in this verse and also in v. 30, though there a different term for *despise* (*bzh) appears. Honoring one's own sons more than Yahweh, thus reversing the priority of devotion, and despising the divine commandment go side by side in the lives of sinful men. In fact, in the Ten Commandments, worshipping God only is the first commandment; next after it is honoring one's parents and treating one's fellow human beings as images of God.

The phrase *the first part* possibly refers to vv. 15-16. For most of the sacrifices of which the priest partook, as those in Lev. 6:15-16; 7:3-5, 31, part is to be burned before the priests receive their share. The phrase *my people* is literally "to my people." The emphasis here seems to be on *my* people, thus accusing Eli as Yahweh's priest (v. 28) of dereliction of duty in not interceding (cf. v. 25) for His people.

158. Lit., "give a kick," *bʿṭ + *b;* this is a metaphorical use of "to kick" (Deut. 32:15); so *HALOT,* p. 142, "ausschlagen"; "verschmähen" (*HAL,* p. 136); cf. "scorn" (NIV); "kick at" (NASB); "maliciously trample upon" (JPS). McCarter, following the LXX, reads *wlmh tbyṭ . . . srt ʿyn* "Then why do you look . . . with a selfish eye?"; also "look with greedy eye at" (NRSV).

159. Caquot and de Robert, p. 49.

160. Wellhausen, p. 48; McCarter, p. 87.

30 The formula *the oracle of the Lord (nᵉʾūm-YHWH)* appears 254 times, mostly in the later Prophets and Psalms, and only here in 1-2 Samuel. This verse is notable in that it repeats the formula twice. The man of God very solemnly announces God's judgment on Eli and his family. The expression *forever* is almost the same as "all the time" in v. 35; note that God's eternal promise can be changed, but never completely abandoned.

The formula *far be it from me! (ḥālîlā(h) llî)* is an adversive exclamation, literally, *ad profanum,* which refers to the foregoing statement. It occurs 21 times in OT; 11 times in Samuel![161] But it is only here that the Lord speaks this formula. This shows how determined the Lord's judgment was and how severe his anger was at the dishonor which the priestly family had brought on him.

In *For those who honor me I will honor, kî* states the reason for the utterance "far be it from me!" According to Olyan,[162] the rest of the phrase illustrates "the ideal expectations of reciprocal honor" in the covenant relation as expressed here by Yahweh who is "the suzerain par excellence in Israel"; see also on 2 Sam. 19:6. As a faithful observer of this covenant, the Lord will surely honor those who honor him and set their minds on "his kingdom and his justice" before everything else (Matt. 6:33; see NEB).

The contrast here is not between "blessing" *(bᵉrākāh)* and "cursing" *(qᵉlālāh)* but between "honoring" and "being dishonored"; simply, God honors those who honor him. Such "reciprocal honor" emphasizes the interpersonal relationship between the two parties.

31-34 Eli has broken the covenant, and his punishment is given in words similar to those of covenant curses. (Curses were a common sanction in ancient treaties.[163])

31 The eschatological formula *Behold the days are coming* appears for the first of 21 times in the OT, 19 times in the later Prophets; the only other occurrences are v. 31 and 2 K. 20:17. With this formula, the prophet announces that the day of judgment is coming when Yahweh will so completely destroy Eli (lit., *cut off* Eli's *arm*) and his priestly household that everyone will die young and there will be no *old man in* the *house.*

32 The MT text *ṣar māʿôn* is often taken as "corrupt" (BDB, p. 865). Various translations have been suggested: for example, "you will see the distress of My dwelling" (NASB); "you will see distress in my dwelling"

161. 1 Sam. 2:30; 12:23; 14:45; 20:2, 9; 22:15; 24:6; 26:11; 2 Sam. 20:20 (x 2); 23:17.

162. S. M. Olyan, "Honor, Shame, and Covenant Relations in Ancient Israel and Its Environment," *JBL* 115 (1996) 205.

163. See R. P. Gordon, "Curse, Malediction," in *NIDOTTE,* 4, p. 491-93; D. Stuart, "Curse" in *ABD,* I, pp. 1218-19 and its bibliography.

(NIV); "in distress you will look with greedy eye on . . ." (NRSV); "You will gaze grudgingly at all the bounty" (JPS); "You will even resent the prosperity . . ." (REB). One might compare the phrase *ṣar mā'ôn* with *māqôm ṣār* "narrow place" (Num. 22:26) or the expression "the place is small/limited/crowded *(ṣar)*" (2 K. 6:1; Isa. 49:20) and, taking it as a construct chain of <adj. cstr. + noun gen.>, translate as *a decline of my dwelling* (lit., "narrowing of [my] dwelling"). Thus, the expression refers to a "shrinkage of the size of Yahweh's temple." It is interesting to note that the "prophets" of Mari are concerned with the prosperity of the temple rather than the welfare of the people;[164] in the ancient world the temple was a center of the economy as well as religion. Therefore, when the society prospered, the temple usually did too. But, here the decline of the temple despite the prosperity of society is announced as the judgment of God upon the priestly family.

Not only the temple-shrine but also the priesthood will shrink as the judgment of Yahweh on Eli. Hence, there will be *no old man* because everyone in the priestly family will die young.

33 *All but one man of you shall I cut* is literally "a man I shall not cut of you." The syntax of this clause is understood variously; cf. "Yet I will not cut off every man of yours from My altar" (NASB); "The only one of you whom I shall not cut off from my altar shall be spared" (NRSV); "Every one of you that I do not cut off from my altar will be spared" (NIV); "I shall not cut off all your offspring from My altar" (JPS). This *man* probably refers to Abiathar, who escaped when Saul killed the priests of Nob (22:17-20). (See also 1 K. 2:27b.)

So that I may wear out your eyes and cause your life to waste away is literally "to wear out your eyes and to cause your life to waste away." This is a result rather than a purpose phrase. A difficult problem is deciding who or what wears out Eli's eyes. NRSV and NIV take the "one" as the subject; JPS connects this infinitive clause with the latter half of the verse. NASB transforms it as intransitive: "that your eyes may fail from weeping and your soul grieve." Since the Lord is the ultimate cause of sending diseases (see below on Lev. 26:16; Deut. 28:65), he is probably the agent of "wear out" and "cause to waste away."

Wear out your eyes and cause your life to waste away are two expressions that describe symptoms of illness or disease. Here, "eyes" and "life" are a word pair, which often appears in the context of grief or distress as a result of judgment.[165] As R. P. Gordon holds, "the wording is strongly evoca-

164. See A. Malamat, *Mari and the Bible* (SHCANE 12; Leiden: E. J. Brill, 1998).

165. Lev. 26:16; Deut. 28:65; Jer. 13:17; Ezek. 24:21; Ps. 116:8; Eccl. 6:9. RSV follows 4QSam[a] and the LXX to translate "his eyes"//"his heart."

tive of the curse formula"[166] as in Lev. 26:16, "I, in turn, will do this to you: I will appoint over you a sudden terror, consumption and fever that shall waste away the eyes and cause the soul to pine away; also, you shall sow your seed uselessly, for your enemies shall eat it up" (NASB; also Deut. 28:65).

The phrase "die of men" (*mwt *'ănāšîm*) probably means *die by the hand of men,* for Eli's two sons, Hophni and Phinehas, died in war (4:11), and most of his other descendants died by the sword (22:18-20).[167] R. P. Gordon thinks that "by the sword," which is in 4QSam[a] and LXX, has fallen out of MT. Alternatively, the sentence could be translated as "but of all the descendants of your house, men will die." Namely, all the male members of the household, that is, all the priests, will die in God's judgment; compare v. 31 ("so that there may not be an old man in your house"). So, in this translation there is contrast

between "one man" *('îš)* and "all" *(kol);*
between "not cut" and "die";
between Eli's death in old age and the violent premature death

of all but one of his *descendants.* It is difficult to decide which of the two interpretations is better. In any case, the context refers to the distress which will come to Eli and his priestly family as the judgment of God (so *your eyes — your life* (MT), rather than "his"; 4QSam[a], LXX).

34 Eli will not experience most of these deaths, and so God gives him a sign that his descendants will indeed be destroyed. His two sons will die on the same day.

35 As the Lord of history God will appoint *(raise up)* a man to lead his salvation plan toward consummation; see Deut. 18:15 ("The LORD your God will raise up for you a prophet like me").

The phrase *a faithful priest (kōhēn ne'ĕmān)* seems to refer to Zadok, Abiathar's rival and successor under the aegis of the *anointed* Davidic kings (2 Sam. 15:24-37; 1 K. 1:22-39; 2:35); note that in 1 Sam. 3:20 Samuel was "established" as a prophet of the Lord, not as a priest. The *ne'ĕmān* can mean both "faithful" and "enduring"; the former meaning goes with *priest* while the latter sense is reflected in the phrase *enduring house.* This phrase appears several times referring to David (13:14; 25:28; 2 Sam. 7:16; Acts 13:22). And it is used both for a priestly house and for a royal house (see 2 Sam. 7:16). Thus, in the books of Samuel "the roles of priest and king become closely associated."[168]

166. R. P. Gordon, p. 87.

167. Cf. "die in the prime of life" (NASB, NIV); "as ordinary men" (JPS); cf. "by the sword of men" (RSV); "by the sword" (NRSV).

168. J. G. McConville, "Priesthood in Joshua to Kings," *VT* 49 (1999) 86.

The expression *according to that which is in my heart and in my soul* means "as I intend and desire."[169] While the heart is "the seat of the intellect and will," the soul is "the seat of desire and the appetites." The word pair "heart" *(lēbāb)* and "soul" *(nepeš)* appears in many passages: for example, Deut. 4:29; 11:13; Josh. 22:5; Ps. 13:2; cf. Jer. 32:41; Prov. 2:10. The term *my anointed* means my "king" in this context; see already in 1 Sam. 2:10b. According to the NT, Christ is not only a faithful priest but an anointed king (Rom. 1:1-6).[170]

36 Eli's descendants will experience extreme poverty, matching their greed. *Whoever remains in your house* refers to those among the Elide priestly family, the Shilonite priesthood. That is, "the non-Zadokite priests, excluded from the altar, will have to perform menial tasks in order to subsist."[171] The term *'ăgôrat* ("a small piece of silver") is a hapax legomenon. In Official Aramaic, the Akk. loanword[172] *'gr* means "rent; wages, salary; price."[173] The term *'grt* appears in a Punic sacrificial tariff text and is usually identified with Heb. *gērāh,* which is the smallest division of the shekel, one-twentieth.[174]

Thus the chapter ends in a very negative tone with a solemn declaration of the severe judgment on the Shilonite priesthood. The message by *a man of God* (vv. 27-36) serves as the concluding section of the chapter, which began with Hannah's song (vv. 1-10) and the key themes, "Yahweh's holy sovereignty," "reversal of human fortunes," and "kingship." They are followed by a contrasting representation of Eli's sons and the boy Samuel. At the same time, the prophetic message prepares for the prophetic call of the boy Samuel in ch. 3.

6. Call of Samuel as a Prophet (3:1-21)

This chapter is tied to the previous chapter in many ways: not only does v. 1 *(the boy Samuel was ministering to the Lord)* function as a LINK (see "Introduction" [Section VI, B]) to the preceding chapter, repeating the key phrase of 1 Sam. 2:11 and 18, but many terms and themes are recapitulated in this chapter: for example, v. 7 *(Samuel did not yet know the Lord)* to 2:12 *(sons of Eli did not know the Lord);* v. 13 (judgment on Eli's house) to 2:10 (judge) and 31 (cut off); v. 13 (not restraining Eli's sons) to 2:29 ("Why"; cf. 2:23-24); v. 14 ("not be atoned") to 2:25 ("mediate," "intercede"); v. 14 ("sacrifice

169. McCarter, p. 91.

170. R. P. Gordon, p. 88.

171. McCarter, p. 91.

172. S. Kaufman, *Akkadian Influences on Aramaic* (Chicago: University of Chicago Press, 1974), p. 33.

173. See *DNWSI,* p. 11.

174. See *CS,* I, p. 308, n. 34.

. . . offering") to 2:13, 15, 19, 29 (sacrifice). In ch. 2 the Lord sends "a man of God" to Eli as a messenger; in ch. 3 he entrusts his message to the young Samuel, who by the end of the chapter will be established as a renowned prophet of the Lord, thus initiating a new prophetic era in the history of the covenant people. Here the rising destiny of Samuel and the falling destiny of Eli's family appear together. Samuel's first message as a prophet is the doom of his teacher (vv. 11-14).

This section has been often classified form-critically as "a prophetic call narrative," like Exodus 3–4; Isaiah 6; Jeremiah 1; Ezekiel 1; and so forth.[1] However, unlike those other passages, here neither a formal commissioning of Samuel nor a confession of unworthiness for the call appears. Hence, other scholars, such as R. Gnuse, classify it as a "dream theophany," that is, a theophany with an oral message, as in throughout the ancient Near East.[2] However, the fact remains that the divine message came to Samuel while he was awake. Therefore this is not a "dream" theophany in the true sense.

The Discourse Structure of Ch. 3

v. 1 general SETTING
<circumstantial>: Samuel ministering to the Lord before Eli
<NEGative circumstance>: the word of the Lord
<temporal>: "in those days"

vv. 2-3 temporal SETTING: "On that day"
<circumstantial>: "Eli was lying down [participle]"
<parenthetical>: Eli's eyesight
<NEG circumstance>: "the lamp of God"
<circumstantial>: "Samuel was lying down [participle]"

1. See N. Habel, "The Form and Significance of the Call Narrative," *ZAW* 77 (1965) 297-323; B. D. Long, "Prophetic Call Tradition and Reports of Visions," ZAW 84 (1972) 494-500.

2. R. K. Gnuse, "A Reconsideration of the Form-Critical Structure in I Samuel 3: An Ancient Near Eastern Dream Theophany," *ZAW* 94 (1982) 379-90; *The Dream Theophany of Samuel: Its Structure in Relation to Ancient Near Eastern Dreams and Its Theological Significance* (Lanham, Md.: University Press of America, 1984). See U. Simon, "Samuel's Call to Prophecy: Form Criticism with Close Reading," *Prooftexts* 1 (1981) 119-32; V. A. Hurowitz, "Eli's Adjuration of Samuel (1 Samuel iii 17-18) in the Light of a 'Diviner's Protocol' from Mari (AEM I/1, 1)," *VT* 44 (1994) 483-86 for various recent scholarly interpretations; J. G. Janzen; P. Segal; M. Garsiel; Y. Amit; Y. Zakovitch; M. Fishbane; W. G. E. Watson; D. W. Wicke; and W. T. Classen. Also Klein, p. 31; Birch, p. 991.

vv. 4-18 EVENT on "that day"
Lord calls Samuel (vv. 4-14)
Eli calls Samuel (vv. 15-18)

vv. 19-21 Terminus
Samuel established as "a prophet of the Lord"
"the word of the Lord"

The structure clearly shows that in the beginning (SETTING) *the word of the Lord* was lacking in the nation, but at the end (TERMINUS) it was supplied. Thus, the pattern of "lack — lack supplied"[3] is tightly integrated into the discourse structure.

a. Setting (3:1-3)

1 *Now the boy Samuel was ministering to the Lord before Eli.*
And the word of the Lord was rare
in those days;
the vision was not frequent.[4]
2 *On that day,*
when Eli was lying down in his place;
— Now his eyes had begun to become weak
and he was becoming unable to see —
3 *the lamp of God had not yet been extinguished,*
and Samuel was lying down in the temple
where the ark of God was.

1 A new episode of the story begins with the general SETTING, which explains the relationship between Samuel and Eli and the negative situation with regard to *the word of the Lord* (v. 1). This lack is eventually reversed as the Lord reveals himself to Samuel the prophet *by the word of the Lord* (v. 21). This SETTING serves as the overall introduction to the EVENT at a specific time, *On that day,* in vv. 2ff.

The name *Samuel* appears 24 times in this chapter; thus, for the first time Samuel becomes the major figure. Yet *Eli* still appears 17 times, and the Lord 19 times; these three are the agents in this story, though the Lord appears in person only to Samuel. The term *ministering* is a key word for explaining Samuel's relationship with the Lord (also 1 Sam. 2:11; 2:18); see

3. W. G. E. Watson, "The Structure of 1 Sam 3," *BZ* 29 (1985) 92.

4. Or "infrequent" (NASB); "not widespread" (NRSV). For the word order, "there is not" + NOUN + participle, see Isa. 57:1 = Jer. 12:11; 1 K. 6:18; Ezek. 8:12; 9:9.

above on the structure of chs. 1–3. The phrase *the word of the Lord* appears again in v. 21, thus constituting an *inclusio.* The initial section (vv. 1-3), SETTING, corresponds well to the final section (vv. 19-21), Terminus.

Verse 1b seems to be a semi-poetic text, which can be analyzed as follows:

And *the word of the Lord* was rare	3 (10) [3 words, 10 syllables]
in those days;	2 (5)
the *vision* was not frequent.	3 (5)

Here the phrase *in those days* is inserted into perfectly parallel lines (3//3), modifying the bicolon as a whole; it is the X of the AXB pattern (see on 1 Sam. 2:2, 3).

The term *vision (ḥāzôn)* denotes God's revelation, which is the equivalent of *the word of the Lord* (v. 1). It should be noted that the prophetic "vision" is used for the divine message communicated to the prophets, and the message was usually to be delivered to the prophet's audience orally in words. But, sometimes the *vision* was directed to be "written down" (Hab. 2:2). In Amos 1:1; Mic. 1:1; Isa. 2:1; etc., the "vision" is recorded in words. Thus, in the biblical prophecy the "vision" was something to be explained or expressed in words, and its message is more important than the visionary experience of the prophet itself. The rarity of *the word of the Lord* might be construed as a sign of divine disfavor (see Ps. 74:9; Lam. 2:9; Amos 8:11; Mic. 3:6f.).

McCarter translates *ḥāzôn niprāṣ* as "widespread vision," which he takes as "a technical designation of some kind."[5] However, *niprāṣ* seems to function grammatically as a predicate in light of the above parallel structure, where *not frequent* is in parallel with *rare,* the former being a negated antonym of the latter: <A not B> pattern; see on 1 Sam. 1:11; 2:3; 12:20.

2 The phrase *on that day* appears 35 times in 1 and 2 Samuel. Here the SETTING of the story changes from a distant *in those days* (v. 1) to a specific *on that day.* See also on 1 Sam. 21:10.

The participle *was lying down (šōkēb)* is used for both Eli (here) and Samuel (v. 3), denoting their common circumstantial situation, though they were lying down in different places. Since the EVENT of the "day" takes place at v. 4 with the first "narrative tense" *wayqtl,* that is, *wayyiqrā',* vv. 2-3 describe the SETTING (also 1 Sam. 1:1-3). The sentence in v. 2b, which explains Eli's eye condition (see 4:15), should be taken as "parenthetical"; the rest (vv. 2a, 3), which mentions Eli, *the lamp of God,* and *Samuel,* should be taken as "circumstantial," since these three elements are more di-

5. McCarter, p. 97.

rectly or immediately related to "the situation or circumstance" on "that day."[6]

The verbal aspect *he was becoming unable to* (impf.) suggests that the weakening of his eyesight was in progress; at this stage Eli could still see a little; note the pf. in 4:15 ("his eye were fixed and could not see"). Therefore it should be translated not as "could not see" (NRSV), but as "could not see well" (NASB) or "could barely see" (NIV; JPS).

3 Note the contrast between the "darkening" of Eli's eyes and the "light" of God's lamp. Does this note have some symbolic meaning? *The lamp of God had not yet been extinguished,* that is, it was not yet dawn, for the outer compartment of the sanctuary was illuminated by a night lamp (see Exod. 27:20f.; 30:7-8; Lev. 24:1-4). So, it is reasonable to hold with McCarter that the present incident took place "just before dawn."[7] Birch sees here reference "both to the near extinguishing of divine vision in Israel (v. 1b) and to the waning of Eli's literal vision as well as his role as a priestly source of spiritual vision (v. 2)."[8] One might wisely avoid making allegorical interpretation especially in our "post-modern" society in which multiple readings are encouraged and meanings are admittedly created by readers.

Lying down in the temple — Driver suggests that Samuel slept in a chamber contiguous to the "temple";[9] R. P. Gordon cites a Targumic tradition: "and Samuel was sleeping in the court of the Levites and the voice was heard from the temple of the Lord."[10] On "temple," see 1 Sam. 1:9. However, since the ark was kept in the inner place (i.e., "the holy of holies," *d^e^bîr)* at the back of the temple, Samuel must have slept in the main room of the temple *(hêkāl).* Probably he slept there to carry out a task or be on call for some duty.

The *ark*[11] of God appears for the first time in Samuel; the syntax of *'ărôn 'ĕlōhîm* is probably to be explained as a construct with an objective genitive, namely, "the ark for God." It cannot be a chest to put God in; rather, "the ark for God" would mean "the ark for symbolizing God or for his presence on the earth."[12] The mention of the ark here prepares the reader for the narrative in the following chapters.

6. For the distinction between "circumstantial" and "parenthetical," see Lambdin, §132.

7. McCarter, p. 98.

8. Birch, p. 992.

9. Driver, p. 42.

10. R. P. Gordon, p. 89.

11. Here, *the ark of God* (*'ărôn 'ĕlōhîm;* also 1 Sam. 4:11). Cf. *'ărôn hā'ĕlōhîm* (x31), all in Samuel and Chronicles; *'ărôn 'ĕlōhê yiśrā'ēl* (1 Sam. 5:7, 8 [x3], 10, 11; 6:3), all in Samuel; *'ărôn YHWH* (x37), 20 times (e.g., 1 Sam. 4:6; 5:3-4; 6:1) in 1-2 Samuel.

12. See I. Wilson, *Out of the Midst of the Fire; Divine Presence in Deuteronomy* (SBLDS 151; Atlanta: Scholars Press, 1995). See also on 1 Sam. 4:3-4.

b. The Lord Calls Samuel (3:4-14)

After three cycles of a pseudo-dialogue (vv. 4-9), the main part begins:

(1) 4-5 The Lord called → Samuel ran to Eli → Eli denied
(2) 6-7 The Lord called → Samuel ran to Eli → Eli denied
(3) 8-9 The Lord called → Samuel ran to Eli → Eli realized
(4) 10-14 The Lord called → Samuel responded → The Lord revealed his message
— CLIMAX: the longest "direct discourse" in this chapter —
(5) 15-18 Eli called → Samuel responded
→ Eli asked → Samuel reported → Eli accepted

(1) First Call (3:4-5)

4 *The Lord called to Samuel*[13]
and he answered,[14]
"Here I am!"
5 *and ran to Eli and said,*
"Here I am! For you called me."
And he said,
"I did not call. Go back and lie down."
And he went and lay down.

4 *The Lord called* — this is the first action, after a long SETTING (vv. 1-3). We cannot be sure where the Lord called from, possibly from the ark; Samuel answered immediately where he was ("Here I am!" i.e., "Coming!" or "What is it?" [see Gen. 22:7]) before running to Eli and answering again ("Here I am!"). This is more vivid than mentioning Samuel's reply only once.

5 Five *wayqtl* verbs *(and ran . . . and said . . . and he said. . . . And he went and lay down)* follow one after another in this single verse, indicating a very quick tempo in this part of the narrative.

(2) Second Call (3:6-7)

6 *Again*[15] *the Lord called*
"Samuel!"

13. Cf. "Samuel! Samuel!" (NRSV, McCarter), following LXX^B, 4QSam^a, and most commentators. The LXX repeats the name again in v. 6. Such a repetition should not be enforced mechanically on a narrative story like Samuel, though it is not uncommon in the Lord's calling. See v. 10 below.

14. Namely, "Samuel answered"; lit., "he said."

15. *'ôd* is a discourse marker. Here it seems redundant to have both *wayyōsep*

and Samuel arose and went to Eli
and said,
"Here I am! For you called me."
And he said,
"I did not call, my son. Go back and lie down."
7 *— Samuel did not yet know the Lord;*
the word of the Lord had not yet been revealed to him —

6-7 Malamat notes a case of a divine manifestation in Mari where the same dream recurred on two successive nights to an inexperienced boy.[16] *Samuel did not yet know the Lord* suggests that Samuel did not yet have the intimate knowledge of personal relationship with the Lord, though he had been ministering to the Lord (v. 1). In this sentence (v. 7), "to know the Lord" is restated by the parallel phrase "the word of the Lord is revealed." Hence, "to know the Lord" means to know the will of the Lord who reveals himself through his word.

(3) Third Call (3:8-9)

8 *And the Lord called, "Samuel!"*[17] *for the third time*
and he arose and went to Eli
and said,
"Here I am! For you called me."
And Eli realized that the Lord had been calling the boy.
9 *And Eli said to Samuel,*
"Go and lie down.
And if he calls you,
say, 'Speak! Lord![18] *For your servant is listening.' "*
And Samuel went and lay down in his place.

8 Threefold repetition is significant in the Bible (e.g., John 21:15-17) as well as in magical incantations; here it is the Lord, not a man, who repeats three times, and in fact he actually calls Samuel four times. The triple repetition made Eli think seriously of this unusual matter.

YHWH qᵉrōʾ and *ʿôd,* but this construction appears also in 1 Sam. 7:13; 18:29; 23:4; 27:4; 2 Sam. 2:22, 28; 5:22; 7:20; 14:10; 18:22.

16. See A. Malamat, "Intuitive Prophecy — A General Survey," in *Abraham Malamat, Mari and the Bible* (Leiden: E. J. Brill, 1998), p. 76; see A. Malamat, "A Mari Prophecy and Nathan's Dynastic Oracle," in *Prophecy: Essays Presented to Georg Fohrer on His Sixty-fifth Birthday, 6 September 1980,* ed. J. A. Emerton (BZAW 150; Berlin: Walter de Gruyter, 1980), pp. 68-82.

17. Or "the Lord called Samuel."

18. So MT, LXX^L; but McCarter, p. 95, omits this with LXX^B. See v. 10.

The key word *boy* in ch. 2 appears again in this chapter (the only time since v. 1), though *Samuel* has already replaced it in the present section of narrative.

9 *For* is a speaker-oriented *kî;* it means here "the reason why I ask you to speak is because I am listening"; see "Introduction" (Section V, C).

(4) Fourth Call and His Message (3:10-14)

10 *And the Lord came and stood and called as previously,*
"Samuel! Samuel!"
And Samuel said,
"Speak! For your servant is listening."
11 *And the Lord said to Samuel,*
"Now I am going to do a thing in Israel
such that as for everyone who hears it, his two ears will tingle!
12 *On that day,*
concerning Eli, I will establish all that I have spoken
about his house from beginning to end.[19]
13 *And I will tell*[20] *him*
that I am indeed[21] *judging his house forever,*
because of his iniquity in[22] *knowing*
that his sons were bringing a curse upon themselves
but not restraining them.
14 *Therefore, I swear concerning the house of Eli:*
'The iniquity of the house of Eli shall never[23] *be atoned for*
by sacrifice or by offering!' "

10 For the first time it is said that the Lord "came" and "stood" before he called. Until now, only "calling" has been mentioned. Does this mean that the Lord had been calling from a distance and now, finally, came close and

19. So McCarter, p. 94. Lit., "beginning and ending," i.e., "accomplishing my full purpose" (BDB, p. 320). This is a merismatic expression with inf. abs. (Lambdin, §172) rather than inf. cstr. (so BDB) + inf. abs., used as a hendiadys (GKC, §113h).

20. The grammatical form of *w^{e}higgádtî* may be explained either as a <*waw* + pf.>, with a retraction of stress, or as a performative perfect: "I tell him" (= "I tell [you NOW to tell] him"), like "I swear [NOW]" (v. 14).

21. "Judging" is the first word in the sentence and so is emphasized. Normally the participle follows a stated subject: here "I."

22. Or "on a charge of the fact that": *b* + <cstr.n. *ʿăwōn*> + *ʾăšer;* reason for being judged; so "because" (McCarter, p. 96); see 2 Sam. 3:8b "charge me now with a crime concerning this woman" (NRSV).

23. Lit., "not . . . forever."

called? Probably so. It is possible that "the revelation to Samuel involved a vision as well as an audition,"[24] but the vision was not so overwhelming and frightening that Samuel could not listen to God's aural message and comprehend its meaning.

Samuel! Samuel!: see "Abraham! Abraham!" (Gen. 22:11); "Jacob! Jacob!" (Gen. 46:2); "Moses! Moses!" (Exod. 3:4). Such repeated pronunciations of a person's name may have a special significance. God called them at crucial times in their lives.

Speak!: this verse lacks "Lord!" unlike v. 9; repetition with variation is typical of narrative; verbatim repetition is not necessary.

11 The Lord is preparing Samuel to be his messenger, that is, "prophet," by informing Samuel of what he is going to do in Israel.

A thing . . . such that . . . : literally, "a word." God's word = God's matter = God's will. Here *a thing* refers to a disaster or a terrible thing, as conveyed by the man of God in 1 Sam. 2:27-36. The expression *his two ears will tingle (tᵉṣillênāh štê 'oznâw)* also appears in 2 K. 21:12 and Jer. 19:3. While the latter two passages specify "disaster" *(rāʿāh),* the present text reads "a thing" *(dābār).* The use of this phrase in the other two passages does not automatically mean that this verse derives from the late monarchic period, since the corpus we have of surviving ancient Israelite documents is far too limited to determine dates statistically.[25]

12 The phrase *concerning Eli* is here topicalized with the resumptive pronoun *his* later in the sentence.[26] Verse 19, "let none of his words fall to the ground," rather supports our interpretation; note the contrast between "to establish" and "demolish" (i.e., "rise" vs "fall"). In 2 Samuel 7, God says he will "establish" David's house, but here the establishment of God's word means the destruction of Eli's house.

All that I have spoken includes, but is not necessarily limited to, 2:27-36, as R. P. Gordon notes.[27]

13 *Judging* here means "punishing." It has "an ironic touch,"[28] since

24. McCarter, p. 98.

25. Cf. McCarter, p. 98.

26. McCarter reads the preposition *'el-* (here as "concerning") as *'al* with the LXX *(epi)* and Syr., Targ., Vulg. He notes the frequent interchange between the two prepositions in MT Samuel, thus translating "against"; also cf. "fulfill against" (JPS; NRSV) and "carry out against" (NASB; NIV). While the Qal of *qwm is collocated with *'al* and often refers to "the one who rises against," which is paired with "enemy" *('yb)* in Hebrew as well as in Ugaritic, the Hi. construction here with the object *all that I have spoken* (see on 1 Sam. 1:23) would mean "to establish" (lit., "cause to rise"), and the preposition *'el* (MT) is most naturally to be taken as "about, concerning." See Fisher, *RSP* 1, p. 98.

27. R. P. Gordon, p. 89.

28. R. P. Gordon, p. 90.

the judge will be judged; compare Eli "judged" Israel (4:18) and "the Lord judges" the earth (2:10).

Were bringing a curse upon themselves — "to themselves" is a case of <Tiq. soph.>, that is, "corrections of scribes," where a phrase that could be considered blasphemous was altered. The original text may have read *ʾlhym* (see LXX), "(were blaspheming) God" (NRSV),[29] which was changed to *lāhem* "to them." In Hebrew this meant just leaving out the initial *aleph.* Close parallels are Exod. 22:28 and Lev. 24:15, and there are similar other cases involving removing or inserting an *aleph.* Zipor,[30] however, accepts the possibility that the *ʾalep* was omitted accidentally.

JPS's and NASB's translation "rebuke" for our *restraining* (also NRSV; NIV) would contradict 2:22-25, where Eli rebuked his sons.

14 Here "the doom of the house of Eli is sealed by an awful oath of disinvestiture."[31] *I swear* is a performative verb with the first person perfect of "to swear" (Ni. *šbʿ) as in Gen. 22:16; 2 Sam. 19:7; Jer. 22:5; etc.; compare "have I sworn."[32] See on 1 Sam. 20:42.

The term *be atoned* is a Hit. of *kpr. Three foundational meanings have been proposed: (a) cover, (b) ransom or (c) wipe away.[33] Eli's house had despised *the sacrifice and offering* (2:29), and hence these things will not have any efficacy on their behalf. Though normal or inadvertent sins of priests could be expiated by offering (Lev. 4:3-12), Eli's sons had sinned defiantly, and their guilt could not be removed (Num. 15:30f.; cf. Heb. 10:26).[34] Note that in 2:25 a relationship with men can be established through mediation and intercession. For "sacrifice" + "offering," see 1 Sam. 2:29.

c. Eli Calls Samuel (3:15-18)

15 *And Samuel lay down till morning and opened the doors of the*
house of the Lord — Samuel was afraid to tell Eli what he saw —
16 *and Eli called Samuel:*
"Samuel, my son!"
and he said,
"Here I am!"
17 *and he said,*
"What is the word that he told you?

29. McCarter, p. 96.

30. M. A. Zipor, "Some Notes on the Origin of the Tradition of the Eighteen *tiqqûnê sôp^{e}rîm,*" *VT* 44 (1994) 92.

31. R. P. Gordon, p. 90.

32. McCarter, p. 94.

33. See *NIDOTTE,* II, pp. 689-710. Also see 2 Sam. 21:3.

34. R. P. Gordon, p. 90.

Do not hide it from me!
May God do thus to you and even more
if you hide from me even one word
of everything that he told you!"

18 *And Samuel told him all the words and did not hide any from him.*
And he said,
"He is the Lord.
He will do what pleases him."

15 Samuel *was afraid to tell* about *what he saw.* Although the Hebrew term *mar'āh* is the term for "vision," nothing indicates a visual act by Samuel in the context. As in v. 21, here the Lord revealed himself to Samuel through "words"; note that God's revelation through voice was clearly communicated to Eli by words. Here Samuel is playing his role as the prophet of the Lord for the first time by delivering God's message as the one who *was called* by Him, *received* His message, and *was sent* as His messenger.[35]

16 The phrase *and Eli called Samuel* (lit., "and Eli called Samuel and said") is a direct sequel to the motion *opened the doors* (v. 15), since *Samuel was afraid . . .* is subsidiary to the main line narrative. Eli was ready to call him as soon as he heard Samuel open the doors, as if he were eagerly waiting for him. Note also the dialogue pattern (see also on 1 Sam. 9:6, 9; 20:2; 28:2) here:

16a A said to B
16b and he (B) said
17 and he (A) said

17-18 "The formal, ritualistic nature" of Eli's words has been compared by Hurowitz to a newly published text ("a diviner's protocol") from Mari. This is "an oath of loyalty and professional conduct to be taken by diviners to king Zimri-lim."[36] According to Hurowitz, "Not only are the content and circumstances similar, but the language of the diviner's oath and of Eli's adjuration of Samuel are strikingly alike."[37] Verse 17 can be compared with the Mari text:

. . . .

[In whatever extispicics] will be performed and I obser[ve,]

35. For a useful summary of the recent studies in prophets and prophecy, see R. P. Gordon, ed., *"The Place Is Too Small for Us": The Israelite Prophets in Recent Scholarship* (SBTS 5; Winona Lake, Ind.: Eisenbrauns, 1995). See also the commentary on v. 20.

36. Hurowitz, "Eli's Adjuration of Samuel," p. 489.

37. Hurowitz, "Eli's Adjuration of Samuel," p. 490.

[Any evil and not go]od entrails which I observe
[to Zimri-lim my lord] I will tell and will not conceal.

Hurowitz suggests that in Israel too prophets may have been called upon to take an oath to reveal all they were told.[38] It is possible that Eli is drawing upon such an oath formula. However, here Eli is adjuring Samuel, not taking an oath himself. Since no one had realized before that Samuel was a prophet, Samuel himself would hardly have taken such an oath.

17 The entire verse constitutes a chiasmus: *that he spoke to you* (A) — *hide it from me* (B) — *hide from me* (B′) — *that he spoke to you* (A′).[39] At the center of this chiastic structure comes the oath formula, *May God do thus to you and do so again if.* This is "a conventional form of adjuration which does not specify the penalty for non-compliance; a gesture may have been enough."[40]

18 The phrase *did not hide* is a negated antonym of *told;* see the commentary on v. 1. The expression can be rightly compared with the Akkadian phrase *lu aqabbi la akattamu,* "I will tell and will not conceal," in the above "diviner's protocol" from Mari.[41]

Once the message is confirmed as from the Lord, Eli accepts God's sovereign will.

d. Terminus (3:19-21)

19 *And Samuel grew up. The Lord was with him and let none of his words fall to the ground.*
20 *And all Israel, from Dan to Beersheba, knew that Samuel was established as a prophet of the Lord.*
21 *And the Lord continued to appear in Shiloh, for the Lord revealed himself to Samuel in Shiloh by the word of the Lord.*

19 The last verses, vv. 19-21, constitute the TERMINUS of the entire discourse of ch. 3. For *grew up,* see 2:21. After this first experience as a prophet of the Lord, Samuel kept growing, preparing to become a mature prophet both physically and spiritually.

38. Hurowitz, "Eli's Adjuration of Samuel," p. 491.

39. See E. J. Revell, "The Repetition of Introductions to Speech as a Feature of Biblical Hebrew," VT 47 (1997) 94, n. 7. This chiastic structure has already been noted by Watson, "The Structure of 1 Sam 3," pp. 90-93; J. P. Fokkelman, IV; Hurowitz, "Eli's Adjuration of Samuel," p. 488: "the interrogation and adjuration are tightly bound together with a chiastic formulation."

40. R. P. Gordon, p. 90; also McCarter, p. 99. See on 1 Sam. 20:13, also 14:44 and 2 Sam. 3:9. See Driver, pp. 44-45, for a complete list of occurrences of this formula.

41. Hurowitz, "Eli's Adjuration of Samuel," pp. 483-97.

Let none of his words fall to the ground: literally, "did not cause any of his entire words fall to the ground." *His words* means Samuel's words (cf. 9:6) and hence refer to the Lord's words. Thus, he could be known as a prophet (Deut. 18:21-22). This is the negated opposite of "establish his word" in v. 12. See also 1 Sam. 9:6. On the relationship between the prophet and the word of Yahweh, see Amos 3:8; Jer. 20:8-9.

20 *From Dan to Beersheba* refers to the traditional limits of Israel to the north and south (cf. 2 Sam. 17:11).

There are two main views on the etymology of *prophet (nābî').* (1) A *passive* interpretation, "one who is called," based on Akkadian verb *nabû,* "to call by name, to call to duty" and used especially of the calling of men by gods. Albright and others explain Hebrew *nābî'* as "one called to duty by a god."[42] (2) An *active* interpretation: (a) "the speaker,"[43] like Aaron for Moses in Exod. 7:1; or (b) "one who calls/invokes," suggested by Fleming[44] and based on Emar texts; see 1 Sam. 12:17. The term *nabû* also appears once in the Mari texts in *ARMT,* XXVI.216.1-13, 3′-9′, a reference to "the prophets *(nabû)* of the Hanum." There, the *nābû*'s main task is said to be "to predict in security matters."[45] Those designated as *nābî'* in OT are Abraham, Moses, Gad, Nathan, Ahijah, Jehu, Elisha, Jonah, Isaiah, Jeremiah, Hananiah, Habakkuk, Haggai, Zechariah, Elijah, Shemaiah, Iddo, Oded, and Samuel, as well as the prophetesses Deborah and Hulda.[46] Whether the biblical *n^ebî'îm* were "ecstatics" or not is still debated.[47]

Prophets and oracles existed outside Israel from before the time of Moses, but as far as we know, there is nothing to show they were concerned with the religious, ethical, and social problems that the major prophets of Israel dealt with.[48]

42. McCarter, p. 99.

43. S. Shaviv, "*nābî'* and *nāgîd* in 1 Samuel ix 1–x 16," *VT* 34 (1984) 111; T. L. Fenton, "Deuteronomistic Advocacy of the *nābî':* 1 Samuel ix 9 and Questions of Israelite Prophecy," *VT* 47 (1997) 35.

44. D. Fleming, "*Nābû* and *Munabbiātu:* Two New Syrian Religious Personnel," *JAOS* 113 (1993) 175-83; "The Etymological Origins of the Hebrew *nābî';* The One Who Invokes God," *CBQ* 55 (1993) 217-24.

45. M. Anbar, "Mari and the Origin of Prophecy," in *Kinattūtu ša dārâti: Raphael Kutscher Memorial Volume,* ed. A. F. Rainey (Occasional Publications No. 1; Tel Aviv: Tel Aviv University, 1993), p. 2.

46. See *HALOT,* p. 662.

47. See on 1 Sam. 10:5. On the older designation for prophet, "seer" *(rō'eh),* see on 9:9. On the verbal forms, see on 10:5. For Mari prophets, see R. P. Gordon, "From Mari to Moses: Prophecy at Mari and in Ancient Israel," in *Of Prophets' Visions and the Wisdom of the Sages,* ed. H. McKay and D. J. A. Clines (JSOTSS 162; Sheffield: Sheffield Academic Press, 1993), pp. 63-79; most recently Malamat, "Intuitive Prophecy," pp. 59-82.

48. See R. P. Gordon, p. 91; McCarter, p. 99.

21 The phrase *the word of the Lord* here and in v. 1 forms an *inclusio*. Together with the appearance of the phrase in v. 7, this emphasizes the importance of God's word, which the prophet, the messenger of God, is called to communicate. Therefore, for the biblical prophets, their messages are more important than their experiences, though the latter are not ignored if they bear God's message as in the case of Hosea. Note that the term *vision* (v. 1) no longer appears in the final verse, though it mentions that *the Lord continued to appear.* Another key word here is *revealed,* which appears in v. 7 as well as in 1 Sam. 2:27. Thus, because of the prophet Samuel, Shiloh changes from a place of infrequent vision to one known for its prophet. But in the next chapter, Israel and the cult centered at Shiloh pass through a dark period.

We now see Samuel at the point towards which the whole story has led, from the time before his birth by God's action, through the notes of his growing up. He had served God as a child in the temple, but now he serves all Israel as a prophet.

B. STORY OF THE ARK OF GOD (4:1–7:1)

The biblical narrative suddenly changes to the Philistine campaign against Israel. Not only was Israel defeated in the battle, but the ark of the Lord was also captured and Eli's two sons, as well as Eli, died. The ark was brought into enemy territory (ch. 5), but the Philistines sent it back to Israelite territory after they suffered greatly because the "hand of Yahweh" was heavy on them (ch. 6). Even though the ark was captured, Yahweh was not vanquished. He was certainly the Lord even in the enemy territory.

It is often held, with Rost,[1] that the story of the capture of the ark of God originally constituted an independent "Ark Narrative" — the account of the installation of the ark in Jerusalem in 2 Samuel 6 was part of this narrative; see "Introduction" (Section III, A, 1). "If so," R. P. Gordon holds, "the obvious connections between ch. 4 and what precedes make it unlikely that 4:1b represents the start of the original 'Ark Narrative,' whatever else may be said on the subject."[2] As Miller and Roberts[3] argue, the original story of the

1. L. Rost, *Die Überlieferung von der Thronnachfolge Davids* (Stuttgart: W. Kohlhammer, 1926) = *Das kleine Credo und andere Studien zum Alten Testament* (Heidelberg: Quelle und Meyer, 1965), pp. 119-253; *The Succession to the Throne of David* (Sheffield: Almond, 1982).

2. R. P. Gordon, p. 92.

3. P. D. Miller, Jr. and J. J. M. Roberts, *The Hand of the Lord: A Reassessment of the "Ark Narrative" of 1 Samuel* (JHNES; Baltimore: Johns Hopkins University Press, 1977). See on 1 Sam. 5:1, 6 for the ancient Near Eastern parallels.

ark, if such an independent story existed, probably included the section of 1 Samuel 2 which deals with the corruption of Eli's house, but not 2 Samuel 6. Besides, the account in 2 Samuel 6 is certainly from a later perspective than that in 1 Samuel 4–6, and the same location is referred to by two different geographical names, Kiriath-jearim (6:21) and Baalah of Judah (2 Sam. 6:2) in the two accounts. Therefore, it is difficult to prove that there existed an independent "Ark Narrative" as an originally single story.

As discussed below, 1 Sam. 4:1a functions as a link, initiating a new section while referring back to the preceding episode in ch. 3. On chs. 4–6 as an embedded discourse in the wider narrative chs. 1–7, see ch. 1.

1. Capture of the Ark (4:1-22)

All Israel acknowledged that "Samuel was established as a prophet of the Lord" (1 Sam. 3:20), and his word, which was the word of the Lord (3:21) through him, eventually spread all over Israel (4:1a). But it seems that his prophetic office did not yet influence political matters. Eli was still the judge who ruled Israel. Samuel's role as "judge" is first mentioned in 1 Sam. 7:6, at least twenty years later.

At this point one would naturally expect an account of the influence of Samuel as the officially established prophet of Yahweh (see 3:20), but the narrator instead directs the audience's attention to another officially established institution, the priestly family at Shiloh and its near extermination as prophesized by the Lord in 1 Sam. 2:31-34 and 3:12-14. This is as if the author/narrator aims to remove Eli and his family before concentrating on Samuel. All these things resulted in the capture of the ark of the Lord, the symbol and guarantee of the divine presence. Such a disaster had never happened in the history of the covenant people Israel. Certainly this was one of the darkest times for them. This also gives the background for Samuel's success.

a. Defeat of Israel (4:1-11)

1 *Around the time when*[4] *the word of Samuel spread through Israel,*[5] *Israel marched out to meet the Philistines for war and encamped by Ebenezer, while the Philistines encamped at Aphek.*

2 *Then the Philistines deployed themselves to meet Israel and the*

4. Lit., "and it was." The *wayhî* introduces a temporal verbless clause here. There is no need to reconstruct the text in favor of the LXX's longer text: "Eli grew very old, and his sons continued to act more and more wickedly in the presence of Yahweh" (McCarter, p. 102); see below.

5. Lit., "the word of Samuel [was] to all Israel."

battle broke out. Israel was defeated before the Philistines and about four thousand men were slain[6] *in battle lines in the field.*

3 *The people came to the camp, and the elders of Israel said,*
"Why did the Lord smite us today before the Philistines?
Let us take from Shiloh
the ark of the covenant[7] *of the Lord*
so that he/it may come among us
and save us from the hand of our enemies!"

4 *So the people sent a messenger to Shiloh and carried from there the ark of the covenant of the Lord of Hosts who sits*[8] *on the cherubim. Eli's two sons, Hophni and Phinehas, were there with the ark of the covenant of God.*

5 *When the ark of the covenant of the Lord came to the camp, all Israel shouted aloud, and the earth roared.*

6 *When the Philistines heard the noise of shouting, they said,*
"What[9] *does this great shouting*
in the camp of the Hebrews mean?"[10]
and learned that the ark of the Lord[11] *had come to the camp.*

7 *Then the Philistines were afraid, for they thought*[12] *that God had come to the camp, and said,*
"Alas for us!
For nothing like this has happened before.
8 *Alas for us!*
Who can deliver us from the hand of these mighty gods?
These are the gods
who struck Egypt with all plagues in the wilderness.
9 *Strengthen yourselves*
and be courageous, O Philistines,
or you must serve the Hebrews
as they have served you!

6. Lit., "they slew" impersonal passive.

7. McCarter omits "covenant" *(b^e^rît)* four times in vv. 3-5. S. D. Walters, "Review of P. Kyle McCarter, *I Samuel,* AB 8 (Garden City: Doubleday, 1980)," *JBL* 101 (1982) 437, wonders if McCarter is guided here by his presumption "that the ark as cherub throne is incompatible with the ark as covenant repository."

8. Yahweh is seated as the king; hence, "enthroned" (NRSV; NIV).

9. Heb. *meh* (spoken by the Philistines also in 1 Sam. 6:2; 29:4), rather than the standard form *māh,* might be a northern dialect; also in 1:8; 4:14; 15:14. See on 1:8.

10. Lit., "What is the sound of this great shouting?"

11. The expression *the ark of the Lord* appears here for the first time in Samuel; most instances are in 1 Samuel 6 and 2 Samuel 6; cf. "the ark of God" in 1 Sam. 3:3.

12. Lit., "said."

You must be courageous and fight!"
10 *So the Philistines fought.*
And Israel was struck and fled, every man to his own tent.
And the slaughter was very great,
thirty thousand infantry fell from Israel.
11 *As for the ark of God, it was captured; and Eli's two sons, Hophni and Phinehas, died.*

A war between the Israelites and the Philistines broke out somewhere between Ebenezer and Aphek. When Israel was defeated, with 4,000 men slain, the leaders of Israel thought that they could utilize the ark of God to acquire divine help in this crisis. However, contrary to their plan, the ark was captured by the Philistines and carried away to their country. From then on the real agent in the story is the ark itself. Both the Israelites and the Philistines were controlled by the ark. McCarter holds that "the theological purpose of the ark narrative as a whole" is to deal with the problem of "How can the Philistines have defied the power of Yahweh and prevailed?" The narrative affirms that "Yahweh was in control of the events from the beginning. . . . The ark was captured because Yahweh had chosen to abandon Israel on account of the wickedness of the Elides."[13]

1 The half verse *wayhî d^{e}bar-š^{e}mû'ēl l^{e}kol-yiśrā'ēl* (lit., "and the word of Samuel was to all Israel") is often grouped with the preceding chapter by scholars (so Hertzberg, McCarter, Klein, R. P. Gordon, Birch, etc.) and the NRSV. However, if *wayhî* is a simple expression at the end of the section, to be translated as "and the word of Samuel was toward all Israel," it is redundant given 3:19-21. And if this *wayhî* clause is indeed a temporal expression here, it would be strange to use it at the end of a section, for the last few verses of ch. 3 have already turned to the TERMINUS, which ends describing the relationship between Samuel and Yahweh in Shiloh, but this verse gives the impression that it is the start of new background information.

Rather than being a part of ch. 3, the *wayhî*-clause could be an example of a "transitional technique" (see "Introduction" [Section VI, B]), presenting the SETTING for the following event, linking a new episode with the previous episode. Thus, this link is a link of the A/aB type, in which key words (a) such as *word, Samuel,* and *all Israel* that appeared in the previous episode (A: ch. 3) are repeated at the beginning of the second episode (B: ch. 4). We would like to propose the following translation: *Around the time when the word of Samuel came toward all Israel.*

By the time of the present event, *all Israel* knew that Samuel "was es-

13. McCarter, p. 109.

tablished as a prophet of the Lord" (3:20) and his word was all over Israel (4:1). However, Samuel had not yet assumed his judgeship (see 7:6), for Eli the priest was alive, judging Israel (see on v. 18). There is no hint in the text that the Israelites marched out at Samuel's command or advice. When the "elders" decided to bring "the ark of the covenant of the Lord" from Shiloh (v. 3), Eli, the priest and judge, probably agreed with the decision, for his two sons accompanied the ark (v. 4), though his anxiety about the ark of God (v. 13) suggests that he had reservations. It seems, however, that Samuel the prophet of the Lord was not involved.

Then, where was Samuel? The narrative keeps silent about him until 7:3. The tragedy of this incident is that the people depended on political leaders (i.e., the elders) who too lightly sought help from a cultic object, the "ark of God," and did not seek the word of the Lord from his prophet. So 4:1a is timely preparation (SETTING) for the coming story (EVENT) in v. 1b onward. The implication of this verse as a whole, therefore, would be: "Though the word of Samuel was recognized throughout Israel, the people went out for battle without asking the will of the Lord through his prophet."

The verb "go out" *(yṣ')* is used with a military sense: hence, *marched out.*[14]

Here *the Philistines* make their debut in the books of Samuel. The earliest known attestation of the name Philistine *(Prst)* in extra-biblical texts is in the list of the "Sea Peoples" written in Egyptian in the temple of Rameses III at Medinet Habu in Thebes (the twelfth century B.C.). They settled along the coast of Canaan in the Early Iron I period and formed a pentapolis of Ashdod, Ashkelon, Gaza, Ekron and Gath. They posed a serious threat to the Israelites who lived in the eastern mountain areas. See "Introduction" (Section IV, B).

Ebenezer and *Aphek* lay at the southern end of the plain of Sharon, to the west of the hill country of Ephraim. The Philistines were interested in expanding their political power north of their territory. The location of *Ebenezer*[15] is unknown, but modern ʿIzbet Ṣarṭah [MR146-167] is an often-cited candidate. It is located 10 miles east of Tel Aviv on the road leading up to Shiloh. About 2 miles to the west of ʿIzbet Ṣarṭah, across the Aphek Pass, lies Tel Aphek.[16] *Aphek* (Gk. Antipatris; Arab. Tell Ras el-ʿAin [lit., "head of the spring"]) is located about 8 miles east of Tel Aviv [MR143-168]. As the

14. See *HALOT,* p. 425. For the word pair *bw'-yṣ'* as a military term, see the detailed study by A. van der Lingen, "*bw'-yṣ'* (to go out and to come in) as a Military Term," *VT* 42 (1992) 59-66.

15. For the etymology and the names with "stone," see on 1 Sam. 7:12.

16. See I. Finkelstein, "ʿIzbet Ṣarṭah," in *NEAEHL,* pp. 652-54. Cf. the maps in M. Kochavi, *Aphek-Antipatris: Five Seasons of Excavation at Tel Aphek-Antipatris (1972-1976)* (Tel Aviv: Tel-Aviv University, Institute of Archaeology, 1977), pp. 3, 10.

Arabic name suggests, it is a place with abundant water, situated near/at the sources of the Yarkon River, on the important access route the *Via Maris,* which had to come inland to this point because the river created a marsh in the coastal plain.

Aphek is first mentioned in the nineteenth-century B.C. Egyptian Execration Texts and is known also from the Assyrian records. It was of great military and commercial importance from earliest times.

Since the Yarkon River was the northern boundary of Philistia, there was a Philistine stronghold there from which they marched out to fight against the Israelites in the hill country (see 1 Sam. 29:1); a Philistine city has been excavated there.[17] The name Aphek may be related to A-pe-ke-e, a city in the kingdom of Pylos, from which the Philistines are said to have come,[18] though its Semitic etymology (cf. *'āpîq* "stream issuing from a spring"; see *HALOT,* p. 80) is more likely.

2 The basic meaning of the verb *deployed themselves* (*ʿrk) is "to arrange in order" for accomplishing a useful purpose.[19] Here, the troops draw up battle lines (Gen. 14:8; Judg. 20:20; etc.). It usually appears in a military context in Samuel: "to draw up in battle array to meet *(liqra't).*"

Another term, *broke out* (*tiṭṭōš:* lit., "loosened itself"; here in *nṭš, Qal, "intransitive"), is also used in a military sense as in Niphal (e.g., 2 Sam. 5:18, 22; Judg. 15:9 "spread out"). According to Tidwell,[20] the verb suggests "a dispersal of troops for some purpose." McCarter's translation "and the battle lines were deployed"[21] is not adequate, since the verb in the present context seems to refer to a certain action between the deployment and the defeat ("smitten").

About four thousand or "about four units" from *'elep* (pl. *'ălāpîm*) can mean (1) "thousand(s)," (2) "clan(s)" (1 Sam. 10:19; 23:23), or (3) "(military) unit(s)," i.e., "troops." Humphreys[22] recently suggested that "the average number of military men (aged over 20) per troop was about 10," while on the other hand McCarter has surmised "(perhaps) some twenty to fifty-six

17. See M. Kochavi, "Tel Aphek," *IEJ* 22 (1972) 238-39; *Aphek-Antipatris;* "Aphek," in *OEANE 1* (1997), pp. 147-51; O. Margalith, "Where Did the Philistines Come From?" *ZAW* 107 (1995) 106-7, n. 32.

18. Margalith, "Where Did the Philistines Come From?" 107.

19. See V. P. Hamilton, in *NIDOTTE,* 3, p. 536.

20. N. L. Tidwell, "The Philistine Incursions into the Valey of Rephaim (2 Sam. v 17ff.)," in *Studies in the Historical Books of the Old Testament,* ed. J. A. Emerton (VTS 30; Leiden: E. J. Brill, 1979), pp. 190-212.

21. McCarter, p. 8.

22. C. J. Humphreys, "The Number of People in the Exodus from Egypt: Decoding Mathematically the Very Large Numbers in Numbers I and XXVI," *VT* 48 (1998) 211.

men."[23] Scolnic, however, totally rejects the third possibility and accepts only "thousand" or "clan."[24] In the present context the term seems to be used in its first meaning.[25]

3 *The elders of Israel (ziqnê yiśrā'ēl)* were a group of senior tribal leaders, seventy in Num. 11:16-17, who were entrusted with important decisions (see also Exod. 18:13-27; Deut. 1:9-13). Here, they took the initiative in bringing the ark of the Lord from Shiloh while Eli was still officially the judge. At a later time, the elders of Israel took the initiative in demanding a king of Samuel the judge (1 Sam. 8:4). Even after the monarchy was introduced, the elders seem to have been influential with the king, as may be inferred from Saul's words to Samuel, "I have sinned; yet honor me now before the elders of my people and before Israel, and return with me" (15:30). See also on 2 Sam. 3:17. Thus, the elders of Israel were the representatives of the "congregation" *('ēdāh)*[26] and held special authority in deciding crucial political matters, especially when the leader of Israel, whether a judge or a king, did not prove himself to be adequate. In this sense, as Weinfeld notes, the judge was "a sort of deputy" of the *'ēdāh* or of the tribe.[27]

Why did the Lord smite us? Here the Israelites assume that Yahweh himself is the one who smote them and that their defeat was not brought about by chance. It seems they did not expect their defeat. Yet, they did not seek the words of the Lord through his servant the prophet but through a religious object, *the ark.* Strangely enough, throughout the narrative, Samuel keeps silence at this national crisis.

The collocation *take + the ark* is a key phrase in this ark narrative. The Israelites "took" (1 Sam. 4:3) the ark to the battlefield but it "was taken" (4:11, 17, 19, 21, 22) by the Philistines who "took" (5:1, 2) it to their city but eventually "took" (6:8) it back to Israel. The narrator probably conveys that the people treated this sacred object without respect as an instrument through which victory might be attained. Surely, the covenant people had lost the

23. McCarter, pp. 105, 107.

24. B. E. Scolnic, *Theme and Context in Biblical Lists* (SFSHJ 119; Atlanta: Scholars Press, 1995), pp. 26-28.

25. See on 1 Sam. 4:10; 6:19; and 10:19.

26. Weinfeld thinks that the congregation gave way in some respect to the monarchy since the term "appears for the last time in the Bible's historical literature in connection with Jeroboam's coronation" (1 K. 12:20); see M. Weinfeld, "Zion and Jerusalem as Religious and Political Capital: Ideology and Utopia," in *The Poet and the Historian: Essays in Literary and Historical Biblical Criticism,* ed. R. E. Friedman (HSS 26; Chico, Calif.: Scholars Press, 1983), pp. 75-76.

27. See Weinfeld, "Zion and Jerusalem as Religious and Political Capital," pp. 75-76. See H. Reviv, *The Elders in Ancient Israel* (Jerusalem: Magnes, 1989). See also on 1 Sam. 11:3.

sense of awesomeness toward God's holy presence. On the practice of capturing the enemy's gods in the ancient Near East, see on 5:1.

The phrase *the ark of the covenant of the Lord ('ărôn bᵉrît YHWH)* appears only in this chapter (4:3, 4, 5) in Samuel.[28] The "ark" already appeared in 3:3 ("the ark of God"). Here "the ark of the covenant of the Lord" can be explained grammatically either as (1) "the ark for the covenant of Yahweh" or as (2) "the Ark-of-covenant for symbolizing Yahweh"; "the ark-of-covenant" signifies here "the ark for keeping the covenant tablets." Moses was commanded by the Lord to put the tablets of the covenant into the ark (Exod. 25:16; Deut. 10:5; cf. 1 K. 8:9).

Not only was the ark a repository for the covenant, it was also "Yahweh's footstool or podium" (1 Chr. 28:2; also Ps. 99:5; 132:7; Lam. 2:1), "above which was the divine throne itself, flanked in the manner characteristic of Canaanite royal thrones by a pair of winged sphinxes or cherubim."[29] Thus, the ark was the visible sign of the holy presence of Yahweh whose real throne is on high above the heavens.[30] Exodus 25:22 says "I will be known to you there; I will speak to you from above the cover *(hakkappōret)* between the two cherubim which are over the ark of the testimony about. . . ."[31]

The conception of the ark as a visible sign of Yahweh's presence gave a military importance to the ark, as seen in Num. 10:33-36 and Joshua 3–4, 6; it functioned as a battle palladium for the armies of Israel; it showed that the Lord was present and fighting for Israel. This understanding is certainly behind the present story. That the ark would inevitably grant victory is a persistent idea which even the present story has not been able to dispel.

The term *covenant* (*bᵉrît;* an old NW Semitic term; see Ugar. *brt*) appears here for the first time in Samuel. It appears thirteen times in the two books: four times in the phrase "the ark of the covenant" and elsewhere to refer to a treaty between a king and a city (1 Sam. 11:1), to a compact between a king and the people (2 Sam. 3:21; 5:3), to the covenant between David and Jonathan (1 Sam. 18:3; 20:8; 23:18), to the agreement between David and Abner (2 Sam. 3:12-13), and to "an everlasting covenant" between God and David (23:5). To refer to the ark, the elders of Israel could have said simply "the ark of God" as in 1 Sam. 3:3, but they use the full description here, that

28. The other twenty-seven occurrences are mainly in historical writings (see Num. 10:33; Deut. 10:8; Josh. 3:3, 17; 1 K. 6:19; Jer. 3:16; 1 Chr. 15:25; 2 Chr. 5:2, 7; etc. The similar phrase *'ărôn bᵉrît hā'ĕlōhîm* "the ark of the covenant of God" appears only in historical books: i.e., Judg. 20:27; 1 Sam. 4:4; 2 Sam. 15:24; 1 Chr. 16:6.

29. McCarter, p. 108.

30. See D. T. Tsumura, "*šmym — Heaven, Sky, Firmament, Air," in NIDOTTE,* 4, pp. 160-66.

31. Also Exodus 37; Ezek. 1:22-26; 10:1. On the "cherubim," see on v. 4.

is, *the ark of the covenant of the Lord.* It may be that the elders wanted to reaffirm the status of Israel as the covenant people of Yahweh. McCarter omits all four occurrences of "covenant" in 4:3-5. Yet this is "not textual criticism, but textual improvement, with the commentator's literary sense the standard."[32]

The subject of the verb *come* is purposely ambiguous in Hebrew; did the elders mean *he* or *it*? If "he," they view the ark as representing the divine presence. However, "it" is preferable, for it was seemingly the cultic object, not Yahweh himself, that they put their trust in; they may have thought that the Lord smote them because they had not trusted in the ark and neglected it. Or perhaps they just thought that the ark of the Lord would perform a miracle, and so they tried to use it magically. Later, Jeremiah refers to the day when the covenant people of God will no longer remember "the ark of the covenant of the Lord," for Jerusalem itself will be called "the throne of the Lord" (see Jer. 3:16-17).

The term *hand* here is literally "palm" (cf. "hand" in 1 Sam. 4:8). "Palm" symbolizes more concretely than "hand" that they are under the control (or grasp) of the enemy.

4 To *carry* the ark is the proper method of moving it (see 2 Sam. 6:13; cf. 2 Sam. 6:3; also Deut. 10:8; Josh. 3:6; 6:6; 1 K. 2:26).

The phrase *the Lord of Hosts who sits on the cherubim* is the full title for Yahweh, the sovereign King of the universe; with this full title, the narrator ironically hints at the people's confidence in the ark rather than in Yahweh whom the ark symbolizes (see 2 Sam. 6:2). For *the Lord of Hosts,* see on 1 Sam. 1:3.

The *cherubim* appear often in the iconography of the ancient Near East; they are hybrid figures with animal and human characteristics often pictured at palace entrances or other royal places, as the much-quoted carving on an eleventh-century Byblos royal coffin and on an engraved ivory.[33]

5 The roaring (*hwm) of the earth like thunder must have sounded like a real threat to the Philistines, since images of roarings of the earth as well as raging storms signify destruction in descriptions of actual battles.[34] However, the roaring of the earth is not necessarily the same as an earthquake

32. Walters, "Review of McCarter, *I Samuel* (1980)," pp. 437-38.

33. See T. N. D. Mettinger, *The Dethronement of Sabaoth: Studies in the Shem and Kabod Theologies* (Lund: C.W.K. Gleerup, 1982), p. 21. On the cherub-throne iconography of Shiloh and later Jerusalem, see F. M. Cross, Jr., *Canaanite Myth and Hebrew Epic* (Cambridge, Mass.: Harvard, 1973), chs. 2–3. On the cherubim in general, see Mettinger, in *DDD,* pp. 362-67, 1736; C. Meyers, "Cherubim," in *ABD,* I, pp. 899-900.

34. See D. T. Tsumura, "The So-called 'Chaos Tradition' behind Psalm 46," *Evangelical Theology* 11 (1980) 95-96 [Japanese with an English summary]. Also on 1 Sam. 7:10.

(see on 1 Sam. 14:15). Here, it points to the overconfidence of the covenant people in the cultic object. They trusted in the ark of the Lord rather than the word of the Lord.

6 *Hebrews (ʿibrîm)* is used here by non-Israelites of the Israelites in a pejorative sense (also v. 9; 13:19; 14:11; 29:3).[35] The term also occurs in reference to the Israelites in a foreign context or in their relation to non-Israelites (see 13:3, 7; 14:21)[36] and in descriptions of a fellow slave who became temporarily a "foreigner" in his own society.[37] However, the Hebrew word formation as a gentilic *(ʿibrî)* suggests that it is a patronymic based on the name of Eber *(ʿēber),*[38] the great-grandson of Shem (Gen. 10:21-25; 11:10-17). So, in the biblical traditions, "Hebrew" is an *ethnic* term (see Gen. 14:13) distinct from *religio-political* designations such as "Israel," "sons of Israel," etc.[39] See on 13:3b.

The background and origin of this term is disputed, however.[40] There are references in the second millennium to a group of people called *ʿāpiru* (Akk. *Ḫabiru,* Egy. *ʿpr.w* and Ugar. *ʿpr*), but there is no scholarly consensus about who they were, or about their connection with the "Hebrews." They apparently were nomadic people living near cities who sometimes tried to seize land, or they were bands formed from various outcast groups.[41] They were a "social group" apparently made up of people who had abandoned urban life to become "gypsies." Among them were probably escaped slaves, debtors, fugitives from lawsuits, and the generally disaffected.[42]

It may be that the terms "Hebrew" and *Ḫabiru,* etc., are cognates and denote one who "crossed over" from urban to "nomadic" life. A. R. Millard thinks that the biblical use derives from the second millennium use, which suits Joseph and others well, taking a more particular meaning when Habiru in general had disappeared from the Fertile Crescent at the end of the Late Bronze Age.[43]

35. Also Gen. 39:14, 17; 41:12; Exod. 1:16, 19; 2:6, 7.

36. Also Gen. 14:13; 40:15; 43:32; Exod. 1:15; 2:11, 13; 3:18; 5:3; 7:16; 9:1, 13; 10:3; Jon. 1:9.

37. Exod. 21:2; Deut. 15:12; Jer. 34:9, 14.

38. Note that in Ebla there was a king named Ebrium, which could be a cognate of the Hebrew name *Eber.* However, no identity between the two is involved.

39. See McCarter, p. 240.

40. See H. Cazelles, "The Hebrews," in *POTT,* pp. 1-28.

41. See G. E. Mendenhall, *The Tenth Generation: The Origins of the Biblical Tradition* (Baltimore: Johns Hopkins University, 1973), ch. V; N. P. Lemche, "Ḫabiru," in *ABD,* III, pp. 6-10.

42. W. Zwickel notes the important role that *Habiru* had taken for establishing the Davidic kingdom; see "Der Beitrag der *Ḫabiru* zur Entstehung des Königtums," *UF* 28 (1996) 751-66.

43. Personally suggested.

7 From the narrator's viewpoint, *'ĕlōhîm* must be singular, hence God; so, the verbal form, *bā'* ("had come") is singular (cf. "Gods" [McCarter, p. 102]). R. P. Gordon explains: "the Philistines regard the Ark as the equivalent of an image, which is exactly how they treated it when it came into their hands (cf. 5:2)."[44]

Alas for us is the cry of woe conventionally uttered in the face of sudden peril.[45]

8 Note that the word *'ĕlōhîm* is plural in this context (with plural adjective and pronoun: *these mighty gods*) where a polytheistic viewpoint is put in the mouths of the Philistines. They must have heard about the great saving works of Yahweh against the Egyptians — geographically Philistia and Lower Egypt are not far apart.[46] Philistia was the first part of Canaan that an Egyptian would mark.

In Exodus the plagues occurred in Egypt, not *in the wilderness;* hence, McCarter translates: "and with pestilence," reading *ûbĕmō-deber.* On the other hand, R. P. Gordon holds the view that the LXX translation "*and* in the wilderness" may preserve a better reading.[47] However, the MT's imprecise expression itself might support the idea that the Philistines heard about the Lord's saving acts both in Egypt and in the wilderness. It is noteworthy that the "Deuteronomistic" history here draws its "theological impetus" from the Pentateuchal materials (see Num. 10:33-36) other than Deuteronomy (also 6:6).[48]

9 For the expression *Strengthen yourselves and be courageous,* see 1 K. 2:2: "Be strong, be courageous/show yourself a man (*hyh + *l*^e*'îš:* lit., become a man)" in David's charge to Solomon. A similar expression to *be courageous* (lit., "become men") may be seen in an Amarna letter (EA 289:26-30), if the reading is correct ("Be men [*lū amīlātunu!*] . . . and let us break with Jerusalem!"[49]), as well as in 2 Sam. 13:28 ("Be strong; be brave!" [*hyh + *libnê-ḥāyil*], lit., "Become sons of strength!"); also 2 Sam. 10:12. In this context is a sorites in which A *(strengthen yourselves)* — B *(be courageous),* B *(be courageous)* — C *(fight)* constitutes a gradation.[50]

You must serve. Here it was not so much a question of land as a question of who would serve whom. Note Goliath's words in 1 Sam. 17:9.

44. R. P. Gordon, p. 95.

45. See McCarter, p. 106, for bibliography.

46. For the Exodus pattern in this part of the narrative, see D. Daube, *The Exodus Pattern in the Bible* (London: Faber & Faber, 1963).

47. R. P. Gordon, p. 95.

48. J. G. McConville, "Priesthood in Joshua to Kings," *VT* 49 (1999) 75.

49. So McCarter, p. 106. However, W. L. Moran, *Les Lettres d'el Amarna* (LAPO 13; Paris: Éditions du Cerf, 1987), p. 518 rather reads this obscure text as "Soyez tous les deux une protection" *(lu-ú 2 ṣíl-la-tu-nu).*

50. See D. T. Tsumura, "Sorites in Psalm 133, 2-3a," *Biblica* 61 (1980) 416-17.

10 Because the Philistines fought courageously, the Israelites were massacred by them and sustained a loss of *thirty thousand infantry.* On the meanings of the term *thousand* (*’lp), see on v. 2. Israel did not have an effective chariot force until the time of Solomon (1 K. 4:26), although David may have experimented with it (2 Sam. 8:4).

To flee *to his own tent* is not simply to retreat, but to abandon military service altogether. McCarter notes that this phrase appears in several different places. In Judges 20:8, they vow not to return “every man to his own tent,” that is, not to break off the battle. In 1 Sam. 13:2, Saul keeps three thousand men and sends “every man [of the rest] to his own tent.” In 2 Sam. 20:1 and 1 K. 12:16 “Every man to his own tent, O Israel” means that the army will no longer serve the Judahite king.[51]

11 Very unexpectedly, the ark of Yahweh *was captured* (lit., “was taken”) by the Philistines. The verb “to take” is the key term in this narrative; see on 1 Sam. 4:3 and 5:1. It was totally unthinkable for the covenant people that the ark of the Lord *be captured* (see Num. 10:35-36). In addition, the priests who served by the ark died in war. This was certainly the first experience in the history of God’s people that was diametrically opposite the glorious Exodus experience. See below on “Ichabod” (v. 21).

The Hebrew word order “and Eli’s two sons died, Hophni and Phinehas” is unusual. However, *Hophni and Phinehas* is not simply an addition but the intended conclusion of the paragraph, for it is here that the sign specified in 1 Sam. 2:34 is given concerning the impeachment of Eli’s house.

Nothing is reported about what happened to Shiloh after this defeat, but the fact that Eli’s descendants are in Nob in chs. 21 and 22 may indicate that the Philistines destroyed it soon after this battle (see Jer. 7:12-14; 26:6; Ps. 78:60-64). Traces of destruction have been found at the site; see on 1 Sam. 1:3.

b. Death of Eli (4:12-18)

12 *And a Benjamite ran from the battle line and came to Shiloh on that day. His clothes were torn and dirt was on his head.*
13 *And he arrived. — Right at that moment Eli was seated on the chair beside the road*[52] *waiting anxiously, for his heart was*

51. McCarter, p. 107.

52. Also “near the road” (Caquot and de Robert). The K. *yk drk* is a case of <distant regressive total assimilation>: *yak derek* ← *yad derek* (Q.). Note that Ugar. *yd* “hand” sometimes means “(together) with”: e.g., *yd mqmh* “together with its place” (*KTU* 1.14 II 1) and *yd bth* “with his house” (*KTU* 4.659:2). See *UT,* §19.1072; *PLMU,* p. 38; *TO,* p. 511, n. d; Rainey, in *RSP* 2, p. 84. McCarter thinks that the MT is “patently corrupt” (p. 111) and translates: “atop the gate watching (the road)”; he explains that “the ‘hands’ of a city gate are the two parallel walls which form the sides of the gateway . . .”

anxious about the ark of God. — As for the man, he entered the city to inform (them). And all the city cried out.

14 *And Eli heard the noise of shouting and said,*
"What is this noise of tumult?"
Just then the man quickly came and informed Eli.

15 *— Now Eli was ninety-eight years old; his eyes were fixed*[53] *and could not see.*[54] *—*

16 *And the man said to Eli,*
"I am he who came from the battle line.
As for me, from the battle line I fled today."
And he said,
"What happened, my son?"

17 *And the messenger answered:*
"Israel fled before the Philistines.
Not only was a great slaughter among the people
but also your two sons, Hophni and Phinehas, died
and even the ark of God was captured."[55]

18 *As soon as he mentioned the ark of God, he fell from upon the chair backwards toward*[56] *the side of*[57] *the gate.*

(p. 114). But see v. 18. Althann proposed a case for "consonant sharing": i.e., the final *aleph* of *hakkissē'* is shared by the following word *yak,* thus becoming *'ēyk* "how," and hence, "how he was watching the road!"; see R. Althann, "Northwest Semitic Notes on Some Texts in 1 Samuel," *JNSL* 12 (1984) 30. However, not only is the syntax awkward, but there is no strong "phonetic" reason why this consonant is to be shared; neither the spelling *yod* nor the vowel /a/ can be satisfactorily explained. See D. T. Tsumura, "Scribal Errors or Phonetic Spellings? Samuel as an Aural Text," *VT* 49 (1999) 403-6 on the difference between "shared consonants" and "consonantal *sandhi*."

53. Lit., "arose," *qāmāh:* old form of pf. 3 f.pl. <qatalā> (see *UT,* p. 70, n. 3; J. Barr, *CPTOT,* p. 30). Here, *'ênâw* refers to his two eyeballs.

54. Cf. McCarter, p. 111: "the mention of his blindness . . . seems to contradict the statement in v 13 . . . that he was watching the road." Hence, McCarter omits the entire verse as an expansion, "although it is found in all witnesses"; see Walters, "Review of McCarter, *I Samuel* (1980)," *JBL* 101 (1982) 437. But see on v. 13.

55. On the expression *was captured,* see on 1 Sam. 4:3, 11. See also on 1 Sam. 5:1 for the common act of "capturing enemy's gods" in the ancient Near East.

56. The term *toward* (*bᵉ'ad,* usually "behind") is often emended to *'al-yad* or *bᵉyad.* However, in the light of *KTU* 1.23:70, "open [a opening] for (lit., toward) them" *(pth . . . b'dhm),* one might possibly translate *bᵉ'ad* here as "toward" or "to." Then no emendation (see *HALOT,* p. 141) is necessary. When A opens a door for B, i.e., toward B, B will be temporarily *behind* the door. On the other hand, A closes (*sgr) the door "toward" himself (e.g., Isa. 26:20) after getting in *or* A closes the door from outside "toward" B (e.g., 2 K. 4:21).

57. Or "next to" (lit., "the hand of"). Cf. Akk. *idu* "side" (a prepositional use; *CAD,* I-J, pp. 13-14); Arabic *lada(y)* "in front of" (lit. "to hand of"); see *UT* §19.633.

And his neck was broken and he died, for the man was old and heavy.
He had judged Israel for forty years.

Now, the stage changes from the battlefield to Shiloh where Eli the old priest-judge was eagerly waiting the result of the battle. There a reporter came from the field with news. This section has some structural similarity to the report of Saul's death in 2 Sam. 1:2-4. Some have said the similarities are due to use of a common repertoire of literary motifs.[58] However, the similarity between these two episodes has been somewhat overstated. Messengers behaved in similar ways in real life, and there were recognized ways to respond to disasters (see 2 Sam. 1:11-12), and thus there is no need to posit a common literary motif. For other examples of messengers, see 2 Sam. 1:2-16; 18:19-33; Job 1:13-19.[59]

As R. P. Gordon aptly explains, "the narrator skillfully creates an air of suspense in the build-up to Eli's death, partly by means of narrative retardation (*e.g.,* v. 15) and partly by repetition of the verb 'come' (vv. 12, 13 (twice), 14)."

12-13 *Came to. . . . And he arrived. . . . he entered.* Though all three verbs are from the same root (*bw' "to come"), their meanings differ according to context. *Came to Shiloh* is a transitional clause which follows the movement verb *ran.* This clause provides a SETTING for the subsequent action *he arrived.* Between *he arrived* and *he entered* comes a clause which explains the situation of Eli at that moment.

Benjamin's territory was between Jerusalem and Bethel. Saul was a Benjamite, and rabbinic traditions identified this messenger as Saul.[60] Why do they mention the messenger was a Benjamite? Is this to prepare for the debut of Saul? Yet it will take another five chapters before the young Saul enters upon the stage (1 Sam. 9:1). This messenger just happened to be a Benjamite and has nothing to do with Saul.

The messenger *ran* a distance of nearly 20 miles. *His clothes were torn and dirt was on his head* — these are the traditional signs of grief.[61] Tearing clothes was the normal reaction to grief or horror in the Old Testament. In Samuel, this practice occurs in reaction to a death or humiliation (2 Sam. 1:2, 11; 3:31; 13:19, 31; 15:32) or as part of a mourning rite (3:31).

58. McCarter, p. 113; see also D. M. Gunn, "Narrative Patterns and Oral Tradition in Judges and Samuel," *VT* 24 (1974) 290-92.

59. See S. A. Meier, *The Messenger in the Ancient Semitic World* (HSM 45; Atlanta: Scholars Press, 1988) on "messengers" in the ancient Near East.

60. See McCarter, p. 113.

61. See E. F. de Ward, "Mourning Customs in 1, 2, Samuel," *JJS* 23 (1972) 6-12.

Later, it is referred to as the appropriate response upon hearing the condemnatory word of God (2 K. 22:11; Jer. 36:24). In the New Testament, it is a reaction to hearing blasphemy (Matt. 26:65; Acts 14:14).

Putting dirt or ashes on the head or sitting in dirt or ashes, often in conjunction with tearing the clothes, was similarly a reaction to calamity (2 Sam. 13:19; 15:32; Josh. 7:6; Isa. 47:1; Job 2:12f.; Est. 4:1-3) and a sign of penitence or supplication (Neh. 9:1; Job 42:6; Dan. 9:3).[62] In one of the Ugaritic Baal myths (*KTU* 1.5:VI:14-15), on the sad news of Baal's death, El pours "dirt of mourning" *(ʿmr un)*//"dust of humiliation" *(ʿpr pl<u>t</u>t)* on his head and covers himself with "a girded garment" *(mizrt)*.[63]

13 *Right at that moment (wᵉhinnēh)* introduces an explanatory clause describing Eli's present situation (see above). With the insertion of this clause between the two actions, that is, *arrived* and *entered,* of the messenger, by slowing down the flow of narration, the narrator succeeds in bringing about a sense of suspense and expectation in the audience's (reader's) mind. The term "watching" is here used metaphorically as in Ps. 5:3; Hab. 2:1, for *waiting anxiously,* for Eli could not see (v. 15). "It is ironical that Eli should fear for the Ark when it was capable of striking terror in the hearts of Israel's enemies (cf. vv. 7f.)."[64]

The Hebrew word order of *entered the city to inform* is "came to inform in the city," with the phrase to *inform* interrupting the verbal phrase *entered the city* ("came in the city"). He entered the city, but Eli could not see him and was unaware he had come until he heard the noise.

While it is true, as Spina says, that the *chair* here may not be ordinary furniture but furniture "symbolic of his priestly and ruling office,"[65] it may be too much to read his falling *from upon the chair* as a metaphor for his deposition (v. 18).

14-15 The syntax of *Just then the man* (*wᵉhāʾîš:* lit., "As for the man") is noteworthy. This man didn't come in response to Eli's question. He happened to come at just the right time. By this time Eli's eyesight was totally gone (*could not see;* pf. *yākôl;* cf. the imperfect *yûkal* in 1 Sam. 3:2). As R. P. Gordon notes, the reference to Eli's age and eyesight at this point "slows up the movement of the story, just as it probably was intended to do." Therefore, "to treat the verse as interpolative is to miss the point (*pace* Smith, McCarter)."[66]

62. De Ward, p. 7.

63. D. Pardee, in *CS,* I, pp. 267-68.

64. R. P. Gordon, p. 96.

65. F. A. Spina, "Eli's Seat: The Transition from Priest to Prophet in 1 Samuel 1–4," *JSOT* 62 (1994) 71.

66. R. P. Gordon, pp. 96-97.

16 The subject *(the man)* and the object *(Eli)* are restated here since the flow of discourse, the main line narrative "the man . . . informed Eli . . . and said," is interrupted by v. 15. The normal sequence would be "informed and said."

I am he who. . . . As for me . . . is the man's self-introduction to the blind Eli. The repetitious expression, with variation of the first person personal pronouns, reflects the real situation when someone tries to explain something to a totally blind person. The blind and aged Eli anxiously asks: *What happened* (so NIV; JPS; lit., "what was the word/matter"; also in 2 Sam. 1:4).

17-18 The messenger responds to Eli with the bad news of Israel's defeat. The phrase *and even* marks the climax, though without the particle *gam.* It is distinguished from two preceding states: a great slaughter and the death of Eli's two sons. "Four clauses, climaxing in the mention of the *Ark,* sum up the day's calamities."[67] It is the ark that Eli is concerned about (as in v. 13), more than the defeat of Israel or even the death of his sons. So, *as soon as he mentioned the ark of God* (v. 18), Eli fell down from the chair. McCarter translates *the side of the gate* (lit., "the hand of the gate") as "over the gate-tower" and explains that Eli fell "over the 'hand' of the gate," that is, over the wall to the street below. But, if Eli had fallen from the wall to the street below, he would have died regardless of his old age and weight (see v. 18b). However, the gate here does not necessarily refer to the city-gate.

A short summary statement about Eli's judgeship closes the section. The verb *šāpaṭ* means "to rule" as well as "to judge" (see *UT,* §19.2727 and on 1 Sam. 8:5; see also *šāpiṭu* ["governor"] of the Mari texts).[68] Eli may have acted in a similar fashion to the minor judges in Judges. Also, Deut. 17:8-13 suggests that priests were involved in deciding appellate law cases.

c. *Birth of Ichabod (4:19-22)*

19 *As for his daughter-in-law, the wife of Phinehas, she was pregnant and about to give birth.*[69] *And she heard the news concerning the fact that the ark of God was captured and her father-in-law and her husband were dead. And she crouched down and gave birth, because her pains turned upon her.*

67. R. P. Gordon, p. 97.

68. *CAD,* Š/1 (1989), p. 459.

69. I.e., the preposition *l* + f. inf. cstr.: *lālat* ← *lā-latt* ← *lā-ladt* (> *lā-lédet*); cf. *yālādt* (v. 20). McCarter takes it as a "scribal omission" of *d* and says: "A contracted form of the infinitive written phonetically is conceivable but unexampled elsewhere in Biblical Hebrew." However, on Ugar. *ylt* (*yld), see Caquot and Sznycer, *TO,* I, pp. 477-78, n. d. There are many phonetic spellings in both books of Samuel; see Tsumura, "Scribal Errors or Phonetic Spellings?" 390-411.

20 *About the time of her death, the women attending her spoke:*
"Do not be afraid, for a son you have borne!"
But she did not answer or pay attention.
21 *And she called the boy "Ichabod," saying,*
"Glory was exiled from Israel!"
in reference to the capture of the ark of God and to her father-in-law and her husband.
22 *And she said,*
"Glory was exiled from Israel!
For the ark of God was captured."

The section urges the readers to think about whose "glory" was gone: Israel's glory or God's glory. For Phinehas's wife, the loss of the ark meant the loss of "Israel's glory." But the apparent exile of the ark was not the defeat of Yahweh himself; rather he revealed his glory even in the place of exile, as is shown in the following chapters. God is certainly the one who does wonders behind the human sight.

19 This episode begins by introducing the participant in terms of the relationship to the major figure in this context — as the *daughter-in-law* of Eli — rather than as *the wife of Phinehas.* Such a technique in narrative discourse to identify a participant in terms of another has been discussed recently by L. J. de Regt.[70]

For *she crouched down (wattikraʿ),* see Dan. 10:16 (metaphorically). Women sat or squatted during labor. This labor was apparently premature due to shock.

20 Compare the account of the birth of Benjamin and death of Rachel in Gen. 35:17-18.

Two suggestions have been made as to why she did not answer. One is that she was too despondent to pay attention, and the other is that the words comforted her and so she paid no heed (to her affliction). However, her pessimistic comment in the following verse rather supports the first view.

21 As Hannah does (1 Sam. 1:20; also 2 Sam. 12:24a), so here too the mother names the boy, though the death of her husband forced her to. One cannot help note the contrast; the one child is named with hope and gratitude "because from the Lord I have requested him," while the other with despair "[for] Glory was exiled from Israel!" The use of *naʿar* also suggests the sharp contrast in the destinies of Samuel and Ichabod.

70. L. J. de Regt, "The Order of Participants in Compound Clausal Elements in the Pentateuch and Earlier Prophets: Syntax, Convention or Rhetoric?," in *Literary Structure and Rhetorical Strategies in the Hebrew Bible,* ed. L. J. de Regt, J. de Ward, and J. P. Fokkelman (Assen: Van Gorcum, 1996), pp. 83-84.

The name *Ichabod (ʾî-kābôd)* means "Where is Glory?"[71] It mourns for Israel without the presence of God. Like Jezebel *ʾîzebel,* it is in the same form as *iy zbl,* that is, Jezebel *ʾîzebel* "Where is the Prince?" (*KTU* 1.6 IV 5),[72] a lamentation for the storm god Baal in the Ugaritic mythological texts. Note that in Phoenician and Ugarit, "Prince" refers to the storm god Baal. Ichabod's brother was Ahitub, the father of Ahijah and Ahimelech, the priests; see on 1 Sam. 14:3.

The term *was exiled (gālāh)* does not simply mean "has departed." Note that in the ancient Near East the idea of "exile" is not limited to that of people (2 Sam. 15:19); even idols were exiled (see below on 1 Sam. 5:1). Hence, the use of this term does not necessarily presuppose the Babylonian exile. In fact, it is somewhat forced to connect this incidence with the departure of glory from the temple as imaged in Ezek. 10:18, as Birch does.[73] In fact, Amos uses this term for the exile of non-Israelite people by other nations (e.g., Amos 1:5, 6; 5:5).

"The death of the grandfather is balanced by the birth of a grandson, but the cheerless event brings no hope to the cursed family."[74]

22 *For* denotes "the reason why I said this is. . . ." In v. 21b the explanation is given from the narrator's viewpoint, but here it is given from the woman's viewpoint.

This episode ends with the pessimistic statement by Phinehas's wife: *Glory was exiled from Israel!* But, contrary to her judgment (i.e., "Glory is gone"), Yahweh is going to demonstrate his glory in the land of Philistia, as seen in the following chapters.

2. The Ark in Philistia (5:1-12)

The Philistines captured the ark and brought it to Ashdod, where they set it up in the temple of Dagon, their chief god. In doing so, they probably intended to indicate that Dagon had conquered Yahweh at Ebenezer, and that now Yahweh was to worship Dagon. However, when no humans were present, the true power was shown. The statue of Dagon was found prostrated before the ark in a position of adoration, and the next night, it was mutilated and defiled. Thus, "the ark of Yahweh [had] become a costly trophy"[1] for the Ashdodites. Yahweh also struck them with tumors. So, they sent the ark to Gath, but a great panic followed it to Gath, and then to Ekron. Since the

71. See Ugar. *iy* "Where is/are?" (*UT* §19.143).
72. Gibson, *CML*², p. 78, n. 6.
73. Birch, p. 997.
74. McCarter, p. 116.
1. McCarter, p. 124.

"deadly panic" (v. 11) was in all the cities, all the Philistine lords decided to return the ark of Yahweh to its place.

Who controls history? This story asserts that Yahweh's sovereignty extends even to the temple of Dagon. Certainly, even though the ark was *captured,* Yahweh was not vanquished. The Lord God himself had brought about the events, removing the ark from Shiloh and displaying his power outside Israel as he had once before in Egypt to teach the Israelites he could not be used. Chapter 6 has allusions to Exodus (see Exod. 9:15-16). The story is not without its humor, however.

It is asserted that this chapter is full of textual problems. According to McCarter, "both MT and LXX are seriously disturbed throughout." He believes that the repeated and mingled references to plague, mice, tumors, and panic make it impossible to determine the original text.[2] However, as will become clear later, those "disturbances" of the text are often imaginary, and the real issue is linguistic rather than textual or orthographical.[3]

a. The Ark in Dagon's Temple (5:1-5)

1 *Now the Philistines had captured the ark of God*
and brought it from Ebenezer to Ashdod.
2 *The Philistines took the ark of God*
and brought it to the house of Dagon
and set it beside Dagon.
3 *And the Ashdodites arose early the next day.*
Then, Dagon was fallen to the ground on his face
before the ark of the Lord.
And they took Dagon and put him back to his place.[4]
4 *And they arose early in the morning on the next day.*
Then, Dagon was fallen to the ground on his face
before the ark of the Lord.
Dagon's head and the palms of his hands were cut off on the threshold;[5]
only Dagon remained on it.
5 *Therefore, the priests of Dagon and all who come to the house of*

2. McCarter, p. 118.

3. See D. T. Tsumura, "Scribal Errors or Phonetic Spellings? Samuel as an Aural Text," *VT* 49 (1999) 390-411; "List and Narrative in I Samuel 6,17-18a in the Light of Ugaritic Economic Texts," *ZAW* 113 (2001) 353-69.

4. I.e., "on his pedestal."

5. So BDB, p. 837; or "lower sill, doorstep" (*HALOT,* p. 619); or "podium" (KB). See H. Donner, "Die Schwellenhüpfer: Beobachtungen zu Zephanja 1,8f.," *JSS* 15 (1970) 42-55. See Zeph. 1:9.

Dagon will not tread on the threshold of Dagon in Ashdod, until this day.[6]

This section constitutes a coherent discourse unit, with repetition of key words and phrases (i.e., "Dagon" x10; "the ark" x4; "the house of Dagon" x2; "the ark of the Lord" x2) and the presence of such literary techniques as *inclusio* ("Ashdod" in vv. 1 and 5; "the house of Dagon" in vv. 2 and 5), *framing* ("they arose early on the morrow" in vv. 3 and 4), and repetition with *climax* (i.e., v. 3 and v. 4). Such a repetitive style makes it possible to analyze this prose narrative as if it were poetic,[7] and these highly poetic features would explain why the subject "the Philistines" is repeated after the SETTING (v. 1) at the beginning of v. 2, where the main line narrative discourse (EVENT) surely begins. The *progression* of verbs in vv. 1-2 is noteworthy: (v. 1) "took" — "brought"; (v. 2) "took" — "brought" — "set." Verse 5 clearly marks the TERMINUS of this section.

1 The narrative agent, the one who "takes" (see on 4:3, 11 for this key word) the ark of God, changes here from the Israelites to the Philistines, and the stage, which had moved from Shiloh to Ebenezer, now moves to Philistia. Thus, the narrator's viewpoint has changed from the Israelite side to the Philistine side: in ch. 4 the Israelites "took" (v. 3) the ark, which "was taken" (v. 11); here the Philistines "take" the ark and "bring" it (i.e., make it come) to Ashdod. This transitional verse, which functions as the SETTING for the EVENT (vv. 2ff.), prepares the audience for the new stage with a new viewpoint. For the change of viewpoint in terms of "go" and "come," see "Introduction" (Section VI, D).

The practice of capturing an enemy's gods was common in warfare in the ancient Near East and is often mentioned in documents such as the Assyrian royal inscriptions,[8] a newly published text of Ninurta-kudurru-uṣur, literary texts from the reign of Nebuchadnezzar I, and the "Marduk Prophecy."[9] The Hittite historiography, "Proclamation of Anitta of Kuššar," mentions carrying off the cult statue of an enemy's deity to its own home city.[10] It was

6. For the phrase *until this day* (also 1 Sam. 6:18b), see on 8:8; "Introduction" (Section III, B, 1).

7. See "Introduction" (Section VII, B).

8. M. Cogan, *Imperialism and Religion: Assyria, Judah, and Israel in the Eighth and Seventh Centuries* B.C.E. (Missoula, Mont.: Scholars Press, 1974), pp. 118-21.

9. P. D. Miller, Jr., and J. J. M. Roberts, *The Hand of the Lord: A Reassessment of the "Ark Narrative" of 1 Samuel* (JHNES; Baltimore: Johns Hopkins University Press, 1977); also *CS,* I, p. 481; see V. A. Hurowitz, "Temporary Temples," in *Kinattūtu ša dārâti: Raphael Kutscher Memorial Volume,* ed. A. F. Rainey (Occasional Publications No. 1; Tel Aviv: Tel Aviv University, 1993), pp. 40-41.

10. Hoffner, in *CS,* I, p. 183.

understood that a people whose gods were in enemy hands was completely conquered.[11]

The modern site of *Ashdod* is Tel Ashdod, located about 3.5 miles south of modern Ashdod, which is inland from the Mediterranean Sea [MR117-129]. It had a major seaport in the Late Bronze and Iron Age and is first mentioned in the Ugaritic texts of the Late Bronze Age: *aḏḏd* (*UT* §19.98). The city was the center of maritime trading in goods such as tin as well as a center of the textile industry, including purple-dyed garments.[12] Its first occurrence in the Bible is Josh. 11:22, where Ashdod is mentioned as one of the three cities where the Anakites survived; the other two cities were Gaza and Gath. It was one of the Philistine Pentapolis, along with Gaza, Ashkelon, Gath and Ekron (see 6:17).

2 The MT mentions *the Philistines* again, but McCarter and the NIV omit it. It should be kept here as the stated subject of the first of three consecutive *wayqtl*s, which initiate a new unit of discourse, a sub-paragraph.

With this verse, the main EVENT begins. The three consecutive actions in the main line of the story are expressed by the three *wayqtl* verbs, *took . . . and brought . . . and set . . .*, the first introduced by a *waw initial* (hence, untranslated; see also 13:2) and the rest by a *waw sequential;* see "Introduction" (Section VI, A). Though the first two actions "took" and "brought" are repeated from v. 1, the emphasis is on the last verb ("set"), that is, placing the ark of Yahweh beside the Philistine god Dagon.[13] In this way the Israelite Yahweh was supposed to have come under the control of Dagon, the god of the conqueror.

Dagon is the Canaanite name of the native West Semitic deity, Dagan, known from Early Bronze Age Mesopotamia and northern Syria. He was a major deity in Ebla and Mari and was the head of Emar's pantheon.[14] In Ugarit, Dagan is the father of the storm god Baal; one of the two temples in Ugarit was dedicated to him, though he himself plays no active role in the Ugaritic myths.[15] His cult is attested "from Early Bronze Age Ebla in northern Syria to Roman Gaza at the southern extreme of the Philistine Plain."[16] See "Introduction" (Section IV, C, 2, b).

11. See also McCarter, p. 24.

12. See M. Dothan, "Ashdod," in *NEAEHL,* pp. 93-102.

13. See Gen. 2:7-8, 19 for other cases where the last verb of the verbal sequence is emphasized; see D. T. Tsumura, *The Earth and the Waters in Genesis 1 and 2: A Linguistic Analysis* (JSOTSS 83; Sheffield: Sheffield Academic Press, 1989), pp. 119-20. See also 1 Sam. 1:20; 7:10; 13:2; 30:18; 2 Sam. 5:8, 9-10; etc.

14. See *CS,* I, p. 431; D. E. Fleming, "The Israelite Festival Calendar and Emar's Ritual Archive," *RB* 106 (1999) 17.

15. See D. E. Fleming, "Baal and Dagan in Ancient Syria," *ZA* 83 (1993) 88-98.

16. McCarter, p. 121.

Two major etymologies have been suggested: (1) Medieval Jewish commentators (Rashi, Kimchi) explained its meaning as "fish" (*dg), but this folk etymology is no longer accepted. (2) Others say it is from "grain" (*dagan),[17] and this would make him a vegetation deity. But Healey is cautious about positing this etymology, for the connection with "grain" is secondary and based on the coincidence of the West Semitic word for grain.[18]

Since Dagon is Semitic and the Philistines were not, they presumably adopted Dagon sometime after their arrival, but how soon is not known. Biblical writers clearly consider Dagon as the Philistines' national god, however (Judg. 16:23; 1 Chr. 10:10). Worship of Dagon at Ashdod still continued around 50 B.C. (cf. 1 Macc. 10:83-85; 11:4).

3 The next morning, to their surprise, the Philistines in Ashdod found that their god Dagon had fallen to the ground before the ark of the defeated deity Yahweh. The phrase *on his face* implies that Dagon was "in a position of adoration"[19] of Yahweh. Here, the phrase *the ark of the Lord* (also v. 4; see 4:6) is used instead of *the ark of God* (vv. 7-11); see on 3:3. Is there a conscious contrast between Yahweh and Dagon in using the former? Probably there is. The narrator might be hinting that the real issue here is warfare between two deities. Note that "before the ark of the Lord" is almost the same as "before the Lord" (see 1:12).

4 In the following morning the Ashdodites again found that Dagon had fallen to the ground, and this time his hands were cut off. Wiggins[20] connects this passage with a "common wartime practice to collect the heads or hands of the fallen to demonstrate victory" and refers to the "heads" *(riš)* and "palms" *(kp)* mentioned in the Baal Cycle (*KTU* 1.3:II:7-13). He sees here a trace of a mythological story of battling deities. However, what the goddess Anath collects in the Ugaritic text are the "heads" and "palms" of human warriors, not of the god who is her enemy. She is simply following a common wartime practice, not creating a mythological prototype. The cutting-off of Dagon's *head*[21] and *palms* in our story is the result of his defeat in war. These

17. J. J. M. Roberts, *The Earliest Semitic Pantheon* (Baltimore: Johns Hopkins University Press, 1972), pp. 18-19, nn. 95-105. For a good summary of this deity, see Healey, in *DDD,* pp. 407-13.

18. Healey, in *DDD,* p. 410; also J. F. Healey, "Grain and Wine in Abundance: Blessings from the Ancient Near East," in *Ugarit, Religion and Culture: Proceedings of the International Colloquium on Ugarit, Religion and Culture, Edinburgh, July 1994: Essays Presented in Honour of Professor John C. L. Gibson,* ed. N. Wyatt, W. G. E. Watson, and J. B. Lloyd (Münster: Ugarit-Verlag, 1996), p. 70.

19. McCarter, p. 124.

20. S. A. Wiggins, "Old Testament Dagan in the Light of Ugarit," *VT* 43 (1993) 270-71.

21. On "Dagon's head," see W. Zwickel, "Dagons abgeschlagener Kopf (1 Samuel v 3-4)," *VT* 44 (1994) 239-49.

"powerless severed palms of Dagon" might be contrasted with Yahweh's "oppressive hand" in 5:6-12.[22]

The LXX translation, "only Dagon's spine was left," seems to suggests that a word such as "body" or "trunk" has fallen out of the MT before *dgwn*.[23] The NIV translates: "only his body remained." However, the MT as it is, that is, *only Dagon,*[24] stands for the main part of the statue. The pronoun "it" refers to "the place" or "pedestal" of Dagon (v. 3), not to "the threshold" (v. 4). So, the MT is not "meaningless."[25]

5 Temple thresholds were considered especially worthy of respect because they separated sacred and common areas. (Compare the importance of the door posts, which marked the entrance to a home, in Israel [e.g., Exod. 12:7; 21:6; Deut. 6:9].) The narrator makes the observation that the Philistines still to the time of the writing bear witness to the humiliation of their god. R. P. Gordon remarks that the mention of the custom in connection with this incident is "perhaps as much satirical as aetiological."[26] This custom is said to have survived, "at least in Gaza, into the first centuries A.D."[27]

b. The Hand of the Lord (5:6-12)

6 *And the hand of the Lord was heavy on the Ashdodites. And he devastated them and struck them with swellings (tumors) — both Ashdod and its environs.*[28]

7 *And the men of Ashdod saw that this was so, saying,*[29]
"The ark of God of Israel should not stay with us,
for his hand is hard[30] *upon us and upon Dagon, our God!"*

22. A. F. Campbell, *The Ark Narrative (1 Sam 4–6; 2 Sam 6): A Form-Critical and Traditio-Historical Study* (SBLDS 16; Missoula, Mont.: Scholars Press, 1975), p. 86.

23. See McCarter, p. 119; R. P. Gordon, p. 99.

24. So Caquot and de Robert, p. 85.

25. McCarter, p. 119.

26. R. P. Gordon, p. 99.

27. McCarter, p. 122, citing M. Delcor, "Jaweh et Dagon ou le Jahwisme face à la religion des Philistines, d'après 1 Sam. V," *VT* 14 (1964) 149.

28. McCarter thinks that LXX's longer text is "correct in introducing the mice early" and restores the following text after v. 6: "He brought up mice upon them, and they swarmed in their ships. Then mice went up into their land, and there was a mortal panic in the city" (McCarter, p. 117). However, as he admits, "the textual problems that center on this verse are extensive and probably insoluble." J. B. Geyer ("Mice and Rites in 1 Samuel v–vi," *VT* 31 [1981] 296) holds that "4QSam^{a}, ignoring the 'second' plague (mice), is strong evidence in favour of the MT."

29. *w*^{e}*'ām*^{e}*rû:* <*waw* + pf.> functioning here almost as inf. *lē(')mōr.*

30. A variant of "heavy" in v. 6.

8 *And they sent a messenger and summoned all the Philistine lords*[31]
to them and said,
"What shall we do to the ark of the God of Israel?"
and they said,
"To Gath let the ark of the God of Israel go on!"
and they moved on the ark of the God of Israel.
9 *After they moved it, the hand of the Lord was in the city with a*
very great panic, and he struck the men of the city, from the
young to the old.
And swellings broke out on them.
10 *And they sent out the ark of God to Ekron. When the ark of God*
came to Ekron, the Ekronites shouted, saying,
"They have moved the ark of the God of Israel to me
to kill me and my people!"
11 *And they sent a messenger and summoned all the Philistine lords*
and said,
"Send the ark of the God of Israel away!
And let it go back to its place and not kill me and my people!"
For a deadly panic was in all the city; the hand of God was very
heavy there.
12 *As for the men who did not die, they were struck with tumors.*
And the cry of the city for help went up to the heavens.

Yahweh afflicts the Ashdodites by striking them with *tumors*. The panic-stricken Philistine people decide to send the ark of Yahweh around their cities, from Ashdod to Gath, then to Ekron. In this way, the God of Israel marches through the enemy territories victoriously.

6 The expression *the hand of the Lord* (*yad YHWH;* also 5:9; cf. "the hand of God" in 5:11) is first used with regard to the Egyptians in Exod. 9:3: "the hand of the LORD will bring a terrible plague on your livestock in the field" (NIV); see on 1 Sam. 12:15. For the expression *the hand . . . was heavy* and its opposite *lighten his hand* (1 Sam. 6:5), Greenfield notes the Akkadian idioms *kabtat qāssu* "he afflicted" (lit., "his hand was heavy") and its opposite *lišaqqil qāssu* "he will lift his hand."[32]

Note that diseases were often considered to be brought about by the

31. **sarn* > *seren* "lord"; also 1 Sam. 29:2. The term is probably Philistine and therefore non-Semitic in origin; see Gk. *tyrannos* "[absolute] ruler, tyrant" and Hieroglyphic Hittite *tarwanas,* a title of Neo-Hittite rulers. See McCarter, p. 123; Gordon, *PLMU,* p. 32 on *srnm;* K. L. Younger, Jr., in *CS,* II, p. 164, n. 4.

32. J. C. Greenfield, "The Root *šql* in Akkadian, Ugaritic and Aramaic," *UF* 11 (1979) 325.

"hand" of a particular deity (see Ashurbanipal's illness "with the hand of god").[33] Hurowitz compares Yahweh's sending diseases with "the famine and civil strife which Marduk bestowed upon his Elamite captors according to I 18–II 11 of the Marduk Prophecy."[34] Yahweh's most common weapon was the plague, though of course he could use other means (2 Sam. 24:13). The only way people could protect themselves was to appease the offended deity.

The term *swellings* (*ʿŏpālîm:* MT, Ketib; also Deut. 28:27), originally "hills, mounds," came to be used euphemistically for referring to tumors, as "swellings, that is, hill-shape growths," for it was often abominable to pronounce the actual name of the disease. Subsequently, the term seems to have experienced a further semantic change to an abominable sense, that is, *taboo,* "swollen parts of the body" such as "buttocks" (cf. LXX: 5:9). Hence, the MT introduced, in Qere, the more straightforward term *ṭᵉḥōrîm,* "tumors." The use of this term as Qere is not a "euphemism"[35] but rather a clarification. For one thing, the term *ṭᵉḥōrîm* is more specific and concrete than "swellings." Thus, both *ʿŏpālîm* and *ṭᵉḥōrîm* refer to "tumors," whose collocation with "mice" has led most commentators to identify the disease as bubonic plague.[36]

McCarter thinks that the phrase *both Ashdod and its environs* is appended "in rather clumsy apposition" to *ʾōtām* "them." However, this information seems to be original and intentional, for a city and its vicinity are treated as one unit in the story, as is specified in 6:18 ("both fortified cities and [their] unfortified villages"); see below on 6:18.

The plague was certainly endemic to coastal areas, "where infected rats might arrive by ship," and "a connection between rats and pestilence was recognized in early times." However, the MT does not mention "mice" until

33. I. Starr, ed., *Queries to the Sungod: Divination and Politics in Sargonid Assyria* (SAA IV; Helsinki: Helsinki University Press, 1990), p. 256; J. E. Curtis and J. E. Reade, eds., *Art and Empire: Treasures from Assyria in the British Museum* (London: The Trustees of the British Museum by the British Museum Press, 1995), p. 205. See also *KTU* 2.10 ("The hands of gods *yd ilm* were very strong like the death").

34. Hurowitz, "Temporary Temples," p. 41, n. 8; see also J. J. M. Roberts, "The Hand of Yahweh," *VT* 21 (1971) 244-51. See also 2 Samuel 24; Hab. 3:5; also Exodus 9.

35. E. Tov, *Textual Criticism of the Hebrew Bible* (Minneapolis: Fortress, 1992), p. 63.

36. G. R. Driver, "The Plague of the Philistines (1 Samuel v,6–vi,16)," *JRAS* (1950) 50-52; B. Brentjes, "Zur 'Beulen' — Epidemie bei den Philistern in 1. Samuel 5–6," *Altertum* 15 (1969) 67-74; J. Wilkinson, "The Philistine Epidemic of I Samuel 5 and 6," *ExTi* 88 (1977) 137-41; J. V. Kinnier-Wilson, "Medicine in the Land and Times of the Old Testament," in *Studies in the Period of David and Solomon and Other Essays: Papers Read at the International Symposium for Biblical Studies, Tokyo, 5-7 December, 1979,* ed. T. Ishida (Tokyo: Yamakawa-Shuppansha/Winona Lake, Ind.: Eisenbrauns, 1982), pp. 362-63. It has also been taken as having a connection with dysentery (Josephus; BDB, p. 377) or to hemorrhoids (Tov, p. 63).

6:4-5, where golden mice are mentioned as the images of tumors. As McCarter rightly notes, "the narrator of the present account is not suggesting any *causal* relationship between the mice and the misery of the Philistines, for he credits the afflictions of Israel's enemies solely to Yahweh."[37] The "golden mice" were then probably made, not because mice or rats were the cause of pestilence, but because "tumors" and "mice" have a similarity in form; see on 6:11. This view may be supported by Geyer, who concludes that only "one" plague is involved here, one of tumors, and that the mice were "an offering to the deity" but never "a plague."[38]

7 *God* (*'ĕlōhîm:* pl.) is here presented from the Philistine viewpoint where "the god(s) of Israel" is contrasted with "Dagon, the god(s) of the Philistines." The Philistines view Yahweh only as "the god of Israel," just as Dagon was their god. On the other hand, the biblical author sees even the history of the Philistines as under Yahweh's control (e.g., Amos 9:7). The phrase *the ark of God of Israel* appears in the mouths of the Philistines five times out of six; the other time is in 6:3.

8 In this critical moment of their history *all the Philistine lords,* which refers to the lords from all the pentapolis, gather to discuss how to deal with the ark of the Israelite "God." First, they decide to send it off to Gath, another member of the Philistine pentapolis. It was the city of Goliath (17:4, 23) and of King Achish (21:10-15; 27:2-12); see also Ittai and the 600 Gittim (2 Sam. 15:18). The identification of the city is still debated and unresolved. Rainey and others suggest Tel eṣ-Ṣâfī [MR135-123], located on the southern bank of Wadi Elah, where it enters the Shephelah. It is about 12 miles east of Ashdod and about 6 miles west of Azekah.[39] Another identification (by Albright and others) is Tel 'Erani (Tel Gath [MR129-113]), located on Nahal Lachish, north of modern Qiryat Gat.[40] One might note, with Rainey, that "the whole idea of a 'southern Gath' is contradicted by the story of David at Ziklag," for if Gath had been in the south of Philistia, David's report to Achish in 1 Sam. 27:7-12 would have been easy to check.[41]

The city name *Gath* is emphasized by its being placed before the verb.

37. McCarter, p. 123.

38. Geyer, "Mice and Rites in 1 Samuel v–vi," pp. 296-97.

39. See A. F. Rainey, "The Identification of Philistine Gath: A Problem in Source Analysis for Historical Geography," *EI* 12 [Nelson Glueck Memorial Volume] (1975) 69*-70*; E. Stern, "Zafit, Tel," in *NEAEHL,* pp. 1522-24; W. M. Schniedewind, "The Geopolitical History of Philistine Gath," *BASOR* 309 (1998) 69-77.

40. See B. Brandl, "'Erani, Tel," in *OEANE,* 2, pp. 256-58.; T. Dothan, "Philistines: Early Philistines," in *OEANE,* 4, p. 310. However, S. Yeivin, "'Erani, Tel," in *NEAEHL,* pp. 417-19, 421-22, criticizes this identification.

41. See Rainey, "The Identification of Philistine Gath," p. 71*. See also J. P. J. Olivier, *NIDOTTE,* 4, pp. 651-52; J. D. Seger, *ABD,* II, pp. 908-9.

It may be that they decided to transfer the ark to Gath away from the seacoast, from which the mice, the carriers of pestilence, were supposed to have come. Even if they did not associate the plague with the mice, they might have associated it with the coastal region. This may be the reason why the ark was not sent to Ashkelon and Gaza, two other cities on the seacoast.

9-10 When the Lord starts fighting for his people, he often throws the enemy into a *panic* (or "tumult, confusion") (as in 7:10; 14:15; cf. Zech. 14:13). Here, *the hand of the Lord* is extremely active among the Philistines wherever the ark is moved. The entire people were struck by *a very great panic,* because *swellings broke out on them.*

So, they sent the ark off to *Ekron,* another city of the Philistine pentapolis. The modern site of *Ekron* is most probably Tel Miqne (Arab. Khirbet el-Muqannaʿ), one of the largest Iron Age sites [MR136-131] in Israel and the largest industrial center for the production of olive oil known from antiquity. Ekron is 22 miles southwest of Jerusalem. It is on the western border between Philistia and Judah, on the edge of the inner coastal plain, the frontier zone that separated Philistia and Judah.

It overlooks the ancient network of highways leading northeast from Ashdod to Gezer and inland via Nahal Sorek to Beth-Shemesh.[42] The city is also mentioned in 6:16, 17; 7:14; and 17:52 along with various other places in the OT. Extra-biblical references to Ekron *(ʾam-qa-(ar)ru-(na))* first appear in the eighth- and seventh-century records of the Neo-Assyrian kings. Its conquest by the Assyrians in 701 B.C. is described in the royal annals of Sennacherib. Esarhaddon called upon Ikausu, king of Ekron, to provide building materials for his palace in Nineveh. In 667 B.C., Ashurbanipal required Ikausu to support his military campaign against Egypt and Ethiopia.[43] For "Ikausu," see on 21:10. The city is associated at a later date with the worship of Baal-zebub (2 K. 1:2).

Daube thinks that *me and my people* is strange for a group to say and believes it reflects passages such as Pharaoh's exclamation in Exod. 8:8. But R. P. Gordon thinks it could be idiomatic. He says, "As the ark moves on to *Gath* and then to Ekron (v. 10), the story begins to read like a parody of a victory tour, in which the roles of victor and vanquished are reversed." This is certainly a triumphant march of the ark of Yahweh through enemy territory from one city to another.

11-12 The Ekronites request the Philistine lords to send the ark away and return it to *its place.* The term *its place (mᵉqōmô)* refers to a shrine

42. T. Dothan and S. Gitin, "Miqne, tel," in *OEANE,* 4, p. 30; T. Dothan and S. Gitin, "Miqne, tel (Ekron)," in *NEAEHL,* pp. 1051-59.

43. See T. Dothan and S. Gitin, "Ekron" in *ABD,* II, pp. 415-22. See also 1 Sam. 17:52. See Ekron inscription in *CS,* II, p. 164.

like Ugar. *aṯr;* Akk. *ašru* "a holy place or shrine"[44] or, as in v. 3, "the pedestal upon which a cultic image resided in its sanctuary."[45] Note that "kings such as Esarhaddon, Assurbanipal and Cyrus tell how they returned captured gods to their home towns."[46]

The expression *a deadly panic* (*m^e^hûmat māwet,* lit., "panic of death") denotes "a panic which brings death" rather than simply an example of the superlative use of *māwet.*[47] For the expression *the cry of the city for help went up to the heavens* (v. 12), cf. Exod. 2:23; 3:7, 9; etc.[48] Sacerdotal knowledge of the proper course of action will come to their aid.

3. Return of the Ark (6:1–7:1)

The ark of the Lord stayed in Philistia for seven months, and during that period the Philistine people were afflicted with *a deadly panic* (5:11). Some were killed, and some were *struck with tumors* (5:12) because *the hand of God was very heavy* in all five Philistine cities — Ashdod, Gaza, Ashkelon, Gath, and Ekron; see 6:17. The people sought advice from their *priests* and *diviners* about how to deal with the ark of Yahweh. These religious authorities ordered the Philistines to put the ark on a *new cart* (6:7) with "five golden mice" as *compensation* and return it to the God of Israel.

The account in this chapter may possibly reflect some details of Philistine original practices and can be compared with non-Canaanite Hittite rituals against plague.[1] However, the Philistines adopted the Canaanite god Dagon as their major god probably soon after their settlement in the land of Philistia; see the commentary on 1 Sam. 5:2. Hence, one would expect that the Philistines in Philistia had become highly Canaanized by the time of Samuel[2] and that these "Philistine" religious practices in ch. 6 were common Canaanite practices reflecting East Mediterranean religious and cultural traditions.[3]

44. See D. T. Tsumura, "The Interpretation of the Ugaritic Funerary Text KTU 1.161," in *Official Cult and Popular Religion in the Ancient Near East,* ed. E. Matsushima (Heidelberg: C. Winter, 1993), pp. 40-55.

45. McCarter, p. 124.

46. Hurowitz, "Temporary Temples," p. 41, no. 7.

47. G. Brin ("The Superlative in the Hebrew Bible: Additional Cases," *VT* 42 [1992] 115-18) adduces additional evidence for this interpretation in [*m*]*hwmt yhw*[*h*] of 4QSam^a^. Cf. "a trembling by God" in 1 Sam. 14:15.

48. See D. T. Tsumura, "*šmym* — Heaven, Sky, Firmament, Air," in *NIDOTTE,* pp. 160-66.

1. *ANET,* p. 347; *CS,* I, pp. 161-62; see McCarter, p. 138.

2. See "Introduction" (Section IV, A).

3. For the East Mediterranean cultural traditions common to Greek and Hebrew civilizations, see C. H. Gordon, *The Common Background of Greek and Hebrew Civilizations* (New York: W. W. Norton, 1965).

a. Priests and Diviners (6:1-9)

1 *And the ark of the Lord was in the country of the Philistines for seven months.*
2 *And the Philistines called the priests and the diviners, saying,*
"What shall we do to the ark of Yahweh?
Let us know how we can send it away to its place!"
3 *And they said,*
"If you are sending the ark of the God of Israel,
you shall not send it away empty-handed
but surely return him compensation.
Then you will be healed
and it will be known to you[4]
why his hand did not turn aside from you."
4 *And they said,*
"What is the compensation that we should return to him?"
And they said,
"According to the number of the Philistine lords,
five golden swellings,[5] *namely,*[6] *five golden mice.*
For the plague is the same to each of them, namely, to your lords.
5 *You shall make images of your swellings,*
namely, images of your mice, which are ruining the land,
and give them to the God of Israel as a tribute.[7]
Perhaps he will lighten his hand from upon you
and from upon your gods and your land.
6 *And why do you harden your hearts*
as Egypt and Pharaoh hardened their hearts?
Was it not that
when he dealt harshly with them,
they sent them away and they went away?

4. *wᵉnôdaʿ* (*waw* + Ni. pf. 3 m.s.); = you will know (why . . .). McCarter treats this phrase as "corrupt" and, based on LXX and 4QSam[a], he translates: "When you have been ransomed" (McCarter, p. 129). For a defense of the MT and a suggestion for a different etymology, see D. W. Thomas, "A Note on *wĕnôdaʿ lākem* in I Samuel VI 3," *JTS* 11 (1960) 52. Recently Emerton rightly rejected his etymology; see J. A. Emerton, "A Further Consideration of D. W. Thomas's Theories about *yādaʿ*," *VT* 41 (1991) 147. However the MT, Ni. of *ydʿ "to know," is acceptable as it stands in the light of the similar construction in Ezek. 13:12, where an interrogative clause constitutes the subject of the passive verb: "will it not be said to you, 'Where is the whitewash you smeared on it?'" (NRSV).

5. K: *ʿply zhb;* Q: *ṭᵉḥōrê zāhāb* "tumors." See 5:6 for Ketib/Qere.

6. *Waw* explicative; see vv. 5, 11, 18.

7. *kābôd;* usually "honor" or "glory"; see McCarter, p. 133.

7 *And now, prepare*[8]
one new cart and two milch cows[9] *that have never been yoked*[10]
and bind the cows to the cart
and drive their calves[11] *home away from them!*
8 *And you shall take the ark of Yahweh*
and put it on the cart.
As for the golden objects,
which you return him as compensation,
you shall place them in the pouch beside it (= the ark)
and send it off, and it will go.
9 *And watch!*
If it goes up on the way to his territory, toward Beth-shemesh,
it is he who brought this great disaster to us;
but if not,
then we shall know that it was not his hand that struck us;
it was an accident that happened to us."

1 For *seven months,* which covers the time from the arrival of the ark at Ashdod (see 1 Sam. 5:1) to the present time, the ark stayed in Philistia. The *seven* implies that the suffering of the Philistines had reached the maximum limit. The expression *the ark of the Lord* (see on 4:6; 5:3, 4) is used in this episode both by the Philistines (vv. 2, 8; translated as "the ark of Yahweh"; see on v. 2) and by the men of Beth-shemesh, as well as by the narrator. To them the ark is the ark of Yahweh, the god of the nation Israel, while, on the other hand, to the biblical author it is the earthly throne of God who controls the course of the universe, even the history of Israel's enemy the Philistines.

In the phrase *the country of the Philistines (śᵉdēh pᵉlištîm;* also 27:7, 11), the term *śādēh* denotes either "country" (so NRSV; NASB) or "territory" (JPS; NIV) of the nation, both urban and rural.[12]

2 The Philistine people call on the religious authorities. One would have expected the rulers to have summoned the priest and diviners a lot ear-

8. Lit., "take and make."

9. *pārôt ʿārôt,* lit., "cows for suckling, giving suck"; this is a construct chain with an objective genitive.

10. Lit., "which a yoke has not gone up on them (*-hm:* 3 m. pl.)." But, "cows" is f. pl. The suffix could be an "archaic dual form" (McCarter, p. 135) in the light of Ugaritic 3 c. du. possessive suffix *-hm* (*UT,* §6.10); see Hubbard, *Ruth,* p. 99, n. 15. Cf. J-M, §149*b.* Note the assonance of [*ʿ-l*] in vv. 6b-7.

11. Lit., "their (3 c. du.) sons."

12. E.g., "the territory of the Amalekites" (Gen. 14:7), "the country of Edom" (32:4; etc.), "the country of Moab" (Ruth 1:1; etc.), "the country of Aram" (Hos. 12:13 [ET 12]).

lier. However, since the rulers already knew the probable cause and remedy for the plague, they had probably consulted with them earlier but had not decided to act on their suggestion till now. To send the ark of Yahweh back would be to acknowledge a religio-political defeat, and such a decision would not be made lightly, especially since there were apparently some who did not believe the link between the ark and the plague was proven beyond a reasonable doubt (vv. 3, 9). But now they admit defeat and ask the priests how to go about sending the ark back.

The Philistines presumably use the proper name "Yahweh" in contrast with Dagon, hence the present translation "the ark of Yahweh" rather than "the ark of the Lord." Note that the same term or expression can mean different things according to the speaker and hearer; see, for example, "the righteous" meaning slightly different things in Hab. 1:4, 13, and 2:4 according to the pragmatic situation: that is, who uses the term to whom, in what situation.[13]

As known from Ugaritic examples, *priests (khnm)* were a class of "priests" in ancient Canaan, alongside the *qdš*-priests.[14] One cannot be sure whether the narrator used this terminology specifically for the *khn*-priests or as a general term for religious practitioners other than "diviners" in the Philistine society. Most likely the phrase *the priests and the diviners* denotes the religious authorities of that society as a whole.

The verbal root *qsm[15] of *diviners* mainly means "to predict (without any reference to the means used)." Here it is used for a practice occurring outside Israel. It refers to a "fortune teller, oracle priest" among the Philistines or in general (Deut. 18:14), or to Balaam (Josh. 13:22). The noun *qesem* "prediction, survey of future events" also appears as a phenomenon outside Israel, where it is characteristically associated with the pagan prophet Balaam (Num. 22:7; 23:23). On consulting a spirit of the dead *('ôb),* see 1 Sam. 28:8. However, the OT hardly mentions the mechanics of divination;[16] it is more concerned with discouraging its practice in Israelite society (see Deut. 18:10-14).

3 The religious professionals warn them not to send the ark away *empty-handed,* i.e., "without a gift"; see the phrase with a verb "send" *(šlḥ),* that is, "send someone away empty-handed" in Gen. 31:42; Deut. 15:13; Job 22:9. One may note the obvious parallel between this and the Exodus tradi-

13. See D. T. Tsumura, "The Problem of Righteousness in Habakkuk," in *Evangelical Theology* 22 (1991) 50-70 [Japanese], v-viii [English summary].

14. See J.-M. de Tarragon, *Le Culte à Ugarit: D'après les Textes de la Pratique en Cunéiformes Alphabétiques* (Paris: J. Gabalda, 1980), pp. 134-35.

15. *HALOT,* p. 1115.

16. See F. H. Cryer, *Divination in Ancient Israel and Its Near Eastern Environment: A Socio-historic Investigation* (Sheffield: Sheffield Academic Press, 1994).

tion (see Exod. 3:21f.).[17] However, the comparison with that tradition has been somewhat overemphasized.

A *compensation* (or "indemnity" [JPS]; *'āšām;* Ugar. *aṯm* [*UT* §19.422]; cf. "guilt offering" in NRSV; NIV; etc.) in Leviticus 5 and 14 is an offering substituted for an unclean person.[18] According to Milgrom,[19] the *'šm*-sacrifice expiates for "desecration," the *ḥṭ't*-sacrifice[20] for "contamination." Besides, the word *'šm* also denotes "penalty, reparation." In the present passage the *'āšām* is "a monetary reparation" (Milgrom) or "compensation paid as protection against further suffering."[21]

There is an on-going debate on the meaning of this term between Milgrom, who takes it to mean "to have a bad conscience, to feel guilty," and Schenker, who interprets it "to be liable, responsible." While Schenker holds that the Bible distinguishes "a malicious will" from "a will without malice," which must compensate for what it could not do, Milgrom holds that no person can be liable "if neither he nor anyone else is aware of what he has done." In our text, according to Schenker, the city of Ashdod was "unaware of the guilt it had contracted by bringing the ark of the Lord into the temple of Dagon. . . . It is in the light of subsequent calamities that the Ashdodites became aware of having committed a grave fault that they had to repair by votive offerings called **אשׁם**." Schenker concludes that "in ancient Israel one could be *'liable and responsible'* for a fault of which one is not conscious because, conscious or not, the person who has offended God has to compensate for the offense."[22] However, Schenker seems to read a biblical idea into the Philistine attitude and to impose a general sense into this particular case.

The Philistines may have thought that Yahweh was angry with his land, and thus allowed them to remove his ark, as we find in other ancient texts. For example, Mesha, the king of Moab, held that Omri, the king of Israel, "oppressed Moab for many days, for Kemosh was angry with his land" (Moabite Stone, lines 5-6).[23]

4 The people were advised to return to the God of Israel *compensa-*

17. See also D. Daube, *The Exodus Pattern in the Bible* (London: Faber and Faber, 1963).

18. McCarter, p. 133; also see A. Marx, "Sacrifice de Réparation et Rites de Levée de Sanction," *ZAW* 100 (1988) 183-98.

19. J. Milgrom, "Further on the Expiatory Sacrifices," *JBL* 115 (1996) 513; also *Cult and Conscience: The Asham and the Priestly Doctrine of Repentance* (Leiden: E. J. Brill, 1976).

20. See N. Kiuchi, *The Purification Offering in the Priestly Literature: Its Meaning and Function* (Sheffield: JSOT Press, 1987).

21. McCarter, p. 133.

22. A. Schenker, "Once Again, the Expiatory Sacrifices," *JBL* 116 (1997) 697.

23. See *CS,* II, 137.

tion, namely, *five golden mice.* These golden objects function as (1) "a compensatory sacrifice, carrying away the contamination from Philistia and with it the suffering."[24] But at the same time, they are (2) a payment of tribute "to the God whose property has been violated."[25] *According to the number of the Philistine lords* takes the term *number (mispār)* as adverbial. On the sympathetic principle, the number has to exactly correspond to that in the real situation. *Five* is the number of the lords of the pentapolis — Ashdod, Gaza, Ashkelon, Gath, and Ekron (see v. 17).

Why did they send "mice"? For both the narrator and the audience, the real concern was not the mechanical cause of the disease, but rather its result and cure. The MT of 1 Samuel 5 does not even hint that the disease was caused by mice but only by Yahweh. Therefore, making and sending off the golden mice was "sympathetic magic" whose purpose was to get rid of the disease itself, not to get rid of mice as the cause of the disease.[26] But it seems that a metal lump similar to a "hill" (*ʿōpel*)-shaped tumor would also be considered similar to the shape of a mouse, especially if there was already some association between the disease and mice. So, it seems that in this account the golden objects are referred to alternatively as "tumors" or "swellings" or "mice" because the mice represent the tumors.[27]

The objects are *golden* to make them valuable as compensation to appease the god whom they had offended.

Namely <u>five</u> golden mice (waḥămiššāh ʿakbᵉrê zāhāb). In other words, just five golden objects are sent. Most translators take the *waw* here as meaning "and," and translate something like "five gold tumors and five gold mice" (NRSV; also NIV; NASB; JPS; McCarter).[28] McCarter[29] thinks that this "contradicts" v. 17 and hence omits this MT phrase "and five golden mice" as an expansion, based on LXX^{B} and 4QSam^{a}. Miller-Roberts similarly take v. 4 as secondary since they think it was an "insert based on 6:5, but in hopeless conflict with 6:18. The story originally had five buboes and an indefinite number of rats."[30] However, *waw* can also be explicative,

24. McCarter, p. 133.

25. R. P. Gordon, p. 101.

26. See D. T. Tsumura, "List and Narrative in I Samuel 6,17-18a in the Light of Ugaritic Economic Texts," *ZAW* (2001) 353-69.

27. See J. B. Geyer ("Mice and Rites in 1 Samuel v–vi," *VT* 31 [1981] 300-301) on the Hittite ritual of Ambazzi, where the sorceress sent a mouse off with a string as part of a sympathetic ritual.

28. Also in v. 5, "images of your tumors *and* images of your mice."

29. McCarter, p. 129.

30. P. D. Miller, Jr. and J. J. M. Roberts, *The Hand of the Lord: A Reassessment of the "Ark Narrative" of 1 Samuel* (JHNES; Baltimore: Johns Hopkins Univ. Press, 1977), p. 54. Also R. P. Gordon: "Whereas there are five *golden tumours* . . . , it seems to be im-

"namely. . . ." If we recognize that use here and in v. 5, 11, 18, all the problems disappear.[31]

5-6 The antecedent of *which (are ruining the land)* is probably *swellings* rather than *mice,* though most translations translate it "mice": for example, "your mice that ravage the land" (NRSV; NASB). However, see 5:12: "they were struck with tumors," which has no reference to the mice at all. As far as the MT is concerned, the text never mentions "mice" as a plague; the "mice" were an offering to the deity.[32]

The expression *lighten his hand* is the opposite of "he afflicted" (lit., "his hand was heavy": Qal *kbd); see on 5:6. The term *harden* means literally "to make heavy" (Pi. *kbd). The expression "to make the heart heavy" besides here appears only in the context of Exodus (Exod. 7:14; 8:15; etc.). For the Philistines' knowledge of the Exodus, see on 4:8 above. The root *kbd also appears in 5:6, 11, where *the hand of the Lord* was heavy, as well as in 6:5 *(tribute: kābôd).* There may be a sort of play on words in speaking of "not making the hearts heavy" when the hand of Yahweh was "heavy"; he may lighten his hand if they give him a tribute.

7 The Philistine priests now suggest that the people prepare a brand new cart, driven by two cows, on which they shall put the ark with the golden objects and send it off to observe the direction in which the cart will go. The present account and the description of a Hittite plague ritual have a certain similarity — the latter involved sending a ram off toward the territory of an enemy god, as noticed by Miller-Roberts.[33] However, whether this similarity is due to the possible connection of the Philistines with Anatolia is not certain.

The *cart* might be compared with "the wagon of Dagan" used in the procession during the Zukru-festival of ancient Emar.[34] The *cart* for this Philistine ritual, however, has to be *new,* that is, previously unused, and ritually clean. And the *milch cows that have never been yoked* would go wherever they pleased since they had not been trained. As R. P. Gordon notes, "it confirms the absence of human interference in their movements." Also, under normal circumstances the cows would naturally head back home to their offspring.[35]

---

plied that the number of golden *mice* was greater, to take account of the full number of Philistine settlements" (p. 103). For a different view, see the general discussion of the mouse images and mouse plagues in the excursus by F. Schicklberger, *Die Ladeerzählung des ersten Samuel-Buches: Eine literaturwissenschaftliche und theologiegeschichtliche Untersuchung* (FB 7; Würzburg: Echter, 1973), pp. 108-17.

31. See also on the relationship between the list and the narrative in vv. 17-18a.

32. Geyer, "Mice and Rites in 1 Samuel v–vi," p. 297; see above (1 Sam. 5:6).

33. Miller and Roberts, *The Hand of the Lord,* p. 55.

34. See *CS,* I, p. 435.

35. See *KTU* 1.6:II:6-7 on cow-calf relationship. In the Sumerian Cylinder A of Gudea, there is an expression "Like a cow that keeps its eye on its calf"; see *CS,* II, p. 427.

Hence, "only a strong impulse from a superior power" would send them off away from home toward Beth-shemesh. "If that happened the Philistines' miseries could confidently be attributed to the Israelites' God."[36]

McCarter thinks that the cows were chosen "as sacrificial animals intended to carry off the contamination from the Philistines" and to ascertain "whether or not Yahweh was in fact involved in the plague (v. 9)."[37] However, there is no hint that the cows themselves were considered contaminated carriers.

8-9 The origin of the term *pouch* (*'argaz;* only here and 1 Sam. 6:11, 15), also translated as "saddlebag" (*HALOT,* p. 84) or "box, chest" (BDB, p. 919), and its Philistine connection are moot.[38] The phrase *his territory* (lit., "border, boundary") refers to the border between Dagon's territory and Yahweh's.

The name *Beth-shemesh* (lit., "house of the sun"; cf. Ir-shemesh, "city of the sun" in Josh. 19:41) evidently preserves the tradition of Canaanite solar worship. It is identified with modern Tel er-Rumeilah [MR147-128], which is located 12 miles to the west of Jerusalem. The site has produced archaeological evidence of Philistine influence. Beth-Shemesh was an Israelite town during the period of the Judges, but "the material culture at the site is indistinguishable from that of its Philistine neighbor, Timnah."[39] It is located along the inner reaches of the Sorek valley, which is the most direct route from the Philistine Plain to Israelite territory. So, if the cart proceeds toward Beth-shemesh, that would be a sure sign for the Philistines that the Israelite god Yahweh brought this disaster to them. If not, it was just an accident that happened to them. The term *accident (miqreh)* refers to something which people cannot foresee; here the Philistines appear to envisage the Israelite God and "accident" as the two possible and contrasting causes for the plague.[40]

36. R. P. Gordon, p. 101. For an example of many ivory carvings of a "cow and calf," see J. E. Curtis and J. E. Reade, eds., *Art and Empire: Treasures from Assyria in the British Museum* (London: The Trustees of the British Museum by the British Museum Press, 1995), fig. 097. For a similar theme, see the Akkadian wisdom: "He was moaning like a donkey foal separated (from its mother)" (Foster, in *CS,* I, p. 485).

37. McCarter, p. 134.

38. See Geyer, "Mice and Rites in 1 Samuel v–vi," p. 303.

39. A. Mazar, *Archaeology of the Land of the Bible, 10,000-586 B.C.E.* (New York: Doubleday, 1990, 1992), p. 312; see W. G. Dever, "Beth-shemesh," in *OEANE 1,* pp. 311-12.

40. On this term in Qohelet and elsewhere, see P. Machinist, "Fate, miqreh, and Reason: Some Reflections on Qohelet and Biblical Thought," in *Solving Riddles and Untying Knots: Biblical, Epigraphic, and Semitic Studies in Honor of Jonas C. Greenfield,* ed. Z. Zevit, S. Gitin, and M. Sokoloff (Winona Lake, Ind.: Eisenbrauns, 1995), pp. 159-75.

b. The Ark to Beth-shemesh (6:10-16)

10 *And the men did so.*
And they took two milch cows and bound them to the cart; as for their calves, they shut them up[41] *in the house,*
11 *and put the ark of the Lord on the cart and the pouch with the golden mice, which were the images of their tumors.*
12 *And the cows went straight*[42] *on the way on the Beth-shemesh road;*[43] *on one highway they went while lowing*[44] *and did not turn aside to the right or the left. The Philistine lords were following them up to the border of Beth-shemesh.*
13 *At Beth-shemesh they (= people) were reaping the wheat harvest in the valley, and they lifted up their eyes and saw the ark and rejoiced in seeing it.*
14 *As for the cart, it came to the field of Joshua, a Bethshemeshite,*[45] *and stood at the place where there was a great stone. They split up the wood of the cart; and the cows they offered as a burnt offering to the Lord.*
15 *Now it was the Levites who brought down the ark of the Lord and the pouch attached to it in which were the golden objects and set them up on the great stone. On the other hand, the men of Beth-shemesh offered burnt offerings and made sacrifices on that day to the Lord.*
16 *As for the five Philistine lords, they saw it and returned to Ekron on that day.*

41. kālû ← <*sandhi*> — kāl^{e}'û. See D. T. Tsumura, "Vowel sandhi in Biblical Hebrew," *ZAW* 109 (1997) 575-88; cf. GKC, §75qq.

42. וַיִּשַּׁרְנָה; *yšr Qal. Note that BHS (sic L) has וַיִשַּׁרְנָה */wayiššárnāh/*, confirmed by *The Leningrad Codex: A Facsimile Edition,* which is a phonetic spelling derived from the expected form וַיִּשַּׁרְנָה */wayyiššárnāh/*, which may have come from *wayyiyšarnāh* (GKC, §71; see also הַשֵּׁן 7:12). Here, the */y/* can be explained as assimilated to the following contiguous consonant, as is the case with */n/* (see GKC, §71). But this is not a Pi. form, which would be */way-yaššárnāh/* < */way-y^{e}-yaššárnāh/*, though McCarter expects Pi. with *derek,* "to go straight ahead" (literally, "straighten one's way") here. However, the MT has the preposition *b-* before *derek,* which cannot be the object of the piel verb; McCarter (p. 136) seems to miss that fact. As for the gender of the verb, whose subject is f. pl. ("cows"), McCarter proposes here to see "an archaic dual verb form of common gender (cf. Gordon, *UT* §9.15)" (McCarter, pp. 135-36) in view of the dual suffixes in vv. 7, 10. See also 2 Sam. 4:1.

43. Or "toward Beth-shemesh."

44. See *g't* "lowing (of plough-oxen)" (*KTU* 1.14 III 18); *CS,* I, p. 335; *TO,* p. 522, n. u.

45. *bêt-haššimšî,* cf. Šimšôn, Šipiš (Ebla); an otherwise unknown Joshua.

10-12 The Philistine people did as told by their priests. The cows went on toward Beth-shemesh straightway. As for the calves, they *shut them up in the house,* presumably after they drove them home away from their mother (see v. 7).

Verse 11 is literally "and put the ark of the Lord on the cart *and* the pouch *and* the golden mice *and* the images of their tumors." McCarter says that "All witnesses here append lists of the other items to be sent back with the ark (the box, the golden tumors, the golden mice), but the lists are at variance in arrangement and completeness."[46] Hence, McCarter omits everything after *the ark* as not likely "original." However, it makes sense if the three *waws* ("and"s) are interpreted differently as "and," "with," and "which is." The translation *with* (lit., "and"), taking the noun with *ʾt* as adverbial, is possible from the context and content; the golden mice were to be put inside the pouch; see v. 15. As in vv. 4, 5, 18 the last *waw* should be taken as explicative, hence *which were* or "namely." Note that only here the order of "tumors" — "mice" is reversed: *the golden mice,* which are "the images of their tumors." This explains that the images were "mouse-shaped" golden items and that the golden mice were made to symbolize their tumors.

In the phrase *the images of their tumors (ṣalmê ṭᵉḥōrêhem),* here, as in v. 17, *tumors* is expressed straightforwardly. It equals the Qere of 5:6 and other places where it is "taboo" to pronounce the Ketib *(*ʿŏpālîm),* and hence the Qere is suggested. See on 5:6.

According to a recent study by Tidwell, the term for *highway* (v. 12) refers to "the approach road which ascended from the base of the mound or hill on which cities in ancient Palestine stood to the main gate of the city on the mound."[47] Such approach roads have been excavated in Beth-shemesh, Gibeon (see 2 Sam. 20:8), and other sites (see also in 2 Sam. 20:12 (x2), 13). However, the term in this context must be referring to a "highway" between two cities and, hence, to a fairly long, gradual ascension from the *valley* (v. 13) in the case of Beth-Shemesh.

13 The time was May/June during *the wheat harvest.* The people at Beth-shemesh were happily harvesting the wheat. One might imagine the contrastive and even comical scene: the Israelites at Beth-shemesh *rejoiced in seeing* the ark, while the dressed-up Philistine lords following the new cow-driven cart were anxious and solemn.

The *valley (ʿēmeq)* refers to a place between two mountains or cities (see *KTU* 1.3:II:6) and is thus sometimes translated as "plain"; see the Valley of Sorek, cf. Judg. 16:4. The idiom *lifted up their eyes and saw* (Gen. 13:10;

46. McCarter, p. 130.

47. N. L. Tidwell, "No Highway! The Outline of a Semantic Description of *mesillâ*," *VT* 45 (1995) 251-69.

18:2; 22:4; 2 Sam. 13:34; 18:24; etc.) appears frequently in Ugaritic literature also (e.g., *nšy* + *ʿn* + *ʿyn* [*KTU* 1.10:II:27, 14]; *nšy* + *ʿn* + *ph* [1.4:II:12; 1.17:V:9; 1.19:II:28-29; etc.]).

14-15 The cart and the golden objects were placed on the *great stone,* which served as an altar; see v. 18. The expression *a burnt offering* appears for the first time in Samuel (see Lev. 1:1-17; 6:2-6 [ET 9-13]; 9:1-24; etc.). Usually male cows were sacrificed (Lev. 1:3, 10; 4:23 *zākār tāmîm* "a male without defect"; 22:19 *tāmîm zākār).*

Many commentators take v. 15 as a secondary verse inserted by "a fastidious scribe who insisted that the Ark must have been handled by Levites";[48] see Num. 3:27-32; Deut. 10:8. The Levites are mentioned only twice in the books of Samuel (here and 2 Sam. 15:24). Does this mean that they were never active in Israel in this period? Judges refers to Levites in chs. 17–18 and ch. 19. The lack of reference to an event is not proof that the event did not occur; note the long silence of Samuel between chs. 4 and 7. As R. P. Gordon holds, "it is unlikely that the Levites were introduced here merely because of the special status of Beth-shemesh,"[49] which is listed among the levitical cities in Josh. 21:16. It can be reasonably assumed that there was a continued priestly tradition at Beth-Shemesh, just as there was at Shiloh (1 Samuel 1–4) and Nob (see 1 Samuel 21–22) during the pre- and early monarchic days.

The temporal order [chronology] is reversed here, since this verse refers back to the time before the wood of the cart is split up in v. 14. The offering of sacrifices is mentioned in both verses. What is emphasized in v. 15 is not so much what they did as who did what. It was the Levites who brought down the ark from the cart and set it up on the great stone, while the people of Beth-shemesh offered the sacrifices probably by the hand of priests.

The word order, *waw* + S + pf., expresses the contrast between "Levites" and "people": hence, *On the other hand.*

16 Ekron is the city most recently afflicted and also the nearest to Beth-shemesh. On this city, see on 5:10.

The phrase *on that day* is mentioned again; see v. 15. Such a repetition signals the TERMINUS of the present episode. The returning of the five lords to Ekron marks the closing of this episode.

c. Summary Statement (6:17-18a)

17 *Now these are the golden tumors, which the Philistines returned to the Lord as compensation:*

48. See McCarter, p. 136.
49. R. P. Gordon, p. 102.

for Ashdod *one*
for Gaza *one*
for Ashkelon *one*
for Gath *one*
for Ekron *one*

18a *namely, the golden mice*
(according to) the number of all the Philistine cities belonging to the five lords, that is, both walled forts and (their) surrounding villages.[50]

McCarter thinks that vv. 17-18 are an "appendix," "probably . . . an addition to the account providing the results of a later audience's analysis of the curious components of the *ʾāšām* [compensation]." Similarly, Caird, following Smith, takes the list section as "an interpolation after the manner of the priestly code or of the Chronicler."[51] But they say it is an addition because they do not understand how lists are used in biblical narratives. The list in v. 17 is an integral part of the original narrative, and v. 18a is the restatement of the same information in summary form with further detail.[52] Therefore, as discussed below, the initial *waw* in v. 18 is to be taken as *explicative* and translated "namely."

17 The phrase *these are (wᵉʾēlleh)* is the title of a list as in Gen. 2:4 or 2 Sam. 6:19. There are a number of list formulas used in the ancient Near East.[53] Lists like this one, where the name of each item is followed by "one," can be found also among Ugaritic economic texts such as *KTU* 4.5 + 4.19, 4.209.[54] Many lists give the total at the conclusion. In our list, the total is not stated, but adding up the numbers gets "five," the number predicted by the expression "the five Philistine lords" in the preceding verse.

As in v. 11, here the more specific term *ṭᵉḥōrîm* is used for *tumors.* The use of *ṭᵉḥōrîm* is expected here in the title of a list formula since a list tends to be more straightforward in the choice of terms than a narrative. This is in line with the metaphorical use of *ʿŏpālîm* in the earlier narrative section.

50. *kōper happᵉrāzî,* lit., "a village of the hamlet-dweller" or "a village of the peasantry"; cf. BDB, p. 826: "villages of . . ." (pl.). See *CAD,* K, p. 190: *kapru* "village," "farm," "settlement," or suburban agglomerations around cities.

51. Caird, p. 911; also Smith, p. 47.

52. See D. T. Tsumura, "List and Narrative in I Samuel 6,17-18a in the Light of Ugaritic Economic Texts," *ZAW* 113 (2001) 353-69.

53. See Tsumura, "List and Narrative in I Samuel 6,17-18a," pp. 355-58.

54. Tsumura, "List and Narrative in I Samuel 6,17-18a," pp. 359-60. There are also lists in Ugaritic economic texts, with the heading of *spr* "list, document" (cf. Gen. 5:1). These lists date from the mid-second millennium B.C., and so lists in this form certainly do not have to be "late."

For *Ashdod* see on 5:1. *Gaza (ʿazzāh)* is first mentioned in Gen. 10:19 in the OT. It appears with Gath and Ashdod in Josh. 11:22 and with Ashkelon and Ekron in Judg. 1:18. It was once identified by F. Petrie as the modern Tell el-ʿAjjul, but as Kempinski[55] has suggested, that site was actually the city of Sharuhen (Josh. 19:6). Gaza was probably located within the confines of the modern Gaza.[56]

Ashkelon is first mentioned in the Bible in Judg. 1:18, together with Gaza and Ekron; the city is known from the story of Samson (Judg. 14:19; etc.) and in David's elegy for Saul and Jonathan (2 Sam. 1:20), along with Gath. It is located [MR107-118] on the Mediterranean seacoast 40 miles south of Tel Aviv. Astride fertile soil and fresh groundwater, it is ideally suited for irrigation agriculture and maritime trade. Its "convenient harbor and its ancient tradition of excellence in crafts and industry" gave the city "a preferred position" among the capitals. There was an excellent temple of the god Ptaḥ, the Great Prince of Ashkelon, which is mentioned in the twelfth-century B.C. ivory plaques uncovered at Megiddo. The city is also mentioned in the nineteenth-century B.C. Egyptian Execration Texts. During most of LB Age, Ashkelon remained under Egyptian suzerainty.[57] About 1175 B.C. the first Philistines arrived, and Ashkelon became a member of the Philistine Pentapolis.

For *Gath,* see on 5:8. For *Ekron,* see on 5:10. It is listed last, for it is the nearest to Israel and the last city where the ark of Yahweh stayed.

18a In a narrative into which a list is integrated, both list and narrative normally deal with the same items. Therefore, it seems reasonable that in our text the items in 18a are the same as those dealt with in v. 17. This means that the initial *waw* in v. 18a is probably to be taken as *waw explicative* as in 17:40 and elsewhere, and thus translated as *namely* (see on vv. 4, 5, 11 [above]; 5:9; 17:40; 28:3).[58] Here, the author gives a narrative explanation of the list formula in v. 17.[59]

As already discussed in 6:4, the number of *mice* should be "five." *The number . . .* here is also "five." The total number of Philistine cities has already been implied by the expression *the five Philistine lords* in v. 16 as well

55. See A. Kempinski, "ʿAjjul, Tell el-," in *NEAEHL,* pp. 52-53; A. Ovadiah, "Gaza," in *NEAEHL,* pp. 464-67.

56. See J. P. Dessel, "ʿAjjul, Tell el-," in *OEANE,* 1, pp. 38-40.

57. See L. E. Stager, *Ashkelon Discovered: From Canaanites and Philistines to Romans and Moslems* (Washington, D.C.: Biblical Archaeology Society, 1991); "Ashkelon," in *NEAEHL,* pp. 103-12; D. Schloen, "Ashkelon," in *OEANE,* 1, pp. 220-23.

58. See D. W. Baker, "Further Examples of the *waw explicativum,*" *VT* 30 (1980) 129-36.

59. Cf. the relationship between lists and narrative in OT and other literatures; see Tsumura, "List and Narrative in I Samuel 6,17-18a," pp. 360-69.

as the expression in v. 4: *According to the number of the lords of the Philistines, five gold tumors, namely, five gold mice.* Thus, the author had no need to repeat the number "five" here. A fortified city and the unfortified villages of its vicinity were treated as one unit (see below). Hence, the total number of the golden mice should be "five."

The expression *both walled forts and (their) surrounding villages (mē'îr mibṣār wᵉʿad kōper happᵉrāẓî)* is literally "from a fortified city and till an unfortified village."[60] It is certainly a merismus and contrasts "fortified" and "unfortified," not "city" and "village." In Deut. 3:5 "unwalled villages" (RSV/NIV) *ʿārê happᵉrāẓî* appears in opposition to the walled/fortified cities; thus, an unfortified "city" refers to an unfortified "village."

This merismatic expression refers to the entire area within the city limits, which include both the walled or fortified city and the surrounding villages associated with it[61] rather than both (1) fortified towns and (2) unwalled villages outside of city limits.[62] A similar expression can be noted in the Assyrian annals of Sennacherib III:13-14, et al.: "46 of his strong cities, that is, fortresses and the countless small villages in their vicinity."[63] Here too the merismatic expression "fortresses and the countless small villages in their vicinity" refers to the makeup of the political city unit. Also, in the expression "both Ashdod and its environs" (1 Sam 5:6), a city and its vicinity are treated as one unit in the story.[64]

To summarize, v. 17 is a list of an <item + "one">-type pattern, and v. 18a gives a supplementary explanation of the items in the list. The total number of golden items involved is five. So, in this narrative five gold mice, which stand for tumors, were sent by the Philistines to Israel as a compensation and a tribute. The compensation was made not just for the cities proper, but for the cities and their environs, that is, for the whole land of the Philistines.

60. See 1 Sam. 7:14; 15:3; 22:19; 2 Sam. 6:19 ("from man to woman" = both men and women); "both Ashdod and its environs" (1 Sam. 5:6).

61. In his third campaign Sennacherib mentions "Great Sidon" and "Small Sidon," which refer to the metropolitan area and the fortified acropolis, respectively; see Gordon, *PLMU,* p. 40, n. 43.

62. Cf. "This long sentence covers Philistia in its entirety not only with '*all* their cities' but also with the well-known merismus . . . of 'fortified towns and unwalled villages'" (J. P. Fokkelman, IV, p. 287).

63. *46 ālāni-šu dannūti bīt dūrānī u ālānī ṣeḫrūti ša limētišunu ša nība la išû* (Annals of Sennacherib, III:13-14, et al.).

64. Also see Josh. 15:45; 10:39.

d. The Ark to Kiriath-jearim (6:18b–7:1)

18b *As for the great platform of Abel on which they laid the ark of the Lord, it is in the field of Joshua, the Bethshemeshite, until this day.*

19 *And he smote some of the men of Beth-shemesh,*
for they looked into the ark of the Lord.
And[65] *he smote among the people seventy men,*
that is, every five people out of a thousand.
And the people mourned,
because the Lord smote some of the people severely.

20 *And the men of Beth-shemesh said,*
"Who can stand before the Lord, this holy God?
To whom will it go up from us?"

21 *and sent messengers to the inhabitants of Kiriath-jearim, saying,*
"The Philistines have returned the ark of the Lord.
Come down and take it up to you!"

1 *And the men of Kiriath-jearim came and took up the ark of the Lord and had it come to the house of Abinadab on the Hill; and his son Eleazar they consecrated to keep the ark of the Lord.*

18b After specifying the total number of golden mice, both in a list and a summary, the narrator refers back to the place where the ark of Yahweh was placed: the great stone (6:14), though naming it this time, *the great platform of Abel.*

As for *ʿad ʾābēl haggᵉdôlāh,* most modern translations (e.g., NRSV; NASB; JPS; NIV), supported by modern commentators (e.g., R. P. Gordon) as well as by the LXX, emend *ʾābēl* to *ʾeben* and translate the phrase as "the great stone" or the like. However, this translation would require the restoration of an article for "stone" and an adequate explanation of the term *ʿad.* If the term *ʿad* is the feminine noun "platform" (see Ugar. *ʿd*)[66] in construct followed by a proper name, the translation *the great platform of Abel* is the most natural one; see also "the stone Ezel" *(hāʾeben hāʾāzel)* in 20:19 and "the stone Ezer" in 7:12. For the proper name "Abel" (so KJV), see the GN "Abel of Beth-maacah" (2 Sam. 20:14, 15, 18). De Ward thinks that if Abel-Haggedolah is a proper name like Abel-Meholah and Abel-Keramim, it may have denoted a place for mourning *(ʾbl)* "even before it came to be associated

65. Note that the usage of the two *wayqtl* (*wayyak . . . wayyak* "and he smote . . . and he smote . . .") is not sequential but a kind of "poetic" repetition; in the first "why" is explained, while in the second "how many" is stated.

66. For "platform" or "dais," see Ugar. *ʿd* (Gibson, *CML*², p. 154; cf. *UT* §19.1814 *"throne room"*).

with the disaster at Beth-shemesh (1 Sam. 6:14, 18)."[67] However, the name "Abel" here in v. 18 is probably prolepsis;[68] this mournful incident (v. 19) gave rise to the name by which it was known at the time of the narrator.

The phrase *in the field of Joshua, the Bethshemeshite* is a recapitulation of the phrase "to the field of Joshua, a Bethshemeshite" in v. 14, where the "great stone" is mentioned. Verses 14 and 18b thus form a *frame.*

The formula *until this day* contrasts with "on that day" in vv. 15 and 16 (also 1 Sam. 5:5; 2 Sam. 6:8). The position of this phrase in the Hebrew text is unusual and exhibits the phenomenon of inversion: literally, "And the great platform of Abel on which they laid the ark of the Lord (is) until this day in the field of Joshua, the Bethshemeshite." This note, given by the author of this section, probably goes back to the time when the ark was still in Beth-Shemesh. On this phrase "until this day," see further on 8:8-19 and "Introduction" (Section III, B, 1).

19 *He/it smote:* YHWH or the ark smote. Whichever pronoun is the subject, the agent is the Lord, who brings destruction "even in Israelite territory."[69]

As McCarter notes, *looked into,* instead of "saw" (LXX), may reflect "an attempt to account for the smiting by appeal to cultic taboos (cf. Num 4:15, 20; so Hertzberg, pp. 60-61)." The action would imply the opening of the ark, which would indeed be shocking.

Seventy men, that is, every five people out of a thousand. MT *šibʿîm ʾîš ḥămiššîm ʾelep ʾîš* has been translated as "70 men, 50,000 men," which equals "50,070 men" (NASB) or "seventy men among the people and fifty thousand men" (JPS). This seems an impossibly large number for a town with probably a few thousand inhabitants. Hence, RSV; NEB; NIV omit "fifty thousand men" *(ḥămiššîm ʾelep ʾîš)* as a later addition, though the majority of LXX manuscripts, including LXX^L, support the MT reading. This omission is almost universally accepted and has recently been reaffirmed by Fouts.[70] On

67. E. F. de Ward, "Mourning Customs in 1, 2, Samuel," *JJS* 23 (1972) 6.

68. For "prolepsis" see on 17:52.

69. R. P. Gordon, p. 103. Cf. McCarter, p. 131, on textual problems: "The beginning of the verse is defective in MT. . . . Most commentators prefer LXX^B. . . . 'But the sons of Jeconiah did not join in the celebration with the men of Beth-shemesh when. . . .'" But Walters thinks it more likely "that the sons of Jeconiah belong to an alternate form of the narrative, and are a tendentious presence in the text to be explained in terms of Hellenistic Judaism"; see S. D. Walters, "Review of P. K. McCarter, *I Samuel: A New Translation with Introduction, Notes, and Commentary* (Garden City, N.Y.: Doubleday, 1980)," *JBL* 101 (1982) 438. The lack of the phrase "the sons of Jeconiah" in MT should not be taken as a textual corruption.

70. D. M. Fouts, "Added Support for Reading '70 men' in 1 Samuel VI:19," *VT* 42 (1992) 394.

the other hand, Allis supports the MT and takes it to mean "50 out of 1,000"[71] (also see 2 Sam. 8:2, "2 out of 3"). However, *ḥămiššîm* could be a form with an enclitic *mem (as šᵉnêm ʿāśār)* following an ordinal *ḥămîšî /ḥămiššî* "fifth,"[72] rather than "fifty"; see on 2 Sam. 15:7. If this is correct, there would be two possible explanations: (1) "one fifth of the clan"[73] (see Lev. 27:32 "every tenth one"; see 1 Sam. 10:19 "clans"; also Judg. 6:15; 1 Sam. 23:23) or (2) "5 out of [every] 1,000 (or clan)." If (1) is the case, the clan has 350 men; if (2) is correct, then the total population of the city would be 14,000 (or 14 clans).[74] The Mari letters attest to a West Semitic word *lîmum,* "a clan or a tribal unit." Malamat sees a semantic parallel to this term in the biblical Hebrew *'elep* since *lîmum* and *'elep* both mean "a clan" and "1,000."[75]

The term *mourned* (*'bl* here and 2 Sam. 11:27; 13:37; 14:2; 19:2) refers to mourning for the dead.

Here the agent is finally specified as *the Lord* at the end of the verse after two ambiguous clauses: *he/it smote — he/it smote — the Lord smote.* This is a skillful way of showing that though the ark was the direct agent, it was really the Lord who struck the people; cf. *the hand of the Lord* (5:6, etc.). However, the ark is not simply a box; it is the seat of royal and holy presence where the Lord of Hosts meets the people, powerfully manifesting himself.

20 The phrase *stand before* (or "wait upon") is often used specifically of priests attending in a sanctuary or "before the ark" as in Judg. 20:28. Compare Samuel's ministering before the Lord *(mᵉšārēt)* in 1 Sam. 2:11, 18; 3:1. But it can also mean "withstand," as in Exod. 9:11, where the Egyptian magicians were not able to stand before Moses. "In this case the men of Beth-shemesh would be acknowledging the overwhelming power

71. O. T. Allis, "The Punishment of the Men of Bethshemesh," *EQ* 15 (1943) 307.

72. See BDB, p. 332 for *ḥămîšît / ḥămīšît* "a fifth part."

73. Fractions were often used in the ANE. For the literary device of expressing totality by using fractions such as $\frac{1}{3} + \frac{1}{4} + \frac{1}{5} + \frac{1}{6} + \frac{1}{7}$ ($\doteqdot 1$) in Keret epic (*KTU* 1.14:I:16-21), see *UT,* pp. 49-50; also D. T. Tsumura, "The Problem of Childlessness in the Royal Epic of Ugarit," in *Monarchies and Socio-Religious Traditions in the Ancient Near East* (Wiesbaden: Otto Harrassowitz, 1984), pp. 11-20.

74. The term *'elep* means either "thousand" or "group" (family, clan, troop, team, etc.); see C. J. Humphreys, "The Numbers in the Exodus from Egypt: A Further Appraisal," *VT* 50 (2000) 323. Cf. "troops," so C. J. Humphreys ("The Number of People in the Exodus from Egypt: Decoding Mathematically the Very Large Numbers in Numbers I and XXVI," *VT* 48 [1998] 211), who concludes: "the average number of military men (aged over 20) per troop was about 10." Yet see B. E. Scolnic, *Theme and Context in Biblical Lists* (Atlanta: Scholars Press, 1995), pp. 26-28: "thousand" or "clan," not "a military unit"; see on 4:3.

75. A. Malamat, "A Recently Discovered Word for 'Clan' in Mari and Its Hebrew Cognate," in *Solving Riddles and Untying Knots,* p. 179.

of Yahweh, rather than overlooking the obvious expedient of hiring a priest."[76]

On the "holiness" of God, see on 2:2. While the people of Beth-shemesh used the same attribute *(holy)* of Yahweh as did Hannah, the implication is different in the two cases. While on the one hand Hannah acknowledged Yahweh as the intimate and yet sovereign Lord of Hosts, these people somehow lacked the proper attitude toward God, not honoring and reverencing the holy One. The addition of *this* makes their relationship with God sound more superficial and exhibits a popular conception of *qādôš* "holiness," that is, "taboo." As it was one of the darkest eras of the history of ancient Israel, it is no surprise to find that the spiritual condition of the covenant people was at such low ebb. In light of this, Hannah's "prayer" sticks out. Now the time is ripe for Samuel's new ministry. God has not forgotten his people even in the darkest time.

21 The modern site of *Kiriath-jearim* is Tel el-ʿAzhar, 8 miles northwest of Jerusalem and about 15 miles east-northeast of Beth-shemesh; it means "City of the Forests." It was a strategic location, on a hill at the juncture of the boundaries of Judah, Dan, and Benjamin. On the basis of its alternative names Baalah (Josh. 15:9), Kiriath-baal (Josh. 15:60), and Baale-judah (2 Sam. 6:2), one might conjecture that this city was formally connected with Baal worship.[77]

6:21–7:1 The usage of the *wayqtl*-verbs *(sent . . . came . . . took up . . . let it come)* describes the movement vividly, as the narrator's viewpoint changes: (1) "sent" from Beth-shemesh to Kiriath-jearim; (2) "came" from Kiriath-jearim to Beth-shemesh; (3) "brought up" from Beth-shemesh; and (4) "let it come" to Kiriath-jearim. Now, the narrator's viewpoint is at Kiriath-jearim.

7:1 The name *Abinadab* appears for the first time.[78] Two sons of Abinadab besides Eleazar were later priests, Ahio and Uzzah (2 Sam. 6:3-8; 1 Chr. 13:7-11).

As in Ramah, *the Hill* could be outside of the city enclosure (see on "Ramathaim" in 1 Sam. 1:1). There, "the high place" was presumably on the hilltop (see 9:25), outside "the city." This possibly refers to a particular quarter of Kiriath-jearim. According to Aharoni, *the Hill* was the older Benjaminite town which was distinguished from a later, adjoining Judahite settlement.[79]

76. R. P. Gordon, p. 103.

77. R. P. Gordon, pp. 103-4. See on 2 Sam. 6:2. See J. Blenkinsopp, "Kiriath-jearim and the Ark," *JBL* 88 (1969) 143-56.

78. "Nadab," a son of Aaron, appears in Exod. 6:23. For the Semitic root *ndb,* see J. P. Weinberg, "The Word ndb in the Bible: A Study in Historical Semantics and Biblical Thought," in *Solving Riddles and Untying Knots,* pp. 365-75.

79. Y. Aharoni, "The Province-List of Judah," *VT* 9 (1959) 228-29.

Eleazar is also the name of Aaron's son (Exod. 6:23, 25; Num. 3:2; etc.); the names Abinadab and Eleazar were probably common in the levitical family.

This is the only place where this verb *keep (šmr)* appears with "the ark" of the Lord. Does it mean "to protect, to look after"? Even though the ark is safely back in Israel and a priesthood is provided to "keep" it, the people's relationship with the Lord remains unchanged. They are not giving due respect to their covenant Lord but instead have worshipped foreign gods and goddesses for twenty years (see 7:2ff.). However, the Lord is preparing the people's heart to hunger spiritually for him, and he is quietly working through the life of Samuel, his chosen servant.

C. JUDGESHIP OF SAMUEL (7:2-17)

Some twenty years have passed since the ark came to Kiriath-jearim; during that period the Israelites forgot their God and served *the foreign gods and goddesses* (v. 3). It took a long time for them to repent and come back to the Lord; for his part he waited patiently and silently for them to feel their spiritual hunger and return to him. Samuel, after a long break, finally took a responsible role in leading *all the house of Israel* (v. 2) to repentance. He also took the crucial role in striking the Philistines (vv. 5-12). He set up *the stone Ezer,* saying, *"Up to this point/time the Lord helped us!"* (v. 12). Samuel *judged* Israel throughout his life, and during his time, *the hand of the Lord was upon the Philistines* (v. 13), protecting Israel from them.

Scholars are sharply divided in opinion about how to place the present section (7:2-17) in the framework of the story of Samuel. According to McCarter, this chapter, with its victory over the Philistines, is the climax of the account of Samuel's boyhood and prophetic commission. It is a pivotal moment in the political situation in Samuel, the description of a situation where there is no need for kingship.[1] Thus, he sees the present chapter as "the climax of the preparation" for the moment when the Israelites will approach Samuel and demand a king (1 Samuel 8).

R. P. Gordon, on the other hand, says that ch. 7 deals with the beginning of "the uncomfortable question of legitimacy" of kingship and conveys that when everything is under the control of God through his chosen judge, "to ask for a king . . . would be an impertinence." He thus sees a greater continuity between ch. 7 and 8 than McCarter does, and he takes the contrast between these chapters as intentional. Samuel is here at his height and can be compared with Moses in Exodus 17–18 as being prophet, priest, and

1. McCarter, p. 148.

judge.[2] Hertzberg similarly takes ch. 7 as "a factual, and above all as a theological introduction to the whole section [of chs. 7–15]."[3]

Nevertheless, from a literary and discourse grammar point of view, ch. 7 seems to be a terminal literary unit. The narrative of Samuel's life has reached a conclusion; it summarizes his role and prepares for the next episode. Verses 13-17 move toward the TERMINUS of the story of Samuel as shown by the phrases "all the days of Samuel" (v. 13) and "all the days of his life" (v. 15). The very last verse with its reference to Ramah, foreshadowing Ramah as the setting of ch. 8, exhibits a linkage, Ab/B pattern (see "Introduction" [Section VI, B]), thus preparing for the next episode with some continuity. However, as a literary unit the story ends with the final verse of ch. 7. Chapter 8 is an independent chapter which functions as a transition to the story of Saul (chs. 9ff.).

1. After Twenty Years (7:2-4)

2 *From the day when the ark stayed in Kiriath-jearim many days*
passed; twenty years passed. And all the house of Israel
lamented after the Lord.
3 *And Samuel said to all the house of Israel, saying,*
"If, with all of your heart, you are going to return to the Lord,
put away the foreign gods and goddesses from your midst
and fix your heart on the Lord and serve him alone
so that he may deliver you from the hand of the Philistines!"
4 *And the sons of Israel put away gods and goddesses and served the*
Lord alone.

2-3 The Philistines kept oppressing Israel even after the ark of God returned to Israelite territory. It took another *twenty years,* nearly half a generation, for the Israelites to be freed from them. By this time Samuel had become a fully mature servant of the Lord.

2 The phrase *the house of Israel,* which appears for the first time in Samuel (x8), refers to the entire land. They *lamented after* (so NRSV; NASB) the Lord, namely, "mourned and sought after" him (NIV). On the basis of Aramaic Targum, Barr suggests the meaning of "follow after, be devoted."[4] The prepositional phrase *'aḥărê YHWH* has a resultative force, like *min* "away from, without" in v. 8.

3 At last Samuel appears! The last mention of him was in 4:1.

2. R. P. Gordon, pp. 105-6.
3. Hertzberg, p. 66.
4. J. Barr, *CPTOT,* pp. 264-65.

Where had he been during the national crisis? He was unnoticed during these dark decades. The narrator may be suggesting that Samuel's long absence, at least on the national political scene, itself hints at the darkness of this era; see on 4:1. But now the time is ripe for God, the Lord of history, to bring him back to the main stage.

In Hebrew, the phrase *with all of your heart* has been moved to before the nucleus of the sentence and thus emphasized. The phrase points to the importance of the "will" in the act of "repentance," in returning to the Lord. While this is sometimes taken as a Deuteronomistic cliché, such a general expression can occur at any place in the Bible.

"To return" (*šwb) here is the act of "repentance," that is, a change of direction back to the Lord. Three things are commanded: (1) to turn aside from idolatry; (2) to fix the heart on the Lord; and (3) to serve him alone (see Deut. 6:4ff.; Josh. 24:14f., 23; Judg. 10:6-16). Naturally, not only the change of direction but the direction to which one turns, that is, towards the Lord, and the subsequent relationship with him, are emphasized.

To *put way the foreign gods and goddesses* means to reject all rivals to God (Ps. 16:2, 4; cf. Judg. 10:16). The phrase *the foreign gods (ʾĕlōhê hannēkār;* see Judg. 10:16; Jer. 5:19; Deut. 31:16) and *goddesses (hāʿaštārôt)* make a merismus referring to the totality of idols. The latter term (lit., "the Astartes") with the article is used as a generalized term for "goddesses."[5] See on v. 4 (below); also on 1 Sam. 12:10; 31:10. In the Hebrew word order, the phrase *from your midst* breaks up the merismatic phrase *the foreign gods and goddesses* (lit., the gods of the foreign and the Astartes), thus constituting an A X and B pattern (see "Introduction" [Section VII, C] and on 6:11).

Deliverance is a synonym of salvation. God will *deliver* his people from the power (lit., "hand") of the oppressors into fellowship with him; this is the theme of the entire Bible. See v. 8 on "to deliver/save from the hand of the Philistines."

4 So the Israelites did as Samuel commanded: they (1) turned aside from idolatry and (3) served the Lord alone. The second command, (2) to fix the heart on the Lord, is not mentioned but can be assumed. This is a summary statement, which mentions the first and the last items, merismatically referring to the entire action.[6] By their repentance the Israelites thus fulfill "the third element in that scheme of apostasy-oppression-repentance-deliverance which is outlined for the period of the judges (Judg. 2:11-23)."[7]

5. Note that Akk. *ištaru* "goddess," plural *ištarātu* "goddesses," often appears in parallel with *ilu* "god"; see *CAD,* I-J, pp. 272-73.

6. See D. T. Tsumura, "The Unity of Psalm 51," *Exegetica* 2 (1991) 35-48 on Ps. 51:20-21 [ET 18-19].

7. R. P. Gordon, p. 106.

The phrase *gods and goddesses ('et-habbᵉʿālîm wᵉ'et-hāʿaštārōt;* lit., "the Baals and the Astartes"; also 12:10) is interpreted variously: for example, "the Baals and the Astartes" (NRSV); "the Baals and the Ashtaroth" (NASB); "their Baals and Ashtoreths" (NIV). Baal is the Canaanite storm god, sometimes called Hadad; Baal worship had been a constant temptation from the very beginning of Israel's settlement process as seen from the Baal-Peor incident (Num. 23:28).[8] Astarte corresponds to the Ugaritic fertility goddess *ʿṯtrt* (*UT* §19.1941).[9] See also on 31:10 for the Philistines' "temple of Astartes."

Male-female pairs of divinities are known in the Ugaritic mythology, such as "El and Asherah"[10] and "Baal and Anat."[11] But here in Samuel, Baal is paired with Astarte. At Emar's western temples, also, the storm god called Baal is paired with the goddess Aštart.[12]

The plural nouns "Baals" and "Astartes" sometime refer to various manifestations of Baal or Astarte in local cults, but here, as in Judg. 10:6 and 1 Sam. 12:10 and most places in the OT, the plural forms seem to stand for gods and goddesses in general. So, from the present context, the idiomatic expression "the Baals and the Astartes" is the equivalent of *the foreign gods and goddesses* in v. 3.

2. Samuel at Mizpah (7:5-12)

5 *And Samuel said,*
"Gather all Israel at Mizpah,
and I shall pray to the Lord for you!"[13]
6 *And they gathered*[14] *at Mizpah and drew water and poured it before the Lord; and they fasted on that day and said there,*

8. See on Baal-Peor in *DDD,* pp. 279-81 (K. Spronk). See "Introduction" (Section IV, C, 2, c).

9. For Astarte *(ʿaštōret),* see *HALOT,* p. 899. For Canaanite goddesses, see P. K. McCarter, Jr., "Aspects of the Religion of the Israelite Monarchy: Biblical and Epigraphic Data," in *Ancient Israelite Religion: Essays in Honor of Frank Moore Cross,* ed. P. D. Miller, Jr., P. D. Hanson, and S. D. McBride (Philadelphia: Fortress, 1987), p. 144.

10. Asherah is not mentioned in Samuel. On Asherah, see R. S. Hess, "Asherah or Asherata?" *Or* 65 (1996) 209-19; N. Wyatt, "Asherah," in *DDD,* pp. 183-95.

11. For the goddess Anat, see P. L. Day, "Anat," in *DDD,* pp. 62-77.

12. See Fleming, *CS,* I, p. 439, n. 37; also "Introduction" (Section IV, C, 2, c).

13. *For you* (m. pl.), i.e., "for you (A) and all Israel (B)." Some MSS have "for them," which excludes those (A) who would gather them (B).

14. Ni. intrans. signifies here a middle voice. *They* (v. 6) and *you* (v. 5) are coreferential; these people includes both those (A) who gathered (trans.) all Israel and those (B) who were gathered.

"We have sinned against the Lord."
And Samuel judged the sons of Israel at Mizpah.
7 *And the Philistines heard that the sons of Israel had gathered themselves*[15] *at Mizpah.*
And the Philistine lords went up against Israel.
And the sons of Israel heard and were afraid of[16] *the Philistines.*
8 *And the sons of Israel said to Samuel,*
"Do not be silent and distant from us,[17]
not[18] *crying to the Lord our God.*
And he will save us from the hand of the Philistines!"
9 *And Samuel took one suckling lamb and offered it as a wholly burnt sacrifice to the Lord.*
And Samuel cried to the Lord for Israel.
And the Lord responded to him.
10 *— Now while Samuel was offering the sacrifice, the Philistines had drawn near for the battle with Israel. —*
And the Lord thundered loudly[19] *against the Philistines on that day and confused them and they were struck before Israel.*
11 *And the men of Israel marched out of Mizpah and pursued the Philistines and struck them up to the place under Beth-car.*
12 *And Samuel took a stone and set it between Mizpah and Jeshen*[20]
and called its name the Stone Ezer and said,
"Up to this point/time the Lord helped us!"

5-6 Samuel summons all Israel at Mizpah to intercede to the Lord for the people's sins. Thus, Samuel's judgeship officially begins at Mizpah.

15. Hith.; cf. Q. (trans.) in v. 5; Ni. (intrans.) in v. 6; and Hith. here.

16. Lit., "from before."

17. Lit., "from us." Note that the basic meaning of the preposition *min* is "distancing." Cf. McCarter, p. 145: "Do not refuse to cry out for us. . . ."

18. Privative *min;* or "being away from" (lit., "from"); "so as not to . . ." (BDB, p. 583) — a prepositional phrase as a resultive phrase, as in v. 2 ("after the Lord").

19. Lit., "a loud voice."

20. MT *haššēn;* cf. "the sons of Jashen" yāšēn (2 Sam. 23:32). McCarter (p. 142) and R. P. Gordon (p. 108) support "Jeshanah" (NRSV), on the basis of LXX *tēs palaias* and Syr. *yšn,* which is the name of a town on the border between Judah and Israel *y^{e}šānāh* (2 Chr. 13:19). "It has been identified with Isanas, the site of a victory of Herod the Great (Josephus *Ant.* 14.458) and modern Burj el-Isânah, ca. 17 miles N. of Jerusalem" (McCarter, p. 146). However, the MT may be explained as an example of phonetic spelling: *haššēn* < *hayšēn* < *hay-y^{e}šēn.* See 1 Sam. 6:12: *wayiššarnāh* < *way-yiššarnāh* < *way-yiyšarnāh.* For an example of the semi-vowel [y] assimilating to the following consonant in Ugaritic *-yt-* > *-tt-,* see *UT,* §9.33; D. Sivan, *A Grammar of the Ugaritic Language* (Leiden: E. J. Brill, 1997), pp. 150-51.

Mizpah is probably modern Tel en-Naṣbeh [MR170-143], 7.5 miles northwest of Jerusalem; not Nebi Ṣamwil (5 miles northwest of Jerusalem). It was a place of assembly for "all Israel" in Judges 20–21 and 1 Sam. 10:17-27. Samuel is said to have gone yearly on a circuit from Bethel to Gilgal to Mizpah to judge Israel (v. 16). Later, Saul was appointed king here; see on 10:17. In the monarchical period its major importance was as Judah's northernmost border fortress; it was fortified early in the ninth century by Asa as a result of his disputes with Baasha of Israel (1 K. 15:16-22).[21]

6 For *drew water and poured it,* see also 9:11. In light of the command-obedience pattern, this water ritual must have something to do with the preparation for Samuel's intercessory prayer for the people ("I shall pray for you") before the Lord. McCarter mentions the Egyptian water ritual at Hierapolis, where "twice a year water was drawn from 'the sea' and poured out in the temple." He notes the "evidence for a connection between the water libations and the hope for sufficient rainfall."[22] De Moor also connects the ritual in this verse with a well-known rain-charm.[23] However, as McCarter himself admits, the relationship of the rain-charm ritual and our incident is not clear.

In the present context, "pouring," instead of drinking, the water and "fasting" are connected, and both acts were done *before the Lord.* R. P. Gordon takes this water pouring as the act of "the self-denial of the occasion as the participants solemnly proclaimed their abstention from even this necessity of life" and accepts here "a fertility significance, in that the God of Israel, and not Baal or Ashtart (*cf.* v. 4), is acknowledged as the true source of life and fertility."[24] Though in 2 Sam. 23:16 David poured out water to the Lord in response to the loyalty of his three brave warriors, the pouring out of water in our passage is for a penitential purpose. For their part, the people fasted and confessed their sin (on this term see 2:25) on that day "there" (at Mizpah).

For the first time Samuel's activity as a judge is mentioned (see v. 15), though he was primarily the prophet of the Lord (see 3:20) and his word had authority all over Israel (4:1). The following war against the Philistines and the subsequent victory as the result of Samuel's "crying to the Lord" (v. 9) proved that Samuel was the real leader-judge in Israel now after the death of Eli and the destruction of Shiloh. Ishida prefers to call Samuel the "seer-*šopeṭ*" or the "prophet-*šopeṭ*."[25] Note that Saul similarly needed to prove

21. See P. M. Arnold, "Mizpah" in *ABD,* IV, pp. 879-81.

22. McCarter, p. 144.

23. See J. C. d. Moor, *An Anthology of Religious Texts from Ugarit* (Leiden: E. J. Brill, 1987), p. 134, n. 45 for bibliography.

24. R. P. Gordon, p. 107.

25. T. Ishida, *The Royal Dynasties in Ancient Israel: A Study on the Formation and Development of Royal-Dynastic Ideology* (Berlin: de Gruyter, 1977), p. 34.

himself to be a real leader by gaining the victory over the Ammonites in ch. 11. For a justification of leadership both "divine" election and "human" proof are often required in the ancient heroic narratives or historiography.

7-9 The Philistines hear about the Israelite gathering at Mizpah and decide to attack Israel. The frightened people ask Samuel to pray to the Lord for their deliverance. Samuel sacrifices and prays to the Lord, who responds to his supplication for the people.

8 Unlike the later elders of Israel who request a king (ch. 8), the sons of Israel here ask Samuel to pray that the Lord may save them from the hand of the Philistines. Note that "to save" *yšʿ (also 4:3; 9:16; 2 Sam. 3:18) is a synonymous variant of "to deliver" *nṣl (see vv. 3, 14), and these two constitute a "word pair" in Hebrew (see, e.g., Jer. 15:20; Ps. 7:1; 33:16; etc.). The people did believe that salvation and deliverance came from the Lord himself. Believers constantly need to depend on God's saving acts even after their repentance.

9 For *suckling lamb (ṭᵉlēh ḥālāb,* lit., "lamb of milk"), see 6:7 ("cows for suckling"). Note that an animal can be sacrificed after it is eight days old (see Exod. 22:30; Lev. 22:27).

As a wholly burnt sacrifice (*ʿôlāh kālîl,* lit., "a burnt offering (and) a whole sacrifice") is an adverbial use of a hendiadys conjuncted asyndetically, that is, without a conjunction; see Ps. 51:19 (the same phrase with the conjunction *waw*)[26] and Punic *kll* in the "Sacrificial Tariff."[27] The second term is more specific (Deut. 33:10), not a "gloss";[28] *ʿôlāh* was originally a general term, meaning simply "an offering" (Gen. 8:20f.; cf. Lev. 1). R. P. Gordon notes here a merging of the ideas of expiation and intercession, "since a basic function of the *burnt offering* was to make atonement (Lv 1:4; cf. 2 Sa 24:25; Jb 1:5; 42:8)."[29]

The expression *Samuel cried to the Lord for Israel (zʿq . . . bʿd . . .)* appears only here. The sense is obvious; Samuel is pleading to God as an intercessor. He is "a general who makes war by prayer." McCarter comments: "The intercessory role of the prophet and his special function in holy warfare were two important aspects of the prophetic view of leadership."[30]

The Lord *responded to* (lit., "answered"). But it does not simply refer to a verbal action in a dialogue; it implies action in response to Samuel's "cry." This action is specified in the sentence after the parenthetical information in v. 10, that is, "And the Lord thundered. . . ."

26. See Tsumura, "The Unity of Psalm 51," 35-48.
27. *CS,* I, p. 306.
28. McCarter (p. 141) takes *kālîl* after *ʿôlāh* as "redundant."
29. R. P. Gordon, p. 107.
30. McCarter, p. 149. Also Birch, p. 1018, n. 55.

10 The first half of this verse is a SETTING, giving the background information. The flow of the narrative discourse is interrupted by the insertion of this parenthetical clause. The mainline event is resumed by the next *wayqtl* expression, *And the Lord thundered.* The interruption in the flow of discourse is a literary device to "slow down" the tempo; see "Introduction" (Section VI, C and VII, C). After the phrase *And the Lord responded to him,* one would naturally expect a remark about how he responded. However, the insertion of the parenthetical information keeps the audience in suspense. In fact, that parenthetical information itself is a vivid description of the current situation: while the Israelites were standing still, watching Samuel sacrifice, the Philistines kept marching closer and closer. Then the narrator begins a new narrative unit, a sub-paragraph initiated by the *wayqtl* followed by the same stated subject: "And the Lord thundered. . . ." In this way the narrator explains more specifically how the Lord responded to Samuel. Since the NRSV; NASB; NIV do not take v. 10a as parenthetical, they are obliged to translate the initial *waw* as "but"; however, that is not a suitable rendering.

For the expression *the Lord thundered,* see also 2:10 and 12:17. Is this a metaphor, that is, did the Lord respond to Samuel with a thunder-like loud sound? Or, did the Lord use actual "timely" providential thunder *against the Philistines?* In either case it describes the Lord's special intervention into a specific fact in human history as the lord and judge.[31] Some scholars immediately take expressions like this to mean that the event is unhistorical. However, Assyrian records also mention divine intervention in battles, and no one claims that those are unhistorical.

In the ancient Near East, battle is often described in terms of a storm, while, on the other hand, storms are described using war language.[32] In the Bible also, the language and imagery of the storm theophany are used for the divine activities in the texts, such as Exod. 19:16; Psalms 18 (= 2 Samuel 22), 29; Habakkuk 3; see on 2:10.[33] The use of storm language in the Old Testament is, therefore, not necessarily an allusion to Baal myths or the like, as is often advocated by scholars.[34] Biblical authors could use expres-

31. On the idea of historical events as governed by divine power in the ancient Near East, see B. Albrektson, *History and the Gods: An Essay on the Idea of Historical Events as Divine Manifestations in the Ancient Near East and in Israel* (Lund: C.W.K. Gleerup, 1967), pp. 24-41.

32. See D. T. Tsumura, "The So-called 'Chaos Tradition' behind Psalm 46," *Evangelical Theology* 11 (1980) 95-96; "'The Deluge' *(mabbûl)* in Psalm 29:10," *UF* 20 (1988) 351-55. See note 73 in ch. 2.

33. For a description of the storm theophany in Canaan and Israel, see F. M. Cross, Jr., *Canaanite Myth and Hebrew Epic* (Cambridge, Mass.: Harvard University Press, 1973), pp. 147-94.

34. E.g., J. Day, "Echoes of Baal's Seven Thunders and Lightnings in Psalm and

sions similar to Canaanite myths to describe the same natural phenomena metaphorically.[35]

The term *confused* occurs first in Exod. 14:24, where the Lord threw the Egyptian army into confusion (also in Exod. 23:27; Josh. 10:10; Judg. 4:15). See especially 2 Sam. 22:15 (= Ps. 18:15) and Ps. 144:6, "where the term is used to describe the effect upon the enemy of Yahweh's lightning ('arrows') in a storm theophany context."[36]

11 The verb *yṣ' (lit., "to go out") is here used in a military sense, *marched out.* The chronological difficulty is: When did they march out? Was it while the Lord was thundering? After the Lord confused them? After the Philistines were struck?

(9) the Lord *responded* to [Samuel]
(10) the Lord *thundered . . . confused . . .* they were struck" (Ni. *ngp)
(11) the men of Israel *marched out . . . pursued . . . struck"* (Hi. *nkh)

This is a series of three clauses starting with a *wayqtl* and stating the subject, not just implying it by the verb. Such clauses or sentences are not necessarily in chronological order. Note that the Israelites participated in the battle, that is, *struck* (v. 11) the Philistines, while from another perspective the Philistines *were struck* by the Lord *before Israel* (v. 10).

Therefore, in our case, the "marching out" of the Israelites (v. 11) was not necessarily after the Philistines were "struck" (v. 10); the Philistines' being struck and the Israelites' striking of them (v. 11) probably refer to the same event. This understanding may be supported by the fact that the Lord's responding to Samuel (v. 9) and his thundering and confusing (v. 10) refer to the same event; see above. So, McCarter's view that "the Israelites have nothing to do but take up the pursuit of the Philistines as they rush precipitously into the hills"[37] places too little weight on the responsibility of the Israelites. Here is another example of the problem of God's sovereignty and human responsibility. Though God acts according to his sovereign will, human beings

Habakkuk 3:9," *VT* 29 (1979) 143-51. See Tsumura, "'The Deluge' *(mabbûl)* in Psalm 29:10," pp. 351-55; "Ugaritic Poetry and Habakkuk 3," *TynB* 40 (1988) 24-48; *Creation and Destruction: A Reappraisal of the Chaoskampf Theory in the Old Testament* (Winona Lake, Ind.: Eisenbrauns, 2005), which is the second, enlarged edition of *The Earth and the Waters in Genesis 1 and 2: A Linguistic Study* (JSOTSS 83; Sheffield: JSOT Press, 1989).

35. See also M. Weinfeld, "Divine Intervention in War in Ancient Israel and in the Ancient Near East," in *History, Historiography and Interpretation: Studies in Biblical and Cuneiform Literatures,* ed. H. Tadmor and M. Weinfeld (Jerusalem: Magnes, 1983), pp. 141-42.

36. McCarter, p. 146.

37. McCarter, p. 149.

have the responsibility of acting by trusting in God's actions at the right moment.

The place-name *Beth-car* appears only here. Its location is unknown, and it cannot be Bethel, a few miles north of Mizpah, since it is difficult to see in *Bêt-kār* a corruption of *Bêt-'ēl;* it is probably to the west of Mizpah in the general direction of Philistia.

12 *The stone Ezer* (*'eben hā'āzer;* or "Ebenezer"; lit., "(the) Stone of Help")[38] is the name of the stone which Samuel set up between Mizpah and Jeshen. There is also a town or city by that name located near Aphek, where Israel was earlier defeated by the Philistines (4:1; 5:1), but there is no reason to identify these as one and the same.[39] Perhaps Samuel named the stone after the place-name "Ebenezer" with the earlier experience in chs. 4–5 in mind so that the people might always be reminded of God's special help (*'ēzer*) in this time and at this place. The name "the stone Ezer" is not unusual as a place-name,[40] and it is certainly a reminder of God's powerful intervention in the history of Israel as well as her former failure at the other "Ebenezer."

Up to this point/time or "Thus far" (*'ad-hēnnāh*) has both spacial and temporal significances. While McCarter accepts only a spacial meaning ("To this point") for this context, R. P. Gordon takes it as temporal and explains that "until this point in Israel's history Yahweh has been her helper."[41] Both interpretations are not only possible but also probably intended by Samuel.

3. Samuel Judges (7:13-17)

13 *And the Philistines were subdued; they did not enter the territory of Israel again. — The hand of the Lord was upon the Philistines all the days of Samuel. —*

14 *And the places which the Philistines had taken from Israel returned to Israel from both Ekron and Gath; their*[42] *vicinities Israel recovered*[43] *from the hand of the Philistines. — There was peace between Israel and the Amorites. —*

15 *And Samuel judged Israel all the days of his life.*

38. Cf. *hā'eben hā'āzel* "the stone Ezel" (1 Sam. 20:19); *'ad 'ābēl hagg^{e}dôlāh* "the great platform of Abel" (6:18).

39. Cf. McCarter, p. 146.

40. For other place-names with "stone," see also *'eben bōhan* "the stone of Bohan" (Josh. 15:6; 18:17); *'eben hazzōḥelet* "the stone Zoheleth" (1 K. 1:9).

41. McCarter, p. 146; R. P. Gordon, p. 108.

42. I.e., Ekron and Gath.

43. Lit., "delivered"; also 1 Sam. 7:3; see on 7:8.

16 *It was his custom*[44] *to go around yearly from Bethel to Gilgal and then to Mizpah and to judge Israel at all these places.*
17 *But his return was to Ramah, for there was his house and there he judged*[45] *Israel.*
And he built there an altar to the Lord.

The transition toward the TERMINUS began with v. 13 after the final EVENT about what Samuel did: *And Samuel took . . . (wayqtl)* in v. 12. His final word, "Up to this point/time the Lord helped us!" is a timely discourse closing that event. After v. 13 the narrative twice goes off the main line with parenthetical clauses. The key phrase *all the days of . . .* bridges this chapter and ch. 8, which refers to Samuel's old age. First, this phrase appears in a parenthetical clause (v. 13b), hence as background information, and then in the summary statement about Samuel's life: "And Samuel judged Israel all the days of his life" (v. 15). Such repetition prepares the audience for the next section where Samuel is already an old man, a long time having passed between the events in the two chapters. McCarter notes this is "an editorial transition from the close of the account of Samuel's career . . . to the events of c 8,"[46] though he sees this transition starting only in v. 15, not v. 13.

13 Because of the victory in the previous section, the Philistines did not trouble Israel for many years. "Samuel's military career is summarized and concluded in a formulaic pattern known from the Book of Judges. . . . Judg. 3:30; 4:23-24; 8:28; 11:33b. The subjugation of an enemy is expressed by the verb 'humble' (Judg 4:23; 1 Sam. 7:13) or 'be humbled' (Judg. 3:30; 8:28; 11:33b)."[47] Note that the phrase *the hand of the Lord* again (see 5:6) refers to Yahweh's control of Israel's enemy.

14 The phrase *both Ekron and Gath* (lit., "from Ekron to Gath") could mean (1) up to the border between Ekron and Gath; (2) the area between Ekron and Gath — from Mizpah, Ekron comes first, then Gath — the geographical situation suggests "from Ekron as far as Gath" (*ištu . . . adi . . .* "from . . . to . . .");[48] or (3) both Ekron and Gath; see on 6:18. The third interpretation probably fits the context best; the sense is that the places returned both from Ekron and from Gath; namely, "their vicinities" were recovered to Israel. To put it differently, it describes the part of the border area that was

44. <*waw*+pf.>; see "repeated action in the past" (GKC, §112t).

45. On the long vowel *ā* with *mûnāḥ,* see GKC, §29I N. For a detailed description of *špṭ,* see *HALOT,* pp. 1622-26.

46. McCarter, pp. 147-48.

47. McCarter, p. 147.

48. A. F. Rainey, *Canaanite in the Amarna Tablets: A Linguistic Analysis of the Mixed Dialect Used by the Scribes from Canaan,* 4 vols. (HbO; Leiden: E. J. Brill, 1996), vol. 3, p. 12.

freed from Philistine control. "The writer's point is that all such cities were controlled by Israel during Samuel's lifetime, and that the Philistines were confined to a minimal home base."[49] On Ekron, see on 5:10; on Gath, see on 5:8.

The Amorites were the pre-Israelite population of ancient Canaan (see also 2 Sam. 21:2); the term is used here in the widest sense, referring to the totality of indigenous inhabitants. The Israelites subdued the Philistines while having a peaceful relationship with the Amorites. In other words, Israel was safe both internally and externally. McCarter holds that such a situation is "a part of the careful negative preparation for the people's demand for a king."[50] R. P. Gordon also notes: "The somewhat idealized picture of domestic stability and of territorial integrity is manifestly intended to demonstrate the sufficiency of the old theocratic order which is about to be called in question. To that end, no account is taken of Philistine garrisons in Israelite territory (cf. 10:5; 13:3), nor of the confrontations between the Israelites and Philistines that were a feature of Saul's reign (cf. 14:52)."[51]

15-16 *Samuel judged* (see v. 6) *Israel all the days of his life;* see 14:52; 15:35. This summarizes Samuel's life in one sentence. The phrase *go around* (v. 16; lit., "go and surround"), a verbal hendiadys interrupted by the temporal phrase *yearly,* is a summary of Samuel's activities as judge. From his hometown Ramah, he visited three cities, Bethel, Gilgal and Mizpah, all in or around the district of the Benjamite clans. Malamat compares Samuel's annual activities at four major towns, including his hometown Ramah (see v. 17), with those of Asqudum, the chief diviner of Mari, who visited four towns "in order to perform extispices there for the well-being of their inhabitants." As he notes, "the mention of just *four* cities in the circuits of each one of the diviners may not be coincidental," since a "quarter" of places in Mari documents indicates "a stable, administrative unit or district."[52]

Bethel appears for the first time in Samuel; other occurrences are 10:3; 13:2; 30:27; it does not appear in 2 Samuel. According to Judg. 20:27, at that time, "the ark of the covenant of God" was there. The modern site is Beitin, about 10 miles north of Jerusalem, located at the intersection of major highways — the mountain ridge road and the main road leading from Jericho to the Coastal Plain.[53] It was one of the most important sacred sites, being associated with the tradition of the patriarchs (see Gen. 35:15). It was "tradi-

49. McCarter, p. 147.

50. McCarter, p. 147.

51. R. P. Gordon, p. 108.

52. A. Malamat, "Episodes Involving Samuel and Saul and the Prophetic Texts from Mari," in *Mari and the Bible* (Leiden: E. J. Brill, 1998), p. 102.

53. H. Brodsky, "Bethel," in *ABD,* I, pp. 710-12.

tionally Benjaminite (Josh. 18:22) but in fact Ephraimite throughout most of its (Israelite) history, serving as one of the two principal sanctuaries of the northern kingdom (1 K. 12:29)."[54]

Gilgal also appears for the first time in Samuel. The site is not yet identified. It was the place "on the east border of Jericho" where Joshua and the Israelites camped after crossing the Jordan River (Josh. 4:19; etc.). Later, "the angel of the Lord went up from Gilgal to Bokim" and warned the Israelites about their apostasy (Judg. 2:1f.). This ancient city was a cult center, an important shrine, and place of sacrifice in the Benjaminite district. To there Samuel ordered Saul to go down and wait on God after his private anointing (see 10:8), and the people "made Saul king there before the Lord" (11:15). But it was also there that Saul's perpetual kingship was rejected (13:8-15) and finally abandoned (15:23). It was the place where David went after crossing the Jordan River on his return to Jerusalem (2 Sam. 19:15, 40). Later, in the eighth century, Amos (4:4; 5:5) and Hosea (4:15; 9:15; 12:11) denounced it as an active cult center.

17 *But his return was to Ramah,* that is, his final place was Ramah; cf. "But he always went back to Ramah" (NIV). For *Ramah,* see on 1:19.

The expression *he built . . . an altar* indicates that Samuel added another sacred location, Ramah, to the traditional three: Bethel, Gilgal, and Mizpah. However, "these sites should not be understood to signal stories preserved around separate shrines, but rather the whole sequence assumes a landscape of several sacred locations."[55] The reference to the altar here is a good background information which anticipates the story of the meeting of Saul and Samuel in 9:11f.

The term *there* is repeated three times in this verse, as if it prepares the audience toward the following story, the SETTING of which is again "there," that is, in Ramah (see 8:4). For this linking technique, see the introduction to this section, 7:2-17.

Thus, the narrator summarizes Samuel's era: Israel was secure and stable both externally and internally under the judgeship of Samuel, *for the hand of the Lord* was on the Philistines and there was *peace between Israel and the Amorites.* Samuel's annual visit to Bethel, Gilgal, and Mizpah from his home town Ramah gave the people confidence and trust in God and in Samuel's leadership. In the next episode, however, the readers will know,[56] the people of Israel senselessly request a new institution of kingship, rather than a new judge, despite Samuel's opposition.

54. McCarter, p. 148.

55. D. E. Fleming, "A Break in the Line: Reconsidering the Bible's Diverse Festival Calendars," *RB* 106 (1999) 171.

56. McCarter, pp. 151-52.

II. — TRANSITION TO THE MONARCHY — (8:1-22)

"APPOINT US A KING" (8:1-22)

This chapter is among the most significant in the historical books of the Old Testament, marking the transition from judgeship to kingship in ancient Israel. This change was made possible by "the will of the two protagonists, the people of the time and the Lord himself."[1] Though Samuel was reluctant to listen to the people's request for a king, he was compelled to institute a new office. Samuel, the last judge, thus became the "kingmaker."[2] Here, too, it is the Lord who providentially guides the history of his covenant people, though somewhat negatively.

When the Israelites realized that Samuel had become old and his two sons were corrupt judges (vv. 1-3), they requested a new institution instead of a new judge, for they thought that a human king like those of other nations had the promise of bringing stability and prosperity to the nation. This was certainly a decisive moment in determining the future of the covenant people as a nation. It was indeed "the change from the kingship of God to the kingship of man."[3]

But why did the people want to have a king instead of a new judge? Did the people consider the institution of monarchy necessary to cope with a new military threat from the Philistines (v. 20)? From one aspect, the monarchy can be certainly seen as "the Hebrew response to the Philistine stimulus."[4] The Philistine presence nearby, together with the Ammonite expansion (see on 12:12), had been a constant threat to the Israelites.

However, as seen in ch. 7, the pre-monarchical institution of judgeship was completely adequate, and even ideal, for the covenant people. So, their insistence upon changing to a new system was a strange denial of this plain fact. McCarter sees the people as motivated by desire or covetousness,

1. Hertzberg, p. 71.

2. See also R. P. Gordon, "Who Made the Kingmaker? Reflections on Samuel and the Institution of the Monarchy," in *Faith, Tradition, and History: Old Testament Historiography in its Near Eastern Context,* ed. A. R. Millard, J. K. Hoffmeier, and D. W. Baker (Winona Lake, Ind.: Eisenbrauns, 1994), pp. 255-69.

3. M. Tsevat, "The Biblical Account of the Foundation of the Monarchy in Israel," in *The Meaning of the Book of Job and Other Biblical Studies: Essays on the Literature and Religion of the Hebrew Bible* (New York: Ktav, 1980), p. 77.

4. C. H. Gordon, *The Common Background of Greek and Hebrew Civilizations* (New York: W. W. Norton, 1965), p. 18; also W. E. Evans, "An Historical Reconstruction of the Emergence of Israelite Kingship and the Reign of Saul," in *Scripture in Context II: More Essays on the Comparative Method,* ed. W. W. Hallo, J. C. Moyer, and L. G. Perdue (Winona Lake, Ind.: Eisenbrauns, 1983), p. 77.

not necessity. They were not content with what they had and started looking for a change.[5]

Others see a socio-political cause for this demand. Within Israel itself, together with the growth in population, there arose economic, agricultural, and political problems.[6] One might yet add religious and ethical problems in society too, as this chapter indicates. The moral and ethical problems of the covenant people cannot be treated as if they were distinct from the religious and theological problems that concern the people's relationship with their covenant God.

It may be that Samuel himself had contributed to the lack of trust in God by appointing his own sons as judges (see below, on v. 1), instead of waiting on God to raise up a judge acceptable in his eyes. In fact, the office of a judge was never hereditary like the priestly one. When Gideon was requested by the people to rule over them, he turned down that request, saying "I will not rule over you, nor will my son rule over you. The Lord will rule over you" (Judg. 8:23). It may be that the people had grown used to seeing the person of Samuel without seeing the God who, though unseen, was king behind him controlling history. When Samuel became old and unable to control the behavior of his own sons, the situation seemed to them to be totally desperate. They too did not want to wait for God to act to raise up someone to judge or lead in battle as the need arose; they wanted someone on hand (see 1 Sam. 8:19-20). So, they requested a king "like all the (other) nations" (v. 5). The same mistake is repeated by the people of God in the modern age as they lose sight of Him who rules as the real king of universe; see "Introduction" (Section IX, A).

Thus, this was not simply a request for a socio-political transformation; it was a serious religious offense against Israel's sovereign God. Since Yahweh the creator had been the king from the beginning, the request for a human king was the rejection of God who had been "ruling over them as a king" (v. 7), namely, the rejection of theocracy. This was an extremely crucial decision made by the people of God, and it would be dangerous for them to become like other nations where a completely different religious system

5. McCarter, pp. 160-61.

6. For example, R. B. Coote and K. W. Whitelam, "The Emergence of Israel: Social Transformation and State Formation Following the Decline in LB Trade," *Semeia* 37 (1986) 107-47; I. Finkelstein, "The Emergence of the Monarchy in Israel: The Environmental and Socio-economic Aspects," *JSOT* 44 (1989) 43-74; see however Gordon, "Who Made the Kingmaker?" in *Faith, Tradition, and History,* pp. 257-60. On the historical problems of the emergence of the monarchy in ancient Israel, see most recently P. McNutt, *Reconstructing the Society of Ancient Israel* (London: SPCK, 1999). See also A. Alt, "The Formation of the Israelite State in Palestine" [1930], in *Essays on Old Testament History and Religion* (Garden City, N.Y.: Doubleday, 1966, 1968), pp. 225-67.

dominated the monarchy.[7] See "Introduction" (Section IV, C) on the Canaanite religion.

PLACE OF 1 SAM. 8 IN THE LITERARY STRUCTURE

There are basically two positions about the place of this chapter in the literary structure of the earlier part of 1 Samuel. Scholars such as Tsevat, McCarter, and Halpern take this chapter as the start of "the story of the foundation of the monarchy in Israel," though Tsevat sees its end at 12:25,[8] while the other two see the end at ch. 15.[9] Other scholars perceive a continuity between ch. 7 and ch. 8.[10] However, as observed in the last chapter, ch. 7 is best taken as the concluding chapter of the preceding section, the "Story of Samuel" (ch. 1–7), based on discourse analysis. At the same time, since ch. 9 opens with an "introductory" formula similar to that of ch. 1,[11] it is reasonable to take ch. 8 as a transitional section from both literary and historical perspectives: literarily, at the transition point from the story of Samuel to the story of Saul; historically, changing from the judgeship to the kingship.

Taking these observations into account, the literary structure of the earlier chapters of 1 Samuel is thus:

1:1–7:17	"Story of Samuel" with the embedded story of "the Ark of God" (4:1–7:1)
8:1-22	— transition to the monarchy —
9:1–15:35	"Story of Saul"

7. See further on vv. 11-18 on the historicity of this narrative. Also M. D. Guinan, "Davidic Covenant," in *ABD,* II, pp. 69-72.

8. Tsevat holds that the narrative from 1 Samuel 13 onward, even to the end of 2 Kings, "stands under the sign of [the] disquieting question . . . what chance has the untried institution? Will it work, will it last?"; Tsevat, "The Biblical Account of the Foundation of the Monarchy in Israel," p. 99. On the negative appraisal of Saul's reign right from the beginning, see on 13:1 (below).

9. McCarter, p. 152; B. Halpern, *The Constitution of the Monarchy in Israel* (Chico, Calif.: Scholars Press, 1981); also Birch, p. 1022.

10. Hertzberg, p. 65; R. P. Gordon, p. 105; "Who Made the Kingmaker?" p. 257.

11. Based on the similarity between 1 Sam. 1:1 and 9:1, van Zyl "organizes his discussions around the two themes of Yahweh as God (ch 1–8) and Yahweh as directing the story of people and nation (ch 9–31)." See R. P. Gordon's review of A. H. van Zyl, *1 Samuel: vol. 1–vol. 2* (Nijkerk: Callenbach, 1988-89), in *VT* 42 (1992) 576.

1. Aged Samuel and His Two Sons (8:1-3)

1 *When Samuel grew old, he appointed his sons as judges of Israel.*[12]
2 *The name of his firstborn son was*[13] *Joel*
and the name of his second was Abijah;
(they were) judges in Beersheba.
3 *But his sons did not walk in his ways and looked for unjust gain*
and took bribes and thus perverted justice.

1-3 In the first three verses, the main sentences do not start with *wayqtl* followed by a stated subject. Therefore they constitute the SETTING for the EVENT starting in v. 4; the *wayqtl* expressions in vv. 1-3 are "sequential," not "initial"; see "Introduction" (Section VI, A).

1 When Samuel grew old — this implies that a long time has passed since the last EVENT narrated, the victory over the Philistines in 1 Sam. 7:12. By now, not only has Samuel grown old, but his two sons have been judges long enough so people know their (poor) quality.

It was unusual for a judge to appoint his own sons as judges, for judgeship was not hereditary. In fact, Gideon refused the suggestion that he establish a dynasty; see Judg. 8:22-23.[14] Though Eli "judged" (1 Sam. 4:18) Israel for forty years, his sons are never said to have judged. (Their priesthood was of course hereditary.) It may be that the narrator calls the audience's attention to this new development, that is, "a hereditary succession,"[15] in the political history of ancient Israel. R. P. Gordon sees here Samuel's "little dynastic experiment."[16] This "experiment" of Samuel's was certainly a breach of the old practice of waiting for the divine appointment of a new judge and was possibly a cause of his family problems. It certainly foreshadows the problems of hereditary kingship in obviating divine choice. Note that the term *he appointed* (*śym) is used again in v. 5 for "appointing" a king.

2 Since the *name* designates the personality which should character-

12. *šōpᵉṭîm lᵉyiśrā'ēl:* non-restrictive meaning: "judges of Israel"; cf. *šōpṭê yiśrā'ēl* "the judges of Israel" (Num. 25:5; 1 Chr. 17:6); *šōpēṭ yiśrā'ēl* "the judge of Israel" (Mic. 4:14). See on *kōhănîm laYHWH* "priests of the Lord" (1 Sam. 1:3).

13. The *wayhî* (lit., "and it was") clause here serves as either an explanatory clause or a subordinate clause that has a tighter connection with the following verse, v. 3, than with the preceding one; hence, another possible translation would be one with the sense, "Though they had good names, they did not live up to them." See "Introduction" (Section V, A) on the topicalizing function of *wayhî.*

14. See M. Weinfeld, "Divine Intervention in War in Ancient Israel and in the Ancient Near East," in *History, Historiography and Interpretation: Studies in Biblical and Cuneiform Literatures,* ed. H. Tadmor and M. Weinfeld (Jerusalem: Magnes, 1983), p. 86.

15. Hertzberg, p. 71.

16. R. P. Gordon, p. 109.

ize the holder, one might see an irony here. Samuel's sons did not deserve their good names, *Joel* and *Abijah.* Both contain short forms (*yô* and *yāh*) of the divine name Yahweh. The name *Joel* means "Yahu is God." *Abijah* means "My father is Yah."[17]

Why did they operate out of *Beersheba,* the traditional southern extreme of Israelite territory (see 3:20)? Beersheba, the ancient holy place associated with the patriarchs, may have been one of the cultic centers in this day, though Samuel's activities were in or around the traditional territory of the tribe of Benjamin. Later, in the eighth century B.C., Amos denounced this place, together with Bethel and Gilgal, as one of the cultic centers to which the people should not go and worship (Amos 5:5).

3 While judges were supposed to be "incorruptible" (see Exod. 18:21; Deut. 16:19) and Samuel himself could claim that he was impeccable in this regard (12:3-5), his two sons are reported not to have followed his example. Although, unlike Eli, Samuel kept faithful to his God, his two sons were perverting justice *(mišpāṭ);* note that Eli's two sons did not know the *mišpāṭ* of the priests (2:13).

The expression *inclined after* (*nṭh + *'aḥărê:* lit., "stretch [one's hand] after . . .") is a brachylogy, an intentional omission of a key word or phrase for a stylistic purpose.[18] This verse progresses toward a climax; (a) inclination toward unjust gain → (b) taking of bribes → (c) thus "perverting justice." *Unjust gain (beṣa'),* that is, ill-gotten gain,[19] and bribe *(šōḥad)* form a word pair which also appears in Isa. 33:15 and in reverse order in Ezek. 22:12-13.

The expressions *lqḥ + *šōḥad* ("to take a bribe"[20]) and *nṭh (Hi.) + *mišpāṭ* ("to pervert justice") appear as a paired expression also in Prov. 17:23 and in reverse order in Deut. 16:19. Note that the opposite of *mišpāṭ* ("justice") is *ḥāmās* ("violence") in Hab. 1:2-4; from the prophet's perspective "injustice" is equivalent to "violence," and social ethics and religious practices are tightly intertwined in the prophetic messages.[21] On misuse of the office of judge, see Amos 5:7, 10-12. When a religious leader perverts justice, society dies out hopelessly.

17. Cf. Abiel "My father is God" (1 Sam. 9:1). Ugar. *ab-* names appear in such names as *abmlk, abršp,* and *abrm;* see F. Gröndahl, *PTU,* p. 86. The element "father" is a frequently occurring divine epithet. See Tallqvist, *AGE,* pp. 1-2.

18. See "Introduction" (Section VII, D).

19. On this term, see most recently P. J. Harland, "**בצע**: Bribe, Extortion or Profit?" *VT* 50 (2000) 310-22.

20. Also see on 1 Sam. 12:3. Hittite "Instructions to Commanders of Border Garrisons" (*CS,* I, p. 224) mentions: "Let no one take a bribe."

21. See L. Epzstein, *Social Justice in the Ancient Near East and the People of the Bible* (London: SCM, 1986); M. Weinfeld, *Social Justice in Ancient Israel and in the Ancient Near East* (Jerusalem: Magnes, 1995).

2. The Elders' Request for a King (8:4-6a)

4 *And all the elders of Israel gathered and came to Samuel at Ramah*
5 *and said to him,*
"Lo! you have grown old;
but your sons have not walked in your ways.
Now, appoint us a king to judge us like all the (other) nations!"
6 *And the matter was evil in Samuel's eyes because they said "Give us a king to judge us!"*

Wellhausen posited two sources concerning the kingship in Samuel, one source favorable to the monarchy (9:1–10:16 and 11:1-11), and the other unfavorable to it (8:1-22; 10:17-27; and 12:1-25). According to him, disillusionment with the monarchy, once conceived of as the zenith of Israel's history, was an aftereffect of the destruction of the Judaean kingdom, which led to anti-monarchic tendencies in the literature of the period.

However, a growing number of recent scholars, such as Crüsemann,[22] are firmly against this commonly accepted view.[23] According to Crüsemann, the "anti-monarchic" passages and the traditions in Judges 6–9 and 1 Sam. 8:11-17 are not the work of the Deuteronomistic redactor at the time of the fall of the Judaean kingdom but a polemic against the monarchy composed by circles familiar with the burdens of taxation and conscription. Crüsemann thus dates the anti-monarchic trend from the Solomonic period. However, these verses do not necessarily apply to Solomon's reign, since "what is given is nothing more than a general sketch of the ways of kings in and out of Israel, and in almost any period."[24]

Weinfeld suggests a much earlier date for this political tension. He holds that though the literary crystallization of the pro-monarchic and the anti-monarchic traditions took place in the tenth century, the ideological struggle had been in process since the times of Gideon (see Judg. 8:22-23; on Gideon's son Abimelek, see Judg. 9:22) and Saul, and even from before the conquest, for example, among the Hivite Gibeonite cities (Joshua 9): "these cities were clearly acquainted with the monarchic system, but opted against it — most probably as a result of their own antimonarchic ideologies."[25]

22. F. Crüsemann, *Der Widerstand gegen das Königtum. Die antiköniglichen Texte des Alten Testamentes und der Kampf am den frühen israelitischen Staat* (Neukirchen-Vluyn: Neukirchener, 1978).

23. See also G. E. Gerbrandt, *Kingship according to the Deuteronomistic History* (Atlanta: Scholars Press, 1986); D. M. Howard, Jr., "The Case for Kingship in Deuteronomy and the Former Prophets," *WTJ* 52 (1990) 101-15.

24. R. P. Gordon, *1 & 2 Samuel* (OTG; Sheffield: JSOT Press, 1984, 1987), p. 44.

25. See M. Weinfeld, "(Review of) F. Crüsemann, *Der Widerstand gegen das*

Thus, there may have been division of opinion from the very beginning in the history of Israel. While one might safely assume that the author certainly had different sources of information and opinions with regard to the monarchy in his contemporary society, the distinction between the positive and the negative attitudes toward the monarchy has been somewhat overemphasized. We have to admit though that the socio-political reality during the era of Saul must have been much more complicated than the impression given by the biblical text — and it is this complicated situation and context that gives the modern reader an impression that different sources existed. But the differences are not necessarily an indicator of different sources but of different attitudes of both God and the people who were confronted with the idea of human kingship in ancient Israel.

4 Now *all the elders of Israel* came to Samuel. Samuel was thus "the first judge in the Bible who was accorded truly national status";[26] see 3:20; 4:1; 7:3, 5; etc. On *Ramah,* see on 1:19; 7:17. During the premonarchic era the *elders of Israel* were the representatives of the people or "congregation" *(ʿēdâ);* see 4:3. However, with the establishment of the monarchy "sovereignty passed from the 'congregation of the Lord' and the assembly of God, to the king."[27] Therefore, the request for a king would mean a fundamental change in the socio-political structure and a major transformation in Israel's life and religion.

5 The elders' request for a king is, at least in their words, based on Samuel's old age and the ill behavior of his sons:

> "Lo! you have grown old;
> but your sons have not walked in your ways.
> Now, appoint us a king to judge us like all the (other) nations!"

They appear to tell Samuel that these problems would be solved if they had a king over them. If they were seeking a stable leadership through hereditary succession like the monarchy, Samuel had already established it by appointing his sons as judges. Were they hoping that the monarchical system would solve moral looseness such as bribery? Probably not. Rather, these facts were simply pretext for demanding a king *like all the (other) nations.*

Samuel had appointed judges; now the elders want him to appoint a

---

Königtum: Die antiköniglichen Texte des Alten Testamentes und der Kampf am den frühen israelitischen Staat (Neukirchen-Vluyn: Neukirchener, 1978)," *VT* 31 (1981) 105; also "Zion and Jerusalem as Religious and Political Capital: Ideology and Utopia," in *The Poet and the Historian: Essays in Literary and Historical Biblical Criticism,* ed. R. E. Friedman (HSS 26; Chico, Calif.: Scholars Press, 1983), p. 87.

26. Bergen, p. 112.

27. Weinfeld, "Zion and Jerusalem as Religious and Political Capital," p. 85.

king. "If he could *appoint* once (v. 1), he could do it again (v. 5)."[28] The people here request a new institution instead of a new judge. While the people wanted a "king" *(melek),* God will give them a *nāgîd* (see 9:16). Tsevat sees a clear distinction between these two terms, "king" and "regent," in 1-2 Samuel, with the possible exception of 1 Sam. 15:1–16:1. According to him, "the ruler is called *ngyd* when his bond or subordination to God is preeminent, *mlk* when the origin of his position and the base of his power lie in the people."[29] Regardless of the terms, however, the human king in the biblical conception was simply a (vice-) regent or deputy of the heavenly King; see "Introduction" (Section IX, A).

The verb *špṭ can mean either "to govern" or "to judge"; hence, *a king to judge us (melek lᵉšopṭēnû)* could be translated "a king to govern us" (NRSV; also JPS); cf. "a king to lead us" (NIV); also vv. 6, 20. Note that in v. 9 the term "rule over" *yimlōk* is used instead of "to judge"; thus, the two terms *špṭ and *mlk are synonymous.[30] To be sure, "judging" was one of the main duties of a king in the ancient world. Kings in other nations, such as in the city-state Ugarit, were supposed to judge justly the cases for widows and orphans (e.g,. Keret[31]); in the story of David and Absalom, judging was one of the king's major responsibilities (2 Sam. 14:1-17; 15:2-6). Absalom said, "If only I were appointed judge *(šōpēṭ)*" (15:4). A king judged the people to sustain "order" in the society.[32] See v. 20 for Yahweh's function as a warrior-king.

For *like all the (other) nations (kᵉkol-haggôyim),* see also v. 20; Deut. 17:14; Ezek. 25:8. The people wanted to become like all the other nations, but God had called them uniquely to be his people, under his especial care. But they are exchanging their true glory for status in the eyes of the world. Just as the Israelites were the people of a God who is unique and incomparable with any other god (see on 1 Sam. 2:2); so they were supposedly incomparable with any other nations: that is, "a kingdom of priests and a holy nation" (Exod. 19:6), "set apart for service to their divine monarch."[33] So, what they hoped to do was exactly to throw away their special status as the chosen people of God in order to identify themselves with the nations of this world.

28. R. P. Gordon, p. 110.

29. Tsevat, "The Biblical Account of the Foundation of the Monarchy in Israel," p. 93.

30. See Ugar. *mlk* "king" — *ṯpt* "judge, ruler" in *KTU* [UT] 1.3:V:32 [*'nt*:V:40], 1.4 [51]:IV:43-44. See most recently T. Ishida, *History and Historical Writing in Ancient Israel: Studies in Biblical Historiography* (SHCANE 16; Leiden: E. J. Brill, 1999), pp. 41-44 for a detailed discussion of the meaning of the word *špṭ* in the West Semitics.

31. See *CS,* I, p. 342.

32. D. J. Wiseman, "Law and Order in Old Testament Times," *Vox Evangelica* 8 (1973) 5-21.

33. Bergen, p. 113.

The same phrase, *like all the nations,* appears in a similar context in Deut. 17:14-15: "When you enter the land which the Lord your God gives you, and you possess it and live in it, and you say, 'I will set a king over me like all the nations who are around me,' you shall surely set a king over you whom the LORD your God chooses; one from among your countrymen you shall set as king over yourselves; you may not put a foreigner over yourselves who is not your countryman."

While the text in Deuteronomy is similar to our passage and some claim that it was "inspired by the tradition about Saul's coronation,"[34] it should be noted that there are differences in the key statements. For example, Deuteronomy insists that the king be an Israelite, a non-issue in the Samuel account. In the Samuel passage, conscription of sons and daughters is forecast, while the Deuteronomy passage forbids multiplication of horses. But though the Samuel passage could be the realization of the situation envisioned in Deuteronomy (in 10:20 only Israelites are involved in the lots), it is hard to think that the traditions recorded in Samuel were the source of the Deuteronomy passage. Kingship in Canaan was known to Israel from the beginning of the settlement; there were kings of city-states such as Adonibezek of Jerusalem (Judg. 1:5). There were also many examples outside of Israel, including the Egyptian kingship[35] as well as the nearby kingdoms of Aram, Moab, and Ammon. It was not surprising, then, that the writer of Deuteronomy would consider the possibility that someday a monarchy might be created in Israel.

6a *The matter was evil in Samuel's eyes* is a more literal translation than "But the thing displeased Samuel" (NRSV). If the passage in Deuteronomy approved of — or at least did not object to — the people's appointing a king "like all the (other) nations," and Samuel himself knew this passage, Samuel's displeasure would have been at the attitude of the elders who requested a king and the reason for their request, rather than toward the fact that they requested a king. Samuel probably took the request not only as "a personal betrayal" but also as a rejection of the God-given institution of judgeship. The fact that the Israelites had been content with the institution of judgeship shows that they admitted that God ruled over them as a king (see v. 7; also Judg. 8:23). Now, the people reject this fact of theocracy and demand a human king. At issue was not simply a personal attack on Samuel.

34. Weinfeld, "Zion and Jerusalem as Religious and Political Capital," p. 87.

35. See H. Frankfort, *Kingship and the Gods: A Study of Ancient Near Eastern Religion as the Integration of Society and Nature* (Chicago: University of Chicago Press, 1948, 1978). Also on v. 11 (below).

3. The Lord's Answer to Samuel (8:6b-9)

6b *And Samuel prayed to the Lord.*
7 *And the Lord said to Samuel,*
"Listen to the voice of the people about[36] *whatever they are saying*[37] *to you,*
for it is not you that they have rejected;
but[38] *it is me they have rejected*
from ruling over them as a king!
8 *Like all the deeds that they have done*
from the day when I brought them up from Egypt to this day,
they have abandoned me and served other gods;
thus they are doing to you too.
9 *Now, listen to their voice; only*[39] *you shall legally declare to them the right of the king who will rule over them!"*

6b *And Samuel prayed to the Lord:* that is, Samuel appealed to the God whom he served; see 1:10. Samuel must have known about his sons' problems, and he did not make any excuse for them; he simply brought the matter to the Lord. He had identified himself with the Lord's cause so much that he felt that he himself had been rejected.

7 Since Samuel had an intimate relationship with the Lord, both as a judge who functioned as an intermediary between the people and God and as the prophet of the Lord who reported the words of the Lord to the people (v. 10), *the Lord said to Samuel* (the Lord responded to Samuel and commanded him) to *listen to* everything *(kōl)* that the people demanded of him. This is not so much his positive order as his negative permission, or concession. The reason is — *for* is the speaker-oriented *kî* of reason (see "Introduction" [Section V, C]) — that the people have rejected their covenant God who has been their king. The issue is not between the people and Samuel, but between the people and their God. So, the Lord is saying that he would be responsible for the consequences.

Rejecting the Lord meant to reject him as king. Thus, the people who demanded a human king "to judge" them — such as all the other nations had — were in the eyes of the Lord rejecting him who has been king forever,[40] for Yahweh has been the sovereign King of the universe, *the Lord of Hosts who*

36. Or "with regard to": *lamed* of specification (W-O, §11.2.10d).

37. Impf. of repeated actions.

38. *kî* = *kî ʾim;* also Gen. 17:15; 45:8; 2 Sam. 20:21.

39. *ʾak kî;* the former is "exclusive," the latter is "assertative"; Andersen, p. 170.

40. For the idea of the god's eternal kingship in Canaan, see "Introduction" (Section IX, A); M. Z. Brettler, *God Is King* (Sheffield: Sheffield Academic Press, 1989).

sits on the cherubim (4:4). Note that Yahweh is *ruling as a* sovereign *king* not only over Israel but also over the Philistines (see 7:13: *The hand of the Lord was upon the Philistines all the days of Samuel,* etc.). He has been king even from before the Flood forever (Ps. 29:10).[41] Therefore, the people's demand for a human king was the rejection of this eternal king. See also 10:19; 12:12. On the kingship of Yahweh, see Psalms 49, 93, 96–99.

8 Referring to the Exodus, Yahweh here once again claims that he is the Lord of the covenant people. On the phrase *to this day,* see "Introduction" (Section III, B, 1).

The word pair *abandoned* and *served* also appears in Josh. 24:16, 20; Judg. 2:13; 10:10, 13; 1 Sam. 12:10; Jer. 5:19. This pair usually appears in the context of apostasy. While God sanctions the king, he warns that the appearance of the king "opens a new way to apostasy from the first commandment."[42] In other words, Israel had rejected Yahweh as their king (Num. 14:11).

9 The expression *legally declare (hāʿēd tāʿîd wᵉhiggadtā lāhem;* lit., "certainly bear witness to them and inform to them") is a hendiadic expression, that is, an expression where two words are used to refer to one thing, with a legal meaning. The verb "to bear witness" (*ʿwd) is a denominative verb from the noun *ʿēd* "witness."[43] Aharoni takes it to mean "to establish a legal relation *with respect to* one's legal partner" rather than "to warn," which he thinks sounds too negative; cf. "solemnly warn" in NRSV; NASB.[44]

The term *mišpaṭ* in *mišpaṭ hammelek* is usually understood to mean *right of the king* or "rule" with regard to king's rights like that of the priests (2:13; Deut. 18:3); see on 1 Sam. 2:13. However, Hertzberg rejects this sense and rather takes it to mean "conduct," that is, the conduct of the king towards Israel, which will be of right "because of his elevation to the throne," for he thinks that "the rights of the king" means "the limits to be set to the powers of the king to put a check to the danger of *anomia* (1 John 3:4)."[45] McCarter translates *mišpaṭ hammelek* as "the justice of the king"; he explains it as "the way he will exercise his authority as judge."[46] R. P. Gordon accepts both

41. See D. T. Tsumura, "'The Deluge' *(mabbûl)* in Psalm 29:10," *UF* 20 (1988) 351-55.

42. Hertzberg, p. 73.

43. See *HALOT,* p. 795.

44. See Arad 24:18-19 ("to adjure and to warn you"); Deut. 32:46; 8:19; also Gen. 43:3; Exod. 19:21; 1 K. 2:42; Jer. 11:7; Neh. 13:21; see Y. Aharoni, *Arad Inscriptions* (JDS; Jerusalem: Israel Exploration Society, 1981), p. 48.

45. Hertzberg, p. 73. Similarly, see "ways" (NRSV); "practices" (JPS); "procedure" (NASB); "what sort of king will govern" (NEB); "what the king . . . will do" (NIV).

46. McCarter, p. 157. See F. Langlamet, "Les récits de l'institution de la royaut* (I Sam., VIII–XII)," *RB* 77 (1970) 186, n. 46.

"ways" and "justice" as the meaning here.[47] On the basis of its literary genre as a "manual" type (see below), we would rather take its meaning to be "rule" or "right," though the use of the term *mišpaṭ* here possibly has a "derogatory tone"[48] or "an element of satire"[49] in the wordplay involving *mišpaṭ* and the related terms (vv. 5, 9). See below (v. 11) and on 10:25.

While the term *rule over (yimlōk)* is a synonymous variant of *to judge* in v. 5, the emphasis here seems to be on ruling as king *(melek)* rather than on doing justice to the people as judge. McCarter, who sees here and in v. 5 a wordplay[50] involving the root *špṭ, seems to ignore this difference. The elders asked for a king to judge the people justly in v. 5; but here the Lord urges Samuel to inform them of the "right" of the king so they will be ready to face the new situation in which a king will rule over them as Yahweh's representative on earth.[51] While a king could be still a just judge, the change of title from "judge" to "king" in ancient Israel would bring a new social structure, the monarchy, in which a king fundamentally "rules over" rather than "judges" the people. This structural change will be described in the following verses (vv. 11-17).

4. "The Right of the King" (8:10-18)

10 *Samuel reported all the words of the Lord to the people who asked*
for a king from him.
11 *He said:*
"This will be the right of the king
who will rule over you.
Your sons he will take,
assigning them for himself to his chariot and his cavalry,
and they will run before his chariot;
12 *and (he will) appoint[52] (them) for himself*

47. R. P. Gordon, p. 110.

48. Ackroyd, p. 72.

49. Baldwin, p. 85.

50. McCarter, p. 157.

51. See B. Albrektson, *History and the Gods: An Essay on the Idea of Historical Events as Divine Manifestations in the Ancient Near East and in Israel* (Lund: C.W.K. Gleerup, 1967), p. 51.

52. *wᵉlāśûm:* lit., "and to put"; "He will appoint for himself . . . from them" (McCarter). Following S. R. Driver, McCarter explains: "[the inf. cstr.] derives its tense value from its position in continuation of *yiqqaḥ,* 'he will take', and carries an implication of purpose" (p. 158). However, the inf. cstr. here functions like an inf. abs., as a substitute for a finite verb; note that in a discourse dealing with regulations (cf. Leviticus 1) the agent is often *defocused,* since it is understood from the context, and the action *fo-*

(to be) captains of thousands and captains of fifties
and to plough for him and to harvest for him,
and to make the weapons and the chariot equipment for him.
13 *Your daughters he will take*
as perfumers, cooks, and bakers.
14 *The best of your fields, vineyards and olive groves*
he will take and give to his officials.
15 *Your seeds and your vintage he will tithe*
and give them to his officers and his officials.
16 *Your servants and maidservants*
and the best of your calves and donkeys
he will take, and they will be made to do his work.[53]
17 *Your small cattle he will tithe.*
And you yourselves will become his servants.
18 *Though you will cry out on that day*
because of your king whom you have chosen for yourselves,
the Lord will not answer you on that day."

10 As the prophet of Yahweh, Samuel reported the entire message from Yahweh to the people. *šʾl (asked for)* is a key term (root) in the books of Samuel; see on 1:28. Note that while Hannah asked a son directly from the Lord in her prayer in 1 Samuel 1, the people asked Samuel for a king (v. 5). Scholars (McCarter, p. 157; R. P. Gordon, p. 110; etc.) are keen to note here a wordplay involving the root *šʾl and "the requested one" *(šāʾûl),* that is, Saul.

11-18 The section, which is a "procedural" discourse,[54] is not a narrative description of deeds of a king. As a literary genre, it is more like a "manual" that explains what a king would do normally to conscript military and administrative personnel. It simply lists the king's rights according to the

---

cused. Similarly, an unmarked verbal form, the infinitive form, is used here for the prescriptive discourse about the "right of the king"; see above (v. 11) on focusing on the object by topicalization. Another example would be v. 16.

53. *They will be made to do his work: w^{e}ʿāśāh limlaʾktô;* lit., "and he will make (them) for his work"; BDB, p. 795: "use." The MT uses "a rather curious construction" (McCarter, p. 155); cf. ועשׂו (4QSam^{a}) and ἀποδεκατώσει "he will tithe" (LXX). McCarter prefers the MT to 4QSam^{a} as *lectio difficilior* (p. 155). A. F. Rainey translates as "put them to his own work" since in Ugarit "the crown demanded certain services from the people" ("Institutions: Family, Civil and Military," in *RSP* 2, p. 94). The 3 m.s. verb in a basic stem (i.e., the "unmarked" form) would be translated as impersonal passive, thus defocusing the agent, in the "manual" type discourse; hence, "be made" (see below on vv. 11-18).

54. See R. E. Longacre, "Building for the Worship of God: Exodus 25:1–30:10," in *Discourse Analysis of Biblical Literature: What It Is and What It Offers* (Atlanta: Scholars Press, 1995), p. 23.

rule, or regulations, in a monarchic society. The same type of discourse can be noted in ritual texts of the ancient Near East. For example, see the Hittite ritual texts in *CS,* I, pp. 61-67, as well as Leviticus 1–7.

Thus, 1 Sam. 8:11-17 simply presents the "right of the king" to the people who requested a king to *rule over* them, unlike Deut. 17:14-17 which warns against having a great number of horses, wives, silver, or gold, none of which is mentioned in the above passage, though it does imply the existence of a cavalry. What it describes is the contemporary reality of the monarchical regime known to the people from the Canaanite examples.[55] References to the duties and levies also appear in the context of formal exemptions and release from tax and service in Mesopotamian, Hittite, Ugaritic, and Alalakh royal documents from the second half of the second millennium.[56]

Verse 18, *Though you will cry out on that day . . . , the Lord will not answer you on that day,* does not deal with any present corruption of the monarchy, but it warns about the possible oppression of the people by a future king. These were all familiar from city-states long before Israel's time.

There is no reason why the present passage could not have come from the time of Samuel.[57] Therefore, contrary to what is often said, the model for this chapter does not have to come from a later time.

11 *The right of the king (mišpaṭ hammelek)* is concerned with only social, not religious, aspects. It should be noted that at the time the institution of kingship was introduced in Israel, the institution of priesthood had long been firmly established. In other words, the kingship in Israel began separately from the priesthood.[58] On *mišpaṭ,* see above (v. 9).

55. See T. Ishida, *The Royal Dynasties in Ancient Israel: A Study on the Formation and Development of Royal-Dynastic Ideology* (Berlin: W. de Gruyter, 1977), p. 30; also I. Mendelsohn, "Samuel's Denunciation of Kingship in Light of Akkadian Documents from Ugarit," *BASOR* 143 (1956) 17-22.

56. See Weinfeld, *Social Justice in Ancient Israel and in the Ancient Near East;* "(Review of) F. Crüsemann, *Der Widerstand gegen das Königtum . . . ,*" p. 101.

57. S. Talmon, "'The Rule of the King': 1 Samuel 8:4-22," in *King, Cult and Calendar in Ancient Israel* (Jerusalem: Magnes, 1986), pp. 53-67. As for the kingship in "other nations," see Frankfort, *Kingship and the Gods* on Egyptian and Mesopotamian kingship; S. M. Maul, "Der assyrische König — Hüter der Weltordnung," in *Priests and Officials in the Ancient Near East,* ed. K. Watanabe (Heidelberg: C. Winter, 1999), pp. 201-14 on Assyrian king as the "Huter der Weltordnung"; T. Kleven, "Kingship in Ugarit (KTU 1.16 I 1-23)," in *Ascribe to the Lord: Biblical and Other Studies in Memory of Peter C. Craigie,* ed. L. Eslinger and G. Taylor (Sheffield: Sheffield Academic Press, 1988), pp. 29-53, and D. T. Tsumura, "Kings and Cults in Ancient Ugarit," in *Priests and Officials in the Ancient Near East,* pp. 215-38 on Ugaritic kingship; also D. E. Fleming, "A Limited Kingship: Late Bronze Emar in Ancient Syria," *UF* (1993) 59-71.

58. On the problem of "sacral" kingship in ancient Israel, see A. R. Johnson, *Sacral Kingship in Ancient Israel* (Cardiff: University of Wales, 1967); Albrektson, *History*

Your sons, the object of the verb *take,*[59] is here focused; also *Your daughters* (v. 13) and others; see below. In a "procedural" discourse of regulations, the object is often focused and hence the agent of the following actions is *defocused* and understood: in this case "the king"; see, for example, Lev. 7:2-4. Notice the following *itemization:*[60]

(11) Your sons (with the particle *'et*)
(13) Your daughters (with *'et*)
(14) The best of your fields, vineyards, and olive groves (with *'et*)
(15) Your seeds and your vintage
(16) Your servants and maidservants
and the best of your calves and your donkeys (with *'et*)
(17) Your small cattle
And you yourselves.

The two words *mrkbh* (v. 11) and *rkb* (v. 12) for chariot are interchangeable and often appear side by side (e.g., Judg. 4:15; 5:28; 1 K. 22:35; 2 Chr. 9:25; 35:24). Egyptian chariots are referred to in Genesis, Exodus, and Joshua, and Canaanite ones in Joshua 11 and Judges 4. While it was David who first introduced chariots into the kingdom, Solomon increased them; see 1 K. 4:26; 10:26-29.[61] Therefore many scholars see here a retrojection of the Solomonic military situation. However, charioteers were a well-known special military class in ancient Canaan from the Late Bronze Age onward (cf. Akk. *mariyannu;* Ugaritic *mryn;* see *UT,* §19.1551: "noble chariot-

---

and the Gods, p. 51, n. 45; G. W. Ashby, "Sacral Kingship in Israel: Samuel/Kings and the Royal Psalms Compared," in *Studies in the Succession Narrative (27th/28th Pretoria OT Society Congress 1984/6),* ed. W. van Wyk (Pretoria, 1986), pp. 19-28; H. Cazelles, "Sacral Kingship," in *ABD,* V, pp. 863-66; "Royauté sacrale," in *DBSup* 10, pp. 1056-77. On the distinction between the religious *ensik* and the non-religious, socio-political *lugal* in the early Sumerian city-states, see P. Steinkeller, "On Rulers, Priests and Sacred Marriage: Tracing the Evolution of Early Sumerian Kingship," in *Priests and Officials in the Ancient Near East,* p. 112, n. 33. See Ps. 2:6; 45:6; 89:27; etc. Also on 2 Samuel 7.

59. For the key phrase *take, assigning,* see J. C. Greenfield, *"našû-nadānu* and Its Congeners," in *Essays on the Ancient Near East in Memory of Jacob Joel Finkelstein,* ed. Maria De Jong Ellis (Hamden, Conn.: Connecticut Academy of Arts and Sciences, 1977), p. 90; Mendelsohn, "Samuel's Denunciation of Kingship," pp. 17-22.

60. See D. T. Tsumura, "List and Narrative in I Samuel 6,17-18a in the Light of Ugaritic Economic Texts," *ZAW* (2001) 353-69 on the list formula; see also on 1 Sam. 6:17.

61. See Y. Ikeda, "Solomon's Trade in Horses and Chariots in Its International Setting," in *Studies in the Period of David and Solomon and Other Essays: Papers Read at the International Symposium for Biblical Studies, Tokyo, 5-7 December, 1979,* ed. T. Ishida (Tokyo: Yamakawa-Shuppansha, 1982), pp. 215-38.

warrior").[62] There is no reason Samuel could have not foreseen that a king would someday want chariots and men to man them.

On *they will run before his chariot,* see 2 Sam. 15:1 ("Absalom provided for himself a chariot and horses, together with fifty men to run before him") and 1 K. 1:5 (Adonijah's chariot runners). It was the custom for the royal chariot to be escorted by a team of runners. In 1 Sam. 22:17 (also 1 K. 14:27f.; 2 K. 10:25) "runners" refers to bodyguards in the king's court.

12 In MT thousands *('ălāpîm)* and fifties *(ḥămiššîm),* both masculine forms, may be representing the entire range of units: namely, "tens" (f. *'ăśārōt)* — "fifties" (m. *ḥămiššîm)* — "hundreds" (f. *mē'ôt)* — "thousands" (m. *'ălāpîm).*[63] So, these captains are military officers of varying rank. Exodus 18:21 and Deut. 1:15 mention the appointment of "officers" (NRSV) or "chiefs" (JPS) over thousands, hundreds, fifties, and tens, but they were chosen to "judge" (*špṭ) the people rather than to be military captains. The *fifties* as an administrative body might be compared with the *Ḫamša'u*-men in Emar texts and the Old Assyrian *ḫamištu.*[64] These "captains" might be permanent, trained professionals commanding the units of thousands conscripted as needed. Saul wanted David as his "eternal servant"; see on 18:2. In these contexts, the term *'elep* cannot mean "a troop" with about ten men, as Humphreys[65] suggests for the cases in Numbers.

Both *to plough* and *to harvest* are the object phrases of the verb *appoint;* these expressions, which refer to the beginning and end of the agricultural cycle, constitute a merismatic pair, referring to the entire process of agriculture. Hence, the addition of "and grape-gathering" (McCarter, p. 155), based on the "Lucianic" LXX, is not necessary.

Verse 12 as a whole could be taken as constituting a <war> — <peace> — <war> structure. At the same time the verse seems to refer to the professions of three classes in society: soldiers — farmers — artisans.

13 *Your daughters* is also focused and itemized; see above on v. 11. Both *perfumers* and *cooks* are *nomen professionalis:* <*qattāl*>-type nouns. The *perfumers (raqqāḥôt)* here refer to female professionals. Though Ackroyd noted that the term might be "a euphemism for 'concubines,'"[66] this is not likely; see *ben-hāraqqāḥîm* (lit., "the son of the perfumers") in Neh. 3:8, where "son" means a member of a group of professionals as in

62. See Rainey, "Institutions: Family, Civil and Military," pp. 106-7.

63. Cf. LXX: "thousands" and "hundreds" (so Josephus *Ant.* 6.40); 1 Sam. 22:7 ("as captains of thousands and as captains of hundreds").

64. See D. Fleming on Emar rituals in *CS,* I, p. 430, n. 34; also p. 438.

65. C. J. Humphreys, "The Number of People in the Exodus from Egypt: Decoding Mathematically the Very Large Numbers in Numbers I and XXVI," *VT* 48 (1998) 196-213.

66. Ackroyd, p. 72.

b^e^nê hamšōr^e^rîm (Neh. 12:28) "the companies (lit., sons) of the singers"; see the Ugaritic phrase *bn šr*[*m*] "singers" (lit., "sons of singers") in *KTU* 1.23:2.

14 A king *will take* (confiscate) private property and *give* it to his trusted servants; see 1 Sam. 22:7, where Saul pleas for loyalty among his officials on the basis of this "kingly" practice.

The word *ʿăbādâw* means *his officials* here — see "his courtiers" (NRSV; JPS), "his attendants" (NIV) — rather than "servants," which gives the impression of menial work. The king's servants are high-ranking officials as in the seal inscription *ʿbd yrbʿm* "servant of Jeroboam" (*HALOT,* p. 775; *CS,* II, p. 200). See 2 K. 22:12 = 2 Chr. 34:20; 2 K. 25:8; also Israelite (and other Northwest Semitic) inscribed seals with this title after proper names. These members of the court received land-grants from the king, who in turn confiscated them from the people, as is known in the societies such as ancient Ugarit: for example, "From this day Niqmaddu son of ʿAmmiṯtamru, king of Ugarit, has taken up the estate (house + field) of PN1 . . . and has given it to PN2, his servant *(ardišu),* in perpetuity. In the future no one shall take it from the hand of PN2 forever. (It is) a gift of the King" (RS 16.247:1-14), cited by Rainey in *RSP* 2, p. 97. This is "the most cogent" text, since "the recipient is called lú IR-*šu (ardišu),* 'his (the king's) servant.'"[67] In a number of Hittite land-grant documents from the "Middle Hittite" period (fifteenth and fourteenth centuries B.C.), it is attested that a king gave estates and landed property (including gardens, woods, meadows, and sometimes the personnel belonging to them) to his officials of various ranks and responsibilities either as a reward for services rendered or as a means of ensuring loyalty.[68]

15 *Tithe* (lit., "to take the tenth part of"; denom. from *ʿeśer* "ten") is, as in Ugarit, a royal tax on agricultural products.[69] It is different from the tithe for the religious institutions (Deut. 14:22-29; 26:12-15), "itself ultimately based on the model of a feudal society with Yahweh as king."[70] On the "fifth," see on 6:19.

The term *sārîs* here refers either to *officers* or to "eunuchs" (NEB; REB) and appears with the other term *officials* or "trusted servants." It is a loanword from Akkadian (Assyrian) *ša rēši,* "one at the head, officer." As the Assyrian merismatic pair, "eunuchs (= beardless officers)" *(ša rēši)* and "bearded offi-

67. Rainey, "Institutions: Family, Civil and Military," p. 98.

68. See T. Bryce, *The Kingdom of the Hittites* (Oxford: Clarendon, 1998), p. 92, n. 85.

69. See Rainey, "Institutions: Family, Civil and Military," p. 96. On the non-literal use of this term, see J. M. Baumgarten, "On the Non-Literal Use of *maʿăśēr/dekatē,*" *JBL* 103 (1984) 245-51.

70. McCarter, p. 158.

cers" *(ša ziqni)*[71] would refer to the court officials in general; the present expression, *l^{e}sārîsâw w^{e}la'ăbādâw,* could also refer to the king's officials in general, though the term *sārîs* by itself can mean etymologically "eunuch."[72]

16 The position of the term *the best (haṭṭôbîm)* in *w^e'et-baḥûrêkem haṭṭôbîm w^e'et-ḥămôrêkem* (lit., "your good calves and your donkeys") is puzzling. While in NASB and JPS this adjective is translated as modifying only the preceding noun, NRSV and NIV translate "the best of your cattle and donkeys." The latter is better supported since it seems that the adjective (lit., "the good") modifies the coordinated nouns "your calves and your donkeys" as a whole, but, following the "A X and B" pattern, is inserted between the nouns; see "Introduction" (Section VII, C).

For *calves (baḥûrêkem),* NASB and JPS translate "young men" while NRSV, followed by many, translates "your cattle," emending it to *b^{e}qarkem* based on LXX; BDB, p. 133; *HALOT,* p. 118. R. P. Gordon thinks that the "young men" are covered in vv. 11f.[73] However, if the Akkadian cognate *būru* ("young calf")[74] is taken into consideration, the Hebrew term could refer to any "young" being, either animal or man; see also on *pārîm* (1:24). Then, Weinfeld's consideration "that in some near eastern documents of release and exemption the royal work-force is represented by the triad slave, oxen, and asses" fits the MT text as it stands;[75] compare "oxen" — "asses" as a paired expression in the Ugaritic texts RS 15.114:14, 16.188 rev:3′.[76]

17 The context requires the translation of *'bd* as *servants* or "slaves" rather than "subjects" (as in vv. 14-15). This is the climax of the "rights of the king." All that the people have and they themselves are subject to arbitrary use by the king. Probably labor corvées would be the most onerous form of this "slavery" (1 K. 5:13-16; 12:4, 18). The writer of 1 Kings is careful to distinguish between conscription and actual slavery (1 K. 9:22).

71. See K. Deller, "The Assyrian Eunuchs and Their Predecessors," in *Priests and Officials in the Ancient Near East,* pp. 303-11.

72. See 2 K. 9:32 and Assyrian reliefs, which often describe both bearded and beardless officers; see *Art and Empire: Treasures from Assyria in the British Museum* (London: British Museum, 1996), Figs. 014 and 016. Cf. H. Tadmor, "Was the Biblical *sāris* a Eunuch?" in *Solving Riddles and Untying Knots: Biblical, Epigraphic, and Semitic Studies in Honor of Jonas C. Greenfield,* ed. Z. Zevit, S. Gitin, and M. Sokoloff (Winona Lake, Ind.: Eisenbrauns, 1995), p. 320. On the significant role that eunuchs played in Assyrian society and administration, see A. K. Grayson, "Eunuchs in Power: Their Role in the Assyrian Bureaucracy," in *Vom Alten Orient zum Alten Testament: Festschrift für Wolfram Freiherrn von Soden zum 85. Geburtstag am 19. Juni 1993,* ed. M. Dietrich and O. Loretz (Neukirchen-Vluyn: Neukirchener, 1995), pp. 93-94.

73. R. P. Gordon, p. 111.

74. *CAD,* B, pp. 340-41.

75. R. P. Gordon, p. 111.

76. See Rainey, "Institutions: Family, Civil and Military," pp. 93, 95.

18 *Because of* (lit., "from before") — Israel's oppression will come from her king, not from the enemies as in the time of the Judges.

The combination of "cry out" (*zʿq) and "answer" (*ʿnh) appears only in 1 Sam. 7:9; Mic. 3:4; and Hab. 2:11 besides this verse. The root *ṣʿq, the bi-form of *zʿq, appears with *ʿnh twice (Isa. 46:7; Job 35:12). Unlike Mic. 3:4 ("Then they will cry to the LORD, but he will not answer them"), this verse does not mention explicitly to whom they cry out. This could be intentional, for Samuel is probably saying ironically that the people will cry out to the Lord eventually, though they are supposed to cry out to their chosen king. This is the final word of warning from Samuel to the people who request the king. But the people refuse to listen (v. 19).

5. People's Demand for a King (8:19-22)

19 *The people refused to listen to (the voice of) Samuel,*
and they said:
"No! But a king shall be over us!
20 *And we also shall be like all the (other) nations;*
our king shall judge us
and go out before us
and fight our battles."[77]

77. *wᵉnilḥam 'et-milḥămōtēnû.* In our verse, the Niphal verb accompanies an object marker *'et,* followed by the cognate accusative or "internal object" (O-int: *milḥămōt*); see D. T. Tsumura, "Niphal with an Internal Object in Hab 3,9a," *JSS* 31 (1986) 11-16. This is not the same as "to fight (Ni.) with/against *('et)* [enemies]" (Josh. 10:25; 1 K. 20:25; Jer. 33:5; 2 Chr. 22:6). It seemingly still preserves the grammatical structure of this idiom on a deeper level; in other words,

LḤM (Ni.) 'et-mLḤMh-nû ←(Ni. trans.)— [LḤM 'et-mLḤMh]-nû

"to fight (Ni.) our battles" = "to fight (Ni.) the fight (O-int) of us against [enemies]" ←(Niphal transformation) "[Vt ("to fight") + O-int ("the fight")] -O ("us") against [enemies]." Put in a general scheme — when A and B fight against each other, i.e., when A fights against B = B fights against A, C comes and fights the fight which A fights against B.

S(C) + [V trans. + O-int] — O(A)
C [fights a fight] A against B
C [fights a fight] with A against B
If C fights a fight together with A against B,
C takes a role as a helper; A remains the major figure.
C fights the fight which A fights against B
Here A and C are fully involved in fighting;
both A and C are the participants in the fight.
C fights a fight of A against B

21 *Samuel heard all the words of the people and spoke them in the ears of the Lord.*
22 *The Lord said to Samuel:*
"Listen to their voice and make a king for them!"
Samuel said to the men of Israel:
"Go back, each to his own city!"

19 The people would not listen to the word of God; their only concern is "our" interest. The 1 c. pl. "we" is frequently used in the following short speech. The Lord fought his battle before (7:10), but now the people are concerned with their own battle! Instead of the Lord's kingship, they look to the visible human kingship. This is the beginning of new distrust by the Israelites of their covenant God.

20 In v. 5 only *to judge us* is mentioned. Here, the king's function as a warrior is emphasized. As Ackroyd notes, here are three functions of kingship, which emphasize "order and security":[78] (1) *like all the (other) nations* — "to have influence and status"; (2) *our king shall judge us* — to lift "responsibility from local leaders" and provide "a figure-head"; and (3) *go out before us and fight our battles* — to have "a focal person, already accepted and therefore immediately prepared to lead the army against any invader." In the ancient Near East, the two functions of "judge" and "warrior" are interrelated elements of his fundamental task — to establish and maintain order throughout the kingdom.[79]

For *fight our battles,* see "to fight the Lord's battles" (18:17; 25:28) and "to fight our battles" (2 Chr. 32:8).

21-22 Samuel hears the people's request and informs the Lord of it; after he is commanded by the Lord to listen to their voice, Samuel then commands the leaders to go back home. The phrase *the men of Israel ('anšê yiśrā'ēl)* refers to the Israelite army most of the time; but in 11:15 and 2 Sam. 15:6 it is a more general phrase. In our passage it refers to the "elders of Israel" (see 8:4), as in the case of "all the men of Jabesh" (11:1) which is co-referential with "the elders of Jabesh" (11:3); also 2 Sam. 2:4. Note the role of "the men of Israel" during Absalom's rebellion against David (see 2 Sam. 15:6).

Go back: McCarter says: "Exeunt omnes,"[80] so as to introduce a leading actor. The drama is at a point of tension.[81] What will happen next?

78. Ackroyd, p. 73.

79. See T. Ishida, "Solomon's Succession to the Throne of David — A Political Analysis," in *Studies in the Period of David and Solomon and Other Essays,* p. 182; Frankfort, *Kingship and the Gods,* pp. 51-60; Maul, "Der assyrische König," in *Priests and Officials in the Ancient Near East,* pp. 201-14, etc.

80. McCarter, p. 159.

81. Hertzberg, p. 74.

III. "STORY OF SAUL" (9:1–15:35)

The last chapter ended with the Lord telling Samuel to give the people a king and with Samuel ordering the elders to return, "each to his own city." We would next expect to hear how Samuel went about choosing the king. However, while the fate of the nation hangs in balance, the reader is introduced to a story of a young man named Saul who is looking for lost asses. This retardation of the narrative heightens the expectation. The young man apparently has nothing on his mind but farm matters and seemingly does not even know about Samuel. But we see how God sees these events as crucial to the history of the nation. He was clearly guiding by his providence the whole business of choosing the requested king.[1]

A. SAUL MADE KING (9:1–11:15)

1. Lost Donkeys (9:1-14)

a. Kish and His Son Saul (9:1-2)

1 *There was a man from Benjamin,*[2] *whose name was Kish, son of Abiel, son of Zeror, son of Bechorath, son of Aphiah, a Benjamite. He was a powerful person.*

2 *He had a son, whose name was Saul, a fine young man. There was no better man among the Israelites than he. From his shoulder upward he was taller than any of the people.*

1 The narrative begins in a way similar to 1 Sam. 1:1 *(There was a man . . .).* In both, the father of the main *dramatis personae* of the section is introduced with his lineage.

Kish, son of Abiel; that is, Kish, the "grandson" of Abiel ("My father is El"; cf. Abijah in 1 Sam. 8:2). Malamat notes: "Unlike the genealogical lists, and as in narrative and historiographical usage, the sequence of generations here ascends, like the table of ancestors of Shamshi-Adad."[3] Here,

1. See F. Deist, "Coincidence as a Motif of Divine Intervention in 1 Samuel 9," *OTE* 6 (1993) 7-18; V. P. Long, *The Art of Biblical History* (Grand Rapids: Zondervan, 1994). On Saul, see D. V. Edelman, *King Saul in the Historiography of Judah* (JSOTSS 121; Sheffield: Sheffield Academic Press, 1991), reviewed by Knoppers in *JBL* 114 (1995) 131-33; G. N. Knoppers, "Dissonance and Disaster in the Legend of Kirta," *JAOS* 114 (1994) 572-82.

2. = "from the land of Benjamin"; see "a man from the land of Benjamin" (9:16); cf. "from Gibeah of Benjamin" (McCarter, p. 167, following Wellhausen, p. 70).

3. A. Malamat, "King Lists of the Old Babylonian Period and Biblical Genealogies," *JAOS* 88 (1968) 171.

Kish's father, Ner, is omitted. For a detailed discussion of Saul's genealogy, see on 14:50.

Elsewhere the gentilic *a Benjamite,* or "a Benjaminite" (NRSV, JPS, McCarter), is variously expressed as *ben-y*ᵉ*mînî* (9:21); *ben-haymînî* (2 Sam. 16:11; 19:17); pl. *b*ᵉ*nê y*ᵉ*mînî* (1 Sam. 22:7); *'îš y*ᵉ*mînî* (2 Sam. 20:1); but cf. *y*ᵉ*mînî* (1 Sam. 9:4). The present phrase *ben-'îš y*ᵉ*mînî* (lit., "a son of a man of Yaminite") also refers to *a Benjamite,* just as *ben-'ādām* "a son of man" means "a man," like *bn ilm* ("son of gods") for "god" in Ugaritic. Talmon takes this phrase and 2 Sam. 23:20 as examples of "synonymous nouns placed side by side without syntactical coordination."[4]

The phrase *a powerful person (gibbôr ḥāyil),* or "a man of substance" (REB), would refer to "a member of the nobility," especially of "the warrior class, who became the landed aristocracy."[5] This title refers back to Kish, rather than to Aphiah. Saul is thus a member of the ruling class even though he was from a "junior clan of the smallest tribe" (v. 21). The title had originally a military sense, "a mighty warrior," as was the case with Gideon, Jephthah, and others. But its meaning had broadened and had come to refer to men of high social standing with economic power, that is, to aristocrats or wealthy citizens (e.g. 2 K. 15:20), such as Jeroboam (1 K. 11:28) or Boaz (Ruth 2:1). That Kish was a "man of wealth" is supported by the reference to the head servant and donkeys in v. 3.

2 Though Saul's home town is not mentioned here, his usual house was in Gibeah (1 Sam. 10:26; also see on 10:10). However he was buried in his family tomb ("in the grave of Kish his father") in Zela, which is near Gibeon; see on 2 Sam. 21:14. Therefore van der Toorn guesses that Saul's family could have been from the vicinity of Gibeon, since "people are generally buried on the land of their ancestors."[6] Based on this hypothesis he speculates that Saul was related to the Gibeonites, who belonged to "an ethnic strain represented also among the early Edomites"; see 1 Chr. 2:50-55; Genesis 36.[7] However, this seems rather unlikely since Edom was among the enemies Saul fought during his lifetime (see 1 Sam. 14:47), and he killed the Gibeonites as non-Israelites (2 Samuel 21). Moreover, the hypothesis that the Deuteronomist substituted the name "Gibeah" for "Gibeon" because there is "a strong anti-Gibeonite bias" throughout the Deuteronomistic history is highly speculative. On Gibeah and Geba, see 1 Sam. 10:10; 13:2.

4. S. Talmon, "Double Readings in the Massoretic Text," *Textus 1* (1960) 166.

5. C. H. Gordon, *The Common Background of Greek and Hebrew Civilizations* (New York: W. W. Norton, 1965), p. 229, n. 2, and p. 295.

6. K. van der Toorn, "Saul and the Rise of Israelite State Religion," *VT* 43 (1993) 520.

7. Van der Toorn, "Saul and the Rise of Israelite State Religion," pp. 540-41.

The phrase *a fine young man (bāḥûr wāṭôb)* is literally "young and good" (hendiadys). For *ṭôb,* various translations have been suggested: "handsome" (NRSV, NASB, McCarter); "impressive" (NIV); "excellent" (JPS); "in his prime" (REB). This "goodness" is not so much a description of the physical appearance as of the nature and personality of a man; cf. the description of Absalom in 2 Sam. 14:25 as *yāpeh* ("beautiful, handsome"), which entails an external (visual) evaluation. By human judgment Saul seemed to be the ideal person — fine and with a potential for anything, particularly as a leader whom the others would admire and follow.

His physical appearance — *taller* (again in 1 Sam. 10:23) — helped Saul make a good impression on people. R. P. Gordon says, "If a king is to be distinguished by his physical appearance then Saul is every inch a king (cf. 10:23f.)."[8]

b. Kish's Donkeys Lost (9:3-4)

3 *Since some donkeys belonging to Kish, Saul's father, were lost,*
Kish said to Saul, his son:
"Take with you the head servant and, now, go and search for the donkeys!"
4 *He went through the mountain of Ephraim.*
He went through the land of Shalishah,
but they were not found;
and he went through[9] *the land of Shaalim,*
but they were not there;
he went through the land of Yaminite,[10]
but they were not found.

3 After a brief introduction to Kish and his son Saul, the narrative focuses on an incident on a particular day. Kish asks his son to search for his lost donkeys. The phrase *ʾăṯōnôt lᵉqîš* denotes *some donkeys,* not "the donkeys of Kish," which would be *ʾăṯōnôt qîš.* Note also that in 25:7 *hārōʿîm ʾăšer-lᵉkā* means "some shepherds belonging to you" rather than "your shepherds."

8. R. P. Gordon, p. 112.

9. Reading *wayyaʿăbōr* instead of *wayyaʿabrû* on the basis of a few ancient MT mss and some Syriac (S^{AB})and Targum (T^{Buxt}) versions.

10. *yᵉmînî: Yaminite.* McCarter (pp. 174-75) suggests "Jabin," which could have been pronounced "Yamin" as a result of assimilation: *yabin-ii —(partial regressive assimilation)→ *yᵉmînî.* The term seems to be a designation of a district like Shalishah and Shaalim rather than of the tribal group; cf. "Benjamin" (NRSV, NIV, JPS, REB); "Benjamites" (NASB). On "Benjamite"; see 1 Sam. 9:1.

Donkeys often went astray,[11] and their owners went far to seek them. Such incidents must have been frequent, but they are reported "only rarely." Malamat finds such a report in a Mari text.[12]

The phrase *'aḥad mēhannᵉʿārîm* (lit., "one from the servants") probably refers to "the head servant" in the light of the fact that the numeral "one" can also mean "the first" (see Gen. 1:5; *UT* §19.126 [p. 550]) and from the context of the present story. The term servant (*naʿar;* see 1:24; 2:11-21) originally had the meaning of "boy" and "young (adj.)." This servant is not necessarily young, however, judging from his knowledge about the man of God and his words in v. 6. Note that Ziba, *naʿar* of the house of Saul (2 Sam. 19:17), had fifteen sons! "He held the important position of custodian of the personal property of Saul and his family."[13] So the man who accompanied Saul was probably the head servant of Kish's family, even Ziba (also 2 Sam. 9:9). The fact that he is seated with Saul as a guest of honor (v. 22) may also mean that he is not simply a menial.

The term *naʿar* appears in the military sense of "squire"[14] in Arad ostracon no. 110, like Jonathan's "young man" (1 Sam. 14:1) and David's "ten young men" (25:5); *Nearin* "warriors" also occurs in Papyrus Anastasi I.[15] However, the term appears not only in the military sense but also as designating stewardship roles. They were "managers of estates, the men of this rank were also responsible for delivering commodities from the produce of the estate to their masters."[16]

Even though Saul was the son of a powerful man, there was nothing

11. A Hittite law refers to the finding of a stray ox, horse, or mule; see *CS,* II, p. 113.

12. A. Malamat, "Episodes Involving Samuel and Saul and the Prophetic Texts from Mari," in *Mari and the Bible* (Leiden: E. J. Brill, 1998), p. 103.

13. N. Avigad and B. Sass, *Corpus of West Semitic Stamp Seals* (Jerusalem: Israel Academy of Sciences and Humanities, 1997), p. 30. Based on the seals, Avigad and Sass conclude: "In the later period of the monarchy, the title *naʿar* came to signify an established class of officials." See also *CS,* II, p. 200.

14. A. F. Rainey, "Three Additional Texts," in *Arad Inscriptions,* ed. Y. Aharoni (JDS; Jerusalem: Israel Exploration Society, 1981), pp. 122-23.

15. See A. Malamat, "Military Rationing in Papyrus Anastasi I and the Bible," in *Mélanges bibliques rédigés en l'honneur de André Robert* (TICP 4; Paris: Bloud & Gay, 1956), p. 115.

16. Rainey, "Three Additional Texts," pp. 122-23; see also N. Avigad, "New Light on the Naʿar Seals," in *Magnalia Dei: The Mighty Acts of God: Essays on the Bible and Archaeology in Memory of G. Ernest Wright,* ed. F. M. Cross, W. E. Lemke, and P. D. Miller, Jr. (New York: Doubleday, 1976), pp. 294-300; "The Contribution of Hebrew Seals to an Understanding of Israelite Religion and Society," in *Ancient Israelite Religion: Essays in Honor of Frank Moore Cross,* ed. P. D. Miller, Jr., P. D. Hanson, and S. D. McBride (Philadelphia: Fortress, 1987), p. 205.

strange about his going on a donkey search himself. C. H. Gordon compares Saul with King Agamemnon, whom Nestor meets wandering about at night and asks whether he is seeking one of his mules or comrades (*Iliad* 10:84).[17]

4 McCarter thinks the transition from v. 3 to v. 4 in the MT is "much too abrupt" and retains the longer reading here based on LXX^L. Besides, according to him, the MT exhibits "a perplexing mixture of singular and plural verbs." Hence, following Wellhausen and Driver, he reads all verbs as plural with the LXX and Vulgate.[18] However, *w^{e}lō' māṣā'û* does not mean "they did not find (trans. vb.), but *they* [= donkeys] *were not found* (intrans. vb.)."[19] Instead of positing plural verbs uniformly, we should probably posit the singular verb *wayyaʿăbōr* even for *wayyaʿabrû* (see footnote). Thus, v. 4 consists of a general description,[20] *He went through the mountain of Ephraim,* followed by a three-fold repetition of *He went through . . . but they were not. . . .*

Shalishah, Shaalim, and *Yaminite* refer to the hill country of Ephraim. It is difficult to identify these places exactly and to reconstruct the itinerary with relative certainty; hence, most commentators do not try. But McCarter identifies these toponyms as follows:

> "Shalishah" — NE Benjamin or SE Ephraim; it could be the same as Baal-Shalishah (2 K. 4:42) and located in the vicinity of Gilgal.
>
> "Shaalim" — probably to be identified either with "the land of Shual" (1 Sam. 13:17), the region N of Bethel in the central hills, or with Shaalbim (Judg. 1:35; 1 K. 4:9), N of Beth-Shemesh.
>
> "Jabin" — either Timnah, which McCarter thinks is near Ramathaim, or Jabneh, N of Ekron. However, McCarter's identification of Ramathaim is questionable; see on 1:1.[21]

c. Saul and His Servant (9:5-10)

5 *When they entered the land of Zuph, Saul said to the servant who was with him:*
"Come, let us return!

17. Gordon, *The Common Background,* p. 229.

18. McCarter, p. 168; see Wellhausen, p. 70; Driver, p. 69.

19. The intransitive use of the verb *mṣ' can also be found in Gen. 2:20; Num. 11:22 (x2); Judg. 21:14; Neh. 9:32; Isa. 10:10; etc.

20. Z. Kallai's view, referred to by G. Galil, "The Jerahmeelites and the Negeb of Judah," *JANES* 28 (2001) 40. For a similar geographical description, first by a general term, then by detailed explanations, see on 1 Sam. 27:10.

21. McCarter, pp. 174-75. See D. Edelman, "Saul's Journey through Mt. Ephraim and Samuel's Ramah (1 Sam. 9:4-5; 10:2-5)," *ZDPV* 104 (1988) 44-58; N. Na'aman in *DDD,* p. 283.

Otherwise my father may give up the donkeys
and worry about us."
6 *And he said to him:*
"There is a man of God in this city. The man is honored.
Everything he will speak (to you) will surely come true.
Now, let us go there!
Perhaps he will tell us about the journey
on which we have come."[22]
7 *And Saul said to his servant:*
"If we go, what shall we take to this man?[23]
For the bread is gone from our vessels.
There is no gift to take to the man of God.
What is with us?"
8 *And the servant again answered Saul and said:*
"Here is found in my hand a quarter shekel of silver.
If[24] *I give it to the man of God,*
he will tell us about our way."
9 *— Formerly in Israel, when a man went to inquire of God, he used to say: "Come, let us go to the seer!" For the prophet of the present day was formerly called*[25] *"the seer" —*
10 *And Saul said to his servant:*
"Well said! Come, let us go!"
And they went to the city where the man of God was.

5-6 Saul is about to give up and go home when his servant's words urging a final attempt lead him to the true, but to him unknown, goal of his journey.

5 Saul was getting more and more discouraged with the progress of his searching; and thus, as soon as they *entered* the land of Zuph he *said* (pf. . . . pf.; as an "instantaneous aspect"[26]), "Come, let us return." *The land of Zuph* refers to an area of unknown extent. It is the district where Ramathaim,

22. Lit., "our way on which we went"; see "the journey on which we have set out" (NRSV; also NASB); cf. "what way to take" (NIV).

23. See J-M, §167lN; lit., "to the man."

24. For a conditional clause (If . . .) expressed by two *waws*, see J-M, §167b; see also on 1 Sam. 9:7. Cf. "Give . . . !" (second person; LXX). "On the imperative force of the construction, see Driver" (McCarter, p. 169).

25. The syntax of the clause *was . . . called* is noteworthy. The Hebrew word order is: *lannābîʾ hayyôm iqqārēʾ lᵉpānîm hārōʾeh; l*-Agent + V(passive) + AdvPh + S, literally "to the prophet of the present day 'the seer' (S) was formerly called"; i.e., "the prophet was called"; see on 20:13; 2 Sam. 17:16. For other examples, see Gen. 2:23; 2 Sam. 18:18; Isa. 1:26; 32:5; 35:8.

26. J-M, §111d; 166c.

Samuel's hometown, was located. See on 1:1, 19. Here, the independent pronoun *they (hēmmāh)* is used for emphasis; after the repeated singular verb *he went through* in v. 4, the plural pronoun is to remind us of the servant and prepare for the following dialogue. The subject *Saul* is before the verb "said" for emphasis.

6 *He said to him:* that is, his servant said to Saul. There should be no ambiguity in the dialogue pattern of this Hebrew discourse. Generally the expression "he said to him" can be repeated twice without losing track of dialogue: (1) A said to B; (2) he said to him; (3) he said to him; (4) B said to A; see 1 Sam. 3:16. Now is the time for the servant to speak up and make "a critical intervention";[27] he was able to give "the right information and the requisite item (v. 8)" at the right moment. The Lord was certainly engineering the circumstances behind all these matters.

"This city" in the land of Zuph was presumably Ramathaim, also known by its shorter name, Ramah.

A man of God (ʾîš-ʾĕlōhîm) is "a man who serves God"; see below and on 28:7. As in 2:27, the only other occurrence of the phrase in the books of Samuel, it is synonymous with prophet. Samuel is first an anonymous figure, referred to here as *a man of God* and later as *the seer* (vv. 9, 11); the narrator first calls him *Samuel* in v. 14. We are not informed at what stage Saul learned the seer's name. Is it possible, as R. P. Gordon notes,[28] that "Saul's ignorance and Samuel's anonymity represent by a kind of metonymy the young man's complete unawareness of what lies ahead of him"? Probably. The audience, however, would immediately have realized the identity of the man of God of Zuph.

His word *will surely come true (bôʾ yābôʾ),* as in Hab. 2:3 "it will surely come true [= be fulfilled], it will not delay." See 1 Sam. 3:19b ("[the Lord] let none of his words fall to the ground"); Deut. 18:22a ("If the prophet speaks in the name of the Lord but the thing does not come about or come true *(lōʾ yābôʾ),* that is the thing which the Lord has not spoken").

The verb *tell* (Hi. *ngd) frequently appears in this story. McCarter thinks this frequent use is "one of the techniques employed to heighten the fundamental irony of a young man's unknowing quest for a kingdom."[29] However, it is the role of a prophet to "tell" the message of God; the frequent occurrence of the verb *ngd could be a wordplay on the term *nāgîd,* as Shaviv notes.[30] But this verb has nothing particularly to do with Saul's ignorance or "innocence." In fact, in ch. 19, the chapter in 1-2 Samuel where this

27. R. P. Gordon, p. 113.
28. R. P. Gordon, p. 113.
29. McCarter, p. 176.
30. S. Shaviv, "*nābîʾ* and *nāgîd* in 1 Samuel ix 1–x 16," *VT* 34 (1984) 111.

verb is most frequent, it simply relates that someone informs someone else of something; nobody's "ignorance" is emphasized.

7 Was the verbal form "we shall bring" *(nābî')* — *(what) shall we take* — originally correlated with the term *nābî',* "prophet," by folk etymology? Curtis thinks so, for a prophet was supposedly "the one to whom we bring a gift to obtain an oracle."[31] However, since the term "seer" is consistently used by Saul and his servant as well as Samuel himself (vv. 11, 18, 19) and is said to be an older terminology for "prophet," any folk etymology would presumably have occurred with regard to the usage of "seer" rather than "prophet." Shaviv takes it as a wordplay, following Vischer and Buber, and holds that the repeated use of the root *bw', meaning "to come," in vv. 7 and 9 is purposeful.[32]

The term *gift (tᵉšûrāh)* is a *hapax legomenon.*[33] It was once explained as "traveler's gift," something to do with travel or journey.[34] However, it has been translated as "interview fee" (Paul;[35] R. P. Gordon, p. 113) and "gift (of greeting)" (McCarter, p. 176), on the basis of *šwr "see." It can be reasonably compared with the Akkadian term *tāmartu,* "gift of greeting," a commonly used derivative of *amāru,* "see."[36] It was customary to take a gift when one went to seek the help of a seer (see 1 K. 14:3; 2 K. 5:5, 15; 8:8). On "a gift," see also 1 Sam. 2:20 *(šᵉ'ēlāh),* 10:27 *(minḥāh),* 25:27 *(bᵉrākāh),* and 30:26 *(bᵉrākāh).* C. H. Gordon notes that gifts were an integral part of social intercourse in the ancient world as reflected in the epics. They were given to friends, guests, and almost anyone whom one wished to treat honorably or have good relations with. A traveler away on a long journey was expected to bring home many gifts (*Odyssey* 11:355-361).[37]

8 The niphal verb *nimṣā'* in *Here is found in my hand* seems to emphasize by defocusing the agent the impersonal situation, that is, "it is found," not "I found." So, the money turned up almost miraculously. But the narrative's emphasis implies that the whole situation has been providentially guided by God. Now "nothing can stand in the way of Saul's meeting with Samuel."[38]

31. J. B. Curtis, "A Folk Etymology of *nābî',*" *VT* 29 (1979) 491-93. See McCarter, p. 176.

32. Shaviv, "*nābî'* and *nāgîd,*" pp. 108-10.

33. See H. R. (Chaim) Cohen, *Biblical hapax legomena in the Light of Akkadian and Ugaritic* (SBLDS 37; Missoula, Mont.: Scholars Press, 1978), p. 24.

34. See BDB, p. 1003; Jastrow, p. 1703.

35. S. M. Paul, "1 Samuel 9,7: An Interview Fee," *Bib* 59 (1978) 542-44.

36. See *HALOT,* p. 1802; A. Malamat, "Parallels between the New Prophecies from Mari and Biblical Prophecy: II. Material Remuneration for Prophetic Services," NABU 1989/89 (1989) 63-64.

37. Gordon, *The Common Background,* pp. 272-73.

38. R. P. Gordon, p. 113.

A quarter shekel of silver weighs about 2.8 grams, since 1 shekel = 11.4 grams.[39]

9 This verse appears to be out of place. Hence, it has often been moved to either after v. 10 (e.g., REB; Dhorme; McCarter; Fenton) or after v. 11 (e.g., R. P. Gordon) where the term "seer" is first used. However, the interpolation of the gloss between Saul's question (v. 11) and the maidens' reply (v. 12), as Fenton notes, would destroy the literary effect.[40] On the other hand, while the hypothesized order vv. 8-10-9 seemingly causes the "least disruption to the narrative,"[41] it still leaves the real question unsolved: Why does the term "seer" instead of the phrase "the man of God" appear here?

Another way of looking at this unusual order would be to take it as a "literary insertion" (see "Introduction" [Section VII, C]), where the narrator deliberately inserted v. 9 into the dialogue pattern (see v. 6) to interrupt the flow of discourse and delay Saul's response. Such a slowing down effectively raises the audience's expectation following the long dialogue discourse — two cycles of Saul's speaking and his servant's responding. Since asking the "man of God" (v. 8) about their way is the same as inquiring of "God" (v. 9), the present comment is inserted here. After this interruption (v. 9), the subject "Saul" is reintroduced in v. 10 as the primary agent in this narrative, the servant being put into the background. Thus, the position of v. 9 in the present location is not totally out of place.

v. 5	Saul said to his servant:
v. 6	And he said to him:
v. 7	And Saul said to his servant:
v. 8	And the servant again answered Saul and said:
v. 9	
v. 10	And Saul said to his servant:
	And they went to the city where the man of God was.

For *to inquire of God* (*drš + *ʾĕlōhîm*), see Exod. 18:15; etc.; cf. + YHWH (Gen. 25:22; Amos 5:6; Ps. 34:4; etc.). Note that in 1 Sam. 28:7 Saul wanted to "seek (a divine will) through" a medium. So, he went to "a woman who serves Lady of the *ʾob*-spirits *(Baʿalat ʾôb;* see on 28:7). A

39. A. Millard, *Treasures from Bible Times* (Tring: Lion Publishing, 1985), p. 116; also R. B. Y. Scott, "Weights and Measures of the Bible," *BA* 22 (1959) 22-40; A. F. Rainey, "Royal Weights and Measures," *BASOR* 179 (1965) 34-36; Y. Ronen, "The Enigma of the Shekel Weights of the Judean Kingdom," *BA* 59 (1996) 122-25. See also *ANEP,* fig. 776a-f.

40. See T. L. Fenton, "Deuteronomistic Advocacy of the nābîʾ: 1 Samuel ix 9 and Questions of Israelite Prophecy," *VT* 47 (1997) 24-25.

41. McCarter, p. 169.

prophet in Israel is "a man of God," that is, "a man who serves God." It may be that the purpose of v. 9 is to explain that to go to "a man of God" in order "to inquire of God" was the same as "to go to the prophet." See above (v. 6) and on 2:27.

The term *the seer (rō'eh)* was apparently outmoded to the narrator, but that does not mean that *nābî'* was a later term. Fenton holds that *nābî'* "belong to the most ancient stratum of Hebrew known to us."[42] This is supported by the existence of *nb' in Emar Akkadian of the second millennium B.C.[43]

d. They Meet Guides (9:11-14)

11 *As they were going up the ascent to the city, they met some girls coming out to draw water. And they said to them:*
"Is the seer here?"[44]

12 *They answered them:*
"He is. He is ahead of you. Hurry now! For just today he has come (back) to the city, because there is a feast today for the people on the high place.

13 *As you come to the city, you will find him before he goes up to the high place to eat, for the people will not eat until he comes, for it is he who blesses the sacrifice; after that, the guests will eat.*
So now go up, for, as for him, at this right moment you can find him."

14 *So they went up to the city. As they were entering the city, Samuel was just coming out toward them to go up to the high place.*

11-14 Until this moment the narrative tempo (see "Introduction" [Section VI, C]) has been rather slow, but now, it speeds up; the girls use such terms as "Hurry now," "just today," "today," "now," and "at this right moment."

11 The phrase *the ascent to the city (ma'ălēh hā'îr)* suggests that the city was located on the top of the hill for defensive purposes. The ascent normally led to the complex structure of the city gate. See 6:12 on "approach road."

The girls were descending the path to the well or spring outside of the city walls *to draw water* (*š'b; cf. 7:6; 2 Sam. 23:16), for it was the duty of women to fetch water daily (see Ugar. *šibt* "a woman who draws water" in

42. Fenton, "Deuteronomistic Advocacy of the nābî'," p. 33.

43. See D. Fleming, "*Nābû* and *Munabbiātu:* Two New Syrian Religious Personnel," *JAOS* 113 (1993) 175-83; "The Etymological Origins of the Hebrew *nābî':* the One Who Invokes God," *CBQ* 55 (1993) 217-24.

44. Not "Is there a seer here?"

KTU 1.12:II:60, 1.14:III:9, V:1);[45] normally they went in the evening (see Gen. 24:11).

12 *Today he has come (back) to the city:* if Saul had arrived one day before, he would have been too early. "Again the overruling of providence is evident, for the two travelers have arrived just in time for a feast at which, unaware of it as they are, Saul will be guest of honour."[46] The fact that Samuel had only just come does not imply this city was not his home in view of the servant's words in v. 6 and the description of his traveling in 7:16-17. Hence, the translation "he has come back to the city" may be preferable; see on 10:13.

The *feast* (*zebaḥ* = Ugar. *dbḥ* "feast"; usually "sacrifice") was "a small, local celebration of a kind which must often have taken place in Israel."[47] In 20:29, it referred to "a family feast" (see below).

The *high place (bāmāh)* is usually associated with pagan Canaanite practice.[48] Here it is outside of the city wall (see v. 14), a hill or an artificial platform on which a local shrine is located.[49] The high places are condemned by Deuteronomic theology which emphasizes a single, central place of worship. Therefore the expression "high places" often carries "a negative connotation, suggesting non-Yahwistic, syncretistic, or at least illicit cultic practice."[50] However, the present passage has no hint of a pagan connection, not so much because of its ancient origin as because of its association with Samuel, the prophet of the Lord (3:20). When Samuel urged the people to "turn aside the foreign gods and goddesses from your midst" in 7:3, those pagan religious cults must have been performed on those high places. Even after Solomon's temple was built in Jerusalem, the high places played a major part in the religion of Israel, especially on a popular level throughout its history; see 1 K. 3:2.[51]

13 Worshipers shared in eating the "peace" or "fellowship" offerings; see on 1:4 for "the sacrificial banquet" of Elkanah's family. The phrase

45. Gibson, *CML*², p. 85, n. 5.

46. R. P. Gordon, pp. 113-14.

47. R. P. Gordon, p. 114.

48. See *HALOT,* pp. 136-37; cf. Ugar. *bmt* "back (of an animal or person)" (*UT* §19.480).

49. See W. F. Albright, "The High Place in Ancient Palestine," in *Volume du Congrès. Strasbourg 1956* (SVT 4; Leiden: E. J. Brill, 1957), pp. 242-58; R. de Vaux, *Ancient Israel,* vol 2: *Religious Institutions* (New York: McGraw-Hill, 1961), pp. 284-88; W. B. Barrick, "The Funerary Character of 'High-Places' in Ancient Palestine: A Reassessment," *VT* 25 (1975) 565-95; A. Biran, "Sacred Spaces: Of Standing Stones, High Places and Cult Objects at Tel Dan," *BAR* 24 (1998) 38-45, 70.

50. McCarter, p. 177.

51. On the difference between official religion and popular religion, see E. Matsushima, ed., *Official Cult and Popular Religion in the Ancient Near East* (Heidelberg: C. Winter, 1993).

blesses the sacrifice appears only here in the OT. Note that the main role of Samuel, the prophet and judge of Israel, was to say "grace" before the people ate, while the priestly role of slaughtering animals was taken by others; see v. 24 ("butcher").

At this right moment (k^ehayyôm): also "at once" (NASB); "right away" (JPS); "immediately" (NRSV); cf. "about this time" (NIV). From the context, the preposition *k-* here should be taken as indicating an exact point in time.

14 McCarter changes the text *entering the city* (lit., "coming in the midst of the city") and translates "into the midst of the gate" in the light of v. 18,[52] but this is not necessary. The phrase "in the midst of the city" does not necessarily mean the center of the city. Note that in Ugaritic *b* "in" and *bqrb* "in the midst of" are synonymous (e.g., *KTU* 1.4 V 64-65, VI 44-45), and here *qrb* does not mean "center" either.

2. Saul's Meeting with Samuel (9:15-27)

a. The Lord's Revelation to Samuel (9:15-17)

15 *Now, the Lord had revealed*[53] *to Samuel one day before Saul arrived, saying:*
16 *"Tomorrow about this time I will send you a man from the land of Benjamin and you shall anoint him as prince over my people Israel, and he will deliver my people from the hand of the Philistines, for I have seen my people, because their cry has reached me."*
17 *The moment Samuel saw Saul, the Lord answered him:*[54]
"Here is the man about[55] *whom I spoke to you.*
This man shall rule over my people."

15-17 This section proves that the whole business of choosing Saul was by God's will and guided by his providence. Each step of Saul's journey to search for the donkeys was directed by the hand of the Lord. Except for Samuel, nobody, including Saul, knew about God's decision to choose Saul as *prince* over his people Israel.

52. McCarter, p. 169.

53. Idiom: "to uncover the ear of s.o." = "to reveal to s.o." (BDB, p. 162). On the meaning of idioms, see "Introduction" (Section VII, D).

54. w+NP(S)-VP(pf.) . . . w+NP(S)-VP(pf.): *The moment Samuel saw Saul, the Lord answered him.* The syntax denotes immediacy; see also v. 5. J-M, §166c: "two instantaneous actions."

55. Not in Hebrew; see J-M, §158i: "With the verbs of saying, the preposition meaning concerning is regularly omitted. . . ."

15 The disjunctive clause, *Now . . .*, with the subject *the Lord* put in front of the verb (pf.), formally introduces the main agent, the Lord, in the following section. Until now he has hidden behind the human events, engineering Saul's circumstances.

Samuel is informed by the Lord beforehand about Saul's arrival. The audience now knows that the earlier, disappointing search for the donkeys was guided by the hand of the Lord. In ch. 8 it was Samuel who informed the Lord of the people's demand for a king; here, it is the Lord who takes the initiative in informing Samuel of Saul's coming. On both occasions, Samuel as the prophet is the intermediary between the people and the Lord — representing both.

16 The verb *anoint* (*mšḥ) can take as its object cultic items such as a pillar (Gen. 31:13), an altar (Exod. 29:36; 40:10), or a tent (Exod. 30:26; 40:9) or a person such as the high priest (Exod. 28:41; 29:7; Lev. 6:13[20])[56] or a king (Judg. 9:8; 1 Sam. 15:1; 2 Sam. 2:4; 1 K. 1:34). They were anointed as a sign that they were set aside for a divinely chosen task. The act of anointing refers to "rubbing or smearing with a sweet-smelling substance" — animal fat or vegetable oil.

According to Fleming, while anointing was an essential part of everyday life in the ancient Near East, it especially marked "a variety of transitions in status." For example, anointing with oil marks "various changes in legal relationships," such as women upon betrothal.[57] In Israel, however, the act of anointing was first of all a royal rite; the king was "the anointed one" or "messiah" of Yahweh (see on 2:10b). The anointing rite was believed to impart something of the divine sanctity to the king. Thus, Saul is told "the spirit of the Lord will rush upon you" after he is anointed (10:6; cf. 10:10); and "the connection between unction and inspiration is drawn even more closely in David's case (see 16:13)."[58] See ch. 16 on the anointing of kings in the ancient Near East.

The term *prince* — or "the leader (of Israel, appointed by Yahweh)" (*HALOT,* p. 668) — appears here for the first time in the OT. It is often asserted that its Hebrew term *nāgîd* is an archaic passive form, *qatīl*-type, of *ngd, meaning "the one proclaimed, designated" (Mettinger; also Shaviv)[59] or "one who is made known, singled out, designated (for office)" (McCarter). However, not every *qatīl*-type noun has a passive force as

56. On the anointing of priests, see most recently D. Fleming, "The Biblical Tradition of Anointing Priests," *JBL* 117 (1998) 401-14.

57. Fleming, "The Biblical Tradition of Anointing Priests," pp. 405-7.

58. McCarter, p. 178.

59. See T. N. D. Mettinger, *King and Messiah: The Civil and Sacral Legitimation of the Israelite Kings* (CB: OT Series 8; Lund: C. W. K. Gleerup, 1976), pp. 151-84; Shaviv, "*nābî*" and *nāgîd*," p. 112.

māšîaḥ "the anointed one" does; in fact, some have classified *nāgîd* as an active "Part. neben dem Zielstamme" (Brockelmann)[60] or "Sager" (Barth). See on 3:20 for an active explanation of *nābî'* as "one who invokes" rather than "one who is called." We must admit that the etymology has not yet been explained satisfactorily.[61]

According to McCarter,[62] *nāgîd* is a title attributed to a king "*before* he begins to reign (9:16; 10:1; 25:30). When applied to a reigning king the reference is to his designation as *nāgîd* before becoming king." While the term may have *referred* to the king-designate or "crown prince" during the monarchic period, it simply *means* "the leader" of Yahweh's people in the present context since Saul's father was not a king. As a crown prince was usually expected to prove himself as his father's successor by being successful in battle (e.g., Nebuchadnezzar[63]), so Saul was chosen as a "military commander" for the people of Israel; in ch. 11 he will prove to be worthy of this title when he fights against the Ammonite Nahash. In fact, despite Mettinger's claim that the term was "probably not used in the pre-monarchic period as a title denoting the leader of the people,"[64] one may hold that the title *prince* or "leader" goes back to premonarchical times "when it referred to the commanders of the Israelite tribal militia."[65] The term was originally "the title of a person who was designated to be ruler either by Yahweh or by the reigning monarch" but later came to stand for king, ruler, chief priests, and chief officials, namely, "the appointee as the head of a certain group or organization."[66] Since God remained the true king, the title might well have meant "regent."[67]

The particle *kî* appears twice in the last part of v. 16: *for . . . because. . . .* The first *kî* explains the reason why "I" say to you "you shall anoint him . . . ," while the second is the cause of "my" seeing. The words of the Lord recall those used in calling Moses. "And now the cry of the Israelites has reached me. . . . I am sending you to Pharaoh to bring my people the Israelites out of Egypt" (Exod. 3:9).

60. Brockelmann, *GVG,* §138d.

61. See T. Ishida, *History and Historical Writing in Ancient Israel: Studies in Biblical Historiography* (SHCANE 16; Leiden: E. J. Brill, 1999), p. 58, n. 9.

62. McCarter, pp. 178-79.

63. See "The Babylonian Chronicle" (on 605 B.C.) in *CS,* I, p. 467.

64. Mettinger, *King and Messiah,* p. 183.

65. R. P. Gordon, p. 114.

66. Ishida, *History and Historical Writing in Ancient Israel,* pp. 65-66.

67. M. Tsevat, "The Biblical Account of the Foundation of the Monarchy in Israel," in *The Meaning of the Book of Job and Other Biblical Studies: Essays on the Literature and Religion of the Hebrew Bible* (New York: Ktav, 1980), pp. 92-93. On the difference between "king" and "regent," see on 1 Sam. 8:5.

17 The verb *rule over* (*yaʿṣōr;* or "govern") normally means "to hold back, restrain" through the following semantic change: "to hold back" > "to restrain oneself" > "to rule."[68] McCarter's suggestion to translate it as "muster"[69] does not fit the context.

b. Saul Meets Samuel (9:18-21)

18 *And Saul approached Samuel in the middle of the gate and said:*
"Tell me where the house of the seer is."
19 *And Samuel answered Saul:*
"I am the seer. Go up before me to the high place
and you shall eat with me today.
I will send you off in the morning.
As for everything which is in your heart
I will tell you [about it].
20 *As for the donkeys lost to you these three days,*
do not be concerned about them,[70] *for they are found.*
And for whom is the longing[71] *of all Israel?*
Is it not for you and all the household of your father?"
21 *And Saul answered:*
"Am I not a Benjamite,[72]
one of the smallest tribes of Israel?[73]
And is my family not[74] *the humblest*
among all the families of the Benjamin clans?
Why do you speak to me in such a way?"

18 The phrase *in the middle of the gate* reflects faithfully the elaborate structure of the gate of a walled city in ancient Israel during the Iron Age.

68. *HALOT,* pp. 870-71, citing H. Seebass, "Tradition und Interpretation bei Jehu ben Chanani und Ahia von Silo," *VT* 25 (1975) 182: "to hold back (those in the military camp prepared for the war of Yahweh)."

69. McCarter, p. 179.

70. Third m.pl. for the feminine noun, *ʾătōnôt,* in plural. This has been explained as an example of "gender neutralization," which is a characteristic of the spoken Hebrew dialect; see G. A. Rendsburg, *Diglossia in Ancient Hebrew* (AOS 72; New Haven: American Oriental Society, 1990), p. 44; see also 2 Sam. 1:24.

71. *ḥemdat* ← *ḥmd "desire, delight"; see *DCH* I, p. 388: *ḥmdt ʾrṣm "desire* [i.e., thing desired] *of their land"* (4QDibHam[a] 1.4:11).

72. *ben-yᵉmînî;* lit., "a son of Yeminite" (see v. 1).

73. *šibṭê yiśrāʾēl;* here *šēbeṭ* refers to a "tribe," a direct subdivision of "people" Israel; see below on *šibṭê binyāmīn.*

74. *hălôʾ* modifies both clauses.

The gate was used for all public business — as a meeting place, as a market place, and as a courtroom. The LXX's understanding "in the midst of the city" (so 4QSam^a) misses the point, for Samuel was about to leave the city when Saul entered it.

20 Again a nonverbal phrase *the donkeys* is in front of the main verb; thus, *everything which is your heart* in v. 19 and *the donkeys* are put in a sharp contrast. Samuel is going to tell Saul about more important matters than the lost donkeys. Saul may have had political matters in his heart.

The expression *the longing of all Israel* (*kol-ḥemdat yiśrā'ēl;* lit. "all the longing of Israel") has been interpreted variously: "And for whom is all that is desirable in Israel?" (RV; Driver, p. 74); "And on whom is all the desire of Israel?" (KJV); see BDB, p. 326. McCarter omits *kol* of this phrase and translates: "the riches of Israel."[75] However, the phrase may be a instance of the "AXB pattern" (see "Introduction" [Section VII, C]), a grammatical expression in which *ḥemdat* "longing" is inserted between the elements *kol* "all" and *yiśrā'ēl* "Israel" of the construct chain *kol-yiśrā'ēl* without affecting the construct relationship: *kol-ḥemdat yiśrā'ēl* → *ḥemdat kol-yiśrā'ēl.* It would mean "the longing of all Israel." Such unusual examples have been noted by Hebrew grammarians.[76] This understanding can be supported by the similar phrase in normal word order, *ḥemdat kol-haggôyim* (Hag. 2:7) "the desired of all nations" (NIV).

The expression *the longing of all Israel* refers to the people's desire (or "coveting" like Exod. 20:17; 34:24; Josh. 7:21) for a king "like all the (other) nations" in 1 Sam. 8:5, 20. Saul is to become a king just as all Israel longs for. He will "judge" them and "go out" before them and "fight" their battles "like all the (other) nations." As R. P. Gordon writes, "Saul is to become the focus of Israelite hopes against the reality of Philistine aggression."[77]

All the household of your father: cf. "all your ancestral house" (NRSV, JPS). Samuel is hinting here that Saul and his household are the hope of Israel.

21 Saul's answer suggests that he understood not only the meaning of the phrase "the longing of Israel" *(ḥemdat yiśrā'ēl)* but also Samuel's implication that he is the one who is to become their future king or designated "prince."

Am I not . . . ? — "Self-deprecation of this sort belongs to a worthy line of tradition which includes Moses (Exod. 3:11) and Gideon (Judg. 6:15)."[78]

75. McCarter, p. 170.

76. E.g., Williams, §30; see D. T. Tsumura, "Literary Insertion (AXB Pattern) in Biblical Hebrew," *VT* 33 (1983) 469, n. 7.

77. R. P. Gordon, p. 115.

78. R. P. Gordon, p. 115.

But Saul's father Kish was, in fact, a "powerful person" (1 Sam. 9:1). Though Benjamin was the smallest tribe and a short time ago had almost been wiped out by its wickedness and stubbornness (Judges 19–20), it lay in a strategic location between north and south; Jerusalem was in traditionally Benjamite territory. One should note that Saul of Tarsus was from this tribe (Phil. 3:5).

The exact meaning of *family (mišpāḥāh)* depends on the context. *mišpāḥāh* can refer to "people" (Amos 3:2) as well as to "tribe, clan, family." The phrase *Benjamin clans (šibṭê binyāmīn)* literally means "the tribes of Benjamin," but since Benjamin is one of the *tribes of Israel* (see above), the phrase is usually emended to "the tribe of Benjamin" (NRSV; JPS; NASB; NIV), by correcting the plural to the singular. McCarter translates, following LXX^{B}, "and from the humblest clan of all the tribe of Benjamin."[79] However, I would suggest that the phrase *šibṭê binyāmīn* could possibly refer to the *clans* of Benjamin, not *tribes* of Benjamin. If *mišpāḥāh* (usually "family") can refer to "a tribe" (Amos 3:1) in relation to "people" (3:2; see above), and to a clan (see also 1 Sam. 10:21) in relation to "tribe," the term *šēbeṭ* could also refer either to a tribe or to a clan depending on the context. On the relationship of "people" — "tribe" — "clan" — "family," see 10:21.[80]

c. Saul as the Main Guest (9:22-24)

22 *Samuel took Saul and his servant and brought them into the chamber. And he gave them a seat*[81] *at the head of the guests, who were about thirty people.*
23 *And Samuel said to the butcher:*
"Give (him) the portion I gave to you,
the one I told you to set aside with you."
24 *And the butcher took up the thigh and that which was upon it and put them before Saul. Then he (= Samuel) said:*
"Here is that which was kept (for you).[82] *Set*[83] *it before you and eat, because for this appointed time it has been kept for you, that is to say, the people whom I have invited."*
Saul ate with Samuel on that day.

79. McCarter, p. 170.

80. Cf. N. K. Gottwald, *The Tribes of Yahweh: A Sociology of the Religion of Liberated Israel, 1250-1050 B.C.E.* (Maryknoll: Orbis Books, 1979), pp. 327-34.

81. Lit., "place."

82. Lit., "was left."

83. *śym, Qal, impv. or "is set": Qal, pass. ptc. (so McCarter). For banquet themes in Ugaritic literature, see J. B. Lloyd, "The Banquet Theme in Ugaritic Narrative," *UF* 22 (1990) 169-93, esp. 182.

22 The term *the chamber* refers to a room on/near the high place; the same term is used for "various ancillary rooms abutting the temples in Jerusalem (*e.g.* Je. 35:2, 4; Ne. 10:38f.)" (R. P. Gordon, p. 116). Saul and his servants were treated as guests of honor at the head of the guest table.

23 Samuel could order *the butcher*[84] to set aside Saul's portion beforehand, since the Lord had told him on the previous day about Saul's arrival. Thus, this was a well-prepared and planned official meal for Saul with thirty representatives of the people, even though to Saul and his servant, their presence looked almost accidental.

Give (him) — the context requires "him"; Samuel ordered the butcher to give the reserved portion to Saul at that moment. See 1:5 on the idiom *ntn+ *mānāh.*

24 The term *took up* (*rwm) is a technical term for the separation of portions from the sacrifice; the same root *rwm is used in the expression "the thigh of the heave offering" (NASB) *šôq hatt*^{e}*rûmāh* (Exod. 29:27) for the thigh of the priests' portion. Saul is here receiving "tokens of the new status which is about to be conferred upon him."[85]

The expression *that which was upon it (w*^{e}*heʿāleyhā)* is an example of nominalization of a prepositional phrase; C. H. Gordon translates the present phrases as "the thigh and the-upon-it" = "the thigh and the fat on it."[86] The same phenomenon appears also in 17:4 (*champion,* i.e., "the in-between one"); 2 Sam. 19:31 ("the in the Jordan"). McCarter takes this "troublesome" phrase as unoriginal and notes the old suggestion of A. Geiger to read *ʾalyāh,* "a fatty tail," followed by Wellhausen, Budde, Driver, Smith, and also R. P. Gordon.[87] However, the two gutturals /ʾ/ and /ʿ/ are normally distinguished in Hebrew, and the fact that 4QSam^{a} preserves the spelling ʿ should not be ignored.

C. H. Gordon observes in this episode the "proportionate feast" as in the *Odyssey* 8:98; 11:185 [also Benjamin's portion in Gen. 43:34] in which the rank of the guests was indicated by the differing amounts and quality of their servings. Saul got a special cut of meat as a mark of his special future rank. The *Iliad* (1:460-8) talks about thighs wrapped with fat and raw flesh as the special portion at a feast.[88]

The term *appointed time (môʿēd)* again appears in the narrative that describes Saul's failure to obey Samuel's word (13:8, 11).

For the phrase *that is to say* (lit., "to say"), various emendations have

84. The *butcher* was a title of officers in royal courts; see Gen. 37:36; 2 K. 25:8; also see *CS,* II, p. 223, n. 1; p. 367, n. 51.

85. R. P. Gordon, p. 116.

86. See *UT,* p. 58, n. 1.

87. McCarter, p. 170; also R. P. Gordon, p. 116.

88. Gordon, *The Common Background,* p. 241.

been suggested. Also diverse translations such as "since I said I have invited the people" (NASB); "when I said I was inviting the people" (JPS); "from the time I said, 'I have invited guests'" (NIV); and "so that you might eat with the guests" (NRSV) have appeared. Althann suggests taking the verb to mean "to see," like Ugaritic *'mr,* and translates: "look I have called the people."[89] Note McCarter's pessimistic comment on this difficult term: "Precisely what Hebrew reading this reflects is impossible to guess. . . . the conjectures of modern scholars are legion and diverse, but uniformly unsuccessful . . . unsolved."[90]

But, the MT as it stands possibly means *that is to say.* Thus, the *meat which has been kept* for Saul stands for *the people whom* Samuel has *invited.* This ritual symbolism of eating the special part of the meat reserved for Saul must have something to do with Saul's ruling over the people (see 1 Sam. 9:17); for the thirty invited guests, who are probably the nobles of the region and represented the people, to eat with Saul at their head seat could mean their obedience and subjugation to him. As is often the case in the ancient Near East, in spite of his claim to divine endorsement, the "authority [of a king] depended largely on the goodwill and support of a powerful landowning and military aristocracy."[91] Saul, the future king, would certainly need the full support from these other guests who are representing the people.

d. Back to the City (9:25-27)

25 *Then they went down from the high place to the city.*
He (= Samuel) talked with Saul on the roof.
26 *And they arose early.*
At the rising of the dawn-star Samuel called to Saul on the roof[92] *and said:*
"Arise! I will send you off."
And Saul arose and the two of them, that is, he and Samuel, went outside.
27 *When they were going down to the edge of the city, as Samuel said to Saul:*
"Tell the servant to go ahead of us,"
he went ahead.
"As for you, stop now! I will let you hear the word of God."

89. R. Althann, "Northwest Semitic Notes on Some Texts in 1 Samuel," *JNSL* 12 (1984) 31.

90. McCarter, pp. 170-71.

91. T. Bryce, *The Kingdom of the Hittites* (Oxford: Clarendon, 1998), p. 92.

92. K: adverbial usage of a noun, as "to the city" (lit., "the city") in v. 25. Qere with an adverbial/directive *he* — "to the roof"?

25 Samuel and Saul went down from the high place and presumably went up to the city (see 1:1 on the topographical situation of "Ramathaim").

Based on the MT reading, the NIV and JPS (similarly NASB) render *talked with Saul.* On the other hand, McCarter, like NRSV, follows the LXX and translates "they made a bed for Saul on the roof, (26) and he slept"; he thinks that the MT is "plainly inferior."[93] R. P. Gordon similarly holds that the MT is inferior, for he thinks "the private interview does not come until 10:1ff.," and he criticizes the NIV's decision to stay with the MT as betraying "remarkable timidity."[94] However, it is hard to imagine that Samuel and Saul had no private talk until 10:1.

27 Here with *the word of God* Samuel functions as the prophet of the Lord, delivering His message to Saul.

Then the narrative continues in the next chapter.

3. Anointing of Saul (10:1)

1 *And Samuel took the flask of/for oil and poured it on his head and kissed him. And he said:*
"Isn't it that the Lord has anointed you over his inheritance as prince?"

1 This is a private anointing. Later, Saul will demonstrate publicly by lots that Saul was chosen by the Lord, not just by Samuel; see vv. 17-27.

A *flask* filled with oil is used here, but in 16:1 "a horn" is used for anointing David. The ingredients of the "sacred anointing oil" were liquid myrrh, fragrant cinnamon, fragrant cane, cassia and olive oil; see Exod. 30:23-25. On anointing in general, see on 1 Sam. 9:16.

Isn't it that (hălôʾ kî) is an unusual combination of two particles; the only other occurrence in the OT is in 2 Sam. 13:28. Here *kî* introduces a subject clause as in *hăkî*,[1] though J-M thinks that the text is doubtful. McCarter, R. P. Gordon, and others take the LXX as original, believing that the MT lost a good portion of text through haplography.[2] Thus, the NRSV restores a long text between *hălôʾ* and *kî:* "Samuel took a vial of oil and poured it on his head, and kissed him; he said, "The LORD has anointed you ruler over his people Israel. You shall reign over the people of the LORD and you will save them from the hand of their enemies all around. Now this shall be the sign to you that the LORD has anointed you ruler over his heritage." McCarter restores the "origi-

93. McCarter, p. 171.
94. R. P. Gordon, p. 116.
1. J-M, §161j. Cf. 2 Sam. 13:28 "is it not I that command you?" (J-M, §161j).
2. McCarter, p. 171; R. P. Gordon, p. 116.

nal" text from the LXX in the following manner: *hlwʾ mšḥk yhwh lngyd ʿl ʿmw ʿl yśrʾl wʾth tʿṣr bʿm yhwh wʾth twšyʿnw myd ʾybyw msbyb wzh lk hʾwt ky mšḥk yhwh ʿl nḥltw lngyd.* He claims that the MT has lost everything between *hlwʾ* and *ky* owing to haplography triggered by the repeated sequence *mšḥk yhwh (lngyd).* However, if it is haplography, why is *ky* preserved?

Here the pouring of oil *on his head* is specifically mentioned. For the placing of fragment oil on the head, see the Emar ritual text of the "Institution of the Storm God's High Priestess."[3] As ordered in 1 Sam. 9:16 (see also 16:3, 12), Samuel as God's agent pours the oil and announces that the Lord *anointed* Saul in order to give him a new status in his relation to the Lord, namely, as Yahweh's *prince* who rules *over his estate;* see on 9:16.

His inheritance (so NIV; NASB) or "heritage" (NRSV); cf. "people" (JPS), "estate" (McCarter, p. 180). The term *naḥălāh* appears six times in Samuel. In comparison with "(as a prince) over my people Israel" (9:16), Yahweh's "inheritance" here seems to refer to Yahweh's people, Israel. However, the primary meaning of the term is "inalienable, hereditary property" (*HALOT,* p. 687). Both "land" and "heir" are the two items of the divine promise to Abraham (see Gen. 12:7; etc.), and these two terms appear as a word pair in passages like Deut. 9:26-29; Isa. 19:25; Joel 2:17; Ps. 78:71; 94:5. The "land" of Israel was won in the conquest, granted by God to the individuals, then passed down by inheritance. So, Yahweh's *inheritance (naḥălāh)* refers not only to the land but also to his people.

For the term *prince,* compare "ruler" (NRSV; JPS; NASB); "leader" (NIV) (see on 9:16). Saul is now appointed or "designated" to lead or rule *over* Yahweh's *estate* as his vice-regent. Even though Israel has become a monarchy, it still is the Lord's "estate," and so Saul will be king only under God.[4]

4. Return of Saul (10:2-16)

a. Samuel's Prediction (10:2-6)

2 *"When you depart from me today,*
you will meet two men near/toward Rachel's tomb
in Zelzah in the territory of Benjamin
and they will say to you:
'The donkeys for which you went to search are found.
Now, your father has left the matters of the donkeys
and is concerned with you, saying,
"What shall I do about my son?"'
3 *And you shall go on from there further*

3. *CS,* I, p. 427.
4. R. P. Gordon, pp. 116-17.

and come to the Oak of Tabor;
and there three men will meet you,
going up to God at Bethel
— one is carrying three kids;
and one is carrying three loaves of bread;
and one is carrying a bottle of wine —.
4 *And they will greet you*
and give you two loaves of bread;[5]
and you shall accept them from their hand.
5 *After this you will come to Gibeath-elohim,*
where there are Philistine garrisons.
When you come[6] *to the city,*
you will meet a band of prophets
coming down from the high place,
before whom will be harp, tambour, pipe, and lyre
and who will be prophesying.
6 *And the spirit of the Lord will rush upon you*
and you will prophesy[7] *with them;*
and you shall be changed to another person."

This section is a "predictive discourse"[8] in which the verbal form *qtl* (perfect), preceded by *waw,* is dominant (e.g., *ûmāṣāʾtā, wᵉʾāmᵉrû,* . . .

5. The phrase *two loaves of bread (štê-leḥem)* may be an abbreviated form of *štê kikkᵉrôt leḥem* in the light of v. 3 *šᵉlōšet kikkᵉrôt leḥem;* in the latter *kikkᵉrôt* could be masculine, though it is ordinarily a feminine noun. See *HALOT,* p. 473; BDB, p. 503; cf. 4QSamᵃ; LXX, "two wave offerings of bread" (McCarter, p. 172; R. P. Gordon, p. 117).

6. *wîhî kᵉbōʾăkā šām hāʿîr;* *hyh (impf.) preceded by a simple conjunctive *waw.* See R. E. Longacre, "Weqatal Forms in Biblical Hebrew Prose," in *Biblical Hebrew and Discourse Linguistics,* ed. R. D. Bergen (Dallas: Summer Institute of Linguistics, 1994), pp. 70-71.

7. *wᵉhitnabbîtā;* Hith. pf. as III-y verb, with *waw* cons. Note the variable spelling — *nbʾ with/without aleph — in the same chapter: with aleph — vv. 5, 10, 11; without aleph — v. 6, 13. Such variable spellings are a common feature of ancient Near Eastern scribal practice; see A. R. Millard, "Variable Spelling in Hebrew and Other Ancient Texts," *JTS* 42 (1991) 106-15 on the variable use of vowel-letters in Hebrew and other ancient texts. See D. T. Tsumura, "Scribal Errors or Phonetic Spellings? Samuel as an Aural Text," *VT* 49 (1999) 390-411.

8. R. E. Longacre, *Joseph: A Story of Divine Providence: A Text Theoretical and Textlinguistic Analysis of Genesis 37 and 39-48* (Winona Lake, Ind.: Eisenbrauns, 1989), pp. 106-11; also "Weqatal Forms in Biblical Hebrew Prose," in *Biblical Hebrew and Discourse Linguistics,* pp. 51-52; "Building for the Worship of God: Exodus 25:1–30:10," in *Discourse Analysis of Biblical Literature: What It Is and What It Offers* (SBL Semeia Studies; Atlanta: Scholars Press, 1995), p. 22. See "Introduction" (Section VI, A).

ûṣālᵉḥāh . . .) as against *wayqtl* in a narrative discourse (see vv. 9-11). The section can be divided into three parts:

	<You will meet>	THEN
2	two men	they will say to you:
3-4	three men	they will give you two loaves of bread
5-6	a band of prophets	the spirit of the Lord will rush upon you

2 For *Rachel's tomb,* see Jer. 31:15, which mentions Rachel's weeping for her children in Ramah, Samuel's home town. According to Gen. 35:16-20, Rachel died and was buried on the road from Bethel to Ephrath (that is, Bethlehem) — "still some distance to go to Ephrath" (48:7) — after giving birth to Benjamin. McCarter thinks that Franz Delitzsch was right in thinking this refers to the Benjamite Ephrathah near Kiriath-jearim.[9] However, before Jerusalem was conquered by David the ridge road southward from Bethel could have been called "the Ephrath road," that is, the road to Ephrath, or Bethlehem (Gen. 35:19 — *derek 'eprātāh;* 48:7 — *derek 'eprāt*) rather than the "Jerusalem road."[10] Therefore, the original location was near Ramah on the "Bethlehem" road. Also see 1:1; 17:12 on "Ephrathite"; and 13:17 on "the Ophrah road." The present-day "Rachel's Tomb" is based on a later tradition.

The name *Zelzah (ṣelṣaḥ)* appears only here. Might it be a non-Semitic name? Because of the "obscure" Hebrew word order, that is, "near/toward Rachel's tomb in the territory of Benjamin in Zelzah," McCarter thinks that the "nearer definition of the location is out of place here, following the foregoing phrases (which a place-name should precede)." Hence, based on the LXX and other Greek MSS, McCarter conjectures *bṣlʿm bmqlwt* (lit., "in their limping on staffs") to be original.[11] However, the unusual sequence could be due to literary insertion, the "AXB" pattern, in which the prepositional phrase ("in the territory of Benjamin") is inserted between the main noun "Rachel's tomb" and the modifier "in Zelzah" of the noun phrase "Rachel's tomb in Zelzah," and the inserted element modifies the noun phrase as a whole. Such a literary phenomenon is not uncommon in a litera-

9. See McCarter, p. 181; F. M. Cross, Jr., *Canaanite Myth and Hebrew Epic* (Cambridge, Mass.: Harvard University Press, 1973), pp. 94-95; M. Tsevat, "Studies in the Book of Samuel: II: Interpretation of I Samuel 10:2: Saul at Rachel's Tomb," *HUCA* 33 (1962) 107-18.

10. Note that *'eprātāh* is "Ephrath" followed by a directive *he,* like *derek timnātāh* (Gen. 38:14) "the way to Timnah" and *derek yᵉraṣṣᵉḥû-šekmāh* (Hos. 6:9) "they murder on the road to Shechem." For the last example, see D. T. Tsumura, "Literary Insertion (AXB Pattern) in Biblical Hebrew," *VT* 33 (1983) 469.

11. McCarter, p. 171.

ture-like narrative, which is essentially to be heard — "aural" — rather than to be read; see "Introduction" (Section VII, B).[12]

3 For *the Oak of Tabor ('ēlôn tābôr),* see other compound names such as "Chisloth-tabor" (Josh. 19:12), "Aznoth-tabor" (19:34).[13] The location is not known; this tree must be near Bethel (see on 7:16). In the OT the oak is mentioned in connection with holy places and cultic activities; see Gen. 12:6; Judg. 9:37; Isa. 6:13.[14]

The phrase *going up to God* may be referring to a kind of pilgrimage (see Exod. 19:3; Deut. 10:10; etc., where Moses "goes up to" God on Sinai).[15] *One is* . . . is a list-like expression, if not a proper list formula; see on 6:17.

4 Judging from the sign or "audience-gift" of two of the three loaves of bread, this is not a "mere passing greetings," especially as these were probably meant to be given in sacrifice and would have been eaten by the priests (Num. 18:11). Saul's portion of the meat at the banquet (1 Sam. 9:24) was also the priest's share, so this indicates the sacredness of his kingship. As Wiseman notes, the bread was to be accepted "since such 'greetings' and gifts were part of the customary diplomatic acknowledgement of a king's new position and authority."[16]

5 The name *Gibeath-elohim* (so NRSV; lit., "the hill of God") and its shorter name Gibeah (v. 10) could refer to a place the same as or near to "Gibeah of Saul" in 11:4, since people *who knew him from before* (v. 11) are there.[17] On Saul's home town "Gibeah," see v. 26.

Most scholars accept it as "Gibeah of Saul" and identify it with the modern Tell el-Fûl [MR172-136], about 3 miles north of Jerusalem; the ancient north-south road ran along the foot of the site to the west. Its location and panoramic view (it rises about 30 m. above the surrounding plain; 862 m. above sea level) have made it an important strategic site; the geological shape of the city gave it the name "Gibeah" (i.e., hill), and the city could be also called "the hill" as in 10:13.[18] On a clear day, from the top of the mound, the

12. On the essential nature of the biblical texts as "aural," see H. van Dyke Parunak, "Some Axioms for Literary Architecture," *Semitics* 8 (1982) 2-4; Tsumura, "Scribal Errors or Phonetic Spellings?" pp. 390-411; S. Hayashi, *Bunshōron no Kisomondai* ("Basic Problems of Discourse Grammar"), (Tokyo: Sanseido, 1998), pp. 249-80 (ch. 12 "Narrative and Speech in Stories").

13. See G. Mussies, "Tabor," in *DDD,* pp. 1565-67.

14. K. Nielsen, "Oak," in *DDD,* p. 1202.

15. McCarter, p. 181.

16. D. J. Wiseman, "'Is It Peace?' — Covenant and Diplomacy," *VT* 32 (1982) 318.

17. See McCarter, pp. 181-82.

18. See P. Lapp, "Tell el-Ful," *BA* 28 (1965) 2-10; Arnold, "Gibeah," in *ABD,* II, pp. 1007-9.

Dead Sea is visible to the southeast; northeast, the view is toward Geba and Michmash; northwest lies Nebi Samwil, and there is a commanding view of Jerusalem sprawled over the hills to the south.[19]

The term (Philistine) *garrisons (n^{e}ṣībê p^{e}lištîm)* here is plural as in 2 Sam. 8:6, 14; compare the singular in 1 Sam. 13:3, 4. Various translations are "outpost" (NIV) and "prefects" (JPS). The plural form probably denotes a composite structure of buildings such as palaces and fortresses, as in Ugaritic *bhtm, mṯbm,* etc.; see *UT,* §19.463. At Tell el-Fûl, the modern site for Gibeah, two fortresses (I and II) have been excavated. While Albright holds that Saul built Fortress I, Alt and B. Mazar have suggested that it was one of a series of Philistine fortresses built to control the principal trade routes.[20] The reason why *Philistine garrisons* is mentioned here is probably that Saul would be empowered by God to deliver his people from them. See on 13:3-4.

The term *ḥebel* (lit., "rope") means here *band,* like "flock/flight (of birds), a band of personages" such as "the band of songstresses" (Ugar. *ḥbl kṯrt* in *KTU* 1.11:6).[21] This "band of prophets" *(ḥebel n^{e}bîʾîm)* is more similar to a group called *āpilum* "answerer, responder" in Mari than to the *muḫḫûm,* an ecstatic or frenetic, in light of the fact that *āpilum,* unlike the other types of prophets, acted occasionally in consort, "in groups similar to the bands of prophets in the Bible."[22] It is often assumed that this band is of a type whose "prophesying" was irrational and ecstatic, but the text only suggests the acts of prophesying in a group with musical instruments. The verbal stem, Hith., of *prophesying (mitnabb^{e}ʾîm)* does not necessarily mean the act is ecstatic, though the prophesying in Israel sometimes accompanied some type of "supernatural" experience. Too much emphasis has been given to this aspect of prophesying; for example, BDB, pp. 611-12. But here as in 19:20, it is the work of the spirit of the Lord that is emphasized; no "pagan" religious actions such as "self-flagellation or mutilation"[23] are mentioned.

Prophecy in the ancient Near East has been the subject of intense scholarly scrutiny. What similarities there are between Israelite prophecy and Canaanite prophecy relate to ecstasy. However, though historians were wont to say that Israelite prophecy was just an outgrowth of Canaanite ecstatic prophecy, it is now difficult to hold this view.[24] For example, *HALOT,* p. 659, is more cautious about the nature of this prophesying; it explains Ni. as "to

19. N. L. Lapp, "Fûl, Tell el-," in *NEAEHL,* p. 445.

20. See N. L. Lapp, "Fûl, Tell el-" in *NEAEHL,* pp. 445-46; B. Mazar, *Biblical Israel: State and People,* ed. S. Ahituv (Jerusalem: Magnes Press, 1992), p. 36, n. 31.

21. *UT,* §19.832.

22. A. Malamat, "Intuitive Prophecy — A General Survey," in *Mari and the Bible* (Leiden: E. J. Brill, 1998), p. 67.

23. McCarter, p. 182.

24. See R. P. Gordon, pp. 117-18; also on 1 Sam. 19:20-21.

be in a prophetic trance, behave like a *nābî*'" (10:11; 19:20; etc.); Hith. as "to exhibit the behaviour of a *nābî*'" (Num. 11:25; 1 Sam. 10:5; 18:10; 19:20; etc.). In these descriptions the terms "ecstasy" and "ecstatic" are wisely avoided, especially since the terms have been used without a careful definition. Wilson suggests that they may have been in some kind of trance, for music is often used for inducing trances, but he points out that these prophets can still walk and play instruments, though the ones prophesying and those performing may not have been the same individuals since the performers were "before them," so it could not have been a deep trance.[25] See on 19:20. On a "prophet" *(nābî')*, see 3:20.

By playing these musical instruments *harp, tambour, double-pipe, and lyre*[26] *(nēbel wᵉtōp wᵉḥālîl wᵉkinnôr)*,[27] their spiritual "experience" is certainly enhanced, if not caused. On a minstrel and a song, see 2 Sam. 23:1. The instrument *tambour* is usually associated with joy and gladness in the Bible; see 18:6; 2 Sam. 6:5; Isa. 5:12.[28]

6 It is noteworthy that the phrase *the spirit of the Lord (rûaḥ YHWH;* also 16:13, 14; 19:9; 2 Sam. 23:2) appears in 1-2 Samuel only in connection with Yahweh's anointed, that is, Saul or David (16:13). Likewise, later it departed from Saul (1 Sam. 16:14), and, in its place, the spirit of Yahweh for disaster came upon him (19:9).[29] Thus, the spirit of Yahweh was given to His anointed that they might fulfill their responsibility as the representative of the people Israel and as the vice-regent of God.

The verb "to rush" (*ṣlḥ) + *spirit (rûaḥ)* appears only in the stories of Samson (Judg. 14:6, 19; 15:14), Saul (10:6, 10; 11:6; 18:10), and David (16:13). The expression does not appear after 18:10. While the onrush of God's spirit usually invigorated the hero's martial spirits — "the hero experiences the spirit as an explosive surge of strength"[30] — the present passage is concerned with endowing the power of "prophecy" (see below). Unlike the normal Canaanite practices, the phenomenon is not artificially manipulated; the spirit of the Lord will rush upon Saul of itself — predicted but not manip-

25. R. R. Wilson, "Prophecy and Ecstasy: A Reexamination," *JBL* 98 (1979) 332.

26. On the harp, see *HALOT,* p. 664. For the most recent study on the lyre, see B. Lawergren, "Distinctions among Canaanite, Philistine, and Israelite Lyres, and Their Global Lyrical Contexts," *BASOR* 309 (1998) 41-68.

27. On these translations, see T. C. Mitchell, "The Music of the Old Testament Reconsidered," *IEJ* (124th year) (1992) 131.

28. Music features as an aid to inspiration in 2 K. 3:15. Also see 16:16; 2 Sam. 6:5. For the musical instruments, see Mitchell, "The Music of the Old Testament Reconsidered," pp. 124-43.

29. See D. T. Tsumura, "'An Evil Spirit from the Lord' in the First Book of Samuel," *Exegetica* 8 (1997) 1-10 [Japanese with English summary].

30. McCarter, p. 182.

ulated. Here, the spirit of the Lord functions as the means by which he takes ordinary people and makes them fit for his service. The onrush of the spirit of the Lord was necessary to dispel any doubts Saul might have of his choice and as a public demonstration that he was now the "prince."[31] The precise nature of Saul's "prophesying" is not specified, but "no negative evaluation is given to it"[32] here or when it occurs in v. 9.

To change to *another person (ʾîš ʾaḥēr)* is not necessarily becoming another person by losing oneself, but rather by being equipped with power to play a new role as Gideon and Jephthah did when the spirit of God came upon them (Judg. 6:34; 11:29). Thus, as Wilson notes, "Saul's possession has to do with his election, not with his becoming a prophet."[33]

b. Samuel's Order (10:7-8)

7 *"When these signs come*[34] *to you, do what your hand finds,*
for God will be with you!
8 *(But) you shall [first] go down to Gilgal before me.*
Soon[35] *I myself am going down to you to offer burnt offerings and to offer peace offerings.*
For seven days you shall wait [on God] until I come to you;
I will let you know what you should do."

7 Samuel now orders Saul to act when the signs come to him. The phrase *these signs (hāʾōtôt hāʾēlleh)* refers to the three preceding matters, that is, the greeting of the two men (v. 2), the gift of two loaves of bread (v. 4), and the onrush of the spirit of the Lord (v. 6).

McCarter explains the phrase *do what your hand finds* as "surrender yourself to any impulse in the assurance that it is of divine origin."[36] But, what is emphasized here by the use of "hand" is not so much Saul's impulse as his ability. The basic presupposition is that the Lord has providentially guided Saul's life this far and from now on he will be with him more closely

31. D. I. Block, "Empowered by the Spirit of God: The Holy Spirit in the Historiographic Writings of the Old Testament," *Southern Baptist Journal of Theology* 1 (1997) 45-47.

32. Wilson, "Prophecy and Ecstasy," p. 333.

33. Wilson, "Prophecy and Ecstasy," p. 333.

34. K. *tbʾynh;* Q. *tābōʾnāh;* here Q., not K., is a phonetic spelling: *tābō(ʾ)nāh* ← *t^{e}bōʾênāh;* see D. T. Tsumura, "Vowel sandhi in Biblical Hebrew," *ZAW* 109 (1997) 583, 587.

35. Lit., "and behold!" This is followed by a participle phrase: "I am about to go down."

36. McCarter, p. 183.

through his spirit and power. The phrase *what your hand finds* may refer either to "a specific opportunity [which] will be provided by the Ammonite attack on Jabesh-gilead (11:1ff.)" or to "the challenge of the Philistine presence" in general (see v. 5). These will be the opportunities for Saul to prove himself as the Lord's anointed who rules over his people. Compare Nathan's answer to David in 1 Chr. 17:2, "Whatever you have in mind, do it, for God is with you" = 2 Sam. 7:3, "Whatever you have in mind, go ahead and do it, for the LORD is with you."

God will be with you: As R. P. Gordon says,[37] God will be present with and aid his anointed king. But for this, it is essential that the spirit of the Lord be with him. The phrase "God/the Lord is with you (s.)/him" appears in the OT with reference to Abraham, Isaac, Joseph, Gideon, Saul, David, Solomon, Hezekiah, and Phinehas. Note that this phrase is used in connection with Saul only this once, in contrast to the many times with David (1 Sam. 16:18; 18:12, 14; 20:13; 2 Sam. 7:3; 1 Chr. 17:2).

8 Many scholars hold that this verse is editorial and is put there secondarily in order to prepare the reader for the account of the rejection of Saul in 1 Sam. 13:7b onward.[38] However, before going into this intricate problem, let us read the MT of this chapter as it stands. The relationship between this section and 13:7b-15 will be dealt with in detail in the discussion of 13:8.

Saul can do whatever his hand finds to do because of God's presence with him. *But* there is one thing he should do before he goes out and fulfills his role as Yahweh's anointed. In the sequence of the preceding impv. (v. 7), the construction <*waw* cons. + pf.> has the imperative force: hence, *you shall go down to Gilgal before me.* We are not told, however, how soon Saul should go down to Gilgal. But Samuel — now at his home town Ramah — was presumably getting ready to start his annual visit to Bethel — Gilgal — Mizpah (see 7:16); so, Saul's visit to Gilgal would need to occur within a few weeks or possibly a few months, but obviously before "Samuel called the people to the Lord at Mizpah" (10:17). There is no reason to think that Saul's visit was postponed until many years later (→ 13:7b), as some claim. In fact, he and Samuel were again at Gilgal when he was officially made king (11:15). Considering the fact that in 13:2 Jonathan could lead his father's troop of one thousand, the events in chs. 10–12 were probably much earlier than those of ch. 13, since Saul at this time was "a fine young man" (9:2), possibly single.

On *peace offerings (zibḥê š^{e}lāmîm;* lit., offerings for peace), compare "fellowship offerings" (NIV) and "sacrifices of well-being" (NRSV; JPS).

37. R. P. Gordon, p. 118.

38. See, for example, McCarter, p. 183; Ackroyd, p. 84; Klein, p. 92; Birch, p. 1068.

Part was burnt, and the rest was eaten by the worshipper (Lev. 3; 7:11-14). This offering must have a function similar to the Ugaritic *šlmm* (see *UT,* §19.2424; cf. Akkadian *hāram ša šalīmim* "the foal of peace" [*CAD,* Ḫ, 118]) in bringing "peace" or "reconciliation" with deities. But it has a completely different significance for the Israelites who accepted only one god Yahweh the Creator and the Lord of the Universe. The sacrificial meals in ch. 1 and ch. 9 would have been the eating of the peace offering. McCarter translates the term as "communion offerings" since, he holds, the meals were eaten in communion with the deity.[39]

It seems to have been the normal practice to offer sacrifices at these sacred places (see on 7:5, 16) — both burnt offerings and peace offerings; see Josh. 8:31; Judg. 20:26; 21:4 (Bethel); 2 Sam. 6:17, 18; 24:25 (Jerusalem).

For seven days you shall wait (šibʿat yāmîm tôḥēl). The command to wait "for seven days" until I come to you could mean one of the following:

[A] "you shall wait for seven days, for seven days from now I will be in Gilgal"
[B] "you shall wait there for my arrival, even if I am as much as seven days late"
[C] "you shall go there seven days before my expected arrival and wait there for the time of my arrival"

But in deciding the meaning of this verse, determining the meaning of "to wait" is important.

The verbs *yḥl "to wait" and *qwh "to wait, hope" appear as a word pair in Isa. 51:5; Mic. 5:7; Ps. 130:5; and Job 30:26. "As with *qwh,* most often, especially in the Psalms, it is God himself that is the explicit object of hope; 3x it is one of God's attributes, viz., his lovingkindness, once his salvation, and once his 'arm.'"[40] Hence, "to wait" in the present context could mean also "to wait on God" in a religious context rather than simply waiting for Samuel's arrival. If this is the case, the seven-day period also must have a religious significance. As a recent study shows,[41] in the OT, the expression "seven days" appears most often in the description of a religious ritual. So, "to wait for seven days" possibly bears a religious significance here, too.

It is noteworthy that LXX translates the verb *tôḥēl* here as *dialeipseis* ("to stop, cease"; also in 1 Sam. 13:8 *dielipen*) which would mean "to stop

39. McCarter, p. 183.

40. D. Schibler, "יחל" in *NIDOTTE,* 2, p. 436.

41. G. A. Klingbeil, "Ritual Time in Leviticus 8 with Special Reference to the Seven Day Period in the Old Testament," *ZAW* 109 (1997) 500-513.

doing something" or "to do nothing." It may be reasonably conjectured that Saul was ordered "to make a seven-day retreat" before becoming engaged in any kingly activity. Since at least the priestly families seemingly observed the Sabbath during the time of Saul (see on 21:6), it is not unreasonable to assume that Samuel also observed the Sabbath.[42] If so, his command to Saul may have had something to do with the observation of the Sabbath. Note also a possible cognate in Ugaritic: *ḥl* "[the king] is clear (of further cultic obligations)."[43] Both the Hebrew and Ugaritic terms may refer to the state of being off duty, that is, doing nothing. See, further, on 1 Sam. 13:8 ("he waited for seven days").

The clause *I will let you know* is better taken to be in sequence to "you shall wait" (so McCarter) rather than to "I come to you" (so NRSV; NIV; etc.).

c. Saul's Departure (10:9-13)

9 *While he was turning[44] his back to go away from Samuel, God gave[45] him another heart. And all these signs came on that day.*
10 *And they came from there to Gibeah, where just at that moment[46] a band of prophets were coming toward him.*
And the spirit of God rushed upon him and he prophesied in their midst.
11 *As for all who knew him from before, they saw him prophesying with the prophets.*
And the people said to each other,
"What in the world[47] happened to the son of Kish?
Is Saul too among the prophets?"

42. For the origin of the Israelite Sabbath, see D. E. Fleming, "A Break in the Line: Reconsidering the Bible's Diverse Festival Calendars," *RB* 106 (1999) 173-74; also "The Israelite Festival Calendar and Emar's Ritual Archive," *RB* 106 (1999) 8-34.

43. See Tsumura, "'An Evil Spirit from the Lord,'" pp. 1-10; "Kings and Cults in Ancient Ugarit," in *Priests and Officials in the Ancient Near East,* ed. K. Watanabe (Heidelberg: C. Winter, 1999), pp. 215-38.

44. *wᵉhāyāh; w+hyh* (pf.); an "abnormal" usage in the sense that it introduces a continuous aspect, hence "while . . . ing," not like *wayhî,* which introduces a past tense; see on 1:12. See Y. Endo, *The Verbal System of Classical Hebrew in the Joseph Story: An Approach from Discourse Analysis* (Assen: Van Gorcum, 1996), p. 184. Longacre takes this expression here to mark "a pivot between Samuel's predictive speech in 10:1-8, and its narrative fulfillment in vv. 10-11"; see Longacre, "Weqatal Forms in Biblical Hebrew Prose," p. 86.

45. Lit., "turned to him" *wayyahăpok-lô.*

46. *wᵉhinnēh;* lit., "and behold"; i.e., "here and now" or "then and there."

47. The emphatic use of *zh;* see W-O, §17.4.3 (p. 313).

12 *And a man who was there*[48] *responded:*
"And who is their father?"
Therefore it became a proverb: "Is Saul too among the prophets?"
13 *And he finished prophesying*[49] *and came back to the hill.*

9-11 This is an abbreviated account of the fulfillment of Samuel's prediction of what would happen to Saul in vv. 2-7. Note that the narrative discourse here is signaled by the *wayqtl* forms, while the predictive discourse is dominated by the *weqtl* forms.[50]

9 The expression *another heart (lēb 'aḥēr)* denotes a new person with a new understanding; compare "another person" *('îš 'aḥēr)* in v. 6.

10 Since the stage, hence the narrator's viewpoint, has changed from Ramah to Gibeah, the verb is *came.* From the narrator's position, "there" refers to Ramah; and so it should be translated as *from there* in combination with the directive "to Gibeah."[51]

For *Gibeah* see on v. 5.

11 Normally *wayhî* is taken as a temporal clause marker and translated as "When . . . saw . . ." (e.g., NRSV; NIV; JPS). However, since *wayhî* here introduces a plural noun, it may function as a topicalizing particle: "as for . . ."; see 11:11 and "Introduction" (Section V, A).

All who knew him from before refers to Saul's neighbors. There is an interval, that is, a space, before the clause *And the people said* in many MSS. This is a new sub-paragraph since it is initiated by *wayqtl* + S. Note that the people here is a much broader term than *all who knew him from before* (so NIV: "they").

The son of Kish . . . Saul is a paired expression (A son of B) and is divided into a parallelism: A // son of B; see on 18:7. Here, the order is reversed.[52]

12 Various interpretations of the question *who is their father?* have been proposed.[53] What is clear from the context is that he is not asking for their father's name, since the office of prophecy is not hereditary like that of priesthood. The term "father" (s.) may refer to their professional leader, just

48. Lit., "from there."

49. Hith. inf. cstr. like III-*h: hitnabbôt;* cf. Ni. for the same action of Saul in v. 11. Ni. of this verb is used only at v. 11 and 19:20 in 1-2 Samuel. See also 19:20-24.

50. Longacre, "Weqatal Forms in Biblical Hebrew Prose," p. 56.

51. Cf. McCarter, p. 172, who translates it in the same way, though based on LXX.

52. See S. Gevirtz, *Patterns in the Early Poetry of Israel* (Chicago: University of Chicago Press, 1963, 1973), pp. 50-52.

53. See R. P. Gordon, p. 340, n. 46; Wilson, "Prophecy and Ecstasy: A Reexamination," p. 333, n. 25.

as the prophets Elijah and Elisha were called "father" in 2 K. 2:12; 6:21; 13:14. According to McCarter,[54] the expression means "And who (but Saul himself) is their leader?" However, the question "Is Saul also among the prophets?" rather suggests that Saul is counted as one of the prophets, not as their leader. See the question "Whose son are you?" in 1 Sam. 17:58; also 17:55.

Therefore (*ʿal-kēn*) is the narrator's remark on one level higher than the preceding dialogue (see "responded"); see also Gen. 2:24.

R. P. Gordon notes that the *proverb* (*māšāl*)[55] itself "need not express a negative evaluation of either Saul or the prophets, though the response of the bystander in verse 12 could be interpreted to the detriment of the latter."[56] This saying is here given its original setting; it reappears in 19:24 in a slightly different nuance with a negative tone. Though "it *was* in common use in the time of the writer," as McCarter notes, "a familiar saying requires no explanation to those who know and use it. . . . The modern reader . . . can only guess at the meaning of the proverb."[57]

13 The term *the hill* (*habbāmāh;* LXX: *eis ton bounon* "into the hill"; Ugar. *bmt* "back" of animal; then "hill") has been variously translated: "hill," "the high place" (NIV; NASB), and "the shrine" (JPS); for this term see on 9:12. Usually it has the religious sense of a "high place" where a shrine is, but here it seems to have the older and non-religious meaning that can be seen in the plural in Deut. 32:13; 2 Sam. 1:19, 25; 22:34 [= Ps. 18:33]; Isa. 14:14; Amos 4:13; Mic. 1:3; Hab. 3:19; Job 9:8. Compare "home" (NRSV), following Wellhausen's emendation.[58]

R. P. Gordon supports the idea that Saul went up to the high place (see v. 5: "coming down from the high place") for a religious purpose and says, "since the ecstatics had recently been to the high place there is no good reason to deny Saul his visit. It is not hard to imagine some private act of devotion in the light of his recent experiences."[59] However, the prophets had come down from the high place, and it is too much to guess that only Saul went up for "private" devotion.

In fact, the verb *came* rather suggests that the narrator's viewpoint has changed; this short sentence *wayyābōʾ habbāmāh* with a movement verb marks the transition to a new stage. As the following section suggests, this hill was the place where Saul's father's house was situated; hence the transla-

54. McCarter, p. 184.
55. See on 2 Sam. 14:1.
56. R. P. Gordon, pp. 118-19.
57. McCarter, p. 183.
58. Wellhausen, p. 75; also McCarter, p. 172.
59. R. P. Gordon, p. 119.

tion: *and came back to the hill;* see 9:12. Note also that in v. 26 Saul's house is said to be at Gibeah, which means "hill." On "Gibeah of Saul," see on 11:4.

d. Saul's Uncle (10:14-16)

14 *And Saul's uncle said to him and his servant,*
"Where[60] *have you been?"*
and he said,
"To search for the donkeys!
As we saw that they were not (anywhere),
we have been to Samuel."
15 *And Saul's uncle said,*
"Tell me what Samuel said to you!"
16 *And Saul said to his uncle,*
"He indeed told us that the donkeys were found."
But of the matter of the monarchy of which Samuel had spoken he told him nothing.

14-15 When Saul came back home on the "hill" (v. 13), *Saul's uncle (dôd),* probably Abner (see on 14:50), asked where Saul had been. When Saul told him that he and his servant were with Samuel, Saul's uncle asked him what Samuel said to him. But why does he, instead of Kish, appear here? It was Kish, Saul's father, who had told them to search for the donkeys (see 9:3). Van der Toorn conjectures that Saul's family, led by his uncle, the head of the clan, was "celebrating a sacrificial banquet at the 'high place.'"[61] However, there is no hint in the text that Saul's clan was holding a family ritual at that time. Others explain the word *dôd* as a designation of a Philistine official.[62] But this view is also a bit forced. It might be conjectured that Saul's fate would be of great concern to his uncle, who would possibly be next in line after Kish and Saul to inherit Abiel's estate (see 9:1). That may be the reason why Saul's uncle, not Kish his father, asked those questions. Or, simply, the uncle happened to be there when Saul and his servant came back home.

The term *hălaktem* normally means "did you go?" but here, from the context, it means *have you been?* The term *wannābô' 'el* literally means "and we came to," but in our context it should be read *we have been to,* not "we

60. 'ān < 'áyin. Note here an unusual contraction of a diphthong. See on 1 Sam. 21:8 (footnote 38).

61. K. van der Toorn, "Saul and the Rise of Israelite State Religion," *VT* 43 (1993) 521.

62. See D. R. Ap-Thomas, "Saul's Uncle," *VT* 11 (1961) 241-45, followed by Ackroyd, Ahlström, Edelman; see van der Toorn, "Saul and the Rise of Israelite State Religion," p. 521, n. 9.

went to" (NRSV; NIV; etc.). Emphasis is given to their being with Samuel rather than just going to Samuel's place.

What Samuel said to you: that is, to Saul and his servant; "you" (pl.); compare s. in LXX; Vulg. Since it was believed that everything Samuel spoke would surely come true (1 Sam. 9:6), Saul's uncle was very much interested in Samuel's words to them.

16 The emphasis *indeed* in Saul's answer sharply contrasts with his silence about his kingship and anointment.

Monarchy or "kingdom" (*mᵉlûkāh;* cf. "kingship" [NRSV; NIV; JPS]) is the same term used later in v. 25 *(mišpaṭ hammᵉlūkāh),* as if foreseeing the event at Mizpah. The whole clause serves as a transition to the following section. R. P. Gordon summarizes as follows: "A short exchange . . . confirms that what has transpired will remain a secret — even to Saul's intimates — until the public declaration of Yahweh's will at the Mizpah convocation (vv. 17-27)."[63]

5. Election of Saul at Mizpah (10:17-27)

17 *And Samuel summoned the people to the Lord at Mizpah*
18 *and said to the sons of Israel,*
"Thus says the Lord, God of Israel:
'It was I who brought Israel up from Egypt
and delivered you from the hand of Egypt
and from the hand of all the kings
who oppressed you.
19 *But you, today, have rejected your God*
who saves you from your miseries and your distresses
and said,
"No![64] *You shall set a king over us!"*
So now present yourselves before the Lord
by your tribes and by your clans!'"
20 *And Samuel made all the tribes of Israel come near.*
And the tribe of Benjamin was taken.
21 *And he made the tribe of Benjamin come near by its clans.*
And the clan of Matri was taken.
And Saul,[65] *son of Kish, was taken.*
And they searched for him, but he was not found.

63. R. P. Gordon, p. 119.

64. MT *lw:* "to him"(?) or a phonetic spelling for *l'.*

65. Before this phrase McCarter, p. 190, reconstructs "So he presented the clan of Matri man by man," based on LXX^{BA}.

22 *And they inquired further of the Lord, (saying)*
"Has the man[66] come here yet[67]?"
And the Lord said,
"There he is hiding himself by the baggage!"
23 *And they ran and took him from there.*
And he took his place among the people; he was taller than all the people from his shoulder upward.
24 *And Samuel said to all the people,*
"Have you seen him whom the Lord has chosen?
For there is no one like him among all the people."
And all the people shouted:
"May the king live!"
25 *And Samuel announced the rules of the monarchy to the people, wrote them in the document, and laid it before the Lord.*
And Samuel sent all the people back, each to his house.
26 *Saul also went back to his house at Gibeah.*
And the band whose hearts God had touched went with him.
27 *But worthless men[68] said,*
"How can this man save us?"
and despised him; they did not bring him any gift.
And he was as one who keeps silent.

17-27 It may seem that this section begins too abruptly with Samuel's summoning the people at Mizpah. However, as noted above, the preceding section ends with a mention of the key word of *hamm^{e}lûkāh* "the monarchy," also used in v. 25. This assembly must have been announced as a response to the demand for a king (ch. 8). It will show publicly that Saul is God's choice, not just Samuel's. But even so, there was some objection to the choice.

17 At the end of ch. 8 Samuel dismissed the elders of Israel who had come to Ramah to request a king; here, he summons (lit., "shouts") the people of Israel before the Lord at Mizpah in order to consult the Lord about his choice of king. The intervening story in 1 Sam. 9:1–10:16 is about the private choice of Saul as a king. The time has come to choose him publicly before the entire population.

In ch. 7 Samuel assembled all Israel at *Mizpah* in order to intercede for the Lord and to judge them; from here the Israelites marched out for a

66. Lit., "a man"; the context requires definiteness.

67. Lit., "again"; so NIV; NASB; also Zech 8:20; or "Is the man still coming here?" Cf. "Did the man come here?" (NRSV); "Has the man come here?" (McCarter, p. 190), following LXX and reading *'ôd* as *'ad.*

68. Lit., "sons of Beliyaal"; see 1:16; 2:12.

battle against the Philistines. In the present instance, too, *Mizpah* plays a crucial role as the politically central city; unlike the cultic center Gilgal, Mizpah was situated at a militarily strategic place, very near the Philistine border.

18 This speech is a typical prophetic speech, contrasting God's goodness with the people's lack of appropriate response. *Thus says the Lord (kōh-'āmar YHWH)* is the so-called "messenger" formula; see on 2:27.

The theme of deliverance from Egypt becomes "the *point d'appui* of many a prophetic remonstrance with the people of Israel (cf. 12:8; Judg. 6:8f.)."[69] See on 2:27; 4:8. *Kings* (*mamlākôt;* usually "kingdoms") is a f.pl. noun but is treated as m.pl, as accompanied by m.p. participle *(hallōḥăṣîm);* hence the word here refers to "kings."[70]

19 *So now present yourselves before the Lord:* after this denunciation of their request for a king, the people probably expected the Lord to reject their request. But instead the Lord specifies how to choose a king: a specific person is to be selected using lots in an elimination process. This method is also used to find the person who has committed a sin that affects the nation, as Achan in Josh. 7:16-18 or Jonathan in 1 Sam. 14:40-42. Here, however, it selects the one whom God has chosen to be his king. Even though Israel's attitude toward God is blameworthy, when he accepts their request, he will give them the best.

For *by your clans (lᵉ'alpêkem;* also 23:23; cf. v. 21; lit., "groups," most often "thousands") McCarter reads *wlmšpḥtykm* on the basis of LXX^{B}.[71] However, the Hebrew term as it is can be used as a unit for counting people, referring to a subdivision of "tribe." So *HALOT,* p. 60; see on 6:19.

20 After Samuel informed the people of the entire message of the Lord, he proceeds to the action of choosing one person by elimination. The expression *was taken (wayyillākēd;* also Josh 7:16-18) has the technical meaning "taken" by the lot, which was used for the division of the Promised Land (Josh. 14:1-2; chs. 18, 19, 21); see on 1 Sam. 14:41, 42. Van Dam assumes that the inquiry described here involved the Urim and Thummim, even though these terms do not appear in the context.[72] See on 14:40f.

21 Here *mišpāḥôt* means "clans" rather than "families." In this context the structure of PEOPLE (Israel) — TRIBE (Benjamin) — CLAN (Matri) — FAMILY (Kish) is presupposed; see 9:21. Josh. 7:14 follows "tribe" *(šēbeṭ)* — "clan" *(mišpāḥāh)* — "family, household" *(bayit),* which

69. R. P. Gordon, p. 120.

70. See G. A. Rendsburg, *Diglossia in Ancient Hebrew* (AOS 72; New Haven: American Oriental Society, 1990), p. 77.

71. McCarter, p. 190.

72. C. van Dam, *The Urim and Thummim: A Means of Revelation in Ancient Israel* (Winona Lake, Ind.: Eisenbrauns, 1997), pp. 186, 206.

are "the basic building blocks" of Israelite society. As Hess observes, these terms are used "with a certain amount of fluidity, especially in the case of overlap between clan and family."[73]

The clan of Matri: Shimei (2 Sam. 16:5) probably belonged to this clan.

22 *Inquired further:* see on 14:37. Though *further* (*'ôd:* lit., "again") is used here, this inquiry is not made by the same method of casting lots seemingly used above, for the casting of lots would not give an answer such as *There he is hiding. . . .* Since the answer is introduced by the formula, *the Lord said,* he possibly told the prophet Samuel directly (see 16:7ff.).

One might wonder why Saul was hiding himself by the baggage. It apparently was not because he was a shy and reserved person. Knowing the result of lot-selection process, he made a special effort to hide himself in order not to be found (v. 21) despite the people's first search, probably for fear of accepting a new and responsible position in the crucial phase of the covenant people's history.

23 Sometimes the tallness of Saul is contrasted with the shortness of Athtar in the Baal myth (*KTU* 1.6:I:54-64).[74] He was to be made king in place of Baal, but since his feet were not long enough to touch the footstool and his head didn't reach the top of the back of Baal's throne, he was rejected as king. While physical build is a crucial element in both stories, Saul's height is compared with others while standing *(from his shoulder upward)* and has nothing to do with his fitness to a kingly throne when he sits on it.

Certainly, to the people Saul's height was seemingly the important quality of his potential leadership, and so the narrator reminds the people that he was tall for the second time: *he was taller than all the people from his shoulder upward;* see 9:2.

24 Samuel emphasizes here the divine decision about Saul's choice. His expression is *the Lord has chosen,* while in 12:13 it is said to the people "you have chosen."

For the expression *there is no one like him among all the people,* note Labuschagne's comment: "As part of the coronation ritual this proclamation could have served to protect the new king from possible rivals claiming the throne for themselves. . . . The newly-elected king is called incomparable, because only he, to the exclusion of all others, has a claim to the throne."[75] See on 2:2.

73. R. S. Hess, *Joshua: An Introduction and Commentary* (TOTC; Leicester: Inter-Varsity, 1996), p. 151.

74. See D. Pardee, in *CS,* I, p. 269.

75. C. J. Labuschagne, *The Incomparability of Yahweh in the Old Testament* (POS 5; Leiden: E. J. Brill, 1966), p. 10.

At last Saul is publicly and officially presented and accepted by the people as the *king.* As R. P. Gordon says, "for the first time since his introduction in 9:1f. Saul is called 'king'; significantly, it is the people who acclaim him so."[76]

25 Following the people's acclamation, Samuel performs three consecutive legal actions: he *announced . . . wrote . . . laid. . . .* The discourse structure of this verse consists of two sub-paragraphs, *wayqtl* + S (Samuel) — *wayqtl* — *wayqtl* and *wayqtl* + S (Samuel). The fact that the actions "to announce" — "to write" — "to lay" are in the same sub-paragraph supports the idea that this is a tripartite action. On the importance of "writing" and "confirming" in the legal procedure, see Hab. 2:2.[77]

It was customary that any legal agreement be written down in a *document (sēper)* and confirmed by the seals of the witnesses.[78] Here *Samuel* was the intermediary and witness of the legal agreement between the king and the people. Samuel also *laid* the legal document *before the Lord (wayyannaḥ),* that is, deposited it in a sanctuary. For putting the covenant document *(hāʿēdūt)* into the ark, see Exod. 25:16, 21; 40:20; for putting the book of the law *(sēper hattôrāh)* beside the ark, see Deut. 31:26.

The phrase *the rules of the monarchy (mišpaṭ hammᵉlūkāh)* is also translated as "the ordinances of the kingdom" (NASB); compare "the nature of a king" (NEB); "the regulations of the kingship" (NIV); "the rights and duties of the kingship" (NRSV). See on v. 16 (above). Since *the right of the king (mišpaṭ hammelek)* had been publicly announced by Samuel in 8:9, 11, the *rules (mišpaṭ)* here must be rather on the institution of monarchy, that is, the relationship between the king and the people, concerning which both the newly enthroned king and the people must have "legal" agreement.[79] Hence, this agreement was not only announced verbally by Samuel but also written down and officially deposited at the sanctuary. As seen below, though most people gladly accepted the new king, there were some people who would not acknowledge the institution of monarchy under Saul.

Compare this also with Deut. 17:18, where it is written "When he sits on the throne of his kingdom, he shall write for himself a copy of this law *(hattôrāh)* on a scroll in the presence of the levitical priests." However, "this law" refers to the Deuteronomic laws in general, while on the other hand *the*

76. R. P. Gordon, p. 121.

77. See D. T. Tsumura, "Hab 2,2 in the Light of Akkadian Legal Practice," *ZAW* 94 (1982) 294-95.

78. See "seals" and "bulae," for example, in A. Millard, *Treasures from Bible Times* (Tring: Lion, 1985), p. 112. Also Jer. 32:10-15; Isa. 8:1-2. In 2 Sam. 11:14, 15, *sēper* refers to a letter; see "Introduction" (Section III, C, 5).

79. McCarter, pp. 193-94, also admits the difference in the meaning of *mišpāṭ* in 1 Sam. 8:9, 11 and here.

rules (mišpaṭ) in this verse are more specific regulations or agreements between the king and the people.

It is Samuel who was in charge of the whole business of choosing a king, and he dismissed the people back to their homes as in 8:22. He is still the main figure of authority and is crucial both in choosing the king and determining the constitution.

26-27 In *Saul also* (or "even Saul") the emphasis is on Saul; we would expect him to assume the office of kingship immediately after the people hailed him. But, actually, he went back to his own home town of *Gibeah* ("a hill"; see v. 10 above) and resumed his normal work (see 11:5). It is not until he proves himself adequate as a military leader that he is actually recognized as king, that is, king *de facto;* see 11:15, where the people made Saul king before the Lord at Gilgal. So, as Wellhausen notes, "Saul is at this point only king *de jure;* he does not become king *de facto* until after he has proved himself."[80]

Saul had supporters: *the band (haḥayil)* or "valiant men" (NIV; NASB); "men of worth" (BDB). McCarter reads *bny hḥyl* ("stalwart men") with 4QSam[a] and LXX and compares it with that in 2 Sam. 2:7. These men were a group of people who "felt a divine impulse to join him, perhaps in anticipation of the war of liberation that was bound to come."[81] However, there were also a group of people, *worthless men,* who would not accept his leadership and acknowledge him as king.

And he was as one who keeps silent (wayhî k^emaḥărîš) — "kept silent" (NIV; NASB); "held his peace" (NRSV); "pretended not to mind" (JPS). McCarter, following his mentor Cross,[82] takes the MT *kmḥryš* as a corruption from *kmw ḥdš* "About a month later," based on 4QSam[a] and the Greek text used by Josephus,[83] and assumed that a whole verse is missing before this phrase. Similarly, according to Ulrich, the MT has not only lost the verse but "even conspicuously erred with the residue, placing a confused ויהי כמחריש at the end of chapter 10 instead of the beginning of chapter 11."[84] NRSV, on the other hand, keeps the MT and translates it as "But he held his peace," though it also restores "About a month later" at the top of 11:1, thus assuming that the whole verse is missing after this MT phrase; see on 11:1.

80. See McCarter, p. 196.

81. R. P. Gordon, p. 122.

82. McCarter, p. 191; F. M. Cross, "The Ammonite Oppression of the Tribes of Gad and Reuben: Missing Verses from 1 Samuel 11 Found in 4QSamuel[a]," in *History, Historiography and Interpretation: Studies in Biblical and Cuneiform Literatures,* ed. H. Tadmor and M. Weinfeld (Jerusalem: Magnes, 1983), pp. 155-56.

83. See E. C. Ulrich, Jr., *The Qumran Text of Samuel and Josephus* (HSM 19; Missoula, Mont.: Scholars Press, 1978), pp. 166-70; Cross, "The Ammonite Oppression of the Tribes of Gad and Reuben," p. 149.

84. Ulrich, *The Qumran Text of Samuel and Josephus,* p. 169.

However, as Herbert recently notes, most probably the reading of 4QSam[a] was "originally absent" from the Samuel tradition.[85] The MT reading *And he was as one who keeps silent* explains the personality of Saul well and prepares the audience for the next stage of this drama with expectation.

6. Saul's First War (11:1-13)

The present chapter marks the transition from Samuel's judgeship to Saul's kingship. Here Saul is formally established as king, and so Samuel's leadership must now pass away, though the subsequent chapters show that he was still active in religious matters through prayer and instruction; see 12:23. In this chapter, though, Saul does not yet have complete authority. He needs to invoke Samuel's authority for his mobilization against the Ammonites (see below v. 7), and v. 12 shows that Samuel still plays a crucial role. And it was Samuel who summoned the people to renew the kingship at Gilgal (v. 14). Saul became king as one of the great judges might have become king, accepted by the people after a great victory of deliverance.[1] See the stories of the so-called "major judges" (Judg. 3:7–16:31).

The episode of vv. 1-13 forms a single narrative unit, "Saul's first war," which is embraced by the episode of Saul's election at Mizpah in 10:17-27 and his coronation at Gilgal (11:14-15). The purpose of this episode is "to show that Saul . . . has now become king *de facto* and earned the loyalty of all Israel."[2] However, Saul's kingship is a "limited monarchy"[3] since acceptance by the people is necessary.

This chapter has been generally accepted as "a reliable historical source."[4]

85. E. D. Herbert, "4QSam[a] and Its Relationship to the LXX: an Exploration in Stemmatological Analysis," in *IX Congress of the International Organization for Septuagint and Cognate Studies: Cambridge, 1995,* ed. B. A. Taylor (Atlanta: Scholars Press, 1997), p. 53.

1. R. P. Gordon, p. 122. For continuities between the stories of the "major judges" and those of Saul, see A. Alt, "The Formation of the Israelite State in Palestine," in *Essays on Old Testament History and Religion,* trans. R. A. Wilson (Garden City, N.Y.: Doubleday, 1968), pp. 223-309; also F. M. Cross, Jr., *Canaanite Myth and Hebrew Epic* (Cambridge, Mass.: Harvard University Press, 1973), pp. 219-21.

2. McCarter, p. 205.

3. McCarter, p. 206; Cross, *Canaanite Myth and Hebrew Epic,* p. 234; J. J. M. Roberts, "In Defence of the Monarchy: The Contribution of Israelite Kingship to Biblical Theology," in *Ancient Israelite Religion: Essays in Honor of Frank Moore Cross,* ed. P. D. Miller, Jr., P. D. Hanson, and S. D. McBride (Philadelphia: Fortress, 1987), p. 388. For the limited kingship in Emar, see D. E. Fleming, "A Limited Kingship: Late Bronze Emar in Ancient Syria," *UF* (1993) 59-71.

4. See T. Ishida, *The Royal Dynasties in Ancient Israel: A Study on the Formation*

a. Nahash's Threat to Jabesh (11:1-3)

1 *Now Nahash the Ammonite went up*[5] *and encamped against*
Jabesh-gilead.
And all the men of Jabesh said to Nahash,
"Make a treaty with us so that we may serve you!"
2 *And Nahash the Ammonite said to them,*
"By this means I will make (a covenant)[6] *with you,*
namely by boring out the right eye of every one of you,
and make it a reproach[7] *against all Israel."*
3 *And the elders of Jabesh said to him,*
"Let us alone for seven days
so that we may send messengers into the entire territory of
Israel!
If there is no one to save us, we shall come out to you."

The text 4QSam[a] gives some background information to this episode that does not appear in the MT. Before v. 1, NRSV, following this text, reads:

> *"Now Nahash, king of the Ammonites, had been grievously oppressing the Gadites and the Reubenites. He would gouge out the right eye of each of them and would not grant Israel a deliverer. No one was left of the Israelites across the Jordan whose right eye Nahash, king of the Ammonites, had not gouged out. But there were seven thousand men who had escaped from the Ammonites and had entered Jabesh-gilead.*
> 1About a month later,"

What is the textual history of the above italicized portion? McCarter holds that it was lost in the MT due to scribal oversight and was never in the LXX;[8] see also on 10:27. However, as he himself admits, there is no element in the text to trigger a haplographic omission.[9] For another thing, the MT

---

and Development of Royal-Dynastic Ideology (BZAW 142; Berlin: de Gruyter, 1977), p. 35. For bibliography see F. Langlamet, "Les récits de l'institution de la royaut* (I Sam., VIII–XII)," *RB* 77 (1970) 167, nn. 27-28; McCarter, p. 207, n. 7.

5. Singular, as with the Assyrian king (2 K. 17:5; 18:13); this does not necessarily mean physically "upward."

6. The term *b*[e]*rît* is omitted as a brachylogy. For this literary phenomenon, see König, p. 188; D. T. Tsumura, "Literary Insertion (AXB Pattern) in Biblical Hebrew," *VT* 33 (1983) 474; "Niphal with an Internal Object in Hab 3,9a," *JSS* 31 (1986) 14, n. 10; also "Introduction" (Section VII, D).

7. Adverbial accusative or a double accusative.

8. McCarter, p. 199.

9. But cf. F. M. Cross, Jr., "The Ammonite Oppression of the Tribes of Gad and

does not call Nahash "king" in this episode, but the phrase "Nahash, king of the Ammonites" appears twice in the addition here. It seems more like an addition from 12:12 than an integral part of the whole section. On the difference between *bny-ʿmwn* (4QSam[a]) and *hāʿammônî* (MT) see below.

While it is possible that 4QSam[a] "correctly preserves an entire narrative section lost from all other biblical mss,"[10] another possibility is that the 4QSam[a] section is a later addition. Or, maybe there existed simply more than one version: see, for example, the coexistence in one text of short (abridged) and long (full) versions of Sennacherib's third campaign.[11] Lack of information contained in one of the versions could be drastic to a modern reader who has no other information, but not to the contemporary readers who might have had other information unknown to us. It might be possible that 4QSam[a] got its information from some other version. This information "makes excellent narrative and historical sense,"[12] but this does not give us the right to reform the shorter version into a longer one. The biblical narrator is concerned more with the delivery of the Transjordan Israelites by Saul than with their oppression by Nahash, king of the Ammonites. The demand for a king to rule over them in ch. 8 might have been made in the midst of this Ammonite oppression; see on 12:12.

1 "Now . . .": *wayyaʿal.* Usually *wayqtl* is the verb for the main line discourse of the narrative EVENT. Here, however, *wayyaʿal* (lit., "and he went up"), the *wayqtl* of a verb of "motion," functions as a transitional link between the preceding section and the following one. A new stage on which a new event with new *dramatis personae* will take place is thus introduced (hence *Now*). Such usage can be recognized in Gen. 20:1 ("Now Abraham journeyed from there"); Gen. 34:1 ("Now Dinah . . . went out"); Exod. 2:1 ("Now a man . . . went"); Deut. 34:1 ("Now Moses went up"); Judg. 2:1 ("Now the angel of the LORD went up"); 9:1; 16:1; 1 Sam. 17:1; 20:1; 22:1; 26:1; 29:1; 2 Sam. 5:1. Thus, there is not even a hint in the text of MT that a chunk of narrative is missing before this verse.

There is no information about *Nahash the Ammonite* in the MT except that he was king (12:12) and later maintained a friendly relationship with David (see 2 Sam. 10:2). Cross notes that the MT's omission of Nahash's full title is "the sole exception to the practice" of introducing a reigning king of a

---

Reuben: Missing Verses from 1 Samuel 11 Found in 4QSamuel[a]," in *History, Historiography and Interpretation: Studies in Biblical and Cuneiform Literatures,* ed. H. Tadmor and M. Weinfeld (Jerusalem: Magnes, 1983), p. 153.

10. E. C. Ulrich, Jr., *The Qumran Text of Samuel and Josephus* (HSM 19; Missoula, Mont.: Scholars Press, 1978), p. 169.

11. D. D. Luckenbill, *The Annals of Sennacherib* (OIP 2; Chicago: University of Chicago Press, 1924), pp. 29-34, 68-70.

12. Cross, "The Ammonite Oppression of the Tribes of Gad and Reuben," p. 157.

foreign nation for the first time.[13] However, note that the expression in 4QSam^a and that in 1 Sam. 12:12 are *nāḥāš melek b^{e}nê-ʿammôn,* lit., "Nahash, king of the sons of Ammon"; see also *melek b^{e}nê-ʿammôn* "king of the sons of Ammon" in 2 Sam. 10:1. In this verse (1 Sam. 11:1; MT), though, different phrasing, "Nahash the Ammonite (*hʿmwny:* s. gentilic)" is used. If 4QSam^a is original, it is hard to see why the author would change from calling him *nāḥāš melek b^{e}nê-ʿammôn* to calling him *nāḥāš hāʿammônî* in such a short space, despite Cross's comment that the author could have deliberately ignored Nahash's title "king" in MT. Note that 2 Sam. 10:1 begins the episode concerning "the king of the Ammonites" without stating his proper name, which appears in v. 2 "Hanun, son of Nahash."

Jabesh-gilead is sometimes identified with the site Tel Abu Kharaz, about 22 miles to the south of the Sea of Galilee in Transjordan; however, other sites such as Deir el-Halawe, Miryamim, and Tell Maqlub are also possible.[14] It was "vulnerable to this kind of attack from the Ammonites when they were in one of their expansionist moods."[15] See also 2 Sam. 2:4.

The expression *all the men of Jabesh* refers to the elders of Jabesh (see v. 3); see on 8:22, where *the men of Israel* refers to the elders of Israel (8:4).

The phrase "to make a covenant with" (*krt *b^{e}rît l-;* for *b^{e}rît,* see on 4:3) appears in the OT first in Gen. 15:18. The reason why the verb "to cut" (*krt) is used for this expression is that treaty and covenant ceremonies often involved the symbolic killing of animals;[16] Gen. 15:9-11, 17; Jer. 34:18f. On the covenant between David and Jonathan, see 18:3.

The people of Jabesh-gilead could make an international treaty with the Ammonites on their own initiative. This indicates that the city was independent enough to act as a political entity. And yet the enemy's threat was painful enough to evoke the weeping of "all the people" (v. 4) of Israel, for they shared "a common feeling of close consanguineous bonds"[17] without a "firm political organization to express its solidarity." Such a loose tribal federation was the characteristic feature of the premonarchic era of ancient Israel. The word of Nahash, *a reproach against all Israel* (v. 2), exhibits his knowledge of such a federation and his intention to challenge Israel as a whole.[18]

13. Cross, "The Ammonite Oppression of the Tribes of Gad and Reuben," pp. 153-54.

14. See D. V. Edelman, in *ABD,* III, pp. 594-95.

15. R. P. Gordon, pp. 122-23.

16. See *HALOT,* p. 500.

17. Ishida, *The Royal Dynasties in Ancient Israel,* p. 36.

18. But see D. J. McCarthy, *Treaty and Covenant* (AnBib 21a; Rome: Pontifical Biblical Institute, 1981), p. 58. H. Reviv notes the distinction between "men" and "elders"

The phrase *serve you* shows that Nahash requested a vassal treaty in which the people of Jabesh would pay tributes and serve Nahash, while receiving Nahash's protection against attacks from other foreign powers.

2 According to the tradition preserved in 4QSam^a, Nahash, king of the Ammonites, had been "grievously" oppressing the Transjordan population of Israel, namely, the Gadites and the Reubenites, by the method described here. So, in MT also, the act of *boring out the right eye* is the required method or means[19] for Nahash to make a covenant with the Jabeshites. Instead of "cutting" a treaty with sacrificial animals, he would "cut" it with their eyes. The phrase *b^{e}zō't* ("in this") here thus signifies *by this means,* not "on this condition" (NRSV; NASB; JPS; also NIV), as in Gen. 42:15, 33; Exod. 7:17; Lev. 16:3; Num. 16:28; Josh. 3:10; Isa. 27:9; Ezek. 16:29; and Mal. 3:10. In the words of Jacob's sons to Shechem and his father Hamor (Gen. 34:15), the phrase *b^{e}zō't* also denotes "by this means," though Shechem might have taken it as a condition, "on this condition"; hence, "Only *by this means* will we consent to you: *that* . . . every male among you be circumcised," while Hamor and his son Shechem explain to the men of their city that "Only *on this condition* will the men consent to us . . . : that every male among us be circumcised . . ." (v. 22; NRSV).

Like the right hand, the right eye was considered a crucial part of the body; see Zech. 11:17. Nahash would make it (f.s.),[20] namely, the state of every right eye being bored, "a visible token of shame and humiliation."[21] The term *reproach (ḥerpāh)* is used for cases such as the state of not being pregnant (Gen. 30:23), of marrying the uncircumcised (34:14), of being slaves in Egypt (Josh. 5:9), of being enslaved by the Philistines (1 Sam. 17:26), of Nabal's contemptuous treatment of David (25:39) and of Tamar's being raped by Amnon (2 Sam. 13:13).

3 Nahash must have known the state of federation among Israelite

---

in vv. 1, 3; this he takes as reflective of the bicameral self-government of towns in Mesopotamia and Syro-Palestine in the second and first millennia B.C.; H. Reviv, "Jabesh-Gilead in I Samuel 11:4: Characteristics of the City in Pre-Monarchic Israel," in *The Jerusalem Cathedra: Studies in the History, Archaeology, Geography and Ethnography of the Land of Israel,* ed. by L. I. Levine (Jerusalem: Yad Izhak Ben-Zvi Institute, 1981), pp. 4-8; R. P. Gordon, p. 341.

19. This is a punishment attested also as a curse in Ugaritic; see C. H. Gordon and G. A. Rendsburg, *The Bible and the Ancient Near East,* 4th ed. (New York: W. W. Norton, 1997), p. 184.

20. The f.s. pronoun here refers to the matter or the state described in the preceding clause. A similar case can be seen in Gen. 15:6 where the *it* (f.s) of "and the LORD reckoned it to him as righteousness" (NRSV) refers to the fact that Abram believed the Lord.

21. McCarter, p. 203.

cities; as his own words hint, his real intention was to bring reproach upon *all Israel.* Therefore, his willingness to wait for seven days is due not simply to his "arrogance before Israelite impotence"[22] but also to his calculated policy and devices. He was ready to face resistance from the entire *territory of Israel* (see also v. 7), the territory where the people of Israel were settled.

In premonarchic Israel every local community was governed by the council of elders; reference is made also to the elders of Bethlehem (1 Sam. 16:4) and to those of various cities of Judah (30:26-31). "This was the people's representative organization which exercised supreme authority in the community, especially in the pre-monarchical period."[23] On "the elders of Israel," see 4:3.

This seven-day period[24] may reflect a literary convention as in Joshua 6 and the Keret epic.[25] Fleming holds that, as in Joshua 6, "seven-day intervals belong to the sacred time of a military campaign undertaken by divine command."[26]

The expression *one to save us (môšîaʿ)* reminds us of the "deliverer" (Judg. 3:9, 15) at the time of the judges. The verb *come out (wᵉyāṣāʾnû)* sometimes appears in a military context, with the sense of "to march out" in 7:11; 8:20; etc. There may be a hint of irony here. See also *nēṣēʾ ʾălêkem* (v. 10).

b. Messengers to Gibeah (11:4-9a)

4 *And the messengers came to Gibeah of Saul and told the words*
into the ears of the people.
And all the people lifted their voices and wept.
5 *At just that moment Saul came in after the oxen from the field.*
And Saul said,
"What has happened to the people that they should weep?"
and they reported to him the words of the men of Jabesh.
6 *And the spirit of God rushed upon him when he heard these words.*
And he became very angry.

22. R. P. Gordon, p. 123.

23. Ishida, *The Royal Dynasties in Ancient Israel,* p. 35.

24. For *seven days,* see on 1 Sam. 10:8; G. A. Klingbeil, "Ritual Time in Leviticus 8 with Special Reference to the Seven Day Period in the Old Testament," *ZAW* 109 (1997) 500-513.

25. See D. E. Fleming, "The Seven-Day Siege of Jericho in Holy War," in *Ki Baruch Hu: Ancient Near Eastern, Biblical, and Judaic Studies in Honor of Baruch A. Levine,* ed. R. Chazan, W. W. Hallo, and L. H. Schiffman (Winona Lake, Ind.: Eisenbrauns, 1999), p. 228.

26. See Fleming, "The Seven-Day Siege of Jericho in Holy War," p. 213.

7 *And he took a yoke of oxen and cut it up and sent them into the entire territory of Israel by the hand of the messengers, saying,*
"Whoever is not coming out after Saul and Samuel,
thus should be done to his oxen!"
And the fear of the Lord fell on the people,
and they came out as one man.
8 *And he mustered them at Bezek.*
There were three hundred thousands of Israelites and thirty thousands of men of Judah.
9a *And they said to the messengers who had come,*
"Thus you shall say to the men of Jabesh-gilead,
'Tomorrow deliverance will be yours
at the heat of the sun.'"

4 The messengers are sent from Jabesh to Gibeah to ask for help. The *wayqtl* of a movement verb ("to come") in the plural signals a SETTING (transition): the stage moves from Jabesh to Gibeah with a change in the narrator's viewpoint.

Gibeah of Saul (gibʿat šāʾûl; also in 15:34; 2 Sam. 21:6; Isa. 10:29) is also called "Gibeah of Benjamin" (1 Sam. 13:2, 15; 14:16), "Gibeah of the sons of Benjamin" (*gibʿat bᵉnê binyāmīn,* 2 Sam. 23:29), or simply "Gibeah" (1 Sam. 10:10, 26; 14:2; 22:6). Judges 19–20 alternates between "Gibeah" and "Gibeah in Benjamin." On *Gibeah* see 1 Sam. 10:5. The phrase *Gibeah of Saul* must have originated after Saul was well established as king and Gibeah became the residence of the king, not simply Saul's hometown (10:26); see 15:34.

The distance between Jabesh and Gibeah is about 42 miles, and it might have taken two days to come to Gibeah. According to Judges 21, the men of Jabesh-gilead had not joined the fight against Benjamin, and 400 of the men of Benjamin, probably many of whom were from Gibeah (cf. 20:37 and 21:16), had gained their wives from Jabesh-gilead. Therefore, it would be natural for the messengers from Jabesh-gilead to go to Gibeah.

5 Just at that moment Saul came back from the field *after the oxen.* If they were sheep, he would have come before them; Saul had probably been plowing in the field. C. H. Gordon notes that like Saul, Odysseus was also able to plough with oxen.[27] Note that after Saul came back from Mizpah (1 Sam. 10:26), he did ordinary work at his house even though he was king elect. Now, however, the time is ripe for Saul to make his public debut as the real king.

27. C. H. Gordon, *The Common Background of Greek and Hebrew Civilizations* (New York: W. W. Norton, 1965), p. 242.

6 Even though the expression *the spirit of God rushed upon* is the same in 10:6 and here, the result differs. In 10:10 Saul began prophesying in the midst of the band of prophets; here he was filled with anger and power, like Samson (Judg. 14:6, 19; 15:14), "to undertake heroic feats of arms."[28] Note also the similar experiences of Othniel (Judg. 3:10), Gideon (6:34), and Jephthah (11:29). "Saul appears for the present to have more of the charismatic 'judge' than the constitutional monarch. However, his symbolic act and accompanying message do seem to presuppose a certain amount of authority on his part."[29] Apparently the recipients of the message needed no further identification as to who "Saul" was.

7 Enraged with the news and filled with God's spirit, Saul cuts up a *yoke of oxen* and sends them to the whole country. The combination of *cut up* and *sent* appears also in the treatment of the concubine's corpse in Judg. 19:29; 20:6, where the parts of her body were sent for the appeal for revenge *(talio).* Here the symbolic dismembering of the oxen can be regarded as "a kind of conditional curse."[30] Since all Israelites were obliged to come and help any Israelite in time of military need, *whoever is not coming out* will be cursed. As R. P. Gordon notes, "the threat was directed not so much at the individual's property as at the individual himself."[31]

The expression *into the entire territory of Israel* (see on v. 3) appears also in Judg. 19:29 ("he . . . cut up his concubine, limb by limb, into twelve parts and sent them into the entire territory of Israel") and is rephrased with a synonymous expression "into the entire land of Israel's inheritance (or 'estate')" *(bᵉkol-śᵉdēh naḥălat yiśrāʾēl)* in Judg. 20:6. Polzin notes here that the judicial echoes of Judges 19–21 are "more extensive" than in the practice of dismembering the bodies and dispatching. In both episodes the towns of Jabesh-Gilead and Gibeah are paired. He also notes "some paronomastic rays" between the name Benjamin, which means "right son," and reference to the "right eye." The exact phrase in v. 12 *Give us the men so that we may put them to death!* appears also in Judg. 20:13 and nowhere else. In the light of these similarities Polzin draws conclusions: "Everything in vv 1-11 . . . contributes toward a conscious and deliberate *ignoring* of the monarchic status of Saul in favour of depicting him as someone who, like the judges of old, leads Israel to victory under God's inspiration."[32] However, Polzin's intertextual approach ignores the more immediate context in which the pres-

28. McCarter, p. 203.

29. R. P. Gordon, p. 124.

30. McCarter, p. 203.

31. R. P. Gordon, p. 124.

32. R. Polzin, "On Taking Renewal Seriously: 1 Sam 11:1-15," in *Ascribe to the Lord: Biblical and Other Studies in Memory of Peter C. Craigie,* ed. L. Eslinger and G. Taylor (JSOTSS 67; Sheffield: Sheffield Academic Press, 1988), p. 502.

ent episode is placed. In fact, ch. 10 already anointed Saul as a king *designate.* As anointed prince over Yahweh's estate (10:1) and king elect (10:24), Saul here sends the messengers into the entire territory, that is, "the entire land of Israel's inheritance," to urge Yahweh's people to unite to rescue their brethren in Jabesh-gilead.

The mention of *Samuel* is often explained as redactional and secondary. However, as Ishida argues, Saul rather "exploited Samuel's authority for his mobilization." Far from being impotent, Samuel is the one considered in authority in v. 12, for he still had "official jurisdiction in internal political matters,"[33] and he is the one who took the initiative to go to Gilgal to renew the kingship there (v. 14). The expression *to his oxen* in fact means "even to himself"! See above.

While *the fear of the Lord (paḥad YHWH)* fell upon the enemies of Israel as "a kind of paralyzing dread" in Isa. 2:10, 19, 21 (*//ḥădar gᵉʼônô* "the glory of his majesty") as well as in 2 Chr. 17:10 (McCarter), here in 1 Sam. 11:7, as in 2 Chr. 14:13 [14], it fell upon the Israelites to bring them victory. In 2 Chr. 19:7, the judges were warned to judge carefully with "the fear of the Lord," which is almost the equivalent of "the fear of God" *(yirʼat ʼĕlōhîm)* in 2 Sam. 23:3 — "When one rules over men in righteousness, when he rules in the fear of God"; see also Ps. 19:9 "the fear of the Lord *(yirʼat YHWH)* is pure, enduring forever."[34] For a similar phenomenon, the "great panic" *(mᵉhûmāh gᵉdôlāh)* which fell upon the Philistines, see 1 Sam. 5:9; 14:20; also 5:11.

8 Saul *musters* the armies of both Israel and Judah at Bezek, not mentioned elsewhere. McCarter identifies it with modern Khirbet Ibziq, about 12 miles northeast of Shechem on the western slope of the Jordan Valley opposite Jabesh-gilead.

The entire size of the army was *three hundred thousands of Israelites and thirty thousands of men of Judah:* 300,000 (Israel) + 30,000 (Judah); cf. LXX — 600,000 + 70,000; 4QSam^a — ? + 70,000; Josephus — 700,000 + 70,000. Since numbers tend to become exaggerated, McCarter prefers the smaller figures of the MT. For *thousands,* compare "contingents,"[35] which R. P. Gordon thinks denotes a military unit.[36] Here the distinction between north and south is already noticeable; see 2 Sam. 24:9.

9 Here *they* probably stands for the elders of the Israelites. They

33. Ishida, *The Royal Dynasties in Ancient Israel,* p. 48.

34. On Hebrew *yrʼ,* see M. I. Gruber, "Fear, Anxiety and Reverence in Akkadian, Biblical Hebrew and Other North-West Semitic Languages," *VT* 40 (1990) 411-22.

35. McCarter, p. 204.

36. R. P. Gordon, p. 124; see C. J. Humphreys, "The Number of People in the Exodus from Egypt: Decoding Mathematically the Very Large Numbers in Numbers I and XXVI," *VT* 48 (1998) 196-213.

play an important role as in Jabesh ("men" in vv. 1, 5, 9, 10; cf. "elders" in v. 3);[37] see on 1 Sam. 11:1.

c. Messengers Come Back (11:9b-10)

9b *And the messengers came back and told it to the men of Jabesh*
and they rejoiced.
10 *And the men of Jabesh said,*
"Tomorrow we will come out to you,
and you shall do to us according to everything
that is good in your eyes!"

9b The phrase *And the messengers came back (wayyābō'û hammal'ākîm)* is exactly the same as in v. 4. It denotes the TRANSITION, that is, the change of the stage from Gibeah to Jabesh-gilead. Also, with the verb "came," rather than "went," the narrator's viewpoint has also changed back to Jabesh-Gilead.

10 Here the subject *the men of Jabesh* is stated anew in order to initiate a new subparagraph with a *waw initial* (see "Introduction" [Section VI, A]), despite the fact that the subject is clear from the context. The men of Jabesh are obviously speaking to Nahash.

The expression *come out to you* is intentionally ambiguous,[38] since it can mean either "surrender to you" (NIV; JPS), "give ourselves up to you" (NRSV), or "march out to you" (see on v. 3 above). Though the next verse does not mention the people of Jabesh, it can be surmised that they too joined in the attack on the enemy camp.

d. Saul's Victory over Ammon (11:11-13)

11 *The next day Saul put the people in three divisions.*
And they entered the camp at the morning watch and struck
Ammon until the heat of the day.
As for those who survived, they were scattered; no two of them
were left together.
12 *And the people said to Samuel,*
"Who is the one who said: 'Should Saul rule over us?'
Give us the men so that we may put them to death!"
13 *And Saul said,*
"No man should be put to death this day!
For today the Lord made a victory in Israel."

37. Ishida, *The Royal Dynasties in Ancient Israel,* p. 47.
38. See also Birch, p. 1055.

11 Saul uses the military tactic of dividing the forces into three *divisions* (or "companies"; lit., "heads"; see the Mesha inscription, l. 20),[39] which can be seen also in Judg. 7:16; 9:43; 1 Sam. 13:17 (the Philistines); 2 Sam. 18:2 (David); Job 1:17 (the Chaldeans); also in Mari.[40] Saul's strategy is similar to Gideon's in Judges 7, but somewhat simpler.

Attacking the enemy *at the morning watch (bᵉʾašmōret habbōqer;* also Exod. 14:24), namely, right before dawn, is an effective practice; so also God's help comes "when morning dawns" or "by daybreak" *(lipnôt bōqer;* Ps. 46:5). There were three night watches; in the spring and fall, the morning watch would have been from about 2 a.m. to 6 a.m. Gideon attacked at the "beginning of the middle watch," around 10 p.m. (Judg. 7:19).

As the pl. noun phrase, *hanniš'ārîm,* cannot be the subject of the preceding *wayhî* (3 m.s.), the text is usually taken as corrupt.[41] But the phrase *wayhî* often plays a topicalizing role (hence *As for*), especially when the following nominal phrase is plural; see also on 10:11; 2 Sam. 2:23.

> As for all who knew him from before, they saw him prophesying with prophets. (1 Sam. 10:11)
>
> As for all who came to the place where Asael fell and died, they stopped. (2 Sam. 2:23)
>
> As for certain people who were unclean through touching a corpse and could not keep the passover on that day, they came before Moses and Aaron on that day. (Num. 9:6)

See "Introduction" (Section V, A).

12 After Saul's victory the people are enthusiastic about him. Note that Samuel still plays the crucial role in establishing and promoting kingship in Israel; see above on v. 7.

Should Saul rule over us? — interrogative, as suggested by Driver.[42] On the other hand, McCarter follows LXX and translates "Saul shall not reign." The verse refers to the incident in 1 Sam. 10:27: "But worthless men[43] said, 'How can this man save us?' and despised him; they did not bring him any gift." Thus, these two passages constitute "a bracket," which points up

39. Gibson, *SSI,* 1, p. 81; K. A. D. Smelik, in *CS,* II, p. 138.

40. See G. E. Mendenhall, "The Census Lists of Numbers 1 and 26," *JBL* 77 (1958) 57-58, n. 32; McCarter, II, p. 404.

41. See Smith, p. 80; Stoebe, p. 222.

42. Driver, p. 87.

43. Lit., "sons of Beliyaal"; see 1:16; 2:12.

the importance of this victory in establishing Saul's kingship. He has proven himself a military leader.[44] Thus, Saul has become king *de facto.*

13 Following LXX, McCarter prefers "Samuel" to *Saul.*[45] However, it is more suitable that *Saul* say these words, since Saul is trying to emphasize that the Lord, not he, delivered the people of Jabesh.

7. Making Saul King at Gilgal (11:14-15)

14 *And Samuel said to the people,*
"Now let us go to Gilgal
so that we may renew the kingship there!"
15 *And all the people went to Gilgal and made Saul king there before the Lord in Gilgal and made peace offerings there before the Lord.*
And Saul and all the men of Israel rejoiced very much.

14 It is Samuel, the "king-maker," who summons the people to *Gilgal* (see on 7:16), the place to which he first commanded Saul to go down before him and "wait" for seven days; see 10:8. It is now also the place where he establishes Saul as the king of Israel; at the same time, it will be the place where he rejects Saul's kingship (see ch. 15).

Since Saul had already been proclaimed king at Mizpah (10:17-24), his kingship need not be granted again (cf. "inaugurate the monarchy" [JPS]). So, they needed to *renew*[46] *the kingship* there *(ûnḥaddēš šām hammᵉlûkāh)* or "reaffirm the kingship" (NIV) at Gilgal. However, this renewal of *the kingship* refers not so much to a reaffirmation or confirmation of Saul's own political role as king as to a renewal of "allegiance to the kingship of Yahweh."[47] This view can be supported when the present verse is taken as an integral part of the story. However many critical commentators regard v. 14 as an editorial attempt to harmonize this Gilgal coronation with the preceding Mizpah narrative in 10:17-27. To them v. 14 is in direct contradiction to v. 15 which, as a part belonging to an originally independent tradition together with vv. 1-11, mentions that Saul was made king by the people in Gilgal.[48] On the other

44. McCarter, p. 204.

45. McCarter, p. 201.

46. See *HALOT,* p. 294: "to make anew, restore" (Pi. *ḥdš).

47. J. R. Vannoy, *Covenant Renewal at Gilgal: A Study of 1 Samuel 11:14–12:25* (Cherry Hill, N.J.: Mack, 1978), p. 68.

48. B. C. Birch, *The Rise of the Israelite Monarchy: The Growth and Development of I Samuel 7–15* (SBLDS 27; Missoula, Mont.: Scholars Press, 1976), pp. 56, 59-60. For a useful survey of various views on vv. 14-15, see Vannoy, *Covenant Renewal at Gilgal,* pp. 114-27.

hand, Vannoy, who takes 11:14–12:25 as describing a covenant renewal ceremony at Gilgal, considers vv. 14-15 to be "lead or introductory sentences summarizing the purpose of the Gilgal assembly" before the more detailed account of the ceremony in 1 Samuel 12.[49]

When we take it into consideration that Samuel's summons in v. 14 is for a religious purpose, the Gilgal assembly is the necessary climax of the entire chapter. Thus the purpose of this occasion at Gilgal seems to be to confirm Saul's kingship, which has been formally known though lacking demonstration. It was necessary for *all the people* to acknowledge Saul as the king of Israel before the Lord. If the election of Saul as king at Mizpah was political, the (re)confirmation of Saul as the king at Gilgal would be religious, that is, *before the Lord.* In any official matter, both political and religious affirmations were necessary. So, the "renewal" confirmed the religious dimension of the kingship of Saul.[50] Thus, vv. 14-15 function as a concluding remark, rather than an introduction, in the history of Saul's election as king.

15 The term *the men* refers to a more limited group of people than *the people:* see on 8:22. Here the term *all* appears twice; it emphasizes that the entire population of Israel now agreed to recognize Saul as the king of Israel since he proved himself to be worthy to be their true leader.

The very elaborate repetition in the expression *to Gilgal . . . there before the Lord in Gilgal . . . there before the Lord* marks the TERMINUS, toward the end of the episode. From the literary point of view, the episode of the renewal of Saul's kingship ends with v. 15. In the next verse, 12:1, *wayyo'mer* starts a new episode.

The *peace offerings (šᵉlāmîm)* were shared by the worshippers (see on 10:8) and were thus almost necessary for a feast (Deut. 27:7; 1 Sam. 1:4). Though the name "Samuel" does not appear here, he was certainly present, especially since peace offerings were offered (see 10:8; 13:9). "As a man of

49. Vannoy, *Covenant Renewal at Gilgal,* p. 185; see G. E. Gerbrandt, *Kingship According to the Deuteronomistic History* (SBLDS 87; Atlanta: Scholars Press, 1986), p. 140.

50. D. Edelman ("Saul ben Kish in History and Tradition," in *The Origins of the Ancient Israelite States,* ed. V. Vritz and P. R. Davies [JSOTSS 228; Sheffield: Sheffield Academic Press, 1996], p. 148) summarizes what she sees as the major pattern of the ritual ceremony for the installation of the king, based on both biblical and extra-biblical texts. According to her, this pattern includes (1) anointing; (2) testing; (3) installation. In Saul's case, in 10:1 Saul was anointed in Ramah for the designation as king-elect; in 11:1-11 Saul was tested by the military deed for delivering Jabesh-Gilead from the Ammonites; in 11:14-15 Saul finally had his coronation as king at Gilgal. However, the election of Saul at Mizpah (10:17-27) does not fit into this pattern. See also D. V. Edelman, *King Saul in the Historiography of Judah* (JSOTSS 121; Sheffield: Sheffield Academic Press, 1991). In our understanding, both the election at Mizpah and the reconfirmation at Gilgal constituted the installation, the former being a political installation, the latter a religious one.

official competence, Samuel could appeal to the people for unification under the new regime at a time of crisis."[51]

Both Saul, the king, and the entire population of Israel, his people, celebrated the victory over the Ammonites and the new institution of monarchy. This ceremony at Gilgal may have been one of the standard rites in the king's accession. Some suggest that this was primarily ratification before the Lord or the covenant between the king and the people, though v. 15 does not hint at a "covenant." But to investigate the purpose, we must first decide whether ch. 12 is relevant, and, if so, what ch. 12 means. See below on 1 Sam. 12:1.

B. SAMUEL'S ADDRESS TO ISRAEL (12:1-25)

This chapter marks "the watershed between the end of the period of the judges and the beginning of the age of kingship."[1] Samuel's words in v. 2 speak to this; they contrast the king who *is walking before you* (see on v. 13) and the judge who *has walked before you.* Samuel himself acknowledges the end to his role as the leader of the people.[2] This chapter corresponds, both thematically as well as literarily, to ch. 8, where the people demanded the institution of a monarchy. However, here the people for the first time recognize the evilness of their "asking for a king" (v. 19). But "it is too late. They have their king, and there can be no return to the old way."[3]

The present chapter has been traditionally taken as Samuel's "farewell speech" and compared with that of Joshua (Joshua 24). As McCarter points out, the two speeches renew the Deuteronomic covenant at critical historical junctures. One is at the time of the completion of the conquest and the beginning of Israel's life in the land, and the other, at the end of the age of the judges and the beginning of life under the kings and before the erection of the temple.[4]

Formal aspects of covenant in this chapter have been thoroughly discussed by a number of scholars such as Muilenburg, Weiser, McCarthy, Baltzer, Birch, Vannoy, and McCarter.[5] And they note that this speech shares

51. Ishida, *The Royal Dynasties in Ancient Israel,* p. 48.

1. McCarter, p. 220.

2. See R. Rendtorff, "Samuel the Prophet: A Link between Moses and the Kings," in *The Quest for Context and Meaning: Studies in Biblical Intertextuality in Honor of James A. Sanders,* ed. C. A. Evans and S. Talmon (Leiden: E. J. Brill, 1997), pp. 27-36.

3. McCarter, p. 217.

4. McCarter, p. 220.

5. See J. Muilenburg, "The Form and Structure of Covenant Formulations," *VT* 9 (1959) 347-65; A. Weiser, *Samuel: seine geschichtliche Aufgabe und religiöse Bedeu-*

a number of formal features with Joshua 24. According to Vannoy, for example, the present chapter as a whole is a covenant-renewal ceremony. He finds in ch. 12 some elements of the covenant form such as (1) the appeal to antecedent history (vv. 6-12); (2) the challenge to the basic covenantal obligation of undivided allegiance to Yahweh introduced by the transitional *and now* (vv. 13a, 14a, 15a, 20-21, 24); (3) blessing and curse sanctions (vv. 14b, 15b, 25); and (4) a theophanic sign (vv. 16-22).[6] He concludes that 1 Sam. 11:14–12:25 is "the record of a covenant renewal ceremony held for the dual purpose of providing for covenant continuity at a time of transition in leadership and covenant restoration after abrogation."[7]

However, Knutson denies the presence of "the treaty structure" or of "covenant language" in ch. 12,[8] though he accepts that some parts of the chapter are similar to some treaty elements. Similarly, we think that the chapter mainly deals with Samuel's justifying his past conduct; that is, it is a "negative confession." The formula *The witness is* in v. 5 reflects the actual testimony — before the witnesses — with regard to the matters between Samuel and the people rather than between God and his people, or his servant king. Samuel is here arguing his case with the people before the Lord (v. 7). Despite the formal similarities with covenants, the purpose of the present chapter is to convey Samuel's new role and his relationship with the people rather than God's covenantal relationship with the people. R. P. Gordon holds that whatever the formal structure, Samuel's speeches address the problems of the new covenant which God allows despite the people's foolish demand for a king.[9]

However, too much emphasis has been given by commentators to the new role of the prophet. For example, according to McCarter, ch. 12 marks "the formal initiation of the prophet's new role in the era of the kingdom."[10] However, this chapter is not so much about a change in the role of the

---

tung. Traditionsgeschichtliche Untersuchungen zu 1 Samuel 7–12 (Göttingen: Vandenhoeck und Ruprecht, 1962), pp. 79-94; D. J. McCarthy, *Treaty and Covenant: A Study in Form in the Ancient Oriental Dcuments and in the Old Testament* (Rome: Biblical Institute Press, 1963, 1978), pp. 206-21; K. Baltzer, *The Covenant Formulary in Old Testament, Jewish, and Early Christian Writings* (Philadelphia: Fortress, 1971 [orig. 1964]), pp. 66-68; B. C. Birch, *The Rise of the Israelite Monarchy: The Growth and Development of I Samuel 7–15* (SBLDS 27; Missoula, Mont.: Scholars Press, 1976); J. R. Vannoy, *Covenant Renewal at Gilgal: A Study of 1 Samuel 11:14–12:25* (Cherry Hill, N.J.: Mack, 1978); McCarter, pp. 220-21.

6. Vannoy, *Covenant Renewal at Gilgal,* p. 161.

7. Vannoy, *Covenant Renewal at Gilgal,* p. 178.

8. See F. B. Knutson, "Literary Genre in *PRU IV*," in *RSP* 2, pp. 171-73.

9. R. P. Gordon, p. 126.

10. McCarter, p. 218.

prophet as a change in political leadership in Israel from judgeship to kingship. When Samuel declares and the people affirm that he had taken nothing from the people (vv. 3-4), they are testifying to Samuel's integrity as a judge, not as a prophet, in contrast to his sons who took bribes and perverted justice (see 8:3). Samuel will continue his role as prophet through intercession and instruction. But while Samuel just drops his duties with respect to judgeship, his prophetic duties remain the same. Vannoy sees here "the initiation of a new order of administration of the theocracy in which there is a new division of responsibility among Israel's leaders."[11] So, Samuel continues as prophet, and will again play an important role as king-maker, "for there is a greater king than Saul still to be anointed." Therefore, while Samuel "will no longer be the center of interest in the narrative,"[12] it is not accurate to call the present speech the "farewell address" of Samuel.

1. "Testify against Me!" (12:1-6)

1 *And Samuel said to all Israel,*
"Now, I have listened to your voice,
to everything you said to me,
and have made a king over you.
2 *And now, here is the king walking before you;*
as for me, I am old and hoary
and my sons are here with you.
It is I who have walked before you
from my youth until this day.[13]
3 *Here I am!*
Testify against me before the Lord and his anointed —
Whose ox have I taken? Whose donkey have I taken?
Whom have I defrauded? Whom have I oppressed?
From whose hand have I taken a bribe
and blinded my eyes with it? —
so that I may repay you!"
4 *And they said,*
"You have not defrauded us; you have not oppressed us.
You have not taken anything from anyone!"
5 *And he said to them,*
"The witness is the Lord! The witness is his anointed
with you today.

11. Vannoy, *Covenant Renewal at Gilgal,* p. 178.
12. McCarter, p. 221.
13. On this phrase, see on 1 Sam. 8:8.

For you have not found anything in my hand!"
And it was declared,
"The witness is. . . ."
6 *And Samuel said to the people,*
"the Lord,
who appointed Moses and Aaron
and who brought your fathers up from the land of Egypt!

1-2 Now that a king is firmly established over the people of Israel, Samuel takes initiative in bringing the issue of his own integrity as judge. But, when and where is he speaking? The construction, *wayyō'mer (wayqtl)* + subject, begins a new episode as in Gen. 7:1; 12:1; Exod. 12:1; Num. 26:1; Josh. 8:1; 1 Sam. 15:1, 32; 16:1; 27:1; 2 Sam. 9:1; 1 K. 17:1. But there is certainly "a curious lack of narrative framework for this address. No time or place is given."[14] This speech by Samuel may possibly have been made during the ceremony for the kingship renewal at Gilgal (1 Sam. 11:14-15),[15] but it seems more likely that it was not.

From the discourse grammatical point of view, the previous episode terminated at 11:15 (see above) and a new episode was initiated at 12:1 by the *wayqtl* with a stated subject, and so it seems more likely that this was a different occasion. Possibly it took place at Ramah, the hometown of Samuel and the place where the people first requested a king (see 1 Sam. 8:4-5). The statement, *I have listened to your voice . . . and have made a king over you,* harks back directly to 8:22: "The Lord said to Samuel: 'Listen to their voice and make a king for them!'"; it reminds us of the event at Ramah where the people first demanded a king over them in 8:5. Moreover, *all Israel* does not necessarily refer to exactly the group of people, that is, *all the people and all the men of Israel,* who gathered to make Saul king at Gilgal in 11:15; but it does refer to the entire covenant people in this context.

The expression "to walk before" in v. 2 means "to perform a function on someone's behalf."[16] Here the king's *walking before you* and Samuel's *having walked before you* are consciously contrasted.

3 *Testify against me:* see also 2 Sam. 1:16 "your own mouth testified against you" *(pîkā ʿānāh bᵉkā).* With this legal expression Samuel "protests against his deposition by the people on the grounds that his leadership has been just."[17] This whole verse is a conditional sentence "If you testify against

14. Birch, p. 1060.

15. As suggested by scholars such as Vannoy, *Covenant Renewal at Gilgal;* R. P. Gordon, p. 125; Birch, p. 1060.

16. See McCarter, p. 90, on 2:30.

17. McCarter, p. 213.

me . . . , I will repay you," with a series of questions ("Whose ass have I taken?" etc.) inserted as parenthetical clauses (AXB pattern) between the protasis and the apodosis, as shown in the translation. McCarter supplies another "Accuse me" before the apodosis *so that I may repay* clause, and Klein says the MT lost it through haplography.[18] However, this is not necessary.

Here, the king, Yahweh's *anointed,* is mentioned as "chief justiciary and upholder of the nation's laws";[19] also v. 5. It is sometimes asserted that the addition of the phrase *his anointed* is ironic in view of the king who would "take" (8:11-18) sons and daughters as well as fields and cattle. However, this contrast is unduly emphasized. Samuel is appealing to his integrity without necessarily comparing himself with the king. For one thing, 8:11-18 does not even mention oppression or bribery by the king. Note that the only element common to both passages is the use of the word *lqḥ "to take"; see below.

Ox and *donkey* are the two main large cattle; compare "oxen and donkeys and flocks" (Gen. 32:5; also Exod. 22:4, 9); these terms are used as the representatives of human possessions.

In a similar context Moses uses a different term for "taking": "I have not taken *(nāśā'tî)* one donkey from them, and I have not harmed any one of them" (Num. 16:15b). One extra-biblical example from Hittite documents suffices to illustrate the popularity of such a "negative confession." In the historiographical text "Crossing of the Taurus," Puḫanu, the servant of Šarmaššu, complains how he has been ill-treated or misunderstood, saying

> "What have I done? What?"
> "I haven't taken anything from anyone.
> I haven't taken an ox from anyone.
> I haven't taken a sheep from anyone.
> I haven't taken anyone's male or female servants."
> "Why have you (plural) treated me so and bound this yoke upon me?"[20]

Defrauded and *oppressed* are a word pair, repeated in v. 4; also Deut. 28:33; Hos. 5:11; Amos 4:1. Note that this word pair does not appear in 8:11-17. The expression *taken a bribe (lāqaḥtî kōper;* also Amos 5:12) reminds us of the evil conduct (*lqḥ + *šōḥad* "to take bribe") of Samuel's sons (8:3) rather than "the right of the king" (8:11); see on 8:3. Thus, Samuel contrasts himself with his sons rather than with the king.

The idiom *blinded my eyes with it* (or "covered it up": lit., "darkened/hidden my eyes from it") with the sense "to ignore" appears also in Ezek.

18. McCarter, p. 209; Klein, p. 111.
19. R. P. Gordon, p. 126.
20. Hoffner, in *CS,* I, p. 184.

22:26; Prov. 28:27 ("to close one's eyes to"); and Isa. 1:15 ("to hide one's eyes from"); note that the preposition *b* means "from," as often so in Ugar., in the light of Isa. 1:15 (see *UT,* §10.1, where Gordon translates: "so that I have to hide my eyes from him," i.e., "so that I can't look him straight in the eye"). Nowdays we say that "justice should be blind" meaning blind to the status, etc., of the individuals involved, but the Hebrew expression "blind justice" would mean blind to the truth as in Exod. 23:8, "a bribe blinds the officials, and subverts the cause of those who are in the right" (cf. Deut. 16:19). The LXX translates "a pair of shoes."

4-6 The entire covenant people affirm Samuel's integrity by repeating the same verbs, that is, *defrauded, oppressed,* and *taken,* in the negative. Then, Samuel calls the Lord and *his anointed* as the witnesses, and a legal formula of witnessing is followed.

The word order of the Hebrew text, literally, "Witness is the Lord in you; witness is his anointed today!" (v. 5), is somewhat awkward. But, as our translation shows, the phrases *with you* (X) and *today* (Y) modify both clauses *The witness is the Lord!* (A) and *The witness is his anointed!* (B). Thus, the text reflects the AXBY pattern, in which XY as a whole modifies AB. The text might be paraphrased as follows: "The witnesses are the Lord and his anointed who are with you today!"

The phrase *it was declared* is literally "he said," but used in an impersonal way. NRSV; NASB; and NIV translate it as "they said," apparently implying "the people said," but the present author thinks that it was declared by someone who mediated between Samuel and the people. Note that, based on the versions of the LXX, McCarter takes the MT as the "conflation" of two variants.[21] But, he is forced to assume that the text is conflated in all LXX versions, that is, LXX^A, LXX^B, and LXX^L.

The witness is . . . the Lord (vv. 5-6) — here, as a part of the court procedure, a third person declares the first half of a formula, "witness is . . . ," followed by Samuel's response with *the Lord!* (see Josh. 24:22). Yahweh and his king were declared witnesses to Samuel's integrity in v. 5a ("For you have not found anything in my hand!"). See Ruth 4:11, where "all the people at the gate and the elders" were witnesses. Regardless of whether this is a part of "the covenantal patterning of vv 6-15" or not (see above), Samuel invokes as a witness Yahweh, who led Israel out of Egypt by the hands of Moses and Aaron. Yahweh here stands as witness between Samuel and the people, just as he is invoked as *ʿēd* ("witness") to the parity treaties in Gen. 31:50 and 1 Samuel 20.

Samuel implicitly compares himself with Moses and Aaron in their role of deliverer. Is it intentional that in v. 6 Samuel no longer refers to the

21. McCarter, p. 210.

king, "Yahweh's anointed," as a witness? See the parallel presentation of the two groups in Ps. 99:6, "Moses and Aaron were among his priests, Samuel was among those who called on his name."

The translation *who appointed* for *ʿāśāh* is possible if we assume a brachylogy, that is, an ellipsis of "a term denoting office or function."[22] Outside of the Pentateuch, the pair *Moses and Aaron* (also v. 8) are usually mentioned as the deliverers from Egypt (Josh. 24:5; Mic. 6:4 [with Miriam]; Ps. 77:21 [20]; 105:26). "The point at issue is God's ability to provide deliverers as in the days of the judges."[23]

2. "Behold the King!" (12:7-15)

7 *"And now,*
take your stand that I may argue my case with you before the Lord
by all the righteous acts of the Lord
who has dealt with you and your fathers.
8 *When Jacob went to Egypt,*
your fathers cried out to the Lord.
And the Lord sent Moses and Aaron,
and they brought your fathers out of Egypt
and settled them in this place.
9 *And they forgot the Lord their God,*
and he sold them
into the hand of Sisera, the army commander of Hazor
and into the hand of the Philistines and the king of Moab,
and they fought against them.
10 *And they cried out to the Lord:*
'We have sinned,[24]
for we have abandoned the Lord
and served[25] *gods and goddesses!*
And now,
deliver us from the hand of our enemies
that we may serve you!'
11 *And the Lord sent Jerubbaal and Bedan*
and Jephthah and Samuel,
and delivered you from the hand of your enemies around
and you lived securely.

22. McCarter, p. 215. On "brachylogy," see "Introduction" (Section VII, D).
23. R. P. Gordon, p. 127.
24. On this term see 1 Sam. 2:25; 7:6.
25. For the word pair "to abandon" and "to serve," see on 8:8.

12 *And you saw*
that Nahash, the king of the Ammonites, had come against you
and you said to me,
'No!
For a king should rule over us!'
though the Lord, your God, was your king.
13 *And now,*
here is the king whom you have chosen,
whom you have requested!
See, the Lord has set a king over you!
14 *If you fear the Lord*
and serve him and listen to his voice
and do not show disobedience to the mouth of the Lord,
both you and the king who rules over you
will be following[26] *the Lord your God!*
15 *But if you do not listen to the voice of the Lord*
and show disobedience to the mouth of the Lord,
the hand of the Lord shall be on your entire household!"

7-12 *And now (w*^{eʿ}*attāh)* marks a beginning of a new unit. Many scholars, following M. Noth, say that vv. 6-15 is a unit inserted by a "Deuteronomistic" writer,[27] but when we look at the discourse structure, it is vv. 7-12, not vv. 6-15, that constitute a real unit, forming a résumé of Israelite history. Note that *ʿattāh* appears in this chapter in vv. 2, 7, 10, 13, 16. As R. P. Gordon notes, "Such summaries of salvation-history were an integral part of Israel's worship (e.g. Ps. 78), and are equally at home in the New Testament, where Christ is seen as their end-point and culmination (e.g. Acts 13:17-23)."[28] The element of historical retrospection can be attributed to a covenantal emphasis in the speech, even if one cannot establish a formal covenant structure in these verses. This historical speech is similar to those by Joshua (Joshua 23–24) and Solomon (1 K. 8:12-61).[29]

7 The expression *take your stand* again appears in v. 16. It has a "juridical/law court force" as in Job 33:5; perhaps Ps. 5:5.[30]

26. Lit., "be after."

27. M. Noth, *Überlieferungsgeschichtliche Studien: Die sammelnden und bearbeitenden Geschichtswerke im Alten Testament* (1943; 2d ed., 1957), p. 5; now in English: M. Noth, *The Deuteronomistic History* (JSOTSS 15; Sheffield: JSOT Press, 1981); see Birch, p. 1061.

28. R. P. Gordon, p. 127.

29. See McCarter, p. 214.

30. P. Bovati, *Re-Establishing Justice: Legal Terms, Concepts and Procedures in the Hebrew Bible* (JSOTSS 105; Sheffield: Sheffield Academic Press, 1994), p. 235.

I may argue my case with you (wᵉʾiššāpᵉṭāh ʾittᵉkem), that is, "you and I may argue our case together," renders the Niphal verb's reflexive sense "I may judge myself" (cf. Ps. 9:19, etc., where it is passive).[31] The Ni. verbal form would suggest that Samuel puts himself on trial. Samuel here, though not a judge, takes the role of prosecutor against the people as well as putting himself on trial.

The expression *the righteous acts of the Lord* (*ṣidqôt YHWH;* lit., "righteousnesses of the Lord") appears also in Judg. 5:11; compare "saving deeds" (NRSV). R. P. Gordon thinks that "the required forensic nuance" would support the translation "righteous acts" rather than the RSV's "the saving deeds," and that this phrase "takes account of the fact that God's covenant faithfulness involves disciplinary, as well as salvific, acts (e.g. v. 9)."[32]

The phrase *you and your fathers* refers to "your entire household"; see on 12:15 (below).

8 The plural pronoun in *they brought* signifies that Moses and Aaron acted as the messengers of the Lord, by his authority.

9-11 While the Exodus and the settlement is summarized in one verse (v. 8), the period of the judges is dealt with in more detail in three verses (vv. 9-11). The Lord's saving acts are explained by key terms such as *went — cried out — sent — brought out — settled* in v. 8; *forgot — cried out — sent — delivered — lived* in vv. 9-11. Thus, "the dismal and recurring pattern of apostasy-oppression-repentance-deliverance in the book of Judges (cf. Judg. 2:11-23) is miniaturized here."[33]

9 *Sisera* is the army commander of Jabin, a king of Canaan; see Judges 4–5; Ps. 83:9; etc. The title *the army commander* occurs from Genesis through Judges and is very frequent in Samuel as well as in the ostracon Lachish iii, 14, referring to the commander in chief of Hazor's army. The phrase *the king of Moab* here probably refers to Eglon, who subdued Israel (Judg. 3:12f.). See also 1 Sam. 22:3.

10 *Gods and goddesses (ʾet-habbᵉʿālîm wᵉʾet-hāʿaštārôt;* lit. "the Baals and the Astartes") means "the foreign gods and goddesses"; see on 7:3-4 (above).

11 *Jerubbaal* is another name for Gideon (Judg. 6:32).

For *Bedan,* the LXX and Peshitta have "Barak," which corresponds

31. For *špṭ (Ni) + *ʾet* "with," "A goes to court with B; A has a controversy with B" (Prov. 29:9); "A enters into judgment with B" (Ezek. 17:20; 20:35; 38:22). For *špṭ (Ni.) + *ʾet* (object), "A executes judgment on B" (Isa. 66:16); also Isa. 43:26 (*niššāpᵉṭāh yāḥad;* "let us argue our case together"); see *HALOT,* p. 1626; Bovati, Re-Establishing Justice, p. 49; cf. "I may plead with you" (NASB); "I may enter into judgment with you" (NRSV; also AB); "I am going to confront you with evidence" (NIV).

32. R. P. Gordon, p. 127.

33. R. P. Gordon, p. 127.

nicely to the mention of Sisera in v. 9.[34] As the present author explains elsewhere,[35] the MT form *bᵉdān* might be explained as a phonetic variant of "Barak."[36]

For Samuel to name himself in a speech he delivers (MT and LXX^{B,A}) sounds a little odd; hence McCarter, following LXX^{L} and Syr., reads "Samson," though he accepts that "many critics prefer [Samuel] on the grounds that the reading 'Samson' was substituted to preserve Samuel's modesty (Smith, etc.)."[37] Josephus (*Ant.* 6.90) omits the name altogether. R. P. Gordon comments, "If the speech is a free composition of such things as Samuel was likely to have said on an occasion like this the problem is, of course, less acute (*cf.* 7:13f.). Emendation to 'Samson' is ill-advised."[38]

12 The reference to *Nahash, the king of the Ammonites,* reminds us of the incident in ch. 11 and gives the impression that the demand for a king in 8:5 was a response to the new threat posed by Nahash the Ammonite in 11:1. However, the threat may have existed for some time before Nahash's attack on Jabash-gilead. As mentioned above, Nahash expresses hostility towards all Israel in his demand, and so tension may have existed before ch. 8 and triggered the demand for a king. If the 4QSamᵃ and Josephus preserve a true tradition (see on 11:1), this is even more likely. For the eternal kingship of God, see on 8:7.

13 The expression *And now, here is the king (wᵉʿattāh hinnēh hammelek)* need not refer to the occasion either at the time of the choosing of Saul as king at Mizpah in 10:24 or at the time of the renewal of kingship at Gilgal as depicted in 11:14-15; see above. In the light of v. 2 *(And now, here is the king walking before you),* it is reasonable to think that the king has been ruling over the people for some time.

It is unnecessary to contrast this expression *you have chosen* and the one in 10:24 *(the Lord has chosen)* and take the former as exhibiting "a more negative view of Saul's election," as R. P. Gordon does. For it was the Lord who *has set (nātan)* a king over the people.

14-15 After these words Samuel concludes his official speech by summarizing his admonitions to the covenant people. Verses 14-15 corre-

34. See the recent discussion on this name by H. Jacobson, "The Judge Bedan (1 Samuel XII 11)," *VT* 42 (1992) 123-24; J. Day, "Bedan, Abdon or Barak in 1 Samuel xii 11?" *VT* 43 (1993) 261-64; H. Jacobson, "Bedan and Barak Reconsidered," *VT* 44 (1994) 108-9.

35. D. T. Tsumura, "Bedan, a Copyist's Error?" *VT* 45 (1995) 122-23.

36. Thus, (1) dissimilation of sonorant: *r* > *d, bārāq* > *bādāq;* (2) velarization of [*q*] with nasalization: *q* > ŋ, *bārāq* > *bārāg* > *bārā*ŋ; (3) assimilation of [ŋ] to [*d*] (dental) with pretonic reduction: ŋ > *n, bārā*ŋ > *bᵉdān.*

37. McCarter, p. 211.

38. R. P. Gordon, p. 128.

spond to the blessing and curse sections in an ancient covenant. The stipulations here do correspond to the stipulations in other covenant texts such as Deuteronomy 12–26; Josh. 24:14.

14 The triple exhortation — "to fear," "to serve" and "to obey" — characterizes the basic conditions for a good relationship between God and his people. The expression *show disobedience to the mouth* means "rebel against the commandment" (NRSV; NASB).

Not only the people but also *the king* should be obedient to the Lord; no king in Israel is exempted from obeying the Lord's commandments. Since many modern translations take v. 14b as another protasis ("and if both you and the king . . ."), they are obliged to supply a phrase such as "it will be well" (NRSV); " — good!" (NIV); "well and good" (NEB; JPS). R. P. Gordon explains this as "a syntactical matter (ellipsis), though it is possible to find something ominous in the absence of a 'hopeful apodosis.'"[39] However, we interpret the first half of this verse as having the sense of "if you say [CONTEXT bound] that you will fear the Lord . . . ," what the apodosis intends to convey is clear: even the king *who rules over you* is not exempt from obeying the divine law. See the translation.

15 *The hand of the Lord (yad YHWH),* as the agent of a terrible plague or destruction (Exod. 9:3; Deut. 2:15; Josh. 4:24; Judg. 2:15; etc.; see on 1 Sam. 5:6), will punish the nation if they disobey.

The text reads literally "the hand of the Lord will be on you and on your fathers." This seems strange, as the "fathers" are presumably dead. Thus, many have suggested omitting "on you" and translate "as it was against your fathers" (NASB; NIV; Targum; Peshitta; Stoebe; Vannoy) or "as it did your fathers" (JPS). McCarter reads it differently: "and your king to destroy you," based on LXX^L; compare "your king" (NRSV). However, the phrase probably refers to the *entire household,* as the phrase *you and your fathers* in v. 7 does; see "we/us and our fathers" (Gen. 46:34; 47:3; Josh. 24:17; Jer. 3:25; 44:17), "you and your fathers" (Exod. 13:11; Deut. 28:36, 64; Jer. 7:14; 16:13; et al.; Joel 1:2), and "they/them and their fathers" (Lev. 26:40; Jer. 19:4; 24:10; Ezek. 2:3; 2 Chr. 6:25).

3. "Take Your Stand and See!" (12:16-17)

16 *"Now then,*[40] *take your stand and see this great thing*
which the Lord is going to do before your eyes!
17 *Is it not the wheat harvest today?*

39. R. P. Gordon, p. 129.

40. *gam-ʿattāh* here signals a "high-level" discourse transition, starting a new paragraph; also Gen. 44:10; 1 K. 14:14; Joel 2:12; Job 16:19. See Andersen, p. 165.

I will call to the Lord
that he may give sounds and rain.
And know and see
that the evil which you have done
by asking for a king for yourselves
is great in the Lord's eyes."

16-17 Now, Samuel directs the people's eyes to the divine response toward their evil of demanding a king for themselves.

Since *the wheat harvest (qᵉṣîr-ḥiṭṭîm)* is usually in May-June, the early summer when rain rarely falls, the thunder and rain would be readily acknowledged as the signs of supernatural intervention in response to the prayer of his prophet. McCarter says that God's point is to show the close relationship between the Lord and his prophet Samuel, a relationship with which the people were not content, more than to show his anger.[41] Against McCarter's view, Longman, following Vannoy's theory that ch. 12 is a covenant renewal ceremony, interprets the thunderstorm as the expression of covenant curse rather than of divine omnipotence, for the heavy rainstorm would be damaging to the crop.[42] But Longman's view is rather forced. Verse 17 explains that its purpose is that the people know that their *evil is great in the Lord's eyes.*

The Ugaritic parallel of the phrase *yittēn qōlôt,* "he gives voices," is *ytn ql,* and it refers to Baal's voice, that is, thunder. In Psalm 29, "the voice of the Lord" *(qôl YHWH)* appears seven times and also refers to the thunder. While as a storm god Baal's voice is thunder, Yahweh, who is the creator of the universe, can express himself through natural phenomena, one of which is thunder. Though the expression "to give voice(s)" is the same in both languages, the purpose of using it is totally different. See on 7:10.

The syntax of *kî-rāʿatkem rabbāh ʾăšer ʿăśîtem bᵉʿênê YHWH lišʾōl lākem melek* (lit., "that your evil is great which you have done in the Lord's eyes by asking for a king for yourselves") is somewhat awkward. Compare "that the wickedness that you have done in the sight of the LORD is great" (NRSV); "that your wickedness is great which you have done in the sight of the LORD" (NASB). Since the phrase "in the sight of the Lord" normally occurs in the context of moral judgment, that is, "good" (*ṭôb;* Num. 24:1; etc.), "wicked" (*raʿ;* Gen. 38:7; etc.) or "right" (*yāšār;* Deut. 12:25; etc.), it is best to take that phrase as belonging to the main clause ("your evil is great") rather than to the relative clause ("which you have done"); hence the translation: *that the evil thing which you have done is great in the Lord's eyes.*

41. McCarter, p. 216.

42. T. Longman, III, "I Sam 12:16-19: Divine Omnipotence or Covenant Curse?" *WTJ* 45 (1983) 168-71.

McCarter's translation: "that the evil you have done in requesting a king for yourselves is great in Yahweh's eyes," makes good sense. The final phrase *by asking for a king for yourselves (liš'ôl lākem melek)* is probably to be understood as modifying the verb *'ăśîtem* (you have done) of the relative clause according to the "vertical grammar"; see "Introduction" (VII, A).

In other words, there is a main clause consisting of two phrases:

A: The evil is great	B: in the sight of the Lord

and a relative clause (modifying "evil") consisting of two phrases:

X: Which [evil] you have done	Y: by asking for a king for yourselves.

But instead of the normal order AB XY, the phrases are overlapped in AX// BY.

kî-rā'atkem rabbāh 'ăšer 'ăśîtem	The evil is great which you have done
be'ênê YHWH liš'ôl lākem melek	In the sight of the Lord by asking for a king

Note that v. 19 also supports this syntactical understanding, namely, "to add another evil" *by asking for a king for us.*

4. "Fear the Lord and Serve Him!" (12:18-25)

18 *And Samuel called to the Lord.*
And the Lord gave sounds and rain on that day.
And all the people feared the Lord and Samuel greatly.
19 *And all the people said to Samuel,*
"Pray for your servants to the Lord your God
that we may not die!
For we have added another evil to all our sins
by asking for a king for us."
20 *And Samuel said to the people,*
"Do not fear!
You yourselves have done all this evil.
Only, do not turn away from (after) the Lord
but serve the Lord with all your heart!
21 *For you must not turn away [to go] after the vain idols*
which can neither benefit nor save,
for they are nothing.

22 *For the Lord will not forsake his people*
because of his great name,
since the Lord was willing to make you a people for himself.
23 *As for me,*[43] *may it never happen to me to sin against the Lord*
by ceasing to pray for you!
And I will teach you the way to the good and right thing.
24 *Only, fear*[44] *the Lord*
and serve him in truth[45] *with all your heart,*
for they will see[46] *what great things he has done for you!*
25 *And if you act wickedly,*
both you and your king will be swept away!"

18 When Samuel invokes the Lord, he responds with *sounds and rain.* The entire covenant people are greatly afraid of the Lord and his prophet Samuel. The phrase *feared the Lord* here is not the same as "to fear, serve, and obey" the Lord, as exhorted by Samuel in v. 14. The people simply feared the fact that the Lord actually responded to Samuel's supplication; hence, in v. 20 Samuel tells them not to fear.[47] The people feared *the Lord and Samuel.* In the addition of the name of Samuel one might note that "even under the monarchy there can be no derogation of prophetic authority."[48] To be sure, this is not "a retirement ceremony" for Samuel; his authority as prophet remains powerful.[49]

19 The people ask Samuel to intercede to their covenant God. *Pray for your servants to the Lord;* see 1:10 on the intercessory prayer. One is reminded of the passages in Exodus (20:19; 32:11-13) where Moses mediates for the people. See Jer. 15:1: "Even if Moses and Samuel were to stand before me, my heart would not go out."

Your servants is a humble and courteous way of referring to themselves, instead of *we.* The people for the first time truly humble themselves before Samuel; contrast their attitude toward him in 8:5.

20-25 Samuel responds to the people's request with compassionate yet straightforward admonitions. The "emphatic" pronouns *'attem (you your-*

43. *gam 'ānōkî* (lit., "Also I"). The particle *gam* here appears in an adjunctive clause; see Andersen, p. 164.

44. Impv.: a shorter form; *y*^{e}*r(')û* < *yir(')û* < *yir'û.*

45. *be'ĕmet;* i.e., "truly"; = Ugar. *imt.* Cf. *HALOT,* p. 68.

46. *kî r*^{e}*'û,* impf. 3 m. "impersonal" plural; this is a *sandhi* spelling, *kîr*^{e}*'û* < *kî-r'û* < *kî-yir'û;* rather than impv. See D. T. Tsumura, "Vowel sandhi in Biblical Hebrew," *ZAW* 109 (1997) 585.

47. On Hebrew root *yr',* see M. I. Gruber, "Fear, Anxiety and Reverence in Akkadian, Biblical Hebrew and Other North-West Semitic Languages," *VT* 40 (1990) 411-22.

48. R. P. Gordon, p. 129.

49. Birch, p. 1063.

selves) and *gam ʾānōkî* (*as for me;* lit., "also I") are the key to understanding the structure of vv. 20-25.[50] They certainly contrast the two parties, the people and the prophet. While for the people to ask for a king for themselves was an "evil" (v. 20), for the prophet to cease to pray for them would be a "sin" (v. 23). Here, the intercessory role of the prophet (see v. 19) is confirmed by the prophet himself. At the same time, the repetition of the particle *ʾak (only)* in vv. 20 and 24 marks the central message of the prophet to the people: "you shall fear and serve the Lord in truth with all your heart!" The word pair "to fear" and "to serve" appears also in v. 14.

20 Samuel told the people not to fear, for they "feared the Lord and Samuel greatly" (v. 18). This "fear" is not like that suggested by Ps. 25:14: "The friendship of the LORD is for those who fear him" (NRSV). Here again, *evil* is asking for a king for themselves; see vv. 17 and 19.

The particle *ʾak* (*only;* also v. 24; 18:17; 25:21; see on 1:23) structurally marks the central message of the prophet in these verses; see above.

The second half of this verse shows poetic features. It constitutes a "bicolon," a-b-c//b′-c′-d′, with a stress pattern of 3:3.

> Only, do not turn away from (after) the Lord,
> but serve the Lord with all your heart!

The expression *do not turn away . . . serve* is a <(not A) + B> pattern. Since "to turn away from the Lord" and "to serve the Lord" are antonymous, "do not turn away" is a negated antonym of, and therefore synonymous to, "serve the Lord."[51] In the Deuteronomic laws, "turn away [from the Lord]" means "serve other gods" (Deut. 11:16; also 7:4); in the subsequent books, conversely, "turn aside" from idols is synonymous with "serve" the Lord (Josh. 24:14; Judg. 10:16; 1 Sam. 7:3, 4; 2 Chr. 34:33). These and similar expressions and phraseologies are not necessarily characteristically "Deuteronomistic"; see "Introduction" (III, B, 1).

The repetition of the object "the Lord" here is more poetic than v. 24, where "him" appears.

21 *For (kî)* here is a speaker-oriented *kî* (See "Introduction" [Section V, C]) and explains "the reason why I emphasize the preceding statement by 'Only' *(ʾak)* in v. 20"; see various passages with the sequence, *ʾak . . . kî . . . ,* for example, in Exod. 12:15; Lev. 11:4; Num. 14:9; Deut. 14:7; Josh. 3:4; 1 Sam. 12:24 (see below); 2 K. 22:7; Jer. 3:14; 5:4; Ps. 49:15; 62:5.

The verbal phrase *you must not turn away (w*^{e}*lōʾ tāsûrû)* precedes the particle *kî* for emphasis.

50. So McCarter, p. 216.
51. For "negated antonym," see on 1:11.

The term *tōhû* in this context is translated *vain idols* and *nothing.* The original meaning of this term is "wilderness"; its metaphorical use, "like wilderness," denotes the state that "there is nothing there," hence "emptiness" or "nothingness."[52] Idolatry is just like "nothing," nothing substantial. In other words, it is an empty entity that rewards the one who trusts in it with only vanity or emptiness.

22 The Lord will not deal with his people simply according to whether they act wickedly (v. 25) but because of *his great name.* This is the biblical principle of the divine saving grace or favor. Yahweh's *great name (šᵉmô haggādôl)* signifies his great fame; see Josh. 7:9; 1 K. 8:42; Jer. 44:26; Ezek. 36:23; 2 Chr. 6:32. "Since Israel is known as Yahweh's special people, it would reflect badly on his own reputation if he were to cast them off."[53]

23 Samuel now turns to his own responsibilities as the prophet of the Lord. For the expression *may it never happen to me,* see on 1 Sam. 2:30; 20:2, 9. Intercession *(pray)* and instruction *(teach)* are Samuel's two major roles as the prophet of the Lord, even after the inauguration of kingship.[54]

Here, the items of the construct chain *derek haṭṭôbāh wᵉhayšārāh* are in an objectival genitive relationship, hence, *the way to the good and right thing.* Compare "in the good and the right way" (NRSV; also NASB); "the way that is good and right" (NIV); and "in the practice of what is good and right" (JPS). The phrase "what is good and right in the eyes of the Lord" *(haṭṭôb wᵉhayyāšār bᵉʿênê YHWH)* is an idiomatic expression, which appears in Deut. 12:28; 2 Chr. 14:2 (cf. 2 K. 20:3; 2 Chr. 31:20). The forms are feminine only here.

24 The people are commanded to *only fear . . . serve;* here, two of the triad "fear, serve, obey" (see v. 14) reappear. The repetition of the phrase *with all your heart* here and in v. 20 constitutes an *inclusio.*

For they will see: compare "for consider" (NRSV; NASB). McCarter reads "for you have seen," based on LXX, for he thinks that the MT's "for see!" is "unsuitable."[55] Since the Lord has made Israel the special chosen people for his great name's sake, it will be his special witness to "what great things he has done for it."

52. The term has nothing to do with the concept of "chaos" as the counterpart of "order"; see D. T. Tsumura, *The Earth and the Waters in Genesis 1 and 2: A Linguistic Analysis* (JSOTSS 83; Sheffield: Sheffield Academic Press, 1989), pp. 17-43; also "The Earth in Genesis 1," in *"I Studied Inscriptions from Before the Flood": Ancient Near Eastern, Literary, and Linguistic Approaches to Genesis 1-11,* ed. R. S. Hess and D. T. Tsumura (SBTS 4; Winona Lake, Ind.: Eisenbrauns, 1994), pp. 310-28.

53. McCarter, p. 217.

54. See S. E. Balentine, "The Prophet as Intercessor: A Reassessment," *JBL* 103 (1984) 161-73.

55. McCarter, p. 212. But the MT is a *sandhi* spelling; see above.

25 "Wickedly": "evil" is a key term which appears in vv. 17, 19, 20.

Note that the fate of the king in Israel is one with that of the people (*both you and your king;* see also v. 14). Both the people and the king are obliged to obey the word of the Lord or else both of them will be swept away. Because of disobedience to the word of the Lord, Saul will be rejected from being king over Israel in the following chapter. Samuel's speech to Israel thus prepares the audience for the subsequent course of the narrative.

C. REIGN OF SAUL (13:1–15:35)

Following the description of the transition of leadership from Samuel to Saul in ch. 12, the narrative quickly moves on toward the rejection of Saul. At the very beginning of this section, in v. 1, the narrator seems to emphasize the shortness (i.e., *just for two years*) of Saul's reign in God's eyes. The following three chapters, chs. 13–15, are therefore a build-up toward the climax of choosing David, Saul's *neighbor* (15:28), as God's anointed. From a literary perspective, Saul's rejection and David's rise thus constitute a <not A but B> pattern.[1] As R. P. Gordon comments, "the dominant feeling in chs. 13–15 is not of success, but of failure."[2] Saul is twice rejected by God for his disregard of God's word (see 13:13 and 15:11, 23), despite Samuel's warning to both the people and their *king* not to *act wickedly* (12:25), that is, to disobey the word of God.

1. Saul and the Philistines (13:1-23)

From here Saul is again the main figure in the story. Therefore, in the first verse of the chapter, the narrator summarizes Saul's reign before entering upon the specific events in his life which lead to the end of his kingship from God's perspective; see v. 14.

a. Summary Statement (13:1)

1 *A certain year of age was Saul when he became king,*
and just for two years he ruled over Israel.

1. For example, it was not animals (A) but a woman (B) that was the helpmate to the man in Gen. 2:19-23. See C. H. Gordon, "Build-up and Climax," in *Studies in Bible and the Ancient Near East Presented to Samuel E. Loewenstamm,* ed. Y. Avishur and J. Blau (Jerusalem: E. Rubinstein's, 1978), pp. 29-34.

2. R. P. Gordon, p. 131.

13:1 Summary Statement

1 The narrative of Saul's failure begins with a summary statement, in the manner of the biblical historiography. The verse has been variously interpreted due to its possible textual problem. No age is specified, and the events in the rest of the book certainly covered more than two years. Various translations have been suggested: "Saul was thirty years old when he became king, and he reigned over Israel forty-two years" (NIV); "forty years old . . . thirty-two years" (NASB); ". . . years old . . . two years" (JPS; also NRSV). The entire verse is omitted in most of the LXX mss.[3] See also on 2 Sam. 2:10a, 11.

Most commentators take the view that the text is defective, missing the original numeral(s),[4] since the accession formula here is incomplete when it is compared with other occurrences as 2 Sam. 2:10; 5:4; 1 K. 14:21; 22:42. As for Saul's age of accession, various unsuccessful attempts have been made to supply "original" numerals. For example, NIV uses "thirty" for Saul's age based on LXX^{L}. However, since Jonathan was old enough to have 1,000 troops under his command in v. 2, and since Saul had a grandson before his death (2 Sam. 4:4), Klein thinks that an age of forty (so NASB) or more is plausible.[5] However, since no length of Saul's reign is given except "for two years," one cannot be sure how old Saul was when he died on Mt. Gilboa (ch. 31). The narrative of chs. 9–10 rather suggests that Saul was still young and possibly single when he was made king. JPS, NRSV, McCarter, and Caquot and de Robert do not attempt to restore the numeral.

As for the length of Saul's reign, modern translations vary: for example, "42 years" (NIV); "32 years" (NASB); "2 years" (JPS); "?2 years" (NRSV); "?? years" (McCarter). It is almost certain that the actual length of Saul's reign was more than two years[6] in light of the available data in chs. 9–31. According to Acts 13:21 and Josephus's *Antiquities* (vi. 14. 9), his reign

3. For various suggestions by modern scholars, see Smith, p. 92; R. Althann, "1 Sam 13,1: A Poetic Couplet," *Bib* 62 (1981) 241-42; McCarter, pp. 222-23.

4. G. R. Driver's "abbreviation theory" (G. R. Driver, in *Textus* 1 [1960] 127) that a Hebrew scribe wrote Saul's age on accession with כ for 20 is no longer tenable, since the available evidence suggests such a practice "would not have taken place prior to the Hellenistic period" (A. Millard, "Strangers from Egypt and Greece — The Signs for Numbers in Early Hebrew," in *Immigration and Emigration within the Ancient Near East: Festschrift E. Lipinski,* ed. K. van Lerberghe and A. Schoors [OLA 65; Leuven: Uitgeverij Peeters, 1995], p. 194). Althann's suggestion ("1 Sam 13,1: A Poetic Couplet," p. 244) of taking *bn* as a comparative *b* with an afformative *nun,* translating *ben-šānāh* as "more than a year" is forced, since this verse follows the accession formula (e.g. 2 Sam. 2:10 and others).

5. Klein, p. 122.

6. The number *two (š^{e}tê)* has an unusual spelling and appears only here. Wellhausen, pp. 79-80, Driver, p. 97, Smith, p. 92, and McCarter, p. 222, take it as corrupt. However, the form is not impossible, as Althann argues in "1 Sam 13,1: A Poetic Couplet," p. 242.

was forty years, "though the latter elsewhere suggests twenty (*Ant.* x.8.4)."[7] Noth, on the other hand, supports the number "two" as appropriate "both for the deuteronomistic historian's chronology and for the historical circumstances."[8] According to 2 Sam. 2:10 Ishbosheth, Saul's son, was forty when he became king and is, like Saul, said to have ruled two years. However, he probably reigned over only Israel, the northern part of the country, since the house of Judah followed David (2 Sam. 2:10b). However, Saul certainly reigned over Judah also.

McCarter suspects that "originally the numbers were lacking in both clauses" and translates: "Saul was ___ years old when he began to reign, and he reigned ___ years over Israel." According to him, the figures were not available to the Deuteronomistic historian — "or (if he had them) they were subsequently lost."[9]

This possibility might be supported by the extra-biblical examples. For example, in the Babylonian Chronicles, sometime numerals showing the length of a reign are omitted: for example, in Chronicle 1, i 25, the length of Tiglath-pileser III's reign (18 according to the Assyrian King List iv 24f.) is missing. Grayson holds that the most probable explanation is that "the original author of the chronicle did not know at the moment how many years Tiglath-pileser had ruled. He therefore left a blank space to be filled in later when he had time to make the necessary calculation. He then forgot to do this."[10]

This could have happened in the history writing in ancient Israel, and this may be such a case, as Buccellati[11] holds. Nevertheless, the fact remains that the MT does preserve the numeral "two" for Saul's reign; so, the omission of numerals, if it happened here, would have been only partial. Also, while it would have been difficult for a scribe/author to fill in a numeral after a clay tablet hardened, it would not be too difficult in a Hebrew text written on parchment or papyrus.

There have also been arguments made to keep the MT as it stands. Two suggestions have been made from the literary perspective: (1) epicanation (epicization); (2) a poetic expression. C. H. Gordon compares this with "the statement in Odyssey 19:179 that Minos, when nine years old, ruled Knossos." According to him, this verse says that Saul began to reign when he

7. R. P. Gordon, p. 132.

8. See M. Noth, *The History of Israel* (New York: Harper and Row, 1960), pp. 176-78.

9. McCarter, pp. 222-23.

10. A. K. Grayson, *Assyrian and Babylonian Chronicles* (Texts from Cuneiform Sources; Locust Valley, N.Y.: J. J. Augustin, 1975), pp. 72-73; also A. K. Grayson, "Nota (1 Samuel 13:1)," *BeO* 5 (1963) 86, 110.

11. G. Buccellati, "Nota: I Sam 13,1," *BeO* 5 (1963) 29.

was only one year old and refers to an epic tradition.[12] However, while Minos could have actually started reigning at the age of 9, Saul could not have been one. Althann,[13] in his translation "More than a year . . . even two years . . . ," notes "a parallel between the numbers 'one' and 'two.'" However, since the numeral "one" does not appear here, this is not a good example of "numerical parallelism," x//x + 1 pattern. Another possibility, which is followed here, is that the expression is "ironic."

The phrase *ben-šānāh* means "a year old" (e.g., Lev. 23:18; Num. 29:36; etc.) and usually denotes the age of a sacrificial animal. Since no numeral "one" is used here, it may mean either "a year old" or *a certain age.* The expression *just for two years* is probably given from the author's, hence God's, point of view: Saul was king only for "two years," even though he remained "king" much longer in human eyes; after ch. 13, Saul is no longer "king" in God's sight (see v. 14). However, since the timespan between 11:15 (Gilgal: Saul as a king) and 13:14 (rejection of Saul) must have more than two years if Saul was still young and unmarried in ch. 9–10, "two years" may be an ironic[14] expression for a very short time;[15] note the numeral "two" is the smallest cardinal, for "one" is usually expressed without the numeral "1" in a series of numerical expressions (e.g., Ugar. *ym wṯn* "a day and two (days)" [*KTU* 1.14:III:2, etc.]). But, in 2 K. 8:26 (= 2 Chr. 22:2), "one year" *(šānāh 'aḥat)* appears. See on 2 Sam. 2:10a, 11. Thus, from God's point of view Saul had been king only for a very short period ("a few years"),[16] and the exact age of Saul's accession did not matter to the narrator, since he was already rejected by his God.[17] This is at least another possible way of explaining this *crux interpretum.*

12. See C. H. Gordon, *The Common Background of Greek and Hebrew Civilizations* (New York: W. W. Norton, 1965), pp. 228-29.

13. Althann, "1 Sam 13,1: A Poetic Couplet," pp. 244-45, followed by R. P. Gordon, p. 342.

14. R. P. Gordon explains that the formula here is "ironically incomplete, as if to signal the outcome of Saul's reign!"; R. P. Gordon, *1 & 2 Samuel* (OTG; Sheffield: JSOT Press, 1984), p. 53. In our understanding, the lack of the numerals was intentionally ironic, not "as if. . . ."

15. Note that the number "two" often replaces the indefinite expression "a few." König quotes A. Berliner's comment: "the smallest number that can indicate plurality is two" in Ed. König, "Number," in *A Dictionary of the Bible,* vol. III, ed. J. Hastings (Edinburgh: T. & T. Clark, 1900), p. 562. On the number "three," see on 1 Sam. 20:20.

16. According to Gunn, Saul was doomed from the start, since he was chosen king for the people (see 1 Sam. 8:22 "for them") rather than for God (16:1); D. M. Gunn, *The Fate of King Saul* (JSOTSS 14; Sheffield: Sheffield Academic Press, 1980), p. 125. However, Saul's rejection was based on his disobedience to God's commands (see 13:13-14 and 15:11).

17. Tsevat's view is that "the story of the foundation of the monarchy" ends at 12:25. From 13:1 onward, the "Book of Kingships" (i.e., Samuel and Kings) tests and

b. Saul and Jonathan (13:2-3a)

2 *Saul chose three thousand for himself from Israel:*
two thousand were with Saul at Michmash
which is in the mountain of Bethel,
while a thousand were with Jonathan[18]
in Gibeah[19] *of Benjamin.*
As for the rest of the people, he sent them back each to his own tent.
3a *And Jonathan struck the prefect of the Philistines who was in Geba.*

2 After the summary statement of v. 1, which is a SETTING, the narrative begins the EVENT with a *wayqtl* + <stated subject> *(Saul chose),* just like Gen. 1:3 where the EVENT begins after the SETTING in Gen. 1:1-2.[20] While the SETTING gives the background information to the subsequent EVENT, the following story provides the reason why the narrator provides a poor evaluation of Saul's kingly role.

Saul has divided the three thousand soldiers of his standing army into two groups: two thousand for himself and one thousand for Jonathan. The sequence of numbers *three thousand . . . two thousand . . . a thousand* is not a numerical sequence of 3-2-1, since only "three" is a numeral in Hebrew — the other two are singular and dual nouns. Here, the *thousand* could refer to a military unit,[21] though an actual thousand would not be impossible. "Prior to

---

evaluates the monarchy's lasting value in the history of the covenant people. M. Tsevat, "The Biblical Account of the Foundation of the Monarchy in Israel," in *The Meaning of the Book of Job and Other Biblical Studies: Essays on the Literature and Religion of the Hebrew Bible* (New York: Ktav, 1980), pp. 83-99.

18. *yônātān* in 1 Sam. 14:6, 8; 18:1, 3, 4; 19:1, 2, 4, 6, 7; 20:1; and passim; *yᵉhônātān* elsewhere.

19. On a purely phonological basis, Gk. *gabaa* probably reflects a f.s. noun *gabʿa (*gabʿ with f.s. ending), which is the earlier pronunciation of *gibʿa, while *gabee* is from m.s. *gabiʿ (*gabʿ with an anaptyctic vowel /i/), which later developed to *gibiʿ, the earlier form of *gebaʿ. Both m. and f. forms appear as common nouns ("hill") in Northwest Semitic (e.g., Heb. *gbʿh* and Ugar. *gbʿ*). While in the LXX Gabaa always stands for MT *gbʿh* Gibeah (e.g., 11:4, *gibʿat šāʾûl* Gabaa pros Saoul ["Gibeah of Saul"]; also 10:26; 13:15; 15:34), Gabee stands for either *gbʿh* "Gibeah" (e.g., 13:2, 16; 14:16) or *gbʿ* "Geba" (e.g., 14:5).

20. See D. T. Tsumura, *The Earth and the Waters in Genesis 1 and 2: A Linguistic Analysis* (JSOTSS 83; Sheffield: Sheffield Academic Press, 1989), pp. 85, 162. Also "Introduction" (Section VI, A).

21. See most recently C. J. Humphreys, "The Number of People in the Exodus from Egypt: Decoding Mathematically the Very Large Numbers in Numbers I and XXVI," *VT* 48 (1998) 196-213.

the monarchy, the Israelites looked to their citizen militia in times of crisis, but Saul's establishment of a cadre of *three thousand men* provides Israel with a standing army (cf. 14:52)."[22] The number of Saul's soldiers as "three thousands" here is significant when we are told that only 600 remain with Saul and Jonathan in v. 15.

Saul was at Michmash, which is the modern Mukhmas, located approximately 7 miles northeast of Jerusalem and 3 or 4 miles south of Beitin, ancient Bethel. On the relation between Michmash, Geba, and Gibeah, see on 10:10 and 14:16.

McCarter thinks that the MT, which has been translated as "in Michmash and in the hill country of Bethel," gives the impression that "one thousand was located in each place." He thus translates: "at Michmash in the hill country of Bethel" (following LXX^B). If the *waw* ("and") is taken as *explicative,* meaning *which is* (see 6:18), his interpretation can be supported from the MT as it stands.

Since *har* "mountain" and *gib'āh* "hill" are a word pair in Hebrew,[23] *the mountain of Bethel (har bêt-'ēl)* is almost synonymous to "the hill country of Bethel" (NIV; JPS; NRSV; NASB).

Jonathan is mentioned here for the first time, with no explanation. To judge by this name ("Yah[weh] has given"), Saul worshipped Yahweh as his family god.[24]

On the location of Gibeah (MT: *gib'at binyāmîn;* also v. 15; 14:16), see on 10:10. Note here the use of a fixed word pair, "mountain" and "hill" (see above). Most modern translations have "Gibeah," but McCarter takes it as "Geba" on the basis of LXX *gabaa* (so LXX^L; but LXX^B *gabee*).[25] Arnold explains the alternation of the variant designations, Gibeah and Geba, as reflecting the extensive editorial splicing of southern and northern accounts of the battle. On the other hand, Edelman holds that "the author of the narrative is making a deliberate and concerted effort to equate the two terms for his ancient audience."[26] McCarter virtually gives up on finding a comprehensive

22. R. P. Gordon, p. 132.

23. See Ugaritic pair *ǵr* and *gb'* (see *RSP* 2, p. 449).

24. See K. van der Toorn, "Saul and the Rise of Israelite State Religion," *VT* 43 (1993) 536.

25. McCarter, p. 225. For the view which identifies Gibeah with Geba, see J. M. Miller, "Saul's Rise to Power: Some Observations Concerning 1 Sam 9:1–10:16; 10:26–11:15 and 13:2–14:46," *CBQ* 36 (1974) 157-74; "Geba/Gibeah of Benjamin," *VT* 25 (1975) 145-66.

26. D. V. Edelman, *King Saul in the Historiography of Judah* (JSOTSS 121; Sheffield: Sheffield Academic Press, 1991), p. 702. See D. Edelman, "Saul's Journey through Mt. Ephraim and Samuel's Ramah (1 Sam. 9:4-5; 10:2-5)," *ZDPV* 104 (1988) 44-58.

solution to these problems.[27] In such a situation, individual passages must be dealt with case by case.

3 In this situation Jonathan makes a decisive attack on the Philistine military power. The singular noun *nᵉṣîb* (only here and v. 4) probably refers to a person, either *prefect* (so JPS) or "governor" (NEB), not "garrison" (NRSV; NASB) or "outpost" (NIV), though in the plural the term seems to refer to "garrisons" (10:5; 2 Sam. 8:6, 14); see v. 23 on "garrison" *(maṣṣab).* The assassination of the enemy's governor would have been very effective militarily and probably initiated the long war between Philistia and Israel that lasted throughout Saul's lifetime. See also 10:5.

"Geba": also v. 16.

c. Philistines and the Israelite Troops (13:3b-7a)

3b *And the Philistines heard,*
— Saul blew the horn in all the land —
[one] saying,
"Let the Hebrews hear!"
4 *On the other hand all Israel heard,*
[one] saying,
"Saul struck the prefect of the Philistines
and indeed Israel has become odious to[28] *the Philistines!"*
And the people were summoned (to come) after Saul at Gilgal.
5 *As for the Philistines, they gathered to fight with Israel*
— thirty thousands of chariotry and six thousands of cavalry
and people like the sand on the seashore[29] *in number —*
and came up and encamped at Michmash, east of Beth-awen.
6 *On the other hand, the men of Israel saw how they were in distress,*
for the troops[30] *were hard pressed.*
And the people hid themselves in the caves, in the holes, in the crags, in the underground chambers, and in the pits.
7a *Also some Hebrews crossed the Jordan to the land of Gad, which is Gilead.*

3b After Jonathan's attack on the Philistine *prefect,* the Philistines hear about Saul's movements. The Israelites, however, hear about Jonathan's, in

27. McCarter, p. 225.

28. Ni. "make oneself odious to"; also 27:12; 2 Sam. 10:6; 16:21. See *HALOT,* p. 107.

29. See also 2 Sam. 17:11.

30. *hāʿām;* lit., "the people"; cf. "their army" (NIV).

effect Saul's, attack. MT punctuation suggests: "(3a) And Jonathan struck . . . (3b) and the Philistines heard (about it). As for Saul, he blew the horn . . . , saying." However, the object of the verb "heard" *(wayyišmeʿû)* is probably *[someone] saying Let the Hebrews hear!* as in v. 4; see below.

McCarter thinks that the clause *Saul blew the horn in all the land* is "out of place at this point" and should be placed right before v. 4, since the term "Hebrews" is usually used by foreigners, not by the Israelites.[31] However, R. P. Gordon comments: "The re-ordering of the last two clauses in this verse is unnecessary if we accept the case for literary insertion (AXB) patterns in Biblical Hebrew."[32] This comment is supported by the existence of the expression, "they heard, saying . . . ," in v. 4. What the Philistines heard was *Let the Hebrews hear!* (see below). Just as the direct discourse, *Saul struck . . . and indeed Israel . . . ,* in v. 4 is expressed from the third person's perspective — not phrasing "I struck . . . and indeed you . . ." — so the command *Let the Hebrews hear!* in v. 3b is from the perspective of the Philistines, hence, *the Hebrews.*

Some modern scholars emend the text of MT *Let . . . hear (yišmeʿû)* to *pšʿw* on the basis of LXX *ēthetēkasin* and translate "the Hebrews were in revolt" (NEB; REB); "have revolted";[33] "have rebelled."[34] McCarter thinks that the MT shows "the influence of the intrusive clause about Saul's horn blowing."[35] But *Let the Hebrews hear!* is what the Philistines have overheard, not what they have said or reported (i.e., "The Hebrews have rebelled!" as LXX), just as *Saul struck . . .* is what all Israel have heard. Note that the first speech was delivered by Saul, as the inserted clause *Saul blew the horn in all the land* implies; the latter speech was probably by messengers sent by Saul or other people. Here the two parts of the clause (AB), "one (over)hears (someone) saying" as in Gen. 27:6-7; 1 Sam. 24:10; 2 Sam. 19:2; Isa. 37:9 are separated by a clause telling who spoke (X: "*Saul* blew the horn in all the land"), thus constituting an AXB pattern (see "Introduction" [Section VII, C]).

For a general discussion of the term *the Hebrews,* see on 4:6. It is possible that Saul himself used this expression, and the "Hebrews" here are the group of Israelites who had been serving the Philistines as mercenaries[36] (see 14:21; 29:3). In this interpretation, *Let the Hebrews hear!* would mean "O

31. McCarter, p. 225. On the foreign use of "Hebrews" in the OT, see the comment on 1 Sam. 4:6.

32. R. P. Gordon, p. 342, following D. T. Tsumura, "Literary Insertion (AXB Pattern) in Biblical Hebrew," *VT* 33 (1983) 468-82.

33. McCarter, p. 226.

34. R. P. Gordon, p. 133.

35. McCarter, p. 226.

36. N. K. Gottwald, *The Tribes of Yahweh: A Sociology of the Religion of Liberated Israel, 1250-1050 B.C.E.* (Maryknoll: Orbis Books, 1979), p. 424.

Hebrews, hear and obey (me)." That is, Saul was summoning a certain group of his people, who had been fighting for the Philistines, to join him. Note that the reliefs from Assyrian palaces, such as the Lachish reliefs from Nineveh, depict many non-Assyrian soldiers, wearing a helmet distinct from Assyrian type, fighting for Assyria.[37] Nevertheless, it seems that in the present context the word is used from the Philistines' point of view, and "Hebrews" means almost the same thing as "Israelites"; see v. 19.

4 With the word order *waw*+NP, *all Israel heard* is contrasted with *the Philistines heard* (v. 3b) — hence, *on the other hand.* See also v. 6.

Saul struck — actually by the hand of Jonathan (v. 3a). What Jonathan did for Saul the king is what Saul did. See the similar case where the actions of the Assyrian generals in 2 K. 18:17ff. are credited to their king Sennacherib in his annals (III:18-49).[38] Hence, both v. 3 and v. 4 refer to the one and same attack against the Philistine garrison. However, it is sometimes claimed that these verses belonged to "originally independent traditions," that is, the Saul tradition associated with Gibeah and the Jonathan tradition from Geba.[39] Such a diachronic and tradition-historical approach misunderstands the stylistic characteristics of ancient Near Eastern narratives.

For *Gilgal,* east of Michmash, in the direction of the Jordan, see on 7:16; 10:8; 15:33. Saul's summoning the people to Gilgal, the ancient cultic center, must have had a strategic (military) purpose (see on v. 5) as well as a religious purpose. Saul had been instructed to go to Gilgal and meet Samuel after his private anointing (10:8), and there he had been made king (11:15). Therefore, at this crucial time of the war against the Philistines, Saul might have expected to meet Samuel there to ask for his intercessory prayer and instruction (12:23).

5 The Philistines are said to have gathered with *thirty thousands* (*šᵉlōšîm 'elep;* so NRSV; JPS; NASB; cf. "three thousand" [NIV; McCarter; Klein], following LXX^L; Syr) *of chariotry.* Klein thinks that even 3,000 chariots is far too many considering the terrain at Michmash and Sisera's force of 900 chariots (Judg. 4:3).[40] However, the Philistines probably needed and possessed many more chariots than Sisera of Canaanite Hazor, for they held control over the entire coastal area, that is, the Philistia, through which the major international road, the Via Maris, ran. Alternatively, the phrase could mean

37. See *ANEP,* p. 130.

38. D. D. Luckenbill, *The Annals of Sennacherib* (OIP 2; Chicago: University of Chicago Press, 1924), pp. 32-34. For the most recent study of Senacherib's campaign to Jerusalem, see W. R. Gallagher, *Sennacherib's Campaign to Judah: New Studies* (Leiden: E. J. Brill, 1999).

39. See Klein, pp. 124-25.

40. Klein, p. 126.

"thirty units"[41] of chariotry. According to Yadin, the Philistines had three-man chariots.[42]

According to v. 2, Saul led *two thousands at Michmash.* The Philistines were encamped there with a huge army (see also v. 16). This suggests that Saul had given up Michmash and retreated to the eastern city of Gilgal.

Hosea refers to Bethel ("house of God") as *Beth-awen* (lit., "house of iniquity"; e.g., 4:15; cf. Amos 5:5), but Stoebe (p. 244) is probably right in favoring "Beth Aven to the east of Bethel," near Ai (Josh. 7:2).

6 In contrast (*On the other hand; waw* +NP; also v. 4) to their enemy, the Israelite troops were hard pressed.

How they were in distress (lit., "for/that it was narrow for him"; *kî ṣar-lô;* also 1 Sam. 28:15) means "that they were in trouble" (JPS); "that their situation was critical" (NIV).[43] The term *niggaś* (*were hard pressed;* also 14:24) has often been taken as an ancient variant, which is conflated with *ṣar-lô.*[44] However, two usages of the particle *kî* seems to function differently, that is, *how* and *for.* Also, the term *hāʿām* is used twice in this verse, once referring to the *troops* and another to the ordinary *people.*

Most scholars emend MT *ḥăwāḥîm,* usually translated as "thickets," to *hwrym,* "holes," following the suggestion of Ewald. On the other hand, McCarter keeps the MT as original since it is the *lectio difficilior.* Compare the LXX *mandrais,* "enclosed spaces," "enclosures."[45] However, the MT may be supported by Ugar. *ḫḫ* (*KTU* 1.4 VIII 13) "opening, hole" and mean "holes."[46]

There were many caves in Palestine that could provide a refuge for people in danger. David used caves when hiding from Saul (22:1; 24:3). From the writings on the wall of a cave near Lachish, it seems some people hid there from the Babylonians in 588-586.[47]

7a In the expression *the land of Gad, which is Gilead, waw* is taken as *waw* explicative (which is); see above on v. 2 and compare "the land of Gad and Gilead" (NRSV; NASB; NIV). Note that the lands of Gad and Reuben made up Gilead, the Israelite lands east of the Jordan (see Josh. 13:24-28).

Why the verse uses the word *Hebrews* here is a problem. One possible

41. See the comment on 6:19 (above).

42. Y. Yadin, *The Art of Warfare in Biblical Lands,* 2 vols. (New York: McGraw-Hill, 1963), pp. 250, 336.

43. See BDB, pp. 864, 1126; *HAL,* p. 990; *HALOT,* p. 1058. See also 30:6; 2 Sam. 13:2.

44. McCarter, p. 226.

45. McCarter, p. 226; also R. P. Gordon, p. 133.

46. See Pardee in *CS,* I, p. 264, n. 197; Caquot and Sznycer, *TO,* I, p. 220, n. g. Also see *HALOT,* p. 296.

47. See McCarter, p. 228, for samples and bibliography.

interpretation of the word is that they were Philistine mercenaries, but it is hard to think of a reason why they in particular would have fled clear to the Transjordan.

d. Saul Waits Seven Days at Gilgal (13:7b-9)

7b *As for Saul, he was still at Gilgal, while all the troops went trembling after him.*
8 *And he waited [on God] seven days to the appointed feast when Samuel would be there, but Samuel did not come to Gilgal.*
And the troops scattered from his side.
9 *And Saul said,*
"Bring the burnt offering and the peace offerings to me!"
and offered the burnt offering.

7b-15a It is often held by scholars that at v. 8 the older record of Saul's hostilities with the Philistines is interrupted by the insertion of a separate account of Samuel's accusation of Saul. Some say that 13:8a refers to Samuel's instructions in 10:8, where Saul was told to wait at Gilgal until Samuel arrived.[48] Some scholars even get around the chronological problems by arguing that the historian has chosen to ignore them.[49]

However, the literary link between Samuel's instructions in 10:8 and the incident in 13:8ff. has been somewhat overemphasized. First, many years separate the two events. In 10:8 Saul was a young man, possibly single, still living in his father's house; now in ch. 13 he is king of Israel and has his grown-up son Jonathan. When compared carefully, the following points are common between 10:8 and 13:8-9:

to wait seven days at Gilgal
until Samuel comes = to the appointed time when Samuel appears
to sacrifice the burnt offerings and the peace offerings.

If the act of "waiting" is not simply to wait for Samuel but to carry out a religious activity, as discussed above (see on 10:8), the command "to wait seven days at Gilgal" could have been given to any person at any time. In other words, to wait on God for seven days at Gilgal may have been a religious custom among the Israelites of Saul's time. And if we take into consid-

48. See S. S. Yonick, "The Rejection of Saul: A Study of Sources," *AJBA* 4 (1971) 30-31; Stoebe, pp. 210-11; also H. Donner, "Basic Elements of Old Testament Historiography Illustrated by the Saul Traditions," *OTWSA* 24 (1981) 52.

49. Birch, p. 1071.

eration that Samuel visited Gilgal annually after visiting Bethel (see 7:16), and if he sacrificed both burnt offerings and the peace offerings, the references in 10:8 and in 13:8 are not necessarily to the same occasion. People could "wait on God at Gilgal for seven days" on many occasions. Though Baldwin holds that Samuel may have undertaken "always to come within seven days in any time of crisis," there is seemingly no crisis in 10:8. It is more significant that both events happened at the same place, Gilgal; Saul was about to be rejected at the very place where he was made king in 11:15.

While Birch has underscored the "annalistic style of 13:2-7a, 15b-18, 23," by noting their concrete detail, lack of dialogue, and compact style and has identified vv. 8-14 to be "a prophetic oracle of judgment against an individual," Klein supports Veijola, who has assigned "the present form of vv 7b-15a to a deuteronomistic redaction (DtrN)."[50] However, discourse analysis of vv. 1-23 based on verbal sequences discloses an entirely different understanding of the literary structure:

SETTING (summary statement)

v. 1	NP-NP; AdvPh *qtl* ("[Saul] ruled")

EVENT: what Saul and Jonathan did

v. 2	*wayqtl* ("Saul chose") . . . *wayhy* . . . *qtl* (*hyh) *qtl* ("he sent")
v. 3a	*wayqtl* ("Jonathan struck")

SETTING: contrast between the two groups

v. 3b	*wayqtl* ("Philistine heard") — *qtl* ("Saul blew") — (saying) . . .
v. 4	*w* + NP *qtl* ("all Israel heard") . . . *wayqtl* ("the people were summoned")
v. 5	*w* + NP *qtl* ("[the Philistines] gathered") *wayqtl* ("came up") *wayqtl* ("encamped")
v. 6	*w* + NP *qtl* ("the men of Israel saw") . . . *wayqtl* ("the people hid themselves")
v. 7a	*w* + NP *qtl* ("Hebrews crossed")
v. 7b	*w* + NP (S: "Saul [was]") *w* + NP *qtl* ("all the troops went trembling")

50. Birch, p. 1071; Klein, p. 124. See T. Veijola, *Die ewige Dynastie: David und die Entstehung seiner Dynastie nach der deuteronomistischen Darstellung* (AASF. Series B 193; Helsinki: Suomalainen Tiedeakatemia, 1975), pp. 55-57.

EVENT: what Saul and the troops did
v. 8 *wayqtl* ("he waited")
w + neg. *qtl* ("Samuel did not come")
wayqtl ("the troops scattered")
v. 9 *wayqtl* ("Saul said")
wayqtl ("offered [the burnt offering]")

transition: Samuel came to Gilgal
v. 10 *wayhy* (Temp-phrase) *w-hinne qtl* ("Samuel came")
wayqtl ("Saul went out")

dialogue: between Samuel and Saul
vv. 11-12 *wayqtl* ("Samuel said")
wayqtl ("Saul said")
vv. 13-14 *wayqtl* ("Samuel said")

transition: Samuel went up from Gilgal
v. 15a *wayqtl* ("Samuel arose") *wayqtl* ("and went up")

EVENT: what Saul did: counted the troops
v. 15b *wayqtl* ("Saul counted the troops")
v. 16 SETTING: Israel at Geba and the Philistines at Michmash
vv. 17-18 transition: the Philistine raiders in three groups
vv. 19-22 <embedded discourse> the Philistine monopoly of metal
v. 23 transition: the Philistine garrison came out

Verses 4-7 (five-fold repetition of *w*+NP *qtl*) provide the SETTING of the narrative, followed by two sets of *wayqtl* in v. 8, which initiate the new EVENTs: about what Saul did ("he waited") and what the troops did ("scattered"). The mention of Gilgal in v. 7b refers back to v. 4. Then, in v. 9, another of Saul's actions follows introduced by *wayqtl:* "and offered the burnt offering." Between Samuel's arrival ("came") in v. 10 and his departure ("went up from Gilgal") in v. 15, there is a dialogue between Samuel and Saul. Saul's counting the troops after Samuel's departure (v. 15b) points back to the on-going fact that the troops had been scattering away from Saul (also v. 11, where it is mentioned as Saul's first excuse to Samuel).

These features rather support reading the entire section of ch. 13 as a literary whole, so in the light of this structure it is not warranted to take vv. 7b-15a as a later redaction.

7b Saul had summoned the people to Gilgal earlier (see v. 4) and *he was still* there, despite the overwhelming difficulties. The narrator tries to convey the idea that Saul was desperately seeking God's oracle at this cultic center before fighting against the Philistines so that he waited until the scheduled (appointed) time when Samuel "was supposed to be" (see below) at Gilgal.

The present reference to Gilgal functions as a connection between v. 4 and v. 8; note this is the most frequent GN in this section so far; three times in eight verses and five times (vv. 4, 7, 8, 12, 15) in this chapter.

8 For *he waited [on God] for seven days,* see 10:8 *(seven days you shall wait).* Here, the purpose of his waiting for seven days is probably for consecration (i.e., *waiting on God*) before going out for battle[51] (see 21:4-5).

Recently Klingbeil studied the significance of the "seven days" period in the OT. According to him, in 10:8 Saul "is to offer sacrifices of well-being for seven days" after his appointment as king over Israel. "The question is whether this formed part of the 'official' ceremony of anointing a king or whether it is only a 'casual' temporal specification. The usage of seven days does suggest a cultic relevance."[52] Here, in 13:8, Saul had to wait for seven days for Samuel's arrival in the camp.[53]

The *appointed feast (môʿēd)* here is usually interpreted as "the time set by Samuel" (NIV) or "the time appointed by Samuel" (NRSV). These translations emphasize that the time was specifically set by Samuel. McCarter even supplies *ʾmr* after *ʾăšer,* translating "the time Samuel had

51. See Yonick, "The Rejection of Saul," p. 31, n. 2.

52. G. A. Klingbeil, "Ritual Time in Leviticus 8 with Special Reference to the Seven Day Period in the Old Testament," *ZAW* 109 (1997) 506, n. 22.

53. Other occurrences of "seven days" in 1-2 Samuel are:

11:3 — <Temporal/Historical> — Elders of Jabesh ask for seven days respite;
31:13 — <Cultic> (also 1 Chr. 10:12) — Men of Jabesh bury Saul and his sons and fast for seven days; also Gen 50:10.

According to Klingbeil, 70 out of 85 times the "seven days" period has a cultic (mourning, cleansing, consecration, etc.) significance. Cf. J. Milgrom, *Leviticus 1-16* (AB 3; New York: Doubleday, 1991), p. 234, on the number seven in OT. The significance of the "seven days" period may be as follows:

(1) seven days "in order to be complete"
(2) transitional characteristics — bridge a gap or fulfill a specific purpose
(3) a seven-day period of separation — the *rite of passage* character of the ritual of ordination — transition and separation
(4) the purification aspect of the seven-day periods.

Klingbeil summarizes "the common denominator for the seven day period" as "the transitional character of the associated event(s)" and that period "had to be completed in order for the ritual to be considered consummated." See Klingbeil, "Ritual Time in Leviticus 8," p. 513.

stipulated" (lit., "the appointed time that Samuel had said") on the basis of the LXX, Targ.[54] None of these suggestions is really satisfactory. For one thing, supplying a verb other than the copula in any clause is a speculative business.

Althann, on the other hand, takes *'ăšer* as substantive, "the one who/ which": thus, "the one of Samuel," hence "Samuel's."[55] However, similar syntax, that is, *'ăšer* followed simply by a proper noun, can be seen in 1 K. 11:25: *wᵉ'et-hārā'āh 'ăšer hădād* "the trouble caused by Hadad" (NIV; JPS), "the evil that Hadad did" (NASB). In both cases it is reasonable to assume that the copula is understood after the relative pronoun *'ăšer;* hence, the translation *when Samuel would be there* can be suggested for our passage.

As for the term *mô'ēd* (lit., "the appointed time"), it refers to a date on the established cultic calendar, set by the Lord (see Ex. 9:5; 23:15; Lev. 23:2; etc.) and is translated *the appointed feast.* So, it is likely that everybody knew when Samuel was supposed to be in Gilgal,[56] which he visited annually (1 Sam. 7:16). In fact, the phrase *at the appointed yearly feast* (lit., "the appointed time of the days") is used by Saul later in v. 11. For yearly feasts, see also 20:6. If this is correct, the text has nothing to do with a personal appointment Samuel made with Saul (see 9:24; 13:11; also 20:35).

9 It was probably Samuel's usual practice to offer *the burnt offering and the peace offerings* whenever he visited this cultic center; see 1 Sam. 10:8.[57] What Saul did is what Samuel was supposed to do (see below, v. 13, on the reason of Saul's blame). However, Saul has offered just *the burnt offering,* not yet the peace offerings.

It is often said that Saul's failure in 13:8f. comes from his disobedience to Samuel's command to "wait" back in 10:8, where the flow of the narrative is suspended. Donner even holds that 10:8 "appears to be an annotation to explain which of Yahweh's commands (13:13) Saul actually broke." On

54. McCarter, p. 226.

55. R. Althann, "Northwest Semitic Notes on Some Texts in 1 Samuel," *JNSL* 12 (1984) 31.

56. M. D. Fowler rejects the idea that Gilgal was a shrine of either Israelite or pre-Israelite origins since "although Gilgal in time may have become an important Israelite sanctuary, it is likely that it served Joshua's followers initially as a rest-place following their desert wanderings, and not as a shrine of either Israelite or pre-Israelite origins. The Hebrew text makes no mention of a permanent structure of any kind having stood at Gilgal at the time of the Conquest, apart from the 12 memorial stones erected by Joshua. Nor is the offering of *šelamim* in the narrative of I Sam 11,15 any necessary indication of a permanent cultic site at Gilgal . . ." ("The Meaning of *lipne YHWH* in the Old Testament," *ZAW* 99 [1987] 388, also 390). However, it is reasonable to think that the three cities Samuel visited annually — Bethel, Gilgal, and Mizpah — were cultic centers (see 7:16). For various local cultic places, see 9:12 (Ramah); 16:1f. (Bethlehem); and 15:33 (Gilgal).

57. See McCarter, p. 228.

the other hand, V. P. Long advocates that this is an example of "the *literary* gap created by the *literal* gap between Saul's first charge and its eventual fulfillment."[58] However, Saul's "waiting" seems to have a religious significance, not just to be the act of waiting for Samuel's arrival, as noted above, so it could well have been repeated. The fact that 10:8 and 13:8 both refer to Gilgal does not show that they deal with a continuing event.

e. Saul and Samuel (13:10-15)

10 *When he finished offering the burnt offering, just at that moment Samuel came.*[59]
And Saul went out toward him to greet him.
11 *And Samuel said,*
"What have you done?"
And Saul said,
"When I saw that the troops were scattered[60] *from beside me*
and that, as for you, you did not come
at the appointed yearly feast
though the Philistines were gathering at Michmash,
12 *I thought*[61]
'Now the Philistines will come down to me at Gilgal,
but the favor of the Lord I have not entreated!'
and compelled myself to offer the burnt offering."
13 *And Samuel said to Saul,*
"You have acted foolishly![62]
You have not kept the commandment of the Lord, your God,
which he commanded you!
For,[63] *now,*
the Lord would have established your kingdom over Israel forever!
14 *But, now, your kingdom will not endure!*
The Lord has sought out for himself a man of his choice.

58. V. P. Long, "How Did Saul Become King? Literary Reading and Historical Reconstruction," in *Faith, Tradition, and History: Old Testament Historiography in Its Near Eastern Context,* ed. A. R. Millard, J. K. Hoffmeier, and D. W. Baker (Winona Lake, Ind.: Eisenbrauns, 1994), p. 281.

59. *wᵉhinnēh šᵉmû'ēl bā';* lit., "behold, Samuel came."

60. Qal *npṣ (similar to Ni. *pwṣ); cf. intransitive Hi. in v. 8.

61. Lit., "I said."

62. *niskāltā;* also 26:21; 2 Sam. 24:10.

63. The reason for the preceding utterance: "You have acted foolishly!" For this "speaker-oriented" *kî,* see "Introduction" (Section V, C).

And the Lord has commanded him as prince over his people,
for you have not kept what the Lord commanded to you."
15 *And Samuel arose and went up from Gilgal to Gibeah of Benjamin.*
And Saul counted the troops who were with him, namely, some
six hundred men.

10-12 Saul has just finished offering the *burnt offering* when Samuel arrives at Gilgal. Saul goes out to greet Samuel, and when Samuel asks what he has done, Saul makes excuses which seem totally legitimate: (1) the troops were scattered; (2) Samuel had not come; (3) the Philistines were gathering, even coming down to Gilgal; (4) yet, he had not entreated the Lord's favor. His first concern is that the troops had been scattering away from him; hence, he made this excuse to Samuel. But Saul judged the situation according to what he *saw,* not by faith in the Lord. Note the sharp contrast between Saul here and Jonathan in ch. 14: while Saul is concerned with the reduction in his troops, Jonathan does not concern himself about the great number of the enemy and totally depends upon the Lord (14:6).

11 For the phrase *the appointed yearly feast,* see the comment on v. 8.

12 Saul puts his own thought or judgment over the word of the Lord through Samuel. What he was supposed to wait for was not simply Samuel's physical presence but Samuel's intercession and instruction (12:23). Saul acted according to what he observed, not by what the Lord commanded, though no specific command is mentioned in the context; see on v. 13.

Entreated . . . the favor of (*ḥlh (Pi.) *pānîm*) means "to soften by caressing": to appease, flatter (*HALOT,* p. 317); cf. "make the face of any one sweet or pleasant" (BDB, p. 318). Saul's concern could be "pious or prudential; no king liked going into battle without first seeking favourable omens."[64]

13-14 Saul's disobedience to the commandment of the Lord, whatever it might have been (see below), brought a serious result: the cessation of his kingdom, for in Israel the kingship itself was under the authority of the word of God. Even though David is not anointed until ch. 16, the *man of his choice* has been already been decided by the Lord. While Saul's kingdom will not endure, the kingship of God has been firmly established from eternity; see "Introduction" (Section IX, A). Shortly God will choose another "deputy" for his kingdom.

13 The incident reaches its climax in Samuel's abrupt indictment of Saul, which takes the form of an announcement of judgment.[65]

64. R. P. Gordon, p. 134.

65. Cf. B. C. Birch, *The Rise of the Israelite Monarchy: The Growth and Development of I Samuel 7–15* (SBLDS 27; Missoula, Mont.: Scholars Press, 1976), pp. 82-83.

"You have acted foolishly!
You have not kept the commandment of the Lord, your God,
which he commanded you!"

Here Samuel harshly criticizes Saul's action as foolish. Was it because Saul usurped Samuel's priestly right by offering the burnt offering himself? Samuel does not say so. Or, did Saul break a specific commandment of the Lord? Then, which commandment? No answer is given in the immediate context of ch. 13.

Because of this, many hypotheses have been offered. According to one view (G. E. Wright; Klein),[66] Saul the king was usurping the role assigned to Samuel as the prophet in holy war. Before the introduction of the monarchy, that is, before the transition from judgeship to kingship, it was Samuel the judge who offered sacrifices (7:9). And it was customary to seek God's permission before entering into a holy war (e.g., Judg. 20:23; 1 Sam. 7:9; 14:8-10, 37; 23:2, 4, 9-12; 28:6; 30:7-8; 2 Sam. 5:19, 23). Saul's offering of sacrifices left no room for Samuel to seek God's oracle in preparation for the holy war. It may be that Saul did not offend any specific commandment as in ch. 15; but his lack of trust, going out for war without first seeking God's will through Samuel the prophet, was possibly the real issue here.

Another view is that Saul's fault was in assuming a dual role as king and priest. According to this view, he usurped Samuel's priestly prerogative by precipitately offering the appointed sacrifices (see 10:8). But R. P. Gordon rejects this view on the basis of 14:33-35, where Saul's altar building and sacrifices are favorably noted, as well as on the basis of 2 Sam. 8:18; 20:26; 1 K. 3:3; 8:62f.[67] However, the offense could have been Saul's offering by himself without the agency of priest. In cases of David and Solomon, presumably a priest would have been involved, even if it is not mentioned explicitly; for one thing, David could not have offered a great number of "burnt offerings and peace offerings" by himself any more than he could have pitched a tent for the ark by himself even if the text says "the tent which David had pitched for it" (2 Sam. 6:17). Solomon could not have "offered a thousand burnt offerings" (1 K. 3:4; also 8:63) by himself; an involvement of many priests is reasonably assumed. And, for the private rituals of the royal family, David could appoint his own sons to the priesthood (2 Sam. 8:18), and he had his personal "priest" (20:26).[68] Therefore, in the cases of David

66. See Klein, p. 127.

67. R. P. Gordon, pp. 133-34.

68. Note that in ancient Canaan the king performed some rituals as a priest, especially the royal monthly rituals; however, as far as the extant Ugaritic ritual texts are concerned, in official or national liturgies, it seems that priestly personnel performed the rituals even though the king was present. See D. T. Tsumura, "Kings and Cults in Ancient

and Solomon, there was no necessity for them to offer sacrifice by themselves. But, it is possible that here, in 1 Samuel 13, Saul sacrificed the offerings by himself without priests, though there are priests with him in ch. 14 and they probably would have carried out the sacrifices if it was thought necessary.

The command can hardly have been the one in 10:8, "to wait seven days at Gilgal." That was probably over ten years earlier, and Saul had presumably kept the command, for after that Samuel officially made him king before the Lord at Gilgal (11:15).

If the text does not refer to any specific occasion, the Lord's commandment must have concerned itself with the nature and status of Saul as the king. The king should "carry out" (see on 15:11) the word of God as the representative of the people at all times, especially at the time of going out for a holy war. As the speech of Samuel (12:20-25) shows, the king is to be under the control of God's word, and the dual role of the prophet is to intercede and instruct the king and the people. In this regard, Saul the king is commanded to listen to the word of Samuel the prophet. Therefore, the "foolishness" of Saul might possibly be not so much in his sacrificing the burnt offering as his failure to acknowledge the prophet's higher role as the divine messenger and to listen to the word of God. Rejecting the word of the Lord was the cause of Saul's total rejection from his throne (see 15:11, 13, 19, 22, 23).

The same term *established* (*kwn) is used by Saul for the establishment of Jonathan's kingship (20:31), of David as king (2 Sam. 5:12), of the throne and kingdom of David and his offspring (7:12-13, 16), of God's people (7:24) and of David's house (7:26).

Here is introduced a "new motif" in 1 Samuel which foreshadows the dynastic promise in 2 Samuel 7.[69] Samuel suggests here (1 Sam. 13:13) that an eternal dynasty or kingdom could have been established for Saul if he had kept the Lord's commandment. Note that the idea of an "eternal kingdom" was not foreign to Israel even in the early stage of the monarchy.[70]

14 The expression *your kingdom will not endure (mamlakt^{e}kā lōʾ-tāqûm)* suggests that Saul cannot establish a dynasty, let alone an eternal dynasty (see *forever* in v. 13) — his son will not succeed him. In addition, in 15:23 Saul himself will be rejected from being king.

Ugarit," in *Priests and Officials in the Ancient Near East,* ed. K. Watanabe (Heidelberg: C. Winter, 1999), pp. 215-38. Also "Introduction" (Section IV, C, 4).

69. Birch, p. 1071.

70. See A. Laato, *A Star Is Rising: The Historical Development of the Old Testament Royal Ideology and the Rise of the Jewish Messianic Expectations* (Atlanta: Scholars Press, 1997); "Second Samuel 7 and Ancient Near Eastern Royal Theology," *CBQ* 59 (1997) 244-69. On this theme, see "Introduction" to the commentary on 2 Samuel.

The verb *biqqēš* (*has sought out;* so NRSV; NIV) is "prophetic perfect," though it is sometimes translated as "will seek out" (JPS). The phrase *a man of his choice* (lit., "a man according to his heart") refers to David, described as *"your neighbor" (rēʿăkā)* in 15:28. The term *commanded* (*ṣwh) is repeated twice in this single verse. The Lord requires and so chooses as king one who keeps his commandments. See on 15:28; 18:8. For *prince (nāgîd)* see 9:16.

15 After this declaration to Saul, Samuel leaves Gilgal for *Gibeah.* Following the LXX, the NRSV has: "And Samuel left and went on his way from Gilgal. The rest of the people followed Saul to join the army; they went up from Gilgal toward Gibeah of Benjamin." Recent scholars (McCarter, p. 227, Klein, p. 122, R. P. Gordon, p. 134) take the longer text of LXX as original, claiming the MT suffered "homoioteleuton" (merging). While in the MT it is Samuel who *went up* to Gibeah, in the longer text it is Saul and his army who *went up* to Gibeah. But Samuel might have gone up to Gibeah of Benjamin because the southern route, which leads from Gilgal to Gibeah, was the only safe way to the territory of Benjamin now that the Philistine army had occupied the Michmash area; see v. 16 (below).

"Counted" *(wayyipqōd)* can also be "numbered" (BDB, p. 823; also 11:8; 14:17; 2 Sam 24:2, 4) or "mustered" (McCarter, p. 225). After this sharp denunciation of his conduct by the prophet who had anointed him king over Israel (vv. 13-14), Saul's primary and only concern was the number of troops with which he had to face the enormous Philistine army. His troops now number *six hundred men,* which is only 20 percent of the original number, since the men kept deserting (v. 8b).

f. Philistine Raiders and Garrison (13:16-23)

The literary structure of this entire section is as follows: v. 16 functions as the SETTING, with a participial phrase; then the first *wayqtl* expression *and . . . came out* follows in v. 17; the same verbal phrase *came out* appears in v. 23 after a long embedded discourse (vv. 19-22). Since the verb "to come out" is a movement verb, the phrases in vv. 17 and 23 are still "transitional" to the main EVENT in ch. 14, while they are EVENTs in relation to the preceding SETTING (v. 16). On the "principle of relativity" in discourse structure, see "Introduction" (VI, A). The word *garrison,* a key word of the following chapter, appears in v. 23 as a "linkage" between this section and the following.

SETTING 16 *(Now Saul . . .)*
transitional EVENT
17-18 *(And the raiders came out . . .)*
EMBEDDED DISCOURSE

19-20 *(Now no metal worker is found . . .)*
21 explanatory
22 *(On a day of war . . .)*
transitional EVENT
23 *(And a Philistine garrison came out . . .)*

(1) Raiders Come Out (13:16-18)

16 *Now Saul, his son Jonathan and the troops who were with them were staying in Geba of Benjamin, while the Philistines encamped in Michmash.*
17 *And the raiders came out of the camp of the Philistines in three divisions —*
one division was taking the Ophrah road
toward the land of Shual;
18 *one division was taking the Beth-horon road;*
one division was taking the border road,
overlooking the valley of Zeboim, toward the wilderness.

16 Saul and the Israelite troops are now staying in Geba, while the Philistines on the other hand are in Michmash. Note that at the beginning of the campaign their positions were reversed; see vv. 2-3. Both MT *gebaʿ binyāmīn* and LXX *Gabee Beniamin* clearly point to *Geba,* not Gibeah (v. 15). Geba is situated only a mile or two away from Michmash, separated from it by a deep ravine — a narrow but strategically important pass from the Jordan Valley into the Ephraimite hills. The Philistine army was stationed at the hilltop that overlooks the ravine from the north, while Saul's army was encamped to the south.[71] For Michmash, see on v. 2 and on 14:1.

17 McCarter alters the verbal form *wayyēṣēʾ (wayqtl: came out)* to <*waw*+pf.>, "a converted perfect expressing repeated action in the past," "in view of the succeeding imperfects,"[72] and translates: "From time to time . . . came out." However, this sequence of "imperfects," *yqtl* verbs *(yipneh)* in vv. 17b-18, is a list-like expression of an explanatory discourse type. It is thus a narrative off the main line and uses *yqtl* verbs. As noted above, in the literary structure, v. 23 recapitulates v. 17 and functions as a transition to the following section. McCarter's view that vv. 17-22 is the SETTING and v. 23 is "the story's first verb in the converted imperfect," which begins the action, is

71. McCarter, p. 237. See further H. J. Stoebe, "Zur Topographie und Üerlieferung der Schlacht von Mikmas, 1 Sam. 13 und 14," *TZ* 21 (1965) 269-80, esp. 271-72, 275-76.

72. McCarter, p. 234.

based on his emendation of the *wayqtl* verb *(wayyēṣē')* here; hence, his argument is circular.

The term *the raiders (hammašḥît)* is from the root "to destroy." Such "a mobile professional military unit, which included chariotry" was sent to repress any attempt at rebellion; see also in 14:15. In this way, the Philistines adopted "the Egyptian political system of the previous period"; they also "conscripted auxiliary units from among the local population" (see 14:21) like the Egyptians.[73] For threefold *divisions* (lit., "heads"), see on 11:11. The Philistines sent military units to the north, west, and east in order to raid the surrounding countryside. The use of the numeral "one" without the article in *one division (hārō'š 'eḥād;* lit., "the head one") is typical of a list-like expression; see on 6:17.

The *Ophrah road (derek 'oprāh)* is the road to Ophrah; see on 10:2. Ophrah is listed among Benjamite cities in Josh. 18:23. McCarter identifies it with the Ephron in 2 Chr. 13:19 and the Ephraim in 2 Sam. 13:23; it may be modern et-Taiyibeh, approximately 5 miles north of Mukhmas (ancient Michmash) and 4 miles northeast of Beitin (ancient Bethel). McCarter identifies Shual with "Shaalim" in 1 Sam. 9:4.[74]

18 The name *Beth-horon* probably means "house of the god Horon" (see Ugar. *ḥrn; UT* §19.898), like "Beth-shemesh," which is originally "the house of the god Shemesh." One division went westward, following the road from Bethel to Philistia, which went past *Beth-horon.*

The third division *was taking the border road* which leads to the border of the tribal territory of Benjamin. The *valley of Zeboim* was toward the east or southeast in light of the phrase *toward the wilderness.* McCarter suggests "the Valley of Hyenas," probably the modern Wadi Abu Daba', southeast of Mukhmas.[75]

(2) Philistine Monopoly of Metal (13:19-22)

For the literary structure of this, see above. This embedded discourse serves to demonstrate how great the Lord's victory was through Jonathan (see ch. 14), especially given the paucity of weapons.

19 *Now no metal worker was found in all the land of Israel, for the Philistines thought*
that the Hebrews should not make swords or spears.

73. Mazar, "The Philistines and the Rise of Israel and Tyre," in *The Early Biblical Period,* p. 73; B. Mazar, *Biblical Israel: State and People,* ed. S. Ahituv (Jerusalem: Magnes Press, 1992), p. 34.

74. McCarter, p. 238.

75. McCarter, p. 238.

20 *So all Israel used to go down*[76] *to the Philistines*
to sharpen each one's plowshare, mattocks, axes, or sickles.
21 *— The price was a paim for sickles and mattocks*
and for three picks and for axes
and for fixing the goad —
22 *On the day of war neither swords nor spears were available*[77]
in the hands of all the people who were with Saul and Jonathan;
they[78] *were available to Saul and his son Jonathan.*

19 On the highly developed iron metal industry, see on the Philistines in the "Introduction" (Section IV, B, 2). According to Margalith, *A-pe-ke-e,* a city in the kingdom of Pylos, the "homeland" of the Philistines, was a center of metalworkers and armorers.[79] There are several other references in the Bible to the importance of iron, such as the Canaanite iron chariots in Judg. 1:19 and the mention of the deportation by the Babylonians of "craftsmen and smiths" in 2 K. 24:14, 16. Some Iron Age iron plows have been discovered.[80]

For *the Hebrews,* the expression used by non-Israelite people, see 4:6.

The word pair *swords or spears* appears also in 13:22; 17:45, 47; in reverse order, in 21:8. The fact that the Israelites did not have "swords and spears" suggests that any victory for them would come from the Lord. See David's words to Goliath: "it is not by sword or spear that the Lord saves; for the battle is the Lord's" (17:47).

20 For *sickles* (*maḥărēšātô;* so NRSV; NIV), McCarter reads *ḥrmšw* based on the LXX *(drepanon),* as suggested by Wellhausen, p. 84, and S. R. Driver, p. 104. Compare "colters" (JPS) and "hoe" (NASB). Note a slightly different form for "plowshare" *maḥăraštô* in the same verse.[81]

76. *wayqtl,* denoting a habitual action in the past.

77. *nimṣā';* lit., "were found"; <perfect>, here as a stative/resultative; note that a m.s. verb is followed by a f.s. noun as a subject.

78. Lit., "she" (f.s.) = "sword" (f.)

79. O. Margalith, "Where Did the Philistines Come From?" *ZAW* 107 (1995) 107.

80. On the origins of ironworking in the ancient Near East, see P. R. S. Moorey, "The Craft of the Metalsmith in the Ancient Near East: The Origins of Ironworking," in *From Gulf to Delta and Beyond,* ed. E. D. Oren (Beer-Sheva 8; Beersheva: Ben-Gurion University of the Negev Press, 1995), pp. 53-68.

81. McCarter holds that "the corruption of *ḥrmšw* to *mḥrštw* is easier to understand" (McCarter, p. 234). Recently S. L. Cook, "The Text and Philology of 1 Samuel xiii 20-1," *VT* 44 (1994) 250-54, explained the two terms *maḥăraštô* ("plowshare") and *maḥărēšātô* as "a homonymic phenomenon" from two different forms of the *mem*-preformative nouns, **maqtalt-* form of the verbal root *ḥrṯ ("plow") and **maqtilat-* form of the verbal root *ḥrš ("craft"). According to him, these two terms are placed in the parallel order of v. 20 and v. 21: i.e., "his plowshare" — "his mattock" — "his axe" — **maqtilat-* form of the verbal root *ḥrš ("craft")//**maqtilat-* form of the verbal root *ḥrš

21 The term *pᵉṣîrāh* is a *hapax legomenon,* whose meaning *price* is a guess from context. The term *paim (pîm),* literally, "two mouths, parts" (dual), denotes "two thirds of a shekel."[82] It appears only here in the OT, but a number of inscribed stone weights marked *pym* have been found; their average weight is 7.616 grams. Sharpening anything in the list costs one *paim* weight of silver.

The phrase *three picks (šᵉlōš qillᵉšôn)* has been translated "three-pronged forks" (JPS), "the forks" (NASB), "one-third of a shekel for sharpening" (NRSV; also Klein), "a third of a shekel for sharpening forks" (NIV), "a third of a shekel for picks" (McCarter), and *treis sikloi eis ton odonta* "three shekels for the tooth" (LXX). McCarter holds that both the MT and LXX preserve "corrupt remnants."[83] On the *hapax legomenon qillᵉšôn,* see *HALOT,* p. 1107. For "a three-pronged fork," see *hammazlēg šᵉlōš-haššinnayim* (2:13). It may also mean "became three q. [monetary unit?]."

22 The expression *On the day of war . . .* literally means "So it would happen on the day of war. . . ." It denotes "So whenever there was a battle. . . ." The LXX adds "Michmash," but if "the battle of Michmash" is meant, *wayhy* is to be preferred to *whyh* (so McCarter, p. 235). On this "abnormal" usage of *whyh,* see on 1:12. *Milḥemet,* "war," is in the construct form instead of the genitive; the form appears only here.

(3) The Garrison Comes Out (13:23)

23 *And the Philistine garrison came out toward Michmash[84] Pass.*

23 The term *garrison* (*maṣṣab;* see on 14:1) is similar to *nᵉṣîb* (pl.) in 10:5; 2 Sam. 8:6, 14 (cf. "outpost": McCarter, p. 232). Apparently, while the three divisions went raiding, the garrison, the main body, went to Michmash Pass *(maʿăbar mikmāś),* which connects Michmash and Geba. The term *maṣṣab* is a key word in ch. 14, occurring five times (vv. 1, 4, 6, 11, 15; also cf. 12 [*maṣṣābāh*]); so, in this verse it functions as a transitional technique linking this chapter with ch. 14; Ab/B pattern (see "Introduction" [Section VI, B]).

Thus, the story continues into the next chapter.

("craft") — "the mattocks" — "the forks" — "the axes" — "the goad point." Hence, he translates the last item of v. 20 as "his goad," while the first item of v. 21 as "the plowshares." However, since these two terms are simply the s. and pl. f. forms of the same noun, his solution is not without problems.

82. *ANEP,* fig. 776a; A. Millard, *Treasures from Bible Times* (Tring: Lion Publishing, 1985), p. 116; *CS,* II, p. 209; see T. C. Mitchell, *The Bible in the British Museum: Interpreting the Evidence* (London: British Museum Publications, 1988), Document 37. See "Weights and Measures" in *ABD,* VI, pp. 897-908, esp. "F. Weight."

83. McCarter, p. 235.

84. *mikmāś* (BHS): Michmas.

2. Saul and Jonathan (14:1-46)

This chapter has been noted as one of the finest examples of Hebrew narrative prose: "a masterpiece of narrative storytelling."[1] The account of the war between Saul and the Philistines continues into this chapter with a reference to the "garrison" mentioned in the last chapter. Indeed, McCarter treats 13:16–14:23a as a literary unit, but there is still a formal difference between the two chapters. With the key word "garrison" *(maṣṣab)* in 13:23 appearing in this chapter in vv. 1, 4, 6, 11, 12 *(maṣṣābāh),* 15, the two chapters are linked together by the Ab/B pattern (see above on 13:23).

Chapter 13 began with a negative comment on Saul's reign and kept "a troubled king" Saul, whose dynasty will not continue, as the only main actor; the main stage was at Gilgal, where Saul was once made king before the Lord. Jonathan and Michmash were mentioned in anticipation of ch. 14. Klein sees in these chapters a partial fulfillment of 9:16 ("he shall save my people from the hand of the Philistines"). He also notes that "Jonathan, who replaces Saul as a leader in battle (13:3; 14:1-15) and in the affection of the people (14:45) serves as a transitional figure to David."[2] These observations are certainly reasonable in view of later development of Jonathan's relationship with Saul and David.

When Saul and Jonathan are compared, there is an obvious contrast: Saul constantly concerns himself with the number of his troops, especially with the decrease from 3,000 to 600, while Jonathan is concerned only with whether the Lord will act on his behalf. If the Lord is on his side, numbers do not matter for God saves *whether by many or by few* (v. 6). It is impressive that this incident of Jonathan's act of trust is sandwiched by two incidents of Saul's acts of disobedience in chs. 13 and 15. The narrator thus lucidly contrasts Saul and Jonathan before moving to Saul and David in the subsequent story (chs. 16ff.).

Since among the Israelites only Saul and Jonathan had swords (13:22), the battle of Michmash Pass had nothing to do with armed might. It was the Lord who guided Jonathan's incursion and brought the victory to Israel. This Israelite victory forced the Philistine army to withdraw from the central hill country for the moment at least. However, in the south the Philistines would come back to challenge Saul's army (17:1; 23:1).

After the account of the battle against the Philistine *on that day* (v. 23), summary statements (vv. 47-52) of Saul's military activities, his family, and his general and his recruitment of soldiers close the chapter.

1. Birch, p. 1078.

2. Klein, p. 134; see D. Jobling, "Saul's Fall and Jonathan's Rise: Tradition and Redaction in 1 Sam 14:1-46," *JBL* 95 (1976) 367-76.

a. Jonathan Attacks the Philistine Garrison (14:1-15)

(1) Initial Statement (14:1)

1 *On that day Jonathan son of Saul said to the servant,*[3] *his armor-bearer,*
"Now, let us go across to the Philistine garrison
which is on the other side!"[4]
But he did not inform his father.

1 Verse 1 provides basic information with no waste of words. The following few verses, vv. 2-5, reinforce the role of v. 1, supplementing it with detailed information. Then, v. 6 recapitulates the main theme, expressed in Jonathan's words, with variations and elaborations.

On that day or "On such a day"; cf. "One day" (NRSV; NIV; JPS). The Hebrew phrase *wayhî hayyôm* (see on 1:4) presents the occasion as happening on a specific day understood from the context rather than "one day" or "once upon a time." On what particular day is known from the preceding context (SETTING); it refers to the day when "the Philistine garrison came out toward Michmash Pass" (13:23). Though "the day" does not necessarily refer to the specific day of their coming out, it does refer to the situation resulting from the garrison move. The main part of the Philistine troops had shifted westwards to Michmash Pass, which connects Michmash and Geba, where the Israelite troops were situated (13:16; 14:5). Jonathan must have been well aware that the eastern side was sharply separated by two rock formations between Michmash and Geba (see vv. 4-5) and that the Philistine presence was particularly thin there at that moment. He was certainly ready to cross ("let us go across") over that part of the ravine; see also 13:16.

This section formally introduces Jonathan as the *son of Saul* and in this verse refers to "his father." In 13:2, when Jonathan was first introduced onto the biblical stage, he was not identified, and his relation with Saul was only mentioned in passing in vv. 16 and 22.

Jonathan was not suggesting to his armor-bearer that they do normal scouting; his attempt was more than collecting information of the enemy as is made clear in v. 6. For scouts' activities, see "Instructions to Commanders of Border Garrisons" (*CS*, I, pp. 221-25). The term *garrison (maṣṣāb)* is the key word in this chapter; it probably refers to the main or central part of the Philistine troops.

This verse is particularly conscious of Jonathan's relation with *his fa-*

3. *hanna'ar;* lit., "the young man" or "squire"; see on 9:3.
4. Lit., "off this side-across" (BDB, p. 229).

ther Saul. This prepares for Saul's ignorance in v. 17. Note R. P. Gordon's comment: "Even in the present chapter filial respect and paternal affection are not overwhelmingly present."[5]

(2) Background Information (14:2-5)

2 *— Saul was sitting on the edge of the hill/Gibeah under the*
pomegranate tree which was in the threshing floor;[6] *and the*
troops who were with him were about six hundred men.
3 *Ahijah, son of Ahitub, the brother of Ichabod, son of Phinehas,*
son of Eli, the priest of the Lord at Shiloh, was wearing the
ephod. —
As for the troops, they did not know that Jonathan had gone.
4 *Now, between the passes which Jonathan sought to cross (to go) to*[7]
the Philistine garrison were a cliff[8] *on one side and a cliff on*
the other side: the name of the one was Bozez and the name of
the other was Senneh;
5 *the one cliff [rose] to a crest*[9] *to the north in front of Michmash,*
and the other was to the south in front of Geba.

2-5 Verse 1 is repeated in v. 6 with variations and elaborations (FRAMEWORK), leaving the intermediate verses (vv. 2-5) to give background information (SETTING). According to Klein, "chap. 14 can be described as a battle report in which Jonathan and Saul appear as individuals. Use of dialogue and a deft listing of the cast of characters and topographical information in vv. 2-5 show a high development of the narrator's art."[10]

5. R. P. Gordon, p. 136.

6. "Migron" has been equated with the Wadi es-Swenit by P. M. Arnold, *Gibeah: The Search for a Biblical City* (JSOTSS 79; Sheffield: JSOT Press, 1990); also "Migron" in *ABD,* IV, pp. 822-23. It cannot be the Migron of Isa. 10:28, which is located on the north of Michmash.

7. *ʿl* = *ʾl* (v. 1).

8. Lit., "the tooth of the rock."

9. Or "as a pillar" (see "pillar(?)" in BDB, p. 848; *HALOT,* p. 623), taking *māṣûq* as an adverbial usage of the noun. The only other occurrence is "the pillars/supports of the earth" (1 Sam. 2:8). The term might be compared with the Ugaritic phrase *bṣq* (*KTU* 1.22 I 25) "on the crest"; see T. J. Lewis, "Toward a Literary Translation of the Rapiuma Texts," in *Ugarit, Religion and Culture: Proceedings of the International Colloquium on Ugarit, Religion and Culture, Edinburgh, July 1994: Essays Presented in Honour of Professor John C. L. Gibson,* ed. N. Wyatt, W. G. E. Watson, and J. B. Lloyd (Münster: Ugarit-Verlag, 1996), p. 141. Cf. "a corrupt anticipation of *mṣpwn* (Driver); delete with LXX, OL" (McCarter, p. 235).

10. Klein, p. 133. For other stylistic details, see J. Blenkinsopp, "Jonathan's Sac-

2-3 Verses 2-3a, *Saul was sitting . . . the ephod,* is parenthetical within SETTING (vv. 2-5). These clauses are inserted between two items of background information: that neither Saul (v. 1b) nor his troops (v. 3b) knew about Jonathan's conduct.

2 Saul's camp was situated *on the edge of the hill* or *Gibeah* at that time. The phrase *biqṣēh haggibʿāh* is usually taken as referring to "the outskirts of Gibeah." However, McCarter comments: "Though MT, LXX, and Targ. all point to 'Gibeah,' topographical considerations seem to require 'Geba,' especially in view of v 16 below where Saul's watchmen see the battle raging at Michmash Pass. Gibeah — even on its outskirts — is too far away."[11] However, the distance between Gibeah and Michmash is less than 4 miles, and Saul's watchmen must have been stationed nearer to Michmash. But, the phrase could mean simply *the edge of the hill.* On the Gibeah — Geba problem, see 10:10 and 13:2.

The expression *under the pomegranate tree* may possibly have a "judicial-administrative significance" like "under the tamarisk tree" in 22:6; "under the palm tree of Deborah" in Judg. 4:5.

The phrase *bᵉmigrôn* has been translated as "in Migron" (so NRSV; NIV; NASB; JPS). However, in the light of Akkadian *magrattu* (< **magrān-t-u*) where a court of justice was held in Nuzi,[12] the translation *in the threshing floor* seems to be preferable (so McCarter, Klein, though by reading *bĕmô gōren*[13] or the like). For the ruler sitting on the threshing floor at the city gate, see *KTU* 1.17 V 4-8; 1.19 I 19-25, where Daniel judged the cases of widows and orphans sitting under a great tree in a threshing floor. For such a chair in the threshing floor at the city gate, see Tel Dan; also, in 1 K. 22:10, the kings of Israel and Judah consult the prophets before battle, "dressed in their royal robes . . . sitting on their thrones at the threshing-floor by the entrance of the gate of Samaria" (NIV).

The repetition of *six hundred men* (also 13:15) is a narrative technique, a reminder of the great decrease in numbers (see 13:2), providing background information for the subsequent narrative.

3 Here we are given the genealogy of the priest Ahijah, *who was wearing the ephod.* In the ancient Near East, oracles were normally consulted about military moves. Sometimes oracular priests were assigned to units.[14] In

---

rilege: 1 Sam 14,1-46," *CBQ* 26 (1964) 423-49; F. Schicklberger, "Jonatans Heldentat: Textlinguistische Beobachtungen zu 1 Sam XIV 1-23a," *VT* 24 (1974) 324-33.

11. McCarter, p. 235.

12. See *CAD,* M/1, p. 46: "grain storage place, threshing floor" (OB, and mostly Nuzi); also Gordon, *UT* §19.622.

13. McCarter, p. 235.

14. C. H. Gordon, *The Common Background of Greek and Hebrew Civilizations* (New York: W. W. Norton, 1965), p. 262.

Ugarit, the priests were present "to authorize or forbid military decisions. Their function was accordingly often one of command."[15] Ahijah the priest was with Saul's troops, ready to supply Saul with divine oracles to guide him in conducting the war.

The name *Ahijah* means "My brother is Yah"; the element "brother" is a popular epithet in PN of Northwest Semites.[16] He is the great-grandson of Eli and the brother of Ahimelech, priest of Nob and father of Abiathar (22:9, 11, 12, 20).

	Samuel		Saul	David	
Eli	Hophni				
	Phinehas	- Ahitub	- Ahijah		
			- Ahimelech	- Abiathar	- Ahimelech
					- Jonathan
		- Ichabod			

There are two Ahimelechs in this genealogical chart, namely, "Ahimelech, son of Ahitub" (see 21:1; 22:20) and "Ahimelech son of Abiathar" (2 Sam. 8:17; 1 Chr. 18:16 [MT]).[17] See also on 1 Sam. 21:1.

Ahijah is noted here as wearing the ephod. The term *nōśē’* means basically "carrying," though it is sometimes translated either as "was wearing" (so NIV; NASB; McCarter) or as "bearing" (JPS). Note that the ephod is carried, not worn, eight times in 1 Samuel; David uses it to seek the divine will in 23:9 and 30:7.

For *the ephod (’ēpôd),* see on 2:28. It contained a pocket or compartment for the Urim and Thummim (see on 14:41-42). (The "linen ephod" worn by Samuel [2:18] and by the eighty-five priests of Nob [22:18] is a different, though probably related, item of clothing.) The mention of the ephod here prepares the audience to think that Ahijah was wearing the ephod when he inquired of the Lord in vv. 18-19 and 36-40. Note that vv. 2-3 provides background information (SETTING) since both verses begin with disjunctive *waw,* not *wayqtl.* Hence, it is not necessary to infer, like Klein,[18] that Saul was already seeking an oracle here.

R. P. Gordon notes that v. 3 links the failed house of Eli with the failed house of Saul, whose house also will be destroyed with just one man left; see 2:33.[19]

15. Gordon, *UL,* p. 125.
16. See Tallqvist, *AGE,* p. 6; Gröndahl, *PTU,* p. 92.
17. See R. W. Uitti, "Ahitub," in *ABD,* I, pp. 122-23.
18. Klein, p. 135.
19. R. P. Gordon, p. 136.

4 The name *Bozez (bôṣēṣ)* means "the Gleaming One" (cf. Arabic *baṣṣa,* "glitter, shine, gleam") or "the Miry One" (cf. *boṣ,* "mire"; *biṣṣa,* "swamp"), while *Senneh (senneh)* means "the Thorny One" (cf. *seneh,* "thornbush"; Empire Aramaic *sanya',* "thornbush") or "Bramble-bush" (Exod. 3:2, etc.). These names and the description in v. 5 indicate how humanly impossible the place was to cross.

(3) Jonathan and His Servant (14:6-15)

(a) "Let Us Go Across!" (14:6-7)

6 *And Jonathan said to the servant, his armor-bearer,*
"Now, let us go across to the garrison of these uncircumcised!
Perhaps the Lord may act on our behalf,
for there is no hindrance for the Lord to save,
whether by many or by few!"
7 *And his armor-bearer said to him,*
"Do all that is in your heart!
Lead on!
Here am I with you according to your heart!"

6 Jonathan's courage and faith in the Lord's ability to deliver Israel regardless of circumstances are of the same quality as David's when he fought Goliath by himself (see ch. 17).

The word *uncircumcised* (*ʿrl; also 17:26; 31:4; 2 Sam. 1:20; etc.) refers to the fact that the foreskins of the Philistines were not cut off; see 18:25; 2 Sam. 3:14. This is a standard epithet of ethnic contempt for Philistines in Judges-Samuel (e.g., Judg. 14:3). The Philistines' uncircumcised state is usually regarded as evidence for their non-Semitic (alien) status.[20]

Perhaps is not a sign of Jonathan's doubt in God's ability, but rather a confession that God is not *required* to act for them. Note that he repeats the name of Yahweh twice here — also vv. 6, 10, 12. This hints at his intimate relationship with the Lord and his trust on Him.

Against many critics who defend the MT, McCarter emends *yʿśh* ("act") to *ywšyʿ* "give (us) victory," for he thinks that the emendation, though without textual support, seems "likely in view of *lhwšyʿ,* 'to gain victory,' in the following clause."[21] But in view of the word "act" in v. 45, there seems little reason to emend.

That God can save *by few* recalls Gideon's reducing of his army for

20. See also *ABD,* I, pp. 1025-31 on "circumcision" (R. G. Hall).
21. McCarter, p. 235.

the war against the Midianites (Judg. 7:2-7). God can save even by "one," as he did in the case of David against Goliath (ch. 17).

7 For *Lead on!* or "You go first!" *(nᵉṭēh lāk),* emendation to *lᵉbābᵉkā nōṭeh lô* has been suggested, "Do all that your mind inclines to" (NRSV) or "to devote oneself to" (*HALOT,* p. 693), but the MT as it stands makes good sense.[22] Jonathan's courage and faith gained the full support from his faithful servant. The Lord surely used these men acting by faith with one heart.

(b) "Come Up toward Us!" (14:8-12)

8 *And Jonathan said,*
"Now we are going across to the men
and we shall show ourselves to them!
9 *If they say to us thus:*
'Stay still until we come to you,'
we shall stay where we are and not go up to them;
10 *but if they say thus:*
'Come up toward us!'
we shall go up,
for the Lord has given them into our hand!
This shall be the sign for us."
11 *And the two of them showed themselves to the Philistine garrison.*
And the Philistines said,
"Look! Hebrews are coming out of the holes
where they hid themselves!"
12 *And the men of the garrison*[23] *hailed Jonathan and his armor-bearer:*
"Come up to us so that we may let you know something!"
And Jonathan said to his armor-bearer,
"Come up after me,
for the Lord has given them into the hand of Israel!"

8-10 Jonathan suggests to his servant that they see how the Philistines respond to their appearing before them. If they say *"Stay still until we come to you,"* they will stay; if they say *"Come up toward us!"* this will be God's sign, so they will go up.

9 The expression *If they say thus . . .* is similar to that in Mesopotamian omens; see *CS,* I, pp. 423-25. But, Jonathan is using the sentence in a normal conversation with his servant, not in a ritual.

22. See Stoebe, p. 257 ("Gib dich dran!"); also p. 259 without changing the MT (*HALOT,* p. 693).

23. MT *hammaṣṣābāh;* usually *maṣṣab;* only here with a feminine ending.

10 The MT *ʿālênû* can mean *toward us,* not necessarily "against us"; hence, there is no need to emend the text to mean "to" from LXX as McCarter does.[24] A classic example is *ʿal-melek ʾaššûr* (2 K. 23:29), which was once translated as "against the king of Assyria" (KJV; JPS) but in light of the historical background from the Babylonian Chronicles, it is clear that it means "to the king of Assyria" (NRSV; NASB) or "to help the king of Assyria" (NIV).[25]

The verb *has given* is a "perfect of confidence"; this is an extension of the use of perfect for future actions.[26] *The Lord has given* is exactly the meaning of Jonathan's name. This is certainly not a play on his name by the narrator but Jonathan's faith in the Lord verbally expressed by him. The term *the sign (hāʾôt)* reminds us of Gideon's request for a sign for deliverance of Israel, which was dew alternatively on the fleece and on the ground (Judg. 6:37-40).

11-12 When Jonathan and his servant appeared before the Philistines at the *garrison,* the *men of the garrison* said *"Come up to us. . . ."* So, Jonathan took this as the *sign* that *the Lord has given them* into Israel's control.

Hebrews is a designation for the Israelites, spoken by foreigners; see on 4:6; 13:3. Also below on v. 21.

The expression *nth *byd* "to give (deliver) into the hand (of)" is very frequent in Deuteronomy, Joshua, Judges, Samuel, and Kings but occurs also in other parts of the Old Testament such as Gen. 14:20; Ex. 23:31; Num. 21:34; Jer. 20:5; Ezek. 7:21; Ps. 106:41; Dan. 1:2; Neh. 9:27; 1 Chr. 22:18; 2 Chr. 16:8. It also appears in the Amarna letters (fourteenth century B.C.) and in a building inscription of Nebuchadnezzar II (sixth century B.C.).[27] So, it is not necessarily "Deuteronomistic." See "Introduction" (Section III, B, 1).

(c) Philistines Fall before Jonathan (14:13-15)

13 *And Jonathan went up on his hands and feet, his armor-bearer behind him; and they fell before Jonathan with his armor-bearer killing behind him.*

14 *And the first attack that Jonathan and his armor-bearer made was*

24. McCarter, p. 236.

25. See *CS,* I, pp. 467-68.

26. See T. L. Fenton, "The Hebrew 'Tenses' in the Light of Ugaritic," in *Proceedings of the Fifth World Congress of Jewish Studies, Held in 1969,* vol. 4 (Jerusalem: World Union of Jewish Studies, 1973), p. 37.

27. B. Albrektson, *History and the Gods: An Essay on the Idea of Historical Events as Divine Manifestations in the Ancient Near East and in Israel* (Lund: C. W. K. Gleerup, 1967), p. 39.

against about twenty men, in about a half of a plowing field,
namely, a "yoke" of a field.
15 *And there was a trembling both in the camp and in the field,*
namely, among all the troops; as for the garrison and the
raiders, they also trembled.
And the earth shook and God caused it to tremble.

13 Jonathan and his *armor-bearer* climbed the cliff and killed those Philistines.

For the translation of *and they fell before Jonathan,* McCarter supplies a stated subject and translates: "and when [the Philistines] turned toward [him]" (also NRSV; NIV; JPS), for he thinks MT is "too abrupt."[28] But "they" of *they fell* by context is the Philistines. It is omitted there because specifying the subject unnecessarily would upset the discourse structure; see on "Introduction" (Section VI, A).

The entire paragraph, vv. 13-15, is a description of the state in the Philistine camp after Jonathan *went up,* not an EVENT of who did what. This is recognizable in the following discourse structure:

wayqtl ("And Jonathan went up")
wayqtl (3 m.pl.) ("and they fell")
  ptc. ("killing")
    wayhi ("And the first attack was")
      [*'ăšer*-clause *perf.*]
    wayhi ("And a trembling was")
  perf. ("they also trembled")
wayqtl (3 f.s.) ("And the earth shook")

Here the first *wayqtl* is a movement verb, and hence the description is off the mainline of narrative. The second *wayqtl* ("and they fell") is in the plural, without a stated subject, hence defocusing the agent. The third *wayqtl* is with an impersonal noun ("the earth") as subject, and hence a little off the mainline. In such a structure the second *wayqtl* would not take a stated subject, for who *fell* is obvious from the context. For clarity, an English reader would like to have a subject specified, though a Hebrew reader/audience would not require such specification.

The verb *killed* (*m^{e}môtēt;* Polel, ptc. of *mwt "to die") signifies the act of "dispatching" as in 17:51 (also Judg. 9:54; 2 Sam. 1:9).

14 For the expression *in about a half of a plowing field, namely, a "yoke" of field (k^{e}baḥăṣî ma'ănāh ṣemed śādeh),* various translations have

28. McCarter, p. 236.

been suggested: for example, "within an area about half a furrow long in an acre of land" (NRSV; also JPS); "in an area of about half an acre" (NIV); "like men cutting a furrow across a half-acre field" (REB). McCarter thinks that the MT is "plainly corrupt" and omits this part of the verse.[29] However, *yoke (ṣemed)* is a unit of area measurement; in the Kassite-NB system the Akkadian term *ṣimdu* "yoke" was probably reckoned as the area that could be seeded in "1 day's seeding with the seeder plow."[30] See "Introduction" (Section III, C, 5).

15 The same root of a *trembling (ḥărādāh)* is used for describing the Israelites' reaction in 13:7. The expression *both in the camp and in the field* (lit., "in the camp, in the field," as an asyndeton) is a merismatic expression: "in the camp as well as in the battle-field," referring to the entire unit, wherever it was stationed. Hence, the following *waw* functions as an explicative: *namely* (see on 6:18). With this explanation any awkwardness[31] in the text disappears.

The phrase *the garrison and the raiders* refers to the main body and to the special raiding armies away from Michmash; it refers to the rest of the Philistine army in the area besides the troops "both in the camp and in the field." The phrase *they also* completes the description of the totality of the Philistine army, including the soldiers, the generals at the garrison, and the special troops (i.e., the raiders; see 13:17). Thus, the entire body of Philistines there *trembled.*

For the motif of the earth shaking, *rgz + *'ereṣ,* see also Amos 8:8; Job 9:6; Prov. 30:21; Ps. 77:18 (*rgz + *rʿš).[32] In this context, the earth was shaking, and there was an utter confusion in the Philistine camp.

The phrase *ḥerdat 'ĕlōhîm* (lit., "the trembling of God") means either *a trembling by God,* "a terror from God" (JPS), "a panic sent by God" (NIV) or, taking *'ĕlōhîm* superlatively, "a very great panic" (NRSV), "a great trembling" (NASB).[33] The reference to God suggests that the "trembling" was not caused simply by Jonathan's first attack but by the hand of God; hence, our translation *God caused it to tremble.* Compare "great panic" in 5:9. This clause is a restatement of the first half of the sentence; the two halves constitute a parallelism:

29. McCarter, p. 236.

30. "In a space equal to about half the distance across an acre field, or 15-20 yards [meters]" (Driver, p. 109).

31. See McCarter, p. 236.

32. "The shaking of the heavens," see D. T. Tsumura, "*šmym* — Heaven, Sky, Firmament, Air," in *NIDOTTE,* 4, pp. 160-66.

33. Also, "an awesome convulsion" (McCarter, p. 236). For "the superlative force" of *'ĕlōhîm,* see D. W. Thomas, "A Consideration of Some Unusual Ways of Expressing the Superlative in Hebrew," *VT* 3 (1953) 209-24.

"And the earth shook
  and God caused it to tremble."

Thus, the entire body of the Philistine army was totally confused by the attacks by two men of faith, Jonathan and his servant.

During the First World War, a brigade major in Allenby's army in Palestine succeeded in taking Michmash by copying tactics of Saul and Jonathan according to a report by Major V. Gilbert. The Turks were utterly confused and all were killed or taken prisoner.[34]

b. The Lord Saves Israel (14:16-23)

(1) Saul at Gibeah (14:16-20)

16 *And the watchmen for Saul, who was in Gibeah of Benjamin, saw the multitude melt away, going back and forth.*
17 *And Saul said to the troops who were with him,*
"Check and see who has gone out of us!"
And they checked. Then Jonathan and his armor-bearer were not there.
18 *And Saul said to Ahijah,*
"Bring near the ark of God!"
—for the ark of God was on that day among the Israelites.[35]
19 *Until Saul said this to the priest, the tumult*[36] *in the Philistine camp had been getting greater and greater.*
Then Saul said to the priest,
"Withdraw your hand!"
20 *And Saul and all the troops with him assembled and came up to the battle. Behold, each one's sword was [stuck] into his neighbor, in very great confusion.*

34. See W. Keller, *The Bible as History* (London: Hodder & Stoughton, 1956), pp. 179-80.

35. Lit., "in that day and (in) the sons of Israel" *(wbny . . .) = wbbny;* see v. 47 *(wbbny)* and Cairo Geniza fragment *(wbny).* Phonologically, the present text seems to reflect a process of *assimilation at the word boundary:*

> *hahû(') bibnê* → hahu^{u} bibnê —(assimilation)→ > hahu^{u} ^{u}ibnê — (elision of vowel /i/) → hahû ^{u}bnê → *hahû(') ûbnê*

or

> *hahû(') b^{e}b^{e}nê* → hahū b^{e}b^{e}nê → hahūbbnê → hahû bnê → *hahû(') ûbnê*

36. *hehāmôn;* also 1 Sam. 4:14; cf. the same term for "the multitude" in v. 16. Here the term is <*casus pendens*> "as for the tumult"; it precedes the main *wayqtl;* see "Introduction" (Section V, A).

16-17 When it is reported that the Philistines at Michmash are melting away, Saul at Gibeah checks to see any of his troops went there, and he notices Jonathan is missing.

Normally the phrase *in Gibeah of Benjamin* is understood as modifying *the watchmen* (e.g., NASB; NRSV; NIV; JPS). However, the Hebrew syntax is ambiguous and the phrase could modify the immediately preceding noun, Saul: hence, *who was in Gibeah of Benjamin.* If this understanding is correct, the watchmen were presumably stationed on some hill between Gibeah and Michmash. Within 2 miles of Gibeah there are several hills from which there is an unobstructed view of Michmash, 2 to 3 miles away. McCarter doubts that Saul's watchmen could have had a good view from Gibeah and hence reads the text as "Geba," which is much nearer to Michmash.[37] But this is unnecessary; see 10:10; also 13:2 and on v. 2 (above).

The term *multitude* (*hāmôn;* or "crowd") is to be distinguished from "tumult, confusion" (v. 19), though McCarter thinks that "MT . . . 'confusion', seems to anticipate v 19" (p. 237) and translates it as "camp," based on the LXX.

The expression *melt away, going back and forth (nāmôg wayyēlek wahălōm)* means that the camp was surging; so Wellhausen, p. 89; also "was surging back and forth" (NRSV); "melting away in all directions" (NIV). McCarter, however, thinks that the MT is "untranslatable."[38]

18 Saul, in this emergency, asks his chaplain Ahijah for a divine message but soon, in v. 19, loses patience and interrupts.

On *the ark of God,* see on 3:3. The ark was often carried to the battle as in 4:3; for the military importance of the ark, see Num. 10:33-36; Joshua 3–4, 6. McCarter, based on LXX^{BL}, translates the second half as "(for he was wearing the ephod at that time before Israel)."[39] R. P. Gordon also prefers "the ephod" (also REB; Birch) here for the following reasons: (1) the ark is not normally associated with oracular consultation; (2) the ark was in limbo in Kiriath-jearim during this period (7:1f.; cf. 2 Sam. 6:1-3; 1 Chr. 13:3); (3) oracular decisions were usually obtained from the ephod; and (4) the verb *bring* (Hi. *ngš) occurs twice elsewhere in 1 Samuel in connection with the ephod (23:9; 30:7).[40]

However, the ephod was already being worn by Ahijah (see v. 3) when the ark was brought near there. So, the issue is not the ark or the ephod but both. Saul must have asked Ahijah to inquire of the Lord using the ephod,

37. McCarter, p. 235.
38. McCarter, p. 237.
39. McCarter, pp. 233, 237.
40. R. P. Gordon, pp. 137-38.

before the ark of God. Therefore, Saul's command to Ahijah to *withdraw* his *hand* (v. 19) was probably understood as a command to withdraw it from the ephod, not from the ark. The verb "to withdraw" is used for the ephod twice (23:9; 30:7) in the OT, while it is not used with reference to the ark of God anywhere else in the OT. The ark of God was normally "carried" (*nś'); see on 4:4. It may be that Saul's use of the verb "bring near" hints at his careless attitude toward the ark of God, which symbolizes the presence of the Lord; it is man who should go before His holy presence not the other way around.

But the most obvious difficulty is that the ark was presumably in Kiriath-jearim. However, there is no reason why the ark could not have been brought from Kiriath-jearim for this campaign and then taken back, just as it was brought from Shiloh in ch. 4. For some unknown but special reason, the ark was "among the Israelites" *on that day.*[41] Even to the narrator, who provides the explanatory comment *for the ark of God was on that day among the Israelites,* the existence of the ark there was seemingly very special. He may be trying to convey that the ark was there only *on that day.* The phrase *on that day (bayyôm hahû')* is a key phrase in this chapter, also appearing in vv. 23, 24, 31, 37. By repeating it the narrator emphasizes the specific day, rather than "at that time."

19 Saul's speaking to the priest refers to the preceding verbal action of bringing near the ark of God; hence, our translation supplies *this* as the object of the verb *said.* Note that most modern translations have "While Saul was talking . . ."; in this case emphasis is given to the situation that the tumult was still getting greater when he spoke the next command to withdraw.

Saul's two commands, *Bring near the ark of God* and *Withdraw your hand* (from the ephod), show his attitude toward the divine matters; he treats both the divine object and the divine method rather carelessly. Instead of inquiring of the priest, Saul commands him to do specific things, which are primarily under the authority of the priesthood. He commands Ahijah to seek divine guidance by means of the ephod, but, at a crucial time, he interrupts the consultation. Saul is a person who prays when he should act and acts when he should pray. Such inconsistency is one of Saul's characteristics.

41. S.-H. Kio, "What Did Saul Ask for: Ark or Ephod? (1 Samuel 14.18)," *BT* 47 (1996) 240-46 supports the LXX's "ephod" for a number of reasons, including "the poor state" of the MT. When Saul asked Ahijah *to bring near the ark,* he certainly did not expect him to do so by himself. For Schley's view that Shiloh was still functioning as a priestly city through Ahijah during Saul's time, see R. P. Gordon's criticism in "Who Made the Kingmaker? Reflections on Samuel and the Institution of the Monarchy," in *Faith, Tradition, and History: Old Testament Historiography in Its Near Eastern Context,* ed. A. R. Millard, J. K. Hoffmeier, and D. W. Baker (Winona Lake, Ind.: Eisenbrauns, 1994), pp. 266-68.

20 At last Saul acts; he *came up* to the Philistine camp in Michmash. The term *came* indicates the change of viewpoint from Gibeah to Michmash.

Each one's sword refers to the situation that they killed each other, rather than that they fought each other. Thus, the translation is not "against his neighbor" but *into* his neighbor. R. P. Gordon aptly says: "If the Israelites are ill-equipped (13:22), Philistine weapons — and hands — can do their work for them (cf. Judg. 7:22)."[42]

Here *very great confusion (m^e^hûmāh)* had arisen and the Philistines were killing each other in panic as in the days of Gideon (Judg. 7:22). Like the "great trembling" caused by God (v. 15), this panic is also ultimately from God.

(2) Hebrews and the Men of Israel (14:21-23)

21 *As for*[43] *the Hebrews, who had belonged to the Philistines previously and gone up into their camps all around*[44] *(to side) with them,*[45] *they too turned to side with*[46] *Israel who were with Saul and Jonathan.*

22 *As for all the men of Israel who had been hiding in the hill country of Ephraim, they heard that the Philistines had fled. And they too pursued them closely in the battle.*

23 *And the Lord saved Israel on that day.*
As for the battle, it went across Beth-aven.

21 For *the Hebrews,* see on 4:6; 13:3; 14:11. The term is used by the narrator here, not by the Philistines (so in v. 11), and these Hebrews were possibly the native Israelites "who defected to the enemy in times of distress and who now return as the fortunes of war change again."[47] See on 13:3.

This illustrates well that the meaning of a word depends on its context and its speaker. In this chapter the word *Hebrews* is used both as a pejorative

42. R. P. Gordon, p. 138.

43. Topicalization, with the resumptive pronoun "they" *(hēmmāh).*

44. The term *all around (sābîb)* is taken by BDB (p. 685), McCarter (p. 237) and others as a verbal form *sbbw:* e.g., "turned" (NRSV). Cf. "all around in the camp" (NASB); "in the army from round about" (JPS); cf. "to their camp" (NIV).

45. The term *'immām* (lit., "with them") is resultative, i.e., as the result of their going up into the camp, hence *(to side) with them;* not "to go up with them," but "to go up *into* the camp."

46. Lit., "to be with."

47. McCarter, pp. 240-41; also B. Mazar, "The Philistines and the Rise of Israel and Tyre," in *The Early Biblical Period: Historical Studies,* ed. A. Ahituv and B. A. Levine (Jerusalem: Israel Exploration Society, 1986), p. 73.

term for the Israelites by the Philistines (v. 11) and as a designation for a group of Israelites who had sided with the Philistines (here).

22 The reference to *Ephraim* here indicates that Saul's leadership was not just recognized around Benjamin.

23 *Beth-aven* (also 13:5) is located a few miles to the northwest of Michmash.

The victory was brought about by Yahweh, not by Jonathan or others, though many joined in for the mop-up action. As is in the case of David's fight with Goliath, the battle was surely the Lord's. The Lord could use even a single person or two to do his saving work. The key expression *on that day* (also see v. 18) links the present section with the following, where it is repeated several times: vv. 24, 31, 37. The word order, w-S V, hence *As for the battle,* and the movement verb ("to go across"), and a new location (i.e., Beth-aven) mark a transition in the story. So, v. 23b, rather than v. 23a, is the TERMINATE of the section, while preparing for the following episode.

c. The People Save Jonathan (14:24-46)

From the narrator's point of view Saul was king only for a short time, *only for two years* (13:1), and has already been abandoned by his God because of his disobedience to "what the Lord commanded to him" in 13:13-14. So, whatever he does afterward is not satisfactory in God's sight, though temporarily his individual actions, both political and religious, seem successful on the surface. To be religious was not enough in the sight of the Lord who sees inside the heart (see 16:7).

As McCarter notes, in this section Saul is "not depraved" but even "capable of some success as the leader of Yahweh's people." But being abandoned by his God, "most of what he attempts goes awry," and "his character is flawed by a lack of good judgment and a kind of reckless impetuosity which thwart his own purposes." In his relationship with the Lord he was "rash and presumptuous" and "he tried to manipulate the divine will through ritual formality (14:24; cf. 13:12; 15:15)."[48] In 13:13, he was denied dynastic succession. Here, in the midst of a great and important victory, he manages because of a foolish oath to nearly destroy the person through whom he achieved the victory and through whom his dynasty would have continued and, furthermore, to become at odds with his troops.

48. McCarter, p. 251.

(1) Saul's Ban (14:24-30)

(a) People under Oath (14:24)

24 *Now the men of Israel were in distress*[49] *on that day.*
And Saul had put the people under oath,[50] *saying,*
"Cursed be the man who eats food before the evening
when I avenge myself on my enemies!"
So none of the troops had tasted food.

Verses 24-27a are all the SETTING for the EVENT of 27b, Jonathan's eating the honey. In more detail, though, there is a series of settings followed by an event, which is in turn the setting for another event.

And Saul . . . (wayyō'el šā'ûl): the initial *waw* of <*wayqtl* + "S"> here is sometimes translated as "because" (NIV) or "for" (NASB; JPS).[51] Since the first half of the verse *(Now the men of Israel were . . .)* is the SETTING, this <*wayqtl* + "S"> might be taken as EVENT which occurs in that situation; see "Introduction" (Section VI, A). However, since the verb "to put under oath" is a verb of speech, which accompanies the act of speaking *(saying),* this *wayqtl* in turn functions as a SETTING to the following direct speech. The entire verse (v. 24) can be taken as a SETTING to the following EVENT, which takes place in v. 27b with Jonathan's stretching out the end of his staff. Note that the *wayqtl* in v. 26 *(And the troops came)* is of a movement verb, hence a transition rather than an event. As v. 24 is a setting, it is not necessarily in chronological order. Actually, Saul probably made his oath in v. 20 just before the attack, because once they were attacking it would have been difficult for the troops to know about it. As Jonathan was not there at that time, he did not hear of the oath.

On vow, see 1:11. The word of oath (*'lh) *Cursed be the man* (*'ārûr;* also v. 28; 26:19) is an illocutionary or "performative" utterance[52] and hence has a binding force; if one breaks it, he will be cursed. Only cursing,

49. *niggaś;* or "were in distress" (NIV); also in 1 Sam. 13:6. Cf. "Saul committed a very rash act" (NRSV); "Saul made a great blunder that day" (McCarter, p. 245), on the basis of the LXX.

50. Or, "curse," for in the present context only cursing is involved; see *'lh "curse" (rather than "oath") in Batto, *DDD,* pp. 398-405. On the close connection between *'ālāh* and covenant, see *DDD,* pp. 402-3.

51. NRSV ("He had laid an oath on the troops") is based on the emendation of the text.

52. That means that "the congruence between word and thing derives from the fact that they are uttered by an acceptable person at an acceptable time and in an acceptable manner" (Batto, in *DDD,* p. 402; see also p. 399).

not blessing, is involved in such an oath. Joshua (Josh. 6:26) and the men of Israel at Mizpah (Judg. 21:1, 18) also pronounced such a curse. Saul is the last one mentioned in the OT to utter such a curse.[53] "Saul imposes a fast upon the army in an attempt, apparently, to influence Yahweh by a grandiose gesture of self-denial"[54] in order to continue securing the Lord's help.

The phrase *before the evening* (*'ad-hā'āreb;* lit., "until the evening") refers to "today" (as in v. 28), that is, before the sunset. See on 20:5; 30:17, where "tomorrow or the next day" means after the sunset.

When I avenge myself on my enemies (*weniqqamtî mē'ōyebay;* lit., "and I will avenge . . .") may also be "before I have avenged myself on my enemies!" (NIV).

(b) Jonathan Tastes Honey (14:25-27)

25 *Now all the land entered the forest; there was honey on the surface of the field.*

26 *And the troops came to the forest, which was flowing with honey right there.*[55] *But there was no one who reached his hand (to it and turned his hand) to his mouth, for the people feared the oath.*

27 *But Jonathan had not heard it when his father caused the people to take the oath.*

He stretched out the end of the staff that was in his hand and dipped it[56] *into the comb of honey and turned his hand to his mouth. Then his eyes brightened.*[57]

53. See M. Weinfeld, "Zion and Jerusalem as Religious and Political Capital: Ideology and Utopia," in *The Poet and the Historian: Essays in Literary and Historical Biblical Criticism,* ed. R. E. Friedman (HSS 26; Chico, Calif.: Scholars Press, 1983), pp. 81-85.

54. McCarter, p. 249.

55. *wehinnēh;* the particle *hinnēh* denotes the "real-timeness."

56. With f.s. suffix. Though McCarter thinks that the "MT reads *'otah* by attraction to the feminine noun *yado,* 'his hand'" (p. 246). The f. may be for "staff," which could be feminine in Mic. 6:9 (MT).

57. Q. *wattā'ōrnāh* (Lambdin, §124, Rem. 1). The K. probably reflects a phonetic spelling, from the same root *'wr (cf. v. 29b) as Q.

> *wtr'nh* (K.) *wattōr(')nāh* ←[metathesis of ' (historical spelling) and *r* but same pronunciation]— *wattō(')rnāh* ←*(sandhi)*— *wattāōrnāh* ← *wattā'ōrnāh* (Q.)

So, this is not a "scribal error," i.e., a mistake in the copying of *wtr'nh* /*wattārō(')nāh* by metathesis of ' and *r.* On phonetic spellings, see "Introduction" (Section II, B, 4).

25 *Now . . . :* this is other information about the setting for the event in v. 27b. McCarter, like Driver, takes v. 25 to be "highly corrupt" and, following Wellhausen's "clever" restoration,[58] translates "Now there was honeycomb on the ground."[59] However, the best method of treating a text that looks "corrupt" but for which there is no evidence supporting the corruption is to leave the MT as it is and explain it with minimal speculation.

Most modern translations take the phrase *kol-hāʾāreṣ* (lit., "all the earth") as referring to the people: that is, "all the people of the land" (NASB); "the entire army" (NIV); "all the troops" (NRSV); "everybody" (JPS). Such use can be seen also in "all the earth shall know" (17:46); "all the country was weeping" (2 Sam. 15:23). In the present context, however, "everyone" has been referred to using the phrase *the men of Israel (ʾîš-yiśrāʾēl)* = "the troops" *(hāʿām)* in v. 24. Verse 25 gives background information about "where" rather than "who." Therefore, the phrase *all the land* probably refers to the entire area of that district (see v. 23, "across Beth-aven").

Forest (yāʿar) is sometimes explained as "a honeycomb" (Driver, p. 114; NRSV) or "a stack of beehives" (JPS with a note: "meaning of Heb. uncertain"). However, the simplest solution is to take it as "forest," which is the usual meaning and is followed by the versions except the LXX. Battles often took place in forests; see 2 Sam. 18:6 ("the forest of Ephraim").

Thus, *Now all the land entered the forest (wᵉkol-hāʾāreṣ bāʾû bayyāʿar),* which probably means something like "[as they went along,] the land became forested," is another set of SETTINGs, giving geographical information about the land with respect to the forest and honey, two items relevant to the following EVENT.

26 In the phrase *flowing with honey* (*hēlek dᵉbāš;* lit., "flowing of honey"), *honey* is an objective genitive to the construct noun *flowing;* the agent of this verbal action is "the forest." See *ʾereṣ zābat ḥālāb ûd(ᵉ)bāš* "a land flowing with milk and honey" (Exod. 3:8, 17; etc.). McCarter, who takes MT as "most awkward," translates it as "its bees had left," reading *hālak dĕbōrô,* "with most critics."[60] R. P. Gordon is inclined to think "that MT may be retained if the (implied) subject of *helek* (or *holek*) is the forest: 'and behold, it was flowing with honey.'"[61] Compare the use of the same verb in Joel 4:18 and the following two lines in the Ugaritic text *KTU* 1.6 III 6-7 (//12-13):

> The heavens rain oil, [*šmm. šmn. tmṭrn*]
> the valleys *flow with* honey. [*nḫlm. tlk. nbtm*]

58. Wellhausen, pp. 91-92; Driver, pp. 113-14; J. Barr, *CPTOT,* p. 144.
59. McCarter, p. 243.
60. McCarter, p. 246.
61. R. P. Gordon, p. 343.

McCarter translates the participle *maśśîg* ("reached") as "one who would raise," reading *mšyb* ("return") with LXX, Targ., and OL.[62] However, the expression *reached* is abbreviated here from the full phrase "reached his hand (to it and turned his hand) to his mouth" since it is understood from the context; see v. 27. But it is usually translated as "put his hand to his mouth" (NIV; JPS; NASB; also NRSV).

Another occurrence of the oath *(šᵉbūʿāh)* in Samuel is 2 Sam. 21:7, which mentions "the oath of the Lord" *(šᵉbūʿat YHWH)*. It is noteworthy that David took the oath between him and Jonathan seriously as the one who feared the Lord, while the troops feared the oath itself. In the ancient Near East an oath was taken seriously "inasmuch as it was reckoned to carry divine authority."[63]

27 *He stretched out the end of the staff:* this is the first *wayqtl* of an action verb; all the material in this section (since v. 24) has been preparing for this action.

Physiologically sugar gives a brightness to the eyes (*'wr). R. P. Gordon sees here an assonance between *'arar* ("curse," vv. 24, 28) and *'or* ("be bright," vv. 27, 29). But those two words never appear side by side. Jonathan probably experienced low blood sugar (hypoglycemia). It can be caused by vigorous exercise and lack of food; today it is most commonly experienced as an insulin reaction by diabetics. A symptom occasionally experienced is a "darkening" of the eyes, in which vision is darkened, appearing similar to the darkening of vision when one stands up too quickly. Eating honey would quickly raise the blood sugar level and make vision normally "bright" again.[64]

(c) Jonathan Is Informed of the Oath (14:28-30)

28 *And a man out of the troops responded [to this] and said,*
"Your father indeed caused the people to take an oath, saying,
'Cursed be the man who eats food today!' "[65]
And the troops were exhausted.
29 *And Jonathan said,*
"My father has disturbed the country!
Look! My eyes are brightened

62. McCarter, p. 246.

63. See R. S. Hess, in *CS,* II, p. 330 for the text of the divine oath of Niqmepa from Alalakh. Also see *ANET,* p. 220 for a good illustration of "fear of the oath" in the Nuzi lawsuit; see R. P. Gordon, p. 139.

64. Susan Tsumura drew my attention to this fact.

65. Equals "by the evening" (v. 24).

because I tasted a bit of this[66] *honey.*
30 *How much more so,*[67] *if the troops had indeed eaten today*
of the spoil of their enemies which was found!
For now the slaughter among the Philistines has not been
great."

28 Jonathan is now informed of the oath which Saul ordered the people to make (v. 27). *And the troops were exhausted (wayyāʿap hāʿām)* is a key phrase (= v. 31) here, which could have been spoken either by this man (so NIV; JPS; NRSV) or by the narrator/author. This clause is sometimes considered "disruptive" at this point and hence is often deleted as a gloss (so Wellhausen, p. 92; McCarter, p. 246). However, as Klein holds, "there is no textual evidence for this and the comment does set the context for Jonathan's reply in vv. 29-30 where he lays a serious charge against his father for troubling the land."[68]

29 S. R. Driver takes *disturbed* (*ʿākar;* or "troubled") as an "ominous word" in the Old Testament.[69] It is a key word from Joshua through Kings and is best known from the story of Achan in Joshua 7. Also, in 1 K. 18:17-18, Elijah and Ahab dispute which one of them is the one "troubling" the land.[70] It may also mean more strongly "to bring disaster, throw into confusion, ruin" (*HALOT,* p. 824).

Today is a key word in this section (v. 28 = *that day* [vv. 18, 23, 24, 31, 37]).

Jonathan thus criticizes his father for having brought disaster to the country by his impractical oath. While Saul was stubbornly religious, Jonathan was, by contrast, practically God-fearing.

(2) The Sin of the Troops (14:31-35)

While these verses look like an interpolation since "the momentum of the story is interrupted, and Jonathan is not involved at all," v. 31 repeats the phrase *on that day,* the key phrase connecting the section vv. 24-30 with the preceding section, vv. 1-23 (see above on v. 23). Verses 24-30 concern Jonathan's breaking Saul's oath by eating honey; the present section, vv. 31-35, is concerned with the troops breaking God's commandment by eating meat with blood. The literary structure is thus in three parts: vv. 1-23; vv. 24-30// vv. 31-35; vv. 36-46.

66. See Ugar. *hnd* (*UT,* §19.786) "this."
67. For *How much more so,* see 2 Sam. 4:11; Hab. 2:5.
68. Klein, p. 138.
69. Driver, p. 114.
70. R. P. Gordon, p. 139.

(a) Troops Eat Blood (14:31-32)

31 *And they struck among the Philistines on that day from Michmash to Aijalon.*
And the troops were greatly exhausted.
32 *And the people rushed upon*[71] *the spoil*[72] *and took sheep, cattle and calves and slaughtered them on the ground.*
And the troops ate them with the blood.

31 As in v. 24, this key phrase *on that day* marks a literary connection with v. 23, which mentions Yahweh's victory "on that day."

Aijalon, modern Yalu (MR152-138) on the edge of the hill country, is at least 20 miles west of Michmash.

And the people were exhausted (wayyāʿap hāʿām) is repetition with variation (the addition of *greatly*) of the key phrase in v. 28b, showing a growing degree of exhaustion among the troops.

32 This incident of the people's rushing upon the spoil may have happened "at evening," as R. P. Gordon suggests.[73] This at least hints that the people refrained for a long time from eating but suddenly started eating when the oath had expired (see v. 34). They struck the Philistines "on that day" (v. 31), but this is after that.

The slaying of the animals *on the ground* (*ʾārṣāh;* lit., "to the earth") denotes that they slaughtered animals without a stone. The phrase *with the blood (ʿal-haddām)* means they did not drain it properly. The blood of an animal was the part that made atonement in sacrifices, and therefore blood could not be eaten (Lev. 17:10-14). This prohibition is also referred to in Gen. 9:4; Lev. 7:26-27; 19:26; Deut. 12:15-16.

(b) Saul Builds an Altar (14:33-35)

33 *When they informed Saul, saying,*
"Behold, the troops are sinning[74] *against the Lord*
by eating with the blood!"

71. K: *wyʿś;* Q: *wayyaʿaṭ.* Or "dart greedily (like a bird of prey)" (BDB, p. 743). For the Q., see 25:14 with preposition *b* and 15:19. The K. has been explained as being from *ʿśh "to turn"; see Barr, *CPTOT,* pp. 67, 246-47; Gibson, *CML,* 2d ed., p. 155 (on *ʿšy*).

72. K.: *ʾl-šll;* Q.: *ʾel-haššālāl;* see 15:19; it is possible that the K. is a phonetic spelling (see "Introduction" [Section II, B, 4]) after the *h* dropped out between a "vocalic" *l* and a vowel: *ʾelaššālāl* ← *ʾel-haššālāl.*

73. R. P. Gordon, p. 140.

74. *ḥṭʾym (ḥōṭî(ʾ)m);* a *sandhi-* spelling, with an *aleph* letter.

he said,
"You have acted treacherously!
Roll a large stone to me now!"
34 *And Saul said,*
"Scatter among the people and say to them,
'Each one of you, bring me your own ox and sheep
and slaughter them here and eat;
do not sin against the Lord by eating with the blood!'"
And all the people brought each one his ox in his hand that night
and slaughtered it there.
35 *And Saul built an altar to the Lord; that altar he built as an altar*
to the Lord for the first time.

33-35 When Saul is informed of the troops' sinful conduct, eating animals *with blood,* he commands people to slaughter animals properly and not to *sin against the Lord* by doing such a thing. Saul builds an altar to the Lord *for the first time* in his life.

A *large stone* served as an altar for draining blood from the meat. The blood could not be drained from the animals when they *slaughtered them on the ground* (v. 32).[75] The term *hayyôm* (lit., "the day") in this context denotes temporary immediacy, that is, *now.* There is no need to read *hlm* with the LXX and translate it as "here" (NIV; NRSV; McCarter, p. 247; R. P. Gordon, p. 344). See v. 28 and on 20:5.

34 *And Saul said:* this is an example of "repeated introduction to speech" in which "speech by one character, introduced with a finite form of the verb 'say' ('mr), is interrupted by a second introduction, also using a finite form of 'say.'"[76] See on 16:11.

The phrase *that night* (lit., "the night") means after sunset, which is the next day. Saul's oath forbidding food "before the evening" (v. 24) is no longer in force.

35 *That altar he built as an altar to the Lord for the first time* (lit., "it he began to build an altar to the Lord": *ḥll (Hi.) "to begin"). The word order with the objective "it" *('ōtô)* preceding the main verb is noteworthy. NRSV and NASB (also McCarter, p. 244) translate "it was the first altar that he built to the Lord." NIV translates in a different way: "it was the first time he had done this." R. P. Gordon accepts a possibility that the author gives this as "a slightly reproachful note."[77] It may be that the author emphasizes that

75. McCarter, p. 249. See 1 Sam. 6:14; 2 Sam. 20:8.

76. See E. J. Revell, "The Repetition of Introductions to Speech as a Feature of Biblical Hebrew," *VT* 47 (1997) 96-97, n. 15.

77. R. P. Gordon, p. 140.

this was Saul's first serious attempt to worship the Lord, though he had been rejected as king in the Lord's sight.

(3) Saul Makes Inquiry of God (14:36-46)

The worst result of Saul's oath is that Jonathan is almost killed. Some critics even read into the story hostility between Saul and Jonathan even before David comes on the scene.

(a) No Answer on That Day (14:36-37)

36 *And Saul said,*
"Let us go down after the Philistines by night
and take spoil among them till the light of morning!
Let us not leave a man among them!"
And they said,
"Do whatever is good in your eyes!"
And the priest said,
"Let us draw near to God here!"
37 *And Saul made inquiry*[78] *of God,*
"Shall I go down after the Philistines?
Will you give them into the hand of Israel?"
But he did not answer him on that day.

36 It is presumably the same night as *that night* in v. 34, after they slaughtered the animals on the altar that Saul built. The phrase *till the light of morning* restates *by night.*

37 As in 30:8, two questions are posed here: *Shall I go down after . . . ?* and *Will you give them . . . ?* (see 23:11f). *But he did not answer . . .* here means that God did not give (him) a favorable answer. P. Haupt proposed that "when the verb *ʿnh* refers to an oracular response, it has the technical meaning 'favorable answer.'"[79] The withholding of an answer was a certain indication that Yahweh was displeased; also 28:6.

(b) Saul's Oath (14:38-39)

38 *And Saul said,*
"Draw near here, all the chiefs of the people,

78. *šʾl b-; see 1 Sam. 10:22; also 22:10, 13, 15; 23:2, 4; 28:6; 30:8; 2 Sam. 2:1; 5:19, 23.

79. See P. Haupt, cited by A. M. Kitz, "The Plural Form of *ʾûrîm* and *tummîm*," *JBL* 116 (1997) 410, n. 36.

and examine and see how this sin has come about today!
39 *For as the Lord lives who delivers Israel,*
even if it[80] *is in Jonathan, my son,*
he shall surely die!"
But there was no one who answered him out of all the people.

38 The term *the chiefs* (lit., "corners") is related to "cornerstone." They were supposed to be the "cornerstones" of the nation as in Judg. 20:2 and Isa. 19:13 (of Egypt) (cf. Zech. 10:4 and Ps. 118:22)

39 The oath formula *as the Lord lives (ḥay-YHWH)* appears sixteen times in Samuel; the first occurrence in the OT is Judg. 8:19. It occurs also in Lachish Letter 3:9, as a military oath.[81]

Some scholars such as Whitelam[82] think that Saul was trying to procure Jonathan's death with this oath. However, the narrator keeps a complete silence here. Certainly Saul is concerned with Jonathan as his heir (20:31) even though he had other sons. R. P. Gordon takes this as a case of "the blind, unreasoning consistency of a man whose moral and religious instincts are badly confused."[83]

The expression *he shall surely die! (kî môt yāmût;* also v. 44; 1 Sam. 22:16; 2 Sam. 12:14; 14:14) is first used in Gen. 2:17 (also in the laws: e.g., Exod. 19:12; Lev. 20:2; and passim) but not in Deuteronomy.

The people kept silence when Saul mentioned Jonathan's name in his oath and expressed his willingness to put him to death; by contrast, they surprisingly intervene later in v. 45 to save Jonathan's life.

(c) Jonathan Is "Taken" (14:40-42)

40 *And he said to all Israel,*
"You shall be on one side;
and I and Jonathan, my son, shall be on the other side."
And the people said to Saul,
"Do what is good in your eyes!"
41 *And Saul said to*[84] *the Lord, God of Israel,*
"Give tamim!"[85]

80. M.s. = "the sin" (f.).

81. See *ANET,* 3d ed., p. 322.

82. K. W. Whitelam, *The Just King* (JSOTSS 12; Sheffield: Sheffield Academic Press, 1979), pp. 78, 80.

83. R. P. Gordon, p. 140.

84. Cf. "O Yahweh" (McCarter, p. 247), following the LXX. It is impossible to explain the particle *'el* as deriving from a vocative *lamed.*

85. Cf. "a perfect *lot*" (NASB); "Give me the right answer" (NIV); "Show Thammim" (JPS).

And Jonathan and Saul were taken, while the people were freed.
42 *And Saul said,*
"Decide between me and my son Jonathan!"
And Jonathan was taken.

The lot-casting ceremony here resembles in form and technical vocabulary the cases of Achan (Josh. 7:16-18) and of Saul's election (10:19-21). The actual procedure is apparently as follows: the lots are "cast" (*hippil,* v. 42; see below). They can only answer Urim or Thummin (see on v. 41), according to which one person or group of persons is "taken" (*lakad,* vv. 41-42) or "goes free" (*yaṣa',* v. 41). In the case of Achan and Saul, presumably the tribes were called up one by one until one was taken, but here Saul twice divides those not yet "gone free" into two groups for each lot. After David this practice was apparently not used.[86]

40-41 Saul appeals to the lot-casting procedure to decide who offended the oath. The term *tamim* (*tāmîm;* *tmm; adj. "complete") here is the equivalent of *tummîm,* which means "completeness, Thummim," hence "pronounced whole, acquitted" (McCarter, p. 250). For *'ûrîm,* "accursed, condemned" (*'rr), see 28:6, where "Urim" is mentioned together with "dreams" and "prophets" as a normal way of inquiring God's will. The phrase "to give *tamim*" *(*yhb tāmîm)* may be an idiomatic expression meaning "to give the truth," as in the Akkadian divinatory prayers used in connection with extispicy, divination by examining the condition of the entrails of sacrificed sheep or goats.[87]

Note the NRSV translation, based on the LXX: "O Lord God of Israel, why have you not answered your servant today? If this guilt is in me or in my son Jonathan, O Lord God of Israel, give Urim; but if this guilt is in your people Israel, give Thummim." It is often explained that the MT "suffered a long haplography caused by *homoioteleuton,*"[88] which skips all the material between the first and third occurrences of "Israel."[89] However, the present narrative seemingly purposely gives an abbreviated explanation of

86. See J. Lindblom, "Lot-casting in the Old Testament," *VT* 12 (1962) 164-78; C. van Dam, *The Urim and Thummim: A Means of Revelation in Ancient Israel* (Winona Lake, Ind.: Eisenbrauns, 1997).

87. See Foster, in *CS,* I, pp. 417-18. The phrase "place the truth!" appears in the Akkadian "Prayer to Gods of the Night" as well as in "Diurnal Prayers of Diviners"; see also W. W. Hallo, in *CS,* I, p. 417: "divination demanded and relied on a 'truthful' answer from the deity."

88. McCarter, p. 247.

89. Also A. Toeg, "A Textual Note on 1 Sam XIV 41," *VT* 19 (1969) 493-98; E. Noort, "Eine weitere Kurzbemerkung zu I Samuel XIV 41," *VT* 21 (1971) 112-16.

the procedure of lot-casting (see also on 10:19-20), since the audience was familiar with the practice.[90]

The *urim* and *tummim* are mentioned by name only seven times in the OT (Exod. 28:30; Lev. 8:8; Ezra 2:63; Neh. 7:65 ["Urim and Thummim"]; Deut. 33:8 ["Thummim and Urim"]; Num. 27:21 and 1 Sam. 28:6 ["Urim"]). They may have been two stones of two different colors, a bright color and a dark color,[91] perhaps one representing a positive and the other representing a negative answer, which were kept in the "breastpiece of judgment" of the priest's ephod (see Exod. 28:30; Lev. 8:8). Klein suggests it is significant that their names start with the first *(aleph)* and last *(tau)* letters of the Hebrew alphabet, respectively.[92] Houtman[93] takes the plural forms as *plurales intensitivi* and the combination of the two terms as a hendiadys. On the other hand, Kitz suggests that the plural forms reflect the practice of lot casting in which "the sum of two or three casts of the lots . . . ultimately decides the answer to a cleromantic inquiry," as is reflected in the lot-casting section in the Hittite KIN-oracles as well as in the Akkadian text LKA 137.[94] On the "psephomancy" ritual, that is, divination by means of white and black stones, in the aforementioned text from Asshur, see Horowitz and Hurowitz.[95] After enumerating eight points of contact between the Assyrian psephomancy and the biblical Urim and Thummin, Horowitz and Hurowitz conclude that both are "highly similar and perhaps somehow related."[96]

The reverse order *Jonathan and Saul* may be intentional, for Jonathan

90. W. Horowitz and V. A. Hurowitz, "Urim and Thummim in Light of a Psephomancy Ritual from Assur (LKA 137)," *JANES* 21 (1992) 109, n. 53. See also M. Tsevat, "Assyriological Notes on the First Book of Samuel," in *Studies in the Bible Presented to M. H. Segal,* ed. J. M. Grintz and J. Liver (Jerusalem: Kiryat Sepher, 1964), pp. 77-86; S. Pisano, *Additions or Omissions in the Books of Samuel: The Significant Pluses and Minuses in the Massoretic, LXX, and Qumran Texts* (OBO 57; Freiburg: Universitätsverlag, 1984), who support the MT for different reasons.

91. Hurowitz relates Urim and Thummim to two types of stone, i.e., alabaster and hematite, for the Akkadian word for alabaster, *gišnugallu,* means "great lamp" and corresponds with a possible meaning of *'ûrîm,* while an Akk. nickname of hematite is "truth stone," corresponding with a possible meaning of *tummîm.* See Hurowitz, in *CS,* I, p. 444, nn. 4, 5.

92. Klein, p. 140. For various explanations of their etymologies and physical nature, see Horowitz and Hurowitz, "Urim and Thummim," p. 96, n. 4. See van Dam, *The Urim and Thummim,* pp. 266-69.

93. C. Houtman, "The Urim and Thummim: A New Suggestion," *VT* 40 (1990) 229-32.

94. A. M. Kitz, "The Plural Form of *'ûrîm* and *tummîm,*" *JBL* 116 (1997) 401.

95. Horowitz and Hurowitz, "Urim and Thummim," pp. 98-106.

96. Horowitz and Hurowitz, "Urim and Thummim," p. 114.

is more significant in the narrative context. Note that the order "Saul and Jonathan" occurs some ten times.[97]

Both *taken* (*lkd; also 1 Sam. 10:20; Josh 7:16) and *freed* (*yṣ') are technical terms. Note that *wṣ' in Akkadian has a legal sense: "to become invalid."[98]

42 The term *decide (happîlû;* lit., "cause to fall") here is without an object noun. Usually the verb (*npl) appears with the term *gôrāl* ("lot") as in the phrase "Cast the lot(s)" *npl (Hi.) + *gôrāl.*[99] Here it is a brachylogy, namely, an ellipsis of the understood noun "lots," and the verb *happîlû* by itself keeps the idiomatic meaning "decide" (impv.).[100] McCarter thinks that MT again suffered a long haplography here.[101] Such "text-critical" solutions miss the characteristics of linguistic expressions.

(d) The People Rescue Jonathan (14:43-45)

43 *And Saul said to Jonathan,*
"Tell me what you have done!"
And Jonathan told him:
"I indeed tasted a bit of honey
with the end of the staff which was in my hand!
Here I am! I must die!"
44 *And Saul said,*
"May God do thus and do so again!
You shall surely die, Jonathan!"
45 *And the people said to Saul,*
"Should Jonathan die
who has made this great victory in Israel?

97. See E. J. Revell, "Concord with Compound Subjects and Related Uses of Pronouns," *VT* 43 (1993) 73.

98. *AHw,* p. 1477; cf. J. J. Finkelstein, "Some New *misharum* Material and Its Implications," in *Studies in Honor of Benno Landsberger on His Seventy-Fifth Birthday, April 21, 1965* (AS 16; Chicago: Oriental Institute, 1965), p. 236. See D. T. Tsumura, "'Fulfillment' and 'Abolishment' of the Law: A Meaning of Hebrew *yṣ'," *Exegetica* 11 (2000) 73-79 [Japanese with an English summary].

99. E.g., Isa 34:17; Ezek. 24:6 (Qal); Jonah 1:7 (Hi. and Q.); Ps. 22:18; Prov. 1:14; Esth. 3:7; 9:24; Neh. 10:34; 11:1; 1 Chr. 24:31; 25:8; 26:13, 14 (Hi. and Qal); cf. *šlk (Hi.) + *gôrāl* in Josh. 18:8, 10.

100. The phrase "to cause the lots to fall" became an idiom which means "to decide." Hence, even after the ellipsis of "the lots," the verb *npl (Hi.) keeps this idiomatic sense. Note a similar semantic development: (1) *drk "to tread" + *qešet* "bow"; (2) "to bend the bow" (in order to shoot); (3) "to shoot" (an arrow) in Ps. 58:7; 64:4. See "Introduction" (Section VII, D).

101. McCarter, p. 248.

May it never happen! As the Lord lives,
no hair of his head shall fall to the ground,
for with God he has acted this day!"
And the people rescued Jonathan, and he did not die.

43 When Jonathan was taken, Saul asks him what he has done. Jonathan confesses that he tasted the honey. Here, the prepositional phrase *with the end of the staff (biqṣēh hammaṭṭeh),* modified by the relative clause *which was in my hand ('ăšer-bᵉyādî),* occurs within the nucleus of the sentence (VSO): *I indeed tasted a bit of honey (ṭāʿōm ṭāʿamtî . . . mᵉʿaṭ dᵉbaš).* Such a construction is not impossible in Hebrew narrative, but it is strange; see "Introduction" (Section V, B).

It is hard to tell whether "I must die!" *('āmût)* is a statement or a question here. But whichever, it seems likely that it is spoken in protest, not acceptance, given Saul's insistence in the next verse. Probably Jonathan thought it unbelievable that his eating the honey could be the cause of the oracular silence, and he still does not accept that he should be killed.

44 On the expression *May God do thus and do so again!,* see 3:17; 20:13.

The use of *kî* with the oath formulae *You shall surely die (kî-môt tāmût;* cf. GKC, §149d) can be seen in 2 Sam. 3:9, 35; 1 K. 2:23; 19:2; also 1 Sam. 20:13.[102]

45 At last the people speak up and save Jonathan at this critical moment. Saul had sworn *As the Lord lives* (v. 39) that the man chosen by the lots as guilty would die, and the people here swear "as the Lord lives" that he will not die. David did not keep his oath to kill Nabal and his men when Abigail pointed out the wrong of it, and so at least it was considered that an oath to sin could be broken. The people here obviously think that God spoke much more clearly in the victory than in the lots.[103]

May it never happen! or "Far be it!" See 12:23; 20:2, 9. McCarter thinks this is "superfluous" and a "corrupt dittography of *hy yhwh.*" He omits it with LXX^{B},[104] but that is unnecessary.

The term *rescued* (*pdh; so NIV; NASB; cf. "ransomed" in NRSV; "saved" in JPS) may be related to the sin offering made for a thoughtless oath (Lev. 5:4-13), but more likely it is here used metaphorically, almost as an idiom, to mean "to save or rescue."

102. Driver, p. 118; McCarter, p. 250.
103. R. P. Gordon, p. 141 and no. 39.
104. McCarter, p. 248.

(e) Saul Returns (14:46)

46 *And Saul went up from pursuing the Philistines, while on the other hand the Philistines went to their place.*

Saul returns toward his home at Gibeah. *Went up* means toward the hill, away from the Philistine territory. Compare "go down after the Philistines" (v. 37). This *wayqtl* phrase of movement verb signals a transition, thus terminating the episode.

The phrase *from pursuing* means literally "from after."

3. Summary Statements (14:47-52)

Verse 46 ends with Saul's battle against the Philistines *on that day* (v. 23). The following verses, 47-52, summarize Saul's military activities and his family, "to sum up the many battles through which Yahweh fulfilled the promise of 9:16 and through which Yahweh had showed his own righteousness."[105] The mention of Amalek in v. 48 links the present section with the following chapter (ch. 15), where Saul himself is finally rejected because of his treatment of the Amalekites against God's commandment. Note the contrast between the positive note on his valiant action toward Amalek here and the negative evaluation of his conduct in the following chapter.

a. Saul against His Enemies (14:47-48)

47 *Now Saul had taken rule [over countries] besides*[106] *Israel.*
And he fought against all his enemies around, namely,[107] *against Moab, the Ammonites, Edom, the kings of Zobah, and the Philistines; and wherever he turned he would surge over them.*[108]

105. Klein, p. 143.

106. *ʿal;* like Ugaritic *ʿl,* "by"; see "outside of" (McCarter, p. 255); cf. "over" (NIV; JPS; NRSV; NASB).

107. Asyndeton.

108. *yaršîaʿ;* like a swarm of locusts. The MT form *yaršîaʿ* is usually analyzed as the Hi. of *ršʿ ("to be wicked") and translated as "inflicted punishment" (NIV; NASB), "worsted" (JPS); "put them to the worse" (RSV); cf. "routed" (NRSV). However, McCarter (p. 254) thinks the MT is corrupted and reads *ywšʿ,* "he was victorious," based on LXX^{B}. He says the MT reading arose because "the letters *w* and *r* were especially liable to confusion in scripts of the third and early second centuries B.C." Similarly R. P. Gordon, no. 41 (p. 344) holds that LXX is "almost certainly" original. While this view is very attractive, the MT may rather be explained as a phonetic spelling in the light of similar examples where the consonant /r/ and its contiguous consonant are switched as a metathesis: MT *yaršî^{a}ʿ* ← (metathesis) — */yašrî^{a}ʿ/ (*šrʿ).* The sense of this verb is explain-

48 *And he acted valiantly and struck Amalek and delivered Israel from the hands of its plunderers.*

So far ch. 14 has presented Saul in a mixed light, but this summary is completely favorable. These six kingdoms — *Moab,*[109] *the Ammonites, Edom, the kings of Zobah,* and *the Philistines* as well as *Amalek* — are mentioned also in 2 Sam. 8:12 as tributaries of David.

47 *Now (waw):* compare "After" (NIV; JPS); "When" (NRSV); "Now when" (NASB). For the expression *had taken rule [over countries]: (lākad hammᵉlûkāh;* so NIV), see "to take over the kingship, assume control" (*HALOT,* p. 530). The perfect verb denotes the pluperfect "had taken." McCarter translates "territory," interpreting the Vorlage of LXX^B as *ml'kh,*[110] but this is not necessary.

In the phrase *against all his enemies around,* Hauer sees "a first step in the king's military strategy, to be followed by somewhat indecisive battles in the south and an unsuccessful attempt to secure the north (1 Sam 31)."[111] For *Edom,* see on 21:7.[112] *Zobah* is an Aramaean city-state on the western slope of the Anti-Lebanon mountains. See 2 Sam. 10:6ff.

Saul was able to gain the upper hand over *the Philistines* in the central, hilly region of Israel, but at the end of his reign they were as much a threat as before.

48 Saul *acted valiantly (wayyaʿaś ḥayil)* and *struck Amalek.* The Amalekites are the archetypal plunderers in biblical tradition (Exod. 17:8-16; Num. 13:29; etc.). *Amalek* was the name of a nomadic tribe that inhabited the desert south of Judah, though they are associated with a *city* (see on 1 Sam. 15:5). They opposed Israel's attempts to enter Canaan from the south (Num. 14:41-45), and in several places in Judges they are mentioned as joining with other groups against Israel. They attacked David at Ziklag (ch. 30), and David is said to have subdued them in 2 Sam. 8:12.[113] Here, *Amalek* is mentioned in anticipation of the events of the following chapter, thus constituting a linking element (b) of the Ab/B pattern; see "Introduction" (Section VI, B).

---

able in the light of Ugar. *šrʿ* (*UT* §19.2488 "surging"). Hence, I would translate the verb as "he would surge over them" — like a swarm of locusts. See Tsumura, "Scribal Errors or Phonetic Spellings?" pp. 390-411.

109. For the most recent comprehensive treatment of Moab, see the special issue "The Archaeology of Moab," *BA* 60/4 (1997).

110. McCarter, p. 253.

111. Klein, p. 134. See C. E. Hauer, Jr., "The Shape of the Saulide Strategy," *CBQ* 31 (1969) 153-67.

112. See J. R. Bartlett, *Edom and the Edomites* (JSOTSS 77; Sheffield: JSOT Press, 1989).

113. See B. Becking, "Amalek," *DDD,* pp. 44-45.

b. Saul's Family and His General (14:49-51)

49 *Now the sons of Saul were Jonathan, Ishvi, and Malchishua; the names of his two daughters were — the name of the first-born was Merab,*[114] *the name of the younger, Michal.*
50 *And the name of Saul's wife was Ahinoam, daughter of Ahimaaz. And the name of the commander of his army was Abner, the son of Ner, Saul's uncle.*
51 *— Kish was the father of Saul; and Ner, the father of Abner, was the son of Abiel —*

49 Saul's sons are listed five times in the OT. Among them only *Jonathan* and *Ish-bosheth* play a role in the stories. Their names and the number are not certain:[115]

1 Sam 14:49	Jonathan, Ishvi, and *Malchishua*
1 Sam 31:2	
= 1 Chr. 10:2	Jonathan, Abinadab, and *Malchishua*
1 Chr. 8:33; 9:39	Jonathan, *Malchishua,* Abinadab, and Eshbaal

"Ishvi": *yišwî.* Compare LXX *(Iessiou),* which favors *yšyw.* Many scholars (including Aharoni, R. P. Gordon, and Japhet)[116] explain that *Ishvi* may be a variant form of Ish-bosheth. They would read "Ishvi" *(yišwî)* as *ʾîšyô,* "Man of Yahweh," which they think is an official, theologically corrected variation of *ʾîšbaʿal (ʾešbaʿal),* "Man of Baal" (1 Chr. 8:33; 9:39; etc.) also euphemistically called *ʾîš-bōšet,* "Man of Shame" (2 Sam. 2:8; etc.). However, as there is no textual evidence for *ʾyš-* here, this remains speculation. In any case, this leaves out Abinadab.[117] On the other hand, if Ishvi is neither Ishbaal or Abinadab, this account leaves out two known sons and puts in an unknown one.

50 *Ahinoam.* Note that one of David's wives has the same name; she is distinguished as "Ahinoam of Jezreel" (1 Sam. 25:43; etc.). Saul also had a concubine named Rizpah, by whom he had two sons, Armoni and Mephibosheth (2 Sam. 3:7; 21:11).

Abner (ʾăbînēr): MT has "Abiner" here, elsewhere spelled "Abner"

114. Cf. "Merob" (so 4QSam[a]: *mrwb*) and LXX (Μεροβ).

115. McCarter, p. 256.

116. Aharoni thinks that Ishvi is a distortion of the name *yʾšʾhw* (Josiah) = *ʾšyhw* (Eshiyahu) (note 6: Mazar; BHK; Soggin); see Y. Aharoni, *Arad Inscriptions* (JDS; Jerusalem: Israel Exploration Society, 1981), pp. 32-33. Also see R. P. Gordon, p. 142; S. Japhet, *I & II Chronicles* (OTL; London: SCM, 1993), p. 198.

117. McCarter, p. 254. See also on 7:1.

('abnēr) (e.g., v. 51). Abner held the important position of commander of Saul's army (see 1 Sam. 12:9; 2 Sam. 2:8); he appears often in the stories about Saul (1 Samuel 17, 20, 26). But during the brief reign of Ishbaal (2 Sam. 2:8ff.), he held greater power until he was slain by Joab, commander of David's army (2 Sam. 3:27).

The phrase *Abner, the son of Ner, Saul's uncle* is ambiguous, for in it "Saul's uncle" can refer either to Ner or to Abner. If it refers to Ner, Saul and Abner were cousins. However, if it refers to Abner the son of Ner, Abner and Kish were brothers. The former is possibly supported by 1 Chr. 9:36; 1 Sam. 9:1 (also Josephus, *Ant.* 6.130), where both Saul's father Kish and Abner's father Ner appear to be the sons of Abiel/Jeiel. The latter seems to be supported by 1 Chr. 8:33; 9:39, where Ner is mentioned as the father of Kish, the father of Saul. These two positions are seemingly irreconcilable.[118] However, "Kish" in 1 Chr. 9:36 and Ner's son "Kish" in 1 Chr. 9:39 could be different persons, based on the way the genealogical data are treated in vv. 35-44. For one thing, the narrator first lists ten sons of Jeiel in vv. 36-37; then, after making a brief reference to the last son Mikloth in v. 38, the narrator moves on to trace in detail the lineage of Ner (vv. 39-44), whose first son was Kish, the father of Saul. If this view is correct, the line of Saul may be explained thus:

	- Kish		
Jeiel (= Abiel)	- Ner	- Kish	- Saul
		- Abner	

In this structure, Saul's father, Kish, is the grandson of Abiel; see "Kish, son of Abiel" (1 Sam. 9:1); this is supported by the usage of *ben* which sometimes refers to a grandson.[119] If so, "Saul's uncle" in 1 Sam. 10:14 was probably Abner.[120] There is (another) example in Saul's family of an uncle and nephew with the same name, namely, Mephibosheth (see 2 Samuel 9 and 21).

51 *The son of Abiel* (so NRSV; NASB); compare "sons of Abiel" (NIV; JPS). The above-reconstructed genealogy perfectly supports this translation. Ner was "the son of Abiel," while Kish was the grandson of Abiel.

118. See J. W. Flanagan, "Chiefs in Israel," *JSOT* 20 (1981) 59-60. Flanagan thinks that Ner was elevated to the vertical line above Kish and Saul because of his importance in 1 Chr. 8:33-40 and 9:39-43.

119. So Japhet, *I & II Chronicles,* p. 197. Also A. Malamat, "King Lists of the Old Babylonian Period and Biblical Genealogies," *JAOS* 88 (1968) 171, n. 27.

120. K. van der Toorn, "Saul and the Rise of Israelite State Religion," *VT* 43 (1993) 523 holds that Ner was Saul's uncle.

c. Recruitment of Soldiers for Saul's Army (14:52)

52 *The war against the Philistines was severe all the days of Saul. And whenever Saul saw*[121] *any mighty man or any valiant man, he recruited him for himself.*

52 This verse reminds the audience that the war against the Philistines was not yet over, despite the successful military activities of Saul described in vv. 47-48. It will be only after David succeeds Saul that Israel defeats and subdues the Philistines (2 Sam. 8:1). Humanly speaking, Saul continued to make progress in strengthening Israel's military power and administration. His drastic failure will come not from his mishandling of the people or his enemies, but from his neglect and disobedience to God's word (see ch. 15).

Like 7:15-17, which summarizes Samuel's activities, this verse summarizes the life of Saul with regard to his military activities. Saul recruited any *mighty man (ʾîš gibbôr)* and *valiant man (ben-ḥayil)* for his standing army.[122] These two terms for soldiers do not appear in Ugarit. They may have entered Israel through Aramaean channels, as Rainey suggests,[123] since there is certainly a difference in military terms between LB Ugarit and Iron Age Israel.

This long chapter finally ends with a note about Saul's constant engagement in the severe warfare against the Philistines *all the days of Saul.* He kept busy by establishing external security of the country and by recruiting mighty men. He had never experienced "rest," as David did in 2 Sam. 7:1. Without the prophetic instructions from Samuel (see 12:23), his spiritual condition had gotten worse and worse into the drastic disobedience to God's commandment. In the following chapter, we will read the final rejection of him by the Lord. Because he acts *wickedly,* he will be *swept away* (12:25).

4. Saul and the Amalekites (15:1-35)

Chapters 15–16 are pivotal in 1 Samuel. In ch. 15 the narrator ends his account of the rise of the monarchy in Israel by telling of Saul's failure to obey the Lord's word and his resultant rejection by God. The next chapter, the anointing of David, is the account of a new beginning. Even though Saul remains king among the people and is honored as the Lord's anointed by David, he is now a "rejected king" in God's sight, as is hinted at in 13:1 where the narrator summarizes Saul's reign as lasting only for a "couple of years." In ch. 13, Saul was told he could not found a dynasty because of disobedience; here

121. Taking *wᵉrāʾāh* (*waw* + pf.) as habitual or "frequentative" perfect.

122. See 2 Sam. 2:17, 31; 18:7; etc. where David's warriors form the standing army; see Weinfeld, "Zion and Jerusalem as Religious and Political Capital," p. 78.

123. A. F. Rainey, "Institutions: Family, Civil, and Military," in *RSP* 2, p. 101.

he even more directly disregards the word of the Lord, and the Lord rejects him as king. As R. P. Gordon aptly says, "Saul is dead while he still lives."[1]

The final verse of ch. 15, v. 35a, marks the formal end of the relationship between Samuel and Saul, who have been the major *dramatis personae* since ch. 9. In ch. 9–10, Saul was chosen by the Lord (10:24); here he is rejected, forming an *inclusio*. Ironically, he became king because of the voice of the people asking for a king (8:9, 22; 12:1); now he is rejected because he listened to the voice of the people (15:20, 24). "Democracy is no more acceptable a replacement for prophetic theocracy than is monarchy!"[2]

At the same time the story looks ahead. The statement in v. 35b that Yahweh regrets making Saul king over Israel, with a reference to *the man of his choice* (13:14) and Saul's *neighbor* (15:28), leaves a tension that must be resolved. Saul's rejection here is the background against which the long struggle between Saul and David in the rest of the book must be understood.

Ch. 13 and Ch. 15 — Two Versions of the Same Incident?

The relationship between 13:7b-15a and 15:1-34 has been a main concern of literary critics.[3] Since Wellhausen's *Prolegomena* (1878),[4] there has been a general tendency to view these passages as doublets, that is, as two versions of the same incident. They both report Saul's cultic offense at Gilgal, emphasize the importance of obedience to the word of Yahweh, and are similar in structure. Birch considers each a "prophetic judgment speech to an individual," and says the entire narrative has been influenced by this form.[5]

vv. 1-13 Introduction
vv. 14-21 Accusation
vv. 22-23 Oracle
vv. 24-31 Announcement

On the other hand, there is a clear difference between the two passages. While ch. 13 explains "the failure of Saul to establish a dynasty," ch. 15 explains "the rejection of Saul as king and the subsequent withdrawal of the spirit

1. R. P. Gordon, p. 142.
2. McCarter, p. 270.
3. For example, see S. S. Yonick, "The Rejection of Saul: A Study of Sources," *AJBA* 4 (1971) 29-50.
4. J. Wellhausen, *Prolegomena to the History of Ancient Israel,* trans. Allan Menzies and John Black (original German edition, 1878) (New York: Meridian Books, 1957), pp. 258-60.
5. B. C. Birch, *The Rise of the Israelite Monarchy: The Growth and Development of I Samuel 7–15* (SBLDS 27; Missoula, Mont.: Scholars Press, 1976), pp. 98-103.

from him."[6] McCarter says these two passages are written by the same author as two stages dealing with two different issues in the progressive denunciation of Saul,[7] but one must be careful not to make too much of the difference between these two issues.[8] Both certainly deal with the rejection of Saul by Yahweh because of his disobedience to his commandment (13:13; 15:11). In both, the issue was certainly Saul's obedience to God's commandments.

a. "Go and Strike Amalek" (15:1-3)

1 *And Samuel said to Saul,*
"It was I whom the Lord sent to anoint you as a king
over his people Israel.
Now listen to the words of the Lord!
2 *Thus says the Lord of hosts:*
'I have taken note of what Amalek did to Israel,
what he put against him on the way,
when he was coming up from Egypt.
3 *Now, go and strike Amalek!*
And you shall utterly destroy all that belong to him
and have no compassion on him;
and you (s.) shall put to death both man and woman,
both child and infant,
both ox and sheep,
both camel and donkey!'"

1 Samuel has been silent and out of the stage since he left Saul in 13:15 where he accused Saul of his disobedience to God's *commandment* (13:13). Samuel appears again before Saul with God's personal message to him. *And he said (wayyō'mer)* followed by a stated subject at the beginning of an episode (also v. 32) gives background information (SETTING); see on 12:1. Note that the end of the previous chapter included a link to this chapter (v. 48). This episode is not necessarily the immediate sequel to the battle against the Philistines in ch. 14. Rather, it is natural to assume that some time had passed since "that day" (14:1).

The Hebrew emphasizes "I," hence, *It was I whom. . . .* Samuel was the kingmaker appointed by God and therefore his instructions must be obeyed by the king, who rules over Israel, the covenant people of Yahweh. Saul is here already king, hence *anoint* him *as a king,* instead of "as a prince"

6. Birch, *The Rise of the Israelite Monarchy,* pp. 107-8.
7. McCarter, pp. 270-71.
8. See R. P. Gordon, pp. 145-46.

as in 9:16; 10:1. This change of designation has nothing to do with "a separate literary history for the two accounts."[9]

The phrase *listen to the words of the Lord* here is literally "listen to the voice of the words of the Lord" in MT. This phrase is unusual in Hebrew and seems to be redundant. Hence, Hertzberg suggests that two variants "the voice" and "the words" were combined.[10] McCarter even thinks that the MT resulted from combining two "early variants," *ldbry* "to my words" and *lqwl yhwh* "to the voice of Yahweh." However, since "listen to the voice of some one" (*šmʿ + *leqôl* . . .) is an idiomatic expression which means "listen to, pay attention to, obey" (e.g., Gen. 3:17; etc.) and Job 34:16 has a similar expression (*haʾăzînāh leqôl millāy* "Listen to the voice of my words"), the MT as it stands should be translated as suggested above.

Here, in the very first verse of ch. 15, the issue of obedience to God's commandment comes to the front.

2 *Thus says the Lord* is the so-called prophetic messenger formula; see on 1 Sam. 2:27. Here Samuel conveys the message of *the Lord of hosts* (see 1 Sam. 1:3 and 4:4), the sovereign King of the Universe, to Saul, the human king of Israel.

For the expression *I have taken note of* (*pqd; or "I do remember"), see Ps. 8:4, where the word pair "be mindful of" (*zkr)//"take note of" (*pqd) appears; also note that "take note of" (*pqd) here is a variant expression of "remember" (*zkr) in Deut. 25:17: "Remember *(zākôr)* what Amalek did to you on the way when. . . ." The phrase *on the way* is an adverbial expression in both passages. 1 Sam. 14:48 was a link to this event (for the Amalekites, see on that verse).

This verse refers to the Amalekite attack on Israel from behind at the oasis of Rephidim during the journey from Egypt to Sinai (Exod. 17:8-13) when the Israelites "were faint and weary" (Deut. 25:18). At that time the Lord swore to Moses, "I will utterly blot out the memory of Amalek from under heaven" (Exod. 17:14b). This became a command for Israel in Deut. 25:19: "you shall blot out the memory of Amalek from under heaven." If Saul is to lead the country as king under Yahweh, it is his duty to carry out Yahweh's commands, particularly this command, *go and strike Amalek!* (v. 3). This principle can be applied only to a theocracy in which God is the king, however; human politicians do not have the right to declare vengeance. Amalek was certainly the Lord's enemy which "first and most obviously sought to deny Israel entry into the Promised Land." And "the victory over Amalek is expressly a victory of prayer (Ex. 17:8ff.) and thus of the Lord,"[11]

9. Klein, p. 148.
10. Hertzberg, p. 120.
11. Hertzberg, p. 124.

for the Lord "will have war against Amalek from generation to generation" (Exod. 17:16).

McCarter reconstructs *qrhw* for *śm lw,* translating "when he confronted him," based on the LXX.[12] However, *what he put against him* (lit., "that he put to him") can be taken as in apposition (so JPS) with asyndeton to the preceding phrase, *what Amalek did to Israel.*

3 The expression *utterly destroy . . . and have no compassion* (*w*^{e}*haḥăramtem . . . w*^{e}*lō' taḥmōl* is an <A-not B> pattern, in which the verb *utterly destroy* is followed by a negated antonym.[13] Note that *w*^{e}*haḥăramtem* is normally 2 m.pl. while *taḥmōl* is 2 m.s. The only possible way to unify the number is to explain the former as 2 m.s. + <enclitic *mem*> (cf. *UT,* §11.7) for emphasis.[14]

The verbal phrase *utterly destroy* or "to put under the ban" (*ḥrm;[15] cf. common Semitic **ḫrm,* "be separate, sacred") is attested in extra-biblical texts such as the Moabite Inscription, where king Mesha records that "he put the Israelite city of Nebo under a ban,"[16] and the Ugaritic myth on Anath's warfare *(KTU* 1.13).[17] The original sense "to consecrate or devote" experienced a semantic change to "to utterly destroy" the enemy as well as "to take the possessions as booty."[18] The word *ḥrm is sometimes translated as "curse" in the sense of "a thing banned or made off-limits from society, thus bringing a curse upon the person who breaks the ban and makes contact with it."[19]

In the Bible, it denotes to devote or set aside something as Yahweh's share or booty. Usually all living things — men, women, children, and livestock — were killed, as in this verse and Josh. 6:21; see also 1 Sam. 22:19. In

12. McCarter, p. 260.

13. See v. 9 for another example of the <A–not B> pattern ("spared . . . were not willing to destroy them utterly"); also 1:11; 2:3; etc.

14. McCarter, p. 261, emends the MT to "put (s.) him and everything . . . under the ban" with the LXX.

15. See *NIDOTTE,* #3049.

16. *DOTT,* p. 197; *ANET,* p. 320; now *CS,* II, p. 138. See P. D. Stern, "I Samuel 15: Towards an Ancient View of the War-*ḥerem,*" *UF* 21 (1989) 413-20; M. S. Smith, "Anat's Warfare Cannibalism and the West Semitic Ban," in *The Pitcher Is Broken: Memorial Essays for Gosta W. Ahlstrom,* ed. S. W. Holloway and L. K. Handy (JSOTS 190; Sheffield: Sheffield Academic Press, 1995), pp. 368-86.

17. For a possible parallel in Mari, see A. Malamat, "The Ban in Mari and in the Bible," *Biblical Essays 1966 (= Proceedings of the Ninth Meeting of "OTWSA" Held at the University of Stellenbosch 26th-29th July 1966)* (Potchefstroom: Society for the Study of the Old Testament, 1966), pp. 40-49. However, while the *ḥerem* in the OT applies to the enemy himself, the practice of *asakkum* in Mari is to prevent uncontrolled pillaging and applies only to the booty.

18. See Malul, "Taboo," *DDD,* p. 1562.

19. D. Stuart, "Curse," in *ABD,* I, pp. 1218-19.

Josh. 6:18-19, 24; 7:1, metal was "devoted" by being put in the Lord's treasury — other objects were burnt.[20] According to Deut. 20:10-18, when "distant cities that are at a distance from you . . ." were attacked, people and livestock could be spared as a work force or as plunder, but for cities within Israel, all living things were devoted. The purpose was to prevent syncretism, that is, "lest they teach you to follow all the detestable things they do in worshipping their gods, and you sin against the Lord your God." In the case in this chapter, the ban is based on Deut. 25:19.

R. P. Gordon notes that "the institution of the 'ban,' like the whole concept of the holy war, is far removed from the Christian code of the New Testament and must be seen in the context of the provisional morality of the Old Testament." But, how shall a Christian "slay the Amalekite"? He can find the answer "in keeping with the broad concept of 'spiritual warfare' in the New Testament"; cf. Eph. 6:12.[21] Such an institution certainly reminds us that "it is a fearful thing to oppose the living God."[22]

For the phrase *both man and woman* (lit., "from man to woman"), see on 1 Sam. 6:18 for the merismus. In our case, importantly, livestock, *both ox and sheep,* was put under the ban, as in Josh 6:21, but this was not always the case, as in Deut. 2:34-35; 3:6-7; Josh. 8:2, 26-27; 11:14. The reference to *camel* is appropriate here, for the Amalekites used camels for raiding, as in 30:17 (see also Judg. 6:5; 7:12).

b. Saul Spares Agag and Livestock (15:4-9)

4 *And Saul summoned*[23] *the people and mustered them at Telaim*[24]
— two hundred thousand = foot soldiers;

20. Most recently Nelson has understood the noun *ḥerem* as "the state of inalienable Yahweh ownership" and an entity in that state, and the verb as "to transfer an entity into the *ḥerem* state" and "to deal with an entity in a way required by its *ḥerem* state," usually by killing or destroying it. See R. D. Nelson, "*ḥerem* and the Deuteronomic Social Conscience!" in *Deuteronomy and Deuteronomic Literature: Festschrift C. H. W. Brekelmans,* ed. M. Vervenne and J. Lust (Leuven: Leuven University Press, 1997), pp. 44-45.

21. See "A Note on the 'Ban,'" in R. P. Gordon, pp. 147-48.

22. Baldwin, p. 113.

23. *wayšammaʿ;* Pi. "cause s.o. to hear," "to assemble." The verbal stem appears only here and 23:8.

24. *baṭṭᵉlāʾîm;* or "with the lambs." McCarter, following Driver, Budde, etc., thinks that the MT ("the lambs") should be read as *ṭēlāʾîm* and suggests a possible identification with Telem *ṭelem* (GN in Josh. 15:24) — cf. BHS, BDB: *ṭēlā(ʾ)m?* However, the MT as it is can be explained as a bi-form of *ṭelem. ṭᵉlāʾîm* (MT) → *ṭᵉlā+îm* → *ṭᵉlām.* = "Telam" (Klein, p. 144; cf. Driver, p. 122). This is similar enough to *ṭelem* ← *ṭalm- (Aramaic name; see BDB, pp. 378-79). If this identification is possible, "it was a city in the

ten thousand = the men of Judah.

5 *And Saul came up to the city*[25] *of Amalek and lay in wait*[26] *in the wadi.*

6 *And Saul said to the Kenites,*
"Go, depart, go down from among the Amalekites,
lest I destroy you[27] *with them.*
It was you who did kindness to all the sons of Israel
when they went up from Egypt."
And the Kenites departed from among Amalek.

7 *And Saul struck Amalek from Havilah up to Shur, which is on the border of Egypt.*

8 *And he captured Agag, the king of Amalek, alive, but all the people he utterly destroyed with the edge of the sword.*

9 *And Saul and the people spared Agag and the best of the small and large cattle, namely, the fat ones,*[28] *and the lambs and all that*

Negeb of uncertain location but not far from the Negebite Ziph (*not* the Ziph of 23:14, etc.), modern Khirbet ez-Zeifeh, some 32 miles due S of Hebron" (McCarter, p. 266). See 1 Sam. 27:8.

25. Cf. "cities" (LXX).

26. McCarter translates "and lay in wait," reading *wy'rb* (i.e., *wayyeʾĕrōb*) on the basis of the LXX, while explaining the MT as "and struggled" (p. 261). According to him, "some critics have attempted to recover a defectively written *Hip'il* of *ʾrb (wayyāreb < wayyaʾărēb)* [from MT] meaning 'he prepared an ambush.'" However, the MT form might be explained as a *sandhi* spelling; see "Introduction" (Section II, B, 4). Hiphil could be taken as an internal hiphil (e.g., Ps. 1:3).

27. *ʾōsīp^{e}kā;* lit., "I gather you up": so BDB, p. 62, NASB. < *ʾsp Qal, 1 c.s.: /*ʾōsip-kā́/* ←(*shwa's* rule; without ʾ)— */ʾō(ʾ)s^{e}p^{e}-kā́/* — (accent shift) — */ʾō(ʾ)sḗp-^{e}kā/* (not Hi. of *ysp, */ʾōsīp^{e}kā/* "I add you," as McCarter suggests). See *KTU* 1.14 [UT Krt]:18 (*yitsp* — gathering by Reshef); see *CS,* I, p. 333. Cf. "I sweep you away" (McCarter, p. 261, followed by Klein, p. 146), based on *sph.

28. *hammišnîm;* "fatlings" (NASB; NRSV); also Targ.; Syr.; "the fat calves" (NIV); also LXX: *kai tōn edesmatōn* "and the victuals" (McCarter, p. 262). McCarter translates it as "the fat ones," reading *haššĕmēnîm* or *hammišmannîm.* Note that one Hebrew ms reads *whšmnym* (BHS); MT *hammišnîm* could mean "the doubles" or "the double portions" (McCarter); cf. "the second-born" (JPS). However, most probably the metathesis of two consonants, *m,* a sonorant, and *š,* resulted in the MT *mišnîm,* which is a phonetic variant of *šimnîm. The latter could probably be a shortened form of *šimanîm, the plural form of *šimn- > *šemen* "oil, fat."

> *šimanîm cf. *š^{e}mānîm, š^{e}mānêkā* (Song 1:3), *mišmannê hāʾāreṣ* (Gen. 27:39)
> —(*sandhi* of vocalic /m/ and /a/)→ *šimnîm
> —(metathesis)→ *mišnîm*

If the above explantion is correct, the MT *mišnîm* is a phonetic variant of the term *šimanîm, which normally changes to *š^{e}mānîm* in the standard vocalization of Tiberian Hebrew.

was good; they were not willing to destroy them utterly. As for all the property despised[29] *and worthless,*[30] *they utterly destroyed it.*

4 Saul listens to the Lord's order to *utterly destroy* the Amalekites and their belongings and puts it into action. He first summons and musters the soldiers at Telaim. Klein thinks that 210,000 is too large in comparison with Saul's army, which "numbered anywhere from 600 up to 3,000 (1 Sam. 13:2, 15)."[31] However, such a number is not impossible, since, as noted above, this chapter did not necessarily follow directly after that great victory over the Philistines (14:23, 31; see on 15:1); it may have been several years later, during which Saul's army must have grown greatly. The point here is that Saul had enough manpower to outnumber Amalek. It may be that such a large army together with the divinely justified purpose and command (vv. 2-3) was a temptation for Saul not to trust on God's help. Compare the view that *eleph* here should denote a "military unit"; see on 6:19.

The expression = *the men* is in a list style; see on 6:17-18a; 25:18; adverbial, with the particle *'et.*

As in 11:8, the army of Judah is mentioned here separately. Judah acted separately from the rest of Israel at various times during the United Monarchy (after Saul's death, during Absalom's rebellion, after Solomon's death) and was obviously a separate unit in Israel. But the presence of the Judahite Jesse's sons in Saul's army and Saul's search for David in Ziph (23:19-24; 26:1-4) suggest that Judahites in general considered themselves part of the kingdom. In this campaign it is not surprising that Judah was heavily involved, as Amalek was near Judah and must have been particularly subject to their raids.

5 As the Amalekites lived in the desert, it seems surprising to have a reference to their "city." However, while *city ('îr)* certainly implies a place more substantial than an encampment, it does not have to refer to a "city." In Deut. 3:5 *'ārê happ^{e}rāzî* refers to "unwalled villages"; see on 1 Sam. 6:18a.

29. *n^{e}miḇzāh* ←(vowel reduction)— *nimiḇzāh* ← (anaptyxis) — *nimbzāh* ← (with *m*-glide) — *niḇzāh* (Ni., ptc., f.s. *bzh).

See D. T. Tsumura, "Scribal Errors or Phonetic Spellings? Samuel as an Aural Text," VT 49 (1999) 408-9. Cf. "grammatical *monstrum*" (Driver, p. 124); "the unintelligible text" (McCarter, p. 262; also Klein, p. 146); "some kind of scribal error" (see *NIDOTTE,* 1, p. 629 for various unsuccessful attempts to solve this problem). See "Introduction" (Section II, B, 4).

30. *nāmēs* (*mss) Ni., ptc., m.s. "wasted" (BDB, p. 588); or *nāmēs* ←(vowel *sandhi*)— *nāme'es* (*m's). Cf. Ni., ptc., f.s. *nim'eset* "worthless, lit., rejected" (BDB, p. 588; McCarter, p. 262).

31. Klein, p. 149.

The term *wadi* probably refers to the Wadi/Brook of Egypt as in Ezek. 47:19; 48:28. It was the traditional southern boundary of the land, as in Num. 34:5; Ezekiel; etc. It is the Wadi el-ʿArîshel, which flows into the Mediterranean about 50 miles south of Gaza.

6 Saul shows favor to *the Kenites,* "a Midianite phratry," who were a tribe of metalworkers (the name means "smith") in the desert south of Israel and Judah. They lived among the Amalekites at the time of the Israelite settlement, according to the LXX of Judg. 1:16.

The term *kindness (ḥesed)* means "loyalty, faithfulness, goodness"[32] as expressed by a deed loyal or faithful to the other party in appreciation of the latter's goodness (see 2 Sam. 2:5). There is no biblical account of this "kindness," but Moses' father-in-law was Kenite (Judg. 4:11), and he came to meet Moses after the attack of the Amalekites (Exod. 17:8–18:12). Their "kindness" is sharply contrasted with the evil conduct of the Amalekites (see Deut. 25:18). David also did not raid them during his Ziklag period (1 Sam. 27:8-10; 30:29). However, there is not enough ground for postulating an actual treaty relationship or alliance between Israel and the Kenites.[33] See on 2 Sam. 2:5.

7 After the Kenites left, Saul attacks the Amalekites. The location of *Havilah* (so MT, LXX; also in Gen. 25:18 with *Shur*) is unknown. *From Havilah up to Shur* is the extent of the Ishmaelite territory in Gen. 25:18. McCarter[34] reconstructs "from the Wadi," for it was "at the Wadi" (see v. 5 above) that Saul *lay in wait* while warning the Kenites, but his emendation has no textual basis. Shur refers to a wilderness region in northwest Sinai, on the eastern border of Egypt; see 1 Sam. 27:8.

Saul's victory is reported only briefly because what Saul did after the victory is more important to the narrator.

8 Saul captures the Amalekite king Agag alive; he may have thought kings should get special consideration, just as Ahab spared Benhadad as his "brother" (1 K. 20:30-34). *Agag,* mentioned only here and Num. 24:7, is either a name or a title, like "Pharaoh"[35] or "Achish" (see on 1 Sam. 21:10). The fact that Haman in Esther is called the "Agagite" (Esth. 3:1; etc.) might possibly show that Agag had become almost "the type of the enemy of Yahweh and his people."[36]

9 The phrase *Saul and the people spared* means that they did not "utterly destroy." This was in direct disobedience to the divine command in

32. See *NIDOTTE,* 2, pp. 211-18; also T. Ishida, *The Royal Dynasties in Ancient Israel: A Study on the Formation and Development of Royal-Dynastic Ideology* (BZAW 142; Berlin: de Gruyter, 1977), p. 109.

33. See McCarter, p. 266.

34. McCarter, p. 261.

35. R. P. Gordon, p. 144.

36. Hertzberg, p. 125.

v. 3. The purpose of this war was not to gain spoil but to fulfill God's ancient command. The ban was not something to be applied lightly as one pleased. Here, Saul showed no respect and regard for the awesome institution of the ban for "partial fulfillment is not a possibility"[37] in the logic of ban.

Saul thus interpreted the command of the Lord in his own way: that was the root of his problem. Hertzberg notes: "It was his sin that he waged this war after the fashion of other wars; that was regarded as a profanation of the realm of the holy."[38]

The phrase *the small and large cattle (haṣṣō'n wᵉhabbāqār)* is a merismus, referring to all the cattle; also v. 15.

Modern translations differ among each other in their understanding of the syntax of the phrase, literally, "the best of the sheep and the cattle and the fatlings and the lambs and all that was valuable." The question is how far the scope of "best" extends. For example, "Agag, and the best of the sheep and of the cattle and of the fatlings, and the lambs, and all that was valuable" (NRSV); "Agag and the best of the sheep and cattle, the fat calves and lambs — everything that was good" (NIV); "Agag and the best of the sheep, the oxen, the second-born, the lambs, and all else that was of value" (JPS). However, the *waw* (*namely;* lit., "and") before "the fatlings" is here explicative, as in 6:18. In other words, the structure here supports the interpretation of taking the fat ones (= "best cattle") as in apposition to the best of small and large cattle (also v. 15), that is, "the best cattle, both large and small, and the lambs and all that was valuable."

c. The Lord's Word to Samuel (15:10-11)

10 *And the word of the Lord came to Samuel, saying,*
11 *"I regret that I have made Saul king,*
for he has turned away from following me
and has not carried out my words."
And Samuel was angry; and he cried out to the Lord all the night.

10 The formula, "And the word of the Lord was to PN," also appears in 2 Sam. 7:4. It is used eighty-three times in the OT, most frequently in the prophetic books. The Lord here takes initiative in conveying his own regret.

11 The verbal phrase *I regret (niḥamtî)* is a performative perfect, and the Ni. pf. 1 c.s. of this verb appears one other place in a performative utterance with Yahweh as the speaker, in Gen. 6:7. In both places, Yahweh ex-

37. R. W. L. Moberly, "'God is not a human that he should repent' (Numbers 23:19 and 1 Samuel 15:29)," in *God in the Fray: A Tribute to Walter Brueggemann,* ed. T. Linafelt and T. K. Beal (Minneapolis: Fortress, 1998), p. 119.

38. Hertzberg, p. 126.

presses regret for his previous actions, his making Saul king or his creation of man; the function of the language used here is thus *emotive* as well as performative. Yahweh's "regret" (or "repentance") is anthropopathic; "yet it conveys an important truth about a God who is not impassive or static, but dynamic in his interaction with his creation."[39] The verb (Ni.) itself is a key word in this chapter and reappears in v. 35 as well as twice in v. 29 ("change one's mind"). It is also used in other passages when God is moderating his judgment (2 Sam. 24:16).[40]

Carried out (*hēqîm;* lit., "made it stand") or "established." It is the king's responsibility as the representative of the people to carry out God's word. In 13:13 Saul was "foolish" not to listen to the Lord's word; here the much stronger expression "turned away from following me" is used.

Since the subjects of the two verbs are different in the expression *And Samuel was angry; and he cried out* (lit., "it burned to/with regard to Samuel and he cried"), the two actions are not sequential. Samuel was probably angry at Saul.[41] What exactly caused Samuel's crying out *to the Lord all the night* is not certain. However, it suggests that as the prophet of the Lord he feels God's inner feeling, the divine *pathos*,[42] violently.

d. Samuel and Saul (15:12-31)

(1) Saul Erects a Monument (15:12)

12 *And Samuel rose early in the morning to meet Saul.*
And it was told Samuel,
"Saul has gone to Carmel;
he is now erecting a monument for himself!
And he turned and passed on
and went down to Gilgal."

12 Early in the morning Samuel rose and went out to meet Saul, but he was informed that Saul had gone to Carmel to erect a *monument* for his victory.

39. R. P. Gordon, p. 144.

40. R. P. Gordon, n. 49 (p. 345).

41. For the various possible explanations of Samuel's anger, see D. M. Gunn, *The Fate of King Saul* (JSOTSS 14; Sheffield: JSOT Press, 1980), pp. 146-47; R. P. Gordon, p. 345, no. 50.

42. Heschel explains the experience of the prophet in Israel as "a fellowship with the feelings of God, a *sympathy with the divine pathos,* a communion with the divine consciousness which comes about through the prophet's reflection of, or participation in, the divine pathos"; see A. J. Heschel, *The Prophets: An Introduction* (New York: Harper & Row, 1962), p. 26.

McCarter thinks that the expression *rose early in the morning to meet Saul* (lit., "rose early to meet Saul in the morning") has the force of "rose early *and went* to meet" *Saul in the morning* (so LXX). However, we take the phrase *in the morning* as modifying the verb "and he rose early," rather than "to meet." The normal word order is . . . "NP(S) rose early in the morning": for example, Gen. 19:27; 1 Sam. 1:19; etc. See also on 1 Sam. 29:11.

Carmel, not the mountain in the north, is a small town in Judah near Maon. The modern site is Tel el-Kirmil, about 7 miles south of Hebron. It was situated at a convenient place for Saul to stop on his return from the Amalekite expedition; Nabal and Abigail were from there (see 25:2a; Josh. 15:55).

At Carmel Saul erected a *monument* (*yad;* lit., "hand"; see 2 Sam. 18:18; *HALOT,* p. 388) probably to commemorate his victory over Amalek, a common practice of kings in the ancient Near East. Then he went to Gilgal, the cultic center of Israel. For Gilgal, see on 7:16.

(2) "I Have Carried Out the Word of the Lord" (15:13-16)

13 *And Samuel came to Saul.*
And Saul said to him,
"Blessed are you of the Lord!
I have carried out the word of the Lord."
14 *And Samuel said,*
"Then what is this bleating[43] *of small cattle in my ears,*
and the lowing[44] *of the large cattle which I am hearing?"*
15 *And Saul said,*
"From the Amalekites they have been brought,
for[45] *the people spared the best of the small and large cattle*
in order to make a sacrifice to the Lord, your God;
but the rest we have utterly destroyed."
16 *And Samuel said to Saul,*
"Stop! Let me tell you
what the Lord said to me last night."
And he said[46] *to him "Speak!"*

This episode takes place at Gilgal. Here Saul was confirmed as king (11:14-15), and here his rejection was announced (13:7-15) and will be announced again.

43. Lit., "voice."
44. Lit., "voice."
45. *'ăšer;* it functions like a <speaker-oriented *ky*> (see "Introduction" [Section V, C]); cf. McCarter, p. 267.
46. Q.; cf. *wy'mrw* (K.).

13 When Samuel arrives at Gilgal, Saul greets Samuel with the formula *Blessed are you of/by the Lord!* (*brk, pass. ptc. + NP (S) + *laYHWH*); this formula also appears in 23:21; 2 Sam. 2:5; as well as in Khirbet el-Qom Inscription[47] and Aramaic inscriptions.[48] With the words *I have carried out* (*hăqîmōtî;* see v. 11) Saul deceives himself. Though Saul acted religiously, he actually did *not listen to the voice of the Lord* (v. 19). The phrase *the word of the Lord* is the key phrase in this chapter; see vv. 11, 19, 22, 23.

14 The poetic feature of Samuel's reply here and in vv. 22 has been noted.[49]

> "Then what is this *bleating* of small cattle in my ears,
> and the *lowing* of the large cattle which I am hearing?"

Here, the merismatic expression *the small cattle and large cattle (haṣṣō'n wᵉhabbāqār)* in v. 9 is broken up into the word pair *small cattle* and *large cattle* in the parallel structure.[50]

15 Here Saul, who has been "rejected" as king in the judgment of the narrator, makes his excuses for not killing all the animals. Several of the phrases are particularly instructive: (1) the impersonal passive construction *they have been brought;* (2) *the people spared;* (3) *the best . . . to sacrifice;* (4) *to the Lord, your God;* (5) *the rest we have utterly destroyed.* Saul excuses himself by saying that (a) the animals were brought back to sacrifice to "the Lord *your* God," and (b) in any case, it was the idea of "the people." This was probably not completely false. Verse 9 says "Saul and the people spared," and since they went to Gilgal, they probably intended to sacrifice at least some of the animals at this cultic center. However, sacrifice and the "ban" are not the same thing;[51] the "ban" is the total destruction, devoting everything to Yahweh as his share, while sacrifice usually provides portions for men. God had not asked for a cultic sacrifice. Saul also was involved in the decision (cf. Adam and Eve's attempt to evade responsibility in Genesis 3).

Instead of specifying who "brought" these cattle, Saul neutralizes his responsibility with the impersonal passive construction: they have been brought (lit., "they have brought them"). If his conscience had been com-

47. *CS,* II, p. 179, n. 3.

48. *CS,* II, p. 187, n. 1.

49. On the poetic nature of Hebrew prose, see "Introduction" (Section VII, B).

50. For the phenomenon of literary "break-up," see E. Z. Melamed, "Break-up of Stereotype Phrases as an Artistic Device in Biblical Poetry," *Scripta Hierosolymitana* 8 (1961) 115-53; D. T. Tsumura, "Literary Insertion (AXB) Pattern in Biblical Hebrew," in *Proceedings of the Eighth World Congress of Jewish Studies, 1981, Division a: The Period of the Bible* (Jerusalem: World Union of Jewish Studies, 1982), pp. 1-6; "Literary Insertion (AXB Pattern) in Biblical Hebrew," *VT* 33 (1983) 468-82.

51. See also Hertzberg, pp. 127-28.

pletely clear about bringing the animals, he would probably have said "I" (or at least "we") have "brought" and "spared." Note he said "I have carried out" (v. 13) and "we have destroyed" (v. 15).

He says they had *spared the best of the small and large cattle,* but in v. 9 God had specifically commanded the small and large cattle to be utterly destroyed. Only that which was not the best of the cattle, Saul destroyed utterly; this is a totally inadequate treatment of God's command of the ban toward the Amalekites, which requires the dedication of everything to the Lord by utterly destroying all.

The Lord your God. Such a use of pronoun "your" suggests the nature of Saul's personal relationship with his God; he does not speak of "our God." While Yahweh was his God too, Saul emphasized that his duty had been to Samuel's God. By doing so, he again tries to lighten his own responsibility as the representative of the people.

(3) "Because You Have Rejected the Word of the Lord" (15:17-23)

17 *And Samuel said,*
"Though little you are in your eyes,
are you not the head of the tribes of Israel?
And the Lord anointed you king over Israel.
18 *And the Lord sent you on a mission,*[52] *saying:*
'Go and utterly destroy the sinners, the Amalekites,
and fight with them till they are exterminated!'[53]
19 *But why did you not listen to the voice of the Lord,*
rushing upon the spoil,[54]
and doing the evil in the eyes of the Lord?"
20 *And Saul said to Samuel,*
"Because[55] *I listened to the voice of the Lord,*
I went on the mission on which the Lord sent me
and brought Agag the king of Amalek,
but as for the Amalekites I utterly destroyed them.

52. Lit., "send in a way."

53. Lit., "till they exterminate them"; <impersonal passive> (so NRSV; NASB); cf. "you exterminate" (so LXX; NIV; JPS). McCarter explains that MT has "what seems to be a mixture" of the reading *'d klwtk 'tm,* based on LXX, and the reading *'d klwtm,* suggested by Wellhausen, p. 100; Driver, p. 126; and Smith, p. 138. Or, the MT's *kallôtām 'ōtām* could be a distant regressive total assimilation from *kallôtāk 'ōtām:* "you exterminate them."

54. *'el-haššālāl;* see on 1 Sam. 14:32 (Q.).

55. *'ăšer;* lit., "that." Cf. GKC, §157c, which holds that *'ăšer* introduces direct narration here as well as in 2 Sam. 1:4. See on 2 Sam. 1:4.

21 *And the people took small and large cattle from the spoil,*
the choicest of[56] *the things devoted to destruction*
to sacrifice to the Lord your God at Gilgal."
22 *And Samuel said,*
"Does the Lord have delight in burnt offerings and sacrifices
as much as in obeying the voice of the Lord?
Behold, obedience is better than sacrifice;
attentiveness than the fat of rams!
23 *For rebellion is the sin of divination;*
presumption[57] *is wickedness and idolatry.*[58]
Because you have rejected the word of the Lord,
he has rejected you from being king!"[59]

17 Samuel purposely uses here a phrase very similar to that which Saul once used about himself. Even though Saul thinks that he is "from the smallest of the tribes of Israel" (9:21), he should not forget that he is the king, who is *the head of the tribes of Israel.* Samuel reminds Saul here again (see v. 1) that the Lord *anointed* him *king over Israel.* Why should Saul, as God's anointed, yield to the people's opinion?

18 The term *sinners* is the only example of substantive use of the root *ḥṭ' ("to sin"; see 2:25; 15:24) in Samuel. It is unusual to use this word for a foreign nation, but among the distant nations, the Amalekites seem to have aroused special hatred, and even the ban was applied to them. Compare "the sin of the Amorites" (Gen. 15:16).

19 The central issue here is Saul's disobedience to the word of God: he did *not listen to the voice of the Lord* (see vv. 11, 13, 22, 23). It is implied that he let greed (or perhaps popularity with the people) stand in the way of obedience.

The verb "to rush upon" is a denominative verb from *'ayiṭ* "bird of prey"; Ugar. *'ṭ;* see 1 Sam. 14:32 (Q). While Saul was trying to put blame on the people, Samuel accused Saul, "the head of the tribes of Israel" (v. 17), of the entire responsibility here ("you [s.] rushed upon").

The phrase *doing the evil in the eyes of the Lord* appears in Num. 32:13; Deut. 4:25; Judg. 2:11; 3:7; as well as Kings (e.g., 1 K. 11:6; 14:22; etc.). The structure puts "not listening to the voice of the Lord" parallel to

56. Cf. "the best of" *mêṭab* (vv. 9, 15) of small and large cattle, which refers to "the fat ones" (v. 9).

57. *hapṣar;* usually as Hi. inf. abs.; "to urge, press"; lit., "to display pushing" (i.e., arrogance, presumption, "pushiness"); see on *wayyipr^{e}ṣû* (1 Sam. 28:23).

58. *'āwen ût(^{e})rāpîm;* a hendiadys which refers to "wicked" idolatry; cf. "the wickedness of idolatry" (McCarter, p. 263), following LXX^B.

59. *mimmelek;* lit., "from a king"; cf. *mihyôt melek* (v. 26).

"doing the evil in the eyes of the Lord"; also, the contrast between Saul's own judgment ("in his eyes" in v. 17) and the Lord's judgment is to be noted here. Surely, to ignore God's word is a very evil thing in his judgment.

20-21 Saul's excuse here is much the same as in vv. 13 and 15. However, in v. 20 the first person prevails; "I" Saul did such and such, even bringing Agag to Gilgal. But in v. 21 he still tries to put blame on "the people." But from the narrator's, hence Yahweh's, viewpoint, it was "Saul and the people" who acted (v. 9).

22-23 As in the other prophetic passages, Samuel is not here denying the total system of sacrificial offerings itself. The prophets indeed attacked the abuses of the sacrificial system (see Isa. 1:11-15; 66:3; Jer. 7:21-22; Hos. 6:6; Amos 5:21-22; Mic. 6:6-8), but as 1 Sam. 2:29 says, "sacrifice and offering" are commanded by the Lord. In the present occasion, Saul was specifically commanded to perform the "ban" against the Amalekites, the enemy of the Lord. No sacrifice, whatever the best it may be, can substitute for obedience to this command as God's anointed king. As Baldwin puts it, "no ceremonial can make up for a rebellious attitude to God and his commandments, because obstinate resistance to God exalts self-will to the place of authority."[60]

At this central point of the chapter, both verses constitute "poetic" prose, which exhibits characteristic features of parallelism; see "Introduction" (VII, B). O'Connor classifies vv. 22-23 as a "poem" together with 1 Sam. 2:1-10; 15:33; 18:7 = 21:11 = 29:5; 24:14; 2 Sam. 1:19-27; 3:33-34; 20:1; 22:2-51; 23:1-7.[61]

		Stress (Syllables)	
v. 22	*haḥēpeṣ laYHWH*	2 (6)	Does the Lord have delight
	b^{e}ʿōlôt ûz^{e}bāḥîm	2 (7)	in burnt offerings and sacrifices
	kišmōaʿ b^{e}qôl YHWH	3 (7)	as much as in obeying the voice of the Lord?

In this three-line parallelism "burnt offerings and sacrifices," a merismatic expression (see 1 Sam. 6:15; Jer. 7:22; 17:26), are contrasted to the obedience to the Lord. "YHWH" appears both in the first and the third lines.

	Stress (Syllables)	
hinnēh š^{e}mōaʿ mizzebaḥ ṭôb	4 (9)	Behold, obedience is better than sacrifice;
l^{e}haqšîb mēḥēleb 'êlîm	3 (8)	attentiveness than the fat of rams!

60. Baldwin, p. 115.

61. M. O'Connor, "War and Rebel Chants in the Former Prophets," in *Fortunate the Eyes That See: Essays in Honor of David Noel Freedman in Celebration of His Seventieth Birthday,* ed. A. B. Beck et al. (Grand Rapids: Eerdmans, 1995), pp. 324-25.

The same thought is expressed differently in this two-line parallelism. The phrase *the fat of rams* is a ballast variant to *sacrifice.* The parallelism as a whole means: "obedience, namely, attentiveness, is better than sacrifice, namely, the fat of rams."

		Stress (Syllables)	
v. 23	*kî ḥaṭṭa'ṯ-qesem merî*	3 (7)	For rebellion is the sin of divination;
	w^{e}*'āwen ût*^{e}*rāpîm hapṣar*	3 (9)	presumption is wickedness and idolatry.

Here, a construct chain "the sin of divination" (a of b) is in parallel with a hendiadys "wickedness and idolatry" (a′ + b′), with the elements a and b corresponding to a′ and b′, respectively. Thus, the parallelism conveys "one thought through two lines" (see "Introduction" [VII, A]): i.e. "rebellion and presumption" is the wicked sin which directly opposes the sovereignty of the Lord. In other words, Saul's disobedience to the word of the Lord is as wicked as idolatry or divination, which seeks the will of no-god.

	Stress (Syllables)	
ya'an mā'astā 'et-d^{e}*bar YHWH*	4 (10)	Because you have rejected the word of the Lord,
wayyim'ās^{e}*kā mimmelek*	2 (8)	he has rejected you from being king!

Here, Saul is told that the Lord *has rejected* him *from being king;* this is the direct opposite of v. 17: *the Lord anointed you king.* This happened to Saul because he *rejected the word of the Lord.* Obedience to God's word is thus of prime importance to the king who is his vice-regent.

22 As in Ps 1:2 (= *thelēma* "will" in LXX), the *delight (haḥēpeṣ)* refers to the thing which preoccupies one's thought and will. The Lord himself does not need the sacrifices like gods and goddesses in other religions. Rather, the people need sacrifices in order to approach the holy God; see Leviticus chs. 1–5. Hence, *sacrifice* without *obedience* as well as *the fat of rams* without *attentiveness* would make this holy God no-god.

Note that fat belongs to Yahweh (Lev. 3:16-17; 7:23-25).

23 The actions *rebellion* and *presumption* are the rejection of the Lord, being equivalent to apostasy. Does this verse "foreshadow"[62] the story of Saul's visit with "the witch of Endor" in 1 Samuel 28? This verse may suggest that Saul already has tried to wipe out divination as something condemned by God. Divination (*qesem;* Ezek. 13:23; pl. Deut. 18:10; 2 K.

62. Zakovitch, cited by A. Frisch, "'For I feared the people, and I yielded to them' (I Sam 15,24) — Is Saul's Guilt Attenuated or Intensified?," *ZAW* 108 (1996) 101, n. 15.

17:17)[63] is consistently prohibited in the Bible (cf. Deut. 18:10 and 2 K. 17:17), but Saul himself later resorts to it (1 Sam. 28:8). See also on 6:2. However, consultation by using the Urim and Thummim was quite acceptable; see on 14:40-42.

The term *idolatry* (*tᵉrāpîm;* lit., "teraphim"), always in plural form, appears fifteen times in the OT; here it is used as a term for idols or idolatry, as in 2 K. 23:24. The older, more specific meaning is "household gods" (Gen. 31:19; Judg. 17:5; 1 Sam. 19:13) and "aids to divination" (Ezek. 21:21; Hos. 3:4; Zech. 10:2).[64] See on 19:13 (below). Various etymologies have been suggested: (1) *rp' "to heal";[65] (2) *rph "to sink, relax"; (3) *trp "to sag"; or others. Following Hoffner, T. J. Lewis prefers the Hittite etymology *tarpi(š)* "a spirit which can be either protective or malevolent."[66] Recently Van der Toorn has argued that the *teraphim* were not household deities but rather ancestor statuettes.[67] Also, Lewis regards "teraphim" as "ancestor-figurines which functioned in necromantic practices in particular as well as divinatory practices in general."[68]

The Lord chose Saul in 10:24; now he "rejects" him because Saul has "rejected" the word of the Lord (see also 28:18 "you did not listen to the voice of the Lord"). Earlier, the people had "rejected" God (8:7). "Choosing" is the start of a relationship; "rejecting" is the end (2 K. 23:27; Isa. 41:9).[69]

In 1 Sam. 13:13 any possibility of Saul's dynastic continuance was denied; here, Saul himself is rejected from his throne. While in ch. 13 he seems to have acted under the extreme threat of attack, here he seems to have acted out of greed (v. 19) perhaps aided by presumption, with much less excuse. As Hertzberg puts it, "the instrument which the Lord uses must be completely adapted to his hand."[70]

63. See Stoebe, p. 291.

64. See H. Rouillard and J. Tropper, "TRPYM, rituels de guérison et culte des ancêtres d'après 1 Samuel xix 11-17 et les textes parallèles d'Assur et de Nuzi," *VT* 37 (1987) 340-61.

65. The *teraphim* is sometimes understood as serving as "a protective, or curative, talisman." See T. J. Lewis, "Teraphim," in *DDD,* pp. 1588-1601; Rouillard and Tropper, "TRPYM, rituels de guérison et culte des ancêtres," pp. 340-61.

66. See H. A. Hoffner, "The Hittites and Hurrians," in *POTT,* p. 217; Lewis, "Teraphim," in *DDD,* p. 1589; *CS,* I, p. 172.

67. K. van der Toorn, "The Nature of the Biblical Teraphim in the Light of the Cuneiform Evidence," *CBQ* 52 (1990) 203-22.

68. T. J. Lewis, "The Ancestral Estate (נַחֲלַת אֱלֹהִים) in 2 Samuel 14:16," *JBL* 110 (1991) 603; *DDD,* pp. 1594-95.

69. McCarter, p. 268.

70. Hertzberg, p. 128.

(4) "The Lord Has Rejected You" (15:24-26)

24 *And Saul said to Samuel,*
"I have sinned!
For I have transgressed the command[71] *of the Lord and your words,*
because I feared the people and listened to their voice.
25 *Now, take my sin away!*
And return with me that I may worship the Lord!"
26 *And Samuel said to Saul,*
"I will not return with you,
for you have rejected the word of the Lord
and the Lord has rejected you from being king over Israel."

24-31 McCarter thinks that the story in its present form seemingly has two conclusions: "(1) vv 24-29, in which Saul confesses his sin, asks Samuel to return to Gilgal with him to worship, and is sharply refused; and (2) vv 30-31, in which Saul confesses his sin, asks Samuel to return to Gilgal with him to worship, and is obliged."[72] However, this explanation misses the point in interpreting a narrative discourse. Here, one should note the persistence of Saul and the personal concern of Samuel for Saul and the national order (see v. 31) as well as the transition in the situation between the two occasions of Saul's confession of his sin (vv. 24, 30).

24 This verse is crucially important in this chapter since here Saul shifts from saying he obeyed God to saying he disobeyed God because he obeyed the people. However, he seems not to understand the seriousness of the situation. Sadly, a person who has lost contact with the word of God would not be able to perceive his own condition before God. In order to know himself, one needs to know God.

Here Saul confessed *I have sinned (ḥāṭāʾtî)* to Samuel. The same expression is used also in v. 30 (Saul to Samuel); 26:21 (Saul to David); 2 Sam. 12:13 (David to Nathan the messenger of Yahweh); 24:10, 17 (David to Yahweh).[73] The confession in 1 c.s. pf. *ḥāṭāʾtî* is not in the past tense but rather denotes "I am a sinner because I have sinned." The verb here is a *performative perfect* (see on 17:10). Saul admits here that he has transgressed against the Lord. And he accepts that his transgression of the Lord's command is because he *feared the people* — instead of the Lord. Note that

71. Lit., "mouth."

72. McCarter, p. 268.

73. Cf. "I have not sinned" in 24:12 [11] (David to Saul); "your servant knows that I have sinned" in 2 Sam. 19:21 [20] (Shimei to David).

"The fear of others lays a snare, but one who trusts in the Lord is secure" (Prov. 29:25). Saul *listened to their voice* instead of listening to God's voice! He could not resist the temptation to gain favor by yielding to the people's request. In the biblical principle, democracy contradicts theocracy.

25 Frisch[74] notes the parallel expressions between Saul's confession here *(take my sin away!)* and Pharaoh's in Exod. 10:16-17; in both a king declares to the prophet that he had sinned and asks for forgiveness from the prophet. This might suggest to the readers that Saul was not truly sincere any more than was Pharaoh, who changed his mind the minute the plague was withdrawn. However, this intertextual association is rather forced. Both incidents rather explain the nature of human sinfulness. Instead of being stricken with the awfulness of his sin, which can be taken away by God alone, Saul is concerned with his relationship with the people and their elders; see below.

26 Samuel did not yield to Saul's request to return with him; he refused it for the same reason expressed in v. 23, that is, *you have rejected the word of the Lord.* Samuel now announces the decisive fact that Saul has been rejected by the Lord *from being king over Israel.*

(5) "The Lord Has Given the Kingdom of Israel to Your Neighbor" (15:27-31)

27 *And Samuel turned to go, and he seized the edge of his robe and it tore.*
28 *And Samuel said to him,*
"The Lord has torn the kingdom of Israel[75] *away from you today*
and has given it to your neighbor who is better[76] *than you.*
29 *Surely*[77] *the Splendor of Israel*
does not deceive and does not change his mind,[78]
for he is not a man that he should change his mind."
30 *And he said,*
"I have sinned!
But now, please honor me before the elders of my people
and before Israel!
And return with me and I shall worship the Lord your God."
31 *And Samuel returned after Saul. And Saul worshipped the Lord.*

74. Frisch, "'For I feared the people, and I yielded to them' (I Sam 15,24)," pp. 102-3.

75. *maml^{e}kût yiśrā'ēl;* cf. "the kingship of Israel" (McCarter, p. 264), reading "tentatively" *mlkwt.*

76. *ṭôb;* see on "a fine young man" *(bāḥûr wāṭôb)* in 1 Sam. 9:2.

77. *w^{e}gam;* emphatic.

78. *lō' yinnāḥēm* (so NRSV; NIV; JPS) or "repent."

27 As Samuel decided to go away from Saul, he *seized the edge of* Samuel's robe. For the idiom "to seize the edge/hem of," see Old Aramaic *(ʾḥz bknp)* and Akkadian *(sissikta ṣabātu)* equivalents, as identified by Brauner.[79] The Ugaritic counterpart, *ʾḫd bsʾn,* is identified by Greenstein.[80] This expression refers to a gesture of "supplication, importuning, submission to a superior" (Brauner). Hence, Saul's seizure of the edge of Samuel's robe was "a final, deferential plea for mercy."[81] On "cutting off the skirt of robe," see 24:5.

28 The tearing away of the edge of Samuel's robe is interpreted by Samuel as a sign for the fact that *the Lord has torn the kingdom of Israel away from* Saul. This is "an unintentional acted parable" (R. P. Gordon, p. 146); compare "Ahijah's prophecy to Jeroboam" in 1 K. 11:29-31, where Ahijah tears his robe as a sign the kingdom would be divided.

The term *today* is used in a legal sense: the rejection is final and has already taken effect; see Ruth 4:9-10; Ps. 2:7. In God's sight, he has already "torn" and "given" (pf. 3 m.s.), though the actual realization is yet to come. As God was the true ruler of Israel, he could give and take away human kingship in accordance with his will. That kings could give and then take away property grants is seen in 2 Sam. 16:4, where David gives to Ziba the property he had earlier given to Mephibosheth.[82]

The phrase *your neighbor,* like "a man of his choice" in 1 Sam. 13:14, refers to Saul's successor, not named, but soon to be introduced (see 16:13). Saul was informed again that his dynastic succession would be suspended, for his "kingdom" would not be given to his son, Jonathan; see further the comment on 13:14.

29 Samuel states that the Lord's decision is final and unchangeable, and so there is no use arguing about it or explaining more. The phrase *the Splendor of Israel* (*nēṣaḥ yiśrāʾēl;* see *HALOT,* p. 716), or "the Glory of Israel" (NRSV; NIV; JPS) is an epithet of Yahweh also in 1 Chr. 29:11: "the greatness, the power, the glory, the victory, and the majesty" (NRSV).

79. R. A. Brauner, "'To Grasp the Hem,' and 1 Samuel 15:27," *JANES* 6 (1974) 35-38; followed by McCarter and P. A. Kruger, "The Symbolic Significance of the Hem *(KĀNĀF)* in 1 Samuel 15.27," in *Text and Context: Old Testament and Semitic Studies for F. C. Fensham,* ed. W. Claassen (JSOTSS 48; Sheffield: Sheffield Academic Press, 1988), pp. 105-16. See *CS,* II, p. 370, n. 4.

80. E. L. Greenstein, "'To grasp the hem' in Ugaritic Literature," *VT* 32 (1982) 217; W. G. E. Watson, "Some Additional Word Pairs," in *Ascribe to the Lord: Biblical and Other Studies in Memory of Peter C. Craigie,* ed. L. Eslinger and G. Taylor (JSOTSS 67; Sheffield: Sheffield Academic Press, 1988), pp. 193-94; see *CS,* II, p. 159, n. 24.

81. McCarter, p. 268.

82. C. H. Gordon, *The Common Background of Greek and Hebrew Civilizations* (New York: W. W. Norton, 1965), p. 241.

McCarter thinks the phrase here is a later insertion, since it "may have had currency very late in the biblical period";[83] compare "my splendor/glory/strength" (Lam. 3:18). However, there is no reason to think it could only be late; as in Ugaritic the term *nṣḥ* "success, triumph" appears in parallel with "victory" in *KTU* 1.19: II:36.[84]

The verb "to change one's mind" (*nḥm) appears also in vv. 11, 35 ("regret(ted)"); see on v. 11. Scholars who see a contradiction between "I regret" in v. 11 and the statement here suggest that this verse is a gloss (e.g. McCarter, p. 268). However, in this verse, which is about the future, the main point is that God will not reverse his decision. A similar motif appears in a Sumerian lamentation in which the god Enlil is said "never to alter the word he utters" (*CS,* I, p. 536). However, one should note that the meaning of a word or phrase is decided according to the context in which it appears and the speaker who uses the word;[85] while *nḥm (Ni.) certainly means "to change one's mind" in the present context, the same verb in vv. 11 and 35 refers to God's "regret." While in the former the word is paired with the term "to deceive" and is used relationally, in the latter it functions emotively, expressing God's inner feeling.

Compare the expression *he is not a man that he should change his mind* with Num. 23:19:

> God is not a man, that he should lie,
> nor a son of man, that he should change his mind.

While there is some tension remaining between the statements, it is a basic theological problem: Why does God let things go wrong? God's "repentance" is, however, never comparable with the untruthfulness or occasional shortcomings of men.[86]

30 *I have sinned!* — this is the second time he has confessed. That his main concern is not with his sin can be seen from the following words: *But now, please honor me before the elders of my people. . . .* Instead of honoring God, Saul is concerned with honoring himself. He was unwilling to lose face before the people. Saul ought to have been reminded of the following divine word: "For those who honor me I will honor" (1 Sam. 2:30). "Saul may be using correct religious language, but without the corresponding reality."[87] Note a

83. McCarter, p. 268.

84. See Gibson, *CML,* pp. 116, 153.

85. See D. T. Tsumura, "The Problem of Righteousness in Habakkuk [Japanese with an English summary]," in *Evangelical Theology* 22 (1991) 50-70 [Japanese], v-viii [English summary].

86. See Hertzberg, p. 129.

87. Moberly, "'God is not a human that he should repent,'" pp. 119-20.

sharp contrast between Saul's "confession" and David's repentance in Psalm 51,[88] though in 2 Sam. 12:9 David "despised the word of the Lord" like Saul (1 Sam. 13:13-14; 15:11, 23).

For the relationship between the king and the elders, see on 4:3. Saul, who "feared the people" (v. 24), is now deeply concerned with what the elders, the traditional representatives of the people, think of him. Saul here notes Israel as his people: *my people.* But, as Samuel says in the beginning of the chapter, Israel is Yahweh's people. After some years as the king of Israel, Saul had forgotten that a king in Israel is not the owner of Israel but just a representative of Yahweh's people; both king and people are under the authority of the word of God (see 12:25). Noteworthy is the use of the pronouns *my* people and *your* God (see v. 15), which exhibits Saul's inner condition in his relationship with his God.

All these features exhibit that Saul was simply the king for the people (see 8:22), even though he was chosen by God, while David will be the king whom God chooses for himself (see 16:1). As Birch puts it, "Saul and the people were a conditional experiment that depended on obedience (12:14-15, 25), but Davidic kingship would rest on God's unconditional commitment. God's choice of David would ultimately lead to a new basis for the role of the anointed one."[89] See further on 2 Samuel 7.

31 Samuel, who is a man, changes his mind and stays with Saul. Perhaps it is out of his personal concern for Saul (v. 35), or perhaps out of concern for the national "order" if it were known that the Lord no longer recognized Saul.

The phrase *And Samuel returned* marks the transition of the narrative into the next stage. On the other hand, Saul *worshipped the Lord* without recovering his relationship with his God!

e. Samuel Kills Agag (15:32-33)

32 *Now Samuel said,*
"Bring Agag the king of Amalek to me!"
And Agag went to him cheerfully.[90]

88. For the date and unity of Psalm 51, see "The Unity of Psalm 51," *Exegetica* 2 (1991) 35-48 [Japanese].

89. Birch, p. 1091.

90. *maʿădannōt;* old crux; *mʿdn,* the only other occurrence is Job 38:31. This has been translated either "cheerfully" (NASB); "confidently" (NIV), based on *ʿdn; "with faltering steps" (NEB; JPS); "haltingly" (NRSV), reading *m^{e}ʿōḏannîṯ,* based on LXX^{BL}: τρέμων "trembling" (so Klein, p. 145), probably from the verb *mʿd, "slip, totter." McCarter (p. 264) suggests "in bands, fetters" (see *HALOT,* p. 609), based on Kimchi's view, in light of Job 38:31 where "the word seems to stand in parallelism with a word

And Agag said,
"Surely[91] *the bitterness of death is past!"*
33 *And Samuel said,*
"As your sword has made women childless,
so your mother shall be childless among women!"
And Samuel hewed Agag to pieces[92] *before the Lord at Gilgal.*

32-33 This episode refers back to the incident while Samuel was still at Gilgal (see v. 33). Until v. 31 the narrator dealt with the relationship between Samuel and Saul all the way through to their departure. Now, he comes back to Samuel's dealing with Agag, which must have happened chronologically sometime before Samuel's departure from Gilgal. Such a narrative technique of "dischronologization" is due to the nature of language, which is mono-dimensional, that is, linear, while the actual world events proceed multi-dimensionally. In other words, both Samuel's dealings with Saul and with Agag happened before he left Gilgal. Thus, a linguistic description is bound to trace one after another, mono-dimensionally. See "Introduction" (Section VII, C).

The first word *wayyō'mer* (lit., "and he said"), the verb of speech, marks a background situation, introducing a direct speech, though in *wayqtl* form; see v. 1 (above), 15:1, and "Introduction" (Section VI, A).

Samuel orders Agag to be brought to him and utterly destroys him, thus performing the ban, *before the Lord,* since Saul neglected to do so. C. H. Gordon notes that this is the "obligatory slaying of captured enemy heroes" and calls attention to *Iliad* 6:55-60, which states "that Agamemnon 'rightly

---

meaning 'bands'; it may thus be related by metathesis to the verb *'nd,* 'bind' (Prov 6:21; Job 31:36)." Job 38:31 —

> *hatqaššēr ma'ădannôt kîmāh*
> *'ô-mōšᵉkôt kᵉsîl tᵉpattēaḥ*
>
> "Can you bind the chains of the Pleiades,
> Or loose the cords of Orion?" (NASB; NRSV)
>
> "Can you bind the beautiful Pleiades?
> Can you loose the cords of Orion?" (NIV)

Cf. M. H. Pope, *Job: Introduction, Translation, and Notes* (AB 15; Garden City, N.Y.: Doubleday, 1965, 1973), p. 300; also S. Talmon, "1 Sam. XV 32b — A Case of Conflated Readings?" *VT* 11 (1961) 456-57.

91. *'ākēn;* this is "utterance-initial asseverative" as in Gen. 28:16; Exod. 2:14; Isa. 40:7; etc. See Andersen, p. 185.

92. *wayšassēp;* hapax legomenon with an uncertain meaning; "hew in pieces" (BDB, p. 1043); "cut in pieces" (KB), comparing post-biblical Hebrew *šsp,* "to separate" (see *HALOT,* p. 1609). Cf. *kai esphaxen,* "and (Samuel) slaughtered" (LXX).

advised' (62) Menelaus to slay the captive Adrastus and not spare any Trojan male foetus in the womb";[93] see on v. 3.

32 Agag (three times in this verse) *said:* that is, said to himself, hence "thought" (so NIV: "thinking").

Surely the bitterness of death is past! If *ma'ădannōt* in the previous line means *cheerfully,* Agag thinks the danger of death is past. More negative comments are expressed in the translations such as "Would death have been as bitter as this?" (McCarter, p. 265), following the LXX (lit., "Would the bitterness of death have been thus?"); "Surely this is the bitterness of death" (NRSV). That is, if he was going to die, he wished he had been killed earlier. One might compare the present expression with Old Aramaic *mr ḥy',* "the bitterness of life" (Sefire, I, B:31) which is a euphemism for "the bitterness of death."[94]

33 O'Connor takes this Agag's death sentence to be a poem built in the narrative:[95]

> "As your sword has made women *childless,*
> so your mother shall be *childless* among women!"

The verb *šikkelāh* denotes "to make someone childless," not "to make women barren." Note that the Ugaritic god "Death-and-Evil" in *KTU* 1.23:8 holds the weapon of "childlessness" *(ṯkl),* rather than of "barrenness"; an Aramaic incantation text with a similar motif supports this interpretation.[96]

And Samuel hewed Agag to pieces: McCarter thinks that the LXX translation and the fact that it was done "before the Lord" suggest "sacrificial butchering." He suggests that "cutting" in covenant ceremonies symbolized the punishment of covenant breakers, and therefore the Amalekites at the time of Moses had broken a covenant with Israel.[97] However, as Hertzberg holds, Samuel's action rather "takes the event from the sphere of sacrifice into that of the ban"; see the punishment of Achan in Joshua 7. Instead of Saul, Samuel completed the performance of the "ban" on the Amalekites, devoting Agag their king to the Lord.

The expression *before the Lord at Gilgal* (see on 1 Sam. 1:12) does not necessarily prove that there was a permanent shrine at Gilgal.[98] Neverthe-

93. Gordon, *The Common Background,* p. 265.

94. McCarter, pp. 268-69. See Talmon, "1 Sam. XV 32b," 456-57.

95. O'Connor, "War and Rebel Chants in the Former Prophets," p. 324.

96. See D. T. Tsumura, "A Ugaritic God, Mt-w-Šr, and His Two Weapons (UT 52:8-11)," *UF* 6 (1974) 407-13.

97. McCarter, p. 269; cf. p. 203.

98. So M. D. Fowler, "The Meaning of *lipne YHWH* in the Old Testament," *ZAW* 99 (1987) 390.

less, as Gilgal was one of the holy places which Samuel visited regularly, it is not unreasonable to assume that there was some sort of sanctuary there. See on 13:8.

f. Samuel Returns Home (15:34-35)

34 *And Samuel went to Ramah, but Saul went up to his house at*
Gibeah of Saul.
35 *And Samuel did not see Saul again until the day of his death, for*
Samuel grieved over Saul.
As for the Lord, he regretted that he had made Saul king over
Israel.

34 After completing the ban on the Amalekites at Gilgal, Samuel goes back home to Ramah, while Saul goes to Gibeah. The distance between Ramah and Gibeah is less than 10 miles. This verse is a transition with *wayqtl* of a movement verb "to go," followed by another movement verb in the perfect.

35 This verse is another summary statement at the end of an episode (see 7:15; 14:52; and above). Such a statement concludes the current episode and prepares the audience for the following section. If we take the verb "to see" as having the sense of "to meet," Saul's behavior "before Samuel" in 19:24 cannot be said to contradict this verse. This verse means their relationship has been broken off.

Is this incident symbolic of the conflict between "church and state" that will be the major problem in the later history? One thing is clear in the kingship ideology of the OT: the king should by all means listen to the word of God, who is the Divine King. However, why was Saul judged by the highest possible ideals and condemned harshly by Samuel yet David was not condemned to death after his awful sins of adultery and murder (2 Sam. 12:13)? In other words, why was Saul rejected while David was accepted? We can see in their lives both God's dealings with "righteousness" and "love and mercy"; both dealings will be fulfilled in the person of Jesus Christ who died on the cross. See "Introduction" (Sections IX, C).

The term *grieved over* is a link with the following section; see 1 Sam. 16:1. Samuel grieved even over one with whom he probably had a rather rocky relation. Here we can see a true pastor and prophet who did not rejoice in the wrong. The chapter ends with the Lord's regret; see on v. 11. The phrase *he had made Saul king over Israel* corresponds to the initial statement of Samuel: "It was I whom the Lord sent to anoint you as a king over his people Israel" (v. 1), thus forming an *inclusio.* This final statement itself looks forward to the appointment of a new person "who is better than" (v. 28) Saul as a king in the following chapter.

IV. "STORY OF SAUL AND DAVID" (16:1–31:13)

In the rest of 1 Samuel, God, the Lord of History, providentially guides the lives of two persons, Saul and David, the former's decline and the latter's rise. However, the emphasis is not so much on their political actions as on their internal conditions, that is, their spiritual relationships with God. Saul is "like a man living under a curse." He is "caught up in something larger than himself, something from which he cannot extricate himself, and all his devices go wrong." David is also "caught up in events he cannot control." Then, was Saul "a victim"[1] of tragic fate and David destined to be a success? The subsequent courses of these two men's lives show complexities and avoid any simple deterministic understandings. In David's case "everything seems inevitably to go well, and he advances step by step toward the kingship" by the special favor (i.e., grace) of the Lord who was *with him.* The Lord's presence with David was the secret of his success and is *the theological leitmotif* of the story of David's rise.[2]

The story has been compared with the thirteenth century B.C. Hittite "Apology of Ḫattušsili III."[3] It is regarded as "an apologetic work composed to defend David against slanderous charges of complicity in the deaths of key members of the Saulide family during the early part of his career."[4]

However, strictly speaking, our story is not an "apology," for an "apology" is written in the first person "I," while this story is narrated from the third person. The biblical narrator seems to be much more interested in the destinies of the chosen individuals, Saul and David, rather than in David's "rise" to political power. To him, whether the Lord was with his anointed is more important than what the king or the king-designate achieved in his life. The theological theme of God's presence with David in this part of 1 Samuel is in accordance with the earlier theme of the presence of the ark among the covenant people in chs. 1–7. It is reasonable for the narrator to begin this "Story" (chs. 16–31) by stating that God is present with David through his Spirit, and end it with the death of Saul. See also "Introduction" (Section III, A, 2).

It might be useful for the reader to have an overview of the structure of this entire "Story of Saul and David" (16:1–31:13) at this point.

1. D. M. Gunn, *The Fate of King Saul* (JSOTSS 14; Sheffield: JSOT Press, 1980).

2. See P. K. McCarter, Jr., "The Apology of David," *JBL* 99 (1980) 503-4.

3. *CS,* I, pp. 199-204.

4. R. P. Gordon, p. 149. See H. A. Hoffner, Jr., "Propaganda and Political Justification in Hittite Historiography," in *Unity and Diversity: Essays in the History, Literature, and Religion of the Ancient Near East,* ed. H. Goedicke and J. J. M. Roberts (Baltimore: Johns Hopkins University Press, 1975), pp. 49-62; see also McCarter, "The Apology of David," pp. 494-95.

A. Introduction of David (16:1-23)
B. David and Goliath: Battle at the Valley of Elah (17:1-54)
C. Saul, Jonathan, and David (17:55–18:5)
D. Saul becomes David's enemy (18:6-30)
E. Saul's attempts to kill David (19:1–20:42)
F. David's escape from Saul (21:1–26:25)
   Early escapes (21:1–22:5)
   Saul's massacre of Nob's priests (22:6-23)
   David's further escapes (23:1-14)
   Jonathan, Saul, and David (23:15-29)
   David spares Saul at En-gedi (24:1–25:1)
   David marries Abigail (25:2-44)
   David spares Saul at the hill of Hachilah (26:1-25)
G. David in Philistia (27:1–30:31)
   "Witch of Endor" (28:3-25)
H. Death of Saul and Jonathan (31:1-13)

A. INTRODUCTION OF DAVID (16:1-23)

Exactly where the so-called "History of David's Rise" begins is a matter of debate.[5] McCarter takes the story of David's election and anointing as beginning with 15:35 and forming "a brace with that of Saul's rejection" in ch. 15 and "a prophetically oriented transition to the history of David's rise to power." Hence, he holds that the story of "The Rise of David" does not formally begin until 16:14.[6] However, since 1 Sam. 15:35 is a summary statement of the relationship between Samuel and Saul (see above), it is better to take it as a part of the previous section. It is more reasonable to explain 16:1 as a link that recapitulates the preceding episode, thus constituting "a" of the "Transitional Technique," the A/aB pattern (see "Introduction" [Section VI, B]):

A (15:1-35)/
a (16:1) B (16:2-13).

At the same time, the section (vv. 1-13) as a whole serves as a link between the "Story of Saul" (A) and the "Story of Saul and David" (B), functioning as "a" of the A/aB pattern.

A (9:1–15:35)/
a (16:1-13) B (16:14–31:13)

5. See the bibliographical references cited in the "Introdution" (Section III, A, 2).
6. McCarter, p. 278; also Birch, pp. 1094-95.

This episode of the "anointing of David" (a) refers back to the incidents in Saul's life, that is, the election and rejection of Saul and God's promise to choose someone who will replace Saul (9:1–15:35). Thus, the story focus shifts gradually away from Saul toward David, and this is reflected in the very structure of the narrative discourse.

1. Anointing of David (16:1-13)

Chapter 16 is divided into two sections. In the first section, vv. 1-13, God chooses David; in the second, vv. 13-23, it is Saul who chooses David. The reader knows that the second choice was the result of the first. It will take some time for Saul to know this fact and admit it; see 18:8; 24:20.

a. The Lord Sends Samuel to Bethlehem (16:1-4a)

1 *And the Lord said to Samuel,*
"How long are you going to grieve about[7] *Saul,*
while I myself have already rejected him
from being king over Israel?
Fill your horn with oil!
Go, I will send you to Jesse the Bethlehemite!
for[8] *I have found*[9] *among his sons a king for me."*
2 *And Samuel said,*
"How can I go? When Saul hears, he will kill me!"
And the Lord said,
"A heifer you shall take in your hand[10]
and say:
'To sacrifice to the Lord I have come.'
3 *And you shall invite*[11] *Jesse to the feast,*
for I myself[12] *will let you know what you should do.*
And you shall anoint for me the one whom I tell you."
4a *And Samuel did what the Lord told him and came to Bethlehem.*

7. *mit'abbēl 'el:* <participle>; the preposition *'el* (variant *'al*) here means "concerning, about."

8. This speaker-oriented *kî* explains the reason why the Lord sends Samuel to Bethlehem: "I have found. . . ."

9. Lit., "have seen"; also v. 17. The phrase "to see . . . among (partitive *min* or *b*) . . ." here and in 2 K. 10:3 may mean "to select," but not "to see" by itself.

10. The same expression appears in the context of sacrifice in ancient Ugarit: "take a lamb [in your hand]" (Krt ii 62-79); see *CS,* I, p. 334.

11. Lit., "call" (also v. 5) as a guest; see 1 Sam. 9:13, 22-24.

12. w^{e}*'ānōkî;* lit., "and I."

1 Some time after Saumel departed from Saul, the Lord himself spoke to his prophet. For *And the Lord said* at the beginning of an episode, see on 15:1.

The expressions *grieve about* and *being king over Israel* echo the last verse of ch. 15 and thus are a link with the previous chapter. With the phrase *I myself,* "you" and "I," both expressed by independent pronouns, are sharply contrasted.

The use of the perfect *have already rejected (mᵉʾastîw)* here is in sharp contrast with the participle which describes Samuel's ongoing state of "grieving"; God's thoughts and ways are certainly not those of man (see Isa. 55:8). The Lord has already made up his mind to choose another man suitable for his work. Samuel has no time to waste by grieving about the man whom God has *already rejected.* For the use of the verb "reject," see also v. 7.

The Lord commands Samuel to fill his *horn with oil* and go to Jesse of Bethlehem. Here a *horn* is used for oil, while in 10:1 "a flask" was used; in 1 K. 1:39, Zadok anoints Solomon with a horn.

The name *Jesse* (*yīšay;* cf. *ʾîšay* in 1 Chr. 2:13) debuts in the books of Samuel. It is not common among the Israelites; H. Cazelles suggests an Aramaic connection.[13] Jesse is the grandson of Boaz and Ruth (Ruth 4:17, 22), and in 1 Chr. 2:3-12 he is mentioned as a Judahite of the house of Perez.

The term *Bethlehemite* also appears for the first time in Samuel. Bethlehem was the home of Naomi (Ruth 1:19; etc.). It is in Judah, about 10 miles from Ramah; see 1 Sam. 17:12. When Samuel departed from Ramah (cf. 15:34), he probably took the main north-south ridge road on the highlands of Benjamin and Judah and came to Bethlehem. This is somewhat beyond the limited circuit of 7:16-17.

Klein says that "David is to be anointed king whereas Saul had been anointed prince (cf. 9:16)."[14] However, the text does not make this point. In other passages David is referred to as *nāgîd* "prince" (25:30; 2 Sam. 5:2; 6:21; 7:8), and 1 Sam. 15:17 states that the Lord anointed Saul as "king." David is not officially anointed as king until 2 Sam. 2:4 and 5:3; in fact, the expression "to anoint David as king" never appears in the present chapter (see also on vv. 3, 12). While Saul was chosen because of the people's desire for a king (8:5; 10:24), the Lord chooses this king on his own; so *I have found . . . for me.*

2 No monarch would be pleased to hear of an attempt to appoint a rival successor, as Saul's later actions and 1 Kings 1–2 show.

A heifer is literally "the young female (one) of the cattle" (*ʿeglat bāqār;*

13. H. Cazelles, "Bethlehem," in *ABD,* I, pp. 712-15.

14. Klein, p. 160.

also Deut. 21:3; Isa. 7:21), which is grammatically an <adj. construct>[15] + <genitive> like *naʿar hakkōhēn* "the young (one) of the priest" (2:13).[16] A *heifer* was acceptable as a "peace offering" in priestly law (Lev. 3:1).

While the fulfillment of the commands "fill and go" in v. 1 and "take a heifer" in v. 2 is simply summarized in v. 4a, *Samuel did what the Lord told him and came to Bethlehem,* the fulfillment of three commands *say — you shall invite — you shall anoint* are narrated more in detail in v. 5 ("And he said" — "And he invited") and in v. 13 ("And he anointed"). This also supports the idea that the section ends with v. 13 when Samuel fulfilled his mission and "went (back) to Ramah."

To sacrifice to the Lord, that is, "to worship the Lord"; also v. 5.

3 The Hebrew phrase *bazzābaḥ,* which literally means "in the sacrifice," signifies "at the time of the feast," hence (invite) *to the feast* (also v. 5); see Ugar. *dbḥ* "sacrifice, feast"; see on 1:4. It is possible that there was a sanctuary at Bethlehem in this period.[17]

Here David's anointing is by God's initiative and sovereign will. Even Samuel does not know whom he should anoint until God informs him. Choosing a king is "for the Lord," for the king is the human agent of the Lord, the heavenly King.

4a In the light of <command-fulfillment> structure and from the context, what Samuel did was to fill his horn with oil and take a heifer in his hand. In response to the Lord's command to go, Samuel *came.* The stage is now in Bethlehem, and the narrator's viewpoint has changed; see "Introduction" (Section VI, D).

We can see Samuel's greatness in carrying out the Lord's command despite the possible risk to his life. This teaches us "what mattered was simple obedience."[18]

b. Samuel Chooses David (16:4b-13)

(1) Elders of the City (16:4b-5a)

4b *And the elders of the city came trembling to meet him and said,*[19]
"Is your coming in peace?"

15. See T. Muraoka, "The status constructus of Adjectives in Biblical Hebrew," *VT* 27 (1977) 375-80.

16. See the commentary on 1 Sam. 2:13.

17. See R. P. Gordon, p. 150.

18. Baldwin, p. 121.

19. The verb is 3 m.s. Did a representative of the elders speak *or* is it the equivalent of *lēʾmōr,* which introduces a direct speech? McCarter emends it to pl.; Driver, p. 132, thinks that "a cognate participle" is implied here. This "number discord" could be a sign

5a *And he said,*
"In peace!
To sacrifice to the Lord I have come.
Consecrate yourselves and come with me to the feast!"

4b When Samuel arrived at Bethlehem, *the elders of the city* (*ziqnê hā'îr;* see on 4:3; 11:3; also the city elders of Succoth, Judg. 8:14, 16) received him with *trembling.* It is not clear why they should "tremble." R. P. Gordon suggests they thought Samuel was making a "disciplinary visit."[20] Baldwin explains that their fear may reflect Samuel's reputation and "the loneliness of his position."[21] However, the elders rather felt something serious with Samuel's sudden visit to their city. For the adverbial use of the phrase *in peace,* see Lachish ostracon vi:2.[22]

5a *Consecrate yourselves* (Hith. impv. *hitqaddᵉšû)* is literally "keep one another in a state of consecration" (Num. 11:18; 2 Sam. 11:4; etc.; *HALOT,* p. 1074), in order to worship the holy God; they would probably wash themselves and perhaps also wash their clothes as in Exod. 19:10 and Num. 8:21. Samuel would invite to the feast the people who had carried out this purification and were in a state of ritual purity.

Come with me to the feast, that is, at the time of the feast; also v. 3; cf. "to the sacrifice" (NASB); "and celebrate with me today" (McCarter), following LXX^{BA};[23] "rejoice with me at the sacrifice" (Smith).[24]

(2) The Lord Rejects the Elder Sons (16:5b-11)

5b *And he consecrated Jesse and his sons and invited them to the feast.*
6 *When they came he looked at Eliab and thought*[25]
"Surely, the one before the Lord is his anointed!"
7 *And the Lord said to Samuel,*
"Do not look at[26] *his appearance*
or at his height,
for I have rejected him!

---

of colloquialism; see G. A. Rendsburg, *Diglossia in Ancient Hebrew* (AOS 72; New Haven: American Oriental Society, 1990), p. 80.

20. R. P. Gordon, p. 151.
21. Baldwin, p. 121.
22. Gibson, *SSI,* 1, p. 46.
23. McCarter, p. 274.
24. Smith, p. 144.
25. Lit., "said."
26. Hi. *nbṭ; often paired with *r'h "to see"; Hab. 1:3, 5, 13, etc.

For[27] my way of seeing is not like man's way of seeing,[28]
for the man judges[29] by the eyes,
but the Lord judges by the heart."
8 *And Jesse called Abinadab and made him pass before Samuel.*
And he said,
"Neither this one has the Lord chosen!"
9 *And Jesse made Shammah pass.*
And he said,
"Neither this one has the Lord chosen!"
10 *And Jesse made his seven sons pass before Samuel.*
And Samuel said to Jesse,
"The Lord has not chosen these!"
11 *And Samuel said to Jesse,*
"Are these all of your boys?"
And he said,
"The youngest still remains.
He is shepherding the flock."
And Samuel said to Jesse,
"Send (a man) and get him,
for we[30] shall not leave until he comes here!"

5b-6 Samuel as a priest *consecrated* [= blessed] *Jesse and his sons and invited them to the feast.* This is a summary statement, like Gen. 1:1, of what will happen in the following (vv. 6-13). That the stage is not yet *the feast* is supported by the verb *leave* in v. 11; see below. Jesse's sons appear one after another before Samuel to be consecrated. Verses 6-11 describe exactly how Samuel *consecrated* them as Jesse made his sons *pass before Samuel.* The first is Eliab the eldest son of Jesse (17:13, 28; 1 Chr. 2:13); he is called "Elihu" in 1 Chr. 27:18 [LXX: Eliab].[31]

Surely, before the Lord is his anointed ('ak neged yhwh mᵉšîḥō); cf. Syr. (Peshitta) *'akwāteh dmāryā mšīḥeh* "similar to the Lord is his anointed." Joosten thinks that the Hebrew *Vorlage (kᵉneged yhwh mᵉšîḥō)* of the Syriac is the original, the MT being secondary since *kᵉneged yhwh* "suitable to YHWH" describes "the ideal Messiah" most concisely.[32] However, his argu-

27. Or "because": the reason for the preceding action: "to reject."

28. Lit., "as/that man sees," i.e., "like the way how man sees." This *'ăšer* is almost equivalent to *ka'ăšer.* For various emendations, see J. Joosten, "1 Samuel 16:6, 7 in the Peshitta Version," *VT* 41 (1991) 232, n. 11.

29. Lit., "sees."

30. Inclusive we, i.e., "you and I."

31. On this problem, see McCarter, p. 276.

32. Joosten, "1 Samuel 16:6, 7 in the Peshitta Version," p. 228.

ment remains highly hypothetical. The MT as it is makes good and similar sense. Since here the question is, "Whom will the Lord anoint?" it is likely to mean "the one (who is now standing) before the Lord is his anointed," taking *neged yhwh* as a nominalized prepositional phrase.[33]

7 Like Eliab, Saul's *appearance (mar'ēhû)//height* (lit., "the height of stature") had been noteworthy. See on 9:2; 10:23.

I have rejected him: the Lord had already decided on David before sending Samuel to Bethlehem (v. 1). Or is this perfect verb *performative* (see 17:10), with the Lord rejecting him by uttering "I hereby reject him" to Samuel? The same verb *m's is used in 15:23, 26; 16:1 for the rejection of Saul. According to Mettinger, "Eliab is something of a 'new Saul,' so that in his rejection Saul is denounced in effigy."[34]

My way of seeing is not like man's way of seeing: literally, "(I am) not as man sees." Most of the modern translations supply "the Lord" or "God" as the subject: for example, "The LORD does not look at the things man looks at" (NIV); cf. "For I am not as man sees" (Syr.).[35] However, the MT as it is could be translated "(I am) not," the subject being understood from the immediate context; this is supported by the Syriac version, though Joosten proposes a different Hebrew *Vorlage.*[36] The same phenomenon can be recognized in Hab. 1:5b "(I am) going to do" (NIV; also LXX; NASB; cf. NRSV: "a work is being done"; also JPS), the subject being supplied from the context.

The expression *by the eyes (laʿênayim)* means "by what he sees"; compare "the outward appearance" (NRSV; NASB; NIV); "only what is visible" (JPS). The preposition *by* is a *lamed* of specification; see GKC, §119*u.* Driver[37] mentions a similar expression in Lev. 13:15 and Num. 11:7, though "eye" is singular there. This structurally perfect parallelism can be analyzed on surface:

a (NP) — b (VP) — c (advPh) man judges by eyes
a′ (NP) — b′ (VP) — c′ (advPh) Lord judges by heart

33. For a nominalized prepositional phrase, see also 1 Sam. 9:24. For various emendations of *neged,* see Joosten, "1 Samuel 16:6, 7 in the Peshitta Version," p. 233, n. 22.

34. T. N. D. Mettinger, *King and Messiah: The Civil and Sacral Legitimation of the Israelite Kings* (CB: OT Series 8; Lund: C. W. K. Gleerup, 1976), p. 175. Following Mettinger, McCarter holds that "this episode is reminiscent of the story of Saul's election by lottery (10:17-27a) in a number of ways. . . . [It] is fashioned at least partly in light of 10:17-27 . . ." (p. 277).

35. See Joosten, "1 Samuel 16:6, 7 in the Peshitta Version," p. 229.

36. Joosten, "1 Samuel 16:6, 7 in the Peshitta Version," p. 229.

37. Driver, p. 133.

But, semantically c//c′ are twisted in terms of their possessors: the "eyes" are the eyes of the man who is judging, while the "heart" is the heart of the one being judged, not of the Lord.

The expression *judges by the heart (yir'eh lallēbāb)* literally means "sees to the heart"; the Lord judges man according to the man's heart, that is, his internal condition.[38] Compare "looks at the heart" (NIV; NASB; cf. NRSV: "on"); "sees into the heart" (JPS).[39]

8 *Abinadab* is the second son of Jesse (17:13; 1 Chr. 2:13)

Does the pronoun *he* (the subject of *said*) refer to Samuel or to the Lord? If "he" is Samuel, he is speaking to Jesse. In this case it is possible that Samuel might have told Jesse his real purpose in coming, or just implied a son was to be chosen for some purpose. Or it may be the Lord speaking to Samuel as in v. 7, using the term "the Lord" to refer to himself, as is often the case in prophetic messages. This ambiguity seems to be intentional and increases the suspense.

9-10 *Shammah* is the third son of Jesse (17:13; 1 Chr. 2:13); compare Shimeah *Šimʿāh* (2 Sam 13:3, 32; 21:21 [Qere]), Shimei *Šmʿy* (2 Sam 21:21 [Ketib]), *Šimʿā'* (1 Chr. 2:13; 20:7). See on 2 Sam. 13:3. Thus, Jesse's first three sons are mentioned by name; then the rest of his sons are included in Jesse's "seven sons." Epics seem often to name the first three of a group in order to represent the whole.

The ideal number of sons in a family is *seven:* for example, Job's seven sons (Job 1:2; 42:13), Keret's seven sons (rather than "wives"[40]), Baal's seven sons (or "lads") in *KTU* 1.5:V:8-9, etc., and "seven" good gods (*KTU* 1.23 [*UT* 52]), as well as 1 Sam. 2:5.[41] Ruth, Naomi's daughter-in-law, is said to be to her better than seven sons (Ruth 4:15).

David here comes after the other "seven" sons of Jesse. Hence, the text implies that he was the eighth son (also 17:12), while in 1 Chr. 2:15 he is "the seventh." Which was he? McCarter suggests that the tradition of the number of Jesse's sons was "mixed" or that "seven" is due to "careless fidelity" to the number seven, apparently meaning that the writer carelessly forgot

38. For this saying, see C. R. Fontaine, *Traditional Sayings in the Old Testament: A Contextual Study* (BLS 5; Sheffield: Almond, 1982).

39. Note that "to look at" is usually with prep. *b* followed by object (see BDB, pp. 907-8); cf. Jer. 20:12, without the prep., God as the one who can "probe the heart and mind" *(rō'eh kᵉlāyôt wālēb);* cf. Jer. 17:10.

40. So D. Pardee in *CS,* I, p. 333; but see D. T. Tsumura, "The Problem of Childlessness in the Royal Epic of Ugarit," in *Monarchies and Socio-Religious Traditions in the Ancient Near East* (Wiesbaden: Otto Harrassowitz, 1984), pp. 11-20; J. M. Sasson, "The Numeric Progression in Keret 1:15-20: Yet Another Suggestion," *SEL* 5 (= *Cananea Selecta: Festschrift für Oswald Loretz zum 60. Geburtstag*) (1988) 181-88.

41. See on 1 Sam. 2:5.

to subtract David from the number in v. 10. Others conjecture that Jesse had a son who died.[42]

However, one might argue that David was actually the seventh son (so 1 Chr. 2:15) as well as climactically the "eighth," just as in Mic. 5:5 ("seven shepherds, even eight leaders of men" NIV); Rev. 17:11 ("the beast . . . is an eighth but it belongs to the seven" NRSV). In fact, the number parallelism of "7"//"8" appears in Ugaritic poetic texts such as *KTU* 1.5 V 8-9; 1.12 II 44-45; 1.15 II 23-24; 1.23:66-67; etc.[43] Therefore, the Samuel passages, here and 17:12, probably adopt the practice of epic writing, explaining the number of Jesse's sons as climactically "eight" even though the actual number was seven, while the Chronicle passage follows the usual practice of listing the actual number, that is, seven, of sons by name. It is certainly "worthy of saga," as C. H. Gordon holds, that the youngest son David eclipsed his "seven" older brothers.[44]

Samuel said to Jesse: here for the first time the full information about the speaker and the hearer is given. This formula: "A said to B" is repeated two more times in v. 11.

11 *And Samuel said to Jesse* is a second introduction which interrupts Samuel's speech to Jesse. According to Revell, such "a repeated introduction to speech" is not a work of redactors but a feature of biblical Hebrew, which, like other phenomena of repetition, draws "the attention of the hearer or reader, to mark it as significant."[45] As other examples, he lists 1 Sam. 14:33+34; 17:8+10, 34+37; 26:9+10, 17+18; 2 Sam. 15:3+4, 25+27; 17:7+8.[46]

Are these all of your boys (hătammû; lit., "Are the boys complete?")? Here *hannᵉʿārîm* is translated as "sons" (NIV; NRSV); "boys" (JPS); "children" (NASB). Samuel is looking for *naʿar* ("a boy"), not just another of Jesse's "sons."

The choice of *the youngest* is a motif known elsewhere in the OT (Jacob over Esau, Gen. 25:23; Ephraim over Manasseh, Gen. 48:8-22). C. H. Gordon compares the case where the eighth child, a girl, named *ṯtmnt* (= "Octavia") becomes the senior in *KTU* 1.15:III:16 "I shall make the youngest of them the firstborn."[47]

42. Baldwin, p. 122; Bergen, p. 191.

43. See *RSP* 1, p. 345.

44. See C. H. Gordon, *PLMU,* pp. 35-36; "A Review of U. Cassuto, *The Goddess Anath* (Jerusalem: Magnes, 1951)," *JAOS* 72 (1952) 181.

45. E. J. Revell, "The Repetition of Introductions to Speech as a Feature of Biblical Hebrew," *VT* 47 (1997) 92.

46. See Revell, "The Repetition of Introductions to Speech," p. 97, n. 15.

47. Gordon, *PLMU,* p. 48. On the preeminence of younger siblings, see F. E. Greenspahn, *When Brothers Dwell Together: The Preeminence of Younger Siblings in the*

For *is shepherding the flock,* see Gen. 37:2 "[Joseph] was shepherding the flock with his brothers." Even though kings were often described as shepherds both in Israel and in the ancient Near East, it is probably too much to read into the text a reference to David's future role as a king, as Klein[48] does. 2 Sam. 7:8 seems rather to contrast David's roles as shepherd and king.

Samuel said they would not *nāsōb* until David came. Several suggestions have been made as to the meaning of the verb: (1) "sit down" (NIV; NRSV; NASB); "sit down to eat" (JPS); "sit (lie) at table" (*HALOT,* p. 739); R. P. Gordon takes it to mean to recline at the table;[49] (2) "make a procession around the altar" (Smith, pp. 146-47; Hertzberg, p. 138); (3) "go away" (Stoebe, p. 302). Klein translates it as "we will not go ahead" and explains that this "is intended to be ambiguous."[50] However, *nāsōb* literally means "turn away" or "turn to do something else" (BDB, p. 685); also 15:12, 27. From the immediate context (see on v. 6 above), it seems that both Samuel, the speaker, and Jesse, the hearer, are expected to do something together, that is, that the "we" is an "inclusive we." The most natural interpretation then is that Samuel and Jesse and the rest of the company will leave together, possibly "depart to go to the place where we hold the feast," when the youngest boy arrives.

(3) Samuel Anoints David (16:12-13)

12 *And he sent (a man) and brought him: he was ruddy and with beautiful eyes and good looking.*
And the Lord said,
"Arise and anoint him,
for this is he!"
13 *And Samuel took the horn of oil*[51] *and anointed him in the midst of his brothers.*
And the spirit of the Lord rushed upon David from that day onwards.
And Samuel arose and went to Ramah.

12 Here, for the first time, David is brought into direct contact with Samuel; the only other occasion we are told about is in 19:18.

Hebrew Bible (New York/Oxford: Oxford University Press, 1994), esp. pp. 84-110 (ch. 3: "The Last Shall Be First").

48. Klein, p. 161.
49. R. P. Gordon, p. 151.
50. Klein, p. 161.
51. Construct chain: "the horn for oil" *or* "the horn full of oil."

The adjective *ruddy (ʾadmônî)* is also used of Esau (Gen. 25:25). In the ancient Near East, "red (actually reddish brown) is the color appropriate for men. . . . And two of the most heroic men of the Old Testament, Esau and David, are described as naturally red: showing that they were born to be heroes."[52]

The expression *with beautiful eyes (y^{e}pēh ʿênayim)* literally means "beautiful of eyes," which is grammatically <adj. construct> + <genitive> like *good looking (ṭôb rōʾî;* lit., "good of looking"); also 17:42; Gen. 39:6. The expressions "ruddy countenance" and "beautiful eyes" are used for describing a happy king with a bright face in the ninth-century B.C. "Sun Disk" Tablet from Sippar.[53] McCarter's translation "attractive"[54] is based on a conjectural emendation, and he deletes the expression in 17:42 as based on the present verse! He does not mention Gen. 39:6.

13 This verse is careful not to say David is anointed "king over Israel" (v. 1). To Jesse and other attendees there, the purpose of this anointing may not have been totally clear, even though it took place "in the midst of his brothers." As R. P. Gordon notes, as far as we know for sure, only Samuel knew the purpose of the anointing, which was done in a small group. As there were various purposes for anointing, the others present may or may not have known the significance. Eliab might never have associated David's anointing with his future kingship (see 17:28).

David was anointed (*mšḥ) three times in his life: by Samuel (16:13) here at Bethlehem, by the men of Judah to be "a king over the house of Judah" (2 Sam. 2:4), and by the elders of Israel to be "a king over Israel" (2 Sam. 5:3). On "anointing," see on 1 Sam. 9:16.

For *the spirit of the Lord rushed upon (wattiṣlaḥ rûaḥ-YHWH ʾel-),* see 10:6; 11:6. For both Saul and David, after they were anointed king, the spirit of the Lord came upon them to equip them to carry out their commission. Compare Isa. 11:1-2; 61:1. Just as the spirit of the Lord rushed upon Saul "on that day" (10:9), that is, the day when Saul was anointed, so it rushed upon David *from that day onwards.* The contrast has been too much emphasized between the "spasmodical" aspect of the spirit upon Saul and the "permanent" endowment of the spirit upon David (see 2 Sam. 23:2; also Ps. 51:11). As the following verse (v. 14) notes, the spirit of the Lord had not yet left Saul by *that day.*

Here the name *David (dāwīd)* makes its debut in the Bible. Note that

52. C. H. Gordon, *The Common Background of Greek and Hebrew Civilizations* (New York: W. W. Norton, 1965), p. 231; *The Ancient Near East* (New York: W. W. Norton, 1965), p. 125.

53. *CS,* II, p. 367.

54. McCarter, p. 275.

he has been kept anonymous until now: "Samuel . . . anointed him [= the youngest]" (v. 13a). The first mention of his name in connection with the onrush of the spirit of the Lord is significant and climactic. From now on, David's entire life would have a special relationship with the Lord's spirit (see 2 Sam. 23:2), while by contrast the spirit of the Lord would depart from Saul (v. 14).

David is the only person in the Bible of that name. The meaning of the name has been variously explained: (1) a connection with the Hebrew *dôd,* meaning "beloved," or even "uncle" (Amos 6:10; Hertzberg, p. 139); (2) the shortened form of a personal name whose theophoric element is a sun deity Dodo; however, there is yet no clear evidence that such a deity ever existed in the ancient Near East;[55] and (3) the Akkadian term *dawidum* from Mari, which was previously taken to mean "commander" and connected with the name David, but the Mari word actually means "defeat."[56] At the present time then, (1) is the most promising. The oldest extrabiblical attestation of David is in the ninth-century B.C. Aramaic inscription from Tel Dan.[57]

In the last sentence, two *movement* verbs in *wayqtl* (arose and went) provide background information, here the terminus of the paragraph, vv. 1-13. Samuel presumably went to the place of the feast and ate before he left for Ramah; see v. 11.

D. Block holds that this is "a most significant turning point in the history of Israel and her monarchy — the transfer of divine authority and support from Saul to David."[58] The next section (1 Sam. 16:14f.) is identified by a number of scholars as the beginning of the history of David's rise to power.[59] However, there are many points of contact between the two sections of this chapter. Klein mentions (1) David's being said to be among the flock (v. 11/v. 19); (2) the word "see" being used in the sense of select (vv. 1, 7/vv.

55. See K. A. Kitchen, "A Possible Mention of David in the Late Tenth Century BCE, and Deity *Dod as Dead as the Dodo?" *JSOT* 76 (1997) 29-44.

56. See J. J. Stamm, "Der Name des Königs David," in *Congress Volume: Oxford 1959* (SVT 7; Leiden: E. J. Brill, 1960), pp. 165-68; G. Hoffmann, *David: Namensdeutung zur Wesensdeutung* (BWANT 5/20; Stuttgart: Kohlhammer, 1973). See *HALOT,* p. 215.

57. See "Introduction" (Section III, C, 1); also D. M. Howard, Jr., "David," in *ABD,* II, pp. 41-49.

58. D. I. Block, "Empowered by the Spirit of God: The Holy Spirit in the Historiographic Writings of the Old Testament," *Southern Baptist Journal of Theology* 1 (1997) 51.

59. On the structure of 1 Sam. 16:14–18:30, see A.-F. Campbell, "Structure Analysis and the Art of Exegesis (1 Samuel 16:14–18:30)," in *Problems in Biblical Theology: Essays in Honor of Rolf Knierim,* ed. H. T. C. Sun et al. (Grand Rapids: Eerdmans, 1997), pp. 76-103.

17, 18); (3) the name David being mentioned only at a climactic moment (v. 13/v. 19). Also he notes (4) the references to the spirit of the Lord in both accounts: at the end of the first (v. 13) and at the beginning of the second (v. 14). Despite these similarities, Klein claims that "accounts of the divine (16:1-13) and the royal (16:14-23) selection of David" have "a separate history of tradition."[60]

Especially to be noted is the last point (4), the device of linkage, similar to that noted between the end of ch. 15 and the beginning of the present chapter. We may add further points of similarities between the two accounts:

(5) personal descriptions of David (v. 12/v. 18);
(6) the proper nouns "Jesse" and "Bethlehem," which appear in v. 1 for the first time in the book of Samuel, and "David" reappear in both parts: "Jesse" — vv. 1, 3, 5, 8, 9, 10, 11/vv. 18, 19, 20, 22; "Bethlehem" — vv. 1, 4/v. 18; "David" — v. 13/vv. 19, 20, 21, 22.
(7) the terms such as "David," "spirit," and "Yahweh" function as linkage words (a or b) in transition from one section (A) to another (B):

Ab/B	"David" — v. 13/vv. 19, 20, 21, 22, 23
	"spirit" — v. 13/vv. 14, 15, 16, 23
A/aB	"Yahweh" — vv. 1, 2, 4, 5, 6, 7, 8, 9, 10, 12, 13/vv. 14, 18
	"with the flock" — v. 11/v. 19
	"to see, find" (r'h + *nbṭ) — vv. 1, 6, 7 (x4+1)/vv. 17, 18

It is hard to see how such closely connected accounts could have developed separately over a long period of time. In light of the above observations, the two parts of this chapter may be considered to be tightly integrated.

Here, David, whose name appeared for the first time in the biblical narrative at the end of the A section, "first steps on stage." Saul, on the other hand, appears as "a man abandoned by God." McCarter notes here three themes: (1) Saul is in decline; (2) Yahweh is with David; and (3) Saul is deeply attached to the younger man. He sees also two other themes, both of which "find full expression in our story": David's unshakable loyalty to Saul and Israel and David's military prowess.[61]

60. Klein, p. 165.
61. McCarter, p. 282.

2. David at Saul's Court (16:14-23)

a. Spirit for Evilness (16:14)

14 *Now the spirit of the Lord departed from Saul, and*[62] *a spirit of evil from the Lord began to terrorize*[63] *him.*

14 Now that the spirit of the Lord rushed upon David (v. 13), it *departed from Saul.* The verb "to depart" (*swr) reappears in v. 23, thus constituting *inclusio* in the section, vv. 14-23. While this verse serves as a SETTING for the subsequent EVENT, v. 23 serves as a TERMINUS (summary statement). While previously "the spirit of God/Yahweh" rushed upon Saul so that he might assume his task as the king of Israel (10:10; 11:6/10:6), it now departed from Saul to David. The on-rush of "the spirit of the Lord" onto a new person, David, meant a transfer of "divine favor" from Saul to David, which in the ancient Near East "could change from dynasty to dynasty, or from one branch of a ruling house to another."[64] As for Saul, as the result of the departure of Yahweh's spirit from him, he began to be "terrorized" by another kind of a divine spirit. R. P. Gordon rightly notes that "Psalm 51:11 ('take not thy holy Spirit from me') may well reflect the psalmist's fear of Saul-like dereliction."[65]

The phrase *a spirit of evil* [or *for evilness*] (*rûaḥ-rāʿāh;* also 16:15, 16, 18:10; 19:9) is grammatically a construct chain like *ʾanšê rāʿāh* "men of evil" (Prov. 24:1), that is, "men who do evil to others," not "evil men," which would be *ʾănāšîm rāʿîm,* and also *rûaḥ šeqer* "a spirit of deception," though it is often translated as "a lying-spirit."[66] It does not mean "an evil spirit," with an adjective; see v. 23 and 18:10. Note that the term *rāʿāh* is a f.s. noun ("evilness") here rather than an adjective ("evil").[67] Thus, Block's explanation hits the mark: "a bad Spirit of God . . . is 'bad' because the effects of his possession are negative and destructive for the object."[68] See Excursus (below).

62. Or "and immediately": <perfect> — <*waw* + perfect>: a frequentative force (Driver, p. 134); rather <simultaneity>! The second perfect functions as inchoative (see below: "began to . . .").

63. *biʿătattû:* Pi. *bʿt, perfect, 3 f.s. + obj. suffix *-hû.*

64. Gordon, *The Common Background,* p. 243.

65. R. P. Gordon, p. 152.

66. See McCarter, *DDD,* p. 604; see *DCH,* I, pp. 230-31.

67. *IBHS,* p. 146.

68. Block, "Empowered by the Spirit of God," p. 47.

EXCURSUS: "AN EVIL SPIRIT FROM THE LORD"[69]

The expression "an Evil Spirit from the Lord" gives the impression that God's spirit can sometimes be evil. Various suggestions have been made in order to solve this theological problem. Keil and Delitzsch distinguish between "an evil spirit from Jehovah," which is a "demon" sent by the Lord, and "the Spirit of Jehovah," who is the spirit of the holy God. According to Vriezen, the fact that not only the good but also the evil comes from Yahweh indicates that he holds absolute authority over the evil too.[70] Eichrodt also suggests that "the evil spirit from the Lord" is a spiritual power under God's sovereignty; hence it is not the same as an "evil spirit," in contrast to a good spirit, in a pagan dualism.[71] McCarter accepts that the evil spirit is "from Yahweh" and explains that even it plays "its part in the working out of the divine plan." Klein and R. P. Gordon also hold that the OT tends "to trace both good *and* evil back to Yahweh," thus ascribing evil to the hand of Yahweh in such texts as Deut. 13:2-4; Amos 3:6; 2 Sam. 24:1; Judg. 9:23; 1 Kgs. 22:19-22; Job 2:10.[72]

However, this is not so much a theological as a linguistic problem. The translation "an evil spirit from the Lord" is not adequate for the Hebrew original. We would like to suggest that the phrase *rûaḥ-rāʿāh,* which is usually translated as "an evil spirit," should be taken as a construct chain, "a spirit of evilness (or disaster)," since *rāʿāh* cannot be an adjective in *rûaḥ hārāʿāh* (16:23) and *rûaḥ YHWH rāʿāh* (19:9). This might be supported by the fact that the noun *rûaḥ* is followed by another noun 128 times, in comparison with about 20 times when it is modified by an adjective (according to acCordance). So, *rûaḥ hārāʿāh* and *rûaḥ YHWH rāʿāh* are better translated as "the spirit which brings forth disaster" and "the spirit of Yahweh which brings forth disaster," taking *rāʿāh* as "objective genitive" (or "genitive of effect") as in the cases of *ʾanšê rāʿāh* (Prov. 24:1), which means "men of evil" (i.e., "men who do evil to others"), not "evil men," and *ʾēšet zᵉnûnîm* (Hos. 1:2), which means "a wife of whoredom" (NRSV), that is, "a wife who will, as a result, commit adultery," not "an adulterous wife" (NIV).

69. See D. T. Tsumura, "'An Evil Spirit from the Lord' in the First Book of Samuel," *Exegetica* 8 (1997) 1-10 [Japanese with English summary].

70. Th. C. Vriezen, *The Religion of Ancient Israel* (Philadelphia: Westminster, 1967), p. 81.

71. W. Eichrodt, *Theology of the Old Testament,* vol. II (Philadelphia: Westminster, 1967), p. 55.

72. R. P. Gordon, p. 152; Klein, p. 165. See McCarter, "Evil Spirit of God," in *DDD,* pp. 602-4. See also R. D. Bergen, "Evil Spirits and Eccentric Grammar: A Study of the Relationship between Text and Meaning in Hebrew Narrative," in *Biblical Hebrew and Discourse Linguistics,* ed. R. D. Bergen (Dallas: Summer Institute of Linguistics, 1994), pp. 320-35.

Now a spirit of evil (or, for evilness) arrived "as though rushing into the vacuum Saul's loss of favor has created" (McCarter) and *began to terrorize* him.[73] Hoftijzer aptly explains that this situation is "not only a state of fright, but also a state of being (partly) incapacitated."[74] This spirit is *from the Lord* and hence "will play its part in the working out of the divine plan."[75]

b. Saul Is Informed about David (16:15-18)

15 *And Saul's servants said to him,*
"Now the spirit of God for evilness is terrorizing you![76]
16 *May our lord command your servants before you*
that they may seek a man who knows how to play[77] *the lyre!*
When a spirit of God for evilness comes upon[78] *you,*
he will play it with his hand, and it will be well with you."
17 *And Saul said to his servants,*
"Find for me a man who can play it well and bring him to me!"
18 *And one of the officers*[79] *answered:*
"I have found a son of Jesse the Bethlehemite
who is skillful in playing,
who is a powerful man, a man of war,
and who is prudent in speech and handsome;
for[80] *the Lord is with him!"*

15-17 Noticing that the spirit of evil *is terrorizing* Saul, a group of *his servants* speak up and suggest that Saul command them to find a lyrist. So Saul commands so. The *servants* here refer to high-ranking members of the court, hence "officials" or "advisers"; see 8:14.

Saul's servants use the phrase *the spirit of God,* instead of "the spirit of the Lord" (vv. 13, 14a) here. The narrator already stated in v. 14 that this spirit *for evilness* is "from the Lord." Since the narrator uses both phrases —

73. For the expression *began to terrorize,* see NASB; cf. *HALOT,* p. 147: "to terrify"; "began to haunt" (McCarter, p. 279).

74. J. Hoftijzer, "Some Remarks on the Semantics of the Root bʿt in Classical Hebrew," in *Pomegranates and Golden Bells: Studies in Biblical, Jewish, and Near Eastern Ritual, Law, and Literature in Honor of Jacob Milgrom,* ed. D. P. Wright, D. N. Freedman, and A. Hurvitz (Winona Lake, Ind.: Eisenbrauns, 1995), p. 781.

75. McCarter, pp. 280-81.

76. *m^{e}ḇaʿittek̲ā* < *m^{e}ḇaʿēt-t-ek̲ā* (part. f.s. + suff.).

77. *m^{e}naggēn:* NGN (root?); also 1 Sam. 18:10; 19:9.

78. Lit., "is to"; see on 1 Sam. 19:20.

79. *hann^{e}ʿārîm* (lit., "the young men"), a synonymous variant of "his servants" *ʿăbādâw* (v. 17).

80. Lit., "and. . . ."

the spirit of God — for evilness — 16:23 and 18:10 and *the Lord's spirit for evilness* in 19:9 — not too much emphasis should be given to the difference between these two variant expressions, *pace* Block.[81]

May our lord command . . . that they may seek . . . (lit., "Let our lord speak . . . ! Let them seek . . . !") in v. 16 is grammatically jussive — jussive; hence, "May our lord (= you) command your servants (= us) before you that they (= we) may seek a man who knows how to play the lyre!" Earlier scholars recognized in this sentence "certain unusual features" in Hebrew and emended according to LXX^B: "Let your servants speak in your presence, and (let them) seek out for our lord. . . ."[82] But this is not necessary.[83]

Spinoza said, "Music is good to the melancholy," and all ancient societies used music against demons. The servants thus propose to find a musician to relieve Saul's melancholia and to keep the spirit from troubling him.[84]

It was believed in the ancient Near East that the *lyre (kinnôr)* had divine power, and a deified *knr* is listed in the official pantheon list of ancient Ugarit.[85] However, there is no direct biblical evidence of deification of instruments in Israel.[86] See 1 Sam. 10:5. The fact remains, however, that music has a therapeutic power.

18 One of the officers informs Saul of David, a *skillful* lyrist. Since the Hebrew term *ydʿ ("to know") means to know something well by experience, the phrase *yōdēaʿ naggēn* (lit., "who knows how to play") denotes that the person is *skillful in playing.* See "who is a skillful musician" (NASB); "who is skilled in music" (JPS). On David and his musical ability, see 2 Sam. 23:1 and also v. 23 below. For Saul's recruiting policy, see on 14:52.

The phrase *a powerful person (gibbôr ḥayil)* refers to a member of the ruling class; see 9:1 on Kish. The other phrase *a man of war (ʾîš milḥāmāh)* denotes "a trained fighter." If this phrase refers to David, it contradicts with 17:33 where Saul says to David, "you are young while he has been a man of war from his youth." Hence, scholars usually think, like Klein, that the present part has a different tradition history from ch. 17.[87]

However, the two phrases, *a powerful man* and *a man of war,* may refer to David's family background rather than his own ability ("to play lyre

81. Block, "Empowered by the Spirit of God," p. 51.

82. Wellhausen, p. 102; Driver, p. 135; Smith, p. 149.

83. McCarter, pp. 279-80.

84. McCarter, p. 281.

85. *KTU* 1.47:32; 1.118:31.

86. See N. Wyatt, "Kinnaru," *DDD,* pp. 911-13. For the most recent study on the lyre, see B. Lawergren, "Distinctions among Canaanite, Philistine, and Israelite Lyres, and their Global Lyrical Contexts," *BASOR* 309 (1998) 41-68.

87. Klein, p. 166.

skillfully") and personality ("excellence in speech and form"). He is a son of Jesse, the Bethlehemite, who is a member of the ruling class like Kish and a trained fighter. The information that David was a skillful lyre-player was the primary information necessary to Saul in the present context; all the other items were additional. It may be that the servant either assumed David to be *a powerful man, a man of war* since he was the son of a well-to-do person, several of whose sons were actually engaged in wars (see 17:12-13) or meant that Jesse was *a powerful man, a man of war.*

The phrase *prudent in speech (n^{e}bôn dābār)* means literally "discerning of word": <adj. construct + objective genitive>. Ability to speak well is typical of one type of hero, as Jacob, Joseph, Daniel, Abigail, etc. (cf. Odysseus). Discerning speech is praised many places in Proverbs (e.g., 21:23; 25:15). Being *handsome* (*ʾîš tōʾar;* lit., "a man of form") is another characteristic of the ideal young man in Israel; *tōʾar* is used of the beauty of Rachel (Gen. 29:17), Joseph (39:6), and Abigail (1 Sam. 25:3).

The comment *for the Lord is with him* explains "all of the previous parts: the young man's success, strength, manners, and looks are the result of divine favor" (McCarter, p. 281). This shows that even Saul's servants knew about the intimacy of the God-David relationship! This "most outstanding qualification of David" is notable also in 1 Sam. 17:37; 18:12; 20:13; 2 Sam. 5:10; and 7:3, 9. The expression *the Lord is with him* [= David] now becomes "a kind of leitmotiv running through the stories of David and Saul."[88]

c. David Attends Saul (16:19-22)

19 *And Saul sent messengers to Jesse, saying,*
"Send me David your son who is with the flock!"
20 *And Jesse took*
an ass-measure of bread
and a nod-measure (skin) of wine
and a kid of she-goats — one,
and sent them to Saul by the hand of David, his son.
21 *And David came to Saul and attended him; and he loved him greatly.*
And he became a weapon-bearer for him.
22 *And Saul sent (messengers) to Jesse, saying,*
"Let David attend me,
for he has found favor in my eyes!"

88. McCarter, p. 281.

19-22 Listening to his servants' advice, Saul sends messengers to Bethlehem where the skillful lyrist David, the son of Jesse, resides. In vv. 19-22, people's movements are frequent and at a quick tempo, literally spatio-temporal "transition":

(19) Saul → Bethlehem
(20) David → Gibeah
(21) quick tempo (see below)
(22) Saul → Bethlehem

19-20 In response to Saul's request to send his son David to him, Jesse prepares gifts to the king that David may take with him. The first item in the list of gifts is *ḥămôr leḥem,* literally, "an ass of bread." This has caused trouble from ancient times. KJV explains it as "an ass *laden* with bread." The LXX, followed by McCarter, changes "hamor" to "omer" and translates "an omer of bread."[89] But this is about the size of a modern loaf and would be too small an amount to take to a king as a gift. NEB's "homer," by reading *ḥōmer,* a dry measure, "perhaps originally meaning 'ass-load'" is much more realistic. Nevertheless, such an alteration of the text, however minimal, is not necessary.

The best solution is to recognize that the term *ḥămôr* is a *calque* (loan translation) of the Akkadian *imēru* "ass"-measure of about 80-160 liters.[90] This measure seems to have gone out of use in Israel. Compare the fifth-century ostracon Arad 3:4-5 ("load of a pair of donkeys") *mś' ṣmd ḥmrm* and 2 K. 5:17. The "homer" is how much a donkey can carry (Aharoni).[91]

The term *nō(')d* may be a unit for liquid, hence, *nod*-measure, just as *ass* was a unit for dry measure, or "skin-bottle."

Bread and *wine* are the basic "food and drink," as in Ugaritic texts such as *KTU* 1.23:6. The expression *a kid of she-goats — one (gᵉdî ʿizzîm 'eḥād)* is a list expression; see 1 Sam. 1:24; 6:17.

21 With the verbal phrase *came to,* the stage changes from Bethlehem to Gibeah. Note the subject switches back and forth between David and Saul: *David came to Saul and* David *attended* Saul; *and* Saul *loved* David *greatly. And* David *became a weapon-bearer for* Saul. The tempo (see "Intro-

89. McCarter, p. 280.

90. See D. T. Tsumura, "*ḥămôr leḥem* (1 Sam xvi 20)," *VT* 42 (1992) 412-14. This could be another sign of the oldness of the language of 1-2 Samuel; also 1 Sam. 1:24; 2 Sam. 11:15; see A. Hurvitz, "The Historical Quest for 'Ancient Israel' and the Linguistic Evidence of the Hebrew Bible: Some Methodological Observation," *VT* 47 (1997) 311-14; also "Introduction" (Section III, C, 5).

91. Y. Aharoni, *Arad Inscriptions* (JDS; Jerusalem: Israel Exploration Society, 1981), p. 18.

duction" [Section VI, C]) is very quick, and there are four consecutive *wayqtl* verbs: "came" — "attended" — "loved" — "became" (not a copula "to be," but "to become"), which signify the narrative transition. Recently Wong suggested that David should be the subject of all four verbs; hence "David loved Saul."[92] While this is grammatically possible, semantically a master's "great love" for a subject would induce the "faithfulness" of a subject to his lord. The fourth verb is not in sequence with the preceding actions but rather a consequence of them. See on 17:55 (below).

The term *attended* (*ʿmd + *lipnê;* lit., "stood before ") may refer "either to the initial presentation, as here, or to more permanent service, as in verse 22" (R. P. Gordon, p. 152). NIV translates "entered his service" (v. 21), but "to remain in my service" (v. 22). See on v. 22.

For *he* (Saul) *loved him* (David), compare "Jonathan loved David" (18:1). Saul was greatly pleased with David and *loved him.* Moran pointed out that the language of love can be found in the description of the loyalty and friendship between king and subject as well as the great king and his vassals in the ancient Near East.[93] Following Thompson, McCarter thinks that "the verb 'love' may also have a political nuance here."[94] But, as R. P. Gordon holds, it is unnecessary "to read into loved the connotation of a political or legal commitment."[95]

Presumably Saul would have had more than one *weapon-bearer (nōśēʾ kēlîm),* though David became his special attendant. Hence, NIV and JPS are correct in their translations: "one of his armour-bearers" (NIV) and "one of his arms-bearers" (JPS); cf. "his armor-bearer" (NRSV; NASB). The phrase *weapon-bearer* could be a term for a status in a royal court, and the one who had this title served his lord in various aspects of life both in peace and in war. Compare the close association between Jonathan and his weapon-bearer (14:1) and the loyalty of Saul's weapon-bearer (31:4-6).

22 When Saul sent messengers to Jesse for the first time, he just asked him to send David to him (v. 19); now, he again sends his messengers to Jesse to get his permission to let him serve him. Yet the sense here is not "to remain in the service," as if "to stay without going back" as 18:2 ("Saul . . . did not let him return"). There is no need to distinguish between "enter" and "remain"; see on v. 21.

Here Saul specifically mentions David's own name; later, after he be-

92. G. C. I. Wong, "Who Loved Whom? A Note on 1 Samuel xvi 21," VT 47 (1997) 554-56.

93. W. L. Moran, "The Ancient Near Eastern Background of the Love of God in Deuteronomy," *CBQ* 25 (1963) 78-79.

94. McCarter, p. 281.

95. R. P. Gordon, p. 153.

came hostile to David, he used "the son of Jesse" *(ben-yīšay)* in 20:27; 22:7; etc. On Saul's ignorance of David's family background, if not the name of David, see on 17:55.

d. Summary Statement (16:23)

23 *And whenever*[96] *the spirit of God came to*[97] *Saul, David would take the lyre and play it with his hand; and Saul would be refreshed and be well;*[98] *and the spirit of evil would depart from him.*

23 In a pagan religion, the *lyre* would have been used for "exorcism," but here there is no sign that it was part of any rite. David's ability to play the lyre well comes from the spirit of the Lord: a "gift" of the spirit. David is attested as a musician in the title "the minstrel of the songs of Israel" in 2 Sam. 23:1. He is referred to as the author of several songs as 2 Sam. 1:17-27; 22:1-51; 1 Chr. 16:7-42, and, according to their titles, of a number of psalms.[99] He was credited with setting up the temple musicians in 1 Chr. 6:31, and the eighth-century B.C. prophet Amos says David was an improviser on musical instruments (i.e., he made up new melodies; see Amos 6:5). See also on 1 Sam. 16:16. The Nikkal hymn from LB Ugarit, with full musical notation,[100] illustrates the centuries-long musical history in ancient Canaan before David.

The term *be refreshed* (impersonal 3 m.s. of *rwḥ; see Job 32:20 and Exod. 8:15) is a pun on "spirit" *(rûaḥ).* The very use of this rare term itself might suggest that this verse is a climax and conclusion of this section.[101]

The term *depart* here corresponds to the verb in v. 14, the beginning of this part, and they form an *inclusio.* Thus, v. 23 constitutes the terminus of the episode. So far, ch. 16 has introduced David, giving the answer to the question, Who is God's choice? On the other hand, ch. 17 will give answer to the question about David, What does he do?

96. *waw*+pf. is frequentative.

97. Lit., "was to"; see v. 16.

98. *ṭôb lô;* impersonal 3 m.s.; lit., "it went well with him"; pf., see BDB, p. 373.

99. D. T. Tsumura, "Hymns and Songs with Titles and Subscriptions in the Ancient Near East," *Exegetica* 3 (1992) 1-7 [Japanese with an English summary].

100. See A. D. Kilmer, R. L. Crocker, and R. R. Brown, *Sounds from Silence* (Berkley: Bit Enki Publications, 1976).

101. Bergen thinks that this clause stands as "a statistical pinnacle"; see Bergen, "Evil Spirits and Eccentric Grammar," p. 328.

B. DAVID AND GOLIATH: BATTLE AT THE VALLEY OF ELAH (17:1-54)

The story of David and Goliath is one of the best known in the Bible and among the classics of the world; for Tom Sawyer, David and Goliath were apparently the only two biblical characters he could remember.[1] This is, "in essence, a story of David trusting God and of God delivering David."[2] It is "an outstanding example of the Lord's power to give victory against dramatically overwhelming odds in response to faith and courage."[3] It has been thus one of the most fascinating and encouraging events, not only to the then minor power Israel but also to believers of God in a "postmodern" society.

This event is the clear step by which young David, already chosen and anointed privately and taken up by Saul as a court musician, comes onto the public stage, to be used in the great battle against the fearful Philistines for the divine purpose of salvation. Here, the unseen guiding hand of the Lord is most evidently at work "for good with those who love Him, who are called according to His purpose" (Rom. 8:28). In the context of the wider narrative, David's victory "evoked jealous feelings in Saul, thus indirectly setting in motion the events which fill the rest of 1 Samuel."[4]

The immediately preceding section, 16:14-23, recounted David's introduction to Saul's court. It is often asserted that the present section is based on a different tradition from the previous one since they appear to be contradictory in certain aspects of the narrative. For example, in v. 28 David's eldest brother Eliab seems to be ignorant of David's anointing in the first half of ch. 16; David in this chapter is described as still shepherding his father's flock and as a stranger to Saul (vv. 55-58), while in the second half of ch. 16 David was appointed as the weapon-bearer of Saul (16:21). These "contradictions" appear to be supported by the fact that MT and LXX are so divergent in this chapter.

MT versus LXX

The LXX version is much shorter than the MT; it lacks 46 percent of the MT — 27 out of 58 verses — that is, 17:12-31, 41, 48b, 50, 55-58 are missing.[5] J. Wellhausen, followed by D. Barthélemy, D. W. Gooding, A. Rofé, and van

1. Mark Twain, *The Adventures of Tom Sawyer* (Hartford, Conn.: The American Publishing Company, 1876), chap. 3.

2. Moberly in *NIDOTTE,* 1, p. 648.

3. Baldwin, p. 124.

4. R. P. Gordon, p. 153.

5. See E. Tov, *Textual Criticism of the Hebrew Bible* (Minneapolis: Fortress, 1992), pp. 334-36.

der Kooij, holds the view that the LXX reflects an abridgment of a longer Hebrew text similar to the MT, Targ., Syr., Vulg. On the other hand, McCarter, like Caird, Stoebe, Hertzberg and Klein, thinks that the MT is an expansion of a shorter original text reflected in LXX^{B}.[6]

E. Tov and J. Lust take a different approach. They claim that there were two Hebrew versions of the story. The LXX reflects one older version, "which stands as a literary unit in its own right." The editor of the MT joined this version with a separate and parallel version, leaving "contradictions" (especially 17:55-58 against 16:21) caused by the combination of the two stories.[7]

Similarly, according to Klein, "the David of this account seems to be unaffected by the event of chap. 16," and ch. 17 had a distinct tradition history from ch. 16. Some even suggest that ch. 16 was originally native to Bethlehem,[8] while ch. 17, which deals with the victory over the Philistines, belongs with "military records."[9] From a literary perspective, Alter explains that the "seemingly contradictory versions" — ch. 16 and ch. 17 — are put together by "the characteristic biblical method for incorporating multiple perspectives," "a montage of viewpoints arranged in sequence."[10]

However, these scholars seem to overemphasize the difference of editions, traditions, perspectives, or even theologies between the two "versions." It is arguable that many such differences are only superficial. R. Polzin argues for the MT's integrity on literary grounds by noting repetitions or alternations of verbal forms and dialogue patterns.[11] Bergen notes the author's narrative techniques in lengthening the narrative account by the "inclusion of non-narrative information" such as the description of Goliath and his weapons (vv. 4-7) and the information about David's family (vv. 12-14).[12] Polzin reminds us that "repetition is the mother even of discourse-oriented learn-

6. See D. Barthélemy et al., *The Story of David and Goliath: Textual and Literary Criticism: Papers of a Joint Research Venture* (OBO 73; Fribourg: Éditions Universitaires, 1986); A. van der Kooij, "The Story of David and Goliath: The Early History of Its Text," *ETL* 68 (1992) 118-31; the Introduction ("The Text") of R. P. Gordon's commentary. See "Introduction" (Section II) to this commentary.

7. E. Tov, "The Composition of 1 Samuel 16–18 in the Light of the Septuagint Version," in *Empirical Models for Biblical Criticism,* ed. J. H. Tigay (Philadelphia: University of Pennsylvania Press, 1985), pp. 97-130; Tov, *Textual Criticism,* p. 336. See van der Kooij, "The Story of David and Goliath," pp. 119-20.

8. Hertzberg, p. 136, following Budde.

9. Baldwin, p. 124.

10. R. Alter, *The Art of Biblical Narrative* (London: George Allen and Unwin, 1981), p. 154.

11. R. Polzin, pp. 161-76.

12. Bergen, p. 188.

ing."[13] Certainly, repetitious expressions are typical of a narrative which is fundamentally an "aural" text.[14]

Straight and strict exegetical efforts to read and seek the plain meaning of the text are needed foremost before accepting "inconsistencies" or "discrepancies" in an ancient narrative.

For example, David, though he was appointed to be one of Saul's weapon-bearers, served primarily as a musician at court, unrelated to the present context of war. As discussed above, the phrase "a powerful man, a man of war" (16:18) could refer to Jesse or even just signify that David is from the ruling warrior class of the society. In fact, 17:15 presupposes that David was serving as one of Saul's servants. He could go back and forth between Saul's court and his father's house in Bethlehem — a journey of some 10 miles. Though David appears to be totally unknown to Saul in 17:58, Saul wanted to know David's father's name, namely, his family background. A king would not take note of the name of his servant's father; see on v. 55. As Polzin argues,[15] "to dismiss these verses with a redactional shrug" simply "robs the story of its esthetic brilliance and ideological complexity, even as it severely weakens the drama of reading." See below (v. 28) on the protest of David's brother Eliab.

The narrative does exhibit literary cohesion, with such techniques as literary (or rhetorical) insertion, AXB and AXYB patterns, and repetition. The literary structure of 17:1-54 as a whole is as follows:

Elah	1. Battle in the Valley of Elah (17:1-11)
	a. Philistines and Israel (17:1-3)
	b. Goliath the champion (17:4-11)
	(1) Goliath from Gath (17:4)
	(2) His weapons (17:5-7)
	(3) Challenge to a duel (17:8-11)
Bethlehem	2. David in Bethlehem (17:12-19)
	a. David son of Jesse (17:12-15)
	b. Goliath the champion (17:16)
	c. Jesse sends David to the Valley (17:17-19)
Elah	3. David's victory over Goliath (17:20-54)
	a. David comes to the valley (17:20-23)
	b. Goliath the champion (17:24)

13. Polzin, p. 172.

14. See H. van Dyke Parunak, "Some Axioms for Literary Architecture," *Semitics* 8 (1982) 2-4; D. T. Tsumura, "Scribal Errors or Phonetic Spellings? Samuel as an Aural Text," *VT* 49 (1999) 390-411.

15. Polzin, p. 172.

c. "Who is this uncircumcised Philistine?" (17:25-30)
d. David appears before Saul (17:31-40)
e. Duel between Goliath and David (17:41-51a)
 (1) "For the battle is the Lord's!" (17:41-47)
 (2) David kills Goliath (17:48-51a)
f. The Israelites defeat the Philistines (17:51b-54)

1. Battle in the Valley of Elah (17:1-11)

a. Philistines and Israel (17:1-3)

1 *Now the Philistines gathered their forces for battle, gathering at Socoh of Judah, and they encamped at Ephes-dammim between Socoh and Azekah.*

2 *As for Saul and the men of Israel, they gathered together and encamped in the Valley of Elah. And they deployed themselves*[16] *for battle against the Philistines.*

3 *The Philistines were taking up their position on a hill on one side, and Israel was taking up its position on a hill on the other side, and a valley*[17] *was between them.*

The story begins with some details about the Philistine and Israelite armies, stating their exact locations in *the Valley of Elah.* The *waw,* translated here as *Now* (lit., "and"), is *waw initial* since the first phrase in *wayqtl* is followed by a stated subject *(the Philistines).* For a *wayqtl* at the initial position of discourse, see Lev. 1:1; etc. See "Introduction" (Section VI, A).

Verses 1-3 give the geographical setting of the EVENT which follows. Not only the specific localities, with proper names such as *Socoh, Azekah, Ephes-dammim,* and *the Valley of Elah* (vv. 1-2), but also the physical geography of the location as the *hill* and *valley* (v. 3) provide the necessary information.

Set against this geographical background, the goal of this strategically important battle was certainly to secure the Valley of Elah, the natural point of entry from the Philistine homeland into the hill country of the Saulide kingdom. The battle was thus crucial.

1 The name *Socoh (šwkh)* appears in Paleo-Hebrew script on a royal stamped jar handle.[18] It is located in the Shephelah (i.e., "Lowland") some 14

16. See the note on 1 Sam. 4:2.

17. Heb. *haggay'* "the valley"; see *HALOT,* p. 188; also cf. *'ēmeq* above.

18. See T. C. Mitchell, *The Bible in the British Museum: Interpreting the Evidence* (London: British Museum Publications, 1988), p. 55; A. Mazar, *Archaeology of the Land of the Bible, 10,000 — 586 B.C.E.* (ABRL; New York: Doubleday, 1990, 1992), pp. 456-57.

miles west of Bethlehem toward Philistine territory; the modern site is Khirbet ʿAbbad [MR147-121], near the village of Khirbet Shuweikeh [MR150-090], which preserves the ancient name (see 2 Chr. 28:18). This town was strategically important both to the Israelites and to the Philistines. Both *Socoh* and *Azekah* appear in Josh. 15:35 in a list of the lowland towns belonging to Judah. The narrator specifies *of Judah* to remind the audience that the Philistines were encroaching on the territory of Judah.

Azekah, modern Tell ez-Zakarīyeh [MR144-123], is located about 2-3 miles northwest of *Socoh* and controlled the main road across the Valley of Elah.[19] It is referred to in Lachish ostracon no. 4 ("we cannot see [the signals of] Azekah").[20] See also Josh. 10:10-11; 2 Chr. 11:9.

Ephes-dammim: perhaps a variant of Pas-dammim,[21] which is the site of the exploits of Eleazar, one of David's heroes (1 Chr. 11:13; cf. 2 Sam. 23:9 [cf. Driver]). The exact location is still unknown. McCarter thinks that the modern site may be Damun, about 4 miles northeast of ancient Socoh, but the map on p. 283 of his commentary places Ephes-dammim about 1.5 miles to the west of Socoh. The city's position on the map is more reasonable since it is located on the same hill as *Socoh* and south of *the Valley of Elah,* which runs from east to west. On the other hand, Rainey's suggestion of placing Ephes-dammim at *Kh. ʿAsqalûn,* a mile south of *Azekah,* on the other side (i.e., west) of the north-south valley which is perpendicular to *the Valley of Elah*[22] is less likely, for in this case the Philistine encampment would be on the opposite side of the valley from Socoh, where they first gathered their forces for battle.

2-3 The Philistine and Israelite armies took their positions on each side of the *Valley of Elah* (or "the Valley of the Terebinth"), now called the Wadi es-Sant. It runs westward from Bethlehem, from the hill country of Judah, toward the Philistine cities of Gath and Ekron; see v. 52. It is immediately south of and parallel to the Wadi es-Sarar (the Valley of Sorek). The Hebrew term *ʿēmeq,* "valley," can refer to a plain located between two mountains or hills.

19. See E. Stern, "Azekah" in *ABD,* I, pp. 537-39.

20. See Gibson, *SSI,* 1, pp. 41-43.

21. The original name of *ʾepes dammîm* could have been ʾApsu (?)-dammim; see LXX: Εφερμαειμ or Αφεσδομμειν/μ (BHS). Its variant form *bappas dammîm* (1 Chr. 11:13) might be explained as resulting either from (1) *sandhi: bappas* ← *bᵉʾappas* or from (2) <assimilation>: *bappas* ← *baʾpas.* On *sandhi* and assimilation, see Tsumura, "Scribal Errors or Phonetic Spellings?" pp. 397-403.

22. A. F. Rainey, "The Identification of Philistine Gath: A Problem in Source Analysis for Historical Geography," *EI* 12 [Nelson Glueck Memorial Volume] (1975) 70*, fig. 2.

b. Goliath the Champion (17:4-11)

(1) Goliath from Gath (17:4)

4 *A champion*[23] *of the Philistine camps*[24] *came out; Goliath was his name and he was from Gath.*[25] *His height was six cubits*[26] *and a half.*

With this verse the narrative moves forward after the SETTING in vv. 1-3. *A champion . . . came out* is the *wayqtl* with a stated subject; hence, it initiates a new discourse unit, that is, a subparagraph, like *Now the Philistines gathered* (v. 1); see "Introduction" (Section VI, A). Since the verb *came out* (*yṣʾ) is a *movement* verb, the action is a little off the main line of the story and prepares for the action *stood* in v. 8. Verses 5-7 are an embedded discourse giving a detailed description of Goliath's weapons. Thus, they are inserted in order to slow down the flow of discourse by interrupting the sequence of actions, *came out* and *stood* in vv. 4 and 8.

v. 4	Goliath from Gath	A
vv. 5-7	His weapons	X
vv. 8-11	Challenge to a duel	B

For the literary insertion, or AXB pattern, see "Introduction" (VII, C).

The champion Goliath and his weapons are described here in detail to impress upon the audience the human impossibility of anyone's prevailing against him.

4 McCarter renders the term *bēnayim*[27] as "a certain infantryman" (pl.: "skirmishers" based on 1QM [War Scroll]),[28] but *champion* fits the present context; the term must have experienced a semantic change by the time of

23. So NIV; JPS; NRSV; NASB; *ʾîš-habbēnayim;* lit., "man of the between"; "the man of the intervals"; "of the spaces between (armies), i.e., champion" (*DCH,* I, p. 229d); cf. "man of the two intervals" (W-O, p. 199). The term appears only here in the Old Testament. The term *bēnayim* is an example of nominalization of the preposition *bên,* "between"; see on 1 Sam. 9:24.

24. McCarter emends the term *maḥănôt* to "ranks," based on LXX[B], for he thinks that MT is "out of place" since, as v. 3 shows, "the two armies have already left camp" (McCarter, p. 286). But "from the camps" probably modifies *champion* rather than *came out;* hence, the translation: *A champion of* [lit., from] *the Philistine camps,* i.e., "chosen from among the Philistine camps."

25. *Gath* was one of the Philistine pentapolis; see 1 Sam. 5:8.

26. So MT and LXX[A]; cf. "four cubits" (McCarter; following LXX[BL], Josephus and 4QSam[a]).

27. The term could be an example of nominalization of an adverbial phrase, i.e., the in-between one; see on 1 Sam. 9:24 for other examples. See *HALOT,* p. 140.

28. See *DCH,* I, p. 231b.

the Dead Sea Scrolls. R. de Vaux,[29] who studied "single combat" in the Old Testament (e.g., 2 Sam. 2:12-17; 21:15-22; 23:20) and extra-biblical literatures, explains the *champion* as "a man who steps out to fight between the two battle lines." Hoffner[30] compares it with the Hittite *piran ḫuyanza* "champion." In the Homeric epic, "Paris suggests that Hector set him 'in the midst' to engage in single combat with Menelaus (*Iliad* 3:69), to settle the war."[31] In the Egyptian story, Sinuhe was forced into such a combat.[32]

The term *Goliath* has been explained as a non-Semitic Philistine, or perhaps Anatolian, name which, it has been claimed, is traceable back to *Walwatta,* an older form of the Lydian name *Alyattes,* from a Luvian base *walwi/a.*[33] However, it might be better to compare it with the second millennium B.C. Ugaritic PN *glyt/n* (*KTU* 4.106 18);[34] the name might still have been an originally Anatolian or Aegean name used in ancient Ugarit, however.

The proper name *Goliath (golyāt)* appears only twice in this chapter: vv. 4 and 23 (also in 21:9); elsewhere he is called "the Philistine" — twenty-seven times in 17:1–18:5. 2 Sam. 21:19 has a notice of a battle at Gob in which "Elhanan . . . killed Goliath the Gittite"; also cf. 1 Chr. 20:5. Some have suggested that this ch. 17 account is based on Elhanan's victory, with Elhanan's deed attributed to David.[35] However, one should note that there are too many differences between the two accounts to identify them as referring to the same event. For one thing, the locations of the duels are different. It is possible that the name was an old name for a giant-hero (see Ugar. *glyt*), which is applied here to David's enemy, then later to Elhanan's enemy. See on 2 Sam. 21:19.

Then follows a detailed description of the giant-hero Goliath. McCarter thinks that *six cubits* is an exaggeration.[36] However, the lowering

29. R. de Vaux, *The Bible and the Ancient Near East* (Garden City, N.Y.: Doubleday, 1971), pp. 122-35, esp. 124-25.

30. H. A. Hoffner, Jr., "A Hittite Analogue to the David and Goliath Contest of Champions?" *CBQ* 30 (1968) 220-25.

31. See C. H. Gordon, *The Common Background of Greek and Hebrew Civilizations* (New York: W. W. Norton, 1965), pp. 262-63, who notes that "the Philistine identity of Goliath ties in with the similarity between his title . . . and the Homeric '(champion) in the midst.'"

32. See M. Lichtheim, in *CS,* I, p. 79. Also see J. P. Brown, "Peace Symbolism in Ancient Military Vocabulary," *VT* 21 (1971) 3; also K. Galling, "Goliath und seine Rüstung," in *Volume du Congrès: Genève 1965* (SVT 15; Leiden: E. J. Brill, 1966), pp. 150-69.

33. See Kitchen in *POTT,* p. 67.

34. See W. G. E. Watson, "Ugaritic Onomastics (2)," *AuOr* 8 (1990) 244.

35. H. J. Stoebe, "Die Goliathperikope 1 Sam. XVII 1–XVIII 5 und die Textform der Septuaginta," *VT* 6 (1956) 397-413.

36. McCarter, p. 286.

of the number in some versions seems to be deliberate; when one considers the huge size of his weapons (note that his *cuirass* weighed 126 pounds; see v. 5), *six cubits* makes better sense.[37] Since the cubit is about eighteen inches, being the distance from a man's elbow to the tip of his middle finger, and a span is about nine inches, from the tip of the thumb to the tip of the little finger of the splayed hand, *six cubits and a half* (*zāret;* lit., "a span") is about 9 feet 9 inches, about 3 meters. Ford notes that such gigantism likely resulted from a dysfunction of the pituitary gland.[38] W. J. Martin "refers to one John Middleton (c. AD 1600) who is reputed to have been nine feet three inches tall. Middleton is buried at Hale, near Liverpool."[39]

(2) Goliath's Weapons (17:5-7)

5 *A bronze helmet*[40] *was on his head;*
in scale-armor[41] *he was dressed;*
the weight of the cuirass was five thousand shekels and it was of bronze.
6 *Bronze greaves*[42] *were on his shins;*
a bronze dagger was on his back.
7 *The shaft*[43] *of his spear was like a weaver's beam;*
the blade of his spear was six hundred shekels of iron.
And a shield-bearer was going before him.

Instead of moving right into the battle itself, the narration "lingers in detail on the intimidating appearance of the challenger"[44] and on his impressive ar-

37. See van der Kooij, "The Story of David and Goliath," p. 118.

38. J. N. Ford, "The 'Living Rephaim' of Ugarit: Quick or Defunct?" *UF* 24 (1992) 88.

39. R. P. Gordon, p. 346. See on "giants, heroes, mighty men" (R. F. Youngblood) in *NIDOTTE,* 4, pp. 676-78.

40. *kôbaʿ* is also spelled as *qôbaʿ* in v. 38; they are probably variant forms of a non-Semitic foreign term; see Hittite *kupaḫ(ḫ)i* "hat, cap"; Gk. *kumbakhos* (*HALOT,* pp. 463, 1081-82). C. H. Gordon takes the term with its variant form as the Caphtorian word for "helmet," since these spellings can be explained in the light of the fact that Ugaritic *ḥkpt* (*UT* §19.860: "Egypt"; *UT,* p. 543) can also be written as *ḥqkpt* (ʿnt:VI:13) with "foreign palatal intermediate between k and q written both ways."

41. *širyôn qaśqaśśîm;* or "a coat of scale armor" (NIV); "coat of mail" (NRSV).

42. *miṣḥat;* MT: s.; cf. pl. (LXX^{B}; Syr); du. (McCarter, p. 286).

43. *ḥṣ ḥnytw* (K.); cf. *ʿēṣ ḥănîtô* (Q.); see *ʿēṣ ḥănîtô* in 2 Sam. 21:19; cf. McCarter, p. 286, who reads *ʿēṣ,* "wood, shaft," as in 2 Sam. 21:19; so Syr., LXX^{B} *(ho kontos)* and LXX^{L} (*to xylon,* "the wood"). The K. however could be explained as an example of distant assimilation: *ʿēṣ ḥănîtô* → *ḥēṣ ḥănîtô.*

44. Birch, p. 1110.

mor. This detailed description of the giant and his weapons embedded into the narrative builds up the suspense.

K. Galling believes that Goliath's armor and weapon are a collection of pieces of diverse origin which have been assembled by the narrator "for literary effect" in order to show how imposing he was and how mightily God acted through David.[45] However, taking into consideration the high quality of the Philistine material culture (e.g., in Ekron) and also the high degree of cultural and religious borrowing (e.g., worshipping indigenous Semitic deities such as Dagon [see on 5:2] and adopting new Semitic personal names such as Abimelek; see "Introduction" [Section IV, A and B]), the diverse origin of Goliath's armament may not be surprising. As J. P. Brown notes, the general description of Goliath's armor is "contemporary with the *Iliad* and strikingly similar," though the biblical account might not be used for an exact reconstruction of "a Mycenaen hoplite."[46] For one thing, Goliath's weapons could have been imported from northern Syria or Anatolia as well as from Egypt, if not directly from the Aegean. A champion for one-to-one combat would be dressed differently from an ordinary soldier.

Goliath's entire body was well shielded except his face. Therefore, no ordinary sword-wielding warrior could threaten him. However, with his huge and heavy armor, Goliath's movement was naturally slow (cf. David's quick movements in vv. 48-51).

5 Since Goliath's *helmet* was made of bronze, it is not likely to be the feathered headdress of the *Prst* (Philistines) depicted in Medinet Habu reliefs of Rameses III. Galling thinks that Assyrian headgear may have provided the model for this helmet.[47] However, this foreign word *kôbaʿ* (see fn. 40 [above]) is also used for Saul's bronze helmet in v. 38, and in the *Iliad* 10:31 Menelaus's helmet was also made of bronze, so there is no need to look for an Assyrian model. The term might have referred to a substantial bronze helmet from an earlier day.[48]

This *scale-armor* may have been similar to the Assyrian armor in the British Museum.[49] The term *širyôn,* also in v. 38 for Saul's armor, seems to be of non-Semitic origin (Hurrian? known from fifteenth-century Nuzi).[50] It became common in biblical Hebrew as a term for "body-armor covering the entire torso" or "the breastplate alone" as in 1 K. 22:34 = 2 Chr. 18:33f.[51] The

45. See Galling, "Goliath und seine Rüstung," pp. 150-69.

46. Brown, "Peace Symbolism," p. 3.

47. Galling, "Goliath und seine Rüstung," pp. 155, 163; also McCarter, p. 292.

48. See Brown, "Peace Symbolism," pp. 5-6.

49. See Mitchell, *The Bible in the British Museum,* p. 57.

50. E. A. Speiser, "On Some Articles of Armor and Their Names," *JAOS* 70 (1950) 47-49; also *HALOT,* p. 1655.

51. McCarter, p. 292.

term *qaśqaśśîm* ("scales") refers to a well-known type, represented by Pharaoh Sheshonq's (Shishak's) armor from the tenth century B.C.[52] But it is not in the Mediterranean-Aegean style. His bronze *cuirass* weighed *five thousand shekels,* that is, 57 kg. = 126 pounds.

6 The term *greaves* is used in the Old Testament only here and in v. 49. They were "probably made of molded bronze encircling the entire calf, like later Greek greaves, and padded inside with leather" (McCarter, p. 292); they were commonplace in the Aegean world and figure in the panoplies of the Trojan heroes of the *Iliad* (18:613; 19:370; 21:592).[53] The term *kîdôn* is usually translated as "javelin" (NRSV; NIV; JPS) or "dagger" (REB). However, Molin, followed by McCarter, suggests "scimitar," a sword-like weapon for close action, with a handle, a straight piece, and a semi-circular piece, and with a cutting edge on the outer side of the blade.[54]

The phrase *on his back* (so NIV) is literally "between his shoulders" (NRSV; NASB); this is similar to Ugaritic expressions such as *bn ʿnm* "between the eyes," which is equivalent to "on the head" (see *UT* §19.1846), and *bn ydm* "between the hands," which is equivalent to "on the shoulders" (*UT* §19.1072). A "poetic" structure in this verse (see "Introduction" [Section VII, B] on poetic prose) would support this interpretation: that is, *on his shin//on his back.* Note JPS's translation: "slung from his shoulders."

7 For the simile, *like a weaver's beam (kimnôr ʾōrᵉgîm),* there are two explanations: (1) the great mass of this spear is compared to that of a weaver's beam (see Krinetzki[55] and others); (2) this type of spear is like a weaver's heddle rod with "the loops or leashes of cord that were attached to it" — the shaft of his spear was equipped with a thong and ring for slinging like a type of javelin in Greece and Egypt.[56] Since the comparison is with the wooden part (i.e., the shaft) of Goliath's spear, the first explanation seems preferable.

52. See Y. Yadin, *The Art of Warfare in Biblical Lands,* 2 vols. (New York: McGraw-Hill, 1963), I, pp. 196-97; II, p. 354; Galling, "Goliath und seine Rüstung," pp. 161-62.

53. Brown, "Peace Symbolism," pp. 3-4; L. Krinetzki, "Ein Beitrag zur Stilanalyse der Goliathperikope (I Sam. 17:1–18:5)," *Bib* 54 (1973) 191. See the "Warrior" vase from Mycenae in A. Millard, "On Giving the Bible a Fair Go," *Buried History: Quarterly Journal of the Australian Institute of Archaeology* 35.4 (1999) 10; Y. Yadin, *The Art of Warfare in Biblical Lands,* II, p. 354.

54. G. Molin, "What is a *kidon?*" *JSS* 1 (1956) 337; Galling, "Goliath und seine Rüstung," pp. 163-67; McCarter, p. 292.

55. Krinetzki, "Ein Beitrag zur Stilanalyse der Goliathperikope," 191.

56. See Y. Yadin, "Goliath's Javelin and the *mᵉnôr ʾorigîm,*" *PEQ* 86 (1955) 58-69; also *The Art of Warfare in Biblical Lands,* II, pp. 354-55. See also 2 Sam. 21:19.

Six hundred shekels is about 15 pounds, that is, about 6.8 kg. The spear point is made of *iron* (see on 13:19-22), while other armaments are of bronze. The fact that only the spear point was iron is "fitting for the period when iron was newly available and costly."[57]

The *shield (ṣinnāh)* held by the *shield-bearer,* unlike the smaller round shield *(māgēn)* held by hand, is a large standing shield which covers the whole body.[58] It looked almost impossible for anyone to attack Goliath, since his *shield-bearer was going before* him. The narration is from the viewpoint of Goliath, not from that of the Israelite army, hence the verb used is *going.* See "Introduction" (Section VI, D).

(3) Challenge to a Duel (17:8-11)

8 *He stood (firm) and called*[59] *to the ranks of Israel:*
"Why will you march out to deploy yourselves for battle?[60]
Isn't it true
that[61] *I am the Philistine but you are (just) slaves of Saul?*[62]
Select[63] *a man for yourself so that he may come down to me!*
9 *If he can fight with me and defeat me,*
we shall become your slaves.
But if I prevail over him and defeat him,
you will become our slaves and serve us."
10 *The Philistine said:*

57. Millard, "On Giving the Bible a Fair Go," pp. 5-12; "King Og's Bed and Other Ancient Ironmongery," in *Ascribe to the Lord: Biblical and Other Studies in Memory of Peter C. Craigie,* ed. L. Eslinger and G. Taylor (Sheffield: Sheffield Academic Press, 1988), pp. 481-92. Also see "Introduction" (Section IV, A).

58. See *HALOT,* p. 1037.

59. Lit., "called . . . and said to them"; for a similar case, see 19:4; see "Introduction."

60. See vv. 20-21; also v. 2. For "march out" and "deploy," see 4:2.

61. *Isn't it true that . . .:* taking *hălô'* as modifying the whole sentence, *'ānōkî happᵉlištî wᵉ'attem 'ăbādîm lᵉšā'ûl,* thus contrasting "I" and "you."

62. *'ăbādîm lᵉšā'ûl; 'ăbādîm* sometimes means "subjects" as in 8:14, but here in Goliath's insulting speech it means "slaves." Note that the expression is not "the servants of Saul," which would be from *'abdê šā'ûl.*

63. *bᵉrû:* *bry[II] "sich ausersehen"; Akk. *barû* (GMD, p. 173). *HALOT,* p. 155 takes *brh[II] as denominative from *bᵉrît* and explains the present form as Qal impv., meaning "enter into a *bᵉrît* with someone; commission him as your representative." Though BDB, p. 136a takes it as a "scribal error" and McCarter reads *bōrû* (< *brr) based on LXX, the Hebrew root *brh (*bry) is probably a bi-form of *brr "to select" (see 1 Chr. 7:40), since both are originally biconsonantal. Hence, no revocalization is necessary. BHS's remark "Vrs a *bḥr* cf 1 R 18,25" is misleading.

"I (myself) challenge[64] the ranks of Israel today!
Give me a man so that he and I may fight each other!"[65]
11 *When Saul and all of Israel heard these words of the Philistine,*
they were greatly[66] dismayed and frightened.

8 The action continues from v. 4a where Goliath *came out.* Note that the *waw* here is sequential, without a stated subject following the verb *stood (firm).* In other words, the verbal sequence *came out* and *stood* has been interrupted by the insertion of the descriptions of Goliath and his weapons (vv. 4b-7).

Using the definite article *(I am the Philistine),* Goliath contrasts himself as *the* Philistine with the Israelites as slaves belonging to Saul. It is not necessary to read "a Philistine" with LXX.

9 As this was a taunt speech, not a negotiation, it is not surprising that the promise was not kept. So, it is pointless to talk about the Philistines' not keeping this agreement in vv. 52-54.

10 *The Philistine said:* this is an example of "repeated introduction to speech" in which "speech by one character, introduced with a finite form of the verb 'say' (ʾmr), is interrupted by a second introduction, also using a finite form of 'say.'"[67]

The verb *challenge* (*ḥrp) is one of the key words in this chapter (also vv. 25, 26, 36, 45); the repeated use portrays the attitude of the adversary. It implies "not only defiance and provocation but also open contempt."[68] Hence, sometimes it is translated as "reproach"; see v. 26. On this term, see 11:2.

11 The Israelites had sufficient reason to be *greatly dismayed and frightened.* Not only were the Philistine's words of challenge frightening, but his outward appearance, with his towering stature and his perfect equipment, was overwhelming. On top of this, the Philistine army was well trained, organized, and, unlike the Israelites, sufficiently equipped with "modern" weapons. Far from being "uncultivated" *uncircumcised* people, recent archaeological excavations have disclosed they were a highly civilized people, having originated in the Aegean culture. See "Introduction" (Section IV, A and B).

64. The verb in the first person is a performative perfect (as in Ps. 2:7 "I have begotten you") with a declarative force: i.e., "hereby I challenge you!"; see "Here and now I challenge" (REB). See 1:28; 3:14; 15:11, 24.

65. *wᵉnillāḥămāh;* lit., "we may fight together" (exclusive — "we," since the Israelite army, who is the audience in the second person, is not included here); "he and I" will engage in a single combat; see de Vaux, *The Bible and the Ancient Near East,* p. 123.

66. *mᵉʾōd* modifies both verbs, i.e., "dismayed" and "frightened."

67. E. J. Revell, "The Repetition of Introductions to Speech as a Feature of Biblical Hebrew," *VT* 47 (1997) 96-97, n. 15. See on 1 Sam. 16:11.

68. McCarter, p. 293.

2. David in Bethlehem (17:12-19)

With v. 12, the flow of the narrative is suddenly interrupted by the insertion of a new paragraph regarding David and his family in Bethlehem; the battle narrative briefly resumes in v. 16, and then the stage goes back to the scene at Bethlehem again. This complex narrative structure is not due to the careless combination of different source materials but rather exhibits the narrator's sophisticated literary organization of "literary insertion": two strands of dialog, AB and XY, are intertwined in an AXBY pattern (A: 1-11; X: 12-15; B: 16; Y: 17-19); see also Exod. 4:18-23 (A: 18; X: 19; B: 20; Y: 21-23). For another example, see v. 28; for the similar but not identical pattern AXYB, see on 21:1–22:23.

a. David Son of Jesse (17:12-15)

12 *Now David was a son of an Ephrathite who*[69] *was from Bethlehem of Judah and whose name was Jesse and who had eight sons.*
Since the man was in the days of Saul old and had become a senior,
13 *the three oldest sons of Jesse had gone, going after Saul, to the war.*
As for the names[70] *of his three sons who had gone into the war, they were Eliab, the firstborn, and his second (son) Abinadab and the third (son) Shammah.*
14 *David was the youngest, while the three oldest had gone after Saul.*
15 *David was going back and forth from before Saul to shepherd the flock of his father in Bethlehem.*

One has the feeling that the narrator here draws upon a new literary source[71] since David is introduced as if for the first time. However, this abruptness may be a narrative technique. While in 16:1-13 the focus in the narrative was on Jesse and his sons, with the youngest one David introduced as the climax, here David is focused on right from the beginning of the narrative in v. 12: hence, "Now David was. . . ." As for vv. 13-15, Jesse's other sons are mentioned in v. 13 before discussing the main actor David in more detail in vv. 14-15, as is the usual manner of a narrative; see for example Genesis 10 (Japheth, Ham, and then Shem); 11:27-32 (Haran, Nahor, and then Abram).

69. *hazzeh;* lit., "this." Here the demonstrative pronoun is used as a relative pronoun like Ugaritic *hnd* ("this") which consists of *hânâ* ("this" in Syriac) + *d* (*UT* §6.22; 19.786). Cf. Ugar. *d,* Heb. *zû* and Aram. *dî.* McCarter, following S. R. Driver, omits this term as "unacceptable on grammatical grounds," though the omission is "without clear support from the ancient witnesses (cf. Syr.)" (p. 301).

70. Lit., "name" (s.); the three oldest sons are also named in 16:6-9.

71. See van der Kooij, "The Story of David and Goliath," p. 127.

12 The expression *'eprātî* is usually used as a gentilic of Ephraim (see on 1:1; 10:2), but here, as in Ruth 1:2; 4:11; Mic. 5:2; and 1 Chr. 2:19, 24, 50; 4:4, an Ephrathite *('îš 'eprātî)* refers to a man from the Judaean Ephrath, around Bethlehem (see on 16:1).[72] For "Jesse" and "eight sons," see on 16:1 and 10, respectively.

Jesse was *old and had become a senior (zāqēn bā' ba'ănāšîm;* lit. "old (and) came [pf., rather than ptc.] into men"), that is, he had reached the age where he was exempted from civil and military services rather than "advanced among men" (MT as translated by R. P. Gordon) or "a feeble old man" (NEB).[73] Jesse must have retired from his patriarchal responsibility by this time or at least sometime soon after; see on 20:29, where his eldest son has seemingly taken responsibility for the family feast as the fratriarch.[74]

McCarter thinks that the MT has "an impossible combination" and hence suggests two possible reconstructions: (1) *zqn b' bšnym,* "old, advanced in years" (so LXX^{L}; Syr.); and (2) *zqn b'nšym* "old among men." He thinks that the former is preferable.[75] However, the expression *zāqēn bā' bayyāmîm* "was old and advanced in years" with *yāmîm,* instead of *šānîm,* often appears in the OT (Josh. 13:1; also 23:1, 2; Gen. 18:11; 24:1; 1 K. 1:1). Since *'ănāšîm* appears instead of *yāmîm* only in the present passage, the translation "advanced in years" (RSV; JPS; NIV) is often suggested on the basis of emendation.[76] Tentatively, however, the MT might be better translated as *had become a senior;* see "old . . . advanced in years among men" (NASB).

13-15 These verses are said to be very repetitive, "possibly as a result of endeavors to harmonize the different stories" (Ackroyd, p. 141). However, this seemingly repetitive style is due to its literary features such as the literary insertion, AXB pattern, and the list-like expression in v. 13; see below.

13 The verb *had gone (wayyēl^{e}kû)* is the first *wayqtl* verb in the embedded discourse (vv. 12-15); it is sequential to the previous perfect verb *had become (bā').* Both verbs are verbs of "motion"; they are not in the main line of the story; see "Introduction" (Section VI, A). The entire verse thus explains David's family background and prepares for David's errand.

72. See R. L. Hubbard, Jr., *The Book of Ruth* (NICOT; Grand Rapids: Eerdmans, 1988), pp. 90-91 on "Ephrathites from Bethlehem in Judah" (Ruth 1:2).

73. See *HALOT,* p. 1601.

74. See C. H. Gordon, "Fratriarchy in the Old Testament," *JBL* 54 (1935) 223-31; *PLMU,* p. 36.

75. McCarter, p. 301.

76. R. Althann ("Northwest Semitic Notes on Some Texts in 1 Samuel," *JNSL* 12 [1984] 32) suggests rereading the MT as *bě'ab 'ănāšîm* "as a father of men," taking the preposition *b* as *beth essentiae,* following Fenton. No satisfactory solution can be offered through emendations.

McCarter thinks that the phrase *going after Saul (hālᵉkû ʾaḥărê-šāʾûl)* is problematic "not only because it is superfluous but also because *hlkw* appears again immediately below, and the entire sequence *hgdlym hlkw ʾḥry šʾwl* recurs in v 14 below (Driver)." He omits *hālᵉkû,* though admits that the omission is "without clear textual support."[77] However, the phrase here seems to be inserted to slow down the flow of discourse. The phrase "had gone to the war" is split up by the insertion of the clause *going after Saul.*

In this verse the names of Jesse's three oldest sons are given in a list-like expression. It lacks some of the formal list features; compare the list built into the narrative in 6:17.[78] For example, in the phrase *and his second (son),* "his" is added to the numeral, which is more in the manner of a narrative than a list. But, note that LXX^L ("Now *these were* the names . . .") seems to preserve a list formula like Exod. 1:1.

14-15 McCarter thinks that these verses are redactional and designed "to harmonize the two stories, in one of which David is already in the service of Saul while in the other he is still at home with Jesse."[79] It seems, however, that the discrepancy between the two narrative portions has been overemphasized. R. P. Gordon's comment hits the mark: "A verse [= 15] designed to explain how David, who, according to 16:21, had been appointed armour-bearer to Saul, was not in the Israelite camp when Goliath was issuing his challenge." In fact, David was serving as Saul's minstrel, though officially as one of the weapon-bearers at Saul's court (see on 16:21), while shepherding his father's flock intermittently. See Introduction to this chapter (above) and also on v. 33.

The alternation *David . . . Saul . . . David . . . Saul . . .* seems to be intentional, in order to remind the reader of the David-Saul relationship.

b. Goliath the Champion (17:16)

16 *And the Philistine drew near early mornings and evenings*
and took his stand for forty days.

16 This verse is a link with the previous section, providing "a picture of the continuing threat and anxiety" (Ackroyd, p. 141). It is a literary insertion into the narrative of Jesse and David in Bethlehem, reminding the audience that the Philistine is still threatening the Israelite army daily, some 12 miles west of Bethlehem.

77. McCarter, p. 302.

78. See D. T. Tsumura, "List and Narrative in I Samuel 6,17-18a in the Light of Ugaritic Economic Texts," *ZAW* (2001) 353-69.

79. McCarter, p. 303.

c. Jesse Sends David to the Valley (17:17-19)

17 *Jesse said to David, his son,*
"Take for your brothers an ephah[80] *of this parched grain*[81] *and ten loaves of this*[82] *bread and run (with them) to the camp, to your brothers!*[83]
18 *And take these ten cheeses*[84] *to the commander of the thousand;*
and find out about the welfare of your brothers
and bring some token of them,
19 *for they as well as Saul and all the men of Israel*
are in the Valley of Elah
fighting with the Philistines."

17-18 The present episode is sometimes compared with the Joseph story. For example, R. P. Gordon explains: "[David's] errand to the battle-front is a detail reminiscent of Joseph's fact-finding mission to Dothan (Gen. 37:12ff.); in both cases the errand leads to an unforeseen encounter with destiny."[85] However, since the sending a messenger to find out about someone's welfare is such a common experience, the narrator probably was not particularly thinking of the Joseph story.

17 *Parched grain* is "a delicacy prepared by roasting the ears in an iron pan" (Ackroyd, p. 141); see 25:18; 2 Sam. 17:28; Lev. 23:14; Ruth 2:14. Klein thinks that "every detail is meant to underscore the human insignificance of David and his family!"[86] since parched grain was "favorite food for simple people"[87] together with loaves of bread. However, nobody expects to eat gourmet cooking on the battlefield! Roasting was the fastest way to prepare the grain and seems to have been a common food. It could keep for a while and could be eaten without further cooking, and so it was suitable for the battlefield or journeys.[88]

18 The term *'elep* usually means "thousand," but in the present context it probably refers to a military unit; see on 6:19; 18:13.

80. See on 1 Sam. 1:24.

81. *haqqālî':* the root is *qly rather than *ql'; see the annotation *ytyr'* ("superfluous") *'alep* in the *Masora parvum* (Mp); also Ezra 6:15 *(wšyṣy').*

82. *hazzeh* here is not "def. article" + "demonstrative pron."; see above (v. 12). Hence no article is necessary for *leḥem,* though McCarter, p. 302, reads *hlḥm.*

83. McCarter, p. 302, supplies "and give it" *(wtnh)* before *to your brothers* on the basis of LXX. But the phrase should be taken as an apposition to the phrase "to the camp."

84. *ḥărīṣê heḥālāb;* lit., "cuts of milk." The term *ḥărīṣê* is a *hapax legomenon.*

85. R. P. Gordon, pp. 155-56.

86. Klein, p. 177.

87. Krinetzki, "Ein Beitrag zur Stilanalyse der Goliathperikope," p. 192.

88. See *NIDOTTE,* 4, p. 450.

While the word *ʿărubbātām (token,* so JPS; NRSV; some kind of object; cf. "assurance" [NIV]; "news" [NASB]) possibly refers to a kind of pledge or surety, it may stand for "a simple token as proof of well-being and/or the receipt of food";[89] see the rare noun "token, pledge" (Prov. 17:18), which refers to "sureties." Here, the term refers to "some agreed sign of the brothers' continued safety and welfare."[90] Does the "token" stand for the receipt of food or for the proof of well-being of the brothers? The latter seems to be better; the following verse concerns the location of the brothers: "they" (see below).

19 NIV ("They are with Saul and all the men of Israel in the Valley of Elah")and NASB ("For Saul and they and all the men of Israel are in the valley of Elah") take this verse as a continuation of Jesse's speech. On the other hand, JPS ("Saul and the brothers and all the men of Israel were in the valley of Elah") and NRSV ("Now Saul, and they, and all the men of Israel, were in the valley of Elah") take it as the narrator's explanation. While Ackroyd takes this as "another linking and harmonizing verse,"[91] it seems more likely to be the information which David needed before he ran with the goods. See the next note.

For they as well as . . . (w^{e}šā'ûl w^{e}hēmmāh w^{e}kol-'îš yiśrā'ēl b^{e}ʿēmeq hā'ēlāh): the word order of MT "and Saul and they and all the men of Israel were in the Valley of Elah" is unusual. McCarter follows MT and thinks that LXX^{A} (cf. Syr.) seemingly reflects a different Hebrew original wš'wl hw' . . . , "Now as for Saul, he and all the men of Israel, etc."[92] In this case v. 19 would not be a part of Jesse's speech but a narrator's comment. In comparison with other texts,

> *šā'ûl w^{e}kol-'anšê yiśrā'ēl* (11:15)
> *w^{e}šā'ûl w^{e}'îš-yiśrā'ēl* (17:2)
> *šā'ûl w^{e}kol-yiśrā'ēl* (17:11)

šā'ûl in the present text is preposed, for focusing, because of the politeness of Jesse toward the king;[93] the expected logical order would be: *w^{e}hēmmāh w^{e}šā'ûl w^{e}kol-'îš yiśrā'ēl* "for they, and/together with Saul and all the men of Israel," because the context would require information on where *they,* that is, David's brothers, are.

89. J. Hoftijzer and W. H. van Soldt, "Texts from Ugarit Concerning Security and Related Akkadian and West Semitic Material," *UF* 23 (1991) 213.

90. R. Wakely, in *NIDOTTE,* 3, p. 517.

91. Ackroyd, p. 141.

92. McCarter, p. 302.

93. Suggested by S. Tsumura. For a recent study of focus structure, see K. Shimasaki, *Focus Structure in Biblical Hebrew: A Study of Word Order and Information Structure* (Bethesda, Md.: C. D. L. Press, 2002), esp. pp. 56-60.

3. David's Victory over Goliath (17:20-54)

a. David Comes to the Valley (17:20-23)

20 *And David rose early in the morning and entrusted the flock to a keeper and took (the things) with him as Jesse had commanded him. And he came to the entrenchment.*[94] *At that moment the army, which was about to march out to the battle lines, was raising shouts for war.*

21 *Israel and the Philistines deployed themselves,*[95] *battle line against battle line.*

22 *David entrusted the baggage which was with him to the hand of the equipment keeper*[96] *and ran to the battle line and came and then asked about the welfare of his brothers.*

23 *While he was speaking with them, just at that moment*[97] *the champion was going up — Goliath, the Philistine, was his name, from Gath — from the battle lines*[98] *of the Philistines. And he spoke [words] like those [previous] words and David heard.*

20-23 One can see here, in a seemingly ordinary event in the life of David, God's providential guidance, as in Hannah's life (see 1 Samuel 1). Although David, when he went, had no intention of getting into a fight with a Philistine champion, God was preparing him for a dramatic debut in the history of Israel for promoting the divine plan of salvation among the covenant people.

20 "The details — David's early start, his arrival just as the fighting men moved to confront their opposing army, and his disposal of his load at the camp — all lend vividness to the developing climax" (Baldwin, p. 126). This vividness is also expressed by some discourse features. Note that *took . . . with him* (lit., "lifted and went") . . . *came to* . . . signifies the change of viewpoint from "this side" (i.e., Bethlehem) to "that side" (i.e., the Valley of Elah). For *wᵉhaḥayil,* the translation *At that moment the army* (lit., "and the army") might be suggested, since a circumstantial clause provides informa-

94. Or "circumvallation."

95. *wattaʿărōk;* 3.f.s. This feminine singular verb takes "Israel" as its grammatical subject. "Israel" is usually masculine, but it is feminine here and in 2 Sam. 24:9 [not// 1 Chr. 21:5]; also Amos 5:2 *bᵉtûlat yiśrāʾēl* "Virgin Israel," not "The Virgin of Israel." Or is this verb a 3 m.s. <*taqtul*> like (see on 2 Sam. 22:3)? For "march out" and "deploy," see 1 Sam. 4:2; also 17:8.

96. *šômēr hakkēlîm;* cf. "a keeper" (McCarter, p. 302; cf. LXX^{A}); "quartermaster" (NEB).

97. *wᵉhinnēh;* lit., "and lo!"

98. *mimmaʿărkôt* (Qere); cf. *mmʿrwt* (Ketib) "from the bare spaces"; < *ʿrw/ʿry; "from the *caves* (!)" (McCarter, p. 302).

tion about what is going on "at that moment"; hence, the participial phrase *hayyōṣē'* (lit., "the going out") is translated as *which was about to march out.*[99] The word order of *the army . . . was raising shouts* is again unusual, w + NP(S) — w + Vpf. The NP(S) appears before *w*^{e} + perfect to topicalize/focus it in order to give a real time description; also 20:4. See "Introduction" (Section V, A).

21-22 In the verbal sequence *ran . . . and came and asked: wayyāroṣ . . . wayyābō' wayyiš'al,* "came" (i.e., "arrived") is more suitable than "went" from David's viewpoint. David *came* to the battle line where the Israelite army had *deployed themselves* against the Philistines.

23 *The champion ('îš habbēnayim)* here is definite, because he is already known to the reader from v. 4. Nevertheless, note the parenthetical explanation of the champion as *Goliath, the Philistine, was his name, from Gath,* adding to his name *the Philistine,* the term used from now on to refer to him.

Goliath is probably *going up ('ôleh)* to a higher place from where he can stand and shout to the Israelites. Or, perhaps the term should be translated as "coming up," if he is coming toward the Israelite battle lines. Nothing happens by chance. *Just at that moment* — David was led to see Goliath and hear his words of challenge. Behind all these matters God was certainly engineering David's life according to his plan and purpose.

b. Goliath the Champion (17:24)

24 *As for all the men of Israel, whenever they saw the man, they retreated from before him and were very frightened.*

Here *all the men of Israel* is topicalized, appearing before *wayqtl (they retreated).* See v. 20. Note that the topic switches from David to the Israelite army. The phrase *were very frightened (wayyîr*^{e}*'û m*^{e}*'ōd)* recalls the previous situation in v. 11.

c. "Who Is This Uncircumcised Philistine?" (17:25-30)

25 *Men of Israel were saying,*
"Did you (pl.) see this man who is coming up?
Surely to challenge Israel he is coming up!
If there should be a man who defeats him,

99. Cf. Driver, p. 142: "And the host that went forth to the battle array — they shouted in the war." — the construction is "very strained." Hence McCarter, p. 302, changes the MT *hayyōṣē'* to *yōṣē'* and translates: "was just marching out."

the king will make him very rich,[100]
and his daughter he will give him,
and his father's house he will make free in Israel."
26 *And David said to the men who were standing with him, (saying)*
"What will be done for the man
who defeats that Philistine and removes (his) reproach from Israel,
for who is this uncircumcised Philistine that he should challenge the battle lines of the living God?"
27 *And the people spoke to him in the same way, (saying)*
"Thus will be done for the man who defeats him."
28 *And Eliab, his eldest brother, heard when he was speaking to the men.*
Eliab became angry with David and said,
"Why have you come down?
To whom have you entrusted even those few sheep
in the wilderness?
I know your insolence and the willfulness of your heart.
For it is to see the battle that you have come down, isn't it?"
29 *And David said,*
"What have I done now? Isn't that just a word?"
30 *And he turned away from him toward another direction and spoke in the same way. And the people answered him as in the first way.*

25-30 In this episode the pronoun "this" is often used to express derision or amazement;[101] see also vv. 26, 32, 33, 36, 37, etc. In v. 25 it may be used in amazement, and in v. 33 it may be neutral, but David seems to use it derisively. *Did you see this man . . . ?* (v. 25). The people judged the situation by what they saw with their eyes; hence they were *very frightened* (v. 24). Without faith we see only negatively when faced with difficulties; we forget our status as God's people and lose confidence in God. But David saw and judged everything by faith; see below.

25 *Men of Israel were saying:* The MT literally reads "A man of Israel said." However, since the direct discourse *"Did you see . . . ?"* is in plural, it was not directed at David. In fact, David was not informed of what was said in v. 25, as v. 26 shows. Hence, modern translations usually take *ʾîš* as collective: for example, "The Israelites said" (NRSV); "And the men of Israel were saying among themselves" (JPS).

100. *yaʿšᵉrennû* (instead of *yaʿšîrennû*); cf. *taʿšᵉrennāh* (Ps. 65:10). For *make him very rich,* which has the structure of V-O S O-int Adj (cognate accusative with adj), see D. T. Tsumura, "Niphal with an Internal Object in Hab 3,9a," *JSS* 31 (1986) 11-16.

101. Polzin, p. 173.

If there should be (wᵉhāyāh; lit., "and he will be") might be also translated "As for the man," since *wᵉ-hāyāh* here introduces a TOPIC like a "topicalizing" *wayhî* (see "Introduction" [Section V, A]), followed by three resumptive pronouns, "him," "him," and "his."[102]

His father's house (bêt 'ābîw) refers to his extended family, smaller than a tribe or clan. It comprises "all the descendants of a single living ancestor (the head, *rō'š-bêt-'āb)* in a single lineage, excluding married daughters . . . , [but including] male and female slaves and their families, resident laborers, and sometimes resident Levites." It is likely that a *bêt-'āb* could have comprised some 50-100 persons, residing in a cluster of dwelling units.[103]

The term *free (ḥopšî)* means "exempt from" taxes and other obligations to the palace.[104] Akk. *ḫupšu* and Ugar. *ḫpṯ* are the cognate terms which refer to "a particular social class in the lower part of the economic order." But Hebrew *ḥopšî* seems to have a more general meaning (adj. "free") than those cognate terms, and can refer to people of a "free" status; see Exod. 21:2 in reference to persons freed from slavery. Thus, cognates that are socially characterized terms may refer to entirely different items in different societies. Linguistic affinity and historical connection should be carefully distinguished; see also the case of the Habiru and Hebrew problem.[105]

Instead of seeking a cognate term, A. F. Rainey[106] compares Hebrew *ḥopšî* with the Akkadian adjective *zaki.* In the Akkadian texts from Ras Shamra (Ugarit) *zaki* is used to describe an emancipated slave women (RS 16.250:21-22) or a soldier who, because of a brave deed slaying a rebel, has been exempted from service to the palace (RS 16.269:14-16). The latter is a striking semantic parallel to the present passage.[107]

26 *For* in the phrase *What . . . for who is . . . ?* is a speaker-oriented *kî,* that is, "the reason why I asked such a question is"; see "Introduction" (Section V, C). Here David's seemingly casual words open up his future as a royal figure and a prototype of the "Messiah"!

For the rhetorical question, *who . . . that . . . should . . . ?* expressing surprise with the "that"-result clause, see Ps. 8:4. David by faith grasped Go-

102. See Ackroyd, p. 141.

103. See *ABD,* II, pp. 761-68.

104. McCarter, p. 304; A. F. Rainey, "Institutions: Family, Civil and Military," in *RSP* 2, pp. 92, 103-4; D. J. Wiseman, in *Archaeology and Old Testament Study,* ed. D. Winton Thomas (Oxford: Clarendon, 1967), p. 126. Cf. O. Loretz, "Ugaritisch — Hebräisch *ḫb/pṯ, bt ḫpṯt — ḥpšj, bjt hḥpšj/wt,*" *UF* 8 (1976) 129-31.

105. See, for example, H. Cazelles, "The Hebrews," in *POTT,* pp. 1-28.

106. Rainey, "Institutions," in *RSP* 2, p. 104.

107. See also McCarter, p. 304; M. Weinfeld, *Social Justice in Ancient Israel and in the Ancient Near East* (Jerusalem: Magnes, 1995).

liath's challenge as directed toward *the battle lines of the living God,* hence toward God himself, for David was seeing the unseen God and his *battle lines;* see also v. 36.

For the term *uncircumcised (heʿārēl),* see on 14:6; cf. v. 36. Circumcision gave the Israelites a sense of national identity.

The God of Israel is *the living God (ʾĕlōhîm ḥayyîm;* also 17:36) in contrast with "the lifeless idols and venerated nonentities of the nations (cf. Jos 3:10; 1 Thes 1:9)" (R. P. Gordon, p. 156). The phrase is "always used to stress the reality and effectiveness of the god of Israel (Dt 5:26 and esp. Jer 10:10) and most often . . . to censure those who would dare to mock or otherwise revile Yahweh (2 K. 19:4,16 = Isa 37:4,17; Jer 23:36)."[108]

28 Being probably the fratriarch (see on 17:12) and at least ten years the elder, Eliab, the *eldest brother,* was annoyed with, not jealous of, his youngest brother's conduct at this very tense and critical situation. The often suggested resemblance with the Joseph story is somewhat overstated; see Ackroyd, p. 141; Klein, p. 178.

In *I know (ʾănî yādaʿtî)* the subject "I" is emphasized. Eliab is acting as a big brother with authority over his little brother.

Insolence and willfulness of heart (ʾet-z^{e}dōn^{e}kā w^{e}ʾēt rōaʿ l^{e}bābekā) are often used to describe human disobedience to God; cf. Deut. 17:12 and 18:22 (insolence) and Jer. 7:24 (willfulness of heart). But these expressions appear as a pair only here; see "the pride of your heart" *(z^{e}dôn libbekā)* in Jer. 49:16.

29 *Isn't that just a word? (hălôʾ dābār hûʾ)* could be a rhetorical question: "Isn't it a matter of importance?" (Ackroyd, p. 141); cf. "I was only asking!" (JPS), "Can't I even speak?" (NIV; supported by R. P. Gordon, p. 156, as "excellent"). Bergen paraphrases: "What have I done to offend you now? I happen to have been asking about a very important matter."[109]

d. David Appears before Saul (17:31-40)

31 *The words which David spoke were heard*[110] *and reported to Saul, who took him.*
32 *And David said to Saul,*
"Let not any man's heart fall on himself!
Let your servant go and fight with this Philistine!"

108. McCarter, p. 293.

109. Bergen, p. 193.

110. Note that וַיְּשָּׁמְעוּ in Leningrad Codex, confirmed by *The Leningrad Codex: A Facsimile Edition* (Grand Rapids: Eerdmans, 1998), reflects the actual pronunciation: *wayyššām^{e}ʿû* (phonetic spelling) [-*jš*-] < *wayyiššām^{e}ʿû* וַיִּשָּׁמְעוּ.

33 *And Saul said to David,*
"You cannot go to this Philistine to fight with him,
for you are young while he has been a man of war from his youth!"
34 *And David said to Saul,*
"Your servant has been shepherding sheep for his father.
Whenever a lion,[111] *and even a bear,*[112] *would come*[113]
and carry a sheep away from the flock,
35 *I would go out after it and defeat it and rescue it from its mouth.*
If it rose against me,
I would seize (it) with its beard and defeat it and kill it.
36 *Lion and bear alike,*[114] *your servant has defeated them.*
This uncircumcised Philistine shall be like one of them,
for he challenged the battle lines of the living God."
37 *David said,*
"The Lord who rescued me from the hand of the lion and bear,
he will rescue me from the hand of this Philistine!"
And Saul said to David,
"Go, for[115] *the Lord will be with you!"*
38 *And Saul dressed David with his garments and put a breastplate on him, placing a bronze helmet on his head.*
39 *And David girded himself with his (= Saul's) sword over his garments and undertook*[116] *to walk, because*[117] *he had never tried.*
And David said to Saul,

111. *hā'ărî;* lit., "the lion"; the article denotes the generic sense; see Driver, p. 145; McCarter, p. 293.

112. *wᵉ'et-haddôb;* the particle *'et* is used here for emphasis; cf. "with" (GKC, §117k); "a lion or a bear" (McCarter, p. 287), taking *w't* as an intrusion "at the wrong point."

113. *ûbā';* *waw* + pf. 3 m.s.; "habitual or repeated action in the past" (McCarter, p. 293).

114. So McCarter, p. 287; or "Both lion and bear" (Andersen, p. 155); "Either a lion or a bear, whichever it may be" for the MT *gam 'et-hā'ărî gam-haddôb.*

115. *waYHWH;* lit., "and the Lord . . ."; here disjunctive *waw* functions as expressing the reason why he says "go!" (imperative), just like the speaker-oriented *kî:* see v. 36 (above).

116. *wayyō'el lāleket;* BDB, p. 384.

117. I.e., the causal *kî,* which should be distinguished from the "for" (the speaker-oriented *kî;* see "Introduction" [Section V, C]) in David's direct speech, which denotes the reason why I say this. Cf. the difference in the meaning of the causal "for" and the speaker-oriented "for" in the interpretation of "Her sins . . . are forgiven for she loved much" (Luke 7:47). The context dictates that it be a speaker-oriented "for."

"I cannot walk with these, for I have never tried."
And David removed them from upon him
40 *and took his staff*[118] *in his hand*
and chose for himself five smooth stones[119] *from the wadi*
and put them in the shepherd's bag he had with him, namely, in the pouch,[120] *and with his sling in his hand approached the Philistine.*

31 This verse is transitional; the passive and impersonal constructions *were heard* (Ni. 3 m.pl.) and *(were) reported* (lit., "they reported") indicate a transition in a narrative discourse. Note that Ackroyd connects it with the preceding verses, since it provides "a link to the resumption of the previous narrative by bringing David into Saul's entourage."[121] We would rather take this verse as belonging to the following section *(B)* literarily and structurally, thus forming *a* of *A/aB* pattern (see "Introduction" [Section VI, B]), while pointing to the preceding section (A) contextually.

The verb *took* implies a special connotation; see 8:11 for the technical use with a king as the subject.

32 David humbly but confidently expresses his opinion to his master Saul. The phrase *any man's heart (lēb-ʾādām)* is an indirect and euphemistic expression used honorifically for "your heart." The LXX interprets it as "my lord's heart" *(lb ʾdny),* which van der Kooij takes as a secondary "exegetical rendering."[122] The idiom "the heart falls" conveys "the loss of courage."

David uses the phrase *this Philistine* instead of "Goliath" derisively; see on v. 25.

33 Saul uses the term *young* (*naʿar:* adjective; see on 2:13 and 9:3) for David in contrast to the professional warrior, *a man of war (ʾîš milḥāmāh;* see on 16:18). Saul is referring to David's lack of military training and experience rather than his youth. David's reply in vv. 34-36 speaks precisely to this issue.[123] There is no incompatibility between the description of David as being "young" here and being Saul's weapon-bearer (16:21).

34-37 On the rhetorical analysis, see Ceresko.[124]

34 NRSV translates David's answer *rōʿeh hāyāh* as "used to keep

118. *maqlô;* or "stick, rod"; also v. 43 (in plural).

119. *ḥallūqê-ʾăbānîm;* lit., "smooth (adj., cstr.) of stones."

120. *yalqûṭ; hapax legomenon.*

121. Ackroyd, p. 142.

122. On this problem, see van der Kooij, "The Story of David and Goliath," p. 124.

123. See McCarter, p. 293.

124. A. R. Ceresko, "A Rhetorical Analysis of David's 'Boast' (1 Samuel 17:34-37): Some Reflections on Method," *CBQ* 47 (1985) 58-74.

sheep," but, as R. P. Gordon notes, "David . . . has just come from the sheepfold and he still has his shepherd's gear (v. 40)."[125] So, we read *has been shepherding.*

Both lions and bears were common in Palestine during the Israelite period; see the stamp seal with the inscription "the servant of Jeroboam" with a picture of a lion, and Assyrian royal reliefs showing lion hunts.[126]

35 The term *rescue* (*nṣl), together with *yšʿ (*save* in v. 47), is a key word, which occurs at the climax of David's two crucial speeches, to Saul (v. 37) and to Goliath (v. 47). Later, David was also rescued from Saul by Yahweh; see 2 Sam. 12:7; 22:1.[127]

The MT *bizqānô* most naturally means *(in) its beard.* However, based on the LXX, McCarter translates "throat" since bears generally do not grow beards. R. P. Gordon also accepts LXX's "throat" since he thinks "'throat' *(garon)* could easily have been corrupted to *beard (zaqan)* in the Hebrew square script."[128] But as the verbs describing the animal's action are singular, David is probably describing his fight with a lion, which represents wild animals, and is the first of the two animals mentioned.

"If it rose against me (wayyāqom ʿālay) or "In the case that." In vv. 34b-35 the verbal forms *(would come . . . carry . . . go out . . . defeat . . . rescue . . . would seize . . . defeat . . . kill)* are all in <*waw*+perfect> except the present one *rose (against),* which is <*waw*+imperfect>. Hence, *rose* is "off the main line" information.

36 The second half of this verse is almost identical with v. 26b.

For is the reason why I say thus; speaker-oriented *kî,* while in v. 26 *kî* denotes result; see on v. 26 ("who . . . that . . ."). McCarter prefers the longer text of the LXX, since the "MT as it stands seems rather abrupt." Hence, he tentatively assumes that the MT has suffered haplography.[129] However, our understanding of *kî* as speaker-oriented would explain this seemingly complicated grammar well; see "Introduction" (Section V, C).

37 McCarter thinks that *David said* is "an expansion in MT, added to re-identify the speaker of an unusually long speech."[130] However, such an insertion is characteristic of a narrative, reminding the audience of who the speaker is, and is "in accordance with Hebrew idiom."[131] See on v. 10.

125. R. P. Gordon, p. 157.

126. See *ABD,* IV, p. 333.

127. See R. W. L. Moberly, in *NIDOTTE,* 1, p. 648; R. L. Hubbard, Jr., in *NIDOTTE,* 3, p. 143.

128. McCarter, p. 287; R. P. Gordon, p. 157.

129. McCarter, p. 287.

130. McCarter, p. 288.

131. Driver, p. 145.

Here David expresses his faith in God. *The Lord who rescued me . . . will rescue me.* We are reminded of Jonathan's speech of 14:6.

38-39 This is almost a comic interlude — we can picture this youth trying to walk in armor too big for him. But it means that in his fight he is trusting completely on the Lord, not on armaments.[132]

38 Though McCarter holds that *wᵉnātan* ("and he would give") is "syntactically impossible,"[133] the discourse grammatical approach clarifies the problem. The *"giving" (wqtl)* is not sequential to the "main line" of the narrative but interrupts its flow (i.e., *"And Saul dressed . . . and dressed . . ."* [A and B]). The clause *giving . . .* is thus the X of an AX&B pattern (see "Introduction" [Section VII, C]), and the entire verse might be translated as above. This is probably better, especially if the last term *širyôn* should have a more specific meaning than "armor" or "a coat of mail" and refer to a "breastplate" (JPS). See "Then Saul dressed David in his own tunic. He put a coat of armor on him and a bronze helmet on his head" (NIV); cf. "Saul clothed David with his armor; he put a bronze helmet on his head and clothed him with a coat of mail" (NRSV). Longacre would rather see here a chiastic structure: *dressed* — "put" — *dressed.*[134]

Stoebe notes on the basis of the booty list of Tuthmosis III from Megiddo that "even experienced fighters would not necessarily possess a *coat of mail*"[135] or *armor (širyôn);* see on v. 5 (above).

39 *And David . . .:* subject switching here is most natural, though McCarter and NEB emend the subject to "Saul"; see "[Saul . . .] girded [him] with his own sword over his uniform. But David . . ." (McCarter, p. 288); "he then fastened his sword on David over his tunic" (NEB).

For *and undertook to walk,* McCarter translates "after he had tried once or twice to walk" on the basis of LXX^B. He sees "not only corruption by metathesis in the verb (*wy'l* for *wyl'*) but also interference from the succeeding material (*ki l' nsyty* "for I have never practiced")."[136] However his understanding of MT: "and he was willing to walk but (?) had not practiced (wearing armor)" is not accurate, for the particle *ki* most naturally means "for, because."

40 *Wadi (hannaḥal)* is the dry riverbed (see Gen. 26:17) of the Valley of Elah. David picked five smooth stones suitable to his sling.[137]

132. McCarter, pp. 293-94.

133. McCarter, p. 288.

134. R. E. Longacre, "Weqatal Forms in Biblical Hebrew Prose," in *Biblical Hebrew and Discourse Linguistics,* ed. R. D. Bergen (Dallas: Summer Institute of Linguistics, 1994), p. 75.

135. Stoebe, "Die Goliathperikope," p. 408.

136. McCarter, p. 288.

137. For slings, see *Art and Empire: Treasures from Assyria in the British Mu-*

Namely: waw explicativum;[138] hence, there is no need of deleting the *waw* of *ûbayyalqûṭ,* though *bkly . . . lw* is often taken as a gloss to the unique *bylqwṭ.*[139] For *waw explicative,* see 6:4, 5, 18.

Sling (qelaʿ) is a military weapon, common in the ancient Near East; Egyptian evidence goes back to the beginning of the second millennium B.C.[140] Note the slingers, wearing iron helmets and coats of mail, depicted on the reliefs in the royal palaces at Nineveh and Nimrud.[141] Hebrew usages support this meaning,[142] though the Ugaritic counterpart *qlʿ* could mean "shield" on the basis of Akkadian *kabābu* (*ga-ba-bu* in *KTU* 4.63:24, etc.) "shield."[143] According to Judg. 20:16 there were seven hundred left-handed Benjamite slingers, "each of whom could sling a stone at a hair and not miss."

e. Duel between Goliath and David (17:41-51a)

(1) "For the Battle Is the Lord's!" (17:41-47)

41 *And the Philistine, before whom was a man carrying the shield,*
drew closer and closer to David.
42 *And the Philistine looked and saw David and despised him, for he*
was young and ruddy with a handsome look.
43 *And the Philistine said to David,*
"Am I a dog that you come after me with staves?"
And the Philistine cursed David by his gods.
44 *And the Philistine said to David,*
"Come to me so that I may give your flesh
to the birds of the sky and to the beasts of the field!"
45 *And David said to the Philistine,*

---

seum (London: British Museum, 1996), fig. 016; J. Reade, *Assyrian Sculpture* (London: British Museum, 1983), fig. 16.

138. D. W. Baker, "Further Examples of the wāw explicativum," *VT* 30 (1980) 129.

139. Wellhausen, pp. 107-8; Driver, p. 146; Smith, p. 164; McCarter, p. 288; Klein, p. 172.

140. Yadin, *The Art of Warfare in Biblical Lands,* I, p. 159.

141. See *Art and Empire,* figs. 016, 173; *ABD,* IV, pp. 826-31.

142. See *HALOT,* p. 1106.

143. *CAD,* K, p. 1; cf. "sling" in *CAD,* G, p. 1. See Rainey, "Institutions," in *RSP* 2, pp. 99-100. On a possible connection between "to throw, cast" and "to plait, weave," hence between "sling" and "shield" in the Semitic root *qlʿ,* see W. G. E. Watson, "Some Additional Word Pairs," in *Ascribe to the Lord,* pp. 182-83; B. L. Eichler, "On Weaving Etymological and Semantic Threads: The Semitic Root QLʿ," in *Lingering Over Words: Studies in Ancient Near Eastern Literature in Honor of William L. Moran,* ed. T. Abusch, J. Huehnergard, and P. Steinkeller (Atlanta: Scholars Press, 1990), pp. 163-69.

"You have come to me with a sword, a spear and a scimitar,
but I have come to you in the name of the Lord of Hosts,[144]
the God of the battle lines of Israel whom[145] *you have challenged.*
46 *This day the Lord will deliver you up*[146] *into my hand,*
and I will defeat you and cut your head off,
and I will give the corpse of the camp of the Philistines this day
to the birds of the sky and to the wild animals of the land.
And all the earth will know
that there is a God for Israel,
47 *and all this assembly will know*
that it is not with a sword and a spear
that the Lord will save and give you into our hands,
for the battle is the Lord's!"

41-44 Here the actual duel between Goliath and David begins. The sharp contrast between the slow movements of Goliath and the quick ones of David are emphasized by the narrator's manner of description. Since every <*wayqtl* + stated subject> constitutes a new discourse unit (see "Introduction" [Section VI, A]), the verses 41, 42, 43 and 44, all with *the Philistine,* repeat the Philistine's actions in five discourse units. Such a heavy repetition of the unit with the same stated agent suggests his slow movements, in contrast with David's quick ones described by the series of *wayqtl* in the preceding verses, vv. 39b-40: David *removed . . . took . . . chose . . . put . . . approached. . . .*

42 The Philistine looked down on David [literally!] and *despised him,* thinking himself almost perfectly equipped; he trusted in his own ability and his weapons. But his overconfidence in human resources lead to his destruction.

43-44 A duel is usually prefaced by boasting of one's own strength and scorning the enemy's; see v. 8.

43 Goliath mentions only *staves* (*maqlôt;* pl.) since he did not notice David's real weapon. R. P. Gordon notes that "the LXX's 'with a staff and stones' aims at exactitude, but misses the point: the stones are not visible."[147]

Goliath *cursed David by his gods.* They are probably the Canaanite gods such as Dagon (see 5:2) and Astartes (or goddesses in 31:10) whom Go-

144. See 1 Sam. 1:3. For the association with the ark of God, see 4:4.

145. Rather than "which" (REB), for "it is not the Israelite army (v. 10), nor Israel (v. 25), nor even the armies of the living God (vv. 26, 36), but Yahweh himself who has been affronted" (R. P. Gordon, p. 158).

146. *y*^{e}*saggerkā;* lit., "shut up into s.o.'s hand"; the Pi. stem appears only in Samuel (1 Sam. 24:19; 26:8; 2 Sam. 18:28). Phoenician *sgr also means "to deliver s.o. up/over for submission or death"; see B. T. Arnold, in *NIDOTTE,* 3, p. 225.

147. R. P. Gordon, p. 157.

liath presumably adopted. It is assumed here that curses derive their power from the gods.[148]

44 Exposure of corpses to the birds of prey, that is, "eagles and vultures," is a common motif of destruction and curse.[149] Privation of burial was worse than death in Israel; see 31:8-13; 2 Samuel 21; Ps. 79:2-3; Isa. 34:2-3; 66:24; Jer. 7:33; 8:1-2. This horror was also common to the Greeks (see *Iliad* 24, Sophocles' *Antigone*).

45-47 Here begins the longest speech by David against Goliath in this chapter. As R. P. Gordon explains, there are "two factors which made the heroic possible, viz. David's zeal for the reputation of Israel's God — . . . (v. 46) — and his utter trust in God's ability to preserve him against all odds."[150] Though no term such as *bṭḥ ("to trust") appears in this story, the concept is demonstrated throughout.[151]

45 *You . . . but I . . . :* note here the sharp contrast.

The term *sword (ḥereb)* was not mentioned among Goliath's weapons above, but see v. 51. It has the general sense of "sword" and is often paired with "spear"; on the word pair, see on 13:19.

As for the expression *the God of the battle lines of Israel (ʾĕlōhê maʿarkôt yiśrāʾēl),* McCarter thinks that it "reads like a kind of word-by-word paraphrase of *yahweh ṣebaʾot,* understood as 'Yahweh of the armies (of Israel).'"[152] Nevertheless, there is no phrase "Yahweh/God of the armies of Israel" attested in the Bible, while, on the other hand, "the Lord of Hosts, the God of Israel" appears thirty-seven times. Thus, McCarter's view is not well founded.

The phrase *in the name of the Lord of Hosts* expressed well David's complete trust in his God, with "no confidence in the flesh" (Phil. 3:3).

46 The expression *this day (hayyôm hazzeh)* is used twice in this verse for emphasis. The expression was used earlier (v. 10) by the Philistine himself; it often has a legal connotation of certainty and decisiveness as in 15:28: "this very day" in Exod. 12:41; Deut. 2:25; 1 Sam. 12:5; 14:45; 28:18; see also Ruth 4:9; Ps. 2:7 for "today" *(hayyôm).*

Wild animals of the land is a synonymous variant of *the beasts of the field* in v. 44. There are two sets of the variants: *beasts-wild animals* and *field-land.* While it is possible that David's phrase here has a broader meaning than Goliath's in v. 44, we cannot really say along with Klein, p. 180, that there is an "escalation in the contrast."

148. See D. Stuart, "Curse," in *ABD,* I, pp. 1218-19.
149. See, for example, *CS,* II, p. 280.
150. R. P. Gordon, p. 153.
151. See *NIDOTTE,* 1, p. 648.
152. McCarter, p. 294.

The Lord's delivery of Israel has two purposes: one is that the whole world (*all the earth;* see Ezek. 39:23) may *know that there is a God for Israel,* that is, that only Israel has the true God; the other is so that all the people of Israel may know that the Lord saves them by himself (v. 47). It is clear that the Lord can and will save his people, a fact that could have been held in doubt in face of Philistine control over Israel. So, "Be still, and know that I am God" says the Lord of Hosts, for he is the one who "will be exalted among the nations" (Ps. 46:10).

47 *All this assembly (kol-haqqāhāl)* refers to both Israelites and non-Israelites. As the term *qāhāl* can refer to a religious convocation (e.g., Neh. 5:13), some scholars have seen here a reference to the ritual battle of the king against the chaos monster, the forces of disorder and destruction.[153] However, as it quite commonly refers to a group of men at arms (Num. 22:4; Jer. 50:9; Ezek. 16:40; 38:15) the reference does not have to be taken cultically.

God's way of salvation is different from the human method, *not with a sword and a spear.* God accomplishes his plan of salvation in his own way, eventually by Jesus Christ, the Messiah.

For the battle is the Lord's — the battle is the warfare against God's enemy, both spiritual and physical. On Yahweh as "a man of war," see Exod. 15:3; also Isa. 3:2; 2 Samuel 22. To David, as to Paul, this battle was fundamentally spiritual in nature; see Eph. 6:12. One should always be reminded that the Lord's battle is to be fought in God's way, "Not by might, nor by power, but by my spirit" (Zech. 4:6), though the Lord can use human experiences and trainings as with David's case. God used David despite Eliab's misunderstanding (v. 28), Saul's dissuasion (v. 33), and Goliath's despite (v. 42). Therefore, the Lord's battle (also in 18:17; 25:28) is not the same as a "just war" (warfare justified by human judgment) or a so-called "holy war" (a war between two opposing deities and their human armies).[154] See on 31:9.

This phrase *for the battle is the Lord's* occurs between the two successive actions: *save* and *give,* an example of the <AXB> pattern. The AB as a whole, the Lord *will save* (A) *and give you into our hands* (B) corresponds to *the Lord will deliver you up into my hand* (v. 46). Therefore, it is not surprising that as a variant the phrase *for the battle is the Lord's* is inserted.

153. J. H. Grønbaek, *Die Geschichte vom Aufstieg Davids (1. Sam. 15–2. Sam. 5): Tradition und Komposition* (ATDa 10; Copenhagen: Prostant apud Munksgaard, 1971), p. 95.

154. For the distinction between a "holy war" and "Yahweh war," see G. H. Jones, "'Holy War' or 'Yahweh War'?" *VT* 25 (1975) 642-58; T. Sasaki, *The Concept of War in the Book of Judges: A Strategic Evaluation of the Wars of Gideon, Deborah, Samson, and Abimelech* (Tokyo: Gakujutsu Tosho Shuppan-sha, 2001), esp. pp. 20-34, 105-8.

Note that this is the concluding remark of David, and the double use of the divine name Yahweh marks the climax of his speech and constitutes *inclusio* with its double use toward the beginning of his speech (vv. 45-46). The length of David's speech in vv. 45-47 is noteworthy in comparison with Goliath's short speech in v. 44. This contrast is intentional.

(2) David Kills Goliath (17:48-51a)

48 *Now at that moment*[155] *the Philistine began to come nearer toward David;*
so David ran quickly to the battle line toward the Philistine.
49 *And David stretched out his hand into the bag,*
and took a stone out of it,
and slung (it)
and struck the Philistine on his forehead.
When the stone sank into his forehead,
he fell on his face to the ground.
50 *Thus David prevailed over the Philistine*
with sling and stone
and struck the Philistine
and killed him,
though no sword was in David's hand.
51a *And David ran*
and stood by the Philistine
and took his sword
and drew it out of its sheath
and killed him
and cut his head off with it.

48 Just then Goliath *began to come nearer* (lit., "rose up and went and drew near"). The verb *qwm here functions as an inchoative verb[156] together with other motion verbs; see also 1 Sam. 24:8.

The present verse contrasts Goliath's heavy motions (three Hebrew verbs) with David's speedy action. From this expression on, the tempo of the narrative (see "Introduction" [Section VI, C]) increases greatly, as is shown by the successive actions in the sequence of *wayqtl* "narrative" tense:

155. *wᵉhāyāh* usually introduces a temporal clause in present/future tense (see Lambdin, §110), but here the formula refers to the past tense. On this "abnormal" usage of *whyh,* see on 1 Sam. 1:12. Longacre thinks that the expression marks "the substantive action" which will follow; see Longacre, "Weqatal Forms," p. 87.

156. Most recently, see F. W. Dobbs-Allsopp, "Ingressive *qwm* in Biblical Hebrew," *ZAH* 8 (1995) 31-54.

v. 48b	David made haste — ran			
v. 49	David sent → took → slung →	struck (on the forehead)		
v. 50	David	struck →		killed (-sword)
v. 51	David		ran → stood → took → drew →	killed → cut (+sword)

49 As for *miṣḥô,* Deem translates it as "greave,"[157] instead of *forehead,* comparing Testament of Judah 3:1, "sank into his greave," that is, he suggests the stone hit the upper shin or knee at the place left open and unprotected so the knee could move. But this probably would not have knocked a giant down, and certainly would not have left him helpless when David came and took his sword.

The *wayqtl* verbal phrase in Qal, impf. 3 f.s. (*wattiṭbaʿ* "and it sank"), with an impersonal subject, is a little off the mainline narrative where David and the Philistine are the main actors; hence, it should be treated as a subordinate clause, *When the stone sank.*

50 *Thus — wayqtl;* with the verb of state *prevailed.* This verse interrupts the flow of the narrative from v. 49 to v. 51; it is a little off the main line, and the narrator exults over this seemingly impossible victory. Verse 51 returns to the main line of narrative, and the emphasis is again on what David did. Thus, vv. 49-51 constitutes an AXB pattern. By the insertion the quick tempo of the narrative is slowed down "so that the real significance of the day's victory over the Philistines can be underlined" (R. P. Gordon, p. 158).

v. 49 (A)Da-vid sent — took — slung — struck
v. 50 (X) <David prevailed = struck — killed>
v. 51 (B)Da-vid ran — stood — took — drew — killed — cut

Note that in v. 49 David is still on "this" side; in v. 51 he quickly moves toward the Philistine: right after he "struck," he "ran." The narrative communicates to the audience that only with God's help could David have won victory.

51 Verses 5-7 do not say that the Philistine had a *sword* (*ḥereb;* see v. 45), and we know that David had none of his own. Probably the general term "sword" is used here for the Philistine's *kidon,* "scimitar."[158] David cut off his enemy's head "with his own sword," as Benaiah slew his enemy with the enemy's spear (2 Sam. 23:21). Sinuhe also killed the enemy champion with the latter's own battle-axe.[159]

David removed the champion's head as a trophy, as he had said he

157. A. Deem, "'. . . and the stone sank into his forehead': A Note on 1 Samuel xvii 49," *VT* 28 (1978) 349-51.

158. McCarter, p. 294.

159. See Ackroyd, p. 138.

would (v. 46). In the Assyrian relief in Ashurbanipal's court[160] the king celebrates his victory with his wife, with the head of the Elamite king hanging beside the table.

f. The Israelites Defeat the Philistines (17:51b-54)

51b *When the Philistines saw that their hero was dead, they fled.*
52 *And the men of Israel and Judah rose up and raised a shout and chased the Philistines up to the Gai Valley and to the Ekron gates.*
Thus the slain Philistines fell lying on the way to Shaaraim and even up to Gath and Ekron.
53 *And the Israelites returned from hotly pursuing after the Philistines and plundered their camp.*
54 *And David took the head of the Philistine and brought it to Jerusalem, but his weapons he put in his tent.*

51b The Philistine army fled when they saw Goliath killed. The discourse is a little off the main line since the agent of the verb (*wayqtl* 3 m.pl.) is in plural and not one of the main characters, David or the Philistine; see "Introduction" (Section VI, A). Hence, the clause is subordinate and temporal: *so when.* The death of the Philistine champion should have involved their submission to the Israelites; see v. 9. However, the confusion in the Philistine camps gave the Israelites a good chance anyway.

52 The reference to *Judah* here has been taken as being anachronistic. However, it should be noted that there were divisions between Judah and the rest of Israel from the earliest time of Davidic monarchy; see 11:8 and 15:4 and 2 Sam. 20:1.

The Gai Valley is translated variously: "Gai" (JPS); "the valley" (NASB). It possibly refers to the part of the Valley of Elah near the Philistine side; cf. "Gath" (NIV; NRSV; McCarter, p. 290, following LXX^{BL}). From the description *to the Gai Valley and to the Ekron gates,* the Gai Valley seems to refer to the valley which leads to Gath.[161]

Ekron is modern Khirbet el-Muqanna' [MR136-131], which is situated about 5 miles north of Gath; see on 5:10. *šaʿărê ʿeqrôn* is probably a construct chain with an objective genitive, meaning *the Ekron gates,* that is, "the gates for the road to(ward) Ekron," like *šaʿar haggayʾ* "the Valley Gate" (Neh. 3:13; 2 Chr. 26:9), which were located probably somewhere east of

160. See Julian Reade, *Assyrian Sculpture* (London: British Museum, 1983), fig. 102.

161. See C. S. Ehrlich, "Gai," in *ABD,* II, p. 869.

Ekron. Or, it may refer to "the gates of the city of Ekron" like "the gates of Jerusalem" in Jer. 1:15; etc.; cf. Ps. 87:2 ("the gates of Zion").

Thus . . . fell lying (wayyipp^e*lû)* is *wayqtl* but 3 m.pl. with an impersonal subject "slain (adj. m. pl. cstr.) of Philistines" *(ḥal*^{e}*lê p*^{e}*lištîm).* It is off the main storyline; it denotes a state rather than an action. Therefore, it is an explanatory clause.

On the way to Shaaraim — that is, on the road to Shaaraim. Shaaraim is in a list of Judean towns in Josh. 15:36. The exact place is unknown, but Joshua mentions it after Socoh and Azekah, mentioned in v. 1.[162] Since the name literally means "two gates," one might conjecture that there was a double gate (where a Philistine garrison may have been) at the junction where the road to Gath and the road to Ekron meet; cf. LXX: *en tē hodō tōn pulōn* "on the road of the gates." Any Philistine soldiers would try to escape westward toward this place, Shaaraim, where the roads toward "the gates of Ekron" and "the Gai Valley" leading to Gath met; see above. On Gath, see on 5:8.

53 Is the phrase *b*^{e}*nê yiśrā'ēl* meant to refer only to "the men of Israel" given the phrase "the men of Israel and Judah" *('anšê yiśrā'ēl wîhûdāh)* in v. 52? Rather, *the Israelites* refers to the entire covenant people of Yahweh, as in the rest of the chapter.

54 This verse picks up the storyline regarding David from v. 51a. This is exactly what a linguistic description, which is mono-dimensional, does when describing the multi-dimensional real world; see "Introduction" (Section VII, C). After cutting Goliath's head off, he takes it with him while the Israelites are chasing the fleeing Philistines and, eventually, brings it to Jerusalem.

51a	David	killed Goliath		
		cut his head off		
51b			the Philistines	
				fled
52			the Israelites	
				chased
53				returned and plundered
54		took the head		

162. Modern Khirbet esh-Sharia (MR145-124), about a mile to the northeast of Azekah (Klein) is sometimes suggested. Rainey once suggested that Shaaraim is the modern Kh. es-Saʿireh, 5-6 (?) miles east-northeast of Azekah; see fig. 2 of Rainey, "The Identification of Philistine Gath," p. 70*. If so, why does not the narrator refer to it as the way to Beth-shemesh? Later, in 1983, Rainey suggested the region north and west of Azekah in the Valley of Elah (see v. 2). A. F. Rainey, "The Biblical Shephelah of Judah," *BASOR* 251 (1983) 1-22; see C. S. Ehrlich, "Shaaraim," *ABD,* V, p. 1148.

(57) (was brought before Saul, carrying the head)
brought it to Jerusalem
put Goliath's weapons in his tent

The present verse informs the audience of what happened to Goliath's head and weapons; *his weapons* prepares for the incident at Nob in 21:9. Thus, the verse serves as the TERMINUS to the preceding episode.

David's action of bringing Goliath's head *to Jerusalem* has been explained as corresponding "nicely with Saul's head being brought to Dagon's temple and fastened there (1 Chr. x 10)."[163] However, Jerusalem was not "the temple city" yet, even if some find "the resemblance of the deaths of Saul and Goliath" in these texts; see also on 31:10.

Scholars have doubted that David took Goliath's head to Jerusalem since it was not part of Israel until David captured it from the Jebusites (2 Sam. 5:6-9). Hence, they take it as anachronism (Klein, p. 181, etc.) and assume "that Goliath's skull was brought there at a later date" (R. P. Gordon, p. 158).[164] However, it seems strange to split up v. 54 and have it refer to the eventual destiny of the head but only the temporary destiny of the weapons. Other scholars accept that there was a tradition in Jerusalem that Goliath's head was preserved there as a kind of "relic."[165] But there is no clear evidence for this view. One even conjectures that David threw Goliath's head over the walls of Philistine-held Jerusalem. According to Grønbaek, "the reference to Jerusalem resulted from the fact that this story was eventually transmitted there."[166]

It may be *proleptical* history writing;[167] "Jerusalem" here might have referred proleptically to a suburb of Jerusalem, if not the Jebusite walled city itself. By the time of the author/narrator of this episode, the outside of the walled city had been also called "Jerusalem."[168] While one may take the biblical description to be historically true, as referring to the historical fact, the

163. C. Y. S. Ho, "Conjectures and Refutations: Is 1 Samuel xxxi 1-13 Really the Source of 1 Chronicles x 1-12?" *VT* 45 (1995) 91.

164. On this question see J. T. Willis, "The Function of Comprehensive Anticipatory Redactional Joints in 1 Samuel 16–18," *ZAW* 85 (1973) 302-5.

165. Hertzberg, p. 153; McCarter, p. 294.

166. See Klein, p. 181.

167. On "prolepsis" in the narrative, see most recently K. Koenen, "Prolepsen in alttestamentlichen Erzählungen: eine Skizze," *VT* 47 (1997) 456-77; also M. Sternberg, *The Poetics of Biblical Narrative: Ideological Literature and the Drama of Reading* (Bloomington: Indiana University Press, 1985), pp. 321-41; S. Bar-Efrat, *Narrative Art in the Bible* (Sheffield: JSOT Press, 1989), pp. 179-80; J. L. Ska, "Sommaires proleptiques en Gn 27 et dans l'histoire de Joseph," *Bib* 73 (1992) 518-27; "Quelques exemples de sommaires proleptiques dans les récits bibliques," in *Congress Volume: Paris 1992,* ed. J. A. Emerton (Leiden: E. J. Brill, 1995), pp. 315-26.

168. On the city of Jerusalem, see on 2 Sam. 5:5.

description itself has to be from the historian's use of language. No one would claim it as unhistorical if a historian uses the Greek term "Mesopotamia" for the description of the early-dynastic Sumerian society in the third millennium B.C.!

For *his weapons (kēlâw),* see 21:9 where Goliath's sword *(ḥereb golyāt)* is in the sanctuary in Nob.

As for David's *tent,* some scholars have held that the youthful David would have had no tent and so emended the text to read "tent of Yahweh," which they interpret to refer either to the tent shrine at Mizpah or the shrine at Nob; see Hertzberg, p. 154. However, it does not seem unlikely that the champion of the Israelite army was given a tent soon after the battle as a sign that he had been made a ranking military man.

C. SAUL, JONATHAN, AND DAVID (17:55–18:5)

This section begins with a "flashback": *Now . . . he had said* (vv. 55-56), going chronologically backward to the time when David went out to fight with Goliath (see 17:40); see also v. 54. But the story moves forward quickly into new relationships of David with Saul and his family members. Very soon Saul becomes David's enemy, while his son Jonathan and his daughter Michal, together with all Israel, become fond of David (in 18:1-30). Whether 18:1-5 should be treated as the conclusion of the story of "David and Goliath" or as the first episode of a chapter (ch. 18) focusing on David's relationships with Saul and his families is still debated.[169] The present writer rather takes 17:55-56 as the beginning of the section which deals with Saul's new concern with David's background.

1. Saul and David: "Whose Son Are You?" (17:55-58)

55 *Now, when Saul saw David going out toward the Philistine,*
he had said to Abner the army commander,[170]
"Whose son is the young man, Abner?"
and Abner said,
"By your life, O king, I don't know!"
56 *And the king said,*
"Inquire whose son that youth[171] *is."*

169. See Birch, p. 1115.

170. See 1 Sam. 12:9; 2 Sam. 2:8; T. Longman III, in *NIDOTTE,* 3, p. 734. For Abner, see on 1 Sam. 14:50.

171. *hā'ālem;* in v. 55, *hanna'ar.*

57 *So, when David returned from defeating the Philistine, Abner took him and brought him before Saul, with the head of the Philistine in his hand.*

58 *And Saul said to him,*
"Whose son are you, young man?"
And David said,
"The son of your servant Jesse the Bethlehemite."

55-56 When David left Saul to go out toward Goliath (v. 40), Saul had asked Abner of David's background. It is seemingly difficult to reconcile Saul's ignorance of David[172] here with the account in 16:14-23. R. P. Gordon explains this "discrepancy" as having stemmed from "independent traditions concerning David's début at court."[173]

But, it is important to note that Saul's question *Whose son is the young man?* is not "Who is he?" Even if Saul knew David from before, he would not remember David's father's name, for a king would not take note of the name of his servant's father. Saul is asking about David's background — his family and hence his social status, that is, pedigree — so that he may ask his father to let him keep David permanently: "as a life-long (i.e., *eternal*) subject" or "permanently recruited servant" of the king.[174] In fact, 18:2 comments: "And Saul took him on that day and did not let him return to his father's house." Such a question about the relation[175] has the special purpose of getting information about one's personal background. So, the question *Whose son are you?* (v. 58) is almost equivalent of "Where are you from?" or "What kind of family and social background do you have?"[176]

But Abner did not know David's background at all ("By your life, O king,": *ḥê-napš^{e}kā hammelek).* For the oath on the life of the king, see 2 Sam. 14:19; 15:21; cf. 2 Kgs. 2:2, 4, 6; 4:30, where an oath is taken on the life of a prophet.[177] Saul asked him to check who David's father was.

57-58 When David comes back from the duel, Abner takes him to Saul, who asks his background. In all these incidents God on whom David put his trust worked providentially, guiding the whole history of ancient Is-

172. On a general theme of ignorance on Saul's part, see D. Jobling, *The Sense of Biblical Narrative: Three Structural Analyses in the Old Testament (I Samuel 13–31, Numbers 11–12, I Kings 17–18)* (JSOTSS 7; Sheffield: JSOT Press, 1978), p. 25.

173. See further Willis, "The Function of Comprehensive Anticipatory Redactional Joints," pp. 295-98.

174. See 1 Sam. 1:11; 27:12 the Ugaritic expression *ʿbd ʿlm* "an eternal servant."

175. See also the question "Who is their father?" in 1 Sam. 10:12.

176. See also D. M. Howard, Jr. on "David," in *ABD,* II, pp. 41-49; Bergen, p. 199.

177. See on 1 Sam. 14:39.

rael by the hand of *the son of* Saul's *servant Jesse the Bethlehemite* for His plan and purpose.

2. Jonathan and David: Covenant (18:1-4)

1 *When he finished talking to Saul, Jonathan loved*[1] *him like himself, since the soul of Jonathan attached to the soul of David.*

2 *And Saul took him on that day;*
he did not let him return to his father's house.

3 *And Jonathan and David made a covenant, because he loved him like himself.*

4 *And Jonathan took off the robe he had on and gave it to David along with his garments as well as his sword, his bow, and his belt.*

1-4 This is a continuation of the episode in the last part of ch. 17. Here, for the first time, David meets Jonathan, who is attached to and loves David. However, the relationship between Jonathan and David was more than simply on the human level; both of them loved and trusted on the Lord and shared the same concerns and convictions: that the victory is by the Lord for His name's sake; see 14:6 and 17:45-47. See also below on vv. 3-4.

Not only Jonathan (vv. 1, 3) but also his sister Michal (vv. 20, 28) and *all Israel and Judah* (v. 16) and even Saul's servants (v. 22) loved David. On the other hand, Saul's hatred toward David grew greater and greater. Love and hatred toward David is the major theme of this chapter. On Saul's part, anger (v. 8), suspicion (v. 9) and fear (vv. 12, 15, 29) come one after another and go hand in hand.

1 *He finished:* that is, David finished. This shows that the section that follows is a continuation of the previous chapter.

The temporal clause *when he finished,* is followed by two clauses. The main clause is *Jonathan loved him.* In the next clause, *the soul of Jonathan attached to . . . (w^{e}nepeš y^{e}hônātān niqš^{e}rāh),* <Wa+subject> precedes the verb in *qtl,* so the clause is a circumstance.[2] Here, the clause explains the situation on the level of the heart and mind.

The expression *attached to (niqš^{e}rāh)* refers to "inseparable devotion," as in a similar expression in Judah's words in Gen. 44:30 ("as his life is bound up in thc boy's lifc"). Jonathan must have been deeply impressed by David's complete trust in the Lord as he moved quickly and bravely toward Goliath.

1. Ketib *wy'hbw* reflects phonetic spelling; see Berg. II, 23g. Q: *ye'ĕhābēhû* → K: *ye'ĕhābēw* (rather than *ye'ĕhābô).* For the ending *-ēw* instead of *-ēhû,* see Siloam inscription 2 (רעו *rēʿēw;* see Gibson, *SSI,* 1, 23).

2. Gibson, p. 99; also Berg. II, 26.

2 This verse constitutes a poetic bi-colon:

And Saul took him on that day;
he did not let him return to his father's house.

As the phrase *did not let* literally means "did not give," "take" and "not give" constitute an <A not-B> pattern.

While Jonathan loved David (with personal affection), Saul *took* him . . . ; is this to indicate the possessiveness of Saul? Rather, this verb recalls "the right of the king" *(mišpaṭ hammelek)* to take sons and daughters; see 8:11f. According to 16:21, Saul had already "loved" David greatly; he kept his affection for him until he started feeling insecure about his kingship in v. 8.

The phrase *that day* refers to the day of David's victory.

3-4 The singular verb *made* (lit., "cut") suggests that Jonathan took initiative in making a covenant with David. Hence, *and David* virtually means "with David." On the phrase "to make a covenant," see on 11:1.

Jonathan's *covenant* with David was based on his love for him in v. 1; this is literarily supported by the structure of vv. 1-3, in which the flow of discourse between vv. 1 and 3 is interrupted by the insertion of the poetic expression in v. 2. This flow indicates that Jonathan's making a covenant with David was the logical consequence of his loving him. However, they did not necessarily make the covenant "that day." David is probably thinking of this covenant when he laments Jonathan as his "brother" (2 Sam. 1:26), and his covenant influences his conduct with respect to Jonathan's son (2 Sam. 9; 21:7).

McCarter thinks that the statement *Jonathan loved him* [= David] "hints of political loyalty just as it describes personal affection."[3] Yet just the word "love" does not imply an upward-directed political loyalty. (Even politically, "love" was supposed to be both upward and downward directed; see on 16:21.) And the same word is used of Saul, Michal, and the people (see on v. 16), too. However, it certainly was a strong matter of personal loyalty that would not let self-interest get in the way of justice.

To what extent did Jonathan realize here that David, not he, would be the next king? It is hard to tell. We know nothing of what he knew of Saul's rejection or David's anointing. In ch. 20:14, 31-32 he seems to have accepted

3. See also W. L. Moran, "The Ancient Near Eastern Background of the Love of God in Deuteronomy," *CBQ* 25 (1963) 77-87; J. A. Thompson, "The Significance of the Verb Love in the David-Jonathan Narratives in I Samuel," VT 24 (1974) 334-38; "Israel's 'Lovers,'" *VT* 27 (1977) 475-81; P. R. Ackroyd, "The Verb Love — *'āhēb* in the David-Jonathan Narratives — a Footnote," *VT* 25 (1975) 213-21 on the political significance of terms such as "love" between partners of international treaties.

it as a possibility, and in 23:17 he has accepted it as a certainty. But what about here?

Jobling says that the giving of his clothes was "a virtual abdication by Jonathan, the crown prince."[4] There are certainly passages where transferring a garment is a transfer of authority (Num. 20:24-28; 1 K. 19:19-21; Isa. 22:21; etc.).[5] However, it cannot always have been the case, as the other people in this chapter do not seem to have recognized it as an abdication,[6] and so it is hard to go beyond saying that here it was a very strong statement of affection and respect. From v. 3, it seems to be a sign of the covenant between them. But certainly it is the covenantal love that Jonathan had for David that makes him able to accept David as the next king, and, thus, one can look backward and see this gift as a sign of abdication.

In as much as Saul was a "king," in view of the hereditary principle in the ancient Near Eastern monarchies,[7] Jonathan, as the popular, eldest son of a king, was likely to become king. However, there were always dynastic changes (see the history of the Northern monarchy), and Israel was used to inspirational leadership. Thus, Jonathan could not have considered the succession assured if a suitable rival arose. As probable but not assured, he had even more reason than Saul to feel threatened by David. The attitude of Jonathan, the crown prince, was thus remarkable and exhibits his unselfish character and personality. Jonathan *gave* while Saul *took.*

3. Summary Statements (18:5)

5 *And David went out (for battle); wherever Saul would send him, he was successful.*[8]
And Saul appointed him over the men of war.
And it was good in the eyes of the whole people and even in the eyes of the officials of Saul.

4. D. Jobling, *The Sense of Biblical Narrative: Three Structural Analyses in the Old Testament (I Samuel 13–31, Numbers 11–12, I Kings 17–18)* (JSOTSS 7; Sheffield: JSOT Press, 1978), p. 12.

5. F. B. Knutson, "Political and Foreign Affairs," in *RSP* 2, pp. 121-22.

6. Even if the gifts had been given privately, the moment Jonathan stopped using them or David started using them everyone must have known about it, and so it was a public gesture.

7. See T. Ishida, *The Royal Dynasties in Ancient Israel. A Study on the Formation and Development of Royal-Dynastic Ideology* (BZAW 142; Berlin: de Gruyter, 1977), pp. 6-25.

8. Compare Davidson's explanation, "went out *prospering*," imperfect in circumstantial clause (Davidson, §141 Rem 3) with Gibson's imperfect with "distributive nuance" in the past: "wherever S. sent him *he was successful*" (Gibson, p. 74).

5 This verse closes the section ("Saul, Jonathan, and David") which began at 17:55. The following are the summary statements that explain how David was *successful* and accepted by the whole people, both civilians and officials. David is appointed by Saul *over the men of war.*

For *went out (for battle)* in a military sense, see also on v. 13. The *wayqtl* of a movement verb would be transitional, thus giving background information to the following EVENT, here "And Saul appointed." According to discourse grammatical analysis, the narrative flows from *David went out* to *and Saul appointed,* the intervening clause, *wherever Saul would send him he was successful,* being circumstantial or subordinate off-line information. Hence the sense is: "And David marched out for battle, with the result that wherever Saul sent him David was successful. So Saul appointed him over the army." McCarter follows LXX^L for v. 5a and translates: "Then Saul put [David] in charge of the men of war, and he marched out and came in, succeeding in whatever Saul would send him to do." He explains that "MT inverts the order and reads the first clause ambiguously."[9] But, it is LXX^L that could be an unnecessary adjustment. Also cf. NASB; NIV; NRSV.

Every *wayqtl* with a stated subject, here *Saul,* introduces a new discourse unit (see "Introduction" [Section VI, A]), and here the EVENT begins: *And Saul appointed him.* The phrase *over the men of the war,* which means "the one in charge of warriors," is to be compared with "a commander of a thousand" below (see v. 13). David's appointment to be Saul's general met with universal approval. The term *officials,* as in 8:15, refers to the ranking members of Saul's court, who are "his potential rivals."

Verse 5 is a summary paragraph with three sub-paragraphs. The terminus of the paragraph is a sentence with an impersonal subject, *And it was good.* This is the first of three expressions with political overtones; the other two are vv. 16 and 30.

D. SAUL BECOMES DAVID'S ENEMY (18:6-30)

After referring to David's new relationships with Saul (v. 2) and with Jonathan (vv. 1, 3-4) and summarizing David's prosperity (v. 5), the narrator starts mentioning the problems in Saul's relationship with David. David was successful and prosperous and loved by all *for the Lord was with him* (vv. 12, 14, 28) — this is "the theological leitmotiv of the stories of David and Saul" (McCarter, p. 314). But David's very success caused Saul to become jealous and afraid (vv. 12, 15, 29). However, everything Saul does to harm David turns into David's advancement.

9. McCarter, p. 303.

The first section of this part, vv. 6-9, reports that *Saul became very angry* on the very first day of David's victorious homecoming. As in the beginning of ch. 13, here the narrator presents Saul as already wrong in himself and insecure and suspicious toward David. This psychological and spiritual condition was to be expected as the spirit of the Lord had left him and *the spirit of evil* (or *for evilness*) had come right after David's anointing (see 16:13-14). On the very *next day* after the homecoming (v. 10), the same *spirit for evilness* rushed upon Saul, and he tried to kill David with his "spear"; the same thing happens again in 19:9-10. He will later even try to kill Jonathan (20:33). With his rival at his court, Saul becomes increasingly insecure and frantic in devising ways to get rid of David, by his own spear (v. 11) or by the hand of the Philistines (vv. 17, 21, 25). The person whom the Lord rejected chooses his own road to destruction. Without God's mercy all sinners will follow Saul to the same fate.

1. Saul's Anger (18:6-9)

6 *When they were coming (back), namely,*
when David was returning from defeating the Philistine,
the women came out of all the cities of Israel to sing,[10]
the dancing (women) to meet[11] *Saul the king,*
to the accompaniment of tambours and lutes with joy.
7 *And the merry-making women sang antiphonally:*[12]
"Saul slew by[13] *thousands;*
and David by ten thousands!"
8 *And Saul became very angry*
and this thing was evil in his eyes.
And he said,
"They gave David ten thousands,
but[14] *to me they gave just thousands!*[15]
Only[16] *the kingship is not yet his!"*
9 *And Saul came to keep his eye on David from that day onward.*

6 The story goes back chronologically to the point when Saul and David came back home from the battle against Goliath. *When they were coming*

10. MT (Q.); Qal, inf. cstr.

11. Or "toward."

12. Lit., "answered to each other."

13. By: an adverbial *-āw,* not "his." See K. Aartun, "Die hervorhebende Endung -*w*(V) an nordwestsemitischen Adverbien und Negationen," *UF* 5 (1973) 1-5.

14. But: the sentence structure suggests the contrastive meaning.

15. *hā'ălāpîm;* article — definiteness; or "only" (NIV).

16. For this limitative "adverb" (also 21:5), see Andersen, p. 175.

(back), namely — We suggest the translation *namely* here, taking the following clause as apposition with asyndeton (i.e., without a conjunction). According to McCarter,[17] the clause is a "conflate" of two readings: (1) "When they came" and (2) "When David returned from." He thinks that the clause was probably introduced "editorially to smooth over the interpolation of 17:55–18:5." However, the account of David's defeat of Goliath the Philistine and its immediate consequences was terminated in v. 17:54; the present verse (18:6) does not simply represent a return to the events following 17:54. Rather, from 17:55 onward, the focus is on David's relation with those around him, and with 18:6, the narrator starts talking about the problems between David and Saul. This is due to the mono-dimensional nature of descriptive language; see "Introduction" (Section VII, C).

Women in Israel celebrated a victory with singing and dancing and instruments (Exod. 15:20; Judg. 11:34). The second half of this verse is usually translated as "the women came out of all the towns of Israel, singing and dancing, to meet King Saul . . ." (NRSV), taking *lāšîr wᵉhammᵉḥōlôt* (lit., "to sing and the dancing [women]") adverbially. Instead of adopting the shorter text of LXX^L with McCarter,[18] we would rather explain the MT as poetic prose (see "Introduction" [VII, B]) and analyze it as a parallel structure:

> the women came out of all the cities of Israel to sing,
> the dancing (women) to meet Saul the king,
> to the accompaniment of tambours and lutes with joy

Here, *the dancing (women)* is parallel to *the women*,[19] and both are subjects of the verb "they (f.pl.) came out." Such a "vertical" relation is characteristic of parallelism. The third line modifies the infinitive "to sing" in the first line rather than the infinitive "to meet" in the second line. In such a poetic parallelism, the *waw* at the beginning of the second line is no problem because of its "vertical grammar" (see "Introduction" [Section VII, A]). Note that McCarter thinks of the MT as a "conflation." According to him, "the infinitive *lšyr* [to sing] may have been introduced to accommodate the double subject, thus 'women . . . to sing' and 'dancing women to meet Saul.' "[20] But, in our "vertical grammar" of the poetic prose, "the double subject" is not a problem.

For *tambours (tuppîm),* see 10:5. They are small round drums, usually associated with joy and gladness in the OT. The term *lutes (šālīšîm)* is a *hapax legomenon* in the Bible, and its exact meaning is not clear.[21] JPS trans-

17. McCarter, p. 310.
18. McCarter, pp. 310-11.
19. See *hannāšîm hamśaḥăqôt* "the laughing women" (v. 7).
20. McCarter, pp. 310f.
21. See *HALOT,* p. 1525.

lates "sistrums." Both lutes and sistrums are three-stringed instruments. Some translations simply render it "musical instruments" (NRSV; NASB). McCarter says the name is similar to "*šalaštu,* a Mesopotamian lute-like instrument."[22] However, this word is listed neither in *CAD* nor in *AHw.*

To the accompaniment of tambours and lutes with joy is literally "with tambourines with joy *and* with lutes." In some mss "with joy" is prefixed by *waw.* "With joy" probably modifies the whole phrase "with tambourines and with lutes" and is inserted between the two parts of the coordinate phrase (the AX&B pattern; see "Introduction" [Section VII, C]). In our view there is no need to translate it as "with joyful sounds" (Stoebe) by taking *joy* as "an abstract noun used for concrete activity."[23]

7 The phrase *the merry-making women (hannāšîm hamśaḥăqôt;* lit., "the women, who were making merry") is possibly a technical term for professional merry-making women; compare professional wailing women in Ugarit "who put on a proper public show of grief, weeping and wailing *(bky)* and mourning aloud *(spd).*"[24] Etymologically the root *śḥq is related to *ṣḥq "to laugh," the former a result of dissimilation of /s/ to /ś/. Most of the modern translations render it contextually; see on 2 Sam. 6:5.

The expression "answered to each other" refers to an antiphon like that sung at the time of Exodus (Exod. 15:20f.). The Ugaritic cognate *ʿny* appears in the same sense in the context of ritual singing (*KTU* 1.23:12).[25] The Qal stem of this verb (there is no Hith. for this verb) has a reciprocal sense, from the context.

Thousands and *ten thousands* (also v. 8; 21:11; 29:5) is a standard word pair for a very large number; see Deut. 32:30; 33:17; Mic. 6:7; Ps. 91:7; 144:13.[26] By using this ancient word pair, the women seemingly praised both Saul and David as the slayers of a great number of enemies. However, this very comparison, if not contrast, provoked Saul's anger (see below). This "victory chant" may go back "as old as the wars of Saul."[27] Freedman notes that "the very fact that David was accorded equal treatment with the king in the song would be sufficient to arouse the suspicions of any monarch, and especially of one insecure in his position and jealous of his prerogatives."[28]

22. McCarter, p. 311.
23. Klein, p. 188.
24. Pardee in *CS,* I, p. 354, n. 123.
25. See D. T. Tsumura, *The Ugaritic Drama of the Good Gods: A Philological Study* (Ann Arbor: University Microfilms, 1973), p. 39.
26. See M. Dahood, "Ugaritic-Hebrew Parallel Pairs," in *RSP* 1, p. 114.
27. McCarter, p. 312. See S. Gevirtz, *Patterns in the Early Poetry of Israel* (Chicago: University of Chicago Press, 1963), pp. 14-24.
28. D. N. Freedman, "Review of *Patterns in the Early Poetry of Israel,* by Stanley Gevirtz (Chicago: University of Chicago Press, 1963)," *JBL* 83 (1964) 201.

If the word pair were "Saul" and "the son of Kish" (10:11; or "David" and "the son of Jesse"), the parallelism would be a progressive or climactic description of the same person. But here two different people are parallel to each other. The principle of parallelism, that is, "one thru two lines," would point to the meaning: "Both Saul and David slew the enemies by the thousands." However, as Freedman notes, this is "the only example of standard number-parallelism, among all those cited by [Gevirtz], in which there is a significant distinction of subjects: Saul and David."[29]

8 Saul got *very angry,* for he interpreted the song as contrasting himself and David. Saul's use of the term *kingship (hammᵉlûkāh;* or "kingdom") shows that he has now discovered who was meant by his "neighbor" in 15:28; see 13:14; 15:28.

9 The translation *keep his eye on (ʿwn)* is based on Qere *ʿôyēn,* which is a participle of a denominative verb; compare "kept a jealous eye on" (NIV; JPS); "looked at . . . with suspicion" (NASB). The verb is a *hapax legomenon,* but it is known in Ugaritic *ʿyn "to behold" (*UT,* §19.1846)[30] as well as in postbiblical Hebrew.[31] Thus, Saul became suspicious toward David from this early stage of their relationship: *from that day onward.* The tragedy of the one from whom the spirit of the Lord had departed was that he could not praise the achievement of others but simply became jealous of them.

2. Saul's First Attack on David (18:10-11)

10 *The next day*
God's spirit for evilness rushed upon Saul
and he prophesied in the midst of the house,
while David was playing (a harp) with his hand as usual; and the spear was in Saul's hand.
11 *And Saul cast*[32] *the spear,*
thinking
"I will pin David even[33] *to the wall!"*
And David turned aside from before him[34] *twice.*

10-11 The very *next* day, Saul attempted to kill David with the spear while he was playing a harp for Saul. A similar incident is reported in 19:9-10.

29. Freedman, "Review of *Patterns in the Early Poetry of Israel,*" p. 202.
30. See D. Pardee in *CS,* I, p. 333.
31. See Jastrow, pp. 1053-54.
32. *wayyāṭel;* or "hurled." McCarter, p. 303, translates it as "brandished" [but "raised" for 1 Sam. 20:33], reading as *wayyiṭṭōl* on the basis of the LXX.
33. *ûbaqqîr* (lit., "and in the wall"); the *waw* here is an emphatic *waw.*
34. Not "it" (= spear), for "spear" is a feminine noun; see HALOT, p. 333.

Whether or not one decides that this is a "duplicate of the incident" and "modeled on 19:9-10" (Klein, p. 188) is a methodological problem. It is always wise not to get behind the text and identify sources before carefully reading the text itself. A synchronic reading should have priority, not because a diachronic approach is useless to the correct understanding, but because methodologically synchrony has priority, as a diachronic approach involves a hypothesis about composition — this is the axiom of literary-linguistic studies.

McCarter thinks the present incident is "out of place at this point." However, Saul's spiritual and psychological disturbance might have happened more than once. The narrator intends to convey that Saul's problem came to the surface on the very next day after he became jealous. This was his first attempt to get rid of David, the "man of Yahweh's choice" (13:14). From now on his spiritual and psychological disturbance escalates and he keeps seeking a chance to kill David.

10 *The next day* is the next day after David's victorious homecoming. For *God's spirit for evilness,* see on 16:14. On *rushed upon,* see on 10:10. While "prophesying" is viewed positively in 10:10, 13, it is taken negatively here.

Saul's *spear* was almost a symbol of his kingship, and he had it at hand in formal situations (cf. 20:33; 22:6; 26:7). Note the contrast between the harp "*with* [lit., in] *his* [David's] *hand* and the spear *in Saul's hand.* This contrasting picture illustrates well the roles and characters of these two men.

11 Here, *thinking* (*wayyōʾmer;* lit., "and he said/thought" with *waw* consecutive) is simultaneous with "casting" rather than sequential to it.

The verb *pin* (*nkh; lit., "strike") appears also in 26:8, where Abishai asked David to let him pin Saul with the spear to the ground. We are not sure exactly what happened. Did David leave the room twice or just dodge the spear twice? Possibly Saul covered up his murderous attempt by claiming he had thrown the spear as part of David's military training.

3. The Lord Is with David (18:12-16)

12 *And Saul became afraid*[35] *of David, for the Lord was with him,*
while from Saul[36] *he had departed.*[37]
13 *And Saul sent him away from him*

35. On this term *yrʾ (fear, anxiety, and reverence), see M. I. Gruber, "Fear, Anxiety and Reverence in Akkadian, Biblical Hebrew and Other North-West Semitic Languages," *VT* 40 (1990) 411-22.

36. Lit., "from with Saul"; contrasting with "with him [= David]"; also contrasting with "from with him" (v. 13).

37. *sār;* see 1 Sam. 16:14 *sārāh* ("the spirit of the Lord departed from Saul").

and appointed him a commander of a thousand,
and he went out and came in before the people.[38]
14 *And David became successful in all his ways,*[39] *for the Lord was with him.*[40]
15 *And Saul saw that he was very successful and dreaded his face.*
16 *But all Israel and Judah loved David,*
for he was going out and coming in before them.

12-30 Saul now tries indirect ways to reduce David's influence and even to kill him, but they end up giving David even more influence. This entire section is framed by a similar expression *Saul became afraid* of David's face (vv. 12, 29).

12-16 In this short paragraph, David's "leitmotiv," *the Lord was with him* is repeated twice (vv. 12, 14), while Saul's "fear" is also repeated twice, once by *yr' ("to be afraid of"; v. 12) and once by its word pair *gwr ("to dread"; v. 15). David "went out and came in" (vv. 13, 16) before the people, who loved him. The more Saul feared David, who was successful (vv. 14, 15), the more solitary he became. These frequent repetitions of words and phrase give this paragraph "unity" and "coherence."

13 Saul *sent him* [= David] *away from him (waysīrēhû).* Here the same root *swr as *departed (sār)* in v. 12 is used. While the Lord departed from Saul, Saul made David depart from himself. Thus, Saul alienates himself both from the Lord and from David His servant *whom the Lord was with.*

In v. 5, David had been put *over the men of war.* Now he is appointed *a commander of thousand* (*śar-'ālep;* see 8:12; 17:18). Probably he was moved from a position on Saul's staff to that of a field commander, "away from [Saul]," where he would have less opportunity to be at court. As a commander in his own right, though, his victories would become even more noticeable.

The phrase *went out and came in (wayyēṣē' wayyābō')* refers to military leadership and often describes the activity of a soldier in battle; see 8:20; 29:6; 2 Sam. 3:25; 5:2, 24; Num. 27:17; Josh 14:11.

15 The term *dreaded* (*gwr) probably denotes stronger fear than *became afraid of* (*yr'; v. 12); the two words constitute a word pair in Ps. 33:8; 22:23.

16 For *Israel and Judah,* see 17:52. Not only *Judah,* David's own tribe, but also *Israel* became fond of David for his military leadership.

The whole of Israel *loved* (*'hb) David. This love goes "beyond an affectionate response to his personal charisma"; McCarter sees a political con-

38. I.e., soldiers.
39. I.e., "conducts"; cf. "undertakings" (JPS; NRSV).
40. *waYHWH 'immô:* disjunctive *waw* for explaining David's success.

notation here too; see vv. 1, 3. He refers to the Amarna letter *EA* 138:71-73, "Half of [the city] loves [a rebel], and half of it loves my lord!" He sees that in the same way: the nation has given its loyalty to David. However, in the rest of 1 Samuel, that is, during Saul's life, there is no sign of this. Jonathan, Michal, and Saul's officials (see 22:6-8) are willing to protect David against Saul's unjust anger, but there is no sign that they or the people in general gave political loyalty to David rather than to Saul. Saul is, after all, later able to hunt David with his forces. However, their affection and respect is the kind that leads to political loyalty, and so Saul's fear is not totally unjustified. If David had decided to declare himself king, as he did after Saul's death, he probably could have gathered enough support to cause a real civil war. It is David's loyalty that keeps matters calm.

4. David as Saul's Son-in-Law (18:17-28)

This section notes two attempts made by Saul to get rid of David by the hand of the Philistines, using the marriages of his daughters. In other words, the entire section can be divided into two parts:

a. Merab for David (vv. 17-19)
b. Michal as David's wife (vv. 20-28)

The former part (a: vv. 17-19) briefly reports Saul's offer of his older daughter Merab on the condition that David fight bravely against the Philistines. But, Saul has not yet fulfilled his "promise" to give his daughter to the one who defeated the Philistine (see 17:25), due to his anger and suspicion right after the victorious return, and it is not hard for him to change his mind and ignore his promise.

Saul then decides to trap David by his other daughter's genuine love. It is nothing for him to utilize another's goodness for his evil purpose. Saul is not an exception among sinners, however. The second part (b: vv. 20-28) reports his device in detail in a carefully structured (i.e., chiastic) discourse: an ABA' pattern:

(1) A (a) Michal had loved David (20a)
      (b) the matter was right in Saul's eyes (20b)
(2) B Saul's device to kill David by the Philistines (21a/21b-26a)
(3) A′ (b′) the matter was right in David's eyes (26b)
      (a′) Michal loved him (28)

The result was that "Saul saw and knew that the Lord was with David and even Michal the daughter of Saul loved him" (v. 28).

While Talmon sees here a case of "synchroneity" of two events which occurred in practically the same locale, that is, Michal's love for David (vv. 20a, 28b) and Saul's device to kill David (vv. 21a-27),[41] structurally the key expressions *the matter was right in X's eyes* in vv. 20b (A-b) and 26b (A′-b′) correspond to each other, thus framing the inserted section "B," which is vv. 21a-26a.

a. Merab for David (18:17-19)

17 *And Saul said to David,*
"My older daughter, Merab, is here; her I will give to you
as a wife, if only you become a brave man[42] *for me*
and fight the Lord's battles!"
for[43] *Saul thought (said): "Let not my hand be on him; let the hand*
of the Philistines be on him!"
18 *And David said to Saul,*
"Who am I and what is my people, my father's family in Israel,
that I should become a son-in-law of the king?"
19 *At the time to give Merab, the daughter of Saul, to David,*
she was given to Adriel the Meholathite as a wife.

McCarter thinks that the offer of Merab (vv. 17-21) originally belonged to the aftermath of the battle with Goliath.[44] However, vv. 17-19 and its subsequent parts seem to fit in this section which describes Saul's increasing fear and attempts to get rid of David.

Here Merab is finally offered to David in consequence of Saul's promise in 17:25. This section is lacking in the LXX.[45] However, the MT's inclusion of this section is crucial from the literary point of view; it prepares for the following section, that is, "Michal as David's wife" (vv. 20-28).

17 For Saul's *older daughter, Merab,* see 14:49. Saul keeps raising the bar for David's marriage. Now the victory over Goliath is not enough; David must continue fighting. The term *will give* (impf.) is not a performative utterance (e.g., Gen. 15:18 <pf.> = "I (hereby) give," which is usually in perfect; see on 17:10). The Hebrew of *if only you become . . .* is an imperative clause, literally, "Only become . . ."; for "only" see on 1:23. The

41. S. Talmon, *Literary Studies in the Hebrew Bible: Form and Content: Collected Studies* (Jerusalem: Magnes, 1993), pp. 124-25.

42. *ben-ḥayil;* or "a valiant man" (NASB); BDB, p. 121; cf. "stalwart man" (McCarter, p. 306).

43. Disjunctive *waw* for an explanatory clause.

44. McCarter, p. 301.

45. See McCarter, pp. 303, 306.

condition is usually expressed in the reverse order: "Become . . . ! [Then] I will give. . . ."

David's fighting *the Lord's battles* (*milḥămôt YHWH;* see also 17:47; 25:28; cf. Num. 21:14) does not lead to his death but rather is a factor making him eligible for the kingship, according to Abigail (25:28). But, Saul tries to make ill use of David's love for God and destroy him by the hand of the Philistines.

My hand, instead of "I do . . . by my hand," is an impersonal subject, which defocuses the agent. Saul here contrasts his own *hand* with *the hand of the Philistines;* he hopes to evade the responsibility of shedding "innocent blood" (see 19:5) by his own hands. "Saul is more concerned about his personal position than about the nation's security."[46]

18 *Who . . . what . . . that . . . should . . .* is a series of rhetorical questions, followed by *ki* of result (e.g., Ps. 8:4), for self-abasement.[47] The second *mî* is translated as "what" as an English idiom. The phrase *my people* (*ḥayyay:* lit., "my life") is a difficult expression.[48] McCarter, following Wellhausen, p. 111, etc., takes the MT form as a misvocalization of the rare word *ḥayyî,* which he thinks "was glossed by *mišpḥt 'by* 'my father's clan.'" Various suggestions have been made:

(1) "my life" (JPS; NASB)
(2) "my family, kinsfolk" (NIV; NRSV; REB), reading *ḥayyî*[49]
(3) "my condition in life"[50]

The term *a son-in-law* is one of the key words in this section of the narrative; see vv. 21, 22, 23, 26b, 27.

19 After the temporal phrase *At the time . . .* comes a clause with a disjunctive *waw* + independent pronoun, followed by a passive verb, *she was given . . . (wᵉhî' nittᵉnāh . . .).* Such a construction marks the TERMINUS of an episode. See "However, when the time came . . . , she had already been given . . ." (REB); "So when the time came . . . , she was given in marriage to . . ." (NIV; also JPS; NRSV). *Adriel ('adrî'ēl)* could be an Aramaic name, whose Hebrew equivalent would be Azriel ("God is my help"). According to

46. R. P. Gordon, p. 161.

47. See G. W. Coats, "Self-Abasement and Insult Formulas," *JBL* 89 (1970) 14-26.

48. Cf. Arabic expression *kayfa anta wa-ḥayyatu ahlika* "How art thou and those remaining alive of thy family?" (Lane, I, p. 681) = "How are you and the people of your family?"

49. BDB, p. 312 חַי (Arab. *ḥayyu* a group of families united by vital ties); *HALOT,* p. 309; Ewald (cited by K and D, p. 191); McCarter, p. 303.

50. Keil and Delitzsch, pp. 191f.: "the relation in which a person stands to others."

2 Sam. 21:8, he was "the son of Barzillai," and Merab[51] bore him five sons, who were executed by the Gibeonites because of Saul's sin.

As for *the Meholathite,* Meholah or Abel-meholah is either (1) modern Tel el-Maqlub [MR214-201], east of the Jordan (Glueck; McCarter), a few miles east of Tell Abu Kharaz, ancient Jabesh-gilead, on the Wadi Yabis, or (2) Tel abu Sus [MR203-197] (Stoebe) on the west bank of the Jordan, about 23 miles south of the Sea of Galilee.[52]

b. Michal as David's Wife (18:20-28)

(1) A: Michal Loves David (18:20)

20 *Saul was informed that Michal, the daughter of Saul, loved David.*
And the matter was right in his eyes.

20 *Saul was informed that Michal . . . loved David* (lit., "and Michal . . . loved David. And they told Saul").

"Michal": *mîkal;* Saul's younger daughter (14:49).[53]

The expression *the matter was right in his eyes* (also v. 26) is a key expression that forms an *inclusio* with v. 26. Both Saul in v. 20 and David in v. 26 see this marriage proposal as an opportunity for their respective aims. Saul again tries to make ill use of somebody's love to destroy him, this time his daughter's love for David. David on the other hand takes this as an opportunity to become the king's son-in-law. The Lord's presence (v. 28) certainly makes the difference in one's judgment in a situation.

(2) B: Saul Sends Messengers to David (18:21-26a)

21 *And Saul thought:*[54] *"I will give her to him so that she may become a snare to him and the hand of the Philistines may be upon him."*
And Saul said to David for the second time,[55]
"You shall become my son-in-law this time!"

51. So LXX^{L}; MT^{MSS}; cf. Syr. However, the MT and LXX^{B} have "Michal"; cf. J. J. Glück, "Merab or Michal?" *ZAW* 77 (1965) 72-81.

52. See Klein, p. 189.

53. On Michal, see D. J. A. Clines and T. C. Eskenazi, *Telling Queen Michal's Story: An Experiment in Comparative Interpretation* (JSOTSS 119; Sheffield: JSOT Press, 1991).

54. Lit., "said."

55. See S. Talmon, "The Textual Study of the Bible — A New Outlook," in *Qumran and the History of the Biblical Text,* ed. F. M. Cross and S. Talmon (Cambridge, Mass.: Harvard University Press, 1975), p. 363, n. 175.

22 *And Saul commanded his servants,*[56]
"Speak to David secretly[57] *(saying):*
'Now, the king is delighted with you
and all his servants love you!
Now, become the king's son-in-law!'"
23 *And the servants of Saul told these words into the ears of David.*
And David said,
"Does becoming the king's son-in-law appear trifling in your eyes?
As for me, I am poor and humble!"[58]
24 *And the servants of Saul informed him thus: "Such and such David spoke."*
25 *And Saul said,*
"Thus you shall say to David:
'The king has no delight in a bride-price
except [to be paid] with[59] *one hundred foreskins of the Philistines*
in order to avenge himself on the king's enemies.'"
For Saul planned to make David fall into the hand of the Philistines.
26a *And his servants informed David of these words.*

21 Saul attempts to trap David by the hands of his daughter and of the Philistines. So, he requests David to become his son-in-law. The repetition of Saul's request *for the second time* has a literary effect of "build-up and climax,"[60] though it is possibly based on what really happened. This repetition and the contrast between Merab and Michal in their relationship with David are built in the literary expressions of the narrative.

22 This is how Saul made his request to David, that is, through his *servants* as messengers. Note that v. 21b is a summary statement of what will happen in the following (vv. 22-23a); see 16:5b. Saul commands the servants to inform David:

56. Officers; "the high-ranking members of Saul's court" (McCarter, p. 317). See 1 Sam. 8:14; 16:15.

57. *ballāṭ;* cf. *ballāʾṭ* (Judg. 4:21); also cf. root *lʾṭ in 2 Sam. 18:5; 19:5.

58. Hendiadys.

59. Lit., "in"; <*beth instrumenti/pretii*>; so "to be paid" being supplied in the translation.

60. C. H. Gordon, "Build-up and Climax," in *Studies in Bible and the Ancient Near East Presented to Samuel E. Loewenstamm,* ed. Y. Avishur and J. Blau (Jerusalem: E. Rubinstein's, 1978), pp. 29-34.

hinnēh ḥāpēṣ bᵉkā hammelek	Now, the king is delighted with you
wᵉkol-ʿăbādâw ʾăhēbûkā	and all his servants love you!

This is a chiastic parallelism introduced by the particle *hinnēh,* as in Judg. 6:28.[61] The term *is delighted with (ḥāpēṣ),* also used of Jonathan (19:1), is paired with *'hb ("to love") as in Ps. 34:12; 109:17. On *love,* or "are fond of," see on v. 1.

23-24 When David heard Saul's request, he expressed his reluctant feeling toward it because of his poor and humble background. Saul's servants informed Saul of David's response.

25 Saul again sends his servants to inform David of his request: to pay *one hundred foreskins of the Philistines* for the *bride-price.* The term *bride-price* (*mōhar;* also Gen. 34:12; Exod. 22:16) appears also in Ugar. as *mhr*[62] in *KTU* 1.24:19-20, as money paid to the father of a woman whom the payer intends to marry.[63] Note that in *KTU* 1.100:74-76 it appears in parallel with *itnn* "gift." It was usually money, or the equivalent, but as in Gen. 34:11-17, a father could set the price or ask for some condition other than money.[64] Saul suggests "one hundred foreskins of the Philistines" instead of money. On the surface, Saul is graciously willing to accept a poor but valiant suitor, and setting a price like that respects the honor of the people involved better than just letting him have his daughter for free.

The Philistines' *foreskins* were not "circumcised"; see on 14:6. Normally in the ancient Near East, heads or hands were cut off from the slain victims and counted in order to prove that the enemies were slain. C. H. Gordon notes that "the circumcised Egyptians counted their slain foes by heads or hands, except in the case of the uncircumcised Libyans, whose phalli were often amputated for counting."[65]

(3) A′: The Matter Is Right in David's Eyes (18:26b-28)

26b *And the matter was right in the eyes of David. In order to become the king's son-in-law the days had not been fulfilled.*
27 *And David arose and went with his men and slew two hundred men of the Philistines.*
And David brought their foreskins.
And the days were fulfilled to the king for him to become the king's

61. See Andersen, p. 139.

62. Gordon, *UT,* §19.1442: "marriage price"; also *CS,* I, p. 298.

63. A. F. Rainey, "Institutions: Family, Civil, and Military," in *RSP* 2, p. 72.

64. See R. de Vaux, *Ancient Israel,* vol. 1: *Social Institutions,* trans. J. McHugh (New York: McGraw-Hill, 1961), p. 27.

65. Gordon and Rendsburg, *The Bible and the Ancient Near East,* p. 187, n. 6.

son-in-law.
And Saul gave him Michal his daughter as a wife.
28 *And Saul saw and knew that the Lord was with David and that even*[66] *Michal the daughter of Saul loved him.*

26b The expression *the matter was right in the eyes of David* (lit., "the word was right . . .") means that David accepted the terms Saul offered in v. 25.

The MT *wᵉlō’ mālᵉ’û hayyāmîm* ("and the days were not fulfilled"; see *HALOT,* p. 583) can be compared with the Akk. expression *malû "to be full" + *ūmū* "days," which means "the days elapse; the term becomes due; the term is up; the appointed day comes."[67]

Modern translations basically accept the MT and translate "Before the appointed time" (REB); "Before the time had expired" (NRSV); "So before the allotted time elapsed" (NIV). However, since the clause does not appear in LXX^{B} and there is no mention of a deadline in v. 25, McCarter and R. P. Gordon believe it was not in the original.[68] However, the second half of v. 26b corresponds very well to the final clause in v. 27. See below.

27 Here David's "men," presumably the members of his "thousand," are mentioned for the first time.

For *two hundred* the LXX, followed by McCarter, p. 316, has "a hundred." Klein thinks that the fact that David fulfilled the conditions beyond and sooner than necessary (based on his interpretation of v. 26b) means the MT "seems to exaggerate the deed of David."[69] But certainly this over-fulfillment is in keeping with the whole story of David. It seems much more likely that the LXX is trying to harmonize the number with v. 25. It is the case, however, that in 2 Sam. 3:14 David says that he paid one hundred foreskins. His point there, though, may be that he had fulfilled Saul's conditions, and so Michal was legally married to him, and the fact that he had paid more was beside the point.

The clause *waymal'ûm lammelek* (lit., "they filled [Pi.] them [m.pl.] to the king") has been translated in modern translations as, for example, "and (he) counted them [= the foreskins] out to the king" (REB); "and (he) presented the full number [of the foreskins] to the king" (NIV); also HALOT, p. 583. Such an interpretation might be supported by the Akkadian usage of *mullû* "to pay or deliver in full (contracted obligations and fines imposed)."[70]

66. Emphasis, based on the word order: *waw*+ Subj. — Verb.
67. See *CAD,* M/1, p. 180.
68. McCarter, p. 316; R. P. Gordon, p. 347.
69. Klein, p. 321.
70. *CAD,* M/1, p. 181.

Hence, the MT, interpreted as "they filled the foreskins to the king," would mean "the foreskins (as the contracted obligations) were delivered in full to the king." In these translations, however, the masculine plural pronominal suffix "them" is interpreted as referring to the feminine plural noun *foreskins.* While this is not impossible, as in the case of *waygār^{e}šûm* in Exod. 2:17, the masculine plural noun "the days" might be a better candidate in the light of v. 26. If this is the case, the expression might be explained as follows:

"They filled the days to the king" → "the days were fulfilled to the king." If this interpretation is correct, v. 27 and v. 26b correspond to each other chiastically as follows:

v. 26	*To become the king's son-in-law*	and the days were not fulfilled
v. 27	And [the days] were fulfilled to the king	*to become the king's son-in-law*

Thus, *Saul gave him Michal,* but later he gives "David's wife Michal" to Palti (25:44). When David establishes his reign over the house of Judah, he regains her (2 Sam. 3:13). See also 2 Sam. 6:16-23.[71]

28 The clause *Michal the daughter of Saul loved him* is an *inclusio* with v. 20; it is important that Michal is Saul's daughter. As in v. 12, Saul knows the Lord is with David, and he realized that "all Israel," including his son and even his daughter, loves David.

Once again, Saul's strategy has backfired. Instead of killing David, his attempt has given David honor in the eyes of all the people as the king's son-in-law (as in 22:14), has given him someone who will protect him against Saul (19:11-17), and has strengthened his claim as Saul's successor (2 Sam. 3:13-16).

5. Saul as David's Enemy (18:29-30)

29 *And Saul became afraid of*[72] *David even more.*[73]
And Saul became an enemy[74] *to David from that time onward.*
30 *And the Philistine princes marched out.*

71. McCarter, p. 321.

72. Prep. + inf. cstr. *y^{e}rō'* (only other in Josh. 22:25); *lērō'* (MT form): *lērō'* is not a defective spelling of לִירֹא which would be *līrō'*. Rather it is a phonetic spelling (see "Introduction" [Section II, B, 4]) of an older form: *lērō'* ← *layrō'* f← *la+y^{e}rō'. Cf. "irregular, but probably לִרֹא is intended" (GKC, §69n); "Punktationsfehler für *līrō" (B-L, 443i); "infolge der hier auffälligen Defektivschreibung falsch vokalisiert" (Berg II, 126, n. d); "an error for 'līrō'" (McCarter, p. 321).

73. *wayyō'sep;* the root *ysp ("to add") — GKC, §68h; Berg II 171, n. d.

74. Or "stayed/kept hating David"; cf. "became David's constant enemy" (McCarter, p. 301). For *hayah* + participle, see Gibson, p. 138: lit., "was hating David."

And as often as they marched out, David was more successful[75] *than any of the servants of Saul, and his name was very highly esteemed.*

29-30 Saul moved from fearing David (v. 12) to dreading him (v. 15), to fearing him *even more* (v. 29).[76] All Saul's attempts to get rid of him have failed; so, Saul became an enemy to David, who was the most successful servant of Saul and whose name was very highly esteemed.

The section vv. 17-30 ends with a very positive summary similar to that in v. 16 ("all Israel and Judah loved David"). Thus, "the story suits perfectly the purposes of our narrator, who is concerned to demonstrate the legitimacy of David's rise to power and succession."[77]

E. SAUL'S ATTEMPTS TO KILL DAVID (19:1–20:42)

1. Saul Orders That David Be Killed (19:1-7)

In the previous chapter, Saul attempted to kill David indirectly by "the hand of the Philistines" (18:17, 21, 25); now (19:1) for the first time he openly announces his intention to his son Jonathan and his officials, who are fond of David (see 18:1, 3, 16, 22). David's life is now in danger, but the loyalty of Jonathan, the heir apparent to the throne of Israel, toward David is confirmed.

a. Saul Gives the Order (19:1)

1 *And Saul told Jonathan, his son, and all his servants to kill David, but Jonathan, the son of Saul, was greatly fond of David.*

1 This sentence marks an important step in the split between Saul and David. In this section, Jonathan plays a crucial role as a mediator between Saul his father and David his brother-in-law, whom he *was greatly fond of* (*ḥāpēṣ;* also 18:22).

b. Jonathan Informs David (19:2-3)

2 *And Jonathan informed David, saying:*
"My father Saul is seeking to kill you!
Now, be on your guard in the morning!

75. Also vv. 5, 14, 15.
76. Driver, p. 155.
77. McCarter, p. 318, n. 1.

You shall sit in a secret place and hide yourself.
3 *As for me, I will go out and stand beside my father*
in the field where you are;
and I myself will speak to my father on your behalf[1] *and see*
what I should inform you of."[2]

2 Saul's son Jonathan informs David of his father's intent to kill David. Jonathan usually uses the phrase *my father* to refer to Saul (in chs. 14, 19, 20, 23). It is hard to see how else he would refer to him, and thus its use three times in vv. 2-3 has nothing to do with a "poignancy" (Klein)[3] in Jonathan's speech.

McCarter thinks that the order *sit in . . . and hide . . .* in the MT is "illogically inverted," and he thus suggests "and hide and remain . . . ," and renders "Keep hidden in. . . ."[4] However, a word pair (A and B), of which a hendiadys is a part, may sometimes be reversed and retain the same meaning. For example, a word pair such as *ydʿ "to know" (A) and *byn "to understand" (B) may appear in both orders: in A — B (Isa. 1:3b; Ps. 139:2; etc.) and in B — A (Ps. 119:125; Isa. 6:9; Job 28:23; etc.).[5]

Note that 20:19 refers to this occasion when David hid himself.

3 *As for me . . . and I myself . . . :* here Jonathan, who is first aware of the danger, takes the initiative and forms a plan. Compare ch. 20. Jonathan's proposal to see Saul *in the field* where David was hiding is often said to be "a seemingly irreconcilable contradiction." For while David could overhear the conversation between Jonathan and Saul, Jonathan says he will inform David what Saul thinks of him. McCarter assumes "an incomplete mixing of two versions of the plan here."[6] However, whatever the result was, Jonathan would certainly want to discuss it with David. No matter how close David was, it could not be certain that he would hear all the conversation.

c. Jonathan Speaks with Saul (19:4-7)

4 *And Jonathan spoke well of David to Saul, his father:*
"May the king not commit a sin[7] *with regard to*[8] *his servant*
David,

1. Or "about you" (NRSV; NIV; JPS); also in Deut. 6:7; Ps. 87:3; see GKC, §119l.

2. Here the <*waw*+pf.> *w^{e}higgadtî* is used as a substitute for impf.

3. Klein, p. 195.

4. McCarter, p. 321.

5. See M. Dahood, "Ugaritic-Hebrew Parallel Pairs," in *RSP 1* (1972), pp. 197-98.

6. McCarter, pp. 321-22; also Hertzberg, p. 164.

7. *yeḥĕṭāʾ;* on this term, see on 1 Sam. 2:25.

8. *b^{e};* not "against" (McCarter, p. 320).

for he has not sinned against you,
and his deeds are very good toward you!
5 *And he took his life in his hand and defeated the Philistine.*
And the Lord brought a great victory to all Israel.
You saw[9] *it and rejoiced.*
Why do you commit a sin by shedding innocent blood
and killing David without cause?"[10]
6 *And Saul listened to the voice of Jonathan.*
And Saul swore: "As the Lord lives,[11] *he shall not be killed!"*
7 *And Jonathan called David.*
And Jonathan informed him of all these things.
And Jonathan brought David to Saul.
And he was before him as before.

4-5 These two verses constitute an envelope structure; the phrase *commit a sin . . . David* appears both at the beginning and at the end of the section.[12]

4 *May the king . . . :* Jonathan addresses his father formally as king. He makes his plea based not on his own feelings, but on the behavior appropriate to a king.

His deeds are very good = "he has acted consistently with the loyalty he owes his king" (McCarter). McCarter sees political overtones here. According to him, "terms like 'love', 'loyalty', and 'goodness' . . . may carry legal and political nuances in addition to their common meanings. . . . 'good(ness)' describes the proper treatment of one another by partners in a formal political relationship."[13] The act of Jonathan's speaking *well of David* might well be compared with the request of Abdi-ḫepa to the Egyptian scribes to speak good things to his king.[14]

5 The phrase *took his life in his hand* (see also Judg. 12:3; 1 Sam. 28:21) is an idiom meaning "risked his life."

For the expression *by shedding innocent blood (b^edām nāqî),* see Deut. 19:10; 21:8; 27:25. This is particularly associated with the sin of Manasseh (cf. 2 K. 21:16; 24:4). It is of supreme importance for the ruler

9. pf. Without the initial *waw.* Jonathan tries to confirm "it."

10. *ḥinnām;* also 25:31.

11. On the oath formula *As the Lord lives (ḥay-YHWH),* see 14:39.

12. See E. J. Revell, "The Repetition of Introductions to Speech as a Feature of Biblical Hebrew," *VT* 47 (1997) 94, n. 7.

13. McCarter, p. 322. See W. L. Moran, "A Note on the Treaty Terminology of the Sefîre Stelas," *JNES* 22 (1963) 173-77; D. R. Hillers, "A Note on Some Treaty Terminology in the Old Testament," *BASOR* 176 (1964) 46-47; A. Malamat, "Organs of Statecraft in the Israelite Monarchy," *BA* 28 (1965) 34-65.

14. *ANET,* pp. 487-89.

to avoid bloodguilt. Later, Abigail says that if David committed bloodguilt, it would be a burden for him when he became king (1 Sam. 25:30-31).

6 Saul *listened to* Jonathan's words and *swore* that he would never kill David. The narrator repeats "Saul" as the subject to make it clear to the audience that Saul surely agreed with Jonathan.

7 In this one verse, the subject *Jonathan* is repeated for all three verbs, "called," "informed," and "brought"; here, it is Jonathan who plays the major role in interceding for and protecting David. This repetition prepares for the TERMINUS at the final clause: *And he* [= David] *was before him* [= Saul] *as before (k*^{e}*ʾetmôl šilšôm).*

2. David's Victory over the Philistines (19:8)

8 *Again there was a war.*
And David marched out and fought with the Philistines and made a great defeat among them.
And they fled from before him.

8 A new episode, hence a paragraph, begins with this short sentence of SETTING: *Again there was a war.* Then the main subparagraph of the EVENT comes, followed by a short statement of TERMINUS: *And they fled from before him.* Though it is not specifically stated, this victory may have been the impetus for the following flare-up of Saul's anger.

3. Saul's Second Attack on David (19:9-10)

9 *And the Lord's spirit for evilness came to*[15] *Saul while he was sitting in his house with his spear in his hand; David was playing (the harp) with his hand.*
10 *And Saul sought to pin David with the spear even*[16] *to the wall.*
As he eluded Saul, he stuck the spear into the wall. As for David, he fled and escaped that night.[17]

9 Under the influence of the Lord's *spirit for evilness,* Saul attempts to kill David again by pinning him with his spear to the wall; see 18:10-11. For the expression *the Lord's spirit for evilness,* see 16:14; 18:10. There does not

15. Lit., "was to"; see on v. 20.

16. Emphatic *waw.*

17. Cf. McCarter who puts it at the beginning of v. 11, following LXX^{B}: "That same night" (p. 325).

seem to be any real difference in this phrase, used by the narrator also in 16:14, and "God's spirit for evilness," used in 18:10, despite Block.[18]

10 *To pin . . . with . . . to . . . (l^{e}hakkôt baḥănît b^{e}dāwīd ûbaqqîr;* lit., "to strike with the spear into David even into the wall"); also 18:11.

The verb *eluded* (*pṭr) is literally "freed himself from before." McCarter notes that the verb "occurs intransitively only here in Biblical Hebrew. . . . Akkadian *paṭāru* is normally transitive ('loosen, set free, ransom'), but in peripheral Old and Middle Babylonian and notably in the Amarna letters from Jerusalem [it] may mean 'depart' (*EA* 287:46; 289:39) or 'defect' (*EA* 286:8,35; 289:44; 290:12,17-23)."[19]

The verbal pair *fled and escaped* (*nās wayyimmāleṭ;* see vv. 12, 18, where *brḥ is used instead of *nws) is a key phrase in this part of the story, indicating a quick transition of the discourse. Thus, David *fled* and never returned.

4. David Escapes from Saul (19:11-24)

a. David Goes Home (19:11-17)

McCarter thinks that this episode is "a direct continuation" of 18:27 but its "connection was broken in the course of the compilation of the larger narrative of David's rise to power."[20] The present episode is rather to be taken as a direct sequel of David's "fled and escaped" in v. 10. Now, the narrative proceeds along the theme of David's escapes from Saul until Saul himself dies on Mount Gilboa in ch. 31.

(1) Michal Helps David to Escape (19:11-13)

11 *And Saul sent messengers to the house of David to watch him*[21] *and*
to kill him in the morning.
And Michal, his wife, informed David, saying:
"If you do not save your life tonight,
tomorrow you will be killed!"
12 *And Michal let David go down through the window, and he went*
and fled and escaped.
13 *And Michal took the teraphim and put it on the bed while placing a*
quilt of goats' hair at its head-place and covered it with a
covering.

18. D. I. Block, "Empowered by the Spirit of God: The Holy Spirit in the Historiographic Writings of the Old Testament," *Southern Baptist Journal of Theology* 1 (1997) 51.

19. McCarter, p. 325.

20. McCarter, p. 325.

21. *l^{e}šomrô;* "to keep watch over him" (NRSV); cf. "to watch it" (NIV).

11 Saul sends his servants to David's house to kill him, but his wife Michal provides for David's escape. Not only Saul's son *Jonathan* but his daughter *Michal* intervenes as Saul tries to kill David.

12 Michal lets David *go down through the window* just as Rahab helped the spies escape in Josh. 2:15; cf. Paul's similar experience in Acts 9:24-25.

13 The term *teraphim* (*hattᵉrāpîm;* also v. 16) is always in plural form, here referring to one image. The *teraphim* in the house of David and Michal was "of human size and shape." Laban's household idols (which are small enough to sit on) are called his "teraphim" in Gen. 31:19, 34-35; in v. 30 Laban calls them "my gods" *(ʾĕlōhāy).* For its etymologies, see on 15:23.

The term *quilt (kᵉbîr)* is a *hapax legomenon;* cf. "net" (JPS; NRSV); "pillow" (KJV); "cover" or "rug" (NEB). Cf. *kebara,* "sieve," *makber,* "blanket" (only 2 K. 8:15), and *mikbar,* "grating." McCarter posits the meaning of *kbr as "intertwine," and *kabir* as "something intertwined, netted"; hence "tangle."[22]

(2) Saul Sends Men to Capture David (19:14-17)

14 *And Saul sent messengers to capture David, and she said,*
"He is ill."
15 *And Saul sent the same messengers to find David, saying,*
"Bring him up in[23] *the bed to me in order to kill him!"*
16 *And the messengers came; here was the teraphim on the bed with*
quilt of goats' hair at its head-place.
17 *And Saul said to Michal,*
"Why did you deceive me like this and let my enemy go
so that he has escaped?"
And Michal said to Saul,
"It is he[24] *who said to me: 'Let me go! Why should I kill you?'"*

14 *Saul sent messengers:* is this the second time he sent his servants after v. 11 where they came simply to *watch him and kill him in the morning?* We would rather take Saul's sending messengers here as the same incident as that mentioned in v. 11. In other words, chronologically the story goes backward to the point when Saul *sent* his messengers for the first time; see on 17:55. The narrative in vv. 12-13 flows around Michal and her letting David escape.

22. McCarter, p. 326.

23. Or "on"; cf. "from" (McCarter, p. 326): "the preposition *be-* with verbs of motion." But, this motion verb is connected with the other preposition "to."

24. Emphasis with an independent pronoun, *hûʾ,* appearing before a finite verb.

But, the narrative flows here around Saul's messengers and Michal who deceives them, hence her father Saul, by camouflaging, saying "He is ill."

15-16 McCarter emends *Saul* out of this verse, but for the sake of narrative structure, where v. 15 starts a new sub-paragraph by a <*wayqtl* + stated subject>, *Saul* should be retained; see "Introduction" (Section VI, A).

17 *Why should I kill you?* "Or else I shall kill you!"; a use of the interrogative in keeping with good Hebrew idiom (see GKC §150e and especially Driver, p. 158). As Baldwin says, "the involvement of Saul's children in the conflict between him and David intensifies the love-hate relationship."[25]

b. David Goes to Samuel at Ramah (19:18-24)

David visits and gets help from several people — Samuel, Jonathan, and Ahimelech — before taking to the wilderness.

(1) David Informs Samuel (19:18-19)

18 *As for David, he fled and escaped and came to Samuel at Ramah*
and informed him of everything that Saul had done to him.
And he and Samuel went and stayed in Naioth.
19 *And Saul was informed:*
"Behold, David has been found in Naioth at Ramah!"

18-19 David escapes to Ramah where Samuel lives and informs him of what Saul has done to him. Soon, Saul is informed of where David is.

The narrator's viewpoint changes to the new situation, thus, *came.* It is the phrase *fled and escaped* (see v. 12), rather than "he came," that marks the crucial points in the development of the subsequent story of David; note the phrase "fled and came" is used here (to Samuel), in 20:1 (to Jonathan) and in 21:10 (to Achish). According to Grønbaek, each of the visits, which is introduced by *and he came,* constitutes a certain serial unity in the section as a whole (19:18–22:23).[26]

For Samuel's home town of *Ramah,* see on 1:19. It is located only 2 or 3 miles to the north of Gibeah, from which David escaped; it would take less than one hour down the hill on foot. Ramah was the place where Saul first met Samuel (see ch. 9); in this very place David now seeks refuge.

Naioth (Q.: *nāyôt;* K.: *nwyt*); the K. could reflect the original term related to *nāweh* "pasture; abode (of shepherds)," that is, a shepherd's

25. Baldwin, p. 132.

26. See J. H. Grønbaek, *Die Geschichte vom Aufstieg Davids (1. Sam. 15–2. Sam. 5): Tradition und Komposition* (ATDa10; Copenhagen: Prostant apud Munksgaard, 1971), pp. 114, 264.

"camp" pitched outside a city (Jer. 33:12; etc.); also Akkadian *nawum*, "pasturage, steppe," which at Mari refers to the encampments of West Semitic nomadic or seminomadic tribes. The prophetic fraternities of Israel dwell in such settlements.[27]

(2) Saul Sends Messengers to Naioth (19:20-21)

20 *And Saul sent messengers to capture David, and they saw*[28] *the elders of the prophets prophesying, with Samuel standing in charge of them.*
And the spirit of God came upon[29] *the messengers of Saul, and they too prophesied.*
21 *And they informed Saul of it and he sent other messengers, and they too prophesied.*
And Saul again sent messengers for a third time, and they too prophesied.

20 *And Saul sent messengers to capture David:* = v. 14.

The term *elders (lahăqat)* is sometimes translated as "company" (NRSV); "group" (NIV) on the basis of the root *qhl.[30] However, a Semitic root *lhq, on the basis of Ethiopic *l*^{e}*hiq* "old man, elder" and Akk. *lēqû* "foster father" (*CAD,* L, p. 147), might rather be postulated; it is possible to argue with Barr that the word refers to a "group of elders" among the prophets.[31] R. P. Gordon suggests that this feminine term means "eldership."[32] It may refer to an elder like *qōhelet* "a preacher, a teacher." Hence the phrase *lahăqat hann*^{e}*bî'îm* may mean "the elder of the prophets"; but the following pl. participle, *nibb*^{e}*'îm* (*nb', Ni.[33] ptc. m.pl.) requires "the elders of the prophets." Compare 10:5 "a band of prophets" *(ḥebel n*^{e}*bî'îm).*

27. See A. Malamat, "Mari and the Bible: Some Patterns of Tribal Organization and Institutions," *JAOS* 82 (1962) 146.

28. Lit., "and he saw" (*wayqtl,* 3 m.s.); cf. "But when they saw . . ." (McCarter, p. 327), reading the verb as plural, following LXX.

29. *watt*^{e}*hî 'al;* "came upon" (lit., "was upon").

30. The MT is often explained as a "corruption" of *qhlt* through metathesis or as a textual error — "promoted by the preceding infinitive *lqḥt,* 'to arrest'" (McCarter, p. 328); see *HALOT,* p. 521. But, the sonorant /l/ may be transposed with a contiguous consonant, like *wyqlhw* (K.) of 2 Sam. 20:14, which is most likely a metathesis of (Q.): *wayyiqqāhălû — (metathesis)→ wayyiqqāl*^{e}*hû.*

31. Barr, *CPTOT,* pp. 25-26, 231, 270-71.

32. R. P. Gordon, p. 347, n. 45.

33. Cf. Hith. for Saul and his messengers (see below); see GKC, §93oo. The only other passage in 1-2 Sam where the Ni. of this verb is used is 1 Sam. 10:11. Both in 1 Samuel 10 and in the present context both stems, Ni. and Hith., are used synonymously.

The phrase *standing in charge of* (*ʿōmēd niṣṣāb ʿal . . . ;* lit., "standing holding a position over") means "standing in the position of authority"; see Ruth 2:5, 6. Thus, Samuel is presiding over the elders of the prophets. Elisha also was often with a group, though most of the writing prophets make no reference to groups of prophets (though Isa. 8:16 refers to "my disciples").

The work of *the spirit of God (rûaḥ ʾĕlōhîm)* is emphasized here as in 10:6; no techniques used to get into an ecstatic state as in other extra-biblical religious practices are noted; the verbal phrase suggests it was an unexpected event; see below.

In passages other than this event (19:20, 23), this phrase *came upon,* with or without the preposition *ʾel,* is always used for "the spirit of God (for evilness)" (16:16, 23; 19:9) which *came upon* Saul. Prophesying under the special influence of God's spirit as such has no negative element in the Bible.

The phrase *they too (gam-hēmmāh)* also appears in v. 21 (twice), and *he too (gam-hûʾ)* in vv. 22, 23, 24 (twice). Saul's messengers too *prophesied* (Hit.; see below) under the influence of the spirit of God.

The term *prophesied* (*wayyitnabbᵉʾû;* Hit.) appears also in vv. 21, 23, 24; see on 10:13; compare Ni. (above). The stem Hit. does not make this "prophesying" ecstatic. This is sometimes explained as a group ecstasy, but the term "ecstasy" is better avoided or used with restriction for the unusual and seemingly abnormal work of God's spirit. This apparent "ecstasy" must be distinguished from non-Israelite phenomena. Avoiding the term "ecstasy," Parker distinguishes between "possession trance" and "prophecy" in ancient Israel. According to him, Saul's experiences both in ch. 10 and here are the former and have nothing to do with "prophecy."[34] According to Wilson,[35] Saul's behavior in 10:6, 10 may have involved "trance" but was "controlled and not incapacitating." On the other hand, the "prophetic" behavior in 19:18-24 is presented negatively, since the behavior took "a form of *uncontrolled* trance," and Saul lost control of himself (v. 24). Wilson concludes: "the question of prophecy and ecstasy is far more complex than earlier scholars had supposed."[36] See on 10:5.

21 The threefold repetition is characteristic of epic; compare the three companies of fifty sent to arrest Elijah (2 K. 1:9-18) and the three signs of 1 Sam. 10:2-7.

34. S. B. Parker, "Possession Trance and Prophecy in Pre-Exilic Israel," *VT* 28 (1978) 271-85.

35. R. R. Wilson, "Prophecy and Ecstasy: A Reexamination," *JBL* 98 (1979) 331-35.

36. Wilson, "Prophecy and Ecstasy: A Reexamination," p. 337. For a short survey of the problem of "ecstasy," see Wilson, "Prophecy and Ecstasy: A Reexamination," pp. 321-24.

(3). Saul Himself Goes to Naioth (19:22-24)

22 *And he too went to Ramah and came to the big cistern which was in Secu and asked:*
"Where are Samuel and David?"
And someone said,
"Behold, in Naioth at Ramah!"
23 *And he went there, to Naioth at Ramah.*
And the spirit of God came upon him too,[37] *and he went along prophesying until he came to Naioth at Ramah.*
24 *And he too stripped off his garments, and he too prophesied before Samuel and fell, (lying) naked all that day and night.*
Therefore they say,
"Is Saul too among the prophets?"

22 Now Saul himself goes to Ramah to find David. In the phrase *the big cistern (bôr haggādôl),* the noun is without an article, while the adjective has one; hence, the phrase is ungrammatical.[38] Rendsburg, however, notes that the examples of an indefinite noun and a definite adjective are "true adjectival clauses" which are very common in colloquial Arabic.[39] Is it "a communal water source for Ramah" from which the young women coming out of the gate of Ramah in 9:11 drew water? McCarter translates: "at the cistern of the threshing floor that was upon the bare height" on the basis of the LXX.[40] R. P. Gordon holds that the LXX is "attractive both for the sense that it offers and because, unlike MT, it properly takes account of the definite article."[41]

Secu (śekû) is probably an old place-name, otherwise unknown. However, mention of these geographical details suggests this account might be "contemporaneous with the events."[42]

23 The syntax of *he went along prophesying (wayyēlek hālôk wayyitnabbēʾ)* is *wayqtl* + <inf. abs.> *wayqtl.* This is an unusual construction with the second *wayqtl* rather than a second inf. abs. as in 6:12; but there are other examples, such as 2 Sam. 16:13; cf. 13:19.[43]

24 *He too . . . he too . . .* (see v. 20) is an epic repetition. Such a repetition marks the TERMINUS of the present episode. See v. 7.

37. *ʿālâw gam-hûʾ;* lit., "upon him, he too"; see Andersen, p. 156.

38. See GKC, §126x; also J. Levi, *Die Inkongruenz im biblischen Hebräisch* (Wiesbaden: Harrassowitz, 1987).

39. G. A. Rendsburg, "(Review of) J. Levi, *Die Inkongruenz im biblischen Hebräisch,* 1987," *JBL* 108 (1989) 500.

40. McCarter, p. 328.

41. R. P. Gordon, p. 348, n. 46.

42. Baldwin, p. 133.

43. See Driver, p. 160; GKC §113st.

The term *stripped off (wayyipšaṭ)* refers to Saul's abnormality resulting from the work of God's spirit for evilness; see on v. 20. *Naked (ʿārōm)* is not necessarily totally without any clothes. As Driver observes,[44] Saul could have worn his inner tunic and still be described as *naked* (see Isa. 20:2; Mic. 1:8).

In the expression *all that day and night (kol-hayyôm hahûʾ w^{e}kol-hallāylāh;* lit., "all that day and all the night"), *that (hahûʾ)* modifies the hendiadic phrase "all the day and all the night" into which it is inserted, thus constituting an <AX&B> pattern; see "Introduction" (Section VII, C).

For the phrase *Therefore they say . . . (ʿal-kēn yōʾm^{e}rû),* see also on 10:12. This quotation marks the TERMINUS of the present episode. Here, the old proverb (or saying) *Is Saul too among the prophets?* is given a background for the second time. In its original setting, this *mashal* was put in the mouth of the people when they asked "What in the world happened to the son of Kish?" (10:11). The saying was given in the context of surprise, without any contempt or negative tone. But this time the proverb is applied to Saul's new situation and reinterpreted. In 10:10b-13 Saul was endowed with the power of prophecy as the result of the onrush of God's spirit, but now he is in an abnormal condition under the influence of God's spirit ("for evilness"; see v. 20 above). The saying here has a more negative tone than it does in its original context. Parker, to the contrary, takes Saul's experiences in both ch. 10 and ch. 19 as positive; "to question Saul's experience of the trance would be to question his qualifications, and therefore his very legitimacy as king."[45] However, just as the meaning of a word is determined by its use in a particular context, so is the meaning of a *mashal.* Interpretation hinges on the context rather than on the ambiguity of an expression. See on "wise woman of Tekoa" in 2 Samuel 14.

Mettinger notes that 19:18ff. is "a reversal of what 10:1-9 says of Saul's endowment with the Spirit. In both cases the Spirit is a divine manifestation. In 10:1-9 it gives Saul strength to carry out his feat of bravery. In 19:18ff. it works in the reverse: it makes Saul helpless and drives him to strip off his clothes . . . the clothes of a king."[46] R. P. Gordon, following McKane, suggests that "the two occurrences of the proverb represent two different evaluations of Saul vis-à-vis the ecstatics: on the first occasion they were not fit company for him, whereas now he is not fit company for them." This saying is "fraught with irony" when the full story of Saul is told. Others would say that it is "a kind of parody of 10:10-12."[47]

44. Driver, p. 160.

45. Parker, "Possession Trance and Prophecy in Pre-Exilic Israel," p. 278.

46. T. N. D. Mettinger, *King and Messiah: The Civil and Sacral Legitimation of the Israelite Kings* (CB: OT Series 8; Lund: C. W. K. Gleerup, 1976), p. 77.

47. R. P. Gordon, p. 165; McCarter, p. 331. See also Grønbaek, *Die Geschichte vom Aufstieg Davids,* pp. 116-17, 264.

The chapter thus ends with Saul being in a rather negative and hopeless situation. But, for David's part, he is again forced to escape from Saul.

5. David Meets Jonathan (20:1-24a)

Except for Jonathan's brief visit with David at Horesh in the wilderness of Ziph (23:16-18), this is the last time the two are reported to meet. They talk intimately and confirm their friendship. Sensing that he might be separated from David, Jonathan looks beyond the present situation. It is Jonathan who *made a covenant with David's house* (20:16) and asked David's *kindness* toward his house *when the Lord cuts off David's enemies* (v. 15). Jonathan was confident that David his friend would rule over Israel as king; see 23:17. They *swore in the name of the Lord* to confirm the covenant between their descendants (lit., *seed*); see v. 42. His love and friendship were rooted deep in his trust and hope in the Lord's "goodness and mercy" (Ps. 23:6). Unless a friendship is seasoned by a taste of trust in the One who is beyond the two of them, that friendship cannot be "wonderful" (2 Sam. 1:26) as Jonathan's friendship with David was. In turn, David never forgot it and showed special favor to Jonathan's house (2 Sam. 9:1).

a. "What Did I Do?" (20:1-4)

1 *Now David had fled from Naioth at Ramah and came before*
Jonathan and said,
"What did I do? What is my iniquity?
What is my sin before your father
that he should keep seeking my life?"
2 *And he*[1] *said to him,*
"May it never happen! You shall not die!
You know,[2] *my father will not do*[3] *anything great or small*
without revealing it to me.[4]

1. Cf. Syr., LXX, "*Jonathan* said." In the dialogue pattern (see on 1 Sam. 3:16; 9:6) in Hebrew narrative discourse, "he said to him" can follow up to twice after "A said to B." Hence, there is no need to supply the subject.

2. *hinnēh;* lit., "behold!"

3. Q.: *lōʾ-yaʿăśeh.* Ketib *lw ʿśh* may be a phonetic spelling as a result of *sandhi* (see "Introduction" [Section II, B, 4]):

lw ʿśh [*lōʿăśeh*] ←(vowel *sandhi*)— [*lō+aʿăśeh*] ← [*lōʾ-ʾaʿăśeh*] ←(ʾ- //y-)—
[*lōʾ-yaʿăśeh*] *lōʾ-yaʿăśeh* "he will not do"

Note that the 3 m.s. preformative *y-* is sometimes changed to ʾ- for phonetic reasons; see Ug. example *itbd* for *ytbd* in KTU 1.14:I:8.

4. Lit., "he will uncover my ear"; see 9:15.

And why should my father hide this matter from me?
There is no such thing!"[5]
3 *And David still swore:*
"Your father must know[6] *that I have your favor*
and have thought[7]
'Jonathan should not know this matter
lest he be grieved.'
But indeed, as the Lord lives and your soul lives,
there is only about a step[8] *between me and death!"*
4 *And Jonathan said to David,*
"Whatever you yourself say, I will do for you."

1 The *wayqtl* of a movement verb *Now David had fled* marks a transition of discourse; here it initiates a new episode, though David's flight continues throughout the rest of the book. For "fled and escaped," see on 19:12, 18.

Some scholars think that the present episode is chronologically out of order, for "it hardly is likely that David would still need to determine if Saul's intentions toward him were hostile. Nor is it likely that David would be an expected or welcome guest at the king's new moon celebration."[9] Hence, the present story is placed directly after the story of spear (19:9-10).[10] This order is seemingly supported by Jonathan's ignorance of what had happened. McCarter places the present event after David's escape from his house through a window (19:12).[11]

However, Polzin argues, if we take note of Jonathan's straightforwardness in speech and act, together with his naïve ignorance (vv. 2, 9, 16),[12]

5. *'ên zō't;* lit., "there is not this"; cf. "It's not so!" (NIV; also NASB); "It cannot be!" (JPS); "Never!" (NRSV).

6. An emphatic expression: <inf. abs.> + finite verb.

7. Lit., "said."

8. *k^{e}peśaʿ:* The noun step *(peśaʿ)* is a *hapax legomenon,* though its verbal form appears in Isa. 27:4; cf. Aramaic and Syriac cognates (Driver, p. 161). McCarter (p. 335) emends the text, based on the LXX: "he has sworn a pact," since he thinks that the LXX reflects "a more intelligible reading." According to him, "LXX^B has . . . , 'because, as I have said, he is sated,' apparently reflecting *ky k'šr 'mrty nśbʿ;* but the last word can be read instead as *nšbʿ* — hence 'as I have said, he has sworn (an oath). . . .' LXX^L is better still; it omits *k'šr 'mrty,* which may have arisen by expansion. Thus read *ky nšbʿ* with LXX^L." His view, however, is highly speculative, while on the other hand MT is well established textually.

9. Klein, p. 205.

10. Hertzberg, p. 172.

11. McCarter, p. 343.

12. D. M. Gunn, *The Fate of King Saul* (JSOTSS 14; Sheffield: JSOT Press, 1980), pp. 84-85, also talks about Jonathan's naïve comprehension.

David's intriguing complexity and subterfuge (vv. 3, 6-8), and Saul's obliviousness of past events (e.g., v. 26),[13] it is possible to expect a kind of narrative continuity and cohesion in the present story.[14] Nevertheless, Polzin's idea does not solve the chronological "problem," that is, the relation between the present incident and those in the previous chapters. It seems that David had fled Naioth before Saul arrived there, and had been back in Gibeah for some time and things had settled down. Then he *came before Jonathan.* The tense of the first *wayqtl* in the subparagraph (see Introduction, VI, A) is "pluperfect" as in Gen. 2:19.

For *came before Jonathan and said* (MT; lit., "came and said before Jonathan"), McCarter translates "came before Jonathan . . . he said," following "the word order of LXX^{BL}." The main sequence of actions (i.e., movement) is "fled and came," rather than "fled and said"; hence, "he said" is subordinate to the transitional expression "fled and came." Therefore the prepositional phrase "before Jonathan" probably modifies the first verb of "came and said" as in Hab. 2:2, 4a.[15] The MT as it stands can thus be translated as *came before Jonathan and said,* as NRSV; cf. NASB.

Iniquity (ʿāwōn) and *sin (ḥaṭṭāʾt)* are a word pair. David's speech constitutes a good poetic tricolon:

meh ʿāśîtî meh-ʿăwōnî	What did I do? What is my iniquity?
ûmeh-ḥaṭṭāʾtî lipnê ʾābîkā	What is my sin before your father
kî m^{e}baqqēš ʾet-napšî	That he seeks my life?

The two half-lines in the first line, which are connected by asyndeton, that is, without a conjunction, further constitute an "internal parallelism."[16] On the other hand, the conjunction *waw* ("and") appears at the beginning of the second line, though it is unnecessary for a poetic style and hence not translated above. Fokkelman explains these three rhetorical questions to be "a vehicle of sharp reproach."[17] But isn't this triple use of "What is . . . ?" an act of swearing? See below.

13. R. Polzin, pp. 187-90.

14. See also Baldwin, p. 134, n. 134.

15. In Hab. 2:2, the prepositional phrase "on tablets" modifies the first verb of the verbal phrase "write and confirm"; in Hab. 2:4a, the prepositional phrase "in him" modifies the first verb of "is puffed up and not upright" (i.e. <A-not B> pattern). See D. T. Tsumura, "Hab 2,2 in the Light of Akkadian Legal Practice," *ZAW* 94 (1982) 294-95; "An Exegetical Consideration on Hab 2:4a," *Tojo* 15 (1985) 1-26 [in Japanese].

16. See W. G. E. Watson, *Traditional Techniques in Classical Hebrew Verse* (JSOTSS 170; Sheffield: Sheffield Academic Press, 1994), pp. 104-91.

17. J. P. Fokkelman, II, p. 296.

What . . . that . . . (meh . . . kî . . .) is an interrogative clause followed by a "result" clause.

2 The expression *May it never happen!* (*ḥālîlāh;* also v. 9) appears eleven times in Samuel, out of twenty-one times in the OT; see on 2:30. The meaning is "Don't even think about such a thing!"

The expression *my father will not do anything . . . without revealing it to me* reminds us of Amos 3:7, which "portrays Yahweh and the prophets as having a similar intimacy."[18] Also see Gen. 18:17. However, this indicates Jonathan's naïvete of which David is well aware. Hence, David keeps insisting that he knows Saul's intentions.

3 *David still swore* — compare "further" (JPS); "also" (NRSV); "again" (NABS); compare LXX *apekrithē* "replied" — raises the problem of when he swore before. Wellhausen and McCarter emend.[19] However, the triple rhetorical questions in v. 1: "What . . . ? What . . . ? What . . . ?" could be like an oath;[20] for threefold repetition of a question, see John 21:15-17. In that case he still continues swearing here, for it is his life that is at stake, and he will not be so easily convinced.

McCarter thinks that "David would not credit Saul with being concerned with his son's feelings at this point," and he follows LXX^{B}, which he thinks reflects *pn ywʿṣ,* "lest he take counsel."[21] But, the MT *(lest he be grieved)* rather shows David's concern or politeness toward Saul and Jonathan.

On the formulas *as the Lord lives* and *your soul lives,* see 14:39. Here they appear side by side, expressing David's seriousness in his swearing. The same "double" formula appears also in 25:26; 2 K. 2:2, 4, 6; 4:30.

4 *Whatever you yourself say (ma(h)-ttō'mar napšᵉkā) I will do for you (wᵉ'eʿĕśe(h)-llāk):* there are similar expressions in Num. 22:17; Ruth 3:5, 11; 2 K. 10:5. Taking *mah* as an interrogative, McCarter translates the first clause "What do you desire?" reading *mh t'wh npšk,* "What does your soul desire?" on the basis of the LXX.[22] However, the MT as it stands makes a good sense. The clause *I will do for you* (*wᵉ'eʿĕśe(h)-llāk;* lit., "and I will do for you") is a <*wᵉ*+impf.>. Here, the first clause, *whatever you yourself say,* is

18. Klein, p. 206.

19. Heb. *wayyiššābaʿ ʿôd dāwīd wayyō'mer.* According to Wellhausen, pp. 114-15, David has not yet sworn once. Hence, he posits that *ʿwd* arose "from a dittography of *dwd,* which through further corruption gave rise to the new verb." McCarter (p. 335) translates "in reply [lit., made return]," reading *wyšbʿ dwd wy'mr* based on LXX *apekrithē* "replied."

20. Note that the threefold repetition of the names of demons, etc., is also important in the pronunciation of incantations; see, for example, J. A. Montgomery, *Aramaic Incantation Texts from Nippur* (Philadelphia: University Museum, 1913), Text no. 3, etc.

21. McCarter, p. 335.

22. McCarter, p. 335.

the object of the verb *I will do.* The object clause is before the <w^{e}+impf.> as a topic/focus. See the similar construction in 17:20 where the subject is preposed, *w* + NP(S) — *w* + Vpf.; see "Introduction" (Section V, A).

b. "Let Me Hide in the Field" (20:5-11)

5 *And David said to Jonathan,*
"It is the New Moon tomorrow;
as for me, I should surely sit with the king to eat.
But you shall let me go that I may hide myself in the field
until the third evening.
6 *If your father surely misses*[23] *me,*
you shall say,
'David strongly asked for a leave of absence[24] *from me*
in order to run to Bethlehem his city,
for a yearly feast[25] *is there for the entire clan.'*[26]
7 *If he says (thus),*
'Good,'
your servant is safe,
but if he gets very angry,
know that he intends evil.[27]
8 *Show kindness toward*[28] *your servant,*
for it is into the covenant of the Lord with you
that you have brought your servant,
and if there is a guilt in me,
you kill me yourself!
And your father, why should you hand me over to him?"
9 *And Jonathan said,*
"May it never happen to you!
For if I ever learn
that my father intends evil to come upon you,
won't I tell you about it?"

23. *pāqōd yipq^{e}dēnî;* so NIV; NRSV; NASB; cf. "notes my absence" (JPS); also vv. 18, 25, 27.

24. *niš'ōl niš'al mimmennî;* lit., "asked for himself" (Ni.) (BDB, p. 982).

25. *zebaḥ hayyāmîm;* lit., "the sacrifice of the days."

26. So R. P. Gordon, p. 166; rather than "family." The term *mišpāḥāh* can mean "clan, tribe, lineage" and be compared with Punic and Ugaritic *špḥ* "offspring"; see *CS,* I, p. 309, n. 41. See below (v. 29).

27. So McCarter, p. 431: *kāl^{e}tāh hārā'āh mē'immô;* lit., "the evil is determined from him"; for this expression, see 1 Sam. 20:9; 25:17; Est. 7:7. Also, 1 Sam. 20:33 below.

28. *'al:* rather than "with" (McCarter, p. 336, reading *'m,* with LXX, Syr., Targ.).

10 *And David said to Jonathan,*
"Who will tell me about it,
namely, about whether your father answers you harshly?"
11 *And Jonathan said to David,*
"Come, let's go out to the field!"
And two of them went out to the field.

5 In ancient Israel *the New Moon (ḥōdeš),* which is "the beginnings (i.e., the first days) of the months" (see *rā'šê ḥodšêkem),* was a joyous occasion (see Num. 10:10; 28:11) like other festivals, when people offered burnt offerings.[29] It is the day of the new appearance of the moon in the western sky at sunset. For the royal family, the new moon festival was seemingly presided over by the king as the clan head.[30] As the king's son-in-law, David was expected to celebrate it with the king and his crown prince, as was the general Abner.

Since for the ancient Hebrews the day started with sunset, the term *tomorrow* denotes after the sunset of our "today"; see on "by the evening" (14:24). Therefore, the phrase *the third evening (hā'ereb haššᵉlīšît)* refers to "the evening of the day after tomorrow" (NIV) in modern terms. Note that the New Moon festival sometimes lasts for two nights, because the new moon cannot be actually observed in the evening of the first day of the festival in certain months,[31] and in such a case the phrase *until the third evening* would mean "when the festival day is over"; see below on vv. 18, 19. This phrase suggests that David (and in v. 12 Jonathan) knew that the New Moon festival was going to last for two nights in that month. Or perhaps he just was not sure when it would be over, and so he planned to hide for two days just to be sure.

Based on "the old calendar with the day reckoned from dawn to dawn," G. R. Driver[32] reexamined the timetable of the events as presented in

29. See the discussion in Klein, p. 206. On new moons, see W. W. Hallo, "New Moons and Sabbaths: A Case-study in the Contrastive Approach," *HUCA* 48 (1977) 1-18. For Emar evidence, see Fleming in *CS,* I, pp. 438-41. For the most recent treatment on this subject, see O. Keel, *Goddesses and Trees, New Moon and Yahweh: Ancient Near Eastern Art and the Hebrew Bible* (JSOTSS 261; Sheffield: Sheffield Academic Press, 1998).

30. In a ritual from Emar — the Installation of the Storm God's High Priestess — the clan head slaughters one sheep at his house and cooks and serves it. See *CS,* I, p. 428. On the king's relationship with the monthly rituals in Ugarit, see D. T. Tsumura, "Kings and Cults in Ancient Ugarit," in *Priests and Officials in the Ancient Near East,* ed. K. Watanabe (Heidelberg: C. Winter, 1999), pp. 215-38, and the "Introduction" (Section IV, C, 4).

31. See D. T. Tsumura, "'New Moon' and 'Sabbath' in Samuel," *Exegetica* 6 (1995) 77-99 [Japanese with English summary; abstracted in *OTA* 20 (1997) no. 289 (p. 81)]; A. Livingstone, *Mystical and Mythological Explanatory Works of Assyrian and Babylonian Scholars* (Oxford: Clarendon, 1986), p. 39.

32. G. R. Driver, "Old Problems Re-examined," *ZAW* 80 (1968) 175-77.

this narrative. However, besides his decision to take a day as being from dawn to dawn, his failure to recognize that the New Moon festival lasted two days for particular months meant he did not achieve a real solution, though he strove to avoid "emendation which has only fatally obscured the sense"; but see his views on "at nightfall" (v. 19) and "the second" (v. 27).

6 For *a yearly feast,* see also 1:21 and the comment on 13:8, 11. See below v. 29 on "a family feast" *(zebaḥ mišpāḥāh).*[33]

8 *Kindness (ḥesed)* means here "fidelity" in their covenant relationship.[34] See on 15:6; 2 Sam. 2:5. For *the covenant of the Lord (bᵉrît YHWH),* see on 4:3. The covenant between Jonathan and David was a covenant of the Lord, in his name (v. 42) and witnessed by him (v. 23).

9-10 After David's fairly long speech, Jonathan responds: *May it never happen to you!* Though McCarter holds that "none of the efforts [of both MT and LXX] to make sense of [the final clause] has proved convincing,"[35] *Won't I tell you about it? (wᵉlōʾ ʾōtāh ʾaggîd lāk;* lit., "and I do not tell it to you") makes good sense (so NRSV; NIV). Jonathan is still naively supposing that his father Saul would not harm David; hence, *if I ever learn.* David, however, is still cautious about *who will tell* him whether Saul answers Jonathan *harshly.*

11 Here the dialogue between David and Jonathan is interrupted by Jonathan's suggestion that they go out to the field. While the interruption helps David and Jonathan have a change of atmosphere, it also has the literary effect of retarding Jonathan's answer and thus arousing suspense.

c. Covenant between Jonathan's House and David's House (20:12-17)

12 *And Jonathan said to David,*
"By[36] *the Lord, God of Israel,*
I will surely[37] *sound out my father*

33. See M. Haran, *Temples and Temple-Service in Ancient Israel: An Inquiry into Biblical Cult Phenomena and the Historical Setting of the Priestly School* (Winona Lake, Ind.: Eisenbrauns, 1985), pp. 307-8: "the annual family sacrifice"; see the comment on 1 Sam. 1:3. Cf. "a seasonal sacrifice" (McCarter, p. 62).

34. See *NIDOTTE* #2874 (2, pp. 211-18); cf. K. D. Sakenfeld, *The Meaning of Hesed in the Hebrew Bible: A New Inquiry* (HSM 17; Missoula, Mont.: Scholars Press, 1978), pp. 82-84.

35. McCarter, p. 336.

36. Lit. "The Lord, God of Israel," adverbial use; cf. "Yahweh, god of Israel, is witness" (McCarter), reading *ʿd yhwh ʾlhy yśrʾl,* based on Syr. Stoebe "finds MT intelligible as it stands ('By Yahweh, the god of Israel . . .') [and] . . . argues for preferring it as *lectio brevior*" (McCarter, p. 336).

37. *kî* as emphatic.

by this time tomorrow, (or) the third (day),
whether[38] *he is favorable toward David.*
If he is not,
then[39] *I will send a messenger to you and reveal it to you.*
13 *May the Lord do thus to Jonathan and thus again,*
if my father is pleased with the evil (coming) upon you
and yet I do not reveal it to you
and let you go and you do not go in peace!
And may the Lord be with you as he was with my father!
14 *And if I must no longer live,*
you need not show the Lord's kindness to[40] *me that I may not die,*
15 *but you shall never*[41] *cut off your kindness from my house,*
never! even when the Lord cuts off David's enemies,
each from upon the face of the earth!"
16 *And Jonathan made a covenant with the house of David, (saying)*
"May the Lord hold David's enemies responsible for it [= their own destruction]!"
17 *And Jonathan made David swear*[42] *again in his love for him,*
for as he loved himself he loved him.

12 After the break, Jonathan takes the initiative in the conversation. He promises David that he will *sound out* his father Saul *by this time tomorrow (kāʿēt māḥār),* namely, before sunset tomorrow. This expression appears also in Exod. 9:18; 1 Sam. 9:16; 1 K. 19:2; 20:6; 2 K. 7:1, 18; 10:6.

The phrase *(or) the third (day)* (*haššᵉlīšīt;* cf. LXX: *hōs an ho kairos trissōs*) refers to until the sunset of the day after tomorrow, that is, during the festival period; see "by this time the day after tomorrow" (NIV). See on v. 5. McCarter omits "the third (day)," though without textual support.[43] G. R. Driver translates *haššᵉlīšīt* as "for the third time" and explains that this will

38. Lit., "and behold," i.e., the case that; note that "if" *('im)* is not used here. See "as to whether he is . . . or not" (McCarter, p. 333).

39. *If not, then . . . (wᵉlō'-'āz);* cf. "or not. Then . . ." (McCarter, p. 336, grouping *wl'* with the preceding words); cf. "will I not send you . . . ?" (NIV); "shall I not then send . . . ?" (NRSV; NASB); "I will send a message to you at once" (JPS).

40. Lit., "not to do the kindness of the Lord to."

41. *lō' . . . 'ad-'ôlām;* lit., "not . . . forever."

42. *lᵉhašbîaʿ;* Hi.: so NRSV; NASB; NIV ("Jonathan had David reaffirm his oath"); also JPS ("Jonathan . . . adjured him"). Cf. McCarter, p. 337: "Jonathan swore to David," following LXX^{L}; he thinks that the passage refers to Jonathan's oath in vv. 12-13, following Wellhausen, p. 117.

43. McCarter, p. 336.

be the third time to talk over David's case with Saul after the two previous occasions, that is, 19:1-3 and 19:4-7.[44] However, it would be strange to say Jonathan "sounded out" his father in 19:1-3, for there it was Saul who told Jonathan to kill David.

I will send a messenger. This at last is the answer to David's question in v. 10.

13 For *May the Lord do thus to Jonathan and thus again,* see 3:17; 14:44. This is an oath formula by which the speaker put a curse on himself (in 3rd person or in 1st person). Here the third person *Jonathan* is used instead of the pronoun "me" in order to distance himself psychologically; see also on 25:22 (euphemism); 2 Sam. 3:9, 35; 19:13; cf. Ruth 1:17; 1 K. 19:2; 20:10; 2 K. 6:31.

When the vertical grammar (see "Introduction" [Section VII, A]) of the poetic style of the speech is taken into consideration, the logic of Jonathan's speech in vv. 12-13 is as follows:

v. 12 I will surely sound out my father
— whether he is favorable toward you.
If he is not favorable,
then I will inform you.
v. 13 If he is not favorable,
and yet I do not inform you and let you go . . .
may I be cursed!

This translation takes the second part (v. 13), not as an alternative to the condition in the first part, but as an expansion of the promise of the first part "I will inform you" in v. 12.[45]

The expression *my father is pleased with the evil (coming) upon you* is literally "the evil on you is pleasing to my father" with the subject "the evil thing." This indirect[46] expression is euphemistic, expressing the delicate feeling of Jonathan towards his father. This nuance disappears if one accepts McCarter's emendation "my father brings evil."

The expression *may the Lord be with you (wîhî YHWH ʿimmāk)* is the key of this part of the story; see on 16:18; 2 Sam. 7:9. It is significantly spoken by Jonathan, supposedly heir of Saul's kingship. This gives "new clarity to the inevitability of David's succession to the throne."[47] Later in 23:21 Saul

44. G. R. Driver, "Old Problems Re-examined," p. 176.

45. On the syntax of vv. 12f. see Driver, pp. 163-64.

46. Subject with *ʾet* and an intransitive verb might reflect gramatical ergativity; see W-O, §10.3.c.

47. McCarter, p. 342.

himself accepts that David *will surely become king.* The past tense in *as he was with my father (ka'ăšer hāyāh 'im-'ābî)* is important, for Jonathan takes the Lord's presence with Saul as being in the past.

14 With the expression *if I must no longer live (wᵉlō' 'im-'ôdennî ḥāy)*[48] Jonathan is concerned with the possible scenario that the life of the heir apparent would be at risk when somebody else becomes a successor.

The Lord's kindness (ḥesed YHWH); compare "unfailing kindness like that of the LORD" (NIV); "the faithful love of the LORD" (NRSV). This is the only place in 1-2 Samuel where this phrase appears; the only other places are Ps. 33:5; 103:17; cf. Isa. 63:7; Ps. 89:2; 107:43; Lam. 3:22 (in pl.); the phrase seems to be in contrast with "your kindness" *(ḥasdᵉkā)* in v. 15; see below. Compare *bᵉrît YHWH* (v. 8). But the phrase "God's kindness" *(ḥesed Elohim)* appears also in 2 Sam. 9:3 and Ps. 52:8.

Jonathan asks David not to *show the Lord's kindness to* him if he should have to die; he is willing to accept the decision from the Lord. Jonathan may not know what will happen to him, but he knows David will probably become king. On the other hand, he knew that often the members of a previous dynasty were killed by the succeeding one (2 K. 10:1-11; 11:1), and he is asking for David's "kindness" to his descendants "forever" (v. 15) on the basis of "the Lord's covenant" in v. 8; see below on v. 16.

In any case, Jonathan's language is very emotional, hence not logical. One should consider the emotive function of language in such a very personal conversation; see on 15:11. *If . . . if . . .* is more an expression of strong feelings like an oath rather than a logical statement of conditions.

15 The phrase *my house* means "my descendants"; see v. 42 and also 2 Sam. 9:1-13 where David fulfilled his "kindness" to Jonathan's son Mephibosheth; see also 2 Sam. 16:1-4; 19:25-31 [24-30]; 21:7.

A shortened utterance *never! (wᵉlō')* stands for "you [= David] never cut off," which is contrasted with *the Lord cuts off.* With the phrase *even when the Lord cuts off David's enemies (bᵉhakrīt YHWH 'et-'ōyᵉbê Dāwīd),* Jonathan affirms that his "house" does not belong to "David's enemies" and asks David not to destroy his descendants as his enemies.

16 Jonathan takes initiative in making a covenant with David's *house.* The expression *made a covenant with (wayyikrōt . . . 'im;* lit., "cut with") is a brachylogy, with the object noun *bᵉrît* understood; see "Introduction" (Section VII, D).

The phrase *the house of David* later refers to the Davidic dynasty; see 1 K. 12:19; 13:2; etc. In a ninth-century Aramaic monument, the Tel Dan inscription, the phrase "the house of David" appears; see "Introduction" (Sec-

48. McCarter repoints MT *wᵉlō'* to *wᵉlû',* and translates: "If I remain alive, deal loyally with me; but if I die."

tion III, C, 1). In this context, however, the phrase simply refers to David's descendants.

May the Lord hold David's enemies responsible for it! (ûbiqqēš YHWH miyyad 'ōyᵉbê Dāwīd) is literally "and the Lord will seek (it) from the hand of David's enemies," with the initial verbal phrase *wqtl* as imperfect. Here it probably refers to their own destruction. The idiom, "A seek B from the hand of C," means "A hold C responsible for B," as it is in *miyyādî tᵉbaqšennû* (Gen. 43:9) "you may hold me responsible for him" (lit., "from my hand you may seek him") and in *hălô' 'ăbaqqēš 'et-dāmô miyyedkem* (2 Sam. 4:11) "shall I not require his blood from your hand . . . ?"; cf. "require it at the hands of" (NASB); "seek out" (NRSV, following LXX); "requite" (JPS); "call . . . to account" (NIV). Compare "And may the LORD take vengeance on David's enemies" (RSV); see below.

It is often said that the meaning of this is "May the Lord hold David responsible (if David breaches the covenant) and that "enemies of" is a euphemism to avoid cursing David (cf. 25:22 and "enemies of the Lord" in 2 Sam. 12:14). However, the translation "vengeance" (RSV) has no textual support and NRSV no longer supports it, and it does not seem the expression "to seek it from David" would be strong enough to demand a euphemism. As in v. 15, the expression *David's enemies* here refers literally to David's enemies, who would include Saul, the speaker's father. Gunn sees Jonathan's speech as full of irony and naiveté.[49]

17 McCarter compares Jonathan's love to David with "the command of loyalty given to the future vassals of the Assyrian king Ashurbanipal: *ki-i nap-šat-ku-nu la tar-'a-ma-ni,* 'You must love (him) as yourselves!'"[50] However, Jonathan's "love" is more a personal than a political "loyalty"; see on 18:1. "Genuine love, person to person, sealed by a covenant, such as there was between David and Jonathan, provides a most telling model of an unbreakable relationship."[51]

d. "You Shall Spend Three Days" (20:18-24a)

18 *And Jonathan said to him,*
"Tomorrow is the New Moon
And you will be missed for your seat is empty.
19 *And you shall wait three days*

49. Gunn, *The Fate of King Saul,* p. 84.

50. Cited by W. L. Moran, "The Ancient Near Eastern Background of the Love of God in Deuteronomy," *CBQ* 25 (1963) 80; M. Fishbane, "The Treaty Background of Amos 1:11 and Related Matters," *JBL* 89 (1970) 314; see McCarter, p. 342.

51. Baldwin, p. 135.

and come after dark on the working day to the place
where you hid yourself
and stay near the stone Ezel.[52]
20 *As for me, I will shoot three arrows by its*[53] *side*
aiming[54] *toward you*[55] *at a target.*
21 *When I send the boy, (saying)*
'Go and find the arrows,'
if I indeed say to the servant,
'The arrows are on this side of you! Get it!'
come, for you are safe!
There will be nothing wrong,[56] *as the Lord lives!*
22 *But if I say to the lad*[57] *thus,*
'The arrows are on that side of you!'
go, for the Lord will have sent you away!
23 *As for the matter of which I and you have spoken,*
lo! the Lord is between[58] *me and you forever!"*
24a *And David hid himself in the field.*

18-19 Here Jonathan is concerned about the nearer future, *tomorrow,* when David's seat will be empty at the New Moon feast. For *wait three days (weššillaštā;* lit., "do for the third time"), see "When you have stayed for three days" (NASB; also RV); cf. "the day after tomorrow" (NIV; JPS; NRSV);

52. So NIV; NASB; see "the Ezel stone" (JPS); Hebrew *'zl "go" (BDB); So Arab. *'zl "fail, be lacking" (Biella, p. 10).

53. = "stone" (3 f.s.); *ṣiddāh;* note the omission of *mappiq* (also Amos 1:11 שְׁמָרָה); cf. Gen. 6:16; etc. (see GKC, §91e, p. 256).

54. *ᵉšallaḥ-lî;* lit., "to send (it)."

55. *lî;* lit., "to me"; it may be similar to the Akkadian ventive suffixes *-am* and *-nim,* which occur "chiefly with verbs of movement and of sending," often corresponding to English 'here'" (A. Ungnad, *Akkadian Grammar,* trans. by Harry A. Hoffner, Jr. [Atlanta: Scholars Press, 1992], p. 65); see also on 22:5. The meaning here is "in your direction." Cf. G. R. Driver's different explanation: "The ethic dative 'for myself' suggests that what Jonathan is doing is intended for himself, *i.e.,* for his amusement or for practice, and that it has no significance for anyone else"; see "Old Problems Re-examined," p. 177. See also on 22:5.

56. *weʾên dābār;* "there is no danger" (NIV; JPS; NRSV).

57. *ʿelem* = "boy" *naʿar* (v. 21); synonymous variants.

58. *YHWH bênî ûbênᵉkā.* LXX's reading "the Lord is witness between" (cf. NEB) is advocated by E. Finkelstein, "An Ignored Haplography in I Sam. 20:23," *JSS* 4 (1959) 356-57; S. Jellicoe, *The Septuagint and Modern Study* (Oxford: Clarendon, 1968), p. 321. But, the MT is defended by Stoebe, p. 377, as in v. 42; see R. P. Gordon, p. 348, n. 57. See on 1 Sam. 12:5-6. Based on the LXX, McCarter (p. 338) restores before "forever" *(ʿd ʿlm)* "a witness" *(ʿd),* which he thinks had been lost by "haplography."

"On the third day" (Guillaume). McCarter translates "on the third day (of the festival)," repointing the consonantal text of the MT to *wišlīšīt* "and a third."[59] However, the New Moon festival seems to have lasted no longer than two nights. The translation "spend" or "stay" "three days" goes well with "hide myself in the field until the third evening" (v. 5).

The expression *tērēd m^{e}'ōd,* translated here *after dark,* means literally "you/she shall go down well." The verb can be analyzed either as 2 m.s. or as 3 f.s., but most of the recent translations take it as 2 m.s.: "you shall go down"; for example, NRSV; JPS; NASB; etc. As for *m^{e}'ōd* "well," it is translated variously: "a long way" (NRSV); "all the way" (JPS); "quickly" (NASB; RV).[60] NIV seems to translate *tērēd m^{e}'ōd* as "toward evening," which does not explain the function of the verb *tērēd.*

I would like to assume that the MT is correct and suggest another solution to this *crux interpretum,* by taking the verb as a feminine verb, whose subject probably is "the sun" *(šemeš),* omitted by brachylogy (see "Introduction" [Section VII, D]). For the feminine usage in Hebrew, see on 2 Sam. 12:11 ("this sun").[61] *šemeš* also appears with the f. verbs *yārādāh* (Isa. 38:8) and *bā'āh* (2 Sam. 2:24); also in Exod. 22:3. In 2 Sam. 2:24,

> *wayyird^{e}pû Yô'āb wa'ăbîšay 'aḥărê 'Abnēr*
> *w^{e}haššemeš bā'āh w^{e}hēmmāh bā'û 'ad-gib'at 'ammāh*
>
> And Joab and Abishai chased after Abner.
> As the sun set, they came to the hill of Ammah

šemeš appears in the temporal clause *w^{e}haššemeš bā'āh* (lit., "and the sun came, i.e., entered"), which intervenes between two verbs in the flow of discourse "chased . . . and came." In the present verse (1 Sam. 20:19), too, syntactically the clause *tērēd m^{e}'ōd* interrupts, though asyndetically, the flow of two sequential verbal phrases (2 m.s.), "you shall spend three days and come" *(w^{e}šillaštā . . . ûbā'tā).* We might well interpret this clause, *tērēd*

59. Similarly, Klein, p. 202. Baldwin also holds that it was "a three-day festival" (p. 134).

60. Guillaume rereads it as *mā'ōd* and advocates the temporal sense "nightfall" in the light of Arab. *'wd, whose unattested noun *ma'ād,* he explains, "resembles" Arab. *ma'ād* ("evening"); see A. Guillaume, "מְאֹד in I. Samuel xx,19," *PEQ* 86 (1954) 85; also G. R. Driver, "Old Problems Re-examined," p. 177 ("nightfall"). Guillaume translates the whole sentence as "et le troisième jour, tu descendras à la tombée de la nuit" (A. Guillaume, "L'apport de la langue et des traditions Arabes à l'interprétation de l'Ancien Testament," in *L'Ancien Testament et l'Orient* [OBL 1; Louvain: Université de Louvain, 1957], p. 113). However, his argument is highly speculative and phonologically unsound.

61. See D. T. Tsumura, "*šemeš* — sun," in *NIDOTTE,* 4, pp. 185-90.

m^e'ōd "let her (= the sun) go down well," as "wait until it gets dark."[62] Compare *w^ehayyôm rad m^e'ōd* (Judg. 19:11), which seems to refer to the evening, that is, the time when the sun was almost going down (*rad:* Qal, inf. cstr. m.s. of *yrd); see "the day was almost gone" (NIV).[63]

Therefore, what Jonathan suggests here is that David wait till it gets dark on the third day, that is, "until the third evening" (v. 5). David can move easily without being noticed after dark after the festival is over, namely, "on the working day" (see below), not "on the third day of the festival" (McCarter, p. 337).[64]

In the expression,

> *ûbā'tā 'el-hammāqôm 'ăšer-nistartā ššām b^eyôm hamma'ăśeh*
> come to the place where you hid yourself on the working day,

the temporal phrase *on the working day* modifies the verb *come* in the main clause, not the immediately preceding verb *hid* in the relative clause, as it is usually taken. So, David is supposed to come to the stone on the working day; Jonathan does not say that he hid there on the working day. For other examples, see Gen. 1:11-12; 1 Sam. 2:29; 2 Sam. 11:27b; etc.; see "Introduction" (Section V, B).[65] On the secret place where David hid himself previously, see 19:2.

The phrase *b^eyôm hamma'ăśeh* has been translated as "when this trouble began" (NIV); "the other time" (JPS); "earlier" (NRSV); "on that eventful day" (NASB); "on the evening of the feast" (G. R. Driver);[66] "on the day of the deed" (McCarter, pp. 342-43: "since *ma'ăśeh* often comes close to meaning 'crime, wrongdoing' [Gen. 44:15; Neh. 6:14; etc.]"). McCarter, Klein, p. 208, and R. P. Gordon, p. 167, suggest that this refers to one of Saul's attempts to kill David in ch. 19. However, all these suggestions and ambiguities come from an inadequate understanding of the syntax. If this phrase belongs to the main clause rather than to the relative clause, as discussed above, the matter becomes very clear and unambiguous.

The most natural meaning of the phrase *b^eyôm hamma'ăśeh* (lit., "on

62. Note that an idiom often lacks a significant term, in our case, the subject of the verb as a brachylogy; on "brachylogy" see "Introduction" (Section VII, D).

63. Cf. "the day has wandered exceedingly," that is, "the day was long gone" (McCarter, p. 337), taking the verb as *rwd* "wander, go astray, be absent" rather than as *yrd;* also G. R. Driver who posits the same root, "to be restless, unsettled" and interprets "the weather (lit., 'the day') was unsettled (cited by Guillaume, "מְאֹד in I. Samuel xx,19," *PEQ* 86 [1954] 85, n. 4).

64. See Tsumura, "'New Moon' and 'Sabbath' in Samuel," pp. 77-99.

65. See Tsumura, "'New Moon' and 'Sabbath' in Samuel," pp. 77-78.

66. G. R. Driver, "Old Problems Re-examined," pp. 176-77, understands this term as "evening" on the basis of Arab. *'ašâ* "supped."

the day of the work") means "on the day of business,"[67] the day following the New Moon festival; see Amos 8:5. In Ezek. 46:1 "the six working days" *(šēšet yᵉmê hammaʿăśeh)* are contrasted with "the sabbath day" and "the day of the new moon."[68] Therefore, we would like to suggest the translation *on the working day.*

For *the stone Ezel (hāʾeben hāʾāzel;* lit., "the stone the *ʾezel*"), McCarter suggests the translation "that mound," reading *hʾrgb hlʾz,* based on LXX^B; also *hallāʾz* in BDB, p. 229. However, "Ezel" could be a Canaanite DN that is preserved in a geographical name.[69] And the phrase *hāʾeben hāʾāzel* can be compared with "the stone Help" *(hāʾeben hāʿēzer)* in 4:1, which is the geographical name Ebenezer.[70] For the names of stones, see on 7:12.

20-24a Jonathan must have meant that he would come the following morning; see v. 35 ("In the morning"). He will *shoot three arrows* near the stone to signal whether David is *safe* or not. So, David hides himself *in the field.*

LXX treats the phrase *three arrows* as a verb: *trisseusō* "I shall shoot a third time." Wellhausen[71] takes LXX's *Vorlage* as "I shall shoot on the third day," but it is difficult to see how the verb *šlš* could mean "do something on the third day." McCarter takes *šlšt* as "on the third day."[72] G. R. Driver would rather take the MT as it is (i.e., "three arrows") as "a general expression for 'several arrows', since three is commonly used for any small number." He adds: "while a single shot would be suspiciously like a signal, two or three would give the impression of shooting practice."[73] We agree with Driver's explanation.

67. So Luther; LXX *en tē hēmera tē ergasimē;* see also Tsumura, "'New Moon' and 'Sabbath' in Samuel," p. 77.

68. G. R. Driver, "Old Problems Re-examined," p. 177, overlooked this reference.

69. Note also that *izl of Ugar. PN *bn izl* and *izldn* (*UT* §19.121) is probably a Hurrian term which could be a divine name or a month name as in Alalakh Akkadian. Also, ʾAzel in Azazel (Lev. 16:8, 10, 26) "ʿAzel is strong" — suitable for a name of a demon — might be a DN in the light of the Ugaritic phrase "Mot is strong" *(ʿz mt);* cf. Hebrew PN *ʿazmāwet* ("Death is strong") in 2 Sam. 23:31; Neh. 7:28; 1 Chr. 8:36; etc.; *ʿazgād* ("Gad is strong") in Ezra 2:12; Neh. 7:17; etc.

70. Cf. "the stone of Help" in 5:1 *(mēʾeben hāʿēzer)* and 7:12 *(ʾeben hāʿāzer).*

71. Wellhausen, pp. 117-18.

72. McCarter, pp. 337-38.

73. G. R. Driver, "Old Problems Re-examined," p. 177.

6. New Moon Festival (20:24b-34)

a. First Day of the New Moon (20:24b-26)

24b *When it was the New Moon,*
the king sat at the meal[74] *to eat.*
25 *And the king sat on his seat as usual, namely, at the wall seat.*[75]
And Jonathan stood in his place
and Abner sat at Saul's side.
And David's place was empty.
26 *But Saul did not say anything that day,*
for he thought,
"It is an accident that he is not clean;
he must be unclean."[76]

24b-25 The king, Saul, sits at the *wall seat* during the New Moon feast, but Jonathan stands in his place. The phrase *stood in his place (wayyāqom)* is usually translated as "arose . . . ," but here Jonathan "took his position" at the royal banquet table. In the Ugaritic myth *KTU* 1.2:I:21 Baal stood by the side of El during a heavenly banquet. Jonathan may have been standing in attendance ready to serve his father the king.[77]

26 *It is an accident that he is not clean . . . (miqreh hûʾ biltî ṭāhôr hûʾ):* that is, "there must have been an accident which caused him not to be clean" or "perhaps he is not clean." The expression *miqreh hûʾ* appears only in 6:9 besides here. McCarter thinks that the MT is a conflation of two readings *(mqrh hwʾ blty ṭhwr* and *mqrh hwʾ lʾ ṭhwr),*[78] though there is no ancient evidence or tradition. However, 4QSam[b] *ky lʾ ṭhr,* which might be taken as a

74. *ʿl-hlḥm;* (Q.) *ʾel-;* cf. "to the table" (McCarter, p. 338, following the LXX, 4QSam[b]); but 4QSam[b] has no data on this verse, while it preserves v. 27 which reads *ʿl hšlḥn* (F. M. Cross and D. W. Parry, "A Preliminary Edition of a Fragment of 4QSam[b] (4Q52)," *BASOR* 306 [1997] 65).

75. *ʾel-môšab haqqîr;* lit., "to/at the seat of the wall"; McCarter, p. 338, translates "against the wall" *(ʿl hqyr),* with LXX[L]. This wall seat is the highest seat; cf. "the safest place" (Hertzberg, p. 175; Klein, p. 208).

76. *kî-lōʾ ṭāhôr: ky* as an emphatic; see "surely he is not clean" (NASB; NRSV). Cf. 4QSam[b] *ky lʾ ṭhr* (see above).

77. See B. A. Mastin, "Jonathan at the Feast — a Note on the Text of 1 Samuel xx 25," in *Studies in the Historical Books of the Old Testament,* ed. J. A. Emerton (VTS 30; Leiden: E. J. Brill, 1979), pp. 113-24. Cf. McCarter: *wyqdm* "sat opposite" (lit., "was in front") on the basis of the LXX; so "opposite Jonathan" (NIV); "Jonathan sat opposite" (RSV); "Jonathan stood" (NRSV).

78. McCarter, p. 338. See S. Talmon, "Double Readings in the Massoretic Text," *Textus* 1 (1960) 173-74.

passive (Pual) meaning "because he has not been cleansed"[79] in the light of LXX, might argue against McCarter's explanation.

Because the Feast of the New Moon is a ritual feast, which involved sacrifices, one had to be "clean" to participate (Lev. 7:20-21; Num. 9:6). Touching a dead animal, for example, made one "unclean till evening" (Lev. 11:25, 28; etc.). So, Saul thought David must have become accidentally unclean, but he would have become clean by the next evening, when the second day of the feast was held.

b. Second Day of the New Moon (20:27-34)

(1) David's Place Is Empty (20:27-29)

27 *And on the morrow of the New Moon, namely, the second day,*
David's place was empty.
And Saul said to Jonathan his son,
"Why didn't the son of Jesse come, both yesterday and today,
for the meal?"[80]
28 *And Jonathan answered Saul,*
"David eagerly asked of me[81] *[to go] to Bethlehem*

79. E. M. Cook, "1 Samuel xx 26–xxi 5 According to 4QSam^b," *VT* 44 (1994) 443.

80. *'el-hallāḥem;* cf. *'l hšlḥn* (4QSam^b); see on 20:24 which has *'l-hlḥm* (K.; cf. Q.: *'el*). On the variation in prepositions, see on 20:29. McCarter prefers the reading of 4QSam^b, but since *šlḥn* has possibly arisen "because of its appearance in vv. 29 and 34," the MT reading is preferred by Cook, "1 Samuel xx 26–xxi 5," p. 444. Cross and Parry see a "graphic similarity" ("A Preliminary Edition of a Fragment of 4QSam^b," p. 67) between השׁלחן "the table" (4QSam^b) and הַלָּחֶם "the meal" in 1 Sam. 20:27 (MT), especially in the seventh-century cursive script, where "*mem* and *nun* are easily confused." They follow here 4QSam^b (and LXX) instead of MT, but they do not give any satisfactory explanation about the loss of the letter שׁ. If השׁלחן were the original, we must also assume that at some early stage the letter שׁ dropped from the MT tradition, for the letter שׁ is the widest letter in the Qumran scrolls (e.g., in 4QSam^a the average width of *shin* is 3.47mm; cf. the final *nun* as the narrowest letter, 0.99mm; see E. D. Herbert, *Reconstructing Biblical Dead Sea Scrolls: A New Method Applied to the Reconstruction of 4QSam^a* [STDJ 22; Leiden: E. J. Brill, 1997], p. 80), and it is unlikely that it was missed by the eyes of the later scribe. However, on the other hand, it is also possible that the form in 4QSam^b is an intentional change by the scribe in Qumran, for the widest letter שׁ would not have been inserted inadvertently. A recent study (I. Teshima, "Textual Criticism and Early Biblical Interpretation," in *The Interpretation of the Bible: The International Symposium in Slovenia,* ed. J. Krašovec [JSOTSS 289; Sheffield: Sheffield Academic Press, 1998], pp. 165-79) explains intentional changes with relation to the practice of retelling in the early biblical interpretation such as rabbinic midrashim. While it is possible one of the two is nearer to the original form, the variant form did not necessarily occur from miscopying the more original one.

81. *mē'immādî;* cf. *mimmennî* (v. 6).

29 *and said,*
'Please let me go!
for we are having a family feast in the city.
It is he, my brother, who commanded me.
And now, if I find favor in your eyes,
let me get away that I may see my brothers!'
Therefore he did not come to the table of the king."

27 *The morrow of the New Moon, namely, the second day (mimmoḥŏrat haḥōdeš haššēnî)* = 4QSam^b = LXX *(tē epaurion tou mēnos tē hēmera tē deutera)*[82] denotes the second day of the New Moon festival, not "the day after the New Moon" (cf. "on the morrow of [= after] the sabbath" (Lev. 23:11, 15, 16).[83] Our interpretation is in harmony with v. 34, which mentions "on the second day of the New Moon" *(b^eyôm-haḥōdeš haššēnî;* see LXX: *en tē deutera tou mēnos).* Cross and Parry see here "the remnant of a double reading," that is, *mimmoḥŏrat haḥōdeš* and *b^eyôm-haḥōdeš haššēnî.*[84] However, the LXX reflects a faithful translation of MT = 4QSam^b.[85] See on v. 5.

The expression *the son of Jesse,* instead of "David," may be due to Saul's reservation toward David, "perhaps from" contempt.[86] See vv. 30, 31; 22:7, 8, 13. Doeg uses the same expression in 22:9. However, the usages in 25:10 (//David); 2 Sam. 20:1 (//David); and 2 Sam. 23:1 (David son of Jesse) are usual expressions.

28 Jonathan refers to his friend by his name *David,* in contrast to Saul.

[To go] to Bethlehem: (ʿad-bêt lāḥem); compare *lārûṣ bêt-leḥem ʿîrô* "in order to run to Bethlehem his city" (v. 6). Here, some movement verb is to be understood, for such words are often omitted in direct speech.

82. See v. 27: "it came about the next day, the second day of the new moon" (NASB — v. 34: "on the second day of the new moon"). Cf. "the next day, the second day of the month" (NIV "on that second day of the month"); "on the day after the new moon, the second day" (JPS — v. 34: "on the second day of the new moon"); "on the second day, the day after the new moon" (NEB — v. 34: "on the second day of the festival"); "on the second day, the day after the new moon" (NRSV — v. 34: "on the second day of the month").

83. G. R. Driver thinks that the reference here is "to the supper 'on the morrow of the new moon', i.e. to the second day as that following the feast" ("Old Problems Reexamined," p. 177).

84. Cross and Parry, "A Preliminary Edition of a Fragment of 4QSam^b," pp. 63-74.

85. See Keel, *Goddesses and Trees, New Moon and Yahweh,* pp. 102-9, on "the New Moon in the Hebrew Bible." Keel (p. 105, n. 11) prefers the translation "the second day of the new moon" over "the second day of the month" or the "second day of the festival" (Fleming, "New Moon Celebration Once a Year," in *Immigration and Emigration within the Ancient Near East,* p. 64, n. 29).

86. Stoebe, p. 378; R. P. Gordon, p. 168 and n. 59; Klein, p. 209.

29 *A family feast (zebaḥ mišpāḥāh)* is a yearly gathering (see v. 6 on "a yearly feast" *zebaḥ hayyāmîm* "for the entire clan") for an entire family. Since it was seemingly held only once a year, it was a good excuse for missing the monthly ritual in Saul's court. Van der Toorn,[87] following Malamat,[88] suggests that this feast was "partly funerary in character"; he holds that the ancestor cult was an important aspect of domestic religion in ancient Israel. However, there is no real evidence for this, and the nature of this family gathering is not so clear. Greenfield thinks that this *family feast* was possibly held on the New Moon and was a memorial rite for departed ancestors.[89] In view of the non-divine nature of the ancestor in ancient Israel thought, as against the practice of postmortem deification of the dead in ancient Canaan (see "Introduction" [Section IV, C, 2, a]), it is unlikely that this gathering had the features of an ancestor cult of the Canaanite type. See on 1:3.

The term *my brother* (s.) refers presumably to David's eldest brother Eliab (17:28); it does not mean that his father was already dead (see 22:1, 3). It reflects a system of the fratriarchy; his father Jesse had already retired (see 17:12; also Laban's role in Gen. 24:50).[90] Note that McCarter too quickly emends the text to the plural "my brothers" following LXX and 4QSam^{b}.[91]

It is he, my brother, who commanded (w^{e}hû' ṣiwwāh-lî 'āḥî).[92] Cook posits behind MT and 4QSam^{b} a corrupted text such as *'ḥy ṣww ly 'ḥy* (by dittography), which was subsequently "corrected" later.[93] Cross and Parry explain that the MT *w^{e}hû'* is a corruption from *w'ny,* since "*nun-yod* in the early Jewish character is often ligatured and resembles *he* closely."[94] However, the reversal of letters in *(w'ny →) w'h → hw'* is still unexplained, and it may be the plural subject that required the plural verb. For one thing, in direct speech word order and syntax can have some unusual features (see v. 28). It

87. K. van der Toorn, "Ancestors and Anthroponyms: Kinship Terms as Theophoric Elements in Hebrew Names," *ZAW* 108 (1996) 9-10.

88. A. Malamat, "King Lists of the Old Babylonian Period and Biblical Genealogies," *JAOS* 88 (1968) 173, n. 29.

89. J. C. Greenfield, "Aspects of Aramean Religion," in *Ancient Israelite Religion: Essays in Honor of Frank Moore Cross,* ed. P. D. Miller, Jr., P. D. Hanson, and S. D. McBride (Philadelphia: Fortress, 1987), p. 70.

90. On "fratriarchy," see C. H. Gordon, "Fratriarchy in the Old Testament," *JBL* 54 (1935) 223-31; J. Hoftijzer, "Absalom and Tamar: A Case of Fratriarchy?" in *Schrift en Uitleg: Studies van oud-leerlingen, collega's en vrieden aangeboden aan Prof. Dr. W. H. Gispen* (Kampen: J. H. Kok, 1970), pp. 54-61.

91. McCarter, pp. 338-39.

92. The plural verb *ṣww* (4QSam^{b}) suggests that *'ḥy,* which could be either singular or plural, is here pl. "his brothers" in 4QSam^{b} like the LXX; see above.

93. Cook, "1 Samuel xx 26–xxi 5," p. 444.

94. Cross and Parry, "A Preliminary Edition of a Fragment of 4QSam^{b}," p. 67.

may be that David emphatically presents his excuse of not attending Saul's feast by mentioning his brother's authority over him.

To the table of the king ('el-šulḥan hammelek), compare to eat "at the king's table" *ʿal-šulḥan hammelek* (2 Sam. 9:13); also 2 Sam. 9:11; 19:28. This is not an example of "confusion" (Cross and Parry)[95] between *'el* "to" and *ʿal* "at"; "to" is normally used with the verb "to come" *(bā');* see also v. 27.

(2) Saul's Anger against Jonathan (20:30-34)

30 *And the anger of Saul burned against Jonathan and he said to him,*
"Son of a perverse, rebellious woman!
Do I not know that you have been a companion of[96] *the son of Jesse*
to the disgrace of yourself
and to the disgrace of your mother's nakedness?
31 *For as long as the son of Jesse lives in this land,*
you and your kingship shall not be established!
And now, send a servant and bring him to me,
for he should be dead!"
32 *And Jonathan responded to Saul, his father:*
"Why should he be dead? What did he do?"
33 *And Saul cast the spear toward/against him to strike him.*
And Jonathan realized that his father was determined to kill David.
34 *And Jonathan stood up from the table with anger;*
he did not eat the meal on the second day of the New Moon,
for he was pained for David because his father humiliated him.

30 When Jonathan explains why David was missing at the table, Saul gets angry *against Jonathan* and insults him. The term *naʿăwat* ("a perverse

95. Cross and Parry, "A Preliminary Edition of a Fragment of 4QSam[b]," p. 67.

96. "Have been a companion of" *bōḥēr l-;* lit., "allying to" (ptc.); ? IIIבחר (*HALOT,* p. 120; following Dahood, who posits a root, *pḫr, in the light of Akkadian and Ugarit *pḫr* "to assemble, gather"); for the voicing of [p] in Ugaritic, see *UT* §5.28; M. J. Dahood, "Qoheleth and Northwest Semitic Philology," *Bib* 43 (1962) 362; Barr, *CPTOT,* p. 323; W. R. Garr, "On Voicing and Devoicing in Ugaritic," *JNES* 45 (1986) 49-51; D. Sivan, *A Grammar of the Ugaritic Language* (Leiden: E. J. Brill, 1997), pp. 27-28. However, this may be a case of metathesis (so F. Delitzsch, *Die Lese- und Schreibfehler im Alten Testament* [Berlin: Walter de Gruyter, 1920], p. 89) as Qoh 9:4; ybḥr (K) "is joined to," which is a metathesis of *yeḥubbar* (Q). In light of a similar phrase, *ḥābēr 'ānî lekol-'ăšer yerē'ûkā* (Ps. 119:63) "I am a companion of all who fear you," the form *bōḥēr* might be explained as a phonetic variant of *ḥābēr* "companion." Cf. "are in league with" (McCarter, p. 339), reading *ḥbr* with the LXX.

woman") is Ni. ptc. f.s. of *ʿwh: "bend."[97] The expression *son of a perverse, rebellious woman (ben-naʿăwat hammardût;* lit., "son of a perverse woman of rebelliousness!") is an idiom of insult directed toward Jonathan. *Son* in such a phrase denotes a "member" of the special class of people "who forsake those to whom they properly owe allegiance."[98]

The term *nakedness (ʿerwat),* which may refer euphemistically to genitals, is used in a curse: *to the disgrace of your mother's nakedness.* Here the emphasis is on the disgrace or shame which Saul thinks Jonathan has brought upon himself and his family rather than "his mother's genitals, whence he came forth."[99] Note that the nakedness itself is disgraceful to anyone.

31 The phrase *in this land (ʿal-hāʾădāmāh;* lit., "on the land") means "on the ground" in 2 Sam. 17:12. In Deuteronomy this expression normally refers to the land which Yahweh was going to give to his covenant people: for example, 4:40; 11:9; etc. Saul may be here concerned with the land, which the Israelites were given by Yahweh, and his kingship over it. Or, the phrase may be simply an expression "on the earth," that is, "in this world."

You and your kingship shall not be established. Since Jonathan as yet has no kingship, McCarter would rather vocalize the verb *tikkôn* ("shall be established") as *tākîn,* "you will establish," based on *tkn* in 4QSam^b, which is usually parsed as a Hi. stem verb. However, Cook explains the Qumran text as a Niph. verb with a *nota accusativi* and translates "your kingdom shall not be firm."[100] R. P. Gordon notes that this is "a vain appeal to Jonathan's self-interest; for, although Saul spoke truly, Jonathan had already come to terms with the situation (cf. 18:1-4; 20:14f.)."[101] Here the hereditary nature of monarchical rule is more or less taken for granted.[102]

The expression *ben-māwet hûʾ* (lit., "he is [to be] son of death") means *he should be dead;* see 26:16; 2 Sam. 12:5. McCarter changed his earlier view of "a dead man" to "a fiend of hell."[103]

32 Here Jonathan responded to his father with a protest; see on 19:4.

97. McCarter (p. 339) translates the phrase "son of a rebellious servant girl," reading *naʿarat* with the LXX. Also Cross and Parry, "A Preliminary Edition of a Fragment of 4QSam^b," p. 67; cf. "girls" *(nʿrwt)* in 4QSam^b. See Driver, p. 170.

98. McCarter, p. 343.

99. McCarter, p. 343.

100. Cook, "1 Samuel xx 26–xxi 5," pp. 445-46.

101. R. P. Gordon, p. 168.

102. See W. Beyerlin, "Das Königscharisma bei Saul," *ZAW* 73 (1961) 196-97; G. Buccellati, *Cities and Nations of Ancient Syria* (Studi Semitici 26; Rome: Instituto di Studi del Vincino Oriente, 1967), pp. 195-200; T. Ishida, *The Royal Dynasties in Ancient Israel: A Study on the Formation and Development of Royal-Dynastic Ideology* (BZAW 142; Berlin: de Gruyter, 1977), pp. 151-82.

103. McCarter, II, p. 299.

Cook, following McCarter, believes that *'byw wy'mr* ("his father and said") is "expansionistic."[104] However, this construction *responded . . . and said* is idiomatic; see "Introduction."

What did he do? — David asked Jonathan the same question at the beginning of the chapter: *What did I do?*

33 And then Saul tries to kill Jonathan. One might see here a merging of the roles of David and Jonathan.

In the structure *his father was determined to . . . (kî-kālāh hî' mē'im 'ābîw l^e-;* lit., "evil was determined to him by his father"), the verb (*kālāh,* 3 m.s.) does not agree in gender with its subject (*hî',* 3 f.s.). But there are cases where a verb which precedes its subject does not agree with its subject but is in the 3 m.s., that is, the unmarked, form, and this may be an instance of that.[105] McCarter, p. 339, emending *klh* to the f. form *klth* on the basis of the LXX, translates as "the aforesaid evil was determined by his father." See *kāl^{e}tāh* (3 f.s.) followed by *hārā'āh* (f.s.) in 20:7, 9; 25:17; Est. 7:7. See v. 7 (above).

34 As for the term *stood up (wayyāqom),* McCarter translates "sprang up," following 4QSam^b *(wyphz)* and the LXX, which he thinks is "to be preferred as *lectio difficilior*"; also Cross and Parry.[106] Cook also holds that the reading of 4QSam^b is to be preferred over "the MT's colorless *wyqm.*"[107] Nevertheless, the following phrase, *with anger* (*ḥŏrî-'āp;* lit., a burning of nose), gives a dramatic touch.

The clause *for he was pained for David* (see v. 3) is omitted with the LXX by McCarter as "expansive," thus the last *him* = Jonathan.[108] But, the MT as it is makes a good sense, for it explains how closely Jonathan identified himself with David; hence, the final *him* should be David from the context.

7. Jonathan Informs David in the Field (20:35-42)

a. Jonathan Shoots Arrows (20:35-41a)

35 *In the morning Jonathan went out to the field for the appointment with David with a small boy.*
36 *And he said to his boy,*
"Run and find the arrows which I am going to shoot!"

104. Cook, "1 Samuel xx 26–xxi 5," p. 446.
105. For example, see Gibson, §22, 23(b).
106. McCarter, p. 339; Cross and Parry, "A Preliminary Edition of a Fragment of 4QSam^b," p. 68.
107. Cook, "1 Samuel xx 26–xxi 5," p. 446.
108. McCarter, p. 340.

While the boy was running, he himself shot the arrow[109]
to cause it to go beyond him.[110]

37 *And the boy came to the place of the arrow which Jonathan shot.*
And Jonathan shouted after the servant:
"Isn't the arrow on that side[111] *of you?"*

38 *And Jonathan shouted after the boy,*[112]
"Hurry, be quick, do not stand still!"
And the boy of Jonathan gathered up the arrows[113] *and came to his master.*

39 *— the boy did not know anything; but*[114] *Jonathan and David knew the matter —*

40 *And Jonathan gave his weapons to his boy and said to him,*
"Go, bring them to the city!"[115]

41a *The boy came (back to the city).*

35 In the next morning, on the day after the New Moon festival, namely, *on the working day* (v. 19), Jonathan goes with a boy to the field where David is waiting.

36 Jonathan shoots *the arrow* while the boy is running. Though Jonathan in v. 20 says he will shoot three arrows, here only one is mentioned.[116] However, he shot others, as v. 38 says: "the servant gathered up the arrows."

While the boy was running (hanna'ar rāṣ) is asyndetic, that is, there is

109. Cook, "1 Samuel xx 26–xxi 5," p. 447, holds that the form *ḥēṣî (arrow)* in the MT appears only here, "but justifiable (see Driver, p. 172)."

110. *lᵉha'ăbīrô;* cf. "to fly toward the city" (McCarter, p. 340), based on 4QSam^b (Cross and Parry, "A Preliminary Edition of a Fragment of 4QSam^b," p. 68). However, "the city" could be a later expansion.

111. Also 1 Sam. 10:3; 18:9; 20:22.

112. *hanna'ar;* cf. *'lmh* (4QSam^b) "his lad" ('almō), with an archaic suffix, preferred by Cross and Parry, "A Preliminary Edition of a Fragment of 4QSam^b," p. 69, and Cook, "1 Samuel xx 26–xxi 5," p. 448.

113. The Ketib *hḥṣy* (Q. *haḥiṣṣîm)* could be due to consonantal *sandhi* between the final consonant of *ḥiṣṣîm* and the first consonant of *wayyābō':*

ḥiṣṣîm wayyābō' → *ḥiṣṣîm+wayyābō'* → *ḥiṣṣîmwayyābō'*
→ *ḥiṣṣîwayyābō'* → *ḥiṣṣî wayyābō'*

Here, the labial consonant /w/ absorbed another bilabial consonant /m/. See D. T. Tsumura, "Scribal Errors or Phonetic Spellings? Samuel as an Aural Text," *VT* 49 (1999) 390-411.

114. Lit., "only"; this is the use of "outright antithesis"; see Andersen, p. 174.

115. Lit., "the city"; adverbial accusative.

116. Note such a comment: "one arrow only is shot" (Cross and Parry, "A Preliminary Edition of a Fragment of 4QSam^b," p. 71).

no conjunction before *the boy.* The term *rāṣ* is a participle *(running)* rather than a perfect form ("he ran").

37-40 Jonathan shouts after the boy, informing David that the situation is bad for him. The boy does not know anything about Jonathan's secret message to David. Jonathan then sends the boy back to the city.

41a The boy *came (back to the city)* — thus only Jonathan and David were left there, for Jonathan *came back to the city* later (v. 42c below). The purpose for shooting the arrows was presumably so Jonathan could signal David without being seen with him; it seems strange that they should meet here. Some think someone wanted to add a farewell scene, but there is a farewell scene in 23:16-18. R. P. Gordon presumes that "it is a case of strong emotions conflicting with the best laid plans, just as happens in ordinary human experience!"[117]

b. Jonathan Sends David Off (20:41b-42)

41b *As for David, he arose from near the rock and fell on his face to the ground and bowed three times.*
And they kissed each other and wept with each other until David cried louder.
42 *And Jonathan said to David,*
"Go in peace!
since[118] *we,*[119] *the two of us, swore in the name of the Lord, saying,*
'The Lord shall be between me and you,
between my seed and your seed forever!' "
And he arose and went, but Jonathan came back to the city.[120]

41b David comes out *from near the rock* before Jonathan. The term *rock (hannegeb)* has been interpreted in a variety of ways: for example, "the south side" (NASB); "the south side of the stone" (NIV); "his concealment at the Negeb" (JPS); "beside the stone heap" (NRSV). McCarter translates "mound," following LXX (= *h'rgb*). Cross and Parry hold that it is a placename which is corrupt in the MT as in v. 19.[121] The term could be explained as referring to something like a stone or rock in light of Mari Akkadian *nagbu*

117. R. P. Gordon, p. 169.

118. *'ăšer;* = *ki;* cf. "for" (McCarter, p. 343; see also p. 267).

119. *'ănaḥnû;* emphatic use of the independent pronoun; inclusive we.

120. *hā'îr;* cf. *h'yrh* in 4QSam^b; see 1 Sam. 20:41.

121. McCarter, p. 340; Cross and Parry, "A Preliminary Edition of a Fragment of 4QSam^b," p. 72.

(*CAD,* N/1, p. 111: "The word either designates a specific stone or is a geographical term"); compare v. 19 (the stone Ezel); or "spring?"; see Akk. *nagbu* "spring, fountain" (*CAD,* N/1, pp. 108-110). The meaning is uncertain.

The expression *until David cried louder (ʿad-Dāwīd higdîl)* is literally "until David made (his voice) great/magnified." Here "his voice" is omitted as a result of brachylogy; see "Introduction" (Section VII, D). The context requires the comparative sense: *louder.*

42 Jonathan sends David off. The expression *Go in peace!* is not used simply in the sense of "farewell" here. It is "the *conclusio* of successful negotiations," as Wiseman holds.[122] See also v. 13 as well as 1:17; 2 Sam. 15:9. On the expression "to ask the peace" as the mark of initiating diplomatic negotiations, see on 2 Sam. 8:10.

The expression *swore in the name of the Lord* is the same as "made a covenant before the Lord" (1 Sam. 23:18). Jonathan and David later reconfirm their covenant at Horesh (23:18). See vv. 8, 16.

The formula *saying* (lit., "to say"; *lēʾmōr*) introduces a performative utterance here. This act of speaking is the performative utterance for "swearing"; see 3:14. Klein seems to overemphasize "the awkward transition" between v. 42a and v. 42b. "Without 42b there is a smooth connection between v. 42a and 21:1 [v. 42c], and in this form of the text the subject of the sentence in 21:1 . . . would not be necessary."[123] In our translation, however, v. 42 as a whole holds a harmonious unit.

The term *seed* replaced "house" in vv. 15-16. Here again Jonathan takes initiative in making the "eternal covenant" with David and his "seed." On *forever,* see on v. 15.

And he arose and went. . . . In the Hebrew numbering (BHS), this sentence is the first verse of chapter 21, but most translations, except Jewish ones as JPS, have it as the end of v. 42 of ch. 20, following Vulgate; so for ch. 21 the English and Hebrew verse numbering is off by 1.[124] Here, the English, etc., numbering seems to reflect the narrative flow better; this verse constitutes a TERMINUS to the preceding discourse, not a SETTING for the following.

Now it is dangerous for David to go back to the palace with Jonathan. They meet each other only once more, when David is at Horesh; Jonathan comes and encourages David "by God" (23:16-18).

While McCarter thinks that the MT reading *he arose* is "quite

122. See D. J. Wiseman, "'Is it peace?' — Covenant and Diplomacy," *VT* 32 (1982) 323.

123. Klein, p. 205.

124. These two traditions for the chapter divisions have existed throughout the history of the printed edtions; see J. S. Penkower, "Verse Dvisions in the Hebrew Bible," *VT* 50 (2000) 390. See also on 24:1.

unintelligible," Cook, following Barthélemy, prefers the MT to 4QSam[b], LXX ("David arose"), for the unexpressed subject "David" is clear enough from its context.[125] Discourse grammatically, a stated subject "David" would make this sentence a new subparagraph and disturb the narrative flow of this transitional verse, in which Jonathan is taking the initiative.

EXCURSUS: "TWO DAYS FOR THE NEW MOON FESTIVAL"

In the ancient Near East the New Moon festival lasted one day or two, depending on whether a new moon crescent was observable on the first day or the second, that is, normally on the 30th or the 1st day of a month; see above on vv. 5, 18, 27. According to the Assyrian astrological texts,[126] the new moon was observed normally on the 30th day and/or the 1st day, but rarely on the 28th day (text 14) or the 29th day (text 457); the full moon, normally on the 14th or 15th day,[127] sometimes on the 13th or 16th day, but rarely on the 12th day (text 88). If the new moon was on the 1st day, the full moon would be most likely on the 15th or 16th day. Hence, one report (text 343) tells that if the new moon is on the 1st day and the full moon is on the 14th day of the same month, that would be a good omen.

The reason for such a variation may be due to the fact that the new moon in those months was celebrated for two days. In a Ugaritic text, *KTU* 1.104:17-18, "And on the second (?) day of the new moon (?): twice." This situation may be reflected in the following, if the reading of the first "new moon" is correct: 1.104 → [unknown months] 9-10 — new moon (?) — new moon. Thus it is possible that the New Moon was celebrated for two days at the royal palace, presided over by king Saul. It was "an occasion for the reintegration of Saul's household over a meal, probably of a sacrificial victim."[128]

Why was it celebrated for two days? The reason for this depends heavily on the system of the lunar calendar. In 1 Sam. 20:5 David told Jonathan that "tomorrow" was the new moon, presumably since the waning moon[129] had

125. E. M. Cook, "1 Samuel xx 26–xxi 5 According to 4QSam[b]," VT 44 (1994) 449.

126. H. Hunger, *Astrological Reports to Assyrian Kings* (SAA 8; Helsinki: Helsinki University Press, 1992).

127. So, in Ugaritic ritual texts; see Tsumura, "Kings and Cults in Ancient Ugarit," pp. 215-38.

128. J. Gray, "Canaanite Religion and Old Testament Study in the Light of New Alphabetic Texts from Ras Shamra," *Ugaritica* VII (1978) 104-5.

129. On the waning and the new appearance of the moon, see two Emar tablets of rites which focus on observances of the moon's cycle; Fleming, *CS,* I, p. 439. In these rites, the time the moon disappears is called "the time of barring the doors," while the New Moon is "the day of opening the doors" (pp. 440-41).

been noticed in the eastern sky just before sunrise of "today." Then, the next observable moon would have been a new moon in the western sky after the sunset of "the day after tomorrow." This is the reason why the New Moon festival was celebrated for two nights.

This may be explained by the following time schedule.

sunrise — sunset	sunrise — sunset	sunrise —
daytime	daytime	daytime
— TODAY →	← TOMORROW →	← third day →
David and Jonathan NOW		morning
		??till the third evening (v. 5)
		spend three days (v. 19)[130]
Day the moon disappears	New Moon festival	second day of festival (v. 34)
before sunrise	← NO MOON IS VISIBLE →	after sunset
midnight	midnight	midnight
modern: — eve →	← 1st →	← 2nd —

This system may be illustrated by the following example giving the times of the rising and setting of the sun and moon in Tokyo around the time of the new moon and the full moon in the first few months of 1989. The times in parentheses are those of the "astronomical" new or full moon. (The dates in brackets are those using the traditional lunar calendar.) Around the time of the new moon, the moon cannot be seen if the sun is in the sky.

	89/1/7 [11/30]	89/1/8 [12/1]	89/1/9 [12/2]
Sun (rise / set)	6:51 / 16:43	6:51 / 16:44	6:51 /
Moon (rise / set)	6:28 / 15:50 (4:22)	7:20 / 17:01	8:04 /
	(waning moon)	← NO MOON IS VISIBLE →	(new moon)
Cf. David and	"today"	"tomorrow"	"third day"
Jonathan	New Moon Festival	Second day of Festival	

If the New Moon feast in that month lasted for two days with a ceremonial meal each day, the full moon would be observed in the eastern sky shortly before sunset on the 14th day in that month.

	89/1/8 [12/1]	89/1/21 [12/14]	89/1/22 [12/15]
Sun (rise / set)		6:51 / 16:44	6:48 / 16:57
Moon (rise / set)	(4:22)	7:20 / 17:01	16:11 / 6:24 (6:34)
	← NO MOON IS VISIBLE →	(new moon)	(full moon)

130. On the exegetical discussion of 1 Sam 20:19, see my "'New Moon' and 'Sabbath' in Samuel," pp. 77-99.

F. DAVID'S ESCAPE FROM SAUL (21:1–26:25)

In the following two episodes of the present chapter the common theme of deception can be recognized, one at Nob and the other at Gath. Although at Gath David is able to get out, unscathed and thankful (see Psalm 34), his lies at Nob have disastrous consequences (1 Sam. 22:18-19). This is the beginning of David's life as a fugitive.

1. Early Escapes (21:1–22:5)

The macro-structure of these two chapters (21:1–22:23) may be described as follows:

Nob		21:1-9
Gath	(a)	21:10-15
Adullam	(b)	22:1-2
Moab	(c)	22:3-4
Judah	(d)	22:5
Nob		22:6-23

The consequences of the first episode are narrated in the last episode. In between are inserted four episodes, each giving a specific location — Gath, Adullam, Mizpeh of Moab, "the stronghold" (22:4), and Hereth of Judah. Hence, the structure is not a simple *inclusio* or "framing."

McCarter thinks that the two parts of the Nob episode were separated by the insertion of the other episodes "in the course of the compilation of the old narrative of David's rise to power." Among these "narrative scraps," he thinks, only the Adullam episode has "an important place in the development of the larger story," while the narratives about Gath and about Moab and Judah reflect "unrelated traditions about David's early career that were included at this point for want of a better occasion."[1]

However, David's escape to the enemy city of Gath is understandable at that situation (see on 21:10; 27:1). And without that episode, David's choice of Adullam becomes less clear, since it is located between Gath and the hill country that is Saul's territory. It is also about 15 miles due west of Bethlehem (see on 22:1), David's home town, from whence his kinsmen, including his parents (see v. 3), could easily come and join him.

Moreover, the journey to Moab is not out of place, for to take his parents to Moab at this critical time was a very reasonable decision since his aged parents could not endure the life of a fugitive. Note that Ruth, Jesse's

1. McCarter, p. 358.

grandmother (see Ruth 4:21-22), was a Moabite woman. (The journey must have involved a great many ups and downs; see on 22:3.)

Furthermore, the transitional verse 22:5 gives the reason for David's return to Judah, where David and his comrades were reportedly found (v. 6). Neither in Philistia, nor in the cave of Adullam, nor in Moab would he be found easily; Saul would not seek after him in a foreign territory. But if he came back to Judah with his comrades, he would soon be noticed. Thus, the word of the prophet Gad ("You shall not stay . . . come to . . .") in v. 5 was almost a strong command to expose himself in a noticeable place, but he must have had confidence that the Lord would guide his life even in the midst of Saul's territory; see "the territory of Israel" (27:1).

Therefore, the flow of narrative, which is interrupted by the insertion of other episodes (21:10–22:5) and then resumed at 22:6, rather exhibits the mono-dimensionality of a linguistic description of multi-dimensional historical reality; see "Introduction" (Section VII, C).

a. To Nob (21:1-9)

(1) David Requests Five Loaves of Bread (21:1-6)

1 *And David came to Nob,*[2] *to Ahimelech the priest.*
And Ahimelech trembled to meet David and said to him,
"Why are you alone, with no one with you?"
2 *And David said to Ahimelech the priest,*
"The king charged me with a task and said to me,
'Let no one know of anything about[3] *the task*
on which I am sending you
and with which I have charged you!'
So I sent the servants to a certain[4] *place.*
3 *And now, what is there in your charge?*
Give into my hand five loaves of bread, or whatever is there!"
4 *And the priest answered David:*
"There is no common bread in my charge
but there is holy bread (to eat),
if only[5] *the servants have kept themselves from women."*
5 *And David answered the priest:*
"But indeed women have been kept away from us
as formerly whenever I marched out

2. *nōbeh* (also 22:9); with the directive *he;* see GKC, §90*i*.
3. Adverbial accusative.
4. *pelōnî 'almônî*); cf. *palmônî* (Dan. 8:13) ← *pelōnî 'almônî.*
5. A limitative "adverb" (also 18:8); see Andersen, p. 175.

and the vessels of the servants were holy,
even though it was a common journey.
How much more today are they consecrated[6] *in their vessels!"*
6 *And the priest gave him the holy thing, for there was no bread*
there except the Bread of the Presence which had been removed
from before the Lord in order to put hot bread (there instead) on
the day when it was taken away.

1 David first escapes to Nob, where Ahimelech the priest is. The modern site of *Nob* is probably el-ʿIsāwîyeh [MR173-134], just north of Jerusalem and south of Gibeah, Saul's capital. This apparently became "the priestly city" (22:19) after the death of Eli and his sons and the presumed destruction of Shiloh; see also Isa. 10:32; Neh. 11:32.

Ahimelech appears for the first time. He was the son of Ahitub (1 Sam. 22:9; etc.), the brother of Ahijah, Saul's chaplain, and the great-grandson of Eli, the priest of Shiloh (see 14:3). He is the father of Abiathar (22:20; 23:6; 30:7). Some scholars think that Ahimelech could be the same person as Ahijah, the son of Ahitub (14:3), since *melech* may be a divine element like *yah.*[7] However, it seems more likely that Ahijah and Ahimelech were brothers; see on 14:3 (cf. 1 Chr. 18:16). As for the phrase "In the days of Abiathar the high priest" (Mark 2:26), though Abiathar was not yet "the high priest" at that time, a historian could use this title *proleptically.* See 1 Sam. 17:54 on "prolepsis."

The title *the priest* refers to "the chief priest" here.

Ahimelech presumably "trembles" because he realizes that something must be wrong for David to be completely alone. The same verb *trembled* (*ḥrd) is used for the elders of Bethlehem when Samuel came to that city to anoint David (16:4).

2 Because Ahimelech was the brother of Saul's chaplain Ahijah, David was probably not sure whether he could trust Ahimelech and hence made up a story to explain why he was by himself.[8] However, David's deception resulted in the disaster in 22:6-23.

The MT *yôdaʿtî* (here *I sent*), taken as "caused to know" (Po.), is often asserted to be incomprehensible, a corruption, and hence "safely dropped."[9] It has been translated "directed" (NASB; JPS) or "I have told them to meet

6. *yiqdaš;* lit., "it/he is consecrated."

7. See R. P. Gordon, p. 348, n. 65; also Hertzberg, p. 179.

8. So, Baldwin, p. 137.

9. E. M. Cook, "1 Samuel xx 26–xxi 5 According to 4QSam^b," *VT* 44 (1994) 450; F. M. Cross and D. W. Parry, "A Preliminary Edition of a Fragment of 4QSam^b (4Q52)," *BASOR* 306 (1997) 69.

me" (NIV). McCarter suggests "I have made an appointment" (also NRSV), reading *yʿdty* with 4QSam^b and the LXX.[10] However, as Barr suggests, the MT form might be translated as *I sent* or "dismissed" in light of the Arabic *wādaʿ* "say farewell, take leave of, abandon, leave."[11]

3 The number *five* is one unit based on the number of fingers in one hand. Klein, following Stoebe, considers it to be a round number since it is "too much for one man and too little for a whole combat team."[12] However, five would be enough for David and his two or three servants.

4 The phrase *in my charge* (lit., "to the place of my hand") is a compound preposition (Lev. 14:42; Judg. 6:19; etc.) like "from under" followed by a noun. Hence, there is no need to take *ʾel-* as "a corrupt dittograph" as Cross and Parry do.[13]

The term *common (ḥōl)* is the opposite of *holy* in vv. 4-5, just as it is in Lev. 10:10 and the book of Ezekiel.[14] In Ugaritic ritual texts the same term *(ḥl)* describes the state where "the king is clear (of further cultic obligations)" *(ḥl mlk).* The nominal form "holiness" *(qōdeš),* translated here as *holy,* appears only in this context (vv. 4-6) in Samuel. On "holiness" of God, see on 2:2.

The phrase *(to eat)* is understood from the context. Hence, there is no need to supply "the missing apodosis" such as "you may eat of it."[15]

The one condition was that David's *servants* were not ritually unclean through coitus; see Exod. 19:15; Lev. 15:18.

5 Sexual abstinence was a common practice during military operations. "War was regarded as sacred; and the prohibition of women to men engaged in it is wide-spread."[16] Deut. 23:9-14 is concerned with the purity of the camp. The rule of sexual abstinence can be noted in the Qumran *War Scroll* (col. VII,1, 3).[17] See 2 Sam. 11:11, where Uriah the Hittite did not go back home to sleep with his wife during the expedition.

10. McCarter, p. 347.

11. See Barr, *CPTOT,* pp. 21-22.

12. Klein, p. 213.

13. Cross and Parry, "A Preliminary Edition of a Fragment of 4QSam^b," p. 69; so Cook, "1 Samuel xx 26-xxi 5," p. 450.

14. For a possible reference to wine for "profane" *(k-ḥl)* uses, see S. Mittmann, "Sakraler Wein und die Flüssigmaße Hin und Log," in *Ana šadî Labnāni lū allik: Beiträge zu altorientalischen und mittelmeerischen Kulturen: Festschrift für Wolfgang Röllig,* ed. B. Pongratz-Leisten et al. (AOAT 247; Neukirchen-Vluyn: Neukirchener, 1997), pp. 272-73 on *kḥl* (Khirbet el Qom #6; Avigad, *IEJ* 22, 3).

15. McCarter, p. 347.

16. Driver, p. 174; see also G. von Rad, *Holy War in Ancient Israel* (Grand Rapids: Eerdmans, 1991 [orig. 1952]), p. 42.

17. For the *War Scroll,* see Yadin, pp. 290f. See R. P. Gordon, p. 348, n. 68.

There are two interpretations for the *vessels* (*kᵉlê-[hannᵉʿārîm]*)[18] (cf. "things" [NIV]): (1) weapons (Stoebe); (2) "vessels" — a euphemism for genitalia.[19] The second position seems to be preferable, for why would David bring up literal "weapons"? That is not what Ahimelech is concerned about. David's *servants* are no longer mentioned in this episode, but their existence is seemingly assumed in Matt. 12:3-4; Mark 2:25-26; and Luke 6:3-4, where Ahimelech's judgment in "putting mercy before ceremonial law" was endorsed by Jesus.[20]

6 "The priest acted in all innocence, but his generosity had frightful consequences for the whole priestly community at Nob."[21] See below 1 Sam. 22:9-19, esp. 10.

The Bread of the Presence (*leḥem happānîm;* lit., "the bread of the face(s)") was set out "before the Lord," that is, in his presence,[22] in the holy place of the sanctuary each Sabbath. The reference to this "bread" might support the Jewish tradition (see B. Zeb. 118-19)[23] that the ark of God was in the temple of Nob at that time; see on 1 Sam. 22:19; also 14:18. Or, on the other hand, the tradition may have been caused by this passage. According to Lev. 24:5-9, the "Show Bread" consisted of twelve loaves of bread set in two rows on a table "before the Lord"; the twelve loaves symbolized the twelve tribes. Each loaf contained about three liters (12 cups) of flour;[24] so, the loaves were larger than usual loaves. "This bread is to be set out before the LORD regularly, Sabbath after Sabbath" (v. 8). The old bread was to be eaten only by the priests "in a holy place" (v. 9).

David and his men obviously would not qualify to eat the bread, but the rules may have been loosely applied during this period, and Ahimelech was probably bending even the current rules somewhat. But at least he did feel it must not be treated the same as common bread. Birch holds that here "the

18. On the difficulties of the MT, see O. Thenius, p. 99; F. I. Andersen and D. N. Freedman, "Another Look at 4QSam^b," *RQ* 14 (1989) 15-16. Cross and Parry, "A Preliminary Edition of a Fragment of 4QSam^b," p. 69, reads *kl* "all" in light of the LXX and 4QSam^b.

19. Hertzberg, p. 177, comparing the Greek *skeuos;* so already P. A. H. de Boer, "Research into the Text of I Samuel xviii–xxxi," *OTS* 6 (1949) 35.

20. See Baldwin, p. 138.

21. R. P. Gordon, p. 170.

22. On the existence of the practice of incense burning at this time, that is, before the building of the temple, see K. Nielsen, *Incense in Ancient Israel* (SVT 38; Leiden: E. J. Brill, 1986), pp. 104-5. See on 2:28.

23. See K. van der Toorn, "Saul and the Rise of Israelite State Religion," *VT* 43 (1993) 529, n. 31.

24. See G. J. Wenham, *The Book of Leviticus* (NICOT; Grand Rapids: Eerdmans, 1979), p. 310, n. 6.

ordinary boundaries between the sacred and the profane have been collapsed in the face of David's need and God's kingdom, which is coming in David."[25]

This passage is indirect evidence that the Sabbath was observed at the time of Saul, at least among the priestly family.[26]

The phrase *which had been removed (hammûsārîm)* is either a plural ptc., since the priest gave David five of the twelve loaves of the Bread of the Presence, or a s. noun with an enclitic mem. McCarter's view that the "ungrammatical" plural form was caused "by attraction to the preceding word"[27] is unnecessary.

(2) Doeg the Edomite (21:7)

7 — *Now, there, one of*[28] *Saul's servants was on that day kept away before the Lord; his name was Doeg the Edomite and he was the chief leader belonging to Saul* — .

7 *Now, there (w^{e}šām)* is a disjunctive clause and hence parenthetical. This verse prepares for the development of the present incident in 22:9-19.

The term *kept away (neʿṣār)* or "detained" (NRSV; NIV; JPS) means detention "for religious reasons, at the temple or a festival" in postbiblical Hebrew.[29] It is probably "for some ceremonial purpose," because it was *before the Lord.* Various suggestions have been given for the reason why Doeg was there: (1) for making a vow (Mowinckel); (2) for an act of penance (Hertzberg);[30] or (3) for observing a day free of work.[31] Kutsch explains it as to "hold one's self back from work" (Ni. *ʿṣr) = "take a holiday."[32] It may be that Doeg, like Saul in 10:8 and 13:8, had been waiting on God *(before the Lord)* without doing any ordinary work. His retreat could be related to the "seven-day" period for waiting; see on 13:8. For one thing, the fact that *the Bread of the Presence* had been removed *from before the Lord* (v. 6) has something to do with the Sabbath, that is, the special day of the seven-day period.[33] *Doeg (Dōʾēg) the Edomite* may have become Saul's servant after his victory over Edom (14:47).[34]

25. Birch, p. 1140.

26. See D. T. Tsumura, "'New Moon' and 'Sabbath' in Samuel," *Exegetica* 6 (1995) 77-99 [Japanese with English summary].

27. McCarter, p. 348; also Cross and Parry, "A Preliminary Edition of a Fragment of 4QSam^b," p. 69.

28. So McCarter, p. 348; lit., "a man of."

29. See Jastrow, p. 1103.

30. Hertzberg, p. 181; also Baldwin, p. 138 ("some kind of punishment").

31. See *HALOT,* p. 871.

32. E. Kutsch, "Die Wurzel עצר im Hebräischen," *VT* 2 (1952) 65-67.

33. See also McCarter, pp. 349-50.

34. Baldwin, p. 138.

As R. P. Gordon notes, "it was possible for Edomites to "enter the assembly of the Lord" (Deut. 23:7[8]), and there may even be hints, in the Old Testament, of common cultic ties between Israel and Edom."[35]

The expression *the chief leader (ʾabbîr hārōʿîm;* lit., "the mighty (one) of the shepherds") is composed of a constract of m.s. adj. <*qattīl*> followed by a pl. noun *shepherds (rʿym)* as referring to leaders. Hence, a translation such as "the chief of Saul's runners,"[36] based on reading *rṣym* from 22:17,[37] is not necessary.

(3) David Requests a Weapon (21:8-9)

8 *And David said to Ahimelech,*
"Is there any spear or sword here in your charge?
For neither my sword nor my weapons/armor have I taken in my hand, because the word of the king was urgent."
9 *And the priest said,*
"As for the sword of Goliath, the Philistine,
whom you slew in the Valley of Elah,
behold it is wrapped in the garment behind the ephod.
If you would take it with you, take it,
for there is no other except it here!"
And David said,
"There is nothing like it! Give it to me!"

David is obviously not an experienced liar. His statement that there was no time even to get a weapon contradicts his previous statement that there had been time for his men to purify themselves by abstinence, but Ahimelech is not used to deviousness either and does not notice.

8 *Is there (wᵉʾîn)* is an interrogative; see GKC, §150c, n. 3: "Quite exceptional . . . (common in Aramaic)."[38] The word pair *spear or sword* here

35. R. P. Gordon, p. 170. See J. R. Bartlett in *POTT,* p. 246; *Edom and the Edomites* (JSOTSS 77; Sheffield: JSOT Press, 1989).

36. McCarter, p. 348.

37. For "chief, leader" for *ʾabbîr* "bull, stallion," see P. D. Miller, "Animal Names as Designations in Ugaritic and Hebrew," *UF* 2 (1970) 180-81.

38. Is this an Eastern or Bethlehemite dialect? Note the dialectal variants

*ʾayn → ʾa^{i}n → ʾēn (normal contraction)
*ʾayn → ʾa^{i}n → ʾān (contraction; 1 Sam. 10:14, cf. Eblaite)
*ʾayn → ʾa^{i}n → ʾīn (vowel *sandhi;* cf. Akkadian *bītu*)

For vowel *sandhi,* see D. T. Tsumura, "Vowel sandhi in Biblical Hebrew," *ZAW* 109 (1997) 575-88; also "Introduction" (Section II, B, 4). McCarter emends it to *whn hyš* on the basis of the LXX *ide ei estin,* since he thinks the MT is "unintelligible" (p. 348).

is reversed; see 13:19; 17:45. For the phrase *in your charge* (lit., "(at) the place of your hand"), see v. 3. Note that the Philistines put Saul's armour in the temple of the Ashtaroth (31:10).

9 In 17:51 David is said to have killed Goliath with *the sword of Goliath.* See 17:54 on the "weapons" *(kēlâw),* which David kept in his own tent. On the term *ephod,* see on 2:28. If the sword is "behind the ephod," it seems that this *ephod* was not a garment, as the ephod in 14:3 seems to be. It may have been some kind of image such as the golden ephod made by Gideon (Judg. 8:24-27), which became a snare. The Ephraimite Micah made an ephod and teraphim (Judg. 17:5; apparently different items from his "graven image and molten image" in 18:14-20), and Hos. 3:4 says Israel will live "without ephod or teraphim."

There is nothing like it! ('ên kāmôhā). Labuschagne thinks that David called Goliath's sword incomparable "because it was invaluable to him, being the only one available."[39] However, David spoke thus because it was a fine sword, not just simply "available." See on 1 Sam. 2:2; 10:24.

b. To Gath (21:10-15)

10 *And David arose and fled on that day from before Saul and came to Achish king*[40] *of Gath.*
11 *And the servants of Achish said to him,*
"Isn't this David, the king of the land?
Isn't it about him that they answered to each other[41]
while dancing, saying[42]
'Saul slew by thousands;
and David by ten thousands!' "
12 *And David took these words to heart and was greatly afraid of Achish king of Gath.*
13 *And he disguised his judgment in their eyes and acted like a mad man in their hands and made marks*[43] *on the doors of the gate*

39. C. J. Labuschagne, *The Incomparability of Yahweh in the Old Testament* (POS 5; Leiden: E. J. Brill, 1966), p. 110.

40. *Melek;* also 27:2; cf. *srn* "lord" (e.g., 1 Sam. 5:8, 11; 29:2, 7; etc.). Rainey holds that Achish here was called "king" because he was the senior among the five Philistine rulers at that time; see *CS,* II, p. 164, n. 4.

41. *ya'ănû,* "sang antiphonally." See on 18:8.

42. As in 29:5, this phrase is "obligatorily required syntactically, since the quotative frame is a question"; see C. L. Miller, "Introducing Direct Discourse in Biblical Hebrew Narrative," in *Biblical Hebrew and Discourse Linguistics,* ed. R. D. Bergen (Dallas: Summer Institute of Linguistics, 1994), p. 221.

43. K. *wytw;* Q. *waytâw;* Ketib is *twh, Pi. while Qere is from *tyw. BDB,

and let his spittle go down to his beard.
14 *And Achish said to his servants,*
"Lo! Look at this madman! Why do you bring him to me?
15 *Am I in want of madmen that you should have brought this one to act mad before me?*
Should this one come into my house?"

The question has been often asked: why did David go to Achish? Gath was the very hometown of Goliath (see 17:4); no clear reason can be given why he chose that city. One possible reason may be geographic; Gath is just beyond the Valley of Elah, and it is the Philistine city nearest to Bethlehem, his hometown. Topographically David escapes from the ridge of the hill country to the Philistine Plain, some 800 m. (2,600 ft.) down. This horizontal and vertical distance from Saul's territory (see v. 10: "before Saul") eventually leads to David's settling among the Philistines in ch. 27.

However, his initial attempt to seek refuge in Gath is unsuccessful. This episode shows how urgent and unprepared his escape was and how bold he was to go there by himself (cf. 27:2; with 600 men), with Goliath's sword! One thing was clear: David and the Philistines now share a common enemy, Saul, king of Israel. David may have been thinking that Achish might hire him as a mercenary (see on v. 15). Psalms 34, 56 are associated by their superscriptions with this difficult time of David's life. In the midst of the deep trouble, David begins his psalm with the confession "I will bless the Lord at all times" (Ps. 34:1). Such is the confession of the one who trusts in the Lord regardless of the external situation.

On the literary relation between this episode and ch. 27, see on 1 Sam. 27:2.

10 This is the real start of David's life as a fugitive (see *arose and fled*), though he has already fled from Saul's court and his city; see 19:12, 18; 20:1. On the inchoative use of *wayyāqom,* see on 26:5 (*set out and came;* lit., "arose and came"). The expression *and came* signifies the change of the narrator's viewpoint; see on 1:19 and "Introduction" (Section VI, D).

The phrase *on that day* is a phrase to express a transitional EVENT, not necessarily referring to the very day when David escaped from Saul's court or city. See on 3:2; 14:1. *From before Saul* means "from Saul's territory."

Achish (*ʾăkîš;* also 1 Sam. 27:2; 1 K. 2:39-40) is a name which

p. 1063. Cf. "he spat" (McCarter), reading *wayyātop.* According to McCarter "the correct reading is reflected by LXX *kai etympanizen,* 'and he drummed,' representing *wytp,* which however should probably be referred not to *tpp,* 'beat the drum,' but rather to *tpp,* 'spit,' which, though unattested in Biblical Hebrew (but cf. *tōpet,* 'spitting,' in Job 17:6), occurs in (Talmudic) Aramaic" (McCarter, p. 355).

seems to be "Philistine" in origin. That is, it may belong to an originally Aegean-West Anatolian onomasticon. It is found in a list of *kftiw* [Cretan] names in an Egyptian text, and is probably cognate with Anchises, the father of Aeneas (*Iliad* 2:819; 20:215).[44] For strong Aegean affinities in the material culture of the Early Iron Age city at Ekron, see "Introduction" (Section IV, B).

The biblical name *'ākîš* has been identified as the same name as that of Ikausu, a king of Ekron who is listed in an Akkadian text among the twelve kings of the seashore who carried to Nineveh building material for the palace of Esarhaddon, 680-669 B.C.,[45] and in the list of kings who participated in Ashurbanipal's first campaign to Egypt, in 667 B.C.[46] His father Padi is mentioned in the annals of Sennacherib.[47] This identification has been recently confirmed by the seventh-century Ekron inscription,[48] which mentions "Akhayus *('kyš),* son of Padi, . . . ruler *(šr)*[49] of Ekron" (line 1-2).[50]

Achish could be a title or a common name for a Philistine ruler, like "Pharaoh" for an Egyptian king; see on 27:2. Note that "Abimelech" in the title of Psalm 34 may be the Semitic name of *Achish* of Gath in the present incident. The Philistine "king" at Gerar at the time of Isaac (Gen. 26:1) is also called "Abimelech."[51]

For *Gath,* see on 5:8. It is located about 23 miles west-southwest of Nob, in a straight line.

11 Achish's servants notice David right away, who is here called *the king of the land (melek hā'āreṣ).* It may be that they simply recognized him as a "local chieftain" of the Israelite country. Or, since Achish was king of only one "city," they may have used the word "king" differently. Hertzberg explains that "the title, chosen by non-Israelites and enemies, is once again meant to underline the fact that the divine plan is inviolably bound up with

44. See S. Gitin, T. Dothan, and J. Naveh, "A Royal Dedicatory Inscription from Ekron," *IEJ* 47 (1997) 11; V. Sasson, "The Inscription of Achish, Governor of Ekron, and Philistine Dialect, Cult and Culture," *UF* 29 (1997) 627-39.

45. *ANET,* p. 291.

46. *ANET,* p. 294.

47. *ANET,* pp. 287-88; *CS,* II, p. 303.

48. Gitin, Dothan, and Naveh, "A Royal Dedicatory Inscription from Ekron," pp. 1-16; *CS,* II, 164.

49. On this term, see K. L. Younger, Jr., in *CS,* II, p. 164, n. 4. See also 1 Samuel 5.

50. See Gitin, Dothan, and Naveh, "A Royal Dedicatory Inscription from Ekron," pp. 8-11; J. Naveh, "Achish-Ikausu in the Light of the Ekron Dedication," *BASOR* 310 (1998) 35-37. According to Gitin, Dothan, and Naveh (p. 9, n. 29), "the equation Ikausu = *'ākîš* indicates that the vocalization should rather be *Ikayus,* which eventually leads us to *Akhayus,* i.e. *Akhaios* or 'Achaean', meaning 'Greek'." They conjecture "that the biblical *'ākîš* may be a reflection of Akhayus king of Ekron in the seventh century B.C.E."

51. Also see K. A. Kitchen in *POTT,* p. 67.

David."[52] In any case, Achish's officials immediately recognize David as the one who was praised by the couplet of 18:7.

Saul slew by thousands//and David by ten thousands! See 18:7; 29:5. It is interesting to note that the couplet is used by the Philistines in the exact form as in 18:7-8.

12-13 Realizing that he is known to them as their enemy hero, David becomes very much afraid of Achish. So, he behaves as if he were a madman. The expression *disguised his judgment* (*šnh [original *šnw] + *ṭaʿam* "change") means "to disguise one's judgment, sense" or "to play a part, feign madness";[53] also Ps. 34, title. Taking the final *w* of the verbal form *wyšnw* as an object suffix "him," that is, "anticipatory pronominal suffix,"[54] Driver translates "And he changed it, (even) his understanding"; on the other hand, McCarter alters the text to *wyšnh,* based on the LXX.[55] However, the *w* should be taken as a part of the verbal root; see Ugaritic *šnw;* see also on 2 Sam. 14:6. The MT may be thus explained as a shortened form: *wayšannô* < *wayyᵉšannaw* (*šnw, Pi.).

R. P. Gordon notes that "If, as is likely, madness was regarded with superstition, this will have worked to his advantage."[56]

14 With the deictic particle "lo!" the meaning of *ʾîš mištaggēaʿ* (lit., "a madman") should be *this madman,* spoken derisively. The root *šgʿ is occasionally used "to indicate the ecstatic behavior of prophets"; see 2 K. 9:11; Hos. 9:7; Jer. 29:26. The root is also used in Deut. 28:34 to indicate how the curses of the covenant would drive people crazy. In Akkadian, *šegû* refers to "an attitude taken up by lions, dogs, other animals and sometimes by women which may be best described as 'highly aggressive' — the opposite of peaceful."[57] In the same way, David would be a danger to society.[58]

15 *Am I in want of madmen . . . ?* This is a very ironic expression. Had Achish in fact already enough of them? For the term "in want of" (*ḥăsar:* adj. cstr.), see *HALOT,* p. 338. To enter Achish's *house* means to become a mercenary for the Philistines. For now, David is chased away from Achish's house. He will become their warrior later when the time is ripe; see chs. 27; 29.

52. Hertzberg, p. 183.

53. *HALOT,* p. 377.

54. G. A. Rendsburg, *Diglossia in Ancient Hebrew* (AOS 72; New Haven, Conn.: American Oriental Society, 1990), p. 127.

55. McCarter, p. 355.

56. R. P. Gordon, p. 172.

57. D. J. Wiseman, "'Is it peace?' — Covenant and Diplomacy," *VT* 32 (1982) 321. See *HALOT,* p. 1415.

58. Baldwin, p. 139, n. 1.

c. To the Cave of Adullam (22:1-2)

1 *And David went from there and escaped to the cave of Adullam. And his brothers and the entire household of his father heard and went down to him there.*
2 *And there gathered to him every man in straits and every man who had a creditor and every man with a bitter spirit. And he became a chief over them. And about four hundred men were with him.*

1 After being chased away by Achish from Gath, David makes a refuge in *the cave of Adullam* where his family members come down from Bethlehem. The clause *And David went from there* is a *wayqtl* of a movement verb signifying a transition; also in v. 3.

McCarter translates *cave (me*ʿ*ārat)* as "stronghold," following Wellhausen who emends the term to *mṣdt,* since he thinks that it was "probably a well-fortified hilltop like the stronghold of Zion" (2 Sam. 5:7 = 1 Chr. 11:5; cf. 2 Sam. 5:9).[1] However, there is really no justification for changing two letters. Also, this may not have been the "stronghold" in v. 4 (see below on vv. 4, 5). Adullam is listed as a city of Judah in Josh. 15:35, and the cave was probably nearby. Note that the superscriptions of Psalms 57, 142 mention "in the cave," but they may refer to the incident in 1 Sam. 24:4[3].[2]

Adullam ("closed-in place";[3] also 2 Sam. 23:13), modern Tell esh-Sheikh Madhkûr [MR150-117], is situated 10 miles east-southeast from Gath, about 16 miles south-west of Jerusalem. It is half way between Gath and Bethlehem.[4] It was a Judahite fortress city in the Shephelah (Josh. 15:33-35). In 2 Chr. 11:7 it is listed among the "cities for defense," built by Rehoboam in Judah.

David's *entire household* (*kol-bêt ʾābîw* lit., "all the house of his father") are in danger now; they come from Bethlehem to join him at Adullam.

2 There, to David, gather some four hundred men. The phrase *every man in straits (kol-ʾîš māṣôq)* refers to every man "in a hard-pressed situation."[5] *Creditor* means "professional moneylender."[6] For the phrase *a bitter spirit (mar-nepeš),* see on 1:10; cf. "was discontented" (NRSV; NIV). It is used for people like Hannah (1:10), the men of Ziklag (30:6), the homeless Danites (Judg. 18:25), David and his followers fleeing from Absalom

1. McCarter, p. 355; Wellhausen, pp. 123-24.
2. See K.-D. Schunck, "Davids 'Schlupfwinkel' in Juda," *VT* 33 (1983) 110-13.
3. See *HALOT,* p. 792.
4. See *ABD,* I, p. 81.
5. *HALOT,* p. 623.
6. See *HALOT,* p. 728.

("fierce, enraged" in 2 Sam. 17:8), etc. Thus, David becomes the leader of everyone who had suffered some kind of loss or deprivation and was discontented, disenchanted, and mistreated in the society. Therefore, they were passionate for change and were willing to share David's fate and do anything for David; see 2 Sam. 23:17.

d. To Mizpeh of Moab (22:3-4)

3 *And David went from there to Mizpeh of Moab and said to the king of Moab,*
"Please let my parents live[7] *with you until I know*
what God will do to/with me."
4 *And he led*[8] *them into the presence of the king of Moab.*
And they stayed with him all the time that David was in the stronghold.

3 *And David went from there* (= v. 1) is again a transition in the flow of discourse. David went with his elderly parents from Adullam to Mizpeh of Moab presumably by going up to the ridge, down to the Dead Sea, up to the plateau of Moab, and then to the fortress of Mizpeh. This would involve a movement of 0.6 miles down and another 0.6 miles up.

The location of *Mizpeh of Moab* is unknown; probably it was a Moabite royal city. Since Ruth, David's great-grandmother, was a Moabite woman (cf. Ruth 4:13-22), David thought that his elderly parents would be safer here than with him. Compare David with Idrimi of Alalakh, who fled to the people of Emar, his mother's relatives.[9] Note that Moab was one of Saul's enemies (see 1 Sam. 14:47) and would be willing to support any split that would weaken him. However, later, when David became king of Israel, he defeated Moab; see 2 Sam. 8:2.

What God will do to/with me is in keeping with David's faith in God who guides his life providentially, according to His will. David uses here God rather than "Yahweh" in expressing his faith to the non-Israelite king. During this time of hardship and uncertainty, David presumably sang Psalm 57, in which he prayed "Be exalted, O God, above the heavens; let your glory be over all the earth" (vv. 5, 11).

7. *yēṣē';* lit., "go out." McCarter (pp. 355-56) thinks "to go forth" (MT) is "inappropriate to the context." But this may be an abbreviated expression of "to go out and in," which probably means "to live."

8. *wayyanḥēm;* cf. "left" (NRSV; NASB; NIV); also Wellhausen, p. 124; Driver, p. 179; McCarter, p. 356, vocalizing *wynḥm* as *wayyannīḥēm* with Targ., Syr.

9. See "Autobiography of Idrimi" in *CS,* I, p. 479.

4 The *stronghold* here refers to an uncertain location, apparently not in Judah, as in v. 5 Gad instructs him "now, come to the land of Judah." Therefore, it is probably not the same as the cave of Adullam (v. 1). It could be an unspecified place in Moab or the other side of the Dead Sea, possibly Masada. As for the time reference in v. 4, *all the time that David was in the stronghold,* Hertzberg interprets it to mean "all the time until his unsettled life came to an end."[10] Klein would rather hold that David's parents stayed in Moab only for a short time and returned when David went back to Judah.[11] It is hard to determine just how long David's parents resided in Moab.

e. To the Forest of Hereth (22:5)

5 *And Gad, the prophet, said to David,*
"You shall not stay in the stronghold;[12]
now, come to the land of Judah!"
And David went and came to the Forest of Hereth.

5 *Gad, the prophet* was, like Nathan, one of the "court prophets" during David's reign, especially in the census episode; see 2 Sam. 24:11-19 = 1 Chr. 21:9-19; 29:29; 2 Chr. 29:25. Malamat notes that the *muḫḫûm*-prophets of Mari were possibly dependent on the royal court like Gad and Nathan (see on 2 Sam. 7:2).[13] It is not clear whether the prophet Gad was with David at this time. We can assume, however, that Gad was with David at least while David was in the Forest of Hereth; see on 1 Sam. 23:2.

The phrase *said to* may refer to a message delivered through messenger(s), and in this case it probably does. Note that *wayyō'mer* may introduce background, here "transitional," information (SETTING) in a narrative discourse; see "Introduction" (Section VI, A).

As for *now, come (lēk ûbā'tā-llᵉkā;* lit., "go and come to you!"), "to you" functions as something like an Akkadian ventive.[14] Note that the verb

10. Hertzberg, p. 184.

11. Klein, p. 223.

12. Also LXX. McCarter, following Klostermann, reads it as "Mizpeh," for "Adullam was certainly a part of Judah (Josh 15:33-35)" (p. 356).

13. A. Malamat, "Intuitive Prophecy — A General Survey," in *Mari and the Bible* (Leiden: E. J. Brill, 1998), p. 67.

14. See J. Huehnergard, *A Grammar of Akkadian* (HSS 45; Altanta: Scholars Press, 1997), §15.2 (pp. 133-34): "The ventive is essentially a directional element that denotes motion or activity in the direction of, or to a point near, the speaker (or a person being addressed, when the speaker places herself in the location of the person addressed)." See also on 20:20.

"come" is used from the viewpoint of Gad, who was in Judah (east of Adullam *or* west of the *stronghold*) and sent a messenger to David.

The Forest of Hereth is an unknown place. It may be compared with "Kharas," the name of a modern village near Khirbet Qîlā, which preserves the name of ancient Keilah. Wellhausen and others suggest that *Hereth* is an Aramaic variant of *Horesh* (23:15).[15] If this is correct, it is probably modern Khirbet Khoreisa [MR 162-095], about 2 miles from Tel Zîp.

2. Saul's Massacre of Nob's Priests (22:6-23)

This is the closing episode of 21:1–22:23, the consequence of 21:1-9 (David's escape to Nob).

a. Saul in Gibeah (22:6-10)

6 *And Saul heard that David and the men with him were known.*
— Now, Saul was sitting in Gibeah under the tamarisk on the height with his spear in his hand; all his servants were standing by[16] *him. —*
7 *And Saul said to his officials who were standing by him,*
"Listen! Benjaminites!
Is it to all of you yourselves
that the son of Jesse will give fields and vineyards?
Is it all of you that he will make
captains of thousands and captains of hundreds?
8 *For all of you have conspired against me;*
there was no one to reveal (it) to me
when my son made a covenant with the son of Jesse
and there was no one from among you to feel sorry[17] *for me*
and reveal to me
that my son caused my servant to rise against me as an ambush[18] *today."*[19]
9 *And Doeg the Edomite, who was standing by Saul's servants, answered:*
"I saw the son of Jesse.

15. Wellhausen, p. 124; Klein, p. 223.

16. *ʿālâw;* just like Baal who was by the side of *(ʿl)* El at the divine court; see *KTU* 1.2 I 21. JPS's "in attendance upon" is better than "standing around" (NRSV; NIV; NASB).

17. On *ḥōleh,* "to be sorry, think," see Barr, *CPTOT,* p. 326.

18. *leʾōrēb,* "to lie in wait"; ptc. refers to a person who lies in ambush.

19. *kayyôm hazzeh;* lit., "like this day."

He came to Nob,
to Ahimelech, the son of Ahitub,
who inquired of the Lord[20] *for him,*
while giving provisions to him
and giving the sword of Goliath the Philistine to him."

6 Saul was informed of the location of David and his men. Saul was then sitting under the tamarisk tree in Gibeah. The theme of "a ruler sitting in council under a sacred tree" (see on 14:2) is, as McCarter notes,[21] "a stock component of ancient Northwest Semitic narrative art." It is interesting to note with R. P. Gordon that the picture of a king here is "vastly different from the Solomonic ostentation of the late tenth century."[22] The same phrase is used when Saul was buried "under the tamarisk" at Jabesh (31:13).

The *tamarisk* is "a deciduous tree up to 20 feet in height with small, feathery leaves that excrete salt through special glands. . . . The pink flowers are followed by minute seeds. The wood was used for construction and as charcoal. The bark was used for tanning and the leaves as fodder."[23] Abraham planted one at Beersheba and called on the name of "the Lord, the everlasting God" in Gen. 21:33.

Saul also has his spear at hand in 18:10; 19:9; and 20:33. The *spear* symbolizes Saul's "kingship" or "kingly status," just like the "bow" and "mace" in the hands of Assyrian kings.[24]

7 David, despite everything, apparently retains his popularity with Saul's officers (18:5), who are unwilling to give Saul any information about him.

The term *gam (yourselves)* in the expression *Is it to all of you yourselves that. . . . Is it all of you? (gam-lᵉkullᵉkem . . . lᵉkullᵉkem)* functions as a "focusing *gam*"[25] rather than contrasting between the Benjaminites and the Judahites. By these rhetorical questions Saul tries to convey that since the Benjaminites will not have any hope of enriching themselves by feudal grants and appointments if the Judahite David should become king, they have no reason to support him. Saul avoids using the name "David" here out of contempt; nevertheless, he cannot ignore his rival, "the son of Jesse."

20. LXX has "God."

21. McCarter, p. 363.

22. R. P. Gordon, p. 173.

23. I. Jacob and W. Jacob, "Flora," in *ABD,* II, 804-6.

24. D. T. Tsumura, "The 'Word Pair', **qšt* and **mṭ,* in Habakkuk 3:9 in the Light of Ugaritic and Akkadian," in *Go to the Land I Will Show You: Studies in Honor of Dwight W. Young,* ed. J. Coleson and V. Mathews (Winona Lake, Ind.: Eisenbrauns, 1996), pp. 357-65.

25. See Andersen, p. 166.

The expressions *give fields and vineyards* and *make captains of thousands and captains of hundreds* are two of the consequences of the kingship predicted by Samuel (8:14, 12). Rainey notes that Saul's statement here takes for granted that professional warriors would be awarded estates. When David became a military vassal of Achish of Gath, he was given Ziklag, from which he probably gave grants to his troops.[26] See also the note on "mighty man . . . valiant man" (14:52).

8 Saul's suspicion is getting extreme: *conspired against me (qᵉšartem . . . ʿālay).* There is certainly no indication that Jonathan had caused David to *rise up against* Saul. On Absalom's revolt and conspiracy, see on 2 Sam. 15:12.

In the expression *made a covenant* (*bikrot;* lit., "in cutting") only the verb *krt is used; the word *brt* "a covenant," is omitted by brachylogy (see "Introduction" [Section VII, D]) as in 1 Sam. 11:2; 20:16; also 1 K. 8:9 = 2 Chr. 5:10. Saul appears to have learned more about the events described in 19:1-7 and is referring to the loyalty pact between David and Jonathan in 18:3; 20:8.

9 We were informed of Doeg's presence at Nob in 21:1-9.

The phrase *the Edomite* (also 21:7) is used three times (vv. 9, 18, 22) in this episode, probably to point out that it was a foreigner who betrayed David and killed the priests.[27]

Doeg *was standing by* as one of the royal guards; or "presiding over" Saul's retinue; "who was in charge of Saul's servants" (NRSV). It was not impossible that a foreigner like *Doeg the Edomite* should be in charge of the royal house. However, in 1 Sam. 22:7, the verbal phrase, *nṣb ʿl-, refers simply to the physical circumstances at that time: "standing by/around" or "being in the presence of," not necessarily "being in charge of."

Like Saul, Doeg avoids the name "David," using instead the phrase *the son of Jesse.*

10 For the phrase *inquired of the Lord (wayyišʾal-lô baYHWH),* see on 10:22. In 21:1-9 there is no reference to Ahimelech's consulting the Lord for David; hence, Doeg may be lying here. But he is accusing Ahimelech of helping David with the Lord, by inquiring presumably how he could achieve his aim. Not only does Doeg claim that Ahimelech inquired of God's will for David, but he calls the holy bread "provisions," and refers to "the sword of Goliath" — each statement more "military" than the next, increasing the listener's tension, provoking the suspicion that the priest was aiding David in military preparations against who else but Saul.

26. A. F. Rainey, "Institutions: Family, Civil and Military," in *RSP* 2, pp. 100-101.
27. R. P. Gordon, p. 174.

b. Saul Kills the Priests of Nob (22:11-19)

11 *And the king sent a man to call Ahimelech, son of Ahitub, the priest, and all of his father's house, the priests, who were in Nob.*
And all of them came to the king.
12 *And Saul said,*
"Listen, son of Ahitub!"
And he said,
"Here am I, my lord!"
13 *And Saul said to him,*
"Why have you and the son of Jesse conspired against me,
by giving him bread and a sword and consulting[28] *God for him,*
to rise against[29] *me as an ambush today?"*
14 *And Ahimelech answered the king:*
"But who among all of your servants can be trusted[30] *like David,*
the king's son-in-law and a commander[31] *over your bodyguard,*
who is honored in your house?
15 *Is it this time that I began consulting*[32] *God for him?*
Absolutely not!
May the king not accuse[33] *his servant*[34]
and any of my father's house!
For your servant does not know anything big or small
of all this."
16 *And the king said,*
"You shall surely die, Ahimelech,
you and all of your father's house!"
17 *And the king said to the runners who were standing by him,*
"Go around and kill the priests of the Lord!
For even their hand is with David,[35]

28. *wᵉšāʾôl;* inf. abs. in sequence after an infinitive construct, as in 25:26, 33; see GKC, §113e.

29. *ʾel* here is a variant of ʿal, followed by *qwm.

30.: *ʾmn (Ni.) appears in Samuel also at 1 Sam. 2:35 (x2); 1 Sam. 3:20; 1 Sam. 25:28; 2 Sam. 7:16.

31. *sār* for *śār;* cf. *archōn pantos paraggelmatos sou.* In David's own court, Benaiah, son of Jehoiada, was in charge of David's bodyguards (2 Sam. 23:23 = 1 Chr. 11:25). Cf. "is quick to do your bidding" (NRSV); "obedient to your bidding" (JPS).

32. K.: *lšʾwl* inf. abs. (not *šāʾûl;* cf. 13b); Q.: *lišʾol* inf. cstr.

33. *yāśēm bᵉ- dābār;* lit., "put a word in."

34. I.e., "me."

35. I.e., "they have sided with" (NIV); "they are in league with" (JPS).

for they knew that he was fleeing but did not reveal[36] *it to me!"*
But the servants of the king were unwilling to send their hands to fall upon the priests of the Lord.
18 *And the king said to Doeg,*[37]
"You go around and fall upon the priests!"
And Doeg the Edomite went around and he himself fell upon the priests and put to death on that day eighty-five men who were wearing the linen ephod.
19 *As for Nob, the city of the priests, he struck with the edge of the sword both man and woman,*[38] *both child and infant, and bull, ass, and sheep with the edge of the sword.*

11 Saul sends and brings Ahimelech and his priestly family members to Gibeah. The antecedent of *who were in Nob* is *all of his father's house,* rather than "the priests." The distance between Nob and Gibeah is not great — less than a few miles. They came to Gibeah with clear conscience; hence, *all of them came.*

12-13 Saul asks why Ahimelech and David conspired against him. For *conspired against me,* see v. 8. "In his paranoia the deluded king sees conspiracy everywhere."[39]

Here *consulting God* comes after *bread* and *a sword;* in v. 10 the order is "consulting the Lord" — "provisions" — "the sword of Goliath." Also note the variants: "bread" — "provisions"; "God" (also v. 15) — "the Lord."

14-15 Ahimelech's reply shows his complete innocence. He had helped David as the trusted servant of the king in carrying out a mission of the king (21:2, 8). Mabee, who studied this passage as a judicial account, points out that Ahimelech's answer is both a statement denying the heart of Saul's case — that his actions were part of a conspiracy — and part of the narrator's overall care to present David as blameless toward Saul.[40]

Who . . . like . . . ? — David is here considered to be *incomparable*[41] with any other servants of Saul. See also 21:9 and on 26:15; 2 Sam. 7:23.

36. *w*^{e}*lō' gālû 'et-'oznô;* Q.: *'oznî;* lit., "did not uncover my ear"; intentionally hid it from me. Cf. Hi. *ngd. See "Introduction" (Section VII, D).

37. *dwyg* (K.): dôyēg; Q.: dô'ēg; cf. *dō'ēg* in 1 Sam. 21:7. The K. is a phonetic spelling, reflecting the phonetic reality of <palatalization>: [ʼ] → [y].

38. *mē'îš w*^{e}*'ad-'iššāh;* lit., "from man to woman"; also 2 Sam. 6:19; see on 1 Sam. 6:18.

39. McCarter, p. 364.

40. See C. Mabee, "Judicial Instrumentality in the Ahimelech Story," in *Early Jewish and Christian Exegesis: Studies in Memory of William H. Brownlee,* ed. C. A. Evans and W. F. Stinespring (Atlanta: Scholars Press, 1987), p. 29, n. 30.

41. On the *incomparability* of Yahweh, see C. J. Labuschagne, *The Incomparability of Yahweh in the Old Testament* (POS 5; Leiden: E. J. Brill, 1966) and on 2:2.

Ahimelech refers to *David* by his name in contrast with Saul and Doeg, who use "son of Jesse" (vv. 7, 8, 9); see 1 Sam. 20:27.

Bodyguard (mišmaʿtekā) refers probably to "an intimate circle of royal retainers, i.e. a king's bodyguard";[42] see Moabite *mšmʿt* "body of subjects."[43]

16 Despite Ahimelech's declaration of his innocence, Saul sentences him to death. According to Mabee, this judgment is unjust because Saul has not proved his case against Ahimelech. To do so, he would have to first prove David's criminality. "Saul no longer has any legal claim to the throne. How could an unjust judge be king over Israel?"[44]

17 Then Saul commands his *runners* to kill the priests of the Lord. The term *runners (rāṣîm)* refers to palace bodyguards; also on 8:11; 2 Sam. 15:1. The first verb of *Go around and kill (sōbbû wᵉhāmîtû)* is a key term in this chapter; it reappears in vv. 18 (x2), 22; see on v. 22. They probably refused both because of the unjustness of the sentence given by the king, whose duty under God was to uphold justice, and the sacredness of the priests of the Lord. Here the *servants of the king* placed their fear of the Lord above their fear of the king.

18 Nobody except Doeg obeys the king and murders the priests. It may be that "Doeg, as a foreigner and (presumably) a non-Yahwist, has no religious scruple to prevent him from slaying the priests of Nob."[45] But then, why was he "detained before the Lord"? See on 1 Sam. 21:7. It is possible that Doeg's religiosity was only liturgical and formal and that he had neither respect for the priests nor fear of God.

The number of priests, *eighty-five,* is noteworthy; only Eli's family (and Samuel) are mentioned in the accounts in Shiloh.

The *linen ephod* was also worn by the young Samuel; see 2:18.

19 A central temple or a national shrine was apparently situated in Nob under Saul. Thus, it is possible that Ahimelech was then the chief priest there; see 21:1. In any case Nob was certainly the major religious center, *the city of the priests* in Saul's kingdom, where the ark of God could have been kept at least for a while; see 14:18.

Saul treated Nob like some enemy city that had been put under the "ban" (cf. 15:3). Thus, Saul carried out "total destruction" on the priests' city, while neglecting to put the Amalekites under a ban in ch. 15. See also Judg. 20:48; Deut. 13:16-17.[46] When they reject God and his "justice," human beings

42. McCarter, p. 364.

43. Gibson, *SSI* 1, p. 82.

44. Mabee, "Judicial Instrumentality in the Ahimelech Story," p. 31.

45. McCarter, p. 365.

46. See M. Weinfeld, "Zion and Jerusalem as Religious and Political Capital: Ideology and Utopia," in *The Poet and the Historian: Essays in Literary and Historical Biblical Criticism,* ed. R. E. Friedman (HSS 26; Chico, Calif.: Scholars Press, 1983), p. 79, n. 14.

can become cruel, totally destroying innocent people, and at the same time become tolerant toward the evil, letting them live on whether in war or in peace.

The phrase *with the edge of the sword (lᵉpî-ḥereb)* is a poetic repetition; hence, there is no need to omit it with LXX^B as McCarter (p. 363) does.

c. Abiathar Escapes to David (22:20-23)

20 *And one son of Ahimelech son of Ahitub, whose name was*
Abiathar, escaped and fled after David.
21 *And Abiathar informed David that Saul had slain the priests of the*
Lord.
22 *And David said to Abiathar,*
"I knew that day when Doeg the Edomite was there,
that he would surely inform Saul;
I am the one who is responsible for the death of every person in
your father's house!
23 *Stay with me! Do not be afraid!*
For he who seeks my life seeks your life;
surely you are under protection[47] *with me!"*

20 The Hebrew expression *bēn-'eḥād* can mean either *one son* or "the first son," taking the numeral "one" as an ordinal (see on 1 Sam. 1:2; 9:3). Thus, the narrative depicts Saul as the destroyer of the priesthood while David is its protector. Hertzberg regards this as the focal point of the chapter and says: "Whereas Saul is in this way alienating the priests, David gains possession of one, a 'real' priest, of the house of Eli."[48] We learn from 23:6 that Abiathar brought the ephod with him. Thus, the true priesthood and priestly counsel and the divine oracle have officially moved from Saul to David.

Abiathar ('ebyātār) or "Ebyathar" is the son of Ahimelech; see on 14:3. This priest of Yahweh will be associated with David throughout the remainder of his fugitive days (23:6, 9; 30:7; 1 K. 2:26) and for the rest of his life. He will eventually share the position of high priest with Zadok during David's reign; see 2 Sam. 20:25; also 15:24-36; 1 K. 4:4. But, later, Solomon will banish him "from being priest to Yahweh" and send him to Anathoth, because he sided with Adonijah over the succession issue (1 K. 1:7); "thus fulfilling the word of the Lord that he had spoken concerning the house of Eli in Shiloh" (2:27b; NRSV). He is the "only one man" who the Lord promised Eli in 1 Sam. 2:33 would not be cut off from Yahweh's altar.

47. *mišmeret 'attah;* lit., "you are guard/watch"; "protection," f.s., is an abstract noun used adverbially. See *HALOT,* p. 649: "in good care."

48. Hertzberg, p. 188.

Abiathar *escaped and fled* (*mlṭ . . . *brḥ), just like David (see on 19:12). Here, the word order is reversed.

According to 23:6, David was already in Keilah when Abiathar fled to him. This illustrates well the mono-dimensional nature of linguistic description; see "Introduction" (Section VII, C). The narrative traces the Nob incidence and its consequences, including Abiathar's escape to David (of course, he may not have gone directly to him). In 23:1 the narrative moves back to a point when David was not yet in Keilah, somewhere between the Forest of Hereth and Keilah. The narrative will then be focused on David; see 23:1.

21 Abiathar informs David of Saul's murder of the priests. *Saul had slain* by the hands of Doeg. Abiathar must have given David a detailed account of the incident. However, the narrator summarizes it in indirect speech, as *Saul had slain the priests of the Lord.* Here, what Doeg did for Saul is what Saul did. Thus, "Saul is presented as authority for the action."[49]

22 The Hebrew verb *yādaʿtî* in perfect is normally translated as "I know," but here, with a past time indicator *(that day),* it should be translated as *I knew* or "I realized."

When . . . that . . . (kî- . . . kî- . . .), or "since . . . , (that). . . ." The first *kî* clause modifies the preceding phrase "on that day." McCarter takes the MT as "a conflation of longer and shorter readings" and the shorter one as original. However, the shorter text is not necessarily original; see "Introduction" (Section II, B, 3). Moreover, the two *kî* function here differently: the former temporally, the latter as a noun clause indicator.

The independent pronoun *ʾānōkî* "I" is used here for emphasis or contrast, hence, *I am the one who* (cf. "you! go around and fall upon the priests!"). David accepted his responsibility when he was informed of how Doeg went around to slay the priests and others. Note the next comment on "to go around and do."

Is responsible for the death of every person (sabbōtî bᵉkol-nepeš): compare "I am responsible for the death of your father's whole family" (NIV; also JPS). The Qal of *sbb here is an intransitive verb which means literally, "went around with." It may be a shortened form of the key phrase in this episode, "went around [and fell] upon" (see v. 17); David here hints at his responsibility by mentioning only the first part of the key phrase euphemistically. Even though it was Doeg who "went around and fell upon the priests" (v. 18), David acknowledges that it was he who "went around" and *did* that. Does the verb *sbb mean "to go around the area in order to control or occupy" so that the area may become "untouchable," that is, "taboo"? R. P. Gordon holds that the repetition of the term *sbb "would very effectively

49. E. J. Revell, "Concord with Compound Subjects and Related Uses of Pronouns," *VT* 43 (1993) 84.

make the point that David is indirectly responsible for the tragedy."[50] McCarter translates "responsible for," reading *'nky hbty* with LXX^{B}.[51]

23 David asks Abiathar to stay with him. The reference to Abiathar's being *with* David prepares the reader for the subsequent events, in which the former plays an important role in inquiring the will of God for David in ch. 23 and after. As R. P. Gordon notes, this tragic incident "paved the way for the elevation of Jerusalem to the status of chief sanctuary-city in Israel."[52] Thus, through this tragedy God's saving plan is materialized step by step, though the human agents are not necessarily aware of it.

In the present episode we can see another account of "the gradual exposition of the relationship between Saul and David." It contrasts Saul as the destroyer of the priesthood of Nob with David as its preserver who saves "the cult of Yahweh from formal extinction in Israel." The following episodes continue to contrast Saul, who chases David without priestly guidance, with David, who is "guided by the divine oracle at every turn."[53]

3. David's Further Escapes (23:1-14)

a. To Keilah (23:1-13)

The local people inform David of the Philistines' attack on Keilah. David inquires of the Lord about his response, presumably through the prophet Gad (see 22:5), since Abiathar is not with David at this point; see v. 6. Note that David has sought God's will (see 22:15) and been guided by Yahweh even before Abiathar's arrival; see on 22:20. Too much emphasis has been given to Abiathar's arrival as if "the divine oracle is now David's ally to guide him into safety."[1] In 22:5 the prophet Gad had already instructed David to come to the land of Judah. And the spirit of the Lord who had been on David since the time of his anointing (16:13) could have conveyed a divine answer directly, though this would have been exceptional; cf. 2 Sam. 23:2: "The Spirit of the LORD spoke through me; his word was on my tongue."

After Abiathar joined David at Keilah, David consulted the divine oracle through the priest who carried the ephod (v. 9). Thus, David received advice from Yahweh through the prophet and the priest as well as information from the local people. On the other hand, Saul's only help was from local informants; see 1 Sam. 23:7, 13, 19; 24:1; 26:1. Without God's help all highly

50. R. P. Gordon, p. 175. For a defense of the MT, see P. A. H. de Boer, "Research into the Text of I Samuel xviii–xxxi," *OTS* 6 (1949) 43.

51. McCarter, p. 363.

52. R. P. Gordon, p. 172.

53. See McCarter, pp. 366-67.

1. McCarter, p. 371.

sophisticated human effort and information are in vain. Just when everything has finally worked out and Saul is in a position to seize David, he is forced to break off because of a Philistine raid (v. 27), which was doubtless brought about providentially by the Lord to protect David; see on v. 14b. Note that Yahweh no longer answered Saul "even by dreams or lots or prophets" (28:6).

(1) David Inquires of the Lord (23:1-4)

1 *And David was informed,*
"Now, Philistines are fighting against Keilah;
they are plundering the threshing floors!"
2 *And David inquired of the Lord, saying,*
"Shall I go and strike these Philistines?"
And the Lord said to David,
"Go and strike the Philistines
and save Keilah!"
3 *And the men of David said to him,*
"As for us, even here in Judah we are afraid.
How much more so if we go to Keilah
to the ranks of Philistines?"
4 *And David again inquired of the Lord.*
And the Lord answered him:
"Arise, go down to Keilah!
For I am going to give the Philistines in your hand."

1 *And David was informed (wayyaggīdû l^{e}dāwīd;* lit., "they informed David") means that the local people informed David, who was presumably somewhere between the Forest of Hereth and Keilah; see on 22:20 and v. 6 below. Note that Saul also "was informed" by the local people in v. 7.

Keilah is probably modern Khirbet Qîlā [MR 150-113], which is located about 3 miles south of Adullam (see 22:1), some 8 miles northwest of Hebron, and due east of Gath; it seems to appear as "Kelti" in the Amarna letters. Though Keilah is listed among cities of Judah (Josh. 15:44), at that time it was at least near enough the Philistine border to be contrasted with Judah. Also, it is possible that the town is at least Israelite, if not Judahite, because David probably would not have inquired about saving it if it had been unrelated to Israel. He certainly doesn't mind raiding non-Israelite places in ch. 27.

This *plundering the threshing floor* may have occurred at harvest time (Judg. 6:11).

2 David *inquired of* (*š'l b-; 1 Sam. 30:8; 2 Sam. 2:1; 5:19, 23; also

1 Sam. 28:6) of the Lord. This happened before the priest Abiathar arrived;[2] see v. 6 and 1 Sam. 22:20. In the ancient Near East, people inquired of their deities before going out for war. On a military query to the solar god, see Akk. *ša'ālu* "to ask."[3] Here, however, David had no obligation to fight against the Philistines, the enemy of Saul, and, in particular, Keilah was not a Judahite city then; see below. But David could not keep himself away from the trouble just a few miles away, though to others his "military intervention" looked crazy.

The term *save* (*yšʿ: Hi.) is used in 1 Samuel for deliverance by the Lord (e.g., 7:8; 14:23; cf. 4:3) or by a human leader (e.g., 9:16).

3 The phrase *here in Judah* implies that Keilah was not within the Judahite limits at this time; see v. 12.

Though BHS lists no MS variant for the MT reading *maʿarkôt (ranks),* McCarter emends the text to *ʿl yrkty* on the basis of LXX and translates as "deep in the recesses,"[4] which would contrast expressly with *here in Judah.* But, the MT as it is makes good sense. The phrase expresses well "the terror felt by David's men."[5]

4 David inquires of the Lord for the second time. Here *again* signifies that the same inquiry is made twice in order to make it sure that it was indeed the Lord's direction. The same double inquiry was made by Gideon (Judg. 6:36-40), who needed reassurance with regard to the will of the Lord. David was not silenced by the negative advice of his close friends, for he was putting his eyes on the Lord, not the outward circumstances. It is the Lord who would bring victory over the Philistines. Regardless of human conditions God can still use the works of David and his men, for the battle is the Lord's (see 1 Sam. 17:47).

Arise, go down (qûm rēd): The Forest of Hereth (see 22:5) was either at a higher elevation than Keilah or located on a hill; therefore, David and his men were supposed to "go down" from the place where they were; see on vv. 6, 8, 11. The Lord assured David that he will *give* the Philistines *into his hand.*

(2) David Saves Keilah (23:5-6)

5 *And David and his men went to Keilah and fought against the Philistines and carried off their property and struck them severely.*

2. R. P. Gordon, p. 176; cf. Baldwin, p. 142: "[vv. 1-5] David depended on the direction of Abiathar."

3. I. Starr, ed., *Queries to the Sungod: Divination and Politics in Sargonid Assyria* (SAA 4; Helsinki: Helsinki University Press, 1990), p. 351 (Glossary).

4. McCarter, p. 369.

5. Klein, p. 230.

Thus David saved the inhabitants of Keilah.

6 — *When Abiathar, son of Ahimelech, fled to David at Keilah, with an ephod he came down*[6] —

5 Convinced by God's answer, David obeyed God's command and acted by trusting on God's promise *I am going to give the Philistines in your hand* (v. 4). The *wayqtl* followed by a stated subject *David* initiates a new subparagraph. Here, the sentence summarizes the various actions: "went" — "fought" — "drove off" — "struck."

The verb *went* is singular, followed by the compound subject *David and his men.* All the subsequent verbs, that is, "fought," "drove off," "struck" and "saved," are also in the singular. Thus, the narrator "draws attention to actions relevant to the picture of David as a daring and successful leader."[7] Contrast v. 13.

Here *property* means "cattle"; see "livestock" (NRSV; NIV). The presence of Philistine cattle at Keilah has puzzled the exegetes. It may be that the cattle were brought along "to forage for what was left on the threshing floors"[8] or "to transport the grain."[9] No real solution is possible.

6 For *Abiathar, son of Ahimelech,* see 22:20.

Many commentators think that this verse is in "somewhat awkward position" and hence take it as "a gloss added to link Abiathar's use of the ephod in v. 9 with his arrival in 22:20."[10] They thus translate it, by emending in light of the LXX, "Now when Abiathar . . . fled to David, he had gone down with David to Keilah, taking an ephod with him."[11] With this translation this verse certainly serves "to smooth over the transition from vv. 1-5, where the oracle is operated anonymously, to vv. 7-13, where Abiathar is in charge." And it even "prepares the reader for the appearance of Abiathar and the ephod in vv. 9ff and also tightens the connection between the present episode and the foregoing."[12] Nevertheless, this interpretation is based on an emended and "improved" text on the basis of the LXX.

On the other hand, Althann translates the MT: "And it happened that after Abiathar the son of Ahimelech had fled to David, he brought an ephod

6. Rather than "went down," for the narrator's viewpoint must be already in Keilah; see also vv. 8, 11.

7. E. J. Revell, "Concord with Compound Subjects and Related Uses of Pronouns," *VT* 43 (1993) 84.

8. McCarter, p. 371.

9. Hertzberg, p. 191.

10. Klein, p. 229.

11. McCarter, p. 368; also Klein, p. 227; Hertzberg, p. 189.

12. McCarter, p. 372.

to Keilah in his hand," taking the preposition *b* as "after."[13] Yet this interpretation is a little forced. The MT as it stands makes sense, however, since 22:20 does not state where David was when Abiathar joined him.[14] This explanatory (parenthetical) sentence would not lead us to take the incidents in vv. 1-5 as happening after Abiathar's arrival; see v. 2. David must have been directed either by the prophet Gad or through other means.

In Keilah, with Abiathar and the oracular *ephod* (see on 14:3), David has now "a more sure means of ascertaining the will of Yahweh."[15] One might assume that the Urim and Thummim (see 14:41) are employed here, since the answers in vv. 11b and 12b are essentially of the "yes" or "no" type. See on 10:20-22.

(3) Saul Is Informed (23:7-8)

7 *And it was told to Saul that David had come to Keilah.*
And Saul said,
"God has alienated him from himself into my hand,
for he is shut up by entering a city with doors and a bar."
8 *And Saul summoned the entire people to war, to come down to*
Keilah and to besiege[16] *David and his men.*

7 When Saul was informed that David had gone to Keilah, he in haste believed and judged that God had delivered David into his hands. Saul's belief that God was on his side turns out to be wrong. Without God's help and guidance we can certainly misjudge a situation and hold the wrong conviction about God's dealings with us.

The verb *has alienated* (*nikkar;* Pi. *nkr) is a denominative verb from the noun "foreigner" and takes a subject and two types of objects (and so has a valency of 3); that is, A estranges B from A to lead B into C. Compare "has given" (NRSV); "has delivered" (JPS); "has handed him over to me" (NIV); *pepraken* "he sold" (LXX).[17]

For *with doors and a bar (d^elātayim ûb^erîaḥ),* see Judg. 16:3; Jer. 49:31; etc. Sometimes only "a bar," as a *pars pro toto,* is mentioned, as in

13. R. Althann, "Northwest Semitic Notes on Some Texts in 1 Samuel," *JNSL* 12 (1984) 33.

14. See Ackroyd, p. 181.

15. R. P. Gordon, p. 176.

16. *lāṣûr;* lit., "to shut in to . . ."; i.e., "to shut in (the city) with regard to . . . ," with brachylogy of "the city"; see "Introduction" (VII, D) on the brachylogy.

17. See *HALOT,* p. 699. Barr posits the meaning "to acquire, sell" for the root *nkr; see Barr, *CPTOT,* p. 331.

Amos 1:5. Note that Sennacherib besieged Hezekiah in Jerusalem "like a bird in a cage."[18] Note the similar situation in 2 Sam. 20:15ff.

8 The term *summoned* (*šmʿ: Pi.; lit., "cause s.o. to hear," "to assemble") appears only here and 1 Sam. 15:4. In the latter Saul summoned "two hundred thousands = foot soldiers and ten thousands = the men of Judah." Here too we can see Saul's overreaction to David. He summoned the *entire people,* that is, two hundred thousands (?), against David's six hundred men (see v. 13) to *besiege* them in Keilah and *destroy* the city (see v. 10).

(4) David Again Inquires of the Lord (23:9-12)

9 *And David knew that against him Saul was devising evil and said*
to Abiathar, the priest,
"Bring the ephod!"
10 *And David said,*
"O Lord, God of Israel!
Your servant has indeed heard
that Saul is seeking
to come to Keilah,
to destroy the city because of me.
11 *Will the citizens*[19] *of Keilah deliver me up to his hand?*
Will Saul come down
as your servant has heard?
O Lord, God of Israel,
inform your servant!"
And the Lord said,
"He will come down."
12 *And David said,*
"Will the citizens of Keilah deliver me and my men up
to Saul's hand?"
And the Lord said,
"They will deliver (you) up."

9 David recognized that Saul was devising evil against *him* and not against *the Philistines.* The phrase *against him (ʿālâw)* is preposed the nucleus of the sentence for emphasis.

10-11 David's inquiry in a direct speech here is poetic prose (see

18. Note that the expression "like a bird in a cage" often appears in similar contexts in the royal annals of Assyria; see *CS,* II, p. 303, n. 9.

19. *baʿălê* (lit., "lords").

"Introduction" [Section VII, B]), constituting a chiastic structure; hence, there is no need to think that vv. 11-12 are "corrupt."[20]

A *O Lord, God of Israel!*
B *Your servant has indeed heard*
C that Saul is seeking
D to come to *Keilah,*
E to destroy the city because of me.
D′ (11) Will the lords of *Keilah*
deliver me up to his hand?
C′ Will Saul come down
B′ *as your servant has heard?*
A′ *O Lord, God of Israel,*
inform your servant!

10 David uses the full expression *O Lord, God of Israel* in this formal prayer, while humbly approaching God by using *your servant* for himself.

Note that the verb *to destroy* (*šḥt) is a denominative verb from "a pit,"[21] hence, "pit of destruction" (//"Sheol"). It is noteworthy that this verbal phrase is situated in the middle of the chiastic structure.

11 Since the question *Will the lords of Keilah deliver me up to his hand?* does not occur in the 4QSam^b version,[22] McCarter thinks that vv. 11-12 are "corrupt in all witnesses except (apparently) 4QSam^b."[23] Taking the MT as "a dittograph from v 12 incorrectly inserted," he translates: "Now then, will Saul come down as your servant has heard? O Yahweh, god of Israel! Inform your servant!" However, as noted above, vv. 10-11 constitute a unified structure, and there is no reason why one should take a shorter text always as original.

Here the verb *yrd, usually "to go down," must mean *come down,* for it is used from the speaker's point of view and its destination is his place. Possibly the verb *yrd "to go down" is a goal-oriented term like the verb *bw' "to come," which is concerned with the movement "to this place"; see "Introduction" (Section VI, D). See also vv. 4, 6, 8.

12 Why would the citizens of Keilah act so ungratefully towards David? Saul had destroyed Nob on a much lesser pretext, and so he was cer-

20. McCarter, p. 370.

21. See *HALOT,* pp. 1469-71; cf. BDB, p. 1001, which traces the term "pit" to the verb "sink down" *šwḥ.

22. See F. M. Cross, Jr., "The Oldest Manuscripts from Qumran," *JBL* 74 (1955) 171.

23. McCarter, p. 370. See Cross, "Oldest Manuscripts," pp. 173-75.

tainly willing and presumably able to destroy Keilah. From their standpoint, David had gotten them into much more trouble than he had saved them from. The Philistines, after all, had only gone after grain. (See 2 Sam. 20:15ff.)

(5) David Leaves Keilah (23:13)

13 *And David and his men, about six hundred of them, arose and went*
out of Keilah and wandered wherever they could.[24]
When[25] *Saul was told that David had escaped from Keilah, he*
ceased to go out.

13 Accepting the words as the answer from God, David acted accordingly. The phrase *arose and went out* suggests David's immediate action. They *wandered,* trusting on the divine guidance for each step without knowing where to go in the long run. This is typical in the life of believers, who are sojourners in this world. For *six hundred* the LXX has "four hundred," possibly under the influence of 22:2. It is not unreasonable, however, to think that by now the number of David's men had grown by two hundred (cf. 25:13). Here the verbs are plural, in contrast to v. 5.

b. To the Wilderness of Ziph (23:14)

14 *Thus David lived in the wilderness, in the strongholds;*
and he lived in the mountain in the wilderness of Ziph.
And Saul sought after him day after day,[26] *but God did not give*
him into his hand.

14 This verse is a transition from the previous episode of the Keilah incident to the following episode of the Ziph incident. Though McCarter takes this passage as a preface to the story of David's sparing Saul's life in 23:19–24:22, the phrase *the wilderness of Ziph* points to a more immediate context, that is, 23:15–24:1.

The first two clauses have a parallel structure, *the wilderness of Ziph* being a "ballast variant" of *the wilderness* to balance the stated subject *(David)* in the first clause. The repetition of *he lived* and *wilderness* and the cor-

24. *wayyithallᵉkû ba'ăšer yithallākû;* lit., "and they went about where they went about." See 2 Sam. 15:20: ". . . and I am going where I am going," that is, "when I go wherever I may go." For further examples of the idiom in biblical Hebrew and related languages, see Driver, pp. 185-86; also J. A. Soggin, "*wayyithalleku ba'ašer yithallaku,* 1 Samuel 23,13a," in *Old Testament and Oriental Studies* (Rome: Pontifical Biblical Institute, 1975), pp. 235-36.

25. *ûlᵉšā'ûl;* disjunctive *waw* — a chronologically backward movement.

26. *kol-hayyāmîm;* lit., "all the days."

respondence of *strongholds//mountain,* as well as the chiasmus *(wilderness — strongholds//mountain — wilderness),* make the verse "poetic prose" (see "Introduction" [Section VII, B]). David was like Idrimi, who escaped "in the desert" and then "to the land of Canaan."[27]

Ziph is usually identified with Tell Zîp [MR 162-048], situated about 5 miles south-southeast of Hebron, about 12 miles southeast of Keilah. From Keilah to the wilderness of Ziph, David went up eastward toward Hebron on the ridge, and then beyond, toward the more hilly country, which drops down sharply toward En Gedi (see 24:1).

With *but God* the narrator contrasts Saul and God, summing up the theological deduction to be drawn from the account: the Lord was with David, and so God did not give him into Saul's hand.

4. Jonathan, Saul, and David (23:15-29)

a. Jonathan Comes to Horesh (23:15-18)

15 *And David saw*[28] *that Saul had gone out to seek after his life.*
Then David was in the wilderness of Ziph, in Horesh.
16 *And Jonathan, son of Saul, arose and went to David at Horesh and encouraged him by God*
17 *and he said,*
"Do not be afraid!
For the hand of Saul, my father, cannot find you;
it is you who will be king over Israel,
but I shall be next to you.
Even Saul, my father, knows so."
18 *And the two of them made a covenant before the Lord.*[29]
And David stayed in Horesh, while Jonathan went back to his house.

15 David sees that Saul has gone out to murder him. At that time he was wandering in the wilderness of Ziph. The phrase *in Horesh (baḥōršāh)* means "in the Wood." It is probably modern Khirbet Khoreisa, about 2 miles from Tel Zîp. A smaller "woods" or "a grove" was possible around there. According to Hareuveni, in Maon there was probably a grove of pine trees that grew easily in the kind of soil there.[30]

27. See "Autobiography of Idrimi" in *CS,* I, p. 479.

28. *wayyar';* or "learned"; cf. McCarter: "was afraid."

29. On the significance of this phrase *before the Lord,* see R. P. Gordon, p. 349, n. 89.

30. N. Hareuveni, *Desert and Shepherd in Our Biblical Heritage* (Neot Kedumim: Biblical Landscape Reserve in Israel, 1991), p. 33.

16 Jonathan comes to see David and encourages him *by God* (lit., "in God"). One can only guess how dangerous it was for Jonathan at this time to visit David, whose life his father *had gone out to seek after,* but how encouraging Jonathan's visit was to David at this hard time. David needed such encouragement from the one who, like him, trusts on God (see 14:6; cf. 17:47) and lives accordingly. This is the last recorded meeting of Jonathan with David. The next mention of Jonathan is the report of his death in battle at Gilboa (31:2; 2 Sam. 1:4).

The expression *encouraged him (wayḥazzēq 'et-yādô;* lit., "strengthened his hand"; see Neh. 6:9; Job 4:3; Ezek. 13:22; etc.) is used for encouraging the fearful. R. P. Gordon notes that the addition of *by God* is "unique" for this expression in the Old Testament. "David is bidden to consider the power and purpose of God. . . ."[31] Jonathan's friendship with David "in God" was certainly based on his unselfish love and faithfulness to his covenant with David; see 1 Sam. 18:1; 19:1; 20:8, 17, 23, 42.

17 Not only does Jonathan assure David that Saul *cannot find* him, but he accepts that David is the one who will become king of Israel, and he himself is *next to* David. By the expression *but I shall be next to you ('ehyeh-lᵉkā lᵉmišneh),* Jonathan, who is now seemingly more mature and realistic than before (see 20:2), explicitly acknowledges David's *future destiny,* that is, that David will be king over Israel, and expects "nothing more for himself than the position of second-in-command";[32] see 20:13-15. Baldwin aptly comments: "far from being downcast, he remains optimistic about the outcome because he is so sure that the Lord is bringing about a new era, with David at the helm."[33] Jonathan was certainly able to see that the Lord was with David (cf. 18:28). Note the sharp contrast expressed by the use of two independent pronouns: "you" and "I."

On *mišneh (next to),* see Esth. 10:3, where it is said that Mordecai was "second in rank" to King Xerxes. In 2 Chr. 28:7 the expression "second to the king" ("the King's Second-in-Command")[34] appears as a title together with "the king's son" (the crown prince) and "the officer in charge of the palace."

Saul, my father, knows so: this is confirmed by Saul himself later, in 1 Sam. 24:21[20]. Even here Jonathan adds *my father* to *Saul,* admitting the fact that his own father was the enemy of his best friend, trying to kill him; note the narrator's use of *son of Saul* in v. 16. Jonathan repeats the phrase *Saul, my father* both in the beginning and at the end of his short speech. Such a repetition *(inclusio)* not only makes this speech vivid and poetic but, at the

31. R. P. Gordon, p. 177.
32. McCarter, p. 375.
33. Baldwin, p. 143.
34. McCarter, p. 374.

same time, conveys his sincere readiness to accept, not reject, his relationship with his father Saul. Jonathan was convinced that God, whom both he and David trust, will protect David from his father's hand.

18 Then Jonathan and David *made a covenant* (*krt + *b^{e}rît*) — here the earlier "friendship pact" (18:3; 20:8, 12-17, 42) is renewed *before the Lord,* with the Lord as witness, as earlier. So this was a real encouragement to David.

b. Ziphites Inform Saul (23:19-24a)

19 *And Ziphites went up to Saul at Gibeah, saying,*
"Isn't David hiding with us
in the strongholds of Horesh,
namely, in the hill of Hachilah,
which is south of Jeshimon?
20 *And now, according to all the desire of your soul,*
O king, to come down, come down!
It is to us[35] *to deliver him up into the hand of the king."*
21 *And Saul said,*
"May you be blessed by the Lord,
for you have compassion on me!
22 *Go and make sure*[36] *again;*
and know and see the place where his foot is.
Who saw him[37] *there?"*
— For he said/thought, "Toward me he will be indeed shrewd" —
23 *"And see and know every hiding place where he may be hidden;*
and return to me assuredly
and I will go with you.
And if he is[38] *in the land,*
I will search for him in all the clans of Judah."
24a *And they arose and went to Ziph ahead of Saul.*

35. *w^{e}lānû.* McCarter (p. 377) reads *'lynw* with 4QSam^b (cf. Smith) and translates: "It will be our task."

36. *hākînû;* "make firm" → "make it sure"; cf. "make ready" (BDB, p. 466). McCarter reads *hbynw* "with Syr. and a few Hebrew MSS" and translates: "investigate" (p. 377).

37. McCarter takes *Who saw him . . . ? (my r'hw)* as "a corruption of *mhrh,* 'quickly,' as preserved in the *Vorlage* of LXX *(en tachei),*" on the basis of which he restores *hmhrh,* "swift, fleet," with Wellhausen, p. 129, and Hertzberg, p. 192; see McCarter, p. 377.

38. *He is (yešnô)* is "the construction with a suffixed direct object"; see Lipinski, *SLOCG,* §49.23 (p. 479).

19 The Ziphites, though they belonged to the tribes of Judah, came and informed Saul of David's group, for "they may not have welcomed the idea of such a large contingent of freebooters in their neighbourhood."[39] *Ziphites* is here without an article (cf. "the Ziphites" in 26:1). Psalm 54 [title verse] refers to this occasion. The Ziphites were to David "the insolent and ruthless ones" (see Ps. 54:3); for his part he could say "God is my helper" (v. 4).[40]

For the word pair, *strongholds//hill (mᵉṣādôt//gibʿāh),* see v. 14 where "strongholds" *(mᵉṣādôt)* and "mountain" *(har)* are paired. Note that "mountain" and "hill" are paired words in Hebrew and Ugaritic: for example, *ṣûr// ǵr — gbʿ* or *ḫlb.*[41] Hence, read *namely.*

On *Hachilah . . . Jeshimon (haḥăkîlāh . . . hayšîmôn),* see also 26:1. Their locations are not known, but they are probably near Maon (v. 24) and somewhere south and east of Hebron.

20 The phrase *according to all the desire of your soul . . . to come down* means "whenever you wish to come down." *O king* is inserted as a vocative. McCarter thinks that both *ʾwt* and *npš* can mean "desire" and hence "represent a conflation of variants."[42] But the latter term, which can also mean "throat,"[43] refers to the place where desire is located; hence, "desire of a soul" is perfectly acceptable.

21 Saul is so pleased with their willingness to *deliver* David *up* into his hand. *You have compassion on me (ḥămaltem ʿālāy)* are words which a king would not normally speak to his subjects. His authority as a leader of the Israelites has now gone, and he only clings to his position for self-preservation. On this phrase, *ḥml *ʿal,* see also 15:3, 9, 15.

22 *For he said/thought, "Toward me he will be indeed shrewd"* is a parenthetical sentence, supplied by the narrator, since it is interrupting the flow of Saul's speech.

23 The phrase *assuredly (ʾel-nākôn;* lit., "for certain, with certainty") means "with sure information";[44] see "with certainty" (NASB). Compare the same expression in 26:4.

For *clans of (ʾalpê);* so NIV; JPS; cf. "regions" (*HALOT,* p. 60); "thousands" (NRSV; NASB). As in 10:19, ʾelep stands for "a clan"; "military units" would not make much sense here.[45]

39. R. P. Gordon, p. 177.

40. See Baldwin, p. 143.

41. See M. Dahood in *RSP* 1, p. 306.

42. McCarter, p. 377.

43. See *HALOT,* pp. 711-13; *NIDOTTE,* 3, p. 133.

44. McCarter, p. 378; Driver, p. 189.

45. B. E. Scolnic, *Theme and Context in Biblical Lists* (SFSHJ 119; Atlanta: Scholars Press, 1995), p. 33.

c. David in the Wilderness of Maon (23:24b-28)

24b *Then David and his men were in the wilderness of Maon, in the desert south of Jeshimon.*
25 *And Saul and his men went to search.*
And the people informed David (of it) and he went down to the crag and lived in the wilderness of Maon.
And Saul heard and pursued David in the wilderness of Maon.
26 *And Saul went to the one side of the mountain, while David and his men, to the other side of the mountain.*
When David was hurriedly going away from Saul, while Saul and his men were surrounding David and his men to lay hold of them,
27 *a messenger came to Saul, saying,*
"Hurry and go,
for Philistines have made a raid on the land!"
28 *And Saul turned back from pursuing David and went toward the Philistines.*
Therefore they called that place the Crag of the Divisions.

The narrative conveys vividly the situation of David and his group. This vividness, however, comes not from the accumulation of adjectives or adverbs (only *hurriedly*) but from the very simple structure of the narration itself. Note that Saul and David are mentioned repeatedly, indicating that Saul's pursuit of David is very persistent. (The underlined words are stated subjects.)

24.	*Saul*		<u>David</u>			
25.	<u>*Saul*</u>	David	<u>*Saul*</u>	David		
26.	<u>*Saul*</u>	<u>David</u>	<u>David</u>	*Saul*	<u>*Saul*</u>	David
27.	*Saul*					
28.	<u>*Saul*</u>	David				

24b David and his men are in the wilderness of Maon. *Maon (Māʿôn)* is the hometown of Nabal (25:2) and is situated on top of a hill surrounded by grazing fields. It is identified with Tell Maʿîn [MR 162-090], about 7 miles south of Hebron, 5 miles south of Ziph, and 9 miles from Arad. It is in the southeastern mountain district of Judah, together with Ziph (Josh. 15:55). Aharoni suggests that later, at the time of Arad inscriptions, Arad, ʿAnim, and Maʿon were in one administrative district (Ziph).[46] See Arad 25:4.

46. See Y. Aharoni, *Arad Inscriptions* (JDS; Jerusalem: Israel Exploration Society, 1981), p. 51.

25-26 Saul and his men come to search for David, who is informed of it and tries to escape from him. Saul goes *to the one side of the mountain;* David, *to the other.* Saul's army was *surrounding (ʿōṭ^erîm),* or "circling in" (McCarter, p. 378), around the mountain in order to capture David, who was on the other side. "Saul is advancing toward David around the mountain from both directions in a kind of pincer[s] movement. David, though 'hurrying to get away,' is trapped and cannot hold out for long."[47]

27-28 At the right moment, *a messenger came* providentially, although as if by chance. Saul returns to fight against the Philistines. *Therefore* the place is called *the Crag of the Divisions.* The Hebrew phrase *selaʿ hammaḥl^eqôt* can mean either *the Crag of the Divisions* or "Crag of Dissention." The former would signify "Saul and David there parting from the neighborhood of one another,"[48] while the latter would signify "the place where dissenting parties struggled with one another." McCarter rather takes the term not from *ḥālaq* "to divide," but from *ḥālaq* "be slippery, smooth" and explains the phrase as originally meaning something like "Slippery Rock" (see BDB, p. 325) or "Bald Mountain."[49] Klein thinks that "the biblical writer is probably recording only a popular etymology."[50] In the present context, though, the meaning "the crag of the divisions" would fit regardless of any "popular" or "learned" etymologies. The rock was named after this incident in which God divided David and Saul providentially.

Hareuveni says "the story is so exact in its description that I believe it enables us to identify the specific location where the events occurred, called 'Mt. Kholed' on today's maps. This hill has a sharp knifelike ridge about one and a quarter kilometers long, with steep slopes on both sides. . . . While David was on the eastern slope on his way into the wadis leading down to the Dead Sea, Saul, on the other slope divided his force into two flanks 'trying to encircle David and his men and capture them.' . . . Because David's direction lay east through open country, Saul's men could have easily captured David's men."[51] Thus ends one of the most dramatic incidents in 1 Samuel. Behind all these "happenings" one can certainly recognize God's strong hand of guidance in David's life.

47. McCarter, pp. 378-79.
48. Driver, pp. 190-91.
49. McCarter, p. 379.
50. Klein, p. 232.
51. Hareuveni, *Desert and Shepherd in Our Biblical Heritage,* pp. 33-34.

Hinge (23:29)

29 *And David went up from there and lived in the strongholds of En-gedi.*

29 [24:1 Jewish numbering] This verse has been explained either as the end of the present episode or as the beginning of the next episode. In fact, there are two traditions, Jewish and Christian, for the verse division of this text in various printed editions.[1] It could be taken as a transitional sentence: b of the Ab/B pattern, in which the key word "En-gedi" (b) links two episodes (A and B). However, the deictic term "there" (a) does point to the preceding episode (A), referring to the wilderness of Maon. Hence, it seems preferable to take the verse as a "hinge" which connects two sections, that is, ab of A/ab/B pattern.[2]

En-gedi (ʿên-gedî), meaning "spring of the young goat," is the modern ʿAin Jidi [MR187-096], which is situated on the western shore of the Dead Sea about 20 miles east-southeast of Hebron and 12-20 miles northeast of the wilderness of Maon (23:24).[3] Being an oasis, it was a good place for a temporary refuge, and there were caves in the vicinity (see 24:3).

5. David Spares Saul at En-gedi (24:1–25:1)

In this episode David was suddenly put into a position where he could take Saul's life without difficulty, but he did not take advantage of the opportunity. To him the idea of killing Saul was abhorrent. So, this episode answers the question, "Did David attempt to wrest the throne from Saul by violence?" in the negative, "No." This passage, like several others, seems to be an apologetic to answer charges such as those of Shimei (2 Sam. 16:8) that David is guilty of the blood of the house of Saul. As this would have been a problem mostly during and right after David's reign, the document in which this was included was most likely written during that time (see "Introduction" [Section III, A, 2]).

Recent scholars such as Polzin[4] and Birch[5] see in the sequence of chs. 24–26 as it stands a "shift from David as one whose life is endangered to Da-

1. See J. S. Penkower, "Verse Divisions in the Hebrew Bible," *VT* 50 (2000) 389-90. See also 21:1.

2. See H. van Dyke Parunak, "Transitional Techniques in the Bible," *JBL* 102 (1983) 525-48; also "Introduction" (Section VI, B).

3. See "En-Gedi" in *NEAEHL,* pp. 399-405; J. M. Hamilton, "En-Gedi" in *ABD,* II, pp. 502-3.

4. Polzin, pp. 203-15.

5. Birch, p. 1164.

vid as one who spares life."[6] For the literary relationship between the present episode and ch. 26, see on that chapter.

a. Saul Enters the Cave (24:1-3)

1 *When Saul returned from after the Philistines, he was told,*
"Now, David is in the wilderness of En-gedi!"
2 *And Saul took three thousand chosen men from all Israel and went to search for David and his men near*[7] *the rocks of the wild goats*
3 *and came to the sheep-folds by the road, where a cave*[8] *was.*
And Saul entered it to cover his legs, while David and his men were sitting in the innermost part of the cave.

1 Saul probably *returned* from a successful operation against the Philistines (see 23:27-28). He is informed of David's hiding place in the wilderness of En-gedi by the local informant (see 23:19).

2 The *three thousand* is five times the size of David's men (23:13), or three military units (see on 6:19). Here too we see Saul's paranoid reaction toward David, trusting on such a large number of trained soldiers; contrast Jonathan's word: *there is no hindrance for the Lord to save, whether by many or by few* (14:6).

The phrase *chosen men (*'*îš bāḥûr),* which refers to men chosen for warfare or "selected warriors" (see Judg. 20:15, 16, 34; 1 Sam. 26:2; also *bāḥûr* in 2 Sam. 6:1; 10:9), with the establishment of the monarchy may have become a technical term for a selective national army.[9]

The *yā'ēl* (1 Sam. 24:2; Ps. 104:18; Job 39:1) is either the "wild goat" *(capra Sinaitica)* or possibly the Nubian ibex *(capra ibex nubiana).* In the limestone wilderness near En-gedi there are still many ibexes.[10] For this expression *the rocks of the wild goats (ṣûrê hayyᵉ'ēlîm),* Greenfield notes a simile, "like a mountain goat/ibex to its rock," in a Ugaritic text from Ras Ibn Hani:[11] "just as lions are in a lair, so (wild) goats in a rock."

6. Birch, p. 1157, n. 155.

7. So NIV; *'al-pᵉnê;* lit. "on the surface of"; cf. "in front of" (NASB), "in the direction of" (NRSV, JPS).

8. See on 22:1.

9. See Z. Weisman, "The Nature and Background of *bāḥūr* in the Old Testament," *VT* 31 (1981) 449.

10. So W. S. McCullough, "Wild goat" in *IDB,* 4, p. 843; J. W. Vancil, "Goat, goathead" in *ABD,* II, pp. 1040-41.

11. See J. C. Greenfield, "The Hebrew Bible and Canaanite Literature," in *The Literary Guide to the Bible,* ed. R. Alter and F. Kermode (Cambridge, Mass.: Belknap Press, 1987), p. 555; also *CS,* I, p. 301.

3 This is a continuation of the sub-paragraph in v. 2, hence Saul *took . . . and went . . . and came.* Note here that not only the movement of location but also the change of viewpoint of the narrator is reflected in the verbal sequence; see "Introduction" (Section VI, D).

The expression *cover his legs* (*l^{e}hāsēk ʾet-raglâw;* cf. "relieve himself" in NRSV; NIV; etc.) is a euphemism for evacuating the bowels. Nobody, even his personal bodyguard, would accompany him into the cave for this purpose. The term *the innermost part* (*yark^{e}tê;* f.du. cstr.) also appears in Exod. 26:22; Judg. 19:1; 2 K. 19:23; Jer. 6:22; Amos 6:10; etc. A. Cooper notes that *yark^{e}tê* in these passages refers to "the difficulty of access."[12] There, unexpectedly, were hiding David and his men.

b. David Cuts Off the Skirt of Saul's Robe (24:4-7)

4 [MT 5] *And David's men said to him,*
"This is the day of which the Lord said to you:
'Lo, I am going to give your enemies[13] *in your hand!'*
You shall do to him as is good in your eyes!"
So David arose and cut off the skirt of Saul's robe secretly.
5 *— Afterwards David's heart struck him because he had cut off the skirt of Saul —*
6 *And he said to his men,*
"The Lord forbid that I should do this thing to my lord,
to the Lord's anointed, to send my hand on him!
For[14] *he is anointed of the Lord."*
7 *Thus David disagreed with his men about the matter, and did not permit them to rise against*[15] *Saul.*
As for Saul, he arose and went out of the cave on his way.

4 Now is the chance for David to murder his enemy Saul. David's men urge him to act accordingly. No narrative about *the day of which the Lord said to you* is known to us, though the Lord had assured David that he would give the Philistines into his hand in 23:4. As R. P. Gordon comments, "those scholars who try to pinpoint the occasion of an otherwise unmentioned oracle — whether at Bethlehem (16:13) or Nob (22:10), do pay them [= David's henchmen] too much respect."[16]

12. A. Cooper, "Divine Names and Epithets in the Ugaritic Texts," in *RSP* 3, p. 413.
13. K.: *ʾybyk;* cf. *ʾōyibkā* [Q.] "your enemy" (s.).
14. A speaker-oriented *kî;* the reason why I say this; see "Introduction" (Section V, C).
15. *lāqûm ʾel;* i.e., "to attack" (NRSV; NIV; JPS). Here *ʾl* = *ʿl.*
16. R. P. Gordon, p. 179.

McCarter takes *You shall do* as a part of the Lord's speech,[17] but the clause is more likely spoken by David's men who urge him to attack Saul from behind (see v. 6).

The piece of *the skirt of Saul's robe* is a kind of "identity card" (Malamat)[18] and proves that David could have killed Saul if he had so chosen. In Mesopotamia a piece from the hem of clothing was used as a type of authorization; see the various references to "the lock of hair and the hem of the garment" in Mari letters in connection with the verification of prophetic utterances and to the cutting of a hem (in divorce proceedings).[19] These procedures probably had a "legal" significance rather than a "religio-magic" meaning.[20] See below on v. 5.

Klein thinks that this passage echoes Saul's tearing of Samuel's robe in 15:27. However, the two occasions are totally different and the significance of "cutting off" and of "tearing" of the garment is not the same; see on 15:27. If nothing else, in the earlier case, the one who tore the robe would have things torn from him, while in the later, the one whose robe was cut would lose. Symbols must be taken in context.

5 Commentators have been puzzled by vv. 4b-5 since they appear to be "out of place" and logically better *after* v. 7a; hence Smith, Ackroyd, Grønbaek,[21] and NEB/REB reorder these verses. Others, however, keep the MT as it is since there is no textual evidence to the contrary and the relocation is not without its own difficulties.[22] One may rather take vv. 4b-5 as X of the literary insertion AXB pattern, in which X interrupts the natural flow of discourse AB and yet relates itself with AB as a whole. In fact, X breaks into the dialogue between David and his men. Here David's men take initiative and suggest David to act. Readers would expect David's verbal response first. But, unexpectedly, the dialogue is suspended and the result of the dialogue breaks into it. See "Introduction" (Section VII, C).

The expression *David's heart struck him (wayyak lēb-Dāwīd 'ōtô)* means "to regret," and it is paralleled only in 2 Sam. 24:10. It may be that while David *cut off the skirt of Saul's robe* in order to prove that he did not try to kill Saul even though he could have done so (see v. 11), he was later *struck*

17. McCarter, p. 380.

18. A. Malamat, "Intuitive Prophecy — A General Survey," in *Mari and the Bible* (Leiden: E. J. Brill, 1998), p. 78.

19. See J. J. Finkelstein, "Cutting the *sissiktu* in Divorce Proceedings," *WO* 8 (1975) 236-40.

20. See Malamat, "Intuitive Prophecy," p. 78.

21. Smith, pp. 217-18; Ackroyd, pp. 187-88; J. H. Grønbaek, *Die Geschichte vom Aufstieg Davids (1. Sam. 15–2. Sam. 5): Tradition und Komposition* (ATDa10; Copenhagen: Prostant apud Munksgaard, 1971), pp. 164-65.

22. Stoebe, pp. 438-39; McCarter, pp. 383-84.

on the heart because he had cut off the skirt of Saul, for "cutting off a corner of the hem" was often taken as a symbol of disloyalty and rebellion in the second millennium B.C.[23]

6 David respected Saul as *the Lord's anointed (mᵉšîaḥ YHWH)* because Saul was still on the royal throne as king over Israel, even though the spirit of the Lord had already left him (16:14). David acknowledged him as the one "anointed" by the Lord, being endowed of his spirit and hence sacrosanct. The anointed of the Lord should not be killed or even cursed (26:9, 11, 16, 23; 2 Sam. 1:14, 16; 19:21). See on 1 Sam. 2:10; 26:11. David's explanation thus "drew the sting of his men's aggression."[24]

7 The expression *disagreed . . . about the matter (wayšassaʿ . . . baddᵉbārîm;* lit. "tore in two"; "tore to pieces") has been translated as "rebuked" (NIV; JPS), "scolded" (NRSV), "persuaded" (RSV; NASB; following the LXX, Targum), "restrained" (NAB; McCarter, p. 381, following Budde who proposed the reading *wymnʿ*), "reproved severely" (NEB), and "deceived" (Theodotion). See *HALOT,* p. 1609 for various explanations.

R. P. Gordon takes this Hebrew expression *wayšassaʿ* as "a figurative usage" like English "tear in pieces" and "excoriate." He compares this expression with Hos. 6:5 ("I have hewn them by the prophets//I have slain them by the words of my mouth") in which the bicolon uses "hew" and "slay" figuratively in a way similar to "cleave" in this passage. He sees here a possible wordplay: "David cuts off the skirt . . . of Saul's coat, but he afterwards proceeds to "cleave" his men verbally because of their inciting him against Saul."[25] But, this is not a "wordplay" concerning any Hebrew term. For one thing, a wordplay has something to do with the same or similar form with two or more different contents.

The sentence *he arose and went out of the cave on his way (qām mēhammᵉʿārāh wayyēlek baddārek)* is literally "he arose (A) out of the cave (X) and went (&B) into his way (Y)." The normal order of A&B XY is here AX &BY. It is hence unnecessary to read with McCarter "and Saul got up and went on down the road" *(wyqm šʾwl wyrd bdrk)* on the basis of LXX^{B}.[26] The inchoative function of the verb *qwm ("to arise") has been noted already; see on 1 Sam. 17:48; 21:10; 26:5. Thus, this is a transitional sentence, with movement verbs, to the next episode.

Even though David had a good chance to kill Saul, the one who

23. Baldwin, p. 144, n. 1, which cites D. J. Wiseman, "Abban and Alalah," *JCS* 12 (1958) 128-29.

24. Baldwin, p. 145.

25. R. P. Gordon, "Word-play and Verse-order," p. 140. He also refers to the use of *dichotomein* ("cut in two") in Matt. 24:51 and Luke 12:46.

26. McCarter, p. 382.

sought his life, he did not follow the advice of his faithful servants and commit murder (see Exod. 20:13). As the one who feared the Lord, David did not choose the way of self-realization by getting rid of his enemy by himself. In other words, David did not allow himself to disobey God's commandment by interpreting this occasion as God-given opportunity to commit murder. Also, David controlled the situation properly as leader and managed his men so they did not *rise against* his *lord* Saul, for what his men do in his name, or in his place, is the same as what he himself does. Thus, David avoided appealing to a human method and entrusted the matter to God's best judgment, for he feared God; see "In the fear of the Lord one has strong confidence" (Prov. 14:26a).

c. David's Long Speech (24:8-15)

8 *And David arose and went out from the cave from behind and called after Saul, saying,*
"My lord, the king!"
And Saul looked behind him.
And David bowed with his face to the ground and paid homage.
9 *And David said to Saul,*
"Why do you listen to the words of men who say, 'David is seeking your harm'?[27]
10 *This very day your eyes have seen that the Lord gave you today into my hand in the cave.*
Although someone said[28] *to kill you, I pitied you and said,*
'I will not stretch out my hand against my lord,
for he is anointed of the Lord!'
11 *And my father, look!*
Look carefully at the skirt of your robe in my hand!
For when I cut off the skirt of your robe,
I did not kill you!
Know and see
that there is no evilness or wickedness[29] *in my hand*[30]
and I have not sinned against you,
though you are lying in wait to take my life.

27. I.e., "David is seeking to harm you."

28. *w*^{e}*ʾāmar;* or "kept saying" (*waw*+pf.). Cf. "I refused" (McCarter, p. 382), reading *wʾmʾn* on the basis of the LXX.

29. *pešaʿ;* lit., "transgression," from "rebellion against"; see *NIDOTTE,* 3, pp. 706-10.

30. See "no evil is in my hands" (*CS,* I, p. 313).

12 *May the Lord judge between me and you*
and may the Lord avenge me on you!
But my hand shall not be on you!
13 *As the proverb of the ancients*[31] *says,*
'Out of the wicked comes forth wickedness';
my hand shall not be on you!
14 *After whom has the king of Israel come out?*
After whom are you chasing?
After a dead dog!
After a single flea!
15 *May the Lord become a judge*
and judge between me and you!
And may he see and plead my cause
so that he may judge [and deliver] me out from your hand!"

8 David goes out of the cave after Saul and calls him from behind, prostrating himself to the ground. The phrase *arose and went out from the cave from behind,* which is a transitional discourse, is literally "arose (A) from behind (or afterwards) (X) and went out (&B) from the cave (Y)," which follows an AX&BY pattern as in v. 7.

9 Here begins David's long speech to Saul. First, David asks Saul: *Why do you listen to the words of men . . . ?* R. P. Gordon comments: "David himself has just rejected *the words of men* where they would have brought him into conflict with the purposes of God (vv. 5f.)."[32]

In view of frequent examples of inner-dynastic strife and bloodshed in the ancient royal courts, it is understandable that some misunderstood or even deliberately slandered David, claiming that he as Saul's son-in-law was *seeking Saul's harm.* For a Hittite example, see the autobiography of King Telipinu (ca. 1500 B.C.), who reports his attempts to put an end to the court struggles in the Hittite Empire which had lasted nearly 100 years.[33] Most

31. *haqqadmōnî;* taking the s. form as collective; so *HALOT,* p. 1071 ("the forefathers"). Or, it may be that the *sandhi* spelling of *haqqadmōnî mērᵉšāʿîm* represents a pl. ending *haqqadmōnîm;* see D. T. Tsumura, "Scribal Errors or Phonetic Spellings? Samuel as an Aural Text," *VT* 49 (1999) 404-6. The plural form is now supported by 4QSam[a] [*hqd*]*mnyym.* However, M. Held ("Marginal Notes to the Biblical Lexicon," in *Biblical and Related Studies Presented to Samuel Iwry,* ed. A. Kort and S. Morschauser [Winona Lake, Ind.: Eisenbrauns, 1985], p. 95, n.16) thinks that the singular form is supported by OB (Mari) formula: "As the ancient proverb which says" (*ARM* I, 5:10-11). Nevertheless, to translate the Hebrew text, like the Mari formula, as "As the ancient proverb says," one would need to repoint *mᵉšal* to the absolute *māšāl* with a preferred article *ha(m)-.*

32. R. P. Gordon, p. 180.

33. See *CS,* I, p. 196.

members of the court were favorable to David (1 Sam. 18:5 and 22:8), though someone apparently did tell Saul something in 22:8. Perhaps David tactfully avoids accusing Saul directly though he knows that Saul's own jealousy was the major cause of the present trouble.

10 David explains that he has no intention of killing Saul, though he had an opportunity to do so and some of his men urged him to do so. One may note the contrast between the expression here, *the Lord gave* [Saul] . . . *into* [David's] *hand,* and *but God did not give* [David] *into* [Saul's] *hand* (23:14). Here the positions of Saul and David are reversed.

The verb *I pitied (wattāḥos;* 3 f.s.) is literally "(my eye) looked upon with compassion" with a brachylogy of the f.s. subject, "my eye." It is unnecessary to restore *ʿyny* ("eye"), since body terms are often omitted from idiomatic expressions. So, its absence is not due to accidental "loss" in textual transmission. See "Introduction" (Section VII, D).

11 David shows *the skirt* of Saul's robe as the proof for his integrity. For *And my father, look! Look carefully . . .* McCarter translates simply "Look . . . ," preferring the short text of the LXX *(kai idou = whnh).* He explains the MT as "a conflation of variants (*wʾby rʾh* and *gm rʾh*) of which LXX *whnh* is a third."[34] However, here the term *father* is an "honorific" title as in 2 K. 5:13; see "my son" in v. 16.

The verb *lying in wait* (*ṣōdeh;* cf. "hunting" in NRSV; NIV) is translated "premeditated" (NRSV) or "do intentionally" (NIV) in Exod. 21:13.

12 David calls the Lord as their judge. The expression *May the Lord judge between me and you* appears also in v. 15 and in Gen. 16:5. C. H. Gordon notes the Homeric example of swearing oaths by a god: "later we will fight again until a god judges between us, and gives victory to one side or the other" (*Iliad* 7:377-78, 396-97). Thus, "oaths were taken seriously, often because the deities would avenge false or broken oaths sworn in their names."[35] David here as in 26:10 leaves his vengeance to the Lord (Deut. 32:35 [Heb. 10:30]; Ps. 94:1-2). Like Macbeth, he thought "if chance [or God] will have me king, then chance will crown me without my stir" (Shakespeare, *Macbeth* I.3.143), but unlike Macbeth, he was firm against the temptation to "help" God along.

With the expression *my hand shall not be on you* (also in the next verse), David makes it plain that he has no intention of using any kind of violence against Saul.

13 David quotes an ancient proverb. Held thinks that the proverb *Out of the wicked comes forth wickedness* is problematic and can "hardly be

34. McCarter, p. 382.

35. C. H. Gordon, *The Common Background of Greek and Hebrew Civilizations* (New York: W. W. Norton, 1965), p. 257.

viewed as a proverb in the strict sense," for he thinks the MT seems to include only "the moral of a proverb"; the proverb itself was "accidentally omitted."[36] However, the point of this proverb is: "deeds express dispositions."[37] David implied that if he were an evildoer, Saul would have been long dead. This proverb seemed to be well known both to David and Saul and to the reader,[38] and in form recalls Samson's riddle (Judg. 14:14). As Fontaine puts it, "David, technically in the inferior position, uses indirection to force his superior to subscribe to his own (David's) interpretation of the situation."[39]

14 The phrase *a dead dog (keleb mēt)* denotes self-abasement; see 2 Sam. 9:8; 2 K. 8:13 (esp. LXX *ho kuōn ho tethnēkōs*); it is also used for contempt (2 Sam. 16:9). McCarter thinks that "the emphasis seems to be more on insignificance than anything else. 'Dog' or 'dead dog' as a term of self-disparagement is found also in Akkadian . . . [as well as] in the Lachish letters."[40]

The phrase *a single flea (par'ōš 'eḥād;* or "one flea"), also in 1 Sam. 26:20, is another expression of self-abasement. The point here is that "there is nothing Saul can gain by all his searching and contriving."[41]

15 David has no chance of justice from the one the Lord has sent to execute his justice, that is, the king, so he must appeal above the king to the Lord. The expression *judge me out (wᵉyišpᵉṭēnî)* means "do justice for me so that I may escape from your hand"; compare "vindicate me against" (NRSV; JPS); "deliver" (RSV; NASB); "vindicate me by delivering me from" (NIV). With these words David ends his long speech.

d. Saul's Response (24:16-22)

16 *When David finished speaking these words to Saul, Saul said,*
"Is this your voice, my son David?"
And Saul raised his voice and wept

36. Held, "Marginal Notes," p. 95, n.18.

37. R. P. Gordon, p. 180.

38. On proverbial insertions in the epic context in ancient Mesopotamia, see W. W. Hallo, "Proverbs Quoted in Epic," in *Lingering Over Words: Studies in Ancient Near Eastern Literature in Honor of William L. Moran,* ed. T. Abusch, J. Huehnergard, and P. Steinkeller (Atlanta: Scholars Press, 1990), pp. 212-17. For this saying, see C. R. Fontaine, *Traditional Sayings in the Old Testament: A Contextual Study* (BLS 5; Sheffield: Almond, 1982), pp. 109-27.

39. Fontaine, *Traditional Sayings in the Old Testament,* p. 120. See 2 Samuel 12 and 14 for similar "strategies" by Nathan and the "wise woman" of Tekoa.

40. McCarter, pp. 384-85, on the expressions "dog," "dead dog," and "stray dog" in the courtly language in the ancient Near East.

41. Baldwin, p. 145.

17 *and said to David,*
"You are more righteous than I,
for you have rendered me this good,[42]
but I have rendered you evil.
18 *But you have informed (me) today*
that you have done good to me,
in that the Lord delivered me up[43] *into your hand*
but you did not kill me.
19 *'And if/when a man finds his enemy,*
will he send him away with good?'
May the Lord reward you with good
for[44] *what you have done to me this day!*
20 *And now, I know that you will surely become king*
and the kingdom of Israel will be established in your hand.
21 *And now, swear to me by the Lord*
that you will not cut off my seed after me
and that you will not destroy my name from my father's house!"
22 *And David swore to Saul.*
And Saul went back to his house, while David and his men went up to the stronghold.

16 After this long speech by David, Saul responds to him with tears, which he probably sheds from self-pity rather than repentance. On the phrase *my son David,* see on 24:11. Its use exhibits Saul's ambivalent feelings.

17-18 The term *righteous (ṣaddîq)* appears here for the first time in Samuel; see 2 Sam. 4:11; 23:3. Von Rad explains David's "righteousness" as faithfulness to the relationship existing between Saul and David.[45] However, the term seems to have the forensic sense of being "in the right."[46]

For the expression *rendered . . . good . . . evil . . . good,* see also Gen. 50:15, 17; Isa. 63:7; cf. 3:9; Prov. 3:30; 31:12. The terms *good* and *evil* are certainly key words for describing David's relationships with Saul and Nabal; see on 25:21.

19 Saul apparently cites a proverb of his own, and acknowledges that David's goodness to him is beyond common sense. Only one who fears the Lord can act like David in such a situation.

42. *haṭṭôbāh;* lit., "the goodness."

43. *sgr (Pi.) appears only in Sam.; 1 Sam. 17:46; 24:19; 26:8; 2 Sam. 18:28.

44. *taḥat . . . 'ăšer;* lit., "in the place that."

45. G. von Rad, *Old Testament Theology,* vol. I: *The Theology of Israel's Historical Traditions* (New York: Harper and Row, 1962 [orig. 1957]), p. 373. See *NIDOTTE,* 3, pp. 744-69 (#7405).

46. R. P. Gordon, p. 181.

The phrase *this day* is inserted into the phrase *taḥat 'ăšer* like X of the <AXB pattern>: *taḥat hayyôm hazzeh 'ăšer* . . . (lit., "in the place" *this day* "that") ← *taḥat 'ăšer . . . hayyôm hazzeh* [ABX]. Read "in the place that" . . . *this day.* Note that McCarter reads *'šr 'śyth hywm* and translates "(the goodness) you have done today."[47] But this is unnecessary.

20 Saul finally admits *(now, I know)* that David will surely become king and *the kingdom of Israel* will be established in his hand, as Jonathan had already acknowledged. And, like Jonathan, Saul asks David to spare his family (20:13b-16). Birch thinks that this is "one of the climactic moments of the history of David's rise."[48] However, the problem with this interpretation is that nothing seems to come of this moment.

21 Like his son Jonathan in 20:42, Saul exacts from David an oath of protection for his descendants. David fulfills this promise when he brings Mephibosheth, Jonathan's son, under royal protection; see 2 Samuel 9.

For the expression *my seed . . . my name (zarʿî . . . šᵉmî),* see "sons and descendants" in *CAD,* Z, p. 94; also in curses, see p. 95. On "seed," see 1 Sam. 1:11; 2:20 (above); on "name," see on 2 Sam. 14:7. This expresses the continuation of Saul's line. On "kingdom — name — seed," see Tukultininurta, 266: LUGAL//MU//NUMUN; also on "name — seed," see MU//NUMUN in "Eridu Genesis" and others.[49] See also on the meaning of the name "Samuel" (1 Sam. 1:20). Thus, the "seed" and the "name" are a synonymous word pair and in such a context refer to one's descendants.

22 David swears to Saul with regards to his future dealings with Saul's house.

Saul goes back to Gibeah, while David and his men go up to the stronghold. The verb *went up ('ālû)* is plural. According to Revell, "when the verb following a compound subject is plural, ignoring the status of the singular component as principal [=but the main item in the compound subject (here "David") is singular], the clause is often terminal."[50] Thus, this sentence is a TERMINUS. See on 2 Sam. 20:10 where the verb is singular. *The stronghold* is either the one at Adullam (1 Sam. 22:1; etc.) or the stronghold of Masada; see on 22:4. If they went to Adullam, they would literally have gone up from En-gedi at 210 m. (680 ft.) below sea level up to Hebron at 930 m. (3,040 ft.) and then down to Adullam at 350 m. (1,160 ft.). G. R. Driver explained that the verb "to go up" here signifies the movement toward "a

47. McCarter, p. 383.

48. Birch, p. 1159.

49. T. Jacobsen, "The Eridu Genesis," *JBL* 100 (1981) 525 and n. 16. Also in the "Sun Disk" Tablet of Nabu-apla-iddina (*CS,* II, p. 368).

50. E. J. Revell, "Concord with Compound Subjects and Related Uses of Pronouns," *VT* 43 (1993) 77.

northerly direction" since it actually refers to going downhill which is inexact.[51] However, the narrator's viewpoint is from En-gedi, and hence the verb "went up" rather than "came down" is used. See the commentary on 23:11.

e. Death of Samuel (25:1)

1 *And Samuel died; and all Israel gathered and lamented for him*
and buried him in his house in Ramah.
And David arose and went down to the wilderness of Paran.

1 Samuel died at this time (see also on 28:3), and so the present explanation is inserted here. With his passing there is no way David and Saul can be reconciled. This may be the reason why David escaped further south, even to "the wilderness of Paran"; see below.

The subject of the sentence in v. 1a switches from 3 m.s. *(Samuel)* to 3 m.pl. *(all Israel)*. This switch makes these latter clauses a little off the main line of narrative discourse. Hence the main line of discourse continues from *Samuel died* to *David arose. . . .* Verse 1 as a whole is transitional, reporting Samuel's death and David's further escape in consequence. Those who alter *Paran* in the second half (see below) to "Maon" tend to divide v. 1 and take v. 1b as the beginning of the new episode on "David and Abigail" (vv. 1b-44).[1] However, according to discourse structure, such an alteration of the text is unnecessary.

The term *spd ("lament") appears here for the first time in Samuel; also in 1 Sam. 28:3; 2 Sam. 1:12; 3:31; 11:26. See Ugar. *mšspdt* "wailing/mourning women" (*KTU* 1.19:IV:10); see on 1 Sam. 18:7. Here, a public *mispēd* (wailing, lament) was made for Samuel[2] (also 28:3), though this term itself does not appear in Samuel. For consistency, *spd is translated as "to lament," while *'bl is translated as "to mourn" (cf. 6:19), since *spd seems to be a more specific action than *'bl, as 2 Sam. 11:26-27 shows. The former term appears often alongside "weeping" (*bky) and "wailing" (*yll), like the present passage, describing lamenting at the time of the burial. As the following parallelism shows,

In all the squares there shall *be wailing (mispēd);*
and in all the streets they shall say, "Alas! alas!" (Amos 5:16)

*spd refers to a vocal action (also Jer. 22:18; 34:5).[3]

51. G. R. Driver, "On עלה 'went up country' and ירד 'went down country'," *ZAW* 69 (1957) 76.

1. Hertzberg, p. 198; also Ackroyd, p. 191; Baldwin, p. 146.

2. See E. F. de Ward, "Mourning Customs in 1, 2 Samuel," *JJS* 23 (1972) 15.

3. For other terms for expressing grief, see de Ward, "Mourning Customs in

Samuel was buried *in his house.* In ancient Ugarit the burial was performed *in* the house and the people of Ugarit worshipped their ancestor spirits.[4] But it is very unlikely that the people worshipped the dead Samuel, and burial in one's house was unusual in Israel.

And David arose and went down . . . (wayyāqom dāwīd wayyēred) — on the inchoative use ("to begin") of the verb *qwm, see on 1 Sam. 26:5. David is sometimes compared with Idrimi of Alalakh, who was forced out of his kingdom to take refuge with the *Habiru.*[5]

Since *the wilderness of Paran* usually refers to the area northeast of the Sinai peninsula (see Gen. 21:21; Num. 10:12; etc.) and the following episode occurs in Carmel, which is in the wilderness around the city of Maon, some follow the LXX^{B} and read "Maon" (NIV; Hertzberg, p. 199; McCarter, p. 388), though MT *Pā'rān* is the *lectio difficilior* and therefore ought to be preferred.[6] If "the stronghold" in 1 Sam. 24:22b is Masada (see on 22:4-5) or a place near there, it would not have been difficult for David and his men to go down southward from there to *the wilderness of Paran.* In this case, "Paran" could be located in the southern end of the Arabah; see Deut. 33:2; Hab. 3:3; see *HALOT,* p. 909.

6. David Marries Abigail (25:2-44)

As in the previous episode, here too David refrains from violence against his enemy. The present story is sandwiched between two episodes (chs. 24; 26) which tell how David spared Saul when he had a chance to kill him; it deals with the same issue, whether vengeance will be David's or the Lord's. In the last chapter, David desired the Lord to avenge him against Saul (24:12). In this chapter God avenges him speedily (v. 39). In the next chapter, perhaps having learned from this event, David is much more specific that God will somehow avenge David (26:10). Taking his own revenge would make him unfit to carry out God's mission for him (25:30-31).

The present episode, however, differs from other two episodes in that in this one it is David who wishes vengeance, and it is the words of another that pull him back. A woman of "noble character" (NIV; *'ēšet ḥāyil:* Prov.

1, 2 Samuel," pp. 15-16. On mourning in Aramaic religion, see J. C. Greenfield, "Aspects of Aramean Religion," in *Ancient Israelite Religion: Essays in Honor of Frank Moore Cross,* ed. P. D. Miller, Jr., P. D. Hanson, and S. D. McBride (Philadelphia: Fortress, 1987), p. 71.

4. See "Introduction" (Section IV, C, 2, a).

5. For example, see N. P. Lemche, "David's Rise," *JSOT* 10 (1978) 11-12.

6. Smith, p. 220, comments: "The historical improbability of David's going so far into the wilderness is not a sufficient reason for changing the text."

31:10) points out the error of his ways and the way he must go to be acceptable for his calling.[7]

The present episode also shows that this woman Abigail became David's wife because she was a prudent and godly woman, and there was no wrongdoing involved. By his marriage to the widow of an important man of the Hebron area, David would have become a prominent figure in the heartland of Judah. David certainly does not plan it this way — he is just after some provisions for a feast — but it turns out that he is developing a power base. After the death of Saul, he first becomes king in Hebron (2 Sam. 2:1-4). Here again, God's unseen hand of guidance is clearly recognizable in the life of the man who has been chosen according to God's purpose (Rom. 8:28). Though Birch thinks that David's character in the present incident "foreshadows" his seeking to kill Uriah and to marry Bathsheba in 2 Samuel 11,[8] David's motive for killing the man is totally different. In the latter it was to cover up his sin of adultery, while in the former it was to avenge an insult.

a. Nabal in Maon (25:2-3)

2 *There was a man in Maon; his business was in Carmel. The man was very rich and had 3,000 sheep and 1,000 goats. When he was shearing his sheep in Carmel,*

3 *— Now the man's name was Nabal; his wife's name was Abigail. The woman was of good intelligence and beautiful in appearance, but the man was coarse and ill-behaved; he was a Calebite*[9] *—*

2 Unlike 1:1 and 9:1, this episode of a rich man in Maon begins without the introductory phrase *wayhî* ("And it was"). For *Maon,* see 23:24. This man had business in *Carmel,* a town in Judah; this is not Mt. Carmel up north; see on 15:12. Here Saul erected a monument after his victory over the Amalekites (15:12); see also Josh. 15:55. The name means "a fertile land"; the word may be explained as a *sandhi* form of *kerem+'el* ("a magnificent orchard"; lit., "orchard of god"; see Gordon, *UT,* §19.163): *karmel* ← *karmu+'ēl;* see "Introduction" (Section II, B, 4).

The Hebrew of *3,000 sheep and 1,000 goats* is literally "sheep 3,000 and 1,000 goats," which is in chiastic word order. Sheep shearing was traditionally a time of festivity (cf. 2 Sam. 13:23-24) as well as of work.

7. R. P. Gordon, p. 181.
8. Birch, p. 1165.
9. *kālibbî* (Q.); cf. *klbw* (K.).

3 The verse is parenthetical with "its disjunctive syntax."[10] See 1 Sam. 1:4b-7a above.

The man's name is given here as *Nabal* (see v. 25); the adjective *nabal* means "foolish, senseless, esp. of the man who has no perception of ethical and religious claims, and with collat. idea of *ignoble, disgraceful"* (BDB, pp. 614-15); *HALOT,* p. 663. Levenson argues this was not his real name but was used to indicate his character.[11] This is possible, but unproven. It is not impossible that his name was of different origin but was homonymous with the adjective. The name *Abigail* means "(my) father was delighted"; see *HALOT,* p. 4. For a variant spelling, see on v. 32 (note).

In v. 2, *a man . . . The man . . .* can be seen in "the narrator's art,"[12] which focuses on a *very rich* man. In v. 3, *man . . . wife . . . woman . . . man . . .*, being a chiasm, AB/BA, emphasizes the contrast between this man and his wife. He is clearly not worthy of her. The phrases *of good intelligence, beautiful in appearance* and *ill-behaved* (lit., "great as to discretion," "beautiful as to form," "evil as to his doings") are all cstr. of adj. followed by a genitive. On such epexegetical genitives, see W-O, p. 151.

Caleb figures in the Exodus account as one of the scouts who was willing to take the land (Numbers 13–14). In Num. 13:6 he is the representative from Judah, but in other places he is referred to as a Kenizzite (Num. 32:12; Josh. 14:6), a descendant of Esau through Kenaz (Gen. 36:11). The Kenizzites apparently became part of the tribe of Judah. Caleb was given the land around Hebron in Judah (Josh. 14:6-15). Because *Calebite* and "dog" *(keleb)* are similar in Hebrew, the narrator might have used the expression *a Calebite* as meaning "the Calebite type," who is "rough, stubborn and thoughtless."[13] But it might also indicate Nabal's status as being from the most prominent clan in the area.

b. David Sends to Nabal (25:4-8)

4 *David heard in the wilderness that Nabal was shearing his sheep.*
5 *And David sent ten young men.*
And David said to the young men,
"Go up to Carmel!
And when you come to Nabal,
ask after his peace in my name
6 *and say thus to my brethren:*

10. McCarter, p. 396; see Lambdin, §132.

11. J. D. Levenson, "1 Samuel 25 as Literature and History," *CBQ* 40 (1978) 13-14. For various proposals, see *HALOT,* pp. 663-64.

12. Baldwin, p. 147.

13. Hertzberg, p. 202.

'May you (s.) have peace!
May your house have peace!
May all that belong to you have peace!
7 *And now, I have heard that you are having sheep shearing.*
Now, some shepherds belonging to you[14] *were with us*[15].
We did not humiliate[16] *them;*
nor was anything missed from them
all the days they were in Carmel.
8 *Ask your young men*
and they will tell you.
And may these young men[17] *find favor in your eyes,*
for on a good day we have come.[18]
Give whatever your hand can find to your servants
and[19] *to your son, David!' "*

4 *David heard* is the first main clause after the temporal clause *When he was shearing* . . . in v. 2. David and his men were already *in the wilderness* of Maon; they must have moved northward from the wilderness of Paran; see v. 1.

5 McCarter omits the subject "David" (twice), following the LXX.[20] However, the repetition of *David,* a "stated subject" after three *wayqtl* (*heard* [v. 4]; *sent and said* [v. 5]), probably reflects the narrator's intentional emphasis of "who," that is, agent focusing. While the second and the third "David" are unnecessary for comprehension, in a discourse structure like this the repetition can be effective.

And David sent ten young men. And David said to the young men. If the meaning were "And David sent ten young men, saying," the second "David" and the second "young men" would have not been necessary. The expected Hebrew sentence would be: *wayyišlaḥ dāwīd ʿăśārāh neʿārîm wayyōʾmer lāhem.* However, the narrator here first makes a summary statement that David sent ten young men to Nabal; see on 16:5b. Then, he gives a detailed description (vv. 5-8) of how David sent them to Carmel where *Nabal was shearing his sheep* (v. 4).

For *sent . . . ask after his peace* (*šlḥ . . . *šʾl *le-šalôm;* also 2 Sam.

14. I.e., "some of your shepherds."

15. McCarter, p. 392, adds "in the wilderness" after this, following the LXX.

16. *heklamnûm;* Hi pf., see GKC, §53p.

17. Lit., "the young men"; here in distinction to "your young men" in the earlier part of the verse.

18. *bānû* is a phonetic spelling of *bāʾnû.*

19. McCarter, p. 392, omits the phrase *to your servants* as "secondary," taking LXX^B as "original."

20. McCarter, p. 392.

8:10; 1 Chr. 18:10), see *šlḥ lšlm . . . "greet" (lit., "send concerning the welfare of . . .") in Arad 16:1-2; 40:2; etc.[21]

Ten suggests that David was requesting a substantial amount of food from Nabal, but as they could hardly have carried food for six hundred men (v. 13), David could not have used this as a normal means of provision. In this context the term *young men* (see 1 Sam. 9:3) has a military connotation, hence, "warriors," as in 2 Sam. 2:14 (below) and in Papyrus Anastasi I where the Egyptian scribe uses the technical term *Nearin* for the rebel warriors in southern Canaan.[22]

6 The MT *leḥāy,* here, "brethren," a "most perplexing and uncertain word,"[23] has been explained either as (1) a greeting formula "to the one who lives" (pausal form of *laḥay;* so G. R. Driver)[24] or "to the living" (Wiseman)[25] or as (2) "to my brothers" (for *lĕ'eḥāy;* so Smith, p. 223; cf. Vulgate). Wellhausen emends the text to *lĕ'āḥî,* "to my brother," which would refer to Nabal.[26] However, the MT form as it stands can be explained as an example of vowel *sandhi* of the word *lĕ'eḥāy* "to my brothers" as the result of the loss of an intervocalic aleph.[27]

lĕ'eḥāy → *lĕeḥāy* → *leḥāy*

The term "brothers" (so Vulg.) here means "fellow countrymen" (e.g., Gen. 29:4); note that the term "brother" can refer to "any male member of the *mišpāḥāh*"[28] and is used as "a term of address between correspondents of equal status or professional colleagues";[29] note that the phrase "your brother"

21. Y. Aharoni, *Arad Inscriptions* (JDS; Jerusalem: Israel Exploration Society, 1981).

22. See A. Malamat, "Military Rationing in Papyrus Anastasi I and the Bible," in *Mélanges bibliques rédigés en l'honneur de André Robert* (TICP 4; Paris: Bloud & Gay, 1956), p. 115.

23. S. R. Driver, p. 196.

24. See G. R. Driver, "A Lost Colloquialism in the Old Testament (I Samuel XXV.6)," *JTS* 8 (1957) 272-73, and NEB's translation "All good wishes for the year ahead!"; also see NIV "Long life to you!"

25. See D. J. Wiseman, "'Is it peace?' — Covenant and Diplomacy," *VT* 32 (1982) 318 for a possible Akkadian parallel.

26. Wellhausen, pp. 131-32.

27. See D. T. Tsumura, "Vowel sandhi in Biblical Hebrew," *ZAW* 109 (1997) 587.

28. F. I. Andersen, "Israelite Kinship Terminology and Social Structure," *BT* 20 (1969) 38.

29. R. Contini, "Epistolary Evidence of Address Phenomena in Official and Biblical Aramaic," in *Solving Riddles and Untying Knots: Biblical, Epigraphic, and Semitic Studies in Honor of Jonas C. Greenfield,* ed. Z. Zevit, S. Gitin and M. Sokoloff (Winona Lake, Ind.: Eisenbrauns, 1995), p. 60.

in Arad 16:1 is used for addressing one of the same rank; also 2 Sam. 19:12 "You are my kin (lit., my brethren)." However, in v. 8 David refers to himself as "your son." Wiseman thinks that this is "an instance of negotiation with an invitation to Nabal to enter into a regulated covenant with David."[30]

One should note that this verse preserves a greeting formula that is not recorded elsewhere in the Old Testament but is preserved in a text like *KTU* 1.161:31-34, which concludes a funerary liturgy with a repetition of "Peace!" *(šlm)* to King Ammurapi and his household.[31] For *you . . . your house,* see also "Your brother A greets B and your house" (Arad 16:1-3).[32]

7 Here, David is saying that since he was "keeping the peace and had never attacked Nabal's interests, David was entitled to Nabal's tribute." In other words, "a band of outlaws could be a force to be reckoned with in a given district in Israel and impose the payment of 'protection money' on private citizens."[33] David's band spontaneously protected Nabal's flock.

8 The phrase *on a good day (ʿal-yôm ṭôb)* refers to a special time of feasting; see Esth. 8:17; 9:19, 22; compare also Zech. 8:19. Here it refers to feasting at the time of sheep shearing. See on 2 Sam. 13:23.

For *your son (binkā),* see above (v. 6) on *my brethren.* This is the language of negotiation. David is speaking politely and humbly to this powerful man. See "son" in 2 K. 8:9; 16:7.

c. Nabal Responds (25:9-11)

9 *And the young men of David came and spoke to Nabal in*
accordance with all these words in the name of David and took
a rest.
10 *And Nabal answered the young men of David:*
"Who is David? And who is the son of Jesse?
Today there are many servants
who break away each from their masters!
11 *Shall I take my bread and my water,*
and my meat that I have cooked for my shearers
and give to the men whom I don't know where they are from?"

30. Wiseman, "Is it peace?" p. 318.

31. See D. T. Tsumura, "The Interpretation of the Ugaritic Funerary Text KTU 1.161," in *Official Cult and Popular Religion in the Ancient Near East,* ed. E. Matsushima (Heidelberg: C. Winter, 1993), pp. 40-55; *CS,* I, p. 358.

32. On similar formulas in Canaanite letters, see Aharoni, *Arad Inscriptions,* p. 31.

33. C. H. Gordon and G. A. Rendsburg, *The Bible and the Ancient Near East,* 4th ed. (New York: W. W. Norton, 1997), p. 189.

9 David's young men probably *spoke* indirectly, for they first talked to Nabal's servants, who informed Nabal of David's message; see below.

David's young men, that is, messengers, *took a rest (wayyānûḥû)* while waiting for the answer from Nabal. Compare "waited" (NRSV; NIV); "stopped speaking" (JPS). A similar case can be noted in the phrase "(the messengers) will rest *i-nu-ḫu-ma* in Mari for two days" (ARM 5 26:17).[34] Note that McCarter emends the text and translates: "he behaved arrogantly" *(wypḥz)*. Also Cross and Parry comment: "In earlier orthography the *nun* and *pe* are easily confused, as are *waw* and *zayin*."[35] However, this forces them to assume the subject switches here instead of in v. 10; McCarter discards the subject, "Nabal," and translates as "[He] made his reply," though there is no textual support for it.

10-11 Even if David had helped (v. 16), Nabal had not asked for his help. Yet, as R. P. Gordon says, "Nabal speaks like one of the later rebels against Davidic rule (compare v. 10 with 2 Sam. 20:1), and therein, from the viewpoint of the narrative, lies his real fault."[36] He answers David's polite request not just with refusal but with contempt.

10 As Wiseman holds,[37] the question *Who is David?* is "a formal rejection" of David's implied invitation to Nabal to enter into a regulated covenant with him.

11 While "bread" and "wine" are a word pair in the OT (Gen. 14:18; Deut. 29:6; Prov. 4:17; 9:5; etc.) as well as in Ugaritic (*KTU* 1.23:6, 71-72), *bread* and *water (mêmay)* also appear in Exod. 34:28; Deut. 9:9; 1 K. 13:8; Isa. 30:20; etc. So, there is no need to alter the text from "water" to "wine," based on the LXX.[38]

d. David Gets Ready to Fight (25:12-13)

12 *And the young men of David turned back to their way and returned and came (i.e., arrived) and informed him of all these things.*
13 *And David said to his men,*
"Each of you, gird on your sword!"
And each of them girded on his sword.
And David also girded on his sword.
And about four hundred men went up after David, while two hundred stayed with the baggage.

34. *CAD,* N/1, p. 147.

35. McCarter, p. 393; F. M. Cross and D. W. Parry, "A Preliminary Edition of a Fragment of 4QSam^b (4Q52)," *BASOR* 306 (1997) 68.

36. R. P. Gordon, p. 183.

37. Wiseman, "Is it peace?" p. 318.

38. See McCarter, p. 393; also see Driver, p. 198.

12 David's *young men* come back and report to him on everything. The verb *came* suggests that the viewpoint changes here; hence, it means "arrived." On this use of "to come," see 1 Sam. 20:1.

13 David acts quickly. He commands his men to get ready to attack Nabal. David's group of four hundred have already left the place where the rest stayed *with the baggage.* Attack seems almost unavoidable. Suddenly the narrative shifts to Abigail's side, leaving the readers in suspense until v. 20, which mentions again *David and his men.*

e. Abigail Is Informed (25:14-17)

14 *Now to Abigail, the wife of Nabal, one of the young men spoke, saying,*
"David sent messengers from the wilderness
to greet our master and he flew at[39] *them.*
15 *But the men were very good to us;*
and we were not humiliated and we did not miss anything
all the days we went about with them
while we were in the field.
16 *They were a wall by us both night and day*
all the days we were with them shepherding the sheep.
17 *And now, know and see what you should do,*
for evil is determined to our master and on all his house!
He is so ill-natured that no one can speak to him."[40]

14-17 Now, an unnamed young man of Nabal informs Abigail, the wife of Nabal, of his master's rudeness to David's messengers. As in the case of Saul, Nabal's family and servants side with David.

14 *Now* implies that the following episode is a flashback, located at the point of transition;[41] also vv. 21-22. David's purpose in sending messengers was *to greet* (lit., "to bless"). He sought good from Nabal, but he instead received insults: *he flew at them.*

15-17 The young man reports to her how good David's men were to them, protecting them and their sheep *both night and day.* He urges his mistress to consider what she should do about David and his men.

39. *wayyāʿaṭ.* So McCarter, p. 393; also R. P. Gordon, p. 183. See Driver, p. 198, on various attempts by ancient versions to translate it. The same verb appears in 15:19, where it is translated as "rushed upon."

40. Lit., "from speaking to him."

41. See S. Bar-Efrat, "Some Observations on the Analysis of Structure in Biblical Narrative," *VT* 30 (1980) 160. Also see "Introduction" (Section VII, C) on the monodimensionality of linguistic description.

17 For the expression *evil is determined to our master,* see 20:7, 33 above. The phrase *ill-natured* (*ben-bᵉlîyaʿal;* so NRSV) is literally "the son of Beliyaal" or "a son of worthlessness." See on 1:16 for possible etymologies (also 10:27; 2 Sam. 20:1).

f. Abigail Gets Ready (25:18-19)

18 *And Abigail hurried and took*
two hundred (loaves of) bread,
two skins of wine,
five dressed[42] *sheep,*
five seahs of parched grain,
a hundred[43] *(bunches of) raisins*
and two hundred (cakes of) figs
and put them on asses
19 *and said to her young men,*
"Go on before me!
I am coming after you!"
But her husband Nabal, she did not tell.

18-19 Here, when David is about to ruin himself, the Lord protects him, almost in spite of himself, by the actions of Abigail, who acts to protect her household. She has the perception to see David's future, unlike her husband.

She quickly takes action and prepares a present in answer to David's request in v. 8 (cf. Jacob's gift in Gen. 32:3-21 to Esau, who was coming with four hundred men) and probably as tribute to the future king.

Malamat[44] made an interesting comparison between this list of Abigail's presents[45] and that in Papyrus Anastasi I, in which an Egyptian military scribe from the reign of Ramses II (1290-1224 B.C.) gives a vivid picture of the food supply to the Egyptian expeditionary force to Palestine. These food supplies were most probably "distributed in Palestine itself and were obviously derived from local produce." According to his analysis,

42. K. *ʿśwwt;* cf. Q. *ʿăśûyōt.* See GKC, §75v.

43. Cf. "one omer" (McCarter), based on "LXX: *gomor hen* = *ḥmr ʾḥd*" (p. 393). But if the LXX is *gomor,* its *Vorlage* would be *ʿmr* "omer"; see on 16:20.

44. Malamat, "Military Rationing," pp. 117-21.

45. On lists with items preceded by numerals, see D. T. Tsumura, "List and Narrative in I Samuel 6,17-18a in the Light of Ugaritic Economic Texts," *ZAW* (2001) 353-69.

Number of soldiers	*Item*	*Total Quantity*	*Field Ration*
Egypt: 5,000	Small cattle	120	$\frac{1}{42}$ head
	Cakes	1,800	$\frac{1}{3}$ loaf
	Loaves of flour	300	$\frac{1}{16}$ loaf
	Wine	30	$\frac{1}{166}$ wineskin?

Abigail's gift can be analyzed as follows:

Israel: 600	Small cattle	5	$\frac{1}{120}$ head
	Bread	200	$\frac{1}{3}$ loaf
	Parched corn	5 seah	$\frac{1}{120}$ seah
	Wine	2 nebel	$\frac{1}{300}$ wineskin
	Raisins	100	$\frac{1}{6}$ cluster
	Figs	200	$\frac{1}{3}$ cake

There are similarities between the two "menus," and there is "no difference between the bread rations issued to the Egyptians and the Israelites respectively, totaling in each instance one-third of a loaf," though there are differences in other items. Since neither list mentions the length of time the supplies were intended to last, there is no sure basis for comparing their quantities. But, "they give us an idea of the diet of an ancient army encamped in Palestine and living off the country."[46]

Here the amount of bread is written without the term for loaf, just as in 2 Sam. 16:1 and in Arad Inscription 2:4, "and 300 (loaves of) bread"; but note the cases where the word is used (e.g., 1 Sam. 10:3; Jer. 37:21).[47]

The *seah* is a dry measure equaling about $\frac{1}{3}$ of an *ephah,* about 15 liters. Hence, *five seahs* would be about a bushel.[48] For *parched grain (qālî),* see 17:17.

g. Abigail Meets David (25:20-23)

20 *Right at that moment when*[49] *she was riding on the ass and going down in the cover of the mountain — then David and his men were going down toward her — she met them.*

46. Malamat, "Military Rationing," p. 120.

47. Aharoni, *Arad Inscriptions,* p. 15.

48. See R. B. Y. Scott, "Weights and Measures of the Bible," in *The Biblical Archaeologist Reader,* vol. 3, ed. E. F. Campbell, Jr. and D. N. Freedman (Garden City, N.Y.: Doubleday, 1970), p. 352; also see "Weights and Measures" in *ABD,* VI, pp. 897-908.

49. *w^{e}hāyāh.* On this "abnormal" usage of *whyh,* see on 1:12. See R. E. Longacre, "*Weqatal* Forms in Biblical Hebrew Prose," in *Biblical Hebrew and Discourse Linguistics,* ed. R. D. Bergen (Dallas: Summer Institute of Linguistics, 1994), pp. 87-88.

Right at that moment: things did not happen by chance. Here, David and Abigail meet each other for the first time. Readers should know that the Lord was guiding everything in David's life providentially according to his plan and purpose, though David himself did not know that this incident would lead to his marrying this prudent, God-fearing woman.

Parenthetical Clause (25:21-22)

21 — *Now David had said,*
"Only[50] in vain have I guarded
all that belonged to this man in the wilderness;
nothing was missed from all that belonged to him.
And he returned me evil instead of good!
22 *May God do thus to David's enemies and thus again,*
if I leave from all that belongs to him, by the morning,
one wall-pisser!" —
23 *And Abigail saw David and quickly went down from upon the ass.*
And she fell down before David on her face and bowed to the ground.

21-22 These two parenthetical verses are a flashback *(Now David had said),* which is located at the point of transition; see on v. 14.

21 *He returned me evil instead of good:* Compare Prov. 17:13: "Evil will not depart from the house of one who returns evil for good" (NRSV).

22 For the oath formula *May God do thus to . . . (kōh-yaʿăśeh ʾĕlōhîm),* see 1 Sam. 20:13 (note); also 3:17; 14:44. Like 20:13 and 2 Sam. 3:9, the third person is used for referring to the speaker. Such a use of the third person for indirect expressions of the first person can be recognized also in Psalms (e.g., 61:7-8).

This is probably David's overreaction toward Nabal. In 1 Sam. 24:7, when he had an opportunity to take revenge against Saul, David avoided appealing to a human method and entrusted the matter to God's hand. Now, however, he seems to have lost control over his feelings and behavior. Even David needs God's gracious intervention on such occasions. God sent Abigail to him at the right time.

McCarter omits the term *enemies (ʾōyᵉbê)* as an "expansion," which he thinks is "surely a deliberate attempt to distort the original meaning. The threat is never carried out, and a scribe has changed David's words to protect him (or his descendants!) from the consequences of the oath."[51] However,

50. *ʾăk;* see on 1 Sam. 1:23.
51. McCarter, p. 394.

this is an example of the *euphemistic addition* by the author as appears in 2 Sam. 12:14 and as is common in the ancient Near East.[52]

The expression *wall-pisser* (*maštîn b^{e}qîr;* lit., "one who urinates in a wall")[53] is a stereotyped formula which refers to all the male members of a household. It always refers to the killing of all males of a group; see v. 34 below and 1 K. 14:10; 16:11; 21:21; 2 K. 9:8.

23 This verse catches up with v. 20. When Abigail sees David, she quickly gets off the ass and prostrates herself on the ground. The phrase *before David* (*l^{e}'appê dāwīd;* lit., "to the face [dual of "nose"] of David") appears only here. It is not necessary, however, to exchange *pny* and *'py* on the basis of the LXX.

h. Abigail's Long Speech (25:24-31)

24 *And she fell down at his feet and said,*
"With me myself, my lord, is the guilt!
Let your maidservant speak to you![54]
Listen to the words of your maidservant!
25 *Let not my lord put his mind*
on this ill-natured man, on Nabal,
for as his name is, so is he;
his name is 'Foolish' and foolishness is with him.
But as for me, your maidservant,
I did not see my lord's young men whom you sent.
26 *And now, my lord, as the Lord lives and your soul lives,*
the Lord withheld you from entering into bloodguilt[55]
and gaining victory for yourself with your own hand.[56]
And now, may your enemies, those who[57] *seek evil for my lord,*
be like Nabal!

52. See R. P. Gordon, p. 167, on 20:16; R. Yaron, "The Coptos Decree and 2 S XII 14," *VT* 9 (1959) 89-91; M. Anbar, "Un euphémisme 'biblique' dans une lettre de Mari," *Or* 48 (1979) 109-11; C. McCarthy, *The Tiqqune Sopherim and Other Theological Corrections in the Masoretic Text of the Old Testament* (OBO 36; Freiburg: Universitätsverlag, 1981), pp. 189-91. For the "euphemistic addition of 'enemies,'" see K. A. Kitchen, *Ancient Orient and Old Testament* (Chicago: Inter-Varsity Press, 1966), p. 166. However, 20:16 is not this phenomenon; see on 20:16.

53. Cf. "one male" (NASB; NRSV; NIV). Also in v. 34.

54. *b^{e}'oznêkā;* lit., "in your ears."

55. So McCarter, p. 395; *mibbô' b^{e}dāmîm;* lit., "from entering into blood."

56. *w^{e}hôšēa' yād^{e}kā lāk;* lit., "your hand's gaining victory to you"; see v. 31 (below).

57. *w^{e}hambaqšîm; waw* explicative; see 6:18.

27 *And now, as for this gift*
which your handmaid has brought to my lord,
let it be given to the young men,
those who go about with my lord![58]
28 *Forgive the offense of your maidservant!*
For the Lord will certainly make for my lord an enduring house,[59]
because my lord is fighting the Lord's battles
and no evil is found in you all your days.[60]
29 *In case a man should rise up to pursue you*
and to seek your life,
the life of my lord shall be tied up with the Lord your God
in the Document of the Living;
but the lives of your enemies he shall sling away
from the hollow of the sling.
30 *And when the Lord does to my lord*
according to all the good things he has promised of you
and appoints[61] *you as a prince over Israel,*
31 *this thing should not become to you a tottering,*[62]
that is, a stumbling of heart to my lord,
that is, shedding blood in vain
and my lord's gaining victory for himself.
And when the Lord does good to my lord,
may you remember your maidservant!"

24-31 Abigail prostrates herself at David's feet and gives a long speech. Her speech can be compared with that of two other wise women in Samuel: the wise woman of Tekoa (2 Sam. 14:2) and the wise woman of Abel of Beth-maacah (2 Sam. 20:16-19). However, Abigail's wise words — the longest speech in this chapter — and her prudent and quick actions saved David from committing a great sin of *shedding blood in vain.* She perceived the Lord's guiding hand in the life of the future *prince over Israel* (v. 30), thus

58. *b^{e}raglê 'ădōnî;* lit., "in the legs of my lord"; cf. "at my lord's heels" (McCarter, p. 394).

59. Cf. "a sure house" (NRSV); "a secure house" (McCarter, pp. 398-99); "a lasting dynasty" (NIV); also in 2:35.

60. *miyyāmêkā;* lit., "from your days."

61. *w^{e}ṣiww^{e}kā;* lit., "to command"; see Neh 7:2; Arad 3:3 ("to appoint someone commander").

62. The MT reading *a tottering (pûqāh),* though unusual, should be preferred to 4QSam^{c} reading *lnqm,* "for vengeance." McCarter (pp. 394-95) prefers the MT as *lectio difficilior.*

admitting that "the Lord withheld you from entering into bloodguilt" (v. 26). Without God's grace, not only can no one be forgiven of his past sins, he cannot be protected from committing further sins.

24 The independent pronoun "I" *('ănî)* is used for emphasis (hence, *myself*), and is not "a corrupt dittograph of *'dny"* (McCarter, p. 394). This is the polite way of initiating a conversation with a superior.

Some argue that in the phrase *With me myself, my lord, is the guilt, guilt (he'āwōn)* does not refer to either "Nabal's misbehavior or David's danger of blood-guilt (v 26)" but is "simply a part of the conversations of courteous and respectful behavior." According to McCarter, p. 398, the meaning is simply, "Let any burden of blame that might arise from our conversation rest upon me and not you!" A similar case can be noted in 2 Sam. 14:9, which reads:

> "On me and on my father's house, O my lord the king, be the guilt
> but may the king and his throne be innocent!"

But it seems that there is more to it here. If she means Nabal's guilt, she is asking him to let her take the blame instead of Nabal. But she knows that David can hardly kill a deferential woman who has brought him provisions and speaks about how God has prevented him from bloodshed, so by this and her words in vv. 26 and 31 she effectively prevents him from harming her household.

Let your maidservant speak to you! see the similar words of the wise woman from Tekoa in 2 Sam. 14:12.

25 For *ill-natured man* (lit., "the man of the Beliyaal"), see on 1:16 (Excursus). *His name is "Foolish" and foolishness is with him (nābāl šᵉmô ûnᵉbālāh 'immô;* see v. 3) is a play on words, like *kî nābāl nᵉbālāh yᵉdabbēr* "for fools speak folly" (Isa. 32:6).[63] In the Bible the fool is godless; see Ps. 14:1. There are various speculations about the origin of this personal name and whether it really did mean "fool" in the beginning or is a "play of homonyms";[64] see also on v. 3.

26 McCarter thinks that this verse is "clearly out of place," for he interprets it as assuming "(1) that David has already been restrained from assaulting Nabal personally, and (2) that Nabal has already met his downfall." Hence, he repositions v. 26 between vv. 41 and 42.[65] However, Abigail was probably observing his reaction to her presence, and could tell he was inclining towards restraint. Also, taking his agreement for granted is a good rhetorical ploy. The reference to Nabal can be taken either as a prophecy of his

63. See Levenson, "1 Samuel 25," pp. 13-14; McCarter, p. 398.
64. See *HALOT,* pp. 663-64.
65. McCarter, p. 394.

death or as just a curse of folly upon David's enemies. If she says God has kept David from bloodshed, it would be rather difficult for him to keep on with his intention.

For the double formula of oath *as the Lord lives and your soul lives,* see 20:3.

The "bloodshed" appears also in vv. 31, 33; also 2 Sam. 16:7-8; 21:1. The avoidance of bloodguilt was of supreme importance even to Saul as the ruler of Israel (see 19:5); so, this was the key issue to David in his relationship with Saul. Hence, whether David spares or kills Nabal has "its symbolic aspect" since David is preparing for his future kingship (see vv. 30f.). However, in the case of Bathsheba, David "did indeed incur blood-guilt";[66] see Ps. 51:14; 2 Sam. 11:14-21. See also on v. 31. It is noteworthy that *entering into bloodguilt* and *gaining victory for yourself with your own hand* are closely associated here (also v. 33). Compare v. 31: *shedding blood in vain* and *gaining victory for himself.* Surely the one who fears God should avoid gaining victory for his own sake with his own hand.

27 Abigail brought a *gift* (*b^erākāh* "blessing"; also 30:26, see the commentary on 9:7) to David, just as her husband Nabal sent away David's messengers who came "to salute, bless" (*lĕbārēk;* v. 14) him. "Though she speaks as a 'handmaid' to her *lord,* Abigail is master of the situation."[67]

28 *Forgive the offense of your maidservant!* can be a polite expression which means "forgive me for speaking further,"[68] rather than an acceptance by Abigail of her husband's liabilities. But, it is probably more than a polite expression. As Baldwin notes, "she does not dare to imply that David is dependent on her gift, and fears lest he be offended and refuse to accept it even for his men. Such need as he has is merely temporary, for Abigail is convinced that the Lord will make him *a sure house.*"[69]

For here is the speaker-oriented *kî,* which explains "the reason why I say this to you"; see "Introduction" (Section V, C). The expression *an enduring house (bayit ne'ĕmān)* is to be compared with *the everlasting covenant* (2 Sam. 23:5). Both expressions are deeply rooted in Nathan's dynastic oracle recorded in 2 Samuel 7, especially v. 16.[70]

David has been fighting *the Lord's battles* (*milḥămôt YHWH;* also 18:17) since he came into the public eye. See the commentary on "Yahweh war" in 17:47.

29 As for the phrase *biṣrôr haḥayyîm,* there have been two different

66. See R. P. Gordon, p. 185.
67. Baldwin, p. 151.
68. McCarter, p. 398.
69. Baldwin, p. 151.
70. See R. P. Gordon, p. 185.

views: (1) *the Document of the Living* (so Tur-Sinai, McCarter, p. 399). According to N. H. Tur-Sinai,[71] *ṣĕrôr* here and in Job 14:17 refers to a document tied up with a string and sealed with a lump of clay (*bullae*[72]); see *ṣārar,* "tie up [a document]," in Isa. 8:16 (*HALOT,* p. 1058 on *ṣrr^{I}). It is probably the equivalent of the "Book of the Living" in Ps. 69:29[28], which refers to the heavenly book "in which all living people are recorded; exclusion from it means death (Exod. 32:32, 33)."[73] (2) The phrase can mean "the bundle of the living" (so NRSV; NIV; NASB; also JPS: "the bundle of life") or "the bag of life" (see Stoebe, p. 450; *HALOT,* pp. 1054-55). R. P. Gordon explains: "David's life is kept as securely as the tally stones in a shepherd's bag."[74] This explanation would neatly contrast David's life with the *lives of* David's enemies, which the Lord will *sling away* like sling-stones. However, Eissfeldt rather finds its background in the practice of counting cattle using counting stones (see *HALOT,* p. 1055). While it is still hard to decide on the meaning, the first view, which has more support from cognates, seems preferable, for the meaning "the bundle/bag of the living" is yet to be clarified etymologically by earlier cognates (so far, only Aram. and Arab.).

30 Here, Abigail "looks forward to the time when God will have fulfilled his covenanted promises to David in relation to the throne."[75] The expression "to speak/promise a good thing about . . ." may refer to a treaty relationship between a vassal and his lord; see the extra-biblical evidence[76] as well as 1 K. 12:7 and 2 K. 25:28; also 2 Sam. 7:28.

For *a prince over Israel (nāgîd ʿal-yiśrāʾēl),* see 9:16; 10:1; and esp. 13:14. Grønbaek holds that it presents David as Saul's legitimate successor.[77]

31 Here, the f.s. demonstrative pronoun *this (zōʾt),* that is, "the following," refers to the fact *(that is)* of *shedding blood in vain and my lord's gaining victory to himself.*

McCarter holds that *heart* should be omitted with LXX^{B} and 4QSam^{c}

71. N. H. Tur-Sinai, *The Book of Job: A New Commentary,* rev. ed. (Jerusalem: Kiryath Sepher, 1967), pp. 240-41.

72. For *bullae,* see, for example, T. C. Mitchell, *The Bible in the British Museum: Interpreting the Evidence* (London: British Museum Publications, 1988), p. 76 (Document 39); N. Avigad and B. Sass, *Corpus of West Semitic Stamp Seals* (Jerusalem: Israel Academy of Sciences and Humanities, 1997).

73. McCarter, p. 399.

74. R. P. Gordon, pp. 185-86.

75. R. P. Gordon, p. 186.

76. A. Malamat, "Organs of Statecraft in the Israelite Monarchy," in *The Biblical Archaeologist Reader,* vol. 3, ed. E. F. Campbell, Jr. and D. N. Freedman (Garden City, N.Y.: Doubleday, 1970), pp. 195-98.

77. J. H. Grønbaek, *Die Geschichte vom Aufstieg Davids (1. Sam. 15–2. Sam. 5): Tradition und Komposition* (ATDa 10; Copenhagen: Prostant apud Munksgaard, 1971), p. 176.

and suspects that *mkšwl (lb),* "a stumbling block (of the heart)," arose originally as a gloss to the preceding word *a tottering.*[78] However, the *waw* at the beginning of the phrase is an *explicative waw* (see also v. 26), thus solving the problem of repeating the two synonymous phrases, *to you* and *to my lord.* The phrase *a stumbling of heart (ûl^{e}mikšôl lēb),* probably means an unstable state of the heart because of the blame, with "of heart" being a subjective genitive, rather than an obstacle which causes the heart to totter or stumble, treating the genitive as an objective genitive.

See on v. 26 for the importance of a king's (or a future king's!) avoidance of bloodguilt. Vengeance was to be left to the Lord.

The phrase *my lord's gaining victory for himself (ûl^{e}hôšîaʿ 'ădōnî lô;* see on vv. 26, 33) has been translated with "my lord's hand,"[79] reading *yd* before *'dny* with the LXX. But this is not necessary, for here is an example of a "lack of person agreement in respectful address structures."[80]

i. David's Response to Abigail (25:32-35)

32 *And David said to Abigail,*[81]
"Blessed be the Lord, God of Israel,
who has sent you this day to meet me!
33 *Blessed be your judgment; blessed be you*
who prevented[82] *me this day from entering into bloodguilt*
and gaining victory for myself with my own hand!
34 *But indeed the Lord, God of Israel, lives,*
who withheld me from doing evil to you!
For, if you had not made haste and come[83] *to meet me,*

78. McCarter, p. 395.

79. McCarter, p. 395.

80. See Contini, "Epistolary Evidence of Address Phenomena," p. 66.

81. *la'ăbîgal;* <pausal form> *'ăbîgal* < *'ăbîgayil* (v. 23); a variant form in 2 Sam. 3:3: <*'ăbîgail*> → *'ăbîgal* (Ketib; not *'ăbîgēl*) and *'ăbîgayil* (Qere) ← *ayi > ai > a (vowel *sandhi*). Note that G. A. Rensburg ("Monophthongization of *aw/ay* > *ā* in Eblaite and in Northwest Semitic," *Eblaitica* 2 [1990] 109) cites these examples of Abiga(i)l as a monophthongization of *ay* > *ā.* But since the vowel remains short (*/a/*) even in a pausal form, this is rather an example of vowel *sandhi.* The name *'ăbîgal* also occurs in 2 Sam. 17:25 as the name of David's sister.

82. *k^{e}lītīnî:* a short form of k^{e}li'tî-nî "you (f.sg.) prevented me" (*kl'); see *HALOT,* 475; Lambdin, §189 (a).

83. MT K.: *wtb'ty;* Q.: *wattābō't.* Smith, p. 228, explains this form as "a mongrel form, having both the preformative of the imperfect, and the ending of the perfect"; see GKC, §76*h.* C. R. Krahmalkov ("The Enclitic Particle TA/TI in Hebrew," *JBL* 89 [1970] 218-19) holds that the MT form ends with an enclitic particle known from Amorite and Amarna Akkadian texts; see McCarter, p. 395.

by the light of morning not one wall-pisser
would have been left for Nabal!"
35 *And David took from her hand what she had brought for him.*
But to her he commanded,
"Go up to your house in peace!
See, I have listened to your voice and lifted up your face!"

32-35 David, practically quoting her words, agrees that she was entirely correct. He also sees the Lord's guiding hand in all these events, that is, in his sending Abigail to prevent David *from entering into bloodguilt* as well as *from doing evil to* Abigail.

33 For the phrase *and gaining victory for myself with my own hand* (lit., "and my hand's gaining victory to me"), see above vv. 26, 31. *hôšēaʿ* (inf. abs.) in v. 26 and here functions as if it were an inf. cstr. (see also *šātōh* in 1:9); the only other occurrence of this term is Jer. 11:12 (emphatic).

34 If Abigail had not come, David would have killed every male member of Nabal's household.

35 David receives the gifts from Abigail and commands her to go back home. *Go up . . . in peace!* is more than a conventional salutation here, for he means he will not attack her household. The expression *lifted up your face* means "granted your request!"; see Gen. 19:21 and Job 42:8-9.

j. Death of Nabal (25:36-39a)

36 *And Abigail came to Nabal — he was just having a banquet in his house like a king's banquet. Nabal's heart was merry, for he was very drunk — but she did not tell him anything, small or great, until the morning light.*
37 *And in the morning when the wine had gone out of Nabal*
his wife told him these things.
And his heart died within him; he became a stone.
38 *In about ten days,*
the Lord struck Nabal and he died.
39 *And David heard that Nabal was dead and he said,*
"Blessed be the Lord,
who conducted the case of my insult by the hand of Nabal;
as for his servant, he withheld him from evil;
as for Nabal's evil, the Lord turned it back to his head!"

36-37 When Abigail comes back home, her husband Nabal is having a banquet fit for a king and has gotten *very drunk.* So she does not tell him anything until next morning, *when the wine had gone out of Nabal.* R. P. Gordon sees here a word play: Nabal is treated "as a *nebel* ('wine-skin')."[84] *And his heart died within him:* Nabal probably had a stroke (due to brain hemorrhage) rather than a heart attack. This view explains the phrase *he became a stone* better.[85]

38 It is stated that "the Lord struck Nabal." One may assume that the Lord will eventually strike Saul too.

39 *My insult* or "my reproach": on the term *ḥerpātî,* see on 11:2. David recognized that the Lord vindicated him and that since he had not taken vengeance on his own behalf, the Lord had done it for him.

k. Abigail Becomes David's Wife (25:39b-44)

39b *And David sent (a messenger) and said to Abigail that he would take her as his wife.*
40 *When the servants of David came to Abigail at Carmel and spoke to her, saying,*
"David sent us to you to take you as his wife,"
41 *she arose and bowed down with her face to the ground and said,*
"Here is your maidservant as a handmaid
to wash the feet of my lord's servants!"
42 *And Abigail hurriedly arose[86] and got on the donkey and went after David's messengers, with her five maids going behind her. And she became his wife.*
43 *Since David had taken Ahinoam (as a wife) from Jezreel, both of them became his wives.*
44 *Now Saul had given David's wife Michal, his daughter, to Palti,[87] the son of Laish, who was from Gallim.*

39b-41 When David informs Abigail through a messenger of his desire to marry her, she immediately accedes to his request.

41 *She arose and bowed down:* Abigail acts here as politely as if David himself were present. She is quite happy to marry him. Nabal may have been the clan chieftain of the Calebites.[88] It cannot be certain whether she (or David) inherited Nabal's property.

42 *Abigail* from Carmel became the mother of David's little-known

84. R. P. Gordon, p. 186.

85. See J. V. Kinnier-Wilson, "Medicine in the Land and Times of the Old Testament," in *Studies in the Period of David and Solomon and Other Essays,* ed. T. Ishida (Tokyo: Yamakawa-Shuppansha/Winona Lake, Ind.: Eisenbrauns, 1982), p. 364.

86. Lit., "made haste and arose"; a verbal hendiadys.

87. *palṭî;* cf. the longer form "Paltiel" (2 Sam. 3:15).

88. Levenson, "1 Samuel 25," pp. 26-27.

second son, Chileab (so 2 Sam. 3:3) or Daniel (so 1 Chr. 3:1). As no mention is made of him in the later squabbles, he probably died young.

Abigail *got on . . . and went* (lit., "and rode on the donkey, with her five maids going behind her, and went"). The verb *rkb basically signifies "the act of mounting and taking one's position upon something."[89] This is so especially when it appears before the verb of horizontal movements. The verbal phrase *rkb + *hlk, "to ride on . . . and go" (A & B), denoting two sequential actions (also 2 Sam. 19:26), is interrupted by the insertion of the circumstantial phrase "with her five maids going behind her" (X). The order here follows the AX&B pattern; see "Introduction" (Section VII, C). See "Abigail quickly got on a donkey and, attended by her five maids, went with David's messengers" (NIV). See on 2 Sam. 6:3.

43 For *Ahinoam . . . from Jezreel,* see 2 Sam. 2:2; also 1 Sam. 27:3; 30:5. Her hometown Jezreel was in Judah, near Maon, Ziph, and Carmel (cf. Josh. 15:55, 56). She became the mother of Amnon, the eldest son of David (2 Sam. 3:2; 1 Chr. 3:1). David's marriages to Ahinoam and Abigail were possibly politically motivated: they were decisive steps on the way to the throne. While Ahinoam was the name of Saul's wife (see 14:50), it is inconceivable that she and this Ahinoam are the same person. Since Ahinoam is always mentioned before Abigail and became the mother of his eldest son Amnon, it is likely that David had married her before he married Abigail.[90]

44 For David's marriage to Michal, see 18:27. Saul probably hoped to weaken David politically. David had not divorced her, however, so he could ask for her back (2 Sam. 3:12-16) when negotiating with Abner to become king of Israel. *Gallim (gallîm)* is an unknown town; if it is the same as the Gallim of Isa. 10:30, it is located somewhere north of Jerusalem.[91]

Behind all these events in the lives of David and Abigail, including the human initiatives, the reader of the narrative will recognize the hand of the Lord working for good with those who are called according to his purpose.

7. David Spares Saul at the Hill of Hachilah (26:1-25)

The similarity between this episode and that in the cave near En-gedi in ch. 24 has been noted by scholars. In both episodes David was given an opportunity to kill Saul, which he refused to use. In both events God was directing the courses of David's and Saul's lives behind the scene according to his purposes.

Many scholars have thought that ch. 24 and ch. 26 are variants of the

89. See W. B. Barrick, "The Meaning and Usage of RKB in Biblical Hebrew," *JBL* 101 (1982) 500.

90. Baldwin, p. 153.

91. McCarter, p. 400.

same original story. Some believe that ch. 24 is the older, others that ch. 26 is. But no definite answer has been given with regard to their relative dating.

Certainly the two episodes have a similar outline, which Koch describes as follows:[1]

(1) David was in the wilderness fleeing from Saul;
(2) he had an opportunity to kill his pursuer;
(3) someone suggested that this opportunity had been provided by Yahweh;
(4) because David respected the anointed of Yahweh, he refused to kill Saul;
(5) he nevertheless took a piece of evidence that showed what he could have done;
(6) Saul recognized David's innocence and superiority.

However, the similarity has been somewhat overemphasized. There are many basic differences between them.

(1) the wilderness of En-gedi ↔ the wilderness of Ziph
(2) Saul appeared before David ↔ David sent spies to locate Saul
(3) Saul was by himself ↔ Saul was with Abner and his soldiers
(4) David took the skirt of Saul's robe ↔ David took Saul's spear and water jar
(5) David called Saul behind him outside of the cave ↔ David called Abner and the soldiers from a distance
(6) Saul acknowledged David as the divinely appointed king to be ↔ Saul simply prays for blessing on David

Klein also notes that in ch. 24, after the event, "the account consists of a speech by David to Saul (vv. 10-16) and a response by Saul to David (vv. 17-22)," while in ch. 26, "after David escaped from Saul's camp he spoke to Abner (v 14a), Abner responded (v 14b) and David replied again to Abner (vv. 15-16). Then Saul (vv. 17a, 21, 25a) and David (vv. 17b-20, 22-24) engage in a two-way conversation."[2] In this episode there are no "explicit statements about David's future and overt or extreme demonstrations of his innocence and piety and of Saul's abjection."[3]

1. K. Koch, *The Growth of the Biblical Tradition: The Form-Critical Method* (New York: Charles Scribner's Sons, 1969), p. 142; see Klein, p. 236, who notes many more similarities between the two.

2. Klein, p. 238.

3. McCarter, p. 409.

A number of commentators explain the similarities between the two as the result of "a degree of assimilation in their early transmission-history."[4] However, the similarities illustrate the nature of the relationship between David and Saul, while, on the other hand, the differences show that there were two distinct occasions when David acted similarly toward Saul.

This is the last encounter between David and Saul. After this incident David will leave "the territory of Israel" (27:1) and serve the Philistines and return only after Saul is dead.

a. Ziphites Inform Saul (26:1)

1 *And the Ziphites came to Saul at Gibeah to say,*
"David is hiding in the hill of Hachilah,
which is before[5] *Jeshimon!"*

1 *And the Ziphites came,* which is a *wayqtl* of a movement verb (see on 11:1) in 3 m.pl. form, is certainly a transitional expression. The stage has changed and participants other than the two major figures, David and Saul, provide background information; see "Introduction" (Section VI, A).

Here, the phrase *the Ziphites* is with an article since it refers to the same Ziphites as those in ch. 23 (*Ziphites* in 23:19 is without an article). The Ziphites here again attempt to assist Saul by bringing information about David, who is *hiding in the hill of Hachilah.* All of David's movements were monitored carefully by them and other local people. In the initial verses, "Saul" and "David" appear alternatively:

v. 1	Saul	David			
v. 2	Saul	David			
v. 3a	Saul				
v. 3b	David	Saul			
v. 4	David	Saul			
v. 5	David	Saul	David	Saul	Saul

This alternation certainly suggests the relationship between Saul the pursuer and David the pursued. A similar alternation of David and Saul can be seen also in 23:24-28. For *the hill of Hachilah,* see on 23:19.

4. See R. P. Gordon, p. 178.

5. *'al-pᵉnê;* lit., "on the faces of"; or "opposite" (NRSV); "facing" (JPS); cf. BDB, p. 818. The phrase cannot mean "east of" since 1 Sam. 23:19 explains it as "south of Jeshimon." See also on 15:7.

b. Saul Goes to the Wilderness (26:2-3a)

2 *And Saul arose and went down to the wilderness of Ziph — with him were three thousand chosen men*[6] *of Israel — to seek David in the wilderness of Ziph.*

3a *And Saul encamped by the road in the hill of Hachilah, which was before Jeshimon.*

2 Saul goes down to the wilderness to pursue David. The phrase *the wilderness of Ziph* is repeated twice in this verse because of a poetic repetition in a three-line parallelism of an AXB pattern.

> And Saul arose and went down to the wilderness of Ziph
> — with him were three thousand chosen men of Israel —
> to seek David in the wilderness of Ziph.

Note that the second line is an inserted parenthetical clause. See "Introduction" (Section VII, B) on the poetic nature of narrative. Also in v. 3b *the wilderness* appears twice. The repetition of the key terms usually provides the SETTING information. Saul still had *three thousand chosen men,* the same number he had on the last expedition (see 24:2).

3a In the Hebrew word order, "And Saul encamped in the hill of Hachilah which was before Jeshimon by the road," the phrase *by the road* appears to be a part of the relative clause. But this is another case in which a relative clause is inserted into a main clause; see on 2:29 and "Introduction" (Section V, B). So, *by the road* modifies the main verb, *encamped;* so NIV; NEB; REB; cf. NRSV ("Saul encamped on the hill of Hachilah, which is opposite Jeshimon *beside the road*").

c. David Goes to Saul's Camp (26:3b-5)

3b *Now David was staying in the wilderness and saw that Saul had come after him to the wilderness.*

4 *And David sent spies and learned that Saul had definitely come.*

5 *And David set out and came to the place where Saul was encamped.*

And David saw the place where Saul and Abner, son of Ner, the commander of his army were lying — Saul was then lying in the entrenchment, while the soldiers were encamped around him —

3b With this verse the order of "Saul — David" is reversed, and now it is David who is the main figure. The heavy repetition of the stated subject *Da-*

6. Or "selected warriors"; see on 1 Sam. 24:2.

vid indicates, despite the frequent use of *wayqtl,* that the whole section, vv. 3b-5, is a SETTING for the following EVENT (vv. 6ff.)

4 The phrase *'el-nākôn* can be translated either "definitely" (as in 23:23) or "to a definite place." Driver thinks one would expect a place-name here since it immediately follows *bā' (had come).*[7] McCarter even suggests reading "to Hachilah" in light of *eis sekelag* "to Ziklag" (LXX^L), which he takes as "probably a corruption of *eis (h)echelath = 'l ḥkylh.*" This would certainly fit in the context (see v. 3a). However, his solution is too speculative.[8] If it should indeed refer to a GN, the unknown name "Nacon" would be the most natural candidate.[9]

5 The phrase *set out and came* (lit., "arose and came"; also in 2 Sam. 14:31; Num. 22:14; 1 K. 11:18; 2 K. 9:6; 10:12) is less common than the phrase "arose and went," which appears thirty-four times in the OT (thirteen times in Samuel). The reason is that while in "arose and went" the narrator's viewpoint is still at the starting point, in "arose and came" the viewpoint (see "Introduction [Section VI, D]) has moved between the two actions, that is, "to arise" and "to come." The latter could be explained as an abbreviation of "arose and went and came," which appears in Judg. 19:10 and 1 K. 14:4. But, note the unusual expression "and he arose and came and went to Samaria" *wayyāqom wayyābō' wayyēlek šōm^erôn* (2 K. 10:12).

David saw how well Saul was protected with Abner as his bodyguard and the soldiers encamped all around him. The repetition of the phrase *the place where* in this verse is a "poetic" literary repetition; see "Introduction" (Section VII, B). On *Abner, son of Ner,* see 14:50.

d. David and Abishai (26:6-12)

6 *And David asked Ahimelech the Hittite and Abishai, the son of Zeruiah, the brother of Joab, saying,*
"Who will go down with me to Saul, to the camp?"
And Abishai said,
"I! I will go down with you."

7 *And David and Abishai came to the soldiers at night; there Saul was lying asleep in the entrenchment, his spear thrust into the ground at his head,*[10] *while Abner and the soldiers were lying around him.*

7. Driver, p. 205.

8. McCarter, p. 405; see also R. Thornhill, "A Note on *'l-nkwn,* 1 Sam. xxvi 4," *VT* 14 (1964) 462-66 for the same conclusion.

9. On "Nacon" (2 Sam. 6:6), see McCarter, II, p. 164.

10. *mr'štw* (K.) = *m^era'ăšōtāw:* the suffix *-āw* is adverbial rather than pronominal; cf. pronominal suffix "his" *-âw* of *m^era'ăšōtâw* (Q.); see on 18:7. Cf. *HALOT,* p. 631.

8 *And Abishai said to David,*
"God has delivered[11] *your enemy into your hand today!*
Now let me pin[12] *him with the spear even*[13] *to the ground*
with one stroke, so that I may not (need to) do it again to him!"
9 *And David said to Abishai,*
"Do not destroy him!
For who has stretched out his hand against the Lord's anointed[14]
and is still innocent?"
10 *And David said,*
"As the Lord lives,[15] *the Lord himself will surely strike him,*
whether his day comes and he dies
or he goes down into war and perishes!
11 *The Lord forbid that I stretch out my hand against the Lord's anointed!*
Now, take the spear and the water jar which are by his head
and let's get out of here!"[16]
12 *And David took the spear and the water jar from by Saul's head*[17]
and they got away. No one saw, no one knew, no one awoke. For all of them were sleeping, because a deep sleep from the Lord had fallen upon them.

6 David asks Ahimelech and Abishai if one of them will go down to Saul's camp with him. Abishai volunteers. The Hebrew of *asked . . . , saying* is liter-

11. The verb *sgr (Pi.) "to deliver up to" appears only in Samuel (1 Sam. 17:46; 24:18; 2 Sam. 18:28).

12. *nkh; lit., "strike"; see 1 Sam. 18:11, where Saul tried to pin David to the wall with his spear.

13. Emphatic *waw.* Cf. McCarter, p. 405: "a misdivision" of *waw* — "his spear."

14. See on 24:6. For Abishai's words about Shimei, who cursed David, "the Lord's anointed," see 2 Sam. 19:21.

15. See 14:39 on this formula.

16. *w^{e}nēlăkāh llānû;* lit., "let us go to us"; BDB, p. 231.

17. For the phrase *from by Saul's head (mēra'ăšōtê šā'ûl),* Wellhausen, p. 137, Driver, p. 207, and McCarter, p. 406, read "at his head" *(mmr'štyw)* with the LXX, taking the MT as having suffered the loss of the first *m-*. But the MT form can be explained either as having experienced the following phonological change:

mēra'ăšōtê ← *mimra'ăšōtê* ← *mimm^{e}ra'ăšōtê* ← *minm^{e}ra'ăšōtê*

or as an example of a consonantal *sandhi;*

hmmym mr'šty ← *hmmymmr'šty* ← *hmmym* + *mmr'šty*

For consonantal *sandhi,* see D. T. Tsumura, "Scribal Errors or Phonetic Spellings? Samuel as an Aural Text," *VT* 49 (1999) 404-6.

ally "answered and said . . . , saying." While the phrase "answered and said" is normally translated as "answered" (see v. 14; "Introduction"), here no question has been asked. The phrase is better translated *asked* as the context requires.

Ahimelech the Hittite is mentioned nowhere else; he was probably a mercenary. The name Ahimelech is a common West Semitic name[18] like Abimelech, a name that was used for some Philistine kings (e.g., Gen. 26:1; Ps. 34, title). *Abishai, the son of Zeruiah, the brother of Joab,* appears for the first time. He was one of the three sons, Abishai, Joab and Asahel, of David's sister Zeruiah (1 Chr. 2:16; 2 Sam. 2:18), and thus David's nephew. Actually, though the phrase "son(s) of Zeruiah" appears frequently, her relation to David is never mentioned in Samuel, though the original audience must have known it. The name of her husband is not mentioned, but he had a grave in Bethlehem (2 Sam. 2:32). It is likely that he died young, especially since it was unusual for a man to be known by his mother's name. See also 2 Sam. 3:30; 21:17; and 23:18; etc. Abishai is also introduced here as *the brother of Joab.* For Joab, see on 2 Sam. 2:13, where Joab himself appears on the stage for the first time.

7-8 David and Abishai come at night to the camp where the soldiers are and find Saul *lying asleep in the entrenchment.* While either a plural or singular verb can be used before a compound subject, the use of the singular "came" here emphasizes the fact that David, the initial component of the compound, is the principal actor.[19] The *spear* of Saul at his head was for his protection. But in Abishai's hand it could have become the means of Saul's destruction, and thus Abishai suggests that David let him *pin him [Saul] with the spear.* As in the case at En-Gedi (ch. 24), it is suggested to David that this is the God-given opportunity to kill Saul; see 24:4.

9 To "destroy" (*šḥt, Hi.) Saul, who is king and *the Lord's anointed,* is abominable. As in ch. 24, David is sure that it is wrong to harm "the Lord's anointed." See on ch. 24, especially v. 7.

As for *has stretched out . . . and is still innocent (šālaḥ . . . wᵉniqqāh)* or "has stretched out . . . and remains blameless," McCarter thinks that the first verb was originally the *yqtl* verb *yšlḥ* and that the preformative *y* has fallen out because of haplography. He translates: "who can raise his hand";[20] see also "who can . . ." (NASB; NIV; NRSV). However, two *perfect* verbs are simply conjuncted (Qal pf. + Ni. pf.), with the second pf. having a stative meaning in a Ni. stem; hence, the translation adds *still* to the second verb.[21]

18. Gröndahl, *PTU,* pp. 86-87.

19. See E. J. Revell, "Concord with Compound Subjects and Related Uses of Pronouns," *VT* 43 (1993) 75.

20. McCarter, p. 405.

21. See "the frequentative perfect consecutive" (*waw*+pf.) after a perfect (GKC, §112*h*).

10 *And David said* is an example of "repeated introduction to speech" in which "speech by one character, introduced with a finite form of the verb 'say' ('mr), is interrupted by a second introduction, also using a finite form of 'say.' "[22] See on 16:11.

The Lord himself will surely strike him: David is probably thinking of his recent experience with Nabal; see 25:36-39a. The verb *perishes* (*sph, Ni.) is in parallel with "to die" (*mwt) only here and with "to perish" (*'bd) only in Amos 3:15. Note, however, "to die" (*mwt) is often paired with "to perish" (*'bd) (e.g., Ps. 41:5; 49:10; etc.).[23] These three terms constitute a so-called "formula system,"[24] sharing the same semantic field.

11 The relative clause *which are by his head* here comes after the first noun phrase, *the spear,* but it modifies the total phrase *the spear . . . and the water jar,* thus constituting the AX&B pattern: A (the spear) X (which are by his head) &B (and the water jar). The construction may be compared with [A&B]X in vv. 12, 16.

v. 11 *’et-haḥănît ’ăšer m*^{e}*ra’ăšōtâw* (Q.) *w*^{e}*’et-ṣappaḥat hammayim*
the spear which (is/are) by his head and the jar for water
v. 12 *’et-haḥănît w*^{e}*’et-ṣappaḥat hammayim mēra’ăšōtê šā’ûl*
the spear and the jar for water by the head of Saul
v. 16 *ḥănît hammelek w*^{e}*’et-ṣappaḥat hammayim’ăšer m*^{e}*ra’ăšōtâw* (Q.)
spear of the king and the jar for water which (was/were) at his head

Also see Gen. 2:9 for the same <AX&B pattern>.[25]

12 As with Saul in 22:21, David is here stated to have done something that he ordered someone else to do, that is, *David took.*[26] The repetition of three short clauses — *No one saw, no one knew, no one awoke* — after the *wayqtl* of a movement verb (*and they got away;* lit., "and they went to them") — signals the TERMINUS of the present episode.

The phrase *a deep sleep from the Lord (tardēmat YHWH)* implies that the Lord intervened in order to aid David. God also imposes a *tardēmat* in Gen. 2:21; 15:12; and Isa. 29:10.

22. See Revell, "Concord with Compound Subjects," pp. 86-87, n. 15.

23. Cf. Dahood, in *RSP* 3, p. 119.

24. W. R. Watters, *Formula Criticism and the Poetry of the Old Testament* (BZAW 138; Berlin: Walter de Gruyter, 1976).

25. See D. T. Tsumura, "Coordination Interrupted, or Literary Insertion AX&B Pattern, in the Books of Samuel," in *Literary Structure and Rhetorical Strategies in the Hebrew Bible,* ed. L. J. de Regt, J. de Waard, and J. P. Fokkelman (Assen: Van Gorcum, 1996), pp. 117-32. See "Introduction" (Section VII, C).

26. See Revell, "Concord with Compound Subjects," p. 84.

e. David and Abner (26:13-16)

13 *And David crossed over to the other side and stood on the top of the mountain at a distance, with a big space*[27] *between them.*
14 *And David called to the soldiers and Abner, son of Ner, saying,*
"Will you not answer, Abner?"
And Abner answered:
"Who are you that have called to the king?"
15 *And David said to Abner,*
"Are you not a man?
And who is like you in Israel?
And why did you not watch over your lord, the king?
For one of the soldiers entered to destroy the king,
your lord!
16 *This thing you have done is not good!*
As the Lord lives, surely you (pl.) are dead men,
you who did not watch (pl.) over your (pl.) lord, the Lord's anointed!
And now, see where the king's spear and the water jar[28]
which were by his head are!

13-14 David crosses over to the other side of the valley and shouts to Abner, the commander of Saul's army. Abner responds.

A relative pronoun *that ('ăšer)* is omitted after *you ('attāh):* "you who have called." McCarter translates the MT as "Who are you? You have called to the king" and explains it as follows: the MT was corrupted from the text which was the *Vorlage* of LXX^A, which is itself a conflation of the two readings which are supposed to lie behind LXX^L and the Syr. version, respectively. They in turn are "expansive readings" from the original short text behind LXX^B, "Who is it that calls?"[29] Surely such a detailed textual reconstruction is highly speculative. For one thing, the principle — "the shorter, the original" — is not always correct.[30]

The phrase *to the king* is lacking in the LXX. Cryer questions whether the MT is correct, seeing that it was to Abner, not to the king, that David was shouting, and David does not actually speak to Saul until later

27. Lit., "place."

28. *wᵉ'et-ṣappaḥat hammayim;* McCarter, p. 406: "and *where* . . . ," reading *w'y* for MT *w't.*

29. See McCarter, p. 406.

30. See J. R. Lundbom, *Jeremiah 1–20: A New Translation with Introduction and Commentary* (AB 21A; New York: Doubleday, 1999), and "Introduction" (Section II, B, 3).

(v. 17b).[31] However, David called to Saul's "soldiers" as well as to Abner in v. 14, so he may have included in his call something like "Hey, you men of Saul!" Abner is treated by David as the representative of Saul's army. Therefore the phrase "to the king" in Abner's mouth is not necessarily out of place.

15 David questions Abner's responsibility, asking, *Are you not a man?* Abner is incomparable to any other man in Israel — *Who is like you in Israel? (mî kāmôkā bᵉyiśrā'ēl)* — for only he was entrusted with the task of protecting the life of the king. See also 22:14; 2 Sam. 7:23; cf. 1 Sam. 2:2.

In fact two men, David and Abishai, not *one,* went in. Cryer thinks that "this discrepancy cannot be explained away by claiming that the singular refers to Abishai's plea to be allowed to do away with king Saul (v. 8)."[32] However, the "discrepancy" is only superficial, since "one" here denotes "a certain one" as in 2 Sam. 18:10; etc.; see on 1 Sam. 1:1. David makes his expression purposely vague, to avoid counting himself among those who sought "to destroy the king."

16 For the expression *dead men (bᵉnê-māwet;* lit., "sons of death"), see 20:31; 2 Sam. 12:5. That is, "You (pl.) deserve to die!"[33] David is here accusing not only Abner but also the entire body of soldiers, who did not *watch over* (pl.) their lord. It is understandable that Abner does not answer David.

f. Saul and David (26:17-25)

(1) Saul Speaks (26:17a)

17a *And Saul recognized David's voice and said,*
"Is this your voice, my son David?"

(2) David Responds (26:17b-20)

17b *And David said,*
"It is my voice, my lord the king!"
18 *and said,*[34]
"Why is my lord chasing after his servant?
For, what did I do and what evil is there in my hand?

31. F. H. Cryer, "David's Rise to Power and the Death of Abner: An Analysis of 1 Samuel xxvi 14-16 and Its Redaction-Critical Implications," *VT* 35 (1985) 387.

32. Cryer, "David's Rise to Power and the Death of Abner," p. 387.

33. Later McCarter changed his view ("dead men," p. 404) to say the phrase means "a fiend of hell" (II, p. 299), but that really does not seem to fit here.

34. See on v. 10 for "repeated introduction to speech."

19 *And now,*
may my lord the king listen to the words of his servant!
If it is the Lord who has instigated you against me,
may he accept an offering,
but if it is men,[35]
may they be cursed before the Lord!
For they have driven me out today
from having a share in the inheritance of the Lord, saying,
'Go, serve other gods!'
20 *And now, let my blood not fall to the ground*
away from the Lord's presence!
For the king of Israel has come out
to seek a single flea
just as he chases the partridge in the mountains!"

17-19 As Abner keeps silent, Saul now speaks up, asking if it is David's voice. David responds and asks why Saul is *chasing after* him. The humble expression *may my lord the king listen to the words of his servant* often appears in administrative letters of the ancient Near East (e.g,. Ugarit, Amarna, etc., also in 25:24). In 24:11 David addressed Saul as *my father.* Here, too, he keeps his sincerity toward the Lord's anointed.

The verb *accept (yāraḥ)* of v. 19 literally means "to smell"; compare "be appeased by" (JPS). Hence, *may he accept an offering* means "let him smell the pleasing scent of an offering (exactly as in Gen. 8:21) and assume a more favorable disposition toward me."[36] What David is saying is this: if this matter comes from the Lord, may he have compassion on me. But if it is from men, *may they be cursed before the Lord!* For they would let me have no share in *the inheritance of the Lord.*

The phrase *naḥălat YHWH* means *the inheritance of the Lord* or "heritage" (NRSV); "possession" (JPS). It primarily refers to the "inalienable, hereditary property" (*HALOT,* p. 687), and this meaning is supported by the Akkadian *niḫlatum* in Mari.[37] However, *naḥălāh* can also designate the people of Israel as Yahweh's special community — or both the land and the people.[38] McCarter earlier explained "Yahweh's estate" as his personal plot of land, that is, Israel. However, he later changes his view, following Forshey,

35. *bᵉnê hā'ādām;* lit., "the sons of the man."

36. McCarter, p. 408.

37. See A. Malamat, "Mari and the Bible: Some Patterns of Tribal Organization and Institutions," *JAOS* 82 (1962) 143-50; T. J. Lewis, "The Ancestral Estate (נַחֲלַת אֱלֹהִים) in 2 Samuel 14:16," *JBL* 110 (1991) 598, n. 5; also the Ugaritic phrase *arṣ nḥlth* "his inherited land" (lit., "the land of his inheritance") in *KTU* 1.3 VI 16.

38. Lewis, "The Ancestral Estate," pp. 598-99.

who argues that the expression here refers primarily to "the political and religious community," not the land itself.[39] Forshey finds "no significant evidence to connect the root to tribal inheritance practices."[40] As Lewis notes, "while *naḥălāh* does not always refer to patrimony, Forshey does a disservice in implying that it is to be totally dissociated from inheritance in every context."[41] As in 1 Sam. 10:1, the term *naḥălāh* here seems to refer both to Israel as the inherited land and to the people as the covenant community. See the commentary on 10:1. Also see on 27:1; 2 Sam. 14:16; 20:19; 21:3.

While "ancestor worship and the ultimate ancestral ownership of the land" went together traditionally, as Brichto notes, "in biblical religion, not the ancestors but God is the ultimate owner of all property." Thus, "if formerly to enter a proto-Israelite family was to enter its ancestral cult and to enter its cult was to enter the family, *now* to enter the *'am* of YHWH was to enter the worship of YHWH and vice versa."[42]

Serve other gods: This reflects the common Near Eastern idea that a god could be worshipped only on its own soil (2 K. 5:17), also perhaps the corporate nature of worship. Israel as the inheritance of the Lord here refers to the worshipping community. This does imply the "limitation of the worship of YHWH," not "a limitation of YHWH's power to his own small area of sovereignty."[43] Certainly 1 Samuel 4–6 presents God as being able to work in Philistia, and other episodes show him as protecting David in his dealings with Achish, and in 23:27 we even get the impression that God caused the Philistines to attack.

Therefore, to chase David away from the Lord's *inheritance* so that he may have no share in it and force him to *serve other gods* is a capital offense against the Lord of Israel who owns the land of Israel and rules his people Israel through his vice-regent the king. Those who commit this sin (see v. 21) should be *cursed before the Lord.* This is what David is conveying to Saul *the king of Israel* (v. 20).

20 For the expression *a single flea (par'ōš 'eḥād),* see also 1 Sam. 24:14.

There is a wordplay between the term *qōrē',* a participial form of *qr', hence meaning "calling," and a "partridge, calling-bird." "David is standing on a mountain (v 13) calling (v 14), and he compares Saul's pursuit of him to the hunting of 'the caller' in the mountains. Specifically the play revolves

39. See McCarter, II, p. 346.

40. H. O. Forshey, "The Construct Chain *naḥalat YHWH/'elōhîm,*" *BASOR* 220 (1975) 51-54.

41. Lewis, "The Ancestral Estate," p. 607.

42. H. C. Brichto, "Kin, Cult, Land and Afterlife — A Biblical Complex," *HUCA* 44 (1973) 11.

43. See Brichto, "Kin, Cult, Land and Afterlife," p. 31, n. 48.

upon Abner's question in v. 14 . . . 'Who are you, O caller?' Thus in David's reply he wryly compares himself to 'the caller' hunted in the mountains."[44]

(3) Saul Speaks (26:21)

21 *And Saul said,*
"I have sinned! Return, my son David!
For I will not do evil to you any more,
because you regarded my life as precious[45] *today.*
Truly I have acted foolishly and gone very much astray!"

21 For the term *I have sinned,* see on 15:24. David, probably very sensibly, ignores Saul's promise in these words; see 27:1.

(4) David Responds (26:22-24)

22 *And David answered:*
"Here is the spear, O king![46]
Let one of the young men come over and take it!
23 *It is the Lord who returns to each man*[47]
his righteousness and faithfulness.
While the Lord has given you today in (my) hand,
I was not willing to send my hand into the Lord's anointed.
24 *And now, as I valued your life*[48] *today,*
so the Lord will value my life and deliver me from all danger."

22 David acts wisely in asking Saul to send a single soldier to come over and get his spear.

23-24 Two terms *righteousness* and *faithfulness* are used as a pair in Ps. 40:11[10]; 143:1. David fully trusted in the Lord's justice. Even though David did good to Saul and is to expect good from Saul in return, David put his trust only on the Lord who *will value* his *life and deliver* him *from all danger.* See 24:6, 10 on David's respect for the Lord's anointed.

44. McCarter, p. 408. See W. S. McCullough, "Partridge," in *IDB,* 3, pp. 661-62.

45. *yāqᵉrāh napšî bᵉʿêneykā;* lit., "my soul is precious in your eyes."

46. *hḥnyt hmlk;* MT, Qere: *ḥănît hammelek* "the spear of the king," like LXX; 4QSam^a.

47. Lit., "the man."

48. *gādᵉlāh napšᵉkā . . . bᵉʿênāy;* lit., "your life is great in my eyes"; see v. 21 for a similar expression.

(5) Saul Returns (26:25)

25 *And Saul said to David,*
"Blessed are you, my son David!
In whatever you do, you will surely succeed!"
And David went to his way, while Saul returned to his place.

25 The expression *in whatever you do, you will surely succeed! (gam ʿāśōh taʿăśeh wᵉgam yākōl tûkāl)* denotes the same thought as the narrator's remark in 18:14 *(And David became successful in all his ways),* though here it is differently worded and put in the mouth of Saul.[49] Saul knows that David *will surely succeed,* namely, he *will surely become king* (24:20).

The *wayqtl* of a movement verb *(And David went)* signals here a TERMINUS of the episode. This is the last occasion for David to see Saul; he will never see him again. After this David escapes to the land of the Philistines.

G. DAVID IN PHILISTIA (27:1–30:31)

The new episode begins with *wayyōʾmer,* as if the dialogue continues from the preceding episode. However, as the previous episode terminated with a transitional phrase, *wayqtl* of a motion verb, 27:1 is the start of a new episode, even though it begins with "And X said," like other episodes such as 12:1. See on 12:1.

The present section, ch. 27, is the beginning of the account of David's sojourn at Ziklag in 1 Samuel 27–30, which is interrupted by the "Witch of Endor" episode in ch. 28. Many hold that this Ziklag section has a highly apologetic tone, as do the accounts where David spares Saul. It certainly seems to emphasize that David only went to Philistia as a last resort, and that in Achish's service he did not attack Israel, but only Israel's enemies.

Regardless whether this account as a whole was written as such an apologetic, it certainly reports "David's ingenuity and ability to succeed in the most hostile circumstances."[1] He was busy in learning from his future enemy various techniques in military and administrative organization. The Philistine culture was at that time much advanced in comparison with the Israelite and Judean cultures; see "Introduction" (Section IV, B). A comparison of pottery from the two areas exhibits the far greater advancement of the Philistine civilization,[2] including cultural traditions such as music.

49. On the use of *gam . . . wᵉgam . . . ,* see Andersen, p. 159.
1. McCarter, p. 416.
2. See, for example, the bichrome Philistine pottery found in Ekron. See

<Relationship between 27:1ff. and 21:10-15>

Since the present episode does not refer to David's previous visit to Gath in 21:10-15, the two episodes have often been explained as duplicate accounts that yet contradict each other. The text in 27:2ff. shows no hint of Achish's previous meeting with David. Hence, many scholars have suggested that the previous account was introduced secondarily as a "'corrective' to 27:1ff, where the future king of Israel is depicted in the embarrassing role of a Philistine-hired mercenary."[3] However, the episodes do not seem to have much in common except that in both David went to Gath and that both episodes portray "the duping of Achish."[4] It is difficult to see how ch. 21, which describes David as behaving like a madman, could be a corrective of chs. 27–30. In ch. 21 he went to Gath alone and apparently anonymously. He was recognized and escaped through a trick. Here, he and a large group of men with their families formally enter Achish's service, presumably after a process of negotiation. Probably Achish here is thinking that David would certainly be a useful servant, and also that a "divide and conquer" tactic would be useful against the enemy in Israel.[5] It is possible that the Achish Ben-Maoch (27:2) in this chapter is a different person than the "Achish" of ch. 21 (see below). But even if he is the same Achish, he could have seen David's feigning in ch. 21 as a sign of the quick wit of a warrior rather than as something to hold a grudge about.

1. David and Achish (27:1-12)

a. Escape to Gath (27:1-4)

1 *And David said to himself,*[6]
"Soon, one day[7] *I may be swept away*[8] *by the hand of Saul!*

T. Dothan and M. Dothan, *People of the Sea: The Search for the Phiistines* (New York: Macmillan, 1992), plate 5; A. Millard, *Treasures from Bible Times* (Tring: Lion Publishing, 1985), p. 104.

3. McCarter, p. 358.

4. R. P. Gordon, p. 171. See F. Crüsemann, "Zwei alttestamentliche Witze: I Sam 21:11-15 und II Sam 6:16, 20-23 als Beispiele einer biblischen Gattung," *ZAW* 92 (1980) 215-27.

5. B. Mazar, "The Philistines and the Rise of Israel and Tyre," in *The Early Biblical Period: Historical Studies,* ed. A. Ahituv and B. A. Levine (Jerusalem: Israel Exploration Society, 1986), p. 74.

6. *wayyōʾmer dāwīd ʾel-libbô;* lit., "said to his heart."

7. NRSV; NASB *(yôm-ʾeḥād);* cf. "One of these days" (NIV); "Some day" (JPS); "Any day now" (McCarter).

8. *sph Ni. impf.; "be destroyed" (NIV); "perish" (NRSV; JPS).

There is nothing left for me except to escape[9]
to the land of the Philistines.
Then Saul may give up on me
without seeking me any longer
in all the territory of Israel
and I may escape from his hand."

2 *And David and the six hundred men who were with him set out and crossed over*[10] *to Achish*[11] *Ben-Maoch, king of Gath.*

3 *And David, with his men, stayed with Achish in Gath, each man with his household and David with his two wives, Ahinoam the Jezreelite and Nabal's wife Abigail the Carmelite.*

4 *And it was told to Saul that David had fled to Gath, and thus he no longer*[12] *sought him.*

1 Sometime after David saw Saul off, he thinks that *soon* he may be *swept away* by Saul. If he escapes to the Philistine land, Saul may give up on him. The phrase *the territory of Israel (g^ebûl yiśrā'ēl)* refers to "the inheritance of the Lord" (26:19). To escape to the land of the Philistines probably meant that David would have no share in "the inheritance of the Lord." One of the reasons for his move may have been practical: David and his men could not keep on the run in the wilderness of Judah with their families (v. 3).

2 It is possible that "Achish" is not a personal name, and that the reason why the "Achish" here is called by the proper name "Ben-Maoch" is that "Achish, the king of Gath" *('ākîš melek gat)* in 21:10 and this *Achish Ben-Maoch king of Gath ('ākîš ben-mā'ôk melek gat)* were different people. An inscription found in Ekron refers to the king as "Akhayus," the same word as "Achish," and Naveh has recently argued that in Iron Age Philistine cities "Achish" may be "the official name" or appellation for the Philistine kings;[13] see on 21:10. Thus, the Achish in 21:10 and the Achish in 27:2 might have the same appellation but be different people. That may be the reason why the "Achish" is called by a proper name "Ben-Maoch" here. This might be sup-

9. Lit., "I have no good thing except that I certainly escape." McCarter, p. 412, reads *ky 'm 'mlt,* lit., "except that I escape" on the basis of LXX^{BL}.

10. Or "began crossing over"; lit., "arose and crossed over." For this inchoative use of the verb *qwm, see 26:5; F. W. Dobbs-Allsopp, "Ingressive *qwm* in Biblical Hebrew," *ZAH* 8 (1995) 31-54.

11. On possible etymologies of "Achish," see 21:11.

12. *ywsp* (K.) in Hi. impf. expresses "habitual action in the past"; cf. *yāsap* (Q.) in Qal pf. See Driver, p. 210; McCarter, p. 412.

13. J. Naveh, "Achish-Ikausu in the Light of the Ekron Dedication," *BASOR* 310 (1998) 35-37.

ported by the following examples, in which the title "Pharaoh" is sometimes followed by a proper name and sometimes not:

"Pharaoh king of Egypt" (Gen. 41:46; Exod. 6:11; Deut. 7:8; 11:3; 1 K. 9:16; 2 K. 17:7; Isa. 36:6; Jer. 25:19; Ezek. 29:2, etc.);
"Pharaoh Neco king of Egypt" (2 K. 23:29; Jer. 46:2; 2 K. 23:33, 34, 35)
"Pharaoh Hophra king of Egypt" (Jer. 44:30).

Whether Achish is a title or not, *Ben-Maoch (ben-māʿôk)* can be a proper name like "Ben-Ammi" (Gen. 19:38), "Ben-Oni" (Gen. 35:18), "Ben-Hadad" (1 K. 15:18; 2 K. 6:24; Jer. 49:27; Amos 1:4; 2 Chr. 16:2, 4), "Ben-Zoheth" (1 Chr. 4:20), "Ben-Hail" (2 Chr. 17:7). Compare Achish Ben-Maakah *(maʿăkâ)* in 1 K. 2:39.

3-4 David and his men stay in Gath with their family members. On *Ahinoam* and *Abigail,* see 25:42-43. Saul is informed of their move to Gath, so he stops seeking David's life.

b. David at Ziklag (27:5-12)

5 *And David said to Achish,*
"If I have found favor in your sight,
let a place be given[14] *to me in one of the cities of the field,*
so that I may live there!
Why should your servant live in the royal city[15] *with you?"*
6 *And Achish gave him Ziklag on that day.*
— Therefore Ziklag has belonged to the kings of Judah to this day —
7 *And the number of the days when David stayed in the field of the Philistines was a year and four months.*
8 *And David, with his men, went up and made raids on the Gashurites, the Gezerites,*[16] *and the Amalekites,*[17] *for they*[18] *were*

14. Lit., "they will give" or "let them give."

15. *ʿîr hammamlākāh;* lit., the city of the kingship.

16. *wᵉhaggizrî* (Q.). Note that *whgrzy* (K.) is a metathesis of the normal form which preserves a phonetic spelling; hence, both forms are acceptable; see D. T. Tsumura, "Scribal Errors or Phonetic Spellings? Samuel as an Aural Text," *VT* 49 (1999) 390-411. McCarter, p. 413, thinks that the Gezerites are not appropriate here since they lived "much too far N." He omits them, with LXX^B.

17. See 1 Sam. 14:48.

18. F.pl. = "these three peoples."

inhabiting the land which is from of old[19] *toward Shur,*[20] *even up to the land of Egypt*

9 *— and David used to strike the land, though he would not keep any man or woman alive, and take sheep, cattle, donkeys, camels, and garments — and returned and came to Achish.*

10 *And Achish said,*

"Where did you make a raid today?"

And David said,

"Toward the Negeb of Judah, namely, toward the Negeb of the Jerahmeelites and to the Negeb of the Kenites."

11 *— and no man and woman would David keep alive to bring to Gath,*

for he thought,[21]

"They might inform about/against us, saying 'Thus did David!'"

Such was his custom[22] *all the days he lived in the field of the Philistines —*

12 *And Achish trusted David, saying,*

"He has become utterly abhorred among his people Israel!

And he will become an eternal servant to me!"

5 David asks Achish to give him a city other than the royal city to live in. David does not mean a specific location with the term *a place;* he rather requests for "some other safe haven for himself and his entourage than the royal capital."[23] He thus could act freely, without interference. Asking land of a lord was not an unusual practice. The feudal practice of giving servants of the king land seems to have occurred in Israel (22:7), as well as among the Philistines.[24]

6 Achish grants Ziklag to David. From David's point of view, Ziklag had the advantage of being far from Saul's territory and isolated enough from the Philistine pentapolis not to be under observation by them. Its disadvantage was that it could become the target of attacks by desert bands such as the Amalekites; see 30:1. The exact location of *Ziklag* is, how-

19. Professor Rainey called to my attention the Moabite phrase *m'lm* "from of old" (Mesha, line 10). See "from ancient times" (NIV; NASB); "Olam" (JPS). Many emend it to "Telam" (*miṭṭēlām;* so NRSV; Femi; BDB, p. 762; *HALOT,* p. 799) on the basis of LXX: *Telam.* Also see 1 Sam. 15:4 (above).

20. See on 15:7.

21. *lē'mōr;* lit., "to say."

22. *mišpāṭô;* cf. "his practice" (NRSV; NIV).

23. D. F. Murray, "mqwm and the Future of Israel in 2 Samuel vii 10," *VT* 40 (1990) 315, n. 33.

24. See McCarter, p. 414.

ever, unknown; the site may be the modern Tell esh-Sherîʿah [MR119-088], about 20 miles east-southeast of Gaza on Naḥal Gerar (Wadi esh-Sherîʿah) and thus some 35-40 miles southwest of Tell eṣ-Ṣâfī (Gath; see on 5:8). It has long been identified with Tell el-Khuweilfeh [MR137-087], approximately 14 miles north of Beersheba, but since that tell seems to be located within the territory of Judah rather than that of the Philistines, this view assuredly has some difficulties.[25] Ray's idea that Ziklag could mean "the man of the Tsikel"[26] is utterly impossible, for Egyptian scribes used the ṯ for Northwest Semitic *samek,* never *ṣadeh.*[27] Ziklag is, however, listed among the Judahite cities in Josh. 15:31 as belonging to the Negeb province.

For the phrase *to this day,* see "Introduction" (Section III, B, 1). The land grants were "permanent and inalienable," and Ziklag was "a special crown property in Judah"[28] in the time of the editor, who put in this historical comment, which probably dates from the time of the Divided Monarchy in view of the plural noun phrase *the kings of Judah.* Then the question arises: When during the time of the Divided Monarchy? Halpern notes: "Given settlement patterns in the Negev, no such statement could be made after the early ninth century, and probably not after Shishaq's campaign [925 B.C.]." See 1 K. 14:25, which mentions Shishaq's campaign as occurring in "the fifth year of King Rehoboam." It seems that Hezekiah had controlled the area of Tell esh-Sherîʿah (Ziklag?) for a short time; see 2 K. 18:8; 1 Chr. 4:39-43.[29] But, later, in the seventh century B.C., that area was dominated by Assyria. Halpern concludes that the text "makes an assertion consistent only with a tenth-century date."[30] If we count Solomon among the "kings of Judah," the phrase *to this day* could refer, as the earliest possibility, to the time of Rehoboam of the late tenth century B.C. Rehoboam's time is certainly a time when the editor might emphasize the fact that the city belonged to the southern kingdom of Judah.

7 On *a year* (*yāmîm;* lit., "days"), see 29:3.[31] *A year and four months* is the total period during which David served Achish, both in Gath

25. See A. F. Rainey, "Ziklag," in *ISBE,* IV, p. 1196; W. R. Kotter, "Ziklag," in *ABD,* VI, pp. 1090-93.

26. J. D. Ray, "Two Etymologies: Ziklag and Phicol," *VT* 36 (1986) 355-58.

27. See Y. Muchiki, *Egyptian Proper Names and Loanwords in North-West Semitic* (SBLDS 173; Atlanta: Scholars Press, 1999), pp. 317-18; also A. F. Rainey (personal communication).

28. McCarter, p. 414.

29. See A. F. Rainey, "Negeb," in *ISBE,* III, p. 513.

30. B. Halpern, "The Construction of the Davidic State: An Exercise in Historiography," in *The Origins of the Ancient Israelite States,* ed. V. Vritz and P. R. Davies (JSOTSS 228; Sheffield: Sheffield Academic Press, 1996), p. 75.

31. Driver, p. 210.

and Ziklag. During this period David built up relationships with the Israelites in the south, that is, with Judah; see 30:26-31.

8 While David served Achish as his subject, he learned much about the art of war from his Philistine associations.[32]

*The Gashurites (hagg*ᵉ*šûrî)* are geographically associated with the Philistines in Josh. 13:2; compare other "Geshurites" of the Transjordanian state of Geshur (Deut. 3:14; Josh. 12:5; 13:11; 2 Sam. 3:3).[33] It may be that there was some historical connection unknown to us between the two groups.

9 The *wayqtl* expression *and returned* is in sequence with the previous action "made raids" (v. 8); hence, the earlier part of v. 9 is a parenthetical clause with a habitual sense *w-qtl.*

10 For the meaning *where* for Hebrew *'al,* see Akkadian *al(i)* "where?" (*CAD,* A/1, pp. 338-39); compare "Against whom" (NRSV; McCarter, p. 413) from the LXX.

The Negeb of . . . (ʿal-negeb . . .) refers to southern districts of Palestine, which correspond to today's northern Negeb, the district east and west of Beersheba and north of Kadesh-barnea.[34] The *Negeb of Judah* refers to the general area, not only that which centers around Beersheba (see 2 Sam. 24:7; 2 Chr. 28:18) but also that which encompasses all the towns listed in Josh. 15:21-32, that is, the southernmost towns of the tribes of Judah in the Negeb toward the boundary of Edom.[35] Hence, *waw* before *toward the Negeb of the Jerahmeelites* is a *waw explicative* and should be translated "namely."[36]

The singular *hayyarḥm*ᵉ*'ēlî* הַיַּרְחְמְאֵלִי (sic L) is used collectively, hence, *the Jerahmeelites;* many MSS have *hayy*ᵉ*raḥm*ᵉ*'ēlî.* Its territory may have been toward the south of Beersheba; in 30:29, Jerahmeel is described as an independent tribe like the Kenites. It is later incorporated into Judah; see 1 Chr. 2:9, 25-27.[37] The element *yrḥm* in GN "Arad of Beth-*yrḥm*" mentioned in the victory list of Shoshenq (= biblical Shishaq) may be a shortened form of *Jerahmeel.*[38]

For *the Kenites (haqqênî),* see on 30:29.

11 This verse is parenthetical. The reason why David did *not keep any man or woman alive* (v. 9) is that he feared that they *might inform* Achish of his conduct.

12 David succeeds in gaining the complete trust of his Philistine

32. See C. H. Gordon, *The Common Background of Greek and Hebrew Civilizations* (New York: W. W. Norton, 1965), p. 18.

33. See B. Mazar, "Geshur and Maacah," *JBL* 80 (1961) 18-21.

34. See Rainey, "Negeb," pp. 511-13.

35. McCarter, p. 415.

36. G. Galil, "The Jerahmeelites and the Negeb of Judah," *JANES* 28 (2001) 40.

37. McCarter, p. 415.

38. Rainey, "Negeb," p. 512.

master, who is convinced that David will become *an eternal servant* to him. For the expression *become utterly abhorred (hab'ēš hib'îš),* see BDB, pp. 92-93; *HALOT,* p. 107. The Ni. ("odious to be hated") appears only in Samuel (1 Sam. 13:4; 2 Sam. 10:6; 16:21) and only figuratively.

The phrase *eternal servant,* both in Hebrew *(ʿebed ʿôlām)* and Ugaritic (*ʿbd ʿlm* in *KTU* 1.14 III 23; cf. 1.5 II 19-20), denotes a life-long slave or "eternal vassal" (also 2 K. 16:7). There were two kinds of slaves in the OT: while "the native (Hebrew) slave" had the right to go free in the seventh (or sabbatical) year, the "eternal slave" (Deut. 15:17; Job 40:28 [41:4]) never became free of his master.[39]

Thus, David is completely accepted by Achish as his servant; see 28:2, where Achish promises David that he will become his lifelong *bodyguard.*

2. The Philistines Gather for War (28:1-2)

1 *In those days the Philistines gathered their troops*[1] *for war,*[2] *to fight with Israel.*
And Achish said to David,
"You should surely know
that you and your men are to march out with me into the camp."
2 *And David said to Achish,*
"Then you yourself will know[3] *what your servant can do!"*
And Achish said to David,
"Then I will appoint you as my bodyguard for life!"[4]

1 The temporal phrase *In those days* initiates a new paragraph. This incident must have happened some time after David's activities described in ch. 27. Achish ordered David to march out with him *into the camp* where all the Philistine troops gather, presumably at Aphek (see 29:1).

2 *Then . . . Then . . .* Here the term *lākēn* is used both by David and by Achish, though with a slightly different nuance, and its repetition adds to the conversation a tense and delicate atmosphere. Achish emphasizes the importance of David's marching out with him: *You should surely know* (v. 1). David takes this command as an opportunity to show what he *can do.* The

39. Also on 1 Sam. 1:11; 17:55; 18:2; 2 Sam. 8:2. See Gordon, *The Common Background,* p. 201.

1. *maḥănêhem;* lit., "their camps"; also 29:1. Cf. "their armed camps" (NASB); "their forces" (NRSV; JPS; NIV).

2. *laṣṣābāʾ;* lit., "to the army"; this is probably taken as a resultative; cf. "call . . . to duty" (McCarter, p. 414).

3. *ʾattāh tēdaʿ;* cf. "you may now learn" (LXX).

4. *kol-hayyāmîm;* lit., "all the days."

narrator probably uses repetition of “who said to whom” to convey the tense situation of this dialogue: *And Achish said to David* (v. 1), *And David said to Achish* (v. 2), and *Achish said to David* (v. 2). In a normal dialogue pattern, the last two expressions would be phrased as “he said to him”; see on 3:16; 9:6, 9; 20:2; etc.

Achish appoints David as his life-long *bodyguard (šōmēr l^{e}rō’šî;* lit., “a keeper of my head”). This is a specific position at court, while *an eternal servant* (27:12) refers to the status of the king’s subjects.

<“Witch of Endor”> (28:3-25) [embedded story]

Now the stage changes to the other side, namely, to the Israelite camp. The present episode, however, is out of place chronologically. Here, in this chapter, the Philistines are already at Shunem in Jezreel and Israel is encamped on the mountain regions of Gilboa. However, at the beginning of the next chapter, ch. 29, the Philistine forces are assembled at Aphek in the Sharon, far south of the plain of Jezreel, and go up to Jezreel only in v. 11, and Israel is still encamped “at the spring in Jezreel” (v. 1), at the foot of Mt. Gilboa. Therefore, chronologically, this section follows ch. 30.

Various reasons for the present unchronological order have been suggested. Budde and others have supposed that this episode was once removed from its original context just before ch. 31 “by a Deuteronomically oriented editor who was offended by its content (cf. Deut. 18:10-12).” But, later, another editor restored it at the wrong place in the narrative. Against this view, Smith points out that it ignores “the fact that this account was written with the scene of Saul’s death in mind.”[5] McCarter also points out that Samuel’s speech in v. 18 about Saul’s failure in the Amalekite incident in ch. 15 may serve as “a kind of *praeparatio* before the account of David’s punishment of the Amalekites in cc 29-30.”[6]

A closer look at the narrative, however, seems to show a sophisticated use of the technique of narrative discourse. Since language is monodimensional in contrast to the multi-dimensional reality of life (see “Introduction” [Section VII, C]), some narrative descriptions may be “dischronologized,” that is, put chronologically out of order[7] with the author using an organizing principle other than chronology. In this case, the narrator’s concern is mainly on the *dramatis personae,* that is, Saul and David, and not on the geographical positions of the armies.

5. Smith, p. 238.

6. McCarter, p. 422.

7. W. J. Martin, “‘Dischronologized’ Narrative in the Old Testament,” in *VTS* 17 (Leiden: E. J. Brill, 1969), pp. 179-86.

If we trace just a spatio-temporal order, the "right" order would be:

	29:1	29:11/30:1	28:4	31:1ff.
Philistines	Aphek →	Jezreel →	Shunem →	Gilboa
David			/Ziklag →	
Israelites (Saul)	Jezreel →			Gilboa [Endor] →

However, the narrator has already dealt with David and his relationship with his Philistine lord Achish in ch. 27. So, when the Philistine troops gather to fight with Israel, the narrator describes the situation from the viewpoint of the Philistines and David in 28:1-2; see "Introduction" (Section VI, D). Then suddenly, but not unexpectedly from the narrator's viewpoint, the episode of Saul and the "Witch of Endor" in 28:3-25 interrupts the flow of discourse. The story of David and Achish resumes in 29:1–30:31, but in 31:1 the account of Saul comes back. Thus, the narrator alternates the episodes centered on David and those centered on Saul.[8]

David	28:1-2 (A) → 29:1–30:31 (B)
Saul	28:3-25 (X) → 31 (Y)

This alternating pattern (AXBY) is used throughout the biblical narrative; see on 17:12-19.

Thus the overall story tells us that the last battle between Saul and the Philistines at Gilboa was initiated by the Philistines, with whom David was then associated, but that David did not participate in the battle. On the other hand, Saul and his sons and much of the Israelite army perished in the battle.

In the present episode, 28:3-25, Saul seeks the Lord's will through a female necromancer, even though he recognized necromancy as wrong and had even forbidden it. Later historians particularly condemned this (1 Chr. 10:13). This story is not concerned with ancestor worship, however, since it has nothing to do with Saul's ancestors.[9] It should be also noted that this biblical episode is much briefer and less elaborate than Mesopotamian texts of necromancy.[10]

Through this séance Saul only learns that his rejection has come to a

8. For a different analysis, see S. Talmon, *Literary Studies in the Hebrew Bible: Form and Content: Collected Studies* (Jerusalem: Magnes, 1993), pp. 127-30.

9. For the differences among the terms "ancestor worship," "cult of the dead," and "necromancy," see "Introduction" (Section IV, C, 3).

10. See, e.g., I. L. Finkel, "Necromancy in Ancient Mesoopotamia," *AfO* 29/30 (1983/84) 1-17. See T. J. Lewis, "Dead," *DDD,* p. 436.

head (*tomorrow you and your sons shall be with me* in v. 19). Thus, the story "depicts the futility of conjuring the dead, since this results in an announcement of death; to speak with the dead is to join the dead."[11] So, this story does not support the view that God sometimes uses even pagan religious practices for his own purpose. Rather, something very unusual even from the perspective of the female necromancer occurred through God's power. The situation, rather than the practice of necromancy, was used for God's purpose to declare his judgment on Saul.

EXCURSUS: TECHNICAL VERBAL EXPRESSIONS

When Saul saw the Philistine army, he was greatly afraid and inquired of (*š'l *b-*) the Lord by legitimate means such as dreams, Urim, and prophets (v. 6). Since he did not receive any answer from the Lord, he turned to the unlawful practice of making inquiry through (*drš *b-*) a female necromancer (v. 7). He wanted her to call (*qr' *l-;* cf. v. 15) Samuel so that Samuel would tell him what he should do in the present crisis. He thus asked the woman to divine by (*qsm *b-*) the *'ôb*-spirits and bring up (*ʿlh [Hi] vv. 8, 11) Samuel, who had been dead and buried for some time (v. 3).

Thus, the present narrative carefully distinguishes five verbs that refer to modes by which humans inquire of the divine will:

(1) *š'l *b-* (v. 6) "make inquiry of"
This expression is used for Saul's inquiry (*š'l + *šā'ûl*) of the Lord; it is the normal verb for legitimate inquiries of God: for example, 1 Sam. 10:22; 14:37; 22:10; 23:2; cf. Akk. *šâlu,* "to ask gods (such as Šamaš) for an oracle" (*CAD,* Š, p. 278). It is probably related etymologically to Sheol.[12]

(2) *drš *b-* (v. 7) "seek through"
The verb is used often positively in the phrase "seek the Lord" (Deut. 4:29; 1 Chr. 22:19; Ps. 9:10; etc.), but with the preposition *b-,* it is usually used to indicate consulting "ghosts and gods" (e.g.,

11. P. D. Miscall, *1 Samuel: A Literary Reading* (Bloomington: Indiana University Press, 1986), p. 172.

12. Sheol is often suggested to be "a place of inquiry referring to the practice of necromancy" (T. J. Lewis, "Dead, Abode of the," in *ABD,* II, p. 102; also see H. M. Barstad, "Sheol," in *DDD,* pp. 1452-57). Oppenheim compares the role of the *šā'iltu*-priestess in Mesopotamia with the woman here; see T. J. Lewis, *Cults of the Dead in Ancient Israel and Ugarit* (Atlanta: Scholars Press, 1989), p. 112, n. 32. Since the Akkadian *šā'ilu* "diviner" is associated with *mušēlû eṭemmi* "one who brings up the spirits of the dead" in the lexical texts, this diviner who "asks" in a process accompanied by a certain type of incense probably practiced necromancy; see *CAD,* Š/1, pp. 111-12.

2 K. 1:2f.) and "never occurs in a context where priests inquire of God."[13]

(3) *qr' *l*- (v. 15) "invoke" (lit., "call to")
This phrase can be compared to the Ugaritic verb *qr',* which appears in *KTU* 1.161 with the technical meaning of "to invoke" the spirits of the dead, that is, *rpum* and *mlkm.*[14]

(4) *qsm *b*- (v. 8) "divine by"
This is the most common term for divination and tends to refer to the whole complex of illicit magical and divinatory practices in ancient Israel (e.g., Deut. 18:14; 1 Sam. 6:2; etc.).[15]

(5) *ʿlh [Hi] (vv. 8, 11) "bring up"
This verb can be compared with Akk. *šūlû* for denoting the function of the Mesopotamian sun god Šamaš as a *psychopompe* who "has the power and authority to bring up *(šūlû)* a ghost from the Underworld." See on 1 Sam. 2:6.[16]

a. Setting (28:3-4a)

3 *Now Samuel had been dead*
and all Israel had lamented[17] *for him and buried him in Ramah, his city.*[18]
As for Saul, he had driven[19] *the necromancers and mediums out of the land.*
4a *And the Philistines assembled, came and encamped at Shunem.*

3 *Now . . . As for Saul . . .* denotes the SETTING of the following EVENT (v. 4b), giving information necessary to understand the story.

Samuel had already been buried sometime ago (25:1), and hence *had*

13. J. Lust, "On Wizards and Prophets," in *Studies on Prophecy: A Collection of Twelve Papers* (VTS 26; Leiden: E. J. Brill, 1974), p. 139.

14. On "dead spirits" *(rᵉpāʾîm),* see *HALOT,* pp. 1274-75; also D. T. Tsumura, "The Interpretation of the Ugaritic Funerary Text KTU 1.161," in *Official Cult and Popular Religion in the Ancient Near East,* ed. E. Matsushima (Heidelberg: C. Winter, 1993), pp. 40-55.

15. Lust, "On Wizards and Prophets," p. 141, n. 2.

16. See F. H. Cryer, *Divination in Ancient Israel and Its Near Eastern Environment: A Socio-historic Investigation* (JSOTSS 142; Sheffield: Sheffield Academic Press, 1994), for "divination" in ancient Israel and in the ancient Near East.

17. *spd: see on 25:1.

18. *ûbᵉʿîrô;* lit., "and in his city"; *waw* here is explicative; see GKC, §154a, cited by D. W. Baker, "Further Examples of the wāw explicativum," *VT* 30 (1980) 136; also 6:18.

19. *swr, Hi. "to turn aside."

been dead (*mēt;* pf. as stative). This verse does not inform us of his death; it just reminds us of it.

The Mosaic laws forbade as abominations *(tôʿēbōt)* mediums, wizards, and necromancers, who consult the spirits of the dead (Deut. 18:11; Lev. 19:31; 20:6, 27). The very need for such prohibitions is an indication that the problem of necromancy and of religious practices related to the dead was widespread in ancient Canaan. The reason Saul opposed these magical practices is presumably because he himself was well aware of "its assumed efficacy," on which the biblical prohibition to magic was based.[20] The present verse is evidence for such Canaanite cults in the land of Israel during Saul's days. Later history also evidences the existence of those abominations in Israel (e.g., Isa. 8:19; 29:4; 2 K. 21:6; 23:24). Saul's action of driving these pagan practices out of the land of Israel indicates that he remains a faithful Yahwist, at least on the surface (see v. 6). It is clear that Saul had already driven them out before the present crisis occurred. This verse seems to be strong evidence of the existence of the prohibition at this time as it is unlikely that a later editor would have made up something good about Saul.

The term *necromancers ('ōbôt)* also appears in vv. 7, 8, 9.[21] There are basically three usages of *'ôb* in the Old Testament, (a) "an *'ôb-* spirit"; (b) "necromancy"; and (c) "necromancer." The *'ôb-* spirit refers to "the spirit of a dead person" in general, like the Akk. *eṭemmu,*[22] rather than to "the deified spirit of the ancestors";[23] note that Samuel was not Saul's ancestor. "Necromancy" is the practice of invoking the dead and divining by an *'ôb-* spirit, and a "necromancer" is a person who practices necromancy.[24]

The term *mediums* (*yiddeʿōnîm;*[25] lit., "(all-) knowing") occurs eleven times in the OT, always in parallel with *'ôb* and as a hendiadys. Twice it refers to the practice of necromancy (2 K. 21:6; 2 Chr. 33:6); the other nine times it refers to the practitioner, but never to the "spirit" itself. Therefore, it

20. See H. C. Brichto, "Kin, Cult, Land and Afterlife — A Biblical Complex," *HUCA* 44 (1973) 7.

21. *'ôb* occurs seventeen times in the OT; for etymology, see H. A. Hoffner, Jr., "Second Millennium Antecedents to the Hebrew 'ob," *JBL* 86 (1967) 385-401; also in *CS,* I, pp. 164, 170; J. U. R. Ebach, "Unterweltsbeschwörung im Alten Testament: Untersuchungen zur Begriffs- und Religionsgeschichte des *'ob,*" *UF* 9 (1977) 57-70; "Unterweltsbeschwörung im Alten Testament. II," *UF* 12 (1980) 205-22.

22. See T. Abusch, "Eṭemmu," in *DDD,* pp. 588-94.

23. J. Tropper, "Spirit of the Dead," in *DDD,* p. 1528.

24. See Tropper, "Spirit of the Dead," in *DDD,* pp. 1524-30; Lewis, "Dead," in *DDD,* pp. 421-38.

25. The nominal pattern of this term is like *qadmônî* "east of, earlier" and *'admônî* "reddish"; see B-L, p. 501y.

probably refers not to "the knowledgeability of the dead"[26] but to that of the medium.

4a The phrase *came and encamped,* rather than "went and encamped," indicates that the narrator's viewpoint is in the north. See 20:1 and "Introduction" (Section VI, D) on the "and came and did" structure. The Philistines *encamped at Shunem* (modern Sôlem [MR181-223]), which is on the southern slope of the Nebī Dahī (the so-called "Hill of Moreh"). On the geographical transition in these chapters, see above.

b. Events (28:4b-23)

(1) No Answer from the Lord (28:4b-6)

4b *And Saul gathered all Israel, and they encamped on (the) Gilboa.*
5 *And Saul saw the Philistine camp; his heart feared and trembled*[27] *very much.*
6 *And Saul inquired of the Lord, but the Lord did not answer him, even by dreams or Urim or prophets.*

4b-5 Saul gathers all his army on Mount Gilboa. When he sees the Philistine camp from the mountain, he is greatly afraid of the enemy.

6 So, Saul *inquired of* (*š'l *b-*)[28] the Lord with regard to the battle against the Philistines. But the Lord did not answer, that is, reveal his will, to Saul. In v. 16 the reason is given that the Lord has turned away from him.

For dreams as a method of legitimate revelation, see Genesis 20, 31 and Num. 12:6; 1 K. 3:5; etc.; see on 1 Sam. 3:7. "Even Jeremiah regarded the dreamer as a distinct type of prophet (Jer 27:9), though he belittled this medium, contrasting it with 'the word of God' and associating it with false prophets . . . (Jer 23:28)."[29] These three methods — dreams, Urim, and prophets — were normally used in Israel when seeking divine guidance. Three means of inquiring of the deity, that is, "omen," "dream," and

26. J. Tropper, "Wizard," in *DDD,* p. 1706.

27. *wayyērā' wayyeḥĕrad;* a verbal hendiadys, taking "his heart" *(libbô)* as their subject.

28. See C. H. Gordon, *The Common Background of Greek and Hebrew Civilizations* (New York: W. W. Norton, 1965), p. 86, n. 1; "Eblaitica," *Eblaitica: Essays on the Ebla Archives and Eblaite Language* 1 (1987) 24; see notes on 23:2 for a military query to a deity in Assyria.

29. See A. Malamat, "Intuitive Prophecy — A General Survey," in *Mari and the Bible* (Leiden: E. J. Brill, 1998), p. 75. On dream-revelations in Mari, see Malamat, "Intuitive Prophecy," pp. 74-76; also *CS,* I, p. 426.

"prophet," are also found in the Plague Prayer of Muršili II.[30] On Urim, see on 14:41. For prophets, see on 3:20.

(2) "Search for Me a Woman" (28:7-8a)

7 *And Saul said to his servants,*
"Search for me a woman who serves the Lady of the 'ob-spirits
so that I may go to her and seek (the divine will) through her!"
And his servants said to him,
"There has been found a woman who serves the Lady of the 'ob-spirits in En-dor!"
8a *And Saul disguised himself and put on different clothes and went with two men.*

7-8a Saul asks his servants to search a female necromancer so that he may inquire the Lord's will through her. McCarter translates *'ēšet ba'ălat-'ôb* (lit., "a woman of lady of *'ōb*-spirit") as "a ghostwife" and explains the MT form as a conflation of two terms referring to a female necromancer, namely, *'št 'wb,* "ghostwife," and *b'lt 'wb,* "ghostmistress." Based on the LXX he is inclined to take *'št 'wb* as the original.[31] However, the phrase seems to mean a woman who serves the Lady of the *'ōb*-spirits; see Excursus (below). In other words, a female necromancer is a woman who serves the Lady of the netherworld and communicates with spirits of the dead.

On the term *'ôb,* see above (v. 3). C. H. Gordon notes that "Odysseus consulted his [the prophet Teiresias's] departed spirit in Hades (*Odyssey* 10:490-5; 11:89-137) much as Saul had the ghost of the Prophet Samuel called up from Sheol."[32]

The term *drš here with the preposition denotes not seeking God himself (as in Amos 5:4, 6; etc.) but seeking the divine will through a medium. It seems that the act of "seeking" is more emphasized than the object which is sought. For the phrase *seek through* (lit., "in"), compare "made inquiry to" in v. 6.

En-dor ('ên dôr) appears also in Josh. 17:11; it is modern Khirbet eṣ-Ṣafṣafe [MR187-227], 4.5 miles northeast of Shunem, where the Philistines were encamped.[33] Therefore, it was on the other side of the enemy's camp

30. Malamat, "Intuitive Prophecy," p. 75, n. 39, which cites *ANET,* pp. 394b-95a. See also B. Albrektson, *History and the Gods: An Essay on the Idea of Historical Events as Divine Manifestations in the Ancient Near East and in Israel* (Lund: C. W. K. Gleerup, 1967), p. 117, n. 6. Cf. "a dream . . . an oracle . . . a prophet" (*CS,* I, p. 159).

31. McCarter, p. 418.

32. Gordon, *The Common Background,* p. 260. On "Hades," see S. Dalley, "The God *Šalmu* and the Winged Disk," *Iraq 48* (1986) 85-101.

33. See D. V. Edelman, "En-dor," in *ABD,* II, pp. 499-501.

from Gilboa, where he and his army were. Saul disguises himself and goes there with two servants.

(3) "Divine for Me" (28:8b-12a)

8b *And they came to the woman at night.*
And he said,
"Divine[34] for me by 'ob-spirits
and bring up for me the one whom I order you to!"
9 *And the woman said to him,*
"You must know what Saul did, that is,
he exterminated the necromancers and mediums[35] from the land.
Why are you striking at my life to kill me?"
10 *And Saul swore to her by the Lord, (saying)*
"The Lord lives! No guilt shall fall on you about this matter!"
11 *And the woman said,*
"Whom shall I bring up for you?"
And he said,
"Bring up Samuel for me!"
12a *And the woman saw Samuel and shouted in a loud voice.*

8b Note the change of the movement verbs from *went* (8a) to *came* here; it signifies the change of viewpoint of the narrator.

Since necromantic rituals regularly took place *at night* (28:8; Isa. 45:18-19), Saul went to the necromancer at night. It was the appropriate time for consulting the spirits of the dead.[36] And it was also the time when the solar deity was supposedly active in the underworld as "the lord of the spirits of the dead" (*bēl eṭemmi* in Akk.); see "Excursus" (below).

The verb *qsm ("to divine") is the basic term for the act of divination and elsewhere refers to the practices of foreign diviners or false Israelite prophets; in Deut. 18:10 the practitioners of divination are condemned as abominable. Here, Saul asks the woman to divine by the *'ob*-spirits, that is, by contacting the spirits of the dead. Since Yahweh would not answer him by

34. *qosŏmî-nā'* (Q.; see GKC, §10h); *qswmy-* (K.; see GKC, §46e).

35. *yidde'ōnî;* MT has a singular form, which McCarter thinks has lost *-m* before the succeeding *min,* "from." However, the form has resulted from consonantal *sandhi,* i.e., the fusion of two contiguous consonants: *hayyidde'ōnîm min-* → *hayyidde'ōnî min-;* see D. T. Tsumura, "Scribal Errors or Phonetic Spellings? Samuel as an Aural Text," *VT* 49 (1999) 401.

36. Lewis, "Dead, Abode of the," in *ABD* II, p. 103; also Lewis, *Cults of the Dead in Ancient Israel and Ugarit,* p. 114.

other, legitimate methods, Saul appeals to this "abominable" practice which he himself has prohibited in Israel. See also on 15:23.

Saul asks the female necromancer to *bring up* (*ʿlh [Hi.]) the spirit of a dead person from the underworld (see v. 13). Note that the Mesopotamian sun god Šamaš is described as *šūlū* "the one who brings up" the spirits of the dead *(eṭemmu)*.[37]

9 *Why are you striking at my life to kill me?* — this is a rhetorical question; the woman is not asking the reason but "accusing" Saul of endangering her life.[38] See also v. 12b.

10 For the oath formula, *The Lord lives!"* see 14:39. It is certainly ironic that Saul uses this formula while seeking guidance from the spirit of the dead, though he himself may not have been aware of the contradiction.

11 The word *Samuel ('et-šᵉmû'ēl)* appears before the verb for emphasis.

Some scholars have argued that there is a literary and logical confusion in vv. 10-12. They say the introduction of Samuel in v. 11 appears to disrupt the natural flow of the narrative and leave the woman's recognition of Saul in v. 12b "without explanation." Hence, McCarter explains that the woman originally brought up an "anonymous ghost" and that Saul's "imperious tone" in v. 10 gave him away, and that vv. 11-12a are "secondary." However, in v. 8 Saul specifically says "bring up for me the one whom I order you," so McCarter would have to emend that away also.[39] Certainly vv. 8-11 flow naturally as they are.

Note that there is no description of the "invoking." Perhaps it is because it was so illicit that the writer did not want even to mention the actual act.

12a *And shouted in a loud voice;* (12b) *And the woman said:* the Hebrew text, *wattizʿaq bᵉqôl gādôl wattō'mer hā'iššāh,* does not mean "the woman shouted in a loud voice, 'Why . . .'" as in 12:10. Since every *wayqtl* followed by a stated subject constitutes a sub-paragraph (see "Introduction" [Section VI, A]), there is a break between the two sentences. This suggests that something about Samuel's appearance surprised the woman. Something unexpected might have happened outside her control after Saul asked her to bring up Samuel in v. 11b.[40] One might surmise that some unknown thing

37. Also note the expression ". . . pulls the deity up from the pit" in Hittite; see *CS,* I, pp. 164, 174.

38. See K. M. Craig, Jr., "Rhetorical Aspects of Questions Answered with Silence in 1 Samuel 14:37 and 28:6," *CBQ* 56 (1994) 230; L. J. de Regt, "Discourse Implications of Rhetorical Questions in Job, Deuteronomy and the Minor Prophets," in *Literary Structure and Rhetorical Strategies in the Hebrew Bible,* ed. L. J. de Regt, J. de Waard, and J. P. Fokkelman (Assen: Van Gorcum, 1996), p. 57.

39. McCarter, p. 421.

40. Beuken holds that she lost the "initiative" between v. 11b and v. 12 and "all of

happened before she *shouted in a loud voice* (v. 12a) and before she turned to Saul again in v. 12b.

This was certainly an extraordinary event for her. It may be that the ordinary divining powers were not employed this time. Or, rather a power stronger than her divining powers might have been at work in bringing up the spirit of Samuel.[41] Even if the spirit was brought up by her actions (see v. 15: "you disturbed me"), it might not have appeared or acted like the spirit(s) of the dead, like *'ôb* or *r^{e}pā'îm,* which she was comfortable handling as a necromancer.

It should be noted that Samuel's "coming up from the underworld" is "presented as an actual event, not a dream or a vision, even though dreams are explicitly mentioned by Saul."[42]

(4) "I Saw Gods Coming Up" (28:12b-14a)

12b *And the woman said to Saul,*
"Why have you deceived me? You are Saul!"
13 *And the king said to her,*
"Do not be afraid! For what have you seen?"
And the woman said to Saul,
"I saw gods coming up from the underworld."[43]
14a *And he said to her,*
"What is his appearance?"[44]
And she said,
"An old man is coming up. He is wrapped in a robe."

12b One can only surmise how the woman knew her customer was Saul. Certainly this realization would cause her fear (v. 13). It may be that as the spirit arose she heard it call on Saul by name. This let her know who Saul was and caused her to cry out.

13 The term *'ĕlōhîm* (pl.: lit., "gods"), translated as "a divine being" (NRSV; NASB; JPS) or "a spirit" (NIV), takes here a plural predicate *'ōlîm* ("coming up": part., m.pl.). So, it means "gods" or "divine beings" who are far from being on par with Yahweh. Hence, *'ĕlōhîm* in this necromantic situa-

a sudden sees Samuel before her. That explains her loud cry (v. 12)." See W. A. M. Beuken, "I Samuel 28: The Prophet as 'Hammer of Witches,'" *JSOT* 6 (1978) 8.

41. See Miscall, p. 168; also L. J. Wood, *The Holy Spirit in the Old Testament* (Grand Rapids: Zondervan, 1976), p. 139.

42. Miscall, p. 171.

43. *hā'āreṣ;* lit., "earth." See N. J. Tromp, *Primitive Conceptions of Death and the Nether World in the Old Testament* (Rome: Pontifical Biblical Institute, 1969), pp. 23-46.

44. *to'ŏrô;* LXX has "What do you know?"

tion/context refers to what the woman called "gods," that is, the spirits of the dead or a "preternatural being"[45] like Ugaritic *rpim — ilnym* and *ilm — mtm* (*KTU* 1.6:VI:46-48) or *ilu,* which refers to the deceased, in the ancient Near Eastern texts.[46] While the woman seems to have represented the Canaanite or pre-Israelite religious traditions, the Israelite king Saul, who is still a seeker of (the words of) Yahweh, expects his prophet Samuel to appear with a message from their God and in v. 14 asks her what *his* (sing.) appearance is. C. H. Gordon notes that "Daniel wants to inter Aqhat in the right tomb: one for slain heroes who become gods of the earth. The word 'gods' is similarly used for departed spirits including that of the heroic figure Samuel, brought up by the Witch of Endor."[47] Another biblical example of the use of *'ĕlōhîm* which can be interpreted as referring to the dead *(mētîm)* is Isa. 8:19, where the prophet Isaiah mocks the people's desire to consult mediums.[48] Lewis also notes a parallel use of these terms in Ps. 106:28 *(mētîm)* and Num. 25:2 *('ĕlōhîm),* where the daughters of the Moabites invite the people of Israel to eat the sacrifices to dead ancestors.[49]

14a For *old (zāqēn),* McCarter reads *zqp* "erect," based on the LXX, since he thinks it to be preferable as a *lectio difficilior.* However, the MT makes good sense and is most natural. The term "an old man" could be an "epithet" for a prophet; Malamat notes in a Mari text that an "old man" was dwelling in the tent-shrine of Dagan.[50]

The *robe (mᵉʿîl)* was the characteristic garment of Samuel (15:27; cf. 2:19). Saul must have recognized Samuel on this basis. Note that in tombs of ancient Israel the bodies of select individuals, including women, were wrapped with a cloak over their dresses and jewelry.[51]

45. T. J. Lewis, "The Ancestral Estate *(naḥălat 'ĕlōhîm)* in 2 Samuel 14:16," *JBL* 110 (1991) 602-3; "Ancestor Worship," in *ABD* I, p. 241.

46. See Lewis, "The Ancestral Estate," pp. 600-602. On Nuzi and Emar, see K. van der Toorn, "Gods and Ancestors in Emar and Nuzi," *ZA* 84 (1994) 38-59. See on 2 Sam. 14:16.

47. Gordon, *The Common Background,* p. 166.

48. See Lewis, "The Ancestral Estate," p. 602; E. M. Bloch-Smith, "The Cult of the Dead in Judah: Interpreting the Material Remains," *JBL* 111 (1992) 220-21.

49. On the *teraphim* as ancestor statuettes, see K. van der Toorn, "The Nature of the Biblical Teraphim in the Light of the Cuneiform Evidence," *CBQ* 52 (1990) 203-22; also see on 15:23.

50. A. Malamat, "Episodes Involving Samuel and Saul and the Prophetic Texts from Mari," in *Mari and the Bible* (Leiden: E. J. Brill, 1998), pp. 103-4.

51. See Bloch-Smith, "The Cult of the Dead in Judah," p. 218.

(5) Saul and Samuel (28:14b-19)

14b *And Saul knew that he was Samuel and bowed down face to the ground and paid homage.*
15 *And Samuel said to Saul,*
"Why did you disturb me by bringing me up?"
And Saul said,
"I am in great distress![52]
For the Philistines are fighting with me,
but God[53] *has turned away from me and no longer answers me*
either through prophets or by dreams.
So I have invoked[54] *you to let me know what I should do."*
16 *And Samuel said,*
"But why do you inquire of me
while the Lord has turned away from you
and become your adversary;[55]
17 *and the Lord has done for himself*[56] *as he told (you) through me;*
and the Lord has torn the kingship from your hand
and given it to your neighbor David?
18 *As you did not listen to the voice of the Lord,*
namely, you did not execute his hot anger against Amalek,
therefore, the Lord did this thing to you this day
19 *so that the Lord might*[57] *give even Israel (who is) with you*
into the hand of the Philistines
— tomorrow you and your sons shall be with me —
(so that) even the camp of Israel the Lord might give
into the hand of Philistines!"

14b It is important to note that Saul did not worship Samuel as a divine being when he appeared. He spoke to the apparition just as he had spoken to the

52. On the idiom *I am in great distress (ṣar-lî m^e'ōd),* see 13:6.

53. *wē'lōhîm;* cf. "gods" (v. 13).

54. *wā'eqrā'eh.* For a full discussion of the anomalous form of the MT, see Stoebe, p. 486; see also GKC, §48d. See above (Excursus).

55. *'ārekā* is possibly an "Israelian," rather than Aramaic, form; see G. A. Rendsburg, "Morphological Evidence for Regional Dialects in Ancient Hebrew" in *Linguistics and Biblical Hebrew,* ed. W. R. Bodine (Winona Lake, Ind.: Eisenbrauns, 1992), p. 70. Cf. "to be with your neighbor" (McCarter, p. 419), based on the LXX. The existence of the "Aramaic" form itself does not make the narrative late. See *HALOT,* p. 876.

56. *lô;* so "for Himself" (JPS); cf. "you" (NRSV; McCarter), based on the LXX. This could be a "ventive" as in Akkadian; see on 20:20. McCarter, p. 419, thinks that the MT lost *k* before the following word (*k'sr,* "just as").

57. *w^eyittēn; w^e+yqtl;* purpose clause; cf. "Moreover" (NASB; NRSV).

prophet during his lifetime. To Saul, Yahweh was still his only God, and Samuel spoke with Saul as the prophet of Yahweh. The narrator also refers to the apparition as "Samuel," not as "gods" or a ghost.

15 The term "to disturb" (*rgz) appears also in Isa. 14:9, where Sheol is said to be "stirred up" and the shades *(r^{e}pāʾîm)* to be roused. Its Phoenician cognate often refers to the violation of tombs in sarcophagus (i.e., sepulchral) inscriptions which were written as warnings against grave robbers: for example, the fifth-century epitaph of King Tabnit of Sidon.[58] Note that the expression "those who disturb a god" (Job 12:6), which is in parallel with "robbers, looters," means "grave robbers."[59]

We are not told how Samuel appeared, but, as Beuken holds, there is no question that it is Samuel himself who speaks here.[60] In his speech in vv. 16-19 Samuel uses the divine name, Yahweh, seven times, while Saul said "God" once.[61] The author certainly intends us to believe it is really Samuel — only he would have been able to give that message — and we have to assume that God permitted the witch to call Samuel up in this case even though he might not normally have allowed it.

In the phrase *either through prophets or by dreams,* the Urim is not included as in v. 6 ("even by dreams or Urim or prophets"), and the others are in reverse order. This is merismatically used, referring to the methods other than the medium.

16 Samuel's answer only reinforces God's judgment against Saul: *the Lord has turned away from you.*

17-18 These verses certainly refer to the story of Saul's rejection in 15:1-34. Here Saul's "neighbor" (15:28), to whom the kingdom of Israel was to be given, is mentioned by name, *David.* The very reason of Saul's rejection is repeated here again: that he *did not listen to the voice of the Lord* (see 15:11, 22-23).

19 McCarter explains this verse as "corrupt in all witnesses, conflating two versions of one clause."[62] However, as discussed in the "Introduction" (Section VII, B), this is poetic diction with an <AXB pattern>, and the first and the third lines constitute a <chiasmus>:[63] a-b-c//b-a-c

w^{e}yittēn YHWH gam ʾet-yiśrāʾēl ʿimm^{e}kā b^{e}yad-p^{e}lištîm	A
ûmāḥār ʾattāh ûbāneykā ʿimmî	X
gam ʾet-maḥănēh yiśrāʾēl yittēn YHWH b^{e}yad-p^{e}lištîm	B

58. *KAI* 13.4, 6, 7; *CS,* II, p. 182.
59. McCarter, p. 421.
60. Beuken, "I Samuel 28," p. 5.
61. See Miscall, p. 169.
62. McCarter, p. 419.
63. See also Andersen, p. 164.

"so that the Lord might give even Israel (who is) with you
into the hand of Philistines
— tomorrow you and your sons shall be with me —
(so that) even the camp of Israel the Lord might give
into the hand of Philistines!"

Note that the third line expresses the same meaning as the first, only replacing "Israel (who is) with you" by "the camp of Israel."[64]

You and your sons shall be with me. In other words, Saul will join the community of the dead[65] by entering the netherworld, Sheol, which seems to have been the abode both of the righteous and the rejected.

(6) Saul Falls Down (28:20-23)

20 *And Saul immediately fell down full length[66] to the ground and was very much frightened by the words of Samuel, and there was even no strength in him, for he had not eaten any food all the day and night.*
21 *And the woman came to Saul and saw that he was greatly terrified and said to him,*
"Now, your maidservant listened to your voice,
and I took my life in my hand[67] and listened to the words which you spoke to me.
22 *Now, then, you also, listen to the voice of your maidservant*
and let me put before you a morsel of bread.[68]
And eat it,
so that strength may be in you,
for you must go on your way."
23 *And he refused, saying,*
"I won't eat."
And his servants and also the woman urged him, and he listened to their words[69] and arose from the ground and sat on the couch.

64. Similarly, but not exactly in the same way, Revell sees here an envelope structure, ABBA. See E. J. Revell, "The Repetition of Introductions to Speech as a Feature of Biblical Hebrew," *VT* 47 (1997) 94, n. 7.

65. McCarter translates: "you are going to fall along with your sons," on the basis of LXX^B. He thinks that the MT has a defective text; see p. 419. Perhaps the LXX^B author did not like the idea that Saul and Samuel would go to the same place after death.

66. *mᵉlōʾ-qômātô;* lit., "full of his height."

67. *wāʾāśîm napšî bᵉkappî;* i.e., "I risked my life"; see on 19:5.

68. *pat-leḥem;* also 2:36.

69. Lit., "voice."

20 Saul was frightened because of the death sentence *tomorrow you and your sons shall be with me* (v. 19). It is not a normal death, as "gathered to his kin" or "sleeps with one's fathers," but a tragic death to come "tomorrow." Thus, Saul "did himself no good by doing what he had decreed to be unlawful. God's word stood and could not be altered."[70] It is to be noted that he did not try to avoid the battle the next day.

Saul *had not eaten any food,* probably to purify himself as preparation for meeting Samuel. He was a very "religious" person as seen in the earlier episodes, even though he had already been rejected by the Lord; see 15:22-23. What matters for us however, is not whether our conduct is religiously proper or not, but to know what the will of the Lord is for us and to act accordingly.

23 Here "rejecting" and "saying" are simultaneous, hence: *And he refused, saying.*

The underlying root of *urged (wayyipr^{e}ṣû)* would be *pṣr rather than *prṣ; the MT form resulted from metathesis; for this root, see on 15:23; 2 Sam. 13:25.[71]

c. Terminus (28:24-25)

24 *Since the woman had a stall-fed calf*[72] *in the house, she quickly slaughtered*[73] *it and took some flour and kneaded*[74] *it and baked it to unleavened bread*

25 *and served Saul and his servants. So they ate and arose and went away that night.*

24-25 In these two verses nine *wayqtl* verbs are used: *watt^{e}mahēr wattizbāḥēhû wattiqqaḥ . . . wattālāš wattōpēhû . . . wattaggēš . . . wayyō'kēlû wayyāqūmû wayyēl^{e}kû. . . .* The sequence describes consecutive actions in a very fast tempo; see also 1 Sam. 17:48-51 and "Introduction" (Section VI, C). This leads to the TERMINUS of this episode. Saul and his servants go back to Mount Gilboa *that night.*

70. Baldwin, p. 164.

71. See Driver, p. 218; F. Delitzsch, *Die Lese- und Schreibfehler im Alten Testament* (Berlin: Walter de Gruyter, 1920), p. 90. For metathesis which involves the consonant /r/, see Tsumura, "Scribal Errors or Phonetic Spellings?" pp. 406-8.

72. *'ēgel-marbēq;* cf. "fatted" (NRSV), "fattened" (NIV; NASB). Elsewhere the expression appears "only metaphorically (Jer. 46:21; Mal. 3:20 [English 4:2])" (McCarter, p. 421).

73. *zbḥ; lit., "sacrificed." Note that in a Ugaritic text a deity himself *slaughters,* not *sacrifices:* "El slaughters game in his house" (*CS,* I, p. 303).

74. *wattālāš;* so in 2 Sam. 13:8 (Qere).

24 The translation *to unleavened bread (maṣṣôt)* reflects that the noun is interpreted as a resultative object.

EXCURSUS

1. 'ēšet ba'ălat 'ôb (lit., "a woman of lady of 'ōb-spirit")

The meanings of *'ôb* were discussed above (see on v. 3). It is also important in this story to know exactly what *'ēšet ba'ălat 'ôb* means and to what it refers. The phrase has been interpreted in various ways.

(1) "A Woman Who Has an *'ôb*-spirit"

For example, "a woman who has a familiar spirit" (NEB; REB). Here, the first term *'ēšet* (cstr.) is taken to be in apposition to *ba'ălat 'ôb,* and the phrase is translated as "a woman, a possessor of an *'ôb*-spirit"; for example, "(woman) who has a spirit = necromancer";[75] "a woman that hath a soothsaying spirit."[76] Compare "a woman who has a pit" — "cavern woman."[77]

(2) "A Woman Who Practices *'ôb*"

For example, "a woman who is a medium" (RSV; NIV). The syntax is similar to (1) but *'ôb* is taken as meaning "necromancy," the act of conjuring the spirits of the dead, rather than the spirit itself. So, the phrase can be translated as "a woman who is a female necromancer" like *ba'ălat k^ešāpîm* (Nah. 3:4); "a woman who practices magic," that is, "sorceress."

(3) "A Woman of an *'ôb*-spirit"

This view takes *'ēšet* as "a *suspended* construct state" (S. R. Driver).[78] Recently McCarter suggested, based on the LXX, that the phrase is a conflation of *'ēšet 'ôb* "a ghostwife" and *ba'ălat 'ôb* "ghostmistress."

However, I would like to propose another possibility, which treats the syntax of the two noun phrases *'ēšet* (cstr.) and *ba'ălat 'ôb* (see below) differently. According to this, the latter noun phrase is an objective genitive, that is, "a woman for *ba'ălat 'ôb,"* like *'ebed YHWH* "servant of the Lord" and *'îš 'ĕlōhîm* "a man of God." Hence, the phrase may be translated as "a woman who serves *ba'ălat 'ôb.*"[79]

75. J-M, §129j (p. 469).
76. GKC, §128u (p. 418).
77. Beuken, "I Samuel 28," p. 7.
78. Driver, p. 214.
79. Tsumura, "The Interpretation of the Ugaritic Funerary Text KTU 1.161," pp. 40-55.

2. *baʿălat ʾôb as a Solar Goddess*

The phrase *baʿălat ʾôb* might mean the "Lady of *ʾôb*-spirits," referring to the sun goddess in her infernal phase, that is, during the night, for it is similar to the phrases *bēl eṭemmi* (GIDIM) "the Lord of the spirits of the dead"[80] and *bēl mīti* (LÚ.UG$_x$) "the Lord of the dead,"[81] which are epithets of Šamaš, the sun god in Mesopotamia.[82]

It is noteworthy that like the Mesopotamian Shamash, the Ugaritic solar goddess Shapshu played the important role of *psychopompe,* that is, the one who brings the spirit of the dead up or down. In text 1.161, a Ugaritic text for the funeral of king Niqmaddu, it is very likely that she went down to the underworld with the newly dead king,[83] as she does in the Baal myth, where she helped Anat bury the dead Baal, searched him out in the netherworld, and restored him to his throne from the realm of the god of death (*KTU* 1.6).[84] Thus, the solar deity in daily travel from west to east through a subterranean tunnel during the night took with him or her "the spirits of the deceased as well as the offerings for those already dwelling in the nether world."[85]

It may be that in the ancient "popular" religion in Israel the solar goddess assumed the role of *psychopompe* as she did in ancient Canaan, since as she had to go through the earth at night from west back to the east, she could bring spirits back with her.[86] It would be no surprise if the sun goddess were the patron deity of the female necromancer in this chapter. Therefore I would like to suggest that *ʾēšet baʿălat ʾôb* means a "woman who serves the Lady of the dead spirits," "the Lady" referring to the sun goddess as ruler or guide of the spirits in the netherworld.

80. *CAD* E, p. 398.

81. *CAD* M/2, p. 141.

82. Cf. "Herrscher: der (Toten-) geister": *šar eṭimmē, bēl šēdi, bēl mīti* (Tallqvist, *AGE,* pp. 458-59); also PN, [d]UTU-*mi-tam-ú-ba-li-iṭ* Šamaš-Revives-the-Dying (*CAD* M/2, p. 141). See Lewis, *Cults of the Dead in Ancient Israel and Ugarit,* p. 38.

83. I.e., Niqmaddu III; see I. Singer, "A Political History of Ugarit," in *Handbook of Ugaritic Studies,* ed. W. G. E. Watson and N. Wyatt (HbO; Leiden: E. J. Brill, 1999), pp. 691-704.

84. See J. F. Healey, "The Sun Deity and the Underworld: Mesopotamia and Ugarit," in *Death in Mesopotamia* (Copenhagen: Akademisk, 1980), pp. 240, 242, n. 14; Lewis, *Cults of the Dead in Ancient Israel and Ugarit,* p. 38. This chthonic (= netherworld) nature of the solar deity might suggest that the dedication of the shrine in the month of "the Sacrifice of the Sun" in Pyrgi, an Etrurian city, has a funerary character; see *CS,* II, p. 184, n. 4.

85. J. C. de Moor, "Rāpiʾūma — Rephaim," *ZAW* 88 (1976) 330.

86. See Tsumura, "The Interpretation of the Ugaritic Funerary Text KTU 1.161," pp. 40-55.

3. The Philistine Rulers and David (29:1-11)

On the relationship between this episode and the preceding ones, see above on ch. 28. This is the B section of the AXBY pattern in chs. 28-31; it resumes the story which was suspended after 28:2. As Bar-Efrat observes,[1] the narrative of David and Achish at Aphek is made up of two dialogues, vv. 3-5 and vv. 6-10, *framed* by the two short narrations in vv. 1-2 and v. 11.

a. Setting (29:1-2)

1 *And the Philistines assembled all their forces at Aphek, while Israel were camping at the spring in Jezreel.*

2 *Now the Philistine lords were advancing by hundreds and by thousands, while David and his men were advancing in the rear with Achish.*

1 The Philistine forces were now at Aphek, about 30 miles north of Gath, but still about 40 miles short of Shunem. Aphek was a strategic place for the Philistines to gather before advancing toward the north. On *Aphek,* see 4:1. Note that in 28:4 the Philistines were already at Shunem. For the relationship between the order of discourse and the geographical situation, see above on ch. 28.

The *spring* probably refers to the spring of Harod *(ʿên ḥărōd),* southeast of the city of Jezreel at the foot of Mount Gilboa; here Gideon encamped against the Midianites (Judg. 7:1).

2 Here the Philistine army marches in a very orderly manner, *by hundreds and by thousands.* On the term *lords,* see 5:8.

b. Philistine Rulers and Achish (29:3-5)

3 *And the Philistine rulers said,*
"What are these Hebrews?"
And Achish said to the Philistine rulers,
"As you know, this is[2] *David, the servant of Saul the king of Israel, who has been with me now for over a year.*
I have not found in him anything (wrong)
from the day when he defected[3] *to me*[4] *to this day."*

1. S. Bar-Efrat, "Some Observations on the Analysis of Structure in Biblical Narrative," *VT* 30 (1980) 158-59.

2. *hălô'-zeh . . . ;* lit., "Is this not . . . ?"

3. *noplô;* so McCarter; lit., "fell." For the sense "fall away, defect" in other biblical passages, see McCarter, p. 427.

4. Supplied from the context; cf. LXX: + *pros me.*

4 *And the Philistine rulers got angry with him.*
And the Philistine rulers said to him,
"Make the man return
that he may go back to the place you have appointed him!
Let him not go down with us into the battle;
let him not become an adversary[5] *to us in the battle!*[6]
With what can this man make himself acceptable to his master?[7]
Is it not with the heads of these men?
5 *Isn't this the David about whom they answered each other while dancing, saying,*
'Saul slew by thousands;
and David by ten thousands'?"

3 The Philistine rulers get upset with David and his men marching with their soldiers. Here the *rulers (śārîm)* is synonymous to *lords (s^erānîm)* in v. 2; 5:8, though usually *śārîm* refers to "rulers" or "officials" lower than "king" *melek* (e.g., Amos 1:15) or "ruler" *šôpēṭ* (e.g., Amos 2:3).[8] There is no need to distinguish between "commanders" and "lords" (see below). In fact, the Ekron inscription gives evidence that *śar* was the title of the ruler of a Philistine city.[9]

The expression *What . . . ?* means "What are they doing here?" rather than "Who are they?" The Israelites were usually called *Hebrews (ʿibrîm)* by the Philistines; see 4:6; 13:3; 14:11.

Achish speaks well of David before the rulers. The expression *zeh yāmîm ʾô-zeh šānîm* (lit., "now for days or now for years") refers to a period of over a year. According to 27:7, it had been a year and four months. Compare *zeh yāmîm rabbîm* "for many days" (2 Sam. 14:2; etc.). McCarter thinks that this expression is a conflation of two synonymous variants,[10] but it seems to be a good idiomatic phrase.

4 This verse appears to be ambiguous as to whether the Philistine rulers *got angry with* David or with Achish. If with Achish, however, the second appearance of *the Philistine rulers* is probably unnecessary. The MT, which has the same stated subject *the Philistine rulers,* might rather support that they *got angry with* David and appears better discourse grammatically. McCarter omits the second subject, based on the LXX; as does NIV; cf.

5. *śāṭān;* also 2 Sam. 19:23.
6. Cf. "in [our own] camp" (McCarter, p. 425), based on LXX^B.
7. Plural form.
8. See K. A. Kitchen, "The Philistines," in *POTT,* p. 69.
9. See *CS,* II, p. 164.
10. McCarter, p. 425.

NRSV; NASB; JPS. However, it does seem much more likely that they would "get angry" with Achish's stupidity than with David's possible actions. Perhaps the repetition of *the Philistine rulers* implies a conference among them after which they speak.

The phrase *the place you have appointed him* refers to Ziklag; see 27:6; 29:10; 30:1.

The term *heads* in such a context reminds us of the Assyrian reliefs that depict counting the heads of enemy soldiers. The phrase *these men* (*hāʾănāšîm hāhēm;* lit., "those men") is probably a euphemistic expression for "us."[11] R. P. Gordon has called attention to the euphemistic use of the Aramaic expression "that man" *(hhwʾ gbrʾ)* in Sokoloff's dictionary *(DJPA)*.[12]

5 The expression *answered each other* refers to antiphonal singing; this song was first sung in 18:7 and is quoted by the Philistines in 21:11. Here, the song is again quoted by the Philistines. Though David was called "the king of the land" in 21:11, here it is Saul who is called *the king of Israel* (v. 3).

c. Achish and David (29:6-10)

6 *And Achish called David and said to him,*
"As Yahweh lives, you are surely just!
Your marching in and out of the camp with me is acceptable
in my judgment,[13] *for I have not found any evil in you*
from the day you came to me to this day,
but in the lords' judgment you are not acceptable.
7 *And now, go back in peace!*
You shall not do evil in the judgment of the Philistine lords."
8 *And David said to Achish,*
"What have I done? What did you find in your servant
from the day I entered your service to this day,
that I should not come and fight with the enemies of my master,
the king?"
9 *And Achish answered David:*
"I know that you are acceptable in my judgment
like God's messenger.
But the Philistine rulers have said,
'He shall not go up with us into the battle!'
10 *And now, get up (s.) early in the morning*

11. See M. A. Zipor, "Some Notes on the Origin of the Tradition of the Eighteen *tiqqûnê sôpᵉrîm*," *VT* 44 (1994) 96; also Num. 16:14.

12. At the OT Seminar of Cambridge University (May, 13, 1998).

13. *Lit.*, "good in my eyes."

with the servants of your master[14] *who have come with you!*
You shall get up (pl.) early in the morning
and go as soon as you have light!"[15]

6-7 The oath formula *As Yahweh lives (ḥay-YHWH)* is often used in the Bible; see 14:39. It seems strange that Achish the Philistine ruler uses this name. One possibility is that the narrator put this formula in his mouth even though he actually had used a different formula such as "As Dagon lives," words which the narrator wanted to avoid using. However, to polytheistic people, to make an oath in the name of gods other than the gods they normally serve is not unthinkable. So, this Philistine king made an oath by David's god either "as a matter of courtesy"[16] or because he believed that David was really *just* and hence swore by his god *Yahweh* (translated so rather than as "the Lord").

Here the Philistine *lords* (v. 7) presumably means "the other Philistine rulers" for he was the lord of Gath.

McCarter says that *seren* in vv. 2 and 7 refers to the lords or rulers, and *śar* in vv. 3, 4 and 9 refers to the military commanders. According to him, "Both Achish and the Philistine lords have found David worthy; it is the Philistine commanders who object to his participation (cf. v 9)." He holds that in v. 6 the "MT confuses the conversation thoroughly by inserting *l'* ["not"] so that David's questions in v 8 are pointless in MT."[17] Supporting the shorter text of LXX^{B}, which lacks *oux* ("not"), he translates: "And also in the opinion of the Philistine lords you are a good man." However, no reasonable explanation can be offered either for the supposed insertion of *lō'* in MT by dittography or for its loss in a variant Hebrew *Vorlage* by haplography.[18] In other words, there are no grounds to emend MT by excising *lō'*. Nor is there any strong reason why we should distinguish between the Philistine "lords" and "commanders" in this context.

8 *I entered your service: hāyîtî l^{e}pāneykā;* literally, "I was before you." As McCarter explains, "To be before someone is to be in full view and eligible for critical appraisal; as in 3:1, for example, it also suggests a position of service."[19]

"That I should . . ." is a result clause, *or* the reason for the question "What . . . ?": "Why won't you let me come and fight with the enemies of my master, the king?" It is a rhetorical question.

14. Plural form.
15. *w^{e}'ôr lākem;* lit., "and light is to you"; or "as soon as it is light" (NIV; JPS).
16. McCarter, p. 427.
17. McCarter, p. 426.
18. See D. G. Deboys, "1 Samuel xxix 6," *VT* 39 (1989) 217.
19. McCarter, p. 427.

The phrase *my master* (s. form) may refer either to Achish or to Saul. On the surface it refers to Achish, and he takes it as meaning such, but the reader may suspect that it actually refers to Saul. The judgment of the Philistine lords was probably very wise.

9 The expression *like God's messenger (kᵉmal'ak 'ĕlōhîm)* is used in referring to David by the wise woman of Tekoa (2 Sam. 14:17) and Mephibosheth (2 Sam. 19:27). McCarter thinks that this comparison is inappropriate here, for "it elsewhere applies to David as having the judicial insight of a divine being."[20] Hence, he omits the phrase with LXX^B. However, one phrase can have a slightly different meaning according to the speaker and the context; to Achish, David had been an acceptable and faithful servant *like God's messenger.*

10 McCarter performs elaborate reconstruction of the text, based on LXX^B, since he thinks that "MT has suffered a long haplography in this verse."[21] Similarly, the RSV translates: "Now then rise early in the morning, you and the servants of your lord who came with you, and go to the place that I appointed for you. As for the evil report, do not take it to heart, for you have done well before me. Start early in the morning, and leave as soon as you have light." However, the repetitive style (*get up* in s. and pl.) can be characteristic of the narrative story, which has poetic features; see "Introduction" (Section VII, B).

> "And now, get up (s.) early in the morning
> with the servants of your master who have come with you!
> You shall get up (pl.) early in the morning
> and go as soon as you have light!"

While in the first sentence it is emphasized that David should go back with "the servants" of his master, that is, David's own men, in the second sentence it is emphasized that they should leave as soon as it is light.

d. Terminus (29:11)

11 *And David, with his men, got up early in the morning to go and return to the land of the Philistines, while the Philistines went up to Jezreel.*

11 The verbal phrase *went up,* a *qtl* perf. of a movement verb, is off the mainline narrative story and points to TERMINUS of this episode; see "Introduction" (Section VI, A). The geographical transition of David and his men from

20. McCarter, p. 426.
21. McCarter, p. 426.

Aphek to *the land of the Philistines* and of the Philistine troops from Aphek to Jezreel prepares for the next two episodes, David and the Amalekite raid on Ziklag (30:1-31) and Saul at Mount Gilboa (31:1-13). Chronologically, however, the present episode is followed directly by 28:3-25.

Here again God providentially engineers the course of David's life by His sovereign will so that he does not have to fight against Saul. David was led back to Ziklag where a hard trial was waiting for him and his men.

4. Amalekite Raid on Ziklag (30:1-31)

When David and his men left Aphek and came back by God's providence to Ziklag, they found that Ziklag was burned and their wives, sons, and daughters had been taken prisoner by the Amalekites. David and his men attacked the raiding band and recovered their families and property. By this act he showed himself a champion also of the Judahite towns in the Negeb. Upon returning to Ziklag, David sent gifts from the plunder to the elders of Judah (vv. 26-31). This event certainly prepares for David's election as king of Judah later in Hebron (2 Sam. 2:4).

a. Raid on Ziklag (30:1-8)

(1) The Amalekites Raid Ziklag (30:1-2)

1 *When David and his men came to Ziklag on the third day, the Amalekites, who had made a raid on the Negeb and on Ziklag, had struck Ziklag and burned it with fire*
2 *and had taken prisoner the women who were in it*[1] *from the youngest to the oldest, though they had not killed any, and had driven them off with them and gone on their way.*

1-2 This section begins with "a flashback" by the narrator relating what had happened at Ziklag before David returned from Aphek.[2]

1 The phrase *David and his men* functions as a link between the present episode and the previous one; cf. 29:11. The movement verb "came" and the geographical term Ziklag as well as the temporal expression *on the third day* all provide the background information necessary to the following EVENT.

1. Cf. "the women and all who were in it" (NRSV; NIV; NASB). McCarter (p. 431) also follows LXX^{B}, translating similarly. "Of the women and everyone else who was there."

2. See S. Bar-Efrat, "Some Observations on the Analysis of Structure in Biblical Narrative," *VT* 30 (1980) 160.

The phrase *on the third day* means "after three days." Three days are "a very reasonable amount of time" for David and his men to march back from Aphek to Ziklag (Tel Sherîʿah).[3]

David had raided the Amalekites from Ziklag (27:8).

(2) David Enters the City (30:3-6)

3 *And David and his men entered the city, which was now burned*[4] *with fire; their wives, sons, and daughters had been taken prisoner.*

4 *And David and the troops with him raised their voices and wept until there was no strength in them to weep.*

5 *— Now David's two wives, Ahinoam*[5] *the Jezreelite*[6] *and Abigail, the wife of Nabal the Carmelite, had been taken prisoner —*

6 *And David was in great distress,*[7] *for the troops spoke of stoning him because the souls of all the troops were bitter,*[8] *each concerning his sons and daughters.*

And David strengthened himself in the Lord, his God.

3-6 In this paragraph, when the subject of *wayqtl* is stated (as in vv. 3, 4, 6b), it is "David" who is the subject and, hence, the major actor in this episode. David faces a great trial with the loss of his beloved wives. Even his men *spoke of stoning him* because of this severe hardship. In this situation David strengthened himself in the Lord, his God. Only the intimate relationship with his personal God gave him strength in such a critical time. Baldwin thinks that Psalm 25 could have been composed at a time like this (see esp. vv. 16-17).[9]

6 Death by stoning (*sql) is referred to both in Greek epic (*Iliad* 3:57 "donning a coat of stone," a euphemism for death by stoning) and the Hebrew Bible.[10] In this critical situation *David strengthened himself in the*

3. M. Kochavi, *Aphek-Antipatris: Five Seasons of Excavation at Tel Aphek-Antipatris (1972-1976)* (Tel Aviv: Tel-Aviv University, 1977), p. 11.

4. Lit., "and behold, it was burned."

5. See 1 Sam. 25:42-43.

6. *yizreʿēlît;* the phonetic spelling without *aleph.*

7. *wattēṣer lᵉdāwīd mᵉʾōd;* lit., "it (f.sg. = the matter) was narrow for"; see *HALOT,* p. 1058; BDB, p. 864; see 2 Sam. 13:2; see also 1 Sam. 13:6; 28:15 with adjectival forms. Driver, p. 222: "This use of the fem., especially with words denoting a mental condition, is particularly common in Syriac."

8. *mārāh nepeš;* for this Hebrew expression, see 1:10; 22:2.

9. Baldwin, p. 167.

10. C. H. Gordon, *The Common Background of Greek and Hebrew Civilizations* (New York: W. W. Norton, 1965), p. 267.

Lord: *ḥzq (Hit.) *baYHWH*. To "strengthen oneself" may carry implications "both of taking courage and of consolidating one's position vis-à-vis some group of people (2 Sam. 3:6)."[11]

(3) David Inquires of the Lord (30:7-8)

7 *And David said to Abiathar, the priest, son of Ahimelech,*
"Bring me the ephod!"
And Abiathar brought the ephod to David.
8 *And David inquired of the Lord, saying,*
"Shall I pursue after this band? Can I overtake it?"
and he said to him,
"Pursue! For you can surely overtake and rescue them!"

7 *Abiathar* (see on 22:20) has been with David since the Nob massacre, and he carried the *ephod* (see 14:3).

8 David *inquired* (see 23:2) of Yahweh's will, asking, *"Shall I pursue after this band? Can I overtake it?"* Two similar questions are asked in 14:37; cf. 23:9. But the verbs for "pursuing" are different: here *rdp, there *yrd *'aḥărê.*

b. Pursuit of the Amalekites (30:9-25)

(1) To Wadi Besor (30:9-10)

9 *And David went with the six hundred men who were with him and came to the Naḥal Besor, where*[12] *those who would be left would remain.*
10 *And David pursued with four hundred men.*
And two hundred men who were too exhausted to cross[13] *the Naḥal Besor remained.*

9-10 Both verbs *went . . . came . . .* (*hlk . . . *bw' . . .) are *yqtl* of motion verbs; hence, the verse is transitional and provides background information (SETTING) for the following EVENT. The stage has moved from Ziklag to Naḥal Besor, and thus the narrator's viewpoint has changed; see "Introduction" (Section VI, D).

The *Naḥal Besor (naḥal habbᵉśôr)* is possibly the modern Wadi Ghazzeh,[14] one of the two major wadis of the western Negeb. This is the first

11. McCarter, p. 435.

12. Disjunctive *waw.*

13. *mēʿăbōr;* cf. "on the other side of (the Wadi)" (LXX^B).

14. McCarter, p. 435. See L. F. DeVries, "The Brook Besor," in *ABD,* I, pp. 679-80.

major wadi southwest of Tell esh-Sheriʿāh (ancient Ziklag?); see the commentary on 27:6.

The phrase *those who would be left would remain (wᵉhannôtārîm ʿāmādû)* is sometimes regarded as being "out of place at this point, anticipating 10b." McCarter thinks that "the extensive confusion exhibited by LXX in vv 9 and 10 must have developed partly out of uncertainty about the size of David's force and partly out of the intrusion of these words."[15] However, the verse as a whole seems to constitute a SETTING, which gives necessary information for the following EVENT, namely, David's pursuit *with four hundred men* (v. 10a). The clause "those who were left remained" prepares the audience for the new STAGE.

(2) David Finds an Egyptian (30:11-15)

11 *And they found an Egyptian in the field and took him to David.*
And they gave him food and he ate; and they gave him water to drink.
12 *And they gave him a slice of fig-cake and two bunches of raisins and he ate. And his spirit revived,*[16] *for he had neither eaten food nor drunk water for three days and three nights.*
13 *And David said to him,*
"To whom do you belong? Where are you from?"
and he said,
"I am an Egyptian lad,
the slave of an Amalekite.
My master abandoned me,
for I have been ill for these three days.[17]
14 *We made a raid on the Negeb of*[18] *the Cretans,*[19]
on the territory of[20] *Judah and on the Negeb of Caleb,*
but Ziklag we burned with fire."
15 *And David said to him,*
"Can you take me down to this band?"
and he said,
"Swear to me by God

15. McCarter, p. 431.

16. Lit., "returned to him."

17. *hayyôm šᵉlōšāh;* or "three days ago" (NRSV; NIV; JPS).

18. See on 1 Sam. 27:10.

19. *hakkᵉrētî;* or "the Cherethites."

20. Lit., "that which belongs to" (NRSV; NASB); cf. "the Negeb of" (JPS); "the territory belonging to" (NIV).

that you will not kill me or hand me over to my master,
and I will take you down to this band!"

11-13 David finds an abandoned Egyptian slave who belonged to an Amalekite master. He gives him food and water, not so much from his compassion and kindness (so Bergen, p. 277) as in order to get crucial information from him. The slave's spirit revives from being ill for three days and nights without eating and drinking. Though the phrase *and two bunches of raisins* is sometimes omitted with LXX^B, one should note that v. 12 as a whole is a detailed description of v. 11b, which simply mentions that the man who was found was given food and water.

14 The Egyptian lad provides the information that the Amalekites made raids on the Negeb and burned Ziklag. The term *Cretans* (or "Cherethites") was at times a synonym for the Philistines (see Ezek. 25:16; Zeph. 2:5). Since the latter is known as of Aegean origin, the "Cherethites" (see later on 2 Sam. 8:18) are to be related to "Cretan"[21] and probably to be equated with the Caphtorim of Deut. 2:23.[22] Therefore, *the Negeb of the Cretans (negeb hakkᵉrētî)* refers to the southern, Philistine part of the Negeb or perhaps the part of it where Ziklag is located.[23] *The Negeb of Caleb (negeb kālēb)* is south of Hebron,[24] the Calebite capital; see Josh. 15:19; Judg. 1:20; 1 Sam. 25:3.

15 David asks the lad to take him to the Amalekite band, to his master. The Egyptian lad asks David to *swear . . . by God. God* here could mean "gods" in the mouth of an Egyptian.

(3) David Strikes the Amalekites (30:16-20)

16 *And he took him down, and there they were, scattered*[25] *all over the*
land, eating, drinking, and celebrating because of[26] *all the great*
plunder which they had taken from the land of the Philistines
and from the land of Judah.
17 *And David struck them from dawn until evening, even to after*

21. See M. Delcor, "Les Kéréthim et les Cretois," *VT* 28 (1978) 409-22; B. Mazar, *Biblical Israel: State and People,* ed. S. Ahituv (Jerusalem: Magnes, 1992), p. 23; also *ABD,* I, pp. 898-99. See 2 Sam. 8:18.

22. See A. F. Rainey, "Negeb," in *ISBE,* III, p. 512.

23. See 2 Sam. 8:18; 15:18; 20:7, 23; 1 K. 1:38, 44.

24. A. F. Rainey called to my attention the fact that the hills south of Hebron are different from those around Hebron (personal communication).

25. *nᵉṭūšîm;* cf. "they were spread out all over the ground" (NRSV); "lounging" (McCarter, p. 432).

26. Lit., "in" or "with."

sunset. No one escaped from them except four hundred young men,[27] *who got on*[28] *the camels and fled.*

18 *And David rescued all that the Amalekites had taken; and his two wives David rescued.*

19 *And nothing was lacking to them, from the youngest to the oldest, from sons and daughters to the plunder, to all that they had taken for themselves; everything David recovered.*

20 *And David*[29] *took all the sheep and the cattle, which*[30] *were driven*[31] *ahead of the other property; and they said: "This is David's plunder!"*

16 The Egyptian lad takes David and his men to the place where the Amalekites are *celebrating* their great plunder. The term *celebrating (ḥōgᵉgîm)* connotes the sense of "'behaving as at a *hag* or gathering of pilgrims,' i.e. enjoying themselves merrily."[32]

17 The term *nešep* "twilight" can refer either to the morning twilight, that is, dawn, or to the evening twilight, that is, dusk; see *HALOT,* p. 730; BDB, p. 676. Whichever position one may take with regard to "twilight," the usual English translation "until the evening of the next day" (NRSV; NIV; JPS) would give an impression that the battle lasted at least one full day, a day and a night. However, the term *moḥŏrāt* (lit., "the morrow") would refer to "after sunset," since a new day begins at sunset; see the discussion on 20:5. With this understanding, the battle most probably lasted from dawn to after sunset of the same day in modern terms.

Probably David waited until dawn and then attacked, for if he had attacked at night it would have been too easy to kill his own family or for the Amalekites to escape unseen. Attacks at dawn are common in warfare; see 1 Sam. 11:11, etc. as well as Mesha stela, line 15 ("from the break of dawn").[33]

The MT *lᵉmoḥŏrātām* (translated as *even to after sunset*) is usually taken as meaning, literally, "to their next day." However, the suffix *-ām* could be an enclitic mem functioning adverbially. McCarter would see here "a corrupt condensation of the reading of LXX^{L}" whose *Vorlage* he suggests to be

27. On *na'ar* with the military sense of "warriors," see on 25:5; 2 Sam. 2:14.

28. Lit., "ride on" or "mount"; see on 25:42.

29. Cf. "He also took" (McCarter, p. 432), following LXX^{B}.

30. The relative clause without *'ăšer.* The order of the verbal forms, *qtl . . . wayqtl . . .*, suggests that "they drove before . . ." is not in the same storyline as, and hence sequential to, "they said."

31. Lit., "they drove"; impersonal passive; so NRSV.

32. Driver, p. 223.

33. See *CS,* II, p. 138.

(w)lmḥrt wtmytm "of the next day. He put them to death."[34] Collins's view that "their next day" means the Amalekites' next day, that is, "soon after sunset in the evening, following the start of their [i.e., the Amalekites'] new calendar day,"[35] is a little forced, for the start of the calendar day seems to be at sunset also among the ancient Israelites during David's time. Besides, it seems strange that they would bring up something as irrelevant as the Amalekites' calendrical system here. See also 14:24 where "by the evening," that is, before sunset, means "today."

18 By repeating *And David* here and also in v. 20, the narrator emphasizes that David was the major figure, as if the only agent. This repetition of the subject is a discourse grammatical device, indicating the beginning of a discourse, not necessarily the beginning of an event, for every *wayqtl* followed by a stated subject initiates a new sub-paragraph. The two halves of this verse constitute a parallelistic structure, a-b-c/c′-a′-b′, with a chiasmus:

> And David rescued all that the Amalekites had taken;
> and his two wives David rescued.

The first half is a general statement; the second a specific one. This also is a poetic feature of Hebrew narrative prose; see "Introduction" (Section VII, B).

19 *From sons and daughters to the plunder* (lit., "to sons and daughters from the plunder"): LXX^B here has "from the plunder to sons and daughters" instead of the MT "to sons and daughters from the plunder." McCarter thinks that "there is little basis for choosing between these arrangements," but, following Driver, he insists on moving the Masoretes' disjunctive accent *(zaqep)* from *wmšll* to *wbnwt* if the MT is retained. However, a similar poetic feature might be recognized here, as above (v. 18).

> And nothing was lacking to them,
> from the youngest to the oldest,
> to sons and daughters from the plunder,
> to all that they had taken for themselves;
> everything David recovered.

The reversal of the prepositional phrases, that is, "from . . ." and "to . . . ," is possibly a chiastic construction: "from . . . to . . ."//"to . . . from. . . ." If so, there is no strong reason why one should transpose the MT's accent.

20 Then David takes all the sheep and the cattle while his men say:

34. McCarter, p. 432. For other various suggestions for emendation, see N. Collins, "The Start of the Pre-exilic Calendar Day of David and the Amalekites: A Note on 1 Samuel 30:17," *VT* 41 (1991) 203-10.

35. Collins, "The Start of the Pre-exilic Calendar Day," p. 208.

"This is David's plunder!" In contrast to Saul's case (see ch. 15), David could keep his plunder as his own.

(4) David Comes Back to Wadi Besor (30:21-25)

21 *And David came to the two hundred men who had been too*
exhausted to go after David and whom they had made stay in
the Naḥal Besor, and they came out to meet David and the
people that were with him.
And David approached the people and asked after their peace.
22 *And every evil and worthless one of the men who had gone with*
David answered:
"Because they did not go with us[36]
we shall not give them any of the plunder we recovered
except for each man's wife and children.
Them they may take and go."[37]
23 *And David said,*
"You shall not act like this, my brothers,
about[38] *the thing which the Lord has given us!*
He has watched over us
and has given into our hand the band who came against us!
24 *Who would listen to you about this matter?*
For[39] *the share of the one who stayed by the baggage shall be*
the same as the share of the one who went down to the battle;
they should share together!"
25 *From that day onward he made it a statute and custom*[40] *for Israel,*
until this day.

21 The pronoun "they"[41] of MT *they had made stay* refers to the four hundred men, while "they" of *they came out* refers to the two hundred men who

36. Lit., "me"; "us" emends to *ʿmnw* "with us" after several Hebrew versions.

37. *w^{e}yinhăgû w^{e}yēlēkû; w^{e}* + impf; as a result sentence; or as a purpose clause like "that they may lead them away and depart" (NASB). Other translations (e.g., NRSV; NIV) connect these verbal phrases with the preceding noun phrase: "except that each man may take his wife and children, and leave" (NRSV).

38. *ʾēt;* or "concerning with," an adverbial accusative; cf. "after what Yahweh has given us" (McCarter); see McCarter, p. 433, for various suggestions about this part of v. 23; some take *ʾt* . . . as the object of *ʿśh. See also 31:11.

39. Speaker-oriented *kî,* denoting the reason why I ask you this rhetorical question. See "Introduction" (Section V, C).

40. *l^{e}ḥōq ûl(^{e})mišpāṭ;* cf. "a fixed rule" (JPS).

41. Cf. McCarter, p. 432: "he had posted," reading *wayyōšîbēm* "with five MSS of MT and LXX^{B}."

stayed. The context guides the reader to the correct reading. In the same manner, "the people" and "their" in the last sentence of v. 21 *(And David approached the people and asked after their peace)* refer to the two hundred men (so LXX). A similar example can be noted in 31:7 ("the men of Israel"). However, McCarter, who thinks that the MT misunderstood the objective particle *'et,* translates the clause "as David approached *with* the soldiers," and he takes this "people" as "the soldiers" who went with David, for "the first part of the verse indicates David is with 'the soldiers' *(h'm)* already, not approaching them." However, a new paragraph begins with this clause, which is *wayqtl* followed by a stated subject, "David." Here the focus is on David's asking about the peace of those who remained; this is the best way of explaining the verbs, "approached" and "asked," as singular, and the discourse flows smoothly.

David's asking their peace could be "more than a routine greeting, to show that there was no hostile feeling towards them, despite the criticism of them by those engaged in the battle."[42]

22 The expression *evil and worthless (rāʿ ûbᵉlîyaʿal)* is a hendiadys, translated as "worthless and evil" in LXX^{B}; see *'îš habbᵉlîyaʿal* (25:25; 2 Sam. 16:7; also 20:1). *Worthless* is literally "Beliyaal" (see on 1:16) and is also used of the men who opposed Saul in 10:27.

23 The plunder is that which *the Lord has given us.* David honors his God Yahweh to whom alone victory belongs, for he *has watched over* them. The phrase *into our hand* modifies the main verb *has given,* though the appositional phrase *habbā' ʿālênû,* "the one who came against us," intervenes.

24-25 David divides his plunder evenly among those who stayed by the baggage and those who went down to the battle. The MT *wayśīmehā* ("and he made it") should be preferred to the LXX ("it became") as *lectio difficilior.* The phrase "to make an ordinance" also appears with Moses (Exod. 15:25; 21:1) and Joshua (Josh. 24:25).

The term *custom (mišpāṭ)* might be compared with the Akkadian *šipṭu* "ordinance," which appears in a Mari letter (ARM II 13) in connection with spoils of war. In this letter the writer complains to his overlord of "unjust distribution of spoils" by the army officers. In order to prevent this wantonness "the writer invoked the taboo, proclaiming the misdeed to be a violation of the *asakku* of the gods, the king and his viceroy."[43] Here David establishes regulations for the distribution of spoils. This would become *mišpāṭ* of Israel.

As in Gen. 47:26, the formula *until this day (ʿad hayyôm hazzeh)* is

42. See D. J. Wiseman, "'Is it peace?' — Covenant and Diplomacy," *VT* 32 (1982) 319.

43. A. Malamat ("The Ban in Mari and in the Bible," *OTWSA* 9 [1966] 42) explains the Akkadian idiom "eating of the *asakku*-plant" as corresponding to the biblical concept of the violation of the *ḥerem* ("ban"). See on 15:3.

used in a legal context; the ancient law is still operative in the day of the narrator. The expression should not be taken particularly as "Deuteronomistic"; see "Introduction" (Section III, B, 1).

c. Gifts to the Elders of Judah (30:26-31)

(1) Narrative (30:26)

26 *And David came to Ziklag and sent (items) from the plunder to the elders of Judah, to his neighbors,*[44] *saying,*
"Here is a gift[45] *for you*
from the plunder of the enemies of the Lord!"

26 This is the narrative part which precedes the list. *The elders of Judah (ziqnê yᵉhûdāh),* to whom David sent gifts, are probably the same as the "men of Judah" who anoint David king over the house of Judah in 2 Sam. 2:4. These gifts are from plunder of "the enemies" of Yahweh, the God of Israel.

"The wisdom, diplomacy, and generosity of David are again shown in that he sent a share of the booty to the elders of Judah, his own tribe, for it was these elders that some day were to make him king, before the other tribes of Israel would accept his sovereignty."[46]

(2) List (30:27-31)

27 *for those in Bethel*
for those in Ramoth-negeb
for those in Jattir
28 *for those in Aroer*
for those in Siphmoth
for those in Eshtemoa
29 *for those in Racal*[47]
for those in the Jerahmeelite cities[48]
for those in the Kenite[49] *cities*

44. *lᵉrēʿēhû.* McCarter conjectures that MT was corrupted early from *lʿryw* "according to its cities" and translates: "city by city" (McCarter, p. 433).

45. *bᵉrākāh:* see 9:7; 25:27; cf. LXX^B, which omits "a gift for you."

46. C. H. Gordon and G. A. Rendsburg, *The Bible and the Ancient Near East,* 4th ed. (New York: W. W. Norton, 1997), p. 191.

47. *rākāl;* see J. M. Hamilton, "Racal," in *ABD,* V, p. 605; cf. LXX: "Carmel" (so McCarter, p. 436).

48. *ʿārê hayyᵉraḥmᵉʾēlî;* south of Beersheba? See on 27:10.

49. *haqqênî;* also in 27:10. Cf. "the Kenizzites" (McCarter, p. 434), following LXX^B and 4QSam^a *hqnzy.*

30 *for those in Hormah*
for those in Bor-ashan
for those in Athach
31 *for those in Hebron,*
that is,[50] *for all the places that David and his men went around.*

27-31 These verses constitute a list formula; see on 1 Sam. 6:17-18a; 25:18.[51] The content of the list is announced in a narrative heading (v. 26), itemized in a list (vv. 27-31a), and then summarized in a narrative summary (v. 31b). David distributes the plunder among a number of large and small cities in the vicinity of Hebron.

27 *Bethel (bêt-'ēl)* is an unknown city in Judah, not the famous Bethel, north of Jerusalem. Compare "Beth-zur" (LXX^{B}).

According to Aharoni, *Ramoth-negeb (rāmôt-negeb)* is the modern Ḥorvat ʿUzza, approximately 5 miles south-southeast of Tel Arad, and is a strategic point on the border with Edom, *that is,* in the southeastern border area of the Judean Negeb.[52] However, the town is probably better identified with modern Tell ʿIra (Khirbet el Gharra) [MR 148-071].[53] It is located on a high, flat-topped hill in the Beer-sheba valley.

Jattir (yattīr) is identified with modern Khirbet ʿAttir [MR 148-062], about 12 miles south-southwest of Hebron; it is a levitical city (Josh. 21:14) in the Judean hills (Josh. 15:48).

28 *Aroer (ʿărōʿēr)* has been associated with *ʿArʿarah,* approximately 12 miles southeast of Beersheba. McCarter thinks that the MT shows "the influence of the name of the well-known Transjordanian city (Num 32:34; etc)."[54] However, since the use of such a common name, which means "crest of a mountain" or "juniper," for various places is not unusual,[55] it is unnecessary to assume the influence of another Aroer on this place-name.

Siphmoth (śipmôt) is not mentioned elsewhere; the site is unknown.

Eshtemoa ('eštᵉmōaʿ) is identified with modern es-Semuʿa, about 8 miles south of Hebron near Carmel and Maon; it is a levitical city (Josh. 21:14) in the Judean hills (Josh. 15:50).[56]

50. Explicative *waw;* see on 6:18a.

51. See D. T. Tsumura, "List and Narrative in I Samuel 6,17-18a in the Light of Ugaritic Economic Texts," *ZAW* (2001) 353-69.

52. Y. Aharoni, *Arad Inscriptions* (JDS; Jerusalem: Israel Exploration Society, 1981), pp. 146-47.

53. See *ABD,* III, pp. 446-48.

54. McCarter, p. 434.

55. See *ABD,* I, pp. 399-400.

56. See *ABD,* II, pp. 617-18.

30 The location of *Hormah (ḥormāh)* is not known, though it was listed as belonging to Simeon in Josh. 19:4. Like nearby Ziklag, it is listed as one of the Judean cities belonging to the Negeb province (Josh. 15:30).

Bor-ashan (bôr-ʿāšān) has been known as "Ashan," modern Khirbet ʿAsan, a few miles northwest of Beersheba. It was a levitical city of Judah (Josh. 21:16 LXX^B^) in the Shephelah (Josh. 19:7; cf. 15:42).[57]

Athach (ʿătāk) occurs only here. Most scholars connect this with Ether in Josh. 15:42, where LXX^B^ has *ithak,* and 19:7, where *ʿtr* is associated with *ʿšn* (see above). McCarter takes it as modern Khirbet el-ʿAter, approximately 15 miles northwest of Hebron. But, the LXX evidence is not without problems: see LXX^B^ *noo;* LXX^L^ *negeb;* LXX(MSS) *nombe.*[58]

31 *Hebron (ḥebrôn)* appears here for the first time in Samuel; it was formerly called *qiryat 'arbaʿ* (Gen. 23:2) [MR 159-103] and is located about 19 miles south-southeast of Jerusalem and about 23 miles northeast of Beersheba. It was the place where Abraham built an altar to the Lord (Gen. 13:18). It was a city of refuge and a levitical city (Josh. 21:13; 1 Chr. 6:57). Hebron was the major city of the Judean Hills south of Jerusalem and the old Calebite capital (see on 25:3); the city reached its zenith between the eleventh century and the end of the tenth century B.C.[59] David's two wives, Abigail and Ahinoam, came from its vicinity, that is, Carmel and Jezreel, respectively (see 25:42-43). The fact that this list ends with Hebron points toward David's being proclaimed king there and his choosing it as his capital before the capture of Jerusalem (2 Sam. 2:1-4).

The list as a whole functions as a transitional LINK between David's time as an outlaw and his anointing as king over Judah in Hebron (2 Sam. 2:4). In the intervening section of 1 Samuel 31–2 Samuel 1, the narrative catches back up to the battle between the Philistines and Saul in the Jezreel Valley, at Shunem and Gilboa (see 28:4).

In summary, we can see the hand of the Lord working in all these matters, preparing David to be the future king, the prototype of the Messiah.

H. DEATH OF SAUL AND JONATHAN (31:1-13)

The present episode describes the final battle between the Philistines and Saul. Having dealt with David's story in ch. 30, the storyline now joins together the account of Saul, which was broken off at the end of ch. 28, and that of the Philistines, which was broken off at the end of ch. 29, at Mount Gilboa.

57. See *ABD,* I, pp. 476-77.
58. See McCarter, pp. 434, 36.
59. See A. Ofer, "Hebron," in *NEAEHL,* pp. 606-9; also *ABD,* III, pp. 107-8.

The Philistines pursue and kill Saul's sons, and Saul also finally kills himself. Israel's kingship is thus suspended. Not only the reigning king but also most of his heirs are gone. What will happen now?

1 Sam. 31:1-13//1 Chr. 10:1-12

Most commentaries since Noth's *Überlieferungsgeschichtliche Studien* (1943) have taken the dependence of 1 Chr. 10:1-12 on 1 Sam. 31:1-13 for granted. However, dissident views have been expressed recently. For example, McCarter holds that "the text of the synoptic passage in 1 Chr. 10 seems to hark back to a shorter, more primitive version of the account at many points."[1] Most recently, C. Y. S. Ho compared these two passages in detail and suggested that "the Chr did not seem to know any form of 1 Sam. xxxi that we have."[2] On the other hand, as Zalewski holds, the Chronicler's negative evaluation of Saul in 1 Chr. 10:13-14 is "properly understood against the background of Saul's sins in the books of Samuel."[3] The matter of interdependence between the two is still moot, and each case should be treated individually in detail; see on v. 6.

Unlike the Chronicle passage, our episode presents Saul's death simply as the solemn fact, without making any reference to Saul's guilt, that is, his inquiry of the "ghost." As Hertzberg puts it, "All is described with great solemnity, even reverence."[4]

1. Saul's Three Sons Fall (31:1-2)

1 *Now the Philistines were fighting*[5] *with Israel.*
And the men of Israel fled from before the Philistines and fell wounded on Mount Gilboa.
2 *And the Philistines pursued*[6] *Saul and his sons.*
And the Philistines struck Jonathan, Abinadab,[7] *and Malchishua, the sons of Saul.*

1. McCarter, p. 440.

2. C. Y. S. Ho, "Conjectures and Refutations: Is 1 Samuel xxxi 1-13 Really the Source of 1 Chronicles x 1-12?," *VT* 45 (1995) 82-106.

3. S. Zalewski, "The Purpose of the Story of the Death of Saul in 1 Chronicles x," *VT* 39 (1989) 456. For a detailed discussion of the meaning of the "addendum" (1 Chr. 10:13-14), see Zalewski, pp. 456-60.

4. Hertzberg, p. 231.

5. Cf. "fought" (McCarter, p. 440; following LXX; 1 Chr. 10:1).

6. *wayyadb*^{e}*qû:* also 1 Sam. 14:22; 1 Chr. 10:2; instead of *wayyadbîqû* (Judg. 18:22); GKC, §53n explains that the *î* appears weakened to *shwa* "in the Aramaic manner" and lists other similar examples. Note that 1 Chr. 10:2 has *dbq . . . *'aḥărê.*

7. See on 1 Sam. 14:49. Cf. 1 Sam. 16:8 (the second son of Jesse).

1 *Now the Philistines (ûpᵉlištîm) were fighting,* a disjunctive clause with a participle, provides a SETTING for the following EVENT. It continues the storyline with regard to the Philistines from 29:11; note the triple repetition of "the Philistines" in vv. 1-2, which also marks the setting. The Philistines had been Saul's constant enemy, *fighting with Israel,* from the beginning of his reign (13:5; see also 9:16) to the end.

The participle ("were fighting") emphasizes the simultaneity of action; while David was pursuing (*rdp; 30:8) the Amalekite band, the Philistines were pursuing (*dbq; v. 2) Saul and his sons.

Gilboa (MT *hglbʿ;* cf. 1 Chr. 10:1 *glbʿ*) was the site of the Israelite camps (28:4), but now the Philistines have come out of their camp at Shunem and are pursuing Saul and his sons on Mount Gilboa.

2 In this verse *the Philistines* is repeated twice as the plural subject of *wayqtl,* that is, pursued and struck. Such repetition of the stated subject and the plural forms of the verbs in the two *wayqtl* mark these verses as functioning as SETTING for the following EVENT; see "Introduction" (Section VI, A). Three of Saul's sons die here in keeping with Samuel's words in 28:19. His son Ishbosheth is not mentioned, and Saul's general Abner also somehow escaped from the deadly battlefield; see 2 Sam. 2:8.

2. Saul Dies (31:3-6)

3 *And the battle became severe on Saul.*
When he was found by certain archers, he writhed greatly in fear of the archers.[8]
4 *And Saul said to his armor-bearer,*
"Draw out your sword and pierce me through with it,
lest these uncircumcised should come
and pierce me through[9] *and deal with me harshly!"*[10]
But his armor-bearer was not willing, for he was very afraid.
And Saul took the sword and fell on it.
5 *And his armor-bearer saw that Saul was dead, and he also fell on his sword, and he died with him.*

8. *wayyāḥel mᵉʾōd mēhammôrîm;* cf. "and he was wounded in the belly" (McCarter), following LXX^{B}, whose "Hebrew correspondent seems impossible to determine with certainty" (p. 440).

9. *ûdᵉqārūnî;* McCarter thinks that the phrase "and run me through" is "out of place here and should be omitted; so I Chr. 10:4" (p. 440).

10. *wᵉhitʿallᵉlû-bî;* also 1 Sam. 6:6; "Saul is afraid of being tortured before he dies" (McCarter, p. 443).

6 *And Saul died with his three sons and his armor-bearer, also with all of his men*[11] *on that day together.*

3 As the subject is the impersonal word "battle," the first sentence with the *wayqtl* verb is off the mainline narrative; thus, it is a SETTING. Since the next sentence begins with a *wayqtl, wayyimṣā'ūhû* (lit., "and they found him") with a plural noun as the subject, it is also off the mainline of the story according to the "principle of relativity" (see "Introduction" [Section VI, A]) in narrative discourse: so, "When."

He was found by certain archers (wayyimṣā'ūhû hammôrîm 'ănāšîm baqqāšet; lit., "the archers men with the bow found him"; also LXX). McCarter takes this as a conflation of variants and translates: "The archers . . . with their bows."[12] However, the indefinite noun *'ănāšîm* ("men") seems to be the subject of the verb *(wayyimṣā'ūhû)* as in Gen. 37:15 (*wayyimṣā'ēhû 'îš* "a man found him"), and the clause is to be understood as passive in meaning. This may be another example of AXB, in which X ("men") is inserted into a phrase "the shooters with bow" (= "the archers"); hence, the underlying structure would be *'ănāšîm hammôrîm baqqāšet* "(certain) men, i.e. the shooters with bow." See 1 Chr. 10:3 *(hammôrîm baqqāšet).*[13]

4-5 This narrative contradicts the Amalekite's report of Saul's death in 2 Sam. 1:6-10. The easiest explanation is that the Amalekite was lying in hopes of currying favor with David. See on 2 Sam. 1:6-10.

Saul did not want the *uncircumcised* Philistines either to shame him or to torture him, as they had done with Samson; so, he ordered his armor-bearer to kill him. But his faithful armor-bearer was unwilling to do so. He also killed himself when he saw Saul dead.

6 Instead of "his armor-bearer, also (with) all of his men," 1 Chr. 10:6 has "all his household" *(kl-bytw).* Thus, the Chronicler's interest is in the providential work of the divine hand over Saul and his family rather than in an exact description of the historical event.[14] 1 Chr. 10:6 is usually taken as an "abridgment" of 1 Sam. 31:6.[15] Others regard the MT's "gloss" as based on Chronicle's reading.[16] McCarter, after comparing the MT of 1 Sam. 31:6 with LXX^{B} and 1 Chr. 10:6, concludes: "a primitive form of the present verse, not reconstructible from the evidence of I Sam 31:6 alone, may have been: *wymt š'wl wšlšt bnyw yhdw,* 'So Saul and his three sons died together.'"[17] He has re-

11. *'ănāšâw;* i.e., Saul's officials; cf. "the men of Israel" (v. 7).
12. McCarter, p. 440.
13. For various views, see Stoebe, p, 521.
14. See Zalewski, "The Purpose of the Story of the Death of Saul," p. 462.
15. E.g., Driver, p. 229.
16. E.g., Klein, p. 286.
17. McCarter, pp. 440-41.

cently supported Chronicle's reading of "all his household," which he thinks is equivalent to "Saul and his three sons" in light of the fact that only "Jonathan, Ishvi, and Malchishua" (1 Sam. 14:49) are mentioned as Saul's sons.[18] Ho therefore takes Saul's household list as a possible source of 1 Chr. 10:6. Compare 1 Chr. 8:33; 9:39, where four men are listed as Saul's sons; see on 14:49.

The available evidence does not allow us to make a final decision about the dependence of 1 Chr. 10:6 on our text; it is always possible that the author of Chronicle had access to other information.

3. The Israelites Flee (31:7)

7 *And the men of Israel*[19] *who were on the other side of the valley and who were on the other side of the Jordan*[20] *saw that the men of Israel had fled and that Saul and his sons had died, and they abandoned the cities and fled.*
And the Philistines came and lived in[21] *them.*

7 Here the first *men of Israel* refers to the Israelite people and the second to the Israelite soldiers. See 30:21 for a similar example where the same word refers to two different referents within a verse: "the people (who went with David)" and "the people (who stayed)."

The phrase *the other side of the valley (ʿēber hāʿēmeq)* refers to the other side of the Valley of Jezreel, that is, the northern side, viewed from Mount Gilboa where Saul and his sons died. Lilley holds that the reference is clearly not to Transjordan and "probably not to Galilee, but to the hills south of Jezreel and to the upper Jordan valley."[22] He therefore thinks that the rendering "beside" for *ʿēber* is definitely indicated. However, with McCarter, we rather take it to refer to "the Israelites who lived N of Jezreel in the southern reaches of the Galilean hills."

As the result of Saul's defeat, the Philistines came and lived in those deserted cities in northern Israel, around the Valley of Jezreel. It is important to note with Hertzberg that the central hill country, which Saul's son Ishbosheth and Abner would soon control, is not mentioned here.[23]

18. Ho, "Conjectures and Refutations," pp. 85-87.

19. *ʾanšê-yiśrāʾēl;* i.e., the Israelite people; cf. "all the men of Israel" (1 Chr. 10:7).

20. McCarter excludes the reference to those *who were on the other side of the Jordan* as "unquestionably expansive" (p. 441), since this phrase is missing in 1 Chr. 10:7, which has only "who were in the valley" *(ʾăšer bāʿēmeq).*

21. Or "occupied."

22. J. P. U. Lilley, "By the River-side," *VT* 28 (1978) 168.

23. Hertzberg, p. 232.

4. The Philistines Expose Saul's Corpse (31:8-10)

8 *On the next day the Philistines came to strip the slain and found Saul and his three sons fallen on Mount Gilboa.*
9 *They cut off his head and stripped off his armor and sent (messengers)*[24] *into the land of the Philistines around to bring tidings to*[25] *the house of their idols and to the people.*
10 *They deposited his armor*[26] *in the temple of Astartes,*[27] *but his corpse*[28] *they thrust on the wall of Beth-shan.*[29]

8 On the next day the Philistines find the corpses of Saul and his three sons. Ho, comparing 1 Chr. 10:8, holds that the numeral "three" was added here, "stressing that only three sons of Saul, not all of them, were killed, as there are still death stories of other sons of Saul to be told in Samuel."[30] But the numeral has already been used in v. 6, and the shorter text is not always "original." One could also argue that 1 Chr. 10:8 ("his sons") resulted from the loss of the numeral.

9 In all ancient versions as well as 1 Chr. 10:9, 10 Saul's beheading is referred to, but McCarter thinks that the varied ways it is referred to show it is "secondary."[31] It may be, as Williamson points out, that the difference between 1 Chr. 10:10 and our text (MT) is due to the difference in perspectives: in 1 Sam. 31:10 "the Philistines' treatment of Saul's body" is the main theme, while 1 Chr. 10:10 is more concerned with "the fate of his head."[32]

Note that in the Assyrian reliefs depicting the battle at the Ulai River, the head of the Elamite king Teumman was cut and sent off to King

24. McCarter revocalizes the MT as qal since he says the MT form (Pi.) would mean "and sent [Saul's head and armor]"; so Driver, p. 229. However, the context requires the meaning *and sent (messengers);* but cf. *HALOT,* p. 1515.

25. *bśr (Pi.); see "to carry the good news to the houses of their idols and to the people" (NRSV). Following LXX and 1 Chr. 10:9, McCarter takes only "their idols" as object of *lbśr* (p. 441).

26. See 1 Sam. 21:8.

27. See on 1 Sam. 7:4.

28. *gᵉwîyātô;* without head; cf. 1 Chr. 10:10 (*glgltw* "his head").

29. *bêt šān;* also 1 Sam. 31:12; 2 Sam. 21:12; this form appears only in Samuel; it is a *sandhi* spelling of *bêt šᵉʾān* (Josh. 17:11, 16; Judg. 1:27; 1 K. 4:12[x2]; 1 Chr. 7:29); see D. T. Tsumura, "Vowel sandhi in Biblical Hebrew," *ZAW* 109 (1997) 585. Cf. 1 Chr. 10:10 *bêt dāgôn* ("in the house of Dagon") instead of *bᵉḥômat bêt šān.* See on 1 Sam. 17:54.

30. Ho, "Conjectures and Refutations," p. 89.

31. McCarter, p. 441.

32. See Ho, "Conjectures and Refutations," p. 90.

Ashurbanipal at his palace.[33] Saul's head was presumably deposited in the Astartes temple together with his armor; see v. 10 and 1 Chr. 10:10.

The phrase *their idols* means the gods of the Philistines. The war was thought to be a "holy war" between the gods of two opponent peoples; see on 17:47.

10 Almost all scholars[34] emend the MT *ʿštrwt* (f.pl.) to *ʿštrt* (f.sg.) based on the LXX *to astarteion.* However, grammatically plural names are attested in such DN as *bʿlm* ("Baals") and *ǵrm* ("Mountains") in the Ugaritic pantheon list (*KTU* 1.118:5-10, 18) and *ilm nʿmm* ("Good gods") in the Ugaritic "myth and ritual" text (*KTU* 1.23:1, 23, 60). The fact that Saul's weapons were offered as tribute to *Astartes* possibly points up to her nature as a war-goddess like Mesopotamian Ishtar.[35]

In 2 Sam. 21:12 also it is said that the Philistines had "thrust" Saul's body on the wall of Beth-shan.

Beth-shan is located at the junction [MR197-212] of two important roads: the east-west road from the Jezreel Valley to Gilead and the north-south road in the Jordan Valley. The site was occupied almost continuously from the Late Neolithic to the Early Arab periods. It was an old Canaanite city, which was under Egyptian control from the fifteenth century to the thirteenth century B.C. and under Philistine control in the twelfth century. It guarded the east end of the Valley of Jezreel.[36] Two temples have been unearthed from the eleventh-century level V, one for the god Resheph and the other for the goddess Antit.[37]

5. The Jabeshites Bury the Corpses (31:11-13)

11 *And the inhabitants of Jabesh-Gilead*[38] *heard of it, that is, about what*[39] *the Philistines did to Saul.*

12 *And all their warriors arose and went all night and took Saul's corpse*[40] *and his sons' corpses from the wall of Beth-shan and*

33. See D. Collon, *Ancient Near Eastern Art* (London: British Museum Press, 1995), p. 150.

34. See McCarter, p. 441.

35. A. Cooper, "Divine Names and Epithets in the Ugaritic Texts," in *RSP* 3, p. 406.

36. See A. Mazar, "Beth-shean," in *NEAEHL,* pp. 214-23.

37. T. C. Mitchell, "Bethshean," in *IBD,* I, p. 190; R. W. Hamilton, "Beth-shan," in *IDB,* 1, pp. 397-401.

38. See on 1 Sam. 11:1.

39. *ʾēt ʾăšer . . . ;* adverbial accusative; see 1 Sam. 30:23 (above).

40. *geᵉwîyat;* a body without the head; see v. 9. McCarter thinks that *gûpat* ("corpse") in 1 Chr. 10:12, which appears nowhere else, is "likely to have been original"

came back to Jabesh and burned[41] *them there.*
13 *They took their bones and buried them under the tamarisk*[42] *in Jabesh and fasted seven days.*

11-13 "A friendly light dawns over the horrible picture at the end."[43] When the people of Jabesh-Gilead heard that the Philistines had thrust Saul's corpse onto the wall of Beth-shan, they rendered kindness for kindness to Saul, who had rescued them from Nahash the Ammonite at the beginning of his career (11:1-11); see also 2 Sam. 2:4. Later, however, David moved the bones (2 Sam. 21:12-14).

12 The men of Jabesh-Gilead *burned* the corpses of Saul and his sons prior to burial. The burning of the deceased's bones was usually considered an awful crime in the OT (see Amos 2:1). However, here it is considered to be an honorable act. C. H. Gordon notes that "variant forms of this custom are attested throughout Indo-European epic: Indic, Greek, Anglo-Saxon and Icelandic. Hittite and Homeric burial have much in common. . . . The burnings of Saul and Hector were thus linked by Hittite custom overland, even as they were presumably linked by Philistine custom imported by sea."[44] This burning of the bodies of Saul and his sons was "to guarantee that the bodies would not be exposed again"[45] rather than to avoid "a risk of infection from the quickly decomposing bodies."[46]

13 A ritual of seven days *(šibʿat yāmîm)* is also attested in the Ugaritic funerary ritual preserved in *KTU* 1.161.[47]

---

and is replaced here "by a more familiar term (under the influence of v 10?) that was graphically quite similar" (McCarter, p. 442).

41. From the common Semitic *šrp "to burn" (see Ugar. *šrp).* To posit another meaning for the root *śrp in the light of *srp, "to anoint" (see on *śrp^{II}; *HALOT,* pp. 1359-60), is somewhat forced; cf. Hertzberg, p. 233.

42. *tamarisk (hāʾešel)* is replaced by "oak" *(hʾlh)* in 1 Chr. 10:12; hence "oak" (NRSV; NASB; JPS); "the terebinth" (McCarter). McCarter thinks that the tamarisk is "a far more frequently mentioned tree and therefore less likely to have been original to the account" (p. 442). But statistics do not decide originality. McCarter seems to have two principles: (1) the shorter text is always the more original; (2) the less frequent term is more original. However, frequency could be just an accident.

43. Hertzberg, p. 233.

44. C. H. Gordon, *The Common Background of Greek and Hebrew Civilizations* (New York: W. W. Norton, 1965), p. 269; also p. 18.

45. H. C. Brichto, "Kin, Cult, Land and Afterlife — A Biblical Complex," *HUCA* 44 (1973) 37, n. 58.

46. Baldwin, p. 171.

47. See D. T. Tsumura, "The Interpretation of the Ugaritic Funerary Text KTU 1.161," in *Official Cult and Popular Religion in the Ancient Near East,* ed. E. Matsushima (Heidelberg: C. Winter, 1993), pp. 40-55. For a detailed study of a seven-day period for a

The honorable death of the tragic hero Saul was courteously treated by the people who had been greatly benefited from his heroic leadership against their enemy. "So Saul's life ends not in dishonour, but in honour, as befits the Lord's anointed."[48] In the next chapter, the death of Saul and his son Jonathan will be the theme of the most moving elegy in the Bible, sung by David the "neighbor" of Saul and the "friend" of Jonathan.

Thus, the First Book of Samuel ends with Saul's death. But this is not the end of the story. Readers would wait for the subsequent narrative with great expectation for the establishment of the throne of David, the very prototype of the future King, the "Lord's anointed" (Messiah), through whom the divine plan of salvation would be fulfilled.

---

ritual in the OT, see the recent work of G. A. Klingbeil, "Ritual Time in Leviticus 8 with Special Reference to the Seven Day Period in the Old Testament," *ZAW* 109 (1997) 500-513.

48. Hertzberg, p. 234.

INDEX OF SUBJECTS

INDEX OF MODERN AUTHORS

INDEX OF SCRIPTURE REFERENCES

INDEX OF FOREIGN WORDS

HEBREW

AKKADIAN

ARABIC

ARAMAIC

SUMERIAN

PUNIC/PHOENICIAN

SYRIAC

HITTITE/ANATOLIAN

EGYPTIAN

ETHIOPIC

GREEK